中国版权年鉴

CHINA COPYRIGHT YEARBOOK

2017

中国版权年鉴编委会 编

中国人民大学出版社
·北京·

2016 年 1 月 18 日，国家版权贸易基地（越秀）在广东省广州市举行“首批授权法律服务机构授牌仪式及维权专家聘请仪式”。（国家版权贸易基地（越秀）供图）

2016 年 1 月 27 日，由中国版权杂志社、中国版权产业网主办的“网络音乐版权保护与商业模式”研讨会在北京召开。会议就当前我国网络音乐产业的现状、网络音乐版权保护和商业模式，特别是收费模式、分配模式等进行了研讨。（摄影 / 赵培育）

2016年2月24日，在由中国版权保护中心（CPCC）主办的以“尊重原创　传统再造”为主题的2016年CPCC中国版权服务年会开幕式上，“2015年CPCC十大中国著作权人”评选结果揭晓。（摄影/史博文）

2016年3月11日，推进使用正版软件工作部际联席会议第五次全体会议在北京召开。会议传达了国务院副总理汪洋关于软件正版化工作的重要批示，对2015年推进使用正版软件工作进行了总结，并讨论审议了2016年工作计划。（摄影/郁致原）

2016 年 4 月 19 日，国务院新闻办公室举行新闻发布会，国家新闻出版广电总局（国家版权局）副局长阎晓宏（右一）介绍 2015 年中国知识产权发展状况，并答记者问。（摄影 / 郁致原）

2016 年 4 月 20 日，江苏省版权局发布了 2014 年度江苏省版权产业的经济贡献调查结果。2014 年，江苏省版权产业增加值突破 5 000 亿元大关，达 5 407.83 亿元，占当年江苏省 GDP 的 8.31%。（摄影 / 万进萍）

2016 年世界知识产权宣传周期间，山西省版权管理部门在部分市的城市广场、图书馆门前、主要街区以举行版权宣传活动启动仪式、摆放宣传展板、发放宣传资料、现场解答问题等多种方式，宣传版权法律知识。（摄影 / 郝子谋）

2016 年 4 月 23 日，四川省版权局、成都市文广新局、锦江区政府联合举办四川地区 2016 年世界读书与版权日活动启动仪式，活动现场为中小学生及文创产业单位作品创作者代表颁发作品登记证书。（摄影 / 王志坚）

2016 年 4 月 23 日，广西壮族自治区版权局在广西民族大学举办广西纪念世界知识产权日版权进校园活动。（摄影 / 杨训国）

2016 年 4 月 26 日，国家版权局在京举办中国网络版权保护大会。工信部、公安部、国家网信办等相关部门负责人及来自版权产业界的代表，共同探讨了“数字网络发展与版权保护”等热点话题。（摄影 / 郁致原）

2016年4月26日，2016中国网络版权保护大会与会领导为部分获得2015年度查处侵权盗版案件有功单位及个人荣誉的版权执法人员进行颁奖。（摄影 / 郁致原）

2016年4月26日，2016中国网络版权保护大会发布了2015中国网络版权保护年度报告。（摄影 / 郁致原）

2016 年 4 月 26 日，北京市版权局组织开展了以“大局观　使命感　新起点”为主题的世界知识产权日宣传周主题活动暨第六届音乐版权保护与产业发展论坛。邀请来自行业协会、唱片公司、音乐网站、法律服务机构、学术研究机构的专家学者以及音乐人代表对如何加强数字音乐版权保护，推动付费下载，建立音乐产业发展的新模式和新机制等方面进行交流探讨。（摄影 / 赵晓鹏）

2016年4月26日，河北省新闻出版广电（版权）局组织开展了“保护版权　鼓励创新”校园签名宣传活动。河北省政协副主席段惠军，省新闻出版广电（版权）局局长李晓明、副局长王智，石家庄市政府有关领导，河北外国语学院师生及省内主要新闻媒体的记者，著作权人代表等 2 000 余人参加了签名活动。（摄影 / 李冬群）

2016年4月26日，为推动版权保护在辽宁全省文博系统中的广泛开展和深化普及，辽宁省版权局在沈阳故宫举办沈阳故宫博物院版权工作站揭牌仪式。（摄影/田大鹏）

2016年4月27日，山东省版权局考察山东版权示范单位——淄博市华光陶瓷集团有限公司。（摄影/高睿）

2016年5月23—25日，由世界知识产权组织（WIPO）与中国国家版权局主办，韩国文化体育观光部与中国陕西省版权局协办的“版权和相关权热点问题亚太地区研讨会”在西安举行。（摄影/赖名芳）

2016年6月13日，四川省版权局、四川省国资委联合检查组对9家省属国有企业软件正版化工作情况进行检查验收，图为检查组听取四川省能源投资集团有限责任公司软件正版化工作汇报。（摄影/王志坚）

2016 年 7 月 7 日，吉林省版权局举办 2016 年度省级机关单位软件正版化工作培训，85 家省级党政机关单位相关负责人参加了培训。（摄影 / 田庆权）

2016年7月12日，国家版权局联合国家网信办、工信部、公安部在京召开新闻发布会，宣布正式启动“剑网 2016”专项行动，突出整治三类作品、重点查处四个平台、规范巩固三个成果。（摄影 / 郁致原）

2016年8月15日，四川省版权局、成都市版权局、成都市龙泉驿区版权局组成联合检查组，对中国（成都）艺库文创产业园区（四川省版权示范园区、全国版权示范园区）版权示范创建工作实施检查考核。（摄影/王志坚）

2016年8月26日，国家版权局副局长阎晓宏（右一）在京会见了英国能源及知识产权国务大臣娜薇尔·露芙（左一）女男爵一行。双方回顾了《中英版权战略合作谅解备忘录》签署以来的工作成果，并就版权立法、执法、产业发展、集体管理等问题交换了意见。（摄影/郁致原）

2016 年 9 月 19 日，网络文学版权保护研讨会在北京举行，国家版权局就发布加强网络文学作品版权管理有关通知征求意见，中国网络文学版权联盟宣布成立。（摄影 / 郁致原）

2016 年 10 月 25 日，天津市版权局召开天津市版权示范单位、示范园区授牌会议。向获得荣誉称号的 7 家企业颁发了“版权示范单位、示范园区”牌匾。（摄影 / 张倩）

2016年11月18日，《人民日报》、《经济日报》、人民网、新华网、中央电视台等17家中央媒体记者与重庆市文化市场行政执法总队、市版权局以及重庆日报报业集团就版权工作进行了学习交流。（摄影/熊明）

2016年11月25日，由中国版权协会主办的第九届中国版权年会在京举行。第三届中国版权卓越成就者奖、中国版权最具影响力企业奖颁奖仪式同时举行。（摄影/郁致原）

2016年11月30日，国家版权局在京召开“网络广告联盟服务版权保护工作座谈会”，通报了国家版权局规范网络广告联盟版权秩序的有关工作情况，调查确定了第一批侵权盗版网站“黑名单”，大型网络广告联盟发起《网络广告联盟版权自律倡议》。（摄影／郁致原）

2016年12月5—6日，2016年国际版权论坛在广州举行。本届论坛由世界知识产权组织（WIPO）与中国国家版权局共同主办，以“版权 创新 发展”为主题，旨在汇集海内外版权界杰出代表，共同探讨版权与创新在文化与经济发展中的作用以及如何促进和保护创新以推动版权产业发展，共同为推动国际版权多元化合作进行了深入探讨和交流。（摄影／郁致原）

2016年12月5日上午，第六届中国国际版权博览会在广州开幕。本届博览会以“展示版权成果、促进版权保护、引领产业发展”为主题，由国家新闻出版广电总局（国家版权局）主办，广州市人民政府、广东省新闻出版广电局（版权局）承办，主宾国为英国。（摄影/郁致原）

2016年12月5日，中国国家新闻出版广电总局（国家版权局）副局长阎晓宏（左一）、世界知识产权组织副总干事王彬颖（右一）在第六届中国国际版权博览会上为获得“2016中国版权金奖作品奖”的获奖者颁奖。（摄影/郁致原）

2016年12月6日，在全国版权社会服务工作交流会上，国家版权局与会领导为获得“全国版权示范单位”称号的单位授牌。（摄影 / 郁致原）

2016年12月22日，国家版权局、国家网信办、工信部、公安部在京联合召开“剑网2016”专项行动总结会。来自全国31个省（区、市）版权局、4个直辖市文化市场执法总队的相关负责人以及几十家版权从业企业代表参加了会议。（摄影 / 郁致原）

中国版权年鉴

2017

（总第九卷）

中国版权年鉴编委会　编

中国人民大学出版社
·北京·

图书在版编目（CIP）数据

中国版权年鉴. 2017/中国版权年鉴编委会编. —北京：中国人民大学出版社，2018.1
ISBN 978-7-300-25578-1

Ⅰ.①中… Ⅱ.①中… Ⅲ.①版权-中国-2017-年鉴 Ⅳ.①D923.41-54

中国版本图书馆 CIP 数据核字（2018）第 031312 号

中国版权年鉴 2017（总第九卷）
中国版权年鉴编委会　编
Zhongguo Banquan Nianjian 2017

出版发行　中国人民大学出版社
社　　址　北京中关村大街 31 号　　**邮政编码**　100080
电　　话　010－62511242（总编室）　010－62511770（质管部）
010－82501766（邮购部）　010－62514148（门市部）
010－62515195（发行公司）　010－62515275（盗版举报）
网　　址　http：//www.crup.com.cn
http://www.ttrnet.com（人大教研网）
经　　销　新华书店
印　　刷　涿州市星河印刷有限公司
规　　格　210 mm×297 mm　16 开本　　**版　　次**　2018 年 1 月第 1 版
印　　张　37.25 插页 61　　**印　　次**　2018 年 1 月第 1 次印刷
字　　数　1 234 000　　**定　　价**　300.00 元
广告经营许可证　京海工商广字第 0086 号

《中国版权年鉴2017》编纂委员会

#《中国版权年鉴》特约编辑

（以姓氏笔画为序）

万进萍　江苏省版权局版权管理处主任科员
马永志　广西壮族自治区版权局版权管理处处长
王丹若　中国文字著作权协会办公室主任
王志坚　四川省版权局版权管理处副处长
王培舒　吉林省版权局版权管理处处长
王新民　陕西省版权局版权管理处调研员
左图强　重庆市版权局版权管理处处长
卢文俊　湖北省版权局版权管理处处长
史文霞　中国电影著作权协会秘书长
付成久　青海省文化和新闻出版厅政策法规（版权）处副调研员
朱严政　中国音乐著作权协会信息宣传部主任
朱宝祺　中国摄影著作权协会副总干事
闫　石　黑龙江省版权局版权管理处主任科员
闫　平　文化部政策法规司法制处处长
孙　悦　中国版权协会秘书长
孙　雷　全国人大教科文卫委员会文化室副主任
严庆荣　浙江省版权局版权处处长
李冬群　河北省版权局版权管理处主任科员
李安庆　辽宁省版权局版权法规处处长
杨　剑　安徽省版权局版权管理处处长
杨建新　新疆维吾尔自治区版权局版权管理处副处长
邱建宏　福建省版权局版权管理处处长
邹建华　中国音像著作权集体管理协会常务理事长兼总干事
沈　欣　广东省版权局版权管理处副调研员
宋　亮　湖南省版权局版权管理处副调研员
宋晓明　最高人民法院知识产权审判庭审判长
张　雯　云南省版权局版权管理处处长
张有立　国家版权局版权管理司综合处处长
张百忍　西藏自治区版权局版权管理处处长
张露娜　天津市版权局版权管理处处长
赵　杰　国家版权局版权管理司执法监管处处长
郝　炜　内蒙古自治区版权局版权管理处主任科员
郝　辉　宁夏回族自治区版权局版权管理处副处长
郝子谋　山西省版权局版权管理处主任科员

夏　玲　甘肃省版权局版权管理处处长
徐　梅　贵州省版权局版权管理处副处长
高　睿　山东省版权局版权管理处主任科员
商　超　工业和信息化部信息化和软件服务业司软件产业处处长
韩　露　中国版权保护中心办公室科员
焦艳娜　河南省版权局版权管理处副主任科员
曾伯林　海南省版权局版权处副处长
阙米秋　江西省版权局版权管理处处长
薛　彬　上海市版权局版权管理执法处处长

《中国版权年鉴》编辑部

主　　编： 于慈珂
副 主 编： 段玉萍　白连永　孟　超
编辑部主任： 侍海诗
策划编辑： 王宏霞
责任编辑： 彭理文　王　喆
执行编辑： 刘　刘　李泓阅
装帧设计： 池海玉
广告经营： 肖　力　李玉彬

编纂说明

一、《中国版权年鉴》由国家版权局组织编纂，中国人民大学出版社、中国人民大学国家版权贸易基地编辑出版，是我国唯一全面系统反映全国版权创造、运用、保护和管理基本概貌的大型专业性工具书。本年鉴于2009年创刊，逐年编纂，连续出版，每年一卷，2017年卷为第九卷。

二、本卷年鉴主要汇辑2016年全国版权保护与版权相关产业发展的综合概况、动态信息、文献资料和统计数据，港澳台版权信息及国际版权动态。

三、本卷年鉴采用分类编辑法。根据2016年我国版权创造、运用、保护和管理的基本情况与主要特点，采用类目、分目和条目三个层次的结构，以文章、条目、条文和图表的形式表述。全书共设14个类目，分列38个分目或次分目。

四、本卷年鉴在延续前八卷编纂总体框架下，为实现年鉴的整体性和在有限篇幅里反映高度密集有效信息，对年鉴内容进行了必要的补充及调整，使之方便读者查阅。

1. 特辑：刊登《国务院关于印发"十三五"国家知识产权保护和运用规划的通知》、《国务院办公厅印发〈国务院关于新形势下加快知识产权强国建设的若干意见〉重点任务分工方案的通知》和《国务院办公厅关于印发知识产权综合管理改革试点总体方案的通知》。

2. 专文：刊载国家新闻出版广电总局局长、国家版权局局长聂辰席《在"全球创作者论坛"上的书面致辞》，国家新闻出版广电总局副局长、国家版权局副局长阎晓宏《版权：仍然任重道远》，中南财经政法大学知识产权研究中心主任吴汉东《经济新常态下知识产权的创新、驱动与发展》。

3. 版权工作概览：全面记录2016年我国各级版权行政管理部门、版权司法审判机构及版权管理与社会服务组织开展的版权工作概况。

4. 版权扫描：翔实记载2016年全国版权相关立法、司法、行政管理、宣传教育、交流研讨、社会管理与服务、国际交流与合作、产业发展等方面的动态信息及港澳台版权信息。

5. 版权相关产业与版权贸易：反映2016年我国新闻出版、数字出版、广播电视、电影、软件、动漫、网络游戏等版权相关产业的基本状况与发展趋势，收录《2015年中国版权产业的经济贡献》、《2016年中国新闻出版产业分析报告》及《2016—2017年中国数字出版产业年度报告》等。

6. 典型案例选编：刊登2016年全国著作权司法保护典型案件、2016年度全国打击侵权盗版十大案件、2016年度部分省（自治区、直辖市）著作权典型案件和行政执法典型案件。

7. 法律法规及规章文件：汇辑2016年国家新闻出版广电总局（国家版权局）印发的版权相关工作文件。

8. 年度发布：主要介绍第五届"世界知识产权组织版权金奖（中国）"获奖名单、2016年中国网络版权保护年度报告、2016年度查处侵权盗版案件有功单位及个人、2016 CPCC十大中国著作权人、2016年（第九届）全国大学生版权征文获奖名单、第十五届输出版引进版优秀图书推介活动获奖名单，以及2016年中国版权十件大事。

9. 理论研究：集中反映2016年全国版权领域的理论研究成果。对2016年中国著作权法理论现状进行了梳理和回顾，并特别转载了反映版权界热点问题的11篇学术论文。同时对2016年出版的著作权相关图书进行了简要介绍。

10. 统计资料：收集2016年与版权登记、版权保护、版权管理和版权贸易有关的统计数据，以及新闻出版产业、广播影视产业和软件产业的统计资料。

11. 名录：刊登版权行政管理部门、版权公共服务机构、版权协会、著作权集体管理组织、版权相关行业协会、版权代理公司、国家级版权交易机构及知识产权教学与研究机构最新的通信联络信息。

12. 国际版权动态：作为附录介绍2016年国外版权法律制度发展的最新动向，包括立法与行政、司法判例及业界动态。

13. 索引：采用内容分析和主题词检索的方式，按汉语拼音字母顺序编制本卷内容的主题索引。

14. 宣传广告：以彩色图文展现2016年版权管理相关的重要活动，并宣传展示版权示范城市及版权相关企事业单位。

五、本卷年鉴中所载内容无特别说明外，均按时间先后顺序排列；涉及各省（自治区、直辖市）的内容，均以全国行政区划为序。因组稿条件有限，本卷年鉴未包含香港特别行政区、澳门特别行政区和台湾省的版权工作概况及相关统计数据。

六、本卷年鉴配备双重检索系统：书前刊有详细目录，书后备有内容索引。

七、本卷年鉴中全国版权统计数据由国家版权局版权管理司、国家新闻出版广电总局规划发展司、工业和信息化部信息化和软件服务业司、国家新闻出版广电总局发展研究中心提供；各省（自治区、直辖市）版权局的统计数据由相关版权局领导确认。

八、本卷年鉴同时出版纸质版和电子版（光盘），其中电子版采用多媒体和全文检索技术，并随纸质版附赠；同时发行纸质版和电子版，其中电子版通过国家版权交易网（www.copyrightmall.com）等数字化平台发行。

九、本卷年鉴在组稿和编辑过程中，得到了国家版权局版权管理司、国家新闻出版广电总局规划发展司、中国人民大学知识产权学院、工业和信息化部信息化和软件服务业司、国家新闻出版广电总局发展研究中心、地方版权局版权管理处及其他版权相关单位的大力支持和帮助，在此一并谨致谢意。

十、因为编辑部人员的水平和能力所限，本卷年鉴中定存有疏漏与错误之处，诚请版权界同仁和广大读者给予批评、指正。

目　录

特　辑

国务院关于印发“十三五”国家知识产权保护和运用规划的通知（国发［2016］86号） 3

国务院办公厅印发《国务院关于新形势下加快知识产权强国建设的若干意见》重点任务分工方案的通知（国办函［2016］66号） 14

国务院办公厅关于印发知识产权综合管理改革试点总体方案的通知（国办发［2016］106号） 21

专　文

在“全球创作者论坛”上的书面致辞　国家新闻出版广电总局局长　国家版权局局长　聂辰席 27

版权：仍然任重道远　国家新闻出版广电总局副局长　国家版权局副局长　阎晓宏 28

经济新常态下知识产权的创新、驱动与发展　中南财经政法大学知识产权研究中心主任　吴汉东 32

版权工作概览

2016年全国版权工作 39

2016年全国版权行政管理工作　国家版权局版权管理司 39

2016年全国版权司法保护工作　最高人民法院知识产权审判庭 42

2016年地方版权工作 45

北京市　赵晓鹏 45

天津市　张　倩 46

河北省　李冬群 48

山西省　郝子谋 50

内蒙古自治区　郝　炜 52

辽宁省　李安庆 54

吉林省　王培舒 56

黑龙江省　闫　石 58

上海市　王　骞 60

江苏省　万进萍 61

浙江省　严庆荣 63

安徽省　汪闻敏 65

福建省 郑开辟 67
江西省 钟　娜 69
山东省 高　睿 72
河南省 焦艳娜 75
湖北省 张　威 76
湖南省 宋　亮 78
广东省 沈　欣 79
广西壮族自治区 杨训国 82
海南省 曾伯林 84
重庆市 汤裕洁 86
四川省 王志坚 88
贵州省 徐　梅 91
云南省 王　成 92
西藏自治区 周祥祎 93
陕西省 王新民 95
甘肃省 夏　玲 95
青海省 付成久 98
宁夏回族自治区 郝　辉 100
新疆维吾尔自治区 杨建新 101

2016 年版权公共服务机构与社会服务组织工作 103
中国版权保护中心 张文娟 103
中国版权协会 王自强 108
中国音乐著作权协会 张　群 110
中国音像著作权集体管理协会 李　婧 113
中国文字著作权协会 张洪波 115
中国摄影著作权协会 朱宝祺 119
中国电影著作权协会 史文霞 121
中国互联网协会网络版权联盟 陈　颖 122

版权扫描

版权界动态 129
立　法 129
中摄权协受邀参加国务院修法研讨会 129
国务院同意建立知识产权战略实施工作部际联席会议制度 129

司　法 129
《奔跑吧兄弟》官微涉著作权纠纷 129
北京三男子因架设“私服”侵犯游戏《笑傲江湖 OL》著作权罪被判刑 130
四川省阆中市审结两起制售盗版音像制品刑事案 130
手游《幻想江湖》被判侵犯著作权 130
“大头儿子”著作权案二审央视胜诉 131
海淀法院：影视聚合平台盗链行为不属于合理使用 131

手游公司擅用金庸小说内容被判侵权　131
乐动卓越起诉昆仑万维“MT 游戏”侵权，法院判决昆仑万维停止不正当竞争行为　132
《QQ 阅读》借势营销《明妃传》被叫停　132
音乐剧《断桥》版权之争结束　133
银川破获全国首起手游侵犯著作权案　133
漫画《蜡笔小新》遭盗播　权利人起诉　133
擅用金庸武侠作品元素　游戏公司败诉赔偿百万元　134
网店售卖画像复制品侵权　卖家被判赔偿著作权人 4.5 万元　134
齐白石后人与湖南美术出版社著作权系列纠纷案达成和解　134
首例电竞直播侵权案终审宣判　135
百度云盘擅传《金陵十三钗》被判赔偿　135
爱奇艺诉华数传媒侵权索赔 30 万元　135
《开心消消乐》游戏引发系列权利纷争　136
导航地图侵权案新进展：第三方公司称奇虎已获授权　136
三男子印刷逾 25 万册高仿盗版教辅书　案值超 700 万元　137
迪士尼等起诉国产动画电影《汽车人总动员》侵权　137
《中国好声音》版权纠纷激化　影响唐德影视业绩　137
《九层妖塔》侵权案宣判：未侵犯保护作品完整权　138
天津 IPTV 被诉侵权　遭索赔 2 000 万元　138
“童话大王”郑渊洁声讨网络店铺侵权　139
乐视诉电视猫“盗链”侵权获赔 50 万元　139
“哆啦 A 梦”诉《叮咚小区》侵权败诉　140
蜻蜓 FM《香火》被判侵权　140
五起《漫画帮》著作权侵权案宣判　141
4 家游戏公司被指侵犯金庸作品改编权　141
《女医·明妃传》陷版权纠纷　掌阅告阅文索赔 100 万元　141
华为被诉侵犯漫画作品版权　142
作家刘心武诉世纪超星侵权　142
胡巴款定制 T 恤引发侵权纠纷　142
页游《青云志》被诉侵犯《诛仙》游戏改编权　143
侵权网站 BT 天堂站长被刑拘　143
《美人制造》著作权纠纷案宣判　143
《芈月传》编剧署名纠纷案一审宣判　143
青岛“5·16”非法期刊经营案告破　144

行政管理　144
国家版权局 2016 年共发布七批重点（影视）作品预警名单　144
北京查获特大网络销售盗版图书案　144
五部门联合下发通知：严打高校周边复印店盗版活动　145
四川省发布《关于加强互联网领域侵权假冒行为治理的实施意见》　145
国家版权局公布 2015 年中国版权十件大事　146
安徽省版权局下发《关于开展广播电视节目版权专项检查活动的通知》　146
《吉林省加强互联网领域侵权假冒行为治理实施方案》下发　146
推进使用正版软件工作部际联席会议第五次全体会议在京召开　146

上海召开推进使用正版软件工作会议 147
合肥开展“2016 扫霾”专项突击检查行动 147
北京“12318”查扣非法出版物、盗版光盘逾 200 万件 147
《2016 年全国知识产权系统执法维权工作方案》印发 147
《2015 年北京知识产权保护状况白皮书》发布 148
2015 年中国知识产权发展状况发布会举行 148
国务院办公厅印发《2016 年全国打击侵犯知识产权和制售假冒伪劣商品工作要点》 148
国家版权局奖励查处侵权盗版案件有功单位及个人 149
辽宁省版权局与京版十五社反盗版联盟签署战略合作协议 149
国家版权局公布打击侵权盗版年度十大案件 150
江苏省镇江市警方破获特大网络制售盗版图书侵权案 150
重庆市文化委、公安局协作打击侵权盗版 150
北京市 2016 年国家机关软件正版化工作全面启动 150
国家新闻出版广电总局发布通知规范移动游戏管理 151
广电总局发布《关于进一步明确进口用于出版的音像制品审批工作相关要求的通知》 151
国家新闻出版广电总局发出《关于大力推动广播电视节目自主创新工作的通知》 151
内蒙古鄂托克旗开展侵权盗版及非法出版物集中销毁活动 152
四部门启动“剑网 2016”专项活动 152
粤港保护知识产权合作专责小组第十五次会议在广州召开 152
聂辰席任国家新闻出版广电总局局长、国家版权局局长 153
北京市版权局再次联合业内企业打击侵权盗版手游 153
阎晓宏赴上海美术电影制片厂调研 153
国家版权局发布《关于加强网络文学作品版权管理的通知》 153
《关于完善产权保护制度依法保护产权的意见》发布 153
国家新闻出版广电总局引入水印技术，强化电影版权保护 153
“剑网 2016”专项行动总结会在京召开 154
国家版权局等四部门通报 21 起“剑网 2016”专项行动典型网络侵权盗版案件 154

宣传教育 155
四川为蜀绣作品免费登记著作权 155
公众号著作权侵权投诉文字作品超六成 155
第四届青岛市版权年会暨版权培训会日前召开 155
江苏泰州开展摄影作品著作权保护培训 155
阅文集团报告显示“90 后”网络作家逐渐崛起 155
2015CPCC 十大中国著作权人评选揭晓 156
长沙市举办网络著作权行政执法培训班 156
武汉开展高校版权专题辩论赛 156
广西举行版权进校园活动 156
“创意广州·梦想飞翔”2016 版权宣传活动在穗举行 157
《2015 年中国网络版权保护年度报告》发布 157
“十二五”期间中国完成软件著作权登记 92 万余件 157
宁夏举办全区党政机关软件正版化工作培训班 158
2016 版权宣传周宣传资料发布 158
国际版权贸易培训班在京举办 158
《2016 体育创业白皮书》关注电竞媒体赛事版权 158

成都在全国率先培训出“双证”文创人才 159
2016 年全国作品登记工作培训班在京举行 159
中国版权协会 2016 年第一期版权培训班成功举办 159
《2015 年新闻出版产业分析报告》发布 159
“助力原创　保护版权”全球公共艺术倡议行动启动 160
第八届中国国际影视动漫版权保护和贸易博览会闭幕 160
山东省即墨市启动首届优秀版权作品大赛 161
国家版权局率 17 家中央媒体记者学习交流重报集团版权维权工作 161
多位文艺创作者获“中国版权卓越成就者”奖 162
2016 中国版权金奖在广州颁发 162
“深圳版权金奖”举行颁奖典礼 162

交流研讨 163
“影视创作从依法保护原创开始”座谈会在京举办 163
“网络音乐版权保护与商业模式”研讨会在京召开 163
“互联网环境下传统出版版权保护与国际版权贸易高级研修班”在沪举办 163
2016 CPCC 中国版权服务年会在京举行 163
首届中国知识产权保护高层论坛举办 164
版权人沙龙聚焦互联网内容平台版权保护与管理 164
三家著作权集体管理组织走进清华研讨热点话题 165
中国网络版权保护大会在北京召开 165
版权相关热点问题媒体研修班在北京开班 165
互联网版权保护与运营新媒体论坛在京举行 166
2016 移动互联网创新大会关注版权开发 166
“一带一路”知识产权高级别会议召开 167
“保护视听表演对文化和创意产业发展的重要性圆桌会议”在京举行 167
中日著作权研讨会在沪举行 168
“APP 及广告联盟相关版权侵权问题研讨会”在京举行 168
2016 年 BIBF 国际版权贸易高级研修班在京举行 169
“一带一路”高峰合作论坛推版权输出 169
2016 中国互联网法治大会在京召开 169
2016 第一届“文化+”新创意新业态新经济论坛举办 170
“大数据安全·互联网新闻出版和数字资产沙龙”举行 170
标准推广与标准版权保护推进会在厦门举行 170
第九届中国版权年会在京召开 171
国家版权局召开“网络广告联盟服务版权保护工作座谈会” 171
2016 年全国版权社会服务工作交流会在广州召开 172
AIPPI 中国分会版权热点论坛举行 172

社会管理与服务 173
四川部分市实行作品登记免费服务 173
中国出版协会六届六次常务理事会召开 173
国家版权贸易基地（越秀）打造版权综合服务平台 173
《老爷车中国行》羊城举行版权授权仪式 173
安徽省版权保护协会选举换届 174

广东省新闻出版广播影视（版权）工作会议在穗举行 174
民进中央召开两会新闻通气会　拟提交版权相关提案 174
移动 APP 第三方证书签名与版权登记联合服务平台正式上线 174
江西省成立首家知识产权仲裁中心 175
江苏张家港推两项版权评审奖励办法 175
北京版权保护协会成立“网络工委” 175
长沙市举办网络著作权行政执法培训班 175
京津冀知识产权发展联盟正式成立 176
广西：下放版权登记权限　桂林人可在本市申请版权 176
“版权云北京之夜暨 426so 平台上线周年庆”在京召开 176
广州首聘版权咨询专家 177
版权师培养计划在京启动 177
中国版权保护中心 DCI 体系再拓新应用 177
烟台建立山东首个著作权纠纷诉调对接机制 177
百度关闭文学类贴吧清查盗版侵权获国家版权局肯定 178
重庆版权交易中心揭牌 178
陕西建成线上代理版权登记平台 178
中国版权保护中心西南版权登记大厅在成都开业运行 178
中国版权协会艺术品版权工作委员会成立 179
首个民族文化版权交易中心落户顺义 179
上海宝山区版权服务工作站揭牌 179
数字版权保护技术研发工程应用在京签约 180
文著协与《读者》签订稿酬收转协议 180
中国版权协会与冠勇科技签署战略合作意向书 180
中国出版数字资源国际交易平台启动 180
少儿出版反盗版联盟在北京成立 181
“西部丝路版权交易平台”在京正式启动 181
“2016 剑网行动·原创文字作品保护月”正式启动 181
重庆文创协会版权登记服务中心成立 181
全国“版权云”体验店授牌仪式在太原举行 181
成都市建立首批版权服务工作站 182
苏州市吴江区成立首个市级版权工作站 182
摄著协推出“摄影家银行卡”加强摄影作品版权保护 182
苏州市版权培训基地揭牌成立 182
深圳罗湖区政府与中国版权保护中心签约设立粤港澳版权登记大厅 183
河北省版权局、河北省版权保护中心在曲阳设立版权服务站 183
中山市设立版权专项资金 184
首个国家网络版权产业研究基地落户腾讯 184
数字版权保护技术研发工程竣工 184
第十五届输出版引进版优秀图书推介活动名单公布 185

国际交流与合作 185
中以签署文学和翻译领域合作谅解备忘录 185
2016 新德里世界书展中国代表团版权贸易成果丰硕 186
阎晓宏率代表团访问埃及并参加开罗国际书展 186

中捷建立战略伙伴关系共同保护知识产权 186
中国图书受突尼斯读者欢迎 187
中国展团重磅亮相博洛尼亚童书展 187
外文出版社伦敦书展版权输出成绩显著 187
“数字环境下影视产业版权保护圆桌会议”在北京举行 187
中英探索建立双语侵权举报平台 188
2016 美国书展中国展团盛装参展 188
第十二届中韩版权研讨会在韩举行 188
“版权和相关权热点问题亚太地区研讨会”在西安举行 188
中韩图书版权交易会在南昌举行 189
中俄两大电影节在俄签署战略合作仪式 189
蔡赴朝会见世界知识产权组织总干事高锐一行 189
中美著作权最新发展研讨会在京召开 190
阎晓宏会见查德·康斯坦德、洪伟典一行 190
“2016 中韩出版合作论坛”在京举行 190
阎晓宏会见英国能源及知识产权国务大臣娜薇尔·露芙一行 191
第 29 届莫斯科国际书展中俄出版机构达成多项合作 191
467 种中国新书亮相第 23 届东京国际书展 191
《婴儿画报》《幼儿画报》向美国输出版权 192
华中国际版权高峰论坛聚焦现代版权产业发展 192
首个中国主题图书翻译出版中心在蒙古国成立 192
德化经验 全球共享 192
中国出版亮相罗马尼亚 193
全球创作者论坛在京举办 193
2016 年国际版权论坛聚焦“版权 创新 发展” 194
逾 6 800 万美元国际动漫版权合作协议在苏州签署 194
中罗文字著作权集体管理组织展开合作 194

产业发展 194
万达 35 亿美元并购美国传奇影业 194
国产电影全球发行平台启动 195
唐德影视购买好声音版权 195
爱奇艺与 20 世纪福克斯合作拓展网络版权 195
美团猫眼电影首推电影票在线改签 覆盖近 2 000 家影院 195
县城影院呈现超速度增长势头 195
熙颐影业收购国际版权销售公司 196
南北两大影视版权交易平台达成战略合作 196
天涯社区携手中大中文系打造全国大学生影视剧本创作平台 196
腾讯“芒种计划”打造媒体生态圈 196
华人文化入股好莱坞 196
光影音乐网站正式上线 196
中国取代美国成为最大文化产品出口国 197
阿里巴巴 238 亿元收购优酷土豆所有股份 197
楚楚街与乐视斥资亿元共建音乐产业新生态 197
中南传媒搭建 IP 全版权运营平台 197

艺恩咨询发布《2015—2016 中国电影产业报告》 198
750 部电视剧亮相 2016 春季北京电视节目交易会 198
IFPI 2016 全球音乐报告发布 198
2015 年中国游戏产业规模达到 1 407 亿元 198
中超天价版权催生“网台联动” 199
2015 年专利、商标、版权质押融资达 931.72 亿元 199
北京国数与北青社合力打造数字产业服务平台 199
第十二届中国国际动漫节交易额逾 151 亿元 199
阿里影业投资大地影院 199
乐视票务平台多元运营挖掘体育赛事版权价值 200
中国资本拿下英国足球版权巨头 200
中国电影衍生品产业联盟成立 200
腾讯、微影 8 500 万美元投资韩国 YG 娱乐 200
腾讯泛娱乐开发深挖儿童出版内容版权价值 200
豆瓣阅读开卖原创故事作品影视改编权 200
暴风体育获得中超新媒体版权 201
我国出版版权输出总量 8 年增 3 倍 201
腾讯 86 亿美元收购 Supercell，开拓网游大时代 201
北京打通动漫游戏产业链 201
乐视成立 CDLA 产业联盟 201
掌阅科技与时尚集团开展版权合作 202
我国数字出版产业规模突破 4 400 亿元 202
一铭软件推动中国—东盟基础软件生态合作 202
百度开放云助力国家新闻出版打造智能数字出版体系 202
乐视 20 亿美金收购美国最大智能电视厂商 202
今日头条战略投资东方 IC 203
“哈利·波特”系列电子书首次在中国发售 203
乐视云发布多款云产品 203
版权为桥——有声出版火起来 203
第 23 届北京国际图书博览会闭幕 204
中国网络文学版权联盟成立 204
青岛出版集团成功并购日本渡边淳一文学馆 204
第九届中国国际漫画节落幕 204
第九届中国家纺画稿交易会在南通举行 205
《2016 中国音乐产业发展报告》发布 205
阿里巴巴海外购得独家版权 205
首份产经媒体融合发展报告发布 205
网络游戏反盗版和产业保护联盟在京成立 206
人民网与各党报新媒体发起党报新媒体版权联盟 206
大优酷与东方梦工厂达成顶级家庭娱乐内容版权合作协议 206
我国视频付费市场规模突破 10 亿元大关 206

港澳台版权信息 207

香　港 207

知识产权署推出有关版权保护新电视宣传短片 207

香港海关侦破“点对点”发放怀疑侵权电视节目案件 207
香港海关打击分发侵权课程教材 207
香港政府建议修订《仲裁条例》 207
泛珠三角区域深化知识产权合作协议 208

台 湾 208
出口视听著作及代工激光唱片不用申请核验文件 208
2016 海峡两岸知识产权法学论坛成果报道 209

澳 门 209
澳门贸促局促中小企业利用知识产权优势勇闯内地市场 209

版权相关产业与版权贸易

2015 年中国版权产业的经济贡献 中国版权产业经济贡献调研课题组 213
2016 年中国新闻出版产业分析报告 国家新闻出版广电总局 218
2016—2017 年中国数字出版产业发展报告 中国数字出版产业年度报告课题组 246
2016 年中国广播电视产业发展报告 国家新闻出版广电总局发展研究中心 252
2016 年中国电影产业发展报告 国家新闻出版广电总局发展研究中心 263
2016 年中国动漫产业发展报告 牛兴侦 269
2016 年中国软件产业发展概况 孙占峰 朱 振 277
2016 年中国网络游戏市场分析 易观智库 283

典型案件选编

2016 年全国著作权司法保护典型案件 295

2016 年度打击侵权盗版十大案件 303

“剑网 2016”专项行动 21 起典型案件 306

部分省（区、市）公布的 2016 年度著作权典型案件 309
北京 309
天津 309
辽宁 310
吉林 310
黑龙江 311
上海 312
江苏 313
浙江 313
安徽 314
福建 315
河南 316

湖北 316
湖南 319
广东 319
广西 320
海南 320
云南 321
新疆 321

2016 年地方著作权行政执法案件 322
河北省 322
辽宁省 323
吉林省 323
上海市 325
江苏省 328
安徽省 329
江西省 329
山东省 331
湖北省 333
湖南省 333
四川省 335
陕西省 336
青海省 337

法律法规及规章文件

规章文件 341
关于废止部分规章和规范性文件的决定
（中华人民共和国国家版权局令第 12 号） 341
关于开展打击网络侵权盗版“剑网 2016”专项行动的通知
（国版发［2016］2 号） 341
关于规范作品登记证书的通知
（国版函［2016］1 号） 343
关于印发《2015 年推进使用正版软件工作总结》
和《2016 年推进使用正版软件工作计划》的通知
（国版函［2016］2 号） 344
国家版权局关于奖励 2015 年度查处侵权盗版案件有功单位及有功个人的决定
（国版函［2016］4 号） 349
国家版权局关于公布 2015 年度全国打击侵权盗版十大案件的通知
（国版函［2016］5 号） 359
关于禁止未经授权通过网络传播中央电视台 2016 年春节联欢晚会的通知
（国版办发［2016］3 号） 361
关于 2015 年全国著作权登记情况的通报
（国版办发［2016］4 号） 362
关于国家版权监管平台（二期）第一阶段著作权登记项目运行有关事项的通知

（国版办发［2016］5号） 363
关于做好2016年推进软件正版化有关工作的通知
（国版办发［2016］7号） 364
关于公布第一批全国版权执法监管培训师资库人员名单的通知
（国版办发［2016］8号） 365
关于印发《正版软件管理工作指南》的通知
（国版办发［2016］13号） 366
关于“剑网2016”专项行动第一批网络侵权盗版案件查办情况的通报
（国版办发［2016］15号） 366
关于同意在深圳市腾讯计算机系统有限公司设立“网络版权产业研究基地”的复函
（国版办函［2016］41号） 367
关于印发《2016年全国新闻出版（版权）打击侵权假冒工作要点》的通知
（新广出办函［2016］198号） 368

年度发布

第五届“世界知识产权组织版权金奖（中国）”获奖名单 373
2016年中国网络版权保护年度报告 377
2016年度查处侵权盗版案件有功单位及个人 387
2016年中国版权十件大事 398
2016 CPCC十大中国著作权人 400
2016年（第九届）全国大学生版权征文获奖名单 403
第十五届输出版、引进版优秀图书推介活动获奖名单 407

理论研究

2016年著作权法研究综述 向 波 415

2016年著作权热点问题研究 424
民间文学艺术作品的保护机制探讨 管亨鹰 424
从知识产权司法需求论我国民法典的编纂 李 琛 427
竞争与垄断：我国著作权集体管理组织的模式选择 林秀芹 黄钱欣 431
论著作权法语境中的作品结构
——以中小学教辅对教材进行“结构性使用”为例 卢海君 436
实用艺术作品交叉保护的证成与潜在风险之化解 吕炳斌 440
比较与选择：互联网环境中作品复制权的重构
——以临时复制为视角 孟兆平 443
论二次创作的著作权法规制与保障 唐 艳 447
论体育赛事现场直播画面的著作权保护
——兼评“凤凰网赛事转播案” 王 迁 451
避风港原则前沿问题研究
——以“通知—删除”作为诉讼前置程序展开 徐 明 457

美术作品的表达及其实质相似的认定　杨雄文　王沁荷　460
网络著作权侵权中“直接侵权主体”判断的规范构成
——以“私人复制例外”的合法范围确定为中心　张　鹏　464

2016 年著作权相关图书简介　468

统计资料

2016 年中国版权统计资料　479
2016 年全国作品登记情况统计　479
2016 年全国版权合同情况统计　480
2016 年全国版权执法情况统计　481
2016 年版权输出地汇总表　481
2016 年版权引进地汇总表　482

2016 年中国新闻出版产业统计资料　483
2016 年全国各地区图书出版总量　483
2016 年全国各级报纸出版数量　484
2016 年全国各地区各类期刊出版的种数、印数、总印张、总金额（1）　486
2016 年全国各地区各类期刊出版的种数、印数、总印张、总金额（2）　488
2016 年全国各地区录音制品出版品种、数量及发行总量（按载体形式分类）　490
2016 年全国各地区录像制品出版品种、数量及发行总量（按载体形式分类）　492
2016 年全国新华书店系统、出版社自办发行单位出版物发行进、销、存情况　494
2016 年全国图书、期刊、报纸进出口情况　495
2016 年全国音像、电子出版物、数字出版物进出口情况　495

2016 年中国广播影视产业统计资料　496
2016 年全国广播电视发展主要指标一览表（1）　496
2016 年全国广播电视发展主要指标一览表（2）　498

2016 年中国软件产业统计资料　500
2016 年全国软件产业统计数据　500

名　录

版权行政管理部门　503
版权公共服务机构　507
版权协会　508
著作权集体管理组织　511
版权相关行业协会　512
版权代理公司　512
国家级版权交易机构　513
知识产权教学与研究机构　514

附录：国际版权动态

综　述 519
著作权在数字时代的保护与限制
——2016年国际著作权法制发展回顾 519

2016年国际版权动态 527
立法与行政 527
2016年度美国版权政策概览 527
欧盟委员会（COE）保护表达自由和隐私的网络中立指南 527
欧盟法院：链接到盗版内容的行为本身不侵犯著作权 528
英国提议加强网络知识产权保护 528
欧盟有权批准《马拉喀什条约》的意见或将被打破 529
澳大利亚生产力委员会提倡合理使用，重新激起版权大战 530

司法判例 531
威秀集团与福斯电视台为屏蔽盗版网站提起诉讼 531
澳大利亚联邦法院认定数字数据信号不受版权保护 532
美国：联邦版权法不能取代对商业秘密的保护 532
纽约州法院：天狼星公司无须向1972年之前的音乐的表演者付费 533
日本“扫描书籍”营业者，因涉嫌侵犯著作权被逮捕 533

业界动态 534
知识共享组织：版权的另一面是什么？ 534
贝宝出于版权问题考量停止支持VPN和智能DNS服务提供商的支付功能 534
知识产权及创新等事项被纳入TRIPs理事会例会议程 535
联合国教科文组织关于文化贸易的报道 535
《我们要战胜一切》歌曲版权争议 536
WIPO召开知识产权及发展里程碑会议 536
世界知识产权组织传统知识委员会同意就修订的草案做进一步讨论 537
新西兰音乐产业要求改变TPP中的版权条款 537
美国《数字千年版权法》对网络服务提供商提出的避风港版权代理新要求 538
图书馆和档案馆呼吁WIPO成员制定避风港规则 538
俄罗斯网络盗版力争上游之下的力量角逐 540
澳大利亚学校因避风港计划出错而违反TPP版权规则 540
知识共享组织在WIPO：支持更公平的教学研究版权政策 541
WIPO：追续权——纠正版权收入不平衡的方式 542
WIPO对自身所有出版物使用知识共享许可 542
欧盟理事会同意消除电子商务地域屏蔽 543
关于ASKA的未发表歌曲的作曲泄露问题之著作权法上的思考 543
音乐产业集团一致呼吁特朗普的支持 544
未确定的盗版索赔不应导致切断互联网 544
USTR谴责窃取流媒体资源的行为，新的“恶名市场”报告点名阿里巴巴 545

索　　引

索引　546

宣传广告

2016 版权工作展示
广告

Contents

Specials

Notice of Printing and Issuing Plan for Protection and Application of Intellectual Property Rights in the 13th Five-Year Plan by the State Council (Guo Fa [2016] No. 86) 3
Notice of Key Task-Assigning Plan of Printing and Issuing *Several Opinions on Accelerating the Building of a Powerful Power of Intellectual Property in the New Situation* by GOSC (Guo Ban Han [2016] No. 66) 14
Notice of Printing and Issuing Overall Plan for Pilot Reform Project of IPR Management by GOSC (Guo Ban Fa [2016] No. 106) 21

Special Articles

Written Speech at World Creators Forum
Nie Chenxi, Director of the State Administration of Press, Publication, Radio, Film and Television of the People's Republic of China (SARFT) and Director of National Copyright Administration of the P. R. C. (NCAC) 27
Copyright: Still a Long Way to Go
Yan Xiaohong, Deputy Director of SARFT and Deputy Director of NCAC 28
Innovation, Drive and Development of Intellectual Property under New Normal Economy
Wu Handong, Director of Intellectual Property Research (IPR) Center, Zhongnan University of Economics and Law 32

Copyright Work Overview

National Copyright Work in 2016 39
National Copyright Administration Management Work in 2016
Copyright Management Division, NCAC 39
National Judicial Protection of Copyright in 2016
Intellectual Property Division, Supreme People's Court of China 42

Local Copyright Work in 2016 45
Beijing Zhao Xiaopeng 45
Tianjin Zhang Qian 46
Hebei Li Dongqun 48

Shanxi Hao Zimou 50
Inner Mongolia Autonomous Region Hao Wei 52
Liaoning Li Anqing 54
Jilin Wang Peishu 56
Heilongjiang Yan Shi 58
Shanghai Wang Qian 60
Jiangsu Wan Jinping 61
Zhejiang Yan Qingrong 63
Anhui Wang Wenmin 65
Fujian Zheng Kaipi 67
Jiangxi Zhong Na 69
Shandong Gao Rui 72
Henan Jiao Yanna 75
Hubei Zhang Wei 76
Hunan Song Liang 78
Guangdong Shen Xin 79
Guangxi Zhuang Autonomous Region Yang Xunguo 82
Hainan Zeng Belin 84
Chongqing Tang Yujie 86
Sichuan Wang Zhijian 88
Guizhou Xu Mei 91
Yunnan Wang Cheng 92
Tibet Autonomous Region Zhou Xiangyi 93
Shaanxi Wang Xinmin 95
Gansu Xia Ling 95
Qinghai Fu Chengjiu 98
Ningxia Autonomous Region Hao Hui 100
Xinjiang Uygur Autonomous Region Yang Jianxin 101

Public Copyright Service Institution and Social Copyright Service Organization Work in 2016 103
Copyright Protection Center of China Zhang Wenjuan 103
Copyright Society of China Wang Ziqiang 108
Music Copyright Society of China Zhang Qun 110
China Audio-Video Copyright Association Li Jing 113
China Written Works Copyright Society Zhang Hongbo 115
Images Copyright Society of China Zhu Baoqi 119
China Film Copyright Association Shi Wenxia 121
China Copyright Union of Internet Society Chen Ying 122

Copyright Scanning

Trends in Copyright Undertakings 129
Legislation 129

ICSC Invited to Participate in the State Council Seminar on Amending the Laws and Legislation 129
The State Council Approving of the Establishment of an Inter-Ministerial Joint Conference System for the Implementation of the Intellectual Property Strategy 129

Judicial 129
Running Man's official Weibo Involving Copyright Disputes 129
Three Men in Beijing Sentenced Due to Infringement on Copyright of *Swordsman OL* by Setting Private Server 130
Two Criminal Cases of Producing and Selling Pirated Audio-Visual Products Concluded in Langzhong City, Sichuan Province 130
Mobile Phone Game *Jianghu*'s Infringing Copyright Brought into a Verdict 130
CCTV Winning the Second Trail of the "Big Head Son" Copyright Case 131
Beijing Haidian District Court: Hot Linking on Film and Television Platforms Is Unreasonable Use 131
Mobile Phone Games Company Declared Copyright Infringement Due to Using Jin Yong's Novel Content without Permission 131
Locojoy Filing Lawsuit Against Kalends' "MT Games", Accusing It of Copyright Infringement; The Court Judging Kalends to Stop Unfair Competition 132
QQReader's Improper Marketing of *The Imperial Doctress* Asked to Stop 132
The Copyright Dispute of the Musical *Broken Bridge* Ended 133
First Mobile Phone Games Copyright Infringement Case Cracked Down in Yinchuan 133
Copyright Owner of the Comic *Crayon Shinchan* Sued for Pirated Broadcasting 133
Game Company Ordered to Pay Millions of Yuan Due to the Use of Martial from Work of Jin Yong Without Permission 134
Online Shop Seller Who Sells Portrait Replicas Ordered to Pay 45,000 Yuan to the Copyright Owners Due to Copyright Infringement 134
Decendants of Qi Baishi and Hunan Fine Arts Publishing House Reaching a Settlement over Copyright Disputes 134
First Case of IPR Infringement of Live Broadcast of Electronic Games Finally Judged 135
Baidu Cloud Disk Sentenced to Compensation Due to the Uploading of *The Flowers of War* Without Permission 135
iQiYi Suing Wasu 300,000 Yuan for Infringement 135
The Game of *Happy Eliminating Animals* Triggering a Series of Disputes 136
New Developments in Navigation Map Infringement Case: Third-party Company Said Qihoo Has Been Licensed 136
Three Men Printed More than 250,000 Copies of High-quality Pirated Reference Books with Value of Over 7 Million Yuan 137
Disney and Other Proprietors Suing Domestic Animation Movie *The Autobots* for Infringement 137
The Voice of China Copyright Dispute Intensified to Impact the Performance of Talent Film and Television 137
Chronicles of the Ghostly Tribe Infringement Judgment: No Infringement on the Integrity of the Protected Works 138
Tianjin IPTV Sued for 20 Million Yuan in Claim of Infringement 138

Famous Fairy Tales Writer, Zheng Yuanjie, Denouncing Online Shop Infringement 139
LeTV Suing More TV for "Hotlinking" Infringement; Compensated for 500,000 Yuan 139
"Doraemon" Failing in Prosecuting *Ding Dong District* for Infringement 140
Dragonfly FM's *Incense* Adjudicated as Infringement 140
Five *Manga Group* Copyright Infringement Cases Closed 141
Four Game Companies Accused of Violating Adaptation Rights of Jin Yong's Works 141
Against Copyright Infringement of *The Imperial Doctress*, iReader Suing China Reading for 1 Million Yuan 141
Huawei Sued for Infringing Comics Copyrights 142
Author Liu Xinwu Suing Beijing Superstar for Infringement 142
Huba T-shirts Causing Infringement Disputes 142
Webpage Game *The Legend of Chusen* Accused of Infringing Adaptation Rights of *Zhu Xian* Game 143
BT Heaven Webmaster Detained for Infringement 143
The Case of *Cosmetology High* Copyright Dispute Adjudicated 143
First Trial of *The Legend of Miyue*'s Screenwriter Signature Dispute Adjudicated 143
Qingdao "5 • 16" Illegal Journal Dealing Cracked Down 144

Administration 144
NCAC Releasing Seven Pre-Warning Lists of Key Film and TV Shows in 2016 144
Serious Online Sale of Pirated Books Cracked Down in Beijing 144
Five Major National Administrative Divisions Jointly Issuing Notice on Cracking Down on Pirate Activities in Copy Shops around Universities 145
Sichuan Province Releasing *Implementation to Strengthen the Governance of IPR Infringement and Counterfeiting on the Internet* 145
SCAC Announcing Top 10 Events on China's Copyright in 2015 146
Anhui Copyright Administration Office Issuing *Special Inspection on Radio, Television Program Copyright Activities* 146
Implementation of Strengthening the Governance of Infringement and Counterfeiting in the Internet in Jilin Province Issued 146
Fifth Plenum of Inter-Ministerial Joint Meeting Held in Beijing to Encourage Use of Licensed Software 146
Work Conference to Encourage Use of Licensed Software Held in Shanghai 147
2016 Brooming Inspection Campaign Launched in Hefei 147
Beijing "12318" Seizing More than 2 Million Pieces of Illegal Publications and Pirated Optical Discs 147
Work Plan on National IPR System Law Enforcement and Safeguarding Rights (2016) Issued 147
Beijing White Paper on Intellectual Property Protection (2015) Launched 148
2015 China IPR Development Conference Held 148
General Office of the State Council Issuing *Key Points of National Campaign to Crack Down IPR Infringement and Manufacture and Sales of Counterfeit and Fake Commodities in 2016* 148
NCAC Rewarding Organizations and Individuals Contributing in Infringement and Piracy Cases 149

Strategic Cooperation Agreement Signed Between Liaoning Copyright Administration Office and Beijing Anti-Piracy Alliance 149
NCAC Announced Annual Top 10 Cases against Infringement and Piracy 150
Serious Online Sale of Pirated Books Cracked Down in Zhenjiang, Jiangsu 150
Chongqing Municipal Cultural Commission and Public Security Bureau Working Together to Crack Down on Infringement and Piracy 150
Work on Use of Authorized Software in State Organs Launched in Beijing, 2016 150
SARFT Issuing Notice Regulating Management of Mobile Games 151
SARFT Releasing *Notice on Further Clarifying Relevant Requirements of Examination and Approval of Audio-Video Product Imports* 151
SARFT Issuing *Notice on Vigorously Promoting Independent Innovation of Radio and Television Programs* 151
Centralized Destruction Activities of Piracy and Illegal Publications Launched in Etuokeqi, Inner Mongolia 152
Four Departments Launching "Sword Net 2016" Special Action 152
15th Meeting of Guangdong-Hong Kong Special Working Group for Promoting IPR Cooperation Held in Guangzhou 152
Nie Chenxi Appointed Director of SARFT and NCAC 153
Beijing Copyright Administration Office, Joining Hands with Publishing Enterprises, to Crack Down on Infringement and Piracy Mobile Phone Games 153
Yan Xiaohong Surveying and Studying in Shanghai Art Film Studio 153
NCAC Releasing *Notice on Strengthening Copyright Management of Internet Literary Works* 153
Opinions on Improving the System of Property Rights Protection to Protect Property Rights According to Law Issued 153
SCAFT Introducing Watermarking Technology to Strengthen Protection of Movie Copyright 153
Summary Meeting of "Sword Net 2016" Special Action Held in Beijing 154
Four Departments Including NCAC Announcing 21 Typical Network Infringement and Piracy Cases in "Sword Net 2016" Special Action 154

Publicity and Education 155
Registering Copyright for Shu Embroidery Works for Free in Sichuan 155
Complaints on Weixin Public Accounts' Infringement of Written Work Copyrights Exceeding 60% 155
Fourth Qingdao Annual Copyright Conference & Copyright Training Conference Held 155
Photography Copyright Protection Training Carried Out in Taizhou, Jiangsu 155
China Reading Group Report Showing "Post-90s" Network Writers' Uprising 155
2015 CPCC China Top 10 Copyright Proprietors Revealed 156
Online Works Copyright Administration and Law Enforcement Training Organized in Changsha 156
University Copyright Special Debate Competition Carried Out in Wuhan 156
Activities of Bringing Copyright Knowledge into Campus Organized in Guangxi 156
2016 Copyright Promotion Activity— "Creative Guangzhou, Dream Flying" Held in Guangzhou 157

Annual Report on China Internet Copyright Protection (2015) Released 157
Over 92,000 Software Copyrights Registered during the 12th Five-Year Plan 157
Party and Government Organs Software Authorization Training Organized in Ningxia 158
Promotional Documents of 2016 Copyright Promotion Week Released 158
International Copyright Exchange Training Course Held in Beijing 158
White Paper on Sports Entrepreneurship (2016) Focusing on Copyrights of Electronic Gaming Media Events 158
Chengdu Took the Lead Training Talents with Double-Certificate (Certificate of Academic Competence and Certificate of Professional Competence) 159
2016 National Work Registration Program Held in Beijing 159
First Session of Copyright Training Class of China Copyright Association Held in 2016 159
Report on the Press and Publication Industry Analysis in 2015 Released 159
The Global Public Art Initiative "Encouraging Original Works, Protecting Copyright" Started 160
The 8th China International Film and Television Cartoon Copyright Protection and Trade Fair Ended 160
First Outstanding Copyright Works Competition Launched in Jimo City, Shandong Province 161
Case of Copyrights Protection by Chongqing Newspaper Group Studied by Reporters from 17 Central Media Organized by NCAC 161
Literary Creators Won "China's Remarkable Achievements in Copyright" Award 162
2016 China Copyright Gold Award Presented in Guangzhou 162
Award Ceremony Held to Present "Shenzhen Copyright Gold Award" 162

Exchanges and Discussion 163
Seminar of Film and Television Creation Starts from the Original Works' Protection According to Law Held in Beijing 163
Seminar of Online Music Copyright Protection and Business Model Held in Beijing 163
Advanced Seminar on Traditional Copyright Protection and International Copyright Exchange under Internet Environment Held in Shanghai 163
2016 CPCC China Copyright Service Annual Meeting Held in Beijing 163
First High-level China Intellectual Property Protection Forum Held 164
Copyright Protection and Management of Internet Content Platform Focused at Copyright Salon 164
Buzz Generated from Three Copyright Group Management Organizations in Tsinghua Research 165
China Internet Copyright Protection Conference Held in Beijing 165
Media Seminar on Hot Issues Related to Copyright Held in Beijing 165
Internet Copyright Protection and Operation of New Media Forum Held in Beijing 166
Copyright Development Focused During 2016 Mobile Internet Innovation Conference 166
"Belt and Road" High-level Meeting on Intellectual Property Rights Held 167
"Round-table Conference on the Importance of Protecting Audiovisual Performances in the Development of Cultural and Creative Industries" Held in Beijing 167
Sino-Japanese Copyright Seminar Held in Shanghai 168

APP and Network Alliance Symposium on Copyright Infringement Held in Beijing 168
2016 BIBF International Copyright Exchange Senior Seminar Held in Beijing 169
Copyright Licensing Promoted During "Belt and Road" Summit Forum 169
2016 China Internet Law Conference Held in Beijing 169
2016 First Cultural + New Creation New Industry New Economy Forum Held 170
Big Data Security • Internet Press Publication and Digital Asset Salon Held 170
Standard Promotion and Standard Copyright Protection Promotion Held in Xiamen 170
Ninth China Copyright Annual Meeting Held in Beijing 171
"Network Advertising Alliance Service Copyright Protection" Forum Held by NCAC 171
2016 National Copyright Social Service Exchange Conference Held in Guangzhou 172
AIPPI China Branch Copyright Hot Spots Forum Held 172

Social Management and Services 173
Free Copyright Registration Service Provided in Some Cities of Sichuan 173
Sixth Round of Sixth Standing Council of China Publishing Association Held 173
National Copyright Trade Base (Yuexiu) to Create a Comprehensive Copyright Service Platform 173
Copyright Authorization Ceremony of *Classic Cars Challenge China* Held in Yangcheng 173
General Election Carried by Anhui Province Copyright Protection Association 174
Guangdong Province Press and Publication Radio, Film and Television (Copyright) Working Conference Held in Guangzhou 174
DPP to Submit Copyright Proposals During NPC and CPPCC, Announced at Press Briefing 174
Mobile APP Third-party Certificate Signing and Copyright Registration Joint Service Platform Officially Launched 174
First Intellectual Property Arbitration Center Set Up in Jiangxi Province 175
Two Incentives for Copyright Review Promoted in Zhangjiagang, Jiangsu Province 175
"Network Working Committee" Set Up by Beijing Copyright Protection Association 175
Online Works Copyright Administration and Law Enforcement Training Organized in Changsha City 175
Beijing-Tianjin-Hebei Intellectual Property Alliance Formally Established 176
Guangxi: Copyright Registration Rights Delegated to Facilitate Guilin People for Copyright Application in Guilin 176
"Copyright Cloud Beijing Night and 426so Platform Online Anniversary" Held in Beijing 176
Guangzhou First Hires Copyright Consulting Experts 177
Copyright Teacher Training Program Started in Beijing 177
New Applications in DCI System Developed in China Copyright Protection Center 177
First Copyright Dispute Resolution System Established in Yantai, Shandong Province 177
Literary Tieba Shut Down by Baidu to Clear Off Piracy Infringement, Approved by NCAC 178
Chongqing Copyright Exchange Center Unveiled 178
Online Proxy Copyright Registration Platform Built in Shannxi 178
China Copyright Protection Center Southwest Copyright Registration Hall Opened in Chengdu 178

Art Copyright Work Committee of China Copyright Association Established 179
First National Culture Copyright Exchange Center Set Up in Shunyi 179
Shanghai Baoshan District Copyright Service Station Set Up 179
Agreement of Digital Copyright Protection Technology R&D Engineering and Applications Signed in Beijing 180
Payment Agreement Signed Between China Written Works Copyright Society and *Readers* 180
Strategic Cooperation Agreement Signed Between Copyright Society of China (CSC) and FIRST BRAVE 180
China Publishing Digital Resources International Exchange Platform Launched 180
Anti-Piracy Alliance Established by Juvenile & Children's Publishing House in Beijing 181
"Western Silk Road Copyright Exchange Platform" Officially Launched in Beijing 181
"2016 Internet Sword Campaign • Original Writing Works Protection Month" Officially Launched 181
Chongqing Cultural and Creative Association Copyright Registration Service Center Established 181
Opening Ceremony of National "Copyright Cloud" Experience Store Held in Taiyuan 181
First Batch of Copyright Service Stations Established in Chengdu 182
First Municipal-level Copyright Work Station Set Up in Wujiang District, Suzhou City 182
"Photographer Bank Card" Introduced by ICSC to Strengthen Copyright Protection of Photographic Works 182
Copyright Training Base Unveiled in Suzhou City 182
Agreement Signed Between Shenzhen Luohu District Government and the China Copyright Protection Center to Build a Guangdong, Hong Kong and Macao Copyright Registration Hall 183
Copyright Service Station Set Up in Quyang by Hebei Copyright Administration Office, Hebei Copyright Protection Center 183
Zhongshan City Set Up Funds for Copyright 184
First National Network Copyright Industry Research Base Settled in Tencent 184
Digital Copyright Protection Technology R&D Project Completed 184
List of the Fifteenth Session of Exported and Imported Version of the Outstanding Books Promotion Announced 185

International Exchange and Cooperation 185
MOU Signed Between China and Israel on Cooperation in Literature and Translation 185
Fruitful Results Achieved by Chinese Delegation in 2016 New Delhi World Book Fair 186
Delegation Led by Yan Xiaohong Visited Egypt and Attended the Cairo International Book Fair 186
Strategic Partnership Established Between China and Czech to Jointly Protect Intellectual Property 186
Chinese Books Popular Among Tunisian Readers 187
Chinese Delegation Made Debut at Bologna Children's Book Fair 187
Great Achievement by Foreign Language Press in Copyright Licensing during London Book Fair 187
Round-table Conference on "Film and Television Industry Copyright Protection in

Digital Era" Held in Beijing 187
China and Britain Explored to Establish Bilingual Infringement Reporting Platform 188
Chinese Exhibitors Attended 2016 American Book Fair 188
Twelfth China-South Korea Copyright Seminar Held in South Korea 188
Asia Pacific Seminar on Hot Issues of Copyright Held in Xi'an 188
China and South Korea Book Copyright Fair Held in Nanchang 189
China and Russia Film Festival Strategic Cooperation Ceremony Held in Russia 189
Cai Fuchao Meets with WIPO Director General Gao Rui and His Delegation 189
Sino-US Seminar on the Latest Development of Copyright Held in Beijing 190
Yan Xiaohong Meets with Chad Constand and Hong Weidian 190
"2016 China-South Korea Publishing Cooperation Forum" Held in Beijing 190
Yan Xiaohong Meets with Lucy Neville-Rolfe, Secretary of State for Energy and Intellectual Property of the United Kingdom and Her Delegation 191
Many Cooperation Reached Between China and Russia Publishing Institutions during 29th Moscow International Book Fair 191
467 New Chinese Titles Shown at 23rd Tokyo International Book Fair 191
Copyright of *Baby Illustrated* and *Preschool Pictorial* Exported to the United States 192
Development of Modern Copyright Industries Focused at Huazhong International Copyright Summit 192
First Chinese Theme Book Translation and Publishing Center Established in Mongolia 192
Global Sharing of Dehua Experience 192
China Publishing Works Exhibited in Romania 193
Global Creators Forum Held in Beijing 193
"Copyright, Innovation and Development" Highlighted at 2016 International Copyright Forum 194
International Copyright Cooperation Agreement Worth Over 68 Million Dollars Signed in Suzhou 194
China and Rome Cooperate in Copyright Group Management 194

Industrial Development 194
Merger and Acquisition of Legendary Pictures Made by Wanda at Total Amount of 3.5 Billion Dollars 194
Global Distribution Platform for Domestic Movie Launched 195
Copyright of The Voice of China Bought by Talent Film and Television 195
iQiYi Works with 20th Century Fox Film Corporation to Develop Online Copyright 195
Online Movie Ticket Alteration Service Firstly Introduced by Meituan MaoYan Movie in Nearly 2,000 Theaters 195
County Cinemas Growing Rapidly 195
International Copyright Sales Company Purchased by Bliss Media 196
Strategic Cooperation Reached Between Two Major Film and Television Copyright Trading Platforms from North and South 196
Tianya Community Works with Department of Chinese Language and Literature, SYSU to Create a Platform for Film and TV Script Writing for College Students in China 196
"Mangzhong Plan" Made by Tencent to Create a Media Ecosystem 196

Chinese Culture Group Becomes Shareholder of Hollywood 196
Light and Shadow Music Website Officially Launched 196
China Replaced the United States as the Largest Exporter of Cultural Products 197
Alibaba Spent 23.8 Billion Yuan to Buy All Shares of Youku and Tudou 197
Billions Invested by Chuchujie and LeEco to Build New Music Industry Ecol 197
China South Publishing & Media Group (CNS) Building IP Comprehensive Copyright Operation Platform 197
China Film Industry Report (2015−2016) Released by EN Consulting 198
750 TV Series Showed on Spring 2016 Beijing TV Fairs 198
IFPI 2016 Global Music Report Released 198
China Game Industry Values Reaching 140.7 Billion Yuan in 2015 198
The Sky-High Cost on the Copyright of Chinese Football Association Super League (CSL) Leading to "Linkage Between the TV Station and Network" 199
In 2015, Patents, Trademarks and Copyright Pledged Financing Amounting to 93.172 Billion Yuan 199
BJND and YNET Together Creating a Digital Industry Service Platform 199
The 12th China International Animation Festival Transaction Volume Reaching More than 15.1 Billion Yuan 199
Alibaba Pictures Group Limited Investing Dadi Digital Cinema 199
LeEco Ticket Platform Exploring the Value of the Copyright of Sporting Events in Many Aspects 200
British Football Copyright Giant Acquired by Chinese Capitalists 200
Derivative Production Alliance Founded by China Film 200
Tencent, Microfilm Investing in South Korea YG Entertainment with 85 Million Dollars 200
Tencent Joy Entertainment Development Digging Deep Children's Publishing Content Copyright Value 200
Douban Reading Starting Selling Original Story Television Adaptation Rights 200
The New Media Copyright of CSL Acquired by Storm Sports 201
The Total Number of Licensed Copyright in China Increasing by 3 Times in Eight Years 201
Tencent Acquiring Supercell with 8.6 Billion Dollars, Opening Up the Era of Online Games 201
The Animation Game Industry Chain Opened in Beijing 201
CDLA Industry Alliance Founded by LeEco 201
iReader Together with Fashion Group to Carry Out Copyright Cooperation 202
The Value of China's Digital Publishing Industry Exceeding 440 Billion Yuan 202
China-ASEAN Basic Software Ecological Cooperation Promoted by Emind Soft 202
Baidu Opening Cloud Helped National News Publishing to Create Intelligent Digital Publishing System 202
LeTV Acquiring the Largest US Smart TV Manufacturers with 2 Billion Dollars 202
Imagine China Invested by Toutiao Strategically 203
The Harry Potter Series E-books on Sale in China for the First Time 203
A Variety of Cloud Products Released by LeEco Cloud 203
Copyright as Bridge-Audio Books Getting Popular 203
The 23rd Beijing International Book Fair Ended 204

China Network Literature Copyright Alliance Established 204
Japan Watanabe Junichi Literature Museum Successfully Merged and Acquired by Qingdao Publishing Group Successfully 204
The 9th China International Cartoon Festival Ended 204
The 9th China Textile Painting Fair Held in Nantong 205
2016 China Music Industry Development Report Released 205
Alibaba Acquiring Exclusive Rights Overseas 205
The First Report of Industrial and Economic Media Convergence Development Released 205
Anti-Piracy and Industrial Protection Alliance of Network Game Established in Beijing 206
A New Media Copyright Alliance Launched by People's Daily Online and New Media of the Party Newspapers 206
Youku and Oriental Dream Works Reaching a Top Home Entertainment Content Copyright Agreement 206
China's Pay-Per-View Video Market Topped the Record of 1 Billion Yuan 206

Hong Kong, Macao and Taiwan Copyright Information 207
Hong Kong 207
A New Promotional Video on Copyright Protection Launched by Intellectual Property Department 207
A "Point-to-Point" Case of Suspected Infringement of TV Programmes Detected by Hong Kong Customs 207
Hong Kong Customs Cracking Down on Distribution of Infringement Course Materials 207
Hong Kong Government Proposing to Amend *Arbitration Regulations* 207
Pan-PRD Regional Deepening IPR Cooperation Agreement 208

Taiwan 208
No Need to Apply for Verification Documents for Licensed Audio-Visual Works and CD OEM 208
2016 Cross-Strait Intellectual Property Law Forum Achievements Report 209

Macao 209
SMEs Urged by MIPIM to Take the Advantages of Intellectual Property to Develop the Mainland Market 209

Copyright Industry and Trade

China Copyright Industry Contribution to Economy (2015)
Research Group on China Copyright Industry Contribution to Economy 213
2016 China Publishing Industry Analysis Report
National Administration of Press and Publication, Radio, Film and Television 218
2016—2017 China Digital Publishing Industry Development Report
China Digital Publishing Industry Annual Report Research Group 246

2016 China Radio and Television Industry Development Report
Development Research Centre, National Administration of Press and Publication, Radio, Film and Television 252
2016 China Film Industry Development Report
Development Research Centre, National Administration of Press and Publication, Radio, Film and Television 263
2016 China Animation Industry Development Report Niu Xingzhen 269
2016 China Software Industry Development Report Sun Zhanfeng, Zhu Zhen 277
2016 China Online Game Market Analysis Enfodesk 283

Selected Typical Cases

Typical Cases of China Copyright Judicial Protection in 2016 295

Top 10 Cases of Infringement and Piracy Combated in 2016 303

21 Typical Cases in "Sword Net 2016" Special Campaign 306

Typical Cases in Some Provinces (Autonomous Regions and Municipalities) in 2016 309
Beijing 309
Tianjin 309
Liaoning 310
Jilin 310
Heilongjiang 311
Shanghai 312
Jiangsu 313
Zhejiang 313
Anhui 314
Fujian 315
Henan 316
Hubei 316
Hunan 319
Guangdong 319
Guangxi 320
Hainan 320
Yunnan 321
Xinjiang 321

Local Copyright Enforcement Cases in 2016 322
Hebei 322
Liaoning 323
Jilin 323
Shanghai 325

Jiangsu 328
Anhui 329
Jiangxi 329
Shandong 331
Hubei 333
Hunan 333
Sichuan 335
Shaanxi 336
Qinghai 337

Laws and Regulatory Documents

Regulatory Documents 341

Decision on Repealing Some Regulations and Normative Documents (No. 12, National Copyright Administration of the People's Republic of China) 341

Notice on Launching the "Sword Net 2016" Special Campaign Against Online Infringement and Piracy (Guo Ban Fa [2016] No. 2) 341

Notice on Regulating the Registration Certificate of Works (Guo Ban Han [2016] No. 1) 343

Notice on Issuing the *Summary of Promoting the Use of Genuine Software in 2015* and the *Plan for Promoting the Use of Genuine Software in 2016* (Guo Ban Han [2016] No. 2) 344

NCAC's Decision on Rewarding the Units and Individuals in Helping Seizing Infringement and Piracy Cases in 2015 (Guo Ban Han [2016] No. 4) 349

NCAC's Notice on Publishing the Top 10 Cases of Cracking Down on Infringement and Piracy in China in 2015 (Guo Ban Han [2016] No. 5) 359

Notice on Prohibiting the Unauthorized Online Distribution of CCTV Spring Festival Gala (Guo Ban Ban Fa [2016] No. 3) 361

Circular on Copyright Registration in China in 2015 (Guo Ban Ban Fa [2016] No. 4) 362

Notice on the Operation of the Copyright Registration Item in the First Stage of the National Copyright Regulatory Platform (Session Ⅱ) (Guo Ban Ban Fa [2016] No. 5) 363

Notice on Promoting Software Application in 2016 (Guo Ban Ban Fa [2016] No. 7) 364

Notice on Publishing the First List of the National Staffing of Regulatory Trainers for Copyright Law Enforcement Administration (Guo Ban Ban Fa [2016] No. 8) 365

Notice on Issuing the *Guidelines for the Management of Genuine Software* (Guo Ban Ban Fa [2016] No. 13) 366

Circular on the First Batch of Network Infringement and Piracy Cases Investigation in "Sword Net 2016" Special Campaign (Guo Ban Ban Fa [2016] No. 15) 366

Reply on Consent to Establish "Research Base of Network Copyright Industry" in Shenzhen Tencent Computer System Co. , Ltd. (Guo Ban Ban Han [2016] No. 4[illegible]) 367

Notice on Issuing *The Key Points of* 2016 *National Publishing (Copyright) Campaign Against*

Copyright Infringement (Xin Guang Chu Ban Han [2016] No. 198) 368

Honors and Awards

The 5th Winners of WIPO Gold Award (China) 373
2016 Annual Report on China Internet Copyright Protection 377
2016 Meritorious Units and Individuals for Investigation of Infringement and Piracy Cases 387
2016 Top 10 Events of Copyright in China 398
2016 CPCC Top 10 Chinese Copyright Owners 400
2016 (the 9th) Winners' List in National College Students Copyright Essay 403
The 15th Winners' List in Promotion of the Outstanding Licensed and Acquired Titles 407

Theoretical Research

Review of 2016 Copyright Law Research Xiang Bo 415

2016 Research on Hot Issues of Copyright 424
Protection Mechanism of Folk Literature Works Guan Yuying 424
Discussion on the Compilation of Civil Code of China from Judicial Demands of Intellectual Property Li Chen 427
Competition and Monopoly: The Mode Selection of Collective Management Organization of Copyright in China Lin Xiuqin, Huang Qianxin 431
Discussion on the Structure of Works in the Copyright Law
—Case Study of "Structural Use" of Teaching Materials in Primary and Secondary Schools Lu Haijun 436
Proof of Cross Protection of Practical Artwork and Resolution of Potential Risks Lü Bingbin 440
Comparison and Choice: The Reconstruction of the Repoduction Right of Works in Internet
—From the Perspective of Temporary Repoduction Meng Zhaoping 443
On the Legal System and Protection of the Dericative Works Tang Yan 447
On the Copyright Protection of the Live Broadcasting Image of Sports Events
—Also Comment on "Phoenix Events Rebroadcasting Case" Wang Qian 451
Research on the Frontier Problems of Safe Harbor Principle
—Taking "Notice-Delete" as a Litigation Prelude to Expand Xu Ming 457
The Identification of the Expression of Art Works and Its Substantive Similarity Yang Xiongwen, Wang Qinhe 460
The Normative Constitution of the "Direct Infringement Subject" in the Network Copyright Infringement
—Centering on the Legal Scope of "Private Copying Exceptions" Zhang Peng 464

Introduction of Copyright Books in 2016 468

Statistics

China Copyright Statistics in 2016 479
National Works Registration Statistics in 2016 479
National Copyright Contract Statistics in 2016 480
National Copyright Law Enforcement Statistics in 2016 481
Summary of Copyright Exports in 2016 481
Summary of Copyright Imports in 2016 482

China Press and Publication Industry Statistics in 2016 483
The Total Number of Books Published in Various Regions of the Country in 2016 483
The Number of Newspapers Published at All Levels in China in 2016 484
The Number of Types, Prints and the Total Number of Printed Sheets and Amount of Various Journals Published in Various Regions of the Country in 2016 (1) 486
The Number of Types, Prints and the Total Number of Printed Sheets and Amount of Various Journals Published in Various Regions of the Country in 2016 (2) 488
Variety, Quantity and Distribution of Audio Products Published in Various Regions of the Country in 2016 (Classified by Carrier) 490
Variety, Quantity and Distribution of Video Products Published in Various Regions of the Country in 2016 (Classified by Carrier) 492
Distribution, Sales and Storage Conditions of Publications in National Xinhua Bookstore System and Publishing House's Own Distribution Unit in 2016 494
National Import and Export of Books, Journals and Newspapers in 2016 495
National Import and Export of Audio-Video, Electronic and Digital Publications in 2016 495

China Broadcasting and Television Industry Statistics in 2016 496
Table (1) of the Main Indicators of the National Radio and Television Development in 2016 496
Table (2) of the Main Indicators of the National Radio and Television Development in 2016 498

China Software Industry Statistics in 2016 500
National Software Industry Statistics in 2016 500

Name List

Copyright Administration Department 503
Copyright Public Service Institutions 507
Copyright Associations 508
Copyright Collective Management Organizations 511
Copyright Industry Associations 512
Copyright Agencies 512
National Copyright Exchange Institutions 513

National Intellectual Property Teaching and Research Institute 514

Appendix: International Copyright News

General 519

Copyright Protection and Limitations in the Digital Age
—Review of International Copyright Law Development in 2016 519

International Copyright News, 2016 527

Legislation and Administration 527

United States Copyright Policy Overview, 2016 527
Council of Europe (COE) Supports the Network Neutrality for Expressing Freedom and Privacy 527
EU Court: Linking to Pirated Websites Does Not Infringe Copyright 528
Britain Proposes to Strengthen Protection of Internet Intellectual Property 528
That EU Is Competent to Ratify *Marrakesh Treaty* Might Break Standstill 529
Australian Productivity Council Promotes Reasonable Use of Copyright, Which Reignited the Copyright War 530

Judicial Cases 531

Village Roadshow and Fox Television Filed a Lawsuit Seeking to Block Piracy Websites 531
The Federal Court of Australia Concluded that Digital Data Signals Was Not Copyrighted 532
The United States: Federal Copyright Law Can't Replace the Protection of Trade Secrets 532
New York State Court: Sirius Did Not Have to Pay for the Music Performers Before 1972 533
Japanese "Scan Bookstore" Operator, Arrested on Suspicion of Copyright Infringement 533

Industry News 534

Knowledge Sharing Organization: What Is the Other Side of the Copyright? 534
PayPal Stopped Support for VPN and Smart DNS Service Providers due to Copyright Issues 534
Issues such as Intellectual Property and Innovation Were Included in the Agenda of the Regular Meeting of the TRIPs Administrative Committee 535
UNESCO's Report on Cultural Trade 535
The Song of *We Shall Overcome* Copyright Disputes 536
WIPO Held an Intellectual Property and Development Milestones Meeting 536
WIPO Traditional Knowledge Committee Agreed to Further Discuss the Revised Draft 537
The New Zealand Music Industry Called for Changing the Articles of the TPP 537
New Requirements of U. S. DMCA for Safe Harbor Copyright Agent by Internet Service Providers 538
Libraries and Archives Called for Member States of WIPO to Make Safe Harbor

Rules 538
Online Piracy is Common in Russian, the Retailers Strived to Compete 540
Australian Schools Violated TPP Copyright Rules Due to Their Mistakes in Safe Harbor 540
Knowledge Sharing Organizations at WIPO: Supporting More Equitable Teaching Research Copyright Policies 541
WIPO: Right of Pursuit—To Correct Imbalance in Copyright Revenue 542
WIPO's all Publications Were Allowed for Knowledge Sharing 542
EU Council Agreed to Eliminate Geographical Block of E-Commerce 543
Thoughts on Copyright Law Concerning Leaks of ASKA's Unpublished Songs 543
Groups in the Music Industry Called for Trump's Support 544
Undetermined Claims of Piracy Should Not Shut Down the Internet 544
USTR Condemned the Theft of Streaming Resources, and the Updated Report of "Notorious Markets" Noted Alibaba by Name 545

Index

Index 546

Publicity and Advertisement

Display of Copyright Works in 2016
Advertisement

版权

特辑

TE JI

国务院关于印发“十三五”国家知识产权保护和运用规划的通知

国发〔2016〕86号

各省、自治区、直辖市人民政府，国务院各部委、各直属机构：

现将《“十三五”国家知识产权保护和运用规划》印发给你们，请认真贯彻执行。

国务院

2016年12月30日

（此件公开发布）

“十三五”国家知识产权保护和运用规划

为贯彻落实党中央、国务院关于知识产权工作的一系列重要部署，全面深入实施《国务院关于新形势下加快知识产权强国建设的若干意见》（国发〔2015〕71号），提升知识产权保护和运用水平，依据《中华人民共和国国民经济和社会发展第十三个五年规划纲要》，制定本规划。

一、规划背景

“十二五”时期，各地区、各相关部门深入实施国家知识产权战略，促进知识产权工作融入经济社会发展大局，为创新驱动发展提供了有力支撑，进一步巩固了我国的知识产权大国地位。发明专利申请量和商标注册量稳居世界首位。与“十一五”末相比，每万人口发明专利拥有量达到6.3件，增长了3倍；每万市场主体的平均有效商标拥有量达到1 335件，增长了34.2%；通过《专利合作条约》途径提交的专利申请量（以下称PCT专利申请量）达到3万件，增长了2.4倍，跻身世界前三位；植物新品种申请量居世界第二位；全国作品登记数量和计算机软件著作权登记量分别增长95.9%和282.5%；地理标志、集成电路布图设计等注册登记数量大幅增加。知识产权制度进一步健全，知识产权创造、运用、保护、管理和服务的政策措施更加完善，专业人才队伍不断壮大。市场主体知识产权综合运用能力明显提高，国际合作水平显著提升，形成了一批具有国际竞争力的知识产权优势企业。知识产权质押融资额达到3 289亿元，年均增长38%。专利、商标许可备案分别达到4万件、14.7万件，版权产业对国民经济增长的贡献率超过7%。知识产权司法保护体系不断完善，在北京、上海和广州相继设立知识产权法院，民事、刑事、行政案件的“三合一”审理机制改革试点基本完成，司法裁判标准更加细致完备，司法保护能力与水平不断提升。知识产权行政保护不断加强，全国共查处专利侵权假冒案件8.7万件，商标权、商业秘密和其他销售假冒伪劣商品等侵权假冒案件32.2万件，侵权盗版案件3.5万件。全社会知识产权意识得到普遍增强。

同时，我国知识产权数量与质量不协调、区域发展不平衡、保护还不够严格等问题依然突出。核心专利、知名品牌、精品版权较少，布局还不合理。与经济发展融合还不够紧密，转移转化效益还不够高，影响企业知识产权竞争能力提升。侵权易发多发，维权仍面临举证难、成本高、赔偿低等问题，影响创新创业热情。管理体制机制还不够完善，国际交流合作深度与广度还有待进一步拓展。

“十三五”时期是我国由知识产权大国向知识产权强国迈进的战略机遇期。国际知识产权竞争更加激烈。我国经济发展进入速度变化、结构优化、动力转换的新常态。知识产权作为科技成果向现实生产力转化的重要桥梁和纽带，激励创新的基本保障作用更加突出。各地区、各相关部门要准确把握新形势新特点，深化知识产权领域改革，破除制约知识产权发展的障碍，全面提高知识产权治理能力，推动知识产权事业取得突破性进展，为促进经济提质增效升级提供有力支撑。

二、指导思想、基本原则和发展目标

（一）指导思想。

全面贯彻党的十八大和十八届三中、四中、五中、六中全会精神，以邓小平理论、"三个代表"重要思想、科学发展观为指导，深入贯彻习近平总书记系列重要讲话精神，紧紧围绕统筹推进"五位一体"总体布局和协调推进"四个全面"战略布局，牢固树立和贯彻落实创新、协调、绿色、开放、共享的发展理念，认真落实党中央、国务院决策部署，以供给侧结构性改革为主线，深入实施国家知识产权战略，深化知识产权领域改革，打通知识产权创造、运用、保护、管理和服务的全链条，严格知识产权保护，加强知识产权运用，提升知识产权质量和效益，扩大知识产权国际影响力，加快建设中国特色、世界水平的知识产权强国，为实现"两个一百年"奋斗目标和中华民族伟大复兴的中国梦提供更加有力的支撑。

（二）基本原则。

坚持创新引领。推动知识产权领域理论、制度、文化创新，探索知识产权工作新理念和新模式，厚植知识产权发展新优势，保障创新者的合法权益，激发全社会创新创造热情，培育经济发展新动能。

坚持统筹协调。加强知识产权工作统筹，推进知识产权与产业、科技、环保、金融、贸易以及军民融合等政策的衔接。做好分类指导和区域布局，坚持总体提升与重点突破相结合，推动知识产权事业全面、协调、可持续发展。

坚持绿色发展。加强知识产权资源布局，优化知识产权法律环境、政策环境、社会环境和产业生态，推进传统制造业绿色改造，促进产业低碳循环发展，推动资源利用节约高效、生态环境持续改善。

坚持开放共享。统筹国内国际两个大局，加强内外联动，增加公共产品和公共服务有效供给，强化知识产权基础信息互联互通和传播利用，积极参与知识产权全球治理，推动国际知识产权制度向普惠包容、平衡有效的方向发展，持续提升国际影响力和竞争力。

（三）发展目标。

到 2020 年，知识产权战略行动计划目标如期完成，知识产权重要领域和关键环节的改革取得决定性成果，保护和运用能力得到大幅提升，建成一批知识产权强省、强市，为促进大众创业、万众创新提供有力保障，为建设知识产权强国奠定坚实基础。

——知识产权保护环境显著改善。知识产权法治环境显著优化，法律法规进一步健全，权益分配更加合理，执法保护体系更加健全，市场监管水平明显提升，保护状况社会满意度大幅提高。知识产权市场支撑环境全面优化，服务业规模和水平较好地满足市场需求，形成"尊重知识、崇尚创新、诚信守法"的文化氛围。

——知识产权运用效益充分显现。知识产权的市场价值显著提高，产业化水平全面提升，知识产权密集型产业占国内生产总值（GDP）比重明显提高，成为经济增长新动能。知识产权交易运营更加活跃，技术、资金、人才等创新要素以知识产权为纽带实现合理流动，带动社会就业岗位显著增加，知识产权国际贸易更加活跃，海外市场利益得到有效维护，形成支撑创新发展的运行机制。

——知识产权综合能力大幅提升。知识产权拥有量进一步提高，核心专利、知名品牌、精品版权、优秀集成电路布图设计、优良植物新品种等优质资源大幅增加。行政管理能力明显提升，基本形成权界清晰、分工合理、责权一致、运转高效、法治保障的知识产权体制机制。专业人才队伍数量充足、素质优良、结构合理。构建知识产权运营公共服务平台体系，建成便民利民的知识产权信息公共服务平台。知识产权运营、金融等业态发育更加成熟，资本化、商品化和产业化的渠道进一步畅通，市场竞争能力大幅提升，形成更多具有国际影响力的知识产权优势企业。国际事务处理能力不断提高，国际影响力进一步提升。

"十三五"知识产权保护和运用主要指标

指标	2015年	2020年	累计增加值	属性
每万人口发明专利拥有量（件）	6.3	12	5.7	预期性
PCT专利申请量（万件）	3	6	3	预期性
植物新品种申请总量（万件）	1.7	2.5	0.8	预期性
全国作品登记数量（万件）	135	220	85	预期性
年度知识产权质押融资金额（亿元）	750	1800	1050	预期性
计算机软件著作权登记数量（万件）	29	44	15	预期性
规模以上制造业每亿元主营业务收入有效发明专利数（件）	0.56	0.7	0.14	预期性
知识产权使用费出口额（亿美元）	44.4	100	55.6	预期性
知识产权服务业营业收入年均增长（%）	20	20	—	预期性
知识产权保护社会满意度（分）	70	80	10	预期性

注：知识产权使用费出口额为五年累计值。

三、主要任务

贯彻落实党中央、国务院决策部署，深入实施知识产权战略，深化知识产权领域改革，完善知识产权强国政策体系，全面提升知识产权保护和运用水平，全方位多层次加快知识产权强国建设。

（一）深化知识产权领域改革。积极研究探索知识产权管理体制机制改革，努力在重点领域和关键环节取得突破性成果。支持地方开展知识产权综合管理改革试点。建立以知识产权为重要内容的创新驱动评价体系，推动知识产权产品纳入国民经济核算，将知识产权指标纳入国民经济和社会发展考核体系。推进简政放权，简化和优化知识产权审查和注册流程。放宽知识产权服务业准入，扩大代理领域开放程度，放宽对专利代理机构股东和合伙人的条件限制。加快知识产权权益分配改革，完善有利于激励创新的知识产权归属制度，构建提升创新效率和效益的知识产权导向机制。

（二）严格实行知识产权保护。加快知识产权法律、法规、司法解释的制修订，构建包括司法审判、刑事司法、行政执法、快速维权、仲裁调解、行业自律、社会监督的知识产权保护工作格局。充分发挥全国打击侵犯知识产权和制售假冒伪劣商品工作领导小组作用，调动各方积极性，形成工作合力。以充分实现知识产权的市场价值为指引，进一步加大损害赔偿力度。推进诉讼诚信建设，依法严厉打击侵犯知识产权犯罪。强化行政执法，改进执法方式，提高执法效率，加大对制假源头、重复侵权、恶意侵权、群体侵权的查处力度，为创新者提供更便利的维权渠道。加强商标品牌保护，提高消费品商标公共服务水平。规范有效保护商业秘密。持续推进政府机关和企业软件正版化工作。健全知识产权纠纷的争议仲裁和快速调解制度。充分发挥行业组织的自律作用，引导企业强化主体责任。深化知识产权保护的区域协作和国际合作。

（三）促进知识产权高效运用。突出知识产权在科技创新、新兴产业培育方面的引领作用，大力发展知识产权密集型产业，完善专利导航产业发展工作机制，深入开展知识产权评议工作。加大高技术含量知识产权转移转化力度。创新知识产权运营模式和服务产品。完善科研开发与管理机构的知识产权管理制度，探索建立知识产权专员派驻机制。建立健全知识产权服务标准，完善知识产权服务体系。完善"知识产权＋金融"服务机制，深入推进质押融资风险补偿试点。推动产业集群品牌的注册和保护，开展产业集群、品牌基地、地理标志、知识产权服务业集聚区培育试点示范工作。推动军民知识产权转移转化，促进军民融合深度发展。

四、重点工作

（一）完善知识产权法律制度。

1. 加快知识产权法律法规建设。加快推动专利法、著作权法、反不正当竞争法及配套法规、植物新品种保护条例等法律法规的制修订工作。适时做好地理标志立法工作，健全遗传资源、传统知识、民间文艺、中医药、新闻作品、广播电视节目等领域法律制度。完善职务发明制度和规制知识产权滥用行为的法律制度，健全国防领域知识产权法规政策。

2. 健全知识产权相关法律制度。研究完善商业模式和实用艺术品等知识产权保护制度。研究“互联网+”、电子商务、大数据等新业态、新领域知识产权保护规则。研究新媒体条件下的新闻作品版权保护。研究实质性派生品种保护制度。制定关于滥用知识产权的反垄断指南。完善商业秘密保护法律制度，明确商业秘密和侵权行为界定，探索建立诉前保护制度。

专栏1　知识产权法律完善工程

推动修订完善知识产权法律、法规和部门规章。配合全国人大常委会完成专利法第四次全面修改。推进著作权法第三次修改。根据专利法、著作权法修改进度适时推进专利法实施细则、专利审查指南、著作权法实施条例等配套法规和部门规章的修订。完成专利代理条例和国防专利条例修订。

支持开展立法研究。组织研究制定知识产权基础性法律的必要性和可行性。研究在民事基础性法律中进一步明确知识产权制度的基本原则、一般规则及重要概念。研究开展反不正当竞争法、知识产权海关保护条例、生物遗传资源获取管理条例以及中医药等领域知识产权保护相关法律法规制修订工作。

（二）提升知识产权保护水平。

1. 发挥知识产权司法保护作用。推动知识产权领域的司法体制改革，构建公正高效的知识产权司法保护体系，形成资源优化、科学运行、高效权威的知识产权综合审判体系，推进知识产权民事、刑事、行政案件的“三合一”审理机制，努力为知识产权权利人提供全方位和系统有效的保护，维护知识产权司法保护的稳定性、导向性、终局性和权威性。进一步发挥司法审查和司法监督职能。加强知识产权“双轨制”保护，发挥司法保护的主导作用，完善行政执法和司法保护两条途径优势互补、有机衔接的知识产权保护模式。加大对知识产权侵权行为的惩治力度，研究提高知识产权侵权法定赔偿上限，针对情节严重的恶意侵权行为实施惩罚性赔偿并由侵权人承担实际发生的合理开支。积极开展知识产权民事侵权诉讼程序与无效程序协调的研究。及时、有效做好知识产权司法救济工作。支持开展知识产权司法保护对外合作。

2. 强化知识产权刑事保护。完善常态化打防工作格局，进一步优化全程打击策略，全链条惩治侵权假冒犯罪。深化行政执法部门间的协作配合，探索使用专业技术手段，提升信息应用能力和数据运用水平，完善与电子商务企业协作机制。加强打假专业队伍能力建设。深化国际执法合作，加大涉外知识产权犯罪案件侦办力度，围绕重点案件开展跨国联合执法行动。

3. 加强知识产权行政执法体系建设。加强知识产权行政执法能力建设，统一执法标准，完善执法程序，提高执法专业化、信息化、规范化水平。完善知识产权联合执法和跨地区执法协作机制，积极开展执法专项行动，重点查办跨区域、大规模和社会反映强烈的侵权案件。建立完善专利、版权线上执法办案系统。完善打击侵权假冒商品的举报投诉机制。创新知识产权快速维权工作机制。完善知识产权行政执法监督，加强执法维权绩效管理。加大展会知识产权保护力度。加强严格知识产权保护的绩效评价，持续开展知识产权保护社会满意度调查。建立知识产权纠纷多元解决机制，加强知识产权仲裁机构和纠纷调解机构建设。

4. 强化进出口贸易知识产权保护。落实对外贸易法中知识产权保护相关规定，适时出台与进出口贸易相关的知识产权保护政策。改进知识产权海关保护执法体系，加大对优势领域和新业态、新领域创新成果的知识产权海关保护力度。完善自由贸易试验区、海关特殊监管区内货物及过境、转运、通运货物的知识产权海关保护执法程序，在确保有效监管的前提下促进贸易便利。坚持专项整治、丰富执法手段、完善运行机制，提高打击侵权假冒执行力度，突出打击互联网领域跨境电子商务侵权假冒违法活动。加强国内、国际执法合作，完善从生产源头到流通渠道、消费终端的全链条式管理。

5. 强化传统优势领域知识产权保护。开展遗传资源、传统知识和民间文艺等知识产权资源调查。制定非物质文化遗产知识产权工作指南，加强对优秀传统知识资源的保护和运用。完善传统知识和民间文艺登记、注册机制，鼓励社会资本发起设立传统知识、民间文艺保护和发展基金。研究完善中国遗传资源保护利用制度，建立生物遗传资源获取的信息披露、事先知情同意和惠益分享制度。探索构建中医药知识产权综合保护体系，建立医药传统知识保护名录。建立民间文艺作品的使用保护制度。

6. 加强新领域新业态知识产权保护。加大宽带移动互联网、云计算、物联网、大数据、高性能计算、移动智能终端等领域的知识产权保护力度。强化在线监测，深入开展打击网络侵权假冒行为专项行动。加强对网络服务商传播影视剧、广播电视节目、音乐、文学、新闻、软件、游戏等监督管理工作，积极推进网络知识产权保护协作，将知识产权执法职责与电子商务企业的管理责任结合起来，建立信息报送、线索共享、案件研判和专业培训合作机制。

7. 加强民生领域知识产权保护。加大对食品、药品、环境等领域的知识产权保护力度，健全侵权假冒快速处理机制。建立健全创新药物、新型疫苗、先进医疗装备等领域的知识产权保护长效工作机制。加强污染治理和资源循环利用等生态环保领域的专利保护力度。开展知识产权保护进乡村专项行动，建立县域及乡镇部门协作执法机制和重大案件联合督办制度，加强农村市场知识产权行政执法条件建设。针对电子、建材、汽车配件、小五金、食品、农资等专业市场，加大对侵权假冒商品的打击力度，严堵侵权假冒商品的流通渠道。

专栏2　知识产权保护工程

开展系列专项行动。重点打击侵犯注册商标专用权、擅自使用他人知名商品特有名称包装装潢、冒用他人企业名称或姓名等仿冒侵权违法行为。针对重点领域开展打击侵权盗版专项行动，突出大案要案查处、重点行业专项治理和网络盗版监管，持续开展“红盾网剑”、“剑网”专项行动，严厉打击网络侵权假冒等违法行为。开展打击侵犯植物新品种权和制售假劣种子行为专项行动。

推进跨部门跨领域跨区域执法协作。加大涉嫌犯罪案件移交工作力度。开展与相关国际组织和境外执法部门的联合执法。加强大型商场、展会、电子商务、进出口等领域知识产权执法维权工作。

加强“12330”维权援助与举报投诉体系建设。强化“12330”平台建设，拓展维权援助服务渠道。提升平台服务质量，深入对接产业联盟、行业协会。

完善知识产权快速维权机制。加快推进知识产权快速维权中心建设，提升工作质量与效率。推进快速维权领域由单一行业向多行业扩展、类别由外观设计向实用新型专利和发明专利扩展、区域由特定地区向省域辐射，在特色产业集聚区和重点行业建立一批知识产权快速维权中心。

推进知识产权领域信用体系建设。推进侵权纠纷案件信息公示工作，严格执行公示标准。将故意侵权行为纳入社会信用评价体系，明确专利侵权等信用信息的采集规则和使用方式，向征信机构公开相关信息。积极推动建立知识产权领域信用联合惩戒机制。

（三）提高知识产权质量效益。

1．提高专利质量效益。建立专利申请质量监管机制。深化专利代理领域改革。健全专利审查质量管理机制。优化专利审查流程与方式。完善专利审查协作机制。继续深化专利审查业务国际合作，拓展“专利审查高速路”国际合作网络。加快建设世界一流专利审查机构。加强专利活动与经济效益之间的关联评价。完善专利奖的评审与激励政策，发挥专利奖标杆引领作用。

专栏3　专利质量提升工程

提升发明创造和专利申请质量。在知识产权强省、强市建设和有关试点示范工作中强化专利质量评价和引导。建立专利申请诚信档案，持续开展专利申请质量监测与反馈。

提升专利审查质量。加强审查业务指导体系和审查质量保障体系建设。完善绿色技术专利申请优先审查机制。做好基于审查资源的社会服务工作。构建专利审查指南修订常态化机制。改进审查周期管理，满足创新主体多样化需求。加强与行业协会、代理人、申请人的沟通，形成快捷高效的外部质量反馈机制，提高社会满意度。加大支撑专利审查的信息化基础设施建设。

提升专利代理质量。深化专利代理领域“放管服”改革，提高行业管理水平。强化竞争机制和行业自律，加大对代理机构和代理人的执业诚信信息披露力度。针对专利代理机构的代理质量构建反馈、评价、约谈、惩戒机制。

提升专利运用和保护水平。加快知识产权运营公共服务平台体系建设，为专利转移转化、收购托管、交易流转、质押融资、专利导航等提供平台支撑，提高专利运用效益。制定出台相关政策，营造良好的专利保护环境，促进高质量创造和高价值专利实施。

2．实施商标战略。提升商标注册便利化水平，优化商标审查体系，建立健全便捷高效的商标审查协作机制。提升商标权保护工作效能，为商标建设营造公平竞争的市场环境。创新商标行政指导和服务监管方式，提升企业运用商标制度能力，打造知名品牌。研究建立商标价值评估体系，构建商标与国民生产总值、就业规模等经济指标相融合的指标体系。建立国家商标信息库。

3．打造精品版权。全面完善版权社会服务体系，发挥版权社会服务机构的作用。推动版权资产管理制度建设。建立版权贸易基地、交易中心工作协调机制。充分发挥全国版权示范城市、单位、园区（基地）的示范引导作用。打造一批规模化、集约化、专业化的版权企业，带动版权产业健康快速发展。鼓励形成一批拥有精品品牌的广播影视播映和制作经营机构，打造精品影视节目版权和版权产业链。鼓励文化领域商业模式创新，大力发展版权代理和版权经纪业务，促进版权产业和市场的发展。

4．加强地理标志、植物新品种和集成电路布图设计等领域知识产权工作。建立地理标志联合认定机制，加强我国地理标志在海外市场注册和保护工作。推动建立统筹协调的植物新品种管理机制，推进植物新品种测试体系建设，加快制定植物新品种测试指南，提高审查测试水平。加强种子企业与高校、科研机构的协作创新，建立授权植物新品种的基因图谱数据库，为维权取证和执法提供技术支撑。完善集成电路布图设计保护制度，优化集成电路布图设计的登记和撤销程序，充分发挥集成电路布图设计制度的作用，促进集成电路产业升级发展。

（四）加强知识产权强省、强市建设。

1．建成一批知识产权强省、强市。推进引领型、支撑型、特色型知识产权强省建设，发挥知识产权强省的示范带动作用。深入开展知识产权试点示范工作，可在国家知识产权示范城市、全国版权示范城市等基础上建成一批布局合理、特色明显的知识产权强市。进一步探索建设适合国情的县域知识产权工作机制。

2．促进区域知识产权协调发展。推动开展知识产权区域布局试点，形成以知识产权资源为核心的配置导向目录，推进区域知识产权资源配置和政策优化调整。支持西部地区改善创新环境，加快知识产权发展，提升企业事业单位知识产权创造运用水平。制定实施支持东北地区等老工业基地振兴的知识产权政策，推动东北地区等老工业基地传统制造业转型升级。提升中部地区特色优势产业的知识产权水平。支持东部地区在知识产权运用方面积极探索、率先发展，培育若干带动区域知识产权协同发展的增长极。推动京津冀知识产权保护一体、运用协同、服务共享，促进创新要素自由合理流动。推进长江经济带知识产权建设，引导产业优化布局和分工协作。

3. 做好知识产权领域扶贫工作。加大对边远地区传统知识、遗传资源、民间文艺、中医药等领域知识产权的保护与运用力度。利用知识产权人才优势、技术优势和信息优势进一步开发地理标志产品，加强植物新品种保护，引导注册地理标志商标，推广应用涉农专利技术。开展知识产权富民工作，推进实施商标富农工程，充分发挥农产品商标和地理标志在农业产业化中的作用，培育一批知识产权扶贫精品项目。支持革命老区、民族地区、边疆地区、贫困地区加强知识产权机构建设，提升知识产权数量和保护水平。

（五）加快知识产权强企建设。

1. 提升企业知识产权综合能力。推行企业知识产权管理国家标准，在生产经营、科技创新中加强知识产权全过程管理。完善知识产权认证制度，探索建立知识产权管理体系认证结果的国际互认机制。推动开展知识产权协同运用，鼓励和支持大型企业开展知识产权评议工作，在重点领域合作中开展知识产权评估、收购、运营、风险预警与应对。切实增强企业知识产权意识，支持企业加大知识产权投入，提高竞争力。

2. 培育知识产权优势企业。出台知识产权优势企业建设指南，推动建立企业知识产权服务机制，引导优质服务力量助力企业形成知识产权竞争优势。出台知识产权示范企业培育指导性文件，提升企业知识产权战略管理能力、市场竞争力和行业影响力。

3. 完善知识产权强企工作支撑体系。完善知识产权资产的财务、评估等管理制度及相关会计准则，引导企业发布知识产权经营报告书。提升企业知识产权资产管理能力，推动企业在并购重组、股权激励、对外投资等活动中的知识产权资产管理。加强政府、企业和社会的协作，引导企业开展形式多样的知识产权资本化运作。

专栏 4 知识产权强企工程

推行企业知识产权管理规范。建立政策引导、咨询服务和第三方认证体系。培养企业知识产权管理专业化人才队伍。

制定知识产权强企建设方案。建立分类指导的政策体系，塑造企业示范典型，培育一批具备国际竞争优势的知识产权领军企业。实施中小企业知识产权战略推进工程，加大知识产权保护援助力度，构建服务支撑体系，扶持中小企业创新发展。

鼓励企业国际化发展。引导企业开展海外知识产权布局。发挥知识产权联盟作用，鼓励企业将专利转化为国际标准。促进知识产权管理体系标准、认证国际化。

（六）推动产业升级发展。

1. 推动专利导航产业发展。深入实施专利导航试点工程，引导产业创新发展，开展产业知识产权全球战略布局，助推产业提质增效升级。面向战略性新兴产业，在新材料、生物医药、物联网、新能源、高端装备制造等领域实施一批产业规划类和企业运营类专利导航项目。在全面创新改革试验区、自由贸易试验区、中外合作产业园区、知识产权试点示范园区等重点区域，推动建立专利导航产业发展工作机制。

2. 完善“中国制造”知识产权布局。围绕“中国制造 2025”的重点领域和“互联网+”行动的关键环节，形成一批产业关键核心共性技术知识产权。实施制造业知识产权协同运用推进工程，在制造业创新中心建设等重大工程实施中支持骨干企业、高校、科研院所协同创新、联合研发，形成一批产业化导向的专利组合，强化创新成果转化运用。

3. 促进知识产权密集型产业发展。制定知识产权密集型产业目录和发展规划，发布知识产权密集型产业的发展态势报告。运用股权投资基金等市场化方式，引导社会资金投入知识产权密集型产业。加大政府采购对知识产权密集型产品的支持力度。鼓励有条件的地区发展知识产权密集型产业集聚区，构建优势互补的产业协调发展格局。建设一批高增长、高收益的知识产权密集型产业，促进产业提质增效升级。

4. 支持产业知识产权联盟发展。鼓励组建产业知识产权联盟，开展联盟备案管理和服务，建立重点产业联盟管理库，对联盟发展状况进行评议监测和分类指导。支持成立知识产权服务联盟。属于社会组织的，依法履行登记手续。支持联盟构筑和运营产业专利池，推动形成标准必要专利，建立重点产业知识产权侵权监控和风险应对机制。鼓励社会资本设立知识产权产业化专项基金，充分发挥重点产业知识产权运营基金作用，提高产业知识产权运营水平与国际竞争力，保障产业技术安全。

5. 深化知识产权评议工作。实施知识产权评议工程，研究制定相关政策。围绕国家重大产业规划、政府重大投资项目等开展知识产权评议，积极探索重大科技经济活动知识产权评议试点。建立国家科技计划（专项、基金等）知识产权目标评估制度。加强知识产权评议专业机构建设和人才培养，积极推动评议成果运用，建立重点领域评议报告发布机制。推动制定评议服务相关标准。鼓励和支持行业骨干企业与专业机构在重点领域合作开展评议工作，提高创新效率，防范知识产权风险。

专栏5　知识产权评议工程

推进重点领域知识产权评议工作。加强知识产权主管部门与产业主管部门间的沟通协作，围绕国家科技重大专项以及战略性新兴产业，针对高端通用芯片、高档数控机床、集成电路装备、宽带移动通信、油气田、核电站、水污染治理、转基因生物新品种、新药创制、传染病防治等领域的关键核心技术深入开展知识产权评议工作，及时提供或发布评议报告。

提升知识产权评议能力。制定发布重大经济活动评议指导手册和分类评议实务指引，规范评议范围和程序。实施评议能力提升计划，支持开发评议工具，培养一批评议人才。

培育知识产权评议服务力量。培育知识产权评议服务示范机构，加强服务供需对接。推动评议服务行业组织建设，支持制定评议服务标准，鼓励联盟实施行业自律。加强评议服务机构国际交流，拓展服务空间。

6. 推动军民知识产权转移转化。加强国防知识产权保护，完善国防知识产权归属与利益分配机制。制定促进知识产权军民双向转化的指导意见。放开国防知识产权代理服务行业，建立和完善相应的准入退出机制。推动国防知识产权信息平台建设，分类建设国防知识产权信息资源，逐步开放检索。营造有利于军民协同创新、双向转化的国防科技工业知识产权政策环境。建设完善国防科技工业知识产权平台，完成专利信息平台建设，形成更加完善的国防科技工业专利基础数据库。

（七）促进知识产权开放合作。

1. 加强知识产权国际交流合作。进一步加强涉外知识产权事务的统筹协调。加强与经贸相关的多双边知识产权对外谈判、双边知识产权合作磋商机制及国内立场的协调等工作。积极参与知识产权国际规则制定，加快推进保护广播组织条约修订，推动公共健康多哈宣言落实和视听表演北京条约尽快生效，做好我国批准马拉喀什条约相关准备工作。加强与世界知识产权组织、世界贸易组织及相关国际组织的交流合作。拓宽知识产权公共外交渠道。继续巩固发展知识产权多双边合作关系，加强与“一带一路”沿线国家、金砖国家的知识产权交流合作。加强我驻国际组织、主要国家和地区外交机构中涉知识产权事务的人才储备和人力配备。

2. 积极支持创新企业“走出去”。健全企业海外知识产权维权援助体系。鼓励社会资本设立中国企业海外知识产权维权援助服务基金。制定实施应对海外产业重大知识产权纠纷的政策。完善海外知识产权信息服务平台，发布相关国家和地区知识产权制度环境等信息。支持企业广泛开展知识产权跨国交易，推动有自主知识产权的服务和产品“走出去”。继续开展外向型企业海外知识产权保护以及纠纷应对实务培训。

专栏 6　知识产权海外维权工程

健全风险预警机制。推动企业在人才引进、国际参展、产品和技术进出口、企业并购等活动中开展知识产权风险评估，提高企业应对知识产权纠纷能力。加强对知识产权案件的跟踪研究，及时发布风险提示。

建立海外维权援助机制。加强中国保护知识产权海外维权信息平台建设。发布海外知识产权服务机构和专家名录及案例数据库。建立海外展会知识产权快速维权长效机制，组建海外展会快速维权中心，建立海外展会快速维权与常规维权援助联动的工作机制。

五、重大专项

（一）加强知识产权交易运营体系建设。

1. 完善知识产权运营公共服务平台。发挥中央财政资金引导作用，建设全国知识产权运营公共服务平台，依托文化产权、知识产权等无形资产交易场所开展版权交易，审慎设立版权交易平台。出台有关行业管理规则，加强对知识产权交易运营的业务指导和行业管理。以知识产权运营公共服务平台为基础，推动建立基于互联网、基础统一的知识产权质押登记平台。

2. 创新知识产权金融服务。拓展知识产权质押融资试点内容和工作范围，完善风险管理以及补偿机制，鼓励社会资本发起设立小微企业风险补偿基金。探索开展知识产权证券化和信托业务，支持以知识产权出资入股，在依法合规的前提下开展互联网知识产权金融服务，加强专利价值分析与应用效果评价工作，加快专利价值分析标准化建设。加强对知识产权质押的动态管理。

3. 加强知识产权协同运用。面向行业协会、高校和科研机构深入开展专利协同运用试点建立订单式发明、投放式创新的专利协同运用机制。培育建设一批产业特色鲜明、优势突出具有国际影响力的专业化知识产权运营机构。强化行业协会在知识产权联合创造、协同运用合力保护、共同管理等方面的作用。鼓励高校和科研机构强化知识产权申请、运营权责，加大知识产权转化力度。引导高校院所、企业联合共建专利技术产业化基地。

专栏 7　知识产权投融资服务工程

建设全国知识产权运营公共服务体系。推进知识产权运营交易全过程电子化，积极开展知识产权运营项目管理。加快培育国家专利运营试点企业，加快推进西安知识产权军民融合试点、珠海知识产权金融试点及华北、华南等区域知识产权运营中心建设。

深化知识产权投融资工作。优化质押融资服务机制，鼓励有条件的地区建立知识产权保险奖补机制。研究推进知识产权海外侵权责任保险工作。深入开展知识产权质押融资风险补偿基金和重点产业知识产权运营基金试点。探索知识产权证券化，完善知识产权信用担保机制，推动发展投贷联动、投保联动、投债联动等新模式。创新知识产权投融资产品。在全面创新改革试验区引导创业投资基金、股权投资基金加强对知识产权领域的投资。

创新管理运行方式。支持探索知识产权创造与运营的众包模式，鼓励金融机构在风险可控和商业可持续的前提下，基于众创、众包、众扶等新模式特点开展金融产品和服务创新，积极发展知识产权质押融资，促进“互联网＋”知识产权融合发展。

（二）加强知识产权公共服务体系建设。

1. 提高知识产权公共服务能力。建立健全知识产权公共服务网络，增加知识产权信息公共服务产品供给。推动知识产权基础信息与经济、法律、科技、产业运行等其他信息资源互联互通。实施产业知识产权服务能力提升行动，创新对中小微企业和初创型企业的服务方式。发展“互联网＋”知识产权服务等新模式，培育规模化、专业化、市场化、国际化的知识产权服务品牌机构。

2. 建设知识产权信息公共服务平台。实现专利、商标、版权、集成电路布图设计、植物新品种、地理标志以及知识产权诉讼等基础信息资源免费或低成本开放共享。运用云计算、大数据、移动互联网等技术，实现平台知识产权信息统计、整合、推送服务。

专栏 8　知识产权信息公共服务平台建设工程

建设公共服务网络。制定发布知识产权公共服务事项目录和办事指南。增加知识产权信息服务网点，加强公共图书馆、高校图书馆、科技信息服务机构、行业组织等的知识产权信息服务能力建设。

创建产业服务平台。依托专业机构创建一批布局合理、开放协同、市场化运作的产业知识产权信息公共服务平台，在中心城市、自由贸易试验区、国家自主创新示范区、国家级高新区、国家级经济技术开发区等提供知识产权服务。在众创空间等创新创业平台设置知识产权服务工作站。

整合服务和数据资源。整合知识产权信息资源、创新资源和服务资源，推进实体服务与网络服务协作，促进从研发创意、知识产权化、流通化到产业化的协同创新。建设专利基础数据资源开放平台，免费或低成本扩大专利数据的推广运用。建立财政资助项目形成的知识产权信息和上市企业知识产权信息公开窗口。

3. 建设知识产权服务业集聚区。在自由贸易试验区、国家自主创新示范区、国家级高新区、中外合作产业园区、国家级经济技术开发区等建设一批国家知识产权服务业集聚区。鼓励知识产权服务机构入驻创新创业资源密集区域，提供市场化、专业化的服务，满足创新创业者多样化需求。针对不同区域，加强分类指导，引导知识产权服务资源合理流动，与区域产业深度对接，促进经济提质增效升级。

4. 加强知识产权服务业监管。完善知识产权服务业统计制度，建立服务机构名录库。成立知识产权服务标准化技术组织，推动完善服务标准体系建设，开展标准化试点示范。完善专利代理管理制度，加强事中事后监管。健全知识产权服务诚信信息管理、信用评价和失信惩戒等管理制度，及时披露相关执业信息。研究建立知识产权服务业全国性行业组织。具备条件的地方，可探索开展知识产权服务行业协会组织“一业多会”试点。

（三）加强知识产权人才培育体系建设。

1. 加强知识产权人才培养。加强知识产权相关学科专业建设，支持高等学校在管理学和经济学等学科中增设知识产权专业，支持理工类高校设置知识产权专业。加强知识产权学历教育和非学历继续教育，加强知识产权专业学位教育。构建政府部门、高校和社会相结合的多元知识产权教育培训组织模式，支持行业组织与专业机构合作，加大实务人才培育力度。加强国家知识产权培训基地建设工作，完善师资、教材、远程系统等基础建设。加大对领导干部、企业家和各类创新人才的知识产权培训力度。鼓励高等学校、科研院所开展知识产权国际学术交流，鼓励我国知识产权人才获得海外相应资格证书。推动将知识产权课程纳入各级党校、行政学院培训和选学内容。

2. 优化知识产权人才成长体系。加强知识产权高层次人才队伍建设，加大知识产权管理、运营和专利信息分析等人才培养力度。统筹协调知识产权人才培训、实践和使用，加强知识产权领军人才、国际化专业人才的培养与引进。构建多层次、高水平的知识产权智库体系。探索建立行业协会和企业事业单位专利专员制度。选拔一批知识产权创业导师，加强创新创业指导。

3. 建立人才发现与评价机制。建立人才引进使用中的知识产权鉴定机制，利用知识产权信息发现人才。完善知识产权职业水平评价制度，制定知识产权专业人员能力素质标准。鼓励知识产权服务人才和创新型人才跨界交流和有序流动，防范人才流动法律风险。建立创新人才知识产权维权援助机制。

（四）加强知识产权文化建设。

1. 加大知识产权宣传普及力度。健全知识产权新闻发布制度，拓展信息发布渠道。组织开展全国知识产权宣传周、中国专利周、绿书签、中国国际商标品牌节等重大宣传活动。丰富知识产权宣传普及形式，发挥新媒体传播作用。支持优秀作品创作，推出具有影响力的知识产权题材影视文化作品，弘扬知识产权正能量。

2. 实施知识产权教育推广计划。鼓励知识产权文化和理论研究，加强普及型教育，推出优秀研究成果和普及读物。将知识产权内容全面纳入国家普法教育和全民科学素养提升工作。

专栏 9 知识产权文化建设工程

*加强宣传推广。*利用新媒体，加强知识产权相关法律法规、典型案例的宣传。讲好中国知识产权故事，推出具有影响力的知识产权主题书籍、影视作品，挖掘报道典型人物和案例。

*加强普及型教育。*开展全国中小学知识产权教育试点示范工作，建立若干知识产权宣传教育示范学校。引导各类学校把知识产权文化建设与学生思想道德建设、校园文化建设、主题教育活动紧密结合，增强学生的知识产权意识和创新意识。

*繁荣文化和理论研究。*鼓励支持教育界、学术界广泛参与知识产权理论体系研究，支持创作兼具社会及经济效益的知识产权普及读物，增强知识产权文化传播的针对性和实效性，支撑和促进中国特色知识产权文化建设。

六、实施保障

（一）加强组织协调。各地区、各相关部门要高度重视，加强组织领导，明确责任分工，结合实际细化落实本规划提出的目标任务，制定专项规划、年度计划和配套政策，推动规划有效落实。加强统筹协调，充分发挥国务院知识产权战略实施工作部际联席会议制度作用，做好规划组织实施工作。全国打击侵犯知识产权和制售假冒伪劣商品工作领导小组要切实加强对打击侵犯知识产权和制售假冒伪劣商品工作的统一组织领导。各相关部门要依法履职，认真贯彻落实本规划要求，密切协作，形成规划实施合力。

（二）加强财力保障。加强财政预算与规划实施的相互衔接协调，各级财政按照现行经费渠道对规划实施予以合理保障，鼓励社会资金投入知识产权各项规划工作，促进知识产权事业发展。统筹各级各部门与知识产权相关的公共资源，突出投入重点，优化支出结构，切实保障重点任务、重大项目的落实。

（三）加强考核评估。各地区、各相关部门要加强对本规划实施情况的动态监测和评估工作。国务院知识产权战略实施工作部际联席会议办公室要会同相关部门按照本规划的部署和要求，建立规划实施情况的评估机制，对各项任务落实情况组织开展监督检查和绩效评估工作，重要情况及时报告国务院。

国务院办公厅印发《国务院关于新形势下加快知识产权强国建设的若干意见》重点任务分工方案的通知

国办函［2016］66 号

各省、自治区、直辖市人民政府，国务院有关部门：

《〈国务院关于新形势下加快知识产权强国建设的若干意见〉重点任务分工方案》已经国务院同意，现印发给你们，请认真贯彻执行。

各有关部门要按照分工方案要求，进一步分解细化涉及本部门的工作，抓紧制定具体措施。涉及多个部门的工作，牵头部门要加强协调，相关部门要密切配合。各省、自治区、直辖市人民政府要加强组织领导，落实责任，结合实际制定实施方案和配套政策。要充分发挥全国打击侵犯知识产权和制售假冒伪劣商品工作领导小组作用，加强知识产权保护，调动各方积极性，形成工作合力。国务院知识产权战略实施工作部际联席会议办公室要加强工作统筹，协调解决重大问题，加强对有关政策措施落实工作的指导、督促、检查，切实推动各项措施落实。

国务院办公厅

2016 年 7 月 8 日

（此件公开发布）

《国务院关于新形势下加快知识产权强国建设的若干意见》重点任务分工方案

为落实《国务院关于新形势下加快知识产权强国建设的若干意见》（国发［2015］71 号），根据各相关部门职责，对各项重点任务作如下分工。

一、推进知识产权管理体制机制改革

（一）研究完善知识产权管理体制。

1. 完善国家知识产权战略实施工作部际联席会议制度，由国务院领导同志担任召集人。（知识产权局负责）

2. 积极研究探索知识产权管理体制机制改革。（中央编办、知识产权局、工商总局、版权局负责。列第一位者为牵头部门，下同）

3. 授权地方开展知识产权改革试验。鼓励有条件的地方开展知识产权综合管理改革试点。（知识产权局、中央编办、工商总局、版权局负责）

（二）改善知识产权服务业及社会组织管理。

4. 放宽知识产权服务业准入，促进服务业优质高效发展，加快建设知识产权服务业集聚区。（知识产权局、工商总局、版权局负责）

5. 扩大专利代理领域开放，放宽对专利代理机构股东或合伙人的条件限制。（知识产权局负责）

6. 探索开展知识产权服务行业协会组织“一业多会”试点。完善执业信息披露制度，及

时公开知识产权代理机构和从业人员信用评价等相关信息。(知识产权局、工商总局、版权局负责)

7. 规范著作权集体管理机构收费标准，完善收益分配制度，让著作权人获得更多许可收益。(版权局负责)

(三) 建立重大经济活动知识产权评议制度。

8. 研究制定知识产权评议政策。完善知识产权评议工作指南，规范评议范围和程序。围绕国家重大产业规划、高技术领域重大投资项目等开展知识产权评议，建立国家科技计划知识产权目标评估制度，积极探索重大科技活动知识产权评议试点，建立重点领域知识产权评议报告发布制度，提高创新效率，降低产业发展风险。(知识产权局、发展改革委、科技部、工业和信息化部、工商总局负责)

(四) 建立以知识产权为重要内容的创新驱动发展评价制度。

9. 将知识产权产品逐步纳入国民经济核算，将知识产权指标纳入国民经济和社会发展规划。(统计局、发展改革委、知识产权局、工商总局、版权局负责)

10. 在对党政领导班子和领导干部进行综合考核评价时，注重鼓励发明创造、保护知识产权、加强转化运用、营造良好环境等方面的情况和成效。(中央组织部、知识产权局、工商总局、版权局负责)

11. 探索建立经营业绩、知识产权和创新并重的国有企业考评模式。(国资委、中央组织部、知识产权局负责)

12. 按照国家有关规定设置知识产权奖励项目，加大各类国家奖励制度的知识产权评价权重。(知识产权局、人力资源社会保障部、工商总局、版权局负责)

13. 发布年度知识产权发展状况报告。(知识产权局、农业部、工商总局、质检总局、版权局、林业局负责)

二、实行严格的知识产权保护

(一) 加大知识产权侵权行为惩治力度。

14. 提高知识产权侵权法定赔偿上限，针对情节严重的恶意侵权行为实施惩罚性赔偿并由侵权人承担实际发生的合理开支。(高法院、农业部、文化部、海关总署、工商总局、质检总局、版权局、食品药品监管总局、林业局、知识产权局、法制办按职责分别负责)

15. 进一步推进侵犯知识产权行政处罚案件信息公开。(全国打击侵权假冒工作领导小组办公室、农业部、文化部、海关总署、工商总局、质检总局、版权局、食品药品监管总局、林业局、知识产权局负责)

16. 完善知识产权快速维权机制。(知识产权局负责)

17. 加大国际展会、电子商务等领域知识产权执法力度。(农业部、文化部、海关总署、工商总局、质检总局、版权局、食品药品监管总局、林业局、知识产权局按职责分别负责)

18. 开展与相关国际组织和境外执法部门的联合执法，加强知识产权司法保护对外合作。(高法院、高检院、公安部、司法部、农业部、商务部、文化部、海关总署、工商总局、质检总局、版权局、食品药品监管总局、林业局、知识产权局按职责分别负责)

(二) 加大知识产权犯罪打击力度。

19. 依法严厉打击侵犯知识产权犯罪行为，重点打击链条式、产业化知识产权犯罪网络。(公安部负责)

20. 进一步加强知识产权行政执法与刑事司法衔接，加大涉嫌犯罪案件移交工作力度。(全国打击侵权假冒工作领导小组办公室、高检院牵头，高法院、公安部、农业部、文化部、海关总署、工商总局、质检总局、版权局、林业局、知识产权局负责)

21. 完善涉外知识产权执法机制，加强刑事执法国际合作，加大涉外知识产权犯罪案件侦办力度。(全国打击侵权假冒工作领导小组办公室、公安部、商务部、海关总署、工商总局、

质检总局、版权局、知识产权局、贸促会负责）

22. 加强与有关国际组织和国家间打击知识产权犯罪行为的司法协助，加大案情通报和情报信息交换力度。（司法部、高法院、高检院、公安部、海关总署、工商总局、质检总局、版权局、知识产权局负责）

（三）建立健全知识产权保护预警防范机制。

23. 将故意侵犯知识产权行为情况纳入企业和个人信用记录。（发展改革委、人民银行牵头，工商总局、版权局、知识产权局等负责）

24. 推动完善商业秘密保护法律法规，加强人才交流和技术合作中的商业秘密保护。（工商总局、法制办负责）

25. 加强海关知识产权执法保护。建立收集假冒产品来源地相关信息的工作机制，发布年度中国海关知识产权保护状况报告。（海关总署、工商总局、知识产权局、邮政局负责）

26. 加强大型专业化市场知识产权管理和保护工作。（工商总局、质检总局、版权局、知识产权局按职责分别负责）

27. 发挥行业组织在知识产权保护中的积极作用。（全国打击侵权假冒工作领导小组办公室负责）

28. 运用大数据、云计算、物联网等信息技术，加强在线创意、研发成果的知识产权保护，提升预警防范能力。（知识产权局、网信办负责）

29. 加大对小微企业知识产权保护援助力度，构建公平竞争、公平监管的创新创业和营商环境。（工业和信息化部、公安部、司法部、农业部、商务部、文化部、人民银行、海关总署、工商总局、质检总局、版权局、林业局、知识产权局、网信办、邮政局按职责分别负责）

30. 开展知识产权保护社会满意度调查。（中央综治办、知识产权局按职责分别负责）

（四）加强新业态新领域创新成果的知识产权保护。

31. 完善植物新品种、生物遗传资源及其相关传统知识、数据库保护和国防知识产权等相关法律制度。（科技部、环境保护部、农业部、林业局、知识产权局、法制办、国防科工局、中央军委装备发展部按职责分别负责）

32. 适时做好地理标志立法工作。（农业部、工商总局、质检总局、法制办按职责分别负责）

33. 研究完善商业模式知识产权保护制度和实用艺术品外观设计专利保护制度。（知识产权局、高法院牵头负责）

34. 加强互联网、电子商务、大数据等领域的知识产权保护规则研究，推动完善相关法律法规。（全国打击侵权假冒工作领导小组办公室、中央综治办、高法院、工业和信息化部、公安部、农业部、商务部、文化部、海关总署、工商总局、质检总局、版权局、食品药品监管总局、林业局、知识产权局、法制办、网信办负责）

35. 制定众创、众包、众扶、众筹的知识产权保护政策。（知识产权局负责）

（五）规制知识产权滥用行为。

36. 完善规制知识产权滥用行为的法律制度，制定相关反垄断执法指南。（发展改革委、商务部、工商总局、知识产权局、法制办按职责分别负责）

37. 完善知识产权反垄断监管机制，依法查处滥用知识产权排除和限制竞争等垄断行为。（发展改革委、商务部、工商总局按职责分别负责）

38. 完善标准必要专利的公平、合理、无歧视许可政策和停止侵权适用规则。（质检总局、知识产权局、工业和信息化部、高法院负责）

三、促进知识产权创造运用

（一）完善知识产权审查和注册机制。

39. 建立计算机软件著作权快速登记通道。（版权局负责）

40. 优化专利和商标的审查流程与方式，实现知识产权在线登记、电子申请和无纸化审批。（工商总局、知识产权局按职责分别负责）

41. 完善知识产权审查协作机制。（中央编办、工商总局、知识产权局按职责分别负责）

42. 建立重点优势产业专利申请的集中审查制度，建立健全涉及产业安全的专利审查工作机制。（知识产权局、工业和信息化部负责）

43. 合理扩大专利确权程序依职权审查范围，完善授权后专利文件修改制度。（知识产权局、法制办负责）

44. 拓展“专利审查高速路”国际合作网络，加快建设世界一流专利审查机构。（知识产权局负责）

（二）完善职务发明制度。

45. 鼓励和引导企事业单位依法建立健全发明报告、权属划分、奖励报酬、纠纷解决等职务发明管理制度。（知识产权局、教育部、科技部、工业和信息化部、农业部、国资委、林业局、中科院负责）

46. 探索完善创新成果收益分配制度，提高骨干团队、主要发明人收益比重，保障职务发明人的合法权益。按照相关政策规定，鼓励国有企业赋予下属科研院所知识产权处置和收益分配权。（知识产权局、科技部、教育部、财政部、农业部、国资委、中科院、国防科工局负责）

（三）推动专利许可制度改革。

47. 强化专利以许可方式对外扩散。研究建立专利当然许可制度，鼓励更多专利权人对社会公开许可专利。（知识产权局、法制办负责）

48. 完善专利强制许可启动、审批和实施程序。（知识产权局负责）

49. 鼓励高等院校、科研院所等事业单位通过无偿许可专利的方式，支持单位员工和大学生创新创业。（教育部、科技部、财政部、知识产权局、中科院负责）

（四）加强知识产权交易平台建设。

50. 构建知识产权运营服务体系，加快建设全国知识产权运营公共服务平台。（知识产权局、财政部、教育部、科技部、工业和信息化部、国资委、中科院、国防科工局、中央军委装备发展部负责）

51. 创新知识产权投融资产品，探索知识产权证券化，完善知识产权信用担保机制，推动发展投贷联动、投保联动、投债联动等新模式。在全面创新改革试验区域引导天使投资、风险投资、私募基金加强对高技术领域的投资。（人民银行、工商总局、版权局、知识产权局、银监会、证监会按职责分别负责）

52. 细化会计准则规定，推动企业科学核算和管理知识产权资产。（财政部、知识产权局负责）

53. 推动高等院校、科研院所建立健全知识产权转移转化机构。（知识产权局、教育部、中科院、国防科工局负责）

54. 支持探索知识产权创造与运营的众筹、众包模式，促进“互联网＋知识产权”融合发展。（知识产权局、发展改革委、工业和信息化部、证监会负责）

（五）培育知识产权密集型产业。

55. 探索制定知识产权密集型产业目录和发展规划。运用股权投资基金等市场化方式，引导社会资金投入知识产权密集型产业。加大政府采购对知识产权密集型产品的支持力度。（知识产权局、发展改革委、财政部负责）

56. 试点建设知识产权密集型产业集聚区和知识产权密集型产业产品示范基地，推行知识产权集群管理。（知识产权局、发展改革委负责）

（六）提升知识产权附加值和国际影响力。

57. 实施专利质量提升工程，培育一批核心专利。加大轻工、纺织、服装等产业的外观设计专利保护力度。（知识产权局负责）

58. 深化商标富农工作。(工商总局、农业部负责)

59. 加强对非物质文化遗产、民间文艺、传统知识的开发利用,推进文化创意、设计服务与相关产业融合发展。(文化部、版权局、知识产权局按职责分别负责)

60. 支持企业运用知识产权进行海外股权投资。(知识产权局、工业和信息化部、国资委负责)

61. 积极参与国际标准制定,推动有知识产权的创新技术转化为标准。(质检总局、工业和信息化部、知识产权局、国防科工局负责)

62. 支持研究机构和社会组织制定品牌评价国际标准,建立品牌价值评价体系。支持企业建立品牌管理体系,鼓励企业收购海外知名品牌。(质检总局、商务部、工商总局、国资委负责)

63. 保护和传承中华老字号,大力推动中医药、中华传统餐饮、工艺美术等企业"走出去"。(商务部、文化部、卫生计生委按职责分别负责)

(七)加强知识产权信息开放利用。

64. 建立财政资助项目形成的知识产权信息披露制度。(知识产权局、科技部、财政部负责)

65. 加快落实上市企业知识产权信息披露制度。(证监会、知识产权局、工商总局负责)

66. 规范知识产权信息采集程序和内容。(知识产权局、工商总局、版权局负责)

67. 完善知识产权许可的信息备案和公告制度。(知识产权局负责)

68. 加快建设互联互通的知识产权信息公共服务平台,实现专利、商标、版权、集成电路布图设计、植物新品种、地理标志等基础信息免费或低成本开放。(知识产权局、发展改革委、农业部、工商总局、质检总局、版权局、林业局负责)

69. 增加知识产权信息服务网点,完善知识产权信息公共服务网络。(知识产权局、工商总局、版权局负责)

70. 推进专利数据信息资源开放共享,增强大数据运用能力。依法及时公开专利审查过程信息。(知识产权局、发展改革委负责)

四、加强重点产业知识产权海外布局和风险防控

(一)加强重点产业知识产权海外布局规划。

71. 加大创新成果标准化和专利化工作力度,推动形成标准研制与专利布局有效衔接机制。研究制定标准必要专利布局指南。(质检总局、知识产权局、商务部负责)

72. 围绕战略性新兴产业等重点领域,建立专利导航产业发展工作机制,实施产业规划类和企业运营类专利导航项目,绘制服务我国产业发展的相关国家和地区专利导航图。(知识产权局、发展改革委、工业和信息化部负责)

73. 编制发布相关国家和地区专利申请实务指引。(知识产权局负责)

(二)拓展海外知识产权布局渠道。

74. 推动企业、科研机构、高等院校等联合开展海外专利布局工作。鼓励企业建立专利收储基金。(知识产权局、教育部、工业和信息化部、财政部、商务部、国资委、中科院、国防科工局、贸促会负责)

75. 加强企业知识产权布局指导,在产业园区和重点企业探索设立知识产权布局设计中心。(知识产权局、科技部、工业和信息化部、国资委负责)

76. 分类制定知识产权跨国许可与转让指南,编制发布知识产权许可合同范本。(知识产权局、商务部负责)

(三)完善海外知识产权风险预警体系。

77. 建立健全知识产权管理与服务等标准体系。(知识产权局、质检总局负责)

78. 支持行业协会、专业机构跟踪发布重点产业知识产权信息和竞争动态。制定完善与知识产权相关的贸易调查应对与风险防控国别指南。完善海外知识产权信息服务平台,发布相关

国家和地区知识产权制度环境等信息。建立完善企业海外知识产权问题及案件信息提交机制，加强对重大知识产权案件的跟踪研究，及时发布风险提示。（工业和信息化部、商务部、工商总局、知识产权局、贸促会按职责分别负责）

（四）提升海外知识产权风险防控能力。

79. 研究完善技术进出口管理相关制度，优化简化技术进出口审批流程。（商务部负责）

80. 完善财政资助科技计划项目形成的知识产权对外转让和独占许可管理制度。（商务部、科技部牵头，财政部、知识产权局负责）

81. 制定并推行知识产权尽职调查规范。支持法律服务机构为企业提供全方位、高品质知识产权法律服务。（司法部、工商总局、版权局、知识产权局负责）

82. 探索以公证方式保管知识产权证据、证明材料。（司法部、高法院、工商总局、版权局、知识产权局负责）

83. 推动企业建立知识产权分析评议机制，重点针对人才引进、国际参展、产品和技术进出口等活动开展知识产权风险评估，提高企业应对知识产权国际纠纷能力。（知识产权局、商务部牵头，工业和信息化部、国资委、贸促会负责）

（五）加强海外知识产权维权援助。

84. 制定实施应对海外产业重大知识产权纠纷的政策。（商务部、知识产权局牵头，工业和信息化部、海关总署、工商总局、质检总局、版权局、贸促会负责）

85. 研究我驻国际组织、主要国家和地区外交机构中涉知识产权事务的人力配备。（中央编办、外交部、财政部、商务部、工商总局、知识产权局、贸促会按职责分别负责）

86. 发布海外和涉外知识产权服务和维权援助机构名录，推动形成海外知识产权服务网络。（商务部、工商总局、知识产权局、贸促会按职责分别负责）

五、提升知识产权对外合作水平

（一）推动构建更加公平合理的国际知识产权规则。

87. 积极参与联合国框架下的发展议程，推动《TRIPs协定与公共健康多哈宣言》落实和《视听表演北京条约》生效，参与《专利合作条约》、《保护广播组织条约》、《生物多样性公约》等规则修订的国际谈判，推进加入《工业品外观设计国际注册海牙协定》和《马拉喀什条约》进程。（外交部、环境保护部、农业部、商务部、海关总署、工商总局、版权局、林业局、知识产权局、贸促会按职责分别负责）

（二）加强知识产权对外合作机制建设。

88. 加强与世界知识产权组织、世界贸易组织及相关国际组织的合作交流。深化同主要国家知识产权、经贸、海关等部门的合作，巩固与传统合作伙伴的友好关系。（知识产权局、商务部、外交部牵头，农业部、文化部、海关总署、工商总局、质检总局、版权局、林业局、贸促会负责）

89. 推动相关国际组织在我国设立知识产权仲裁和调解分中心。（知识产权局、外交部、司法部负责）

90. 加强国内外知名地理标志产品的保护合作，促进地理标志产品国际化发展。（农业部、商务部、海关总署、工商总局、质检总局按职责分别负责）

91. 积极推动区域全面经济伙伴关系和亚太经济合作组织框架下的知识产权合作。（商务部、知识产权局、外交部、工商总局、质检总局、版权局负责）

92. 探索建立"一带一路"沿线国家和地区知识产权合作机制。（知识产权局、商务部牵头，外交部、发展改革委、工商总局、质检总局、版权局、贸促会负责）

（三）加大对发展中国家知识产权援助力度。

93. 支持和援助发展中国家知识产权能力建设，鼓励向部分最不发达国家优惠许可其发展急需的专利技术。（知识产权局、外交部、科技部、商务部负责）

94. 加强面向发展中国家的知识产权学历教育和短期培训。（知识产权局、外交部、教育部、人力资源社会保障部、商务部负责）

（四）拓宽知识产权公共外交渠道。

95. 拓宽企业参与国际和区域性知识产权规则制修订途径。推动国内服务机构、产业联盟等加强与国外相关组织的合作交流。（知识产权局、外交部、工业和信息化部、商务部、贸促会负责）

96. 建立博鳌亚洲论坛知识产权研讨交流机制，积极开展具有国际影响力的知识产权研讨交流活动。（知识产权局、商务部负责）

97. 建立具有国际水平的知识产权智库。（知识产权局负责）

六、加强政策保障

（一）加大财税和金融支持力度。

98. 运用财政资金引导和促进科技成果产权化、知识产权产业化。（知识产权局、科技部、财政部负责）

99. 落实研究开发费用税前加计扣除政策，对符合条件的知识产权费用按规定实行加计扣除。（财政部、税务总局负责）

100. 制定专利收费减缴办法，合理降低专利申请和维持费用。（财政部、发展改革委、知识产权局负责）

101. 积极推进知识产权海外侵权责任保险工作。（保监会、知识产权局负责）

102. 深入开展知识产权质押融资风险补偿基金和重点产业知识产权运营基金试点。（财政部、知识产权局牵头，工业和信息化部负责）

（二）加强知识产权专业人才队伍建设。

103. 加强知识产权相关学科建设，完善产学研联合培养模式，在管理学和经济学中增设知识产权专业，加强知识产权专业学位教育。加大对各类创新人才的知识产权培训力度。（教育部、知识产权局负责）

104. 鼓励各地引进高端知识产权人才，并参照有关人才引进计划给予相关待遇。探索建立知识产权国际化人才储备库和利用知识产权发现人才的信息平台。（中央组织部、知识产权局负责）

105. 鼓励我国知识产权人才获得海外相应资格证书。进一步完善知识产权职业水平评价制度，稳定和壮大知识产权专业人才队伍。选拔培训一批知识产权创业导师，加强青年创业指导。（知识产权局、人力资源社会保障部负责）

（三）加强宣传引导。

106. 广泛开展知识产权普及型教育，加强知识产权公益宣传和咨询服务，提高全社会知识产权意识。（中央宣传部、知识产权局、教育部、文化部、工商总局、版权局、网信办负责）

国务院办公厅关于印发知识产权综合管理改革试点总体方案的通知

国办发［2016］106号

各省、自治区、直辖市人民政府，国务院各部委、各直属机构：

《知识产权综合管理改革试点总体方案》已经国务院同意，现印发给你们，请认真贯彻执行。

国务院办公厅

2016年12月30日

（此件公开发布）

知识产权综合管理改革试点总体方案

推进知识产权综合管理改革是深化知识产权领域改革、破解知识产权支撑创新驱动发展瓶颈制约的关键，对于切实解决地方知识产权管理体制机制不完善、保护不够严格、服务能力不强、对创新驱动发展战略缺乏强有力支撑等突出问题具有重要意义。按照《国务院关于新形势下加快知识产权强国建设的若干意见》（国发［2015］71号）和《中央全面深化改革领导小组2016年工作要点》要求，为充分发挥有条件的地方在知识产权综合管理改革方面的先行探索和示范带动作用，制定本方案。

一、总体要求

（一）指导思想。全面贯彻党的十八大和十八届三中、四中、五中、六中全会精神，深入贯彻习近平总书记系列重要讲话精神，围绕统筹推进“五位一体”总体布局和协调推进“四个全面”战略布局，牢固树立和贯彻落实创新、协调、绿色、开放、共享的发展理念，按照党中央、国务院决策部署，深化知识产权领域改革，依法严格保护知识产权，打通知识产权创造、运用、保护、管理、服务全链条，构建便民利民的知识产权公共服务体系，探索支撑创新发展的知识产权运行机制，有效发挥知识产权制度激励创新的基本保障作用，保障和激励大众创业、万众创新，助推经济发展提质增效和产业结构转型升级。

（二）基本原则。

——问题导向。集中资源和力量破解制约知识产权支撑创新驱动发展的难题，因地制宜，实施知识产权综合管理，实行严格的知识产权保护，提升知识产权管理水平。

——紧扣发展。紧贴经济转型发展的重大需求，以改革促发展，充分发挥专利、商标、版权等知识产权的引领作用，有效发挥自主品牌消费对经济增长的拉动作用，激励创新创业，推动供需结构升级。

——统筹推进。统筹中央改革部署与地方改革需求，在有条件的地方开展知识产权综合管理改革试点，及时总结提炼，形成可复制经验，适时推广实施。

——大胆创新。注重顶层设计与基层探索相结合，突破妨碍知识产权发展的思想观念制约，尊重基层首创精神，激发全社会创新活力，允许多种类型、多种模式的改革探索和试验。

（三）试点布局和试点期限。根据国家实施创新驱动发展战略总体部署和重点区域发展战略布局，结合地方知识产权事业发展水平和创新驱动发展对知识产权综合管理改革的需求，选择若干个创新成果多、经济转型步伐快、发挥知识产权引领作用和推动供需结构升级成效显著的地方，开展知识产权综合管理改革试点。改革试点地方选择条件：（1）经济发展步入创新驱动转型窗口期，创新资源和创新活动集聚度高，专利、商标、版权等知识产权数量质量居于全国前列；（2）设有或纳入国家统筹的国家自主创新示范区、国家综合配套改革试验区、全面创新改革试验区、自由贸易试验区等各类国家级改革创新试验区和国家战略规划重点区域，或设有知识产权法院的地方；（3）知识产权战略推动地区经济发展成效显著，知识产权管理体制和市场监管体制机制改革走在前面，知识产权行政执法力量较强，知识产权行政执法效能突出。具体试点地方由国家知识产权局会同工商总局、新闻出版广电总局（国家版权局）等部门尽快研究共同确定。试点期限为 1 年。

（四）工作目标。通过在试点地方深化知识产权综合管理改革，推动形成权界清晰、分工合理、责权一致、运转高效、法治保障的知识产权体制机制。通过深化简政放权、放管结合、优化服务改革，实现知识产权行政管理更加顺畅、执法保护体系进一步完善、知识产权市场监管和公共服务水平明显提升，有力促进大众创业、万众创新，加快知识产权强国建设，为全面建成小康社会提供有力支撑。

二、主要任务

（一）建立高效的知识产权综合管理体制。鼓励多种类型、多种模式的改革探索。科学划分知识产权部门政策引导、公共服务、市场监管职责，探索有效可行的知识产权管理体制机制。按照推进综合执法的要求，减少层次，提高效率，有效避免多层次多头执法。按照实行严格的知识产权保护的要求，结合综合行政执法体制改革，整合优化执法资源，统筹知识产权综合行政执法，避免出现版权执法的重复交叉。加强知识产权工作领导协调机制以及商标战略实施、软件正版化等工作机制建设，做好与知识产权司法工作特别是知识产权法院的衔接。

（二）构建便民利民的知识产权公共服务体系。坚持法定职责必须为、法无授权不可为的原则，大力推行知识产权权力清单、责任清单、负面清单制度，并实行动态管理。加大知识产权领域简政放权力度，强化依法行政，坚持放管结合，合理减少审批和管理事项。放宽专利代理机构准入条件限制，加强知识产权服务机构事中事后监管，完善执业信息披露制度。整合知识产权公共服务资源，优化知识产权公共服务供给，实现知识产权信息等各类服务的便利化、集约化、高效化。加强统筹规划和行业管理，完善知识产权交易市场。加强知识产权维权援助服务，完善知识产权维权援助机制，构建体系完备、运转高效的知识产权维权援助网络。

（三）提升综合运用知识产权促进创新驱动发展的能力。探索支撑创新发展的知识产权运行机制，构建促进市场主体创新发展的知识产权服务体系。建立健全知识产权评议、专利导航机制，完善知识产权风险预警体系，提升区域创新发展决策水平。统筹制定实施知识产权密集型产业促进政策，培育知识产权密集型产业成为新的经济增长点。指导市场主体综合运用专利、商标和版权组合策略，全方位、立体化地保护产品、技术、工业设计等的知识产权。引导市场主体综合运营知识产权，促进知识产权领域军民融合发展，加快药品等领域过期专利技术的有效应用，提升知识产权价值，加速知识产权转化运用。

三、组织实施

（一）加强组织领导。国家知识产权局要牵头会同工商总局、新闻出版广电总局（国家版权局）等部门加强对知识产权综合管理改革试点工作的指导，统筹协调改革试点中的重大政策问题。各试点地方要建立由政府主要领导负责的协调推进机制，将知识产权综合管理改革试点工作纳入重点改革任务，因地制宜研究制定改革试点具体实施方案，积极推进落实改革试点任务。各试点地方具体实施方案应于试点地方确定后两个月内印发实施。

（二）强化政策保障。针对改革试点任务部署和需求，各有关部门要积极研究制定支持改革试点的政策措施。各试点地方政府要按照改革任务要求，研究制定配套政策措施，做好与有关部门的衔接和协调，形成工作合力。

（三）做好评估推广。国家知识产权局要会同工商总局、新闻出版广电总局（国家版权局）等部门做好试点地方改革推进的督促检查和考核评估工作。根据改革试点评估情况，对取得实质效果和成功经验的改革举措，及时提出推广建议，报国务院批准后在更大范围推广。

各有关部门和地方要按照本方案精神，统一思想，密切配合，强化全局和责任意识，勇于创新，主动改革，积极作为，抓好落实，确保改革试点工作取得实效。要及时总结、宣传改革试点进展和成效，加强试点地方工作交流，强化舆论引导，营造有利于知识产权综合管理改革的良好社会环境。

成都市版权局

概况：2016年成都版权工作围绕服务于成都市建设国家中心城市的目标和双创工作大局，以深化全国版权示范城市建设为主线，着力健全版权生态服务系统，成绩斐然。

版权登记与资助：改革创新作品登记，建立全市作品登记数据库，2016年共完成作品登记41 127件，其中，一般作品登记27 330件，是2015年的11.18倍，计算机软件著作权登记13 797件，较2015年增长61.1%；优化软件著作权登记资助审批流程，全年共受理软件著作权登记资助5 796件共329.09万元，分别较2015年增长82.4%和37.2%。

软件正版化深入推进：一是健全了全市机关软件正版化考核机制，首次将党委、政府、人大、政协等机关使用软件正版工作纳入考核体系；**二是**深化软件正版化服务工作，编印《成都市机关单位使用正版软件知识手册》2 000余册，开展专题培训10余场次，开设“正版软件工作服务站”微信公众平台；**三是**调研全市正版软件使用情况，完成《成都市使用正版软件情况调研报告》和《成都市政府机关使用正版软件管理办法》；**四是**如期完成20家市属国企总部、20家县级国企正版化任务。2016年全市采购正版软件4 443套933.8万元。

版权公共服务与管理：一是在16个区（市）县建立29个版权服务工作站，初步构建了公共服务网络；**二是**指导成都市版权协会换届并完善组织管理机制，成立了成都市创意产业联合会以打造创意设计产业发展平台；**三是**完成《2015年成都版权产业统计调查分析研究报告》《2015年成都市计算机软件著作权登记情况分析报告》《游戏作品版权价值评估体系研究报告》《成都市版权工作服务于创新型城市和文创中心建设纪实与展望》等专题调研，深入分析版权重点领域发展状况和探索版权价值实现路径，并出台《优秀版权作品和版权示范单位（园区、工作站）奖励管理办法》《版权示范单位和示范园区（基地）评选管理办法》《版权服务工作站管理办法》；**四是**推进成都国际版权交易中心建设。

版权知识宣传：创新宣传模式，以需求为导向，多措并举，全年开展专题培训54次，3 260余人参训；在新媒体设立版权宣传专区，覆盖范围500万人次，曝光3 239.5万余次，点击量达276万次；在“4・23”世界图书与版权日、“6・1”著作权法实施纪念日及创交会等重大活动现场设置版权登记服务10余次，宣传报道480余次。

中国版权金奖：巩固发展全国版权示范城市成果，在世界知识产权组织与国家版权局首次设立“中国版权金奖・管理奖”之际，成都市版权局荣获我国版权领域的国际性奖项——“中国版权金奖・管理奖”，同时中国艺库文化产业园和成都音像出版社有限责任公司还分获“全国版权示范园区（基地）”和“全国版权示范单位”称号。2016年成都市版权局还荣获第六届中国国际版权博览会“金慧奖’最佳组织奖。

创新版权服务　深化示范创建

——创新发展中的张家港版权工作

近几年来，张家港市版权部门以“全国版权示范城市”荣誉为动力，不断创新服务内涵，深化示范创建成果，取得了显著的成绩。

一、版权示范单位、园区创建成效明显，国家级、省级数量居全国县（市）首位

目前，张家港市共有江苏国泰新点软件有限公司、张家港市金陵纺织有限公司、江苏东渡纺织集团有限公司等3家全国版权示范单位，数量居全国县级市首位；共有1家江苏省版权示范园区、7家江苏省版权示范单位，数量居全省首位；共有24家苏州市版权示范单位，数量居苏州县市（区）首位。

二、版权宣传常态化、体系化，全民版权认知度提升

2016年共受理一般作品著作权登记超20 000件，年均增长率超过50%。全市版权工作站总数增至17家，促进了版

● 江苏东渡纺织集团有限公司

● 张家港市金陵纺织有限公司

● 张家港软件（动漫）产业园创建“全国版权示范园区”动员会议

权咨询、版权宣传、版权登记等管理和服务职能向基层延伸。开展“我的版权故事”和“青少年版权作品大赛”等活动，统筹指导“推重点”等方式，深入开展版权宣传进机关、进校园、进企业、进社区、进媒体、进市场“六进”活动。

三、版权精品成果丰硕，获奖位居全省、县市前列

在2016年苏州市优秀版权奖评选中，张家港市作品《迪拜精致点心盒》和《一盅缘》荣获一等奖（共5个一等奖），作品《我要努力去长大》荣获二等奖，“二金一银”的佳绩高居苏州县市（区）之首，并创张家港获奖历年之最。此外，还有4件作品获江苏优秀版权奖。

2016年张家港市侵犯盗版制品及非法出版物集中销毁活动

四、版权执法屡破大案要案，连续三年获评国家级有功单位

深入开展“双打”和“剑网”专项行动，先后破获了朱某某侵犯著作权案、“3·4”侵犯著作权案、“2020KK”电影网侵犯著作权案和风雨文学网侵犯著作权案等一系列较有影响力的大案要案，年年荣获全国查处侵权盗版案件有功单位和有功个人奖项。张家港市文广新局荣获2015年度全国查处侵权盗版案件有功单位二等奖，张家港市文化行政综合执法大队获评2015年度全国查处侵权盗版案件有功单位三等奖和2016年度全国文化市场重大办案单位。查处的风雨文学网侵犯著作权案位列2016年度全国打击侵权盗版十大案件之首。

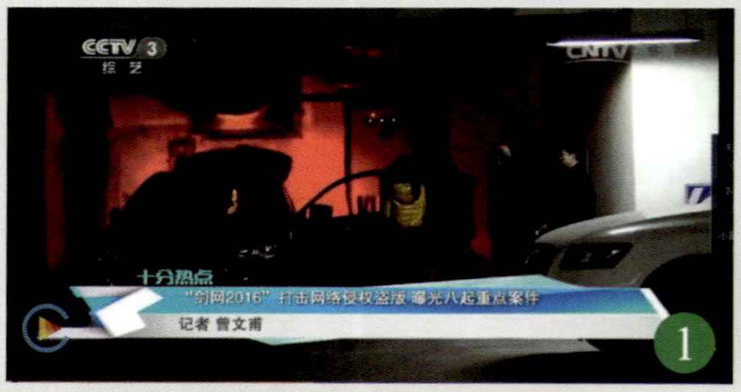

五、转型升级实现新突破，版权产业规模发展态势喜人

2016年，张家港市版权产业保持喜人发展态势，版权产业增加值占地区生产总值比重达7.3%，境内上市企业18家，其中文化企业6家。张家港软件（动漫）产业园成功获批国家影视网络动漫产业园，实现营业收入5.75亿元，税收7 718万元。2家公司分别获评2014年、2015年中国版权最具影响力企业。张家港幸运金属工艺品有限公司荣获“CICE金慧奖・优秀企业奖”。

7

8

9

10

11

图片注释

①“风雨文学网涉嫌侵犯著作权案”入选全国“剑网2016”专项行动首批网络侵权盗版案件。 ②张家港市动漫企业参加第十二届中国杭州国际动漫节。 ③苏州市优秀版权奖一等奖作品《迪拜精致点心盒》。 ④张家港市文广新局荣获2015年度全国查处侵权盗版案件有功单位二等奖、张家港市文化行政综合执法大队荣获2015年度全国查处侵权盗版案件有功单位三等奖。 ⑤张家港市开展“4・26”版权保护宣传活动（照片）。 ⑥大唐丝绸文化产业园。 ⑦苏州市优秀版权奖一等奖证书。 ⑧苏州市优秀版权奖一等奖作品《一盅缘》。 ⑨苏州市优秀版权奖二等奖作品《我要努力去长大》。 ⑩“2015年中国版权最具影响力企业”奖。 ⑪2016年国家版权局金慧奖优秀企业。

2016年12月5日上午，国家新闻出版广电总局副局长、国家版权局副局长阎晓宏亲临第六届中国国际版权博览会张家港展会指导工作

即墨市文化市场行政执法局

国家版权局副局长阎晓宏、山东省版权局副局长钟华视察广州版博会即墨市展馆

即墨市组团参加第三届青岛东亚版交会

2016年，即墨市把强化版权管理、促进版权产业发展作为推动全市经济、科技、文化和社会建设的重要环节来抓，建立了完善的版权管理工作体系，为促进经济增长和文化发展提供了有力保障。

一、高度重视版权，组织领导到位

将创建全国版权示范城市工作纳入市委工作要点和政府工作报告。2016年2月，召开了全市创建全国版权示范城市工作动员大会，成立了由市长任组长的领导小组，全市范围内的创建工作正式启动。

二、健全工作队伍，强化资金保障

为扎实做好版权工作，即墨市在文化市场行政执法局内增设了版权保护执法科，核定编制5名。每年安排200万元专项经费，用于版权宣传、培训、执法、登记、奖励等相关工作。

三、突出管理服务，培育壮大产业

（一）重点打造纺织服装产业龙头。在淘宝网“中国质造”平台建立童装、内衣等产业带，2016年针织童装网络销售额突破50亿元，连续两年居全国县级市之首。

（二）聚力发展商贸物流业。立足国家“一带一路”倡议，打造即墨国际陆港，建设跨境贸易电子商务产业园、济铁综合物流园、华骏物流园和半岛国际汽车贸易城“三园一城”。

（三）影视、雕塑产业聚力突破。2016年，成功引进举办第二届中国大学生微电影大赛，并确定即墨市为大赛永久举办地。连续举办五届中国・青岛（即墨）国际雕塑艺术节，使雕塑艺术成为引领时代、展现创意的重要载体。

（四）重点培育高端会展业。出台了《关于加快会展业发展的实施意见》，成功举办了中国（青岛）国际海洋科技展览会、中国国际渔业博览会、中国服装大会等12个会展活动，吸引了100多个国家、2 100余家企业参展，会展业发展进入快车道。

2016年12月5日即墨市人民政府荣获“中国版权金奖·管理奖”

即墨市组团参加第六届版博会，获4个优秀组织奖和1个优秀设计奖

即墨市7家单位（园区）荣获“山东省版权示范单位（园区）”荣誉称号

评选表彰2016年即墨市优秀版权工作站

2016年9月8日举行即墨市第一届优秀版权作品大赛启动仪式

2017年1月11日举行即墨市第一届优秀版权作品大赛颁奖仪式

召开即墨市版权登记工作推进会议

即墨市召开创建全国版权示范城市工作调度会议

四、坚持主动服务，鼓励版权创造

在各镇、各相关部门成立了专门的版权管理工作办公室，研究制定了《即墨市版权登记资助奖励办法》，对登记的计算机软件作品实行每件600元的补助。2016年6月，即墨市取得了山东省县级市首例版权登记初级审核、证书打印权限。全市全年实现版权登记7 000余件，占山东省年登记总量的十分之一。

五、打击侵权盗版，规范市场秩序

通过加强执法部门的横向联系与纵向沟通，形成了“宣传教育、监督防范、查处打击”三位一体的工作态势。自2012年来，即墨市累计荣获全国查处侵权盗版案件有功集体二等奖1次、三等奖3次，荣获有功个人二等奖4人次、三等奖4人次。

六、发挥示范作用，大力推广正版

自2011年即墨市党政机关率先完成软件正版化以来，即墨市已逐年完成环保产业、家装设计、星级酒店行业和国有企业的软件正版化。2016年确立了“扩面增量、量质并举、企业主体、协调联动”的企业软件正版化推进思路，并对年内软件正版化项目总投入20万元以上且软件正版率50%以上的辖区企业实施资助。

七、加强宣传引导，营造良好氛围

通过组织开展全市中小学生“知识产权日”创作活动和全市优秀版权作品大赛征集评选活动，设计制作系列版权宣传品，在市内公交站牌和户外塔式广告牌上设置版权公益广告，在电台开设版权服务专题栏目等举措，形成了人人关心、参与创建全国版权示范城市的良好局面。

主动走进企业开展版权登记培训

国家版权局于慈珂司长进行版权知识讲座

举办2017年“世界知识产权日”创作大赛颁奖暨“绿书签”系列宣传活动启动仪式

山东省版权局副局长谢宁到即墨北安中学指导版权工作

制作了连环画、优盘、笔记本、签字笔等一批版权宣传品

制作出版了“知识产权日”创作大赛获奖作品集和“护苗2017”活动绿书签

德化县版权保护工作情况汇报

一、德化县基本情况

德化是千年古县，位于福建省中部、泉州市北部，后唐长兴四年(933年)置县，取名“德化”，有“以德化民”之意。县域面积2 232平方公里，户籍人口33.6万，辖18个乡镇、214个行政村（社区）。2016年，全县实现GDP194.8亿元，增长6.2%；一般公共预算总收入15.63亿元，一般公共预算收入10.95亿元。德化有以下五个特色：

世界陶瓷之都。德化的陶瓷制作始于新石器时代，德化与江西景德镇、湖南醴陵并称我国三大古瓷都，是民窑的典型代表。德化陶瓷以“白”见长，瓷雕技艺享誉天下，早在宋元时期就成为“海上丝绸之路”的重要出口商品，被誉为“中国白的故乡、瓷艺术的摇篮”，被列入国家首批非物质文化遗产保护项目。现有陶瓷企业2 600多家，从业人员10多万人，2016年产值199.5亿元，是全国最大的陶瓷工艺品生产和出口基地、国家级出口陶瓷质量安全示范区，获评中国瓷都、中国民间文化艺术之乡、中国陶瓷历史文化名城，荣膺全球首个“世界陶瓷之都”。2015年5月26日，作为首届中法文化论坛的活动之一，以“德化·中国白——文化交流的使者”为主题的中国德化陶瓷艺术展在北京隆重举行，开启了“一带一路”中国白再出发的新启程，成为中欧文化艺术交流的新平台。

最佳生态旅游县。素有“闽中屋脊”之称的戴云山脉主峰（海拔1 856米）绵亘境内，森林覆盖率78.4%，居泉州市首位；空气质量接近国家一级标准，环境空气质量综合指数排名全市第一，饮用水源水质达标率100%。拥有“五区两园”（戴云山国家级自然保护区、岱仙湖国家级水利风景区、石牛山国家4A级旅游景区、九仙山国家4A级旅游景区、云龙谷国家3A级旅游景区、石牛山国家地质公园、石牛山国家森林公园）7块“国”字号生态旅游品牌，获评全国绿化模范县、国家生态县、国家生态文明建设试点示范区、中国最佳生态旅游县。

大城关发展典范。上世纪80年代末开始实施“大城关”发展战略，率先撬开城镇化大门，2016年城区建成区26平方公里、人口21.3万，常住人口城镇化率74.1%，集中了全县三分之二多的劳动力、经济总量、税收和95%的中小学生，开创了以“大产业、大城关、大生态”为主要特点的“大城关”发展模式，被中央党校作为典型案例编进课题丛书，被列为福建省首个统筹城乡发展试点县、新型城镇化试点和国家智慧城市试点县。

电子商务百佳县。2016年，全县电子商务运用企业6 700多家，交易额达到70.8亿元，占据全国80%的网上茶具销售市场。拥有3个淘宝镇、11个淘宝村，是全国最大的陶瓷电子商务产业基地；连续两年位列“中国电子商务百佳县”第9位、全省第2位；连续三年跻身全国大众电商创业最活跃十佳县；入围阿里全国“2016年跨境电商创业最活跃的25个县”；被列入国家电子商务示范基地；获评福建电子商务示范县、中国电子商务百佳县和百强县。

特色农业示范县。优越的自然生态环境孕育了“三黑三黄三宝”等生态安全绿色农产品（“三黑”指黑鸡、黑羊、黑兔；“三黄”指黄花菜、德化梨、茶油；“三宝”指棘胸蛙、黄花远志、淮山），拥有黑鸡、黑兔、淮山、黄花菜、十八学士茶花等5个国家农产品地理标志，获评中国早熟梨之乡、中国油茶之乡、中国竹子之乡。

二、德化县陶瓷版权保护开展情况

德化历经千年风霜，今天依然窑火不熄、蓬勃发展，得益于世界知识产权组织以及国家、省、市版权部门的关心、指导和支持，得益于德化历届县委、县政府一以贯之重视版权保护，得益于德化人民以传承传统技艺为己任，积极主动加强版权保护，促进了陶瓷产业健康有序发展。在福建省做到“五个第一”，即获得全省第一个版权就地办理省级权限，发布全省第一份陶瓷产业知识产权保护状况白皮书，成立全省第一个县级版权协会，设

2016年11月德化经验在瑞士日内瓦向全球推广

立全省第一个县级版权咨询服务公司和知识产权庭，成立全国第一个陶瓷知识产权保护教育基地。获评福建省知识产权强县、福建省首个版权示范园区、全国版权保护示范单位、国家知识产权强县工程试点县、中国版权金奖·保护奖，圆满完成世界知识产权组织和国家版权局“全球第二个版权保护优秀案例示范点”调研项目，于2015年6月和2016年11月先后在中国厦门和瑞士日内瓦的世界知识产权组织总部发布《版权保护促进中国德化陶瓷产业发展的研究》（中英文版），向全球推广中国德化在陶瓷产业版权保护方面成功做法，让全世界共享“德化经验”。目前，德化版权保护建立并形成了行政+司法+协会 “三位一体”的版权服务保护体系。

一是政府主导。⑴实施知识产权战略。扎实创建国家知识产权强县工程试点县，出台版权登记奖励措施，鼓励社会加大创新力度，积极申请版权和专利，提升产业版权保护能力，营造促进陶瓷产业转型升级的版权保护环境。2011年以来，累计兑现版权保护、鼓励创新、品牌打造等奖励政策9400万元，冠福家用、佳美集团、恒忆股份、万旗非金属先后被认定为国家知识产权优势企业，双旗山矿业等5家企业被列入省级知识产权优势企业，22家企业被确定为市知识产权试点、示范企业。⑵健全版权执法机构。2011年12月成立县版权局，2011年5月组建文化市场综合执法大队，配备8名执法人员，加强版权执法监管，及时保护被侵权企业合法权益。2011年以来，共受理侵权盗版案件72件，涉案金额1 568万元，受理案件全部调处结案。⑶加强宣传教育引导。建设县陶瓷版权展示中心，建成全国首个陶瓷知识产权保护教育基地，编写版权教育读物，开展版权教育进校园活动，建立常态化宣传教育机制，教育引导企业经营者增强版权保护意识，营造良好社会氛围。

二是司法保护。作为福建省4个具有知识产权案件管辖权的基层法院之一，县法院始终把保护版权作为服务地方经济发展的重要工程来抓，在全省首推“1小时”诉前证据保全机制，推行行政司法诉调对接机制。自2014年成立知识产权审判庭以来，该院共审结知识产权案件177件、诉前证据保全案件84件，其中著作权纠纷案件140件，为企业挽回经济损失9 000多万元。德化通过推行县法院、检察院、公安局、版权局保护知识产权联席会议制度和联合执法机制，有效维护了陶瓷创新成果、促进了企业创新驱动、推动了产业转型升级。

三是协会推动。成立县陶瓷同业公会、电子商务协会，制定行业维权公约；成立福建省第一个县级版权协会，内设版权登记服务中心、版权咨询中心、版权调解中心和版权交易中心四个中心，就地为德化陶瓷企业办理版权登记，充分调动了企业自主权利、行业自律、自我服务的积极性。拥有版权协会会员366家，占全县陶瓷企业总数的22.2%。自2001年开展版权登记以来，免费为企业登记8万多件，2011年以来每年登记量以20%的速度

2017年6月6日全国人大常委会副委员长陈竺到企业调研《著作权法》实施情况

增长，仅2016年版权登记数就占全省登记总量的40%；提供咨询服务1 000多人次，调解版权纠纷100多起，开展版权交易680多宗，有省市级版权登记重点保护企业近60家。

由于政府和企业在版权保护工作上达成了共识，形成了合力，德化陶瓷产业和县域经济得到了良性发展。一是激发了陶瓷企业创新。版权保护推动了陶瓷技艺的传承和创新，企业更加重视开发拥有自有知识产权的新产品，提高市场占有率。据不完全统计，每年投入创新资金3亿元以上，年开发新产品2万多件，现在德化每天都有200多件新产品问世。专利申请量、专利授权量、每万人发明专利拥有量每年都成倍增长，2016年新增专利申请2 316件，授权1 412件，申请量同比增长57.8%，每万人发明专利拥有量4.67件。有效国内注册商标总量达3 233件、国际注册商标总量达22件；知名商标总量达50件、著名商标总量达37件、中国驰名商标总量达6件、地理标志商标总量达2件，驰名商标、地理标志商标数量居全省山区县前列。连续六届获评全国科技进步先进县。二是推动了陶瓷产业发展。陶瓷产品推陈出新，市场份额显著提升，转型升级步伐加快，推动德化陶瓷产业逆势发展。全县陶瓷产值从2010年的82.38亿元增加到2016年的199.5亿元，年均增长15.9%；出口交货值从2010年的67.38亿元增加到2016年的137.6亿元，年均增长12.6%。创造就业岗位10多万个，陶瓷产业成为德化的民生产业。德化日用工艺陶瓷产业集群被评为中国百佳产业集群。三是促进了“三赢”发展。由于陶瓷版权得到有效保护，激发了陶瓷企业创新，稳定了十多万陶瓷从业工人的经济收入，促使社会安定稳定，注重生态环境保护，德化走上了经济、社会、生态“三赢”的“大城关”集约型科学发展道路。

三、下一步工作思路

德化陶瓷版权保护工作虽然取得了一定的成效，但也存在着版权侵权认定的难度较大、个别企业版权保护意识还不够浓厚等问题。下一步，德化将着重抓好如下三个方面：一是加大版权宣传力度。开展版权进校园、进企业等系列活动，进一步营造版权保护浓厚氛围，提升公民和企业版权保护意识。二是加大版权维权力度。建立长效机制，进一步完善行政+司法+协会 “三位一体”版权保护体系，形成合力。三是加大版权服务力度。充分发挥县版权登记服务中心作用，做好代理作品版权登记工作。每年组织开展一次版权创意大赛，激发企业创新意识。组织版权企业参展“版博会”，让优秀版权企业“走出去”，打响“世界瓷都”品牌。

四、建议意见

1．建立全国版权作品检索系统。参考国家专利检索及分析系统，开发面向公众的便于操作的版权检索系统，将全国版权数据进行统一汇总，打破地域界限，实现版权登记全国联网化。

2．建议成立版权作品司法鉴定机构。为版权管理部门提供版权作品抄袭、剽窃和未经授权的改编、复制行为的鉴定服务。

3．设立中国陶瓷版权保护基金。由各级政府和基金拨款成立，主要用于中国陶瓷版权文化交流、活动开展、人才培养等项目。

2016年11月德化经验在瑞士日内瓦向全球推广

2014年1月10日德化县版权协会成立大会

2012年4月26日在德化陶瓷学院举行陶瓷侵权作品现场销毁活动

2017年6月6日全国人大常委会副委员长陈竺到企业调研

2016年4月21日举办德化陶瓷产业电子商务知识产权保护讲座

德化县版权协会版权登记服务中心

2016年4月21日在德化县尚思小学举办以“保护版权、拒绝盗版、自主创新、从小做起”为主题的陶瓷侵权产品现场销毁活动

2013年4月25日在德化陶瓷学院举行“知识产权、知识宣传”活动

2013年4月25日在德化陶瓷学院举行“保护知识产权——我们共同努力”千人签名活动

山东省政协副主席郭爱玲（左二）、国家新闻出版广电总局（国家版权局）版权管理司司长于慈珂（右二）、山东省新闻出版广电局（版权局）局长司安民（左一）、青岛市文化广电新闻出版局局长李明共同按下开馆启动按钮

第三届“青岛·东亚版权创意精品展示交易会”

由山东省新闻出版广电局（版权局）、青岛市人民政府主办，山东省版权协会、青岛市文化广电新闻出版局承办，青岛市文化市场行政执法局为执行单位的第三届“青岛·东亚版权创意精品展示交易会”（以下简称第三届“东亚版交会”）于2017年4月16日在青岛国际会展中心圆满落下帷幕。

山东省政协副主席郭爱玲，国家新闻出版广电总局（国家版权局）版权管理司司长于慈珂，青岛市副市长栾新，马来西亚拿督、马来西亚山东商会会长李卫，山东省新闻出版广电局（版权局）局长司安民，山东省新闻出版广电局（版权局）副局长谢宁，山东省新闻出版广电局（版权局）副局长钟华，辽宁、江苏、河南、安徽、湖北、广东、江西等省市以及部分版权示范城市代表等出席开馆仪式及相关活动，并为“城市传媒杯”国际青少年动漫大赛获奖选手颁奖。

为期三天的第三届“东亚版交会”以“版权推动发展，创意成就梦想”为主题，吸引了国内外300余家高端版权属性企业参展，全面展示了新闻出版、动漫游戏、影视音乐、艺术美术、工业设计等方面的最新版权创意成果，实现工业版权、出版、影视、动漫等22项签约，实现版权项目交易额39亿元，比第二届增长了95%。

《人民日报》、新华社、中央电视台、《中国新闻出版广电报》、《大众日报》、山东电视台、《青岛日报》、青岛电视台及新华网、中国网、腾讯、网易、半岛网、青岛新闻网等进行了全程报道。

近几年来，青岛市以建设创新型城市为目标，大力实施创新驱动战略，不断加强版权监管执法，完善版权保护体制机制，着力推进版权创意产业发展，取得明显成效，为提升城市自主创新能力和核心竞争力做出了积极贡献。先后荣获“全国版权示范城市”、世界知识产权组织“版权保护金奖”和“版权推广运用金奖”等称号，即墨市进入争创版权示范城市行列，2013年国家级的青岛国际版权交易中心正式落户青岛。

山东省政协副主席郭爱玲、国家新闻出版广电总局（国家版权局）版权管理司司长于慈珂参观展会

2017第三届“东亚版交会”主要亮点如下：

由国际动画协会中国分会承办的“城市传媒杯”国际青少年动漫创意作品大赛由青岛城市传媒股份有限公司、青岛奥美克医疗科技有限公司、青岛任缘印刷包装有限公司、青岛新华印刷有限公司赞助支持。从2016年4月份开始，国际动画协会中国分会通过国际动画协会（ASIFA）和国际青少年动画工作组（AWG）的国际化权威资源渠道，在全球青少年动漫爱好者中广泛征集原创动画及漫画

与会领导参观展会

市民积极参加展会活动

开幕式现场

作品，共收到来自日本、法国、美国、俄罗斯、马来西亚等17个国家和地区的作品近2 000部。通过初评、终评，最终，37部作品获得最佳动画短片、最佳剧情漫画奖、最佳绘本或插画奖等九项大奖。

马来西亚作为本届展会的“主宾国”参展，组织本国文化、设计、出版、旅游等版权属性企业组团参展，在展会现场设立“马来西亚馆”，展位面积108平方米，参展期间马来西亚方面与青岛本地企业及展会参展商进行多项经贸和版权贸易洽谈。

新闻出版展区活动精彩纷呈，“从失乐园到我永远的家——纪念渡边淳一逝世三周年文学作品展”亮相展区，著名翻译家林少华先生现场为作品展揭幕，渡边淳一代表作《失乐园》、获得直木奖的作品《光与影》等与读者见面。国内美食特色书店“BC MIX”专门在会展现场搭建了展区，让参展观众在现场品尝咖啡与特色美食。此外，还举办了“文化青岛 美丽崂山”——《世界的青岛多语绘本》推介会、《环球少年地理》地球大发现之旅、《心目中的海洋》知识讲座、“中日小学生书法作品展”等多场特色活动。

由中国版权协会、青岛市人民政府、山东省新闻出版广电局主办的“互联网形势下的版权产业发展”高峰论坛成功举办。腾讯视频维权总监刘政操，北京外国语大学法学院副院长、教授丛立先，百度版权中心副主任易镁金，青岛出版集团副总编辑高继民，海尔集团知识产权总监王建国等专家学者围绕更好地推动互联网环境下的版权保护机制升级，营造鼓励知识创新和保护版权的社会环境，助推“互联网+版权”产业健康有序快速发展进行了精彩演讲和经验交流。同时，还举办了“东亚文化科技金融论坛”，论坛围绕金融、版权交易、文化产业为主体进行了演讲和交流。

动漫游戏板块得到了腾讯、世界Cosplay大会等方面大力支持，腾讯《魔游纪》成为亮点。举办红龙NCE动漫嘉年华展，涵盖了动漫、游戏和VR虚拟现实相结合的多项主题活动，腾讯视频也对本届展会有关内容进行全程直播。同时，展会期间，还举办了世界Cosplay大会华东赛区选拔赛。

“黄海电影”借势青岛打造世界电影之都的历史机遇，携手中影股份、星光国际、天河盛宴、看购网等影视投资机构，共同打造国产精品电影制片的联合舰队，展会上《一夜暴富》和《火牛阵》两部投资共计1.5亿元人民币的电影项目进行签约，并举办了青岛网络大电影《女神联盟》上线发布会，“青岛制作”“青岛创作”将成为国产优质电影的新标签。

国家级版权协会和集体管理组织齐聚青岛，中国版权协会、中国出版协会、音著协、音集协、文著协、摄著协、影著协、国际唱片业协会、国际设计协会、世界动画协会等国家级或国际版权组织作为第三届“东亚版交会”的支持单位齐聚青岛，现场为参展商提供版权服务和支持，搭建版权交流交易平台。

新闻出版展区现场

新闻出版展区青岛出版集团纪念渡边淳一逝世三周年文学作品展现场

展会现场

中国国家新闻出版广电总局（国家版权局）版权管理司司长于慈珂（左一）、世界知识产权组织版权发展司司长高航（右一）为获得“保护奖”的获奖单位颁奖，徐州市文化广电新闻出版局（版权局）局长高成富（左四）在领奖台上领奖

徐州市版权局荣获“中国版权金奖”

近年来，徐州市大力实施版权强市战略，促进版权产业健康发展，着力加大版权保护力度，精心组织“剑网行动”，2014年以来查处侵权盗版案件28起，其中刑事案件12起，行政案件16起，抓获犯罪分子30多人。市版权局连续两年被国家版权局评为打击侵权盗版有功单位一等奖，其中江苏“放放电影网”侵犯著作权案、江苏“速酷电影网”侵犯著作权案，分别入选全国2014年、2015年打击侵权盗版十大案件。2015年全市荣获国家版权局表彰有功单位一等奖3个、二等奖1个，有功个人一等奖3人、二等奖6人。在查办案件中，市版权局深入了解案件特点、难点，按照证据要求逐条、逐起分析证据，提出补充侦查建议20余条，较好地帮助公安机关制定针对性较强的侦查方向和侦查方案，为案件的成功查办积累了宝贵的经验。2015年以来，市版权局为配合公安机关办案签发鉴定协调函273份，与上海外文出版社、京版十五社反盗版联盟等95家出版单位建立打击侵权盗版合作关系，要求出示侵权盗版出版认定书352份，出示非法出版物鉴定书35份，电子出版物鉴定书17份，为市检察院和市中级人民法院审判著作权案量刑提供了法律依据。

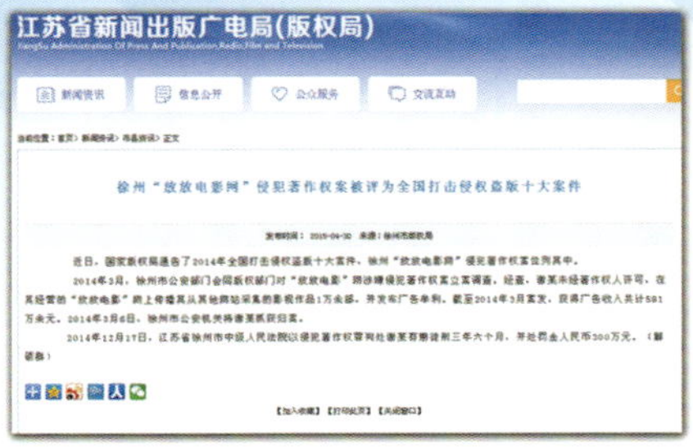

“放放电影网”侵犯影视著作权案被评为2014年度全国打击侵权盗版十大案件

2014年、2015年徐州市版权局均荣获“全国查处侵权盗版案件有功单位一等奖”

中国版权金奖

中国外文局

在2016年8月第23届北京国际图书博览会（BIBF）上刘云山同志（中）视察中国外文局展台

中国外文出版发行事业局，又称中国国际出版集团（China International Publishing Group，CIPG），是承担党和国家书、刊、网络对外宣传任务的新闻出版机构，是中国历史悠久、规模宏大的专业对外传播机构。

中国外文局是在毛泽东、周恩来、陈毅等老一辈无产阶级革命家的亲切关怀和直接领导下创办的，前身是成立于1949年10月的中央人民政府新闻总署国际新闻局。全局拥有近3 000名职工，其中包括近百名外国专家。下属20个机构，包括7家出版社、5家杂志社，以及中国网、中国国际图书贸易集团公司、对外传播研究中心、翻译资格考评中心等单位，在美国、加拿大、英国、德国、法国、比利时、俄罗斯、埃及、南非、墨西哥、秘鲁、土耳其、日本、中国香港等国家和地区设有24个海外分支机构，形成了涵盖翻译、出版、印刷、发行、互联网和多媒体业务、理论研究及社会事业等领域的事业格局。每年以40余种文字出版5 000余种图书、编辑近30种多语种期刊、运营30余家多语种网站，书刊发行到世界180多个国家和地区，网络受众遍及世界各地。中国外文局对外传播的信息，全面反映了中国悠久的历史文化，真实展现了中国改革开放取得的新进展、新成就，为增进中外理解和友谊发挥了积极作用。

中国外文局版权输出情况

2016年外文局输出图书版权640种，比上年同期增长16.8%，其中数字版权输出数量较上年有大幅提升。版权输出以汉语教学、历史文化、少儿、文学艺术、社会科学、政治法律等内容和题材的图书为主；输出国家和地区24个，包括美国、英国、新加坡、俄罗斯、黎巴嫩、印度、德国等，输往欧美发达国家有338种图书，输往“一带一路”沿线国家有290种图书。

向世界说明中国

2016年1月第24届印度新德里世界书展期间，中国外文局副局长陆彩荣（左三）出席《摆脱贫困》英文版海外推介会

2016年10月第68届法兰克福国际书展中，中国外文局副局长方正辉（左一）与出席嘉宾为《中国关键词》多语种版图书全球首发揭幕

2016年4月第43届伦敦国际书展期间，新世界出版社与阿拉伯科学出版社就《一带一路：中国崛起后给世界带来了什么？》等书的版权输出举行签约仪式

使命 奉献

外文局组织机构介绍

局属单位

> 中国互联网新闻中心(中国网)
> 中国国际图书贸易集团有限公司
> 融媒体中心
> 对外传播研究中心
> 北京周报社
> 今日中国杂志社
> 人民画报社
> 人民中国杂志社
> 中国报道杂志社
> 外文出版社有限责任公司
> 新世界出版社有限责任公司
> 华语教学出版社有限责任公司
> 新星出版社有限责任公司
> 中国画报出版社有限责任公司
> 海豚出版社有限责任公司
> 朝华出版社有限责任公司
> 翻译专业资格考评中心
> 教育培训中心
> 信息技术中心
> 服务中心

主管协会

> 中国翻译协会
> 中华全国世界语协会

海外机构

> 和平图书有限公司（中国香港）
> 华媒（美国）国际集团（旧金山）
> 常青图书（美国）有限公司（旧金山）
> 中国书刊社（旧金山）
> 长河出版社（旧金山）
> 德国中国图书贸易有限公司（法兰克福）
> 中国网伦敦工作站（伦敦）
> 中国网墨西哥工作站（墨西哥城）
> 北京周报社北美分社（纽约）
> 北京周报社非洲分社（约翰内斯堡）
> 今日中国杂志社中东分社（开罗）
> 今日中国杂志社拉美分社（墨西哥城）
> 今日中国杂志社秘鲁代表处（利马）
> 人民画报社莫斯科分社（莫斯科）
> 人民中国杂志社东京支局（东京）
> 常青图书（英国）有限公司（伦敦）
> 光华书店（伦敦）
> 国图集团公司东京联络事务所（东京）
> 长城书店（布鲁塞尔）
> 法国百周年出版社（巴黎）
> 法国凤凰书店（巴黎）
> 长城书店（洛杉矶）
> 中国图书贸易（加拿大）有限公司（多伦多）
> 华语教学出版社伦敦分社（伦敦）

传承 创新

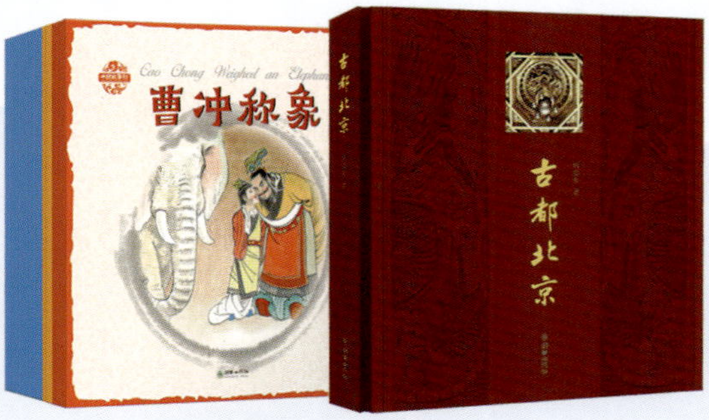

朝华出版社

新世界出版社

海豚出版社

中国画报出版社

华语教学出版社

外文出版社

新星出版社

中国人民大學文化科技园

RENMIN UNIVERSITY OF CHINA CULTURE AND SCIENCE PARK

国家版权贸易基地
创意产业技术研究院

版权

国家版权贸易基地
中关村版权争议调解中心
版权评估中心

园区

创业服务与孵化器
艺术授权与创意产品
文化企业服务

数据

中国省市文化产业发展指数
中国文化消费指数
中国文化企业品牌价值TOP50排行榜

平台

文化部国家文化产业项目服务平台（www.ccipp.org）
国家文化消费服务平台（www.whtianxia.com）

联系我们

地址：北京市海淀区中关村大街甲59号文化大厦
电话：010－82503001
网址：www.cspruc.com
邮箱：cspruc@cspruc.com

企业公众号　　人大文创

中国出版集团

中国出版集团公司总裁、党组副书记——谭跃

谭跃，江苏南京人，现任中国出版集团公司总裁、党组副书记，中国出版传媒股份有限公司董事长，中国出版协会副理事长。曾任江苏省南京市文化局副局长兼文物局局长，江苏省委宣传部副部长兼省文明办主任、省哲学社会科学界联合会党组书记，凤凰出版传媒集团党委书记、董事长。

谭跃同志2005年10月至2011年8月担任凤凰出版传媒集团董事长，带领经营管理团队将凤凰出版传媒集团打造成全国第一个资产规模和销售收入双超百亿的出版企业，实现集团旗下两家企业在A股成功上市。2011年8月就任中国出版集团公司总裁后，谭跃同志带领中国出版集团围绕“建设国际著名出版集团”的战略定位，制定并实施以“三六构想”为核心的集团长远发展战略目标，即通过实施内容创新、品牌经营、集团化、数字化、国际化、人才强企“六大战略”，实现建设“现代化、大型化、国际化”国际出版传媒集团的“三化目标”。在谭跃同志领导下，中国出版集团在“十二五”期间的各项指标实现持续较快发展，位居全国领先地位，连续9年入选“全国文化企业30强”；连续4年入选“全球出版业50强”，列前15位；两度入选“亚洲品牌500强”，并在2015年列第331位；入选“2016年中国品牌500强”，列第29位。四次荣获“中国图书对外推广计划”综合排名第一，荣获伦敦书展首次也是唯一的主席大奖“国际出版卓越奖”和三个提名奖，荣获“阿富汗总统特别勋章”和两项吉尼斯世界纪录，逐步成为国际出版业聚焦中国出版的标志性企业。同时，集团在“五个一工程”奖、中国出版政府奖、“中国好书”榜、国家出版基金项目、图书零售市场占有率、版权输出等12项主要出版指标上位居全国第一。

谭跃同志曾获“新中国60年百名优秀出版人物”“2009CCTV中国经济年度人物”“2012中国文化产业年度人物”“2014年度中国十大出版人物”“第三届中国版权卓越成就者”等荣誉称号，入选中宣部“四个一批”人才、“全国新闻出版行业领军人才”，享受国务院特殊津贴。

谭跃同志对行业发展的重大问题进行了比较深入扎实的理论思考，形成了有分量有影响的学术成果，发表《中国出版业发展的五大趋势》《深入学习贯彻十八大精神 努力探索中国出版集团特色发展道路》《传统文化需要当代表达》《呼唤匹配中国道路的学术表达》《践行社会主义核心价值观 努力铸就品牌出版风格》《出版国际化的主要思考》《扩大文化影响 打造数字集团 保持稳健增长》《商务印书馆：丰碑一样的文化坐标》等多篇论文。

努力建设国际著名出版集团

中国出版集团是适应出版业改革发展的需要，经中共中央、国务院批准，于2002年4月9日成立的中央级出版机构。2004年3月25日，国务院授权成立中国出版集团公司。2011年12月28日，中国出版传媒股份有限公司成立。

中国出版集团是中国最大的大众出版和专业出版集团，被业界和读者赞誉为中国出版“国家队”。集团每年出版图书1.9万余种，在全国图书零售市场占有率为7.5%左右，连续15年位居全国第一；出版期刊报纸58种；每年音像、电子、网络等出版物2 000余种。进出口各类出版物20多万种，书报刊进口和出口分别占据全国市场份额的62%和30%。2016年集团资产总额近200亿元，净资产和营业总收入均逾100亿元，迈上全国为数不多的“三百亿集团”台阶。

集团自2008年以来连续9年入选“中国文化企业30强”，在全国文化企业中名列前茅。2013—2016年连续4年入选“全球出版业50强”，其中2014年位居第14位，名列国内出版企业之首。两次入选“亚洲品牌500强”，是唯一入选的国内出版企业；首次入选“2014中国经济最具发展潜力企业”，位居年度入选企业之首，也是唯一入选的文化企业；首次入选“中国品牌500强”并位列第29位。

过去五年，集团资产总额、销售收入双双翻番，利润总额逼近翻两番，在中国出版政府奖、中宣部“中国好书”、总局“大众喜爱的50种图书”、国家出版基金项目、全国各类重要媒体榜单、中国图书对外推广计划等12个主要指标中名列全国第一，荣获伦敦书展“国际出版卓越奖”、阿富汗总统特别勋章、两项吉尼斯世界纪录，对外输出版权3 368种，逐步成为世界关注中国出版的标志性企业。每年年销量10万册以上的图书达60多种，《老生》《长征》《抗日战争》《布谷鸟的呼唤》《北鸢》《极花》《重读先烈诗章》《哈利·波特与被诅咒的孩子》等热销市场。

集团的战略目标是：大力推进内容创新、品牌经营、数字化、集团化、国际化、人才强企战略，在2020年基本建成国际著名出版集团。

ZIZHU

上海紫竹高新技术产业开发区

SHANGHAI ZIZHU HI-TECH INDUSTRIAL DEVELOPMENT ZONE

上海紫竹高新技术产业开发区位于上海的西南角，是集科研、人才、资本、产业等优势，运用市场化运作方式而设立的新型高新技术产业开发区。以集成电路与软件、新能源、航空、数字内容、新材料和生命科学等六大类产业作为主导产业，自2002年成立以来，紫竹高新区在国家版权主管部门、上海市版权主管部门的支持和指导下，依托“中国（上海）网络视听产业基地”，在版权领域开展了大量工作，在知识产权托管、理论研究、知识产权尽职调查等方面特色鲜明、成效显著，先后获评“全国版权示范园区（基地）”“中国版权影响力企业”“国家知识产权试点园区”“上海版权示范园区（基地）”“上海市知识产权示范园区”等称号，知识产权托管理论成果《智财管家——高新区知识产权托管探索与实践》于2016年11月由北京大学出版社正式出版发行，该书的发行，对更好地发挥高新区这一平台作用，支持知识产权和网络视听版权工作更好地开展具有特别的意义。

图片注释

①紫竹高新区鸟瞰风貌 ②“双创中的知识产权”——高新区知识产权运营与保护论坛 ③《智财管家——高新区知识产权托管探索与实践》封面 ④中国（上海）网络视听产业基地风貌 ⑤全国版权示范园区（基地）铜牌 ⑥国家知识产权试点园区铜牌

版权

专文

ZHUAN WEN

在“全球创作者论坛”上的书面致辞

国家新闻出版广电总局局长　国家版权局局长　聂辰席

今天，国际作者作曲者协会联合会（CISAC）的贵宾和全球数十个国家的创作者、政府官员、专家学者代表集聚北京，参加由国际作者作曲者协会联合会和中国知识产权法学研究会共同举办的“全球创作者论坛”，这是国际版权界的一大盛事。首先，我谨代表中国国家新闻出版广电总局、国家版权局，向论坛的召开表示祝贺！向长期关心和支持中国版权事业的新老朋友们表示热烈的欢迎和衷心的感谢！

国际作者作曲者协会联合会（以下简称联合会）有着90年历史，成员遍及123个国家和地区的239个创作者协会，领域涵盖音乐、戏剧、文学、音像、摄影和视觉艺术等门类，致力于为数百万创作者提供权利认证和保护，在国际上有着广泛的影响力。近年来，联合会非常重视发展与中国的密切关系：2014年，联合会将原设于新加坡的亚太区总部迁至中国，成为第一家将区域总部设在中国的著作权国际组织；2016年，中国著名导演、编剧贾樟柯先生当选为联合会副主席。中国音乐著作权协会作为联合会会员，在其框架之下已与全球60余个著作权集体管理组织签订了相互代表协议。应该说，联合会近年来的工作，有效地加强了中国创作者的权益保护，提升了中国的著作权集体管理水平，促进了中外文化交流和版权合作。

创作是文化之本，文化让世界多彩，版权把创作与文化连接起来。版权保护制度源于“保护创作者”最直接的精神和利益诉求，越来越多的国家重视版权在提高民族创新能力、转变经济发展方式、提高国家核心竞争力方面的积极作用。改革开放以来，中国逐步建立了一整套既符合中国实际又与国际规则相接轨的版权法律体系，确立了具有中国特色的司法审判和行政执法并行的版权法律救济制度，版权国际交流与合作不断深化，版权环境和秩序日益好转，版权市场机制基本形成，版权产业健康发展，2014年版权产业对国民经济贡献率已达7.28%。这些成绩的取得，既凝结着中国广大版权工作者的心血和智慧，也包含着国际社会，包括国际作者作曲者协会联合会等国际组织，以及在座国际友人的关心和支持。借此机会，我代表中国国家新闻出版广电总局、国家版权局，再次向各位多年来对中国版权事业的关注和支持表示感谢！

当然，我们不能忽视的是，中国的版权保护制度还面临着许多困难和挑战。比如，中国的著作权集体管理起步较晚，我了解到，今天有代表出席的法国戏剧作者和作曲者协会已有240年的悠久历史，而我国几家著作权集体管理组织才刚起步。中国的版权制度正在解决发达国家甚至许多发展中国家已经解决了的传统环境下的问题，还将与世界各国共同应对新技术、新形势带来的诸多挑战。中国政府保护版权的立场是坚定的，态度是坚决的，成效也将越来越显著！随着中国经济发展进入“新常态”，以及创新型国家和知识产权强国建设的逐步实施，速度变化、结构优化、动力转换等突出特征逐步呈现，经济社会发展将更多依靠创新作为发展动力，将更多依靠包括版权在内的智力成果的创造与运用，基于作品的创作、传播和社会公众的消费而形成的版权产业，必将迎来蓬勃发展的新时期。我们愿意借鉴国际社会版权保护与产业发展的成功经验，共同探讨互联网环境下发挥版权制度的功能与优势，促进国际版权交流，同时，我们也愿意更加主动积极地开展版权贸易，向世界介绍中国版权优秀成果。我相信，联合会等国际版权组织利用自身的优势和经验，在版权国际舞台必将发挥更大的作用！

让我们共创国际版权事业的美好未来！祝本次全球创作者论坛圆满成功，祝贺国际作者作曲者协会联合会九十岁生日，祝愿各位朋友北京之行吉祥如意！

谢谢大家。

版权：仍然任重道远

国家新闻出版广电总局副局长　国家版权局副局长　阎晓宏

党的十八届五中全会提出的“创新、协调、绿色、开放、共享”五大发展理念，为我们做好“十三五”期间版权工作指明了方向。“十二五”期间，我国版权工作在各方面都取得重大进展，但是客观冷静分析我们所处的国际、国内环境，在“十三五”期间，版权仍然任重道远。

一、从自身发展来看我国当前版权保护的形势

从国内自身发展来看，我国著作权的保护历程不是很长，但是发展很快，我们的评价是处于整体快速上升阶段。

第一，从法律制度建设来看，当前，我国文化领域的立法都在加快，版权的法律制度建设在文化领域一直都是领先的。经过改革开放以来三十多年的努力，我国已经基本形成了较为完备的既符合中国国情又与国际规则相衔接的版权法律体系，即我们所说的“一法六条例”，我们还加入了《世界知识产权组织版权条约》（WCT）、《世界知识产权组织表演和录音制品条约》（WPPT）等与版权相关的重要国际条约，为全面推进版权保护奠定了法律基础，为保护作品的创造、运用和传播提供了制度保证。

第二，从法律实施情况来看，我国实行司法与行政并行的保护体系。近年来，很多法院成立了专门的知识产权庭，北京、上海、广州还成立了专门的知识产权法院；版权行政执法力度也不断加强，查办了一大批大案要案，侵权盗版乱象大为改观，开始从无序走向有序。尤其是在互联网领域，自2005年以来，国家版权局联合公安部、工信部（2008年后网信办加入）连续11年开展打击网络侵权盗版专项行动，共查办网络侵权案件5 064起，依法关闭侵权盗版网站2 789个，移送司法机关追究刑事责任案件447件，相继查处了天线视频、番茄花园、思路网、快播、射手网字幕组等一批侵权盗版大案要案，在国内外引起关注。同时，通过开展网络重点监管工作，极大改变了网络视频、音乐版权混乱的局面，视频、音乐网站正版率大幅提高，得到了权利人、使用者和社会各方面的广泛认同。此外，对网络环境中的版权热点难点，国家版权局高度关注并依法予以治理，譬如网络转载新闻作品、网盘服务、应用程序APP、体育赛事节目转播中的版权保护等等。下一步，我们将继续加强执法，旗帜鲜明地打击各类网络侵权盗版，特别是对恶意的、规模性的侵权盗版行为，必须追究其刑责。

第三，从权利人的维权来看。近年来，著作权作品登记量逐年提高，权利人的主动维权意识显著增强，如著名作家莫言，以及今天演讲的音乐家叶小钢主席等都对版权有着很深的理解。此外，著作权集体管理制度的确立在维护权利人权益方面发挥越来越大的作用。这一制度能够有效地降低交易成本，在我国建立以后总体发展不错，近年来促使权利人收入不断增加，但在分配的规范性和透明性上仍需要进一步改进和加强。

第四，从版权价值的实现来看。衡量版权治理成效最根本的标准，是权利人的权利是否得到尊重，是否能够拿到报酬。同时也要看权利人的作品能不能得到比较好的传播，以及在这个传播过程中，作品的社会效益及相关产业的价值能否实现。但是不是给权利人的钱越多越好？也不是。要实现一个平衡，就是权利人和使用者都能受益。如果是使用者传播机构这一方非常强势，就会对权利人的权利进行一定的限制甚至剥夺；还有一种就是权利人非常强势，使用者传播机构处于一个非常可怜的位置。这两种情况个别地或者局部地在中国都有，但是从整体上来看，我认为目前在中国，还是权利人这一方相对处于一个比较弱势的位置。

二、从国际比较来看我国版权面临的问题和挑战

从国际比较上来看，目前我国版权保护仍处于

矛盾和纠纷高发阶段，仍然存在很多问题和挑战，总体特征仍然是保护不足，而发达国家在知识产权领域却处于垄断和滥用阶段。

第一，国际规则正在悄然发生变化。多年来，版权领域最重要的两个国际公约，一个是《与贸易有关的知识产权协定》（TRIPs 协定），另一个是《伯尔尼公约》，这两个多边国际公约，可以使发展中国家与发达国家在一个相对透明和公平的平台上发表自己的看法，在国际谈判中发挥了十分重要的作用。现在多边的规则受到了挑战，由美国主导的 TPP（跨太平洋伙伴关系协议），还有美国和欧盟合作的 TIPP（跨大西洋贸易与投资伙伴关系协定），这两个由少数发达国家参与的协定几乎将全球 70% 以上的贸易纳入囊中，这将实际上改变当前的 WTO 贸易体系。这个问题是非常需要关注的。

第二，著作权的法律制度调整在加快。随着科技的发展，我们已经进入了互联网、移动互联网、大数据时代，法律制度要根据生产传播方式的变化而变化、调整。换言之，法律存在适用性问题，法律制度也存在改进和创新的问题。所以，我们著作权的法律调整也在加快。前面我讲在国内文化领域，版权制度建设从自身发展看是比较快的，但在国际上，与日本、欧盟、韩国以及我国的台湾地区、香港地区比较的话，我们著作权的立法、修法是滞后的。我国《著作权法》自 1990 年颁布以来，已经 25 年了，没有进行大的修订，只有 2001 年和 2010 年的两次局部修订，而不少发达国家的著作权法一两年就会修订一次。当然，从整体上来讲，我们 1990 年《著作权法》的水平还是比较高的，是一部比较完备的法律，但是毕竟发展到现在，面临新形势和新技术带来的很多问题，要修订的地方也是比较多的。前几年，国家版权局已会同有关部门，启动了《著作权法》的第三次修订工作。目前，国务院法制办正在向社会征求意见，集思广益，以凝聚权利人、产业界、法律界和社会各界的共同智慧。《著作权法》的第三次修订也引起了社会的广泛关注。现在条件基本都就绪了，国务院法制办连续三年把著作权法修订列为立法一档，全国人大现在也把著作权立法作为全国人大立法的预备项目，我们也期待着这次修法尽快完成。

第三，我国仍处于知识产权纠纷高发期。近年来，我国在专利、商标、版权等重要知识产权领域发展很快，总体水平有了很大提高，但与美、日、韩、欧等世界知识产权强国与地区相比，在很多方面还存在不小的差距。另外，随着技术的不断进步，新问题、新挑战层出不穷，我们的判断是在一段时间内，我国仍将处于知识产权纠纷的高发期。据统计，近几年法院的知识产权诉讼持续上升，其中著作权民事诉讼案件的比例最高。以北京为例，2014 年各级法院共办理知识产权民事案件 11 332 件，其中著作权案件 8 953 件，占 79%。而著作权案件中，网络案件又占一半以上。

三、关于对未来发展趋势的分析

在今后创新、协调、绿色、开放、共享的发展进程中，智力成果在推动社会进步、经济发展方面所发挥的作用将更加突出，而另一方面著作权的纠纷和矛盾也更加凸显，这就决定了我们仍然要将版权保护放在版权工作的重要位置。创造良好的版权保护环境，仍将是“十三五”版权工作的重点。

第一，创新及创新成果的运用将更为重要而紧迫，版权在其中的作用将更加凸显。

“十三五”时期，我国经济发展将表现出速度变化、结构优化、动力转换等重要特点，经济社会发展将更多依靠创新作为发展动力的驱动，将更多依靠包括版权在内的智力成果的运用，将更多依靠以版权作为基础资源的版权产业的发展。

从目前开展的版权的经济贡献率调查来看，2014 年我国版权产业的经济贡献率已超过了 6%，而上海、北京和深圳三个城市已达到了两位数。这个数字超过了文化产业，原因在于文化和版权产业统计方法不同，范围、口径也不同。但文化的内核是版权，在文化产业发展中，版权的基础性、资源性作用将越来越凸显、越来越重要，特别是在传播方式正在发生革命性变化的今天，实现版权的价值，最重要的是依靠更多的优秀作品。现在的图书、电影和电视剧每年都增长很快，但真正能够实现两个效益统一的好作品，仍然是少数的，这样的一个规律让我们认识到挖掘版权的价值，重点就是要创造出好作品、掌握好作品，然后在这个基础上才能去制作和传播好作品，以推动文化产业和事业的大发展。

第二，在创新过程中，资本对版权作品的控制力在提高。

鉴于版权在创新发展过程中的基础性、资源性作用，其越来越受到资本的关注，目前很多电信运营商和平台商都正在进入或即将进入内容领域，对优秀作品和版权资源的竞争正在逐渐加剧。我们常说要重视国家文化安全，实际上国家应该首先通过资本来控制版权资源，而不仅仅限于出版传播机构。在新技术环境下，这个问题将更加凸显。党的十八大提出传播正能量、唱响主旋律，贯彻落实党中央的这一要求，需要有大量的优秀作品在平台上投送。近年来，我们在基础设施和平台建设上投入很大，但如果缺乏对版权资源的投入和控制，后果将十分严重。其次，要注意实行国家调控和引导，对竞争过度集中的地方要进行调控，防止形成恶性竞争，恶性竞争对权利人、对企业、对传播者和消费者都不利；对一些新的领域，国家要加强政策和资金引导，使版权能够为文化发展提供一个很好的支撑。

第三，在新形势下，版权保护力量更需加强。

近年来，我国的版权保护力度不断加强，版权环境有了很大提升和改善，但总体来说我们的保护还是不够的。在“十三五”时期，国家鼓励大众创新、万众创业，推动创新成果转化，版权保护的任务将更重，版权保护力量也须进一步加强。目前，版权领域的刑事执法、行政执法和民事诉讼并存，这是当下我国的国情所决定的，但是存在着执法队伍专业化水平不高、执法能力相对薄弱的情况。今后需要进一步推动版权领域的执法改革，进一步推动刑事、行政执法衔接合一。应当根据我国正处于版权矛盾纠纷高发期这样的现实，进一步加强版权执法力量，提高版权执法人员的专业化水平。版权刑事执法最具威慑力。

现在达到刑事门槛的案件多，而版权刑事执法队伍相对薄弱，可以考虑学习借鉴韩国和我国香港地区的版权执法和管理经验，推动建立专业的版权执法警察队伍。

四、关于建立网络版权新秩序的几点看法

互联网的产生和发展，改变了世界也改变了中国，改变了人类的生存、生活方式，但是也为二十多年前相对落后的中国，在互联网领域实现快速健康发展，提供了难得的机遇。在建立网络版权新秩序的实践中，也有几点看法与大家交流：

第一是版权和法律、经济的关系。版权和法律的关系是不言而喻的，版权是因创作而产生的权利，是受法律保护的。而版权与经济的关系容易被我们忽视或者不愿意提及。事实上从著作权制度的诞生就能够看出，正是复制有利可图这个经济上的动因催生了现代版权制度。其实三百年过去，现在也是一样，经济上的动因、利益的调整与分配驱动法律的修改和调整。捅破这层窗户纸，有利于理性科学地看待网络中出现的各种问题，有利于推动建立网络新秩序，有利于激励创新、激励好作品不断涌现，同时也有利于降低社会网络治理成本。在世界知识产权组织的指导下，中国开展了版权对中国经济和社会发展中的贡献调研，这个调研不是要替代其他的社会统计，而是要让人们清楚地看到版权不仅对文化发展有贡献，对经济发展也有贡献，这有助于人们认识版权的价值，认识不同类型作品的不同价值，也认识到同一类型的作品因质量优劣而价值不同。这无论对于创新发展，对于社会进步，对于公众享有更好的文化作品，对于政府管理，都是很有意义的。

第二是版权和文化的关系。版权和文化之间有天然的血缘关系，虽然文化远远早于版权制度产生，但是版权制度产生以来，所有的有价值的文化作品都不可避免地要打上版权的烙印。我们既不能抽象地谈版权，也不能抽象地谈文化。任何版权都是一定作品的版权，比如书的版权，影视的版权，音乐的版权等等。脱离了具体的作品就没有版权。而文化也不是抽象的文化，也一定有它的表现形态，如文字作品的表现形态，视听艺术的表现形态，音乐会演唱会，电影电视等等。我曾经就版权和文化的关系请教英国创意产业先驱霍金斯先生，他在黑板上画了一个洋葱，然后告诉我，版权就是这个洋葱的内核，而洋葱就是文化。这个表述虽然不一定很严谨，但是很形象生动。前几年的情况是搞科技的人不愿意谈专利，而搞文化的人不愿意谈版权。现在已有很大改观，但重视程度仍不到位。

第三是要处理好加强保护与防止垄断和滥用的关系。在当前，我国仍然是版权保护不足，要加强保护。这是我们的工作方针，这一点是坚定的。加强保护是为了鼓励创新，为创新发展提供一个良好的有秩序的市场环境。但是从国际范围看也要注意另一种倾向，就是美国等发达国家着力抬高知识产权的保护门槛。版权和其他知识产权都有一个前期投入和后期回报的平衡的问题，如果不保护，投入创新拿不到回报不行，但是一次投入无期限、无限制，垄断市场和价格的回报，也不是人类创造和发展知识产权的本来意义。因此知识产权和版权都有一个既要防止保护不够、损害创新，也要防止垄断和滥用的问题。

中国的著作权保护起步比较晚，还存在许多矛盾纠纷和不足，特别是表现在互联网领域，但是我们有信心和能力，依法治理网络环境中的多类侵权问题，认真履行国际承诺，在世界贸易组织与贸易

有关的知识产权协定的框架下，在世界知识产权组织《伯尔尼公约》、WCT、WPPT 等国际条约的框架下，广泛深入地进行多双边国际版权交流与合作，推动建立国际版权合作新秩序，推动建立网络环境下的更加健康有序的版权制度，以惠及广大的创作者、使用者和社会公众。

（本文系作者在第八届中国版权年会上的发言，发表时略有删减）

经济新常态下知识产权的创新、驱动与发展

中南财经政法大学知识产权研究中心主任　吴汉东

当前，我国经济发展进入新常态，实施创新驱动发展战略成为时代主题。在国家创新政策体系中，知识产权为创新发展战略目标实现提供了重要的制度支撑和法律保障。从一定意义上讲，经济新常态下的创新驱动发展就是知识产权驱动发展。

一、经济发展中的创新现象与创新发展中的法律保障

创新是经济发展的基本现象。创新是指人们在生产力、生产关系和上层建筑全部领域中进行的创造性活动，既包括知识创新（含科技创新、文化创新、产业创新、产品创新等），也包括制度创新（含法律创新、政策创新、体制与机制创新等）。在发展理论中，经济增长、知识创新与法治建设应是一个相互作用、相互促进的协调机制。经济增长对社会变革起着决定性作用，它带来了社会物质财富的快速增长，也引起了社会生活方式的巨大变化。在知识创新、经济发展、法治建设的协调体制中，经济处于中轴的地位，知识与法律为之进行曲线偏向摆动。其中，知识进步是经济增长的动力机制，法治建设则是经济增长的保障机制。新制度经济学派将技术进步和制度演变都看成一种创新过程。

20世纪初，经济学家熊彼特在《经济发展理论》一书中首先提出了“创新理论”。在他看来，创新是在生产体系中引入生产要素和生产条件的新组合，包括引进新产品、采用新技术、开辟新市场、控制原材料新供应来源和实现新企业组织。熊彼特将创新作为其经济发展理论的核心，认为经济发展的基本现象是创新[①]。20世纪50年代以来，诺斯、科斯等学者在熊彼特创新理论的基础上，分析了制度创新的需求与供给，研究了知识创新与制度创新的关系、国家的制度创新职能以及制度创新在经济发展中的作用，从而构建了系统的制度创新学说。对于制度经济学而言，制度创新一般是指制度主体通过新的制度构建以获得追加利益的活动，它是关于产业制度、产权制度、企业制度、经济管理制度、市场运行制度等各种规则、规范的革新[②]。可以认为，在新制度经济学派那里，“技术进步和制度演变都看成是一种创新过程”[③]。

知识产权制度作为财产非物质化革命的法律文明，表明了“制度创新”的本质属性。在近代法的发展过程中，知识产权制度与企业法人制度的建立，是“现代产权制度建立的标志”[④]。知识产权法作为制度创新的产物，在经济学意义上是一种激励和规制创新活动的新制度“供给”，而在法律层面被喻为私权领域的财产“非物质化革命”，其基本功能是：为创新活动进行产权界定并提供激励机制；为创意产业进行资源配置并提供交易机制；为创造性成果进行产权保护并提供市场规范机制。

知识产权制度是创新发展的基本保障，具有实现“知识创新”的法价值目标。知识产权制度在一个国家的法律体系中，起着激励和保护知识创新、促进和推动创意产业发展的重要功能，所以很多学者称之为“创新之法”“产业之法”。创新这一概念是对知识经济全面而精要的解释，可以视为知识产权制度的基本价值范畴[⑤]。创新价值体现在知识产权政策制定与立法活动之中。知识产权制度以基于创新所产生的社会关系为主要调整对象，体现了尊重创新、保护智力成果、规制知识经济市场秩序的主旨。创新价值目标的实现，在法律规范设计中主要表现在以下三个方面：一是知识产权保护与私人创新激励机制。知识产权制度是一种对知识产品有

---

① 约瑟夫·熊彼特．经济发展理论［M］．叶华，译．北京：中国社会科学出版社，2009：85.

② R. H. 科斯，等．财产权利与制度变迁［C］．胡庄君，译．上海：上海三联书店，上海人民出版社，1994.

③ 汪丁丁．制度创新的一般理论［J］．经济研究，1992（5）：69-80.

④ 刘凤朝．论技术创新与制度创新的互动：以知识产权制度的创立和发展为例［J］．科学技术与辩证法，2000（2）：57-60.

⑤ 陈谊，汪天亮．试论知识产权法的价值定位：创新［J］．行政与法（吉林省行政学院学报），2004（9）：118-120.

效的产权制度选择。这一制度通过授予发明创造者以私人产权，为权利人提供了最经济、有效和持久的创新激励，保证了创新活动在新的高度上不断向前发展，从而促进了创新成果所蕴藏的先进生产力的快速增长。二是知识产权限制与社会创新发展机制。知识产权的限制，是对权利人专有权利的行使限制，其功能在于通过对产权的适度限制，平衡权利人与社会公众之间的利益，确保社会公众有接触和利用知识产品的机会。三是知识产权运用与创新成果交易机制。知识产权运用是连接知识产品创造者、传播者和使用者之间的法律纽带，旨在规制不同主体的产权交易行为，促进知识产品的动态运用和精神财富的流动增值，其主要制度就是授权使用、法定许可使用和合理使用。

对我国而言，经济发展开始进入新常态，从表面上看是经济增长减速换挡，但是从本质上看则是发展动力的转换和重塑，一个显著的变化就是要素的规模驱动力减弱，经济增长将会更多地依赖科学技术的进步。近年来，我国科研投入大幅提升，自主创新能力不断提高，科技进步对于经济发展的驱动作用也正在加强。2015 年我国研发经费投入 1.4 万亿元，占 GDP 的 2.1%，以知识产权为核心的创新指标得到较快发展：科技创造能力提升，跻身于发明专利申请大国，连续 4 年位居世界第一；品牌创建能力提高，商标注册申请量连续 14 年位居全球第一；文化创新能力增强，版权产业发展势头良好，对经济发展的贡献率已达到 7%左右。我国信息技术、生物医药、高端装备制造、新能源等新兴产业迅速崛起，在国际市场份额中逐渐提高。而同期中国 GDP 的增速一直保持在 7%左右，仍然处于中高速增长，我国经济总量从入世前的世界排名第 6 位跃升至第 2 位；2015 年我国国内生产总值为 68.91 万亿元。当下中国经济发展正处于“爬坡过坎”的关键阶段，已经进入经济发展的增速换挡期、风险凸显期和升级机遇期。在这一转型发展阶段，打造中国经济升级版，实现从世界大国向世界强国的转变，关键在于改变经济发展动力、提高经济发展质量，其基本路径就是发挥知识产权激励和保障创新发展的制度功能。

二、科技创新、产业创新与知识产权产业发展

进入新世纪以来，世界经济结构发生深刻变革，第四次国际产业转移已经开始启动[①]。在各国政府的积极推动下，新技术革命步伐加快，第三次工业革命初见端倪[②]。习近平总书记对此做出了精辟分析：“新一轮科技革命和产业变革与我国加快转变经济发展方式形成历史性交汇。”经济新常态的基本要求是，经济发展的动力应来源于创新驱动，经济发展的方式需进行结构性改革。经济新常态的出现，其动因是科技革命，其表现是产业创新。产业创新是以科技革命为引擎的。科技发展的智能化、数据化、网络化、绿色化以及科技中心多元化、科技生产一体化，成为新一轮全球科技革命的显著特点。我们看到，无论是美日欧等传统经济体，还是中俄印等新兴经济体，都在发动本国（地区）的科技革命，抢占全球创新的制高点，将信息网络、生物技术、清洁能源、新材料与先进制造等作为研发投入最集中的领域。科技专家预测，全球创新中心正由大西洋向太平洋扩散，由欧美走向亚太。未来的 20 到 30 年间，北美、东亚、欧洲三大世界科技中心将鼎足而立，主导全球创新格局。新一轮技术革命将带来世界各国的产业变革，这在科技领先型国家中将会表现得特别明显。

改革开放 30 多年来，我国经济发展道路从传统的资源、资本驱动正走向创新驱动。迈克尔·波特的“地区经济发展阶段理论”认为地区经济发展具有四个阶段：生产要素导向阶段、投资导向阶段、创新导向阶段和财富导向阶段。一国在经济欠发达时，其经济增长的动力主要依赖基本生产要素；在经济初等发达阶段，投资是驱动经济增长的主要动力；在创新导向阶段，也就是向中等发达国家和发达国家迈进的过程中，产权化的创新成为经济增长的主要驱动力[③]。目前我国已进入工业化中后期，正处于寻找新的经济增长点的关键时刻。从经济发展新常态到供给侧经济结构性改革，表明我国宏观经济调控的思路发生了重大转变。就整个宏观经济来说，从生产到流通再到消费，是一个供给与需求各处一端的完整链条。在过去的 30 多年间，中国经济一直保持较高的增长率，且主要是依靠需求侧的拉动，即倚重“投资、消费、净出口”这三驾马车。不断扩大的投资在拉动经济高速增长的同时，也带来供需之间的不平衡，产生了经济结构性矛盾，其重要问题就是一些行业的产能过剩。就国际制造业占比而言，中国生产、出口产品占据第一的有 250 种，其中化纤占

① 中国国际经济交流中心课题组. 打造中国经济升级版［M］. 北京：人民出版社，2013：6-7.

② 杰里米·里夫金. 第三次工业革命［M］. 张体伟，等译. 北京：中信出版社，2012.

③ 迈克尔·波特. 国家竞争优势［M］. 李明轩，等译. 北京：华夏出版社，2002：533-547.

41%、粗钢占44%、玻璃占50%、水泥占60%、电解铝占70%。生产如此规模数量的产品，造成了GDP指数的上扬，但没有足够的消费，从而导致产能过剩。行业产能过剩的表现是：产品价格指数下滑，企业盈利能力下降，行业供给超过需求。2008年前，我国行业产能过剩达20%左右，而现在产业利用率不到70%，存在较严重的产能过剩。从实质上讲，产能过剩是低端产能过剩，其背后的要害问题是产业创新乏力。供给侧改革将聚焦生产要素的有效供给和利用，旨在通过创新驱动、解放生产力、提高效率来促进经济发展。

产业创新和变革的重要任务，就是调整产业间要素配置的结构，也就是通常说的产业结构调整和优化，要让资源更多地流向有需求、有前途、有效益的产业类型和经济形态。知识产权是产业创新和发展的核心制度。在全球范围内，各国政治家、企业家以及战略科学家一直密切关注新一代技术革命带来的发展机遇，充分挖掘知识产权对经济发展的引领作用，以适应新的产业革命并形成新的竞争优势。2011年世界知识产权组织发布《世界知识产权报告——创新面貌的变化》，明确指出：拥有知识产权已成为创新企业战略核心。依赖于知识产权的知识市场日益增长，全球知识产权交易额的增速已超过全球GDP的增长率。知识产权将企业的创新、研发、制造和营销等有效地联结起来，既可以引领创新创业发展，又能够推动传统产业转型升级。产业创新的过程和结果是知识产权密集型产业的发展。在发达国家，现代经济整体依赖于某种形式的知识产权，与专利、版权、商标相关联的知识产权密集型产业是本国经济的支柱。可以认为，知识产权本身就是一种产权化的创新，构成了经济增长的原动力。在某种意义上讲，创新驱动就是知识产权驱动，知识产权密集型产业是实现上述创新发展的内在要求和外在表现。

知识产权密集型产业是一种特殊的产业分类，在外延和范围上与高科技产业、创意产业、战略性新兴产业等有交叉重叠之处。从其产业本质特征而言，它以法定权利作为相关产业命名，突出了该类产业中的知识产权构成：一是知识产权要素的高密集性。该类产业是以专利、商标、版权等无形资产要素组合，依靠知识产权的专业服务和质量管理而发展。二是知识产权保护的高依赖性。该类产业是以权利的存在为基础，以权利的保护为后盾，依赖健康有序、公平开放的法治环境而生存。三是知识产权价值的高成长性。以知识产权为实质的创新与经济增长之间具有正相关性，知识产权本身成为知识经济时代财富创造的主体资源。知识产权密集型产业这一概念的提出，先是在美国（2012年），后是在欧盟（2013年）。而在我国，2015年国务院发布的《关于新形势下加快知识产权强国建设的若干意见》，以“培育知识产权密集型产业”为专项任务，提出了“规划指引”“市场投入”“政策扶持”“示范引导”“管理服务”等知识产权密集型产业发展的若干措施。各国发展态势表明，知识产权密集型产业已然成为拉动世界经济增长的主导力量。我国供给侧改革的要义，在于改变依赖资源和投资驱动的传统经济发展模式。知识产权强国建设的一个重要任务，就是以知识产权密集型产业作为经济结构性改革的新“供给”。具体而言，首先要提升创新主体的知识产权运用能力，引导和支持企业提高知识产权创造质量和运用效益，将知识产权优势转化为产业优势，促进产业转型升级，提升产业层次和企业竞争力。同时，要完善高校和科研院所知识产权管理规范，充分调动高校和科研单位人员转化运用知识产权的积极性，承接和盘活高校和科研院所知识产权资产，促进高校、科研院所知识产权转移转化。其次，要推进知识产权与产业的深度融合，充分发挥知识产权对于科技创新和产业发展的支撑、导航作用，不断推动全面创新，更多靠产业化的创新来培育和形成新的经济增长点，把创新落实到创造新的增长点上，把创新成果变成实实在在的产业活动。最后，要加快产业集聚区建设，努力建成一批产业链完善、创新能力强、特色鲜明的战略性新兴产业集聚区，通过知识、技术、资本和产业转移带动和引领周边区域知识产权密集型产业的发展。

三、知识产权事业发展新常态：目标与任务

经济新常态的形成，有赖于知识产权事业同步进入新常态。在新形势下，知识产权的有效转化和运用，对于提高经济发展质量、转变经济发展方式具有特别的意义和作用。知识产权作为激励和保障创新的制度产品，其本身只是一种独占性的法律授权。知识产权只有与市场经济相结合，进行转化和运用，才能成为企业和产业经营中的“正资产”①，产生经济社会发展的正能量。

① 在会计管理和资产评估那里，知识产权是一项期待收益的无形资产，依据知识产权的商业转化情形，企业资产负债表对知识产权的记载有正资产、零资产与负资产之分。刘玉平. 基于知识产权视角的无形资产评估问题研究［J］. 中国资产评估，2008（2）：13-15.

知识产权转化和运用的基本方式有：（1）知识产权的“产业化”（industrialization）。知识产权的产业化，是指将知识产权所保护的知识、技术、信息等应用到生产经营活动之中，使之转化为有益的生产力，成为企业有价值的无形资产。产业创新须以科技创新为前提，科技创新是以产业创新为目的。知识产权的产业化，意味着科技创新成果与现实生产力的有机结合，这是实现创新驱动发展和建设知识产权强国的必然要求。知识产权的生命在于实施，知识产权的产业化是以知识、技术、信息的充分实施为基础。无论是研发者的自行实施，多个研发者以及研发者与投资者的共同实施，还是研发者将创造成果转让他人实施，都是实现知识产权产业化的重要途径。（2）知识产权的“商业化”（commercialization）。知识产权的商业化，则是指将知识产权作为商品转让给他人或者许可他人使用，是知识产权转化运用的一种间接方式，也是知识产权转化为经济效益的重要途径，其主要表现为知识产权转让和知识产权许可两种交易模式。在知识产权的商业化过程中，创造成果的交易价格往往由自身价值、买方情况、卖方情况和权利转让方式四大类因素所决定，其中创造成果的自身价值无疑是核心要素。（3）知识产权的“资本化”（capitalization）。知识产权的资本化，即为知识产权投资和知识产权收购的运营问题，目前主要表现为专利运营。在专利技术资本化的过程中，专利不再仅仅是技术和权利的代名词，更是市场主体的一种竞争资本。近年来，随着企业间专利交易的不断发展，一种新的专利经营主体 NPE（non practicing entities，即“非专利实施实体”），在专利运营中扮演重要角色，该类实体本身不进行产品的生产或销售，而是投资创新和收购专利，专门从事专利技术的资本化运营活动。

我国知识产权的有效运用，受制于创新水平不高、创新成果商业价值较低以及知识市场发育不尽完善等诸多问题。就知识产权构成而言，具有大而不强、多而不优的特点，存在效益与贡献不足的弊端。现就数量、结构、质量、效益四大要素构成分析如下：（1）数量规模相当可观。2015 年，发明专利申请量首次突破百万件，达 110.2 万件，占全球有效申请量的近三分之一。同年，受理商标注册申请 280 万件，商标累计有效注册量达到世界第一。（2）结构布局不尽合理。在世界知识产权组织划分的 35 个技术领域中，中国主体发明专利拥有量高于外国来华发明专利拥有量的有 28 个，但在光学、发动机、运输、半导体、基础通信程序、音像、医学等 7 个领域与国外存在差距；在包括电影、电视、音乐、图书的版权产业领域，本土市场的占有率尚可，但国际竞争力较弱。2010 年，我国出口的版权产品在国际市场份额为 4.66%，与美国（18.74%）、德国（10.69%）、法国（33.81%）和英国（13.38%）等存在较大差距；中国是商标注册大国，但出口产品 90%左右是贴牌加工，有世界影响力的中国商标为数不多。（3）质量水平参差不一。中国在 3D 打印、纳米技术、机器人工程等少数尖端前沿领域表现强劲，但在大多数核心技术领域的创新总体偏少。2010—2013 年中美日韩四国专利技术流动数据表明，中国仍是最大的技术输入国，其中 95%的高档数控系统、80%的高档芯片、近 100%的大型发动机依赖进口。（4）实施效益有待提升。具有商业价值（其要素包括市场竞争优势、技术应用价值和产业化前景）的专利总量不足，对产业发展贡献不力。据统计，2015 年备案专利合同标的平均仅为 50 万元。综上所述，我们需要调整知识产权构成要素，强调以绩效为核心的知识产权政策导向。过去我们较多注重数量和规模，但现在更多要强调质量和水平，考虑结构和布局，着力实施和效益。这里有几项具体指标，似可作为知识产权制度产品的重点“供给”：核心技术专利的拥有量、发明专利的域外布局、专利技术的应用率和产业化率；版权产品在国际市场的占有率、版权产业对 GDP 的贡献率；商标的附加值构成、知名品牌的拥有量及其在国际市场的影响力；等等。总体来说，知识产权的“供给”，应致力于提升创新型国家的综合发展实力。

对于当下中国而言，知识产权制度建设的本身，就是一场以制度创新促进知识创新、以法治建设保障创新发展的伟大社会实践。在经济新常态下，知识产权制度被赋予推动国家创新发展的功能和使命。认识新常态，适应新常态，引领新常态，是当前和今后一个时期我们经济发展的大逻辑。因此，围绕着经济新常态，知识产权事业发展的各项工作，包括知识产权的制度建设和战略实施，都需要与时俱进，做出相应的调整和充实。质言之，知识产权事业新常态，即是以法治化国家建设和创新型国家形成为目标，依靠知识产权的数量、质量、效益的综合提升和有效运用，不断提高国家科技创新力、文化软实力、经济发展力和国际核心竞争力。

（本文原发表于《法学》2016 年第 7 期）

版权工作概览

BAN QUAN GONG ZUO GAI LAN

2016年全国版权工作

2016年全国版权行政管理工作

国家版权局版权管理司

2016年，全国各级版权行政管理部门认真落实党中央、国务院关于新形势下加强版权工作有关要求，以十八大及十八届三中、四中、五中、六中全会精神为指引，坚持体制机制创新，围绕中心，服务大局，各项工作取得显著成绩。

一、版权执法监管工作成效显著

（一）深入开展打击侵权盗版专项行动

一是扎实推进“双打”工作。按照国务院关于打击侵犯知识产权和制售假冒伪劣商品专项行动的工作部署，国家版权局印发《2016年全国新闻出版（版权）打击侵权假冒工作要点》，部署打击侵权假冒重点工作。全年全国各级版权行政执法监管部门共检查经营单位878 013家，取缔违法经营单位6 243家，查获地下窝点325个，行政处罚3 065起，移送司法机关版权行政案件189件，收缴各类盗版品1 291.97万件。

二是联合开展“剑网2016”专项行动。国家版权局联合国家互联网信息办公室、工业和信息化部、公安部开展打击网络侵权盗版“剑网2016”专项行动，对网络文学侵权盗版、APP侵权盗版、网络广告联盟等进行专项整治。专项行动期间，各地共查处网络行政案件514件，行政罚款467万元，移送司法机关刑事处理33件，涉案金额2亿元，关闭网站290家。

（二）科学强化版权重点监管

一是继续推进国家版权监管平台建设，完成平台二期第三阶段主要建设任务。

二是加强网络文学作品版权管理。印发《关于加强网络文学作品版权管理的通知》，建立网络文学作品版权监管“黑白名单制度”，要求网络服务商建立“通知—删除”等四项工作机制，先后查处了江苏苏州“风雨文学网”等侵犯著作权案。

三是开展“春晚”、国产电影专项保护。印发《关于禁止未经授权通过网络传播中央电视台2016年春节联欢晚会的通知》，对“央视2016春晚”网络传播进行专项保护。在中秋国庆期间，对《湄公河行动》等国产优秀电影进行专项保护。

四是加强网络视频领域版权重点监管。对20家大中型视频网站继续进行版权重点监管，要求主动下线授权到期和无授权文件的影视剧；进一步完善公示、约谈、警示制度；推动权利人方与网络服务商建立版权保护合作机制；适时公布重点影视作品预警名单，全年共公布七批共计284部作品。

（三）健全执法工作体系

一是召开中国网络版权保护大会，发布《2015年中国网络版权保护年度报告》和“2015年度全国打击侵权盗版十大案件”，聚焦“体育赛事节目与版权保护”等主题进行了广泛深入讨论。

二是创新执法培训工作。将各地版权执法监管经验丰富的50名同志列入第一批全国版权执法培训师资库。举办四期全国版权执法监管培训班，对全国各省（区、市）的1 295名基层版权执法监督人员进行了培训。

三是开展执法奖励工作。下发《关于奖动2015年度查处侵权盗版案件有功单位及有功个人的决定》，对在2015年度查处侵权盗版案件工作中做出突出贡献的195家有功单位及215名有功个人给予奖励，有效激发了相关执法部门打击侵权盗版的积极性。

二、软件正版化工作稳步推进

（一）加强研究部署，明确目标任务

召开推进使用正版软件工作部际联席会议第五

次全体会议，全面总结2015年推进使用正版软件工作，明确2016年推进使用正版软件工作任务。向国务院报送了《关于2015年推进使用正版软件工作情况的报告》，向各省（区、市）印发了《关于印发〈2015年推进使用正版软件工作总结〉和〈2016年推进使用正版软件工作计划〉的通知》。

（二）加强指导协调，推进长效机制建设

印发《关于做好2016年推进软件正版化有关工作的通知》，指导各省（区、市）完善软件正版化工作责任制度、加强计算机软硬件采购源头管理，督促各省（区、市）开展软件使用情况全面自查，健全软件正版化工作责任人信息库、落实软件正版化工作主体责任。

（三）创新督查方式，加强督促检查

会同部际联席会议成员单位组织了10个督查组，随机抽查了32家中央和国家机关、10个省（区、市）的60家省级机关、20家国有企业和20家金融机构的1 316台计算机，实现对中央和国家机关软件正版化工作检查全覆盖。改进督查方式，首次利用第三方专业机构资源、软件检查工具等技术手段，对安徽、江苏、山东的省级政府机关软件正版化工作进行了全面检查，共检查单位155家、计算机6 554台，提高了督查效率，扩大了督查的深度和广度。

（四）研究编制指南，推进软件使用管理规范化

经广泛深入调研、反复征求意见和建议，编制印发《正版软件管理工作指南》，为各地各部门提供了操作性较强的正版软件管理工作制度范本和台账范本，为推进软件正版化工作规范化标准化奠定了重要基础，成为各地区、各部门规范软件使用管理的重要抓手。

（五）开展国产软件应用试点，推广使用国产软件

组织召开国产软件应用试点启动会，在贵州黔西县、山西平顺县和宁夏盐池县开展国产软件应用试点工作，指导参与试点的政府机关加强软件正版化工作制度建设和软件使用管理台账建设，建立健全软件正版化工作长效机制。

（六）加强宣传培训，营造良好舆论氛围

会同部际联席会议成员单位举办4期政府机关软件正版化工作培训班，对6个省的全部省级机关软件正版化工作责任人进行了培训。会同国资委、银监会等单位举办3期企业软件正版化工作培训班，组织编写《软件正版化专刊》，制作印发漫画形式的软件正版化工作公益宣传海报。通过国家版权局网站和微博、微信等方式及时宣传软件正版化工作成果，推广各地区、各部门典型经验做法，营造使用正版软件的良好舆论氛围。

三、版权社会服务水平显著提升

（一）加强版权行政审批及监管工作

一是按照国务院行政审批制度改革要求，全面实施行政审批事项一个窗口受理，做好“新闻出版行政审批预审查预受理平台”项目相关工作。

二是召开著作权集体管理组织工作会议，参与审核5家集体管理组织的年检报告，参加中国音像集体管理组织理事会议，妥善协调解决著作权集体管理组织与相关利益方之间的矛盾与纠纷。

三是召开涉外著作权认证机构在华代表处通气会。

四是完成版权相关法规和规范性文件清理工作。梳理废止2个法规、7个规范性文件。

（二）有序推进著作权登记工作

一是下发《关于规范作品登记证书的通知》，要求各地版权局启用新版证书并统一签章。著作权登记继续保持平稳增长态势，全年登记总量突破200万件，其中作品登记159.96万件，计算机软件著作权登记约41万件，质权登记327件。

二是下发《关于国家版权监管平台（二期）第一阶段著作权登记项目运行有关事项的通知》，要求各地版权局使用监管平台开展作品登记工作并报送数据。

三是举办两期“全国作品登记工作培训班”。

四是协调推进制定《军用计算机软件著作权登记工作暂行规则》进程。

（三）扩大版权工作社会影响力

充分利用各种渠道加强宣传，扩大版权工作的社会影响。

一是在“4·26”世界知识产权宣传周期间，通过举办数字环境下的影视产业版权保护圆桌会议、中国网络版权保护大会及制作布设宣传海报等形式，提升版权工作的社会影响力。

二是建立版权舆情监测信息专报制度，针对国家版权局重点工作、版权敏感热点问题开展舆情监测和分析工作，出版9期《网络版权舆情动态》，及时提供版权舆情信息服务。

三是利用新媒体加强版权宣传工作，国家版权局官方网站发布信息1 284条，制作“2016中国版权金奖”等6个宣传专题，“中国网络版权保护大会”专题荣获“2016年度中央国家机关网站特色栏目”奖。官方微博发布信息211条；官方微信公众

账号累计发布60期共计103条图文消息，被评为“2016年度中国优秀政务微信”；新闻客户端“头条号”发稿441篇，总展示量达1亿次以上。

四是举办三期“版权媒体热点问题研修班”，中央主流媒体《人民日报》、新华社、中央电视台等40多家新闻媒体记者参加了培训，取得良好效果。

四、版权产业持续发展壮大

（一）举办第六届中国国际版权博览会

12月5—7日，在广州市成功举办第六届中国国际版权博览会。博览会期间，举办了中国版权金奖颁奖仪式、国际版权论坛、全国版权社会服务工作交流会、中国音乐版权保护论坛、粤港澳版权保护交流合作论坛、中国当代艺术品版权成果拍卖会等多项主题活动。中国、英国、美国、法国以及世界知识产权组织、国际唱片业协会等众多国际组织共212家单位参展，来自文学艺术、科技和管理等领域的1 000多位嘉宾出席博览会。博览会观众达到5万多人次，创下历届版权博览会之最。

（二）设立颁发中国版权金奖

为表彰在版权发展与保护方面做出突出贡献的个人和单位，建立长效版权激励机制，国家版权局申请设立“中国版权金奖”纳入政府常设评比达标表彰活动序列并获得批复。经过申报和评选，在第六届中国国际版权博览会上颁发了6个作品奖、5个推广运用奖、5个保护奖、4个管理奖共计20个中国版权金奖，有力促进了版权创作、运用和保护。

（三）开展全国版权示范创建工作

下发《关于加强对全国版权示范城市、示范单位和示范园区（基地）管理的工作要求》，协调各地版权局上报候选名单，经过评审选出18个全国版权示范单位、6个全国版权示范园区（基地），在全国版权社会服务工作会议上予以授牌。

（四）开展系列版权产业调研工作

加强对版权产业的监测和分析，为制定版权产业发展相关政策提供理论依据。

一是发布2014年中国版权产业对国民经济贡献的调查报告，并继续开展2015年度调研工作，调查显示，2014年我国版权产业增加值已占全国GDP的7.28%。

二是推动具备条件的上海、江苏、山东、广东东莞等地版权局开展本地版权产业对国民经济贡献的调查统计工作。

三是开展“国有出版企业版权资产管理研究”。

五、国际交流合作不断深入

（一）继续加强国际版权多边话语体系建设

一是巩固加强与世界知识产权组织（WIPO）的良好合作关系，参加WIPO各委员会和地区会议，参与《保护广播组织条约》等国际条约的磋商，完成福建德化版权保护优秀案例示范点调研，在WIPO总部举办中国德化陶瓷版权保护优秀成果展和《版权保护促进中国德化陶瓷产业发展的研究》（英文版）首发仪式，与WIPO合作举办2016国际版权论坛及数字环境下的影视产业版权保护圆桌会议等重要会议。

二是与全国人大、外交部等部门，共同推动《视听表演北京条约》早日生效。

三是参加WTO对华贸易政策审议和我对其他国际贸易政策审议工作。

四是参加亚太经合组织（APEC）知识产权专家组会议，积极应对有关版权事务。

（二）进一步加强版权双边交流合作

积极应对中美商贸联委会（JCCT）以及中美战略经济对话（SED）项下版权工作，在《中美版权战略合作备忘录》项下就2017年召开体育赛事版权研讨会达成一致。在《中英版权战略合作备忘录》项下邀请英国作为2016年中国国际版权博览会主宾国，确定双方2017年合作计划，就第八次中英经济财金对话版权案文达成一致。参与中欧知识产权工作组对话及中俄、中巴知识产权工作组会议。举办第12届中韩版权研讨会、中日著作权政府间会谈及研讨会。积极参与中澳、中韩、中日韩、区域全面经济合作框架协议（东盟10+6）、中国与格鲁吉亚、中美投资协定和中欧投资协定等自贸区谈判以及中国与欧亚经济联盟经贸合作协议谈判等工作。

（三）跟踪研究国际版权发展态势

依托以中南财经政法大学知识产权研究中心为主体的国家版权局国际版权研究基地，了解国际版权发展情况，研究有关版权问题，委托该基地编写《国际版权动态》。完成“各国知识产权机构设置情况调查报告”等多个研究成果。同时，加强版权对外宣传工作，对重点国家的政府和业界主动、公开、透明地介绍我版权保护的情况，为涉外版权应对工作营造良好的国际环境。

2016 年全国版权司法保护工作

最高人民法院知识产权审判庭

2016 年，人民法院深入学习贯彻习近平总书记系列重要讲话精神和治国理政新理念新思想新战略，牢固树立“四个意识”，切实贯彻实施国家知识产权战略和国家创新驱动发展战略，紧紧围绕“努力让人民群众在每一个司法案件中都感受到公平正义”的目标，忠实履行宪法和法律赋予的审判职责，全面实施“司法主导、严格保护、分类施策、比例协调”的知识产权司法保护基本政策，为建设知识产权强国和世界科技强国提供有力的司法保障。

一、案件特点

2016 年，人民法院知识产权著作权案件审判工作呈现出下列四个新特点：

案件数量再创新高。2016 年，人民法院新收知识产权民事、行政和刑事案件数量大幅增加，其中，一审案件 152 072 件，比 2015 年上升 16.80%。知识产权民事一审案件上升幅度最为明显，达到 24.82%。北京、上海、江苏、浙江、广东五省市法院收案数量一直保持高位运行态势，新收各类知识产权案件数合计 107 011 件，占全国法院的 70.37%。其中，广东同比上升 22.36%，上海同比上升 20.74%。山东、福建新收各类知识产权案件同比增幅也均在 20%以上。其他一些省份也一改往年案件数量偏少的状况，如贵州法院随着工业强省、城镇化带动战略的推进，案件数量增长迅猛，同比上升了 58.20%。重庆法院的知识产权案件数量也大幅攀升，全年新收知识产权案件数量同比上升 57.85%。湖南、安徽法院知识产权一审案件数量也增长迅速，分别同比上升 52.02% 和 45.40%。

审理难度逐步增大。网络著作权侵权案件仍然突出并出现新情况。此类案件除表现出传统网络著作权侵权案件的一般性特征外，又出现一些新态势，使著作权审判不断面临新挑战。如新商业模式下网络著作权侵权案件的法律适用问题，特别是涉及信息网络传播行为认定的问题，继续成为著作权审判实务与理论界最为关切的问题。影视作品保护新问题层出不穷。此类案件除涉及传统的修改改编与原创作者的权利冲突之外，还出现了抄袭剽窃、合理使用、共有权利人侵权纠纷以及作品角色的衍生保护等问题。在互联网环境下，网络产业发展迅速，新的网络功能和新的商业经营模式不断推出，当事人举证和人民法院采信证据异常困难。

审判质效稳中向好。一是再审率大幅下降。2016 年，地方各级人民法院审结的知识产权民事一审案件虽然同比上升 30.09%，但是二审案件的改判发回重审率为 5.94%，与上一年基本持平，再审率下降 45.00%。地方各级人民法院民事一审案件调解撤诉率达到 64.21%，二审案件调解撤诉率达到 27.44%，取得了良好的法律效果和社会效果。上海法院知识产权民事案件调撤率为 73.92%。山东法院知识产权民事一审案件调撤率达到 69.70%。天津三级法院上下联动，积极发挥司法能动性，在查清案件事实的基础上，圆满调解了涉齐白石作品的数百起著作权纠纷案，使双方当事人历经十余年的纠纷全部得以化解。江西法院创新调解方式，引导 20 多家文化传媒公司与集体管理组织签订著作权许可使用合同，化解了社会矛盾，规范了版权市场秩序，降低了社会成本。二是结案数量大幅上升。重庆法院审结一、二审知识产权案件数量同比上升 62.74%；湖南法院审结知识产权一审案件数量同比上升 48.79%；广东法院审结知识产权民事案件数量同比上升 42.82%；江苏法院审结知识产权民事一审案件数量同比上升 30.80%。

赔偿力度有所提升。人民法院逐步探索将市场价值作为知识产权赔偿数额计算的参考，依法加大对关键核心技术和知名品牌的保护力度。通过对律师费等诉讼合理支出在赔偿额中单独计算和推进适用惩罚性赔偿等措施，使赔偿数额与知识产权市场价值相适应。

二、发挥审判职能，公正高效审理著作权案件

（一）妥善审理著作权民事案件，维护权利人合法权益

一年来，人民法院加强知识产权民事审判工作，严格保护知识产权，给权利人提供充分的司法救济。2016年，地方各级人民法院共新收和审结知识产权民事一审案件136 534件和131 813件，分别比2015年上升24.82%和30.09%，一审结案率为83.18%，同比上升0.52%。其中，新收著作权案件86 989件，同比上升30.44%。审结著作权案件84 129件，地方各级人民法院共新收和审结知识产权民事二审案件20 793件和20 334件，其中著作权案件新收12 411件，结案12 134件。共新收和审结知识产权民事再审案件79件和85件，同比分别下降31.30%和25.44%。

2016年，最高人民法院新收知识产权民事案件369件，审结383件，同比基本持平。其中，新收和审结二审案件7件和11件；新收和审结申请再审案件319件和331件；新收提审案件32件，审结32件。

一年来，人民法院审结的具有较大社会影响的知识产权民事案件有：杭州大头儿子文化发展有限公司与央视动画有限公司侵害著作权纠纷案，孙新争与马居奎侵害著作权纠纷申请再审案，齐良末等与湖南美术出版社有限责任公司、天津市超越世纪图书商贸有限公司侵害著作权纠纷申请再审案，上海耀宇文化传媒股份有限公司与广州斗鱼网络科技有限公司侵害著作权及不正当竞争纠纷上诉案，江苏林芝山阳集团有限公司与磊若软件公司侵害计算机软件著作权纠纷上诉案，叶宗轼与浙江冠素堂食品有限公司著作权权属、侵权纠纷上诉案，上海美术电影制作厂有限公司与杭州玺匠文化创意股份有限公司侵害著作权纠纷上诉案，安少康与长江文艺出版社有限公司等侵害著作权纠纷上诉案等。

（二）妥善审理著作权刑事案件，惩治侵犯知识产权犯罪

一年来，人民法院坚持宽严相济的刑事政策，依法运用各种刑事制裁措施，严厉惩治和震慑侵犯知识产权犯罪，保护权利人的合法权益，维护合法有序的社会经济秩序。2016年，地方各级人民法院共新收涉知识产权刑事一审案件8 352件，同比下降23.90%。其中，侵犯著作权罪案件195件，涉及侵犯知识产权的非法经营罪案件1 567件。地方各级人民法院共审结涉知识产权刑事一审案件8 601件。其中，审结侵犯知识产权罪案件3 903件，生效判决人数5 167人；涉及侵犯知识产权的非法经营罪案件1 551件，生效判决人数1 790人。在审结的侵犯知识产权罪案件中，侵犯著作权罪案件207件，生效判决人数274人；销售侵权复制品罪案件4件，生效判决人数2人。

地方各级人民法院共新收涉知识产权的刑事二审案件787件，同比基本持平；审结812件，同比上升3.83%。

三、全面加强对著作权及有关权益的保护

通过明确法律适用标准，加强对著作权人和相关权利人的保护。通过准确划定著作权保护范围和保护强度，合理界定著作权的权属判断标准，明确网络环境下先授权后使用的原则，妥善处理涉著作权集体管理和大规模系列化维权纠纷，全面维护权利人的利益。如最高人民法院在孙新争与马居奎侵害著作权纠纷案中，就对独创性等作品保护要件的含义给予了明晰。

通过依法采取综合手段，加大对侵害著作权行为的惩治力度。在著作权刑事保护上严格执行罚金刑，在民事保护上不断加大损害赔偿力度，增加惩罚性赔偿，积极适用知识产权临时措施。如北京知识产权法院在书生公司系列侵犯著作权上诉案中，全额支持权利人的赔偿额请求。

通过推出典型案例，推动版权文化事业和产业的发展。人民法院在审理与电影作品有关的纠纷、动漫作品纠纷、计算机软件纠纷、网络游戏作品纠纷等与文化创意产业有关的案件中，充分了解行业发展情况，顺应产业发展规律，营造有利于文化艺术产业繁荣发展的法治环境。在最高人民法院2017年公布的著作权典型案例中，有2件涉及动漫形象的保护问题，从一定层面反映了人民法院对文化创意产业保护的力度。

四、完善著作权审判体制和机制

《著作权法》实施之初，我国尚无专门的著作权案件审判机构。1993年8月，北京市高、中两级法院率先成立知识产权审判庭；1995年10月，最高人民法院成立知识产权审判庭，专门审理著作权、专利和商标等知识产权案件。截至2016年底，全国34个省（自治区、直辖市）中，已有224个中级法院、167个基层法院具有著作权案件管辖权。自2014年11月起，北京、广州、上海知识产权法院

相继成立，专门审理其辖区内的著作权二审案件。2016 年 7 月，知识产权民事、行政和刑事案件审判“三合一”在全国法院推行，涉及著作权民事、行政和刑事一审案件由指定的基层人民法院受理。2017 年 4 月 24 日，最高人民法院制定《中国知识产权司法保护纲要（2016—2020）》，对著作权等知识产权案件的管辖布局、审判机构设置做出了明确部署。可以说，著作权等知识产权案件管辖、审判机构等体制机制问题已经基本完善。

五、健全多元化纠纷解决机制

近年来，人民法院的著作权案件呈现逐年增长的趋势，“案多人少”的矛盾日益突出。因此，健全和加强多元化纠纷解决机制建设，对提高知识产权司法质量和效率具有重要的现实意义。北京法院加强与北京市保护知识产权举报投诉服务中心、中国互联网协会调解中心等相关单位的对接，充分调动行政调解、行业调解、人民调解组织的力量，推进纠纷的和解解决。上海知识产权法院与中国互联网协会调解中心、上海市软件行业协会、上海市生物医药行业协会、上海市工商联民商事人民调解委员会、东方公证处等 10 家社会组织和机构建立诉讼与非诉讼相衔接的多元化纠纷解决合作机制，推进诉前调解、诉调对接，形成优势互补、资源共享的多元化纠纷解决机制。福建法院注重发挥行业协会和科技专家的专业技术优势，实施委托调解、行业调解、科技专家调解，发挥协同解决知识产权纠纷作用，公正、有效地解决了一大批案件。内蒙古法院与文化市场行政管理部门沟通协调，尝试从源头解决涉卡拉 OK 经营者著作权纠纷系列案件，初步形成呼和浩特地区版权使用费的三级收费标准。

六、加强审判指导和审判调研工作

推动法律编纂修订工作。积极参与《民法典》《著作权法》的编纂修订工作，提出修改意见并建议将知识产权纳入《民法典》。最高人民法院通过召开研讨会、参加会议、书面意见等多种方式，充分发挥著作权审判的优势，为《民法典》编纂和《著作权法》修改献计献策。

加强法律适用的专题研究。最高人民法院对审理电影作品和以类似摄制电影的方法创作的作品民事纠纷案件适用法律问题以及著作权集体管理制度的相关问题进行调研，参与“标题党”整治工作，为净化网络环境提供法律支持。北京市高级人民法院在调研的基础上形成并发布《北京市高级人民法院关于涉及网络知识产权案件的审理指南》。上海市高级人民法院对“涉深层链接的著作权侵权问题”开展调研。江苏省高级人民法院开展“供给侧结构性改革可能引发的法律问题及司法应对”调研。贵州省高级人民法院完成《黔茶知识产权保护问题研究——模式、问题及对策》调研报告及贵州省重点课题“非物质文化遗产保护”。

发挥案例指导作用。最高人民法院知识产权审判庭定期发布典型案例，编辑出版《知识产权审判指导》《中国知识产权指导案例评注》。最高人民法院知识产权案例指导研究（北京）基地总结案例指导工作的经验，积极开展案例指导研究工作。

2016年地方版权工作

北　京　市

2016年，北京市版权局认真贯彻落实市委市政府的相关工作要求，紧密围绕首都经济建设的新要求新部署，积极推进著作权普法宣传活动，大力开展软件正版化工作，重点提升版权监测评估水平，全方位推进版权保护工作，取得了显著成效。2016年，北京地区作品自愿登记693 421项，占全国的43.35%，同比增长15.38%，连续十四年位列全国第一。版权合同登记10 281项，其中图书（期刊）出版单位引进版权10 090项，涉外电子出版物和计算机软件著作权合同登记191项。北京地区计算机软件著作权登记82 490项，占全国的20.20%，位列全国第二。

一、形式多样，多方参与，着力抓好版权普法宣传活动

（一）基础和声势结合，举办音乐版权保护与产业发展论坛

2016年4月26日，北京市版权局组织开展了以“使命感　大局观　新起点”为主题的第六届音乐版权保护与产业发展论坛，邀请来自行业协会、唱片公司、音乐网站、法律服务机构、学术研究机构的专家学者以及音乐人代表齐聚一堂，就加强数字音乐版权保护，推动付费下载，建立音乐产业发展的新模式和新机制等方面发表真知灼见，形成全行业的版权保护共识。

（二）发力与借力结合，积极探索开展版权师培训计划

4月20日，北京市版权局启动了中国版权师培养计划。该计划采用线上线下一体化的新型学习培训方式，组织国内外一流专家学者线上线下双线授课，面向各级党政机关、企事业单位招生，为各行各业培养版权领域专业人才和领军人物，助推我国版权产业和文化创意产业发展。

（三）主导与参与结合，多方聚力启动文化创作嘉年华

为响应李克强总理“大众创业、万众创新”号召，北京市版权局联合中国人民大学与中国下一代教育基金会青年创业基金于4月25日举办了以“加强版权保护　鼓励校园双创”为主题的世界知识产权日版权系列宣传活动暨2016年北京文化创作嘉年华启动仪式。来自不同领域的专家学者围绕“数字世界中的版权　保护与创新创业”展开精彩探讨，丰富多样的版权进校园活动，吸引了广大青年学子的广泛关注。

二、加强协作，攻坚克难，稳步推进软件正版化工作

2016年是深入巩固和扩大全市国家机关软件正版化工作成果、促进北京市机关软件正版化工作向新常态转变的关键之年，也是深入开展市属国有三级以上企业使用正版软件工作、全面完成市属国有企业软件正版化四年工作规划的收官之年，版权局始终坚持“机制制度为核心，宣传培训为引导，创新服务为措施”的基本原则，确保年度各项工作任务有序推进、圆满完成。2016年的软件正版化工作，呈现出五个新突破：

（一）在推进覆盖范围上有新突破

在实现全市市、区、乡镇（街道）三级机关软件正版化常态化的基础上，联席会议有关成员单位密切联合，经过四年的逐级深入、不断总结、探索创新，基本实现了全市市属国有企业（三级以上）软件正版化，并联合行业相关主管单位，于2016年下半年启动了全市卫生计生系统软件正版化工作。

（二）在政策制度保障上有新突破

市政府办公厅、联席会议办公室先后印发了《北京市政府机关使用正版软件管理办法》《关于明确我市垂直管理机关软件正版化工作机制的通知》等多项制度文件，有效解决国务院、部委级正版化工作政策文件相对宏观、落地困难等问题，为全市软件正版化工作提供了明确的政策依据和行动指南。

（三）在考核评议机制上有新突破

联席会议办公室通过分解相关管理办法和国务院工作要求，结合工作实际，研究建立了一套真正具有可操作性的软件正版化工作考评体系，分门别类、权衡轻重、明确依据，精细化检查考核评分项目、客观化检查考核评分结果，既实现了考核工作的公平公正，又达到了推进工作的作用，同时按年度开展了认真严格的检查考核工作，并将结果以市政府办公厅的名义在全市范围进行通报，实现了考核评议的标准化和制度化，相关工作标准和工作机制被许多省市借鉴和采用。

（四）在工作推进模式上有新突破

针对部分单位和区县正版化工作人力、物力及知识技能的缺乏和不足，将软件正版化工作与政府购买服务相结合，在部分地区和单位采用政府购买服务的方式，委托首都版权产业联盟等第三方专业机构开展软件正版化相关服务，使软件正版化各项基础性工作更加规范化和标准化，使相关单位或辖区的软件正版化工作迈上了新的台阶。

（五）在使用国产软件上有新突破

北京市紧随国家政策要求，广泛推广以场地授权形式，集中统一购买并部署国产办公软件的采购模式，全市80%以上的地区及10余个大型机关和企事业系统，均采取了此种工作模式，节约了大量采购资金并有效促进了民族软件产业的快速发展，彻底打破了国外办公软件在北京市软件正版化工作中占主导地位的局面。

三、提升监测水平，聚焦大案要案，切实加强版权保护工作力度

（一）纲举目张，逐月重点推进监测工作

按月选取具有代表性的重点热门影视17部、电视剧22部、音乐和综艺节目类作品15部，参照网站权重排名有针对性对20家主流视频网站和12家音乐网站开展监测工作。在调取、核实各重点作品权利人权属授权和分销置换的基础上，实现了对各网站的播放和授权情况的完整性监测分析，并将授权播放情况与国家版权局重点预警名单详细对比，较为准确地掌握了北京市版权总体情况。

（二）标本兼治，及时跟进侵权下线处理

在对各网站重点作品授权播放监测评估的基础上，对涉及侵权盗播的网站的盗版侵权情况也做了详细的跟踪调查，并及时发送下线通知和违规警示。为及时整治盗版侵权违法行为，保护权利人合法权益，净化网络版权空间，在有效监测的基础上，按照《信息网络传播权保护条例》的规定向侵权链接所在的网络服务提供者发布了5 000多条侵权下线通知，要求其在24小时之内删除侵权链接，同时加强对侵权下线通知履行情况的跟踪监察，绝大多数网络服务提供者能够及时履行“通知—删除”义务。

（三）重拳出击，协调推进大要案整治工作

2016年7月，北京市版权局正式启动“剑网2016”专项行动，按照国家版权局部署安排，紧密围绕“网络文学转载、网络云盘、移动APP、音乐和广告联盟”五个方面开展相关工作。根据2016年工作重点，结合北京市版权保护的实际工作需要，对网络云存储领域的侵权盗版行为开展了重点整治行动。

（四）多策并举，加大版权行政调解力度

2016年共受理著作权纠纷调解案件225起，其中，行政调解52起，民事调解173起，涉及的范围包括图书出版物、信息网络传播、软件等。经调解，已结案并成功化解矛盾纠纷的案件118起，调解成功率52%以上。行政调解工作有效化解了权利人和使用单位的矛盾，并促成双方良好的合作关系。

（赵晓鹏）

天　津　市

2016年，天津市版权局全面贯彻落实中央和市委、市政府有关部署，结合新形势、新任务、新要求，突出责任意识和担当精神，将进一步加强软件正版化长效机制建设、打击网络侵权“剑网2016”专项行动作为当年的重点工作，同时，加强了版权行政监管及推进版权产业发展，在加强软件正版化长效机制建设，净化网络版权环境，保护权利人的合法权益，积极开展版权宣传等方面取得了显著成绩。

一、继续完善天津市软件正版化长效机制建设

1. 强化软件正版化工作的基础性工作建设。核实天津市70个部门政府机关软件正版化负责人信息库，并进行了全面的核实补充完善。完善了市、区两级政府机关使用正版软件数据库。天津市、区两级共计864个政府机关，共有工作人员59 801人，计算机56 959台。安装使用正版软件分别为：操作系统52 646个，办公软件42 522个，杀毒软件56 751个。完成了天津市130家企业软件正版化工作情况的信息统计。

2. 加强软件正版化工作宣传和培训。组织召开软件正版化工作培训4期，参加培训的人数近200人；制作《天津市正版软件管理工作手册》，并下发到天津市政府机关及企事业单位。

3. 开展软件正版化工作检查。对天津市6家国有企业软件正版化工作进行检查；圆满完成国家督察组对天津市软件正版化工作的督导检查。推进使用正版软件工作部际联席会议第七督查组对天津市的软件正版化工作进行督导检查，检查了6个市级政府机关、2家国有企业和2家银行的软件正版化工作完成情况，天津市推进软件正版化工作得到了第七督查组的充分肯定。

4. 落实长效机制建设。按照推进使用正版软件工作部际联席会议第七督查组的反馈意见和市政府要求，督促整改落实，汇总整改情况报送市政府；开展软件正版化工作考核，组织了4个考核小组，对天津市10个市级政府部门和4个区政府软件正版化工作进行了考核，共抽查180台计算机。经过考核情况汇总，2016年度软件正版化工作考核结果为：4个市级政府部门和3个区政府为A级；5个市级政府部门为B级；1个市级政府部门和1个区政府为C级。

二、打击网络侵权，开展“剑网2016”专项行动

1. 启动天津市“剑网2016”专项行动。制定“剑网2016”行动方案；成立“剑网2016”专项行动协调小组；召开动员部署会，加强联动形成合力。

2. 加强宣传培训，提高版权保护意识。“剑网2016”协调小组共同组织召开加强网络监管培训，天津市53家市重点监管网站负责人参加会议；在“剑网2016”专项行动期间，利用简报、局政务网等形式进行宣传，《天津日报》、国家版权局网站等媒体对天津市“剑网2016”专项行动多次进行宣传报道。

3. 组织联合执法检查、净化网络版权空间。实地检查了3家网站，重点检查了网站各栏目的版权情况。

4. 对外公布了六批重点影视作品预警名单。在天津市版权局政务网进行发布，并将预警名单发送给天津市53家重点监管网站，要求其立即进行自查自纠。指定专人加大网上检查力度，查找侵权线索，确保网络版权健康发展。

三、版权行政监管

1. 完成4起涉嫌侵权盗版案件中侵权制品的认定工作。天津市版权局对涉嫌盗版的17种图书和2种光盘进行了认定，并出具了认定意见，为案件的进一步审理提供了依据。

2. 开展2次版权执法检查。联合相关单位，对南开大学、天津大学及其周边20余家复印店开展了两次执法检查。

3. 加强对天津市重点网站的日常监管。向53家重点监管网站转发国家版权局公布的三批重点影视作品预警名单，强化日常监管，及时查找问题，确保天津市网络环境的健康。

4. 保护著作权人权益，调处版权纠纷3件。

四、开展2016年市版权示范单位和示范园区（基地）评选活动

天津市版权局起草下发了《关于开展2016年天津市版权示范区县、示范单位和示范园区（基地）申报工作的通知》，完成了4个区县9家单位申报材料的初步审核。对9家申报单位进行了实地考察，确定企业的版权资源和版权保护工作成果。成立专家评审小组，由社会不同层面的版权专家对9家企业的材料进行评审，给出9家参评单位全部通过的评审意见。

市版权局党组召开会议，对市版权示范评选工作进行最终审定，经过会议讨论决定，对9家申报企业再通过天津市市场主体信用信息公示系统进行查询，确定最终结果。经查询，颐博数码科技有限公司、方正汇智（天津）彩色印刷股份公司等7家参评单位通过最终审核，并在版权局政务网进行入选公示。在公示期间，没接到对名单有异议的电话、邮件。

组织召开天津市16个区版权局、各区拥有版权资源的企业代表、市版权保护专家、获奖企业及部分媒体参加的天津市版权示范单位（园区）授牌会议，向7家单位授予了牌匾。不断挖掘企业亮点，为扩大影响力做宣传推广，联系了《中国新闻出版广电报》记者对意库文化创意产业园进行了采访，并做专题报道。

五、版权行政管理工作

1. 2016年，完成涉外图书出版合同审核登记320个；完成涉外电子出版物和计算机软件著作权审核、认证42个，其中电子出版物审核、认证13个；完成作品自愿登记审核发证440件。

2. 完成了“2016年中国版权金奖评选活动提名推荐”组织上报工作。

六、开展版权宣传工作

1. 开展“4·26”世界知识产权宣传周活动。监制了1200张宣传海报和20个易拉宝，在天津市各大公共资源地张贴；与滨海新区版权局联合开展街头宣传活动，发放印有版权宣传口号的便签本及印有版权宣传标语的自来水笔，印制了各类优秀图书名录在本次宣传周发放。

2. 以“4·23”世界读书日、“4·26”世界知识产权日及4月29日至5月3日的春季书展为主题，录制《公仆走进直播间》节目。

3. 借助2016年春季书展的平台，继续延展版权宣传周活动，设立法律咨询、版权咨询等咨询台，为公众提供免费咨询服务。

（张　倩）

河　北　省

2016 年，河北省各级版权行政部门按照国家有关部门的安排和部署，进一步巩固政府机关和企业软件正版化工作成果，严厉打击各领域侵权盗版行为，积极创建版权示范单位和园区（基地），引领版权相关企业参与国际展会，不断提高版权服务能力，取得了显著成效。

一、继续抓好政府机关和企业软件正版化成果的巩固工作

一是加强工作部署。制定了《河北省 2016 年推进使用正版软件工作实施方案》，对 2016 年的工作进行了统一部署。转发了《关于做好 2016 年推进软件正版化有关工作的通知》，就完善长效机制、明确目标任务、落实主体责任等三方面工作做出部署，提出了具体要求。及时召开了全省版权工作会议，河北省新闻出版广电局（版权局）局长李晓明、副局长王智出席会议，并传达学习了国家版权局相关会议精神，部署了全省软件正版化重点工作。

二是加强制度建设。河北省版权局联合省财政厅、省公共资源交易监督办公室共同制发了《关于进一步加强计算机软硬件采购源头管理工作的通知》，对今后各单位新采购计算机软硬件的计划、预算、采购等工作进行了源头管控，严防盗版软件流入政府机关。及时转发了由国家版权局出台的《正版软件管理工作指南》，要求各地、各单位贯彻落实，开展好软件正版化工作。

三是开展督查考评。2016 年下半年，河北省版权局分别组织开展了督导检查和考核评议活动，先后督查了 3 个设区市、6 个县级政府的部分机关，完成了 96 家省直单位和 13 个市政府、11 个县政府的考核工作，形成了情况通报，推动了工作的开展。

四是推进企业软件正版化工作。河北省国资委印发了《2016 年推进监管企业使用正版软件工作实施方案》，加快推进省国资委监管企业软件正版化工作进度。下半年其对部分监管企业进行了软件正版化工作培训和督导检查。石家庄市国资委召开了北国商城、常山纺织集团股份有限公司等 12 家国有企业参加的座谈会，并组织人员对企业上报的情况进行了认真的核查。2016 年 1 月、12 月，全国打侵办考核组分别对河北省 2015 年度、2016 年度包括软件正版化在内的打侵工作进行了检查，现场查看资料和听取汇报，并实地抽查了邯郸、石家庄等市部分单位的计算机，对河北省软件正版化工作的考核均给予了满分。国家版权局在对全国 2016 年度软件正版化工作进行总结时，也给予了河北省满分的评价，并进行了通报表彰。

二、认真开展互联网领域和传统领域中的打击侵权盗版行动

一是组织开展“剑网 2016”专项行动。按照国家要求，河北省版权局会同省网信办、省通信管理局、省公安厅等部门联合制发《河北省打击网络侵权盗版“剑网 2016”专项行动方案》，在全省突出整治未经授权非法传播网络文学、新闻、影视等作品的侵权盗版行为，重点查处通过智能移动终端第三方应用程序（APP）、电子商务平台、网络广告联盟、私人影院（小影吧）等平台进行的侵权盗版行为，进一步规范网络音乐、网络云存储空间、网络转载新闻作品的版权秩序。专项行动期间，河北省版权局主动监管互联网站 8 000 多家（次），先后查处了“指导网”“云腾网”等侵权假冒案件，处理涉嫌侵权盗版违规网站 17 个，注销违规网站备案 11 个，取消违规网站接入 7 个，列入黑名单管理 5 个。

二是加强源头管理。河北省版权局协同新闻出版行业监管部门，对各类印刷复制企业进行专项整顿，确保了全国“两会”、暑期和国庆等重要时间节点印刷复制企业和出版物市场的安全稳定。

三是加大出版物市场监管力度。制定了《河北省新闻出版广电局 2016 年打击侵权假冒工作方案》，对全年“双打”工作进行了安排部署。协同新闻出版行业监管部门采取多种方式，对盗版重大题材、畅销、常销图书及教材教辅、影视、软件等出版物进行了重点查缴。对繁华街区、旅游景点、交通枢纽、学校周边等重点部位进行清查并定时巡查。加大对节假日、早晚市等游商地摊活跃时段的巡查和打击力度，坚决取缔游商地摊。

四是加大版权执法力度。先后查处了保定市霍某某侵犯著作权案、石家庄市张某某侵犯著作权案、衡水市王某某和霍某某侵犯著作权案、赵某某等人侵犯著作权案、衡水运输集团有限公司汽车驾驶员培训学校侵犯著作权案等侵权盗版案件。在国务院考核组的考核中，版权执法工作成绩为满分并获得加分。

三、加强版权宣传、教育和培训工作，提高公众的版权意识

一是重视知识产权保护宣传周宣传活动。2016 年 4 月 23 日至 26 日，河北省版权局组织电台、电视台、报纸、网络等新闻媒体，在积极宣传国家版权局制作的“世界知识产权日”主题——“数字创意、重塑文化”系列版权宣传海报的同时，还在25个频道全天24小时滚动播出由河北省版权局、省版权保护中心与石家庄市文广新局联合制作的版权公益广告宣传片《创作即有版权　版权创造财富》，取得了良好的社会效果。在“4·26”世界知识产权日当天还组织开展了“保护版权、鼓励创新”校园签名宣传活动。河北省政协副主席段惠军，省新闻出版广电（版权）局局长李晓明、副局长王智，石家庄市政府和市版权局有关领导及工作人员，河北外国语学院师生及省内主要媒体记者、著作权人代表等2 000余人参加了签名活动。另外，河北省版权局利用媒体对外公布了2015年度全省10起侵权盗版案件，受到社会广泛关注。

二是加强日常宣传。充分利用《中国版权年鉴》、《河北新闻出版广播影视年鉴》、《河北省知识产权保护状况》白皮书、《软件正版化在中国》等出版物的地位及影响，积极总结全省版权保护经验，通过文字、图片等形式，全面展示版权保护成果，不断扩大对外宣传。

三是加强软件正版化工作培训。2016年上半年，河北省版权局组织省使用正版软件工作领导小组相关成员单位有关负责人一起，参加了2016年国家版权局组织的政府机关软件正版化培训会议，并参加了座谈发言。在全省版权工作会议前夕，省版权局专门为参会代表编发了软件正版化知识介绍材料，并进行了专业知识讲座和业务培训。12月份，河北省版权局专门召开会议，对参加全省政府机关软件正版化考核评议工作11个考核组的考核成员进行了政策、专业知识讲解和业务培训。石家庄、衡水、秦皇岛等市及时召开培训会议，邀请河北省版权局专业人员与会传达国家会议精神，讲解《正版软件管理工作指南》和软件正版化检查方法，当地还编发了软件正版化文件选编和工作手册。廊坊、沧州等地先后举办了“软件正版化业务培训”，聘请专业人士讲解版权常识、政策法规、技术规范等业务知识。2016年，省、市、县三级政府先后完成230余次培训，参训人员达1万余人次。

四是推荐宣传了查办案件的有功单位和个人。2016年4月20日，国家版权局印发《关于奖励2015年度查处侵权盗版案件有功单位及有功个人的决定》，河北张某某等印制盗版图书案专案组、河北华宁印刷厂侵犯著作权案专案组、河北叶某销售侵权复制品案专案组、河北省版权局版权处、河北张某等侵犯《热血传奇》网络游戏著作权案专案组、河北省衡水市文化市场行政执法大队等涉及的19家单位及22名个人分别获奖。

四、加大版权示范城市、示范单位、示范园区（基地）建设及版权登记和服务推广工作，促进版权产业发展

一是推进开展版权示范城市、示范单位、示范园区（基地）建设。印发了《河北省版权局贯彻落实〈关于加强全国版权示范城市、示范单位和示范园区（基地）管理工作要求〉的通知》和《河北省版权示范城市、版权示范单位管理办法》，强力推进全省版权示范城市、示范单位和示范园区（基地）的创建和管理工作。2016年6月下旬，河北省新闻出版广电局（版权局）副局长王智带队就创建全国版权示范城市工作赴廊坊市进行了实地调研，专门听取了廊坊市政府创建全国版权示范城市工作情况汇报，到乐聪公司、华夏幸福大厂影视创意园区、大厂微软游戏中心等单位实地考察。经过调研，河北省版权局同意廊坊市政府创建全国版权示范城市的申请，并已上报国家版权局审批。同时河北省版权局对君乐宝、汉佳、中科恒运三家公司以及乐聪科技创意园区上报的有关申请材料进行了审核，经会议审定后，分别授予了“河北省版权示范单位”和“河北省版权示范园区”称号。

二是强化版权服务功能。河北省版权局有关领导带领省版权保护中心人员两次赴保定市曲阳县调研该县版权产业发展情况，讲解版权知识，撰写调研报告，并帮助解决版权产业发展中存在的问题。在此基础上，河北省内第一个以单项产业为主体的版权服务站在曲阳县石雕产业中设立。该站直接针对石雕产业的著作权人和著作权单位提供版权服务，简化登记程序，加快登记速度，提供版权咨询，维护主体权益，得到了当地政府和企业的广泛认可。截至2016年底，已有200余件作品正在预审当中。2016年，河北省版权保护中心还与省内六家文化、出版、报刊单位签署了《版权顾问协议书》，并提供了切实有用的版权服务，解决了顾问单位的困惑，保障了著作权人和版权产业单位的正当权益，全年未发生投诉事件。2016年，河北省版权部门先后为省内各出版社登记外国及港澳台图书出版合同88件，为社会公众登记美术、文字和音乐等作品372件。

三是助推版权产业发展。2016年12月5日至7日，省版权局组织全省11家单位的300多件作品参加了由国家新闻出版广电总局（国家版权局）主办的第六届中国国际版权博览会，并获得了多项丰硕成果。河北省版权局局长李晓明高度重视参展工作，多次对参展工作做出指示，省版权局副局长王智亲自带队参展。展会期间，国家新闻出版广电总局、国家版权局副局长阎晓宏出席并见证了河北省的版权项目签约仪式，专程视察了河北省展台，对近年来河北省版权工作给予了充分肯定。博览会上，河北省版权局推荐的电视剧《海棠依旧》荣获我国版权界最高奖项“中国版权金奖”，是全国六个获奖作品之一。《知之深　爱之切》等一批作品获版博会颁发的“金慧奖”。河北省版权局获得最佳组织奖。展会期间，河北省组织了版权签约仪式，签约金额达10.2亿元，为此次版权博览会各参展省份之最，其中华夏幸福分别与派格控股有限公司、金海岸公司签订了版权作品投资项目，签约投资金额分别为8亿、2.1亿元人民币；乐聪科技分别与广州小鸡快跑公司、广州唯诺冠公司签约，授予两公司三眼猫品牌形象版权作品的使用权，签约金额各500万元人民币。此外，河北省的展台设计、参展作品展示了河北版权产业发展成果，展现了河北的文化自信，对推动全省版权产业的发展起到了积极作用。

（李冬群）

山　西　省

2016年，山西省版权局坚持创新管理方式、依法依规行政、全面从严监管和注重实际效果的原则，着力加强版权监管保护力度，有效拓展版权宣传教育范围，突出注重打击侵权盗版和软件正版化工作，扎实开展版权公共服务体系建设，版权市场环境得到有效改善，版权管理和服务能力显著提高，版权工作的社会影响明显增强，全省版权工作取得积极成效。

一、注重版权生态保护建设，创新开展版权管理执法工作

山西省版权局不断提高工作标准、加大打击力度、丰富监管方式，以打促防，打防结合，力求保持对侵权盗版不法分子和违法行为的持续高压态势。

（一）加强领导，整合执法资源形成监管合力

切实发挥局“双打”领导小组办公室的职能作用，多次召开会议、下发文件对全省版权领域“双打”工作进行部署，要求加强版权监管源头治理，开展印刷复制发行企业大检查、大整顿、大治理工作，突出重点领域、重点环节、重点位置、重点对象的整顿工作，狠打快打、聚焦重点、追根溯源、强力查办，保持对生产、销售侵权盗版制品违法行为的持续有效打击。同时，特别注重“双打”数据统计与信息宣传统筹工作，以求全面掌握工作情况，有效反映工作动态。

（二）集中力量，全面整顿传统出版物市场秩序

组织版权、“扫黄打非”、印刷、发行、传媒等部门，坚持日常巡查与抽查暗访相结合，先后开展了全省冬季出版物市场整治行动、“秋风2016”专项行动、“净网2016”专项行动、“护苗2016”专项行动、教材教辅专项整治行动、云盘专项整治行动、印刷复制企业整治行动等全省性的集中统一行动，坚持每月重点抽查和每季全面检查，基本完成了全省绝大部分县区的明察暗访和通报问题“回头看”，下发《出版物市场巡查暗访友情告知书》14份，当面反馈问题30多个。全省全年查处较大侵权盗版案件52起。

（三）创新理念，继续加强网络版权环境治理

在7月至11月与省互联网信息办公室、省通信管理局、省公安厅共同组织开展第十二次打击网络侵权盗版专项治理“剑网行动”，以查办网络侵权盗版案件为抓手，加强网络版权监管，加大版权执法力度，保障权利人合法权益，营造网络版权良好生态。突出整治未经授权非法传播网络文学、新闻、影视等作品的侵权盗版行为，重点查处通过智能移动终端第三方应用程序（APP）、电子商务平台、网络广告联盟、私人影院（小影吧）等平台进行侵权盗版的行为。

（四）转变方式，推动案件办理规范化建设

下发了《山西省新闻出版广电局关于加强新闻出版广电系统“双打”工作信息共享平台管理应用工作和行政处罚案件信息公开工作的通知》，要求各级版权管理部门做好“双打”行政处罚案件信息公开工作和“双打”信息共享平台管理应用工作，实现信息共享，完善网上办案，提高工作效率。

二、注重版权舆论环境建设，持续加大版权宣传教育力度

“4·26”知识产权宣传周期间，围绕“加强知识产权保护运用、加快知识产权强国建设”的宣传主题，组织全省各级版权管理部门大范围、多角度、创新性地开展各类版权宣传活动，努力在全社会营造“尊重知识、尊重版权、崇尚创新、诚信守法”的良好舆论氛围。

（一）版权宣传进媒体活动

晋中、朔州、忻州等地的市级广播、报纸、电视和晋中部分县级媒体利用播放版权公益广告、开

设专栏等方式宣传版权知识；太原、晋城、阳泉等市利用公交移动媒体和城市核心区域的楼宇LED播出版权宣传片达1 750余次。太原新闻网、太原在线、龙城热线、三晋热线等网站大力宣传版权相关法律法规和相关知识。

（二）版权宣传进机关活动

山西省版权局设计制作版权宣传漫画（3种，共计15 000张）给100余个省级政府机关和各市市级政府机关，组织学习《政府机关使用正版软件管理办法》等相关文件，在全省各级政府机关形成了学正版、用正版、防盗版的良好氛围。

（三）版权宣传进企业活动

太原市、晋中市、朔州市、忻州市、吕梁市在各县（区）电脑城、书店或影剧院悬挂宣传条幅、张贴宣传海报、解答版权问题；大同市利用短信平台开展针对性宣传，发送3 000条以保护版权为主题的宣传短信给全市出版、发行、印刷、网吧等重点区域。

（四）版权宣传进校园活动

山西省版权局在山西大学开展版权宣传活动，发放版权宣传海报1 300余张、版权宣传品1 800余件，解答各类版权法律问题80余个；太原市印制18万册《小学生漫画版权读本》发放给全市10县（区）各小学学生，做到版权宣传从娃娃抓起。

（五）全省知识产权街头集中宣传活动

晋中、朔州、晋城、阳泉、运城等市在城市广场、图书馆门前、主要街区以举行版权宣传活动启动仪式、摆放宣传展板、发放宣传资料、现场解答问题等多种方式，宣传法律知识。

（六）侵权盗版和非法出版物集中销毁行动

组织全省11个市同时举行了侵权盗版及非法出版物集中销毁活动，销毁侵权盗版光盘音像制品、非法图书报刊及电子出版物等各类侵权盗版及非法出版物16.8万余件。

三、注重重点版权扶持保护，全力推进软件正版化工作

（一）加强政府机关使用正版软件工作长效机制建设

全面落实《政府机关使用正版软件管理办法》的有关规定，下发了《山西省2016年推进使用正版软件工作实施方案》并严格组织实施，巩固政府机关使用正版软件工作成果。

一是落实工作责任。下发了《关于报送省级机关单位软件正版化工作责任人的通知》，完善更新省级政府机关软件正版化责任人数据库。督促各市更新各单位责任人数据库，推进明确软件正版化工作责任部门和责任人，将软件正版化工作成果巩固情况与具体责任人挂钩。

二是加强考核管理。由省政府办公厅下发了《山西省政府机关使用正版软件工作考核办法（试行）》，对全省各级党政机关、人大、政协、法检两院、民主党派、人民团体正版化工作责任落实情况、软件正版化工作实施情况、软件安装使用情况、软件资产管理和长效机制建设情况等方面进行考核，对于工作出现问题的单位和责任人严肃追究责任。

三是试点国产软件。山西省平顺县是国务院推进使用正版软件部际联席会议确定的全国三个国产软件应用试点县之一，2016年10月，山西省版权局在平顺县全面启动了一铭操作系统和金山办公软件等国产软件应用试点工作。

四是组织业务培训。2016年11月17日，组织召开全省政府机关使用正版软件工作培训会议，重点在《正版软件管理工作指南》和《山西省政府机关使用正版软件工作考核办法（试行）》、软件检查工具使用等方面对全省108个省级政府机关和11个市版权局的分管领导和工作人员进行培训。

五是开展审计工作。由山西省审计厅督促各级审计部门围绕政府机关软件资金预算编制、软件采购实施和软件资产管理情况进行审查，重点关注经费保障是否到位，资金使用是否合规，采购程序是否规范，采购需求是否符合资产配置标准或实际工作需要，是否及时建立和完善软件资产管理制度。

（二）逐步推进省属国有企业和全省银行系统、民营企业使用正版软件工作

1. 有序开展省属国有企业和全省银行业软件正版化工作

在企业软件正版化工作过程中，要求各企业加强对软件正版化工作的重视，主要领导切实加强组织协调、全面履行工作职责，认真组织抓好调查摸底、资金落实、软件采购、督促检查、资产管理、信息报送等关键环节，确保按时完成企业软件正版化工作任务。

（1）银行业金融机构。山西银监局扎实推进软件正版化工作。一是于2016年修订了《山西银监局计算机软件管理办法》和《山西银监局正版软件管理台账》，进一步规范了软件资产管理制度。二是积极组织辖内各法人银行业金融机构推进软件正版化工作。对辖内银行机构开展了软件正版化工作培训，并组织辖内法人机构开展软件正版化自查工作，辖内银行业金融机构软件正版化率比2015年提高5百分

点。三是山西省银监局多次约谈正版化工作推进缓慢的山西省农村信用社联合社，并对其下达了监管意见，责令其制定全省农合机构软件正版化工作整改计划并报银监局审核后执行，定期汇报工作进展。

(2) 省属国有企业。在山西省版权局与省国资委联合下发了《关于做好推进省属国有企业使用正版软件工作的通知》，全面启动全省省属国有企业使用正版软件工作的基础上，省国资委对全省省属国有企业正版化工作进行了督促，对工作中发现的问题提出了整改意见，要求加大省属国有企业软件正版化工作进度，加快软件采购安装工作，确保按时完成任务。

2. 继续推进新闻出版行业企业软件正版化工作

山西省积极推进新闻出版行业二级企业软件正版化工作。省版权局组织通过软件资产管理和制度建设深入推进企业软件正版化工作，全面提高新闻出版行业软件正版化工作规范程度和管理使用水平。

四、完善版权公共服务，以服务促管理、促规范

在版权公共服务体系建设中，山西省版权局特别注意加强作品版权登记工作，努力为广大著作权人提供可靠便捷的版权保护服务，为版权贸易的不断拓展保驾护航。全年完成作品版权登记350余件，完成版权贸易合同备案46件。总计答复著作权方面的社会咨询近180人次，调解多起著作权纠纷，版权工作的社会影响逐步显现。推动成立了山西省版权保护中心，努力将其建成版权服务、版权保护、版权交易、对外展示、宣传教育等版权服务的主要渠道。

（郝子谋）

内蒙古自治区

2016年，内蒙古自治区版权局在自治区党委、政府的正确领导下，紧紧围绕党和国家工作大局，认真贯彻落实自治区党委、政府和国家版权局的各项工作部署，全面推动各项工作落到实处，不断创新工作方式，以培养提升良好版权环境、促进版权相关产业繁荣发展为目标，大力推进软件正版化，加强版权行政执法监管，坚持开展版权法律知识宣传教育，提升版权公共服务能力，各项工作取得显著成绩。

一、深入推进使用正版软件工作

1. 政府机关软件正版化工作

拟订《内蒙古自治区推进政府机关使用正版软件工作考核评价实施细则》。按照自治区党委政府年度考核工作领导小组《关于印发〈盟市厅局党政领导班子2016年度考核指标〉的通知》（内考发［2016］1号）要求，政府机关软件正版化工作仍将纳入对盟市厅、局党政领导班子2016年度考核指标体系，并由自治区版权局进行软件正版化考核工作任务分解和监控评价。为此，自治区版权局拟订了《内蒙古自治区推进政府机关使用正版软件工作考核评价实施细则》，经各盟市及联席会议成员单位征求意见并修改完善后，经自治区版权局党组研究审议，于5月底前报自治区考核办。

开展软件正版化年度考核督查工作。根据自治区盟市厅、局党政领导班子年度实绩考核工作安排，内蒙古自治区将软件正版化工作年度考核工作与督促检查工作相结合，由自治区推进使用正版软件工作联席会议16个成员单位组成8个考核组，按照新修订的《内蒙古自治区推进政府机关使用正版软件工作考核评价实施细则》，分四大类13个考核项目对各盟市和区直政府机关单位软件正版化工作进行考核检查。

推进内蒙古自治区软件使用管理标准化。向自治区各厅局、各盟市转发了国家版权局制定的《正版软件管理工作指南》，按照《指南》要求，推进各级政府机关建立包括软件采购、入账、保管、领用、安装、卸载、更换、核销、技术支撑等在内的软件使用管理制度，形成信息全面、动态更新的软件管理台账，规范各级政府机关软件使用和管理的标准化。

2. 全面开展内蒙古自治区国有企业软件正版化工作

按照自治区版权局2016年工作重点安排，自治区版权局联合自治区国资委于2016年4月开展了全区国资委监管国有企业软件正版化调研工作，了解掌握内蒙古自治区直属国有企业软件正版化情况现状，成立了由自治区版权局、国资委及内蒙古电力集团、包钢集团等六部门组成的推进区属企业使用正版软件工作联席会议。

6月，自治区版权局与自治区国资委联合制定了《推进自治区直属企业使用正版软件工作实施方案》及《软件正版化工作进度安排表》，按照“一企一策”的方式，分户下达各企业软件正版化年度推进目标，细化工作任务，全面推进自治区国有企业软件正版化工作。

3. 建立全区各级政府机关软件正版化责任人数据库

2016年，自治区版权局建立了自治区、盟市、旗县区三级机关单位软件正版化工作具体责任人数据库，推动各级机关单位部门责任人切实抓好本机关单位使用正版软件，包括预算、采购、管理、检查、审计、宣传、培训、考核、台账登记等各项工作任务。

二、加大版权执法工作力度

1. 有效开展打击侵犯知识产权和制售假冒伪劣商品专项行动。按照国家版权局和自治区“双打”专项行动领导小组要求，严格落实案件信息公开和版权执法信息月报制度，全面掌握全区版权执法案件进展情况及重要成果。协调自治区版权局科研所在自治区版权局官方网站开辟“双打”工作专栏，将涉及各盟市的“双打”工作情况链接在自治区版权局官网，上报国家版权局和自治区“双打”办的同时向社会公示。

2. 积极开展“剑网2016”打击网络侵权盗版专项工作。7月，按照国家版权局“剑网2016”专项行动部署，召开全区“剑网2016”专项行动电视电话会议，制作打击网络侵权盗版专项行动公益公告，运用多部门网络专项治理协作机制，针对网络音乐、网络云存储空间、智能终端APP、网络广告联盟以及网络文学等重点领域实施立体布控，全面清查，打击网络侵权盗版行为。

截至2016年10月底，全区共办理版权案件31起，比2015年全年增加近20%，其中移交公安机关案件2起（含2016年拟移交案件），有效地净化了内蒙古自治区版权环境，维护了著作权人权益。

三、组织版权宣传培训教育

2016年，内蒙古自治区版权局始终将宣传教育工作贯穿于版权执法监管和管理服务之中，建立起版权宣传、教育和培训的常态机制。

（一）版权宣传工作落到实处

按照国家版权局、自治区知识产权协调指导办公会议要求，自治区、盟市、旗县三级版权部门上下联动，统一步骤，围绕第16个“4·26”世界知识产权日，开展了形式多样、内容丰富的版权宣传活动。活动期间，召开了面向自治区主要媒体参加的宣传工作协调会议，向媒体记者通报了内蒙古自治区版权工作情况。开展了侵权盗版及非法出版物集中销毁活动，并在呼和浩特市设立全国集中销毁活动分会场暨全区集中销毁活动主会场。利用国家版权局提供的“4·26”世界知识产权日宣传素材，结合内蒙古自治区版权工作情况，制作了LED视频，在自治区版权局楼宇LED屏及楼宇电梯口进行播放，并在市区16辆公交车上进行了为期一周的循环播放。印制“4·26”世界知识产权日宣传海报和易拉宝，在自治区版权局办公大楼各显著位置摆放。“4·26”期间，《内蒙古日报》《内蒙古法制报》《北方新报》《内蒙古晨报》等媒体，从普及版权知识、提升版权社会认知度、打击侵权盗版和加强版权保护等方面进行了多层面、多角度的宣传报道，为内蒙古自治区版权保护工作营造了良好的社会氛围。

（二）版权培训工作进一步加强

2016年，自治区版权局共组织举办各类版权培训班5次，共300余人次参加了培训，无论是培训次数，还是培训人数，均创历年之最。

1. 6月，组织24名各盟市版权执法人员参加国家版权局在郑州举办的全国版权综合执法培训班（第二期），提升基层版权执法队伍的业务水平和执法能力。

2. 6月，组织内蒙古自治区作品登记服务机构参加国家版权局举办的全国作品登记工作培训班，从深化版权公共服务能力建设，规范作品登记和加强作品登记工作人员队伍建设出发，不断提高内蒙古自治区作品登记质量，扩大作品登记覆盖面。

3. 7月，与自治区国资委共同组织举办了有120人参加的区属国有企业使用正版软件培训，推动企业在编制软件采购预算，规范软件采购、建立软件资产台账，软件使用安装管理等方面，建立软件正版化长效工作机制。

4. 依托京蒙合作对口支援项目，自治区版权局于2016年10月8日至15日，在北京印刷学院举办了本年度全区政府机关软件正版化工作培训班和全区版权行政执法工作培训班。按照国家版权局对软件正版化工作、“剑网2016”打击网络侵权盗版专项行动具体要求，结合内蒙古自治区实际，重点就提高内蒙古自治区政府机关软件正版化工作水平、政策措施，全面提升版权执法工作队伍的理论水平和业务能力等进行了培训。

四、提升版权公共服务能力

1. 版权作品登记情况

自1994年国家版权局制定实施《作品自愿登记试行办法》以来，内蒙古自治区按照该办法组织开展了全区作品自愿登记工作，截至2016年底共登记版权作品2 138件，其中，2016年已登记134件。

2. 网络版权公共服务平台项目建设情况

2016年，内蒙古自治区版权公共服务平台项目建设工作已基本完成，该平台处于试运行阶段，待该服务平台项目完成后，将实现与国家版权局、盟市版权管理部门网上互联互通，规范工作程序；实现侵权盗版网上监控、取证、执法等功能，加大版权保护工作水平和工作力度；作品登记、合同备案网上办理，实现作品登记信息实时发布、在线传输、实时统计；将为海量版权作品提供展示平台，为获取有价值版权作品的使用者提供便捷授权通道，促进内蒙古自治区版权贸易和版权产业繁荣发展。

（郝　炜）

辽　宁　省

2016年是“十三五”规划的开局之年，辽宁版权工作紧紧围绕辽宁省版权局党组确定的“工作落实年”总体要求，真抓实干，勇于探索，突出重点，狠抓落实，主要工作如下：

一、围绕中心，全力推进北方国家版权交易中心项目申报工作

2016年初以来，根据辽宁省版权局党组的部署，全力做好北方国家版权交易中心项目前期论证和调研工作，组织召开项目论证会，指导辽宁出版集团研究制定项目可行性报告。

二、多措并举，全面提升政府和企业正版化工作水平

1. 组织召开辽宁省政府使用正版软件工作领导小组成员单位联络员会议，全面总结了2015年正版化工作情况，审议讨论了2016年推进使用软件正版化工作实施方案，部署年度正版化工作任务。

2. 为进一步推动软件正版化工作深入开展，鼓励先进，树立典型，组织开展了全省政府机关软件正版化工作先进单位和先进个人表彰工作，经过层层推荐和集中评定，辽宁省共评选出正版化工作先进集体50个、先进个人80名。

3. 组织召开辽宁省直机关软件正版化业务培训。分三批组织召开了省直机关软件正版化工作业务培训，共有178家省直机关的257名正版化责任部门负责人和技术人员参加了培训。着重部署各单位做好本单位软件正版化查缺补漏、软件使用与管理、建立软件台账、纳入资产管理等长效机制建设工作。

4. 扎实推进企业软件正版化工作。辽宁省版权局联合省国资委举办了全省推进国有企业软件正版化工作部署暨业务培训会议，邀请国家版权局版权司领导及有关方面的专家进行专题授课。2016年，分批次、分行业组织召开了三期企业软件正版化业务培训，来自辽宁省的金融保险、勘察设计、商业服务等重点行业的100余家企业相关部门负责人参加了培训。

5. 组织开展国有企业和政府机关软件正版化督导检查。联合辽宁省国资委组成省政府督查组，2016年6月至9月分两个阶段对26家省属国有企业推进软件正版化工作情况进行了实地督导检查，并对存在的问题进行了梳理汇总，以省政府使用正版软件工作领导小组名义印发了督查通报。10月下旬，抽调省政府使用正版软件工作领导小组有关成员单位人员，组成4个督查组，对39家省直机关、14个市30个县区级政府机关软件正版化工作进行督导检查。

三、加强版权执法，提升版权监管水平

1. 及时发布央视春晚版权预警。2016年1月，根据国家版权局的通知要求，及时部署各市版权局及省内主要网站，对本地区主要网络服务商发出针对“央视2016春晚”的版权预警提示，加强版权监管力度，在辽宁省范围内未出现盗播、盗版情况。

2. 满分成绩通过了国家对辽宁省“双打”工作中版权项目的现场考核。

3. 深入推进辽宁全省新闻出版广电和版权领域打击侵权假冒工作和“剑网2016”专项行动。根据国家四部委的统一部署，由辽宁省版权局牵头，起草制定了《辽宁省打击网络侵权盗版“剑网2016”专项行动实施方案》，召开了辽宁省打击网络侵权盗版“剑网2016”专项行动工作会议，全面启动了辽宁省打击网络侵权盗版“剑网2016”专项行动。据统计，截至2016年11月底，已成功查办两起重大网络侵权案件，分别给予罚款15 000元、没收涉案服务器1台的行政处罚。两起案件在结案后已及时在官方网站予以行政公开。

4. 举办全省基层版权执法业务培训班。为开展加强全省版权执法监管工作，进一步提高基层版权执法人员的政策水平和业务能力，举办了全省版权执法业务培训会，各市、县基层版权执法人员80余人参加培训，邀请了省通信管理局、省内知名版权法律方面的律师讲授了网络管理、互联网法律法规等知识，来自基层一线的版权执法业务骨干讲授了网络侵权盗版案件的查办工作情况等。

四、强化版权宣传，提升政策水平和业务能力

1. 部署知识产权宣传周期版权集中宣传工作。组织各市版权局结合各地实际，通过举办启动仪式、参与读书节活动、授权揭牌、城市中心宣讲、咨询、发放宣传品、展览等形式组织开展了集中宣传活动。为配合版权集中宣传活动，4月初开始，各市版权局组织全市版权执法人员开展了版权执法行动，重点对各地出版物发行单位、印刷企业、校园周边复印和打印店进行了检查，打击盗印中小学教辅材料行为。

2. 组织开展第五届辽宁省全民读书节版权集中宣传活动。为全面做好第五届全民读书节暨庆祝“4·23”世界图书与版权日版权宣传活动，在第五届全民读书节开幕式主会场公共活动区域设立版权宣传与咨询服务台，设立大型版权宣传展示板 5 块，组织版权专家、志愿者，为广大读者以及参展商提供版权法律宣传与咨询服务，现场发放宣传材料 2 000余份，吴尚之、范卫平等国家新闻出版广电总局及辽宁省领导亲临展位参观指导。

3. 举办“辽宁省集中销毁侵权盗版及非法出版物销毁活动”及版权宣传活动。2016 年 4 月 21 日，联合“扫黄打非”办公室在沈阳浑南区亿丰时代广场举行了辽宁省侵权盗版及非法出版物集中销毁活动。在仪式现场，联合省知识产权局和沈阳市版权、文化执法、知识产权、法院等相关部门举行了版权宣传活动，张贴宣传海报，发放宣传材料，设立咨询台，开展知识产权宣传、投诉案件受理等活动。

4. 组织开展版权保护进园区系列主题讲座。组织网络版权专家赴东北地区最大的互联网企业沈阳盘古网络技术有限公司开展以互联网条件下加强版权保护为主题的版权保护进园区系列讲座、论坛。

5. 设立沈阳故宫博物院版权工作站。在第 16 个世界知识产权日当天，在沈阳故宫举办辽宁省版权局沈阳故宫博物院版权工作站揭牌仪式，推动了版权保护在全省文博系统中的广泛开展和深化普及。

6. 2016 年 4 月，举行京版十五社反盗版联盟与辽宁省版权局战略合作协议签字仪式及版权保护工作座谈会，并达成了战略合作协议，举行了战略合作协议签字仪式。

7. 联合拍摄系列版权宣传公益广告。为更好地宣传普及版权知识，进一步提升公众版权保护意识，辽宁省版权局联合省知识产权局、省工商局、辽宁广播电视台组织策划拍摄了版权公益系列宣传片。

8. 组织参加国家版权局举办的系列培训。2016 年 3 月份，辽宁作为 6 个试点之一，参加了国家版权监管平台软件正版化平台试运行培训，协助国家版权局进行对平台的调试，此项工作辽宁走在了各省前列。5 月，组织省经信委等 6 家单位的正版化工作负责人，参加国家版权局举办的第一期地方政府机关软件正版化培训班，根据会议安排，辽宁省就扎实推进省属企业软件正版化工作在培训会上做了交流发言。7 月，组织辽宁省 98 家 112 名省直机关单位的正版化工作负责人参加由国家版权局举办的 2016 年政府机关软件正版化工作培训班。7 月下旬，组织 14 个市及绥中、昌图县的基层版权执法人员共计 20 人，参加国家版权局举办的 2016 年第三期版权执法培训。

此外，参加了辽宁省政府新闻办举办的辽宁省知识产权保护状况新闻发布会、辽宁省知识产权宣传周启动仪式，辽宁省高级人民法院组织的 2016 年省知识产权司法保护座谈会，并就推进软件正版化，助力创新发展做了发言。

五、促进版权贸易，推动版权产业发展

1. 召开图书出版单位版权贸易座谈会。为充分展示辽宁形象，加强版权交流，进一步推动全省版权贸易快速发展，联合辽宁省版权局出版管理处先后在沈阳、大连召开了两片区图书出版单位版权贸易工作座谈会。通报了近五年来全省图书版权贸易情况；传达了国家有关加强中国出版“走出去”及版权贸易的有关政策措施，并对做好版权贸易工作提出要求。

2. 召开版权工作站工作座谈会。2016 年 9 月初，组织辽宁省内 10 余家省版权局版权工作站召开工作座谈会，总结交流了各设站单位版权业务发展情况，就如何进一步提高各单位版权创造、运用、保护、管理及服务能力，扎实推进辽宁版权产业发展进行了讨论。

3. 组织参加第 23 届北京国际图书博览会。组织辽宁出版集团有限公司、北方联合出版传媒有限公司及所属出版社、大连理工大学出版社、东北财经大学出版社、大连出版社等 12 家出版单位，参加在北京举办的第 23 届北京国际图书博览会，积极协助各出版单位认真做好参展图书书目选编、展位选择、展台装饰及会务保障等工作。展会期间，共签订版贸协议及达成版权合作意向百余项。

4. 组织推荐参评 2016 年“中国版权金奖”活动。根据国家版权局的部署，辽宁全省共报送“丝绸之路与石窟艺术”丛书等 5 个作品、《小王子》AR 技术童书等 3 个项目参评。

5. 积极筹备第六届中国国际版权博览会的参展工作，组织协调辽宁各市及省文联、辽宁出版集团、沈阳故宫博物院等部门认真做好第六届版博会的参展工作，及时协调组委会联系展位预订、展场搭建装修、展品精选等筹备组织工作。

六、开展版权示范，推动版权公共服务体系建设

为贯彻落实国家版权局“十三五”规划，进一步提升自主创新能力，推动版权示范更好地服务全省经济社会发展，结合辽宁省工作实际，2016 年初，制定出台了规范性文件《辽宁省版权示范城市、示范单位、示范园区（基地）管理办法》，印发全省实施，全面启动全省版权示范工作。

在国家版权局发布的《关于奖励 2015 年度查处侵权盗版案件有功单位及有功个人的决定》中，辽宁省共有 5 个单位、5 名个人获奖。

2016 年度，辽宁省共办理作品自愿登记 8 244 件，审核涉外著作权合同登记 262 件，办理著作权合同备案登记 5 件。

（李安庆）

吉　林　省

2016 年，吉林省各级版权行政管理部门在吉林省委、省政府和国家版权局的领导下，学习贯彻落实党的十八届五中、六中全会精神和习近平总书记系列重要讲话精神，围绕推进“一三三九”工作方略，坚持加强版权保护、推动产业发展的工作主线，不断创新，认真履职，进一步强化和规范版权社会监管，提高版权社会化服务水平，积极探索新形势下加强版权保护的工作举措，持续推进版权相关产业的健康发展，为全省经济社会发展提供更为有力的支撑。

一、加强协调配合，规范执法，版权行政监管工作成效显著

2016 年，吉林省版权局认真履行执法监管职责，组织和指导全省各级版权执法机关开展版权侵权案件查处和执法监管工作，取得良好的工作效果。全省 2016 年度共 15 个单位和 12 个人（专案组）获国家版权局查处侵权盗版有功单位和有功个人的奖励，获奖数量居全国前列，吉林省版权局版权管理处获有功单位一等奖。

2016 年，吉林省版权管理部门多措并举，版权行政监管工作取得良好成效。

1. 统一领导，加强指导，打击侵权盗版形成合力

通过案件预报机制，吉林省版权局定期协调、调度各级版权执法机关的案件查处工作，通过督办、转办等方式及时督促、指导各地的版权执法工作；严格落实全省版权执法案件月报制度，及时总结上报国家有关部门，通过多种途径和信息平台对全省执法案件进行信息公开。各市、县级版权执法机关按照省版权局的统一要求，组织了对印刷复制企业的专项执法检查，查办多起案件，针对校园周边复制、发行盗版教材活动多发的现象开展了阶段性集中治理，查处多家复印社和小书店；配合“扫黄打非”部门开展了“秋风 2016”专项行动，多部门协同工作，打击侵权盗版，有效地遏制了侵权违法活动。为加强对各市县级版权执法机关行政执法工作的指导，提高办案质量，吉林省版权局还结合实际对部分地区的文化综合执法机构一线执法人员多次开展版权执法专题业务培训，培训总计达 80 人次。2016 年，吉林全省共立案查处涉及版权侵权的行政处罚案件 64 件，移送司法机关 1 件，没收盗版图书、教辅材料 15 000 余册，罚款总计 43.7 万元。

2. 省级版权机关积极履行主体责任，查办典型、重大侵权案件

在领导和组织全省版权行政执法工作的同时，吉林省版权局坚持亲自查办案件，提高版权执法工作的社会影响。经认真调查核实，依法对中国移动通信集团白山移动公司《智慧白山》手机 APP 未经许可播放视频作品的网络侵权行为做出了行政处罚。这也是吉林省内首次查处聚合类手机移动客户端网络侵权行为，具有典型的示范作用。对“就爱网”未经许可传播网络文学作品的侵权行为进行了深入调查，经核实有关网站备案信息及相关当事人，确定其为冒用他人名义备案的非法网站，并协调省通信管理局申请对该网站予以技术屏蔽处理。对国家版权局移交线索进行督办的“梨树文学网”涉嫌侵权行为立案调查。此外，吉林省版权局还根据属地管理原则，向相关市、县级版权执法机关移交 4 起涉嫌侵权的案件线索，并进行督办。

3. 组织开展“剑网 2016”专项行动，严厉打击互联网领域侵权盗版行为

根据国家版权局的统一要求，2016 年 7 月末，吉林省版权局、省互联网信息办公室、省公安厅、省通信管理局联合印发了《吉林省 2016 年打击网络侵权盗版专项治理“剑网行动”工作方案》，对吉林省第十二次打击网络侵权盗版专项治理“剑网行动”进行了部署。根据“剑网 2016”行动的工作实施方案和责任分工，吉林全省各级版权执法机关围绕重点工作任务，结合本地实际开展案件查处工作，通过对网络侵权行为的集中治理，极大地净化了网络空间。吉林省版权局将网络文学网站和手机 APP 移动客户端侵权作为专项治理的重点，对该领域的网站进行重点监测，及时发现案件线索，立案查处重点、典型网络侵权案件。共立案查处网络侵权案件 3 件，结案 2 件，其中做出行政处罚 1 件，申请予以

局制定了《正版软件政府集中采购管理办法》，其中规定，“完善采购方式，实行硬件软件同步采购，采购人不得采购未预装正版操作系统的计算机，并对需要购置的办公软件和杀毒软件一并做出购置计划”，“交货时，使用单位必须验证新购计算机是否预装正版操作系统，查看正版软件授权协议及安装介质，防止侵权盗版软件产品进入政府采购渠道”。

二是注重使用管理。各地各单位将软件资产纳入本单位资产管理体系，建立软件使用管理制度和软件台账，将正版软件授权文本以及种类、型号、数量等存档备案，做到专人负责、台账齐全、管理严格、使用有序。抓好软件事后监督与使用监督的问题，保证软件使用者不擅自安装卸载正版软件，充分发挥正版软件的使用价值，从根本上保证软件正版化工作的长效性，巩固软件正版化工作成果。

三是注重长效管理。甘肃省“双打”工作领导小组各成员单位按照各自职责，分别就软件资产管理、采购资金预算、软件采购、管理审计、年度考核等相关内容建立了制度，形成长效管理体系。甘肃省审计厅下发了《关于进一步加强政府机关正版软件采购经费及资产管理审计的通知》；省电子政务办制定了《甘肃省政府机关软件正版化工作与信息化工作相结合实施方案》；省机关事务管理局制定了《甘肃省省级行政事业单位软件资产管理办法》；省公共资源交易局制定了《正版软件政府集中采购管理办法》等。

四是注重考核评议。甘肃省的软件正版化工作历年都被列为“双打”的重点工作，纳入“双打”考核体系，每年由国家“双打”考核组来现场考核，对软件正版化工作进行规范化常态性考核管理。2016 年，甘肃省版权局起草了《甘肃省软件正版化工作实施意见》《甘肃省机关软件正版化考核办法》，对考核范围、考核内容、考核标准、考核结果进行了全面细化。这两个规范性文件均已于 2016 年底前上报甘肃省政府，这两份文件为甘肃建立软件正版化工作的考核机制从顶层设计上提供保障。

3. 企业同步“三推进”

甘肃省企业软件正版化工作着力推进国有企业、金融机构和新闻出版行业企业。

一是推进国有企业。2016 年 7 月，甘肃省国资委下发了《关于开展 2016 年省属监管企业软件正版化实施工作督查的通知》，对 2016 年的国有企业软件正版化进行了部署。白银公司、八冶集团、华亭煤业等 10 家企业已完成软件正版化工作任务。从 2016 年 11 月开始，甘肃省版权局对省属 10 家国有企业软件正版化工作进行了抽查。

二是推进金融机构。2016 年 7 月，组织人员对金融机构软件正版化工作进行了抽查。抽查了中国银行、甘肃银行、兰州银行，华龙证券、海通证券、华龙期货，太平洋保险、安邦财保、平安保险等金融机构，每家机构抽查了 6 台计算机。抽查结果显示，金融机构对使用正版软件工作很重视，各单位软件正版化率都比较高，基本实现了 100%。

三是推进新闻出版行业企业。2016 年 7 月，甘肃省版权局组织人员实地抽查了甘肃省新闻出版行业企业包括读者集团本部、甘报集团本部、飞天出版集团本部以及这 3 家企业下属的 6 家二级企业，共抽查 9 家企业。抽查结果显示，行业企业均按照国家版权局对新闻出版行业企业使用正版软件的要求，建立了软件资产管理长效工作机制，完成了软件正版化工作目标。

二、开展“剑网 2016”专项行动

甘肃省版权局联合公安部门、互联网信息管理部门、通信部门联合下发“剑网 2016”专项行动的通知，制定了专项行动工作方案。各市（州）按照甘肃省的安排，积极组织开展专项行动，及时与相关部门沟通协作，加强对主要网站的监管，持续对侵权网站保持高压态势。

据不完全统计，2016 年，甘肃省各级行政执法部门共受理侵权案件 9 起，行政处罚结案 2 起，移交司法机关 3 起，调解处理 1 起，另行起诉 1 起，正在办理 2 起。

三、版权法律服务水平稳步提高

1. 提高作品著作权登记的效率

加大了作品著作权登记工作宣传力度，提高登记工作效率，为权利人提供优质、快捷的服务。2016 年甘肃省版权局受理作品登记 215 件，为历年之最。与此同时，甘肃省版权局注意强化诸如版权纠纷调解、作品登记、版权贸易合同的指导、版权咨询等工作。与兰州新区党群工作部联系，为其推介兰州新区提供法律服务；2016 年 12 月，甘肃省版权局首次组织读者集团等出版单位负责人赴广州参加了第六届中国国际版权博览会，为推进甘肃省版权贸易开了一个好头；积极与文化集市负责人联系，力图通过提供版权法律服务促使甘肃版权产业再上新台阶。

2. 加大对著作权的宣传力度

以“双打”、“4·26”保护知识产权宣传周为平台，创新形式，深入宣传版权保护的措施和成效。制作“保护版权、促进创新”的宣传条幅，在 4 月

21 日组织现场万人签名活动，甘肃省委常委、宣传部部长梁言顺等领导带头签名；配合甘肃省高级法院，召开了省知识产权司法与行政保护座谈会；制作宣传挂图，在 4 月 23 日“世界读书日”的全民阅读启动仪式现场进行宣传展示；甘肃广电总台策划制作了一批尊重、保护知识产权的公益宣传广告，并在宣传周期间集中播出，进一步丰富了保护版权宣传方式。

（夏　玲）

青　海　省

2016 年，青海省版权局在省委、省政府的领导下，按照国家版权局的工作部署和要求，在省版权局党组的正确领导和国家版权局领导的有力指导下，围绕法制建设、版权管理和推进全省政府机关及企业软件正版化等工作，把握重点，认真谋划，精心实施，圆满完成了各项工作任务。

一、法制建设稳步推进

（一）着力推进依法治省加快法治政府建设。为贯彻落实党的十八大和十八届四中、五中全会以及中共中央、国务院《法治政府建设实施纲要（2015—2020 年）》和省委省政府关于全面推进依法治省和深入推进依法行政加快建设法治政府两个《实施意见》精神，为推进局系统依法治省各项工作任务的落实，制定印发了青海省版权局《2016 年依法治省工作要点》、《2016 年深入推进依法行政加快建设法治政府工作要点》和《任务台账》，明确了主要目标和具体任务，并就工作任务进行了逐项分工，设定完成时限，落实到具体处室。

（二）积极提升依法行政能力。将依法行政能力提升纳入年度培训目标和任务，整理了涉及文化新闻出版（版权）方面现行有效的法律、法规、规章以及规范性文件，编印了《文化新闻出版（版权）法律法规汇编》；4 月份，举办了规范性文件制定报备培训班；5 月份，举办了全省文化新闻出版（版权）依法行政能力提升培训班。

（三）积极开展法治宣传教育。制定印发了局系统《2016 年普法依法治理工作要点》，4 月 20 日在青海大学举行了青海省“版权进校园”主题宣传周启动仪式，5 月 31 日在新宁广场参加了《青海省法制宣传教育条例》集中宣传活动。

（四）全面完成了全省文化新闻出版（版权）系统行政执法人员资格清理工作。为加强行政执法人员资格管理，促进严格规范公正文明执法，根据省政府法制办《关于开展全省行政执法人员资格清理的通知》，对照“三定”规定认真核查执法主体和执法岗位，核查实际持有行政执法证件的人员，逐个部门、逐项内容积极推进清理工作。据清查，全省文化新闻出版（版权）系统现有行政执法证件人员 236 人，其中，由省政府法制办核发执法证的 22 人，各市（州）、县由省文化市场管理领导小组办公室核发执法证的 214 人。依照清理要求，对不应当持有而实际持有行政执法证件的离岗、临聘、合同制、工勤、执法辅助等 47 人的证件全部予以了收缴并统一注销，并在省政府法制信息网上统一进行公示公开，从源头上推进严格规范公开文明执法。

二、版权服务成效显著

（一）加强宣传，提升公众版权意识。青海省版权局始终把法制宣传普及作为工作的重中之重常抓不懈。充分利用“4·26”知识产权宣传周活动平台，着力加强了著作权法主题宣传普及活动。2016 年，联合青海省教育厅、省“扫黄打非”办公室在全省开展了“拒绝盗版，从我做起——版权进校园”主题宣传周活动。于 4 月 20 日上午，在青海大学举行了启动仪式，1 000 余名高校师生参加了现场宣传活动，并在“拒绝盗版，从我做起”条幅上签名。现场悬挂横幅标语 3 条、展出展板 18 块、散发宣传资料 5 000 余份，集中展示了近年来青海省实施知识产权战略以来取得的显著成效，宣传了开展打击侵犯知识产权和制售假冒伪劣商品专项行动，特别是集中宣传了自 2011 年以来全省各级政府推进软件正版化、版权保护工作取得的成果。同时，充分利用网络媒体进行宣传。在青海民族文化网和微信公众号“大美青海多元文化”等网络平台全面跟踪报道了各项活动。积极营造了以“尊重知识、崇尚创新、诚信守法”为核心的知识产权文化建设氛围，增强了公众的版权保护意识。

（二）开展高校及其周边复印店专项整治。3 月份，青海省版权局与省“扫黄打非”办公室、省教育厅、省工商局等部门联合下发了《关于开展高校及其周边复印店专项治理行动的通知》，部署开展了高校及其周边复印店专项治理行动。3 月 8 日至 15 日，联合成员单位对青海大学、青海师范大学、青海民族大学等 10 所高校校内及其周边的 34 家复印店开展了执法检查，对 4 家违规经营的打字复印店做出停业整顿处理。同时，向院校有关部门通报了检查情况，提出了明确要求，进一步教育引导高校师生提高自觉抵制盗版盗印的意识。

（三）积极开展打击网络侵权盗版“剑网 2016”

专项行动。根据国家版权局、国家互联网信息办公室、工业和信息化部、公安部联合印发的《关于开展打击网络侵权盗版“剑网2016”专项行动的通知》(国版发〔2016〕2号)要求，结合实际，制定下发了《青海省开展打击网络侵权盗版“剑网2016”专项行动实施方案》(青权〔2016〕10号)，对全省开展“剑网行动”做出了安排和部署，明确要求各市、州紧密围绕工作重点积极组织开展查办网络侵权盗版案件。通过专项行动，青海省各网站的版权保护意识得到极大提高，网络作品传播方式更加规范有序。截至2016年底，全省未发生一起网络版权侵权案件，专项行动取得了明显的成效。

(四)开展集中销毁侵权盗版及非法出版物活动。根据全国“扫黄打非”工作小组统一部署，4月21日上午，省“扫黄打非”领导小组、省版权局、西宁市“扫黄打非”领导小组在西宁举行了2016年侵权盗版及非法出版物集中销毁活动。此次活动，全省“扫黄打非”部门集中销毁侵权盗版及非法出版物共计10.2万件。省“扫黄打非”领导小组各成员单位负责同志，省版权局机关处室和下属单位工作人员，西宁市及四区三县“扫黄打非”办公室负责人、文化市场管理执法人员、出版物经营单位代表等参加了销毁活动。

(五)全面推进软件正版化工作。为巩固省、市(州)、县级政府机关软件正版化工作成果，建立健全政府机关软件正版化管理的长效工作机制，建立软件资产管理办法及计算机采购、安装、使用、管理等制度。根据国家版权局《关于印发〈2016年推进使用正版软件工作计划〉的通知》(国版函〔2016〕2号)等文件要求，分别制定印发了《青海省2016年推进使用正版软件工作实施方案》(青软件组办〔2016〕5号)、《关于做好2016年推进软件正版化有关工作的通知》(青软件组办〔2016〕8号)和《关于做好推进企业使用正版软件工作有关事项的通知》(青软件组办〔2016〕9号)。一是加强计算机软硬件采购源头管理。联合省财政厅制定印发了《关于进一步加强计算机软硬件采购源头管理的通知》(青权〔2016〕11号)。二是举办全省软件正版化工作培训班。分别举办了2016年全省党政机关、省属国有企业和民营企业软件正版化工作培训班，对各级政府机关和企业开展正版化软件管理工作，规范使用正版软件行为，提高软件资源使用效率，保障信息系统安全高效运行，推进使用正版软件工作规范化、标准化进行了系统培训。三是加强对软件正版化工作督查考核。11月份部署开展了政府机关、省属国有企业、大中型民营企业和金融机构的软件正版化督查考核工作，首次实现了对69家省直党政机关软件正版化督查考核的全覆盖。

(六)积极开展执法培训工作。为切实提高行政执法人员的法律素质和水平，分别举办了全省文化新闻出版(版权)依法行政能力提升培训、全省印刷复制发行法制培训、全省文化市场综合执法骨干培训、全省网络文化以案施训培训、全省软件正版化工作培训、全省文化市场综合执法及“扫黄打非”业务骨干培训等七期培训班，共有720名文化新闻出版行政管理执法人员参加了培训。同时，先后组织99人次分别参加了由国家版权局举办的版权执法和软件正版化工作培训、上海市文化行政执法总队开展的驻场培训以及河南省和四川省举办的文化市场综合执法及318机制培训班。2016年，全省共计819人次参加了执法培训，有效提升了行政执法人员的执法能力和水平。

(七)加大市场监管力度，规范市场经营秩序。青海省版权局始终坚持日常监管和专项行动相结合，严厉打击各类侵权盗版经营活动。持续组织开展了以抓源头、清市场、打网络、查办大案要案为重点的“双打”行动，有效提升了版权执法监管效能。根据西宁市大通县科技文化和旅游体育局《关于对涉嫌侵权盗版音像制品给予认定的申请》(大科文旅体〔2016〕119号)(大科文旅体〔2016〕127号)，分别对送鉴的316种389张、191种317张音像制品样品进行了鉴定，并出具了认定意见书。根据西宁市城东区科技文体旅游局《关于申请鉴定涉嫌非法销售盗版出版物的报告》(东科文旅办〔2016〕59号)，分别委托湖北省版权局、内蒙古版权局对涉案出版物给予了认定。根据举报，省“扫黄打非”办公室会同印刷发行部门在西宁嘉彩印刷公司查获5种共9 720册未办理印刷委托手续、违规印刷的盗版藏文出版物。依据《中华人民共和国著作权法》第四十八条第一款第(一)项、《中华人民共和国著作权法实施条例》第三十六条和《印刷业管理条例》第三十九条第一款第(三)项的规定，对该印刷企业做出警告并罚款3万元的处罚。

2016年，全省共出动文化市场综合执法人员47 006人(次)，检查文化市场经营单位28 945家(次)，查处违规经营单位300家(次)；查缴各类侵权盗版非法出版物及宣传品共6.4万件，取缔游商摊点94个，有效净化了文化市场环境，规范了市场经营秩序。

(八)认真开展版权服务工作。全年接待来人

（来电）版权咨询 400 余人（次），进行著作权作品登记 70 件，著作权合同备案登记 1 件。

（付成久）

宁夏回族自治区

宁夏回族自治区版权局版权管理处的工作除了日常版权管理和理论学习之外，重点工作有三项，分别是版权执法监管、著作权保护、推进使用软件正版化。2016 年以来，在自治区版权局党组的领导下，版权管理工作坚持“打基础、建制度、抓服务”的工作思路，全处同志团结协作、埋头工作，工作呈现出“3443”的特点，即理论学习做到了三个求实、版权执法监管呈现出四个亮点、软件正版化工作在四个方面有所突破、著作权保护得到了三个提升，现简要汇报如下：

一、理论学习的三个求实

一是学习内容求实。年初制定《版权处党支部学习活动计划》，以习总书记“三严三实”要求为目标，在“两学一做”活动中，全处认真学习《党章》和习近平总书记系列讲话精神，学习廉洁从政各项规章制度。二是学习效果求实。每月两次的学习，坚持做到“三必须原则”，即“学习必须围绕工作，学习必须有利于工作，学习必须服务于工作”，每人撰写心得体会 4 篇。三是活动内容求实。全年，按照一岗双责的要求，加强了党支部建设，共召开理论学习、“两学一做”专题讨论、民主生活会等支部活动 26 次，开展谈心 6 次。

二、版权执法监管的四个亮点

第一个亮点：两次就版权执法监管工作专门给自治区党委常委蔡国英、自治区政府副主席姚爱兴写专报。一是 2016 年 3 月，在国务院“双打”考核中，宁夏打击侵权盗版案件和推进软件正版化工作成效显著，全国排名靠前，宁夏版权局党组书记朱昌平批示由自治区版权局版权管理处向蔡国英常委、姚爱兴副主席报送出版权管理工作专报。二是 2016 年 5 月，版权管理处等 6 个版权执法部门和 9 名执法工作人员在查处侵权盗版案件中，受到国家版权局的表彰奖励，朱昌平书记又一次批示，由自治区版权局版权管理处就此事向蔡国英常委、姚爱兴副主席报送工作专报。

第二个亮点：查处侵权盗版大案。一是协调银川市文广局、公安部门查办广州创思信息技术有限公司《烈焰手游》涉嫌侵犯著作权案。该案涉案金额过亿元，是宁夏多年来查处的最大一起侵犯著作权案，此案已向国家版权局申请列为全国挂牌督办案件。二是指导银川市文广局查处银川商城盗版图书案，此案正在查处中。

第三个亮点：公开案件信息。根据国务院的统一部署，依照“谁执法、谁公开”的原则，依法先后在新闻出版广电局门户网站、宁夏电视台、《宁夏日报》上向社会公开了 2015 年办结的三起侵权盗版典型案例，用实例以案说法，取得了良好的社会效果。

第四个亮点：联动执法，打击侵权盗版行为。2016 年 4 月 21 日，与自治区“扫黄”办、公安等部门联合在银川市光明广场举行了侵权盗版及非法出版物集中销毁活动。销毁侵权盗版制品及非法出版物共计 6.2 万余件，其中侵权盗版音像制品 45 289 张、侵权盗版图书 5 330 册（本）。

7 月份协助国家版权局在自治区召开了全国版权执法工作培训会议和全国“剑网 2016”专项行动工作会议。

三、推进软件正版化工作的四个有所突破

2016 年，在推进全区党政机关使用正版软件工作中，自治区版权局版权管理处以抓好“三个到位”为起点，即组织领导到位、摸底检查到位、意识培养到位；以建立“三个机制”为平台，即建立第一责任人的责任机制、建立督导检查常态化的工作机制、建立“版权局抓总、成员单位牵头、各单位落实”的管理机制；以做好“三个服务”为基础，即版权处做好协调指导服务、联席会议成员单位做好政策支持服务、软件公司做好售后维护服务；建议并协助政府办公厅召开了两次软件正版化推进会，即由政府副主席姚爱兴主持召开的区直机关党政机关软件正版化工作会议和各市县、区推进党政机关软件正版化工作会议；举办了两期培训班，一期全区党政机关软件正版化工作培训班，一期全区国有、民营企业培训班；完成了两次软件正版化督查，一次是区级 34 家党政机关检查，一次是全区各市、县（区）党政机关检查；建立起了软件正版化工作责任人数据库，指导各级政府机关建立起软件正版化工作长效机制；起草印发了《自治区政府机关软件正版化管理办法》《自治区政府机关使用正版软件工作考核细则》等一些管理制度，软件正版化工作得到了国家版权局的赞扬和肯定。5 月 18 日，在武汉召开的全国软件正版化工作会议上，国家版权局安排宁夏回族自治区介绍了软件正版化工作经验；10 月 21 日，国家版权局副局长阎晓宏对自治区软件正版化工作做出批示，肯定了宁夏在推进软件正版化、

建立长效机制方面，工作抓得紧、抓得实。全区软件正版化工作在四个方面有所突破。

一是制度建设上有所突破。在调研的基础上起草印发了《关于规范党政机关软件采购使用有关事项》的通知，组织相关人员在调查论证的基础上，起草并以自治区政府名义印发了《宁夏回族自治区政府机关软件正版化工作管理办法》《自治区政府机关使用正版软件工作考核细则》；指导全区各级政府机关建立了软件采购、使用、资产管理、审计监督、责任追究等制度；首次对软件正版化工作的相关问题提出了明确、系统、规范的管理要求，杜绝了软件市场的混乱现象，此做法被国家版权局在武汉会议上向全国推广。

二是推进范围上有所突破。2016 年，重点在党群口、人大、政协、法检两院、民营企业中开展了软件正版化工作。3 月份举办了 2016 年全区党政机关软件正版化工作培训班，专门针对党群口、人大、政协等部门，就推进软件正版化工作政策措施及长效机制建设等内容进行了培训。11 月份举办了国有、民营企业软件正版化培训。6 月份首次对自治区党委办公厅、组织部、宣传部、纪委、自治区政府办公厅、自治区人大、政协、自治区工会、妇联、团委等部门进行了督导检查，共检查 396 台计算机。9 月份对全区 5 市、22 个市县区进行了软件正版化工作督查，共检查 1 804 台计算机。

三是管理方式上有所突破。先后探索建立了推进软件正版化工作“分级管理、层层负责”的管理模式。建立了全区各级党政机关软件正版化工作责任人数据库。建立了全区计算机使用软件台账，对全区各市、县（区）党政机关、区直各部门的1 070 个单位在用的 42 300 多台计算机使用软件情况进行了全面摸底调查，登记造册。对进入宁夏的软件公司实行了备案制，明确谁供货、谁安装、谁维护的服务原则。公布国家软件采购价格、规范软件市场。协调自治区财政厅出台规定，明确今后党政机关在计算机采购合同中，增加预装正版软件的条款，不得购买 OEM 版（家庭版）的一体机等内容。首次从软件采购源头上、使用行为上进行了规范管理。分层分级分批举办了自治区及各市县软件正版化工作培训班。全年对自治区区直机关和盐池县、永宁县、石嘴山市、中卫市、吴忠市、平罗县、贺兰等县市进行了软件正版化工作培训，为巩固全区党政机关软件正版化工作打下了良好基础。

四是使用国产软件上有所突破。首次将国产操作系统引进宁夏。指导吴忠市、永宁县等市县、区属企业中煤实业公司及全区新华书店安装使用一铭操作系统 V2.0 软件和金山 WPS 办公软件。

8 月份国务院推进使用正版软件工作部际联席会议在贵州召开国产软件应用试点启动会议，确定自治区盐池县为全国三家国产软件应用试点县之一，并予授牌，11 月 11 日，自治区国产软件应用试点工作正式在盐池县启动。

四、著作权保护的三个提升

一是作品登记量的提升。进行了作品登记服务流程的优化改造，简化了作品登记程序、扩大了作品登记覆盖面。全年除了以往登记的摄影、文字和美术作品外，往年登记不多的影视作品、工程设计图、产品设计图、计算机软件著作权登记、涉外著作权合同登记等也有了较大增幅，共计登记 219 件作品，比上年增加 36.8%。

二是版权服务方式的提升。采用了著作权人作品的社会公示，承诺登记办理期限，为老年人、残疾人等特殊群体开辟“绿色通道”等服务方式。著作权人的合法权益得到了进一步的保护，作品登记时间比法定期限缩短一半以上，著作权专有权合同备案及著作权转让合同备案、涉外著作权合同备案等版权工作得到了进一步的发展。同时，也实现了办理著作权业务的零投诉和群众满意度 100% 的目标。

三是宣传形式的提升。2016 年初，自治区版权局版权管理处就制定下发了《关于开展 2015 年版权宣传工作的通知》，明确全年及重要宣传节点版权宣传的目标、任务。全年上报国家版权局各类信息 10 条，在版权局门户网站刊登版权信息 32 条，《宁夏新闻出版广电》刊物使用版权管理处信息 8 条。印制《宁夏版权与你同行》《保护版权从我做起》《您的作品登记了吗》等宣传册 30 000 册，两次组织全区各级版权执法人员走上街头发放宣传册。开展了版权知识进机关、进课堂、进社区、进企业、进家庭、进军营、进机关的“七进”活动，按照普及基层、普及群众的原则，为十个基层单位购买配送了 10 万元的图书。在“4·26”世界知识产权日期间，开展了“数字创意、重塑文化”的主题宣传活动，印制了“尊重版权、保护创作”宣传海报10 000 张，在全区各市县区机关、学校、企业及中心城镇张贴，使版权知识宣传多样化、常态化。

（郝　辉）

新疆维吾尔自治区

2016 年，新疆维吾尔自治区的著作权保护工作以加强宣传服务、狠抓执法监管、有序推进软件正版化为抓手，取得了较好成效。

全年共登记各类作品 920 余件，登记出版外国图书合同 46 件；新疆各出版单位向国外出版机构共输出版权 56 项（含合作出版图书），引进国外版权 44 项。全区各级版权执法部门积极开展“剑网 2016”“清源 2016”“秋风 2016”“固边 2016”等集中行动，严厉打击各类侵权盗版行为，全年共出动执法人员 5 537 人次、执法车辆 1 641 台（次），检查出版物批销店（摊点）和文化用品店 28 855 个，印刷复制企业 26 643 家，取缔摊点 64 个，关闭印刷复制打字店 4 家。收缴非法（盗版）音像制品 164 496 张（盒），图书 369 852 本（册），教辅材料 3 693 册（盒），盗版软件 1 272 张。加大行政与司法衔接力度，全年向司法机关移送严重侵权案件 4 起，其中 3 起案件经人民法院审理，判处侵权人侵犯著作权罪，1 起案件在侦查阶段。新疆版权局对 17 起安装盗版软件案件进行查处，调解结案 12 起；对 9 起侵权案件进行督办，全部予以行政处罚，其中沙湾县某学校侵权案，对侵权单位罚款 21 万元。

深入持久地抓好软件正版化工作，完善长效机制，推进软件正版化工作规范化、标准化，巩固政府机关软件正版化工作成果，加强督促检查和宣传培训，稳步推进国有企业及其他行业企业的软件正版化工作。全年各级政府机关共新购正版操作系统软件 200 多套，办公软件 7 144 套；企业软件正版化稳步推进，自治区级 41 个国有企业中已有 20 家完成了集团本级的软件正版化；启动了事业单位的软件正版化工作。组成检查组，先后对自治区级 44 家政府机关以及伊犁州等 10 个地州市和 10 个县市区开展软件正版化现场检查，共检查计算机超过 800 台。投入资金 68 万元，与乌鲁木齐市、阿克苏地区等 11 个地州市共同举办软件正版化培训 11 期 12 场次，培训人员 2 055 人，提升了全区的政府机关的软件正版化意识，增强了基层政府机关开展软件正版化工作的能力。

做好版权宣传，通过乌鲁木齐晚报社阅报栏、乌鲁木齐市新闻出版局（版权局）、乌鲁木齐电视台公交移动电视等渠道，制作版权宣传海报 1 200 套，在 260 多个公交阅报栏、全市近 900 个社区张贴海报；在 BRT 大容量公交移动电视上制作海报宣传片进行每天 8 次滚动播出，每天约有 30 余万人次观看；在“亚心网”以悬浮广告方式进行宣传，在全社会营造尊重创作、尊重版权的良好氛围。

加强版权对外交流工作，积极组织中俄媒体交流年活动和第二届“中国亚欧出版博览会”，在第二届中国亚欧出版博览会上，共有来自 14 个国家的 23 家出版机构参加，展出国外图书 5 000 余种，举办了出版论坛活动和中外合作出版签约仪式等，取得了良好的社会反响。

（杨建新）

2016年版权公共服务机构与社会服务组织工作

中国版权保护中心

2016年，中国版权保护中心（以下简称中心）在国家新闻出版广电总局和国家版权局的领导下，深入贯彻落实习近平总书记系列重要讲话和十八届三中、四中、五中、六中全会精神，紧紧围绕打造数字化网络化环境下我国规模最大、功能最强、最值得信赖的国家版权公共服务机构的战略目标，面向"十三五"开局之年，在坚持正确的战略发展方向，持续巩固创新积累的基础上，把全面从严治党要求落实到事业单位治理战略布局中，进一步加强顶层设计，提出新要求，展开新布局，以国家创新发展理念为魂，发挥综合版权服务优势，提升版权服务理念，再造科学管理机制，重大项目整合建设和重要业务整合推进成果不断显现，版权服务技术、模式和机制体系化创新全面进入实践应用阶段，版权公共服务核心业务覆盖面进一步扩大，DCI（digital copyright identifier，数字版权唯一标识符）数字版权公共服务体系应用取得全面进展，以创意中国版权服务计划为核心的品牌战略布局逐步清晰，版权市场服务与行业和地区发展融合更加紧密，科学管理体系建设和运行更加成熟有序，构建决策、执行、监督三分的管理结构和运行机制初见成效，在新的发展起点上推动中心版权服务能力、管理机制建设和总体工作布局全面取得了新进展。

2016年，中心各项业务工作均超额完成任务，全年在1 903.84万元财政拨款之外，中心和两个下属公司实现自营收入1.79亿元，上缴软件著作权登记费9 318.51万元。

一、持续扎实推动版权公共服务基础夯实和品质提升，着力拓展DCI数字版权公共服务体系应用覆盖，线上线下互动的版权服务网络逐步形成，互联网环境下的核心版权服务能力进一步增强

1. 扎实抓好核心业务基础建设，全力保障登记工作高效运转，登记量不断再创新高

中心始终将版权登记作为公共服务职能的核心业务，为了有效应对版权登记数量连续多年的迅猛增长，持续加强版权登记基础工作，加大了根据实际情况及时调整优化工作流程、岗位设置、业务分组、表单项目和操作规范的力度，不断优化著作权登记信息管理系统功能，利用自有资金投资建设了著作权登记管理信息系统业务流程再造信息化项目，为连年迅猛增长的登记信息数据处理需求提供保障，多措并举进一步提高了登记工作质量和效率，每名审查员的日接审量同比增加了约100%。

全年共完成软件著作权登记407 774件，同比增长39.48%，登记量首次突破40万件大关，再创历史新高。另外，完成软件著作权转让合同登记49件，软件著作权专有许可合同登记21件，软件登记事项变更或补充登记31 323件，同比增长67.22%；查询软件登记档案55 129件，同比增长22.85%。共完成各类作品著作权登记89 580件/系列，同比增长34.69%，涉及作品146 775件，同比增长23.67%。其中作品登记87 988件/系列，同比增长34.34%，涉及作品139 928件；著作权合同备案1 592件/系列，同比增长57.62%，涉及作品6 847件。共完成出版境外音像制品合同登记1 374件，其中录音制品275件，影视作品833件（涉及信息网络传播权557件），公版影视作品266件。共完成著作权质权登记327件（其中软件著作权质权登记263件、作品著作权质权登记64件），涉及作品1 079件（其中软件1 015件、其他作品64件），涉及主债务金额33.75亿元（其中软件28.59亿元、其他作品5.16亿元）。

按照国家版权局要求，继续扎实规范做好全国作品登记信息统计工作。2016年全年，通过全国作品登记信息库管理平台汇总审核统计，全国作品登记共计1 596 582件/系列。

2. 全面推行微笑服务，实现手机预约和查询，版权登记大厅窗口服务品质进一步提升

高度重视北京东城、西城两个版权登记大厅服务窗口的运营，确保为各类登记申请者提供高效优质的"一站式"的服务。面对越来越常态化的大厅人流量增多情况，为了给申请人提供更加便捷的窗口服务，研发推出了移动互联网端应用——中国版权保护中心微平台，实现了版权登记大厅登记申请全面微信预约，以及办理进度和登记公告信息公开实时微信查询，通过技术手段对办理时间进行科学规划管理，极大方便了申请人，减少了大厅登记申

请人的排队等候时间。同时，大厅在中心率先以推行“微笑服务”为抓手，进一步全面提升服务品质，持续改进服务体验，不断打磨服务细节，进一步提升了窗口服务质量和效率，被评为国家版权总局“敬业廉洁身边事”先进集体。全年仅西城区版权登记大厅就接待各类登记申请者 18 万人次，平均每个工作日 800 多人次，最多时近千人。通过中心微平台成功预约办理登记日均约 600 件，通过微信进行作品著作权公告查询用户月均 3 000 余人次。

3. 深入开展登记数据挖掘，不断拓展服务领域和方式，软件登记信息分析咨询服务又有新突破

持续完善和深化软件著作权登记数据挖掘和分析服务，为软件产业和版权产业发展服务。完成了《2015 年度中国软件著作权登记情况分析报告》，并在持续开展年度分析的基础上，进一步开发和利用全国软件著作权登记信息资源，完成了《“十二五”中国软件著作权登记情况分析报告》，展现了“十二五”期间全国软件登记整体情况，详细介绍了“十二五”期间我国软件著作权登记变化趋势，从软件产品研发的角度，客观地反映了我国软件产业的发展趋势和创新情况，为有关机构和部门制定“十三五”发展规划提供有价值的信息参考。《报告》一经推出就受到媒体和业界的广泛关注，4 月 26 日央视新闻频道《朝闻天下》进行了专题报道，晚间《新闻联播》做了新闻报道，软件登记分析服务的社会影响力不断提高。此外，持续深入开展定制性软件著作权登记数据分析服务，为北京、深圳、武汉、苏州、成都、上海等多地的版权局或相关机构提供了区域软件著作权登记信息分析服务，与国家版权局办公厅签订协议，开展了“十二五”金融软件分析工作，首次实现了从区域分析到行业分析的突破。

4. 继续加强基础建设，努力把握发展机遇，着力推动以 DCI 体系为核心的数字版权公共服务体系投入应用取得全面进展

继续把 DCI 体系建设和应用推广放在核心战略位置，全面推进执行与国家信息中心关于 DCI 服务体系建设工程的合作，着力加大 DCI 体系面向应用的技术及业务运营的投入，持续大力推动 DCI 体系建设，在模式创新、科研攻关、平台搭建和标准制定等方面取得新成果，为全面开展 DCI 体系的应用示范提供坚实的基础平台和运营能力支持。

围绕“确权、授权、维权”不断拓展服务领域，完善服务方式，积极开拓在各个垂直细分领域的嵌入式服务，并取得新进展。一是在继续深化与畅元国讯、华云音乐、新华金融信息交易所、百度糯米、版信通、版库、特创意等等机构合作的基础上，进一步规范合作模式，开拓了与云莱坞、中金数据、知乎、妹夫家等机构在影视剧本版权交易、影视作品版权运营、自媒体问答社区版权运营、自媒体视频和图文作品版权运营方面的 DCI 体系应用合作。通过 DCI 体系的推广，2016 年中心共完成数字作品版权登记 310 264 件，数字作品邻接权登记 467 件，数字作品合同备案业务达 15 499 件。此外，以移动 APP 的安全管理和版权登记作为 DCI 体系向移动互联网推广应用的重要战略切入点，完成了移动 APP 在线登记的有关工作流程、标准和规则的制定，移动 APP 第三方证书签名与版权登记联合服务平台建设已进入测试阶段。

二是稳步推进第三方版权结算体系有关工作，中华版权代理中心音乐版权费用结算平台（华云音乐平台）10 月开始正式投入运营，已为 50 家音乐制作公司和独立音乐人提供了服务，启动了与中国电信爱音乐平台的词曲版权费用结算项目，预计 2017 年初正式开展相关结算服务；CACC 数字阅读版权分发与费用结算服务平台建设已进入测试阶段，以此为依托在数字阅读领域探索建立公开透明的第三方版权费用结算机制；积极推动中国版权交易所的筹建，力争在版权交易结算及相关数据和金融服务领域取得新的突破。

三是网络音视频版权监测平台影响力和服务范围不断扩大，以监测平台为依托的网络快速维权机制运行效率进一步提升，2016 年为腾讯、优酷、哔哩哔哩等提供了多档热门视频节目和音乐作品监测，至 2016 年底，累计监测侵权链接 1 174 055 条，删除侵权链接 1 074 679 条，删除率 91.54%。同时，正在推进与国家计算机病毒应急处理中心和北京市文化执法总队在侵权处理方面的流程对接，以加强中心快速维权的处理效果。

5. 版权鉴定工作方式不断改进，工作效率进一步提升

接受各地公检法司法机关、版权行政机关的委托，全年完成版权鉴定 50 件，涉及计算机软件、游戏、美术、文字等类型的作品共 4 000 余部。其中网络侵权案件鉴定仍然保持逐年增加势态，针对此类鉴定涉及作品数量多、网站内容易更改和需要从技术层面入手等特点，认真研究新情况新问题，积极运用大数据分析等新工具新方法，不断积累工作经验，改进工作方式，提高工作效率，确保了网络侵权案件鉴定工作的时效性和有效性。

6. 中国ISRC（中国标准录音制品编码）中心各项工作顺利开展

不断适应录音制品制作、复制和传播等的新特点，通过行业机构向符合条件的唱片制作公司等机构开放ISRC登记申领资格，全面拓展ISRC登记申领范围，进一步提升了ISRC编码在产业的覆盖面和影响力。2016年全年共完成ISRC申请受理59 821件，其中录音制品52 279件，音乐录像制品7 542件，单日最高受理量约800件；全年共完成编码发放58 652件，平均每工作日发码量233件。同时正式启动加入国际ISRC中心相关程序，加快与国际接轨步伐。

7. 全方位版权宣传交流网络影响力不断扩大，新媒体宣传运营方式作用进一步显现

不断完善中心与著作权人和业界交流、互动的综合平台，成功举办“尊重原创　传统再造”2016 CPCC中国版权服务年会和CPCC十大中国著作权人年度评选活动，央视《新闻联播》连续第二年对有关活动进行了报道，年会的品牌影响力持续提升。依托《中国版权》和《创意中国》杂志，注重策划宣传的导向性和权威性，充分发挥版权前沿理论研究和产业实践指导的作用。成功举办了第八届大学生版权征文活动，共106所高校大学生的1 711篇征文参加了活动，高校参加数创历年新高。成功举办了全国版权经纪人专业实务培训班、数字出版与版权管理培训班、ISRC标准系列培训班和版权登记及代理培训班等6期培训班，在培训中新开设了“贯彻习近平总书记系列讲话精神”专题课程，共525人参加培训。

通过多种媒体形式大力宣传版权公共服务理念，充分利用中心专业理论积累资源优势，不断研究摸索新媒体传播规律，以构建品牌营销新媒体平台和版权社会生态圈的定位，运营好“中国版权服务”微信公众平台，在坚持推送高品质原创版权专业文章的基础上，针对受众需求策划推出了《作品著作权登记信息精选》和《作品著作权登记常见问题答疑系列》等栏目和选题，截至2016年底总订户数达38 233人，推送原创文章230余篇，已跻身国内版权服务类微信第一大号，成为中心重要的新闻发言平台和业务营销推广平台，行业影响力进一步扩大。

二、以品牌战略为统领，从产业链和区域性两个维度入手，加强整合营销和纵深服务，充分发挥全流程综合性版权服务优势，版权市场服务体系建设更加成熟完善

1. 以创意中国版权服务系列计划为核心，进一步整合版权服务资源，创新多种模式助力地区版权产业发展

不断推进创意中国版权服务系列计划实施，塑造中心的全流程版权服务品牌，创意中国县域平台计划在贵州、安徽等地的县域开展了务正道项目和绿金淮北项目，推动创意知本、金融资本与地缘文化质本的全方位对接，积极探索助力全国县域经济转型升级的有效途径；研究推出了版权服务推动文化金融业务产品——“版融宝”，整合内部业务流程，周密衔接合作银行的相关工作流程，为广大权利人提供了较既往时间缩短近一半、费用节约近三分之一、成功率提高近一倍的版权质权融资服务，已面向三家试点企业提供服务，已有3 000万元贷款正处于批贷阶段；开创了“创意孵化器”模式和品牌，依托各地版权登记大厅建设，对接金融、渠道、地方园区各方资源，打造版权创客空间和文化空间，建立多层次的区域版权产业发展促进机制。持续深化与北京市西城区人民政府的合作，积极推进国家数字版权产业基地建设，天桥演艺区专项工作小组为园区发展继续提供专业的版权服务支持，积极参与北京天桥演艺联盟的日常运营。进一步探索在外省市设立版权登记大厅，推进区域版权服务窗口体系建设，支持地方文化创意产业发展，成都的西南版权登记大厅已经正式投入运营，上海市闵行区和深圳市罗湖区版权登记大厅都正在推进建设中。

2. 以全方位全流程综合版权服务为支撑，坚持深入产业链提供专业服务，行业性服务平台不断取得纵深发展成果

不断加强业务资源、服务项目和营销工作的整合协调以及工作流程的衔接，与版权产业价值链紧密融合的全流程、全方位版权服务体系逐步成熟完善，各项业务以点切入，以面支撑，根据行业实际需求积极拓展延伸服务，由单一业务向综合服务拓展的情况显著增加。进一步发挥“影视版权产业联盟”平台的作用，与地方高新区合作共同建设影视衍生品服务平台，通过服装、道具、植入广告等衍生品版权交易、设计开发、制造生产、品牌授权营销的产业集聚区和一体化服务，实现共赢发展；与上海美术电影制片厂建立全面版权代理关系，取得《大闹天宫》等百余部经典作品的版权代理权，并将《葫芦娃》形象授权服装领域，实现了影视衍生品服务平台建设与运营同步推进；根据市场实际问题和需求，与西单商会等机构合作，加强了对接实体商品渠道和实体商品版权保护方案的调研与探索。衍

生品版权服务模式不断完善，积极拓展民族特色文化版权保护与服务，与北京市顺义区人民政府共建的民族特色文化版权保护与展示交易中心，征集民族特色文化原创版权作品 2 000 余件，培育转化输出文化项目 10 余个，推动灶王爷、百顺图等版权衍生品设计研发和市场拓展，组建了“GO 当地”电子商务平台，逐步达成了衍生品版权授权、产品研发、市场拓展的产业闭环，以衍生品版权服务为载体，以线上平台线下实体为保障，促进作品版权保护与价值实现。

3. 以版权资产管理为核心的版权咨询服务取得实质突破，加强版权服务基础理论研究和国外相关实践成果研究，进一步筑牢专业优势

经过多年的探索和积累，版权资产管理咨询服务这一创新性业务在标准编制、工具研发、业务实践等方面全面取得了实质性突破，启动编制了《版权资产管理通用规范》等四个行业标准，开发完成了文化企业版权资产管理终端工具，相关示范应用项目获得中央文资办立项支持，完成和正在进行一些单位的版权资产管理咨询工作。进一步加强了对版权理论研究和前沿信息搜集的组织推动力度，完成了《奥运特许经营研究报告》《设计成果版权保护制度研究》等课题；完成了对《美国版权局实务指南》（第三版）以及美国版权局登记工作各类表单、登记指引、收费标准的翻译，形成了一套较为系统完整的介绍美国版权登记工作的近 80 万字的说明文本；启动了欧盟知识产权局《知识产权对欧洲经济总体影响最新报告》版权和设计部分的翻译工作，不断夯实筑牢中心版权咨询业务的理论支持基础和领先信息优势。

4. 广泛开展版权国际交流与合作，积极服务文化“走出去”战略

不断深化开展版权国际交流与合作的内涵，派员访问了国际 ISAN（International Standard Audio-visual Number，国际标准视听资料号）中心、德国 ISAN 中心、国际奥委会、德国书业协会、韩国著作权委员会等机构，就版权相关法律、版权管理和服务、奥运知识产权保护和维权、数字出版、数字作品版权保护、ISAN 工作等方面内容进行了广泛交流。在第六届香港亚洲流行音乐节上，中心派员就内地著作权保护的最新动态、著作权法修改的进展情况、流行音乐发展态势、音乐版权保护举措以及当今互联网时代音乐版权工作面临的新形势及新特点等与其他亚洲国家和地区有关机构进行了交流。同时，继续发挥中心版权服务综合优势，积极服务文化“走出去”战略，在各大国际书展上围绕独家代理客户组织的 China Day 活动取得经济效益和社会效益双丰收，对外版权贸易和交流成绩显著，以出版版权贸易为例，全年共引进与输出图书 300 本。

三、以落实全面从严治党要求为主线，着力完善基层党建工作机制和事业单位治理机制，持续发挥绩效管理和岗位管理的基础保障作用，从加强监督入手大力推进再造科学管理机制，党的建设、制度建设和管理体系建设水平迈上新台阶

1. 主动适应全面从严治党新常态，进一步强化基层组织建设，全面夯实党建工作基础，不断提升党建工作水平

认真落实全面从严治党主体责任，紧紧围绕中心加强党的建设，深入体会和贯彻思想建党和制度治党紧密结合的工作思路，在党的思想、作风和纪律建设，加强权力制约和监督机制建设，扎实基层组织建设基础，严肃党内政治生活，从严管理干部等方面都取得了新的进展。

认真组织学习贯彻落实党的十八届六中全会精神和习近平总书记系列重要讲话精神，及时发放学习材料，迅速组织部署全体党员开展专题学习，每次班子成员都带头先学一步，通过学原文深入领会精神，再到支部带头引导党员开展学习。积极推进“两学一做”学习教育的开展，各党支部分别组织了 4 次集中学习讨论、4 次专题党课，结合学习讨论主题和重点学习内容，认真组织党员查摆问题，不断提高四个意识。还建立了包含中心全体党员的“两学一做”微信群，围绕学习重点及时发送形式多样的学习材料。

以开展“两学一做”为抓手，全面加强基层党组织建设，根据实际及时调整了支部设置，7 个党支部都已进行支部委员会换届工作。各党支部都开展了党员学习教育“灯下黑”问题专项整治工作，对照查找了在党员学习教育上存在的问题和不足，提出了整改措施，明确了责任人，建立了工作台账和情况月报制度，为进一步加强支部建设各方面工作，有效发挥基层支部战斗堡垒作用奠定了基础。

坚持认真落实党风廉政建设责任制，完成了各层级廉政责任书的签订，抓好责任落实。持之以恒贯彻落实中央八项规定精神不放松，坚持把有关要求纳入考核体系，落实融合到各岗位职责和工作流程中，对照中央八项规定精神进一步建立完善中心 10 余项规章制度，加强了制度落实的日常监督检查。盯紧重要节点严明廉政要求，严防“四风”反

弹，对照国家新闻出版广电总局（国家版权局）机关党委、纪委有关要求，进一步规范了中心党员干部特别是中层干部的离京请假报告制度，制定下发了《关于建立党员干部离京审批制度的通知》。

认真贯彻落实总局直属机关党委各项工作部署和要求，开展了整治“四风”问题“回头看”、党风廉政建设主体责任落实情况“回头看”、贯彻落实中央八项规定精神和纠正“四风”工作自查、党费收缴工作专项检查、基层党组织按期换届检查、党员学习教育情况检查、党员组织关系集中排查、党代会代表和党员违纪违规未给予相应处理情况清理等工作，严格对照有关要求认真细致地做好各项工作，按时将有关工作情况上报总局直属机关党委。

严格执行《党政领导干部选拔任用工作条例》有关要求进行干部选拔、考核、聘任等工作，严格落实个人有关事项报告有关工作要求。

2. 坚持以岗位管理和绩效管理为基点，推动各项管理基础工作不断完善和巩固，日常管理秩序运转更加成熟高效

持续深化细化绩效责任制度体系，基于实践不断优化业绩指标设计，继续完善月度、季度和半年考核等日常考核激励机制，进一步增强了绩效考核的针对性、科学性、公正性，有效发挥了监督指导和激励执行的双重作用。继续巩固岗位管理，坚持在《部门工作手册》和《岗位工作手册》等规范性文件的基础上，以岗定责，不断优化岗位设置，加强岗位管理，专业技术岗位聘用和职工续聘常态化工作机制运行顺利，岗位职责清晰、发展目标明确、岗位竞争有序的工作局面进一步巩固。

在经过多年努力形成了明确的职能定位、清晰的战略规划、明确的业务布局、完善的管理体系、精细的制度规范的基础上，不断加强人才队伍建设和管理团队建设，注重引导干部职工从工作实践中学习提升，持续抓好内部知识经验的挖掘、积累和分享以及职工队伍培训。与专业培训机构合作，重点针对中层管理团队进行了涉及项目管理、营销推广和具体工作技能提升等多个领域的系统性培训，中心管理团队和职工队伍的管理能力和专业素养又有新提升。

3. 积极推动再造科学管理机制，探索构建决策、执行、监督三分的管理结构和运行机制初见成效

从中心长远发展出发，围绕构建决策、执行和监督三分的管理结构和运行机制，把进一步完善规章制度，全面加强内部控制制度体系建设，提高中心事业运行的合规度、规范度作为工作重点。进一步完善了党委会、主任办公会集体决策机制，研究制定了《中国版权保护中心党委议事规则（试行）》、《中国版权保护中心主任办公会议议事规则（试行）》和《中国版权保护中心“三重一大”决策范围（试行）》。持续探索建立以内控为核心的监督机制，聘请专业会计师事务所对中心进行了内控基础情况评价，查找不足和薄弱环节，不断推进内控机制和日常工作的融合；研究制定了《中国版权保护中心内部控制制度》《中国版权保护中心出差审批和差旅费管理办法》《中国版权保护中心国内公务接待管理办法》《中国版权保护中心职工工作餐管理办法》《中国版权保护中心计划生育管理规定》《中国版权保护中心微笑服务规则（试行）》《中国版权保护中心因公临时出国（境）管理办法》《中国版权保护中心外事接待管理办法》等一系列制度规范，大力加强内部监督制度的建设和落实；成立了中心监督委员会，组织编制《中心监督工作办法》；多次组织专题培训，不断深入推动干部职工在监督意识、管理观念上的转变。

4. 切实贯彻落实国家事业单位机构改革有关要求，规范、有序完成事企分开各项工作任务

严格按照事企分开的要求，指导中华版权代理总公司加快建立健全公司治理结构、业务体系和管理机制，研究制定了《关于进一步深化中华版权代理总公司改革实施方案》，明确中心和总公司的管理职责界限，将面向市场的经营性业务转入总公司，推动总公司健全和规范管理制度体系。目前总公司的业务部门和机构人员调整已基本到位，决策机制、业务开展和日常行政、财务、人事管理已全面独立运行。同时，中心各部门持续加强对总公司各项工作的指导和帮助，不断帮助其提升独立运营的能力和各项工作的规范化程度。

5. 不断探索具有自身特色的组织文化建设途径，多方协力推动精神文明建设不断开创新局面

中心精神文明建设工作坚持围绕中心，服务大局，全方位关心职工身心健康，组织开展了形式多样的学习交流、业务实践和文体活动。持续把中心职业操守准则作为中心组织文化建设的一条主线，组织进一步学习探讨了职业操守准则的修改，不断推动准则融入职工思想意识和行为实践。组织“做最好的自己”商务照拍摄活动，用职业形象照展现职工最好的精神面貌，激励大家每天都做最好的自己，始终保持最好的状态。在中心全面推行微笑服务，下发了《中国版权保护中心微笑服务规则（试

行)》,组织“开展微笑服务,提升服务水平”职工培训,进一步增强了职工服务意识,用“微笑服务”的态度全面提升中心服务的品质和体验。从细处着手,发布《关于加强和改进中心环境卫生工作的通知》,推动职工共同营造良好的公共卫生环境。工青妇组织充分发挥自身作用,坚持推动做工间操,结合实际开展了跳绳、拔河、平板支撑、“奔跑吧,版权人!”比赛、舞蹈兴趣小组、编织献爱心活动、庆祝三八国际妇女节大会暨职工论坛演讲演出活动等形式多样、职工广泛参与的文体活动,平均每月、每季度都有文体活动开展。中心工会在 2016 全国新闻出版广电系统工会工作经验交流会上介绍了工作经验。在元旦、春节、五一、七一、十一等重要节假日前,开展了对困难职工、退休职工和党员的走访慰问活动,把组织关怀及时送达给职工群众。通过多方共同努力,营造了积极向上、团结和谐的氛围,为促进中心改革发展稳定发挥了重要作用。

6. 纪检工作进一步贯彻“三转”工作要求,以更加严、实、细的标准发挥职能作用

中心纪委认真履行监督执纪问责职责,不断加强和丰富廉政教育的内容和形式,坚持落实常态化的新提拔干部廉政诫勉谈话制度,建立了每月与一名部门负责人进行廉政谈话的惯例,不断严肃强调廉政纪律和责任担当。把中央八项规定精神的贯彻落实作为监督重点,认真对照有关制度规范,对有关问题严查细究早提醒,积极推动相关工作制度的有效落实和进一步完善,自觉纠正存在的问题和隐患,提醒相关领导和部门准确把握和执行政策,确保各项工作的合规性,使“四种形态”成为工作常态。

(张文娟)

中国版权协会

2016 年,中国版权协会(以下简称协会)在国家新闻出版广电总局(国家版权局)的指导下,积极贯彻落实国家版权工作方针和政策,通过搭建版权相关服务平台,聚集了一大批有影响力、有实力的会员,各项工作取得良好成效。

一、拓展协会业务范围,提高服务会员能力

(一)中国版权协会艺术品版权工作委员会挂牌运行

2016 年 1 月 7 日,中国版权协会艺术品版权工作委员会挂牌运行,雅昌文化集团董事长、中国版权协会副理事长万捷任主任委员,该委员会将向协会会员提供艺术作品鉴定、评估、交易等方面服务,并在净化艺术品行业版权生态环境,促进艺术品反盗维权工作常态化、系统化和制度化等方面发挥作用。

(二)研究筹备“中国版权协会鉴定、监测、调解工作委员会”

整合协会反盗维权、鉴定监测工作机制,研究筹备“中国版权协会鉴定、监测、调解工作委员会”,该委员会拟为协会会员提供鉴定、监测、调解咨询服务。2016 年 8 月,协会引入第三方合作机制,与有关科技机构签署战略合作协议,通过“中国版权协会监测中心”(域名 12426.cn),向会员提供反盗维权网上免费监测服务。

(三)继续做好面向会员的版权培训服务

2016 年 6 月,协会邀请立法、司法、行政、教学科技单位的领导和专家,以及版权产业界的领军人物,向会员介绍版权立法的新动态、司法行政的新情况、技术发展与运用的新趋势、版权产业发展的新特点。200 多位会员参加了培训,通过对理论与实践的双重解读,增强了会员对版权发展规律的总体把握能力,受到会员单位的积极评价。

(四)针对社会热点问题,开展版权研讨活动

在国家版权局和新华社的指导下,中国版权协会与新华社新闻研究所共同举办了“保护新闻作品版权论坛”。新华社社长蔡名照在进行主旨演讲时指出:新闻作品是媒体的核心资产,保护好新闻作品,才能将内容资源转化为版权资产。国家版权局副局长阎晓宏强调:网络媒体转载新闻作品,必须事先得到许可,且支付相应报酬。其他与会嘉宾则呼吁加强对新闻作品的版权保护,研讨会引起了社会的强烈反响。

2016 年初,为适应“互联网+”时代、“大众创业、万众创新”的新形势,中国版权协会与金山公司合作,举办了以“创新与共享”为主题的思享会。会上小米科技公司董事长雷军和中国与世界经济研究中心主任李稻葵博士,以深刻的思想分析和卓越的洞察能力与大家分享了他们对互联网思维和发展的理解和体会。

(五)固化研究成果,及时向会员提供有关版权信息

2016 年初,协会将 2015 年第八届中国版权年会“互联网+时代的音乐——价值挖掘与实现途径”高层论坛的嘉宾发言集结成集为《因乐而动》一书,由人民音乐出版社正式出版,其中涵盖了全国政协

副主席齐续春、世界知识产权组织副总干事王彬颖、著名企业家雷军、著名音乐家叶小钢和高晓松等主讲嘉宾的发言，让更多的会员了解了以上嘉宾对版权保护与产业发展的领悟与思考，帮助会员从更广的领域、更宽的视角、更多的层次了解版权保护的作用和意义。

二、服务会员、服务行业、配合政府，积极开展反盗维权活动

（一）配合政府部门启动的“剑网2016”专项行动，开展版权执法和反盗维权研讨活动

8月，协会主办了“APP及广告联盟相关版权侵权问题研讨会”，分析了APP及广告联盟相关版权侵权的基本现象，研究了移动网络反盗维权的对策。9月，协会在国家版权局的指导下，举办了“网络文学版权保护研讨会”，研讨会上，发布了《网络文学版权联盟自律宣言》，北京掌阅科技有限公司总裁张凌云、阅文集团CEO吴文辉在研讨会上强烈呼吁加强网络文学版权保护，各大网络文学网站纷纷表示，要依法开展网络文学经营活动，自觉遵守国家法律法规，配合政府维护良好的网络文学版权市场环境。

（二）配合国家版权局等部门积极推进软件正版化工作

2016年协会接受国家版权局的委托，在推进软件正版化工作方面主要做了以下三项工作：一是组织培训。2016年协会承办了4期政府机关软件正版化培训班，培训分别在武汉、济南、哈尔滨、北京举办，来自全国31个省（区、市）的政府办公厅、工信厅、财政厅、发改委、版权局等部门的千余名公职人员参加了培训。二是承担正版化项目开发。根据国家版权局的要求，协会研究、论证，并组织制定了“制定软件信用管理标准”，按照招标流程，研发了“建立培训系统及专家库”，相关的项目成果已在正版化工作中得到应用。三是承担软件正版化督查的组织协调工作。根据国家版权局关于开展软件正版化督促检查的工作总署，协会完成了对安徽、江苏和山东三省使用正版软件工作进行督查的组织协调工作，并根据实地检查结果，向国家版权局提交了该三省使用软件正版检查工作报告和有关检查数据资料等。

三、深化海峡两岸版权交流，举办海峡两岸版权保护研讨会

2016年9月，“第九届海峡两岸著作权保护研讨会”在四川成都举行，来自两岸的著作权人、权利人组织、社会团体、产业界的代表，以及专家学者，围绕“著作权法制之新思路”和“数字创意，再塑文化”的主题展开深入的探讨和交流。双方一致认为，在全球网络化趋势下，两岸数字文化产业发展迅速，图书、音乐、美术作品等，几乎所有的版权客体形式都将以数字化的形态出现，两岸著作权保护的思维和目标不仅一致，而且两岸版权产业界的交流与合作进一步加深。通过共同研究对策、相互借鉴经验，一定能够促进两岸版权产业的不断发展。

四、筹备举办第九届中国版权年会

中国版权年会是中国版权界规格最高、规模最大的年度盛会，在中国版权界及社会各界有较大的影响力，到目前已成功举办八届。从过去的经验看，每届年会都是以论坛加年会的方式进行，而且盛况空前。但有不少会员反映，这种方式主要凸显了少数主讲嘉宾，会员参与程度不高，希望年会增加会员沟通交流的机会。根据会员的建议，2016年协会对年会进行了适当改革，将论坛和年会进行分离，年会的形式，是在听取协会工作报告、表彰版权杰出个人和最具影响力单位后，重点放在开展会员间的自由交流互动环节上，使广大会员真正成为版权年度盛会的参与者，并通过互动交流达到交流经验、增进友谊、加强合作、思想融合、共谋创新的目的。当然，协会仍然将继续推动论坛和研讨的举办，只是要与年会做适当的分离。岁末年初，协会将与有关社会团体、行业组织和市场主体合作分别举办以网络、软件、体育赛事等为主题的版权论坛和研讨会，为会员提供研讨分析版权热点问题，谋划版权保护应对之策的平台。

五、加强协会组织建设，促进协会健康有序发展

2016年，中国版权协会根据国家有关社团管理，以及中央巡视组，国家新闻出版广电总局（以下简称总局）人事、党务、纪检等部门的有关管理要求，采取多项措施加强协会组织建设，促进协会健康有序发展。

（一）立行立改，积极落实中央、总局社团巡视整改工作要求

针对2016年中央巡视组和总局关于整顿检查局属社团的工作部署，中国版权协会领导高度重视，专门召开理事长会议研究贯彻落实措施，认真梳理存在问题，积极开展自查自纠，加强完善管理制度，切实做到立行立改：一是按照中央、总局和民政部文件要求，认真贯彻执行中央八项规定精神，及时落实了党政机关干部（含离退休干部）兼职取酬的

清退工作。二是根据中央有关党政干部和公职人员社团兼职的有关规定，按照规定程序，报请总局人事部门批准，办理了部分党政干部和公职人员请辞本协会领导职务的申请。

（二）加强党建工作、发挥党组织政治核心作用

坚持党的领导，在2015年协会成立党支部的基础上，积极开展党建活动，落实总局人事、党务、纪检工作要求，认真开展“两学一做”学习教育活动，明确党组织在社会组织中的功能定位，发挥党组织在协会的政治核心作用，确保协会坚持正确的政治方向。

（三）完善管理制度，落实管理要求

根据总局巡视整改工作要求，协会修改完善了《财务管理制度》、《人事制度》、《行政管理制度》及《文件管理制度》，重新制定《内部控制制度》，细化了管理办法。在制度落实方面，严格按照社会组织分类标准和具体办法开展业务，明确内部分工，落实相关工作第一责任人和具体责任人，确保协会工作有序开展。

（四）清理整合协会内设机构，保持协会运转活力

协会对8个内设委员会进行了全面梳理，凡2013年协会换届以来未开展工作的，进入整顿清理状态，对不具备工作条件和工作基础的拟做出撤并处理，并根据会员的实际需要，增设具有活力、面向社会和市场的内设服务机构。

（五）明确工作计划，加强管理和监督

2016年以来，协会加强了工作计划和管理监督力度，一方面严格落实日常督查，实行周报告、月例会、半年年度总结，定期调度各项工作进度；另一方面健全年度绩效考核工作机制，对协会干部实行绩效考评、利益挂钩，增强党员干部干事创业的责任感、紧迫感和积极性。

（六）加强基础建设，完成协会迁址

在朝阳区南磨房乡政府的大力支持下，协会由海淀区知春路迁入朝阳区中国北京出版创意产业基地先导区，协会的办公条件得到改善。协会将努力为会员提供一个常态化的交流平台，并提供良好的版权咨询服务。

总体来看2016年是协会的发展年，通过搭建版权相关服务平台，协会聚集了一大批有影响、有实力的优秀成员，成为协会不断发展的强劲动力。在国家版权局指导下，在阎理事长的直接领导下，在各会员单位的热情支持下，2016年协会各项工作取得一定成效，开拓了协会发展的新局面。

（王自强）

中国音乐著作权协会

2016年，中国音乐著作权协会（以下简称音著协）在国家新闻出版广电总局（国家版权局）的指导下，积极发展会员，在音乐作品资料管理和许可使用、音乐作品许可使用费分配、音乐作品诉讼维权、信息宣传和国际事务等方面扎实开展工作。

一、会员发展

2016年，中国音乐著作权协会新发展会员数为401，其中词作者126人、曲作者256人、继承人12人、出版公司6家、其他1人。截至2016年底，会员总数达8 502人（家）。其中，在新发展的会员中，较有影响力的个人会员有：杨一博、鄂矛、陈小涛、湘海、丁于、苏运莹、宋宇宁、曾昭玮、颜小健、钱雷；公司会员有：北京石刻欣乐文化有限公司、相信音乐文化传媒（北京）有限公司等。

二、音乐作品资料管理

作为中国大陆地区唯一的音乐作品著作权集体管理组织，音著协通过全球最大的中文音乐作品版权信息系统DIVA（Documentation Innovation Visionary Art）对海量的音乐作品进行管理。DIVA可凭借其强大而完善的数据库处理会员信息、作品资料及版税分配等工作内容。当会员加入音著协时，音著协会在DIVA系统中为每一名会员建立一个专属的权利人识别编码，其中包含会员的姓名、身份证号码、住址、入会身份（词曲作者、继承人或其他著作权人）等个人信息，以及该会员公开发表的音乐作品名称和该音乐作品的详细权利信息，包括音乐的词曲作者、权益人、权利归属和权利比例等内容，这些都是附着在一首音乐作品上的重要法律信息。2009年2月1日，音著协成为ISWC（国际标准音乐作品编码）在中国大陆的唯一代理机构，负责ISWC编码在中国大陆地区的登记、发放和管理等工作。在数字音乐和网络环境下，ISWC编码是一首音乐作品在世界范围内被有效给予辨识、版权保护的“身份证号码”。

截至2016年底，DIVA数据库作品数目达到740万余首，其中音著协会员登记作品为39.2万余首（原创作品314 160首，影视作品65 784首，改编作品7 556首，填词作品5 205首），申请ISWC作品为13.4万余首。主要完成工作如下：

（一）提供版权证据证明，协助法院认定“非法的集体管理组织”

2016年1月，在声影网络科技有限公司诉侨声

娱乐有限公司卡拉OK一案中，音著协为中国音像著作权集体管理协会（以下简称音集协）授权的侨声娱乐有限公司核实并提供了174首会员作品登记版权证明。这些证据资料，有效证实了声影公司为非法的集体管理组织，为法院做出最终判决提供了关键性的证据。

2月，应音集协请求，音著协再次对6万余首音乐作品进行了细致的核查工作，为后续各地法院判决非法著作权集体管理提供了有力证据。此类案件对维护我国著作权集体管理组织的合法性，净化著作权集体管理环境，促进我国著作权集体管理的发展具有重要意义。

（二）署名核查

2016年1月15日起，由湖南卫视重金打造的歌手竞赛节目《我是歌手》第四季共播出十一期。为了尊重音乐著作权人合法权益，保证参赛歌曲署名的正确性，音著协本着认真严谨的工作态度，通过查阅会员登记表跟直接电话联系会员等方式再次确认词曲作者署名；涉及的海外歌曲，直接通过与外国同类协会沟通等多种途径取得联系，及时有效地保证了每期每首歌曲署名的准确无误。

（三）与海外协会进行交流并提供影视作品核查清单

为维护协会会员的海外著作权益，顺利实现海外使用音乐作品的许可收费，为会员的海外版税收益起到保驾护航的作用。资料部在2016年为COMPASS（新加坡词曲版权协会）、JASRAC（日本音乐著作权协会）、MACP（马来西亚音乐著作权协会）、KOMCA（韩国音乐著作权协会）、SIAE（意大利作者协会）等19个海外协会核查了1 200余部影视作品，提供并制作完成了会员作品70余部、870余集，包括电影《天下无贼》《白日焰火》《西游降魔篇》《做头》《步步惊心》、86集电视剧《新水浒传》、76集电视剧《甄嬛传》、66集电视剧《大秦帝国》、47集电视剧《上海滩》、35集电视剧《孙子大传》、28集电视剧《我的美丽人生》、46集电视剧《唐宫燕之女人天下》、99集动画系列片《熊出没》等影视剧资料。

三、音乐作品许可使用工作

2016年，音著协许可总收益约为人民币1.84亿元（含海外收益人民币约622万元），创历年收入新高，较2015年增长8.24%。

（一）表演权许可工作

2016年，音著协表演权许可收益约人民币5 940万元。

1. 现场表演

商业演出一直是音著协许可工作的重点，但是因为演出分散在全国各地，工作人员与演出组织者谈判时频繁受地域差异、场地差异等因素的影响，导致实际收费标准偏低。自2011年起，音著协一直致力于逐步提升许可收费的幅度，同时对拒绝按新标准付费的演出组织者提起侵权之诉。从实践效果来看，在2016年，新的标准已在全国各地逐渐推广开来，同时在诉讼中，法院对音乐著作权人维权的判赔力度也越来越大。

2. 机械表演

2016年，机械表演许可收益较2015年有所减少。主要原因有二：第一，有些背景音乐服务公司在没有获得著作权人许可的情况下，私自向使用者发放授权，搅局版权市场；第二，实体经济衰退，导致部分音乐使用者为了削减成本，不再使用背景音乐。截至2016年底，全国获授权使用音乐的门店约两万家，其中：航空公司背景音乐收费已基本100%覆盖全行业；大型活动如深圳大运会、南京青奥会等均获音著协授权；全国连锁企业沃尔玛、家乐福、麦当劳、肯德基、万豪酒店等继续与音著协保持长期合作。同时，在背景音乐的许可工作中，当遇到较大阻力时，音著协仍然需要依靠相当数量的诉讼、行政处罚等非常规手段，才能实现许可收费。近几年，一些背景音乐服务公司为了扩大自己的市场份额，除提供音乐设计等服务外，还声称拥有相应著作权资源，并对外发放虚假授权。音著协对此也采取了发函交涉、诉讼等手段。整体来看，背景音乐诉讼的结果向有利于著作权人的方向转变，但是取证难、周期长、耗力多、判赔低的问题依然存在。

（二）广播权许可工作

2016年，音著协共实现广播权许可收益约人民币4 159万元。

对于音乐作者、对于音乐著作权集体管理协会而言，广播权许可业务的重要性不言而喻，但是在中国大陆，它一直是音著协“最难攻克的堡垒”。截至2016年底，全国有44家电视台、51家广播电台与音著协签署了音乐作品广播权付酬协议，签约台覆盖了国家级台、多数省级台和少量市级台。但是，广播权许可工作仍存在两个主要问题：一是收费标准偏低，二是许可覆盖率偏低。第一个问题的根本解决还依赖第二个问题的明显改善。数据显示，全国有2 500多家电台、电视台。这些广播组织——特别是数量庞大的市级台、县级台，甚至是个别省级台，从音乐版权保护的角度来看，多数仍在“三无”行列——无视作者权益、无视法律法规、无视行业形象。究其原因，主要是因为这些广播组织存在落后的、不正确的思想观念，缺少基本的版权法律意识，无视他人的著作权利，存在着严重的“依权不依法，依人不依法”的思想。

许多未履行付酬义务的地方广播组织在与音著协的沟通中态度消极、恶劣，以各种理由推诿搪塞。有些电台电视台甚至指责已经付酬的电台电视台过于积极，称“我们至今没交一分钱，音著协也没拿我们怎么样”。持这种态度的广播组织在广电行业内不在少数，它们的所作所为在树立了“违法经营成本”低于“守法经营成本”坏榜样的同时，也是在怂恿业界其他广播电台电视台效仿其违法行为。这对于已经自觉付酬的广播电台电视台造成了极大的不公，严重扰乱市场秩序，破坏行业规范。

为解决以上问题，音著协只有拿起法律武器，为维护权利正义和市场公平而战斗。继 2015 年后，2016 年音著协再次发起 10 场广播权维权诉讼。但音著协进行的诉讼并不是为了获得涉案少量曲目的赔偿，而是希望通过诉讼促使侵权使用者转变意识，自觉获得著作权许可，通过国家倡导的著作权集体管理制度、“行业许可合作模式”整体解决其广播使用音乐作品的合法性问题。目前看，10 场诉讼还不足以实现此目的，有些台音著协已经起诉 2 至 3 次仍然不解决整体付酬问题，还需要继续加大诉讼维权的力度。

（三）复制权及新媒体许可工作

2016 年音著协复制权许可收益约人民币 863 万元，新媒体业务许可收益约人民币 6 845 万元，继续保持快速增长。

1. 复制权业务

音著协在影视、广告、录像、境外使用音乐的许可授权等方面，加大了对单一会员作品的定向服务。

针对工业产品（如儿童玩具、早教机等）内置音乐的情况，音著协在市场调研后，通过向销售终端投诉的方式，促使生产厂家解决著作权问题。

2. 新媒体许可业务

2016 年，音著协继续坚持原有的“主渠道合作”模式，逐步拓展网络直播和网络视频业务。经过这一年坚持不懈的努力，与音著协达成音乐使用许可合作的较大影响力的企业共计 7 家，直播类的有陌陌，视频类的有乐视、爱奇艺、芒果 TV，大型 K 歌类的有唱吧。另外与海洋音乐、今日头条也达成了合作关系，与其他中型企业建立合作关系的共计约 12 家。从许可收入上看，本项业务增长迅速，较 2015 年增长达到 50%。

自 2016 年 2 月至 11 月，音著协就苹果商店上的移动端 APP 产品侵权使用音乐的情况进行了较大范围的调查、投诉和沟通维权工作。据统计，音著协向苹果应用商店共投诉了 166 个移动端 APP，涵盖了众多与音乐相关的类目，包括视频类、FM 广播类、在线试听下载音乐类、手机铃声类、音乐游戏类、育儿教育类、网络直播类等，所投诉的产品多由在国内影响力较大的公司开发和上架。音著协与苹果商店及 APP 开发商来往邮件 2 657 封，被投诉下架的 APP 产品数量为 56 个。

四、音乐作品许可使用费分配

2016 年，音著协面向海内外音乐著作权人分配音乐许可使用费扣除增值税后约 1.197 亿元人民币（其中主要为 2015 年到账的使用费，因修改分配程序，来自互联网的使用费中有 0.25 亿元延迟到 2017 年分配）。其中，来自图书、音像制品、点歌机等的复制权使用费分配金额约为人民币 740 万元，来自互联网的使用费分配金额约为人民币 734 万元，来自卡拉 OK 的使用费分配金额约为人民币 3 002 万元，来自演唱会表演歌曲的使用费分配金额约为人民币 373 万元，来自经营性场所播放背景音乐的使用费分配金额约为人民币 2 431 万元，来自广播电台、电视台的使用费分配金额约为人民币 4 149 万元，来自海外许可的使用费分配金额约为人民币 540 万元。

五、音乐作品诉讼维权工作

2016 年，音著协共办理民事诉讼案件 117 件。通过诉讼方式获得判赔、调解及和解金计人民币 974 万余元，待执行款人民币 133 万余元，诉讼花费总支出为人民币 13 万余元。

重点案例：音著协诉 2015 陈奕迅 Another Eason's LIFE 演唱会南京站、徐州站侵权案，音著协诉北京王府井百货大楼背景音乐侵权案，音著协诉上海宜芝多（龙之梦店）背景音乐侵权案，音著协诉上海龙记香港茶餐厅背景音乐侵权案，音著协诉“咪哒”K 歌产品侵权案，音著协诉上海教育出版社教科书侵权案，音著协诉武汉广播电视台侵权案，音著协诉厦门广播电视集团侵权案（第三次诉讼），音著协诉宁波广播电视集团侵权案（第二次诉讼）。

六、信息宣传工作

2015 年音著协共制作完成《会讯》两期——第 30 期、第 31 期。其他主要工作如下：

1. 建设自身的宣传平台

音著协微信公众号2016年3月开通，面向会员、产业界、学界、政府以及社会公众，通过即时和定期两种方式将会员发展、许可收费、费用分配、对外交流等各项工作全面地展示出来，为社会各界了解音著协主动提供了信息和窗口。

2. 扩大与社会各界的交流与合作

在全社会版权法律意识还有待提高的现实情况下，加强海内外、版权产业界的交流与合作对音著协工作的开展十分必要。为此，音著协不仅积极参加由政府、国际组织、高校、行业组织、著作权集体管理组织举办的各种交流会和研讨会，还单独或合作组织了多次交流活动。

2016年4月21日，音著协与清华大学法学院共同组织了“著作权集体管理热点研讨会”。参会人员中，除了中国音乐著作权协会、中国音像著作权集体管理协会、中国文字著作权协会三家集体管理组织的代表外，还有来自清华大学、北京大学、中央民族大学、德国马普所等高校和研究机构的知识产权专家学者。

3. 组织或参与各类著作权宣传活动

2016年11月28日，音著协参加全球创作者论坛。本论坛由国际作者和作曲者协会联合会（CISAC）和中国知识产权法学研究会共同举办。来自30多个国家的超过200名创作者、政府官员、业界专家和知名人士参加了此次盛大的活动。音著协常务理事李海鹰在“21世纪的著作权集体管理”主题讨论环节做了精彩发言；音著协理事郝维亚和知名会员科尔沁夫、董冬冬、陈曦作为中国大陆地区的词曲创作者代表共同见证了“亚太音乐创作者联盟”（APMA）的成立；音著协副总干事刘平在“集体管理所面临的挑战”主题讨论环节中担当主持。

2016年12月5—7日，音著协参加于广州举办的“2016国际版权博览会”。博览会期间，有多名广州会员及业内人士专程赶赴音著协展区，就其关心的入会、许可收费、版税分配、法律咨询、版权合作等众多问题和现场工作人员进行了深入交流，在拉近双方距离、增加彼此信任等方面起到了良好的作用。

七、国际事务

2016年8月，音著协与蒙古音乐著作权协会（MOSCAP）就音乐著作权的表演权和复制权签订了相互代表协议。至此，音著协已与73家音乐著作权集体管理组织建立了相互代表关系。

（张　群）

中国音像著作权集体管理协会

2016年，在国家新闻出版广电总局（国家版权局）的指导下，在全体会员的支持与配合下，中国音像著作权集体管理协会（以下简称音集协）在新一届理事会的领导下，遵循集体管理的规则，不断理顺机制体制，规范权利管理，积极开展许可业务，在贯彻实施国家版权制度方面取得了成效。

一、提升服务意识，增强会员凝聚力

截至2016年12月31日，音集协共有会员153家，包括278家权利人的权利，其中新入会会员24家，授权曲目总计102 804首。为推进会员发展，音集协大力宣传协会职能，积极提升服务质量。

新歌制作推广是主要服务项目之一，音集协不断制作适合卡拉OK歌厅使用的新歌版本，丰富娱乐市场，2016年共为会员制作新歌487首，并在原有的推广渠道基础上，增加了卡拉OK系统设备及服务商（以下简称VOD）的渠道，使新歌推广已达到卡拉OK市场70%以上，加快了新歌使用的速度，提升了覆盖率。2016年，推广发放新歌累计1 800余首。

为完善授权曲目管理，音集协建立了电子信息档案库、实物光盘硬盘库、视频曲库等信息库，涵盖会员信息的各个方面，能够达到资料翔实准确。同时，音集协为会员提供ISRC申领服务使其获得独立的登记者码，为尚未申请ISRC编码的会员免费提供申请ISRC编码服务，以提高音集协对会员授权作品的版权管理水平。ISRC编码作为使用作品版权唯一标识的国际标准，有利于会员向其他平台包括国外平台开展授权、确权及维权活动。

二、开拓许可业务，促进版权收费

卡拉OK歌厅著作权许可业务是音集协的主营业务，截至2016年12月31日，全国29个省（区、市）开展了许可工作，签约场所共计3 992家，卡拉OK著作权使用费实际到账金额1.7亿元，再创历史新高。

随着卡拉OK行业转型，新型“自助卡拉OK可移动娱乐包房产品”（简称迷你KTV）以更贴近年轻化消费群体、更善用碎片化时间的优势迅速进入市场。2016年，音集协共向三家迷你KTV产品发放了音乐电视作品的放映权许可，在新业务的付费及合作模式上有了更多突破。

智能电视/智能机顶盒端的卡拉OK点唱产品随互联网电视的兴起广受好评。2016年，音集协初探这一新业务领域，以音集协拥有信息网络传播权的歌曲许可产品使用，并在共享大数据平台、新歌推广方面达成合作。

2016 年音集协根据《教科书法定许可使用作品支付报酬办法》，对市面上销售的义务教育教科书及其配盘情况开展了法定许可业务，实现了教科书法定许可业务零的突破。

音集协自 2014 年面向 VOD 服务商开展曲库许可业务，2016 年度使用费 700 余万元。VOD 行业在正版推广、新歌发放、节目制作等方面与音集协达成诸多合作，对规范 VOD 行业秩序有巨大推动作用。

三、打击侵权行为，维护会员权益

为维护权利人利益，提高收费覆盖率，2016 年度，音集协在全国 28 个省（自治区、直辖市）与 133 家律师事务所合作开展了维权活动，发起千余起维权诉讼。维权诉讼的目的是打击侵权行为，促使使用者获得合法许可，建立良好的授权机制，因此，音集协力主达成许可和解。2016 年，和解或调解结案共计 1 150 家，因维权促成签订版权许可合同共计 1 083 份，合同金额合计 4 397 万元，占版权费总额的 28.5%。维权诉讼目前仍是集体管理的重要手段之一，许可付费的法律意识在实体娱乐行业经营中仍需加强宣传，只有在集体管理体制下的诉讼，才能保证手段和目的不发生偏离，使之不成为盈利手段。

除民事诉讼外，音集协还针对侵权歌厅提起 344 例行政投诉，其中 29 家卡拉 OK 歌厅经营者在版权行政、文化执法部门的协调下，与音集协签署了《著作权许可使用合同》，交纳著作权使用费共计 903 446 元。

四、完善著作权使用费分配，规范财务工作

2016 年初，音集协总结分配工作经验，从 VOD 厂商和大型卡拉 OK 连锁歌厅调取点播数据，共 80 万条，经数据规范化，委托第三方独立咨询公司进行分析统计计算，最终出具了《KTV 歌曲点唱调查报告（2015）》，作为许可使用费分配的依据。根据会员章程和会员大会授权，第二届理事会第二次会议审议通过了《2015 年度卡拉 OK 著作权使用费分配细则》及《VOD 商著作权使用费分配办法》。依照上述文件，音集协开展了 2015 年著作权使用费分配工作，共向会员分配卡拉 OK 著作权使用费 4 159 万元、VOD 商著作权使用费 730 万元。分配工作流程完全依照法律、法规和会员章程进行，通过官方网站和微信公众号向社会通报了分配工作，并向版权局提交了分配工作报告，使管理部门、权利人、使用者及社会各界了解情况并予以监督。

五、处理非会员诉讼事务，扼制非法集体管理

近几年，非法集体管理活动的蔓延对歌舞娱乐场所的有序经营、对集体管理制度的执行、对唱片行业的健康发展造成了诸多负面影响，其伴生的商业诉讼也给各省司法审判工作带来了极大负担。2016 年，音集协协助已获得集体管理许可的卡拉 OK 场所处理非会员诉讼共 334 起。合法经营者不堪“累讼”之扰，侵权使用者借非法集体管理逃避侵权责任。为此音集协进行了大量的社会调研，向国家版权局汇报了相关情况，同时，将调研报告呈送最高人民法院。

经过多年的不懈努力，继江苏省高院 2015 年 12 月首例非法集体管理案件判决生效以来，2016 年度陆续有上海知识产权法院、广东省高级人民法院等 17 家法院认定深圳声影网络科技有限公司（以下简称深圳声影）、广州菜之鸟唱片有限公司从事非法集体管理行为。与此同时，国家版权局也正式立案查处深圳声影从事非法集体管理行为。司法审判与行政执法的重拳出击对扼制非法集体管理及其伴生的商业诉讼行为具有重要意义。江苏高院“已向集体管理组织缴费卡拉 OK 歌厅被深圳声影起诉不承担赔偿责任”的判决在最高人民法院再审中获得支持。

六、加强自身宣传建设，扩大海内外合作

音集协始终坚持在“阳光”下办会的理念，遵循公开、透明原则，接受权利人、使用者、管理部门及社会各界的监督，加强信息公开，保证著作权集体管理工作依法依规开展，保障全体权利人的利益得到最大程度实现。

2016 年，音集协编辑、印制和发放了《卡拉 OK 著作权许可收费法律依据及行为规范》手册，向权利人、使用者及相关社会各界宣示音集协卡拉 OK 工作的法律依据、著作权集体管理工作义务、工作流程及监管措施，共向使用者、权利人、管理部门及社会各界累计发放 20 000 余册，收到良好反响。

2016 年，音集协在音集协官网上再次更新发布了《2016 年卡拉 OK 著作权使用费收取标准公告》《著作权许可合同范本及管理办法》《卡拉 OK 版权收费工作地方服务机构名录》《音集协版权许可工作证管理办法》，开放了音集协版权许可工作人员实名查询平台等，新发布了《关于 2015 年卡拉 OK 著作权使用费分配的公告》等信息，将集体管理工作的全过程透明化，同时开放协会邮箱及办公电话接受社会各界监督。同时，音集协开通官方微信公众号，随时向权利人、使用者、社会公众通报音集协工作，全面将音集协党建工作、制度建设、著作权使用费分配工作、法律维权工作、海外著作权组织介绍、会员风采等信息公开。

音集协加入国际唱片业协会后，积极加强海外交流与合作，学习引进海外先进经验，向国际社会展示中国音像著作权工作取得的突出成果，为促进我国著作权事业发展贡献力量。

（李　婧）

中国文字著作权协会

2016 年，中国文字著作权协会（以下简称协会或文著协）在国家新闻出版广电总局（国家版权局）（以下简称总局）的领导下，按照总局的整体工作部署，积极维护会员权利，推广会员作品；深入贯彻实施国家版权局和国家发展改革委颁布的《教科书法定许可使用作品支付报酬办法》和《使用文字作品支付报酬办法》，开拓思路，切实履行报刊转载和教科书“法定许可”稿酬收转的法定职能；探索积极推进会员作品的数字版权授权业务，向数字版权要效益；按照党中央“一带一路”的伟大倡议，全力推进“中俄文学作品互译出版项目”，有条不紊地开展“中白文学作品互译出版项目”，通过版权贸易，推动中国作家作品“走出去”，加强国际交流和国际版权贸易。同时，按照总局党组要求和中直机关工委的统一部署，有条不紊地做好脱钩前的各项准备工作。

一、会员发展

会员是著作权集体管理组织的立足之本。协会成立八年以来，通过坚持不懈地为广大权利人推广作品、收取稿酬、释疑解惑、调解纠纷、诉讼维权，为会员办实事、办好事，树立了良好的社会形象，赢得了会员和其他权利人的信任。截止到 2016 年 12 月 31 日，新增会员 225 人，协会会员总数已达 8 800 人。通过主动寻找作者，主动向权利人核实权利人信息和每月主动转付稿费的形式，联系了众多权利人，许多权利人主动要求加入协会，老会员也纷纷向协会备案新创作的作品。

文著协始终以“让权利人利益最大化”为宗旨，将会员利益放在工作首位，认真处理会员的每一个诉求、每一项委托。针对中国社会科学院外国文学研究所研究员陈忠梅、邹海仑、庄焰等会员十余部翻译作品被某中央级出版社十年间多次侵权出版的问题，文著协高度重视，制定维权方案，多次走访，沟通谈判协商，经过大半年的调解，最终为会员挽回经济损失 20 余万元，同时也促成会员与该出版社达成新的合作。协会工作人员精湛的谈判沟通技巧、敬业的精神让会员深受感动，这些权利人还纷纷介绍一些同行加入协会。

2016 年，协会代表翻译家王永年和王干卿与江苏亲近母语文化教育公司签署版权协议，授权出版王永年翻译的《爱丽丝漫游仙境》和《绿野仙踪》，授权出版王干卿翻译的《爱的教育》。两位翻译家对协会的专业态度、带来的经济收益和协会的协调非常满意。协会还成功代理了梁实秋经典散文集《雅舍小品》《雅舍谈吃》的中文简体字版非专有出版授权，并为其女儿梁文茜送去稿酬。梁文茜曾经是专业精湛的律师，对协会严格遵守“先授权后使用”的著作权授权基本原则高度赞赏。

协会通过完成会员的一件件授权、维权，不但展示了协会团队的专业版权基本功、协调沟通谈判能力，也进一步密切了与会员的关系，使协会团队的整体素质逐渐得到提升。

二、稿酬收取和转付工作

文著协是向著作权人转付报刊转载和教科书“法定许可”使用费的法定机构，因此，“法定许可”稿酬收取和分配工作是协会的法定职能，也是协会工作的重点。协会制定的主动查找作者、主动核实作者信息和转载信息、主动发放转载稿酬的“三主动”方法实行多年，向作者转付报刊转载和教科书选文稿酬，确保把每一笔稿酬发放到真正的权利人手中。“三主动”方法受到广大作者的高度认可和褒奖。

2016 年，经过协会全体员工的努力，文著协收取文字作品版权使用费共计 560 万元，比上一年增长 30%。其中，报刊和教科书“法定许可” 221 万元，版权代理 274 万元，数字版权 30 万元，维权 35 万元。

协会按每月一至两次向会员和其他作者转付稿酬，并向其提供作品使用明细单。2016 年全年共向会员和其他作者转付稿酬 454 万元，平均转付率 83%，其中，教科书和汇编作品转付率超过 90%，数字版权和版权代理转付率 100%。由于文摘类报刊委托转付稿酬的大量文章作者都是笔名或没有署名，查找难度大，所以报刊转载稿酬转付率较低。

在“4·26”世界知识产权宣传周期间，文著协工作人员专程探望了梁实秋、艾青、叶圣陶、严文井、陈伯吹、史铁生等现当代文学名家的权利继承人，为他们送去出版单位近期使用文字作品的稿酬，共计7万余元。协会已经连续八年在“4·26”世界知识产权宣传周期间为老会员上门送稿酬。

著名儿童文学作家、翻译家、教育家陈伯吹的作品深受少年儿童喜欢。他的儿子著名物理学家、中国科学院院士、北京大学原校长陈佳洱于2011年加入中国文字著作权协会，委托协会全权处理陈伯吹的著作权事宜。多年来，协会采取各种措施，努力管理好大师的经典作品，目前已代表陈佳洱与高等教育出版社、当代世界出版社、天津华文天下图书、天天出版社、明天出版社、长江少年儿童出版社、中国少年儿童新闻出版总社、春风文艺出版社、长江文艺出版社、北教小雨文化传媒（北京）有限公司等多家出版社签订作品授权使用协议，授权出版《一只想飞的猫》《绿野仙踪》《骆驼寻宝记》等十余册图书，一年授权单篇使用文章50余篇次，为陈佳洱争取版权收益数十万元。陈佳洱在协会员工送稿酬上门的当天，感动于协会多年来为他做的工作，主动签署独家授权合同，将陈伯吹全部作品中文版权独家授予协会管理。年近九旬的著名儿童文学作家葛翠林也因为协会工作认真负责，主动将全部作品版权独家授予协会管理。

协会对于暂时没掌握联系方式的作者信息，全部公示在协会网站，并通过博客、微博、微信公号等形式向社会公布，鼓励权利人领取。

三、“法定许可”业务

向教科书出版机构和文摘类报刊社宣传普及著作权法“法定许可”规定，签署法定许可稿酬收转协议，收取文摘类报刊和教科书出版社交纳的转载和选文稿费是国家法律赋予文著协的法定职能。协会经过一年的不懈努力，继人民教育出版社、江苏教育出版社之后，2016年，成功与河北教育出版社、北京师范大学出版社、西南师范大学出版社签订了“法定许可”稿酬转付协议并收到这三家出版社向协会交付的教科书使用作品稿酬。

2016年7月，经过多次沟通，协会与读者出版集团有限公司签订了《报刊“法定许可”稿酬收转协议》。根据该协议，《读者》《读者·校园版》《读者·海外版》三本期刊所选用部分文字作品的稿酬，由文著协收取并转付给相关的作者或权利人。《读者》在我国享有盛誉，在消费类期刊月均发行量排行中稳居全国第一、亚洲第一、世界第三，被誉为“中国人的心灵读本”“中国期刊第一品牌”。文著协与《读者》系列杂志签订法定许可稿酬收转协议，表明文著协在落实国家法律规定、履行报刊和教科书法定许可稿酬收取转付的法定职能方面迈出了重要一步。

2016年，协会继续积极向报刊社宣传介绍国家版权局和国家发改委颁布的《使用文字作品支付报酬办法》，先后与《半月选读》《文学少年》等几家杂志社和新加坡名创教育出版社、培生教育出版亚洲有限公司等机构签订了“法定许可”稿酬转付协议，认真执行国家规定的法定许可稿酬标准。

四、版权集体管理业务

（一）数字版权

2016年，协会继续与北京世纪卓越信息技术有限公司（亚马逊中国）、北京掌阅科技有限责任公司、北京世纪超星信息技术发展有限责任公司等机构合作，通过数字新媒体平台推广会员作品，为会员创造收益。截止到2016年12月31日，亚马逊共销售协会会员电子书51 406册，其中会员汪曾祺的《人间草木》销量最大，共计24 018册。

（二）戏剧公开表演权

2016年，文著协与俄罗斯最大的著作权集体管理组织——俄罗斯著作权协会等机构签署公开表演权相互代表协议，与俄罗斯FTM版权代理公司签署合作协议，为国内院团成功引进了《办公室的故事》（作者：埃利达尔·梁赞诺夫，埃米尔·布拉金斯基）、《我可怜的马拉特》（作者：阿尔布卓夫）、《长子》（作者：万比洛夫）等俄罗斯五部经典话剧。这些话剧已陆续在国内上演，产生了良好的市场反响，使俄罗斯戏剧家获取了较为可观的戏剧公开表演权收益，促进了中俄两国戏剧界的交流与合作。

五、版权代理工作

（一）汇编作品授权代理

2016年，协会利用长期积累的会员和作者信息，与人民文学、商务印书馆、二十一世纪、中信、中译、中国妇女、中国戏剧、中国劳动社会保障、长江少儿、山东教育、浙江大学、江苏译林、江西人民、长春、明天、希望、河南人民广播电台、海豚等40余家出版社和民营出版策划机构签订了《汇编作品委托代理协议》，代理解决了100余种汇编作品的作者、译者授权问题，涉及作者、译者逾千人次，文章数千篇次，为作者争取稿酬145万元。

（二）国际版权贸易代理

2016年，协会与日本株式会社公文教育研究会签署版权代理协议，授权该机构在教学过程中以中文简体、繁体使用沈从文、朱光潜等中国作家作品。

协会还为人民出版社、北京十月文艺出版社、江苏译林出版社、黑龙江大学出版社、黑龙江少年儿童出版社等多家出版机构从俄罗斯、德国、塞尔维亚等国引进《巴塔传》、《普京：权力的逻辑》、《神奇的童话》（作者为高尔基，插图作者为俄罗斯当代艺术家）、《课外阅读丛书》（作者为列夫·托尔斯泰，插图作者为俄罗斯当代艺术家）等多部国外图书版权。

与此同时，协会把姜戎、阿来等作家和新世界出版社等出版机构的作品输出到俄罗斯、乌克兰、阿尔巴尼亚等国家。并为韩国、日本、新加坡和我国香港、台湾等地区大部分中文教材选用中文著名作家作品代理解决多位作家授权问题。文著协已经成为中国出版、中国文化“走出去”的一支重要力量、一个重要窗口。

（三）其他领域的版权代理

2016年，协会为北京新世邦文化传媒有限公司解决了即将拍摄的影视剧《北京人在北京》中使用著名诗人海子的诗歌《面朝大海　春暖花开》的版权授权问题，为杭州奥觉广告有限公司解决了即将拍摄的广告片《上好佳鱼果》中使用作者放平的诗歌《小金鱼》的版权授权问题，获得使用者和权利人的好评。

协会还为国家话剧院等机构演出使用俄罗斯话剧剧本中文译本解决多个译者的授权问题。同时，协会积极联系著名作家、编剧等，参加第二届中国影视文学版权拍卖大会（浙江宁波镇海）。

六、“中俄现代与经典作品互译出版项目”成果丰硕

2016年，文著协依然是总局批准的“中俄现代与经典作品互译出版项目”的中方承办单位。在总局领导的亲切关怀和悉心指导下，通过文著协的协调和中俄双方各出版机构以及双方翻译家的努力，“中俄经典与现代作品互译出版项目”结出丰硕的成果。截至2016年底，中方已出版“俄罗斯文库”中的文学作品共计34种，其中2016年新出版20种；俄方已出版“中国文库”中的文学作品共计18种，其中2016年新出版3种。

在2016年8月举办的第23届北京国际图书博览会期间，由中国国家新闻出版广电总局和俄罗斯出版与大众传媒署主办，文著协联合俄方承办机构——俄罗斯翻译学院承办的“中俄互译出版项目”新书发布暨座谈会，邀请了总局进口管理司、中国社科院外文所、中国俄罗斯文学研究会、俄罗斯驻华大使馆、俄罗斯翻译学院和参与中俄互译项目的两国出版机构、译者、俄罗斯作家代表和两国部分媒体参会。与会代表一致认为，“中俄互译出版项目”丰富了中俄两国人文交流的内涵，有助于扩大和加深两国出版界、文学界、翻译界的交流与合作，加深两国人民之间的相互了解。最后，文著协还组织了向俄罗斯驻华大使馆赠送互译项目新书的活动。

在2016年9月举办的第29届莫斯科国际书展期间，由中国国家新闻出版广电总局和俄罗斯出版与大众传媒署主办，中国文字著作权协会和俄罗斯翻译学院承办的“中俄互译出版项目”新书暨俄文专刊发布会在中国展台举行。中国国家新闻出版广电总局、俄罗斯出版与大众传媒署、俄罗斯中国友好协会、中国驻俄使馆、俄罗斯科学院远东研究所、俄罗斯出版商协会、俄罗斯儿童基金会、莫斯科大学、莫斯科人民友谊大学等有关部门的领导、嘉宾，中俄出版机构、作家、翻译家代表和中俄媒体代表近百人参加了本次活动，这是莫斯科书展期间最有影响力的活动之一，在俄罗斯当地产生了不小的社会影响。

与此同时，由总局资助、文著协与俄罗斯翻译学院策划的《“中俄互译出版项目”俄文专刊》由俄罗斯《图书评论》周报正式出版；《“中俄互译出版项目”中文专刊》由中国新华书店总店主办的《国际出版》周报正式出版。两份专刊分别在莫斯科书展和北京国际图书博览会上精彩亮相，这是苏联解体以来中俄两国新闻出版界首次以报纸专刊的形式集中介绍两国文学作品的互译出版盛况。

来自白俄罗斯、土库曼斯坦、哈萨克斯坦、乌克兰、阿尔巴尼亚、罗马尼亚、塞尔维亚、匈牙利、波兰等国的出版商代表对“中俄互译出版项目”很感兴趣，对俄文专刊和中文专刊爱不释手，高度评价了这一项目的最新成果。

在莫斯科书展期间，在文著协的协调安排下，总局莫斯科书展代表团团长、总局进口管理司司长蒋茂凝与俄罗斯出版与大众传媒署副署长弗拉基米尔·格里高利耶夫举行了会谈。蒋茂凝司长代表总局参观了莫斯科中国文化中心，并赠送“中俄互译出版项目”新出版的中俄文图书，中国驻俄罗斯大使馆公使衔文化参赞、莫斯科中国文化中心主任兼中共六大遗址永久纪念馆馆长张中华接受赠书。

七、积极维护权利人的合法权益

2016年，协会为维护广大权利人的合法权益做了一些具体的工作，先后为葛翠琳、毕冰宾、董天佑、常福生、尹维平、匡咏梅、庄焰等权利人成功调解与相关出版机构的版权纠纷，追讨出版单位拖欠的会员稿酬，为权利人挽回实际损失共计 30 余万元，受到权利人的一致好评。文著协以自己的实际行动努力当好权利人的“娘家人”。

会员陈漱渝与某中央级出版社签订图书出版合同五年多，但是出版社拒不履行合同义务，没有如约出版他的三部书稿。这不但使他丧失了最佳出版时机，造成了十余万元的可期待的稿酬损失，还给他的正常退休生活造成了极大的困扰。经文著协多次出面交涉，该出版社向陈漱渝足额支付了出版合同约定的违约金，并向其表达了歉意。陈漱渝先生专门来到协会表达谢意，对文著协尽心尽力、认真负责的工作态度和规范有序、专业到位的版权纠纷处理能力非常赞赏，充分肯定了文著协在维护作者权益方面做出的积极努力。

2016 年“4·26”世界知识产权宣传周期间，协会接到多位会员对中国知网（清华同方科技公司）的投诉，认为中国知网未经其授权，收录他们在期刊发表的大量文章，并通过向海内外高校图书馆等机构销售数据库等形式获得大量收益。协会经过认真核实，第一批统计出协会会员 100 多人的 2 万多篇文章被侵权。协会与中国知网进行了多次沟通，中国知网承认侵权事实，并愿意就赔偿事宜进一步协商。

与此同时，接会员投诉，协会经过调查发现，万方数据科技公司、重庆维普科技公司、北京书生科技公司等公司也存在侵犯多位会员权利的情况，会员反应也比较强烈。

八、参加的重要版权宣传研讨交流活动

2016 年，协会多次参加了与自身业务发展紧密相关的版权宣传研讨交流活动，如 2016 知识产权南湖论坛、2016 年内地与香港澳门特别行政区知识产权研讨会、版权与相关权热点问题亚太地区研讨会、第十二届中韩著作权研讨会、中国国际版权博览会（广州）、第十三届上海国际书展、中国互联网版权保护大会、互联网版权保护与运营新媒体论坛、中国知识产权保护高层论坛、CISAC 全球创作者论坛、中国学术期刊大会、新闻作品版权保护研讨会、新闻出版社团发展座谈会、著作权集体管理修法建议研讨会、“剑网 2016”专项行动座谈会、中俄出版论坛、CCTSS 国际图书系列沙龙等等。通过参加这些活动，并在会上做专题发言，协会积极宣传了自己的职能、宗旨和服务理念，扩大了在社会上的影响，同时有机会虚心学习国内外同行的先进经验和成熟做法。

在 2016 年 3 月全国“两会”期间，文著协协助全国政协委员、韬奋基金会理事长聂震宁完成了《关于加强网络版权保护，促进数字文化创意产业发展的提案》，协助全国政协委员、协会副会长张抗抗完成了《关于提高稿酬个人所得税起征点的提案》和《关于加强整顿教科书编写出版单位侵害著作权行为的提案》。聂震宁委员联合白岩松、李从军、何建明等 32 位全国政协委员联署，聂震宁和张抗抗在全国政协联组会议上分别就上述提案做专题发言，受到政府有关部门的重视和社会关注。

九、国际交往

（一）与罗马尼亚著作权集体管理协会签署合作协议

2016 年 12 月 14 日，文著协总干事张洪波与到访的罗马尼亚著作权集体管理协会主席欧根·乌里卡鲁在鲁迅文学院签署版权合作协议。根据该协议，罗马尼亚著作权集体管理协会将代表文著协在罗马尼亚依法为会员收取中文文字作品影印复制权、表演权、公众传播权等版权使用费。这是文著协继英国、韩国、俄罗斯著作权集体管理组织后签署的第四个国际合作协议，为中文书报刊海外复制权和数字化复制权的授权与收费进一步拓宽了道路。双方还就推动两国政府主管部门建立中罗文学作品互译出版项目，开展图书、影视、戏剧版权贸易，加强人员往来进行了富有成效的会谈。

罗马尼亚著作权集体管理协会（Societate de Gestiune Colectiva a Drepturilor de Autor）是罗马尼亚文字作品著作权集体管理组织，管理文学、艺术和科技作品的复制、表演、演绎、向公众传播等权利，以保护创作者利益、促进文学和文化的繁荣发展为宗旨。文著协和该协会同为国际影印复制权组织联合会（IFRRO）会员。根据罗马尼亚相关法律规定，该协会向复印扫描设备和纸张制造商或进口商、有线电视运营商、公共图书馆等收取文字作品的私人复制、有线电视转播、图书馆公共借阅等该国法律规定的强制补偿金。

中国作协党组成员、书记处书记、副主席兼鲁迅文学院院长、著名诗人吉狄马加（彝族），鲁迅文学院常务副院长邱华栋和北京罗马尼亚文化中心主任鲁博安、罗马尼亚文化学院国家图书中心主任博格丹·波佩斯库等中罗两国友好人士出席了签字仪式。

（二）参加莫斯科国际书展、土库曼斯坦国际书展

2016 年 9 月，按照总局安排，协会分别派工作人员参加了莫斯科书展和土库曼斯坦阿什哈巴德国际书展，举办了“中俄互译出版项目”新书发布会、

新书成果展，发放俄文专刊和协会宣传资料，向参展商、有关媒体展示文著协的工作成果，重点介绍了“中俄互译出版项目”最新成果，帮助国内出版社与海外参展商建立联系，现场洽谈，尽最大可能展示中国文化的魅力，吸引了众多参展观众，获得了良好的参展效果。

（三）参加国际影印复制权组织联合会（IFRRO）年会

2016年8月和11月，协会分别派工作人员参加了在荷兰阿姆斯特丹举办的国际影印复制权组织联合会（IFRRO）全球年会和该组织在澳大利亚悉尼举办的IFRRO亚太区年会，并在会上做了年度工作报告，同时与前来参会的各国集体管理组织代表进行了深入交流，进一步增进了相互了解。

（四）赴塞尔维亚参加“第一届中国—中东欧文化创意产业论坛”

2016年6月，协会总干事张洪波应文化部邀请，参加北京第二外国语学院组织的代表团赴塞尔维亚参加“第一届中国—中东欧文化创意产业论坛”，并做主旨发言。

在塞尔维亚期间，张洪波总干事和代表团主要成员受到了塞尔维亚文化媒体部部长的接见，参观了塞尔维亚著作权集体管理组织、有关媒体机构，双方对著作权集体管理模式进行了较为深入的探讨。同时，还访问了塞尔维亚知名出版机构，与当地汉学家进行了深入交流，展望了中塞开展互译的前景。该次出访为双方签订集体管理相互代表协议、开展互译出版项目打下了良好的基础。张洪波总干事向塞尔维亚文化媒体部部长赠送了上世纪70年代中国出版的《瓦尔特保卫萨拉热窝》老版连环画，并就引进《巴塔传》（巴塔为扮演电影《瓦尔特保卫萨拉热窝》主人公瓦尔特的演员）中文翻译权与对方出版机构达成版权引进意向。这是“第一届中国—中东欧文化创意产业论坛”达成的重要成果，得到了中塞两国大使馆的高度赞扬。

（五）接待乌克兰汉学协会代表团

2016年3月31日，文著协接待了乌克兰汉学协会会长和秘书长一行，双方就推动中乌开展互译出版、文学期刊合作、编写汉乌—乌汉对照字典等问题进行了友好深入的交流。文著协将进一步关注并加强与乌克兰汉学协会的交流，增进中乌两国文化和版权领域的相互了解，开拓合作渠道，为中国文化走出去再添新功。

十、协会获得的荣誉

协会经过多年的辛勤耕耘，在2016年获得了一些荣誉：

1. 2016年4月，经中国知识产权研究会（协会为该研究会理事单位）推荐，经国家知识产权局审核，张洪波总干事入选国家知识产权专家库，成为国家知识产权专家库第二批入库专家。

2. 2016年11月，全国政协常委、中国文字著作权协会会长、中国作家协会副主席陈建功荣获中国版权协会颁发的“中国版权卓越成就者奖”。

3. 2016年12月，中国文字著作权协会荣获国家版权局和世界知识产权组织颁发的“2016年度中国版权金奖·管理奖”，这是该奖项自2008年在华设立以来我国著作权集体管理组织第一次获此殊荣。

十一、脱钩准备工作

按照中央和总局关于行政机关与行业协会商会脱钩的要求，协会多次参加总局和中直机关工委组织的社团脱钩会议和调研活动，向员工传达脱钩文件精神，组织学习领会脱钩的意义，并专门成立脱钩工作组，起草脱钩实施整体方案和外事、党建等分方案，有组织有步骤地推进协会脱钩的各项准备工作。

（张洪波）

中国摄影著作权协会

2016年，是中国摄影著作权协会（以下简称摄著协）积极进取勇于担当，大胆探索摄影版权保护创新工作的一年。这一年，摄著协在国家版权局的领导下，在中国摄影家协会的大力支持下，深入学习习近平总书记系列重要讲话精神。2016年，在会员快速发展的基础上，又实现了历史性突破，5 382名新会员使得摄著协会员总人数接近万人。2016年协会大胆探索、勇于担当，积极工作、不断创新，依据会员代表大会通过的决议，把百万元教科书摄影作品使用费在会员中进行分配。此举被版权界视为重要事件。同时百万元教科书稿酬分配和摄影作品原作讨论，双双入选全国摄影界十大新闻，受到了摄影界的热烈欢迎。2016年，摄著协积极开展中外摄影文化交流，通过举办美国著名摄影家《保罗·卡普尼格罗“直接摄影”原作展》和《迪尔曼·科瑞恩“光之炼金术”摄影原作展》，探索和寻找“摄影原作”形成轨迹，为修改《著作权法》建立追续权制度在摄影业界形成共识。2016年，协会把普及摄影版权保护知识宣传和推广作为一项重要工作任务，从2016年初在新疆做普法宣传开始，连续在重庆、内蒙古、陕西、浙江、贵州、江苏、辽宁、北京等多省市进行巡回演讲，直至把这项专题讲座送到雪地高原的西藏阿里地区，得到了各地摄影界的好评，受到了广大摄影家的热烈的欢迎。

2016 年摄著协工作主要呈现以下几点特色：

一、发展会员又上新台阶

摄著协在连续两年会员发展保持高速增长的基础上，2016 年会员发展工作又上新台阶，全年共发展会员 5 382 人，使得协会会员总人数接近万人。多年来，协会秉承一切为会员着想，切实做好为会员服务的精神，2016 年初大胆简化新会员入会程序，通过网上申请和在线初审等环节方便摄影家申报入会，这一改革既受到了摄影家的欢迎，又提高了发展会员的工作效率。在会员人数不断上升的同时，摄著协还积极做好与会员的联络和服务工作，2016 年协会与相关部门合作启动了建立会员电子档案与信息管理系统工作，该系统建成后除能够做到与会员保持畅通的沟通与联系外，还可以避免由于个体会员流动性强而不好管理和“连长找不到兵”的现象。

二、在国务院修法层面为摄影家力争权利

国务院启动修改《著作权法》工作以来，摄著协多次组织摄影家召开座谈会，积极征集广大摄影家的意见和建议，并把这些意见及时反映到国家相关部门。2016 年 3 月，国务院法制办召开修法专家论证会，摄著协应邀两次出席。在论证会上摄著协以发生在摄影家身上的鲜活案例为例，以国际版权公约和国际社会取得的成功经验为依据，代表摄影家利益明确支持在新的《著作权法（修改草案）》中增加视觉艺术追续权规定。以协会开发并经过市场检验，受到摄影家欢迎的摄影作品限量鉴证为实例，用实物说明摄影作品原作已得到作者、市场和公众的认同，为追续权立法后保护摄影作品做好铺垫。摄著协的意见和例证得到了与会专家们的认同。

三、与金融服务业合作打造为会员服务新手段，启动并实施教科书稿酬分配工作

在著作权集体管理制度下做好摄影版权保护，重在为众多的摄影家征得更多的权利与利益。著作权集体管理组织意在取得摄影家授权后为他们争取到实实在在的经济利益。几年来，摄著协克服困难，努力为摄影家收取了教科书使用摄影作品版税，并积极探索把这些版税最大限度地向摄影家进行转付和分配。摄著协学习和借鉴国内外著作权集体管理组织的经验和做法，把分配不尽的教科书使用摄影作品版税，按协会《章程》经会员代表大会审议通过后，在 2016 年第 16 个世界知识产权日启动了向摄影家分配工作。为做好版税分配，摄著协制定了缜密的分配工作方案，并把参与发起成立中国摄影著作权协会的中国摄影家协会、中国新闻摄影学会、中国人像摄影学会、中国艺术摄影学会、中国民俗摄影协会和中国女摄影家协会的会员纳入被分配对象，引起了摄影界的关注并受到了欢迎。为了把这些版税分配工作做好，摄著协严守公开、公正、透明原则，邀请众多社会媒体举行新闻发布会，在社会舆论和公众的监督下有序进行，做到了使摄影家知道、业界知晓、社会知情，收到了积极和正面的社会效果。

为准确无误地把这些版税分配给会员，摄著协还与中国工商银行合作共同打造为会员服务新手段，设计、开发并向摄著协会员专属发行了“摄影家银行卡”，以此作为分配渠道使教科书版税可直接打入会员银行账户。国家版权局领导对“摄影家银行卡”的发行给予了高度评价，表示这是版权保护领域和金融服务领域业务探索和服务创新的重要举措。“摄影家银行卡”除了分配教科书版税外，还具备保障摄影家金融安全、为摄影家提供理财服务和终身免年费等多项优惠，受到了会员的喜爱和欢迎。

四、积极开展国际摄影文化交流，力促在摄影业界形成对摄影原作的共识

为了配合修改《著作权法》增加视觉艺术追续权，力促在摄影业界形成对摄影作品原作的共识，2016 年 4 月和 11 月，协会在中国美术馆先后举办了直接摄影流派代表人物美国摄影家《保罗·卡普尼格罗“直接摄影”作品展》和《光之炼金术——迪尔曼·克瑞恩铂金印相原作展》，用国际上具有影响力的摄影家“原作展”展现摄影原作的魅力。两个原作展的举办在摄影界产生了热烈反响，使得更多的摄影家对摄影原作有了更深刻的认识和理解，拉近了摄影人对摄影原作共识的距离。两个“原作展”不仅向中国摄影家解读了摄影原作的形成轨迹，摄著协还邀请了保罗和迪尔曼亲临影展开幕现场，用他们几十年的亲身摄影实践和经验与中国的摄影家进行交流，在摄影界产生了很大影响。

除此之外，摄著协还利用 2016 年在黑龙江伊春和贵州都匀进行国际摄影活动的时机，召开中外摄影家研讨会，专题讨论摄影原作问题，从理论和创作实践角度进一步探讨摄影原作。参会中外摄影家发言踊跃，学术气氛十分活跃，一致认为形成对摄影原作的共识，不仅关系到中国摄影家的切身利益，还将影响摄影家的子孙后代，承认摄影作品原作，摄影家将在修法中赢得新的权利。

五、与中国摄协共同举办摄影图片产业专家谈

12月，摄著协与中国摄影家协会和成都市文学艺术界联合会，在成都共同主办了“图片产业发展与摄影版权维护专家谈”活动。本次专家谈活动围绕图片产业发展与摄影版权维护这一主题，就以下问题进行了阐述和探讨：如何坚守艺术理想，用高尚的文艺引领社会风尚，在图片产业中成就自我、实现价值；中国网络平台图片市场的现状与国外情况异同；摄影著作权维护与图片市场的关系；版权在市场中的地位与作用；中国摄影艺术家如何逐渐进入国外艺术市场、渠道；国外市场需要什么风格或内容的作品；中国拍卖行的图片拍卖现状与发展，与国外的异同；传统传媒业中的图片与市场的关系；如何把摄影作品推进市场等。北京视觉中国执行董事、总编辑柴继军，加拿大ifp国际摄影师联盟委员会主席兼艺术总监段岳衡，雅昌文化集团董事长万捷，河南省摄协顾问、时光空间画廊艺术总监姜健，大理国际影会艺术总监、云南省摄影家协会副主席鲍利辉，华辰拍卖有限公司常务副总经理李欣以及摄著协总干事林涛等七位专家代表图片产业、摄影著作权等方面的专家学者做了主题发言。这次座谈会在摄影界产生了重要反响，被称为中国图片产业发展与摄影版权维护的助推剂。

六、加强普法宣传，把著作权保护知识送到天山和世界屋脊

2016年，摄著协加大了普法宣传工作力度，全年在新疆、重庆、内蒙古、陕西、西藏、浙江、贵州、江苏、辽宁、北京等十个省（区、市）进行了十几场普法宣传专题讲座。2016年初随中国文联送欢乐下基层活动，把普法宣传讲座送到了新疆克孜勒苏柯尔克孜自治州和喀什地区。8月又结合深入基层调研，把普法宣传带到了西藏海拔最高的阿里地区。在阿里地区的5天时间，摄著协人员克服高原缺氧走访了札达、普兰和阿里三个市、县进行了四场专题讲座。在阿里摄著协还与当地摄影界建立了工作联系机制，聘任了三名当地摄影家为摄著协的首席代表，把摄著协的工作触角延伸到祖国偏僻、文化较落后的地区。

七、设立最庞大的微信群，利用手机与各地首席代表建立工作交流平台

摄著协由于工作人员数量有限，要在全国范围扩大影响力必须借助各地摄影组织和团体的力量。自摄著协启动各省和地市级城市首席代表工作以来，其为推广普法宣传、发展会员、举办摄影活动、扩大摄著协在全国的影响力发挥了重要的作用。随着各地首代工作的逐步展开，怎样加强与他们的沟通与联络，指导他们做好工作使摄著协颇费周折。2016年，摄著协以手机为平台建立起“中摄权首代”微信群，在中国摄影著作权协会成立八周年之际开通，在开通一周内就有七百余人上线。这个微信群做到了快速发布摄著协相关信息，及时指导各地首代做好工作，并可迅速收到摄著协工作在各地进展情况的信息反馈，真正成为摄著协做好首代工作的抓手。今后摄著协将逐步加强和拓展这两个微信群的功能与作用，借助各地首席代表的地域资源和优势，把摄影著作权保护和推广工作向更深更广发展。

八、职业化标准手册编辑出版，把协会科学化管理推上一个新台阶

2016年，是摄著协成立八周年，经过八年的不断探索与努力，摄著协已经初步摸索出摄影著作权集体管理的工作模式。为了把分散在各个工作环节中的规章和制度加以梳理，并形成指导今后工作的制度性文件，2016年，摄著协编辑了包括摄影版权许可管理制度、会员管理制度、限量鉴证管理制度、信息资源管理制度、首席代表管理制度、行政管理制度和财务管理制度等十个篇目、五十余章节、近六万字的《中国摄影著作权协会职业化标准手册》，作为协会走过八周年的工作和制度总结。这本手册汇集了摄著协八年来从事摄影著作权集体管理工作的探索、实践和经验总结，它对今后指导摄影著作权集体管理业务工作的开展，指导和培训这方面的专业人员具有重要的作用。

（朱宝祺）

中国电影著作权协会

2016年，中国电影著作权协会（以下简称影著协）在党的十八届五中、六中全会精神的指引下，在国家版权局的指导下，围绕巡视整改、社团脱钩以及著作权保护和管理等重点任务，具体开展如下工作：

一、配合做好巡视及整改工作

自2016年4月15日接到国家版权局有关部门通知起，影著协按照中央巡视组要求准备材料并接受相关问询。同时，接受国家版权局巡视组的巡视。5月5日接到国家版权局巡视组整改通知后，影著协按照要求制定整改方案，并于6月完成整改工作。

影著协将巡视工作作为首要政治任务，认真配合巡视组，查找自身问题。除了按照巡视整改要求进行改进外，影著协还以点带面，将问题所涉及的相应内控制度和责任制度进行修订和细化，同时对影著协类似业务进行清理，并按照制度要求进行相应处理。

通过该项工作，影著协全体工作人员不仅提高了政治觉悟，端正了政治态度，而且将党的要求贯彻落实到工作的每一个环节。

二、启动脱钩准备工作

继巡视整改工作完成之后，2016 年 8 月 24 日，影著协参加民政部组织的全国性行业协会商会（第二批）脱钩试点工作培训班。这标志着作为全国第二批、国家版权局第一批脱钩试点单位之一的影著协的脱钩准备工作正式开启。影著协先后向党建、人事、机构、财务、外事等相关管理部门提交调研表格和相关问询材料，报告影著协基本情况。根据国家版权局人事司的部署，经常务理事会决定，影著协于 2016 年 10 月报送脱钩方案及脱钩领导工作小组。2016 年 11 月，影著协脱钩实施方案获得民政部核准。2016 年 12 月，影著协参加人事司组织的第二次脱钩工作会议，明确与各相关司局办理脱钩事务的具体方案。2016 年 12 月，影著协参加进口管理司外事脱钩会议并按要求准备相关材料。

三、继续开拓影著协著作权保护和管理业务

1. 走访会员单位。听取电影权利人代表对影视作品相关司法解释的建议，交流影吧使用电影作品相关情况，争取会员单位的著作权集体管理授权。

2. 针对影吧使用电影作品进行调研。通过参加影吧行业高峰论坛、与影吧经营者交流、拜访 KTV 系统提供商、与相关主管部门沟通、咨询法律专家、关注网络信息等多种方式对影吧使用电影作品情况进行调研并形成报告。

3. 尝试性开展影吧使用电影作品的授权许可工作。2016 年影著协与两家连锁影吧签订电影作品使用协议，并已完成 8 万余元的著作权使用费的分配转付工作。

4. 协助使用者获得电影音频使用许可。在影著协的协调下，北京广播电台与影著协会员单位达成电影音频使用协议，涉及电影作品 30 部。

5. 收到西班牙著作人和音乐人协会转付的著作权使用费 36 608 元。根据西班牙著作人和音乐人协会提供的分配清单，影著协已经基本完成分配清单的翻译、整理、结算、制表、相关说明文件的起草等工作。本次分配涉及电影作品 37 部、导演 29 位、编剧 76 位。

6. 启动电影作品院线期保护工作。鉴于会员单位大部分已经将作品信息网络传播权的维权权利随信息网络传播权一同转让或者与律师事务所合作维权，影著协将维权工作的重点转移至影片首发期间，首先加强电影作品的院线期保护。准确定位影著协角色，协调权利人和相关行政管理部门，汇总电影权利人的作品上映和权利信息，代表其向有关部门申请电影作品版权重点保护。截至 2016 年底已经基本完成相关材料的起草和修改工作。

（史文霞）

中国互联网协会网络版权联盟

2016 年，中国互联网协会网络版权联盟（以下简称联盟）积极开展互联网版权保护相关方面的培训、研究等活动，加强与其他单位的合作，推动网络版权保护的发展。

一、会议活动

（一）第五届首都互联网法律工作者年会暨诉调对接联动机制研讨会

为推动首都互联网行业健康发展，增进首都各界互联网法律工作者之间的交流，2016 年 1 月 22 日，中国互联网协会调解中心与北京人民调解协会联合主办的“第五届首都互联网法律工作者年会暨诉调对接联动机制研讨会”在北京召开。

司法部基层工作指导司、国家新闻出版广电总局版权管理司、工业和信息化部科技司、中华全国人民调解员协会、北京市司法局、北京市社会工作委员会、北京市互联网信息办公室、国务院台湾事务办公室等单位的 10 余位领导；最高人民法院，北京市高级人民法院，北京知识产权法院和北京市人民检察院第一分院、第四分院，及北京市各级人民法院、检察院的近 30 名代表；百度、腾讯、新浪、京东、中搜、乐视、搜狐、阿里巴巴、安存、环球网、风行网、蚂蜂窝等 70 余家互联网企业单位代表共 110 余人参加了此次年会。

会上，国家新闻出版广电总局（国家版权局）版权管理司副司长段玉萍、中华全国人民调解员协会副会长兼秘书长李冰、北京多元调解发展促进会会长翟晶敏、工业和信息化部科技司技术基础处处长常利民分别为本次大会致辞。

与会嘉宾表示调解工作对化解纠纷机制建设起到了非常重要的作用，同时，一致认为中国互联网协会调解中心在互联网纠纷调解工作中，以及诉调对接方面开展了大量的工作，并取得了非常好的成效；这项工作不仅受到互联网公司的大力欢迎，也得到各级法院的充分肯定；知识产权的保护和司法的实践工作是长期的、艰巨的，需要政府、司法和产业界共同的努力去推动和营造良好的知识产权保护环境。

在本次大会上，北京市高级人民法院知识产权庭、北京知识产权法院、北京市人民检察院第四分院等领导分别围绕网络纠纷审理情况、信息网络传播司法保护发展以及检察监督发表演讲。

（二）互联网食药安全法律问题研讨会

2016 年 3 月 11 日上午，由北京市海淀区人民检察院、中国互联网协会调解中心、北京人民调解协会联合主办的“互联网食药安全检企共治平台启动仪式暨互联网食药安全法律问题研讨会”如期召开，本次会议邀请了北京市海淀区人民检察院检察长王伟、副检察长刘惠，北京市海淀区人民法院副院长范君，北京市公安局海淀分局副局长蒋林、赵磊砢与来自海淀区人民法院、北京市公安局海淀分局、海淀区食品药品监督管理局、北京人民调解协会、中国互联网协会调解中心以及互联网企业的代表和媒体代表，共计 70 余人参会。

在中国互联网协会调解中心的推动下，美团外卖、百度外卖、新浪网三家互联网企业分别与北京市海淀区人民检察院签订了《互联网企业食药安全共治协议》，并举行了互联网食药安全检企共治平台启动仪式。

下一步，中国互联网协会调解中心将对互联网食品药品的案件类型及食品药品领域遇到的新型法律问题进行为期一年的研讨。通过网络平台管理，在行政机关、司法系统，以及互联网企业等方面形成有效的联动机制，针对案件中的取证难点、涉网食品药品的法律适用、涉网食品药品纠纷的应对机制及解决机制、商家与电商平台经营跨境食品药品的刑事法律责任，以及《中华人民共和国消费者权益保护法》对“知假买假”的职业打假人的适用范围等内容进行研究。

本次会议，与会嘉宾围绕“食品药品网络经营者如何防范食药犯罪”“涉网食品餐饮实体的线下治理”“电商平台在食品安全监管及经营跨境食品的刑事法律责任”等问题进行了探讨。

（三）第七届首都互联网知识产权保护论坛

2016 年 4 月 28 日下午，由北京市高级人民法院知识产权庭和中国互联网协会调解中心联合主办的“第七届首都互联网知识产权保护论坛”在北京召开。本次论坛的主题为“诉调促进和谐　创新共享发展”。

北京市高级人民法院、北京知识产权法院等北京地区各级人民法院代表，北京市人民检察院四分院、北京市海淀区人民检察院等 50 余名代表，以及百度、乐视、中文在线等 40 余家互联网企业代表，共计 100 余人参加了本次论坛。

会议对北京市 2015 年知识产权司法审判情况和 2016 年司法审判发展趋势进行了回顾和展望。其间，北京市高级人民法院知识产权庭庭长助理潘伟和中国互联网协会副秘书长石现升，分别为论坛进行致辞；北京高级人民法院知识产权庭对《涉及网络知识产权案件审理指南》进行了详细的解读；中国互联网协会调解中心和北京市西城区人民法院就“诉调对接工作”进行了详细的汇报。

会上，北京市东城区人民法院知识产权庭和中国互联网协会调解中心联合发布了《移动互联网环境下文字作品著作权保护问题调研报告》；北京地区各级人民法院代表分别围绕“涉网著作权侵权案件”“涉网络商标侵权案件”“涉网不正当竞争案件”“涉网动漫游戏案件”，以及“以深度链接为视角的聚合平台的经营模式对司法的挑战”等新型商业模式中出现的焦点问题进行了主题发言；百度、乐视等互联网企业围绕“互联网司法规制对产业的影响”及“聚合软件行为分类及其法律责任”分别与与会嘉宾进行了深度交流。

本次论坛既有来自司法一线的案件实证经验分享，还有来自互联网企业的新问题和保护呼声，为促进产业发展，进一步加强首都知识产权保护力度，保障互联网的健康有序发展取得了积极的作用和良好的社会反响。

（四）2016 中国互联网大会暨首届中国互联网纠纷解决机制高峰论坛

中国互联网协会网络版权工作委员会、调解中心和中关村社会组织联合会联合主办的“首届中国互联网纠纷解决机制高峰论坛”于 2016 年 6 月 23 日在北京国际会议中心圆满结束。

最高人民法院司法改革办公室指导处龙飞副处长以互联网时代发展的新背景、新观念和新需求为前提，分析了中国在线纠纷解决机制的六大发展趋势，包括更具开放性的纠纷类型、更具共享性的解纷资源、更具便捷性的解纷服务、更具普遍性的解纷规则、更具综合性的平台建设和更具挑战性的国际化发展方向。最后，龙飞副处长针对在线纠纷解决机制平台建设、解纷方式和解纷服务等方面提出了三点期待，并指出中国在线纠纷解决机制的发展和成果必将为世界 ADR 的发展提供“中国经验”。

中华全国人民调解员协会副理事长兼秘书长李冰以《人民调解在互联网的应用》为题做了深入的分析，指出：互联网纠纷解决对群众申报上来的矛盾纠纷信息第一时间进行了收集、归类，并派遣合适的调解员及时调解处置。对处置情况进行动态跟踪、监控，处置结果在互联网上及时公示公开，群众通过网络可以查询处置结果、相关法律法规，选择人民调解员和了解处置结果。真正实现群众矛盾纠纷及时申报，及时化解，及时结案。把各类矛盾纠纷化解在基层，消灭在萌芽状态。“互联网＋”人民调解工作平台成了群众最快捷、最省时、最有效化解矛盾的平台，成了一线维稳的“消防栓”。

中国互联网协会石现升副秘书长和中国互联网协会调解中心王斌秘书长分别发布《中国互联网行业争议解决办法》《中国互联网纠纷解决平台》。“情理法”平台集“受理、调处、培训、资讯”四大板块于一体，实现与互联网纠纷解决平台衔接，实现诉讼与非诉讼无缝衔接，为当事人合法合理主张提供便利，为调解员提供学习成长的场所。

论坛上，海淀区人民法院中关村法庭、知识产权庭，朝阳区人民法院知识产权庭，中国互联网协会调解中心与中关村社会组织联合会联合发布了《有关网络游戏侵犯知识产权案件的调研报告》《关于网络不正当竞争案件的调研报告》《视频聚合平台运行模式在著作权法规制下的司法认定》。

中国互联网协会调解中心联合科研机构及国信嘉宁数据技术有限公司、杭州安存网络科技有限公司、北京联合信任技术服务有限公司、厦门市美亚柏科信息股份有限公司、杭州天谷信息科技有限公司、北京文章无忧信科技有限公司六家电子数据企业联合发布了中国互联网电子证据专家名单，首批入选专家共 27 人，这些专家将为中国互联网争议解决提供专家意见，为已经建立诉调衔接机制的法院提供专家意见。未来争议解决在诉前和诉中调解中将大量应用电子证据，在司法审判中电子证据将发挥越来越大的作用。

中国互联网纠纷解决机制高峰论坛的成功举办，给中国在线纠纷解决机制的发展趋势做出了规划，为今后互联网纠纷解决机制健康发展奠定了基础。

（五）网规与互联网纠纷争议解决论坛

中国互联网协会网络版权工作委员会、调解中心和中关村社会组织联合会联合主办的“网规与互联网纠纷争议解决论坛”于 2016 年 6 月 23 日在北京国际会议中心成功举办。

本次论坛邀请近 400 人参会，分别为：最高人民法院，北京、浙江、上海、江苏、广东等全国各地法院立案庭、知识产权庭代表；北京地区检察院系统及北京市司法局等政府机构领导；中华全国人民调解员协会，中国消费者协会，首都互联网协会、北京仲裁委、证券业协会、保险行业协会等协会的调解组织；以及奇虎 360、e 签宝、新浪等企业代表。

会上，中国电子商务协会政策法律委员会副主任、网规研究中心主任阿拉木斯介绍了网络纠纷以及大众评审制度等网规的特点，为线上纠纷解决提供了参考价值。新浪人民调解委员会法务经理王烁分享微博诉讼与非诉讼衔接机制的经验。国家信息中心电子数据鉴定中心副主任王笑强围绕电子证据的证明力、电子证据的标准和科研、电子证据在打击网络犯罪中的作用等方面做了详细介绍。奇虎 360 科技有限公司法务副总监许坚针对“互联网＋”时代的纠纷提出倡议。各地法官围绕“知识产权案件的诉调衔接机制”“诉讼与非诉讼衔接机制在纠纷解决中的应用”“诉调对接机制在实践中的应用”等内容展开讨论。论坛为与会嘉宾提供了含金量极高的交流平台，让思维碰撞，共话发展。

（六）网络游戏产业保护论坛暨网络游戏反盗版和产业保护联盟发布会

为应对网络游戏盗版猖獗、恶意山寨、不正当竞争等诸多问题，2016 年 11 月 24 日，由中国互联网协会网络版权工作委员会、网络游戏反盗版和产业保护联盟主办的“网络游戏产业保护论坛暨网络游戏反盗版和产业保护联盟发布会”在北京召开。来自工业和信息化部、国家版权局、国家体育总局等行政机关和相关法院人员出席会议并发言，共同关注游戏知识产权保护及行业发展。

会上，“网络游戏反盗版和产业保护联盟”（以下简称游戏联盟）在北京宣告成立。游戏联盟由腾讯、掌趣、畅游、完美世界、百度、新浪、爱九游、聚力、西山居、欢聚时代、联众、搜狗、乐视、网易、烽火连城等十五家游戏运营企业、独立游戏制作人和游戏平台企业发起成立并授牌。

游戏联盟未来将建立联盟成员之间的绿色通道，简化投诉流程，形成快速便捷的侵权投诉处理机制；共建诉调衔接机制，促进诉讼纠纷快速解决；促进电子证据在司法实践中的采用和认可，通过广泛应用电子证据解决取证难、举证难的问题；启动打击游戏外挂的专项维权行动，打击影响游戏运营安全和公平的“毒瘤”；定期召开研讨会议，探讨游戏新型侵权行为，推动解决维权疑难问题；发布游戏侵权案件调研报告、行业年度知识产权保护白皮书。

与会嘉宾围绕网络游戏产业发展的核心竞争力、发展及保护现状、主要挑战和建议等进行探讨，共话游戏知识产权保护及行业发展。

二、培训活动

（一）互联网纠纷人民调解员培训——调解与诉讼相衔接

为帮助涉网纠纷调解员提高涉网纠纷调解技巧、了解司法确认的要求与流程、完善多元化纠纷解决机制，为大量化解互联网纠纷，培养合格调解员奠定良好的基础，由中国互联网协会调解中心和北京人民调解协会联合主办、新浪人民调解委员会协办的“互联网纠纷人民调解员培训——调解与诉讼相衔接”于2016年5月5日在北京大学圆满结束。参加此次培训的学员有新浪、畅游人民调解委员会调解员，中国互联网协会人民调解委员会调解员，北京大学学员以及搜狗等互联网企业代表，共计20多位学员。

本次培训邀请了北京市海淀区人民法院立案庭副庭长宋硕、北京理工大学法学院教授郑晓静。两位讲师分别以《司法确认的要求与流程》及《ADR在我国的发展》为题进行了讲解。中国互联网协会调解中心首席调解员郭玉忠结合工作中的实际经验，为学员们生动地讲解了《调解程序和技巧》。新浪人民调解委员会副主任谷海燕讲解《涉网微博纠纷处理情况》并与现场学员进行经验交流。

培训结束后，由郑晓静教授和中国互联网协会调解中心共同为20多名学员颁发了调解员结业证书。

（二）互联网纠纷人民调解员培训——调解程序与技巧

为全面提升调解员的调解能力，完善多元化纠纷解决机制，由中国互联网协会调解中心和北京人民调解协会联合主办的“互联网纠纷人民调解员培训——调解程序与技巧”于2016年5月26日在北京圆满结束。参加此次培训的学员有百度人民调解委员会调解员，中国互联网协会人民调解委员会调解员，中国人民大学学员以及合一集团、中文在线、蚂蚁金服等互联网企业代表，共计30余位学员。

本次培训从法学、心理学应用等角度，采取授课与模拟体验等方式对涉网纠纷调解员进行培训。中国互联网协会调解中心调解员培训师蒋丽萍和首席调解员郭玉忠先后进行授课，从调解程序的不同阶段、人民调解工作方法与技巧等方面进行讲解。特别是结合实例，安排现场学员进行分组模拟演练，大大提升了学员的学习兴趣并营造了浓厚的学习氛围。

中国青年政治学院副教授师晓霞以《调解中的心理学应用》为题进行了讲解。通过培训，学员进一步增长了调解业务知识，拓宽了调解工作思路，提高了调解实用技能，对涉网纠纷调解工作起到了积极作用。

三、协议合作

深圳前海合作区人民法院与中国互联网协会网络版权工作委员会、中国互联网协会调解中心建立知识产权保护协作机制。

2016年5月28日，深圳前海合作区人民法院诉调对接中心正式揭牌成立。这一诉调对接中心是专门负责诉前调解和诉中调解的机构，是在前海法院主导下的国际化、专业化、社会化的多元化纠纷解决平台。诉调对接中心将包括中国互联网协会调解中心在内的行业调解组织、商事调解组织及其他境内外调解组织引入法院，建立特邀调解员名册，根据当事人自愿原则，在纠纷受理前委托专门的资深调解员或相关调解组织进行调解，调解成功后由法院审查确认调解协议法律效力，从而灵活、高效地解决民商事纠纷。

四、课题项目

2016年，中国互联网协会网络版权工作委员会和调解中心共发布课题报告4项，分别是《移动互联网环境下文字作品著作权保护问题调研报告》《关于网络不正当竞争纠纷案件的调研报告》《网络游戏侵犯知识产权案件的调研报告》《视频聚合平台运行模式在著作权法规制下的司法认定》。

（一）《移动互联网环境下文字作品著作权保护问题调研报告》

该报告分析了网站、微博、微信、移动应用商店等渠道传播文字作品的经营模式，归纳总结了类型化案件的裁判方法，对案件审理过程中的疑点难点问题进行详细分析，并提出有效的应对举措。

对于微博与微信内容发布者与转发者的法律责任，报告认为，通过微博或微信公众号传播文字作品应受信息网络传播权的规制，发布者应对其发布的内容承担法律责任，如其发布的文字作品系侵权作品，则侵犯了作品的信息网络传播权。对于转发者，用户通过点击微博上的转发按钮进行转发，在转发过程中并未生成新的复制件，并不构成对作品复制权的侵犯。至于转发微博内容的行为是否侵犯了信息网络传播权，目前对该问题仍存在争议，但如果转发微博的目的并不在于传播被转发微博内含有的作品，而是为了对被转发的微博内容发表评论意见，使评论更具针对性，则该转发行为可以构成著作权法上的合理使用。

（二）《关于网络不正当竞争纠纷案件的调研报告》

该调研报告首先对近五年海淀法院审理的网络不正当竞争案件进行了全面梳理，充分展现了此类案件的受理情况、涉案当事人情况、案由分布情况、案件裁判方式、审理期限、诉赔情况变化等。随着互联网行业的不断推进与发展，网络不正当竞争纠纷呈现了许多新的特点，对此，调研报告从争议行为对传统行业的依赖程度、争议行为的复杂程度以及是否可适用类型化不正当竞争行为规定三个维度对此类案件进行了分类并总结不同类型案件的特点，重点分析了传统不正当竞争行为在网络环境下引发的不正当竞争纠纷、经营网络产品或服务过程中引发的不正当竞争纠纷等类型的案件。

在此基础上，调研报告总结了此类案件事实查明及法律适用过程中的难点。事实查明难点包括技术创新与不正当竞争的界线判断存在困难、对涉及商业模式法律保护问题判断存在困难、专家辅助人辅助技术事实查明的作用有限、电子证据的审查和认定标准尚未统一、网络信息的真实性难以查明等；法律适用过程中存在的难点包括《反不正当竞争法》类型化不正当竞争行为规定的适用难点、《反不正当竞争法》一般条款的适用难点、利益平衡原则的考量和适用难点、诉讼禁令的适用难点等，并对突破上述难点进行了分析与建议。在该部分中，调研报告重点阐述了非公益必要不干扰原则的适用、正当商业模式产生的商业利益受法律保护、专家辅助人的制度完善、类型化不正当竞争行为的区别、谨慎适用诉讼禁令的原因等方面的内容。

（三）《网络游戏侵犯知识产权案件的调研报告》

该调研报告在调查游戏产业的发展现状、对辖区乃至全国近年来网络游戏侵犯知识产权典型案例进行梳理的基础上，通过案例研究、数据统计、资料分析、调查走访、专题讨论等方式，梳理、总结目前网络游戏侵犯知识产权案件的类型、特点、产生原因、发展趋势、法律难点、案由选择、实务操作等问题，给出科学、合理的司法对策，解决目前存在的司法救济不到位、诉讼禁令下达难、诉讼进程推进难等问题，并就游戏产业发展中的法律风险防范、纠纷解决策略等提出相关建议。

（四）《视频聚合平台运行模式在著作权法规制下的司法认定》

该报告指出，随着移动智能设备的普及，视频聚合平台发展迅猛。视频聚合平台采用所谓的深度链接技术直接向用户提供视频资源。具体来说，根据其行为手段及所采取的技术手段的不同，视频聚合平台又分为采用一般深度链接手段的聚合平台及采用盗链手段的聚合平台。其中，采用盗链手段的视频聚合平台违背被盗链的视频网站的意志，通过技术破解措施，直接盗链视频网站的资源，达到向用户提供作品的目的。上述盗链行为，应在著作权法上认定为信息网络传播权的直接侵权行为。

五、建立调解工作站

2016年，中国互联网协会调解中心分别在北京市海淀区人民法院和北京市朝阳区人民法院设立互联网纠纷调解室。

海淀法院调解室2016年9月28日至12月15日，共受理诉前案件224件，调解成功85件，在调过程67件；朝阳法院调解室2016年10月至12月，共受理诉前案件147件，调解成功97件，在调过程38件。

（陈　颖）

版权扫描

BAN QUAN SAO MIAO

版权界动态

◆立　法

【中摄权协受邀参加国务院修法研讨会】 2016年2月，国务院法制办召开《著作权法》专题论证会，就国务院第三次修改《著作权法》邀请全国人大、中国社科院、中国人民大学、北京外国语大学、中央电视台、北京相关法院和摄影界的专家、学者进行研讨论证，围绕《著作权法（修订草案送审稿）》中关于作品的分类、作品的界定和各类作品的具体含义等内容听取意见。自国务院启动第三次修改《著作权法》以来，摄影界积极配合深入参与，先后召开了多次研讨会和座谈会，广泛听取摄影家的意见和建议。

中国文联党组成员、副主席，中国摄影著作权协会主席李前光就中国摄影著作权协会提出并被《著作权法（修订草案送审稿）》采纳的延长摄影作品保护期、增加视觉艺术追续权、完善广播权法定许可等三项修法建议，专门召开摄影界座谈会，听取摄影家意见并把这些意见及时反馈到国家立法和主持修法的相关部门。

本次研讨会上，中国摄影著作权协会总干事林涛就什么是摄影作品原作，以及中国摄影著作权协会为配合修法所推出的摄影作品限量鉴证服务发表了意见。参加此次会议的人员认为，有必要再次召开专门的会议，就送审稿中涉及的追续权问题进行深入研讨。

（资料来源：中国摄影家协会网）

【国务院同意建立知识产权战略实施工作部际联席会议制度】 2016年3月30日，国务院为贯彻落实《国家知识产权战略纲要》和《国务院关于新形势下加快知识产权强国建设的若干意见》，加强组织领导和统筹协调配合，深入实施国家知识产权战略，加快知识产权强国建设，同意建立知识产权战略实施工作部际联席会议制度。

联席会议主要职责是在国务院领导下，统筹协调国家知识产权战略的实施和知识产权强国建设工作。包括加强对国家知识产权战略实施和知识产权强国建设工作的宏观指导；研究深入实施国家知识产权战略和加强知识产权强国建设的重大方针政策，制定国家知识产权战略实施计划；指导、督促、检查有关政策措施的落实；协调解决国家知识产权战略实施和知识产权强国建设中的重大问题；完成国务院交办的其他事项。

联席会议由知识产权局、中央宣传部（国务院新闻办）、最高法院、最高检察院、外交部、发展改革委、新闻出版广电总局（版权局）等31个部门和单位组成，知识产权局为牵头单位。

国务院分管知识产权工作的领导同志担任联席会议召集人，协助分管知识产权工作的国务院副秘书长和知识产权局主要负责同志担任副召集人。联席会议办公室设在知识产权局，承担联席会议的日常工作。

联席会议根据工作需要定期或不定期召开会议，由召集人或召集人委托的副召集人主持。成员单位根据工作需要可以提出召开会议的建议。

各成员单位要按照职责分工，深入研究国家知识产权战略实施和知识产权强国建设工作中的重大问题，制定相关配套政策措施或提出建议；及时向联席会议办公室提出需讨论的议题，认真落实联席会议确定的工作任务和议定事项；互通信息，相互支持，密切配合，形成合力，充分发挥联席会议的作用。

（资料来源　新华社）

◆司　法

【《奔跑吧兄弟》官微涉著作权纠纷】 2016年1月，因认为《奔跑吧兄弟》官方微博在未经许可的情况下，擅自使用其作品，原告万女士将浙江广播电视集团、北京微梦创科网络有限公司以侵犯著作权为由诉至法院，索赔55 500元。2016年1月4日，海淀法院表示已受理此案。

原告万女士诉称，其系漫画师、插画师，是新浪微博“养猫画画的随随”的实名认证用户。2014年10月24日，其在个人微博上发布了涉案漫画图片，后发现浙江广电经营的浙江卫视频道所属的《奔跑吧兄弟》官方微博未经许可，擅自在微博中使用涉案漫画作品用于广告宣传，且该广告在使用其作品过程中未署名、未支付报酬并对原作品进行了修改，故万女士认为该行为侵犯了其署名权、修改权、复制权、发行权、信息网络传播权、获得报酬权等著作权。万女士另称，微梦公司作为新浪微博网站的经营者和管理者，并未尽到相应的审查义务，应承担停止侵权、公开致歉的法律责任。万女士认为，二被告的行为构成共同侵权，故将二被告诉至法院，要求法院判令二被告停止侵权、公开致歉并赔偿经济损失及合理支出共计 55 500 元。

（资料来源：《北京晨报》　作者：黄晓宇）

【北京三男子因架设“私服”侵犯游戏《笑傲江湖 OL》著作权罪被判刑】　2016 年 1 月 5 日，三男子因架设游戏私服并收取玩家充值款，被海淀法院认定构成侵犯著作权罪，并判处刑罚。被告人何某、厉某、罗某在网络上相识。2013 年 10 月底，何某通过论坛从一外国人处以 3 万美元的价格购买《笑傲江湖 OL》网络游戏程序。后何某负责运营、租用服务器等，罗某负责编写、修改程序，厉某负责上传服务端、调试客户端登录游戏等。游戏程序修改完成后，三人租用美国、香港的服务器，通过私服论坛进行推广吸引玩家，自 2013 年 11 月起，开始运营《笑傲江湖 OL》私服并通过销售元宝（游戏币）进行营利，收取玩家充值款共计 31 万余元。2014 年 2 月 21 日，完美公司通过内部手段检测到有人利用公司的技术手段在外地开设私服并报警。同年 4 月 15 日、4 月 17 日，何某、厉某被抓获，10 月 21 日，罗某投案自首。后何某、厉某、罗某由各自家属分别代为向完美公司赔偿了 10 万元和 20 万元，完美公司对三人表示谅解。

庭审中，三人对指控的事实和罪名均无异议。法院审理后认为，三人以营利为目的，未经著作权人许可，发行运营其网络游戏软件作品，情节特别严重，其行为均已构成侵犯著作权罪。鉴于三名被告人均系初犯，到案后能积极退赔和弥补被害单位的经济损失，取得被害单位的谅解，具有真诚悔罪的表现，认罪态度较好，最后，法院从轻判处何某、厉某有期徒刑 3 年，缓刑 4 年，罚金 16 万元；判处罗某有期徒刑 2 年，缓刑 3 年，罚金 10 万元。

（资料来源：《北京日报》　作者：高　健　文海宣）

【四川省阆中市审结两起制售盗版音像制品刑事案】　2016 年 1 月，四川省阆中市人民法院依法对阆中市“1 • 20”京泰音像制品店和同乐堂音像制品零售店制售盗版音像制品案件做出判决：赵某某犯侵犯著作权罪，判处有期徒刑 2 年 6 个月，缓刑 3 年 6 个月，并处罚金人民币 15 000 元，没收其盗版音像制品 13 416 张；陈某某犯侵犯著作权罪，判处有期徒刑 2 年，缓刑 3 年，并处罚金人民币 8 000 元，没收其盗版音像制品7 305 张。

经查，赵某某为阆中市人，自 2006 年 8 月起在阆中市关王庙街 10 号经营京泰音像制品店；陈某某为阆中市人，自 2010 年 4 月起在阆中市关王庙街 10 号经营同乐堂音像制品零售店，对外公开出售音像制品。2015 年 1 月 20 日，南充市“扫黄打非”办组织检查组检查时，查获京泰音像制品店用于公开销售的盗版音像制品 4 193 种、13 416 张，查获同乐堂音像制品零售店用于公开销售的盗版音像制品 1 847种、7 305 张。查获的音像制品系赵某某、陈某某违法复制，但因相关职能机构及时查处而未能销售。

（资料来源：《中国新闻出版广电报》　作者：川　为）

【手游《幻想江湖》被判侵犯著作权】　2016 年 1 月，北京市石景山区人民法院审结了一起金庸小说改编网游引发的著作权侵权及不正当竞争纠纷案件，判令广州游爱网络技术有限公司（下称游爱公司）等 3 家公司停止侵权，并赔偿北京畅游时代数码技术有限公司（下称畅游公司）经济损失 35 万余元。

原告畅游公司诉称，其于 2013 年斥资千万元从金庸处获得《天龙八部》《鹿鼎记》等 11 部小说的手机游戏改编权，并先后发布多款相关游戏。游爱公司未经许可，在其开发的移动端网络游戏《幻想江湖》中大量使用了《鹿鼎记》《天龙八部》的故事情节、人物姓名及道具名称，并从中获利，故诉至法院，请求判令赔偿经济损失 500 余万元。

游爱公司等答辩称，被诉游戏未侵犯金庸文字作品及畅游公司相关游戏的著作权。

法院经审理认为，被诉游戏《幻想江湖》中“双双被绑架，小宝营救”“铁面喜欢阿紫”等情节、人物与金庸小说《鹿鼎记》《天龙八部》中相关内容构成实质性相似。这些内容已经超出合理使用的范围，侵犯了畅游公司的改编权，遂判令游爱公司等 3 家公司立即停止侵权并赔偿畅游公司经济损失及合理支出 35 万余元。

（资料来源：《中国知识产权报》　作者：苏　杰）

【"大头儿子"著作权案二审央视胜诉】 2016年2月25日，"大头儿子和小头爸爸"著作权案二审结果公开。根据浙江省杭州市中级人民法院的判决，央视动画有限公司有权行使1995版动画片的全部著作权及动画片中包括但不限于文学剧本、造型设计、美术设计等作品除署名权外的全部著作权；有权在2013版《新大头儿子和小头爸爸》中使用1995版动画片中的人物形象；有权在CCTV、各地方电视台、央视网上进行播放；有权宣传、展览2013版动画片形象；有权许可中国木偶艺术剧院使用2013版动画人物形象进行舞台剧表演等权利。

法院认定，杭州大头儿子公司受让于刘某1994年创作的草图并无载体，且多年来未进行单独发表，没有任何知名度的积累，而央视及央视动画公司的创作团队最终完成了动画角色造型和整部动画片的创作，并使大头儿子、小头爸爸、围裙妈妈成为家喻户晓的知名动画品牌，对人物形象的知名度和影响力有巨大贡献，获得了社会公众的广泛认知，取得了较好的社会效果。并据此驳回了杭州大头儿子公司相关的无理诉求。对此法院表示，无论是动画片，还是木偶剧，均具有公共文化的属性，符合著作权法立法宗旨，鼓励作品的创作和传播。

另一方面，杭州大头儿子公司无法提供请求保护的原作品，无法提供所谓取得著作权作品的载体，其通过受让取得的作品也非作品登记证书中所记载的作品。据此，法院驳回了杭州大头儿子公司其他相关的不合理上诉，认为其缺乏事实和法律依据。

（资料来源：北青网）

【海淀法院：影视聚合平台盗链行为不属于合理使用】 2016年2月，北京市海淀区人民法院就深圳市腾讯计算机系统有限公司诉北京易联伟达科技有限公司侵犯作品信息网络传播纠纷一案做出一审判决。

海淀法院认定影视聚合平台盗链行为不属于合理使用，并非合法链接，而属于侵权行为；易联伟达公司的一系列行为相互结合，导致独家信息网络传播权人本应获取的授权利益在一定范围内落空，给腾讯公司造成了损害，构成侵权，应承担相应的民事赔偿责任。为此，判决被告易联伟达公司赔偿原告腾讯公司经济损失包括合理支出35 000元。

法院经审理认为，该案的关键在于，公证书显示在《快看影视》APP中搜索《宫锁连城》一剧时，界面的网址来源一栏显示相关视频的来源是乐视网，而非直接存放于《快看影视》的服务器，即《快看影视》APP扮演的是视频聚合平台的角色。而乐视网对涉案影视作品的播放是有合法授权的。易联伟达公司据此主张由于自己仅提供搜索链接服务，被链接的视频又是合法的，故其链接行为并不构成侵权。腾讯公司则主张，易联伟达公司进行了选择、编辑、整理、专题分类等工作，同时破坏了乐视网所采取的禁链措施，构成对其独家信息网络传播权的侵害。

海淀法院指出，对视频聚合平台经营者易联伟达公司的相关行为是否构成侵犯著作权的法律判断，需要综合独家信息网络传播权人分销授权的商业逻辑、影视聚合平台经营获利的商业逻辑、影视聚合平台是否仅提供单纯链接服务、影视聚合平台盗链行为的非法性及主观过错、影视聚合平台盗链行为不属于合理使用等因素。易联伟达公司经营的《快看影视》APP并非仅提供链接技术服务，还进行了选择、编辑、整理、专题分类等行为，且主观上存在积极破坏他人技术措施、通过盗链获取不正当利益的过错。易联伟达公司的一系列行为相互结合，实现了在其平台上向公众提供涉案作品播放等服务的实质性替代效果，对涉案作品超出授权渠道、范围传播具有一定控制、管理能力，因此构成侵权。

（资料来源：《法制日报》　作者：王开广）

【手游公司擅用金庸小说内容被判侵权】 2016年2月，5家游戏公司因金庸名著的独家改编权之争而对簿公堂，上海市杨浦区人民法院经审理认定平杰公司侵犯达兴公司的游戏改编权，判决赔偿其经济损失50万元。

达兴公司早在2013年与作家金庸就《笑傲江湖》《神雕侠侣》等4部作品签订了移动终端游戏软件改编授权合同，约定该公司有权以4部小说的名称、故事、人物为蓝本，改编制作专供移动终端用户使用的游戏软件。

2014年5月，达兴公司发现平杰公司自行开发了一款名为《六大门派》的手机游戏。达兴公司认为，平杰公司在未经其授权的情况下，擅自以《神雕侠侣》《笑傲江湖》等小说为蓝本制作游戏，还在宣传该手机游戏时大量使用与金庸小说有关的元素；另有3公司参与了《六大门派》手机游戏的实际运营，并从中获利。达兴公司以侵犯作品改编权、不正当竞争为由，将平杰公司等诉至法院，要求上述4家公司立即停止侵权。

平杰公司辩称，《六大门派》是公司独立创作完成的游戏，并于2014年4月取得了该游戏的软件著作权登记证书，游戏人物名称虽与金庸小说里的人物部分一致，但是脱离了金庸小说的情节，在游戏宣传时，该公司也没有将“改编自金庸作品”作为广告噱头。

另外3家游戏公司均称，自身并非《六大门派》手机游戏的运营商，而是网络服务提供商，游戏收益最终由平杰公司享有，3家公司在涉案游戏上传至平台时，均要求平杰公司提供了相应的软件著作权登记证书，已尽合理审查义务，不应承担侵权连带责任。

杨浦区法院认为，从人物角度来看，《六大门派》游戏人物与金庸小说《笑傲江湖》中的人物名称完全相同。在达兴公司发出侵权函后，平杰公司将游戏人物名称略做改动，但也仅是同音字替换，人物关系仍与《笑傲江湖》完全一致；从故事情节发展来看，涉案游戏与《笑傲江湖》前7章情节发展基本相同；从细节设计来看，涉案游戏中再现了《笑傲江湖》中诸多经典桥段。法院认为，《六大门派》游戏构成对小说《笑傲江湖》前7章的改编行为，但因未涉及另外3部小说的故事情节，所以不构成对其他3部小说独家改编权的侵犯。在游戏广告宣传方面，平杰公司运用了诸多《笑傲江湖》等小说中的元素，对达兴公司开发运营相关游戏产生不利影响，构成不正当竞争。其他3家公司均属于网络服务提供者，从形式上已经尽到了合理注意义务，不承担侵权责任。

（资料来源：《中国知识产权报》　作者：张静露）

【乐动卓越起诉昆仑万维“MT游戏”侵权，法院判决昆仑万维停止不正当竞争行为】　2016年2月，北京乐动卓越科技有限公司诉被告北京昆仑万维科技股份有限公司等企业旗下的移动终端游戏《超级MT》侵权《我叫MT》案尘埃落定。被告被判连带赔偿乐动卓越经济损失50万元，合理支出3.5万元。

乐动卓越公司诉称，其是移动终端游戏《我叫MT Online》《我叫MT2》（统称《我叫MT》）的著作权人，对游戏名称、人物名称享有独占被许可使用权，对人物形象享有美术作品的著作权；被告未经许可，在《超级MT》游戏中使用与《我叫MT》游戏名称、人物名称、人物形象相近的名称和人物，侵犯了乐动卓越公司的著作权。而且《超级MT》游戏抄袭了《我叫MT》游戏的名称，且两游戏的人物名称也十分相似，被告在游戏的宣传过程中，使用与《我叫MT》游戏相关的宣传用语，构成不正当竞争行为。

北京知识产权法院判决认为：由于原告的游戏名称和游戏人物名称不构成作品，且被诉游戏亦未使用乐动卓越公司在其改编作品中的独创性表达，故被告不构成著作权侵权；但是，乐动卓越公司的游戏名称及人物名称构成手机游戏类服务上的特有名称，被告在主观明知的情况下提供被诉游戏的下载及宣传，构成擅自使用原告知名服务特有名称的行为。此外，被告“我叫MT原班人马配音”这一宣传用语，内容亦非客观事实，构成虚假宣传行为。

最终，法院判决各被告立即停止不正当竞争行为，连带赔偿原告北京乐动卓越科技有限公司经济损失50万元，以及合理支出3.5万元。

（资料来源：《北京日报》）

【《QQ阅读》借势营销《明妃传》被叫停】　2016年2月，上海市浦东新区人民法院发出民事裁定书，对阅文集团与掌阅科技产生争议的《女医·明妃传》电子书一事做出裁定，要求上海阅文信息技术有限公司立即停止在《QQ阅读》客户端上销售小说《明妃传》过程中使用“女医明妃传”字样。

掌阅科技作为《女医·明妃传》电子书独家销售平台，于2016年2月16日起上线销售电子书。但早在2016年2月2日，阅文集团就在《QQ阅读》客户端上销售名为《明妃传》的小说，并利用电视剧《女医·明妃传》对该小说进行推广介绍。掌阅科技认为，《明妃传》的小说书名、作者、人物、故事、情节等与《女医·明妃传》系不同作品，与热播电视剧也无任何关系。在原著小说的关注度大幅提升的时期，阅文集团在电视剧开播前夕上架小说《明妃传》，会使消费者误以为其销售的作品即为原著小说，构成不正当竞争。因此要求对阅文集团的行为采取临时禁令措施。

法院认为，阅文集团在销售小说《明妃传》过程中使用了“刘诗诗、霍建华主演：女医明妃传”字样，这种行为易使消费者误以为销售的小说为电视剧《女医·明妃传》的原著小说或与电视剧《女医·明妃传》的原著小说存在一定关联性，造成相关公众的混淆和误认。法院裁定上海阅文信息技术有限公司立即停止在《QQ阅读》客户端上销售小说《明妃传》过程中使用“女医明妃传”字样。

（资料来源：《中国新闻出版广电报》　作者：任晓宁）

【音乐剧《断桥》版权之争结束】 2016年3月，音乐剧《断桥》的版权之争尘埃落定。原告公司杭州断桥文化艺术发展有限公司称，自己是原创音乐剧《断桥》及剧本的版权人。被告浙江翰三甲文化艺术发展有限公司在广东省珠海市某演剧院演出的音乐剧《断桥》，在剧本、音乐、舞台、背景等方面与其享有版权的音乐剧《断桥》完全一致，故认为被告公司的行为侵犯了其著作权，诉至下城法院，要求对方停止侵权、赔礼道歉、赔偿经济损失和合理费用近47万元。

被告则表示，音乐剧《断桥》是由杭州剧院创作并享有合法表演权及经营权，而杭州剧院委托其用于演出经营，故不构成侵权。

法院表示，本案的争议焦点在于原告公司对涉案的音乐剧《断桥》是否享有著作权。关于《断桥》的剧本，庭审中三方均明确其作者为田某。而原告公司提交了作品登记证书，用以证明洪某利用其资源创作完成并发表了《断桥》的剧本。但经法院调查，该主张与查明事实不符。故原告公司不能证明其享有《断桥》剧本的著作权。

关于《断桥》的19首音乐作品，双方均认可19首音乐作品的曲作者为祁某，但原告公司称不清楚词作者是谁。杭州剧院则表示，词作者为剧本创作者田某。经法院比对，其中17首音乐作品含有歌词内容，且歌词内容均包含在《断桥》剧本中，可确认这17首音乐作品的词作者为田某；另2首仅有曲谱、没有歌词的音乐作品作者应为曲作者祁某。

原告公司没能证明祁某和田某的创作是在己方的主持之下完成的，根据《著作权法》的规定，仅凭其提供的作品登记证书是不够的，所以原告对19首音乐作品，也没有著作权。

关于音乐剧《断桥》的作品类型，原告公司主张其为电视作品，表现形式是录制有演出内容的光盘，杭州剧院则对此存有异议。法院认为，音乐剧《断桥》是将剧本结合作曲、灯光、舞美，由导演、制作人、演员等参与，以音乐剧形式在舞台上演出的作品，因此其作品类型应属于戏剧作品。

原告公司将音乐剧《断桥》的演出过程录制成光盘的行为并非创作作品的过程，不因其录制行为而享有音乐剧《断桥》的著作权。

因此，原告公司提交的各项证据未能证明其是戏剧作品音乐剧《断桥》的剧本、19首音乐作品的著作权人，无权主张被告公司侵犯了其著作权。下城法院对此案做出一审判决，判令驳回原告诉请。当事人均表示服从判决，不再上诉。

（资料来源：杭州网　作者：陈少思　夏　法）

【银川破获全国首起手游侵犯著作权案】 2016年4月11日，记者从银川市公安局侵犯知识产权犯罪侦查支队了解到，该支队于2015年11月破获全国首起手游侵犯著作权案，涉案金额过亿元。经过近5个月的侦查取证，该案的侦查工作已进入尾声。

2015年10月19日，上海数龙科技有限公司向知侦支队报案：由广州创思信息技术有限公司研发并运营的手机游戏《烈焰手游》在作品名称、NPC、角色形象名称、地图场景、技能、动画特效等方面存在大量抄袭上海数龙科技有限公司享有著作权的游戏《热血传奇》的情况，广州创思信息技术有限公司的行为涉嫌侵犯著作权。

知侦支队通过调查取证了解到，安徽德力日用玻璃股份有限公司准备以25亿元左右的资产评估价值收购广州创思信息技术有限公司并重组上市，《烈焰手游》的著作权登记人为上海创文信息技术有限公司，即广州创思信息技术有限公司的全资子公司。

知侦支队于2015年10月底对广州创思信息技术有限公司涉嫌侵犯著作权进行立案，以单位犯罪将广州创思信息技术有限公司列为犯罪嫌疑人，并迅速锁定了广州创思信息技术有限公司的实际控制人兼CEO黄某、《烈焰手游》的项目经理李某2名犯罪嫌疑人，经过部署，最终将2人在广州市抓获并采取相应强制措施。

经查证，黄某在明知公司研发的《烈焰手游》对《热血传奇》构成侵权的情况下，仍指使公司员工在《烈焰手游》中运用了大量《热血传奇》的元素。经过初步审计，本案中涉嫌侵权的《烈焰手游》从上线至今的总流水收入近1亿元，知侦支队第一时间对广州创思信息技术有限公司的涉案银行账户依法进行了冻结，共计冻结资金6 000余万元。

（资料来源：《宁夏日报》　作者：李　锦　陶　涛）

【漫画《蜡笔小新》遭盗播　权利人起诉】 2016年4月，北京市石景山区人民法院受理了一起漫画作品《蜡笔小新》引发的侵害作品信息网络传播权纠纷案件。

原告北京某动漫公司诉称，其已经依法取得授权，享有漫画作品《蜡笔小新》中文翻译版在中国大陆地区的信息网络传播权。被告北京某科技公司未经授权，通过互联网在其经营的《魔屏漫画》苹果手机客户端，向用户提供漫画作品《蜡笔小新》

中文版的在线观看及下载服务，侵害了原告对该漫画作品享有的独占性信息网络传播权，给原告造成了经济损失。故诉至法院，请求判令被告北京某科技公司停止侵权并赔偿原告经济损失10万元。

（资料来源：《中国新闻出版广电报》 作者：郑天晓）

【擅用金庸武侠作品元素 游戏公司败诉赔偿百万元】 2016年4月21日，北京知识产权法院终审判决，认定北京普游天下等两家游戏公司行为构成不正当竞争，判决共同赔偿北京畅游时代数码公司100万元。

北京畅游时代数码公司一审起诉称，2013年经金庸授权，其获得了《天龙八部》《鹿鼎记》《书剑恩仇录》等11部作品在中国大陆地区改编为游戏软件的独家移动端游戏软件改编权。2014年，普游公司和微游公司未经许可，在其开发、运营的手机网络游戏中使用了金庸作品中的人物名称、武功或装备及部分情节，并在游戏宣传上自称“云集了‘飞雪连天射白鹿，笑书神侠倚碧鸳’中的枭雄豪杰”。

畅游公司认为，普游公司和微游公司的行为，不正当地降低了制作成本、借助金庸作品的知名度不正当地诱使用户使用，请求判令立即停止不正当竞争行为，消除影响，赔偿各项损失近500万元。

普游公司一审辩称，畅游公司不具备诉讼主体资格，且其开发的游戏软件与金庸作品不一样，其游戏元素来源于凭空想象，是具有独创性的新作品，未构成侵权。微游公司辩称，涉案游戏软件与其无关。

一审法院认定，普游公司和微游公司的行为构成不正当竞争，应对涉案游戏共同承担法律责任，判决其立即停止涉案不正当竞争行为，并停止运营涉案游戏，共同向畅游公司赔偿各项经济损失共计100万元。

随后，普游公司和微游公司上诉至北京知识产权法院。

经审理，法院终审判定撤销了一审停止运营涉案游戏的判决，维持了普游公司等两公司共同向畅游公司赔偿各项经济损失共计100万元的判决。

（资料来源：《京华时报》 作者：杨凤临）

【网店售卖画像复制品侵权 卖家被判赔偿著作权人4.5万元】 2016年4月，法院经审理，认定被告淘宝一卖家侵害了原告著作权人天津画家邹起奎的复制权和信息网络传播权，判令其赔偿原告4.5万元。

邹起奎是天津杨柳青画社画家，先后出版了多部美术作品。在公开出版的《邹起奎画集》中，有周恩来画像、巴达维画像和李显龙画像。淘宝卖家唐裕华在淘宝网经营“北京祥红云天书画院”，并在该店铺中标价售卖周恩来、巴达维、李显龙画像，在商品描述中注明“邹起奎”。截至邹起奎2014年7月31日进行证据保全时，唐裕华的网络店铺中被诉侵权作品的销售记录为零。2014年9月1日，邹起奎致函浙江淘宝网络有限公司，要求其提供包括“北京祥红云天书画院”在内的涉嫌侵害邹起奎著作权的13家网络店铺的相关信息，淘宝公司将上述卖家信息反馈给邹起奎，并删除了相关网页链接。邹起奎随后提起诉讼，请求唐裕华及淘宝公司立即停止侵权并赔偿经济损失。

法院经审理认为，经比对，《邹起奎画集》中的原作品与被诉侵权作品构图及表现内容基本一致，且被诉侵权作品的商品介绍中已标明“邹起奎”，能够认定唐裕华在淘宝网站上标价售卖的被诉侵权作品为邹起奎作品的复制品。未经著作权人邹起奎同意，唐裕华在网络上公开销售邹起奎作品的复制品，应承担相应的侵权责任，但唐裕华在商品介绍中已注明“邹起奎”，未以他人名义署名作品，不存在侵害邹起奎署名权的行为，故认定唐裕华侵害了邹起奎享有的作品复制权和信息网络传播权。淘宝公司提交公证书证明已主动删除淘宝网上相关链接，履行了其对网站的管理义务，淘宝公司不承担赔偿责任。故判决唐裕华赔偿邹起奎经济损失及维权合理费用共计4.5万元。

（资料来源：《今晚报》 作者：孙启明 祖先海）

【齐白石后人与湖南美术出版社著作权系列纠纷案达成和解】 2016年5月6日，齐白石后人与湖南美术出版社有限责任公司著作权系列纠纷案，在天津市第一中级人民法院法官的主持下达成和解协议，由该出版社给付齐白石后人110套《齐白石全集》。

齐良末、齐秉颐、齐来欢、齐展仪诉称，4人系我国著名画家齐白石系列美术作品的合法继承人，湖南美术出版社在没有得到合法授权的情况下，以营利为目的，多年来非法出版发行《齐白石全集》（第五卷）。4人认为上述行为侵犯了涉案作品的著作权，请求判令湖南美术出版社停止侵权并承担赔偿经济损失的责任。

该案经一审法院判决后，湖南美术出版社上诉至天津市一中院，天津市一中院组成5人合议庭，进行公开开庭审理。

开庭后，经法官多次调解，双方连同申诉到天津市高院和正在基层法院审理的322件齐白石作品著作权纠纷案件一并达成和解协议，其中一件案件双方以和解方式结案，其余321件案件，齐良末、齐秉颐、齐来欢、齐展仪申请撤回起诉，湖南美术出版社申请撤回上诉。

湖南美术出版社给付齐良末、齐秉颐、齐来欢、齐展仪110套《齐白石全集》，由齐秉颐代表全体齐白石后人保管和分配给其他齐白石后人；双方在一审法院形成的7件著作权纠纷案件，齐良末、齐秉颐、齐来欢、齐展仪不再申请执行；就齐白石作品及书籍著作权问题互不追究，不再有任何争议。

（资料来源：《法制日报》

作者：张　驰　孙玲姚　泓　冰）

【首例电竞直播侵权案终审宣判】 2016年5月，国内首例电子竞技类游戏赛事网络直播引发的著作权侵权及不正当竞争纠纷案在上海终审宣判。上海知识产权法院对上诉人广州斗鱼网络科技有限公司（简称斗鱼公司）诉被上诉人上海耀宇文化传媒有限公司（简称耀宇公司）著作权侵权及不正当竞争纠纷上诉案做出二审判决，驳回上诉，维持原判。斗鱼公司需赔偿耀宇公司经济损失人民币100万元和维权的合理开支人民币10万元，并在斗鱼网站首页显著位置刊登声明，消除不良影响。

耀宇公司与DOTA2（刀塔2）代理运营商完美世界（北京）网络技术有限公司（以下简称完美公司）签订合作协议，共同打造2015年DOTA2亚洲邀请赛，耀宇公司获得该赛事在中国大陆地区的独家视频转播权。

耀宇公司认为，斗鱼公司未经授权，通过客户端旁观模式截取赛事画面配以主播点评的方式，实时直播该赛事，且在直播时使用了耀宇公司的标识。因此，耀宇公司诉至法院，请求判令斗鱼公司停止侵权，消除影响，赔偿经济损失及合理费用共计821.1万元。

一审法院审理后认为，网络用户仅能在斗鱼公司直播的特定时间段内观看正在进行的涉案赛事，耀宇公司主张被侵害的视频转播权既不属于信息网络传播权，亦不属于其他法定的著作权权利，且比赛画面不属于著作权法规定的作品，故耀宇公司关于斗鱼公司侵害其著作权的主张不能成立，但认定斗鱼公司构成不正当竞争，遂判决其承担消除影响、赔偿经济损失及合理费用共计110万元。

一审判决之后，斗鱼向上海知产法院提起上诉，但二审判决，驳回上诉，维持原判。

有分析指出，专业的游戏直播网站，应当知晓如此大规模的知名赛事转播必须经授权许可。本案的判决结果对规范电竞直播有一定的指导作用。

（资料来源：TechWeb）

【百度云盘擅传《金陵十三钗》被判赔偿】

2016年5月，北京市海淀区人民法院就原告乐视网（天津）信息技术有限公司诉被告北京百度网讯科技有限公司侵害作品信息网络传播权纠纷案做出一审判决，判决认定百度公司经营的百度云网盘服务通过不同方式帮助用户非法传播电影《金陵十三钗》，应当赔偿乐视天津公司经济损失1.4万元。

乐视天津公司享有电影《金陵十三钗》的信息网络传播权。该公司发现，百度公司经营的百度云网盘在其网页版、手机客户端和iPad版的“达人推荐”及“热门资源”中均提供了涉案电影的播放服务。乐视天津公司请求法院判令百度公司赔偿其经济损失及合理开支共计4万元。

法院经审理后认为，百度公司作为百度云服务的提供者，在其网页版和手机客户端中，虽然并未直接上传涉案电影，但作为信息存储空间服务的网络服务提供者，在“达人推荐”页面对明确标注提供“手机电影下载”“手机、平板、iPad、iPhone电影下载”且页面存在大量电影资源的用户进行了推荐，并在iPad版的页面首要位置对未经任何备案的7060影视网进行了推荐和链接。百度公司的这种行为虽然并未直接对电影作品进行推荐和链接，但其所采取的通过对侵权用户及侵权网站进行推荐的方式，客观上增加了涉案作品被侵权传播的机会和可能，主观上具有明显过错，应当承担侵权责任。据此，法院做出上述判决。宣判后，双方均未表示是否提起上诉。

（资料来源：《中国新闻出版广电报》　作者：邹　韧）

【爱奇艺诉华数传媒侵权索赔30万元】 2016年5月，因“华数TV”未经允许提供原告权属作品《重返20岁》的在线播放服务，原告北京爱奇艺科技有限公司以侵害信息网络传播权纠纷为由诉至法院，请求判令被告华数传媒网络有限公司停止侵害、赔礼道歉，并赔偿经济损失及合理费用合计30万元。北京市海淀区人民法院受理了此案。

原告诉称，其经北京奇艺科技有限公司授权，依法享有影视作品《重返 20 岁》在中国大陆地区的独占性信息网络传播权。被告华数传媒网络有限公司为“华数 TV”电视端的运营单位，未经其允许在“华数 TV”上非法向公众提供涉案影视作品的在线播放服务。

原告认为，《重返 20 岁》是花费巨大人力、物力和财力制作的影视作品，截至 2015 年 2 月该作品票房已达 3.5 亿元，刷新了由《分手合约》（1.93 亿元）保持的中韩合拍片最高票房纪录；而被告侵犯了其网络信息传播权，给原告造成了一定损失。故诉至法院，请求法院判令被告立即停止对原告著作权的侵害，停止提供《重返 20 岁》的在线播放服务；赔偿原告经济损失及合理费用合计 30 万元；被告在其平台“华数 TV”上刊登声明，消除影响。本案尚在审理中。

（资料来源：中国经济网　作者：李万祥）

【《开心消消乐》游戏引发系列权利纷争】
2016 年 5 月，因认为古川公司开发的《开心消消乐 2015》等游戏仿冒《开心消消乐》，乐风创想公司以侵犯信息网络传播权、商标权及不正当竞争将古川公司诉至法院，索赔 300 余万元。北京市海淀区人民法院受理了此案。

乐风创想公司发现，古川公司在当乐网、苏宁易购应用商店等多家平台上发布了古川公司开发的、以“开心消消乐 2015”“开心消消消”等命名的网络游戏，古川公司在前述网站中发布的游戏宣传图、游戏图标中使用的绿色藤蔓、卡通动物形象、美术字等元素与《开心消消乐》游戏中的美术作品整体或部分构成相同或实质性相似，侵犯了乐风创想公司的署名权及信息网络传播权。

古川公司在上述游戏的名称、宣传用语、宣传图片、下载及安装页面、游戏内等多处使用了“开心消消乐”“开心消消乐 2015”等与“开心消消乐”注册商标相同或近似的名称或标识，侵犯了乐风创想公司的注册商标专用权。

《开心消消乐》游戏自 2013 年 7 月上线后，具有较高知名度，属于知名商品，古川公司开发的前述游戏名称“开心消消乐 2015”等与“开心消消乐”相同或高度近似，且古川公司在多个平台上，在前述游戏的下载、宣传页面的游戏图标、宣传图片等多处使用了与《开心消消乐》特有的三张装潢图相同或高度相似的图片作为游戏装潢，导致相关公众误认古川公司开发的上述游戏是《开心消消乐》的最新版本、衍生游戏，或与《开心消消乐》属同一系列，其行为已构成不正当竞争。

古川公司还实施了虚假宣传行为，宣称前述游戏是“1.2 亿人都在玩的休闲游戏”“2015 年最火热的消除游戏”等，但事实上前述游戏的用户数量及热门程度远未达到宣称的程度；古川公司在前述游戏的宣传页面易使相关用户误以为前述游戏是《开心消消乐》的新版本，且事实上，上述卡通动物均为《开心消消乐》游戏特有的游戏元素，古川公司开发的游戏中并没有这些元素。

另外，古川公司在前述游戏中以十分隐蔽的方式恶意设置了扣费点，致使许多游戏用户在不知情或未充分意识到的情况下被扣费，由于古川公司从商标、游戏名称、装潢、宣传语等多个角度整体抄袭、模仿，导致相关公众产生混淆，误认为恶意扣费是乐风创想公司所为并向乐风创想公司投诉。

乐风创想公司认为，古川公司实施侵权行为的平台多、下载人数多、侵权时间长、模仿程度高，且侵权恶意明显，因此，起诉要求判令古川公司停止侵权、公开赔礼道歉并赔偿损失 300 余万元。

（资料来源：中国经济网　作者：李万祥）

【导航地图侵权案新进展：第三方公司称奇虎已获授权】　2016 年 6 月 12 日，针对北京四维图新科技股份有限公司（下称北京四维图新公司）与北京奇虎科技有限公司（下称奇虎公司）导航地图侵权纠纷，北京秀友科技有限公司（下称秀友科技）发表声明，称奇虎公司未侵权，并阐述了与各方合作的情况。

因认为奇虎公司未经许可，在向公众提供的导航电子地图、开发的应用软件《360 搜索》中使用其享有著作权的电子地图，误导公众认为奇虎公司提供的地图具有合法来源，北京四维图新公司将奇虎公司起诉至法院，要求奇虎公司停止侵犯著作权及不正当竞争行为，赔礼道歉，消除影响，并赔偿损失 1 亿元，赔偿合理支出 100 万元。北京市海淀区人民法院已受理了此案。随后，奇虎公司回应称，360 地图产品中使用的导航电子地图具有合法来源，全部由拥有导航电子地图制作资质的立得空间集团提供，双方签订了合法有效的许可使用协议，360 为此已经支付了巨额的许可使用费。

秀友科技在其发布的声明中，称自己是立得空间集团旗下一家从事互联网地图服务的专业公司，通过运营 www.ishowchina.com 网站向企业和个人提供地图服务。2014年4月1日，秀友科技与北京四维图新公司签订了为期3年的有关地图数据许可的合作协议，获得了北京四维图新公司地图及相关数据的合法授权，秀友科技向北京四维图新公司支付了许可使用费。2014年4月25日，秀友科技与奇虎公司签订了地图数据服务许可协议，按照上述北京四维图新公司的授权为奇虎公司提供地图数据服务。奇虎公司依照协议约定合法使用相关服务，并支付了许可使用费。秀友科技表示，奇虎公司不存在侵犯北京四维图新公司地图著作权及不正当竞争的行为。秀友科技与北京四维图新公司和奇虎公司分别签订的合作协议已顺利执行2年多，仍然合法有效。

（资料来源：中国知识产权资讯网　作者：窦新颖）

【三男子印刷逾25万册高仿盗版教辅书　案值超700万元】　2016年6月13日，徐州市鼓楼公安分局对外公布一起侵犯著作权案件。江苏省徐州市三名男子依照“顾客”的需求，按照提供的正版书样，印刷出大量盗版教辅书。警方在现场收缴盗版图书5.8万多本，加上已经印刷运出的20余万册，涉案总金额达700余万元。

2016年初，徐州市鼓楼公安分局铜沛派出所刑警中队接到上级交办的一起侵犯著作权案。经蹲点守候、跟踪、多方侦查，警方锁定了位于云龙区骆驼山工业园内的某印刷厂。在随后的侦查过程中，警方顺藤摸瓜来到云龙区刘桥工业园。民警细心观察到在一条排水管道排出的污水中，掺杂着部分碎纸屑。办案队员迅速沿着管道开展工作，一家装订厂进入办案队员的视线。由此，此案涉及的两个窝点全部浮出水面，嫌疑人最终确定。

2016年3月11日，办案民警兵分两路，一路突击检查骆驼山工业园的印刷厂，一路突击检查刘桥工业园里的涉案装订厂。警方在装订厂内现场搜查出各类图书58 000多本，按照书本上标的价格，总额高达160余万元。经清查发现，这些盗版书是高级翻译、雅思之类的英语教辅材料。警方随后将负责印刷的徐某和负责装订的申某控制。

5月中旬，徐某和申某的上线张某投案自首。据张某交代，他是受别人之托，才通过申某找到徐某。其上线将所要印刷图书的正版书样交过来，他再找申某和徐某，由他们印刷、装订。经清点账本，警方发现该厂已经印刷运出20多万本，并通过物流发送出去，涉案总金额达700余万元。

（资料来源：中国新闻网　作者：朱志庚　晨　晓）

【迪士尼等起诉国产动画电影《汽车人总动员》侵权】　2016年6月21日下午，国产动画电影《汽车人总动员》被迪士尼公司和皮克斯公司起诉侵权案在上海浦东新区人民法院公开开庭审理。

迪士尼公司和皮克斯公司是知名动画电影《赛车总动员》《赛车总动员2》的著作权人。电影《汽车人总动员》于2015年7月公映，厦门蓝火焰影视动漫有限公司（以下简称蓝火焰公司）是制片人，北京基点影视文化传媒有限公司（以下简称基点公司）是发行单位，上海聚力传媒技术有限公司（以下简称聚力公司）在PPTV网站向社会公众提供了该电影。

迪士尼公司和皮克斯公司认为，《汽车人总动员》的主要汽车动画形象“K1”及“K2”明显使用和剽窃了《赛车总动员》《赛车总动员2》中“闪电麦坤”及“法兰斯高”的形象，《汽车人总动员》的电影海报与《赛车总动员2》的电影海报亦构成实质近似，侵害了两公司作品的著作权。此外，“赛车总动员”是知名商品特有名称，蓝火焰公司以“汽车人总动员”为电影名称，误导公众，属于擅自使用知名商品特有名称的不正当竞争行为。

迪士尼公司、皮克斯公司将蓝火焰公司、基点公司、聚力公司起诉至法院，请求法院判令该三家公司停止侵权，并要求蓝火焰公司、基点公司连带赔偿两原告公司经济损失300万元；蓝火焰公司、基点公司连带赔偿两原告公司因制止侵权行为而支出的合理费用100万元。该案尚在审理中。

（资料来源：澎湃新闻网）

【《中国好声音》版权纠纷激化　影响唐德影视业绩】　2016年6月23日，唐德影视以灿星公司和世纪丽亮国际文化传媒有限公司（以下简称世纪丽亮）构成了商标侵权行为为由，向北京知识产权法院提起诉讼，请求法院判令两被告停止在歌唱选秀节目的宣传、推广、海选、广告招商、制作播出时使用包含“中国好声音”“The Voice of China”或“好声音”的节目名称和相关商标标识，并要求灿星公司赔偿各项损失共计5.1亿元。

2016年6月20日，在唐德影视缴纳了1.3亿元的保证金后，北京知识产权法院接受了唐德影视方面提交的诉前保全申请，判决灿星公司需停止使用“中国好声音”“ The Voice of China”品牌的宣传。灿星公司表示将提出行政复议。在6月29日的行政复议中，双方继续争辩不休，始终没有达成共识。

《中国好声音》脱胎于荷兰著名的真人秀节目

"The Voice of Holland"。2012年，该节目的中国版权由灿星公司从原荷兰版权所有人Talpa公司引进。灿星公司负责内容制作，浙江卫视提供播出平台，冠名《中国好声音》("The Voice of China")。播出4季后，《中国好声音》的热度和版权价值持续走高。Talpa公司和灿星公司在后续的版权价格上产生了分歧。2016年1月29日，唐德影视用6 000万美元打包价买断了未来5年4季"The Voice of China"的版权。灿星公司认为，原合同应于2018年到期，指责Talpa公司在合同尚未到期就率先毁约、索要高价版权费用。

双方争辩的焦点在于"中国好声音"(zhong guo hao sheng yin)与"The Voice of China"的品牌归属，以及浙江卫视是否可以继续播出《2016中国好声音》。

如果唐德影视败诉，不排除出现浙江卫视《2016中国好声音》和唐德影视为"The Voice of China"寻求国产化并在其他电视台落地并存的情形。

唐德影视一季报显示，公司一季度合并报表后营收6 046万元，而上年同期营收达1.48亿元；一季度扣非后归属母公司股东净利润只有860万元，相比2015年一季度更是大跌71.7%。如果法院在唐德影视2016年财报截止日前做出判决，且唐德影视的诉请获得法院支持，巨额的赔偿将明显改善唐德影视的全年业绩。

（资料来源：《证券市场周刊·红周刊》）

【《九层妖塔》侵权案宣判：未侵犯保护作品完整权】 2016年6月28日，北京西城法院对社会广泛关注的电影《九层妖塔》著作权纠纷案做出一审判决，判令被告中国电影股份有限公司、被告梦想者电影（北京）有限公司、被告乐视影业（北京）有限公司、第三人北京环球艺动影业有限公司在发行、播放和传播电影《九层妖塔》时署名天下霸唱为电影《九层妖塔》的原著小说作者，并就涉案侵权行为刊登声明，赔礼道歉，消除影响，驳回原告其他诉讼请求。

小说《鬼吹灯》的作者张牧野（笔名"天下霸唱"）认为电影《九层妖塔》涉嫌侵犯自己著作权，故于2016年1月4日诉至西城法院，请求法院判令被告立即停止侵权行为，向张牧野公开赔礼道歉、消除影响，并赔偿张牧野精神损失100元万人民币。

针对张牧野的诉讼请求，法院经审理认为，涉案电影《九层妖塔》系根据小说《精绝古城》改编而成。《著作权法》第十二条规定：改编、翻译、注释、整理已有作品而产生的作品，其著作权由改编、翻译、注释、整理人享有，但行使著作权时不得侵犯原作品的著作权。电影《九层妖塔》的权利人在行使权利时，不得侵犯原作品即小说《精绝古城》的著作权，其中当然包括小说作者对于作品享有的署名权。换言之，电影《九层妖塔》权利人在行使权利时，必须为小说《精绝古城》作者张牧野署名，否则即视为侵犯了原告张牧野的署名权。

同时，法院在全面分析使用作品的权限、方式，原著小说的发表情况以及电影作品的特殊规定等因素后，认为本案中认定涉案电影《九层妖塔》是否侵犯原告的保护作品完整权，应当以是否损害原著作者的声誉为构成要件。原告提供的证据不能证明涉案电影的改编、摄制行为损害了小说作者的声誉，因此，电影不构成对原告保护作品完整权的侵犯。判决还特别指出，本案在考虑保护作品完整权的边界时，应当结合《著作权法》的立法宗旨，充分考虑激励创作、促进产业发展和保障大众文化需求之间的关系，在充分尊重、维护小说作者人格尊严和声誉的前提下，亦应充分尊重合法改编者的创作自由和电影作品的艺术规律，促进文化的发展与繁荣，满足社会公众的多元化文化需求。

判决显示，原告张牧野没有提交证据证明涉案行为对其造成严重精神损害，因此，关于其要求赔偿精神损害抚慰金的主张法院不予支持。最终，法院做出了如上判决。

（资料来源：央广网　作者：孙　莹）

【天津IPTV被诉侵权　遭索赔2 000万元】 2016年6月，中央电视台旗下央视国际网络有限公司（下称央视网）控股子公司——爱上电视传媒（北京）有限公司（下称爱上传媒公司）以侵犯著作权及不正当竞争为由，将天津IPTV的运营方天津广播电视台、中国联合网络通信有限公司天津市分公司（下称天津联通公司）以及汇川（天津）商务酒店有限公司（下称天津汇川酒店）诉至北京市朝阳区人民法院，请求法院判令上述3被告停止侵权、天津广播电视台和天津联通公司刊登声明消除影响，并共同赔偿其经济损失2 000万元。

爱上传媒公司认为，天津广播电视台和天津联通公司在未经授权的情况下，通过合作运营的IPTV向用户提供电视"直播"和"回放"服务，内容涉及CCTV1综合、CCTV2财经、CCTV3综艺、CCTV4中文国际、CCTV5体育等32个频道，包含《2016年中央电视台春节联欢晚会》《今日说法》《星光大道》《朝闻天下》等51个节目。

爱上传媒公司代理人、北京高文律师事务所律师孙茂成介绍，2009年4月20日，央视网经中央电视台授权，取得了中央电视台所有频道和节目独占性的通过信息网（包括但不限于互联网、移动平台、IP电视、车载电视等新媒体传播平台）向公众传播、广播的权利。2015年7月1日，央视网将通过IP电视（包括但不限于IPTV等符合国家IPTV定义的商业模式）向公众传播、广播的权利，以独占形式授权给爱上传媒公司。双方约定爱上传媒公司有权针对侵权行为提起诉讼。

爱上传媒公司认为，天津广播电视台和天津联通公司合作运营的IPTV与其构成直接竞争关系。因此，天津广播电视台和天津联通公司未经授权，以IPTV形式向用户提供电视“直播”和“回放”服务，不仅侵犯了爱上传媒公司的著作权，而且违反了公平原则和诚实信用原则，构成不正当竞争，给其造成了巨大的经济损失。

此次天津广播电视台之所以被诉侵权，是由于其没有按照要求与IPTV集成播控总平台对接，未经授权向用户提供中央电视台节目的“点播”和“回放”服务。

（资料来源：《中国知识产权报》　作者：祝文明）

【“童话大王”郑渊洁声讨网络店铺侵权】

2016年6月，被誉为“童话大王”的郑渊洁公开声讨网络店铺销售侵权盗版产品。

多位读者向郑渊洁举报淘宝“Taolive”、天猫“淘生活旗舰店”、天猫“上海美术电影制片厂店”预售舒克和贝塔玩具。郑渊洁在微博上表示，这3家店铺销售的舒克和贝塔玩具是未经授权的侵权盗版产品，已侵犯了其本人的著作权和商标权，3家店铺应立即停止侵权行为并向消费者退还预售款。

郑渊洁在微博中表示，舒克和贝塔是其在1982年9月创作的文学形象。34年来，《舒克和贝塔》书刊总销量超过7 000万册，影响了国内三代孩子。同时，其本人也是舒克和贝塔玩具商标持有人。根据读者举报，上述淘宝3家店铺在宣传文字中介绍，舒克和贝塔玩具由阿里巴巴联合上海美术电影制片厂推出，但事实上，这是未经授权的侵权盗版产品，已经侵犯了权利人的著作权和商标权等相关权利，应当承担相应的法律责任。

郑渊洁还表示，2015年，其本人已授权上海喜马拉雅公司生产销售舒克玩具等相关衍生品，上述3家店铺的行为已经侵犯了上海喜马拉雅公司的相关权益。3家淘宝店铺应立即停止侵权行为，并向消费者退还预售款。另外，消费者在购买到假冒侵权商品时，可根据相关法律向经营者提出赔偿要求。

（资料来源：《中国知识产权报》　作者：姜　旭）

【乐视诉电视猫“盗链”侵权获赔50万元】

2016年7月，因认为电视猫视频软件以“盗链”形式传播影视作品，侵犯著作权、构成不正当竞争，乐视网信息技术（北京）股份有限公司（简称乐视公司）将上海千杉网络技术发展有限公司（简称千杉公司）诉至法院，要求停止侵权，索赔200万元。

乐视公司诉称，该公司对《道士下山》《老严有女不愁嫁》《顾家乐的幸福生活》等三部作品享有著作权。然而，千杉公司经营的电视猫视频（MoreTV）软件，未经授权，故意避开并破坏乐视的保护技术措施，以“盗链”形式在互联网传播、提供上述作品，侵犯了公司著作权。千杉公司还去除了公司播放页面广告及贴片广告，跳过会员收费环节，对该公司经营模式造成严重破坏。其行为吸引了海量用户下载使用其应用软件，获得不法收益，却无偿占用乐视公司带宽资源，增加公司服务器负担，构成不正当竞争。

朝阳法院经审理认定，乐视公司对涉案影视作品享有独占专有信息网络传播权，应受著作权法保护。电视猫软件通过数据解析获取绝对URL地址的行为是对可变参数的破解，该行为是一种非法盗取行为。基于电视猫链接行为的非法性，法院指出该行为不适用网络服务提供者享有的免责条款和承担责任的条件。

同时，千杉公司虽未将涉案作品存储在其服务器上，但其行为显然是将他人服务器作为提供视频资源的存储来源，达到了向用户提供视频资源的目的，其提供的效果与乐视公司完全一样，甚至因无前置广告，效果更优于乐视客户端或网站。据此，法院认定千杉公司的行为系作品提供行为并应承担相应法律责任。

千杉公司破解、盗链行为具有违法性，对乐视公司造成直接损害，其盗链行为与损害后果有直接因果关系，千杉公司具有利用他人享有合法权利的作品获取利益的主观故意。综上，法院认定千杉公司构成侵权，系对乐视公司信息网络传播权的直接侵害，且其行为属于避开或破坏技术措施的行为，构成著作权侵权。

千杉公司通过电视猫软件所提供的，已不仅仅是软件开发服务，其目的旨在向用户提供视频资源，其与乐视公司在服务对象、目的、途径、平台上具有一致性，二者在争取互联网用户方面存在竞争关系、具有直接冲突的竞争利益。

最终，法院结合电视猫用户量、播放时长、市场作品购买费用、流量使用成本、作品市场价值等因素，酌情判断千杉公司立即停止著作权侵权及不正当竞争行为，赔偿乐视公司经济损失 50 万元、公证费 22 040 元。一审宣判后，双方均未明确表示是否上诉。

（资料来源：《法制晚报》 作者：晏 如）

【“哆啦 A 梦”诉《叮咚小区》侵权败诉】 2016 年 7 月，浦东法院对“哆啦 A 梦”诉《叮咚小区》一案做出一审判决，驳回了原告艾影公司的全部诉请。动漫形象“哆啦 A 梦”著作权方发现一个叫《叮咚小区》的应用软件的图形及文字与“哆啦 A 梦”有相似之处，因此双方打起了侵权官司。

经“哆啦 A 梦”卡通形象著作权人授权，艾影（上海）商贸有限公司取得了在中国大陆进行商品授权业务，并在发生侵权行为时采取法律行动等权利。艾影公司诉称，“哆啦 A 梦”卡通形象构成了美术作品，而其身体躯干部位因在剧情中尤为重要，故是该作品独创性的集中体现。同时，其使用的“哆啦 A 梦”文字图形因具有独创性，亦构成美术作品。然而，被告开发、经营的《叮咚小区》应用软件擅自使用了“哆啦 A 梦”形象的诸多要素特征，这侵犯了其享有的作品复制权及改编权，要求赔偿 205 万元损失。

壹佰米公司辩称，著作权侵权认定应以保护作品的独创性为原则，而“哆啦 A 梦”卡通形象的独创性体现在其整体形象，尤其是头部特征，而不是原告所主张的项圈、铃铛、口袋等要素。同时，色彩、视角、形状以及审美习惯所支配的艺术法则等是不受著作权保护的，对该些部分，原告无权主张权利。

法院审理后认为，原告主张权利的“哆啦 A 梦”卡通形象的猫脸造型无疑是该美术作品中最具有独创性的部分，集中体现了该猫型机器人的特质；但躯干部分独创性较低，就其与《叮咚小区》应用软件图形已经剔除了思想以及公有领域部分的相同及相似之处判断分析，尚不足以构成实质性相似。同时，原、被告作品间存在着较多的不同之处与较大的视觉差异，如对原告作品予以保护，将妨碍他人在法律保护范围内的创作自由。被告行为不构成对上述作品复制权的侵害，被告的作品也非基于原告作品所创作产生的新作品，不构成对原告作品改编权的侵害。

（资料来源：中国知识产权资讯网）

【蜻蜓 FM《香火》被判侵权】 2016 年 7 月，上海知识产权法院审结一起上诉人上海麦克风文化传媒有限公司（以下简称麦克风公司）和被上诉人劳某侵害作品信息网络传播权纠纷一案，麦克风公司未经著作权人劳某许可，通过网络提供小说《香火》的在线听书服务，麦克风公司需赔偿劳某经济损失和合理费用共计 1.5 万元。

2015 年 4 月，被上诉人劳某发现，自己所著的小说《香火》被放置在该网站上，供听众在线听书，劳某认为自己并未授权该网站进行在线听书服务，该网站的行为侵害了劳某对该作品享有的信息网络传播权，遂将麦克风公司告上法院，请求法院判令立即停止侵权，下线相关产品并赔偿经济损失和合理费用 5 万元。

麦克风公司在庭审中提出，劳某将涉案作品的电子版权、报刊摘登权、连载权、广播权、影视版权、声像版权以及转授权的权利授予了国文润华公司。此后，国文润华公司通过 4 个公司层层授权。麦克风公司从上海倾听信息技术有限公司（下称上海倾听公司）合法获得了《香火》录音制品的复制权和信息网络传播权。

上海知识产权法院审理后认为，国文润华公司根据该合同获得的是《香火》文字作品的电子版权、报刊摘登、连载权、广播权、影视版权、声像版权及相应的转授权利，而本案系争的《香火》有声读物是根据文字作品制作的录音制品，其本质上已属于不同作品。本案中，上海倾听公司通过层层授权获得了劳某《香火》文字作品的相关授权，并制作了涉案录音制品，根据《著作权法》规定，上海倾听公司拥有了涉案录音制品相关版权，并合法授权了麦克风公司涉案作品的复制权和信息网络传播权。

然而，上海知识产权法院表示，根据《中华人民共和国著作权法》相关规定，被许可人复制、发行、通过信息网络向公众传播录音录像制品，还应当取得著作权人、表演者许可，并支付报酬。

本案中，没有证据表明麦克风公司取得过劳某的许可以及向其支付报酬，因此即使麦克风公司提供的是免费有声读物的收听服务，并没有提供下载，也没有提供商业广告，但是麦克风公司仍然构成对劳某作品享有的信息网络传播权的侵害。

（资料来源：人民网—上海频道 作者：吴心远）

【五起《漫画帮》著作权侵权案宣判】 2016年7月，深圳市南山区人民法院就腾讯计算机系统有限公司诉上海元酷网络科技有限公司著作权权属、侵权纠纷案件做出判决，法院认定《漫画帮》构成侵权，判决被告在判决生效之日起十日内赔偿原告腾讯公司经济损失共计30.2万元，维权合理费用共计2.1万元。

2015年，针对元酷公司旗下《漫画帮》移动端漫画阅读软件未经授权传播《狐妖小红娘》《2B家庭欢乐多》等5部漫画作品，腾讯公司诉至法院。

被侵权的作品《狐妖小红娘》(以下简称《狐》)的点击量在腾讯动漫各排行榜均居前列，该作品由杭州幻想岛文化创意有限公司员工庹新科、樊鹏飞共同创作，并于2013年在腾讯动漫平台网站发表并连载。根据幻想岛公司与两位作者的约定，两位作者对该作品仅享有署名权，而其他著作权归幻想岛公司享有。

2014年4月29日，原告与幻想岛公司签署了《漫画作品授权许可合同》，并随该合同向原告出具了《狐》漫画作品信息网络传播权许可使用证明书及打击盗版的《狐》漫画作品授权证明书，幻想岛公司将其享有著作权的《狐》作品独占许可给原告，且在发现有第三方侵犯漫画作品著作权时，在一定期限内，原告有权单独以自己名义追究侵权行为人的法律责任。

2015年7月，原告发现被告开发并运营的手机APP《漫画帮》中，未经原告许可传播《狐》作品。原告认为，被告作为《漫画帮》软件的开发者与运营者，未经原告同意而在其软件中向用户提供《狐》作品的在线阅读和下载服务，其上述行为已侵害了原告的信息网络传播权，给原告造成了严重的经济损失，应当承担停止侵权、赔偿损失和维权支出的民事责任。

法院经过审理认为，原告经幻想岛公司授权许可，获得涉案作品的专有信息网络传播权，并有权单独以自己的名义提起诉讼。虽然作品是从被链网站的服务器上发出，被告的应用软件没有复制、上传内容，但此时被链网站存储该作品的服务器已形同被告所控制的远程服务器，被告所设置的链接只不过是其向公众传播作品的一个环节而已，被告对整个信息网络传播过程起到了主导作用，已经在实质上替代了被链网站向公众传播作品。因此，被告的行为侵犯了原告就涉案作品享有的信息网络传播权，应立即停止侵权并承担赔偿损失的责任。

鉴于被告已经删除涉案作品链接，实际上停止侵权，原告未举证证明其实际损失或被告的违法所得数额，综合考虑原告作品的类型、知名度、被告侵权程度、侵权行为的情节等因素，法院判决被告在判决生效之日起十日内赔偿原告腾讯公司经济损失9万元，维权合理费用共计0.5万元。

(资料来源：法制网　作者：王开广)

【4家游戏公司被指侵犯金庸作品改编权】 2016年7月，因认为游戏《金庸群侠传》侵犯了金庸作品的著作权，北京畅游天下公司(以下简称畅游公司)以其拥有该作品的改编权为由，将深圳扑雷猫公司(以下简称扑雷猫公司)等4家公司诉至法院并索赔1 100万元。海淀法院已受理该案。

畅游公司诉称，其获得了金庸作品《天龙八部》《鹿鼎记》《雪山飞狐》等11部作品的独家移动端游戏软件改编权，也运营开发该类软件，且有权追诉第三方对金庸11部作品的侵权行为。然而，扑雷猫公司同时研发了《金庸群侠传》，并会同上海月球漫步公司等，4公司共同发行。该款游戏大量内容以金庸作品的情节、人物、武功和装备为蓝本，如使用《鹿鼎记》中的韦小宝、陈近南等角色，使用《天龙八部》中的乔峰、段誉、灵鹫宫、生死符等人物及情节，还使用金庸作品内容做宣传，这严重侵害了畅游公司的权益。

2016年1月26日、27日，畅游公司分别和上海月球漫步公司的关联公司上海黑桃互动网络科技有限公司(以下简称黑桃公司)及其股东庞东升签订赔偿协议并和解，黑桃公司承诺不再利用金庸作品中的任何元素。但协议签订后，畅游公司发现，该款游戏仍在多渠道运营，故诉请海淀法院判令4被告立即停止侵权，赔礼道歉并赔偿经济损失1 100万元。

(资料来源：《京华时报》　作者：张淑玲)

【《女医·明妃传》陷版权纠纷　掌阅告阅文索赔100万元】 2016年7月，浦东法院公开审理了掌阅科技股份有限公司诉上海阅文信息技术有限公司一案。

2016年初，原告认为被告经营的《QQ阅读》客户端上销售的小说《明妃传》在推广中使用了“女医明妃传”等字样，涉嫌侵权和不正当竞争，向上海市浦东新区人民法院提出诉前行为保全申请，并获得法院支持。不久后，掌阅科技又将阅文集团告上了法庭，要求停止侵权并赔偿100万元经济损失。

电视剧、电子书《女医·明妃传》和电子书

《明妃传》均以历史上真实存在的明代女医师谈允贤为主要人物，但两者的故事情节、写作方式、作者等均不同，系不同作品。

电视剧《女医·明妃传》由新丽电视文化投资有限公司、天津唐人影视股份有限公司等联合出品，其编剧也是小说《女医·明妃传》的作者张巍。掌阅科技获得《女医·明妃传》电子小说独家信息网络传播权后，于2月16日在其运营的掌阅小说网《掌阅 iReader》平台上上线。由诸葛公子创作的网络小说《明妃传》为阅文集团签约作品，于2月2日在腾讯读书网《QQ阅读》平台上线。

掌阅科技代理律师称，电视剧和小说属于《女医·明妃传》同一作品的两个表现形式。《女医·明妃传》作品名称是为了区别商品来源，女医和明妃作为谈允贤的身份高度概括了电视剧和小说的内容，具有对应性。掌阅科技经过合法授权，不仅成为《女医·明妃传》电子小说的信息网络传播权人，也享有代原作者进行维权的权利。被告在宣传、推广、销售《明妃传》过程中，使用了“女医明妃传”字样、电视剧《女医·明妃传》海报和字样，甚至称其为《女医·明妃传》原著，在读者中引起了混淆，构成了不正当竞争。

阅文集团称，小说《明妃传》在上线时，电视剧和电子书《女医·明妃传》均未发表，不构成知名商品。公众看到《女医·明妃传》名称时，想到更多的是电视剧，而非该小说。另外，被告是《明妃传》销售者，只是根据作者创作时的名称进行传播，被告不构成使用名称行为，使用名称行为的是《明妃传》小说作者，但是其发表在前，即使构成知名商品特有名称，也是被告《明妃传》小说作者享有，而不是原告。

此外，对于掌阅科技提出的100万元经济损失赔偿，阅文集团也不认同。阅文集团代理律师辩称，被告小说2月2日上架，3月1日下架，原告将人气乘以销售价格作为损失计算依据，但是人气不等于销量，原告提出100万元赔偿要求无依据。

庭审结束后，此案未当庭宣判。

（资料来源：《中国知识产权报》　作者：姜　旭）

【华为被诉侵犯漫画作品版权】 2016年8月16日，因“荣耀6 plus”手机提供《奇拉漫画》软件下载服务，且使用《奇拉漫画》可阅读原告权属作品，原告天津神界漫画有限公司以侵犯信息网络传播权纠纷为由诉至法院，请求判令被告一“荣耀6 plus”的生产者华为技术有限公司、被告二《奇拉漫画》的开发者北京汇文立业文化传播有限公司停止侵权、赔偿损失。海淀法院受理了此案。

原告天津神界漫画有限公司诉称，其系国内最早成立的原创性漫画企业，其漫画作品在国内外有很高的知名度和品牌价值，已被授权至世界众多国家并出版了20多个不同语言版本；《三国演义》漫画作品系其出品，原告依法享有该书包括信息网络传播权在内的著作权。被告一生产的“荣耀6 plus”手机中的“应用市场”可以下载被告二开发的《奇拉漫画》应用程序；且未经原告授权，《奇拉漫画》软件通过手机客户端为用户提供《三国演义6：千里走单骑》漫画作品的在线阅读服务。

原告认为，被告一作为《奇拉漫画》软件的下载平台，理应对《奇拉漫画》非法提供在线阅读服务负有审查义务，二被告已构成共同侵权，严重扰乱了原告作品的正常市场出版秩序，给原告造成了巨大的直接经济损失，应对上述侵权行为承担连带责任。故诉至法院，请求法院判令二被告立即停止侵权，赔偿原告经济损失5万元。

（资料来源：海淀法院网）

【作家刘心武诉世纪超星侵权】 2016年8月，著名作家刘心武以著作权被侵犯为由将世纪超星公司诉至法院，索赔2.7万余元。海淀法院已受理该案。

刘心武诉称，世纪超星公司未经其许可，擅自将他的作品《果实累累》和《刘心武代表作》扫描后上传至世纪超星网站（www.chaoxing.com）传播、出售，通过提供下载和阅读牟取高额利润。

刘心武认为，世纪超星公司的行为严重侵犯了他的著作权，应停止侵权并赔偿经济损失，故诉请法院判令世纪超星公司停止侵权、删除《果实累累》《刘心武代表作》等作品，并赔偿相关经济损失2.7万余元。

（资料来源：《京华时报》　作者：张淑玲）

【胡巴款定制T恤引发侵权纠纷】 2016年8月，安乐（北京）电影发行有限公司以京东商城中的“萤火虫动漫旗舰店”销售的胡巴款定制T恤涉嫌侵权为由，将该网店诉至法院。海淀法院受理了此案。

安乐公司诉称，其是“捉妖记—胡巴系列”美术作品的制作权人，享有胡巴等美术作品的著作权。安乐公司发现“京东商城”中名为“萤火虫动漫旗舰店”的网店中，出售以胡巴人物形象为装饰的指定款T恤。但该网店的行为并未取得其同意或授权，故安乐公司将该网店的营业者北京环亚美讯科技有限公司诉至法院，要求其停止使用胡巴形象，并赔偿其经济损失6万元和维权费用5 000元。

（资料来源：海淀法院网）

【页游《青云志》被诉侵犯《诛仙》游戏改编权】 2016年8月，因认为广州华多网络科技有限公司运营的《青云志》网页游戏大量使用《诛仙》小说中的人物设定、场景，侵犯其获得的《诛仙》小说游戏改编权的独占许可使用权，且利用《诛仙》及其元素进行网络宣传，构成不正当竞争，完美世界（北京）软件科技发展有限公司将广州华多网络科技有限公司起诉至海淀法院，要求其停止制作、宣传、运营及授权他人运营侵权网页游戏《青云志》，消除影响，赔偿损失500万元，赔偿合理支出2 500元。

完美公司称，原告于2006年从小说作家张戬处获得小说《诛仙》及其元素的游戏独占改编权，自2007年起上线发行了《诛仙》《梦幻诛仙2》等系列游戏，为此支付了巨额授权费。2016年7月28日，华多公司运营的《青云志》网页游戏上线，华多公司未经原告许可，在游戏中擅自大量使用了《诛仙》小说人物、场景，如“张小凡”“碧瑶”“陆雪琪”等。华多公司在《青云志》游戏的宣传首页中以大版面并配文字说明的形式突出使用并介绍了主角人物“张小凡”“碧瑶”，在宣传中使用“最大程度还原原著”等宣传语，直接侵犯原告对《诛仙》小说及其元素在游戏领域的独占权利。

完美公司认为，华多公司运营的《青云志》网页游戏大量使用《诛仙》小说中的人物设定、场景，侵犯其获得的《诛仙》小说游戏改编权的独占许可使用权，且利用《诛仙》及其元素进行网络宣传，构成不正当竞争，故向法院提起诉讼。

（资料来源：海淀法院网）

【侵权网站BT天堂站长被刑拘】 2016年9月，提供非法BT和磁力下载的“BT天堂”网站负责人袁某飞在苏州被江苏淮安警方抓获。“BT天堂”网站提供的一万余部国内外影视作品的BT种子和磁力链接，均未经授权，侵犯了他人的影视作品著作权，嫌疑人袁某飞从中非法牟利九十余万元。

“BT天堂”提供的P2P下载模式，使众多网民在获取非法侵权他人作品的同时，又充当着传播扩散的“帮凶”角色。根据我国法律规定，袁某飞以营利为目的，未经著作权人许可通过信息网络向公众传播他人电影、电视作品，涉嫌侵犯著作权罪。警方表示，对于“BT天堂”这类互联网侵权盗版案件，将持续予以打击，进一步净化国内网络空间及网络版权环境。

据警方调查，自2015年6月以来，“BT天堂”网站负责人袁某飞在未经授权的情况下，将从互联网上采集的一万余部涉及国内外影视作品的BT种子和磁力链接，存储放置在自己负责经营和维护的“BT天堂”“迅雷家”“迅雷港”3个影视下载网站上，供网民免费下载播放，以此提高网站流量和人气。高峰时期，该网站日均IP访问量达到60万，日均PV浏览量达到300万。“BT天堂”已成为名副其实的国内“BT”第一站。袁某飞在网站流量和人气大幅度提升后，通过相关广告联盟注册账号并绑定网站域名和银行卡，以投放广告的方式，在短短一年时间内牟利达九十余万元。

（资料来源：中国青年网）

【《美人制造》著作权纠纷案宣判】 2016年11月7日，作家周浩晖诉电视剧《美人制造》著作权侵权案一审宣判，江苏省扬州市中级人民法院认定电视剧《美人制造》不构成对其小说《邪恶催眠师》的抄袭、改编，判决驳回了周浩晖的全部诉讼请求。

《美人制造》是于正制作的古装剧作品，2014年播出时曾引起很大的反响。作家周浩晖状告《美人制造》制作方，称第29集、第30集抄袭了其小说《邪恶催眠师》，其中对于催眠术的理解、主要人物的感情线索、反派的犯罪动机，以及咬人、跳楼、摔杯子的催眠桥段均雷同，要求《美人制造》相关制作公司及于正赔偿83万余元。

扬州市中级人民法院公布了一审判决结果，法院审理后认为，小说《邪恶催眠师》和电视剧《美人制造》第29集、第30集两部作品的故事主线、故事情节、故事结构顺序、人物设置以及人物关系均不相同。两部作品的主要故事内容以及故事结构存在明显差异，完全属于两个不同的故事，不会导致读者和观众对两部作品产生相同、相似的欣赏体验，故两部作品不构成实质性相似，原告关于被告侵犯其作品改编权、摄制权的主张不能成立。法院在判决中驳回了周浩晖的全部诉讼请求。

（资料来源：《京华时报》　作者：许青红）

【《芈月传》编剧署名纠纷案一审宣判】 2016年11月21日，浙江省温州市鹿城区人民法院就编剧蒋胜男诉王小平、东阳市乐视花儿影视文化有限公司编剧署名纠纷案做出一审判决，认为王小平和乐视花儿影视不存在侵权行为，驳回原告蒋胜男的全部诉讼请求。历时一年多的《芈月传》编剧署名纠纷案暂告一段落。

判决书认为，根据乐视公司提交的蒋胜男与王小平、制片人曹平之间的邮件往来内容，可以反映制片方对蒋胜男创作的剧本不满意，多次修改后作品仍不符合要求。法院认为，“总编剧”既不是法律概念，也不是合同约定名词，“原创编剧”并未贬损蒋胜男的身份和贡献。因此法院判决，蒋胜男主张花儿影视公司、王小平在电视剧视频、新闻发布会、新浪微博等处署名“总编剧：王小平”，在新浪微博、优秀作品申报书等处署名“编剧：王小平、蒋胜男”侵害其署名权，没有依据，法院不予支持。

对于案件的判决结果，《芈月传》制片人曹平表示：“希望《芈月传》事件能够成为国内编剧行业的一个案例，透过这次事件让人们看到当前编剧行业的乱象，并有针对性地制定保护编剧劳动成果的条例，促进相关管理标准的完善，为以后类似事件提供参考依据。”

（资料来源：中国知识产权资讯网　作者：姜　旭）

【青岛“5·16”非法期刊经营案告破】　2016年11月，山东省青岛市文化市场行政执法局联合青岛市公安局、青岛市公安局市北分局在陕西当地“扫黄打非”部门的密切配合下成功破获“5·16”非法期刊经营大案，先后在青岛、西安抓获25名犯罪嫌疑人，端掉多处印刷、批销窝点及仓储库房，收缴非法期刊近20万册，打掉一个涉及全国21个省（区、市）、33个地市的非法期刊经营犯罪网络，从源头上清理整治了出版物市场、维护了文化市场安全。

2016年春节前后，青岛市文化市场行政执法局、青岛市市北区综合行政执法局执法人员在日常巡查中发现部分报摊销售非法期刊，有的含有传播政治谣言等方面的违禁内容，性质严重，是历年来从未有过的。对此，青岛市立即启动“扫黄打非”应急机制，成立了由青岛市文化市场执法局牵头，公安多警种、市北区综合行政执法局参与的专案组，动用多种技术侦察手段，持续加大工作力度，迅速锁定了相关犯罪嫌疑人及其印刷、批销窝点，摸清了其活动规律。

鉴于收网时机成熟，5月中旬，青岛市文化市场行政执法局联合公安部门先后在青岛、西安实施联合行动，对该案进行收网，在青岛抓获23名犯罪嫌疑人，收缴非法期刊1.6万余册，在西安抓获2名犯罪嫌疑人，收缴非法期刊15.3万余册，同时，端掉两地多处非法期刊编辑、印刷、批销窝点及仓储库房。收网后，青岛市文化执法部门还开展了为期一个月的报刊市场集中整治，查缴市面上各类非法报刊近万册，进一步净化了市场环境，规范了市场秩序。

经初步审理，西安、青岛两地涉嫌犯罪团伙，近年来共编印并向全国发售非法期刊数百万册，在全国各地有下线经销商40多个。在青岛抓获的犯罪嫌疑人中，有王姓兄弟两人自行组织部分非法期刊编、印、发，尤其是利用“翻墙软件”，从境外网站获取违禁内容，编入其非法期刊并流入市场，造成较恶劣影响。另有2名犯罪嫌疑人通过开办印刷厂，承接印制非法期刊获利。在西安方面，西安市某文化传播公司胡某某等两人自2013年开始雇用他人从境内外网站下载涉政类信息进行编辑，委托陕西西安一地下印刷厂制作、印刷《探索揭秘》《共同关注》《人物真相》《大揭秘》《焦点纪实》等涉政类非法期刊，向四川、山东、云南、江苏、河北、山西等全国21个省（区、市）33个地市进行销售，数量达数百万册，涉案金额上千万元。

（资料来源：《中国新闻出版广电报》　作者：孙长越）

◆ 行政管理

【国家版权局2016年共发布七批重点（影视）作品预警名单】　2016年，国家版权局共公布了七批重点影视作品预警名单。预警名单共包括284部作品，多为热播、热映的影视剧，类型涵盖电视剧、电影、综艺、网络剧、动漫、纪录片，涉及的权利主体有央视网、优酷土豆、爱奇艺、搜狐视频、腾讯视频、乐视网和PPTV等网站，授权形式包括独家授权和原始两种。

国家版权局要求相关单位应对名单内的作品采取以下保护措施：直接提供内容的网站未经许可不得上传预警名单内的作品；用户上传内容的网站应禁止用户上传预警名单内的作品；提供搜索链接的网站应仅提供获得合法授权网站的搜索结果及跳转链接服务；电商网站及应用平台应加快处理预警名单内作品权利人关于删除侵权内容或断开侵权链接的通知。

（《中国版权年鉴》编辑部综合）

【北京查获特大网络销售盗版图书案】　2016年1月15日至18日，北京市文化市场行政执法总队对通州区北京永顺兴望印刷厂和朝阳区半截塔村两个仓库的印刷、存储非法图书情况进行调查，现场查获涉嫌非法出版图书近70万册。此案为全国“扫黄打非”工作小组办公室挂牌督办案件，涉案地域广，涉案金额巨大。主要犯罪嫌疑人张某某、王某某等已被刑事拘留。

2016年1月15日至18日，根据已查明的线索，北京市文化市场行政执法总队对位于通州区的北京永顺兴望印刷厂进行调查，现场查获该厂印刷《家》《春》《秋》《林清玄散文精选·青少卷》等图书所使用的软片4套。该厂负责人承认，上述软片由“10·26”销售盗版图书案主犯王某某提供。此外，北京市文化市场行政执法总队现场查扣涉嫌非法出版图书1万余册。后经调查确认，2015年10月至12月，该厂非法承印王某某委托的《平凡的世界》《骆驼祥子》《幻夜》等涉嫌侵权盗版图书4万余册，获取印刷费5.6万元。随后，执法人员在朝阳区半截塔村两仓库库房内查获涉嫌非法出版图书67万余册，涉及书目种类224种、出版社71家，其中涉及京内印刷企业43家，涉案码洋累计已达3 147.74万元。截至2016年1月，案件仍在进一步侦破中。

（资料来源：《中国知识产权报》　作者：窦新颖）

【五部门联合下发通知：严打高校周边复印店盗版活动】　2016年2月3日，全国“扫黄打非”办公室会同教育部、国家工商总局、国家新闻出版广电总局、国家版权局联合下发《关于开展部分重点城市高校及其周边复印店专项治理行动的通知》。《通知》要求，要以案件查办为着力点，对高校及其周边复印店的盗版复印活动予以严厉打击，有效遏制部分城市高校及其周边复印店盗版复印扩散蔓延势头。

此次专项治理以高校聚集或复印业较为发达的40个城市为重点，其中包括北京等4个直辖市、石家庄等22个省会城市、南宁等4个民族自治区首府城市和10个其他城市。

《通知》要求，各地要将专项治理工作列入2016年“扫黄打非·秋风2016”专项行动，按照部门职责分工和属地管理原则，调查高校及周边复印店存在的问题，依法依规查处从事盗版复印的店铺，关闭无证照经营场所，查办相关案件，落实加强管理和规范的相关措施，教育引导高校师生提高版权保护意识，自觉抵制盗版复印活动。要求各地各相关部门要对属地高校内及其周边的复印店展开一次全面摸查，统计复印店数量，确定重点检查对象，对复印店证照持有情况进行调查。对旨在整合本地复印资源，涉嫌提供盗版复印服务的网站、手机客户端等进行调查。对本地高校及其周边的复印店进行全面深入的检查，切实加强监管力度。要向复印店经营者进行普法教育，要求其依法依规经营。要举一反三，对相关复印店开展定期和不定期检查；对已取消许可审批的城市（北京、武汉、海口）的复印店，要检查其是否持有营业执照，对无照经营的予以依法查处；对未取消许可审批的城市的复印店，同时检查其是否持有营业执照和印刷经营许可证，对未持有印刷经营许可证擅自从事印刷经营的，按照《印刷业管理条例》相关规定予以处理。对从事盗版复印的复印店，依据《出版管理条例》《著作权法》《著作权法实施条例》相关规定，对非法印刷的盗版出版物予以收缴，对从事非法印刷复制活动依法予以处罚。要及时向社会公众公布举报方法，完善电话、网络和信函等举报方式，安排专人受理举报，制作对复印店的专项举报台账，鼓励教师、学生对复印店盗印教材等行为积极举报，确保相关线索能够及时核实、及时查处、及时向举报人反馈，对举报有功人员要落实奖励措施。

《通知》强调，要在专项治理行动中加大案件查办力度。对在清查中发现的线索要深查彻究，达到行政立案标准的必须立案查处，涉嫌犯罪的及时移送公安机关。对复印店电脑中存储大批量教材PDF文档情况进行调查并纳入案件查办。相关高校要加强对高校内复印店管理，积极配合行政管理部门对校内复印店进行执法检查。此外，要结合高校及其周边复印店的实际，建立健全复印店管理工作机制，如复印店黑名单机制、台账管理机制、针对性巡查机制、定期回查机制等。

（资料来源：《中国新闻出版广电报》　作者：赖名芳）

【四川省发布《关于加强互联网领域侵权假冒行为治理的实施意见》】　2016年2月16日，四川省政府办公厅下发《关于加强互联网领域侵权假冒行为治理的实施意见》（以下简称《意见》）。提出要加大打击利用互联网制售假劣商品、网络侵权盗版等互联网领域侵权假冒行为，力争用3年左右时间，有效遏制互联网领域侵权假冒行为。

针对利用互联网制售假劣商品的行为，《意见》提出以农资、食品药品、汽车配件、装饰装修材料、服装鞋帽等商品为重点。在整治中突出电子商务平台监管，督促电子商务企业落实责任，建立完善举报投诉处理机制，配合执法部门反向追溯电子商务平台上的侵权假冒商品经营者。

针对网络侵权盗版行为，《意见》要求加大对网络交易商品中侵害驰名商标、省著名商标、地理标志商标、涉外商标的保护力度，建立健全电子商务平台专利执法检查工作制度，建立电子商务领域专利维权快速通道。

针对利用互联网（移动互联网）运营侵权盗版游戏、动漫、影视等含有著作权的标准类作品等行为，《意见》要求重点查处通过智能移动终端第三方应用程序（APP）、网络云存储空间、网络广告联盟等信息平台实施侵权盗版行为，网络游戏“私服”“外挂”，以及网吧等上网服务经营者未经权利人许可将影视作品等上传至其局域网服务器等行为。

（资料来源：《四川日报》　作者：王域西）

【国家版权局公布 2015 年中国版权十件大事】
2016 年 2 月 25 日，国家版权局在 2016 CPCC 中国版权服务年会闭幕式上公布了“2015 年中国版权十件大事”。2015 年度版权十件大事由《中国版权》杂志和《中国新闻出版广电报》联合评选。

入选的这十件大事分别是：国务院发布知识产权强国建设若干意见，版权强国建设提上日程；国家版权局发布“最严版权令”，网络音乐版权秩序明显好转；第四届“世界知识产权组织版权金奖”颁发，进一步激发版权创新创造活力；“剑网 2015”专项行动成效显著，网络版权生态进一步优化；我国版权产业对 GDP 贡献增至 7.27%，对促进经济社会发展的重要作用日益凸显；国家版权局与世界知识产权组织签署版权合作备忘录，版权国际合作开启新篇章；政府机关软件正版化强化审计和考核，软件正版率明显提升；国家版权交易中心联盟在京成立，共同打造版权交易服务体系；琼瑶诉于正抄袭案终审胜诉，版权司法保护力度不断加大；IP 元年开启，文学艺术领域版权价值迅速提升。

（资料来源：《中国新闻出版广电报》　作者：邹　韧）

【安徽省版权局下发《关于开展广播电视节目版权专项检查活动的通知》】　2016 年 3 月 4 日，安徽省版权局下发《关于开展广播电视节目版权专项检查活动的通知》，对全省各广播电视台制作和播放的广播电视节目版权问题进行专项检查，以打击侵权盗版违法行为，加快推进知识产权强省建设。

《通知》要求，全省各广播电视台要对本单位制作、播出的广播电视节目进行一次全面梳理、检查，厘清版权归属关系，没有取得权利人授权或未支付报酬的，要立即停止制作和播出。对于已经播出的广播电视节目没有取得权利人授权或未支付报酬的，应积极进行整改，并按规定向权利人支付报酬。

《通知》还要求，各地版权管理部门要做好属地广播电视台广播电视节目版权的日常监管工作，及时公开投诉举报电话，大力宣传广播电视台广播电视节目版权管理的法律知识，及时受理权利人和群众举报。公开曝光违法行为和案件查处情况。对辖区内市、县广播电视台的自查情况进行检查，监督整改，维护权利人合法权益，有效打击和震慑版权侵权违法行为。安徽省版权局组成联合督查组对各地自查和检查情况进行专项抽查。

（资料来源：《中国新闻出版广电报》）

【《吉林省加强互联网领域侵权假冒行为治理实施方案》下发】　2016 年 3 月 8 日，《吉林省加强互联网领域侵权假冒行为治理实施方案》下发。《方案》提出，开展打击网络侵权盗版专项行动，强化对网络（手机）文学、音乐、影视、游戏、动漫、软件及含有著作权的标准类作品等重点领域的监测监管，及时发现和查处网络非法转载等各类侵权盗版行为。

吉林省计划用 3 年左右的时间，有效遏制互联网领域侵权行为，初步形成政府监管、行业自律、社会参与的监管格局。为此，《方案》提出以保护商标权、著作权、专利权等知识产权为重点，严厉打击利用互联网实施的侵权违法犯罪行为。加大对销售仿冒知名商标、涉外商标商品的查处力度，维护权利人和消费者的合法权益。

《方案》提出，依托国家版权监管平台，扩大版权重点监管范围，将智能移动终端第三方应用程序（APP）、网络云存储空间、微博、微信等新型传播方式纳入版权监管范围。加强网上专利纠纷案件办理和电子商务领域专利执法维权。

吉林省督促网络服务商落实“通知—删除”义务，对利用网络服务实施侵权假冒行为的网络信息，及时采取删除、屏蔽、断开链接等必要措施。

（资料来源：《中国新闻出版广电报》
作者：张席贵）

【推进使用正版软件工作部际联席会议第五次全体会议在京召开】　2016 年 3 月 11 日，中宣部副部长、国家新闻出版广电总局（国家版权局）局长蔡赴朝主持召开推进使用正版软件工作部际联席会议第五次全体会议。会议传达了国务院副总理汪洋关于软件正版化工作的重要批示，对2015年推进使用正版软件工作进行了总结，并讨论审议了2016年工作计划。

国家新闻出版广电总局（国家版权局）副局长阎晓宏在会上汇报了2015年推进使用正版软件工作进展情况和2016年工作计划。工信部副部长怀进鹏、商务部部长助理童道驰、国务院国资委秘书长阎晓峰、国家工商总局副局长王江平、国家知识产权局副局长贺化、国管局副局长陈建明、国务院法制办副主任袁曙宏、证监会主席助理赵争平、保监会副主席周延礼、中直管理局副局长张放鸣、全国工商联副主席杨启儒以及全国打击侵权假冒工作领导小组办公室副主任柴海涛、财政部及银监会相关部门负责人出席会议，会议审议通过了《2015年推进使用正版软件工作报告》及《2016年推进使用正版软件工作计划》。

（资料来源：国家新闻出版广电总局）

【上海召开推进使用正版软件工作会议】 2016年3月11日，上海市政府召开全市推进使用正版软件工作会议，在对2015年工作进行总结的同时，对2016年工作做出部署。

会议通报，2015年上海推进使用正版软件工作取得新成果。进一步完善了软件正版化长效机制，建立了正版化工作考核评议和责任追究制度；通过政府软件服务中心平台，为市级机关用户搭建一套自助式产品试用和解决方案的综合性环境。截止到2015年11月，该平台共向427家市级预算单位提供在线订购和技术支持服务。与此同时，积极推进国产基础软件应用，国产基础软件的使用数量同比增长45%。

上海市政府副秘书长宗明对2016年上海推进使用软件正版化工作提出六点要求：严格督查，切实推进软件正版化责任落实；建立健全软件正版化工作督察制度；建立推进软件正版化工作信息化管理平台；深入推进企业使用正版软件工作，制定切实可行的工作计划和目标；加大执法力度，开展侵权盗版“剑网2016”专项行动等，严厉打击软件侵权盗版行为；加强宣传培训工作，继续开展年度十大版权典型案件评选与宣传活动，进一步提升版权的社会认知度。

上海市新闻出版（版权）局局长徐炯参加会议，会议由市新闻出版（版权）局副局长蔡纪万主持。来自全市两级政府机关的相关负责人40余人参会。

（资料来源：《中国新闻出版广电报》 作者：金 鑫）

【合肥开展“2016扫霾”专项突击检查行动】 2016年3月14日，为深入开展出版物市场“扫黄打非”工作，查处违禁、侵权盗版等非法出版物，合肥市文化广电新闻出版局综合执法大队在全市范围组织开展了代号为“2016扫霾”的专项突击检查行动。

为了开展好本次集中行动，该市文化市场综合执法大队制定了周密的行动方案。3月14日下午，执法大队联合各区文化执法部门，同步对全市出版物市场展开执法行动，重点对出版物批发分销单位、大型书刊批发市场和校园周边等地进行集中执法检查。执法人员每到一地，都对经营场所出版物进行详细排查，并细致查看进销货清单等票据。同时要求经营单位负责人增强守法意识，加强内部管理，规范进货渠道，并保留进销货清单等相关手续备查，杜绝销售非法出版物的违规行为，切实承担应尽的社会责任。

此次行动，共出动执法人员187人次，检查出版物发行单位近30家，抽样取证涉嫌非法出版物110册（份）。

（资料来源：《中国新闻出版广电报》 作者 邹 韧）

【北京“12318”查扣非法出版物、盗版光盘逾200万件】 2016年3月18日，北京市16个区同步开展“12318健康文化你我他”法制宣传日活动，2016年3月18日是第6个“全国文化市场法制宣传日”。活动主会场设在西城区，其他15个区设立分会场，这是北京市文化执法总队自成立以来首次开展全市规模的集中宣传活动。全市会场设立法规宣传展板近百块，张贴宣传海报2 000多张，发放新修定法规宣传材料3 000多份，多种形式的宣传品1.2万件。活动中，主办方将正版书籍光盘与盗版书籍光盘同时展出，现场教观众如何辨别盗版产品。

“12318”全国文化市场举报热线开通10余年来，北京市已接收文化市场各类举报信息18万余条，根据“12318”热线提供的线索查处案件2 743件，扣押、收缴非法出版物和盗版光盘211.8万余件，罚没款930余万元。

（资料来源：《中国知识产权报》 作者：刘 仁）

【《2016年全国知识产权系统执法维权工作方案》印发】 2016年4月5日，为深入贯彻党中央、国务院关于严格知识产权保护的工作部署，按照全国知识产权局局长会议、局党组扩大会议的要求，结合本系统执法维权工作实际和创新主体、市场主体的现实需求，国家知识产权局印发《2016 年全国知识产权系统执法维权工作方案》(以下简称《方案》)。

《方案》紧紧围绕执法办案这一核心执法工作进行全面部署，明确了全面强化专项行动与办案工作、创新执法体制机制、推进执法队伍与能力建设、加强案件信息公开与信用体系建设工作、强化快速维权与维权援助体系建设、积极拓展和深化重点联系机制、加强执法维权舆论引导与宣传工作等 7 大项重点任务，提出了 24 项具体措施，并细化了各项措施的分工与进度安排。

下一步，国家知识产权局继续坚持分工明确、目标清晰、进度保证、绩效考核的工作推进机制，加强督促检查，适时开展实地督导、落实工作责任，全面推进落实《方案》提出的各项措施，努力提升知识产权领域社会治理能力，积极构建创新发展的良好环境，大力促进新常态下的经济发展。

(资料来源：国家知识产权局网站　作者：关　健)

【《2015 年北京知识产权保护状况白皮书》发布】 2016 年 4 月 14 日，《2015 年北京知识产权保护状况白皮书》正式发布。针对网络侵权行为，北京市初步实现全网络动态监控，并将进一步治理网络未经授权擅自播放音乐作品的行为，2016 年监管首先锁定一万首最流行的音乐“金曲”，三到五年将范围扩大到十万首。

白皮书显示，“十二五”时期，北京市专利申请量和授权量年均增长率分别达到 19.44%和 22.9%。北京市专利申请量和授权量累计达到 58.8 万件和 32.3 万件，分别是“十一五”时期的 2.8 倍和 3.2 倍。截至 2015 年底，北京市每万人发明专利拥有量达到 61.3 件，居全国第一。北京市有效注册商标达到 69.2 万余件，中国驰名商标达到 220 件，北京市著名商标达到 663 件。北京地区软件著作权登记量近 6.4 万项，占全国总登记量的 21.9%。

(资料来源：《北京晨报》　作者：王歧丰)

【2015 年中国知识产权发展状况发布会举行】 2016 年 4 月 19 日，国务院新闻办公室在京举行新闻发布会，介绍 2015 年中国知识产权发展状况。国家知识产权局局长申长雨、国家工商行政管理总局副局长刘俊臣、国家版权局副局长阎晓宏出席发布会并一同回答了记者的提问。

2015 年，国务院印发了《关于新形势下加快知识产权强国建设的若干意见》，对知识产权强国建设做出明确安排。各级政府和有关部门深入推进国家知识产权战略实施，扎实推进知识产权强国建设，知识产权工作取得了新的成就：一是知识产权创造保持了良好的增长势头。在著作权方面，2015 年我国作品著作权登记量再创历史新高，达到 134.8 万件，同比增长 35.9%；计算机软件著作权登记量为 29.2 万件，同比增长 33.63%。二是知识产权法律法规建设稳步推进。国家版权局积极推进《著作权法》第三次修改以及有关法规的修订；发布了《关于规范网络转载版权秩序的通知》《关于规范网盘服务版权秩序的通知》《关于明确涉外著作权合同登记工作性质的通知》等规范性文件，进一步规范了版权秩序。三是知识产权保护力度进一步加大。2015 年国家版权局持续强化打击侵权盗版行为，联合国家网信办、工信部、公安部开展了第 11 次打击网络侵权盗版“剑网 2015”专项行动，对网络音乐、网络云存储空间、智能移动终端第三方应用程序(APP)、网络广告联盟等进行了专项治理。专项行动中，全国各地共查处网络侵权盗版案件 383 起，行政处罚 450 万元，移送司法机关刑事处理 59 件，涉及金额 3 845 万元，关闭侵权盗版网站 113 家，下线侵权盗版音乐作品 220 万首。四是知识产权转化运用进一步加强。国家版权局规范版权交易和流转，推动版权价值的有效实现。2015 年，我国著作权质权登记 606 件，同比增长 22.18%，涉及主债务金额 287 285 万元。五是知识产权重点领域改革稳步推进。国家版权局实现了行政审批事项受理和审查环节的“一站式”服务。六是知识产权对外合作交流深入开展。2015 年国家版权局积极参与多双边版权事务，参与国际条约磋商；与世界知识产权组织(WIPO)合作成功举办了“世界知识产权组织版权金奖”评选活动，签署了国家版权局与 WIPO 版权双边战略合作备忘录。

(资料来源：《中国新闻出版广电报》　作者：赖名芳)

【国务院办公厅印发《2016 年全国打击侵犯知识产权和制售假冒伪劣商品工作要点》】 2016 年 4 月 19 日，国务院办公厅印发《2016 年全国打击侵犯知识产权和制售假冒伪劣商品工作要点》(以下简称《要点》)，强调要结合推动供给侧结构性改革，依法严惩影响创新发展、妨碍公平竞争和侵害消费者合法权益的侵权假冒违法犯罪，为经济社会持续健康发展提供有力保障。

《要点》明确了 7 个方面、27 项重点工作。

一是加大对重点领域的治理力度。着力打击网上销售假冒伪劣商品和网络侵权盗版行为，强化农村和城乡接合部市场监管执法，持续开展中国制造海外形象维护“清风”行动，深入推进软件正版化工作，从生产、流通和消费等方面对侵权假冒行为实施全链条整治。

二是强化行业日常监管。严肃查处制售假药劣药、生产销售不符合国家标准车用燃油、无证出厂销售强制性认证产品等违法行为，开展“防雾霾”商品监督抽查和专项整治；依法查处侵犯知识产权和滥用知识产权等违法行为，加强商业秘密行政保护。

三是加强法规制度建设。推动电子商务法、反不正当竞争法、药品管理法、著作权法、专利法、化妆品卫生监督条例、专利代理条例等法律法规的制定修订工作，健全侵权假冒商品无害化销毁机制。

四是加强部门协同与司法保护。推进行政执法与刑事司法衔接，大力推进行政处罚案件信息公开，推动长三角、京津冀、泛珠三角等地区执法协作；严查侵权假冒犯罪案件背后的职务犯罪，推进知识产权审判民事、行政、刑事“三合一”改革。

五是推动打防结合与打建结合。健全预警防范机制，大力推进信用建设，充分发挥行业自律作用，强化企业主体责任，发挥媒体和社会公众监督作用，推动打击侵权假冒社会共治共享。

六是开展多样化宣传教育。组织各类新闻媒体解读政策措施，树立正面典型，曝光违法犯罪案件；充分运用主流宣传媒体以及微博、微信、移动客户端等新技术手段，扩大宣传覆盖面。

七是做好多双边协作与交流。深化中美、中欧、中俄、中巴（西）、中瑞（士）、中日等知识产权对话交流，加强与非洲、拉美国家和“一带一路”沿线国家的执法合作，完善海外维权援助机制。

（资料来源：新华社）

【国家版权局奖励查处侵权盗版案件有功单位及个人】 2016年4月20日，国家版权局下发《关于奖励2015年度查处侵权盗版案件有功单位及有功个人的决定》，对在2015年度查处侵权盗版案件工作中做出突出贡献的195家有功单位及215名有功个人给予奖励。

国家版权局要求各级版权相关执法部门及广大执法人员要向查处侵权盗版案件有功单位和有功个人学习，进一步加强版权执法监管工作，严厉查处各类侵权盗版行为，有效维护权利人合法权益，积极推动版权相关产业健康发展，为提升我国版权保护水平做出更大贡献。

（《中国版权年鉴》编辑部综合）

【辽宁省版权局与京版十五社反盗版联盟签署战略合作协议】 2016年4月25日，辽宁省版权局与京版十五社反盗版联盟在辽宁签署了战略合作协议。双方将充分发挥版权管理、行政执法的职能作用，以及出版单位在打盗维权工作中的优势资源，密切配合，齐抓共管，全面提升打击侵权盗版的针对性和有效性。这是京版十五社反盗版联盟首次与省级政府执法部门签订战略协议，将是一次有益的尝试。

在这次签订的战略协议中，辽宁省版权局明确提出，将积极组织全省各级版权执法力量，重点加强对印刷企业的监督检查，依法严厉打击各类盗版、盗印等侵犯著作权的违法犯罪行为，做到优先保护，及时保护。还将组织开展经常性出版物市场巡查，重点加强对图书批发市场、出版物集中经营场所、早市夜市、校园周边、仓储物流，以及互联网环节的监管。并组织开展教材教辅集中整治专项行动，切实加大打击中小学校，特别是高校使用盗版教材教辅图书行为的力度。另外，还将在省内高校开展拒绝盗版使用正版的集中宣传教育活动。

京版十五社反盗版联盟将向辽宁省版权局及时提供出版信息，发布重点图书预警信息，提供正版图书样本，提供重点图书防伪情报信息等方面的支持。在涉嫌盗版图书进行鉴定、认证工作等方面，以及执法人员开展市场巡查及执法行动中给予积极配合。同时，还将协助组织开展版权执法人员业务培训，在安排京外印刷项目中将重点向辽宁倾斜，积极支持辽宁印刷企业发展，在优势选题和重点选题对外合作中也会优先与辽宁出版单位对接。

为确保战略合作落在实处，经双方共同研究，将建立联席会议、信息共享、协作配合、联合巡查、鉴定认证、联合培训、合作共赢七大工作机制，并通过全面加强版权执法合作，切实维护联盟成员的合法权益，充分发挥联盟的产业资源优势，通过优势互补，资源共享，实现市场净化、互利共赢、共同发展的战略目标。

辽宁省版权局党组副书记、常务副局长田铁林与京版十五社反盗版联盟秘书长李晶分别代表战略合作双方签署协议书。外语教学与研究出版社、高等教育出版社、人民出版社等33家京版十五社反盗版联盟成员单位代表，辽宁省各市执法队主要负责同志，省内各出版社代表共计80余人参加了签约仪式。

（资料来源：《中国新闻出版广电报》 作者：邹 韧）

【国家版权局公布打击侵权盗版年度十大案件】 2016年4月26日，国家版权局公布了2015年度全国打击侵权盗版十大案件。

在公布的案件中，行政处罚案件和刑事判决案件各占一半。其中获得行政处罚的案件有：北京金图创联国际科技有限公司侵犯信息网络传播权案、广东"DJ020网"侵犯音乐作品著作权案、北京天盈九州网络技术有限公司侵犯文字作品著作权案、"人人影视网"侵犯影视作品著作权案、安徽蒋某等销售盗版图书案。进行了刑事判决的案件有：河北张某某等印制盗版图书案、山东"8·5"制售盗版光盘案、江苏"速酷电影网"侵犯影视作品著作权案、浙江郑某等复制并通过网络销售盗版图书和软件案、四川"风云丝路网"侵犯著作权案。

（资料来源：《中国新闻出版广电报》　作者：邹　韧）

【江苏省镇江市警方破获特大网络制售盗版图书侵权案】 2016年5月26日上午，江苏省镇江市公安局召开新闻发布会，宣布镇江市警方成功侦破了由国家"扫黄打非"办、国家版权局、公安部联合挂牌督办，居全国"扫黄打非""秋风"专项行动十大侵权盗版案件之首的2015年"10·26"特大网络制售盗版图书侵权案，先后摧毁两个制售盗版图书犯罪团伙，抓获涉案成员42人，依法扣押盗版图书120余万册。

2015年9月，镇江市警方根据网民举报线索，在对淘宝"剑锋时代图书专营店"网售图书情况进行初查时发现，该店所售图书明显存在侵犯他人著作权等行为。警方高度重视，迅速组织警力立案侦查。经过长达7个多月的艰苦努力，警方掌握了其盗版图书印制工厂、仓库窝点、分销体系、作案手法等重要情况和证据，揭开了以盗版书商为中心，涉及制版、印刷、销售、物流等多个利益相关"制售一条龙"犯罪的黑色产业链。

"10·26"特大网络制售盗版图书侵权案系江苏公安机关首次成功侦破的网络制售盗版图书案件，也是近年来全国案值最大的网络制售盗版图书案件。由于该案涉及地域广、案情典型、社会影响巨大，被列入全国"扫黄打非""秋风"专项行动十大侵权盗版案件之首。在全国"扫黄打非"办公室、公安部的指导协调下，在北京警方及北京文化执法总队的全力协助下，专案组共打掉售卖盗版图书源头3个，刑拘犯罪嫌疑人14人，清理大型盗版图书仓库5个，摧毁非法印刷厂3个，现场扣押盗版图书120余万册（图书各类达210种、涉及70余家出版社），涉案案值高达5 200余万元，依法扣押及冻结赃款154万元。

（资料来源：《镇江日报》　作者：张　杰　胡冰心）

【重庆市文化委、公安局协作打击侵权盗版】 2016年5月，为严厉打击侵权盗版违法犯罪行为，重庆市公安局与市文化委联合召开打击侵权盗版违法犯罪工作联席会。重庆市公安局党委副书记、副局长刘新宇与市文化委副主任、市版权局副局长雷平签署协作机制，市公安局打假总队、市文化委相关处室负责人，部分民警代表，主城9区文化执法支（大）队长及业务骨干参加了会议。

会上，围绕"打击网络侵权盗版，维护文化版权创新"的主题，双方通报了近年来重庆市文化版权领域行政监管和公安机关刑事执法的相关工作情况，总结回顾了近年来成功侦破的多起互联网侵权盗版大要案件，分析梳理了当前重庆市文化产业发展态势及面临的侵权盗版违法犯罪形势，并就健全完善信息共享、执法协作、案件侦办等协作机制达成共识。

针对近年来侵权盗版网站和智能移动终端第三方应用程序（包含手机APP）非法传播音乐、影视、新闻、游戏、文学、软件、标准化作品等违法犯罪行为有所抬头的势头，市公安局、市文化委将进一步创新监管方式和手段，不定期联合开展综合查处整治行动，加大对互联网侵权盗版的行政处罚和刑事执法力度，依法治理网络空间，净化网络版权环境。

（资料来源：重庆市文化委员会）

【北京市2016年国家机关软件正版化工作全面启动】 2016年5月，北京市国家机关软件正版化工作动员部署会召开，会议对全年各项工作任务做了全面细致部署及明确要求。

"北京市持续深入在市、区、乡镇（街道）三级国家机关推进开展软件正版化工作并积极探索实现全市软件正版化工作的常态化转变。"北京市版权局局长李春良介绍说。2016年北京市国家机关软件正版化工作分为部署宣贯、清查整改、检查验收、总结考核等4个阶段，北京市100余家市级机关和16个区政府都将纳入检查考核范围。

会议分享了软件正版化建设经验，并对全市软件正版化工作的常态化、制度化建设提出建议。在软件采购方面，北京市推广国产软件场地授权集中统一采购的先进经验，在全市超过三分之二的区和部分软件使用量大的市级机关，共计10余万台计算机实现了办公软件的国产化；在工作模式方面，全市部分区和单位通过政府购买服务的方式，充分借助外部力量，委托专业人员和机构开展软件资产清查、授权审核、报表填制等工作，有效提升了工作效率和专业化水平；在督导考核方面，北京市在过去的两年里全面结合软件正版化检查整改先后开展了两轮全市范围各级国家机关的软件正版化常态化检查考核工作，并由市政府对考核结果进行全面通报，为实现北京市软件正版化工作向新常态的转变打好坚实基础。

（资料来源：《中国新闻出版广电报》　作者：王坤宁）

【国家新闻出版广电总局发布通知规范移动游戏管理】　2016年6月2日，国家新闻出版广电总局发布《关于移动游戏出版服务管理的通知》。根据《通知》，总局对移动游戏实施分类审批管理，今后将进一步压缩内容审查时间，提高移动游戏受理和审批工作效率。该《通知》自2016年7月1日起施行。自施行之日起，未经国家新闻出版广电总局批准的移动游戏，不得上网出版运营。

《通知》指出，申请出版不涉及政治、军事、民族、宗教等题材内容，且无故事情节或者情节简单的消除类、跑酷类、飞行类、棋牌类、解谜类、体育类、音乐舞蹈类等休闲益智国产移动游戏，游戏出版服务单位要填写《出版国产移动游戏作品申请表》，报送属地省级出版行政主管部门。省级出版行政主管部门在5个工作日内完成审核工作，总局收到省级出版行政主管部门报送材料10个工作日内，做出是否批准的决定。

申请出版其他类别的国产移动游戏，按照《关于进一步规范出版境外著作权人授权互联网游戏作品和电子游戏出版物申报材料的通知》（简称《规范通知》）和《关于启动网络游戏防沉迷实名验证工作的通知》的要求办理。其中，《规范通知》附件1所列申报材料中第（二）至（六）项变更为提交《出版国产移动游戏作品申请表》。

申请出版境外著作权人授权的移动游戏，按照《规范通知》和《关于启动网络游戏防沉迷实名验证工作的通知》的要求办理。

《通知》要求，移动游戏上网出版运营时，游戏出版服务单位须在游戏开始前、《健康游戏忠告》后，设置专门页面，标明游戏著作权人、出版服务单位、批准文号、出版物号等经国家新闻出版广电总局批准的信息，并严格按照已批准的内容出版运营。

（资料来源：中国新闻出版广电网　作者：尹　琨）

【广电总局发布《关于进一步明确进口用于出版的音像制品审批工作相关要求的通知》】　2016年6月3日，广电总局发布《关于进一步明确进口用于出版的音像制品审批工作相关要求的通知》，《通知》内容如下：

一、根据《音像制品进口管理办法》第十六条的规定，进口用于出版的音像制品应当先行申请著作权合同登记，取得登记文件后方可履行进口音像制品内容审查手续。现根据国发［2016］11号文件规定，进口用于出版的音像制品不再要求申请人提供著作权合同登记文件，改由国家新闻出版广电总局统一委托中国版权保护中心开展合同登记工作。

二、进口用于出版的音像制品审批材料采取“一站式受理”，统一在国家新闻出版广电总局（宣武门办公区）行政受理大厅办理受理工作，提交材料包括：1.《进口录音（像）制品报审表》；2. 版权贸易协议中外文文本草案，原始版权证明书和版权授权书；3. 节目样片（载体形式为CD、VCD、DVD、BD或其他通用载体）；4. 中外文曲目、歌词或对白，其中音乐类节目要求提供音乐专辑介绍、专辑曲目、歌词中文翻译、表演者、演奏者、词曲作者及主创人员简介，影视类节目要求提供剧情梗概、编导人员、演员、制作公司介绍、国际发行及获奖情况；5. 内容审查所需的其他材料。

三、以上所称进口用于出版的音像制品含信息网络出版，在著作权合同登记和认证工作过程中，不向申请人收取任何费用。

（资料来源：新闻出版广电总局网站）

【国家新闻出版广电总局发出《关于大力推动广播电视节目自主创新工作的通知》】　2016年6月20日，国家新闻出版广电总局发出《关于大力推动广播电视节目自主创新工作的通知》（以下简称《通知》），就加强自主创新、引进模式管理、“920”时段编排等做了进一步明确。《通知》要求各卫视要特别注意提高晚间时段自主原创节目播出比重。

《通知》要求各卫视把节目原创作为自主创新工作的核心，只有具有中华文化基因和中国特色、中国风格、中国气派的自主创新节目，才能更好地讲好中国故事、弘扬中国精神。总局将在创新创优节目评选、宣传推介和进入黄金时间等方面优先考虑自主原创节目。

在引进境外版权模式节目备案工作方面，《通知》规定各卫视播出引进境外版权模式节目（包括当年新引进和往年引进的节目），均需提前两个月向省新闻出版广电局备案。2016 年 7 月 1 日起，新开播的引进境外版权模式节目，如未按《通知》要求备案或未如实备案，一经查实，该节目立刻停播，该频道下一年内不允许播出引进境外版权模式节目。

在总局没有下达《通知》之前，“联合研发”一直是节目市场打擦边球的最好方式。而此次《通知》规定，与境外机构联合研发、邀请境外人员担任主创人员或境外人员在节目制作中发挥主要指导作用的节目，如中方未取得完全知识产权，视同引进境外版权模式节目管理，需完整履行备案程序，合并计算。《通知》强调，各卫视每年在 19:30—22:30 开播的引进境外版权模式节目，不得超过 2 档。每个电视上星综合频道，每年新播出的引进境外版权模式节目不得超过 1 档，第一年不得在 19:30—22:30之间播出。

另外，总局希望将“920”时段（即 21:20 时段）作为推动自主创新的重要基地，在不同主题、不同领域开发多样态、差异化的节目，力求电视荧屏丰富多彩。同一档真人秀节目，原则上一年内只播出一季。“920”时段总体上应呈现公益特色鲜明、题材均衡分布、形态相互区别、风格各有千秋的播出效果。

各家卫视表示已收到《通知》，将会严格执行。

（资料来源：《北京日报》　作者：徐颢哲）

【内蒙古鄂托克旗开展侵权盗版及非法出版物集中销毁活动】　2016 年 6 月，由鄂尔多斯市鄂托克旗旗委宣传部、旗文化广播电影电视局主办的侵权盗版及非法出版物集中销毁活动在鄂旗建筑垃圾填埋场开展。

此次活动共销毁盗版光盘 4 000 多张，图书 100 多册，游戏机 1 台。活动的开展不仅是对知识产权保护的宣誓，也是对侵权盗版及非法出版物的一次亮剑，为鄂托克旗文化市场管理工作奠定了基础。

（资料来源：《鄂尔多斯日报》
作者：杨艳秋　巴　拉）

【四部门启动“剑网 2016”专项活动】　2016 年 7 月 12 日，国家版权局联合国家网信办、工信部、公安部在京召开新闻发布会，宣布正式启动“剑网 2016”专项行动，突出整治三类作品、重点查处四个平台、规范巩固三个成果。值得注意的是，“剑网 2016”专项行动还创新监管手段，将建立“黑白名单”制度，即在网络文学、APP、网络广告联盟等领域建立重点保护作品“白名单”库，同时公布侵权盗版互联网企业“黑名单”，旨在通过此种制度树立版权保护典型企业，推进版权领域信用体系建设。

国家版权局版权管理司司长于慈珂通报了“剑网 2016”专项行动的工作部署。专项行动从 2016 年 7 月开始，利用 5 个月的时间，突出整治未经授权非法传播网络文学、新闻、影视等作品的侵权盗版行为，保障有关权利人的合法权益；重点查处通过智能移动终端第三方应用程序（APP）、电子商务平台、网络广告联盟、私人影院（小影吧）等平台进行的侵权盗版行为，维护网络版权正常秩序；进一步规范网络音乐、网络云存储空间、网络转载新闻作品的版权秩序，营造网络版权良好生态。

专项行动要求各地版权、互联网信息内容、通信主管、公安等部门加强监测检查，突出查办案件，创新工作方法，完善工作机制，落实主体责任，加强宣传动员，完成三项重点任务：一是开展打击网络文学侵权盗版专项整治行动，加强对文学网站的版权执法监管力度，严厉打击通过网站、贴吧、微博、微信等方式未经授权非法传播网络文学作品的侵权盗版行为，规范通过浏览器、搜索引擎等方式传播文学作品的行为。二是开展打击 APP 侵权盗版专项整治行动，加强对 APP 上传者和应用程序商店的版权执法监管，加大对聚合类 APP、与网络电视棒及电视机顶盒关联的 APP 侵权盗版行为的打击力度，强化应用程序商店对提供文学、影视、音乐、新闻等作品 APP 上传者的版权监管责任。三是开展规范网络广告联盟专项整治行动，加强对网络广告联盟在版权保护方面的监督管理，推动网络广告联盟落实企业主体责任、建立版权保护工作机制，推动版权执法监管机构与网络广告联盟建立切断侵权盗版黑色经济链条的工作机制，严厉打击故意为侵权盗版提供支持的网络广告联盟。

国家版权局版权管理司副司长段玉萍通报了 2015 年网络视频、网络音乐和网盘领域版权重点监管情况，将不按照要求报送授权文件的优酷网、腾讯视频列入警示名单，责令进行整改，并对做好 2016 年的网络重点监管工作提出要求，将网络文学纳入网络版权重点监管工作。

（资料来源：中国版权产业网）

【粤港保护知识产权合作专责小组第十五次会议在广州召开】　2016 年 8 月 18 日，粤港保护知识产权合作专责小组第十五次会议在广州召开。海关总署广东分署法规处副处长刘阳表示，粤港两地正针对里约奥运会这一特殊时期展开特别行动，严防奥运标识及体育用品侵权行为。

香港知识产权署署长梁家丽在会上指出，2015年以来，粤港两地海关开展了多次联合执法行动，并通过情报交流携手打击两地进出口侵权行为，成效显著。

梁家丽认为，粤港保护知识产权合作专责小组有效地协助粤港两地企业运用知识产权以提升创新能力，从而为开拓海外市场做好准备，也在不同层面为粤港双方的知识产权组织、中介机构、行业协会以及青少年提供了有效的交流平台。

本次会议讨论通过了2016下半年至2017上半年粤港知识产权合作计划及项目。根据合作计划，粤港双方将围绕完善合作机制、加强跨境保护、推进贸易合作、推进交流研讨、完善引导服务、开展宣传教育、加强广东自贸区建设中的粤港知识产权合作等七个方面实施24项合作项目。

（资料来源：中国新闻网）

【聂辰席任国家新闻出版广电总局局长、国家版权局局长】 2016年9月29日，国家新闻出版广电总局召开领导干部会议，宣布中央决定：聂辰席同志任中宣部副部长，国家新闻出版广电总局局长、党组书记，国家版权局局长。蔡赴朝同志不再担任中宣部副部长，国家新闻出版广电总局局长、党组书记，国家版权局局长职务。

（资料来源：国家新闻出版广电总局网站）

【北京市版权局再次联合业内企业打击侵权盗版手游】 2016年10月27日，“2016—2017动漫游戏版权保护新闻发布会”在第十一届文博会新闻广电展区的主舞台上隆重举行。

此次发布会是继2015年以来，北京市版权局与万代南宫梦（上海）商贸有限公司再次合作，旨在打击手游侵权盗版，进一步规范手游领域的版权秩序。

当天下午，北京市版权局与万代南梦宫（上海）商贸有限公司就知名动漫IP《航海王》《龙珠》《火影忍者》《机动战士敢达》《数码宝贝》开展版权保护工作，再次签订战略合作协议。万代南梦宫（上海）商贸有限公司战略部副总裁池沢苗表示，公司对侵权盗版问题非常重视，将持续与北京市新闻出版广电局（北京市版权局）合作，保护IP作品的版权不受侵害，共同打击侵权盗版行为。

（资料来源：北青网）

【阎晓宏赴上海美术电影制片厂调研】 2016年10月，国家新闻出版广电总局（国家版权局）副局长阎晓宏赴上海美术电影制片厂调研，上海市新闻出版局（版权局）局长徐炯、副局长蔡纪万陪同调研。

阎晓宏一行参观了上海电影博物馆，与上海电影集团、上海美术电影厂班子成员进行了座谈。阎晓宏充分肯定了上影集团及美影厂在版权创作、运用和保护方面所做的工作，希望上影集团及美影厂进一步加大版权工作力度，重视版权登记，理清版权资源，不断提升版权的价值。

（资料来源：上海市新闻出版局网）

【国家版权局发布《关于加强网络文学作品版权管理的通知》】 2016年11月14日，国家版权局发布了《关于加强网络文学作品版权管理的通知》。《通知》进一步明确了通过信息网络提供文学作品以及提供相关网络服务的网络服务商在版权管理方面的责任义务，细化了著作权法律法规的相关规定，是国家版权局加强网络文学版权保护的一项重要举措，对规范网络文学版权秩序具有重要的意义。

（资料来源：澎湃新闻网）

【《关于完善产权保护制度依法保护产权的意见》发布】 2016年11月27日，中共中央、国务院发布《关于完善产权保护制度依法保护产权的意见》。《意见》中明确表示，产权制度是社会主义市场经济的基石，保护产权是坚持社会主义基本经济制度的必然要求。其中特别强调要加大知识产权保护力度，“加大知识产权侵权行为惩治力度，提高知识产权侵权法定赔偿上限”，“将故意侵犯知识产权行为情况纳入企业和个人信用记录”。《意见》将知识产权放到了与土地、房屋等“硬件”财产同等重要的位置上，将保护知识产权上升到国家的高度，有望进一步推动版权产业的发展，备受业内人士关注。

（资料来源：中国新闻网）

【国家新闻出版广电总局引入水印技术，强化电影版权保护】 2016年11月29日，国家新闻出版广电总局电影质检所（以下简称质检所）与瑞士NexGuard公司签署独家水印保护授权协议，将运用NexGuard提供的水印版权检测技术，为片方、发行方及影院方提供版权保护服务。自2012年以来，质检所已经尝试通过水印检测技术，查处了200余次盗版侵权行为，其中包括《画皮》《泰囧》《捉妖记》

等热门影片首映场即遭盗录的问题。在正式引入NexGuard数字水印保护之后，质检所对于国内上映影片的保护将覆盖到所有电影播放终端。

水印检测技术是指在视频图像或是音频轨迹中嵌入一些特定信息，一旦发现在电影院使用非法设备拍摄的盗版片源，NexGuard可通过软件检测片源水印信息，一小时内就能精确定位盗版内容出自哪家影院的哪一个场次，大幅提高维权效率，同时减少成本。但保利影业公共事业部总监刘建峰指出，水印检测技术对于打击从电影放映终端流出的盗版片源能起到很好的效果，但是盗版片源的资料来源有很多，水印检测技术并不能一一覆盖，网络上很多高清的盗版资源是从源头母带流出的，还有一些是经营场所私自传播的，这些盗版内容没有进过终端放映，自然也就难以检测到。

（资料来源：《北京商报》　作者：卢　扬　王嘉敏）

【“剑网 2016”专项行动总结会在京召开】 2016年12月22日，国家版权局、国家网信办、工信部、公安部在京联合召开“剑网 2016”专项行动总结会。会议认为，通过5个月的专项治理，网络文学、影视、音乐等领域大规模侵权盗版现象基本得到遏制，版权秩序进一步规范，网络版权环境进一步净化。国家新闻出版广电总局副局长、国家版权局副局长阎晓宏出席会议并讲话。

会议认为，“剑网 2016”专项行动在五个方面取得了显著的工作成效。一是措施有力，集中查办一批网络侵权盗版案件。各级版权执法部门周密部署，靠前指挥，各省（区、市）局发挥带头作用，积极查办案件。专项行动期间，各地共查处行政案件514件，行政罚款467万元，移送司法机关案件33件，涉案金额2亿元，关闭网站290家。二是分类监管，集中开展多个领域的专项整治。针对当前互联网治理的热点和难点，分类开展了打击网络文学侵权盗版专项整治、私人影院专项整治、APP专项整治及网络广告联盟专项整治等行动，取得了较好的效果。三是创新管理，进一步推进网站版权重点监管工作。各级版权执法部门继续加强对大型视频网站、音乐网站、文学网站和网盘企业的版权重点监管，推进约谈、预警工作机制，先后公布7批284部热播、热映的重点作品预警名单，指导网站开展自查整改、严格自律。四是健全体系，夯实版权执法监管基础建设。各级版权执法部门认真贯彻“双随机、一公开”原则，全面推进依法公正监管；加强基层执法培训，进一步强化基层基础建设工作；加强案件督查补贴和执法奖励工作，国家版权局联合相关部门督办4批共计31起侵权盗版大要案件。五是积极构建多元化打击侵权盗版社会共治新格局。不断强化宣传，扩大版权工作社会影响；加强与社团组织的联系，发挥协会、联盟和各类权利人的维权积极性。

阎晓宏在讲话中指出，第十二次“剑网行动”具有三个特点：一是覆盖面更宽，除了巩固上年网络音乐、网络云存储空间、网络转载新闻作品等治理成效，重点整治网络文学和APP商店、网络广告联盟、私人影院等领域版权秩序。二是视角更敏锐，积极响应权利人反映强烈的贴吧、微博、微信及私人影院等领域侵权盗版多发高发的情况，并对转码、深度链接、聚合APP等热点难点问题进行深入研究。三是措施扎实有力，在网络文学、广告联盟、APP等领域推行“黑白名单”制度，建立重点保护作品“白名单”库，公布侵权盗版企业“黑名单”；针对侵权盗版黑色经济链条，严厉整治为侵权盗版提供帮助的网络广告联盟。网络版权治理更加深入有效，版权行政执法的优势越来越受到社会重视。“剑网行动”取得的成绩，为进一步做好新形势下的版权执法监管工作奠定了良好的基础。

会议由国家版权局版权管理司司长于慈珂主持，副司长段玉萍通报“剑网 2016”总体情况。全国“双打”办副主任王胜利、国家网信办网络综合协调管理和执法督查局专项治理负责人贺永强、公安部治安局副局长杨奇、工信部信息通信管理局副巡视员游建青就做好网络执法监管工作分别讲话。北京、福建、辽宁、江苏等省份的地方版权执法部门、网络信息管理部门、通信管理部门及公安机关的代表做了经验交流。来自全国31个省（区、市）版权局、4个直辖市文化市场执法总队相关负责人以及移动、联通、百度、阿里、腾讯等几十家版权从业企业代表参加了会议。

（资料来源：《中国新闻出版广电报》　作者：赖名芳）

【国家版权局等四部门通报21起“剑网 2016”专项行动典型网络侵权盗版案件】 2016年12月22日，国家版权局与国家互联网信息办公室、工业和信息化部和公安部四部门联合开展的“剑网 2016”专项行动已圆满收官。各地区、各部门集中查办了一批网络侵权盗版案件，取得了阶段性成果。国家版权局等四部门通报21起较为典型的网络侵权盗版案件。

21起网络侵权盗版案件分别为：北京“顶点小说网”侵犯著作权案、广西南宁“皮皮小说网”涉嫌侵犯著作权案、重庆“269小说网”涉嫌侵犯著作权案、江苏苏州“风雨文学网”涉嫌侵犯著作权案、四川成都“轻之国度网”“轻之文库网”涉嫌侵犯著作权案、北京《一点资讯》客户端软件侵犯著作权案、江苏常州“99770漫画网”等涉嫌侵犯著作权案、天津“吉吉影院网”涉嫌侵犯著作权案、江苏淮安“BT天堂网”涉嫌侵犯著作权案、江苏镇江“迅播影院网”涉嫌侵犯著作权案、湖北黄石“汇梦影视茶吧”侵犯著作权案、上海《echo回声》客户端软件侵犯著作权案、重庆《音乐一号》客户端软件侵犯著作权案、河北保定卫某某涉嫌侵犯网络游戏著作权案、重庆“8·5”系列侵犯网络游戏著作权案、福建厦门“系统大全网”侵犯著作权案、北京“亿梦春田”等6家淘宝网店涉嫌侵犯著作权案、江苏苏州“12·15”侵犯著作权案、江苏镇江“10·26”侵犯著作权案、江西南昌“6·4”侵犯著作权案、广东佛山“12·23”网络批销盗版图书案。

（《中国版权年鉴》编辑部综合）

◆ 宣传教育

【四川为蜀绣作品免费登记著作权】 2016年1月5日，“川针引线·巧手春晖——四川妇女居家灵活就业成就展”在中国妇女儿童博物馆举办。成都市国际版权交易中心主任黄玲介绍，本次展览中的蜀绣作品将全部进行免费著作权登记。自2016年1月1日起，四川省版权局对全省范围内符合《著作权法》规定的作品（不含计算机软件）予以免费登记。

（资料来源：《中国新闻出版广电报》 作者：赖名芳）

【公众号著作权侵权投诉文字作品超六成】 2016年1月11日，腾讯公司发布《2015微信知识产权保护白皮书》。《白皮书》显示，2014年第四季度至2015年第四季度，微信收到针对微信公众账号的投诉超过2.2万件，其中涉及知识产权的投诉超过1.3万件，占比达到60%；针对微信个人账号的投诉超过1.2万件，其中涉及知识产权的投诉有200多件，比例仅为2%。

从发布的数据看，无论对个人账号还是公众账号，商标侵权的投诉在常见知识产权投诉中是最多的，其次是著作权领域，而针对专利侵权的投诉数量均较少。就微信收到的著作权侵权投诉细分数据看，公众账号涉嫌侵权行为集中在对文字类作品的抄袭上，占比61%，而图片类（占比25%）和视频类（占比14%）相对较少。在个人账号侵权投诉中，著作权侵权的类型呈现了不同的特点：涉嫌侵害摄影作品著作权的投诉占2/3左右，其余1/3由侵害他人电影作品著作权（15%）、文字作品著作权（10%）和美术作品著作权（8%）构成。

（资料来源：《中国新闻出版广电报》 作者：赖名芳）

【第四届青岛市版权年会暨版权培训会召开】 2016年1月21日，青岛市文化市场行政执法局联合青岛市版权保护协会组织召开了第四届青岛市版权年会暨版权培训会。

2015年青岛市在打击侵权盗版、做好公共服务和推进版权产业发展方面取得了新成效。全市共有5个单位、11名个人分别获得了全国打击侵权盗版有功单位和有功个人，查处的4起侵权盗版案件被国家版权局挂牌督办，1起案件被评为全国版权十大案件，成功举办了第二届中国青岛·东北亚版权创意精品展示交易会，山东省版权保护与发展现场会在青岛成功召开，即墨市创建全国版权示范城市获得国家版权局批准。2016年，将努力打造“正版青岛、创新城市”。

（资料来源：《半岛都市报》 作者：王法艳）

【江苏泰州开展摄影作品著作权保护培训】 2016年1月，为满足广大摄影爱好者对摄影作品著作权登记知识的需求，江苏省版权局携手泰州市版权局及泰州市摄影家协会在泰州市开展了“摄影作品著作权登记讲座”等系列培训活动。

随着读图时代的来临，摄影作品的价值日益凸显，同时盗版侵权行为也时有发生。由于侵权情节复杂、举证难等，摄影作品著作权人往往会放弃维权。在此情况下，如何让协会会员充分保护自己的作品，如何进行维权等，成为协会亟待解决的问题。培训会上，泰州市版权局相关负责人表示，泰州市版权局将适应版权保护新形势，加强与行业协会的交流与合作，扩大行业协会在版权保护方面的影响力，推动泰州市文化艺术和科学等繁荣发展。泰州市文联相关负责人认为，应充分发挥行业协会在著作权保护方面的作用，探索建立一套行之有效的版权集体管理制度，促进行业协会的健康发展。

（资料来源：《中国知识产权报》 作者 万进萍）

【阅文集团报告显示“90后”网络作家逐渐崛起】 2016年2月17日，阅文集团发布了《阅文集团2015年原创文学报告》，有一个值得注意的现象是，“90后”网络作家正在大量崛起。数据显示，阅文集团签约作家中，“90后”的作家数量占78%，“80后”占16%，其余年龄段仅占6%。

“90后”网络作家的作品也越来越受欢迎。在体现作品人气程度的销售榜上，“90后”作家在前100名中已经占据28席，其中最年轻的作家年仅19岁。此外，值得注意的是，“80后”作家的构成也日益年轻化，在上榜的53位“80后”作家中，“85后”占据了一半以上。

年轻作家的价值在版权上也开始得以体现。比如阅文集团重点运作的叶非夜等“90后”成功作家作品整体版权价值已经进入千万元的阶层。

（资料来源：《中国新闻出版广电报》　作者：任晓宁）

【2015 CPCC十大中国著作权人评选揭晓】　2016年2月24日，在由中国版权保护中心（CPCC）主办的以“尊重原创　传统再造”为主题的2016 CPCC中国版权服务年会开幕式上，“2015 CPCC十大中国著作权人”评选结果揭晓。

白明、唐镛、刘和平、张威（唐家三少）、汪克、北京数字圆明科技文化有限公司、北京爱奇艺科技有限公司、国创联合控股投资有限公司、上海酷景信息技术有限公司、东阳市乐视花儿影视文化有限公司被评为“2015 CPCC十大中国著作权人”。另外，蒋胜男、速泰熙、中国中医科学院中药研究所、北京匡恩网络科技有限责任公司、广州酷狗计算机科技有限公司和熊猫传媒集团（北京紫媒广告有限公司）荣获专家特别提名奖。

“CPCC十大中国著作权人”年度评选活动是中国版权保护中心于2008年推出的一项面向社会的版权公益宣传活动，目的是“携手创新、保护版权、促进发展、构建和谐”，展示广大著作权人的文化创意和创新成果。凡是在中国版权保护中心进行了作品著作权登记并取得著作权登记证书的著作权人，均可报名参加评选活动。2008年以来，音乐创作表演艺术家叶小钢、关峡、小柯、王太利（筷子兄弟成员之一），服装设计师曾凤飞，动画师黄伟明等17人，中国航天员科研训练中心、中国电影集团公司、中国电视剧制作中心有限责任公司、华谊兄弟传媒股份有限公司、央视动画有限公司等53家单位先后荣获“十大中国著作权人”称号。活动向社会公开推介了上百部具有丰富版权价值的好作品，已成为我国版权领域最权威、最公正、影响力最大的著作权人展示和推广平台。

（资料来源：《中国新闻出版广电报》　作者：赖名芳）

【长沙市举办网络著作权行政执法培训班】　2016年3月11日，长沙市举办了全市网络著作权行政执法培训班。

此次培训邀请了上海市文化市场综合执法局的杨勇处长授课，培训主要就网络著作权行政执法依据、程序，互联网环境下著作权行政执法要求、执法特点以及具体执法技巧等方面进行了详细讲授。杨处长将基础理论知识与真实案例有机结合，紧贴实际、操作性强，对长沙市版权行政执法工作具有指导和借鉴作用。

针对网络著作权行政执法案情复杂、专业知识强、执法人员能力不足的特点，长沙市开展了全系统的培训。此次培训，目的是增强全市版权行政执法人员的法治观念、法律意识，提升版权执法人员的业务水平，为下一阶段顺利开展网络版权执法工作打下良好的基础，同时为长沙建设知识产权强市、推动转型创新发展提供支撑。

长沙市各区县（市）知识产权局、版权局，园区知识产权管理部门有关工作人员共60余人参加了培训。

（资料来源：长沙市政府门户网站　作者：潘　虹）

【武汉开展高校版权专题辩论赛】　2016年3月，由武汉市版权局与湖北高校法学辩论联盟联合主办的第六届湖北高校法学专业辩论赛暨2016年版权专题辩论赛在华中农业大学拉开帷幕。来自武汉大学、华中科技大学、华中师范大学等9所高校的大学生以“版权”为主题进行辩论，活动持续一个月，于4月底结束。这也是武汉市版权局第六次主办大学生版权辩论赛。

（资料来源：《中国新闻出版广电报》
作者：汤广花　薛汉卿）

【广西举行版权进校园活动】　2016年4月23日，为迎接“4·26”世界知识产权日，广西纪念世界知识产权日版权进校园活动在广西民族大学举行，以版权进校园活动为契机，推广普及著作权法，加大知识产权保护宣传力度。

活动仪式上，广西民族大学学生代表向全区高校师生发出拒绝盗版倡议书，号召广大师生了解版权保护的有关知识，尊重知识产权，自觉拒绝盗版。自治区版权管理部门在现场为学生们进行了版权登记，现场受理登记的作品类型多样，包括文字作品、摄影作品、音乐作品、美术作品等。

（资料来源：《广西日报》　作者：秦　雯）

【“创意广州·梦想飞翔”2016版权宣传活动在穗举行】 2016年4月24日，为响应第16个世界知识产权日“数字创意、重塑文化”的宣传主题，由广东省新闻出版广电局（版权局）、广州市文化广电新闻出版局（版权局）和广州市文化市场综合行政执法总队主办的“创意广州·梦想飞翔”2016版权宣传活动在广州图书馆启动。香港特别行政区政府知识产权署代表，主办、承办单位有关领导，版权社会服务机构、文化企业代表，广州部分高校学生以及资深媒体人等约500人出席仪式。

启动现场上，首次公布了《2014年广州市版权产业的经济贡献调研报告》，举行广州版权专家库专家聘任仪式，启动“挥动笔尖重塑精彩”原创图文有奖征集活动。同时，启动现场还首播了三部版权主题宣传片。

（资料来源：《广州日报》 作者：黄丹彤）

【《2015年中国网络版权保护年度报告》发布】 2016年4月26日，中国信息通信研究院发布了《2015年中国网络版权保护年度报告》。《报告》指出，2015年，中国网络版权保护取得重大进展。国家更加重视文化产业和知识产权工作，先后做出一系列重大部署，产业政策环境不断优化，互联网、文化、创意等因素更好融合，深入助推国民经济转型升级。在此大背景下，网络版权保护迎来新任务、新机遇。

《报告》认为，2015年“互联网＋”带来了新一轮互联网产业变革和创新，在“互联网＋”行动计划、建设“数字中国”、发展分享经济的推进下，“跨界”“融合”成为产业发展的新态势。“互联网＋”带来了新一轮互联网产业变革和创新，成为经济增长、结构优化新动力。“IP”成为“互联网＋文化”的发展主线与核心价值，“泛娱乐”生态构建行业全产业链内容布局。

《报告》认为，2015年在“剑网行动”的高压态势和网络版权重点监管工作的积极引导下，我国网络版权环境明显好转；与网络版权纠纷相关的互联网行业竞争规则在实践和司法审判中日渐明晰；权利人采用多种方式积极维权，互联网企业互诉与合作并存。

在立法保护方面，我国深入推进国家知识产权战略，立法和司法解释工作得到加强，网络版权法律体系不断完善。在司法保护方面，2015年全国共有2 118件网络版权相关的民事判决和裁定书，与上年同期相比增长28.3％。在行政保护方面，国家版权局在开展版权行政监管与执法工作中呈现出“监管思路更加清晰、监管重点更加突出、监管措施更加有力、监管效果更加显著”的特点。在社会保护方面，互联网企业版权意识不断提升，以声明为基础，加强自律，加大版权合作力度，保护原创作品，完善版权保护和维权机制。

《报告》认为，2015年，我国网络版权保护虽然取得了重大进展，但是也存在诸多问题和挑战，比如：随着大数据时代的到来，网络作品的使用方式和传播路径发生了重大变革，作品创作向全民化、大众化方向发展，传统“先授权后使用”的许可付酬模式面临挑战；内容产业涉及的利益链条较多，如何平衡版权所有人、网络服务商和广大用户的利益，划出网络服务商承担或者不承担侵权责任的界限，成为困扰立法、司法和行政机关的难题；如何在“互联网＋”环境下加强网络版权执法，更加有效地打击网络侵权盗版行为，更好地维护权利人的合法权益，平衡、协调传统行业利益与鼓励互联网企业创新，仍然是我国网络版权保护面临的长期、复杂、艰巨的任务。

（资料来源：国家版权局网站）

【“十二五”期间中国完成软件著作权登记92万余件】 2016年4月26日，由中国版权保护中心组织撰写的《“十二五”中国软件著作权登记情况分析报告》在京发布。《报告》显示，“十二五”期间，中国共完成软件著作权登记92万余件，登记量是“十一五”期间的3.8倍，增速明显。

《报告》称，个人软件著作权登记量年均增速35.64％，增速超过企业著作权人，物联网软件登记“十二五”增速最快，APP软件登记增长势能最为强劲。凸显国家知识产权战略对中国软件产业创新力爆发的驱动作用，呈现了“十三五”开局之年的产业发展新趋势。

《报告》显示，进入“十二五”以来，中国软件著作权登记量呈现出持续快速增长的发展态势，年均增速高达28.96％。2011年中国软件登记量突破10万件，2014年软件登记量突破20万件，2015年软件登记量近30万件。

此外，《报告》显示，“十二五”期间，北京、广东、上海、江苏、浙江软件著作权登记量稳居全国前五。前五位省市共登记软件61.6万件，约占同期中国登记总量的66.68％。

从“十二五”时期中国软件著作权人登记量排名情况来看，大专院校占据了前10位中的9席。其中，昆明理工大学登记软件 2 904 件，高居全国榜首。

（资料来源：新华社）

【宁夏举办全区党政机关软件正版化工作培训班】 2016 年 4 月，宁夏回族自治区推进使用正版软件工作联席会议办公室在银川举办了 2016 年全区党政机关软件正版化工作培训班。自治区新闻出版广电局（版权局）副局长李宝宁代表自治区推进使用正版软件工作联席会议办公室为培训班做了开班动员讲话。国家版权局版权管理司执法监管处副处长郑良斌就国务院推进软件正版化工作政策措施及推进软件正版化长效机制建设等内容进行了讲解。自治区新闻出版广电局（版权局）版权处调研员张宁学对《宁夏回族自治区政府机关使用正版软件管理办法》进行了解读，吴忠市和盐池县分别介绍了推进软件正版化工作的经验和做法。自治区新闻出版广电局（版权局）版权管理处处长张世明主持培训班并做总结讲话。

会议指出，自治区推进软件正版化工作已由推动落实采购经费、建立相关制度，进入到推动规范使用管理、落实责任到人，巩固工作成果、创新工作方法，完善长效机制、加强宣传培训的新阶段。自治区 2016 年将重点抓好以下工作：一是细化责任，推进责任落实到人；二是加强督查，推进制度落实到位；三是加强监管，维护软件市场秩序；四是广泛宣传，营造良好舆论氛围。

培训班还邀请了一铭软件、金山软件、微软（中国）等企业代表，分别就各自产品的性能、特点、服务形式等做了详细介绍。自治区党委、人大、政府、政协、人民法院、人民检察院、总工会、团委、妇联分管信息化工作的负责人，自治区政府各厅、局、委、办负责办公信息化工作的负责人，各市、县（区）政府办公室负责人，各市、县（区）文广局分管领导，共计 134 人参加了此次培训。

（资料来源：宁夏版权局）

【2016 版权宣传周宣传资料发布】 2016 年 4 月，为贯彻落实《国务院关于新形势下加快知识产权强国建设的若干意见》，加强版权宣传普及，做好 2016 年“全国知识产权宣传周”的相关工作，根据《关于做好 2016 年全国知识产权宣传周版权宣传活动的通知》，国家版权局自 4 月初起集中开展版权宣传活动，并将 4 月 20 日至 4 月 26 日作为版权重点宣传时段。

为此，国家版权局制作了四组版权公益宣传画，发布在国家版权局网站（www. ncac. gov. cn）的《通知公告》栏目。宣传资料可用于版权公益宣传。

（资料来源：国家版权局网站）

【国际版权贸易培训班在京举办】 2016 年 4 月，第三届国际版权贸易培训班在京举办。国家新闻出版广电总局进口管理司副司长赵海云说，对于出版单位而言，加快“走出去”首先要看大势、谋大局、做实事。不论是项目申报，还是谋划未来发展，跟上国家的大势才是发展之道。其次，版贸人才和国际管理人才对于“走出去”至关重要。出版社应进一步加强机构和人才的国际化发展。再次，加强人际人脉的交流，使各国的汉学家、作者和译者为我们所用。此外，出版社要有更开阔的视野，进行跨界融合。

培训班上，有关部门的专家就国际出版趋势和中国出版“走出去”、出版物国际传播与推广重点政策和工程项目等进行了解读。

（资料来源：《中国新闻出版广电报》　作者：范燕莹）

【《2016 体育创业白皮书》关注电竞媒体赛事版权】 2016 年 5 月 18 日，中国体育产业跨界峰会在北京举行，会上发布了《2016 体育创业白皮书》。《白皮书》指出，过去 15 个月，体育创业公司完成了超过 257 次融资，融资规模达到 174 亿元人民币。值得一提的是，《白皮书》对于电竞媒体的赛事版权给予了高度关注。

《白皮书》认为，电竞作为聚焦新兴消费人群的赛事 IP，是体育和游戏娱乐的结合体，其产业链中的每一环节都有爆发的趋势，也是体育产业变现路径最清晰的领域之一。电竞新媒体迎来了发展机遇，这是因为较大直播平台缺乏专业的电竞内容，而用户对这方面的内容有强烈的需求，这为垂直的内容媒体或社区的出现创造了机会。

尽管发展迅速，市场潜力巨大，但《白皮书》同时指出，从全球范围的电竞行业来看，电竞媒体的赛事版权归属尚不清晰。在电竞领域，比如《英雄联盟》的游戏版权归 Riot 等游戏开发商和运营商所有，但由粉丝或流媒体制作的包含比赛内容的视频版权却归粉丝和平台所有。目前开发商尚未注重内容版权，对粉丝生产的内容也缺乏足够的重视。

此次峰会由北京懒熊体育文化有限公司主办，逾千名体育产业界人士参加了此次峰会。

（资料来源：中国知识产权资讯网　作者：侯　伟）

【成都在全国率先培训出“双证”文创人才】 2016年6月1日，在成都市文化广电新闻出版局主办的首届国家级版权经纪“双证”人才与创意企业交流会上，成都首批40名获得文化创意师、版权经纪人资格的成都文创人才获颁“双证”。作为全国首个版权示范城市，成都市又成为全国首个培养出“双证”文创人才的城市。

成都市本着“产业发展，交易先行；交易推进，人才先行”的理念，启动版权经纪人才培训计划，率先举办全国版权经纪人和文化创意师（版权经纪）“双证”培训，参与培训的人才经过考试取得了“双证”。

文化创意师（版权经纪）“双证”培训是由国家人力资源和社会保障部教育培训中心立项运营的项目。旨在增进对版权领域各产业及新媒体版权运营模式的理解，革新我国文化创意领域核心版权人才的经营理念，进而为相关单位实现版权产品深度研发和跨平台、跨行业版权合作提供必要的人才储备。

（资料来源：《成都晚报》　作者：汪　兰）

【2016年全国作品登记工作培训班在京举行】 2016年6月27日，由国家版权局主办的2016年全国作品登记工作培训班在京开班。

作品登记工作是建设版权公共服务体系的重要内容。自1995年《作品自愿登记试行办法》发布实施后，各地版权局陆续开展了此项工作。目前除西藏自治区外，共有30个省级版权局及中国版权保护中心正在从事作品登记工作。据统计，“十二五”时期，全国作品登记量有突破性增长，仅2015年全年，全国共完成作品登记1 348 200件，比2014年的992 034件增长了35.9%。

国家版权局版权管理司副司长汤兆志说，随着社会公众版权意识不断增强，加大版权运用、以版权为核心资产进行融资等方面的需求日益强烈，作品登记工作仍然是国家版权局的重点工作，希望各登记机构以推进作品登记工作为重点，加强版权公共服务能力建设，进一步规范作品登记工作，加强主体责任意识；做好信息报送工作；加强作品登记工作人员队伍建设，不断提高作品登记质量，不断完善作品登记信息统计工作，不断扩大作品登记覆盖面，推进作品登记工作向纵深发展。

培训班上介绍了国内外作品登记工作情况，并对国家版权监管平台著作权登记运行情况以及作品登记、信息统计报送注意事项和常见问题进行说明与解答。来自北京、上海、山东、江苏、福建、湖北6省市的代表发言，与大家交流作品登记工作经验。

中国版权保护中心副主任范继红致辞。本次培训为期两天，中国版权保护中心、各省级版权局版权处负责人以及各地登记机构负责作品登记的人员参加了专题培训。

与会者认为，本次培训不仅有宏观的业务指导，也有各地经验交流，同时还有操作层面的相关业务讲解以及对中国版权保护中心的实地参观，对进一步做好作品登记工作很有帮助。

（资料来源：《中国新闻出版广电报》　作者：赵新乐）

【中国版权协会2016年第一期版权培训班成功举办】 2016年7月8日，中国版权协会2016年第一期免费版权培训班在北京京瑞饭店会议大厅举办，来自中国版权协会会员单位的百余负责人参加了此次培训。

国家新闻出版广电总局副局长、国家版权局副局长、中国版权协会理事长阎晓宏，北京知识产权法院法官芮松艳分别做了题为《版权与文化产业发展》和《著作权典型案例介绍》的报告；国家新闻出版广电总局版权管理司司长于慈珂、北京外国语大学法学院教授丛立先、北京冠勇科技有限公司总裁吴冠勇在会上发表了演讲。

阎局长在报告中强调了版权的基本属性是作者权利，同时指出版权的本质属性还不被社会大众所认知，所以提高和树立版权意识仍然是当前全社会的紧迫任务。

芮法官从作品的实质性近似的判断、古籍典校的问题、合理使用以及网络服务提供行为的侵权认定四个方面展开介绍了著作权纠纷中的典型案件；于司长从版权的本质、版权的规律、版权的保护与运用等方面展开了讲述，系统梳理了我国版权发展历程。

结合当前热点问题，丛立先教授从产业层面和政策制度层面做了题为《传统出版与新兴出版融合中的出版保护与运用》的主题演讲。吴冠勇先生则重点介绍了版权监测保护的产业链，以及版权监测技术及应用。

（资料来源：中国版权产业网　作者：慕　因）

【《2015年新闻出版产业分析报告》发布】 2016年8月8日，国家新闻出版广电总局发布了《2015年新闻出版产业分析报告》。《报告》显示，2015年全国出版、印刷和发行服务实现营业收入21 655.9亿元，较2014年增加1 688.8亿元，同比增长 8.5%。新闻出版服务大局能力持续提升，主题出版、主流媒体传播力影响力进一步彰显。在年度单品种累计印数排名前 10 的书籍中，主题出版书籍占据半壁江山。其中，《习近平关于党风廉政建设和反腐败斗争论述摘编》超过 550 万册，《习近平谈治国理政》超过 400 万册。《求是》平均期印数超过 100 万册，《时事报告》两个版本每期平均印数合计超过 400 万册。《人民日报》、《参考消息》和《环球时报》等报纸平均期印数均超过 100 万份，《人民日报》和《参考消息》稳居年度报纸平均期印数排名前 10 位。

数字出版继续保持高速增长，已成为产业发展的主要增长极。数字出版实现营业收入 4 403.9 亿元，较 2014 年增加了 1 016.2 亿元，增长 30.0%，占全行业营业收入的 20.3%，提高了 3.4 百分点；对全行业营业收入增长贡献率达 60.2%。增长速度与增长贡献率在新闻出版各产业类别中均位居第一。

出版传媒集团整体规模稳步提升。全国 119 家集团共实现主营业务收入 3 001.8 亿元，较 2014 年增加 187.0 亿元，增长 6.6%；拥有资产总额 6 018.1 亿元，增加了 670.2 亿元，增长 12.5%；拥有所有者权益 3 178.1 亿元，增加了 357.5 亿元，增长了 12.7%。共有 16 家集团资产总额超过百亿元。

报刊结构调整进一步深化，报纸出版面临的挑战更趋严峻。报刊专业化、细分化趋势加快。2015 年，平均期印数超过百万册的前 10 位期刊中，《读者》《小学生时代》《知音漫客》《青年文摘》等文摘类、少儿类期刊超过半数。报纸出版出现全方位下滑趋势。报纸出版总印数、总印张分别降低 7.3% 和 19.1%，营业收入、利润总额分别降低 10.3%和 53.2%。43 家报业集团主营业务收入与利润总额分别降低 6.9%与 45.1%，其中 31 家报业集团营业利润出现亏损，较 2014 年增加 14 家。面对严峻挑战，报纸出版单位积极探索业务转型，其中浙报传媒集团股份有限公司、华闻传媒投资集团股份有限公司、浙江华媒控股股份有限公司等单位数字出版、动漫等新业态业务收入实现较大幅度增长，平均净资产收益率均超过 10%，浙报传媒集团股份有限公司数字出版等新业态业务收入已超过传统报刊业务收入。

国民阅读率持续提升，数字化阅读增长较快。2015 年我国各媒介综合阅读率为 79.6%，较 2014 年提高 1.0 百分点；国民图书阅读率为 58.4%，提高 0.2 百分点；数字化阅读方式的接触率为 64.0%，提高 5.9 百分点，增长幅度远高于国民图书阅读率，反映出国民阅读方式正在发生深刻变化。

（资料来源：新闻出版广电总局网站）

【“助力原创　保护版权”全球公共艺术倡议行动启动】　2016 年 8 月 18 日，第八届中国国际影视动漫版权保护和贸易博览会在东莞举行。在开幕当天举办的“中国动画影视高峰会”上，启动了“助力原创　保护版权”全球公共艺术倡议行动。

动漫产业是现在的朝阳产业之一，其产业链涵盖了动画、漫画、游戏、玩具制造业等诸多行业。从根本上说，动漫产业每个链条之间的关系其实质就是一种版权关系，对版权的创造、管理、保护和运用的好坏直接关系到动漫产业的生存和发展，随着我国动漫产业日益壮大，原创动漫被侵权盗版的现象频发、高发，严重影响了产业的健康有序发展，版权问题已经成为动漫产业发展中的核心问题。

“漫博会作为国际级展会，加强版权保护，促进版权贸易一直是办展的宗旨和亮点。”广东省新闻出版广电局（版权局）版权管理处处长张同英说，“本届漫博会我们将有效整合省、市现有的版权行政管理、版权行政执法、版权行业协会和中介组织等各方力量，在总结历届漫博会版权服务成功经验的基础上继续设立版权服务工作站，负责漫博会期间的版权行政执法、版权保护宣传、版权服务管理、版权运用交易等工作，对本届漫博会的参展作品实行‘作品著作权免费登记’，努力为本届漫博会营造良好的版权保护和版权贸易氛围。”

（资料来源：央广网　作者：周　羽）

【第八届中国国际影视动漫版权保护和贸易博览会闭幕】　2016 年 8 月 22 日，为期 5 天的第八届中国国际影视动漫版权保护和贸易博览会（以下简称漫博会）在广东省东莞市闭幕。

本届漫博会共有海内外参展企业 503 家，征集扶持作品 1 539 件，现场入场人数超过 30 万人次，其中专业观众 8 238 人，现场消费和合同、意向成交额 34.6 亿元，受理参展作品著作权免费登记申请 828 宗，现场核发作品著作权登记证书 503 个。漫博会已成为集版权贸易、产业对接、衍生品交易和行业交流于一体的动漫行业高端商贸平台。

广东省版权局、东莞市版权局、广东省作品著作权登记机构等单位派出 46 人的版权服务团队，设立 2 个版权服务工作站、2 个版权执法巡查组，现场为参展、参观企业及参观观众提供一站式专业服务。

本届漫博会继续设立“一对一”商务洽谈区，为动漫企业提供合作交流平台。据不完全统计，展会期间共安排了292宗“一对一”商务洽谈，分别为原创、游戏与渠道、金融、衍生产品等项目搭建对接交流平台。漫博会还举办2016年最具市场潜力动漫原创项目预售——商务配对活动，组织影视动漫、漫画剧本、新媒体、游戏等动漫原创项目进行专场预售。本届漫博会还举办中国动画影视高峰会、品牌授权精准对接会等11场专业活动，力促企业对接合作。

本届漫博会VR产业大热，吸引了来自北京、广州、深圳、东莞等地28家VR/AR企业组团参展，VR展区既赚足人气又引发行业热议。展会期间，举办多场论坛关注VR产业。在松山湖举行的2016中国（松山湖）VR国际论坛，是东莞首次举办VR国际论坛，国内外VR产业专家、开发厂商、应用服务商等齐聚松山湖，重点讨论VR技术应用如何对接家具、服装、房地产、旅游、影视、游乐等传统产业，以及展览展示、电子商务等新兴产业，利用VR技术助推传统产业转型升级的路径。本届漫博会还举办影视互动娱乐投资对接会，现场多位嘉宾看好VR市场，认为VR产业已应用在影视、地产等领域，而在消费端应用预期市场规模巨大。

本届漫博会，多家动漫企业借助漫博会影响力发布最新消息。例如，时代科腾最新动漫作品《飞天少年》举行了首映仪式，《飞天少年》是中国首部航空航天电视动画片，是国家新闻出版广电总局“中国梦”题材的重点项目；东莞本土企业智高文具举行新闻发布会喜报成功登陆“新三板”，将以IP运营为核心，打造一个集动漫文化创意、幼儿教育、少儿连锁体验经营、品牌授权、渠道运营、媒体联盟、文具产品研产销于一体带动的文化创意产业生态平台；东莞市海霖动画制作有限公司制作的东莞首部三维动画电影《吉祥宝宝之我是食神》选择在本届漫博会期间在各大院线上映。

本届漫博会主分会场亮点纷呈，共举办80多场大众活动，吸引超过30万人次入场参与活动，让市民尽享动漫欢乐。

（资料来源：央广网）

【山东省即墨市启动首届优秀版权作品大赛】 2016年9月8日，山东省即墨市创建全国版权示范城市工作领导小组启动即墨市第一届优秀版权作品大赛。大赛以文学艺术和工业设计为分类，分别对即墨市的歌曲、舞蹈、微电影、小品、诗词和工业设计等原创作品进行了生动展示，并现场为作者颁发山东省版权登记证书。

本次版权作品大赛以“版权引领升级，创新推动转型”为主题。大赛自2016年8月起，面向即墨市各界有创意设计能力的个人和机构征集文学艺术类和工业版权类原创作品。凡是文字、美术、音乐、戏剧、曲艺、舞蹈、杂技艺术、摄影、电影或产品设计图、工程设计图、计算机软件均可参赛。作品要求从未公开发表，创造性地使用即墨文化艺术元素，且取得国家或山东省版权登记证书。

即墨市近年来大力开展版权宣传，版权登记作品数量猛增。2016年6月1日，即墨市向山东省版权局申请获得全省县级市唯一的版权登记初级审核、证书打印权限以后，版权登记数量进一步攀升。截至2016年9月，已通过版权登记初审4 000余件。

（资料来源：《中国新闻出版广电报》　作者：刘　冰）

【国家版权局率17家中央媒体记者学习交流重报集团版权维权工作】 2016年11月18日，国家版权局率《人民日报》、《经济日报》、人民网、新华网、中央电视台等17家中央媒体记者就重庆日报报业集团（以下简称重报集团）版权维权工作的有效做法进行学习交流，他们对重报集团在全国报业集团首创新闻作品数字版权维权系统平台给予了充分肯定。

重报集团有关负责人介绍，从2015年开始，重报集团通过建设“新闻内容生产及运营监管平台”，将版权维权系统纳入平台建设的“六大板块系统”之一。该监管平台和版权维护系统项目被国家新闻出版广电总局确立为2015年国家数字化转型升级重点建设项目和改革发展入库重大项目，建设周期两年。经过1年多建设，该平台已于2016年7月试运行。

该版权维权平台系统由版权确权、版权监测、版权维权、报表分析四个模块构成。版权确权模块通过和集团各媒体的采编系统及工作平台进行无缝对接，将其发布的新闻作品嵌入水印进行确权。同时，平台监测系统还可以在全网进行查找疑似作品，将相关作品的数据、信息与确权作品进行比对，并分析统计。而系统的取证功能则会针对侵权作品数据自动生成取证任务，并完成实时在线取证。

“该维权系统可第一时间确权、第一时间固化证据，而且在查找疑似作品时，还可以追踪到对方服务器地址，及时提出预警。可以说，只要启动了这个维权系统，所有互联网上疑似侵权的行为都逃不过它的‘法眼’。”该负责人说。

2014年3月12日，重报集团在旗下媒体及《中国新闻出版报》发布《重庆日报报业集团版权声明》，成为全国率先发声进行版权维护的党报集团，引起社会广泛关注，并受到国家版权局高度重视。重报集团也荣获“2014 中国版权最具影响力企业”称号。

重报集团总裁向泽映在接受采访时表达了重报集团维权的坚定决心。他说，集团以先进技术为引领，创新理念和技术手段，实施的版权保护系统和一系列维权措施，既是对新闻记者采写的新闻作品自身权益的尊重和维护，也是贯彻落实国家新闻出版广电总局关于进一步规范网络转载有关规定的具体措施。

国家版权局版权司执法处处长赵杰说：“这次由国家版权局集中组织中央媒体到重报集团采访调研。重报集团维权的做法是走在全国新闻单位前列的，许多地方值得总结和推广，尤其是数字版权维权系统。这套数字版权维权系统在全国新闻作品版权维权中起到了很好的带头作用，希望重报集团认真总结，让其发挥更大的示范作用。”

（资料来源：《重庆日报》）

【多位文艺创作者获“中国版权卓越成就者”奖】 2016 年 11 月 25 日，在由中国版权协会主办的“第九届中国版权年会”上，作家陈建功、音乐家李海鹰等十人获“第三届中国版权卓越成就者”奖。

获奖者为作家陈建功、中国出版集团公司总裁谭跃、作家熊召政、音乐家李海鹰、音乐人小柯、华东政法大学教授王迁、高等教育出版社社长苏雨恒、北京知识产权法院院长宿迟、北京市版权局副局长王野霏、金山办公软件 CEO 葛珂。他们分别在推动文学艺术创作、版权学术研究、司法保护、版权产业发展和行政管理方面取得了显著成绩，获得各界的高度认可。

在文学艺术创作方面，作家陈建功曾出版《迷乱的星空》《丹凤眼》《北京滋味》《嬉笑歌哭》等多部作品，部分作品还经翻译后在国外出版。作家熊召政曾出版长篇历史小说《张居正》四卷本，并因此获得茅盾文学奖。音乐家李海鹰创作了《七子之歌》《弯弯的月亮》《我不想说》《走四方》等一系列有影响力的音乐作品。小柯是北京奥运歌曲《北京欢迎你》的作曲者，还创作了《归去来》《因为爱情》等多部优秀作品。

（资料来源：《中国知识产权报》 作者：刘 仁）

【2016 中国版权金奖在广州颁发】 2016 年 12 月 5 日，中国版权金奖颁奖仪式作为第六届中国国际版权博览会开幕式上的重头戏，在众人的期待中揭开了面纱。6 个作品奖、5 个推广运用奖、5 个保护奖和 4 个管理奖悉数亮相。

其中作品奖文字作品有 3 个，分别是曹文轩的《青铜葵花》、上海译文出版社出版的《英汉大词典》和海宴的《琅琊榜》，另 3 个是中国电影股份有限公司等制作的电影《狼图腾》、一铭软件股份有限公司设计的《一铭操作系统》和河北电影电视剧制片中心制作的《海棠依旧》。

5 个推广运用奖被外文出版社有限责任公司、深圳市腾讯计算机系统有限公司、江西网络广播电视台、时代出版传媒股份有限公司和宁夏盛天彩数字科技股份有限公司捧走。5 个保护奖由重庆市公安局打击假冒伪劣商品犯罪侦查总队、上海冠勇信息科技有限公司、徐州市版权局、北京搜狐互联网信息服务有限公司和德化县人民政府获得。4 个管理奖则由成都市版权局、中国文字著作权协会、北京中视瑞德文化传媒股份有限公司和即墨市人民政府获得。

“中国版权金奖”是中国国家版权局与世界知识产权组织（WIPO）开展的合作项目，每两年评选一次，是中国版权领域内评选的唯一国际性奖项，也是国内版权领域的最高奖项。“中国版权金奖”的前身是“世界知识产权组织版权金奖（中国）”，已于 2008 年、2010 年、2012 年和 2015 年成功举办了四届，共有 55 个版权相关企业、机构及著作权人获奖，引起国内国际社会广泛关注，收到良好社会反响。

（资料来源：国家版权局网站 作者：邹 韧）

【“深圳版权金奖”举行颁奖典礼】 2016 年 12 月 9 日，第五届“深圳版权金奖”颁奖仪式在鹏城举行。国家版权局版权管理司副司长汤兆志，广东省版权局专职副局长陈春怀以及深圳市司法界、创意文化产业界、深圳市版权协会的代表近 200 人出席了颁奖活动。

第五届“深圳版权金奖”评选于 2016 年 9 月 20 日正式启动，由组委会邀请著名学者、行业专家、专业机构代表组成专家评审团，对本次参赛作品和参选单位进行评审。在奖项设置上立足文化创意产业与版权产业的版权创造、运用、保护与管理，共评选出“版权作品金奖”、“版权运用金奖”、“版权保护金奖”、“优秀版权经理人奖”以及“年度版权登记领衔奖”、“年度软件正版化企业示范奖”六类 30 个奖项，以此来表彰和鼓励在这些领域取得出色成绩的代表。

“深圳版权金奖”评选活动对促进深圳产业发展发挥了引领作用。本次活动由深圳报业集团、深圳广播电影电视集团、深圳市版权协会、深圳新闻网联合主办，得到广东省版权局、深圳市市场监督管理局（知识产权局）及有关部门的支持和指导。

（资料来源：《深圳商报》　作者：苏　兵）

◆ 交流研讨

【“影视创作从依法保护原创开始”座谈会在京举办】　2016年1月15日，中国电影文学学会在京举办“影视创作从依法保护原创开始”座谈会，多位知名编剧与法律界人士围绕“琼瑶诉于正案”进行深入探讨，呼吁行业自律和保护原创。与会者认为，“琼瑶诉于正案”不仅在于原创的胜利，而且警醒每一名创作者，要懂得用法律保护自己的合法权益，在知法懂法的同时，创作更好的作品。

会上，琼瑶委托律师宣读了她的感谢信，表示对大陆的司法环境和知识产权保护力度充满信心。琼瑶表示，500万元赔偿款已悉数收到，按照计划她将把赔偿金用于成立一个面向华语文化的“琼瑶文化基金”，以培养和资助青年学生的原创文化作品，扶持贫困学生等。

中国电影文学学会副会长兼秘书长汪海林表示，在“琼瑶诉于正案”的判决中，看到了法院对专业的高度尊重。法律只是底线，基于行业的处罚则更能促进行业自律。他透露，中国广播电影电视社会组织联合会电视剧编剧工作委员会正在探讨对于正的行业处罚。

北京知识产权法院副院长、“琼瑶诉于正案”审判长宋鱼水认为，行业惯例和法律的互动是非常有价值的。在当前媒介发达的社会环境下，主审法官一方面希望案件审理公开透明，另一方面不希望舆论干预司法。

中国电影文学学会会长王兴东表示，中国电影文学学会将继续秉承“自律、维权、服务、管理”的理念，服务华语电影事业，同时呼吁《电影产业促进法》应加强对原创剧本、编剧权益的保护。

（资料来源：《中国新闻出版广电报》　作者：李　彦）

【“网络音乐版权保护与商业模式”研讨会在京召开】　2016年1月27日，由中国版权杂志社、中国版权产业网主办的“网络音乐版权保护与商业模式”研讨会在京召开。会议就当前我国网络音乐产业的现状、网络音乐版权保护和商业模式，特别是收费模式、分配模式等进行了梳理和分析。

会上，国家版权局版权管理司司长于慈珂介绍说，在2015年国家版权局等四部门开展的“剑网2015”专项行动中，首次把音乐作为重点治理领域，目的就是要规范网络音乐版权秩序，推动并建立一个良好的网络音乐版权生态环境。

正是基于政府所做出的努力，我国网络音乐版权出现了可喜的“基本正版”局面。对此，海洋音乐集团首席内容官姜山希望2016年政府部门继续加大推动和关注有关互联网音乐的正版化工作，同时他们也会在现有成绩的基础上，做好相关的打盗维权工作，并利用这个契机培养用户购买正版的消费习惯和付费习惯，从而促进各个平台共同推动网络音乐付费的商业模式。

研讨会上，与会嘉宾提出，正版并不是终极目标，在正版的基础上让产业有实质性的发展、建立良好的商业模式，让产业链上的相关各方都得到回报、各得其所，并真正推进音乐创作和音乐产业的繁荣，才是根本目标，也是行业下一步的努力方向和工作重点。

（资料来源：《中国新闻出版广电报》　作者：邹　韧）

【“互联网环境下传统出版版权保护与国际版权贸易高级研修班”在沪举办】　2016年1月，上海新闻出版教育培训中心、上海市版权协会联合举办了“互联网环境下传统出版版权保护与国际版权贸易高级研修班”。此次培训班特邀美国出版集团负责人、版权领域资深律师及国内版权专家，围绕互联网环境下的版权保护、版权经营、国际版权贸易等内容展开主题授课。上海市版权局副局长蔡纪万到会致辞，他强调了当前形势下加强对传统出版行业版权保护的重要意义，希望通过培训与交流，促进解决传统出版业面临的版权保护与版权贸易难题，切实提高出版行业版权管理经营水平。上海市以及辽宁、安徽、浙江三省的出版行业、报刊行业的版权部门负责人200余人参加了本次培训。

（资料来源：上海市新闻出版局网站）

【2016 CPCC中国版权服务年会在京举行】
2016年2月24日至25日，由中国版权保护中心（CPCC）主办、以“尊重原创　传统再造”为主题的2016 CPCC中国版权服务年会在京举行。国家新闻出版广电总局副局长、国家版权局副局长阎晓宏出席年会开幕式，并为获得“2015 CPCC十大中国

著作权人”称号的刘和平、张威（唐家三少）等颁奖，希望获得2015 CPCC十大中国著作权人和专家提名奖的获奖者，不断创造更多优秀的版权成果和财富。

阎晓宏对年会的召开表示祝贺。阎晓宏指出，2016年是“十三五”规划的开局之年，也是版权工作加快发展的关键之年。“十三五”期间，我国经济发展将表现出速度变化、结构优化、动力转换等重要特点，经济社会发展将更多依靠包括版权在内的智力成果的运用，将更多依靠创新作为发展的驱动。创新的关键是原创，原创则更多来源于丰富多彩的传统文化。以优秀传统文化为根脉，以原创的优秀作品为中心环节，激发原创动力，释放原创动力，进一步提高原创版权的创造、运用、保护和管理水平，深化对原创版权价值的认识和理解，这既是时代的呼声，也是版权工作的重要内容。举办以“尊重原创　传统再造”为主题的版权服务年会既符合业界期许和诉求，又顺应版权产业繁荣发展的大趋势，具有十分重要的现实意义。

（资料来源：《中国新闻出版广电报》　作者：赖名芳）

【首届中国知识产权保护高层论坛举办】　2016年4月9日至10日，首届中国知识产权保护高层论坛在北京举办。

本届论坛的主题是“保护知识产权、促进创业创新”，论坛希望通过强化知识产权保护意识，营造更好的创业创新环境，支撑创新驱动发展战略实施。

与会者认为，如何用好知识产权保护这个“驱动轮”，促进创业创新，已成为社会各界关注的焦点。我国知识产权保护虽然已经取得显著成绩，但也面临着一系列深层次的矛盾和问题，保护效果与社会期待相比还有一定差距。比如，知识产权行政保护手段不足、能力不强，行政保护与司法保护的衔接也还不够紧密和协调顺畅等。这些问题都需要通过进一步加大知识产权保护工作力度加以解决。

此次论坛共分为1个主论坛和5个分论坛。来自国内外600余名与会代表紧紧围绕“保护知识产权、促进创业创新”这一主题，就专利、版权、商标等领域的知识产权保护热点问题进行了深入交流，共同探索知识产权保护的新路径。

（资料来源：《中国新闻出版广电报》　作者：邹　韧）

【版权人沙龙聚焦互联网内容平台版权保护与管理】　2016年4月21日，由中国人民大学国家版权贸易基地和创意产业技术研究院主办的第36期版权人沙龙在文化大厦举行。本期沙龙主题为“互联网内容平台的版权保护与管理”，来自国家版权局版权管理司、文化部政策法规司的负责人，中国人民大学知识产权学院、北京交通大学法学院的专家学者，以及互联网内容平台和相关企业的代表参加了本期沙龙。沙龙由中国人民大学国家版权贸易基地主任、中国人民大学创意产业技术研究院院长彭翊主持。

在沙龙上，酷酷集团、今日头条、迅雷网络、美好景象、冠勇科技等知名互联网企业代表分别介绍了文字、音乐、视频、图片等内容平台的发展情况，分享了版权保护和管理的模式和经验，多家内容平台针对版权维权的主要技术手段、当前互联网侵权特点，提出建立统一反盗版技术措施的行业标准和新模式，构建版权生态环境和版权保护机制。中国人民大学知识产权学院教授金海军针对各企业提出的问题，分享了其在内容聚合平台研究课题方面的调研成果，以及各国平衡技术创新与内容保护的不同方式。北京交通大学法学院副教授陈明涛则分析了内容聚合平台在内容制作方面涉及的转码、深度链接和分工合作问题，并指出商业维权难的根源在于侵权赔偿过低。在听取企业代表的经验分享和专家学者的相关观点后，文化部政策法规司法制处处长阎平介绍说，近两年来文化部持续关注与扶持知识产权保护工作，并积累了一定的经验，但文化系统在知识产权方面存在着保护意识比较薄弱，保护力度不足，文化领域侵权成本低、举证和维权难度大，知识产权权属不明等问题。针对以上问题，文化部将加强工作指导，提高服务能力，借助“外脑”资源开展理论研究，与文化企业、高校密切合作，继续推动文化知识产权各方面工作。国家版权局版权管理司司长于慈珂在总结发言中指出，经过十多年的“剑网”行动，侵权盗版行为已经得到了很大的遏制，但面临互联网条件下侵权盗版花样不断翻新、版权保护难度不断加大的现状，政府和企业仍需要共同努力，从依法保护、严格保护、适度保护三个方面发力，进一步构建有效的网络版权保护格局。依法保护是指在现有法律框架下，不断完善法律，积极推进第三次《著作权法》修订；严格保护是指不断加大保护力度，对新技术条件下产生的新问题及时解决，并将其作为行政监管工作的着力点；适度保护是指立足国情，在构建网络版权有效保护的格局下，实行适度保护的政策选择。

（资料来源：人大新闻网）

【三家著作权集体管理组织走进清华研讨热点话题】 2016年4月21日，中国音乐著作权协会、中国音像著作权集体管理协会、中国文字著作权协会三家集体管理组织与清华大学法学院共同组织了“著作权集体管理热点研讨会”，就非法集体管理、延伸集体管理、集体管理许可费率等热点问题展开深入研讨。三家集体管理组织分别介绍了集体管理组织的具体实践、各自的运行状况及遇到的困难，专家学者从立法背景、法律机理、国内外借鉴等角度提出了有针对性的观点和建议。

在研讨会上，集体管理组织的代表与学术界的专家学者不断产生观点碰撞和思想交锋，各有坚持又互相理解，取得了很好的效果。研讨会结束后，大家意犹未尽，希望能保持这种经常性的沟通和交流，加深相互理解，增进学术界对版权产业发展及著作权集体管理实务的了解，以便今后能够给予集体管理组织更多的智力支持与法理指导。

中国文字著作权协会负责人张洪波表示，在此之前，3月24日下午，中国音乐著作权协会、中国音像著作权集体管理协会、中国文字著作权协会三家集体管理组织的负责人就曾一起前往中国人民大学，参加由英国驻华大使馆与中国人民大学法学院共同举办的“著作权集体管理制度修法建议研讨会”，就《著作权法》第三次修改过程中著作权集体管理制度的修改完善等问题，阐述了集体管理组织的态度、观点和建议。

另外，中国文字著作权协会等著作权集体管理组织还通过与高校专家学者共同研究课题、开展专题研讨会、邀请专家学者实地调研及授课等方式，增强学术界与集体管理实务界的联系互动。“前不久，我们就邀请德国马克斯·普朗克知识产权法学研究中心的李陶博士来中国文字著作权协会举办了专题讲座。李陶介绍了著作权集体管理的理论架构和制度功能，比较了中德两国文字著作权集体管理在制度及实务上的差异，并对集体管理制度的完善提出了建议。”张洪波说道。

（资料来源：《中国新闻出版广电报》）

【中国网络版权保护大会在北京召开】 2016年4月26日是第16个世界知识产权日，国家版权局当天在北京举办中国网络版权保护大会。工信部、公安部、国家网信办等相关部门负责人及来自版权产业界的代表，共同探讨了“数字网络发展与版权保护”等热点话题。国家新闻出版广电总局副局长、国家版权局副局长阎晓宏出席大会开幕式并致辞。

阎晓宏在致辞中表示，从现阶段看，网络版权保护呈现出三个积极特征：一是版权在互联网生态中的重要作用日益凸显，“互联网+版权”已经成为互联网产业发展的重要模式。二是期待网络版权秩序更加清朗已经成为行业的共识，网络版权治理初见成效。三是网络版权保护迎来了春天。党的十八大以来，党中央、国务院将网络治理和知识产权工作提高到了前所未有的高度。要贯彻中央关于实行严格知识产权保护的战略部署，进一步加大网络版权保护力度，针对网络文学、网络新闻作品转载、智能移动终端第三方应用程序（APP）等网络侵权的热点领域开展专项治理。要始终抓住社会共治这一重要手段，推动构建全社会共同治理新格局，把行业、企业包括社会公众的力量凝聚起来，形成政府有效监管、企业自我约束、行业自律与公众监督相结合的打盗维权新格局。

国家网信办政策法规局局长杨树桢在发言中就如何进一步加强网络版权保护提出五点建议：以观念为先导，不断提高广大网民的网络版权保护意识；以创新为引领，积极鼓励和推动网络版权保护技术创新与发展；以法治为保障，加大网络执法力度；以共治为基础，构建社会各界共同参与、共享的全社会协同治理体系；以开放为动力，加强网络知识产权保护国际交流合作。

工信部信息通信管理局副局长李湘宁表示，工信部将按照“剑网2016”专项行动各项工作要求，形成长效的工作机制，通过加强监督检查、落实企业责任等方式，继续做好打击网络侵权假冒违法违规行为的相关工作。

韬奋基金会理事长聂震宁、乐视网副董事长韩方明、腾讯高级执行副总裁汤道生、世界知识产权组织中国办事处主任陈宏兵、合一集团总裁刘德乐、新华社新闻信息中心主任储学军、中国互联网协会秘书长卢卫、阿里音乐首席执行官宋柯分别做了演讲。

国家版权局在大会上发布了“2015年度全国打击侵权盗版十大案件”，为部分获得“2015年度查处侵权盗版案件有功单位及个人”荣誉的版权执法人员进行颁奖。

（资料来源：《中国新闻出版广电报》 作者：赖名芳）

【版权相关热点问题媒体研修班在北京开班】 2016年4月27日，2016年第一期版权相关热点问题媒体研修班在北京开班。

来自新华社、《人民日报》、《光明日报》、《经济日报》、《科技日报》等近30家媒体的40余名编辑记者经过一天紧张的学习研讨，对版权进行了更深的了解，对于三位老师授课的内容大家感觉受益匪浅。有记者表示，通过此次学习，在今后进行与版权有关的新闻报道时心里更有谱了。

本次媒体研修活动，国家版权局特意选择了专家授课的形式，目的是让更多记者对我国版权保护工作现状以及著作权法律法规知识有更全面、深入的了解。研修活动专门邀请了国家版权局版权管理司司长于慈珂做了题为《数字环境下，中国版权保护现状、政策与措施》的讲解，他从宏观角度全面系统地介绍了我国在版权创造、运用、管理和保护方面的经验和做法。中南财经政法大学法学院、知识产权学院教授熊琦，讲授了在互联网环境下版权面临的新常态、新闻版权的认定以及新闻版权保护等热点问题。北京知识产权法院法官芮松艳则通过以案说法的形式，给大家深入浅出地讲授了在数字环境下新闻作品该如何进行版权保护与传播。

中国新闻出版广电报社社长兼总编辑马国仓在主持研修活动时介绍，从2009年开始，由国家版权局主办、《中国新闻出版广电报》承办的版权相关热点问题媒体研修班，一直以“培训一名记者，将引导一大群读者”为宗旨，先后举办了15期，来自中央几十家主流媒体以及山东、浙江、福建、广东、上海等省市的数百名编辑记者，以“边学习、边调研，边采访、边报道”不断“充电”的形式，不仅学习了版权理论知识，也加强了新闻媒体对版权产业发展的了解与认识，这样的研修学习对编辑、记者们在相关版权事件报道时起到了良好的引导作用。

（资料来源：《中国新闻出版广电报》　作者：邹　韧）

【互联网版权保护与运营新媒体论坛在京举行】

2016年6月1日，针对版权板块举办的互联网版权保护与运营新媒体论坛在国家会议中心拉开帷幕。本论坛是第四届中国（北京）国际服务贸易交易会重要论坛之一。

论坛以“新媒体、新版权、新价值”为主题，探讨互联网环境下各类新媒体在版权开发与运营方面的新思路、新方法。本次论坛由嘉宾演讲和圆桌谈论以及现场签约等环节组成，论坛汇聚了政府领导、协会领导，以及众多的媒体专家和知名媒体人等，与会嘉宾就新媒体环境下版权运营与保护、网络侵权、互联网版权授权模式、版权维权以及新媒体版权价值等主题进行演讲和经验分享。

在此次论坛上，“版权印”与信达财险举办了签约仪式，此举是对版权产业与保险行业结合的有益尝试，推动了金融与文化产业的深度结合。

本次活动上，相关领导对互联网版权快速授权平台“版权印”进行了介绍。“版权印”这一平台巧妙运用互联网技术，将授权交易的入口植入各类媒体自己的网站、微信公众号、微博号等内容发布渠道中，需要转载内容的机构，只要轻点几下鼠标即可在线获得转载授权，极大地简化了媒体内容的授权和获权过程，能够有效促进互联网正版内容的流通，挤压盗版空间。目前，平台的注册媒体机构超过3 300家，收录的媒体原创内容超过4万余篇。数据统计显示，互联网对中国经济的贡献率已高达6.9%。

（资料来源：中国经济网）

【2016移动互联网创新大会关注版权开发】

2016年7月15日至16日，钛媒体联合《商业价值》在北京主办了2016移动互联网创新大会（MIIC 2016），其中版权尤其为与会人员关注，来自电影界、音乐界等的从业人员就内容创业者如何获得资本的青睐、如何实现版权产业化等话题进行了探讨。

知名导演陆川认为，只有优质的电影作品才能吸引资本的目光，因此编剧要潜下心来创作。现在很多编剧因为市场的诱惑，签的电影项目较多，导致其精力分散，无法安心创作。如果电影行业热度消减，编剧们就有可能创作出良好的作品。同时，他认为，资本更重视的是人本身，希望能与内容创业者有很好的交流。

版权的产业化也是与会人员关心的问题。对此，《煎饼侠》《老炮儿》幕后营销公司卓然影业CEO张进认为，这需要从三个方面做工作。其一是挑选版权，作品除了要具有较高辨识度、趣味性强、传统文化元素外，清晰的目标受众也很重要，合家欢电影往往能获得较高票房。其二是品牌的市场定位。要依据上作品的核心元素和受众精准分析，做出一个品牌定位。其三是较高的执行力。通过产品销售和营销推广，培养用户的品牌忠诚度。

张北音乐节创办人李宏杰则从音乐节角度分析如何实现产业化。在他看来，如今中国音乐节市场快速发展，用户黏性很高，但相较国外成熟的音乐节商业模式，中国还有很长的路要走。他建议，中国音乐节可以细分音乐节市场，分析用户需求，优化用户体验，保证音乐节品质，做好商业孵化以及衍生品开发，从而拓宽音乐节市场。

（资料来源：中国知识产权资讯网　作者：侯　伟）

【"一带一路"知识产权高级别会议召开】 2016年7月21日至22日，由世界知识产权组织（WIPO）与中国国家知识产权局、国家工商总局、国家版权局、商务部、北京市人民政府联合主办的"一带一路"知识产权高级别会议在北京举行。中国国务委员王勇、世界知识产权组织总干事弗朗西斯·高锐出席7月21日上午举行的开幕式并致辞。

此次会议的主题为"包容、发展、合作、共赢"。会议旨在落实"一带一路"重大倡议，分享"一带一路"沿线国家依托知识产权促进创新和经济发展的经验，加强"一带一路"沿线国家在知识产权能力建设、基础设施和公众意识提升方面的合作，推动"一带一路"建设深入开展，促进沿线国家和地区的创新发展与繁荣进步。

中国国家知识产权局局长申长雨，国家新闻出版广电总局副局长、国家版权局副局长阎晓宏等出席开幕式。

中国国家版权局版权管理司司长于慈珂在大会举行的"推动国际知识产权法律框架向着更加普惠、包容、平衡的方向发展"主题单元上，做了题为《推动〈北京条约〉早日生效建立公正合理的国际版权制度》的演讲。他代表中国国家版权局表示，2012年6月，WIPO保护音像表演外交会议在北京召开，会议通过了一部新的旨在加强保护视听表演者的国际条约——《北京条约》。中国政府在外交会议后就积极开展条约批准工作，2014年4月24日，中国第十二届全国人民代表大会常务委员会第八次会议通过决定，批准《视听表演北京条约》。同年7月10日，中国国家版权局局长蔡赴朝代表中国政府向高锐总干事递交了关于批准《北京条约》的政府声明，我国正式成为《北京条约》的第五个缔约方。截至2016年7月，全球已有11个国家正式批准或加入了该条约。而根据条约生效条款，需要30个有资格的有关方交存批准书或加入书，条约才能生效。中国作为条约缔结地，愿意与各国携手，共同推进《北京条约》生效进程，为建立公正合理的国际版权制度而努力。

"一带一路"沿线50个国家和地区的知识产权机构、18个驻华使馆、6个联合国驻华机构的120余名嘉宾，以及180余名中方代表参加会议。

（资料来源：《中国新闻出版广电报》　作者：赖名芳）

【"保护视听表演对文化和创意产业发展的重要性圆桌会议"在京举行】 2016年7月22日，由世界知识产权组织（WIPO）与中国国家版权局共同举办的保护视听表演对文化和创意产业发展的重要性圆桌会议在北京举行。此次会议对于推动《视听表演北京条约》（以下简称《北京条约》）早日生效，巩固2012年保护音像表演外交会议成果，促进WIPO各成员国视听表演产业发展具有重要意义。世界知识产权组织副总干事王彬颖，中国国家新闻出版广电总局副局长、国家版权局副局长阎晓宏出席会议开幕式并致辞。

王彬颖在致辞中表示，作为"一带一路"知识产权高级会议的一部分，召开此次圆桌会议具有重要意义。由于2012年6月缔结的《北京条约》涉及视听表演这一非常重要的知识产权领域，因此备受"一带一路"沿线国家的重视。这个条约一旦生效，将会推动"一带一路"沿线国家的文化和创意产业繁荣壮大、促进其经济快速稳定发展。在此次会议召开前，WIPO欣喜地获悉，突尼斯政府已批准加入该条约，成为《北京条约》的第12个缔约方。但是，根据条约生效条款，必须要有30个有资格的有关方交存批准书或加入书，条约才能生效。此次会议将保护视听表演对文化和创意产业发展的重要性作为研讨主题，就是希望WIPO成员国间加强视听表演领域的信息交流与合作，尽快推动更多成员国批准或加入《北京条约》。

阎晓宏在致辞中表示，由中国国家版权局与WIPO共同举办的此次圆桌会议，可以说是双方在中国共同组织的又一次国际版权盛会。《北京条约》从国际立法层面对表演者的权利进行了有效确认和完整保护，结束了表演者权利不能享有完整知识产权保护的历史，也进一步丰富完善了国际知识产权保护体系，对于通过版权保护促进文化产业发展，推进国际知识产权合作具有里程碑式的意义，必将有力地推动影视、音乐等视听领域的知识产权保护水平，使加入方和缔约方的表演者从中受益，进而推动相关文化及创意产业的发展。作为世界上最大的发展中国家，中国在版权保护方面还有很多工作要做。但是，中国政府保护版权的立场是坚定的，态度是坚决的。我们真诚地希望和各国朋友携手努力，在知识产权大家庭中继续保持和发展良好的版权交流与合作，共同推进《北京条约》早日生效。

WIPO文化与创意产业部版权发展司司长高航，中国国家版权局版权管理司司长于慈珂分别主持会议。来自WIPO和"一带一路"数十个国家的高级别官员，中国全国人大、外交部、商务部等相关部门，中国版权协会、中国版权保护中心、著作权集体管理组织、著作权涉外认证机构及北京市版权局等相关版权部门的60余名代表参加会议。会上，WIPO文化与创意产业部版权法司司长米歇尔·伍兹从国际层面上介绍了保护视听表演对文化和创意产业发展的重要性。中国国家版权局版权管理司副司长汤兆志全面地介绍了中国在视听表演领域实施的版权保护政策。蒙古知识产权局局长南吉尔·辛巴特、南非商贸部公司和知识产权局副局长洛里·沃勒则分别介绍了两国在视听表演领域采取的保护措施。

（资料来源：《中国新闻出版广电报》　作者：赖名芳）

【中日著作权研讨会在沪举行】　2016年7月28日至29日，中日著作权研讨会在上海举行。研讨会由中国国家版权局与日本文化厅主办，上海市版权局承办。其间，中日双方围绕各自著作权立法最新进展、打击网络侵权实践、促进版权产业发展，以及开展国际合作等议题进行了政府间工作会谈。

本次研讨会采取实地考察和座谈研讨相结合的形式，双方版权行政管理机构和相关业界就版权行政执法及版权产业发展的最新动态进行了深入交流。以日本文化厅长官官房审议官磯谷桂介为团长的日方代表团先后来到上海冠勇信息科技有限公司和国家版权贸易基地（上海），实地考察了冠勇科技利用海量音视频及图文搜索、云计算、版权大数据可视化分析等领先技术建立的全网版权监测保护体系，详细了解了版权贸易基地依托上海四个中心、文化国际大都市建设以及浦东先行先试、综合改革配套等政策与创新取得的实践成果和积极进展。

国家版权局版权管理司司长于慈珂说，中日两国在网络环境下维护良好的版权秩序、促进产业发展等方面有着共同的需求，面临着一些共同的问题，也存在很多值得互相学习和借鉴的地方。中国近几年实行国家知识产权战略和创新驱动发展战略，版权产业发展驶入快车道。此时，中日两国更应该深入开展交流与合作，共同探讨版权保护和发展之道。

磯谷桂介说，此次研讨会主题明确，形式新颖，高效务实，集中展示了中国近年来在版权执法和产业发展方面取得的成就，希望两国政府和民间组织能在进一步打击盗版，平衡创作者、使用者、传播者之间的利益，促进版权产业发展等方面共同努力，拓展两国版权合作新空间。

中日两国依据2010年《中日版权战略合作备忘录（部级）》，建立版权人才培养和信息交流磋商机制，不定期举办研讨活动，在版权领域开展实质性的交流与合作。中日著作权研讨会是双方开展版权领域合作与交流的有效平台，对于促进两国版权保护和版权产业发展具有重要意义。

（资料来源：《中国新闻出版广电报》　作者：魏　芳）

【“APP及广告联盟相关版权侵权问题研讨会”在京举行】　2016年8月20日，由中国版权协会主办、《中国版权》杂志社承办、互联网视频正版化联盟协办的“APP及广告联盟相关版权侵权问题研讨会”在北京举行。国家版权局版权管理司司长于慈珂出席会议并讲话。

“剑网2016”列出了三项重点任务，本次研讨会即围绕着其中的两项（开展打击APP侵权盗版专项整治行动、开展规范网络广告联盟专项整治行动）而展开，旨在贯彻落实“剑网2016”行动精神，对聚合平台、应用商店及网络广告联盟等所涉相关版权问题展开探讨，以推进相关问题解决、推进产业发展。

会上，各位嘉宾围绕上述热点话题展开了研讨。腾讯公司副总裁、法务部总经理江波作为互联网视频正版化联盟代表，阐述了网络侵权3.0时代的行业规制与法律协同问题。上海市文化市场行政执法总队网络（版权）执法处处长杨勇以自己多年来的执法实践，总结了对网络侵权认定标准的研究。北京市版权局副局长王野霏以《实施“清源行动”切断网络侵权利益链》、北京市高级人民法院知识产权庭庭长助理潘伟以《关于深度链接问题的调研进展》、北京市朝阳区人民法院知识产权庭庭长林子英以《聚合平台的司法规制》、金城同达律师事务所高级合伙人汪涌以《手机视频聚合应用软件的技术特征与法律责任》为题分别阐述了自己的观点。清华大学法学院副院长崔国斌教授则从学术角度对“得形忘意的服务器标准”进行了分析。

国家版权局版权管理司司长于慈珂做会议总结发言，他指出，“剑网2016”重点开展打击APP侵权盗版专项整治行动、开展规范网络广告联盟专项整治行动。要重点针对APP上传者和应用程序商店的版权执法监管，加大对聚合类APP、与网络电视棒及电视机顶盒关联的APP侵权盗版行为的打击力度，强化应用程序商店对提供文学、影视、音乐、新闻等作品APP上传者的版权监管责任。他说，规范网络广告联盟专项整治行动也是2016年的重点。一方面，要加强对网络广告联盟在版权保护方面的监督管理，推动网络广告联盟落实企业主体责任、建立版权保护工作机制；另一方面，推动版权执法监管机构与网络广告联盟建立切断侵权盗版黑色经济链条的工作机制，严厉打击故意为侵权盗版提供支持的网络广告联盟。

研讨会由中国版权协会秘书长、《中国版权》杂志社社长孙悦主持。国家版权局政策法制司司长、中国版权协会驻会副理事长王自强出席会议。来自版权管理部门、权利人组织、院校、互联网企业等单位的近百人出席了会议。

（资料来源：中国版权产业网　作者：肖　虹）

【2016年BIBF国际版权贸易高级研修班在京举行】　2016年8月25日，由国家版权局主办，中国图书进出口（集团）总公司承办的2016年BIBF国际版权贸易高级研修班在北京举行。国家新闻出版广电总局副局长、国家版权局副局长阎晓宏出席并发表主题演讲。

阎晓宏指出，第23届北京国际图书博览会有86个国家和地区的2 400多家出版商参展，其规模、交易活跃度是在10年前无法想象的，这说明中国出版物市场蕴含着巨大的潜力和吸引力，也说明BIBF为中外出版界提供了很好的交流、交易平台。2015年，我国图书出版实现营业收入822.6亿元，同比增长4%；全国共出版图书47.58万种，同比增长6.1%；输出版权10 471种，引进版权16 467种，版权输出品种与引进品种比例为1∶1.6。目前，我国出版业总销售量已位居全球第三，仅次于美国和日本。从纵向上分析，我国出版业发展速度是比较快的，但从横向上跟其他出版强国相比，还存在着一定差距，这既说明我们还需要不断努力，也说明随着经济社会的不断进步，我国传统出版仍存在很大的发展空间。

在谈到数字出版和互联网发展时，阎晓宏强调，2015年我国数字出版营业收入达到4 400多亿元，较2014年增长30%，这说明数字阅读在我国已经成为趋势，同时也说明中国数字出版市场潜力巨大。2015年，总局出台了《关于推动传统出版和新兴出版融合发展的指导意见》，鼓励传统出版向网络空间延伸，推动传统出版和新兴出版实现出版资源、生产要素等的有效整合。这些都为提升国际版权贸易带来了新的发展契机。我们要秉承开放的心态，坚定信心、推动发展，在做好版权输出工作的同时，积极对待引进图书、电影、音乐、软件等版权产业，进一步满足人民群众的文化需求。

就如何做好版权经理人，阎晓宏提出了建议：一是交易的作品要让老百姓喜欢；二是要让交易的作品实现其版权价值增值，使作者获得权益的保障，并推动出版企业进一步发展。他强调，出版界不应盲目追求图书出版品种数量，而更应该注重出版内容质量的提升，这需要版权经理人拥有一双善于挖掘、发现、培育优质版权资源以及能够预判市场反响的慧眼。他希望在“一带一路”倡议背景下，中外出版界同人通过BIBF平台，利用区位、环境与文化优势，开拓国际版权贸易市场，用版权贸易的方式丰富“一带一路”内涵，扩大“一带一路”的影响。

（资料来源：《中国新闻出版广电报》　作者：赖名芳）

【“一带一路”高峰合作论坛推版权输出】　2016年8月25日，以“深化出版合作　实现文化共赢”为主题的第14届北京国际图书节“一带一路”高峰合作论坛活动举行。活动吸引了30余家国内外出版企业。

本次活动是北京市新闻出版广电局为促进“一带一路”沿线国家出版业合作交流而打造的一项品牌文化活动。与会嘉宾共同探讨如何进一步推动双方互惠互利合作，加深中外出版业发展战略交流。论坛现场还举行了一系列签约仪式。如北京时代华语图书股份有限公司与斯里兰卡苏勒瑟出版社就《习近平时代》和《中国梦》两部图书达成出版协议；北京时代华语图书股份有限公司将《习近平时代》和《中国梦》两部图书授权于尼泊尔天利出版社；北京求是园文化传播有限公司与印度GBD出版社签署关于《学习习近平总书记重要讲话》英文版等79部图书的授权出版协议等。

（资料来源：《中国新闻出版广电报》
作者：王坤宁　李婧璇）

【2016中国互联网法治大会在京召开】　2016年10月16日，“2016（第二届）中国互联网法治大会”在北京举办。大会主题为“互联网+时代的创新与治理”。与会嘉宾呼吁社会各界应大力推进依法治网、依法办网、依法上网，为维护网络空间秩序，推进“互联网+”法律的进程，共同营造风清气正的网络清朗空间。全国人大法律委员会副主任委员苏泽林出席主论坛并发表演讲。

大会共设1个主论坛和6个分论坛，不仅聚焦网络法治建设，还共同探讨了网络法治创新新思路。会上，部分嘉宾就如何加强网络内容版权保护发表了各自见解。国家版权局版权管理司副司长段玉萍认为，“互联网+”确实为互联网产业、文化产业提供了很大的空间和动力，但是版权保护也因为“互联网+”的快速发展而遇到了巨大挑战。2016年最新统计的互联网十大应用中，包括了与文化有关的图像、网络新闻、网络视频、网络音乐、网络文学、网络游戏等，然而网络侵权盗版现象也一直存在着。自 2005 年起，国家版权局联合相关部委连续开展了针对网络侵权盗版活动的“剑网”专项行动，网络版权秩序有了一定的好转，但对于“避风港原则”怎么适用、侵权盗版成本比较低、互联网企业从业人员版权意识比较欠缺等问题，仍需要在推进我国互联网法治建设中加以解决。法律出版社社长黄闽说，作为出版人，他认为应更加关注思想与文化的互联网法治建设。互联网法治应注意在完善立法方面回归宪法精神。民主与法制杂志社总编辑刘桂明介绍说，目前最关注的是传统媒体和新媒体如何融合的问题，以及在媒体融合中所产生的知识产权保护与发展问题。

大会还发布了 2016 年优秀“互联网＋法律”创新项目、2014—2016 年中国互联网法治十大影响性案例。会议由中国互联网协会主办，中华全国律师协会、法律出版社支持，北京中律联网络科技有限公司和中闻律师事务所承办。

（资料来源：《中国新闻出版广电报》　作者：赖名芳）

【2016 第一届“文化＋”新创意新业态新经济论坛举办】　2016 年 10 月 28 日，“2016 第一届‘文化＋’新创意新业态新经济论坛”在南京国际展览中心举办。

此次论坛由国家级文化和科技融合示范基地管理办公室主任、中国人民大学创意产业技术研究院院长彭翊主持，江苏省科技厅副厅长蒋跃建出席会议并致辞，知名学术专家、行业专家、投资机构代表、文化产业投资人等近 300 人参加了此次论坛。

本次论坛共分为嘉宾主题演讲及高峰对话两大板块，邀请了行业内的知名专家、学者进行演讲和交流。江苏省科技厅副厅长蒋跃建在致辞中指出：在探索经济新常态的大背景下，进一步加大文化领域的交流能够提炼文化创意与相关产业融合的路径与模式，总结文化产业新业态、新模式、新技术、新产品的成功经验，并提升文化产业发展的质量、效益和竞争力。

在主题演讲环节，国家版权局版权管理司副司长段玉萍、苏宁环球股份有限公司首席文化官陈梁、黑马金融 CEO 陈永进、中文在线集团市场中心总经理刘涵、国家行政学院文化政策与管理中心主任祁述裕、北京天空之城影视有限公司董事长路伟等 6 位嘉宾先后登台，分享各自领域内文化科技融合发展的现状、趋势与思考。

高峰对话环节由中国社科院文化研究中心副主任贾旭东主持，东海瑞京资产管理公司董事长王恒、国家音乐产业促进工作委员会会长汪京京等嘉宾同台对话，围绕文化科技融合发展各抒己见，为南京文化产业发展提供了学术和实践经验的双重支撑。

（资料来源：搜狐新闻）

【“大数据安全·互联网新闻出版和数字资产沙龙”举行】　2016 年 11 月 2 日，百家城市新闻网站“中国数谷”行之“大数据安全·互联网新闻出版和数字资产沙龙”举行。媒体人和专家学者以新闻版权为切入点，围绕以大数据安全为基础的知识产权、数字资产、安全防护和法律维权等进行探讨。

贵州省新闻出版广电局副局长杨庆武认为，随着互联网的快速发展和大数据技术的广泛应用，盗版等违法行为时有发生，保护互联网新闻版权与数字资产，已成为有关部门的重要职能。

贵阳市互联网信息办公室专职副主任潘峰认为，在面对网络安全威胁时，不能因噎废食，要以法治建设推进网络治理，通过信息技术提升网络空间的安全防护能力。

（资料来源：《贵州日报》　作者：杨丰源　李定林）

【标准推广与标准版权保护推进会在厦门举行】　2016 年 11 月 8 日，国家标准版权保护工作组办公室在福建厦门举办了标准推广与版权保护推进会。国家质检总局、国家标准委、人大财经委、最高人民法院、国家版权局、全国“双打”办、公安部、国家认监委以及高等院校、律师事务所等方面的代表参加了会议。

会议总结了一年来版权保护工作，探讨了标准化法修订和标准推广过程中标准公开与版权保护的关系，交流了标准公开与版权保护工作中的新情况，分享了标准版权保护理论研究成果，并就进一步促进标准推广、保护标准版权进行了深入的交流研讨。

国家标准委有关领导指出，我国的标准版权保护工作已形成了国家质检总局、国家标准委、国家版权局、全国“双打”办、公安部、最高人民法院和最高人民检察院等部门共同参与的良好协调工作机制，工作成效显著，得到国际组织的高度认可。一要认真总结标准推广和版权保护工作，结合当前的形势推进标准化工作的创新。二要做好标准的推广和版权保护工作，让标准充分发挥在推动标准互联互通、国际产能合作和产业协作等方面的作用；要做好标准版权保护工作，积极推动中国标准“走出去”。三要进一步加强研究，承接好加快标准化法的修订工作。四要做好标准化推广服务，探索“标准化+”新模式。五要继续发挥联络协调机制作用，在更高水平上做好版权保护和标准的推广工作。

（资料来源：《中国质量报》　作者：徐　风）

【第九届中国版权年会在京召开】 2016年11月25日，由中国版权协会主办的第九届中国版权年会在北京举行。第三届中国版权卓越成就者奖、中国版权最具影响力企业奖颁奖仪式同时举行。国家新闻出版广电总局副局长、国家版权局副局长、中国版权协会理事长阎晓宏做题为《2016版权回顾与展望》的主题发言。

2016年年会在形式上进行了重大创新，以回顾与展望版权工作、表彰年度版权卓越成就者和最具影响力企业为主题，以增强会员互动和行业交流为形式，以期达到交流经验、增进友谊、加强合作、思想融合、共谋创新的目的，成为中国版权界精英汇集、交流合作的大平台。

阎晓宏首先代表国家版权局对获得第三届中国版权卓越成就者奖的陈建功、谭跃等人表示敬意，感谢他们在版权创作、使用、保护、管理方面做出的成就。同时，对获得中国版权最具影响力企业的人民音乐出版社有限公司、荣宝斋出版社等19家单位表示祝贺，希望获奖企业珍惜荣誉、再接再厉。

阎晓宏在主题发言中指出，当前在“创新、协调、绿色、开放、共享”的五大发展理念中，版权的战略意义正在进一步大幅提升。版权作为知识产权的重要组成部分，不仅是文化领域的核心竞争力，也是文化发展的基础性资源和战略性资源。版权并不仅仅停留在传统的书报刊、影视、艺术、表演等文化领域，在计算机软件、建筑外观、纺织品、陶瓷、家具等领域也都有版权的烙印。按照世界知识产权组织的划分原则和标准，目前版权产业对于我国国民经济贡献率已达到7.28%。近年来随着我国版权生态环境的改善，版权秩序从以往的混乱无序逐渐走向有序规范；版权的对抗性在减弱，理性因素大大提升，大量的著作权纠纷通过诉讼、司法调解、法院判决来化解矛盾已成为大趋势；权利与使用、权利人与使用者间的关系更趋于理性，原来的不均衡现象发生了很大转变；版权价值更加受到社会的重视和尊重。他表示，虽然版权在中国仍然是新生事物，但是因其旺盛的生命力，一定会为社会创造出应有的财富和价值。

阎晓宏及中国文联副主席李前光，全国人大常委会原委员、著名音乐家谷建芬，国家新闻出版广电总局原党组成员、中国摄影著作权协会副理事长宋明昌，中国作家协会副主席张抗抗，中国书法家协会主席苏士澍等为获得第三届中国版权卓越成就者奖的个人和中国版权最具影响力企业颁奖。

国家新闻出版广电总局政策法制司司长、中国版权协会驻会副理事长王自强在会上做2016年中国版权协会年度工作报告。国家新闻出版广电总局版权管理司司长于慈珂以及来自版权立法、司法、行政管理等有关部门的负责人，著作权人、权利人组织、版权产业界、版权教学科研、法律事务、新闻媒体代表等300余人参加年会。

（资料来源：《中国新闻出版广电报》　作者：赖名芳）

【国家版权局召开“网络广告联盟服务版权保护工作座谈会”】 2016年11月30日，国家版权局在北京召开“网络广告联盟服务版权保护工作座谈会”，通报了国家版权局规范网络广告联盟版权秩序的有关工作情况，调查确定了第一批侵权盗版网站“黑名单”，大型网络广告联盟发起《网络广告联盟版权自律倡议》。

据通报，国家版权局等四部门2016年7月部署开展的“剑网2016”专项行动把“开展网络广告联盟专项整治”作为2016年的一项重要任务，目的就是要联合主要网络广告联盟，切断专门从事侵权盗版的小网站的非法利益链条，从根本上遏制小网站侵权盗版势头，有效净化网络版权环境，维护网络版权产业的正常秩序。通过建立工作协调机制、广泛征求网络广告联盟意见、积极协调行业主管部门、调查确定侵权盗版网站“黑名单”等措施，专项整治工作已经取得初步成效。下一步，国家版权局计划在征求网络广告联盟意见基础上进一步完善相关工作方案，以维护权利人的合法权益，并为网络广告联盟规避法律风险，促进网络广告联盟良性发展。

国家版权局版权管理司相关负责人强调，近年来，中央下发了一系列文件，要求加快实施创新驱动发展战略、加快知识产权强国建设、完善产权保护制度依法保护产权，都突出强调了“保护”这个关键词。国家版权局将按照中央要求，进一步加强执法投入、加大打击力度，加强与相关部门的执法协作，形成工作合力，加大网络侵权盗版惩治力度，提高侵权盗版成本。此外，国家版权局推动企业落实主体责任，改变单纯依靠政府部门力量加强版权保护的做法，充分发挥行业组织和企业主体作用，推动加强行业自律，畅通投诉举报渠道，把行业、企业包括社会公众的力量凝聚起来，形成政府有效监管、企业自我约束、行业自律与公众监督相结合的版权保护新格局。为此，国家版权局要求网络广告联盟企业强化合法经营意识，加强对所投网络经营者的资质审查，建立健全平台版权保护内部监控管理制度和举报投诉处理机制，履行好违法犯罪线索报告等责任和义务，共同做好网络版权保护工作。

国家工商行政管理总局广告监督管理司王晓东处长出席会议，并对网络广告联盟落实主体责任提出工作要求。首都版权产业联盟联合大型网络广告联盟发出版权自律倡议，表示将积极配合国家主管部门的监管工作，共同维护健康良好的网络版权秩序。

多家大中型网络广告联盟相关负责人、主要权利人代表、主要权利人组织代表、集体管理组织代表以及相关行业协会代表参加了会议。

（资料来源：国家版权局网站）

【2016年全国版权社会服务工作交流会在广州召开】 2016年12月6日下午，国家新闻出版广电总局（国家版权局）在广州召开了2016年全国版权社会服务工作交流会。会议旨在表彰2016年度全国版权示范单位和示范园区，交流各地版权示范创建工作的先进经验，部署下一步版权社会服务的重点工作。国家新闻出版广电总局副局长、国家版权局副局长阎晓宏出席并讲话，广州市人民政府秘书长唐航浩出席并致辞。

阎晓宏在讲话中表示，全国版权示范创建工作开展近十年来，在国家版权局的积极推动下，在各地版权行政管理部门及版权相关单位的共同努力下，已建立起较为完善的全国版权示范城市、示范单位、示范园区（基地）的创建机制，特别是对推动地方区域经济发展、带动版权产业发展发挥了显著作用。阎晓宏指出，互联网时代下的版权与传统意义下的版权使用模式有很大不同，这给版权服务工作带来了全新的挑战。版权管理者要创新思维，努力推进著作权登记、版权价值评估以及全国版权示范创建等一系列基础性工作，真正促进一批高质量的优秀作品转化为社会生产力，特别是各省（区、市）在推动属地创建版权示范城市、示范单位、示范园区（基地）时，要把这一观念融入其中。版权管理部门要进一步提升版权社会服务工作的能力和水平，不断开创新形势下版权社会服务工作的新局面。

交流会上，阎晓宏为湖北广播电视台、长江文艺出版社有限公司等18家获得“全国版权示范单位”称号的单位，为环上大国际影视园区、中国光谷创意产业基地等6个获得“全国版权示范园区（基地）”称号的园区（基地），以及为腾讯公司“网络版权产业研究基地”授牌。

国家新闻出版广电总局（国家版权局）版权管理司司长于慈珂在会上就如何落实好“十三五”时期版权社会服务工作提出了具体要求：要全面建立版权社会服务工作长效机制，创建网络环境下版权社会服务工作的新格局。一是要进一步完善著作权登记制度。进一步梳理涉外著作权登记、著作权合同备案等工作，对著作权登记工作中的相关问题开展调研并提出解决方案。二是推动全国版权示范创建工作上台阶。国家版权局将推动各地版权部门，特别是鼓励西部地区参与创建工作，对已经授予称号的全国版权示范单位和园区基地适时进行督查。三是促进版权产业健康发展。国家版权局将进一步加强对国家版权交易中心、版权贸易基地的指导和规范，推动市场机制的完善，充分发挥其在版权交易、资产评估、融资等市场要素中的积极作用。四是全面提升版权宣传工作水平。各地版权行政管理部门要高度重视版权宣传工作，充分利用各种媒体宣传渠道，注重发挥新媒体的优势，以“4·26”世界知识产权日为契机，积极开展多种形式的版权宣传与交流工作，注重版权对外宣传工作，掌握传播方式，讲好中国故事。他强调指出，“十三五”时期，是版权社会服务工作开创新局面的重要时期，各级版权行政管理部门、版权相关单位要勇于探索，不断实践，坚持“激励创造、有效运用、依法保护、科学管理”的方针，注重在版权社会服务工作中体现社会化的特点，整合运用全社会的力量和资源，全面提升版权创造、运用、保护和管理能力，共同推动版权产业健康发展。

会上，江苏省版权局介绍了版权示范创建经验，湖北省广播电视台、成都（中国）艺库文创产业园区分别代表示范单位、示范园区（基地）介绍了创建经验。

（资料来源：国家版权局网站　作者：邹　韧）

【AIPPI中国分会版权热点论坛举行】 2016年12月11日，AIPPI（国际保护知识产权协会）中国分会版权热点论坛（2016年度）在北京举行。

论坛是由AIPPI中国分会主办，AIPPI中国分会版权专业委员会承办。这是AIPPI首次在中国举办以版权为主题的论坛，会上还发布了2016年度中国版权行业十大热点案件。

论坛由4个主题组成。上午，北京知识产权法院法官冯刚、乐视控股法务部总经理刘晓庆等6位嘉宾，分别围绕“著作权维权难点及解决路径”和“商品化权的司法保护现状及立法建议”2个主题进行研讨。

下午，清华大学法学院副院长、副教授崔国斌，北京市高级人民法院知产庭法官苏志甫等6位嘉宾则围绕“影视改编相关热点知识产权问题”和“著作权侵权损害赔偿问题研究”2个主题发表了自己的看法。

（资料来源：《中国新闻出版广电报》　作者：邹　韧）

◆ 社会管理与服务

【四川部分市实行作品登记免费服务】 2016年1月1日起，四川省成都、泸州、遂宁市全面实行作品登记免费服务，登记范围包括文字作品，口述作品，音乐、戏剧、曲艺、舞蹈、杂技艺术作品，美术、建筑作品，摄影作品，电影作品和以类似摄制电影的方法创作的作品，工程设计图、产品设计图、地图、示意图等图形作品和模型作品，法律、行政法规规定的其他作品（计算机软件著作权除外）。

四川省范围内凡符合《中华人民共和国著作权法》规定的作品都可在以上市区进行免费登记。政策实行后，成都市权利人作品版权登记量骤增，截至1月31日，成都市版权局已受理作品登记505件，较上年同期增长近153%。

（《中国版权年鉴》编辑部综合）

【中国出版协会六届六次常务理事会召开】 2016年1月15日，全国人大教科文卫委员会主任委员、中国出版协会理事长柳斌杰主持召开中国出版协会六届六次常务理事会。会议总结了2015年中国版权协会工作，对2016年的工作做了深入讨论和部署。

会议认为，2015年中国版权协会工作成绩的取得，主要得益于坚持政治担当，牢牢把握为行业服务的导向；得益于坚持改革创新，不断深化体制机制改革；得益于坚持科学发展，服务行业的水平、能力不断增强；得益于坚持依法办会，全面提升管理能力；得益于坚持正风肃纪，不断加强队伍建设。

柳斌杰围绕中国版权协会当前工作提出几点要求：一要深入贯彻学习党的十八大和十八届三中、四中、五中全会精神，贯彻学习习近平总书记系列重要讲话精神，坚持正确的政治方向，遵守政治纪律；二要守住法律的底线，依法办会，照章办事；三要牢记反腐倡廉的高压线不能碰，让反腐倡廉规范化、制度化；四要全力推动出版业改革发展，配合政府部门搞好调研，提出政策建议；五要为会员服务，维护会员的合法权益；六要进一步抓好机关建设，用制度管人、管事；七要开放办会，共同推动中国出版“走出去”；八要做好换届工作，发挥行业协会的桥梁作用。

（资料来源：《中国新闻出版广电报》　作者：章红雨）

【国家版权贸易基地（越秀）打造版权综合服务平台】 2016年1月18日，国家版权贸易基地（越秀）在广东省广州市举行“首批授权法律服务机构授牌仪式及维权专家聘请仪式”。这是该基地打造版权法律服务体系的重要举措。

国家版权贸易基地（越秀）引入版权经纪人模式，提倡优先采用调解、授权解决版权纷争，促进版权交易市场发展。维权专家委员会是华南地区首个国家级的版权法律维权联盟，聚集了华南地区的核心版权专业律师力量，在国家、省、市、区四级政府的指导下，联合文化执法部门和相关社会组织，为维权方提供一体化的专门法律服务，其中包括行政执法、仲裁调解、司法维权等，并设有多种线上线下受理方式。此外，国家版权贸易基地还依托维权专家委员会，整合旗下相关社会资源，与相关权威媒体机构开展合作，创办国内首档针对版权贸易与保护中产生的法律问题的专业电视栏目——《律师话版权》。

国家版权贸易基地（越秀）经国家版权局批准建立，是华南地区首个国家级版权综合性服务平台。该基地以版权交易为核心，以版权保护为特色，致力打造“立足广东、辐射华南、服务全国、面向全球”的版权综合服务平台。

（资料来源：《中国知识产权报》　作者：侯　伟）

【《老爷车中国行》羊城举行版权授权仪式】 2016年1月29日，在广东省广州市国家版权贸易基地（越秀），《老爷车中国行》举行了版权授权签约仪式，著作权人易黎明将该美术作品的品牌Logo授权广东汽车文化促进会举办经典老爷车文化巡回展，国家版权贸易基地（越秀）为该版权授权提供了交易见证及合同备案服务。

《老爷车中国行》于2010年9月16日获得国家版权局颁发的著作权登记证书，登记号为2010-F-

031391。为了传承和再现老爷车文化，《老爷车中国行》著作权人德国德中之窗文化促进会主席（德籍华人）易黎明多次联系广东汽车文化促进会，最终双方达成了此次版权授权合作。

广东汽车文化促进会曾为我国重大的喜庆节日举办过多次老爷车中国行巡展活动。经典老爷车文化巡回展的再次举办，对于传承汽车经典文化，推动社会经济发展和城市经典名片的建设起到积极的作用。

（资料来源：中国知识产权报资讯网　作者：侯　伟）

【安徽省版权保护协会选举换届】　2016 年 1 月，安徽省版权保护协会第四届会员代表大会日前在合肥召开，会议审议通过了协会第三届理事会工作报告和财务报告、章程修改草案及会费收取和管理办法，选举产生了协会第四届理事会成员。

安徽省委宣传部副部长、省新闻出版广电局（省版权局）局长车敦安说，新一届协会要紧紧围绕全省版权业"十三五"规划开展工作，充分发挥参谋助手、桥梁纽带和行业引领作用，进一步加强协会组织建设和内部管理，建设一支高素质的版权从业队伍，培育版权行业企业做大做强，推动国际合作和交流，着力推动知识产权强国和创新型国家建设。

安徽省版权保护协会新一届理事会的下一步工作重点在于着力加强版权社会意识培育、版权争端调解、版权产业交易和版权社会服务等方面。

（资料来源：《中国新闻出版广电报》　作者：汪闻敏）

【广东省新闻出版广播影视（版权）工作会议在穗举行】　2016 年 2 月 2 日，广东省新闻出版广播影视（版权）工作会议在广州召开，广东省副省长蓝佛安出席会议并讲话。

蓝佛安对 2015 年及"十二五"时期广东省新闻出版广播影视版权工作取得的成绩给予了充分肯定，并要求新闻出版广播影视版权工作在"十三五"期间要认识新常态、适应新常态、引领新常态，以高度的政治责任感和使命感，坚持正确舆论导向，加强传播主阵地建设，巩固和提升主流媒体在新形势下的传播力、影响力和引导力，严厉打击非法出版、非法广播电视设备安装和侵权盗版等违法犯罪行为，为改革发展稳定提供有力的舆论支持。

蓝佛安强调，要创新推动文化产业结构调整和转型升级，以"主业＋新媒体"模式做大主业做大规模，推动文化产业向数字化、网络化、智能化和集约化方向发展，培育打造产业基地、集群、园区和创业创客生态圈，逐步由传统业态、单一经营向新兴业态、多元运营的战略性转型。公共服务要突出文化惠民的时代要求，落实好民生工程提质增效，以标准化推动均等化。要适应深化行政管理体制改革新要求，积极推进行政审批标准化建设，探索"互联网＋管理""互联网＋决策服务"新模式，加快构建"一门式""一网式"政务服务体系。

（资料来源：广东省人民政府网）

【民进中央召开两会新闻通气会　拟提交版权相关提案】　2016 年 2 月 19 日，"民进中央与媒体座谈暨两会新闻通气会"在北京召开。民进中央副主席刘新成向媒体介绍民进中央拟提交全国政协十二届四次会议的提案和大会发言等情况。

民进中央拟向全国政协十二届四次会议提交的大会发言共 3 份，党派提案共 38 份，其中包括 11 件重点推荐提案。作为民进中央重点关注的文化出版领域，民进中央有 5 件提案。

针对目前我国视障群体面临的买书难、读书难等难题，民进中央提出了《关于加大盲文出版物出版力度，满足视障群体阅读需求的提案》；面对互联网给版权经营和保护带来的许多新问题以及随着云存储、移动互联网、大数据和人工智能等新技术发展，古籍数字资源如何保护等问题，提出了《关于加强互联网内容版权经营与保护，推动数字出版可持续发展的提案》和《关于启动中华古籍数字化国家工程的提案》。民进中央还针对目前学术造假现象，提出《关于创新文化，推动创新发展的提案》。

（资料来源：《中国新闻出版广电报》　作者：王坤宁）

【移动 APP 第三方证书签名与版权登记联合服务平台正式上线】　2016 年 2 月 25 日，由中国版权保护中心和北京数字认证股份有限公司共同推动，由中华版权代理总公司和北京版信通技术有限公司共同推出的"移动 APP 第三方证书签名与版权登记联合服务平台"正式上线。

为解决移动互联网领域移动 APP 的版权保护与网络安全问题，2015 年 2 月 5 日，中国版权保护中心与北京数字认证股份有限公司签署了战略合作协议，共同推动建设移动 APP 第三方证书签名与版权登记联合服务平台，依托 DCI 体系打造移动 APP 版权与安全综合服务体系。联合服务平台开通了 24 小时 APP 软件著作权在线快速登记通道，移动 APP 开发者不需要去大厅排队，就可以方便、快捷地在线提交版权登记资料，为每个通过版权登记的APP签发版权登记电子证书和作为数字资产唯一身份标识的DCI码。

作为DCI体系在移动APP领域的核心示范应用，联合服务平台构建了版权登记电子证书的应用场景。版权登记电子证书可以嵌入APP中，并经过数字签名和安全加密，不可破解，不可篡改，支持APP版权24小时在线验证。联合服务平台还提供版权监测、侵权报告、维权取证等一系列版权服务，以及安全检测、漏洞扫描、安全加固等增值服务，从而实现对APP版权的有效保护。

（资料来源：《中国新闻出版广电报》　作者：邹　韧）

【江西省成立首家知识产权仲裁中心】 2016年2月26日，南昌市举办仲裁委员会知识产权仲裁中心成立授牌大会。

南昌市仲裁委员会知识产权仲裁中心是在江西省新闻出版广电局（版权局）、江西省司法厅推动和南昌市政府支持下，由江西省出版工作者协会、江西省律师协会知识产权专业委员会联合发起设立的，是南昌市仲裁委员会根据知识产权纠纷专业性、时间性、保密性的特点而专门设置的专业纠纷解决平台。其主要职能是受理和调解、仲裁知识产权纠纷；帮助权利人树立维权意识，推动知识产权的创造、运用、保护和管理；推行仲裁法律制度，引导当事人在合同中约定仲裁条款，为当事人提供仲裁调解服务，维护合法权益，保护创新能力和成果。

江西省版权保护中心主任赖正兵介绍，中心的成立，为当事人解决知识产权纠纷提供了一条司法、行政之外新的有效途径，为江西省知识产权仲裁事业发展提供了广阔空间，进一步推动了江西知识产权保护体系的健全和完善。

（资料来源：《中国新闻出版广电报》　作者：范占英）

【江苏张家港推两项版权评审奖励办法】 2016年3月1日起，江苏省张家港市将正式实施两项版权相关评审奖励办法。《张家港市版权示范单位、示范园区和优秀版权工作站评审奖励办法》和《张家港市软件正版化示范企业评审奖励办法》经市政府第27次常务会议讨论通过。

两办法自2013年发布试行以来，推动了张家港市版权工作的开展。截至2015年底，张家港市拥有各类核心版权的企业400多家。张家港市建立了“政府资助、服务商优惠、企业自筹”相结合模式，全市千余家规模以上企业软件正版化率达到70%以上，每年用于软件正版化的投入近3亿元。2013年以来，国泰新点软件、金陵纺织、东渡纺织等3家企业获评全国版权示范单位。目前，张家港市有江苏省版权示范单位4家、苏州市版权工作示范单位12家，数量居全省首位。

（资料来源：《中国新闻出版广电报》　作者：苏　菊）

【北京版权保护协会成立“网络工委”】 2016年3月11日，北京版权保护协会网络出版工作委员会宣布成立。作为北京版权保护协会的分支机构，北京版权保护协会网络出版工作委员会内的单位有300余家，包含网络游戏、网络文学、网络动漫等国内网络出版的各种细分行业。未来计划按照行业细分成立若干行业办公室，加强细分行业内的企业之间的联系，也将促进跨界合作，推动协会各行业办公室之间的交流，同时推动网络出版业与金融、资本、影视等其他行业深度交流，带动行业蓬勃发展。

成立大会上，北京市新闻出版广电局副局长王野霏表示，在调研中发现，网络出版企业与政府之间，企业与企业之间信息沟通、业务交流、资源互动的愿望十分强烈。搭建工作委员会的平台，是满足企业这种愿望和诉求的举措。

北京市网络出版行业近年来取得了一些成绩。2015年，北京市已经取得国家新闻出版广电总局互联网出版许可证的单位313家，总数位列全国第一；12家单位入选国家新闻出版广电总局认定的首批互联网络文学出版试点单位，总数位列全国第一；8家单位入选国家新闻出版广电总局网络连续型出版物试点单位，总数位列全国第一。北京地区网络出版业产值超过500亿元，占全国的四分之一。

（资料来源：《中国新闻出版广电报》　作者：王坤宁）

【长沙市举办网络著作权行政执法培训班】 2016年3月11日，长沙市举办了全市网络著作权行政执法培训班。

此次培训邀请了上海市文化市场综合执法局的杨勇处长授课，培训主要就网络著作权行政执法依据、程序，互联网环境下著作权行政执法要求、执法特点以及具体执法技巧等方面进行了详细讲授。杨处长将基础理论知识与真实案例有机结合，紧贴实际、操作性强，对长沙市版权行政执法工作具有指导和借鉴作用。

针对网络著作权行政执法案情复杂、专业知识强、执法人员能力不足的特点，长沙市开展了全系统的培训。此次培训，目的是增强全市版权行政执法人员的法治观念、法律意识，提升版权执法人员的业务水平，为下一阶段顺利开展网络版权执法工作打下良好的基础，同时为长沙建设知识产权强市、推动转型创新发展提供支撑。

长沙市各区县（市）知识产权局、版权局，园区知识产权管理部门有关工作人员共60余人参加了培训。

（资料来源：长沙市政府门户网站　作者：潘　虹）

【京津冀知识产权发展联盟正式成立】 2016年3月29日，京津冀知识产权发展联盟在北京成立。该联盟将推动京津冀三地协同发展，提升三地企业的知识产权管理能力，充分调动京津冀优质知识产权服务资源，解决企业发展过程中遇到的与知识产权相关的问题和困难，提升京津冀三地企业在国内外市场的核心竞争力，为本地区企业“走出去”战略保驾护航。

京津冀知识产权发展联盟，是为贯彻落实国家京津冀协同发展战略以及知识产权强国战略，在京津冀三地政府的指导下，由首都知识产权服务业协会、天津科学学研究所和河北省知识产权研究会共同倡议发起的。联盟得到了三地创新型企业和知识产权服务机构的响应，三地共有120家创新型企业和30家知识产权服务机构作为京津冀知识产权发展联盟的发起成员单位。

联盟成立以后将着重进行联盟宣传推广，开展知识产权风险防范培训和重点企业帮扶活动。联盟将依托京津冀丰富的专家资源，定期面向京津冀三地企业开展知识产权风险防范培训，培训内容主要围绕与我国商务往来密切的国家和地区的商业、政策、法律环境等方面的知识产权风险，培训方式主要包括论坛、讲座、沙龙等，并结合实际编制印发风险防范实务指南。对有较大行业影响力、在“走出去”过程中遇到困难的成员企业，联盟将进行“一对一”的专业帮扶活动，组织相关领域的专家和知识产权专业人员与企业对接，提供专家指导和具体解决方案，支撑京津冀企业的国际化发展。

（资料来源：《中国知识产权报》　作者：王　康）

【广西：下放版权登记权限　桂林人可在本市申请版权】 2016年4月4日，广西壮族自治区版权局已决定授权桂林市版权局就近为本市版权（著作权）进行版权（著作权）登记。这也是广西为有效保护知识产权、方便版权（著作权）人进行版权（著作权）登记，进行的版权登记改革。

自20世纪90年代开始实施版权登记以来，20多年来，桂林的著作权人只能向自治区级版权登记部门提出申请。桂林市版权协会会长苏理立介绍，近年来，桂林很多本土知名品牌都曾被山寨，遭受了各种被侵权的困扰，为了维权也耗费了大量人力物力，且因为不良商家的山寨，对正牌商品也造成了不良影响，让人十分惋惜。为了改变这一现状，增强桂林人的版权意识，桂林版权相关部门在打击侵权、申请保护方面都做出了很多努力，其中一项就是申请版权登记的落地。

“这次版权登记权的下放，就是对桂林版权工作的肯定。”苏理立表示，随着版权登记权限的下放，桂林将逐步建立起立体的版权工作体系，建立健全商业“黑名单”制度，真正让侵权售假者“一次违规，寸步难行”。

（资料来源：《桂林晚报》　作者：阳　颜　胡思进）

【“版权云北京之夜暨426so平台上线周年庆”在京召开】 2016年4月20日，以“打击网络盗版　保护知识产权　擎起共同蓝天　共享云上生活”为主题的“版权云北京之夜暨426so平台上线周年庆”在北京召开。主办方中国音像与数字出版协会数字音像工作委员会负责人龙昌明表示：“版权”是文化产业发展的核心，网络盗版、非法传播等侵权现象严重制约了产业的整体发展。“打击网络盗版、保护知识产权”，不仅是文化产业健康发展的根本，也是我国文化繁荣的关键。

主办方邀请了各协会领导上台与到场嘉宾共同见证并启动了《中国数字电影魅力排行榜》。本榜单利用大数据、云计算技术，基于海量监测成果，利用百余部经典电影建设数据模型，结合“版权云标本数据库”数据，从票房总量、口碑指数、保护指数等多个维度进行综合评定，探索性地构建出一套客观公开、操作性强、多维角度的数字电影魅力评价体系。排行榜能对影片的盗版情况起到预警作用。

活动上，中国音像与数字出版协会数字音像工作委员会、北京印刷学院新闻出版学院、北京出版产业与文化研究基地、天擎华媒（北京）科技有限公司四家单位共同推出《2015年境内院线电影网络盗版监测统计报告》。并由北京印刷学院新闻出版学院院长、北京出版产业与文化研究基地主任魏超对报告进行讲解。报告全面分析了全年院线电影上映情况及网络盗版情况，就主要盗版电影传播网站、盗版电影数量、盗版电影版本情况、传播区域、盗版方式、盗版用播放器及传输协议等情况做了重点介绍，对政府监管部门、电影制作单位、电影及互联网产业研究机构以及版权协会等具有参考价值和借鉴意义。

会上，中国电视剧制作产业协会副会长兼秘书长王鹏举代表主办方呼吁影视公司勇敢地站出来反盗维权，呼吁社会各界为建立良好的中国版权生态环境而努力，让更多的版权人相互牵手擎起共同的网络蓝天。

（资料来源：和讯科技）

【广州首聘版权咨询专家】 2016年4月24日，由广东省新闻出版广电局（省版权局）、广州市文化广电新闻出版局（版权局）和广州市文化市场综合行政执法总队主办的“创意广州·梦想飞翔”2016年版权宣传活动在广州图书馆启动，首次聘任7位专家作为广州市版权咨询专家。

现场首次公布的《2014年广州市版权产业的经济贡献调研报告》显示，2014年广州市版权产业的行业增加值为1 576.28亿元人民币，占广州GDP的9.43%。

当天还举行了广州版权专家库专家聘任仪式，首批有7位专家被聘为广州市版权咨询专家，包括广东省高院知识产权庭副庭长、高级法官、博士张学军，广州知识产权法院高级法官、博士郑志柱，华南理工大学法学院、知识产权学院教授孟祥娟，中山大学法学院副教授、广州市政府知识产权专家顾问团成员李颖怡等。同时，还开展了“挥动笔尖，重塑精彩”图文创作征集活动。征集活动期间，还举办了“文化艺术创作与版权保护”等公益性讲座。

（资料来源：《信息时报》 作者：蒋 隽）

【版权师培养计划在京启动】 2016年4月，由中共中央党校中国干部学习网、中国创意产业联盟、首都版权产业联盟共同打造的版权师培养计划在北京启动。这一培养计划旨在为首都乃至全国培养版权专业人才和领军人物，助推我国版权产业发展。首批培养计划于2016年5月开始。

中共中央党校中国干部学习网相关负责人介绍，在有关部委和北京市版权局指导下，培养计划面向各级党政机关、企事业单位招生，采用线上线下一体化（OTO）新型学习培训方式，组织国内外一流专家学者线上线下双线授课。课程全面覆盖版权的知识、政策、商业模式、运营管理、版权贸易及相关前沿问题研讨等。此外，该计划还包含建立创意智库、版权智库、创意论坛、版权论坛等高端平台，为我国创意产业和版权产业发展贡献智力。

（资料来源：中国知识产权资讯网 作者：刘 仁）

【中国版权保护中心DCI体系再拓新应用】
2016年5月10日，华云音乐与Sony/ATV在中国版权保护中心举行了战略合作签约仪式。双方以华云音乐平台为基础，建立音乐版权基础信息库，并与中国版权保护中心携手，在中国标准音像制品编码（ISRC）登记以及数字版权唯一标识符（DCI）体系版权登记方面进行全面的应用合作。

在签约仪式上，华云音乐总裁杨超和Sony/ATV音乐版权公司董事总经理华山就双方长期战略合作相关问题达成一致，并发表了多项规划启动声明。双方的目标是建立一个音乐版权基础信息库，通过与中国版权保护中心联手，来厘清音乐权利，尤其是所涉及的信息网络传播权，使版权方在主张权利时能获得有效支持，让使用者更容易找到正版资源所在，从而降低交易成本和法律风险。信息数据库的建立，使音乐版权信息清晰透明，起到防止假授权、避免重复授权等作用，提高版权交易的可信度。

中国版权保护中心副主任索来军介绍说，DCI体系是中国版权保护中心的自主创新，主要具有数字作品版权登记、版权费结算认证和侵权监测快速维权三大核心功能。其中版权费结算认证即是以第三方专业、中立、权威的定位，为产业提供版权交易结算服务支撑，助力版权运营企业建立透明规范的授权、监测和计费平台，并设计合理的收费机制，打破传统音乐行业管理中的“潜规则”，使所有版税收益的流向透明、易查，破解数字音乐产业的不良竞争现状。

（资料来源：《中国新闻出版广电报》 作者：邹 韧）

【烟台建立山东首个著作权纠纷诉调对接机制】
2016年5月16日，烟台市中级人民法院与烟台市文化广电新闻出版局签署建立了山东省首个著作权纠纷诉调对接机制。相关案件可优先到委员会进行诉前调解，利用委员会专业的行业优势，促进矛盾纠纷及时有效地化解。

著作权案件在烟台中院知识产权案件中占到40%左右。烟台市中院民三庭庭长任广科说，建立著作权纠纷诉调对接机制，可有效利用行政执法人员充足的知识储备和管理经验，做到更加专业地调解，促进矛盾双方纠纷的化解。

烟台市文化广电新闻出版局党委委员、副局长于仁山介绍，著作权纠纷诉调对接机制的建立，在保护知识产权，保护著作权人的权利行使，维护著作权人合法权益中发挥优势。

（资料来源：齐鲁网　作者：卢伟霞）

【百度关闭文学类贴吧清查盗版侵权获国家版权局肯定】　2016 年 5 月 23 日，百度公司发布公告，宣布分批次暂时关闭百度贴吧文学目录下的全部贴吧，全面整顿和清查其中的盗版侵权内容，并开设 2 条发帖投诉举报绿色通道“全民举报吧”和“贴吧曝光台”。百度表示，一旦接到举报，将立即开展清查并在 12 小时内删除相关的盗版侵权内容。这则公告在版权领域及网民中立即“引爆”讨论，同时引起了国家版权局的关注。

国家版权局版权管理司主要负责人表示，2016 年以来，权利人对一些网民利用百度贴吧等网络平台传播未经授权的大量网络文学作品的行为反响强烈。国家版权局对此高度重视，多次组织相关网络企业和权利人研究整治网络文学版权秩序的问题。此次百度公司主动暂时关闭文学目录下的全部贴吧，开展侵权盗版作品排查整顿，这种做法值得肯定，反映了百度公司尊重版权、关切权利人利益的态度。

该负责人希望互联网企业能履行法律规定的义务，强化内部管理机制，主动及时删除、屏蔽侵权盗版作品，不断提升企业版权保护水平。百度公司对盗版网络文学类贴吧“刮骨疗毒”的做法是一个好的开端，期待百度有一个好的整治效果，从而为互联网企业尊重、保护版权起到带头作用。

（资料来源：《中国新闻出版广电报》　作者：赖名芳）

【重庆版权交易中心揭牌】　2016 年 5 月，重庆版权交易中心揭牌仪式在重庆黄桷坪 102 艺术基地举行。该中心重点经营具有重庆特色的版权资源交易及相关服务。

重庆版权交易中心分为版权综合服务大厅、线下版权综合展示厅、互联网交易平台三个部分，采取线上线下相结合的模式。其中，版权综合服务大厅具备版权登记、版权鉴证、版权维护等相关配套服务功能；版权综合展示厅则包括版权作品分类展示、衍生品研发等功能；互联网交易平台通过建设版权作品数据库等八大专业数据库，开发建设集登记、展示、交易等功能于一体的自主交易平台系统。

重庆版权中心负责人表示，该中心作为第四方平台，以“立足重庆、辐射全国、连接世界”为发展目标，通过交易规则约束、信息展示、技术提质等，优化整合版权资源，实现版权资源价值最大化，为重庆文化产业提供一个专业的版权交易平台，助推重庆版权产业发展。

（资料来源：《中国新闻出版广电报》　作者：侯文斌）

【陕西建成线上代理版权登记平台】　2016 年 5 月，由陕西省版权局支持西部国家版权交易中心打造的陕西线上代理版权登记平台正式上线发布，作家王晋康现场通过该平台为自己的原创作品办理了版权登记，并取得了著作权登记证书。

为优化传统代理版权登记流程，缩短审核周期，降低著作权人登记成本，促进陕西全省版权登记工作快速、便捷地开展，在陕西省版权局的支持下，西部国家版权交易中心开发建成了服务于全省著作权人的线上代理版权登记平台。

该平台开通后，广大创作者可以通过中国影视版权交易网方便快捷地注册登录并委托该中心申请办理版权登记。

（资料来源：《中国新闻出版广电报》）

【中国版权保护中心西南版权登记大厅在成都开业运行】　2016 年 6 月 22 日，中国版权保护中心西南版权登记大厅正式启动运行。该登记大厅位于成都天府软件园 G 区成都高新区移动互联创业大厦旁，是中国版权保护中心在中国除北京以外设立的首个直属业务受理中心，可办理中国版权保护中心拥有的所有业务，包括国内外著作权登记、数字版权登记、软件著作权登记信息分析服务、版权法律服务、网络监测取证、作品保管服务、区域版权产业研究咨询服务、版权价值评估咨询服务以及中国标准录音制品编码中心音像版号申领服务和中国数字版权登记支撑服务等。

在功能划分上，西南版权登记大厅搭建了“一大厅”和“两平台”。“一大厅”即登记大厅，“两平台”即中国数字音像产业服务支撑平台和中国游戏产业服务支撑平台——这也是西南版权登记大厅重点拓展发挥的公共服务功能。依托西南版权登记大厅，同时搭建了“音像产业支撑平台”和“游戏产业支撑平台”，为成都高新区音乐音像及游戏产业等文化创意企业提供版权、技术和市场等方面的支撑。

在“两平台”中，中国数字音像产业服务支撑平台包括中国音像版权费用结算中心和中国 ISRC 中心，开展面向互联网及手机网络音乐的登记、盗版监测、维权等一站式版权服务，并通过提供国际标准音像制品编码（ISRC）申领和发放服务，将版权作品与国际对接，搭建音像进出口版权贸易、国际音像文化交流展示的窗口，在保护音乐著作权人合法权益的同时促进数字音乐产业的有序繁荣发展。

中国游戏产业服务支撑平台引进ACTIVSION-Marmalade公司的全球游戏开发平台，为本地游戏企业提供国际顶尖游戏开发引擎的技术培训及支持、国内外游戏渠道的接入、与国际知名游戏企业合作及游戏开发外包服务等，并集合国内外优质资源形成从游戏开发、计费支持、中国销售、终端预装到全球发行的国内领先的完整生态系统，实现对游戏的知识产权保护和盗版打击，最大限度地维护游戏开发公司的经济利益。

中国版权保护中心主任段桂鉴表示，成都作为中国文化重镇之一，是中国知识产权和文化创意产业的重要基地，“西南版权登记大厅开业运行，是中国版权保护中心将国家版权公共服务向重点地区延伸的一项重要尝试，对支撑中国文化创意产业整体发展具有重要示范意义”。

（资料来源：四川新闻网）

【中国版权协会艺术品版权工作委员会成立】 2016年6月29日，中国版权协会艺术品版权工作委员会在京成立。国家新闻出版广电总局副局长、国家版权局副局长、中国版权协会理事长阎晓宏，中国版权协会副理事长、雅昌文化集团董事长万捷，中国版权协会秘书长孙悦，以及靳尚谊、张立辰、杜滋龄、何家英等数十位艺术家代表出席了中国版权协会艺术品版权工作委员会成立发布会。会上，中国版权协会秘书长孙悦宣读了《关于同意成立中国版权协会艺术品版权工作委员会》的批复意见。

雅昌文化集团董事长万捷担任艺术品版权工作委员会主任委员，人民美术出版社总编辑林阳、上海市政协文史委员会副主任祝君波、中国美术家协会副秘书长杜军、中国美术馆副馆长张子康、中国书法家协会副秘书长潘文海、中国工艺美术协会秘书长王山担任艺术品版权工作委员会副主任委员，雅昌文化集团律师仝文担任艺术品版权工作委员会秘书长。中国版权协会艺术品版权工作委员会的办公地点设立在雅昌北京艺术中心。

“从国家的层面来讲，在国家‘十三五’规划中，国家把文化作为支柱产业，但是目前文化产业只占据了全国GDP的3.4%，未来达到5%才能称之为支柱产业。目前的背景下，如果没有知识产权的保护，就很难去实现。这种情况下，我们成立了艺术品的版权保护委员会，看起来是一个领域很窄的方面，但是我们有很多领域的专家和艺术家参与，我们需要有更多的人参与和了解知识产权的保护。”中国版权协会艺术品版权工作委员会主任委员、雅昌文化集团董事长万捷在发布会现场说道。

（资料来源：中国新闻出版广电网　作者：李　彦）

【首个民族文化版权交易中心落户顺义】 2016年6月，中国首家“民族特色文化版权保护与展示交易中心”落户顺义奥林匹克水上公园。《北京青年报》记者从顺义区政府获悉，该中心共有民族文化版权征集中心、管理中心、授权许可中心、体验中心、活动中心五个重要组成部分。每年可征集民族特色文化原创作品1万件，培育转化民族文化特色项目50个。

该中心举办的首个公开日展出了我国著名非物质文化遗产传承人赵广智先生的11件故宫微缩景观作品以及100余件民族文化特色展品，现场达成展品交易30余件。顺义区政府相关负责人透露，中国民族特色文化版权保护与展示交易中心的设立是以国家版权公共服务为载体，整合传统与现代元素，建构新的保护、传承、发展和商业模式。奥林匹克水上公园是顺义新城发展方向的原动力。此次“民族特色文化版权保护与展示交易中心”的落成填补了顺义区在版权保护方面的空白。

（资料来源：《北京青年报》　作者：王　斌）

【上海宝山区版权服务工作站揭牌】 2016年7月15日，上海市宝山区版权服务工作站正式揭牌启用。宝山区副区长秦文波和上海市版权局副局长蔡纪万共同为工作站揭牌。

近年来，宝山区委、区政府围绕“创新驱动发展、经济转型升级”，聚焦结构调整，促进质量型增长、内涵式发展，加紧建设产业互联网实践区，大力推进大数据、云计算、移动互联网、文化创意等新兴产业发展。在“互联网+”的时代背景下，宝山许多企业面临转型升级，对版权登记和服务的需求也不断变化，对知识产权保护的要求也越来越高。

工作站挂牌后将致力于为企业提供版权业务的培训、咨询服务，指导企业健全和完善版权管理的工作机制，协助企业开展版权维权行动。上海市版权局也通过该平台，协助企业加强和提升版权的创造、运营、管理和保护，促进企业版权保护水平和版权管理制度的完善。

（资料来源：新华网上海频道）

【数字版权保护技术研发工程应用在京签约】 2016年7月21日，中国数字出版年会在北京举行，中国新闻出版研究院与一起作业网就数字版权保护技术研发工程应用完成签约。这也是继在2016年深圳文博会上，中国新闻出版研究院与上百家出版单位及相关机构签订数字版权保护技术服务意向书、战略合作协议之后，就数字版权保护技术研发工程应用完成的首个具有实质服务内容的签约。

中国新闻出版研究院基于数字版权保护技术研发工程成果，为一起作业网提供数字内容注册登记、认证查询、侵权追踪等数字版权保护技术服务，并协助一起作业网开展数字内容作品的版权保护、打击侵权盗版行为，为在线教育市场规范提供版权保护技术支撑。双方通过合作，共同推动在线教育领域数字内容资源的版权保护水平，为在线教育行业带来积极示范作用。

（资料来源：《中国新闻出版广电报》　作者：尹　琨）

【文著协与《读者》签订稿酬收转协议】 2016年7月，中国文字著作权协会与读者出版集团有限公司签订了《报刊“法定许可”稿酬收转协议》。

根据协议，《读者》《读者·校园版》《读者·海外版》3本期刊所选用部分文字作品的稿酬，将由中国文字著作权协会收取并转付给相关的作者或权利人。此次中国文字著作权协会与读者出版集团有限公司签订“法定许可”稿酬收转协议，表明中国文字著作权协会在落实国家法律规定，履行报刊和教科书法定许可稿酬收取转付职责方面迈出了重要一步。

中国文字著作权协会成立8年来，一直主动与教科书出版社、报刊社沟通协商，积极推动作者及权利人实现获酬权。截至2016年7月，文著协已经先后与《意林》《知音》《知音文摘》《老友》《语言文字周报》等文摘类报刊，以及人民教育出版社、江苏教育出版社、河北教育出版社等教科书出版单位共计200多家签订了法定许可稿酬转付协议，为广大文字作品权利人收取报刊和教科书法定许可稿酬1 000多万元。

（资料来源：《中国新闻出版广电报》　作者：邹　韧）

【中国版权协会与冠勇科技签署战略合作意向书】 2016年8月20日，中国版权协会与上海冠勇信息科技有限公司在北京举办签约仪式，双方本着服务于会员、服务于社会的宗旨，就数字网络环境下文字、图片、电影、电视剧、音乐等版权作品在线的监测维权开展战略合作，签署战略合作意向书。

针对数字网络环境下侵权盗版的新特点和新形态，建立和完善以技术手段为主要特征的版权监测保护体系，净化版权生态环境，促进中国版权产业链的良性发展，是当下版权产业发展的当务之急。中国版权协会与上海冠勇信息科技有限公司的合作契合了当下版权产业发展的需求。

在签约仪式上，中国版权协会驻会副理事长王自强、冠勇科技董事长吴冠勇代表双方签署《中国版权协会与上海冠勇信息科技有限公司战略合作意向书》，国家版权局版权管理司于慈珂司长出席签约仪式并致辞。

《中国版权协会与上海冠勇信息科技有限公司战略合作意向书》签署后，双方在国家政策、法律、法规许可的范围内，开展版权监测维权并积极探索在鉴定调解等其他业务领域的合作，实现双赢互利。

（资料来源：中国版权协会）

【中国出版数字资源国际交易平台启动】 2016年8月24日，由中国图书进出口（集团）总公司（以下简称中图公司）主办的中国出版数字资源国际交易平台启动暨海外合作签约仪式在北京国际图书博览会现场举行。国家新闻出版广电总局副局长吴尚之、中国出版集团总裁谭跃等出席并讲话。

中国出版数字资源国际交易平台是由中图公司自主研发、专门面向海外机构市场的数字资源交易与服务平台，集资源聚合、搜索、荐购、访问与管理等功能于一身。该平台与国内400余家出版商开展合作，聚合中国出版的多语种优质电子书20万种，涵盖人文、社科、理工、农医等全学科。近年来，中图公司拓展海外数字营销网络，目前已覆盖4万家机构用户和几百万个人读者，打通了进入国际主流阅读市场的道路。本次仪式上，美国哈佛大学图书馆、加州大学伯克利分校东亚图书馆和英国牛津大学图书馆等多家海外客户与中图公司现场签约，开通平台服务。

中宣部、财政部、广电总局相关司局负责人及来自国内出版社和海内外图书馆的100余位嘉宾参加了本次活动。与会者认为，该平台的搭建不仅为海外读者了解中国政治、经济、文化等信息提供了便利，还为中国优秀数字出版物走入海外主流市场，增进多方合作起到了积极的推动作用。

（资料来源：《中国新闻出版广电报》　作者：刘蓓蓓）

【少儿出版反盗版联盟在北京成立】 2016年8月26日，中国出版协会少年儿童读物工作委员会在其主任单位中国少年儿童新闻出版总社举行了少儿出版反盗版联盟成立大会。大会现场，联盟还与阿里巴巴集团签署合作备忘录，决定与淘宝网就少儿图书版权保护工作进行合作，共同抵制少儿出版物盗版问题，并在淘宝平台启动阿里巴巴维权投诉平台。

联盟作为版协少读工委的下设机构，在版协和版协少读工委的指导下开展工作，通过开展市场巡查、网络监督、线索搜集、信息披露、政府联络、法律服务、舆论声援、定时发布盗版侵权黑名单等工作，保护包括著作者和成员单位在内的权利人的著作权及与著作权有关的其他权利。

为了净化市场，为少年儿童守护一方文化净土，联盟向社会各界郑重宣言："一、坚决打击侵权盗版，保护权利人合法权益，维护少儿图书市场的良好秩序；二、强化自身的版权意识和维权意识，加强行业自律，建立打盗维权的长效机制；三、深入推进国家知识产权战略的实施，扎实推进知识产权强国建设。"

联盟的成立引起了政府相关部门的重视，国家版权局版权管理司副司长段玉萍，国家新闻出版广电总局出版管理司副司长许正明、反非法和违禁出版物司副司长汤清淇等分别就联盟今后的工作给出了建议、提出了希望。

（资料来源：中国新闻出版广电网）

【"西部丝路版权交易平台"在京正式启动】 2016年8月，由辰华（北京）版权经纪有限公司牵手西部丝路文化艺术产权交易中心联合主办，"西部丝路版权交易平台"在京正式启动。

该版权交易平台的宗旨是，通过开展文化产品版权交易的模式，推动平台作品版权交易的信息化和网络化，在作者、影视制作公司、娱乐传媒机构之间搭建起小说作品版权推介平台，形成常态化对接与沟通机制，从而挖掘、推广、拓展、保护小说作品版权，提升优秀知识产权价值，活跃小说作品版权交易市场，推动全国范围内影视版权产业的繁荣发展。辰华（北京）版权经纪有限公司的前身和创业班底是一群专业从事交易所及全版权、全产业链开发运营的行业人员，现已涉及数字出版、微电影、动漫、音频、相声、小品、图书等多个领域的产品开发业务，多次为小说、诗歌、漫画、剧本等创作者实现与影视行业的对接提供了一站式便捷版权交易服务。

（资料来源：龙讯财经）

【"2016剑网行动·原创文字作品保护月"正式启动】 2016年9月1日，由中国文字著作权协会（以下简称文著协）发起的"2016剑网行动·原创文字作品保护月"在北京启动，活动为期一个月。

治理网络文学侵权盗版是"剑网2016"专项行动的工作主线。"原创文字作品保护月"活动即意在号召原创媒体机构和原创个人积极主张权益，呼吁社会公众保护正版，呼吁网络内容聚合平台等媒体尊重原创，规范互联网版权秩序。

针对文字作品权利人和产业发展需要，以及网络转载、传播文字作品版权保护的难点，文著协联合东方雍和国际版权交易中心和北京版银科技公司，推出了数字授权许可技术平台"版权印"，创作者或权利人可以通过平台自主完成授权，有效解决互联网内容在网络转载使用中的侵权和维权问题，降低了版权管理和运营的门槛。

（资料来源：新华网　作者：王志艳）

【重庆文创协会版权登记服务中心成立】 2016年9月7日，由重庆市版权局、重庆版权交易中心批准成立的重庆文化创意产业协会版权登记服务中心正式授牌成立。中心的工作是为重庆地区的版权著作和创作人与机构提供版权登记等多项服务，同时在重庆版权交易中心指导下，通过文创基金和众多协作资源平台，为版权著作人提供IP版权孵化和投资与经纪代理，着力打造重庆艺术、文学、音乐和电影与网络影视剧的IP成果。该中心联合同禾基金、一九七八文创机构完成的对重庆IP原创音乐人李波的联孵化投资，正是着力重庆IP发展的具体实践。

重庆文化创意产业协会于2012年正式成立，是重庆文化创意领域的专业服务机构，至2016年9月已经拥有200多家文创机构和个人会员，参与了多个文化创意产业项目的孵化。

（资料来源：华龙网　作者：黄　军　杨正东）

【全国"版权云"体验店授牌仪式在太原举行】 2016年9月9日，全国"版权云"体验店授牌仪式在山西省太原市举行，中国音像与数字出版协会数字音像工作委员会办公室主任武晓芳、监测中心主任姬佩，山西省新闻出版广电局版权处副处长侯广林，传媒处副处长张铁铮出席现场活动，并与泛娱乐场所及行业代表进行了研讨和交流。全国"版权云”体验店授牌，标志着我国泛娱乐经营场所逐步走上规范经营之路。

“版权云”（暨国家数字音像传播服务监管平台）是中国文化（出版广电）大数据产业项目（简称CCDI项目）的核心业务之一，也是我国广电版权领域的重点项目。“版权云”体验店业务，按照先行先试的政策，进行广电版权领域的探索和创新，针对开展影视、音乐、游戏VR等数字内容体验的实体店面提供登记备案、数字正版内容、法律法规等一揽子服务。该业务已在北京、贵州建设大数据基地，并逐步面向全国开展服务。

（资料来源：新华娱乐）

【成都市建立首批版权服务工作站】 2016年9月13日，成都市版权服务工作站授牌仪式暨成都市版权协会换届大会在龙泉驿区洛带古镇举办，成都市29个版权服务工作站诞生。

作为助推创意产业发展的核心要素，版权历来是评估一座城市文化创意行业繁荣与否的晴雨表和分析器，版权服务生态体系的建立，更是城市发展的助推器。作为首批版权服务工作站的代表，来自成都市锦思文化传播有限公司的任梦莹称，企业计划做好区域内版权咨询、登记、孵化等工作，特别是做好音乐艺术类作品的版权服务工作，全力支持成都市音乐产业转型升级。

（资料来源：《成都日报》 作者：王 嘉）

【苏州市吴江区成立首个市级版权工作站】 2016年10月11日，苏州市吴江区首个市级版权工作站揭牌仪式在太湖新城（松陵镇）文体站举行。江苏省版权局版权管理处副处长余列、太湖新城社会事业局局长曹吉华为工作站揭牌。该版权工作站设在太湖新城（松陵镇）文体站内。

太湖新城（松陵镇）辖区内拥有各类版权企业200多家，每年新创版权作品超3 000件，另拥有文艺团队138个，文艺骨干及爱好者6 000多人，具有广泛的版权基础。

太湖新城（松陵镇）文体站自2012年开展版权工作以来，逐步成立了工作班子，明确了专人负责，制定了版权工作制度，版权登记数量逐年提升，版权登记种类不断丰富，辖区内多家优质企业连年获得苏州市版权计划项目扶持资金奖励和苏州市优秀版权奖。在文化与产业融合发展的时代背景下，举行版权工作站揭牌仪式，标志着太湖新城版权工作步上新台阶。

工作站挂牌后，将致力于为企业和个人提供版权业务的培训、咨询服务，指导企业和个人健全和完善版权管理的工作机制，协助企业和个人开展版权维权行动。

（资料来源：《吴江日报》 作者：方 芳）

【摄著协推出“摄影家银行卡”加强摄影作品版权保护】 2016年10月，中国摄影著作权协会（下称摄著协）和中国工商银行在北京举行“摄影家银行卡”发行仪式，国内摄影界首张专属银行卡面世。这是摄著协为加强摄影作品知识产权保护，创新会员服务手段的一项新举措，也是保护摄影家版权和资金安全的一次有益尝试，标志着我国摄影版权保护事业的进步。

在广泛征求摄著协会员和广大摄影家意见基础上，“摄影家银行卡”定位为借记卡，摄著协将通过此卡向会员转付和分配各种形式的摄影作品稿酬和使用费。持有此卡，除了享有普通工商银行借记卡的功能外，摄著协会员还享有一系列优惠政策。同时工商银行还向会员提供各类金融服务。另外，整张卡片在具备金融功能和保护资金安全的同时，更加体现了摄影的行业特色。

国家新闻出版广电总局党组成员、副局长阎晓宏，中国文联党组成员、副主席，摄著协主席李前光，中国工商银行总行党委委员李云泽为“摄影家银行卡”揭牌，并为首批中国摄影著作权协会会员代表颁发了“摄影家银行卡”。

（资料来源：中国知识产权资讯网 作者：姜 旭）

【苏州市版权培训基地揭牌成立】 2016年11月8日，苏州市版权培训基地揭牌暨2016年苏州市版权年会在苏州市会议中心召开，苏州市版权培训基地正式揭牌成立，重点围绕强化版权人才队伍建设、提升版权企业核心竞争力、促进版权中介服务有序发展、为苏州市版权工作建言献策等四个方面推进基地建设，开展培训工作。

建设版权培训基地的目的，一方面是为了通过各方面配合协作，实现版权资源的集聚与叠加，加强版权专业培训，整合现有的苏州市版权人才培训资源、规范培训管理、提高培训质量，为推进苏州市版权工作提供支持和保障；另一方面，更是为了依托版权培训基地这一平台，发挥各方优势和长处，进一步提升苏州市版权智库层次、建强版权执法队伍、优化版权产业布局、提升版权服务能力，全面推进版权创造、运用、保护和管理服务工作，从而助推经济社会更好更快发展。

（资料来源：《苏州日报》　作者：刘晓婷）

【深圳罗湖区政府与中国版权保护中心签约设立粤港澳版权登记大厅】　2016年11月18日，第十八届高交会罗湖展团的重头戏——“罗湖区大梧桐新兴产业带推介会暨项目签约仪式”在高交会上隆重举行。本场活动七个高端项目签约一气呵成，其中首个项目就是《设立中国版权保护中心粤港澳版权登记大厅合作框架协议》，深圳罗湖区区长聂新平、中国版权保护中心主任段桂鉴代表双方签约。深圳市副市长陈彪、罗湖区委书记贺海涛等领导共同见证了这一重要时刻。

中国版权保护中心决定在罗湖设立“粤港澳版权登记大厅”。登记大厅为粤港澳地区各项作品著作权登记、计算机软件著作权登记提供受理、代理、审核和发证服务；后续还合作开展文化创意孵化器建设、国家级版权贸易基地建设，支撑文化创意产业发展。

罗湖区政府与中国版权保护中心的签约，意味着华南地区唯一的版权登记大厅落户罗湖“大梧桐新兴产业带”。协议文本约定，双方在签约基础上充分发挥各自优势，共建文化创意孵化器，打造版权创客空间和文化空间，承办文博会文化版权高峰论坛，建立多层次的区域版权产业发展促进机制，助力深圳新兴产业走向新未来。

版权产业属于现代服务业、生产性服务业的范畴，在都市经济中扮演重要角色。2016年前三季度，罗湖现代服务业增长10.6%，快于GDP增速1.8百分点，占服务业比重为72.1%，同比提高0.5百分点，比全市高1.7百分点；生产性服务业增长8.6%，占服务业比重为66.6%。2016年前三季度，罗湖规模以上新兴产业（七大战略性新兴产业和四大未来产业）增长12.8%，分别高于全市平均水平和全区GDP增速1.6和4百分点。

产业的高端化转型为罗湖版权业等文化产业带来了发展机遇，罗湖区“十三五”规划对激励创新、保护产权做出了明确具体的部署，使版权产业迎来了黄金季，也对其发展提出了更高的要求。

贺海涛表示，激励创新离不开对版权的保护，版权产业的发展离不开对创新性内容的扶植、培育及维护。“十三五”期间，罗湖将加大版权保护力度、有效打击侵权、强化尊重原创、遵守法律和促进产业生态良性发展的意识，塑造版权产业持续健康发展的氛围。围绕《深圳市罗湖区产业发展“十三五”规划》发展版权产业，为优化产业结构、推动罗湖七大产业重点工程建设、提高服务水平、扩大对外影响做出贡献。

在2016年第十一届深圳文博会上，罗湖区依托产业园区集聚发展优势，推出5个分会场、6个活动点、100余项活动。在深圳市评选的文化创意百强企业中，罗湖区占14家，位居全市各区前列。

设置中国版权保护中心粤港澳版权登记大厅这一“国字头”登记大厅，有利于粤港澳地区相关企业、权利人就近登记，提高效率。对于罗湖而言，能够以大厅所在地为依托，实现对影视文化产业、工艺设计产业等文化创意类、计算机软件、信息网络等产业的功能支持。

版权产业作为经济创新发展的重要力量，可以更好地服务文博会，服务整个深圳乃至粤港澳地区的相关企业发展。通过各类活动（宣传、培训、推介等）激发相关企业从版权价值角度来构思和实践企业的新发展，对于围绕版权登记、版权评估、版权投融资、版权交易等一系列版权产业创新经济发展方式也有很好的示范作用。

登记大厅的设立，有利于带来各类版权服务机构和金融机构的入驻，拉动相关行业发展，进一步活跃罗湖经济。

（资料来源：《深圳商报》　作者：颜新华　林苗苗）

【河北省版权局、河北省版权保护中心在曲阳设立版权服务站】　2016年11月24日，河北省版权局在曲阳县举行版权服务站授牌仪式。河北省新闻出版广电局、曲阳县相关管理部门代表以及雕塑行业工艺美术大师，石雕、定瓷等企业代表共计100余人参加活动。

曲阳石雕是河北省传统文化产业的典型代表。近年来，曲阳雕刻产业快速发展，已成为全国雕塑门类最全、品种最多、规模最大的雕塑生产加工基地。随着曲阳石雕创新步伐的加快，诞生了一大批反映燕赵文化特色、凝结劳动人民思想智慧的优秀原创作品。但是在市场蓬勃发展的同时也受到了侵权盗版的侵扰，极大影响了创作者的创新热情和产业健康发展。提高版权保护意识，增强作品的技术及艺术含量，走创新发展之路，成为曲阳雕刻行业的当务之急。此次在曲阳县设立版权服务站，是促进传统版权产业转型升级、创新发展的一个有益探索。

河北省版权保护中心与曲阳县政府签订了《作品著作权登记代办合作协议书》，正式授权曲阳县政府设立版权服务站。该站的设立将为曲阳县 2 000 多家雕刻企业，近 10 万从业人员直接提供作品登记、版权咨询、版权交易、纠纷调解等版权服务。

授牌仪式结束后，河北省新闻出版广电局版权管理部门的负责同志为参会的百余名工艺美术大师、企业代表进行了著作权法讲座和作品登记业务培训，解答个人创作及企业发展中遇到的版权问题。

（资料来源：河北新闻网）

【中山市设立版权专项资金】 2016 年 11 月，根据中山市文广新局出台的《中山市版权专项资金使用办法》，中山市设立版权专项资金，以促进中山市版权事业和产业协调发展。2017 年核定拨款 245 万元，以后将逐年增加。

中山市版权专项资金主要用于资助以下几个方面：一对版权作品和计算机软件登记进行资助。以中山市地址成功登记的一般作品每宗资助 300 元，计算机软件作品每宗资助 800 元，优秀版权作品（市级及市以上获奖作品）全额资助。二是对版权基层服务站和社会版权登记代理机构进行资助。版权基层服务站和社会版权登记代理机构根据登记数量进行补贴资助，每成功登记 1 宗资助 150 元，年终再根据各机构登记情况进行奖励。三是对版权公共服务平台建设项目进行资助。对符合资助条件的版权公共服务平台建设项目一次性支持金额 20 万元。同时对在中山市设立版权交易平台的运营商，按每年实际发生的与中山市企事业单位有关的版权技术交易额的 1% 给予资助。四是对版权优势单位进行资助。对符合资助标准的企业，每家支持金额 8 万元，每年不超过 5 家，连续资助不超 2 年。五是对版权竞赛活动进行资助。资助对象为由市版权局主办或参与的全市版权创意设计大赛等竞赛活动，每次活动资助不超过 10 万元。六是对获得国家或省奖励的优秀版权作品、示范基地（园区）、示范企业等进行资助。

（资料来源：《中山日报》 作者：冷启迪）

【首个国家网络版权产业研究基地落户腾讯】 2016 年 12 月 6 日，在国家版权局主办的 2016 全国版权社会服务工作会上，国家新闻出版广电总局党组成员、国家版权局副局长阎晓宏及与会领导共同为首个国家网络版权产业研究基地落户腾讯主持了揭牌仪式。

据腾讯研究院版权研究中心测算，2016 年底，网络版权产业整体产值将突破 5 600 亿元。随着产业链上下游在视频、动漫等领域以及直播、VR 等新业态持续发力，网络版权产业还将在各细分领域市场拓展新的版图，发展前景更为广阔。

国家版权局 2016 年 10 月份决定在腾讯公司设立“网络版权产业研究基地”，依托腾讯研究院，聚合中外产业界和学术界高端研究资源，共同研究中国网络版权产业的发展以及面临的问题，为政府决策提供研究支持。

作为国内第一家通过正版音乐实现盈利的企业，腾讯目前正在积极探索泛娱乐的发展模式，打通文学、动漫、视频、游戏之间的价值联系，并通过开放平台战略扶持原创，培养广大用户欣赏正版作品的习惯。

承担本次网络版权基地研究任务的腾讯研究院，是腾讯公司于 2011 年成立的社会科学研究机构，旨在依托腾讯多元的产品、丰富的案例和海量的数据，围绕产业发展的焦点问题，通过开放合作的研究平台，共同推动互联网产业健康、有序地发展。腾讯研究院在网络版权保护方面已累计输出了数十万字的研究报告，在政府、司法界和学术界均产生了一定影响。

在本届中国国际版权博览会上，腾讯也同时获得由国家版权局颁发的首届“中国版权金奖”的“推广运用奖”。该奖由国家版权局设立，并与世界知识产权组织共同主办。

自 2005 年起，国家版权局联合国家网信办、工信部、公安部连续 11 年开展打击网络侵权盗版“剑网行动”，针对视频、音乐、软件等重点领域，集中强化对网络侵权盗版行为的打击力度，有效地维护了权利人的合法权益和社会公共利益。

（资料来源：法制网 作者：王开广）

【数字版权保护技术研发工程竣工】 2016 年 12 月 20 日，数字版权保护技术研发工程竣工大会在北京召开，国家新闻出版广电总局副局长孙寿山出席会议并讲话。经过 20 多家单位 5 年时间的协同攻关，国家新闻出版广电总局新闻出版重大科技项目——数字版权保护技术研发工程顺利竣工。该工程已为多家数字出版企业批量注册了版权作品信息，同时也在网络文学侵权追踪中发挥了重要作用。

数字版权保护技术研发工程被列入国家“十一五”与“十二五”时期文化发展规划纲要的重大科技专项。工程共 18 个分包、26 项课题，涵盖技术研究、系统开发、平台搭建、标准制定、总体集成、应用示范等多个方面，参与工程管理、研发和集成任务的单位24家。工程总目标是探索数字环境下的版权保护机制，为出版单位数字化转型提供政府主导的第三方公共服务平台，为数字出版产业发展提供一整套数字版权保护技术解决方案。目前，该工程已经完成了全部预定任务，形成了综合性的数字版权保护技术管理与服务平台。

在研发过程中，工程共申请发明专利41项，登记软件著作权62件，在国内外媒体上发表论文42篇。其中，6项专利申请已获国家授权，1项发明专利荣获第十八届中国专利优秀奖。此外，工程媒体指纹相关技术、数字水印相关技术均获得2015年中国电子学会技术发明一等奖，数字水印相关技术还获得教育部2015年高等学校科学研究优秀成果（技术发明）一等奖。

孙寿山指出，数字版权保护技术研发工程圆满完成了预定任务，取得了多方面的成果。它可以解决我国新闻出版业发展中的版权瓶颈问题，可以确立我国在数字版权保护技术研发中的自主地位，也可以树立我国在知识产权保护方面的良好形象。要从三个方面下大气力抓好工程的应用推广工作：一是要做好相应技术成果的应用推广与宣传工作；二是要做好政策性支持工作；三是要做好后续资金的保障工作。

中国新闻出版研究院作为工程应用推广单位，已与120多家单位签订了技术服务意向书，与一起作业网、华东师大出版社、上海交大出版社等多家单位签订了技术服务合同，并为中文在线、万方数据等数字出版企业批量注册了作品信息，同时也把侵权追踪技术成果应用到了网络文学反盗版实践中。

（资料来源：《中国新闻出版广电报》　作者：王坤宁）

【第十五届输出版引进版优秀图书推介活动名单公布】　2016年12月，由中国出版协会、中国新闻出版研究院、出版参考杂志社联合主办的第十五届输出版引进版优秀图书推介活动圆满结束。推介活动于2016年初启动，国内各出版单位踊跃报名，几乎有版权输出、引进业务的出版社均参加了此项活动。活动推介输出版优秀图书100种，引进版优秀图书78种，推动版权输出、引进的典型人物4名，版权经理人9名。

本次获推介的图书，基本涵盖了国内外相关领域的优秀经典图书，很多图书在销量上都有不俗表现。

本届活动推介的输出版图书呈现以下几个特点：一是选题丰富，题材广泛。主题出版输出成绩喜人，输出图书从不同方面向世界讲述中国故事，如《中共十八大：中国梦与世界》《中国新趋势》《中国未来十年改革之路》。二是输出版科技图书学术价值极高，从系统性、专业性和实用性等不同角度填补了业界空白，如科学出版社的《中国大陆科学钻探工程》、人民卫生出版社的《实用传染病影像学》。三是少儿原创作品受关注，一系列国际化品牌开始涌现，如江苏凤凰少年儿童出版社的《青铜葵花》、浙江少年儿童出版社的“中国原创绘本精品系列”。四是长篇文学佳作纷纷走出国门，获得世界影响力，如中国教育图书进出口有限公司和湖南科学技术出版社版权输出的《三体》三部曲、四川文艺出版社版权输出的《琅琊榜》。五是输出版图书进入越来越多的世界主流国家和地区，彰显了我国文化在国际上愈来愈重要的影响力和话语权。输出由最初的我国港澳台地区扩展到东南亚、中亚，欧美等国家所占比例越来越高。“经典中国国际出版工程”、“丝路书香工程”、中华学术外译项目、“中国图书对外推广计划”等国家资助项目为这些图书的“走出去”搭建了平台。

引进版图书类别和题材百花齐放，社科类图书经典之作层出不穷，思想价值、文化价值、市场价值俱佳，如四川人民出版社的《历史的教训》、浙江大学出版社的《道德的起源：美德、利他、羞耻的演化》。引进版科技类图书，代表着世界科技发展的方向和最高水准，如中国水利水电出版社的《河流演变学》、化学工业出版社的《农药手册》；引进版少儿类图书中，经典之作依然唱主角，如浙江少年儿童出版社的《不列颠百科全书》、二十一世纪出版社的《不一样的卡梅拉》。

（资料来源：《中国新闻出版广电报》　作者：刘宇阳）

◆ 国际交流与合作

【中以签署文学和翻译领域合作谅解备忘录】　以色列时间2016年1月11日至13日，国家新闻出版广电总局副局长孙寿山应以色列外交部邀请，率中国出版代表团出访以色列，并与以色列外交部签署《中华人民共和国国家新闻出版广电总局与以色列外交部在文学和翻译领域的合作谅解备忘录》。该备忘录的签署开启了两国在新闻出版领域交流与合作的新篇章。

1月12日，孙寿山会见了以色列外交部负责文化科技事务的副总司长拉斐尔·甘姆祖。孙寿山表示，近年来中以两国在新闻出版领域的交流交往日益频繁，中国出版界通过参加重要国际书展等多种方式，不断扩大中国与以色列之间的图书版权贸易。据不完全统计，从 2000 年至 2016 年 1 月，中国翻译的以色列文学作品已达到 365 种，这些优秀作品成为中国读者了解以色列历史、文化的重要窗口。中国国家新闻出版广电总局与以色列外交部签署在文学和翻译领域的合作备忘录，将进一步推动中以两国在新闻出版领域特别是文学翻译方面的合作，让两个民族、两国人民通过图书媒介，互学互鉴，更加相亲相近。

（资料来源：《中国新闻出版广电报》　作者：洪玉华）

【2016 新德里世界书展中国代表团版权贸易成果丰硕】　2016 年 1 月 17 日，为期 9 天的 2016 新德里世界书展落下帷幕。其间，作为主宾国参展的中国代表团举办近 70 场文化和出版交流活动，中国出版商同外国出版商共达成 588 项版权协议及 172 项合作意向，版权贸易成果丰硕。

此次中国主宾国活动由国家新闻出版广电总局主办，中国图书进出口（集团）总公司承办。书展期间，《习近平谈治国理政》研讨会成功举办。一大批讲述中国故事、中国梦、中国经济和“一带一路”内容的主题类图书受到印度出版商热捧，《走向人人享有保障的社会》《破解中国经济发展之谜》《中国梦是什么》《中国机遇》《邓小平改变中国——1978：中国命运大转折》《改变世界经济地理的一带一路》等图书现场签订了版权输出协议。中国少儿精品图书展、中国古代出版印刷展、中印文化交流图片展都深受当地观众喜爱，拉近了中印两国人民的距离，加深了印度民众对中国的了解。曹文轩、刘震云、麦家等 9 名中国作家在印举办的多场文学交流活动，以及中印出版发展高峰论坛等活动的举办，加强了中印两国文学界和出版界的沟通与对话，增进了彼此的了解和友谊。

（资料来源：《中国新闻出版广电报》
作者：涂桂林　孙京平）

【阎晓宏率代表团访问埃及并参加开罗国际书展】　2016 年 1 月 26 日至 29 日，国家新闻出版广电总局副局长、国家版权局副局长阎晓宏率新闻出版代表团对埃及进行访问并参加开罗国际书展，进一步拓展中国与埃及以及阿拉伯国家的出版文化交流，推动广电总局“丝路书香工程”全面实施，促进互利合作机制建立，提升中华文化在阿拉伯国家的传播力和影响力。

开罗时间 1 月 27 日，第 46 届开罗国际书展开幕，中国代表团携 500 种 1 200 册优秀图书参展，埃及总理伊斯梅尔参加书展并参观了中国展台，阎晓宏向伊斯梅尔总理介绍了中国代表团的参展情况以及《习近平谈治国理政》一书阿拉伯文版的出版和在埃及的发行情况。1 月 28 日，“丝路上的埃及与中国：埃中关系走向”论坛举行，阎晓宏与埃及文化部部长赫尔米 · 纳木纳出席论坛并致辞，来自中国的张维为、刘震云、王义桅与埃及的多位知名作家、汉学家等进行了交流。阎晓宏在致辞中表示，中埃都是历史悠久的文明古国，两国在经济和文化上都对人类历史做出过突出贡献。2016 年是中埃两国文化交流年，希望中埃两国出版文化领域能够以“一带一路”倡议为契机，共同开启中埃两国出版文化交流互鉴的新篇章。

赫尔米 · 纳木纳表示，“在此次书展上，《习近平谈治国理政》无疑是最耀眼的，这本书使我深受启发，对于中国发展经验、发展道路有了更加深刻的了解，埃及愿意在促进经济社会和文化发展上与中国相互学习，相互借鉴，共同发展”。

在埃及访问期间，代表团还拜会了中国驻埃及大使馆，并与宋爱国大使等进行了会谈；考察了埃及最大的书店——埃及国际图书中心。在考察书店销售情况后，阎晓宏指出，随着“经典中国国际出版工程”“丝路书香工程”重点翻译出版项目的开展，一批中国知名作家学者的优秀作品，如《中国震撼》《一带一路》《手机》等在埃及实现有效落地，受到读者欢迎，有效推动了中华文化在阿拉伯地区的传播。

（资料来源：《中国新闻出版广电报》　作者：刘蓓蓓）

【中捷建立战略伙伴关系共同保护知识产权】
2016 年 3 月 28 日至 30 日，应捷克共和国总统米洛什 · 泽曼邀请，中华人民共和国主席习近平对捷克共和国进行国事访问。其间，中国和捷克两国达成多项重要共识，一致决定建立中捷战略伙伴关系。双方签署了《中华人民共和国和捷克共和国关于建立战略伙伴关系的联合声明》。

根据联合声明，双方决定按照 2004 年《中华人民共和国政府与捷克共和国政府经济合作协定》，充分发挥两国政府间经济联委会机制的宏观指导作用，推动扩大贸易规模和双向投资，促进双边贸易平衡发展。双方将为双向投资创造公平透明、积极友善的政策环境，致力于解决企业界有关市场准入和法规方面的关切。双方将共同努力，保护在捷中国企业和在华捷克企业的知识产权。

（资料来源：《中国知识产权报》）

【中国图书受突尼斯读者欢迎】 2016年4月3日，第32届突尼斯国际书展在孩子们的歌声中落下帷幕，参展的五洲传播出版社与突尼斯库努兹出版社签订了“中国文化”系列的阿文及法文版权输出协议。

此次书展，五洲社携带近200种法文、英文及阿文的图书参展，重点向突尼斯读者展出了“中国文化”系列及“人文中国”系列图书，其中广受欢迎的还有“中国智慧”系列以及讲述“丝绸之路”历史的一系列图书。

多家突尼斯大学图书馆及突尼斯的发行商表示希望能够采购五洲社的书籍，五洲社也与当地的其他出版社达成了10余项版权输出意向。

创办于1982年的突尼斯国际书展是北非地区一年一度的文化盛事，由突尼斯文化和遗产保护部主办。作为突尼斯最重要的多边文化活动之一，书展每年吸引来自世界各地的上千家出版社参展。

（资料来源：《中国新闻出版广电报》 作者：孙海悦）

【中国展团重磅亮相博洛尼亚童书展】 2016年4月4日至7日，第53届博洛尼亚国际童书展在意大利博洛尼亚会展中心举行，中国展团以超大规模参展。

中国展团在26号馆设立336平方米超大联合展台。2016年，中国版协少读工委第三次牵头，中国少年儿童新闻出版总社组织成员单位和少儿出版界表现优异、版权输出实力雄厚的非成员出版单位联合参展。此次中国展团在组成和展位配置上与往年不同：一是专业少儿社占比提高，组团更加专业化；二是组团规模扩大，成员数达到113人，比上年增加约28%，其中作家、插画家人数大幅增加。

本次中国展团参展图书更加具有针对性，更加符合国际规范，适应童书展版权贸易的需求。中国展团共准备了3 300册图书，并制作了英、德等不同语种的外文样书651种计825册。中国展团计划实现图书版权输出540项，同比增长38%。

博洛尼亚插画展是博洛尼亚童书展的重要组成部分，我国之前只有个别插画家的作品在展览上展出。2016年，少读工委组织十几家出版社推选了40位插画家的作品，最终选出朱成梁等3人的作品参展。同时，在中国展团的展位内，还进行了优秀插画作品展示。为增强国外出版界对中国童书原创力量发展状况的了解，此次还将制作《2016年博洛尼亚童书展中国原创插画展作品及作家介绍》画册。

“好故事一起讲——中国图画书与世界的对话”是本次中国展团的活动亮点。对话活动将邀请曹文轩、朱成梁、徐鲁与国外知名出版人、儿童文学作家及插画家等，围绕“生命与哲学的思考”“中国传统文化故事”“和平思考——人类共同的命运”3个主题进行深入探讨，推动国内外作家和插画家的相互理解，进一步加深合作。此外，接力出版社“走进昆虫的奇妙世界——《酷虫学校》全版权推介会”、新蕾出版社“梅子涵少儿文学作品推荐会”、湖南少儿出版社“‘汤素兰图画书系列’（中英双语版）首发式”等活动也在展会期间举办。

（资料来源：《中国新闻出版广电报》
作者：刘蓓蓓 左志红）

【外文出版社伦敦书展版权输出成绩显著】 2016年4月12日，外文出版社携两百余种以英文为主的多语种图书参加2016年伦敦书展，积极开展版权贸易洽谈，版权输出成绩显著。

该社与阿拉伯科学出版社达成版权输出协议，并于书展开幕首日举行了版贸签约仪式，输出“中国经典外文读库”系列《中国古代寓言选》《史记选》《陶渊明诗文选》《杜甫诗选》《长生殿》等14项图书的阿拉伯语版权。

“中国经典外文读库”是外文出版社积数十年之功，在近年重新整合、精心打造的中国经典作品的对外普及性读本系列，在中国文学的外文读本中具有针对性强、选题精当、译文典范、制作精良的特点，获得国外读者和出版同业的高度关注和好评。此次阿语版权的输出，将有助于扩大中国文学在阿拉伯世界的影响，增进阿拉伯读者对中国的了解。

（资料来源：中国网 作者：王志永）

【“数字环境下影视产业版权保护圆桌会议”在北京举行】 2016年4月25日，围绕着世界知识产权组织（WIPO）2016年发布的“数字创意、重塑文化”主题，中国国家版权局与WIPO在北京联合举办了“数字环境下影视产业版权保护圆桌会议”。来自WIPO与中国相关部委、法院、著作权涉外认证机构、著作权集体管理组织的代表以及影视领域权利人和专家学者等60余人参加了专题研讨。与会者研讨了数字时代影视产业发展所面临的版权保护重点和热点问题，探索了版权保护新途径和版权合作新模式，共同呼吁只有切实维护影视作品权利人的合法权益，加大版权执法力度，才能激发影视作品作者的创作热情，催生更多兼具社会效益和经济效益的优秀影视作品。

（资料来源：《中国新闻出版广电报》 作者：赖名芳）

【中英探索建立双语侵权举报平台】 2016 年 4 月 27 日，在中国国家版权局版权管理司司长于慈珂、英国知识产权局版权与执法司司长罗斯·林奇的见证下，百度与在华国际出版商版权保护联盟（IPCC）在北京签署版权保护合作备忘录。

在此备忘录框架下，针对互联网侵权盗版行为，百度将探索建立中英双语的侵权举报平台，并为联盟成员开辟快速反应“绿色通道”，及时有效处理侵权盗版行为。双方将定期进行信息交流和沟通，通过紧密的版权保护合作打击网络侵权盗版。

于慈珂表示，互联网领域的版权保护是世界性难题，中英两国对此有共识也有共同措施，希望通过此次签约进一步加深交流合作、借鉴学习，探索建立好做法、好制度，为攻破这一世界难题贡献中英双方力量。

罗斯·林奇表示，此次合作标志着数字技术正为减少网络侵权提供支持，为中英两国共同面临的知识产权网络侵权问题提供了更加快捷、有效的解决方案，对于在全球范围内建立版权保护体系也是至关重要的。

（资料来源：《中国新闻出版广电报》 作者：李 森）

【2016 美国书展中国展团盛装参展】 2016 年 5 月 9 日，由北京、河南、贵州、江苏、青海、江西、湖南等 11 个省（区、市）41 家单位组成的 2016 美国书展中国展团从北京启程。

2016 美国书展于当地时间 5 月 11 日至 14 日在芝加哥麦考密克展览中心举办。此次书展，中国展团的参展图书共 836 册，其中外文版图书 408 册，均为各出版社精心挑选的近两年出版、适合版权输出的新书。书展期间，中国展团举办了中美出版人交流会、赴芝加哥公共图书馆调研等一系列活动，并邀请中、美两国的出版界人士共同探讨中美出版业深化合作的有关问题。此外，参展单位也举办了一系列出版交流活动。

2016 年的美国书展展期已由往年 3 天专业展览模式调整为 3 天专业展览、1 天图书销售模式。为配合美国书展的转型政策，更好地服务于中国图书“走出去”，展期最后一天的图书销售活动中，中国展团选派了有代表性、有能力的出版社参加。

（资料来源：《中国新闻出版广电报》 作者：杨雅莲）

【第十二届中韩版权研讨会在韩举行】 2016 年 5 月 10 日，中国国家版权局与韩国文化体育观光部在韩国济州岛共同举办了第十二届中韩版权研讨会。双方围绕“促进中韩著作权产业持续发展的合作”这一主题，分别介绍了两国版权产业发展的状况、推动版权产业发展的政策以及版权保护对产业发展的促进作用等情况。中国国家版权局版权管理司司长于慈珂、韩国文化体育观光部著作权政策官金哲民、韩国著作权委员会委员长吴承锺出席研讨会并致辞。中韩两国版权相关企业负责人、版权专家学者近百人参加了研讨会。

（资料来源：国家版权局网站）

【“版权和相关权热点问题亚太地区研讨会”在西安举行】 2016 年 5 月 23 日至 25 日，由世界知识产权组织（WIPO）与中国国家版权局主办，韩国文化体育观光部与中国陕西省版权局协办的“版权和相关权热点问题亚太地区研讨会”在西安举行。

WIPO 版权发展司司长高航在 23 日上午举办的开幕式上致辞。她对中国政府为此次会议所付出的努力表示感谢。她说，互联网为以版权为核心的创意产业带来了巨大的机遇，WIPO 组织召开此次研讨会的目的就是通过提供一个有效的平台，促进亚太各国在版权领域进行经验交流、问题研讨与分析，希望通过两天的讨论，促进亚太地区版权界开展务实合作，共同促进版权市场的持续繁荣发展。

中国国家版权局版权管理司司长于慈珂在致辞中表示，这次会议的召开对于亚太各国从容应对新形势下版权保护面临的挑战和机遇，有针对性地营造良好的版权保护法制环境，促进版权产业健康发展具有重大意义。他强调，中国政府历来重视版权保护，近年来中国国家版权局开展了一系列卓有成效的版权保护的工作：积极推动《著作权法》第三次的修法工作，促使中国的版权法律制度更加完善；强化版权执法监管，进一步规范版权秩序；完善版权社会服务体系，不断提升版权服务水平；全面开展版权宣传培训，提升尊重版权、保护版权的社会意识；与国际社会建立了广泛、深入的版权多边、双边关系，特别是 2012 年《视听表演北京条约》在北京成功签署，体现了国际社会对中国版权工作的肯定和认可。中国将积极承担自己的国际责任，真诚地与各国继续保持和发展良好的版权交流和合作关系，共同努力创造国际版权事业的美好未来。

在为期三天的研讨会上，百余名中外与会者还围绕版权和相关权在国际层面的发展现状、趋势及挑战展开了热烈的讨论。中国、韩国、马来西亚、柬埔寨、孟加拉、蒙古、不丹、印度尼西亚等国代表还分享了各自在版权产业发展、立法和政策、管理、执法等方面的经验和实践。为各国促进版权产业的繁荣发展提出了建设性意见。

（资料来源：《中国新闻出版广电报》　作者：赖名芳）

【中韩图书版权交易会在南昌举行】　2016年5月25日，由江西省出版集团公司、韩国文化体育观光部主办，韩国出版文化产业振兴院、中文天地出版传媒股份有限公司、韩国中小出版协会联合承办的2016中韩图书版权交易会在南昌举办。开幕式上，江西省出版集团公司与韩国出版文化产业振兴院、韩国中小出版企业协会代表签订《图书版权交流合作意向书》，中文传媒与韩国杂志协会代表签订了《业务合作协议书》。

交易会上，中韩两国60余家出版单位参展，展出图书、期刊、电子出版物2 800余种。其中，中文传媒10家出版企业以及人民教育出版社、五洲出版社、山东出版传媒、北洋出版传媒、中南出版传媒等25家出版企业展出图书2 000余种，主要涵盖少儿、人文、教育、美术等产品。据了解，中韩自贸协定正式签署以来，中韩两国的合作空间和贸易领域逐步扩大，江西省内企业与韩国国内企业的贸易合作日益频繁。

此次交易会，除了图书版权贸易交流活动外，还开展了多场中韩学术交流活动。

（资料来源：《江西日报》　作者：钟端浪）

【中俄两大电影节在俄签署战略合作仪式】　莫斯科当地时间2016年6月27日，中国丝绸之路国际电影节与莫斯科国际电影节战略合作签约仪式在莫斯科举行。

陕西省副省长姜锋、国家新闻出版广电局电影局副局长栾国志、陕西省新闻出版广电局局长钱远刚、俄罗斯文化部电影司司长特尔诺夫、莫斯科国际电影节总监谢明娜等出席了签约仪式。

中国丝绸之路国际电影节由国家新闻出版广电总局创办，是“丝绸之路影视桥工程”的重点项目，每年一届，由陕西、福建两省轮流主办。莫斯科国际电影节是俄罗斯（苏联）最大的国际电影节，也是世界上最重要的国际电影节之一。此次两大电影节进行战略合作，旨在就进一步深化中俄影视拍摄合作、中俄电影人互访、中俄影视节目交流达成一致意见。

姜锋在活动中表示，陕西西安是中华民族和华夏文明的重要发源地，也是古丝绸之路的起点。中国丝绸之路国际电影节自2014年举办以来，坚持以电影为纽带，促进丝路沿线各国展开文化交流与合作，同时传承丝路精神，弘扬丝路文化，为“一带一路”建设创造良好的人文条件。

此外，第38届莫斯科国际电影节“中国西部电影展映周”单元活动也于当天启动。《红高粱》《康定情歌》《东北偏北》《郎在对门唱山歌》《遥远的天熊山》等五部西部影片也参加了展映。

（资料来源：中国新闻网　作者：王修君）

【蔡赴朝会见世界知识产权组织总干事高锐一行】　2016年7月19日，中宣部副部长、国家新闻出版广电总局局长、国家版权局局长蔡赴朝在北京会见了世界知识产权组织总干事弗朗西斯·高锐一行，双方就进一步巩固和发展更加积极、务实、友好的合作关系进行了深入交流。国家新闻出版广电总局副局长、国家版权局副局长阎晓宏陪同会见。

蔡赴朝首先表达了对高锐一行的欢迎。他说，世界知识产权组织与中国国家版权局一直保持着密切联系和良好合作，关心和支持中国版权保护事业，在华设立南通家纺、德化陶瓷版权保护优秀案例示范点并进行全球推广，大力支持重要国际版权会议在华举办，并在华颁发“中国版权金奖”。特别是2015年12月，中国国家版权局与世界知识产权组织在华签署了合作谅解备忘录，更是标志着双方迈上版权领域全面开展合作的新台阶。

蔡赴朝表示将尽快推动《视听表演北京条约》早日生效，充分发挥版权在经济发展、科技创新、文化繁荣和社会进步等方面的推动及保障作用。他相信高锐此行将进一步加强双方合作，并促进中国版权事业发展。

高锐感谢中国国家版权局给予世界知识产权组织的大力支持。他说，世界知识产权组织高度重视同中国国家版权局之间的关系，对中国在版权工作领域所取得的进步深感敬佩，也十分感谢中国在《视听表演北京条约》成功缔结和推动其生效方面所做的贡献和努力。他表示，世界知识产权组织将更加紧密地同中国合作，推动包括版权在内的知识产权多边关系健康发展。

世界知识产权组织副总干事王彬颖，国家新闻出版广电总局、国家版权局办公厅主任吴保安和版权管理司司长于慈珂等双方相关负责人参加会见。

（资料来源：《中国新闻出版广电报》 作者：魏 芳）

【中美著作权最新发展研讨会在京召开】 2016年7月20日，“中美著作权最新发展研讨会”在中国人民大学法学院召开。此次会议由中国知识产权法学研究会、美国专利商标局、中国人民大学法学院和中国人民大学知识产权学院共同主办。来自中美两国近百位嘉宾参加了此次会议，共同就中美著作权法的历史、背景、主要内容以及最新发展等相关领域的重要问题开展深入讨论。

本次论坛分上下半场，共设置五个讨论单元，中美两国代表分别就“从学术界的视角看中美著作权法发展”、“内容产业的商标与收益多样性：令百川归海”、“美国著作权法及政策：历史简介与最新发展”、“中国著作权法修改的背景、主要内容及进展”及“中国著作权保护司法与行政发展”等主题发表报告，与会嘉宾围绕这些议题依次进行评议。两国代表积极互动交流，特别是针对版权法如何让文化产业人士和企业受益、如何随着技术的发展进一步调整法律保护方式等问题展开了深入讨论。

本次研讨会得到了一些专家学者及产业界、司法界等的关注。与会嘉宾认为，本次研讨会为进一步推动中国与美国在著作权立法、司法和行政保护方面的共同进步和相关领域的合作共赢提供了坚实的理论基础和沟通平台。中国人民大学知识产权学院院长、中国知识产权法学研究会会长刘春田表示，每年召开这样的会议已经成为惯例，由此延伸出多方位、多领域、更为持久深入的合作，对美国产业界、法律界加深对中国的了解，以及中方对美国发展新趋势的了解都非常有益。

（资料来源：中国知识产权资讯网 作者：朱杉杉）

【阎晓宏会见查德·康斯坦德、洪伟典一行】 2016年7月21日，中国国家新闻出版广电总局副局长、国家版权局副局长阎晓宏在北京会见了来访的环球唱片公司全球法律总裁理查德·康斯坦德及国际唱片业协会（IFPI）亚洲总裁洪伟典一行。双方就如何通过保护版权促进中国音乐市场的发展等共同关心的话题进行了探讨。阎晓宏表示，版权保护的进步带来了中国音乐市场的健康繁荣。

阎晓宏首先对理查德·康斯坦德和洪伟典等一行的到来表示欢迎。他说，近几年来，在国际组织和跨国企业的支持下，中国音乐版权的正版化进展很快，在全球音乐市场的排名也有很大提升。去年中国国家版权局重点对音乐市场进行了治理，下发了《关于责令网络音乐服务商停止未经授权传播音乐作品的通知》，在各大网络音乐服务商的配合下，不到两个月就下架未经授权的音乐作品220余万首，网络音乐的环境得到进一步净化，数字音乐的付费模式也得到了更多用户的认同。

阎晓宏在谈话中提到，网络盗版一直以来都是一个世界性难题。相对于视频内容来说，音乐市场的盗版情况比较严重。阎晓宏强调，中国政府对待盗版问题的态度非常明确。一方面要进行有效监管，对大的网络运营商要加强监管，保持对侵权盗版的高压态势，7月12日，国家版权局已与公安部等四部门启动了“剑网2016”专项行动；另一方面要加大执法力度，尤其是对一些恶意盗版侵权的小网站要加大刑事打击力度。而从音乐网站自身来说，也要积极探索建立更高品质的音乐服务和更便捷的付费音乐模式。

理查德·康斯坦德向阎晓宏及中国国家版权局为促进全球音乐市场所做的努力深表感谢。他说中国的音乐市场在近两年发生了显著的变化，最新数据显示，中国音乐市场已经上升到了全球排名第十位，2015年中国音乐市场销售总额高达1.7亿美元，增长率达到64%，这与中国政府对音乐市场的版权治理是分不开的。他还说，环球唱片作为全球最大的唱片公司，愿促进中国音乐市场发展，并将更多的中国音乐人和艺术家推向国际。

在会谈中，中国国家版权局版权管理司司长于慈珂和政策法制司副司长高思还与来访嘉宾就版权的行政执法、著作权集体管理组织及著作权法第三次修订、广播与公开表演权、“避风港”原则的适用等细节性问题进行了深入交流。

（资料来源：《中国新闻出版广电报》 作者：魏 芳）

【“2016中韩出版合作论坛”在京举行】 2016年8月25日，由五洲传播出版社、韩国出版文化产业振兴院主办的“2016中韩出版合作论坛”在北京国际图书博览会（BIBF）举行。

在本次论坛上，中国新闻出版研究院副院长张立和韩国出版文化产业振兴院院长李基盛等致辞，对中韩两国出版界的合作前景寄托殷切期望。中韩出版界专家还就两国纸书和电子书的合作现状、发展方向等议题进行了深入讨论。论坛上，中国新闻出版研究院、五洲传播出版社和韩国出版文化产业振兴院签署了 MOU 协议，开启中韩出版合作交流之门。

据介绍，目前在中国翻译出版的韩文图书品类繁多。其中，儿童读物最为畅销，深受中国民众的喜爱。从 2013 年到 2014 年，韩国向中国输出的图书版权共有 2 655 件，儿童图书和漫画占绝大部分。

专家表示，中韩两国在学术出版方面的交流已经持续了 20 多年，但在商务出版方面的交流仍需进一步推动。此次“中韩出版合作论坛”将成为推动两国商务出版合作的重要契机。

（资料来源：新华网　作者：孙　琪）

【阎晓宏会见英国能源及知识产权国务大臣娜薇尔·露芙一行】　2016 年 8 月 26 日，中国国家新闻出版广电总局副局长、国家版权局副局长阎晓宏在北京会见了英国能源及知识产权国务大臣娜薇尔·露芙女男爵一行。双方回顾了《中英版权战略合作谅解备忘录》签署以来所开展的交流合作及取得的成果，并就版权立法、执法、产业发展、集体管理等问题交换了意见。

阎晓宏对娜薇尔·露芙再次来访中国国家版权局表示欢迎。他说，自 2010 年 9 月中英签署备忘录后，两国版权交流与合作进入了常态化、制度化阶段。在该备忘录框架下，中国国家版权局与英国知识产权局积极制定 2011 年至 2016 年的工作计划，并开展了许多具体工作，两国版权领域的沟通交流非常活跃。

阎晓宏向娜薇尔·露芙一行介绍了中国国家版权局为落实《国务院关于新形势下加快知识产权强国建设的若干意见》所开展的重点工作。他说，我们当前的任务是为加快知识产权强国建设而努力营造公平、公正的版权生态环境。为此，中国国家版权局联合工信部、公安部和网信办共同开展了打击网络侵权盗版的“剑网”专项行动。在过去 11 年的集中治理过程中，中国网络版权秩序得到了很大的扭转，国内外权利人组织、作品的使用者以及社会公众对此都给予了很高的评价。与此同时，中国国家版权局开展了社会公众版权意识的教育与引导，并加大推进作品登记、评估及贸易，促进作品在良好版权环境中传播，使创作者能够获得合理的报酬。此外，中国国家版权局连续 3 年发布了中国版权产业的经济贡献调研报告，并与世界知识产权组织（WIPO）共同举办国际版权论坛，联合为对中国文化艺术、版权保护、社会和经济发展做出突出贡献的个人或组织颁发“版权金奖”。

娜薇尔·露芙对《中英版权战略合作谅解备忘录》签署以来两国版权领域交流合作所取得的成果表示满意。她说，从 2010 年参加上海世博会到 2016 年参加第 23 届北京图博会，她亲身感受了中国创意产业的蓬勃发展。2014 年，已经有 731 种中国图书通过版权许可的方式被引进到英国，仅次于美国，位居英国图书引进版数量第二。她相信中英合作将促进两国经济增长和创新能力提升，希望两国继续加强在网络版权执法等方面的合作。

（资料来源：《中国新闻出版广电报》　作者：赖名芳）

【第 29 届莫斯科国际书展中俄出版机构达成多项合作】　莫斯科当地时间 2016 年 9 月 11 日，为期 5 天的第 29 届莫斯科国际书展落下帷幕。中国出版代表团在版权贸易、对外推广、行业交流等方面都取得丰硕成果。

书展期间，中国出版单位与国外出版单位达成版权贸易意向 30 余项，中华书局、中国建筑工业出版社、四川新华文轩出版传媒股份有限公司、陕西新华出版传媒集团均与俄罗斯出版单位签署合作协议，接力出版社、高等教育出版社、中国社会科学出版社等单位与俄方进行了深入洽谈。

“以前我们的书主要输出英语国家，没想到在俄罗斯也有市场。”人民交通出版社股份有限公司总编辑韩敏告诉记者，几天来，在与俄罗斯出版同行的交流中发现，俄罗斯读者对中国交通方面的标准、技术也很有兴趣。他期待着在“一带一路”的背景下，中俄双方在交通出版领域的合作可以更深入。

一些中国出版人表示，参加此次活动使他们看到了中国图书在俄罗斯市场的潜力，他们将继续深入调研并在外向型图书出版上有所调整。

（资料来源：《中国新闻出版广电报》　作者：闫　松）

【467 种中国新书亮相第 23 届东京国际书展】　2016 年 9 月 23 日，第 23 届东京国际书展在东京国际展览中心开幕。来自全球 30 多个国家和地区的国际展商代表为书展开幕剪彩。由中国言实出版社、党建读物出版社等 14 家中国出版单位组成的中国展团参展。

本届东京国际书展吸引了 800 多家出版机构，创下了历史最高纪录。为充分利用这一重要文化交流平台，中国展团将展示近两年出版的 467 种 812 册新书，图书内容涉及文学、科普、教育、建筑、传统文化、美术等领域。《习近平谈治国理政》等主题图书将重点展示。这些图书主要涵盖“四个全面”

“中国特色社会主义和中国梦”“经济发展新常态和发展成就”“社会主义核心价值观”“中日友好邦交”等主题，共计 100 册。

书展期间，中国建筑工业出版社、黑龙江美术出版社、黑龙江教育出版社与科学出版社东京株式会社将就《中国古建筑丛书：北京古建筑》《唐代边疆民族与对外交流》《中国手工竹纸制作技艺》等书签订日文版权输出合作协议。中国言实出版社计划与日本出版机构就《中国的海洋》、“了凡四训”系列图书、《东京旧事》等图书签订版权转让协议。

（资料来源：《中国新闻出版广电报》　作者：任晓宁）

【《婴儿画报》《幼儿画报》向美国输出版权】 2016 年 9 月 23 日下午，由中国期刊协会主办、中国少年儿童新闻出版总社承办的“我的报刊　我的童年——《婴儿画报》《幼儿画报》版权输出美国发布会”在第四届中国（武汉）期刊交易博览会现场湖北武汉国际博览会中心举行。《婴儿画报》和《幼儿画报》是国内最早的两份婴幼儿期刊，此次由美国 CM 媒体集团引进至美国，标志着我国少儿出版在国际舞台又迈出了重要一步。截至 2016 年 7 月 1 日，中国少年儿童新闻出版总社图书版权输出已达到 535 种，覆盖 53 个国家和地区。

《婴儿画报》《幼儿画报》围绕幼儿园孩子们日常生活中各个方面切实遇到的小发现，既讲好故事，又塑造形象，还巧妙地融入知识和引发思考。据悉，《幼儿画报》已经在国内数十个省市幼儿园里开展绘本公开课活动，让幼儿们在阅读和游戏中得到锻炼，全面成长。2017 年，《幼儿画报》还要进行改版，选取动人心弦的故事和匹配风格的插画进行组合，每月增加一本绘本刊。

（资料来源：中国知识产权资讯网　作者：刘　仁）

【华中国际版权高峰论坛聚焦现代版权产业发展】 2016 年 9 月 24 日，华中国际版权高峰论坛在武汉举行，海内外专家聚焦现代版权制度及版权产业的发展。

国家新闻出版广电总局版权管理司司长于慈珂说，改革开放以来，我国制定了符合中国国情和国际规则的版权法律、制度体系，确立了司法、行政并行的版权保护制度，在打击侵权方面也取得了较好成效。中国特色版权制度的建立和实施，在规范市场经济秩序、提高创新能力、扩大对外开放等方面发挥了积极的作用。他建议华中国家版权交易中心积极探索，走出一条符合实际、行之有效的版权交易路子，为全国的版权产业发展积累经验。

根据中国新闻出版研究院发布的数字，2014 年中国版权产业对国民经济的贡献率已达到 7.28%，其中核心版权的增加值占全部版权产业的比重达到了 59%，版权产业已成为推动国家经济发展的重要力量。与会者认为，近年来，业界的研究重心由版权保护向版权产业化转变，但我们的日常生活中，社会公众的知识产权保护意识仍较薄弱，从版权保护转向版权产业化，目的是把版权产业做大做强，让更多人加入到这个产业链中，通过产业化享受利益，从而使得整个社会公众的知识产权重视程度得到提高。

湖北省新闻出版广电局副局长胡伟参加论坛并致辞。来自俄罗斯、加纳、韩国及国内高校和知识产权研究机构的专家学者发表了主题演讲。

（资料来源：《中国新闻出版广电报》
作者：汤广花　左尚鸿）

【首个中国主题图书翻译出版中心在蒙古国成立】 2016 年 10 月 1 日，首个中国主题图书翻译出版中心在蒙古乌兰巴托举行的中国蒙古国文化合作启动仪式上正式成立。该中心由中国人民大学出版社和蒙古国立师范大学共同成立。中心将推动做好中国主题图书在蒙古国的出版发行、促进两国版权合作与版权贸易、设立和审定中蒙图书翻译资助项目等工作，旨在搭建中蒙两国新闻出版领域的政府间合作交流平台。

中国国家新闻出版广电总局与蒙古国教育文化科学体育部对中心的成立给予了高度肯定。蒙古国教育文化科学体育部部长扎·巴特索日专程接见了到访的中国人民大学出版社代表团。他表示，中心的成立是蒙中两国文化交流的重要成果，要把中心建成蒙中新闻出版交流的唯一官方平台和重要文化窗口，推动两国图书翻译出版工作取得更大进展。

中国人民大学出版社社长李永强与蒙古国立师范大学校长孟和吉日嘎拉代表两校签署了成立协议。

（资料来源：《中国新闻出版广电报》　作者：范燕莹）

【德化经验　全球共享】 2016 年 11 月 14 日至 18 日，根据世界知识产权组织（WIPO）与国家版权局合作计划，国家版权局在瑞士日内瓦的世界知识产权组织总部举办了中国德化陶瓷版权保护优秀成果展，发布了《版权保护促进中国德化陶瓷产业发展的研究》（英文版），向全球推广中国德化在陶瓷产业版权保护方面成功做法，让全世界共享“德化经验”。WIPO副总干事西尔维·福尔班女士、中国驻日内瓦代表团余蜀昆公参，以及国家版权局版权管理司司长于慈珂出席开幕式并讲话。100个WIPO成员国及60余个国际组织代表参加了上述活动。

WIPO副总干事西尔维·福尔班女士充分肯定了中国德化通过版权保护促进陶瓷产业发展的经验，并表示，版权保护对版权产业发展，乃至一国的经济发展意义重大，“德化经验”对于发展中国家探索版权保护和经济发展的密切关系有重要指导和借鉴作用，此次中国在世界知识产权组织总部举办德化陶瓷版权保护优秀成果展，将进一步推动“德化经验”在全球化范围内得到广泛应用。

于慈珂表示，德化积极引入版权保护机制，打破制约当地陶瓷产业发展的瓶颈，走出了一条有特色的版权保护促进经济腾飞之路。版权保护促进当地经济繁荣、人民富裕的“德化经验”，显示中国的版权工作已从被动的保护阶段转入版权创造、运用和保护并重的阶段，为版权产业发展树立了一个好的典型，这个典型不仅是中国的，也是世界的。我们将推动中国有更多的“德化经验”产生，也希望这一成功经验能够全球共享，特别是在全球新一轮科技革命与产业变革的重大机遇和挑战下，为全球版权保护促进经济发展提供有益的借鉴。

（资料来源：国家版权局网）

【中国出版亮相罗马尼亚】 2016年11月16日至20日，第23届罗马尼亚高迪亚姆斯国际图书与教育展在罗马尼亚国际展览中心举办。这是中国首次以主宾国身份亮相该书展。

此次主宾国活动是“中国—中东欧国家人文交流年”的一项重要活动，是继2016年8月罗马尼亚与其他中东欧国家整体担任北京国际图书博览会主宾国之后，中罗两国出版界再一次共同举办的大型国际出版交流盛会。

书展期间，中国以“阅读中国”为主题，以书为媒，以系列出版交流活动为平台，扩大中罗文化贸易，推动图书版权输出，提升中国图书在罗马尼亚图书市场的影响力和竞争力。来自国内50多家重点出版单位的100多名出版人组成中国代表团参展，展示精品图书约2 000种、3 000册。曹文轩、余华、西川、蓝蓝、徐则臣5名中国作家参加多场文学交流活动，与当地读者面对面交流。

本次中国主宾国活动期间，将策划举办一系列中罗出版文化交流活动，包括中国主宾国开幕式、《习近平谈治国理政》等系列著作推广会、中罗出版发展高峰论坛、中罗作家交流座谈会等30余场活动。

（资料来源：《中国新闻出版广电报》
作者：赵新乐　杜一娜）

【全球创作者论坛在京举办】 2016年11月28日，全球创作者论坛在北京举行。国家新闻出版广电总局局长、国家版权局局长聂辰席在致辞中强调，版权是国家的核心竞争力，中国政府保护版权的立场是坚定的，态度是坚决的。

聂辰席委托国家版权局版权管理司司长于慈珂向大会致辞。他说，全球数十个国家的创作者、政府官员、专家学者集聚北京，参加由国际作者作曲者协会联合会（CISAC）和中国知识产权法学研究会共同举办的全球创作者论坛，这是国际版权界的一大盛事。

聂辰席指出，CISAC有着九十年历史，在国际上有着广泛的影响力。2014年，CISAC将亚太区总部迁至中国，成为第一家将总部设在中国的著作权国际组织；2016年，中国著名导演、编剧贾樟柯当选联合会副主席。中国音乐著作权协会作为联合会会员，在其框架之下与全球60个著作权集体组织签订了相互代表协议。应该说，CISAC近年来的工作，有效地加强了中国创作者的权益保护，提升了中国著作权集体管理水平，促进了中外文化交流和版权合作。

聂辰席强调，版权是国家的核心竞争力。他说，创作是文化之本，文化让世界多彩，版权把创作与文化连接起来。版权保护制度源于“保护创作者”最直接的精神和利益诉求，越来越多的国家重视版权在提高民族创新能力、提高国家核心竞争力方面的积极作用。

聂辰席指出，中国的版权保护还面临着许多困难和挑战。中国的著作权集体管理起步较晚，与发达国家相比，我国几家著作权集体管理组织才刚起步。中国的版权制度正在解决发达国家甚至许多发展中国家已经解决了的传统环境下的问题，还将与世界各国共同应对新技术、新形势带来的诸多挑战。

聂辰席强调，中国政府保护版权的立场是坚定的，态度是坚决的，成效也将逐渐呈现。随着中国经济发展进入新常态，以及创新型国家和知识产权强国建设的逐步实施，基于作品的创作、传播和社会公众消费而形成的版权产业，必将迎来蓬勃发展的新时期。

（资料来源：《法制日报》　作者：张红兵）

【2016 年国际版权论坛聚焦“版权　创新　发展”】　2016 年 12 月 5 日至 6 日，被称为国际版权界盛会的 2016 年国际版权论坛在广州举行。本届论坛由世界知识产权组织（WIPO）与中国国家版权局共同主办，以“版权　创新　发展”为主题，旨在汇集海内外版权界杰出代表，共同探讨版权与创新在文化与经济发展中的作用以及如何促进和保护创新以推动版权产业发展，共同为推动国际版权多元化合作进行深入探讨和交流。中国国家版权局副局长阎晓宏，WIPO 副总干事王彬颖出席论坛开幕式并致辞。WIPO 副总干事西尔维·福尔班在主旨发言中转达了 WIPO 总干事高锐对于 2016 年国际版权论坛的良好祝愿。

在 5 日至 6 日的论坛上，英国知识产权局局长、总审计长肖恩·丹内利、中国国家版权局版权管理司司长于慈珂共同就“版权与创新：版权在文化与经济发展中的作用”议题做了专题演讲。国际音乐创作者理事会（CIAM）主席洛伦佐·费雷罗，中国新闻出版研究院副院长范军就“版权与发展：国家版权政策与战略的重要性”议题分别发表了各自的看法。马来西亚知识产权局版权处处长 Mohamed Fairuz bin Mohd Pilus、韩国著作权委员会首席高级研究员 Kyong-Soo Choe、腾讯集团法务总经理江波、上海冠勇信息科技有限公司 CEO 吴冠勇就“版权与文化繁荣：视听表演的重要性及其对文化和经济发展的贡献”进行了探讨。论坛还举办了以“促进和保护创新以推动发展：政策、战略和最佳实践”为主题的圆桌讨论。越南、肯尼亚等十余个 WIPO 成员国代表参与了讨论。

12 月 6 日，中外嘉宾还实地参观了广州国家版权交易基地和中国艺术品保护交易会。来自世界知识产权组织及英国、俄罗斯、韩国、肯尼亚等 20 多个国家和地区的版权专家、政府主管、企业精英，中国有关政府部门、各省市版权协会等行业组织代表和学界代表共两百余名中外嘉宾出席论坛。

（资料来源：国家版权局网　作者：赖名芳）

【逾 6 800 万美元国际动漫版权合作协议在苏州签署】　2016 年 12 月 14 日，为期四天的 2016 中国苏州动漫国际合作峰会正式落下帷幕。峰会期间，苏州欧瑞动漫有限公司与来自四大洲、8 个国家的 12 家企业正式签署了动漫版权合作协议，签约总金额逾 6 800 万美元，成为中国动漫企业走向国际市场、开展版权合作成果最大的一次贸易行动。

文化部外联局亚非处处长余建表示，本届峰会是国内唯一、国际少有的以动漫版权交易为主题的文化贸易交流活动，摸索出了中国文化由“走出去交流互动合作”向“发展文化贸易互动共赢”转变的新思路。“此类中外联合制片的文化合作模式不仅可以做大服务贸易，而且还能吸引国外合作方参与创意设计和市场开发，有助于推动中国文化更好地开拓海外市场。”

2016 中国苏州动漫国际合作峰会由中国苏州创博会组委会主办，吸引了来自美国、俄罗斯、白俄罗斯、英国、法国、日本、澳大利亚、意大利等 8 个国家的 20 多名影视动漫企业负责人与会。

（资料来源：新华网　作者：陆华东）

【中罗文字著作权集体管理组织展开合作】　2016 年 12 月 14 日，中国文字著作权协会（下称文著协）总干事张洪波与罗马尼亚著作权集体管理协会主席欧根·乌里卡鲁在鲁迅文学院签署版权合作协议。根据该协议，罗马尼亚著作权集体管理协会将代表文著协在罗马尼亚依法为会员收取中文文字作品影印复制权、表演权、公众传播权等版权使用费。

罗马尼亚著作权集体管理协会是罗马尼亚文字作品著作权集体管理组织，总部位于罗马尼亚首都布加勒斯特，管理文学、艺术和科技作品的复制、表演、演绎、向公众传播等权利，以保护创作者利益、促进文学和文化的繁荣发展。根据罗马尼亚相关法律规定，该协会还向设备和纸张制造商或进口商、有线电视运营商、公共图书馆等收取文字作品的私人复制、有线电视转播、图书馆公共借阅等该国法律规定的强制补偿金。文著协和该协会同为国际复制权组织联合会会员。

（资料来源：《中国知识产权报》　作者：刘　仁）

◆ 产业发展

【万达 35 亿美元并购美国传奇影业】　2016 年 1 月 12 日，万达集团并购美国传奇影业签约仪式在京举行。万达集团以不超过 35 亿美元的价格收购传奇影业，这是迄今中国企业在海外的最大一桩文化并购。

传奇影业是美国知名影视制作公司。传奇影业涉及电影、电视、数字媒体以及动漫等业务，曾出品《侏罗纪世界》《蝙蝠侠》《盗梦空间》《环太平洋》《超人：钢铁之躯》等商业大片，其在全球已获得超过120亿美元的票房。

万达集团目前已拥有全球最大的电影院线，2012年以26亿美元控股美国院线AMC娱乐控股公司，2015年收购澳大利亚第二大院线Hoyts集团。

万达集团董事长王健林表示，并购传奇影业使万达影视控股公司成为全球收入最大的电影企业，特别是在中美两个全球最重要的电影市场，万达拥有了更大的影响力。万达打造的电影制作、放映、发行产业链，提升了万达在全球电影行业中的竞争力和话语权。

（资料来源：《中国新闻出版广电报》　作者：刘　巍）

【国产电影全球发行平台启动】　2016年1月15日，“中国电影，普天同映”国产电影全球发行平台在京举行启动仪式，该平台由国家新闻出版广电总局电影局策划指导，华人文化控股集团、华狮电影发行公司共同搭建。

2015年，国产电影海外票房达到27.7亿元，同比增长48.13%，优秀作品不断涌现，海外影响持续扩大。与此同时，中国电影在海外有着雄厚观众基础，成为外国民众了解中国的一个重要窗口。

据了解，2016年春节前后，“中国电影，普天同映”国产电影全球发行平台将全球同步发行星皓影业出品的《西游记之孙悟空三打白骨精》，国内先期上映的《唐人街探案》也将与该片同时在北美、欧洲、亚洲、澳大利亚的50余座主要城市上映。今后，平台的发行规模还将逐步扩展至全球百余座城市。

（资料来源：《中国新闻出版广电报》　作者：杨　骁）

【唐德影视购买好声音版权】　2016年1月20日，公司公告与Talpa签署合作意向书，双方将共同成立合资公司，同时Talpa向唐德影视予《……好声音》（“The voice of…”）节目在整个中国范围，包括香港、澳门和台湾地区使用授权语言（指唐德影视地区使用的所有中国语言和方言）的所有相关独家权利、许可、特权和授权，并向唐德提供相关服务。

（资料来源：中泰证券）

【爱奇艺与20世纪福克斯合作拓展网络版权】　2016年1月28日，视频服务平台爱奇艺与20世纪福克斯电影公司联合宣布进一步拓展合作，在既有海量片库合作的基础上，爱奇艺获得20世纪福克斯未来几年在华所有新片独家网络版权。

新合作达成后，爱奇艺和20世纪福克斯将在既有数百部最大在华片库合作基础上，进一步进行经典影片扩容。对于无缘中国大银幕且能够在华引入的影片，爱奇艺将按照相关管理规定，以最快速度上线播出。

（资料来源：《中国新闻出版广电报》　作者：任晓宁）

【美团猫眼电影首推电影票在线改签　覆盖近2 000家影院】　2016年1月，美团猫眼电影在新版APP中发布了电影票在线改签功能，可为消费者提供电影票在线改签服务，该项产品功能及服务均属业内首创。

这是美团猫眼电影和大众点评电影业务在2015年12月中旬完成整合后的第一次重大产品及服务更新。今后，消费者陆续通过猫眼电影APP、美团网电影频道、大众点评电影频道均可享受电影票在线改签服务。

目前，猫眼的电影票在线改签功能及服务已经获得了全国近2 000家影院的支持，并且支持影院数量还在持续上升中，其中包括万达、大地、CGV等全国性院线。这表明，猫眼与点评在完成电影业务整合实现全国700多家城市5 000多家影院覆盖之后，猫眼与影院合作的深度也在进一步加强。

（资料来源：凤凰娱乐）

【县城影院呈现超速度增长势头】　2016年2月17日，艺恩发布中国县城影院发展统计数据。数据显示，在县城影院数量方面，2015年中国县城影院已达2 635家，近三年县城影院数量复合增长率达45%，是全国影院数量复合增长率的1.8倍；在全国影院数量的占比也逐年走高，由2012年的23%提升到2015年的36%。

调查表明，目前中国县城影院正以“超速度”的增长势头彰显着该区域的市场机遇和活力。以北京红鲤鱼院线为代表的全国性电影院线，凭其独有的跨界服务模式形成了县城影院国内规模最大的格局，并通过在县城市场多年的耕耘和积累，自然形成了“千县千院”的传媒平台——红鲤鱼传媒，成为中国县城市场最大的影院整合营销平台。

（资料来源：《中国新闻出版广电报》　作者：李　彦）

【熙颐影业收购国际版权销售公司】 2016年2月，上海熙颐文化传媒有限公司（下称熙颐影业）收购国际版权销售公司Insiders（局内人公司），成为其主要股东，借此布局影视产品的全球发售渠道。收购完成后，除熙颐影业自身制作的电影外，其他优质中国电影都可通过该渠道发行到北美、欧洲、亚洲等40多个国家和地区。

熙颐影业总部位于上海，在美国洛杉矶设有分部，业务涵盖中外合拍电影的制作、发行，电影国际版权销售等，拥有26部优质英文电影在中国的独家版权。对于熙颐影业收购Insiders的原因，熙颐影业CEO韩薇表示，熙颐影业的战略是“立足本土，放眼全球”，基于此，熙颐影业在几年前就从电影的版权开发、制作到发行等着手进行全球布局。Insiders在电影国际版权销售和发行方面具有很大优势，其股东之一泛欧上市公司Wild Bunch曾成功销售过《一代宗师》的电影版权，深谙中文影片的国际发行之道，并且Insiders的其他股东都是欧洲和北美的影视巨头，它们将成为熙颐影业搭建国际影视平台的战略同盟。

（资料来源：中国知识产权报资讯网　作者：侯　伟）

【南北两大影视版权交易平台达成战略合作】 2016年2月25日，梧桐山影视版权交易有限公司与共和影业有限公司在深圳签署协议，双方结为战略合作伙伴，未来将共同推进影视版权产业化发展，共同组建电影和电视剧版权交易平台，实现优势互补和版权、渠道、资源、资本、数据的整合与共享。

合作协议签署后，华表电影交易中心将在其交易平台上与“剧宝”合作开设电视剧交易专区，梧桐山版权将在“剧宝”电视剧交易平台上与华表电影交易中心合作，搭建电影交易专区；“剧宝”的电视剧海外版权交易将全权委托共和影业代理；梧桐山版权电视剧将在共和影业海外开设的电视平台运营，双方以收益分成模式合作，“剧宝”电视剧海外版权的多语转换将由共和影业承担。

（资料来源：《南方日报》（广州）　作者：胡　明）

【天涯社区携手中大中文系打造全国大学生影视剧本创作平台】 2016年2月，天涯社区网络科技股份有限公司发布公告称，其下属全资子公司海南天涯创业投资有限公司投资参股中大文化创意发展有限公司，携手中山大学中文系剧本创作与研究中心，深度进行学术、产业与资本的合作，以“优质内容创作”为核心，整合优势文化资源，打造全国大学生影视剧本创作平台。

（资料来源：《齐鲁晚报》）

【腾讯“芒种计划”打造媒体生态圈】 2016年3月1日，腾讯公司在北京召开发布会，宣布启动“芒种计划”，打造媒体共赢生态圈。按照这个计划，媒体和自媒体发布、运营的内容，可以通过腾讯企鹅媒体平台，在天天快报、腾讯新闻客户端、微信新闻插件和手机QQ新闻插件等平台渠道进行一键分发，实现优质内容的更多分享。

除了开放平台资源、拓展流量及用户连接外，在商业变现方面，腾讯也表示，将以开放的姿态，给予媒体、自媒体丰厚的激励和补贴政策，共同营造更优质的内容生产新生态，实现共生共荣。

（资料来源：《中国新闻出版广电报》　作者：任晓宁）

【华人文化入股好莱坞】 2016年3月7日，华人文化控股集团宣布入股好莱坞影视制作公司“想象娱乐”。“想象娱乐”由两位屡获奥斯卡金像奖、金球奖、艾美奖的资深影视制作人朗·霍华德和布莱恩·葛瑞泽创立。

华人文化控股集团董事长黎瑞刚表示，通过入股“想象娱乐”，华人文化将携手好莱坞顶尖的制作班底，深入全球影视工业的核心腹地，提升中国在世界影视业界的发言权；也为快速变局中的中国影视业带来世界领先的内容创造力量，共同打造更多优秀的作品，推动中国文化向全球传播。

（资料来源：《中国新闻出版广电报》　作者：杨　骁）

【光影音乐网站正式上线】 2016年3月7日，国内首个以音乐交易和音乐社区两大板块为核心的音乐社交商务平台——光影音乐网站测试版正式上线，成为影视行业内正版授权音乐的又一个线上交易系统。

光影音乐网站拥有一套自主研发的国内首款影视配乐智能检索系统，能够通过识别用户输入的时间节点、动态响度和情绪种类来自动搜索到符合用户需求的配乐素材，用户只需按照操作提示，根据影片的时间点、情绪点和响度来筛选音乐，并且通过在线付款即可得到该素材的正版授权。

国家动漫园的相关负责人表示，音乐创作人可以利用这个平台将作品录入到光影音乐网站的版权库内进行编目分类交易，以供有偿授权给需要的影视和动画制作机构。同时，光影音乐网站还在社区内搭建了一套可以让音乐人协同创作的平台——众乐坊，制作人可以将其作品介绍或展现给其他人。

（资料来源：《中国新闻出版广电报》 作者：刘梦琦 杨 芮）

【中国取代美国成为最大文化产品出口国】 2016 年 3 月 10 日，联合国教科文组织统计研究所就全球文化产品和服务贸易发布最新统计报告。报告显示，在 2004 年至 2013 年期间，尽管全球经历了经济衰退以及电影、音乐等产品在消费者中大规模向基于网络平台服务的转移，文化产品贸易在此期间仍然增长了一倍，显示了文化产业的强劲恢复力。与此同时，中国取代美国成为文化产品的最大出口国。2013 年，中国文化产品出口总额为 601 亿美元，而美国为 279 亿美元。

该报告指出，艺术品和手工制品在全球贸易额最大的 10 类文化产品中排名有所上升。这主要是受到黄金饰品的影响。在经济不稳定时期，黄金饰品通常成为安全的保值产品。2013 年，全球黄金饰品贸易额超过 1 000 亿美元。中国、美国作为黄金饰品的最大出口国，出口额分别为 320 亿美元和 107 亿美元。紧随其后的国家包括印度、马来西亚、泰国和土耳其等。另外，雕像、塑像和绘画等产品在艺术和手工制品类中的份额有所上升，2013 年的贸易额为 190 亿美元。中国、美国和英国为最大出口国，其次为印度、越南和印度尼西亚等国。

报告还指出，音乐、电影和报纸等产品正在逐渐成为文化服务的一部分，但受到数字化制作程序的巨大冲击，这些产品的销售通常以网络订阅的形式为主。音乐和电影的录制品贸易在 10 年中分别下降 27%和 88%。尽管包括报纸在内的印刷制品贸易也出现下降，但书籍作为重要的文化产品，在一些地区同期增长了 20%。

（资料来源：《经济日报》 作者：张 伟）

【阿里巴巴 238 亿元收购优酷土豆所有股份】 2016 年 3 月 14 日，优酷土豆宣布，在特别股东大会上，公司股东已投票批准了公司 2015 年 11 月达成的私有化协议。预计交易于 2016 年 4 月初完成，交易完成后，优酷土豆从纽交所退市。

阿里巴巴对优酷土豆的全资收购于 2016 年 4 月初完成。在 2015 年 11 月 6 日，优酷土豆宣布公司与阿里巴巴达成收购协议，阿里巴巴将以每股美国存托股 27.60 美元的现金收购优酷土豆。排除阿里巴巴已持有的优酷土豆股份，该交易为优酷土豆剩余股份估值 47.7 亿美元。由于优酷土豆账上仍有 11 亿美元现金，因此相当于阿里巴巴以 36.7 亿美元收购优酷土豆剩余股份，约合人民币 238 亿元。

（资料来源：《华西都市报》 作者：杨尚智）

【楚楚街与乐视斥资亿元共建音乐产业新生态】 2016 年 3 月 18 日，知名电商平台楚楚街宣布与乐视生态营销、乐视音乐达成深度合作，双方在 2016 年在音乐、电影、综艺三个维度上达成亿元级的合作，实现版权内容的多元开发和同电商平台的跨界融合。

在音乐的合作上，双方将实现点线面的战略合作。在面上，乐视音乐的黄金营销资源将向楚楚街全面开放，拓宽合作的广度；在线上，乐视音乐打造的韩流垂直频道内容将精准锁定楚楚街目标人群，实现更精准的触达；在点上，双方会通过韩国梦想演唱会等重点项目，借助爆点事件，形成楚楚街与用户的深度互动。

在电影维度上，双方将坚持与品牌共创版权（IP）的内容营销理念，与楚楚街共同投资，从上游参与电影制作，全力打造热门 IP。在综艺节目维度上，双方的玩法则更加深入，不断让楚楚街深度参与到乐视的自有综艺中，将综艺娱乐营销进行到底。

乐视网营销副总裁谭靖颖表示，未来乐视生态营销将和楚楚街一起，继续以内容为入口，不断贴近年轻用户，在音乐、电影、综艺三个维度上实现全面的内容战略合作，协同这三大领域的内容资源、明星资源，促成“购物＋娱乐”的跨界融合，深度挖掘内容的版权价值。

（资料来源：中国知识产权资讯网 作者：姜 旭）

【中南传媒搭建 IP 全版权运营平台】 2016 年 3 月 23 日，中南传媒旗下博集天卷与最世文化在北京举行战略合作签约仪式，这标志着中南传媒以 IP 为核心的全版权运营平台正式启动。

在发布会上，郭敬明宣布了最世文化与博集天卷的首部合作计划：由郭敬明执导并首度参演电影《爵迹》，其同名小说《爵迹》新书四部曲在经过大量修改和调整后，也由博集天卷全新呈现。双方还计划排他合作出品发行最世文化旗下的《最小说》等期刊。本次战略合作关系并非仅限于纸质书出版，对于未来的深度合作，郭敬明坦言：“存在一切的可能性。”

除进一步打造纸质出版品牌外，双方还有意在推进 IP 运营、实现文化传媒领域的共同发展方面进行更深层次的合作。

（资料来源：中国证券网　作者：刘　涛）

【艺恩咨询发布《2015—2016 中国电影产业报告》】 2016 年 3 月 24 日，艺恩咨询发布《2015—2016 中国电影产业报告》。《报告》显示，2015 年中国电影（直接）产业规模首次达到 1 000 亿元人民币，电影关联产业规模超过 3 000 亿元人民币。

艺恩咨询的电影（直接）产业规模的测算范围包括影院和电影项目投资，电影消费测算范围包含电影票房及版权销售、衍生品、海外票房及版权收入，前者在 2015 年占比 34%，后者占比达到 63%。电影关联产业规模的测算范围包含产业投资和产业消费两方面，其中产业投资总额超过 1 500 亿元、产业消费达到 1 500 亿元。

《报告》分析认为，随着国产影片的数量和质量的逐步提升，未来中国电影市场的增长点将逐步由影院、屏幕的投资转向电影本身票房和相关的广告和版权，预计 2016 年电影消费的贡献度同比将增长 4 百分点，提升至 67%，其主要的驱动因素是居民的消费升级以及观影习惯的逐步养成。而中国电影出口比重仅占 3%，依然有较大的提升空间。

（资料来源：《中国新闻出版广电报》　作者：李　彦）

【750 部电视剧亮相 2016 春季北京电视节目交易会】 2016 年 3 月 28 日至 31 日，2016 春季北京电视节目交易会在北京举行。交易会上，750 部电视剧作品、18 部网络剧，以及多部优秀的动画片、纪录片、电视栏目作品集中亮相，来自全国各地和海内外的电视节目制作和播出机构、产业链机构各方代表围绕电视剧、动画片、纪录片、电视栏目等多元的电视节目形态进行研讨。而北京版权保护协会网络出版工作委员会的 13 家网络文学的会员单位参展，成为此届交易会的一大亮点。

此届交易会举行了节目交易、行业表彰、业务论坛、新剧发布会、专项活动等多项精彩主体活动。在电视剧展览交易方面，有纪念红军长征胜利 80 周年的《红色护卫》，抗战剧《巨浪》《黎明决战》《胜算》《铁血军歌》，还有宣扬当代和谐美好生活的《岁月如金》《领养》《酸甜苦辣小夫妻》《拥抱星星的月亮》等，还有动画片《戚继光》《西游记的故事》《最可爱的人》和纪录片《天下第一雄关》《纽带》等优秀文化作品。

（资料来源：中国知识产权资讯网　作者：窦新颖）

【IFPI 2016 全球音乐报告发布】 2016 年 4 月 12 日，国际唱片业协会（IFPI）发布了 IFPI 2016 全球音乐报告。报告显示，2015 年全球音乐产业收入增长 3.2%，数字音乐收入首次超过实体音乐收入。其中，数字音乐收入占行业总收入的 45%，超过实体音乐 39%的占比。报告还显示，流媒体服务收入增长 45.2%，推动全球收入上涨 3.2%；音乐消费全球激增，但“价值差距”依然是艺人和唱片公司收入保持可持续增长的主要障碍。

报告显示全球音乐数字收入增长 10.2%，至 67 亿美元，其中流媒体收入上涨 45.2%，抵消了下载和实体收入的下滑。音乐产业全球总收入增长 3.2%，达 150 亿美元，实现了产业收入 20 年来的首次年度同比增长。在 19 个国家，数字音乐收入在录制音乐市场中的占比过半。

报告指出，在市场逐渐复苏的背后仍然存在着根本性的不足。音乐的消费量达到了历史最高水平，但是音乐消费量的暴增却没有为艺人和唱片公司带来相应的合理回报。其中的深层原因在于市场扭曲造成的“价值差距”，这种“价值差距”阻碍了艺人和唱片公司获得合理的回报。

（资料来源：中国版权产业网）

【2015 年中国游戏产业规模达到 1 407 亿元】 2016 年 4 月 18 日，2016 国际游戏商务大会暨互动娱乐展（IGBC）在北京举办。国际游戏商务大会高峰论坛是此次大会首场重要活动，内容涉及 2016 年中国游戏市场发展，著作权法律法规解读，以及以 VR 游戏、H5 游戏、游戏电竞为代表的产业新动态解读。会上，国家新闻出版广电总局数字出版司巡视员、副司长宋建新表示，2015 年中国游戏产业规模达到 1 407 亿元，5 年间实现翻两番。

宋建新介绍，游戏大国向游戏强国转变的一个重要标志是能否出精品力作，因此，做大做强游戏产业，需要坚持“内容为王”理念，不断向社会供给文化价值高又受市场欢迎的游戏力作，更好地满足广大人民群众精神文化需求。“十一五”“十二五”期间，国家新闻出版广电总局组织实施“中国民族网络游戏出版工程”，游戏企业积极响应，10 年间分 10 批推出了 214 种具有中华民族优秀文化特色、内容健康向上的网络游戏出版项目，引领游戏产业成功打造出游戏出版的“高原”。游戏产业发展如何从“高原”走向“高峰”，是下一步发展必须攻克的课题。目前，国家新闻出版广电总局正在着手组织实施“中国原创游戏精品出版工程”，相关调研工作已经提上工作日程。希望广大游戏企业积极参与，通过产业政策、扶持基金资金等各种优势资源，提升游戏企业创新力，做强我国游戏产业。

（资料来源：中国知识产权资讯网　作者：窦新颖）

【中超天价版权催生“网台联动”】　2016年4月19日，北京星空浩宇体育公司在京宣布，与甘肃卫视、腾讯体育合作，推出“网台联动”的中超观赛互动模式，进一步拓宽球迷的收看和参与渠道。

甘肃卫视已获得2014至2017赛季中超的地方卫视独播权，球迷通过该频道看中超，观赛成本较低。现如今，由于互联网的普及，球迷不只是信息的接收者，还是信息的参与者、制造者。“加之中超版权大幅增值的背景，我们三家合作方决定打造‘地方卫视＋互联网’的中超观赛模式，拉近球队和球迷间的距离，让球迷有更好的观赛体验。”星空浩宇负责人表示，甘肃卫视本赛季每轮中超直播场次已增至4到5场，转播条件和质量也有所提升，今后将在此基础上利用网络平台加强球迷跟比赛的互动。“比如在某场中超比赛期间，球迷可以边看电视直播，边上网加入聊天室、发送弹幕等。”

乐视体育此前以27亿元购得2016和2017赛季中超独家新媒体版权，开始试水“付费看中超”模式。而这次“网台联动”并不向球迷收费，对此，星空浩宇负责人表示，“跟其他媒体相比，我们拿到的资源成本不高，因而会在球迷服务方面投入更多，不向球迷收费”。

（资料来源：《北京日报》　作者：黄志阳）

【2015年专利、商标、版权质押融资达931.72亿元】　2016年4月19日，国家知识产权局局长申长雨在国务院信息化工作办公室新闻发布会上介绍，2015年我国共受理专利申请279.9万件，其中发明专利申请量突破100万件，达到110.2万件，同比增长18.7%，连续5年位居世界首位。2015年，知识产权转化运用进一步加强，全年专利、商标、版权质押融资总额达931.72亿元。

申长雨介绍，2015年国家知识产权局授权的发明专利为35.9万件，位居全世界第二位。受理商标注册申请287.6万件，同比增长25.85%。截至2015年底，我国有效注册商标量突破1 000万件，达到1 034.4万件，连续14年保持世界第一。国家知识产权局、工信部还围绕重点领域，开展专利导航和知识产权分析评议工作，国资委则推动11家央企开展专利运营试点。

（资料来源：《经济参考报》　作者：侯云龙）

【北京国数与北青社合力打造数字产业服务平台】　2016年4月29日，北京国家数字出版基地与北京青年报社（集团），签署战略合作框架协议，并合作成立国数北青数字产业发展（北京）有限公司。双方表示，将聚集和整合各自在数字出版和文化传播领域的优质资源，推动文化产业实现跨界融合式发展。

在战略合作框架协议下，双方计划切实开展四项主要业务。一是建立数字产业媒体宣传平台，为北京国家数字出版基地及行业企业提供媒体宣传服务。二是建设数字出版行业大数据中心，为政府及业界企业提供大数据服务。三是建设数字产业创业创新服务平台，为文创企业和数字出版企业、社团、工作室提供创业创新服务。四是通过开发文化产业创新服务和数字产品，整合业内优质资源，打造细分产业链，促进数字产业的融合发展及转型升级。

北京市新闻出版广电局副局长王野霏表示，此次合作是传统媒体实现转型、数字出版平台化建设水到渠成的产物，为北京国数带来新的发展机遇，也为北青社提供了新的平台。

（资料来源：中国知识产权资讯网　作者：刘　仁）

【第十二届中国国际动漫节交易额逾151亿元】　2016年5月2日，第十二届中国国际动漫节在杭州落幕。此届动漫节共有2 531家中外企业机构、5 300余名展商和专业人士参展参会，实际成交及达成签约交易、意向合作项目948项，涉及金额129.37亿元，动漫节综合消费涉及金额22.26亿元，总计151.63亿元。

此届动漫节以“更国际·更动漫”为主题，设立了1个主会场和12个分会场，围绕会展、论坛、商务、赛事、活动五大板块组织实施了59项活动，共吸引了80个国家和地区参与，其中南非的参展，让动漫节首次实现五大洲全覆盖。截至5月2日下午的初步统计，共有138.15万人次参加了动漫节各项活动，其中主会场35.87万人次。参与国家地区数及办展规模、参与人数、交易金额、节展效益再创新高。

（资料来源：中国知识产权资讯网　作者：窦新颖）

【阿里影业投资大地影院】　2016年5月9日，阿里巴巴影业集团公告称，阿里影业通过旗下子公司认购大地影院 10 亿元人民币可转债。根据认购协议，在约定期限内，阿里影业可将债券本金转为对大地影院的股权投资。同时阿里影业与大地影院还签订了业务合作协议，双方未来将进行电影的营销推广合作，以及共同开发电影相关市场及相关电子商务业务。

大地影院目前是中国最大的连锁影院投资管理公司之一，在全国拥有 313 家影院，共 1 662 个影厅。2015 年，大地影院观影人次达 7 158 万，含税票房收入 22 亿元，同比增长 47%，在全国影院投资管理公司中排名居第二。

（资料来源：《信息时报》　作者：潘敬文）

【乐视票务平台多元运营挖掘体育赛事版权价值】　2016 年 5 月 11 日，乐视体育与永乐文化集团在北京联合宣布，双方将合资创建独立运营的互联网体育票务销售公司乐加乐体育，成立后的新公司将依托上述两家投资公司的优势资源，为俱乐部、联赛、赛事主办方提供包括多重生态服务，深度挖掘赛事商业价值。例如为提供赛事直播服务、制作内容节目、开发智能产品，与乐视体育商城等共同开发版权衍生产品等。此种模式在国内并不多见，有望给体育赛事的多元运营提供新的思路。

（资料来源：中国知识产权资讯网　作者：姜　旭）

【中国资本拿下英国足球版权巨头】　2016 年 5 月 24 日，上海浸鑫投资基金宣布已经完成对国际顶尖体育媒体服务公司 MP&Silva 65%股份的收购。

上海浸鑫投资基金是由暴风科技全资子公司暴风投资与光大证券全资子公司光大资本联合发起成立的基金。

本次收购标的公司 MPS 拥有、管理并行销顶级国际体育赛事版权，其业务覆盖全球 200 多个国家和地区，拥有 90 多个全球赛事版权，每年超过 1 万小时的播放时长，有超过 30 个赛事权利的机构合作伙伴、200 多个全球电视客户以及 40 多种工作语言的国际化团队，截至 2015 年 6 月份的总营业额超过 6 亿美元。

（资料来源：《证券日报》　作者：曹卫新）

【中国电影衍生品产业联盟成立】　2016 年 5 月 26 日，中国电影衍生品产业联盟成立发布会在北京举行。中国版权保护中心与唐山高新技术开发区签订了战略合作协议，将一起打造“全国电影衍生品产业平台”，加速中国电影衍生品开发。

2015 年中国电影获得 440.69 亿元总票房，但拥有千亿级市场需求的电影衍生品产业却处于初级阶段，电影收入的 90%～95%都来自票房和植入式广告，很多国产电影在衍生品的开发上一片空白。与此相比，美国电影衍生品收益却占电影产业收益的 80%，是电影票房收益的 4 倍。

中国电影衍生品产业联盟相关负责人介绍，中国电影衍生品产业联盟的 125 家会员单位涵盖了电影衍生品产业中版权交易、投融资、创意设计、制造生产、市场营销的国内外相关企业，还完成了与美国电影衍生品生产商 ICC 公司等国际机构的签约，中国电影衍生品未来有望在国际进行推广。

（资料来源：《京华时报》　作者：严　絮）

【腾讯、微影 8 500 万美元投资韩国 YG 娱乐】　2016 年 5 月 27 日，腾讯宣布，将联合微影时代向韩国娱乐业巨头 YG 公司注资 8 500 万美元，其中腾讯投资 3 000 万美元，微影时代投资 5 500 万美元，分别获得 4.5%与 8.2%的控股权，成为 YG 公司的第三、四大股东。

YG 成立于 1996 年，是韩国最大的嘻哈音乐公司，旗下艺人有 BIGBANG、2NE1、Se7en、PSY 等，2015 年的销售额仅次于 SM 娱乐达到 1 931 亿元韩币（约合 10.23 亿元人民币），净利润约 239 亿元韩币（约合 1.26 亿元人民币），同比增长 31.2%。

腾讯计划与 YG 娱乐联手打造“中韩娱乐航母计划”，内容包括 YG 公司艺人来华演出以及相关经纪事务等。腾讯官方表示，此次注资后，双方将在音乐领域之外，开拓更多的娱乐领域。

（资料来源：财新网）

【腾讯泛娱乐开发深挖儿童出版内容版权价值】　2016 年 5 月 30 日，腾讯在北京举行“腾讯儿童内容平台开放合作大会”，宣布成立集合线上儿童内容作者以及线下青少年儿童出版机构等优质 IP 创作者资源的“腾讯儿童内容开放平台”，旨在与业内合作伙伴一起推动国内儿童数字内容知识产权开发，共同开拓移动互联网时代青少年儿童数字内容市场的未来。发布会上，腾讯儿童内容开放平台正式同著名儿童文学家曹文轩、迪士尼集团、人民文学出版社、天天出版社等版权方达成内容合作。

（资料来源：中国知识产权资讯网　作者：姜　旭）

【豆瓣阅读开卖原创故事作品影视改编权】　2016 年 5 月 31 日，豆瓣网旗下的豆瓣阅读正式上线了一个新页面——影视改编。这意味着豆瓣作为一个在线原创作品的聚集地，要开始销售和运营自己的原创IP了。

据豆瓣网方面介绍，编剧可以从“待改编的故事作品”中挑选故事，撰写改编剧本大纲。豆瓣阅读会挑选其中优秀的剧本大纲进行集中的展示，并有可能资助编剧把故事变成完整剧本。制片方可以从“待改编的故事作品”中挑选故事，查看豆瓣阅读推荐的改编剧本大纲，与豆瓣阅读接洽版权购买事宜。

（资料来源：《每日经济新闻》 作者：丁舟洋）

【暴风体育获得中超新媒体版权】 在2016年6月7日举办的第一届世界体育产业生态峰会暨暴风体育战略发布会上，暴风集团宣布获得了2016—2017赛季中超联赛新媒体转播权，并成为2016—2017赛季CBA联赛官方合作伙伴、中国男篮国家队官方赞助商，中国女篮官方VR视频合作伙伴。

乐视体育是2016—2017赛季中超联赛新媒体的独家合作伙伴，是唯一拥有全部240场比赛的新媒体平台。暴风体育获得的是每轮一场比赛（央视直播场次）的权益，具体平台为PC端和移动端。

（资料来源：中国新闻网）

【我国出版版权输出总量8年增3倍】 2016年6月7日至8日，“中国图书对外推广计划”工作会议在成都召开。

“推广计划”工作小组成员单位版权输出总量已从2007年的1 132项，增长到2015年的4 375项，增长了近3倍，在国际出版、营销、发行等方面与国际同业的合作不断深化，中国出版业加快“走出去”，进军世界舞台。

为讲好中国故事，传播好中国声音，国家新闻出版广电总局副局长吴尚之透露，总局正在启动实施“外国人写作中国计划”，利用“特贡奖”积累的海外人才资源，请海外知名的作者、译者、出版人，每年创作出版关于中国的主题图书，通过他们把真实而丰富的中国传播到世界各地。与此同时，很多外国友人也主动积极服务中国出版“走出去”，如第九届青年成就奖获奖人艾哈迈德·赛义德（白鑫）获奖之后，在2015年一年之内就为中国出版企业向阿语地区输出版权200多种。

（资料来源：《人民日报》（海外版） 作者：钟 萱）

【腾讯86亿美元收购Supercell，开拓网游大时代】 2016年6月21日，腾讯宣布以86亿美元从日本软银（SoftBank）购入手机游戏《部落冲突》《皇室战争》的开发公司，芬兰游戏公司Supercell。

腾讯方面发布公告称，将斥资86亿美元收购Supercell 84.3%的股权，总对价分三期支付。公告中声明，Supercell的现有管理层将维持独立营运，Supercell将继续以芬兰为总部。

随后，Supercell CEO伊卡·帕纳宁也撰文解释了这笔收购的原因，称在收购完成后Supercell仍将独立运营，总部仍继续留在赫尔辛基。与腾讯的合作，可以让更多的玩家接触到Supercell的游戏。

在中国，腾讯拥有微信、QQ两个覆盖面最广的社交软件，但公司的营业收入大部分来自游戏。收购Supercell公司绝大部分的股份之后，中国的腾讯公司在全球游戏市场中所占的份额达到了13%。

（资料来源：观察者网）

【北京打通动漫游戏产业链】 2016年6月23日，在北京举行的《视听表演北京条约》签署4周年纪念推广活动上，多个由中国创意产业联盟以及首都版权产业联盟面向会员单位广泛征集而来的优秀动漫和游戏项目一一亮相，并进行推介展示。

扶持国产动漫游戏原创，完善产业链条，近年来，北京市在财政政策扶持、动漫游戏版权保护等方面取得了一定成绩。2015年，我国动漫游戏产业总产值为1 400亿元，而北京市的动漫游戏产业产值就达455亿元。

然而，在北京市版权局副局长王野霏看来，国产动漫游戏产业还存在作品总体质量偏低、缺乏相对完整产业链等问题。针对这些问题，北京市在鼓励优秀动漫游戏作品原创、加大版权保护的同时，也在不断完善产业链条，深度挖掘动漫游戏版权价值。

（资料来源：《中国知识产权报》 作者：窦新颖）

【乐视成立CDLA产业联盟】 2016年6月27日，乐视在北京举行“声音的革命”发布会，宣布成立全程数字无损音频标准（CDLA）产业联盟，与产业共同推动数字无损音频接口的标准化进程。会上，乐视发布了CDLA标准的技术白皮书，宣布将与联盟成员携手开展知识产权与技术合作。著名钢琴家李云迪担任CDLA推广大使。

CDLA产业联盟包含4种主体：声音标准机构、硬件厂商、内容平台和音乐人。中国电子技术标准化研究院全国音视频标委会、哈曼国际、fiil耳机、喜马拉雅等机构与企业代表作为合作伙伴参与了联盟启动。

CDLA标准由乐视推出，是希望使智能手机平台的音频传输过程实现无损化。此外，乐视还发布了CDLA标准的技术白皮书，宣布与联盟成员共同推动数字无损音频接口的标准化进程，并将与CDLA产业联盟成员在知识产权与技术上展开合作。发布会上，乐视特别展示了一张CDLA耳机的设计图片，该图片来自其外观设计专利的申请文件。

（资料来源：中国知识产权资讯网　作者：赵世猛）

【掌阅科技与时尚集团开展版权合作】 2016年6月，时尚传媒集团对外宣布，将旗下所有原版原刊全品种杂志的电子版权授权给掌阅科技股份有限公司（下称掌阅科技）。届时，时尚传媒集团在发行纸质版杂志的同时，电子版将同步在掌阅书城首发。自2015年5月在掌阅iReader应用上线杂志频道以来，截止到2016年6月，掌阅科技已经与故事会、知音、爱格、读者等123个国内知名杂志品牌达成授权合作，免费下载电子杂志的品牌达34个，月均下载量超过1 000万。

时尚传媒集团此次将旗下所有杂志的电子版权授权给掌阅科技，不仅是传统媒体对互联网企业的创新性合作，也是寻求数字化转型的新尝试。时尚传媒集团希望借助掌阅科技的渠道、平台，以及分发等方面的优势，增加受众群和提高自身品牌影响力。

（资料来源：《中国知识产权报》　作者：姜　旭）

【我国数字出版产业规模突破4 400亿元】 2016年7月19日，2016中国数字出版年会在北京召开。据《2015—2016中国数字出版产业年度报告》显示，2015年我国数字出版产业整体收入规模为4 403.85亿元，比2014年增长30%。数字出版产业收入在新闻出版产业收入中的比重由2014年的17.1%升至20.5%。其中，互联网期刊收入15.85亿元，电子书49亿元，数字报纸9.6亿元，博客11.8亿元，在线音乐55亿元，网络动漫44.2亿元，移动出版1 055.9亿元，网络游戏888.8亿元，在线教育180亿元，互联网广告2 093.7亿元。

中国新闻出版研究院院长魏玉山指出，移动出版和网络游戏在数字出版总收入中所占比例分别为23.98%和20.18%，两者合计占比为44.16%，接近收入总规模的一半，二者仍然是数字出版收入的主力军。值得引起重视的是互联网期刊、电子书、数字报纸的总收入仅占数字出版总收入的1.69%，这说明传统出版单位在数字化转型升级、融合发展方面仍需加大力度。

（资料来源：人民网　作者：张　贺）

【一铭软件推动中国—东盟基础软件生态合作】 2016年7月22日，由广西软件行业协会、一铭软件股份有限公司主办的"2016中国—东盟基础软件生态战略发展研讨会"在广西南宁举办。国产操作系统厂商一铭软件与东盟各国驻南宁领事馆负责人、众多中国基础软件生态系统高层以及广西壮族自治区行业用户参与了本次会议，共同探讨了中国—东盟基础软件生态合作发展之路。

作为中国—东盟最重要的枢纽，广西正在积极推进中国—东盟信息港建设的各项工作，中国—东盟信息港的南宁核心基地已经启动，致力于打造连接中国与东盟之间的"信息丝绸之路"。在此背景下，此次研讨会的举办获得了高度关注，产业各方在会上纷纷为如何推动中国—东盟基础软件生态协作献计献策。

（资料来源：中华网）

【百度开放云助力国家新闻出版打造智能数字出版体系】 2016年7月25日，百度开放云中标国家新闻出版广电总局国家数字复合出版系统工程公有云服务项目。百度开放云不仅将为支撑国家数字复合工程的大型软件和系统提供性能强大的云计算产品，还将通过大数据处理技术为国家出版行业打造一个智能数字出版体系，助力出版行业的产业升级、技术改造和企业数字化转型。

在本次国家新闻出版广电总局国家数字复合工程中，百度开放云提供了完整的高性能、智能弹性伸缩的基础架构服务，包括云服务器（BCC）、对象存储（BOS）、云磁盘（CDS）、关系型数据库（RDS）等，将支撑整个工程中34个大型软件和系统的流畅运行和安全存储。此外，百度开放云的大数据处理技术，也将运用于其中，为国家出版行业打造一个智能的数字出版体系，帮助出版单位准确把握读者阅读行为和市场需求，制定有效的选题策划、营销发行策略，有效解决数字复合出版所面临的技术难关。

（资料来源：中国网）

【乐视20亿美金收购美国最大智能电视厂商】 美国时间2016年7月26日，乐视旗下的LeEco Global（乐视全球）在美国洛杉矶宣布，耗资20亿美元收购美国最大的电视厂商 Vizio。这笔收购被业内认为是目前全球电视产业史上最大的收购计划，同时也是中国互联网企业走向世界的又一次重大的举措。

本次 LeEco 计划收购对象为 Vizio 及其关联公司 Inscape。数据显示，截至 2016 年第二季度，Vizio 品牌触达北美 8 000 家渠道商的 15 万个货架，分发渠道渗透率高达 83%；累计售出超出 2 200 万台智能电视，每日生产 1 000 亿电视观看大数据，用户累计观看时间超过 50 亿小时。Vizio 拥有一支强大而高效的管理团队，过去五年间净利润稳步增长。Inscape 则是 Vizio 旗下公司，在智能电视大数据方面拥有领先优势。收购完成后，LeEco 将拥有 Vizio 100%股权以及 Insacape 49%股权。

乐视表示，Vizio 管理团队将保持不变，继续在位于加州尔湾的总部负责公司的日常管理运营。同时，为保证公司持续发展和增长，乐视已与其管理层确认了未来三年的业绩激励计划；另外，Vizio 在北美的客服体系保持不变，“我们计划以相同的投入继续进行业务运营，从而为消费者提供最大程度支持”；Vizio 的供应商伙伴保持不变，此前 Vizio 与各方签订的协议所牵涉的主旨和条款也将保持不变。

（资料来源：南方网　作者：叶　丹）

【今日头条战略投资东方 IC】 2016 年 8 月 1 日，今日头条宣布战略投资国内知名图片库东方 IC，这也是图片版权史上少有的交易。今日头条方面介绍，此举是为了进一步加大对原创内容的扶持和对版权内容的保护。

在具体产品层面，今日头条会在大数据、图像分析和个性化算法等方面帮助东方 IC 进行图片新闻的分发。东方 IC 联合创始人匡展宇介绍，东方 IC 图库中的图片数量目前已经过亿，服务国内外上千家媒体及广告客户，过去三年的收入呈明显上升趋势。然而，他也坦陈如今摄影行业主要存在的两大问题——价格低廉和盗版横行。

“今日头条的技术优势和平台优势，不但可以助力东方 IC 大幅提升目前的客户服务能力，更精准地满足市场对图片内容的需求，也可以让图片创作者、摄影师真正有机会获得更好的回报。”今日头条高级副总裁赵添说。

（资料来源：《北京日报》　作者：洪嘉琳　孙奇茹）

【“哈利·波特”系列电子书首次在中国发售】 2016 年 8 月 1 日，阅文集团宣布开始发售 J. K. 罗琳知名的“哈利·波特”系列的电子书版本。这标志着“哈利·波特”系列的电子书首次在中国发售。此外，丛书的中文版和英文版也一同上市。2016 年 7 月 30 日在伦敦首次公演的舞台剧《哈利·波特与被诅咒的孩子：第一和第二部分》的官方脚本，其英文原版电子书也可以购买。

Pottermore 是伦敦哈利·波特电子书和数字有声读物出版商，同时也是 J. K. 罗琳旗下的数字娱乐新闻和电子商务公司。掌阅科技是 Pottermore 选出的中国 5 家发售哈利·波特电子书的零售商之一。其余的 4 家公司是：当当、豆瓣、掌阅、小米。

（资料来源：中国知识产权资讯网　作者：姜　旭）

【乐视云发布多款云产品】 2016 年 8 月 18 日，知名视频云平台乐视云在北京举办年度“卍·乐视云产品发布会”，发布多款云产品，比如，云资源、云视频、云应用、云发行、云营销等，涵盖了媒体、教育、游戏、金融、智能硬件等多个行业。此外，乐视云宣布与全球知名网络解决方案供应商思科集团（Cisco）在数字版权管理（DRM）领域开展深度合作，接下来将推出免费“云版权”产品，为全球商业用户提供全媒体、全终端云版权服务，确保全球优质视频内容的安全流通。据悉，这是思科集团首次与中国公司在数字版权管理领域探索开展合作。

对于双方的此次合作，思科大中华区资深副总裁张力表示，“云版权”的出现，将带给视频版权领域一次新的技术化、生态化革命，能够共同为全球商业伙伴创造前所未有的商业价值。

另讯，发布会的另一看点是，乐视云发布了“云新闻”“云媒体”两款产品，借助手机等移动终端，实现原创视频新闻采编、播放、发稿于一体的新闻生成全流程服务，吸引了业界关注。发布会上，乐视云与财新网达成合作，双方将围绕新闻产业视频化、云化展开深入合作，意在促进传统新闻产业颠覆性的变革。

（资料来源：中国知识产权资讯网
作者：姜　旭　柳雁春）

【版权为桥——有声出版火起来】 2016 年 8 月 22 日，音频分享平台喜马拉雅 FM 与中信出版集团、中南出版集团、上海译文出版社、果麦文化、企鹅兰登等多家国内外知名出版集团在上海签约，就有声改编、IP 孵化、版权保护等方面达成深度战略合作。

喜马拉雅近年加强了其在有声书领域的布局。

除去此次签约，喜马拉雅 FM 已与数十家一线出版商签订独家战略合作协议，并在 2015 年与全球最大的中文数字阅读平台阅文集团达成独家合作，目前已拥有市场上 70%畅销书的有声版权。

喜马拉雅 FM 联合创作人兼联席 CEO 余建军表示，有声书市场的壮大将造福整个产业链，包括上游的作家、出版商，下游的有声改编解决方案提供方、有声书分发渠道等，而良好的版权环境可以促进行业健康发展。对此，上海译文出版社社长韩卫东也表示，传统出版社也一直在探索以纸质为载体的内容是否还有其他方式的呈现来满足读者对阅读的需求，“现在在版权保护方面大家达成了共识，也形成了可盈利的商业模式，我们也是乐见其成的”。

（资料来源：《中国新闻出版广电报》　作者：金　鑫）

【第 23 届北京国际图书博览会闭幕】　2016 年 8 月 28 日，为期 5 天的第 23 届北京国际图书博览会（以下简称图博会）闭幕。经初步统计，本届图博会共达成中外版权贸易协议 5 018 项，同比增长 6.3%。其中，达成各类版权输出与合作出版协议 3 075 项（含合作出版），同比增长 6.5%；达成引进协议 1 943 项，同比增长 5.9%；引进输出比为 1∶1.58。

本届图博会展览规模再创新高，各项核心指标持续稳定增长，世界第二大书展地位更为稳固。其中，书展总面积达到 78 600 平方米，增长 19%；参展的国家和地区达到 86 个，增长 4.8%；参展商达到 2 407 家，增长 4.3%；共有来自英、法、美、韩、日、印度等国的 1 379 家海外出版机构参展，增长 5.7%。中东欧 16 国联合担任本届图博会主宾国。5 天时间里，图博会展览展示了 30 多万种精品图书，举办了 1 000 多场文化交流活动，参展参观人数近 30 万人次。

2016 年图博会共达成各类版权输出与合作出版协议 3 075 项，创历史新高。主题类、少儿类、文学类、文化教育类、经济类、哲学类图书排在输出前列。浙江人民出版社的《中国道路与中国梦想》《中国梦与浙江发展》等主题图书，输出到德国、韩国、俄罗斯、印度、阿尔巴尼亚等国家；中国人民大学出版社的《一个人的聚会》及部分文学类图书输出到哈萨克斯坦、以色列、韩国等国家。广西师范大学出版社在图博会上正式宣布成功收购英国 ACC 出版集团，完成国际化出版发行全产业链布局。安徽时代出版集团与西班牙 Blue Bottle Biz 达成电子图书平台合作协议，实现了数字出版版权贸易。

（资料来源：《人民日报》　作者：张　贺）

【中国网络文学版权联盟成立】　在 2016 年 9 月 19 日召开的网络文学版权保护研讨会上，由 33 家单位共同发起的中国网络文学版权联盟宣布成立，并发布《自律公约》。

33 家联盟成员包括掌阅科技股份有限公司、阅文集团、咪咕数字传媒有限公司、阿里巴巴文学网、北京红袖添香科技发展有限公司、起点中文网等。

联盟成员在会上共同承诺：坚持网络文学正确导向，坚持社会主义核心价值观，大力弘扬主旋律，传播正能量；增强版权保护意识，坚持“先授权、后使用”的版权保护原则，切实尊重网络文学著作权人的合法权利；自觉抵制侵权盗版行为，坚决不用侵权盗版网络文学作品，不为任何侵权盗版网络文学作品提供接入、存储、搜索、链接等网络技术服务；积极配合政府部门开展网络反盗维权活动，努力营造良好的网络文学版权保护社会氛围等。

（资料来源：《中国新闻出版广电报》　作者：赖名芳）

【青岛出版集团成功并购日本渡边淳一文学馆】　2016 年 9 月 20 日，青岛出版集团收购日本渡边淳一文学馆交接仪式在日本东京举行。这是山东省国有文化企业的首例海外并购。

青岛出版集团董事长孟鸣飞在致辞中介绍，青岛出版集团多年来一直把中日文化交流作为重要的出版定位，引进出版过夏目漱石、芥川龙之介、川端康成、小林多喜二、东山魁夷、宫西达也、片山恭一、渡边淳一等多位日本著名作家的书籍，也将《中国针灸史图鉴》和诸多中国美食类图书输出到日本，增进了两国人民间的文化沟通和了解。

（资料来源：中国版权产业网）

【第九届中国国际漫画节落幕】　2016 年 10 月 5 日，第九届中国国际漫画节在广州落幕。据组委会统计，本届漫画节中的动漫游戏展入场观众达 22.5 万人次，比 2015 年增长 12.5%。2016 年首设的专业展共促成交易及潜在交易超过 68.93 亿元，粗略统计参展商营业额同比增长 30%。

本届漫画节上发布了 2016 年“原动力”中国原创动漫出版扶持计划扶持项目，共有 52 个扶持项目和 16 个重点扶持项目。其中，漫画图书类扶持项目 29 个，重点扶持项目 10 个；多媒体动漫类扶持项目 15 个，重点扶持项目 4 个；期刊连载漫画类扶持项目 4 个，重点扶持项目 2 个；民文译制漫画类扶持项目 4 个。此外，启动了动漫金龙奖中国二次元指数。

本届漫画节由国家新闻出版广电总局和广东省

人民政府主办，吸引了阅文集团、腾讯动漫、索尼互娱、漫友文化、天闻角川、网易游戏、盛大游戏、快看漫画等近百个海内外知名动漫品牌参与，展出的漫画图书及衍生品达1万多种，超过500名海内外知名动漫行业嘉宾、漫画家参加了系列活动。

作为国家重点支持的动漫节展，本届首设的专业展吸引了近300个国内外众多知名动漫游戏品牌、逾1 000名专业观众争相参与。在“产业项目推介与交易会”上，包括《我要回家》动漫形象授权在内的9个重大项目现场签约，签约总额达3.57亿元。在以“IP产业化的创新之路”为主题的产业高端论坛——动漫版权交易会暨第十届中国漫画家大会上，动漫业界人士分别从“内容创作、IP运营、产业研究、股权投资”四个方面对动漫IP进行了多维度剖析。

（资料来源：《中国新闻出版广电报》　作者：李　彦）

【第九届中国家纺画稿交易会在南通举行】 2016年10月18日至19日，第九届中国（川姜）家纺画稿交易会在江苏南通举行。共有119家单位参展，参加展示交易的画稿达到1.5万幅。交易会期间，举办了张謇杯·2016中国国际家用纺织产品设计大赛获奖作品颁奖典礼、画稿作品展示交易、2016中国家纺微商论坛等活动。

10月18日上午，张謇杯·2016中国国际家用纺织产品设计大赛获奖作品颁奖典礼上，公布了获奖作品、企业和设计师名单。其中，在15件获得中国家纺好设计奖的作品中，由罗莱家纺选送的大鱼海棠系列产品，通过获得授权，将电影《大鱼海棠》中的人物形象与背景画面等开发成家纺产品。

（资料来源：《中国新闻出版广电报》　作者：李明远）

【《2016中国音乐产业发展报告》发布】 2016年11月8日，《2016中国音乐产业发展报告》在北京发布。《报告》显示2015年中国音乐产业总产值首次突破3 000亿元大关，达到3 018亿元，同比增长5.85%，较2014年提高19.4%。

《报告》认为，“创新、跨界、融合”成为2015年中国音乐产业发展的新气象。

2015年，中国内地实体唱片产值规模为5.59亿元，同比下降9%，新华书店等传统线下渠道实体唱片销售约为4 361.3万张，同比下降23%。中国数字音乐市场规模达498.18亿元，其中PC端音乐市场规模为58.06亿元，同比增长13.4%；移动端音乐市场规模为41.5亿元，同比增加22.8%；电信音乐增值业务为398.62亿元，同比略有下降；网络音乐用户规模达5.01亿，同比增长4.8%。音乐图书出版总码洋为8.3亿元，同比增长10.6%。

中国音乐著作权协会的版权许可收益达到1.7亿元，同比增长24%。2015年度中国音像著作权集体管理协会的总收入达1.55亿元，同比实现11.51%的增长，网络直播的音乐版权问题也开始成为关注重点。

国家音乐产业基地主营业务收入75.91亿元，基地园区利润总额达6.6亿元，其中主营业务利润4.73亿元。

（资料来源：《中国新闻出版广电报》　作者：孙海悦）

【阿里巴巴海外购得独家版权】 2016年11月14日，阿里巴巴集团已和日本电视机构就视频业务签署相关协议。从11月底开始，阿里巴巴集团将获得日本电视台“东京广播公司”提供的部分电影短片的独家版权，并通过旗下土豆网、优酷网等网站播出。

据悉，此次阿里巴巴集团购得的短片内容包括东京广播公司主办的DigiCon 6电影短片大赛中的优秀获奖作品。DigiCon 6电影短片大赛自2000年首次举办至今，影响力逐步扩大，每年都会吸引包括中国大陆、中国台湾、韩国等地区两千多部电影短片参赛，多部获奖短片还曾被美国电影公司购入，并被拍摄成长篇影视作品。

（资料来源：《北京商报》　作者：卢　扬　邓杏子）

【首份产经媒体融合发展报告发布】 2016年11月19日，中国行业报协会发布首份《中国产经媒体融合发展实践报告》。《报告》显示，有36.67%的产经新媒体处于投入阶段，尚未营收；53.33%实现部分营收，但处在盈利初期；仅10%实现收支平衡。这表明在推进产经新媒体与传统媒体融合的过程中，仍然面临诸多问题。

《报告》显示，参加调查的产经媒体普遍意识到了融媒体建设的重要性，其中，46%的产经媒体覆盖“两微一端一站”（微博、微信、移动客户端、官方网站）。

《报告》还在给出的媒介融合趋势与建议中指出，传统纸媒要以人为本，进行技术创新，利用先进传播技术增加媒体的信息生产和服务能力；随着4G技术的大范围应用，可折叠设备、移动智能设备等新型信息传播技术的研发应用，传统媒体应尽早吸引和储备相关技术人才，加大对技术的投入和对技术人才的储备。

（资料来源：《中国新闻出版广电报》 作者：张雪娇）

【网络游戏反盗版和产业保护联盟在京成立】 2016年11月24日，“网络游戏反盗版和产业保护联盟”在北京宣告成立。在当天的网络游戏产业保护论坛暨联盟成立发布会上，来自国家版权局、广电总局、工信部、国家体育总局等行政机关和相关法院人员出席会议并发言，共同关注游戏知识产权保护及行业发展。

据悉，联盟由腾讯、掌趣、畅游、完美世界、百度、新浪、爱九游、聚力、西山居、欢聚时代、联众、搜狗、乐视、网易、烽火连城等15家游戏运营企业、独立游戏制作人和游戏平台企业发起成立。成立该联盟，旨在打击盗版游戏，维护正版游戏权益，促进行业健康发展。联盟成员在其章程中宣布，将建立网络游戏快速维权机制，定期组织联合维权行动，打击遏制盗版侵权行为，建立盗版预警排查机制及快速纠纷调解机制。

腾讯公司法务总监周高见代表联盟成员介绍了联盟下一步的工作计划。第一是建立联盟成员之间的绿色通道，简化投诉流程，形成快速便捷的侵权投诉处理机制；第二是共建诉调衔接机制，促进诉讼纠纷快速解决；第三是促进电子证据在司法实践中的采用和认可，通过广泛应用电子证据解决取证难、举证难的问题；第四是启动打击游戏外挂的专项维权行动，遏制影响游戏运营安全和公平的“毒瘤”；第五是定期召开研讨会议，探讨游戏新型侵权行为，推动解决维权疑难问题；第六是定期发布游戏侵权案件调研报告或行业年度知识产权保护白皮书。

（资料来源：中国知识产权资讯网 作者：姜 旭）

【人民网与各党报新媒体发起党报新媒体版权联盟】 2016年12月15日，2016党报网站高峰论坛在北京举行。论坛主题为“初心与创新——媒体融合时代的党报网站发展之道”。人民日报社副总编辑、人民网董事长王一彪与会并致辞。

王一彪说，未来互联网将向我们展示“连接一切”的能力。为了连接起来，先要联合起来。党报网站要靠内容、靠服务、靠技术、靠实力面向未来、赢得未来。

为加强党报网站间的横向交流与合作、共同推进媒体融合发展进程，人民网与多家党报网站在论坛上签署了党报新媒体版权联盟、地方政务发布平台、移动直播报道联盟、入驻人民日报社数据中心等战略合作协议。

（资料来源：人民网—传媒频道）

【大优酷与东方梦工厂达成顶级家庭娱乐内容版权合作协议】 2016年12月15日，阿里巴巴文化娱乐集团大优酷事业群和东方梦工厂宣布，双方达成为期3年的版权授权合作协议，将梦工场动画的大量顶级家庭娱乐内容在中国大陆地区独家授权给大优酷。梦工场动画的优质电影、电视内容将独家提供给优酷、土豆和天猫魔盒的用户。

此次授权的内容包在体量和内容覆盖方面都是史上最大的一宗，它将进一步丰富大优酷旗下优酷、土豆、天猫魔盒三大平台上的娱乐内容阵容。大优酷希望借此进一步扩展其内容库，强化其作为中国市场上家庭娱乐内容首选平台的领先地位。

首批片库计划于2017年1月上线，其中包括一系列广为观众喜爱的动画电影，如《功夫熊猫》《怪物史瑞克》《驯龙高手》系列。未来还将包括即将上映的“Boss Baby”“Captain Underpants”，以及《驯龙高手3》。另外包括动画电视“Blackstar”“Casper's”，即将上映的“Troll Hunters”也在其中。

（资料来源：中国新闻网）

【我国视频付费市场规模突破10亿元大关】 2016年爱奇艺发布《网络视频个人付费行业白皮书》，数据显示，2015年第三季度，我国视频行业个人付费市场规模突破10亿元大关，达到11.9亿元，同比增幅达256%，较上季度环比增长137%。

白皮书显示，会员大剧、网络大电影的蓬勃发展、模式创新创造了中国视频付费业务的爆发式增长。与此同时，会员的消费人群也正从一二线城市逐渐向三四线城市下沉，华语电影在网络院线持续走俏。可以看出，中国视频会员服务市场的变化折射出了中国网民线上娱乐生活和消费习惯正在发生着巨大变化。

（资料来源：《中国新闻出版广电报》 作者：任晓宁）

港澳台版权信息

◆香　港

【知识产权署推出有关版权保护新电视宣传短片】 2016年4月25日，香港知识产权署推出全新一辑电视宣传短片，以提高市民尊重和保护版权的意识。

最新的电视宣传短片由香港特别行政区政府知识产权署与广东省新闻出版广电局（广东省版权局）首度共同制作，是粤港保护知识产权合作专责小组2015—2016年度的合作项目之一。电视宣传短片邀请香港著名创作歌手周柏豪参与演出，宣扬“支持创作，尊重版权”的信息。电视宣传短片会在香港及广东省两地播放。

4月24日，电视宣传短片的首播仪式由香港知识产权署及广东省新闻出版广电局（广东省版权局）代表在广州共同主持。世界知识产权日定于每年4月26日举行，首播仪式为2016年的庆祝活动之一。

（资料来源：http://sc.isd.gov.hk/gb/www.info.gov.hk/gia/general/201604/25/P201604250335.htm　信息搜集：李泓阅）

【香港海关侦破“点对点”发放怀疑侵权电视节目案件】 2016年10月13日，香港海关版权及商标调查科人员采取行动，侦破一宗涉嫌利用“点对点”技术在互联网分发涉嫌侵权电视节目的案件。行动中，海关拘捕一名二十五岁男子，涉嫌为有关讨论区的管理人，并查获一部电脑及六部硬盘驱动器，总值约二万三千元。

香港海关早前接获线报，指有人在一个香港网上讨论区发放大量涉嫌侵权的海外及本地电视台的节目，供已缴交月费的会员下载，而讨论区的会员分布世界各地。

香港海关人员经调查后采取行动，在葵青区拘捕一名男子，怀疑他为有关讨论区的管理人，并在他的电脑器材内发现大量涉嫌侵权电视节目档案。该男子现正保释候查。

香港海关呼吁市民尊重知识产权，切勿以身试法。根据《版权条例》，任何人士在没有版权拥有人的特许下，分发侵犯版权复制品而达到损害版权拥有人权利的程度，不论是否为获取利益，均属违法，最高刑罚为监禁四年及每件侵权物品罚款五万元。

市民如怀疑有任何侵犯版权的资料，请致电海关24小时热线2545 6182举报。

（资料来源：http://sc.isd.gov.hk/gb/www.info.gov.hk/gia/general/201610/04/P2016100400824.htm　信息搜集：李泓阅）

【香港海关打击分发侵权课程教材】 香港海关于2016年11月23、24日采取行动，打击补习社分发涉嫌侵权课程教材，共检获超过五万页涉嫌侵权课程教材、二十五台电脑、一台打印机和十三台影印机，估计市值约五十八万元。

香港海关早前接获举报，指有连锁式补习社在教学时向学生派发涉嫌侵权课程教材。经调查后，海关人员于11月23及24日搜查位于全港不同地区的十三间连锁式补习社及一间办公室。行动中共检获超过五万页怀疑侵权课程教材、二十五台电脑、一台打印机和十三台影印机，并拘捕六男八女，年龄在二十七至五十五岁之间，分别为补习社董事、负责人及导师。案件仍在调查中，被捕人士现正保释候查。

香港海关版权及商标调查（行动）课监督方永佳11月25日提醒补习社负责人，切勿在未获授权下制作或分发版权作品，作为课程教材。商业机构在使用及分发版权作品前，有责任查究有关的物品或材料并非侵犯版权制品。

根据《版权条例》，任何商业机构，包括补习社，如在业务过程中分发侵犯版权复制品，即属违法，一经定罪，最高可被判每件侵权物品罚款五万元及监禁四年。

（资料来源：http://sc.isd.gov.hk/TuniS/www.info.gov.hk/gia/general/201611/25/P2016112500313.htm?fontSize=1　信息搜集：李泓阅）

【香港政府建议修订《仲裁条例》】 香港政府建议修订《仲裁条例》（第609章），厘清以仲裁方式解决知识产权权利（知识产权）争议的法律状况，借此促使更多当事人在香港透过仲裁方式解决知识产权争议。

香港律政司发言人 11 月 30 日表示，有关修订旨在厘清可透过仲裁解决知识产权争议，以及强制执行涉及知识产权的仲裁裁决，并不违反香港的公共政策。

目前，《仲裁条例》并无针对知识产权争议可否透过仲裁解决的具体条文，而香港亦没有相关的权威性判决。政府相信就此制定具体法例条文，可厘清法律情况及释除任何不明确之处。

发言人说："我们相信有关修订将进一步巩固香港作为主要国际仲裁中心的竞争力，并凸显香港较亚太区其他司法管辖区在解决知识产权争议方面的优势。"

此外，香港政府亦建议修订《仲裁（纽约公约缔约方）令》，以更新 1958 年《承认及执行外国仲裁裁决公约》的缔约方名单，包括将安道尔及科摩罗加入缔约方名单。

载有上述修订的《2016 年仲裁（修订）条例草案》于 2016 年 12 月 2 日刊宪，并于 12 月 14 日提交立法会审议。

（资料来源：http://sc. isd. gov. hk/TuniS/www. info. gov. hk/gia/general/201611/30/P2016113000327. htm? fontSize=1　信息搜集：李泓阅）

【泛珠三角区域深化知识产权合作协议】 2016 年 12 月 13 日，香港特别行政区政府与澳门特别行政区政府及九个泛珠三角区域知识产权管理部门，在江西省南昌市举行的第十一届泛珠三角区域知识产权合作联席会议上，签署了《泛珠三角区域深化知识产权合作协议》（以下简称《深化合作协议》）。九个泛珠三角区域知识产权管理部门分属福建、江西、湖南、广东、广西、海南、四川、贵州、云南等省区。

第一份泛珠三角区域知识产权合作协议于 2005 年在四川省成都市签署，《深化合作协议》旨在推动泛珠三角区域知识产权事业全面发展、充分发挥各方的优势和特色、促进知识产权创造运用、加强知识产权保护及优化知识产权服务，以推动区域经济共同发展。

香港知识产权署署长梁家丽在联席会议代表香港特别行政区政府签署《深化合作协议》。梁家丽表示："泛珠三角区域的合作日渐拓展，有利于深化区域知识产权合作，在新协议、新形势、新方向下，九个省（区）与港澳特区可互补优势，发挥协同效应，进一步强化知识产权保护，促进知识产权贸易和推动高端知识产权服务业的发展。"

根据协议内容，泛珠区域将深化其知识产权合作至以下八个范畴：知识产权强省建设；知识产权保护；知识产权转化运用，促进泛珠三角区域内的知识产权贸易发展；知识产权服务；知识产权信息开发利用；知识产权对外交流合作；知识产权宣传培训；知识产权交流研讨。

（资料来源：http://sc. isd. gov. hk/TuniS/www. info. gov. hk/gia/general/201612/13/P2016121300298. htm　信息搜集：李泓阅）

◆ 台　湾

【出口视听著作及代工激光唱片不用申请核验文件】 2016 年 3 月 1 日起，台湾地区出口含有视听著作的激光影碟（LD）、影音光盘（VCD）、数码影音光盘（DVD）以及 CD 唱片等货品时，将无须再向"智慧局"申请著作权文件核验单，依一般通关程序办理出口即可。因为近年来因网络科技兴起，光盘片已逐渐式微，出口申办案件逐年衰退，考量本地区已有"光盘管理条例"可对本地生产光盘业者于源头加以有效管理，且基于简政便民及遵行 WTO"贸易便捷化协定"致力简化货物通关手续，节省业者的成本负担与降低进出口通关程序的不必要障碍。

1991 年间，为落实对于出口货品著作权的保护，避免盗版品输出造成国际纠纷，针对录像节目带及激光唱片等著作，本地区人于出口时须向前"行政院新闻局"办理授权文件审查，取得出口证明书后，始得出口。嗣后于 2001 年 1 月 1 日因应当时录像节目带已逐渐由光盘取代之趋势，因而调整项目，针对"视听著作光盘"及"代工激光唱片"（即视听著作或录音著作固着之光盘）出口时，应检附著作财产权人授权书向"智慧局"申请核验单，确认出口的光盘并无侵害著作权情事，办理至今。因应时代变迁，此一措施将走入历史。

"智慧局"提醒，虽然以后出口影音光盘片已无须申办著作权文件核验单，但依"著作权法"第 90 条之 1 规定，海关得依职权要求出口人提供出口货物之著作权授权资料，一旦经查获出口人如有侵害智慧财产权之行为者，依据"贸易法"第 17 条第 1 款规定，得予以警告，处新台币 3 万元以上 30 万元以下罚款或停止其 1 个月以上 1 年以下输出、输入或输出入货品，请出口人仍应尊重知识产权并遵守相关法规规定，避免受罚。

（资料来源：https://www.tipo.gov.tw/ct.asp?xItem=615426&ctNode=7127&mp=1　信息搜集：李泓阅）

【2016 海峡两岸知识产权法学论坛成果报道】

2016 年 4 月 7 日，海峡两岸知识产权法学论坛在北京中国人民大学隆重开场，本次论坛上，来自海峡两岸的知识产权界专家、学者、产业代表分别就“两岸知识产权专业法院之现况与展望”、“专利创造性判断之法学方法论”、“知识产权保护模式比较研究”及“台湾保智大队之设计优势与实际运作情形”等专题进行了广泛且深入的探讨，通过加深彼此了解，取得共识，进一步促进两岸知识产权保护联系机制的构建、加大两岸知识产权保护力度、有效维护两岸消费者和经营者的合法权益，从而拓展两岸知识产权及品牌合作空间，推动两岸经贸关系向深入发展。

在第一场“两岸知识产权专业法院之现况与展望”议题中，与会者可充分掌握目前两岸有关知识产权专责法院管辖之事件类型、审理情形等信息；在第二场“专利创造性判断之法学方法论”议题中，就专利创造性判断之法学方法等情形，两岸基于社会价值理念、文化背景不同，以案例对照说明，印象鲜明有趣；在第三场“知识产权保护模式比较研究”议题中，两岸代表对于知识产权保护模式等实务问题，进行深入讨论；在第四场“台湾保智大队之设计优势与实际运作情形”专题演讲中，两岸专家就知识产权专责查缉机构定位及设置提出新思维及观点，精彩又发人深省。

海峡两岸知识产权法学论坛是海峡两岸知识产权法学领域界最高层次的交流平台，透过彼此的对话与互动，对扩大、深化两岸经贸合作，促进两岸产业发展发挥了重要作用。经过一天密集的研讨，官方精辟见解，产业务实对话，充分发挥了会议应具有的前瞻性意义的策略性对话平台功能，双方达成多项具体意见交流，对于两岸经贸发展和产业合作，具有非常重要的历史意义。来自最高人民法院、北京知识产权法院、广州知识产权法院、国台办、台湾“智慧财产法院”、“保安警察第二总队刑事警察大队”的代表及相关官员、两岸知识产权专家学者、产业代表、知识产权代理机构代表等约 100 人与会研讨交流。

在北京期间，海峡两岸商务协会代表团一行先后拜访最高人民法院副院长陶凯元、北京知识产权法院院长宿迟，听取 2015 年中国人民法院审理知识产权案件的情况，以及大陆方面知识产权法院建设和运行、知识产权案件“三合一”改革和第四次专利法修改进展情况。双方并就两岸在知识产权审判有关方面开展合作等议题进行了深入交流。最高人民法院研究室、民三庭，北京知识产权法院，广州知识产权法院，中国人民大学知识产权学院有关负责人陪同会见和座谈。双方代表均表示肯定，海峡两岸知识产权法学论坛是两岸知识产权司法领域交流与合作的重要平台。中国知识产权法学研究会和海商会在推动两岸知识产权领域的民间交流合作和保护两岸企业合法知识产权权益方面做了大量卓有成效的工作。

（资料来源：http://www.ccicsonline.net/web/index.php/210　信息搜集：李泓阅）

◆澳　门

【澳门贸促局促中小企业利用知识产权优势勇闯内地市场】　2016 年 7 月 20 日，“澳门中小企业如何在内地取得知识产权保护研讨会”举行，研讨会旨在通过培训和交流，令澳门企业增强知识产权意识，把握《内地与澳门关于建立更紧密经贸关系的安排》机遇，利用澳门知识产权优势，勇闯内地市场。

本次研讨会由澳门特区政府贸易投资促进局、经济局及中国国际贸易促进委员会驻香港澳门代表处联合主办。会议邀请到多位专家进行分享，内容涉及内地商标申请的流程及策略，如何解决侵权诉讼及商业纠纷等，以加强本地企业对内地知识产权法规及相应保护措施的认识，协助澳门企业及品牌‘走出去”。

“支持中小微企业成长，鼓励各界创新创业”是澳门特别行政区行政长官崔世安在 2016 年度施政报告中提出的目标。为此，澳门特区政府经济财政司辖下的各部门，应中小企业需求，通过举办论坛、培训等，提供相关顾问、中介服务，为其拓展业务给予支持和帮助。

澳门特区政府贸促局执行委员吴爱华表示，国家“十三五”规划提出的创新驱动发展战略，包括深化知识产权改革等内容，对该领域的发展提出了更高要求。未来特区政府将加大对本地中小企业知识产权业务培训，帮助其了解内地及国际市场的最新情况，把握区域经济融合机遇，推动澳门产业适度多元发展。

（资料来源：新华网　杨悦筠　杨　懿
信息搜集：李泓阅）

陕西人民出版社
SHAANXI PEOPLE'S PUBLISHING HOUSE

第四届中国出版政府奖·优秀出版人物奖——惠西平

惠西平，1958年10月出生，陕西甘泉县人，1976年11月参加工作，1982年毕业于西北大学中文系，大学本科学历，文学学士学位，中共党员，编审职称。先后任陕西人民出版社、华岳文艺出版社、太白文艺出版社、陕西科学技术出版社编辑、编辑室主任、副社长、副总编、社长等职，现任陕西新华出版传媒集团股份有限公司党委委员、董事，陕西人民出版社社长、编委会主任。第四届中国出版政府奖·优秀出版人物奖获得者。

从事出版工作35年来，惠西平同志在编辑和领导岗位上成绩斐然，先后被评为新中国60年百名有突出贡献的新闻出版专业技术人员、享受国务院特殊津贴专家、全国百佳出版工作者、全国新闻出版行业领军人才、陕西省人文社会科学领域顶尖人才、陕西出版集团优秀经营管理者，2014年荣获第十二届韬奋出版奖，2017年荣获第四届中国出版政府奖·优秀出版人物奖。现为中国出版协会常务理事、国家出版基金评审委员会评委、中国武侠文学会副会长、陕西省出版工作者协会常务理事、陕西省文化交流协会常务理事、陕西省教育学会副会长、陕西省出版专业高级职务任职资格评审委员会学科组组长、陕西省古籍整理委员会专家组成员。

参与策划及担任编委、主编、出品人的《鼎立南极：昆仑站建站纪实》《这个冬天懒懒的事》《陕北民歌集萃》等多种图书分别获得 “五个一工程”奖、中国出版政府奖、中华优秀出版物奖；《红色档案——延安时期文献档案资料汇编》等11种图书入选国家出版基金资助项目；《丝绸之路大事编年》等7种图书入选“十三五”国家重点图书出版规划。

为积极落实“把红色资源利用好、把红色传统发扬好、把红色基因传承好”的有关精神，惠西平同志主持、带领陕西人民出版社与中国延安精神研究会等部门共同组建成立延安书局，使延安成为弘扬红色文化的精神高地。

2016年度中国十大出版人物——乔玢

乔玢，现任北京出版集团董事长，被誉为“学者型企业家”，有着学者扎实、稳重的风格和睿智、超前的思维，更有着企业家大胆、果敢的冲劲和魄力。2011年担任北京出版集团总经理，2015年任董事长，在领导和经营管理、图书策划、资本运作、资源整合、国际合作等方面开拓创新，带领集团实现跨越式发展，目前集团总资产达到25.4亿元，是转企时的1.9倍，出版效率在中国出版行业位居前列。2016年度中国十大出版人物获得者。

作为集团主要负责人，乔玢带领班子成员积极进取，为从严治党及集团发展劳心费力，认真负责地做了大量工作。从战略高度推进集团改革发展，主持制定北京出版集团“十三五”发展规划，完成北教控股公司“新三板”上市挂牌和融资，使其成为全国率先登陆“新三板”的国有控股图书策划发行企业。探索推动国际合作，主持集团与德国梅尔杜蒙公司共同投资组建京版梅尔杜蒙公司，为拓展国际旅游图书市场打下了基础。支持北教传媒、京版芳草、少儿事业部等产品创新、产业融合、资源整合。一批线上线下互动创新产品脱颖而出，发现并支持北京少年儿童出版社开发国内领先的VR技术与传统图书的融合。

在把握集团战略发展的同时，乔玢亲身参与图书编辑策划，注重精品出版和文化传承积累，主导策划“双效”显著的图书精品，有效提升了图书销售业绩，使北京出版集团在各类图书、媒体奖项上表现出众。

另外，乔玢还积极承担文化传播使命，推动北京出版集团“走出去”，加强出版产品和企业文化输出，先后组织策划香港“京港出版交流活动暨京版集团精品图书展”、新西兰“京版集团图书展”、“京版集团马来西亚精品书展”、广东“南国书香节”主宾省活动、2014上海书展“北京主宾展团”，带队参展、指导筹备“品读北京”2015台湾书展并在两岸出版界引发广泛好评。2016年带队远赴英伦三岛，举行“品读北京 · 北京出版集团精品图书英国巡展暨文化交流活动”，让参与其中的英国读者近距离品读京味文化，了解当代中国社会发展的崭新面貌，进一步提升了集团的影响力。

在全身心投入到工作中的同时，乔玢还关注偏远地区孩子们的阅读情况，2015年北京出版集团与北京电视台联合发起了“带本书，给家乡的孩子们”大型公益活动，活动目前已开展4季，累计在全国建立“爱心图书馆”23座，数百名“捎书信使”将十余万册京版图书送抵全国21个省、自治区、直辖市的100所小学，受益学生近万人。北京出版集团每年举办“世界图书和版权日京版集团纪念讲坛”，每月举办“京版大众文化公益讲座”，还邀请健康专家深入社区、机关，开展健康宣讲活动等，丰富读者文化生活，培养读者阅读习惯。

北京出版集团
BEIJING PUBLISHING GROUP

以文学为载体，"十月作家居住地 · 爱丁堡"投入运营

2015年起，举办“带本书，给家乡的孩子们”大型公益活动

成立十月文学院

北教传媒公司"新三板"上市

北京出版集团是北京市属综合性出版机构，前身为1948年成立的北平大众书店，现已发展成为拥有8家专业出版社、5家杂志社和14家子公司的大型文化企业，培育出北京出版社、北京十月文艺出版社、北京少年儿童出版社、北京美术摄影出版社、北京教育出版社、《十月》、《父母必读》、《少年科学画报》、《十月少年文学》等知名出版品牌，打造了北教传媒、十月文学院、父母必读育儿传媒、京版北美、京版梅尔杜蒙等机构品牌，形象地印证了中国当代出版事业发展与壮大的历史。

北京出版集团始终秉承“崇尚价值以文化人”的出版理念，坚守主业，专注前行，出版了社科、文学、少儿、科学、生活、艺术、教育、音像、期刊等一大批反映中华优秀传统文化和具有鲜明时代特色的精品佳作，锻造了“书山有路步步巅峰”的企业精神。目前，集团共有员工850余人，年生产各类出版物7 000余种，图书期刊获得国家、省部级奖项800余种。2016年生产码洋超过35亿元，出版效率、图书零售市场码洋占有率居全国出版集团前列。

2016年度中国十大出版人物——刘明辉

刘明辉，湖南汨罗人，中共党员，编审，教授，博导，从事出版工作24年，现任大连出版社社长兼总编辑，曾先后任东北财经大学出版社社长兼总编辑、东北财经大学杂志社社长、大连报业集团副社长，2016年度中国十大出版人物获得者。

近年来，刘明辉同志带领大连出版社进行战略转型，进军儿童文学市场，提出了自己的童书出版理念——“保卫想象力”，明确了自己的奋斗目标——打造幻想儿童文学产业基地。按照“一个项目多家合作、一项合作多方资源、一项资源多方利用、一个品牌多家共享”的思路，积极创新体制机制，与战略合作伙伴成功打造了“大白鲸”“八尾猫”“快乐星球”等系列文化产业品牌。其中，仅“大白鲸计划”的参与企业就已超过10家，带动投资逾35亿元，产品形态包括图书、电影、电视、舞台剧、动漫作品、主题公园等，形成以出版社为龙头，上、中、下游多业联动的一条龙产业链。“大白鲸”成为我国文化产业融合发展的知名品牌，在全国出版界起到了引领示范作用，受到地方政府及行业主管部门领导的充分肯定。

围绕幻想儿童文学产业化布局和数字出版发展战略，刘明辉同志主持策划并实施的“‘幻想屋’儿童文学数字出版升级改造工程”、“中国幻想儿童文学新媒体平台建设”和“幻想儿童文学产业化基地建设”等多个项目成功入选国家新闻出版改革发展项目库，并获得中央文化产业发展专项资金支持。

刘明辉同志在图书出版规划、图书质量控制、图书营销创新、财务成本管理、内部控制与风险管理、会计审计等方面均有深入的研究，先后在国家重要刊物发表学术论文、译文350余篇，其中《出版社图书选题风险管理现状调查》获得第五届中华优秀出版物（出版科研论文）奖；主持承担国家自然科学基金2项，国家社会科学基金1项，部级以上科研课题20余项；撰著、主编各种学术专著、教材共87部。

2016年，刘明辉同志策划并担任责编的《百年见证》荣获第六届中华优秀出版物奖，《富民与安居》入选国家出版基金项目，“大白鲸幻想儿童文学读库”等80多种图书入选“十三五”国家重点图书出版规划，《大机车》入选国家2016年主题出版重点出版物选题。

刘明辉同志2007年被评为“全国新闻出版行业领军人才”，2014年入选“全国会计名家培养工程”，2015年入选中国企业财务管理协会“全国企业财务管理领军人才”，2016年入选中国审计博物馆“中国重要审计学专家”。

大连出版社主办的2017“大白鲸”原创幻想儿童文学年度盛典在京举行

大连出版社

大连出版社成立于1988年3月15日，是全国十六家城市出版社之一。做儿童想象力的保卫者是大连出版社给自己的角色定位，是大连出版社全体员工的共同愿景！2012年初，处于战略转型初期的大连出版社提出了自己的童书出版理念——“保卫想象力”，明确了自己的奋斗目标——打造幻想儿童文学产业基地。据此，大连出版社描绘了一张属于自己的地图，探索出坚守主业、强化特色、发展产业的新路子。

近年来，大连出版社着力打造原创幻想儿童文学图书品牌，积累了“大白鲸”金牌作品、“大白鲸幻想儿童文学读库”、《校园三剑客》、《海军陆战队》、《少年冒险王》、“中华原创幻想儿童文学大系”等多个知名品牌，其中，《拯救天才》《古蜀》分别入选2016年、2017年国家新闻出版广电主管部门向全国青少年推荐百种优秀出版物，《拯救天才》《大熊的女儿》双双荣获第十届全国优秀儿童文学奖，《百年见证》获第六届中华优秀出版物奖。

2014年9月，大连出版社被评为“辽宁省传统出版单位数字化转型示范单位”；2015年6月，被授予“全国海洋文化产业示范基地”；2016年6月，被授予“辽宁幻想儿童文学产业基地”；2016年9月，被全国图书馆协会、图书馆报评为“最受图书馆欢迎的少儿出版机构”。

社长兼总编辑刘明辉在第二届幻想儿童文学高层论坛上发言

“大白鲸”金牌作品

“大白鲸”原创幻想儿童文学优秀作品征集活动钻石鲸作品获得者、“90后”作家王君心成为大连出版社签约作家

2017“保卫想象力——‘大白鲸’全国小学生阅读与创作活动”启动仪式

2016年度中国十大出版人物——宗俊峰

2017年1月13日，由中国出版协会主办的中国出版年会在京举行，年会发布了2016年度出版业十件大事、十大人物和30本好书。清华控股成员企业清华大学出版社社长宗俊峰被评为2016年度中国十大出版人物。

作为大学版协的理事长和水木清华的出版掌门，执掌清华大学出版社8年来，宗俊峰无愧于“传播先进文化，推动社会进步”的时代重任。2016年，他带领清华大学出版社加快推进传统出版和新兴出版的融合发展，“文泉书局”“智学苑”“书问”“兆泰源”等4个数字出版平台建设特色凸显、功能不断完善，各项经营指标较上年稳步增长。

2016年，清华大学出版社在宗俊峰的带领下，取得较快发展，多种图书期刊获奖。

2016年4月，清华大学出版社图书《癌症·真相》获中国图书评论学会和中央电视台联合推出的“2015中国好书”奖之科普生活类“2015中国好书”。

2016年11月，2016中国学术期刊未来论坛发布2016年“中国国际影响力优秀学术期刊”名单，清华大学出版社出版的8种期刊入选。

2016年12月，清华大学出版社讲述中国航天人奋斗历程的《嫦娥揽月》荣获第六届中华优秀出版物图书提名奖等奖项。

2016年8月，宗俊峰被国家新闻出版主管部门评为2016年度全国新闻出版行业领军人才。

清华大学出版社是新闻出版主管部门审定的国家一级出版社，是国内领先的综合性教育与专业出版机构，先后荣获“中国出版政府奖先进出版单位”、“全国百佳图书出版单位”、“十一五”国家重点出版规划出版工作先进单位，是新闻出版主管部门和教育主管部门表彰的全国优秀出版社和全国先进高校出版社，累计获得各类图书奖500多项。

在“互联网+”的经济社会发展新形态下，清华大学出版社坚持以先进技术为支撑，内容建设为根本，大力促进数字出版与传统出版深度融合，创新发展的模式，形成新的出版合力，由教育出版向教学资源研发、服务战略转型，致力于为我国文化事业的大发展大繁荣做出更大贡献。

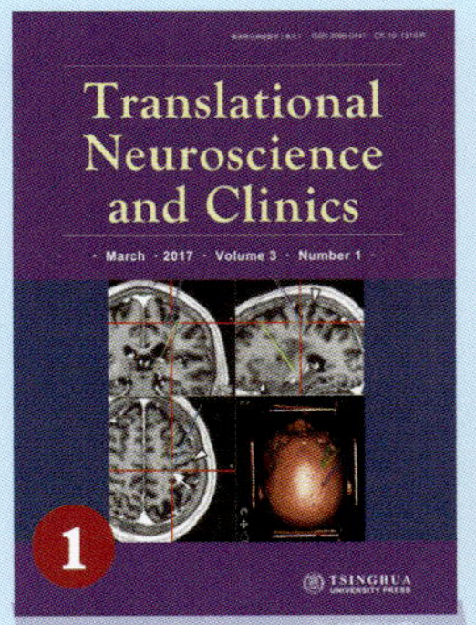

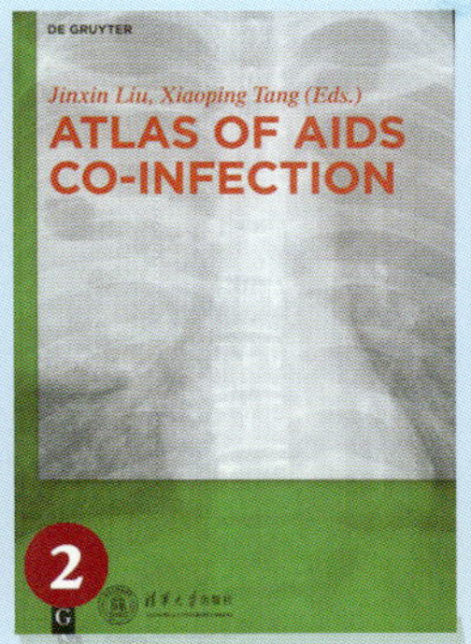

清华大学出版社

清华大学出版社认真贯彻党的出版方针，坚持正确出版方向，坚持全面深化改革，以集团化建设为契机，着力解决出版社转型升级的瓶颈问题，加快推进传统出版和新兴出版的融合发展，各项经营指标较2016年稳步增长，集团化发展稳步推进，以分社为主的各专业出版领域结构趋于合理，呈现螺旋式上升趋势；数字出版平台建设特色凸显、功能不断完善；重点出版项目申报、“走出去”工作卓有成效，作为“中国图书对外推广计划”成员单位，清华大学出版社迄今已有500余项约10个文种的各类图书版权输出到北美、欧洲和亚洲国家，另有200余项图书的中文繁体字版在中国港澳台地区出版发行。通过与多家国际著名出版公司的合作，清华大学出版社外文版学术著作和期刊以及教育和专业图书已销往全世界，进入了国际学术界和教育界的视野。荣获获评“中国图书世界影响力百强出版单位”；入选国家新闻出版主管部门数字出版转型示范单位；多种图书、期刊获得重大奖项；取得良好的社会效益与经济效益；在业界树立了鲜明的清华特色品牌，具有广泛的影响力！

图片注释

①《临床转化神经医学》 ②《艾滋病胸腹部影像诊断图谱》 ③《控制系统计算机辅助设计—— MATLAB语言与应用》（第3版） ④《摩擦学原理》（第4版） ⑤《癌症·真相》 ⑥ 清华大学出版社与爱思唯尔（Elsevier）签约 ⑦ 清华大学出版社社长宗俊峰获评2016年度中国十大出版人物

2016年度中国十大出版人物——于殿利

于殿利，现任商务印书馆总经理。历史学博士，中共十八大代表。北京师范大学、中国传媒大学兼职教授，博士生导师。荣获全国“文化名家暨宣传文化系统四个一批人才”“中国出版政府奖优秀出版人物”“全国百佳出版工作者”“全国新闻出版行业领军人才”等称号。著有《巴比伦与亚述文明》和《巴比伦法的人本观——一个关于人本主义思想的起源》等专著5部，译著2部，在《人民日报》、《光明日报》和《中国社会科学》等报刊上发表论文近百篇。

2010年于殿利任法人代表以来，商务印书馆在他的带领下经营规模不断拓展，社会效益和经济效益业绩屡创新高，进入了跨越式、加速度发展的新时期。

于殿利具有高度的文化自觉和政治自觉，把社会效益放在首位，强化“用思想推动社会进步”的出版理念，带领商务印书馆出版了一系列顺应新时期文化发展要求的优秀作品。除加速出版“汉译世界学术名著丛书”之外，打造了代表中国传统文化集大成者和辞书编纂成就的大型国家出版项目《辞源》（第3版）并实现纸电同步出版，出版了《新华字典》（第11版）、《现代汉语词典》（第6版、第7版）、“中华现代学术名著丛书”、“国际文化版图研究文库”、《中国设计全集》、《中国当代设计全集》、“中国道路丛书”、“自然博物系列丛书”等一系列在思想和学术领域填补空白的作品，展现出百年商务印书馆在瞬息万变的时代“激动潮流”，反映时代之需、国家之需、民族之需的强烈使命感和责任感，取得了巨大的社会反响。

于殿利积极推进出版体制机制改革，率先实施纸电同步出版战略，开启了全媒体融合出版的新局面；他努力践行“五跨”战略，积极推进商务印书馆建立了19家涵盖多种所有制形式的子公司，为开展多种经营开创了道路；他积极坚持国际化品牌发展之路，贯彻“走出去”战略，策划了商务印书馆与众多国际知名出版企业建立战略合作伙伴关系，不断提升商务印书馆在国际出版业的影响力。

于殿利强调“文化决定高度”的企业文化理念，在新时期适时梳理了商务印书馆的企业核心价值观和核心经营理念，并提出了“服务教育、引领学术、担当文化、引领潮流”的新时期企业宗旨。他积极推进各项文化公益活动的开展，积极推动形成了“《新华字典》文化民生工程”惠民政策，惠及全国农村地区义务教育阶段的近亿名中小学生；他坚持致力于公益事业，与央视主播联合组织了多次“放飞梦想的翅膀”公益行动，建设多家“商务印书馆阅读体验店”“商务印书馆价值阅读品牌示范店”，并且在具有深厚历史文化底蕴的乡镇开设商务印书馆“乡村阅读中心”，设立乡村教师助教资金。他为建设书香中国，推广全民阅读做出了突出贡献，使商务印书馆获得了越来越多的社会赞誉。

商務印書館 The Commercial Press

创于1897

使命：昌明教育　开启民智

宗旨：服务教育　引领学术　担当文化　引领潮流

商务印书馆1897年2月11日创立于上海，它的创立标志着中国现代出版事业的开端。数十年间，商务印书馆从一个小小的印刷作坊发展成为一家以出版为主业的文化教育机构，鼎盛时期是亚洲第一、世界前三的出版企业，在全国乃至海外设有36家分馆和千余个销售网点。1954年，商务印书馆总馆迁至北京。2002年中国出版集团公司成立，商务印书馆是成员单位之一。2011年改制为商务印书馆有限公司。

一个多世纪以来，商务印书馆始终秉持“昌明教育，开启民智”的文化使命，竭力继承中华文化，积极传播海外新知，出版图书5万余种，创造了中国文化出版史的辉煌，为近现代中国文化与文明的发展构筑和提供了文化基石与精神给养，与北京大学一起，被誉为中国近现代文化史上的双子星座。代表性出版物《辞源》绵亘百年，历久弥新；《新华字典》、《现代汉语词典》、《牛津高阶英汉双解词典》、“汉译世界学术名著丛书”、“中华现代学术名著丛书”、“世界名人传记丛书”，以及《英语世界》、《汉语世界》等杂志，领风气之先，普惠学林大众。《文津阁四库全书》《新华字典》等被党和国家领导人作为国礼赠送外国宾朋。作为出版业的“中华老字号”，商务印书馆是全国“百佳出版社”和“中国出版政府奖”荣誉称号的获得者，曾经获得“国际白金星质量大奖”和“国家图书奖”，被誉为“工具书王国”和学术出版重镇，是目前中国具有很强实力和影响力的文化出版机构。

商务印书馆“十二五”重点图书

《新华字典》（第11版）

《现代汉语词典》（第6版）

《辞源》（第3版）

《牛津高阶英汉双解词典》（第8版）

《新时代俄汉详解大词典》

“汉译世界学术名著丛书”

“中华现代学术名著丛书”

商务印书馆“十二五”重点图书

“国际文化版图研究文库”

《钱锺书手稿集·外文笔记》

自然博物系列：《发现之旅》(珍藏本)

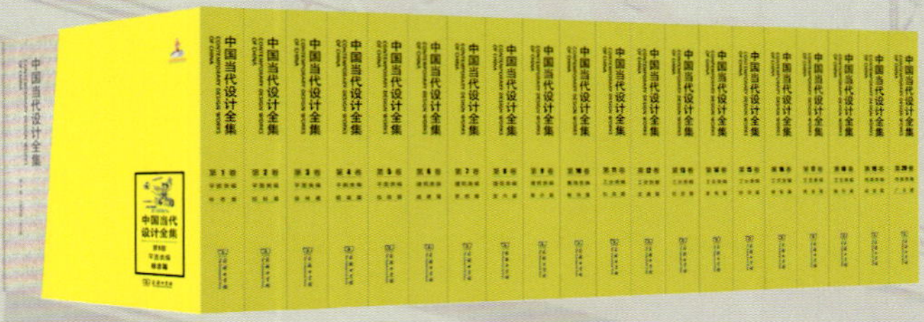

《中国当代设计全集》

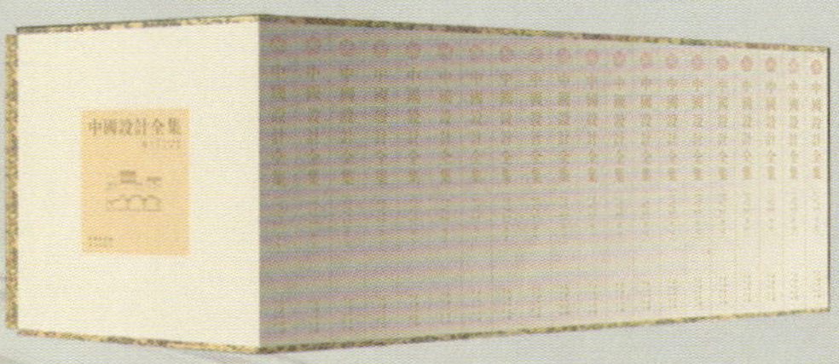

《中国设计全集》

证　书

安晓露

荣获第十五届输出版引进版优秀图书推介活动优秀版权经理人奖。

特发此证，以资鼓励。

中国出版协会国际合作出版工作委员会
中国新闻出版研究院
出版参考杂志社
2016年9月

证　书

商务印书馆有限公司：

贵社出版的《中国特色社会主义审计理论研究（修订版）》荣获2015年度输出版优秀图书奖。

特发此证，以资鼓励。

中国出版协会国际合作出版工作委员会
中国新闻出版研究院
出版参考杂志社
2016年9月

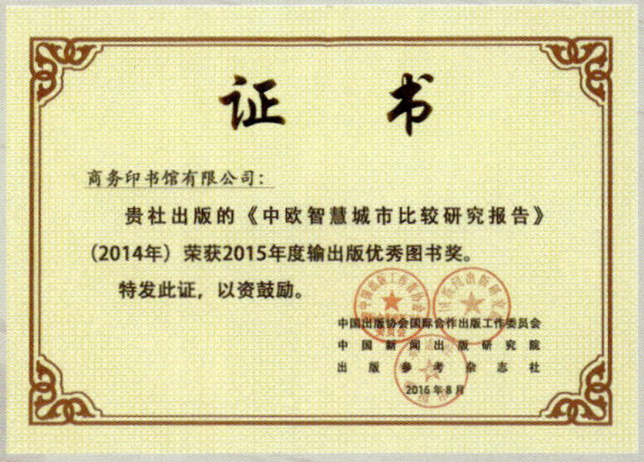

证　书

商务印书馆有限公司：

贵社出版的《中欧智慧城市比较研究报告》（2014年）荣获2015年度输出版优秀图书奖。

特发此证，以资鼓励。

中国出版协会国际合作出版工作委员会
中国新闻出版研究院
出版参考杂志社
2016年8月

证　书

商务印书馆有限公司：

贵社出版的《中国语言生活状况报告（2014年）》荣获2015年度输出版优秀图书奖。

特发此证，以资鼓励。

中国出版协会国际合作出版工作委员会
中国新闻出版研究院
出版参考杂志社
2016年9月

《中国特色社会主义审计理论研究》（修订版）荣获2015年度输出版优秀图书奖

《中国语言生活状况报告（2014）》荣获2015年度输出版优秀图书奖

《中欧智慧城市比较研究报告（2014年）》荣获2015年度输出版优秀图书奖

2016年，商务印书馆引进版权347项，引进图书品种涉及外语工具书和教材、人文社科学术著作和大众文化类图书等，与英、美、德、日等20余个国家的一流出版机构，如英国牛津大学出版社、英国泰勒弗朗西斯集团、德国德古意特出版社、德国施普林格出版社、荷兰威科集团等保持着密切的业务往来。与此同时，商务印书馆积极向德国、英国、韩国、日本、印尼等国家输出语言、社科、管理、文学、对外汉语教学等类别的图书版权，全年输出版权50项，"世界少儿汉语"系列、《汉语图解小词典》（马来语版、越南语版）、《东西文化及其哲学》、《中国公司法案例精读》、《中国救荒史》、《筹资约束与货币理论——蒋硕杰经济科学论文集》等优秀图书顺利实现"走出去"。《中欧智慧城市比较研究报告（2014年）》《中国语言生活状况报告（2014年）》《中国特色社会主义审计理论研究》（修订版）荣获2015年度输出版优秀图书奖；安晓露荣获第十五届（2015年度）"优秀版权经理人"称号。

2016年，商务印书馆参加了第23届北京国际图书博览会、第68届法兰克福国际书展，以及英国伦敦国际书展、美国纽约书展等各种大型的版权贸易和文化交流活动。全年共接待BIBF新参展商代表团、英国牛津大学出版社、剑桥大学出版社、德国施普林格出版社等合作伙伴代表来访100余人次。各项展览和会谈活动推动了商务印书馆的版权贸易工作，扩大了商务印书馆的品牌影响力。2016年，商务印书馆跻身"2015—2016 中国图书海外馆藏影响力出版百强"。

1

2

3

4

5

6

7

图片注释

① 商务印书馆—名创教育出版集团《全球华语大词典》海外出版发行协议签约仪式 ②《新华字典》《现代汉语词典》汉英版合作协议签约仪式 ③《学习牛津3000词》APP发布会 ④ 商务印书馆—Routledge"国家治理丛书"项目合作协议签约仪式 ⑤《牛津中阶英汉双解词典》（第5版）新书发布会 ⑥ 剑桥大学出版社—商务印书馆战略合作协议签约仪式 ⑦ 参加第23届北京国际图书博览会

第三届中国版权卓越成就者奖获得者——苏雨恒

苏雨恒，现任高等教育出版社社长，中国教育出版传媒集团有限公司党组成员，中国职教学会副会长，中国编辑学会副会长，中国高教学会常务理事，中国出版协会常务理事，大学出版社协会常务理事，中国版权协会常务理事。全国新闻出版行业领军人物、第十二届韬奋出版奖获得者。

苏雨恒同志1986年入高教社工作至今，从事教育出版已30余年，是高教社事业不断前行发展的见证人、亲历者。自2011年执掌高教社以来，他高度重视版权的保护和经营工作，始终坚持认为版权是出版社的核心竞争力和重要资源，使得版权在高教社核心竞争力和比较优势建设中的地位得到进一步重视和凸显。在他的带领下，高教社近几年在版权的保护、经营、使用和管理方面均取得了显著的成绩。

在版权保护方面，高教社屡出重拳，多年来不断拓展维权领域。高教社作为发起人，组织成立“京版七社反盗版联盟”，建设打盗维权体系，提升打盗维权成效。2016年，苏雨恒亲自挂帅成立专项小组开展复印教材治理行动，侵权复印教材得到遏制，正版教材发行得以提升。

在苏雨恒的带领下，高教社在版权引进方面坚持“以我为主，本土化设计”，致力于积极引进国外优质教育资源和前沿信息，这些引进版教材、学术著作填补了国内特定图书领域的空白，受到了广大读者的欢迎，在全国高校教育教学改革与发展中发挥了重要作用，同时为高教社创造了良好的社会效益和经济效益。在“走出去”方面，目前，高教社已与包括众多知名出版商在内的全球200多家合作伙伴开展了合作，30个语种版本的国际型产品行销世界60多个国家和地区，海外收入已达数千万元，并获得“世界知识产权组织创意金奖——单位奖”奖项。在我国图书版权贸易多年逆差的困境中，高教社版权输出数量在全国单体出版社中连年名列前茅。

数字化时代，版权的管理和开发面临更多挑战，苏雨恒带领高教人迎难而上，为应对数字化转型升级和版权发展的需要，将“版权业务管理和开发体系”作为推进高教社数字化转型升级“五大体系”之一，利用原有版权合同资源，开发多样化、个性化的版权衍生服务。在发挥传统出版的版权资源优势的同时，高教社借助数字化传播能力，寻求新的发展机遇，逐步实现互联网背景下传统出版业的重大突破，让版权切实成为数字化时代的效益来源。

中宣部负责“马工程”重点教材
咨询委员会委员、审议专家

（以姓氏笔画为序）

王伟光	王沪宁	王晓晖	王梦奎	王维澄
韦建桦	尹汉宁	龙新民	邢贲思	刘永治
刘国光	江 流	汝 信	孙 英	苏 星
李 捷	李卫红	李君如	李忠杰	李宝善
李景田	李慎明	冷 溶	张 宇	张文显
陈宝生	邵华泽	欧阳淞	金冲及	金炳华
周 济	郑必坚	郑科扬	侯树栋	逄先知
逄锦聚	袁贵仁	贾高建	顾海良	徐光春
黄坤明	龚育之	蒋乾麟	韩 震	虞云耀
雒树刚	滕文生	魏礼群		

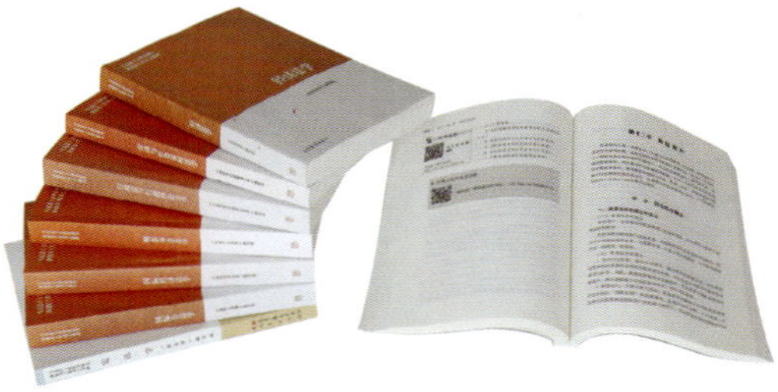

教育部负责“马工程”重点教材
审议委员会委员、审议专家

（以姓氏笔画为序）

马 敏	王一川	王浦劬	韦建桦	朱之文
杜玉波	李 龙	李 捷	李卫红	杨 河
杨圣敏	杨春贵	杨慧林	沈晓明	张 力
陈 炎	陈宝生	林尚立	郑杭生	胡树祥
胡培兆	胡德坤	逄锦聚	娄成武	洪银兴
袁贵仁	顾海良	徐显明	黄 进	韩 震
韩大元	童庆炳	谢维和	雷跃捷	

花繁枝秀香已馥

反映中国特色、中国风格、中国气派
“马工程”重点教材建设成果丰硕

深入推进马克思主义理论研究和建设工程（简称“马工程”）重点教材建设，加快构建适应中国特色社会主义发展要求、立足国际学术前沿、门类齐全的哲学社会科学教材体系，切实推动中国特色社会主义理论体系进教材进课堂进头脑，是贯彻落实十八大以来以习近平同志为核心的党中央对深入实施“马工程”做出的新决策新部署新要求的必然要求，是巩固马克思主义在意识形态领域指导地位的基础工程，是繁荣哲学社会科学的重大举措。

“马工程”重点教材基本覆盖哲学、政治经济学、科学社会主义以及政治学、社会学、法学、史学、新闻学、文学等哲学社会科学专业核心课，充分反映马克思主义中国化新成果、充分反映中国特色社会主义的丰富实践、充分反映本学科专业领域新进展。

高等教育出版社承担了绝大部分“马工程”重点教材的出版任务，目前已出版“马工程”重点教材 50 余种，并不断加大力度，提升“马工程”教材配套的数字资源建设数量和质量，提高线上内容与纸质教材一体化服务教学水平，为加强和改进新形势下高校思想政治工作提供有力支撑。

高等教育出版社

PEOPLE'S EDUCATION PRESS 人民教育出版社

人民教育出版社是教育主管部门所属的一家大型专业出版社，主要从事基础教育教材和其他各级各类教材及教育图书的研究、编写、编辑、出版和发行。人民教育出版社成立于1950年12月1日，首任社长兼总编辑是我国著名文学家、教育家、出版家叶圣陶先生。

为了加强基础教育课程和教材的研究工作，1983年经教育主管部门批准，成立课程教材研究所，与人民教育出版社合署办公，三十多年来，课程教材研究所先后承担了二十八项全国教育科学规划国家、国家教育主管部门重点课题，对基础教育课程、教材和教法进行了深入、系统研究，为全面提升人教版教材和图书的质量提供了有力保障。

2010年12月和2011年3月，中国教育出版传媒集团有限公司和中国教育出版传媒股份有限公司相继成立，人民教育出版社成为核心成员单位。

六十多年来，人民教育出版社在教育主管部门党组的领导下，主持或参与拟定了2000年以前历次中小学各科教学大纲；根据我国教育改革和发展的需要，先后研究、编写、出版了11套全国通用的中小学教材；累计出版各类出版物4万余种，发行量逾600亿册。

截至2014年初，人民教育出版社拥有员工1 000余人，其中主要从事研究、编写和编辑中小学教材任务的社本部有390余人。在社本部，共有博士56人（其中博士后4人）、硕士及同等学历者244人。在教材编写人员中，196人具有高级专业技术职务。作为我国中小学教材编写的“国家队”和“专业队”，人民教育出版社编辑机构设置齐全，共有政治、语文、数学、外语等22个编辑部门。人民教育出版社图书馆是我国中小学教材资料中心，藏有丰富的古今中外教材和其他教育文献。

为了适应市场经济发展和出版体制改革的需要，人民教育出版社围绕编写出版中小学教材的核心业务

人教社第28次全国中小学教材工作会

人教社数字出版工作会

进行内涵式扩展，先后设立了多个社属企业。其中，人教教材中心主要承担人民教育出版社的出版和发行业务；人民教育电子音像出版社主要承担人教版电子音像和其他多媒体出版物的编辑、制作、出版和发行业务；人教云汉数媒科技有限公司主要开发人教电子书包和建设优质数字教育资源，不断推出适合教学需要和市场需求的优质数字产品，实现人教版基础教育教材和教学资源的立体化、数字化和现代化。

改革开放以来，人民教育出版社以促进教育出版事业发展为宗旨，以丰富出版资源为目的，先后承担了联合国教科文组织、联合国儿童基金会、联合国人口基金、联合国开发计划署和世界银行等国际组织的多个项目；还与培生教育出版集团、圣智学习出版集团、日本光村图书出版株式会社、日本教科书研究中心、新加坡教育主管部门、新加坡泛太平洋教育出版有限公司、加拿大灵通教育有限公司、美国莫瑞州立大学、美国陶森大学、俄罗斯国立普希金俄语学院、韩国学中央研究院、韩国课程评估院和马来西亚华文学校“董教总”等二十多个国家及我国港澳台地区的出版机构和教育科研机构开展了广泛的交流与合作，取得了丰硕的成果。

近年来，人民教育出版社经营业绩稳步增长，各项事业持续发展，多次荣获中国出版政府奖、国家图书奖、中国图书奖、国家音像制品奖、国家电子出版物奖、国家期刊奖、中华优秀出版物奖和莫必斯国际多媒体作品大奖赛大奖等数十项荣誉；还先后荣获全国百佳图书出版单位、中国驰名商标、读者最喜爱的出版社、“讲信誉·重服务”出版单位、全国“两基”工作先进单位、全国语言文字工作先进集体、全国环境教育先进单位、全国民族团结进步先进集体、中央国家机关文明单位和北京市纳税百强企业等数百项荣誉。

在自身事业快速发展的同时，人教社始终不忘履行社会责任，坚持回报社会，奉献教育。上世纪八九十年代，人教社积极投身社会公益事业，编写出版培智、视障和听障等特殊教育教材，捐建叶圣陶纪念馆和河北平山希望学校等，大力支援贫困地区和灾区教育事业。自1995年以来，人教社通过捐款、捐物、援建学校等多种方式，向贫困地区、少数民族地区和灾区提供援助近1亿元，先后荣获中华慈善奖、全国教育援藏先进集体、新闻出版行业抗震救灾先进集体等荣誉。在国家教育主管部门等有关部门指导下，人教社还大力支援西部农村现代远程教育工程等重大项目建设，为我国基础教育发展做出了应有的贡献。

北京书展版权合作洽谈

举办书展活动《我是猫王波比克》《数数小狗有几只》新书发布会

重要奖项

圣智学习出版集团访问人教社

人教社主办“剑网2016”网络平台
销售出版物版权保护座谈会

美国书展版权合作洽谈

经过六十多年的发展，人民教育出版社形成了全方位、多样化、系列化、立体化的出版格局。全方位是指人民教育出版社的出版物涵盖了学前教育、基础教育、高等教育、师范教育、职业教育、成人教育、继续教育、民族教育、特殊教育、对外汉语教育等领域；多样化是指同一学科的人教版教材具有多个版本，具备不同风格，体现不同层次，满足不同教学需要；系列化是指各学科人教版教材均以教科书为核心，配以教学参考资料、教学辅助资料和教具学具等；立体化是指人教版出版物具备纸介质、电子音像、多媒体及数字出版物等形态。

如今，人民教育出版社已成为我国中小学教材和教育图书的建设基地，形成了独特的品牌优势、科研优势、人才优势、资源优势和市场优势；并形成了以研究、编写、编辑、出版和发行中小学教材和其他各级各类教材、教育图书为核心业务，以纸介质图书、电子音像和多媒体产品的出版和印制，版权贸易，图书及相关产品的物流服务，数字出版与服务等为辅助业务的经营格局，为进一步做强做大奠定了坚实的基础。

参加土耳其书展与当地机构交流

电影《李雷和韩梅梅》开机，人教社经典教材人物形象走上银幕

前往文字著作权协会就教科书法定许可等问题进行沟通

就图片版权基础知识及图片搜索技巧和方法对全社人员进行培训

回首过去，从借鉴国外经验，研究编写全国通用的中小学教材，到开发立体化中小学教材，提供全套中小学教材解决方案，人民教育出版社见证了我国基础教育发展的风雨历程。展望未来，伴随着我国基础教育和出版体制改革的步伐，人民教育出版社将充分利用中国教育出版传媒集团有限公司和中国教育出版传媒股份有限公司的制度优势、资金优势，建设成为国内一流、世界知名的出版机构，为促进我国教育出版事业的繁荣，为中华民族伟大复兴事业做出更大的贡献。

地址：北京市海淀区中关村南大街17号院1号楼 邮编：100081
电话：010－58758866 传真：010－58758877
网址：www.pep.com.cn 电子邮箱：pep@pep.com.cn

接力出版社
Publishing House

荣膺“第四届中国政府出版奖·先进出版单位奖”

以“创造、传承人类先进文化”为办社宗旨的接力出版社长期以来致力于打造优秀的青少年精神文化产品，不断推出优秀少儿出版物。坚持正确的政治方向和舆论导向，以社会效益为先，成为获“全国百佳图书出版单位”和伦敦书展“国际卓越奖”的出版社。

（一）坚持创新发展，社会效益成果显著

1．荣誉卓著

近年来，接力社荣誉卓著，2007年和2010年接力出版社蝉联第一届、第二届“中国出版政府奖”先进出版单位奖，2010年被评为“全国新闻出版行业文明单位”，2015年，接力出版社继李元君社长获“韬奋出版奖”之后，总编辑白冰获得第十二届“韬奋出版奖”，先后2名领军人物获“韬奋出版奖”。2016年，在伦敦书展和英国出版协会主办的“国际卓越奖”评选中，接力出版社荣获“国际儿童及青少年出版商奖”，是中国率先获得此奖项的出版单位，标志着中国出版企业向国际出版品牌迈进。

2．斩获众多图书大奖

长期以来，接力出版社以传承人类优秀文化、构建民族主流文化为己任，先后有《神脑聪仔》《阿笨猫全传》《巨人的城堡》《小英雄和芭蕾公主》《万物简史》《狼獾河》《黄琉璃》《当着落叶纷飞》《世界儿童文学阅读与经典》《黑狗哈拉诺亥》《我爱大自然》《云朵一样的八哥》等27种图书（或音像电子出版物）获得“五个一工程”奖、国家图书奖、中国图书奖、中国出版政府奖、中华优秀出版物奖等，500多种图书获省部级以上各类奖项，接力社连续八届获“五个一工程”奖。

3．引领市场畅销精品

接力出版社相继推出了包括“淘气包马小跳”系列、“鸡皮疙瘩”系列、“大王书”系列、“第一次发现”系列、“巴巴爸爸”系列、“蓝精灵”系列、“鼹鼠的故事系列”、“暮光之城”系列、“怪物大师”系列、“荒野求生”系列、刘墉励志系列等多种在市场上产生较大影响的品牌畅销图书。其中“淘气包马小跳”系列净销售码洋3.6亿元，“鸡皮疙瘩”系列净销售码洋1.57亿元，刘墉励志系列净销售码洋1.70亿元，“暮光之城”系列净销售码洋1.39亿元，“第一次发现”系列净销售码洋1.17亿元，“怪物大师”系列净销售码洋1.86亿元，“荒野求生”系列净销售码洋1.17亿元。

4．教材教辅稳定增长，完成大教育产品群的构建

接力出版社修订并通过了小学《音乐》《英语》2套国标教材，形成了以国标教材为核心资源，区域教育读物为基本的大教育产品群，尤其是《幼儿适应性发展课程》《小橘子幼儿启蒙读物》《接力宝贝》等幼儿课程资源，完成了产品群的构建，形成区内市场优势，并拓展区外市场。

（二）强调规范出版，建立健全质量保障体系，保证产品质量、工作质量、服务质量上乘

接力出版社始终高度重视图书质量保障体系建设，将质量视为出版社品牌的生命线。近年来，出版社进一步强调出版管理的规范化、制度化、科学化，通过不断规范标准，强化制度、完善管理，严抓图书质量管理，保证图书的精品品质。实施了精品出版战略，起到了完善质量保障体系、加强人才传帮带的作用。

（三）强化企业社会责任，加强思想道德建设，在公益捐赠及推广方面不遗余力

接力出版社自觉承担社会责任，强调文化接力、道德接力。接力出版社长期关注贫困失学儿童，积极参与“希望工程”建设，用自身的出版资源长期支援、帮扶少数民族地区的教育，在广西各少数民族地区建立起了10个未成年人思想道德教育基地，积极向社会图书馆、贫困山区小学捐赠图书，向四川、玉树地震灾区及冰冻灾区捐赠图书及款物。

（四）创新机制，积极探索和推动传统出版与新兴出版融合发展，谋求传统出版的转型升级

近年来，接力出版社创新机制，加快出版产业转型升级。接力出版社向国家文化发展产业扶植基金申报了“中国青少年多媒体阅读推广平台”项目并进入新闻出版改革发展项目库，平台的建成，将使少年儿童图书出版产业与新媒体、新网络结合，实现跨媒体、跨网、跨平台的新技术与少年儿童图书出版产业的融合，为青少年提供全方位阅读服务，强化出版产业链的整合与发展，有力推动传统出版的转型升级。

（五）积极贯彻实施“一带一路”战略，加强文化交流合作，努力扩大版权贸易，为进一步提高中华文化国际传播力、影响力做出积极贡献

接力出版社坚持“让中国孩子和世界孩子同步阅读，让外国孩子感受中国的精彩”的出版理念，为“走出去工程”建立长效机制。多年来，共输出图书（电子书）版权300种（其中英国、美国、法国、瑞典等西方国家超50种，东盟越南、马来西亚近200种，韩国及港澳台地区逾50种），为国际传播中国文化、倾听中国声音发挥了积极作用。2015 年，接力出版社组建接力出版社埃及分社，提高了国际影响力。

（六）健全法人治理结构，规范企业管理，注重企业党建工作。领导班子团结，廉洁自律，作风优良，具有较强的凝聚力和战斗力

长期以来，接力出版社做好人才培养，打造职业化、专业化、社会化的接力团队。坚持以党建促发展，以发展强党建。不断加强政治理论知识的学习，努力提高领导班子的思想政治素质；领导班子成员不断提升业务知识和工作管理水平，自觉深入基层调查研究，认真总结员工的新创造、新经验，增强了领导班子的凝聚力和战斗力，在他们的带领下和全体员工的共同努力下，接力出版社实现跨越发展，迈上新的台阶。

北京大学出版社 PEKING UNIVERSITY PRESS

北京大学出版社把发展版权贸易作为走向世界、融入国际社会、参与国际竞争的重要途径，在版权贸易工作中一直坚持“输出引进并举”的工作思路，并建立了让版权贸易健康发展的长效机制。目前，北京大学出版社已同几十个国家、地区的上百家出版社建立了业务往来。

北京大学出版社在引进版权图书上坚持“为我所需”和“双效并重”方针，坚持社会效益与经济效益并重，引进各种版权3 000余种。北大社组织翻译的一系列高质量的优秀外版图书，如《全球通史》《世界：一部历史》《美国人民》《科学的旅程》《哲学的邀请》《经济学原理》《批评官员的尺度》《轻松学韩语》等，受到读者的广泛欢迎，并多次获得各级图书奖。

近年来北京大学出版社积极响应党中央、国务院的中国文化“走出去”战略，立足于版权输出，整合全社资源，结合本社的发展规划，大力推进本社图书“走出去”工作。北大出版社根据自身的出版特点和优势，将对外汉语教材和人文社科类图书作为版权输出的重点领域，与剑桥大学出版社、荷兰博睿出版社、施普林格出版社等一批国际知名出版社展开深入广泛的合作，共向海外输出版权1 500余种，涉及英语、德语、法语、俄语、泰语、越南语等十几个语种。其中《中华文明史》成功输出了英文版、日文版、韩文版、塞尔维亚文版、匈牙利文版和印地文版，《解读中国经济》成功输出了英文版、日文版、韩文版、德文版、阿拉伯文版、泰文版、吉尔吉斯文版等，出版后在国际市场上产生了良好反响。北大社获得“经典中国国际出版工程”、“中国图书对外推广计划”、“中华文化著作翻译出版工程”、“丝路书香工程”重点翻译资助项目、“外国人写作中国计划”、“中华学术外译项目”等“走出去”项目立项共计120项。

北京大学出版社是“中国图书对外推广计划”工作小组成员单位之一，并被国家商务主管部门、国家文化主管部门、国家广电主管部门、国家新闻出版主管部门联合认定为2007—2008年度、2009—2010年度、2011—2012年度、2013—2014年度、2015—2016年度“国家重点文化出口企业”，2011年因版权输出成绩突出被评为全国“新闻出版走出去先进单位”，2012年获评北京市新闻出版和版权工作先进集体，2013年荣获“中国版权影响力企业”称号。

北大社荣获“中国图书对外推广计划优秀奖”

《解读中国经济》阿拉伯文版新书发布

德古意特出版社来访北大社展台

《解读中国经济》阿拉伯文版亮相阿布扎比书展

北大社与德古意特出版社签署合作协议

中国人民大学出版社

中国人民大学出版社成立于 1955 年，是中华人民共和国成立后建立的第一家大学出版社。作为中国重要的高校教材和学术著作出版基地，人大出版社始终秉承“出教材学术精品，育人文社科英才”的出版理念，实施精品战略。建社 60 多年来已累计出书 25 000 余种，出版了一大批具有文明传播、文化累积价值的优秀教材和学术著作。新世纪以来，人大出版社的优秀出版物获得省部级以上奖项 500 多项，是荣获国家级奖项最多的出版社之一。作为图书、音像、电子、网络和数字出版物等多媒体兼营的大型综合性出版社，人大出版社已成为我国哲学社会科学出版的重镇和旗舰。

多年来，人大出版社致力于搭建国际文化交流平台，极大推动了中外学术文化交流。人大出版社以高端学术著作国际出版为特色，已累计输出图书版权近 2 300 种，涉及 27 个语种，与 30 多个国家和地区的百余家出版机构建立了合作伙伴关系，并在以色列、罗马尼亚、蒙古设立海外分支机构，有效推动中国文化“走出去”。通过搭建国际出版平台，人大出版社倾力打造国家出版名片，努力讲好中国故事、传播好中国声音、阐释好中国特色，不断增强中国文化国际传播的软实力。

新中国的大学出版事业，从这里开始

人大出版社连续 9 届获得“中国图书对外推广计划”版权输出单体出版社排名前两名

刘延东副总理为中国人民大学共建的土耳其首个“中国馆”揭牌，人大出版社出版的《中国之路》《大国的责任》《中国的抉择》等英文版图书在“中国馆”重点展示

中埃文化年中国高等教育展，刘延东副总理视察中国人民大学展台并特别鼓励，人大出版社在“走出去”方面做得很好

人大出版社与尼泊尔白莲花出版社签署合作协议

人大出版社以色列分社揭牌仪式

人大出版社在黎巴嫩举办系列文化活动庆祝两国建交四十五周年

中国—罗马尼亚学术出版合作中心揭牌仪式

人大出版社在美国书展主宾国活动中成绩优异获总局表彰

人大出版社在蒙古设立中国主题图书翻译出版中心

★ 2014 年中国图书评论学会“大众好书榜”
★ 2014 年“中国好书”第十届文津图书奖推荐图书
★ 第十二届向全国青少年推荐百种优秀图书
★ 第六届中华优秀出版物奖

★ 第十二届向全国青少年推荐百种优秀图书

★ 第四届中国科普作家协会优秀科普作品奖

★ 第五届中华优秀出版物图书提名奖

★ 2015 年向全国老年人推荐优秀出版物

★ 2015 年百强报刊 2016 年期刊数字影响力 100 强

人民邮电出版社成立于 1953 年 10 月，是具有 60 多年历史的大型科技出版社。建社以来，始终坚持“立足文化产业、面向现代社会、传播科学知识、服务科教兴国，为走中国特色新型工业化道路服务”的出版宗旨，不断改革进取，目前图书出版领域涵盖信息技术、少儿、经管、摄影、集邮、旅游、心理学、军事、家庭教育等。2016 年出版新书 2 912 种，再版图书 4 742 种，出版物总销售码洋达 16.12 亿元。计算机类、艺术类、摄影类、科普类、美术类、经管类、运动与休闲类、旅游类、少儿类图书的零售市场占有率位居前列。人民邮电出版社还出版《无线电》《集邮》《通信学报》《大数据》《米老鼠》《童趣》等 18 种期刊，年出版音像电子出版物1 000余种，网络出版物1 000余种。

人民邮电出版社近年来荣获了“全国优秀出版社”、“全国百佳图书出版单位”、“全国文明单位”、“中央国家机关文明单位标兵”、“首都文明单位标兵”、“全国新闻出版行业文明单位”、“全国图书对外版权贸易先进单位”、“讲信誉、重服务”出版单位等荣誉称号，成为“数字出版转型示范单位”，并连续三届荣获中国出版政府奖先进出版单位称号。历年来，有数百种图书、期刊和音像电子出版物获得了中国出版政府奖图书奖、中华优秀出版物、向全国青少年推荐百种优秀图书、国家期刊奖等荣誉。

人民邮电出版社拥有遍及全国四通八达的发行渠道和国内外众多的合作伙伴，已发展成为集图书、期刊和数字出版于一体的综合性科技出版大社，为广大读者提供了丰富优质的精神食粮，取得了良好的社会效益。

人民邮电出版社
POSTS & TELECOM PRESS

地址：北京市丰台区成寿寺路 11 号邮电出版大厦
邮编：100164
电话：010－81055137（社长办公室）
010－81055315（总编室）
010－81055059（发行部）
传真：010－81055044
网址：www.ptpress.com.cn
电子邮箱：315@ptpress.com.cn

人民音乐出版社
PEOPLE'S MUSIC PUBLISHING HOUSE

人民音乐出版社1954年建社，六十余年来始终践行“用音乐记录历史，用出版记录音乐”的出版理想，始终坚守“责任第一、质量第一、诚信为本、读者为先”的事业担当，策划出版了多品种、高品质的音乐学术图书、专业乐谱、中小学教材、学术期刊和音像制品，始终注重优秀民族音乐文化的传承和传播，不断推进中国优秀音乐作品版权资源的积累与开发，努力探索中国现当代音乐原创作品版权的保护与运营，积极打造民族音乐文化的重点出版项目，有效推动中国本土音乐的海外传播。多次获得国家新闻出版主管部门、中国出版协会、中国出版集团公司、北京市版权主管部门“输出版优秀图书奖”“优秀走出去奖”等奖项，荣获“全国百佳出版单位”“全国新闻出版行业文明单位”“中直工委先进基层党组织”“首都文明单位”“中国出版政府奖·图书奖”“中国出版政府奖·先进出版单位奖”等荣誉。

2016年11月25日，在中国版权协会主办的第九届中国版权年会上，人民音乐出版社荣获相关荣誉奖项。

青岛出版集团 QINGDAO PUBLISHING GROUP | 城市传媒 CITY MEDIA | 青岛出版社 QINGDAO PUBLISHING HOUSE

兼具系统性、规模性、专业性的
大型儿童文学研究学术丛书

《中国儿童文学名家论集》

- 2017年国家出版基金资助项目
- 荟萃儿童文学理论界10位重量级学者的学术精要

定价：680.00元　出版时间：2017年6月

这是一套具有很高学术价值的理论文丛，汇聚了当下中国儿童文学理论界具有学术影响力的10位中坚学者：吴其南、金燕玉、王泉根、刘绪源、班马、孙建江、朱自强、汤锐、彭懿、方卫平。他们是中国儿童文学学术进程的重要参与者和见证者，其学术贡献更是中国当代儿童文学理论史上重要的一笔。

这套丛书，内容涉及中国儿童文学的历史发展、理论进程、创作思想、作家作品研究、儿童文化产业透析等方面，具有很高的学术价值和史料价值，可作为图书馆馆藏、学术研究、儿童文学爱好者等的藏书。

集团官方微信　青岛微书城

地址：青岛市海尔路182号　邮编：266061　电话：0532-68068608　传真：0532-68068607　网址：www.qdpub.com

时代出版

时代出版传媒股份有限公司于2008年由安徽出版集团以其所持有的出版、印刷等文化传媒类资产在全国率先以出版业务整体上市，目前拥有全资或控股子公司23家，其中有9家出版社。公司成立以来，高度重视版权推广运用，大力实施文化“走出去”战略，把版权作为提高出版竞争力、抢占竞争制高点、推动文化产业发展的重要战略资源，以版权输出提升文化影响力，增进国际文化交流。

近年来，公司不断创新发展模式，积极推进资本合作，积极开发互联网平台，有效促进版权数字化转变，加快版权资源产业化进程，加快“走出去”由简单版权贸易向新媒体、新业态转型，由传统合作模式向多元化国际合作转型的步伐，实现了从产品“走出去”到产业“走出去”、从出版“走出去”到文化“走进去”、从产业项目化到资本国际化的巨大飞跃。

公司先后荣获全国文化体制改革先进单位、国家文化出口重点企业、新闻出版“走出去”先进单位等诸多荣誉，连续8年被评为“国家文化出口重点企业”，连续9年在北京国际图书博览会上版权输出全国领先。近两年，又先后获得中国图书对外推广计划2016优秀奖、2017BIBF优秀版权贸易输出奖，是2016年荣获“中国版权金奖”的地方出版企业。

图片注释

① 第24届BIBF展会上，安徽出版集团暨时代出版举办“唱响主旋律，迎接十九大主题出版物丝路行”盛大签约仪式　② 时代出版传媒广场　③“丝路童书联盟”合作论坛　④ 2016年“一带一路”国际出版联盟签约仪式暨《丝路霓裳》发布会　⑤ 时代出版传媒股份有限公司旗下三家出版社于新加坡友联书局设立“一带一路 共建繁荣”主题书柜

教育科学出版社

全国百佳图书出版单位　国家一级出版单位
中国出版政府奖先进出版单位

联合国教科文组织
教育理念典藏系列

2015 年联合国教科文组织国际高级专家组提交的报告，重新思考不断变化的世界中的教育

《反思教育：向"全球共同利益"的理念转变？》
RETHINKING EDUCATION: TOWARDS A GLOBAL COMMON GOOD?
联合国教科文组织 编 联合国教科文组织总部中文科 译

重申人文主义教育观，对教育再次做出高瞻远瞩的思考
教育和知识是全球共同利益

1996 年由雅克 · 德洛尔任主席的国际 21 世纪教育委员会向联合国教科文组织提交的报告

《教育——财富蕴藏其中》
LEARNING：THE TREASURE WITHIN
联合国教科文组织 编 联合国教科文组织总部中文科 译

教育：必要的乌托邦
学会求知、学会做事、学会共处、学会生存

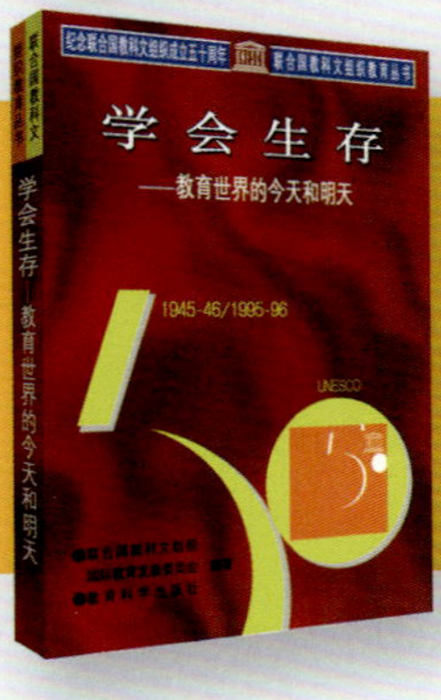

1972 年由埃德加 · 富尔任主席的国际教育发展委员会向联合国教科文组织提交的报告

《学会生存——教育世界的今天和明天》
LEARNING TO BE: THE WORLD OF EDUCATION TODAY AND TOMORROW
联合国教科文组织国际教育发展委员会 编著 华东师范大学比较教育研究所 译

如果我们要学习的所有东西都必须不断地重新发明和日益更新，
那么我们必须强调终身教育和学习化社会

教育科学出版社
ESPH Educational Science Publishing House

地　址：北京市朝阳区安慧北里安园甲9号　邮　编：100101
电　话：(86)-(010)-64989003　64989009
传　真：(86)-(010)-64891796
网　址：http://www.esph.com.cn

教科社微信订阅号

①

浙江教育出版集团

②

③

④

浙江教育出版集团有限公司前身为成立于1983年的浙江教育出版社，2016年1月，经国家新闻出版主管部门批准，变更组建集团，简称浙江教育出版集团。建社以来，始终以“服务教育，繁荣学术，积累文化”为宗旨，主要从事教材、文教读物、科普读物、大众读物以及教育学、心理学等学术著作的出版发行。

30余年来，浙江教育出版集团立足教育，出版了近千种中小学教材，包括600余种国标教材和浙江省九年制义务教育教材，200余种地方教材，以及幼儿教材、培智教材、专题教材等。21世纪初国家课程改革启动，浙江教育出版集团是全国新课标教材13家出版社之一，教材相继在全国十多个省、自治区、直辖市和400多个县区使用，年使用学生数超过1 000万。浙江教育出版集团依托丰富的内容和作者资源，出版了大量的文教读物和大众读物，其中《中国少年儿童百科全书》畅销25年，累计销售400多万套。30多年来，学术出版、主题出版成果丰硕，共获得国家各种图书奖项18个，入选国家出版项目45个。

浙江教育出版集团先后荣获“全国百佳图书出版单位”“中国出版政府奖先进出版单位”等称号。据《2015年新闻出版产业分析报告》，浙江教育出版集团总体经济规模在地方图书出版单位中居前列。

图片注释

① 2016年7月，领导合影　② 国标教材　③ “大国教育战略研究”　④ 《中国少年儿童百科全书》

上海译文出版社

上海译文出版社成立于1978年1月1日，是一家出版有关外国文学、外国哲学社会科学、外国风俗文化的翻译图书，外语工具书，外语语言教材的大型综合性翻译出版社。拥有近十个主要语种的专业外语编辑和大批享誉国内外的优秀译者队伍，每年出版各类图书、音像制品700余种，期刊5种。

在外国文学出版领域，译文社着力良多，声誉卓著。在一百多位诺贝尔文学奖得主中，译文社出版了其中大多数作家的重要作品或代表作；在当代世界公认的一百多位文学大师中，译文社出版了其中60多位的完整作品系列。在哲学社会领域，译文社引进出版的大批优秀读物对学术界的思想解放产生了巨大影响。译文社还出版多语种国内权威而规模较大的双语词典。

早在1993年，上海译文出版社就成为国家宣传主管部门、新闻出版主管部门表彰的16家“全国优秀出版社”之一，并连续荣获“上海市文明单位”称号。2009年又被新闻出版主管部门评为“全国百佳图书出版单位”。2012年被人力资源和社会保障主管部门和新闻出版主管部门授予“全国新闻出版系统先进集体”称号。2013年荣获“2013年中国版权影响力企业”称号。2014年被上海市新闻出版主管部门授予“上海数字出版转型示范单位”称号。2014年译文社社标被评为“上海市著名商标”。2015年被上海市语言文字工作委员会授予“2015年上海市语言文字工作先进集体”称号。2016年译文社的《英汉大词典》（第2版）荣获“2016年中国版权金奖”。

译文社设有专门的版权室，负责处理与版权引进和输出有关各项事务以及打击侵权盗版。目前引进图书约3 500种，输出词典工具书数字权利和文学经典译本300多种，累计收入人民币4 000多万元。在打击侵权盗版方面，译文社也做了大量工作，以维护权利人和出版社的合法权益。译文社版权室因卓有成效的工作实绩获得“2001—2003年度上海市劳动模范集体”和“2007年上海市三八红旗集体”的殊荣。

地址：上海市福建中路193号15—17楼　电话：021-53594508转　邮编：200001　网址：www.stph.com.cn

陕西师范大学出版总社

SHAANXI NORMAL UNIVERSITY GENERAL PUBLISHING HOUSE

1

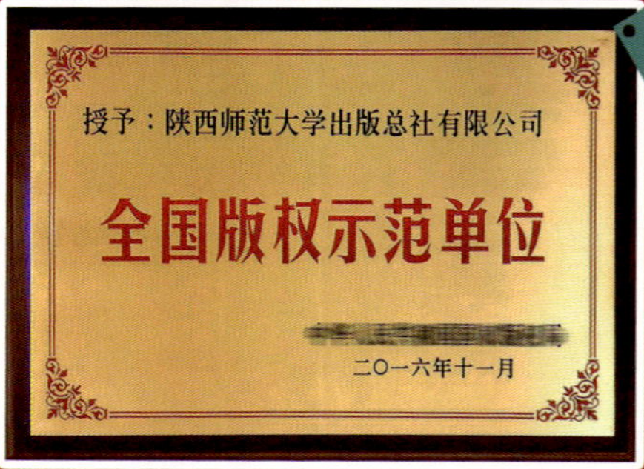

2

3

陕西师范大学出版社成立于1985年，于2010年成立陕西师范大学出版总社，是集图书、期刊、电子音像、数字出版、教育文化服务于一体的综合出版传媒机构。出版的一大批图书荣获“国家图书奖”“中国图书奖”“中华优秀出版物奖”“鲁迅文学奖”“中国好书”等重大奖项。出版的8种“中学教学参考”期刊全部被国家新闻出版广电主管部门评为学术期刊，其中7种入选全国中文核心期刊。

陕西师范大学出版总社有健全的版权保护制度，注重版权宣传教育，努力提升全员版权意识；建立软件正版化管理制度，软件正版化率达100%。积极响应“走出去”战略，不断完善“走出去”考核机制，设立专项奖励，已与俄罗斯、美国、韩国等国家的出版机构建立合作关系，拓展版权业务。引进版权图书两百余种，输出版权图书近百种，国际合作能力显著增强。2015年被陕西省版权主管部门授予“陕西省版权示范单位”称号，2016年被国家版权主管部门授予“全国版权示范单位”荣誉称号。

4 5 6

7

8

图片注释

①2016年总社被国家版权主管部门授予“全国版权示范单位”称号 ②2017年5月，美国南犹他州大学出版社社长理查德·桑德斯博士一行到总社交流访问，签署合作备忘录 ③2016年3月，总社图书《在西北局的日子里》向韩国东文选出版社输出版权 ④《先前的风气》向中国台湾地区九歌出版社输出版权 ⑤《现代口承神话的民族志研究》向中国台湾地区秀威资讯公司输出版权 ⑥《秦朝穿越指南》（台湾版图书更名为《回到秦朝大冒险》）向中国台湾时报文化出版公司输出版权 ⑦总社精品图书 ⑧2016年9月，在俄罗斯莫斯科国际书展上，总社董事长兼社长刘东风（右）与莫斯科俄语出版社社长斯维特兰娜·列米佐娃签订合作互译出版协议

华东师范大学出版社　给您一个智慧的人生

1957 — 2017

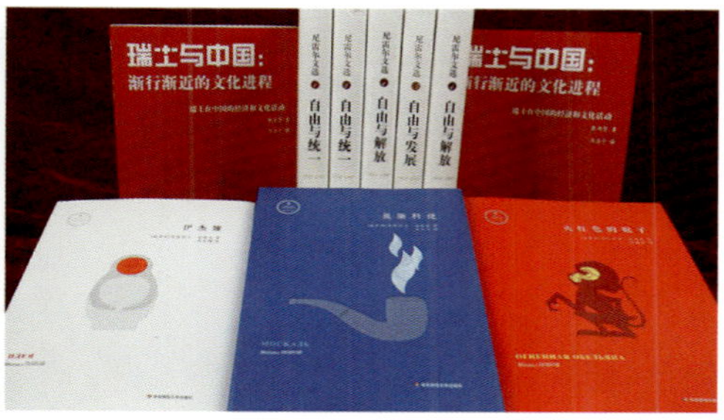

华东师范大学出版社创建于 1957 年 6 月。秉承大夏大学（华东师大前身）的人文精神，依托华东师范大学深厚的学术底蕴，形成了以大教育为出版宗旨的综合性出版特色。

在版权创造、运用、保护和管理等方面，华东师范大学出版社一直处于出版行业的领先地位。以“做有理想、有情怀的出版人，出有社会效益的优质精品图书，以图书出版促进国家文化繁荣，产生良好的社会影响”为社会责任目标，专注于出版精品图书。原创图书屡获嘉奖，其中《中国文字发展史》获第四届中国出版政府奖图书奖。践行“服务外交”的神圣使命，坚持精品、高端的引进策略，译介了大批国外优秀的教育学、心理学及人文社会科学著作，推动了相关学科研究与国际水平的接轨。积极响应新闻出版“走出去”的号召，加强与“一带一路”沿线国家和欧美发达国家一流出版企业的战略合作，逐渐形成了以立体化的多学科优质教育资源“走出去”为主导的版权输出特色。

华东师范大学出版社注册商标“ECNUP”为上海市著名商标，“华东师大版一课一练”注册商标为上海市著名商标。

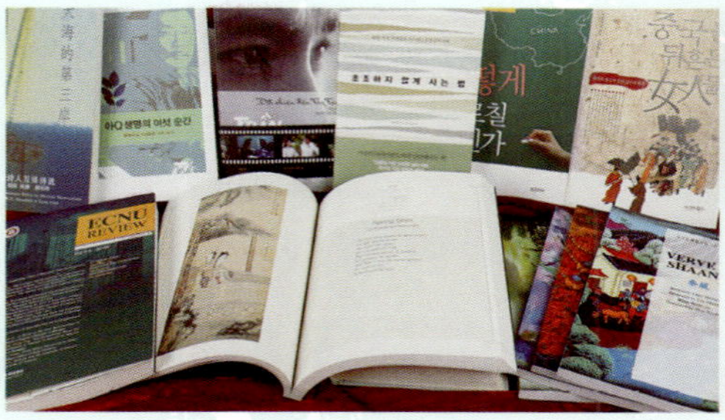

- **全国百佳图书出版单位**
- **全国版权示范单位**
- **上海市知识产权示范企业**
- **第四届中国出版政府奖先进出版单位**
- **全国图书版权输出先进出版单位**
- **上海市版权示范单位**

ECNUP

明天出版社

明天出版社是一家出版少年儿童读物的专业出版社。长期以来，明天出版社一直坚持正确的出版导向、坚持社会效益第一，以向广大少年儿童提供精美的精神食粮为己任，出版了一大批社会效益、经济效益俱佳的精品图书。转企改制后，明天出版社确立了“以内容创意为核心，立足传统图书出版，着眼于全媒体，面向整个文化产业”的战略发展规划，把确保图书的质量、努力为少年儿童打造精品图书作为求生存、谋发展的着力点，抓好原创少儿读物的出版工作，以高质量、高品位、高格调的精品图书赢得读者、赢得市场。近几年，明天出版社一直处于全国同行业领先地位，综合经济实力位居全国少儿出版社第3名，全国少儿图书市场出版社市场占有率第3名。先后被国家新闻出版主管部门评为“全国一级出版社”“全国百佳图书出版单位”，多次被国家人力资源和社会保障主管部门、国家新闻出版主管部门评为“全国新闻出版系统先进集体”。

文学类

《樱花巷的秘密》

“杨红樱成长小说系列”

《消失的请假条》

《我是学霸我怕谁》

《祝你天天都长高》

《宝塔》

《雄鹰飞翔》

《方卫平精选文学读本》

《埃里希·凯斯特纳作品典藏》

低幼类

《秦文君温暖绘本》

《金波花环诗》

《妈妈是地上一朵花》

《金谷粒桥梁书》

知识类

《马小跳发现之旅》

“少年哲学智慧启蒙丛书”

《大嚼科学》

欢迎关注明天出版社微信

联系地址：济南市市中区万寿路19号 联系电话：0531-82098622

曹文轩绘本馆

《烟》

用诗意的语言讲述了一个关于理解和宽容的故事

英国皇家艺术学院艺术学硕士、布拉迪斯拉发国际插画双年展（BIB）金苹果奖得主　郁蓉／图

获奖记录：2015 年陈伯吹国际儿童文学奖绘本奖，塞尔维亚国际书展插画奖，入选 2017 韩国南怡岛国际图画书奖大赛，2017 韩国南怡岛国际儿童插画奖紫岛奖

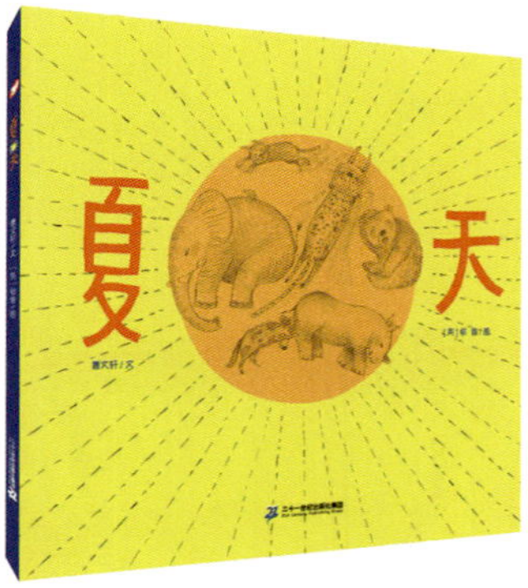

《夏天》

东方哲学＋剪纸艺术，教孩子学会“爱与被爱”的妙趣图画书

获奖记录：原创图画书 2015 年度排行榜 TOP10，2015 十大中国原创新书，入选 2016 年德国国际青少年图书馆“白乌鸦书单”

《鸟和冰山的故事》

安静、单纯却充满力量的故事，带你领悟友情和爱油画的开阔和质感，带你领略艺术之美

信谊图画书奖佳作奖、张乐平绘本奖获得者　弯弯／图

获奖记录：“2016 年不可错过的 15 种好童书”（《中华读书报》评选）

《笨笨驴系列》（第一、二辑）

开启儿童心灵成长之旅

博洛尼亚插画奖得主　王祖民／图

凤凰传媒 PHOENIX MEDIA

江苏凤凰少年儿童出版社有限公司

PHOENIX JUVENILE AND CHILDREN'S PUBLISHING LTD.

江苏凤凰少年儿童出版社是以少年儿童为读者对象的专业出版社，主要出版文学、动漫、低幼、知识、教育等少儿读物，《美术》《音乐》《书法练习指导》等国标教材，以及《东方宝宝》《东方娃娃》《儿童故事画报》《少年文艺》《凤凰动漫》《我爱学》《幼儿100》《七彩语文》《兴趣阅读》等少儿期刊。产品赢得多项国家大奖，在业内和读者中享有良好声誉，被评为“全国百佳图书出版单位”，和海外出版社及版权代理商保持良好合作关系，形成版权输出平台，曹文轩、黄蓓佳、金波、程玮、单瑛琪等一大批名家原创作品走向世界各地，其中《青铜葵花》输出到法国、德国、意大利、英国、韩国、越南、斯洛文尼亚、埃及、日本等13个国家。

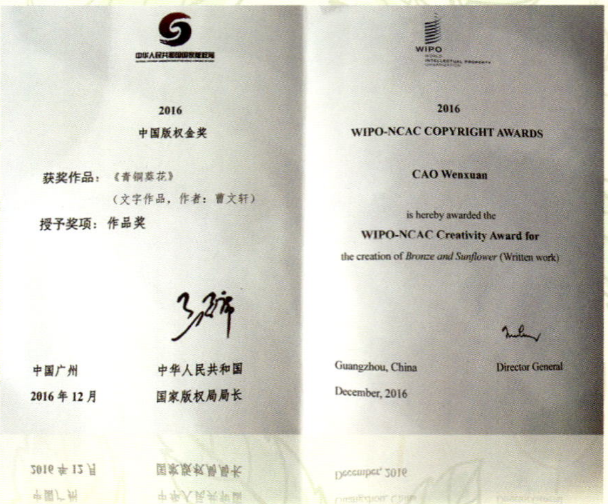

2016

中国版权金奖

获奖作品：《青铜葵花》

（文字作品，作者：曹文轩）

授予奖项：作品奖

中国广州　　中华人民共和国

2016年12月　　国家版权局局长

WIPO

2016

WIPO-NCAC COPYRIGHT AWARDS

CAO Wenxuan

is hereby awarded the

WIPO-NCAC Creativity Award for

the creation of *Bronze and Sunflower* (Written work)

Guangzhou, China　　Director General

December, 2016

2016年《青铜葵花》获得中国版权金奖（作品奖）

敬请关注　新浪微博 weibo.com　江苏凤凰少年儿童出版社 http://weibo.com/jiangsushaoer

地址：南京市湖南路1号A座　邮编：210009　电话：025-83314977

微信公众号

北京大学医学出版社
PEKING UNIVERSITY MEDICAL PRESS

关注医读
获取更多新书信息

打造精品 服务医学

北京大学医学出版社成立于1989年8月，是教育主管部门直属的重点大学出版社。建社20多年来，该社先后荣获国家多次荣誉表彰，并于2009年被新闻出版主管部门评估为“国家一级出版社”，授予“全国百佳图书出版单位”的荣誉称号。该社坚持“学术为本，教材优先”的办社理念，经过多年的耕耘， 已发展成为国内医学教材及专著、译著的重要出版基地。20多年来，该社共出版医学图书4 000余种 ，发行量达4 000余万册。该社以“高质量、高品位、高水平、多层次”的品牌理念， 成为社会信誉度很高的大学出版社。该社先后共有近30套（册）图书各类图书获得出版界各类大奖，包括中国出版政府奖（图书奖）、中华优秀出版物奖、国家图书奖等。自国家出版基金推出以来，该社共有七大项目获得国家出版基金支持。多部著作入选“十二五” “十三五”国家重点出版物出版规划项目、 “三个‘一百’”原创出版工程，多部译著荣获全国引进版科技类优秀图书。

“‘十二五’ 普通高等教育本科规划教材”
“中国高等教育学会医学教育专业委员会规划教材”

《血管生物学》（第2版）
第六届中华优秀出版物获奖图书

“泌尿外科学”
国家出版基金项目

《米勒麻醉学》（第8版）
麻醉学经典教科书

地 址 | 北京市海淀区学院路38号
电 话 | 010-82802230（市场部） 82802495（邮购）
网 址 | www.pumpress.com.cn
邮 编 | 100191

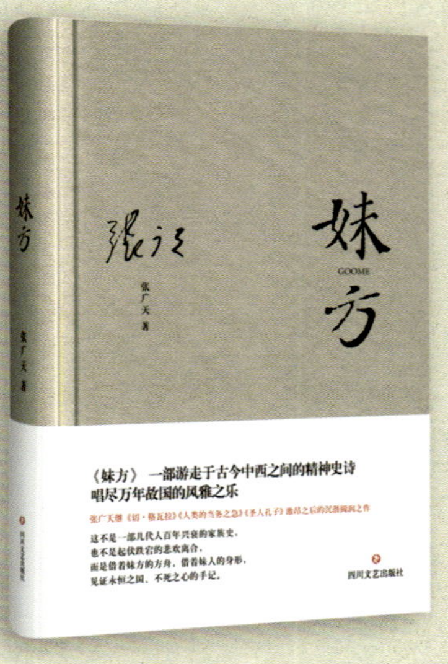

《妹方》

张广天继《切格瓦拉》《圣人孔子》激昂之后的沉潜圆润之作，一部游走于古今中西之间的精神史诗，唱尽万年故国的风雅之乐。

韩少功　侯德健　孟京辉　史　航

孔庆东　李亚伟　韩毓海　张　锰

诚挚推荐

《大地的阶梯》

茅盾文学奖得主阿来非虚构经典，重返嘉绒藏地，对《尘埃落定》的精神探源。有时候，离开是一种更本质意义上的切近与归来。

《阿来的诗》

茅盾文学奖得主阿来完备的诗歌作品集，对阿来多年诗歌创作成就的集中展示。

我的表达是从诗歌开始；我的阅读，我从文字中得到的感动也是从诗歌开始。可以说，诗歌丰富了我的生命，也丰富了我的文学生命。

——阿来

《狗孩格拉》

茅盾文学奖得主阿来长篇少年小说，讲述成长的诗意与苦难，致敬人性温暖之作。

我愿意写出生命所经历的磨难、罪过、悲苦，但我更愿意写出经历过这一切后，人性的温暖。

——阿来

《阿古顿巴》

茅盾文学奖得主阿来写给少年的藏式寓言、成长诗篇。

我也有过一个那样面孔脏污，眼光却泉水般清洁明亮的童年！想起日益远去的童年时光，内心总有一种隐隐的痛楚与莫名的忧伤！

——阿来

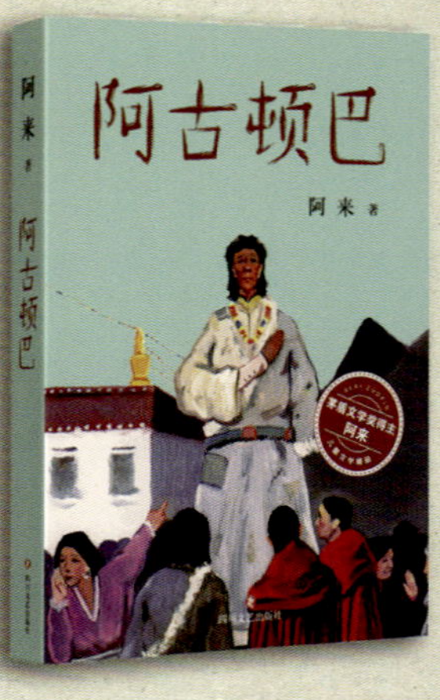

中国版权产业网（www.cncri.com）是中国版权产业领域具有权威性和实用性的专业网站。

网站秉承“**立足版权、服务产业**”的宗旨，依托版权领域权威管理部门、协会团体、司法和研究机构等优势资源力量，深入解析版权产业单位的实际需求，为版权产业相关单位和权利人提供资讯传播、宣传推广、会展培训、公关企划、法律支持、金融和中介代理等诸多专业服务，合作伙伴遍及新闻出版、影视制作、网络视频、动漫卡通、软件游戏、书画艺术、音乐音像以及版权运营、版权服务等诸多版权产业相关领域。

咨询电话：**010-58604520**　　中国版权产业QQ群：**211815826**

扫一扫关注

知网众思 智汇天下

OKMS 机构知识管理与协同创新整体解决方案

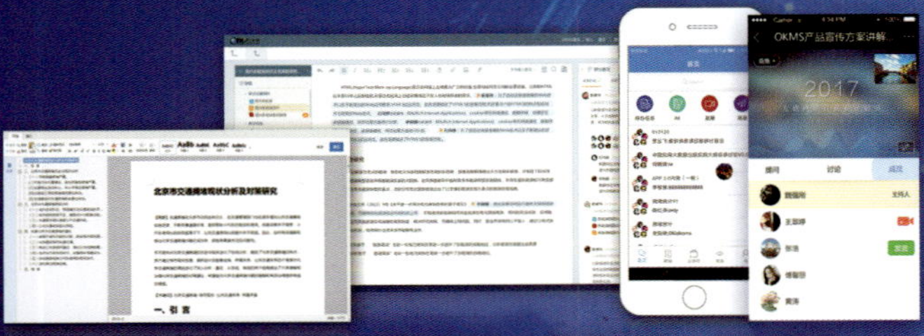

电话：010-62791950
传真：010-62969002-6000
E-mail：okms@cnki.net

知识管理 + 知识服务 + 开放协同 + 知识创新

核心功能

- 机构知识仓库
- 协同研究
- 协同研讨
- 协同创作
- 学习培训
- 即时通信
- 在线直播
- 个人知识管理

应用价值

- ✓ 整合单位内外部知识，统一服务
- ✓ 单位内部业务协同和知识创新
- ✓ 员工学习及岗位技能创新能力培训
- ✓ 信息化基础设施和创新体系支撑

典型用户

构建全媒体、碎片化机构知识仓库，沉淀知识资产

实现机构内外部各种知识资源的一站式发现与获取，为研究和创新提供基础支持

- 整合多维多源知识资源，统一仓储，统一服务
- 异构知识资源混合排序，相互关联
- 机构内部文档实现XML碎片化检索和展示
- 按部门和业务体系进行组织导航
- 内部研究和创新成果可归档和分享

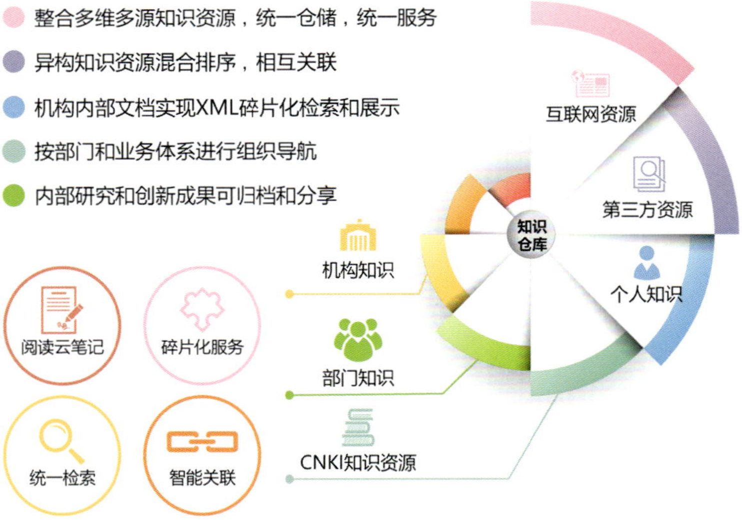

整体解决方案

- 面向决策的智库
- 面向科研管理
- 面向协同创新中心
- 面向企业知识管理
- 面向内容写作
- 面向技术创新

版权相关产业与版权贸易

BAN QUAN XIANG GUAN CHAN YE YU BAN QUAN MAO YI

2015 年中国版权产业的经济贡献

中国版权产业经济贡献调研课题组

一、2015 年中国版权产业经济贡献的主要数据

经过调查测算，2015 年中国版权产业的行业增加值为 50 054.14 亿元人民币，比上年增长了 3 766.33 亿元，增长率为 8.14%①，占全国 GDP 的 7.30%，比上年提高了 0.02 百分点；城镇单位就业人数 1 666.90 万人，比上年增长了 2.19 万人，占全国城镇单位就业总人数的 9.23%，比上年提高了 0.12 百分点；商品出口额为 2 633.36 亿美元，比上年减少了 311.56 亿美元，占全国商品出口总额的 11.58%，比上年下降了 0.99 百分点（见表 1）。

表 1　　2015 年中国版权产业的经济贡献

类型	行业增加值		就业人数		商品出口额	
	数值（亿元人民币）	占全国比重	数值（万人）	占全国比重	数值（亿美元）	占全国比重
核心	30 229.87	4.41%	870.40	4.82%	72.85	0.32%
相互依存	8 966.17	1.31%	412.49	2.28%	2 344.83	10.31%
部分	3 811.12	0.56%	233.18	1.29%	215.67	0.95%
非专用支持	7 046.98	1.03%	150.82	0.84%	—	—
合计	50 054.14	7.30%	1 666.90	9.23%	2 633.36	11.58%

调研数据表明，中国版权产业发展势头良好，行业增加值持续增长，在国民经济中的比重逐步上升，在推动经济发展、优化经济结构中发挥着越来越重要的作用，成为中国经济发展的新引擎。

二、2006—2015 年中国版权产业经济贡献的综合分析

自 2007 年中国国家版权局和世界知识产权组织联合委托中国新闻出版研究院开展“中国版权产业的经济贡献调研”以来，该工作已经走过十年历程，连续对 2006 年至 2015 年十个年度中国版权产业的经济贡献进行了调查研究。通过十年的数据分析可以发现，2006 年至 2015 年中国版权产业的发展势头良好，行业增加值持续增长，占 GDP 的比重稳步提升，吸纳就业人员的能力不断增强，对外贸易规模有所扩大；版权产业的结构得到优化，核心版权产业的作用日益增强；与美国等发达国家的差距逐渐缩小。中国版权产业在推动经济发展中发挥着越来越重要的作用，为“稳增长、调结构、惠民生”做出了积极贡献。具体来看，十年间中国版权产业具有如下几个发展特点：

（一）中国版权产业的行业增加值持续增长，占 GDP 的比重稳步提升

2006 年至 2015 年，中国版权产业的行业增加值从 13 489.33 亿元人民币增长到 50 054.14 亿元人民币，十年间翻了近两番，占 GDP 的比重也从 6.39%提高至 7.30%，十年间提高了 0.91 百分点（见图 1）。

从增速上看，中国版权产业行业增加值的增长速度整体上高于 GDP 的增长速度。2006 年至 2015 年间中国 GDP 的年均增长率为 13.49%，而同期中国版权产业行业增加值的年均增长率为 15.68%，

① 本报告中的所有增长率均为名义增长率，即未考虑价格因素，下同。

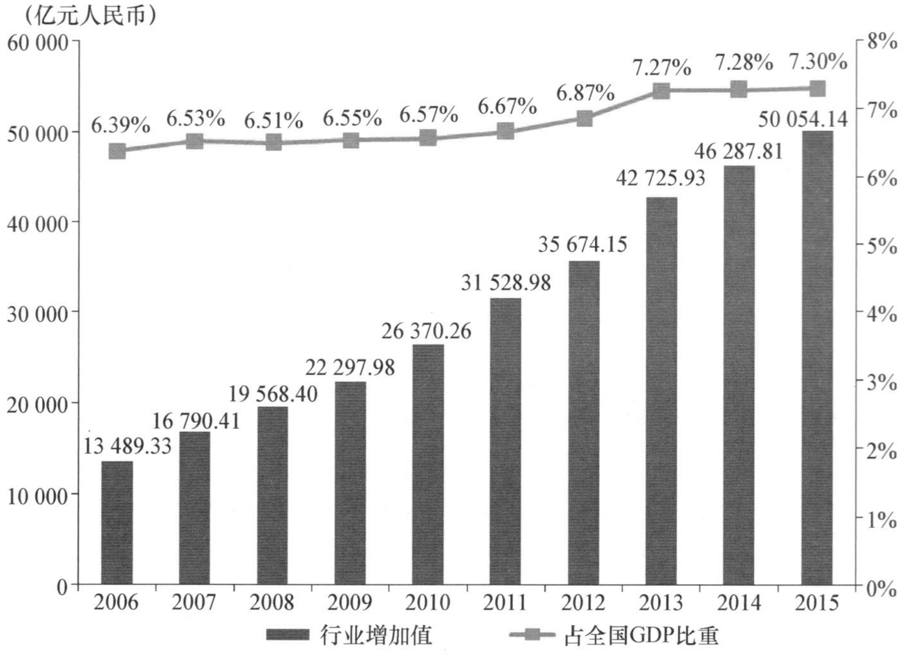

图 1　2006—2015 年中国版权产业的行业增加值及占全国 GDP 比重

高于 GDP 增速 2.19 百分点。特别是中国版权产业中的核心版权产业发展迅速，2006 年至 2015 年间的年均增长率为 18.68%，高于 GDP 增速 5.19 百分点（见图 2）。

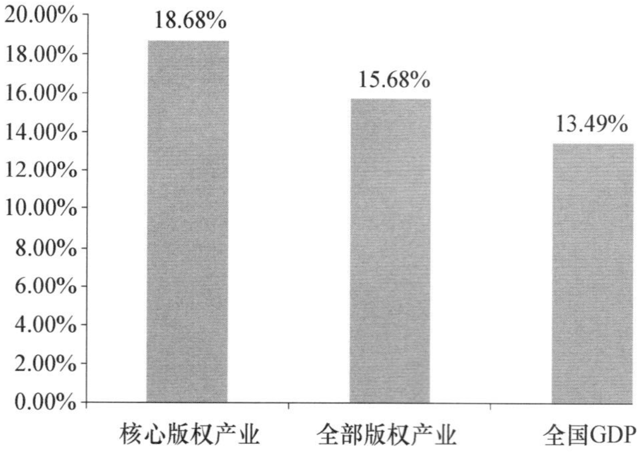

图 2　2006—2015 年中国核心版权产业、全部版权产业行业增加值与 GDP 的年均增长率对比图

（二）版权产业的结构不断优化，核心版权产业的作用更加突出

2006 年至 2015 年，中国版权产业的结构不断优化，核心版权产业在版权产业中的比重显著提高，对经济发展的贡献更加突出。2006 年，中国核心版权产业的行业增加值仅占到全部版权产业的 48%；2015 年，中国核心版权产业行业增加值在全部版权产业中的比重已经达到 60%，十年间提高了 12 百分点（见图 3）。

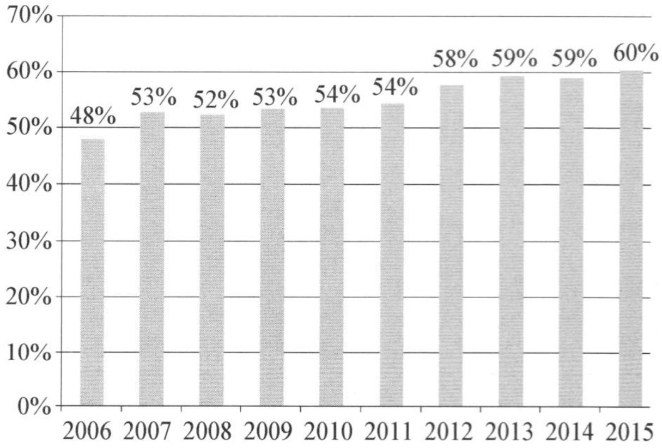

图 3　2006—2015 年中国核心版权产业行业增加值占全部版权产业的比重

核心版权产业与版权的关系最为密切，其比重的提高反映出中国版权产业创新能力和核心竞争力的增强。2015 年，中国核心版权产业的行业增加值突破 3 万亿元，达到 30 229.87 亿元人民币，比 2006 年翻了两番多，已经占到全国 GDP 的 4.41%，比 2006 年提高了 1.35 百分点（见图 4）。核心版权产业成为推动中国版权产业发展的主要力量。

（三）版权产业吸纳就业的能力逐年增强

2006 年至 2015 年，中国版权产业的城镇单位就业人数从 2006 年的 762.92 万人增长至 2015 年的 1 666.90 万人，十年间翻了一番多，占全国城镇单位就业总人数的比重从 6.52%增长到 9.23%，十年间提高了 2.71 百分点（见图 5）。中国版权产业提供就业岗位、吸纳劳动力的能力逐年增强，在推动社会就业、促进社会稳定方面产生了积极意义。

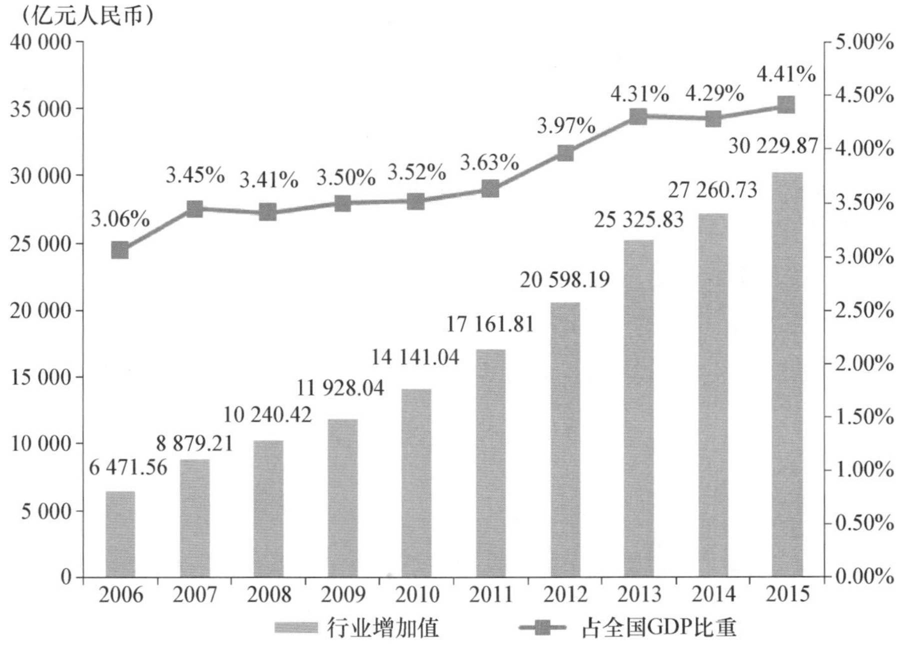

图 4　2006—2015 年中国核心版权产业的行业增加值及占全国 GDP 比重

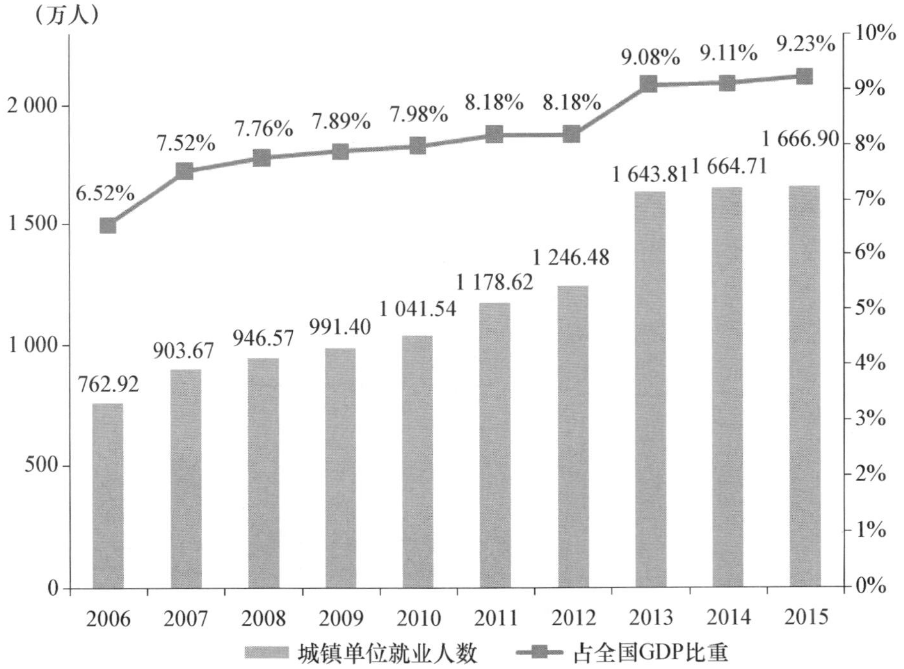

图 5　2006—2015 年中国版权产业的城镇单位就业人数及占全国 GDP 比重

(四) 版权产业的对外贸易规模有所扩大

受全球复杂严峻外贸形势的影响，2006 年至 2015 年中国版权产业的商品出口额时有波动，占全国商品出口总额的比重从 15.40%下降到 11.58%，但出口额仍从 1 492.62 亿美元增长至 2 633.36 亿美元（见图 6），版权产业的出口规模十年间增长了近一倍。

但从出口结构上看，中国版权产业的商品出口以计算机和电视机等视听设备产品相互依存的版权产业为主，这些年来相互依存的版权产业一直占到了全部版权产业商品出口额的 90%左右。而最能反映中国商品国际市场核心竞争力的核心版权产业的商品出口额比重较小，仅占版权产业商品出口额的 3%左右（见图 6）。这反映出中国版权产业的出口以版权附加值较低的商品为主，创新活动较高的核心版权产业在国际市场上的竞争力不足。

(五) 与美国等发达国家的差距逐渐缩小

从国际范围来看，中国版权产业的经济贡献虽然与美国等发达国家相比仍有一定差距，但随着近年来的不断发展，这种差距正在逐渐缩小。

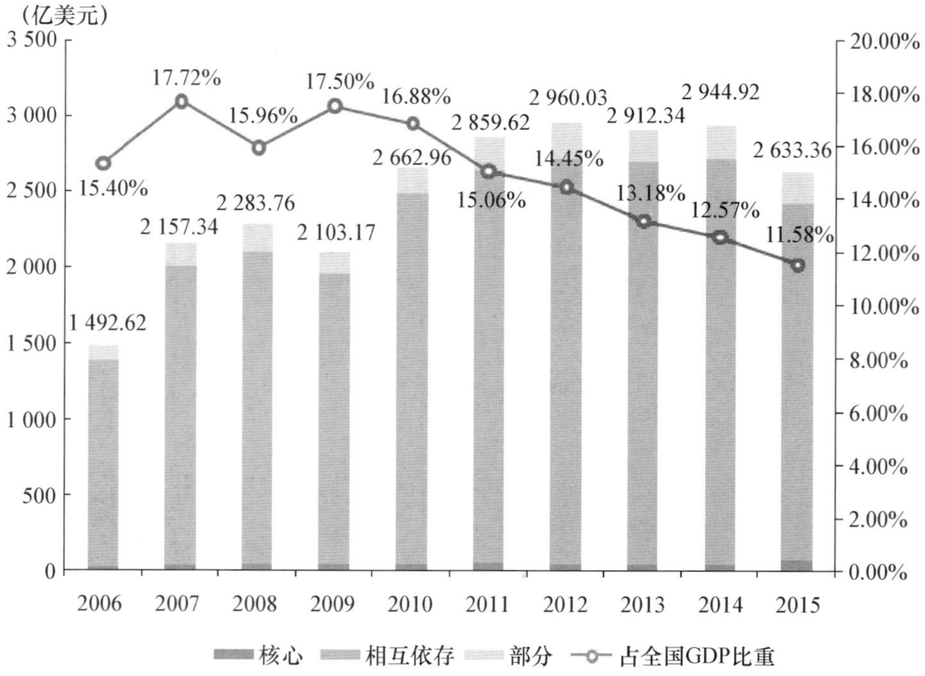

图 6 2006—2015 年中国版权产业的商品出口额及占全国 GDP 比重

2006 年，中国版权产业行业增加值占 GDP 的比重为 6.39%，美国版权产业行业增加值占 GDP 的比重为 11.04%，中国版权产业比美国低 4.65 百分点；其中，中国核心版权产业行业增加值占 GDP 的比重为 3.06%，美国核心版权产业行业增加值占 GDP 的比重为 6.35%，中国核心版权产业比美国低 3.29 百分点。

2015 年，中国版权产业行业增加值占 GDP 的比重已达 7.39%，美国版权产业行业增加值占 GDP 的比重为 11.69%，中国版权产业比美国低 4.30 百分点，十年间缩小了 0.35 百分点；其中中国核心版权产业行业增加值占 GDP 的比重已达 4.41%，美国核心版权产业行业增加值占 GDP 的比重为 6.88%，中国核心版权产业比美国低 2.47 百分点，十年间缩小了 0.82 百分点。详细数据见图 7①。

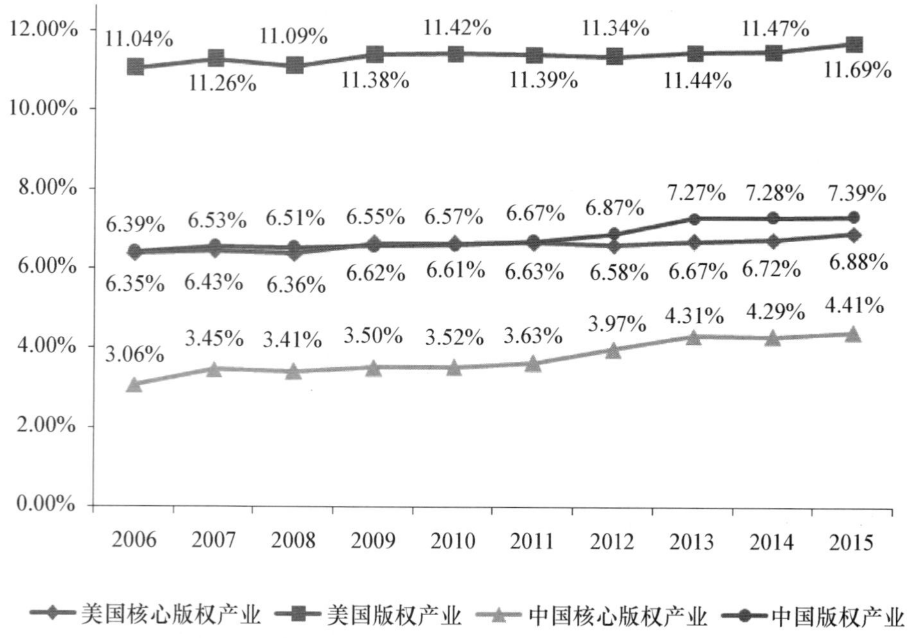

图 7 2006—2015 年中国与美国版权产业行业增加值占全国 GDP 比重的比较

① 美国版权产业 2006 年数据来源于“Copyright Industries in the U. S. Economy：The 2003—2007 Report”，2007 年、2008 年数据来源于“Copyright Industries in the U. S. Economy：The 2011 Report”，2009—2011 年数据来源于“Copyright Industries in the U. S. Economy：The 2014 Report”，2012—2015 年数据来源于“Copyright Industries in the U. S. Economy：The 2016 Report”。

三、中国版权产业经济贡献调研项目的总结与展望

中国版权产业的经济贡献调研项目自2007年起已经走过十年历程。在项目开展过程中，国家版权局的相关领导同志均对项目亲身指导并给予了大力支持，并将此项研究作为连续性项目列入工作议程，每年均为调研项目提供经费支持。世界知识产权组织也为调研工作提供了资助与技术指导，委派美国、新加坡等国专家具体开展指导工作。工业和信息化部、海关总署以及中国电子信息行业联合会、各省市等国家和地方主管部门、行业协会也为调研提供了大量帮助。在调研进行过程中，课题组还积极与有关国际组织、外国研究机构进行了沟通交流，先后走访了美国、加拿大、澳大利亚、新西兰、俄罗斯、匈牙利、芬兰、瑞典、波兰、奥地利、捷克等国和世界知识产权组织总部，开展了版权学习交流活动。

调研项目比较准确地掌握了中国版权产业的基本规模、发展趋势及其在国民经济中的地位与作用，相关成果也被国内外政府机构、研究部门所采用，成为中国政府宏观决策的重要依据。中央领导同志数次做出重要批示，强调要加强宣传与研究，推动版权产业的更大发展。国家版权局有关领导多次在不同场合引用调研数据。国家版权局还将该项目列入《版权工作"十二五"规划》和《版权工作"十三五"规划》中，指出要继续开展版权产业经济贡献调研工作。调研项目成果还曾入选"中国版权十大事件"。世界知识产权组织也对调研工作给予肯定，并将首次调研成果收入其系列出版物向世界各国予以推广。

调研成果在一定程度上展示了中国在版权保护和版权产业发展方面取得的巨大成就，版权产业在推动经济发展、优化产业结构、实施创新驱动发展战略中的重要作用也被越来越多的人所了解，各级地方政府和社会公众对版权产业和版权保护重要性的认识得到进一步提高。

中国新闻出版研究院还先后接受广东、山东、陕西、广州、东莞等地版权局委托，开展了地方版权产业的经济贡献调研项目，这些地方项目的开展印证了版权产业在推动地方经济发展方面发挥的重要作用，特别是在东部发达省市，版权产业已经成为地区经济重要的增长点。

调研也在一定程度上表明，我国版权产业的发展环境日益改善。近年来，版权已经被提升到我国国家战略的高度，版权法律制度正不断完善，司法与行政并行的版权监管工作成效显著，中国版权社会服务体系已基本形成，社会公众的版权意识明显提高，尊重版权、保护版权的社会氛围正逐渐形成，这些都促进了版权产业又好又快发展。

"十三五"时期，中国经济面临提质增效、转型升级的迫切要求，版权产业将会成为经济增长的一个亮点，在实施知识产权强国战略、建设创新型国家中发挥更加重要的作用，中国版权产业的经济贡献调研项目也将成为衡量中国经济创新发展的重要晴雨表。

（本报告为国家版权局委托课题的成果。课题组成员：范军、赵冰、杨昆、郝丽美、刘钊；执笔人为赵冰、杨昆）

2016 年中国新闻出版产业分析报告

国家新闻出版广电总局

一、产业结构分析

1. 经济总量规模

2016 年，全国出版、印刷和发行服务实现营业收入 23 595.8 亿元（见表 1），较 2015 年增长 9.0%；利润总额 1 792.0 亿元，增长 7.8%；不包括数字出版的资产总额为 22 070.3 亿元，增长 6.2%；所有者权益（净资产）为 11 245.5 亿元，增长 6.1%。

表 1　　新闻出版产业结构

产业类别	营业收入			
	金额（亿元）	增长速度（%）	比重（%）	比重变动（百分点）
图书出版	832.31	1.19	3.53	−0.27
期刊出版	193.70	−3.63	0.82	−0.11
报纸出版	578.50	−7.61	2.45	−0.44
音像制品出版	27.51	4.80	0.12	0.00
电子出版物出版	13.20	6.37	0.06	0.00
数字出版	5 720.85	29.91	24.24	3.90
印刷复制	12 711.59	3.81	53.87	−2.66
出版物发行	3 426.61	5.96	14.52	−0.41
出版物进出口	91.52	8.69	0.39	0.00

2. 图书出版总量规模

2016 年，全国共出版图书 50.0 万种，较 2015 年增长 5.1%；总印数 90.4 亿册（张），增长 4.3%；总印张 777.2 亿印张，增长 4.6%；定价总金额 1 581.0 亿元，增长 7.1%。图书出版实现营业收入 832.3 亿元，增长 1.2%；利润总额 134.3 亿元，增长 7.2%。

3. 期刊出版总量规模

2016 年全国共出版期刊 10 084 种，较 2015 年增长 0.7%；总印数 27.0 亿册，降低 6.3%；总印张 152.0 亿印张，降低 9.4%；定价总金额 232.4 亿元，降低 4.3%。期刊出版实现营业收入 193.7 亿元，降低 3.6%；利润总额 25.7 亿元，降低 2.2%。

4. 报纸出版总量规模

2016 年，全国共出版报纸 1 894 种，较 2015 年降低 0.6%；总印数 390.1 亿份，降低 9.3%；总印张 1 267.3 亿印张，降低 18.5%；定价总金额 408.2 亿元，降低 6.0%。报纸出版实现营业收入 578.5 亿元，降低 7.6%；利润总额 30.1 亿元，降低 15.7%。

5. 音像制品出版总量规模

2016 年，全国共出版音像制品 14 353 种，较 2015 年降低 6.6%；出版数量 22 124.3 万盒（张），降低 24.8%。音像制品出版实现营业收入 27.5 亿元，增长 4.8%；利润总额 3.7 亿元，降低 7.1%。

6. 电子出版物出版总量规模

2016 年，全国共出版电子出版物 9 836 种，较 2015 年降低 2.5%；出版数量 29 064.7 万张，增长 35.6%。电子出版物出版实现营业收入 13.2 亿元，增长 6.4%；利润总额 2.4 亿元，增长 4.3%。

7. 数字出版总量规模

2016 年，数字出版实现营业收入 5 720.9 亿元，较 2015 年增长 29.9%；利润总额 427.8 亿元，增长 27.9%。

8. 印刷复制总量规模

2016 年，全国黑白印刷产量 31 517.6 万令，彩色印刷产量 150 688.4 万对开色令；装订产量 33 668.5 万令。印刷复制（包括出版物印刷、包装装潢印刷、其他印刷品印刷、专项印刷、打字复印、复制和印刷物资供销）实现营业收入 12 711.6 亿元，增长 3.81%；利润总额 882.7 亿元，增长 1.2%（见表 2）。

表 2　　印刷复制的内部构成

类别	营业收入			
	金额（亿元）	增长速度（%）	在印刷复制中所占比重（%）	比重变动（百分点）
印刷	12 684.99	3.93	99.79	0.12

续前表

类别	营业收入			
	金额（亿元）	增长速度（%）	在印刷复制中所占比重（%）	比重变动（百分点）
其中：出版物印刷	1 605.46	3.28	12.63	−0.06
包装装潢印刷	9 712.74	4.99	76.41	0.86
其他印刷品印刷	1 084.49	−0.82	8.53	−0.40
复制	26.61	−33.43	0.21	−0.12
合计	12 711.59	3.81	100.00	0.00

9. 出版物发行总量规模

2016年，全国共有出版物发行网点163 102处，较2015年降低0.3%；出版物发行实现营业收入3 426.6亿元，增长6.0%；利润总额282.0亿元，增长8.6%。

10. 出版物进出口总量规模

2016年，全国累计出口图书、期刊、报纸、音像制品、电子出版物、数字出版物数量2 181.69万册（份、盒、张），较2015年增长2.7%；金额11 010.77万美元，增长5.0%（其中，数字出版物出口3 055.3万美元，增长29.1%；全国出版物进出口经营单位累计出口数量1 766.9万册（份、盒、张），增长13.7%；金额6 043.1万美元，增长3.1%）。全国累计进口图书、期刊、报纸、音像制品、电子出版物、数字出版物数量3 118.99万册（份、盒、张），增长10.5%；金额55 911.11万美元，增长2.1%。进出口总额66 921.88万美元（其中，全国出版物进出口经营单位进出口总额61 954.2万美元，增长2.2%）[①]（见表3）。全国出版物进出口经营单位实现营业收入91.5亿元，增长8.7%；利润总额3.3亿元，增长41.5%。

表3　全国出版物对外贸易情况

类型	指标	累计出口	累计进口	总额	差额
图书、期刊、报纸	数量（万册（份、盒、张））	2 169.94	3 108.18	5 278.12	−938.24
	金额（万美元）	7 785.11	30 051.73	37 836.84	−22 266.62
音像制品、电子出版物、数字出版物	数量（万册（份、盒、张））	11.75	10.81	22.56	0.94
	金额（万美元）	3 225.66	25 859.38	29 085.04	−22 633.72
合计	数量（万册（份、盒、张））	2 181.69	3 118.99	5 300.68	−937.30
	金额（万美元）	11 010.77	55 911.11	66 921.88	−44 900.34

说明：差额为累计出口减去累计进口之差。正号表示出口大于进口，存在贸易顺差；负号表示出口小于进口，存在贸易逆差。

11. 版权贸易总量规模

2016年，全国共输出版权11 133种（其中输出出版物版权9 811种），较2015年增长6.3%（其中输出出版物版权增长10.7%）；共引进版权17 252种（其中引进出版物版权17 174种），增长4.8%（其中引进出版物版权增长7.5%）（见表4）。2016年，出版引进版图书15 416种[②]。

表4　出版物对外版权贸易构成　单位：种

类型	引进	输出	总额	差额
图书	16 587	8 328	24 915	−8 259
录音制品	119	201	320	82
录像制品	251	18	269	−233

续前表

类型	引进	输出	总额	差额
电子出版物	217	1 264	1 481	1 047
合计	17 174	9 811	26 985	−7 363

说明：差额为输出减去引进之差。正号表示输出大于引进，存在顺差；负号表示输出小于引进，存在逆差。

二、产品结构分析

（一）整体结构

2016年全国共出版图书、期刊、报纸、音像制品和电子出版物512.5亿册（份、盒、张），较2015年降低6.9%。其中，出版图书90.4亿册（张），增长

① 此数据仅包含全国拥有出版物进口资质的出版物进出口经营单位及部分开展出版物直接出口业务的出版发行单位数据。另据国家统计局公布的数据，2016年全口径出版物出口额34.7亿美元。

② 中国版本图书馆CIP登记数据。

4.3%，占全部数量的 17.6%；期刊 27.0 亿册，降低 6.3%，占 5.3%；报纸 390.1 亿份，降低 9.3%，占 76.1%；音像制品 2.2 亿盒（张），降低 24.8%，占 0.4%；电子出版物 2.9 亿张，增长 35.6%，占 0.6%。

（二）图书结构

1. 书籍

书籍按照内容类型划分为社科人文、科学技术、综合 3 类。

2016 年，全国出版社科人文类书籍共 34.5 万种，较 2015 年增长 7.0%，占书籍品种总数的 84.1%；科学技术类书籍 6.1 万种，增长 5.0%，占 14.9%；综合类书籍 0.4 万种，增长 8.1%，占 1.0%。

全国出版社科人文类书籍 54.5 亿册，增长 8.3%，占书籍总印数的 95.0%；科学技术类书籍 2.6 亿册，与 2015 年基本持平，占 4.5%；综合类书籍 0.3 亿册，增长 15.4%，占 0.5%。

2016 年全国社科人文类书籍单品种平均印数 15 793 册，增加 182 册；科学技术类书籍单品种平均印数 4 241 册，减少 226 册；综合类书籍单品种平均印数 7 511 册，增加 519 册。

2. 课本

课本划分为大专及以上课本、中学课本、小学课本、中专技校课本、业余教育课本、扫盲课本和教学用书 7 类。

2016 年，全国出版中学课本 0.6 万种，较 2015 年降低 6.3%，占课本品种数的 7.2%；小学课本 0.6 万种，降低 8.6%，占 6.4%。中小学课本合计 1.2 万种，占课本品种数的 13.6%，图书品种数的 2.4%（较 2015 年减少 0.4 百分点）。

全国出版中学课本 15.3 亿册，降低 0.4%，占课本总印数的 46.7%；小学课本 13.1 亿册，降低 0.9%，占 40.1%。中小学课本合计 28.4 亿册，占课本总印数的 86.8%，图书总印数的 31.5%（较 2015 年减少 1.6 百分点）。

3. 新版与重印图书

2016 年全国出版新版图书 26.24 万种，较 2015 年增长 0.8%；占图书品种总数的 52.5%，较 2015 年减少 2.2 百分点；重印图书 23.75 万种，增长 10.3%；占 47.5%，提高 2.2 百分点。重印图书与新版图书品种之比由 2015 年的 1∶1.2 变为 1∶1.1。

全国出版新版图书 24.08 亿册，降低 3.8%；占图书总印数的 26.7%，较 2015 年减少 2.3 百分点；重印图书 51.19 亿册，增长 10.9%；占 56.6%，提高 3.4 百分点。重印图书与新版图书总印数之比由 2015 年的 1.8∶1 变为 2.1∶1（见表 5）。

2016 年全国新版图书单品种平均印数 9 178 册，较 2015 年降低 434 册；重印图书单品种平均印数 21 554 册，增加 122 册。

表 5　　新版图书与重印图书品种、总印数结构

类型	品种				总印数			
	数量（万种）	增速（%）	比重（%）	比重变动（百分点）	数量（万种）	增速（%）	比重（%）	比重变动（百分点）
全部图书	49.99	5.1	100.0	0.0	90.37	4.3	100.0	0.0
其中：新版	26.24	0.8	52.5	−2.2	24.08	−3.8	26.7	−2.3
重印	23.75	10.3	47.5	2.2	51.19	10.9	56.6	3.4

说明：全部图书总印数包括新版图书、重印图书和租型图书。

4. 少儿图书

2016 年全国出版少儿图书 4.4 万种，较 2015 年增加 0.7 万种，增长 19.1%；其中新版图书 2.5 万种，增加 0.3 万种，增长 15.0%。

全国出版少儿图书 7.8 亿册（张），增加 2.2 亿册（张），增长 40.0%；其中新版图书 3.8 亿册（张），增加 0.9 亿册（张），增长 28.7%。

2016 年全国少儿图书单品种平均印数 17 825 册，增加 2 658 册；其中新版图书 15 141 册，增加 1 614册。

5. 当年累计印数超过百万册的图书

《习近平总书记系列重要讲话读本（2016 年版）》《习近平关于严明党的纪律和规矩论述摘编》等 109 种图书当年单品种累计印数达到或超过 100 万册。其中，《习近平总书记系列重要讲话读本（2016 年版）》合计超过 5 200 万册，《习近平关于严明党的纪律和规矩论述摘编》超过 600 万册，《全面小康热点面对面》超过 200 万册；《平凡的世界》等 5 种文学图书和《曹文轩纯美小说·草房子》等 5 种少儿图书当年累计印数均超过 100 万册。2016 年单品种累计印数排名前10位的图书如表6所示。

表6　2016年单品种累计印数排名前10位的图书

排名	图书名称	出版单位	新出或重印
1	习近平总书记系列重要讲话读本（2016年版）（32开版）	学习出版社	新出
2	中国共产党章程（平装）	人民出版社	重印
3	上海市民科学健身知识读本	上海科学普及出版社	新出
4	奋发向上　崇德向善（初中生读本）	新世界出版社	重印
5	习近平总书记系列重要讲话读本（2016年版）（16开版）	学习出版社	新出
6	中国共产党章程（红皮烫金版）	中国法制出版社	新出
7	习近平关于严明党的纪律和规矩论述摘编（小字本）	中国方正出版社	新出
8	传承中华文化　共筑精神家园（初中生读本）	新世界出版社	重印
9	水与生命	浙江科学技术出版社	重印
10	关于新形势下党内政治生活的若干准则　中国共产党党内监督条例（国际版）	人民出版社	新出

与2015年相比，当年单品种累计印数超过100万册的图书品种增加41种，排名第10位图书的累计印数较2015年排名第10位的图书增加22万册。

（三）期刊结构

1. 内容结构

期刊按照内容划分为综合、哲学社会科学、自然科学技术、文化教育和文学艺术5类。

2016年，全国出版哲学、社会科学类期刊12.70亿册，较2015年降低3.39%，占期刊总印数的47.08%，提高1.42百分点；文化、教育类期刊6.17亿册，降低4.68%，占22.90%，提高0.39百分点；文学、艺术类期刊2.58亿册，降低20.31%，占9.57%，减少1.68百分点；自然科学、技术类期刊3.69亿册，降低6.65%，占13.69%；综合类期刊1.82亿册，降低7.43%，占6.76%。哲学、社会科学类期刊占期刊总印数比重继续提高，文化、教育类期刊所占比重有所回升，文学、艺术类期刊占比继续减少（见表7）。

表7　　期刊产品结构

类型	总印数			
	数量（亿册）	增长速度（%）	比重（%）	比重变动（百分点）
哲学、社会科学	12.70	−3.39	47.08	1.42
文化、教育	6.17	−4.68	22.90	0.39
文学、艺术	2.58	−20.31	9.57	−1.68
自然科学、技术	3.69	−6.65	13.69	−0.05
综合	1.82	−7.43	6.76	−0.08
合计	26.97	−6.29	100.00	0.00

2. 平均期印数超过百万册期刊

2016年，共有《求是》、《时事报告》大学生版和中学生版、《读者》等10种期刊平均期印数超过100万册。其中，《时事报告》平均期印数超过400万册，《读者》、《特别关注》、《小学生时代》、《青年文摘》和《家庭医生》等文摘类、少儿类、科普类期刊占据半数（见表8）。

表8　2016年平均期印数排名前10位的期刊

排名	期刊名称	刊期	所在省份	2015年排名	排名变化
1	时事报告（大学生版）	半年刊	北京	1	0
2	读者	半月刊	甘肃	2	0
3	特别关注	月刊	湖北	3	0
4	求是	半月刊	北京	5	+1
5	小学生时代	月刊	浙江	4	−1
6	中共中央办公厅通讯	月刊	北京	6	0
7	青年文摘	半月刊	北京	9	+2
8	时事（《时事报告》中学生版）	月刊	北京	8	0
9	家庭医生	半月刊	广东	11	+2
10	半月谈	半月刊	北京	12	+2

与2015年相比，《家庭医生》《半月谈》进入前十，《知音漫客》《意林》退出前十；前10位中，《求是》《青年文摘》排名上升，《小学生时代》排名下降；排名第10位期刊的平均期印数较2015年排名第10位期刊减少3万册；平均期印数超过100万册期刊减少3种；平均期印数和总印数整体继续下降。

（四）报纸结构

1. 层级结构

报纸根据地域层级划分为全国性报纸、省级报纸、地市级报纸和县级报纸4类。

2016年，共出版全国性报纸78.76亿份，较2015年降低0.85%，占报纸总印数的20.19%，提高 1.72 百分点；省级报纸 185.57 亿份，降低 11.56%，占 47.57%，减少 1.21 百分点；地市级报纸 124.93 亿份，降低 10.76%，占 32.03%；县级报纸 0.81 亿份，降低 3.21%，占 0.21%。全国性报纸所占比重继续提高，省级报纸仍占据半壁江山，但比重继续减少；省级和地市级报纸印数下滑加剧，占报纸总印数比重出现下降（见表 9）。

表 9　报纸的层级结构

地域层级	总印数（亿份）	增长速度（%）	比重（%）	比重变动（百分点）
全国性报纸	78.76	−0.85	20.19	1.72
省级报纸	185.57	−11.56	47.57	−1.21
地市级报纸	124.93	−10.76	32.03	−0.52
县级报纸	0.81	−3.21	0.21	0.01
合计	390.07	−9.31	100.00	0.00

2. 内容结构

报纸根据内容划分为综合、专业、生活服务、读者对象和文摘 5 大类。

2016 年，全国出版综合类报纸 250.61 亿份，较 2015 年降低 11.88%，占报纸总印数的 64.25%，减少 1.88 百分点；专业类报纸 106.92 亿份，降低 3.57%，占 27.41%，提高 1.63 百分点；生活服务类报纸 10.63 亿份，降低 15.21%，占 2.72%；读者对象类报纸 17.19 亿份，降低 1.04%，占 4.41%，提高 0.37 百分点；文摘类报纸 4.71 亿份，降低 3.64%，占 1.21%。综合类与生活服务类报纸降幅较大，所占比重有所减少；市场细分更为清晰、读者对象更为明确的专业类与读者对象类报纸降幅较小，所占比重有所提高（见表 10）。

表 10　报纸的内容结构

内容类型	数量（亿份）	增长速度（%）	比重（%）	比重变动（百分点）
综合	250.61	−11.88	64.25	−1.88
专业	106.92	−3.57	27.41	1.63
生活服务	10.63	−15.21	2.72	−0.19
读者对象	17.19	−1.04	4.41	0.37
文摘	4.71	−3.64	1.21	0.07
合计	390.07	−9.31	100.00	0.00

3. 平均期印数超过百万份报纸

2016 年，共有《人民日报》《参考消息》《环球时报》等 25 种报纸平均期印数超过 100 万份，较 2015 年减少 1 种；其中综合类 12 种，减少 1 种；专业类报纸 11 种；读者对象类报纸 2 种。2016 年平均期印数排名前 10 位的综合类报纸详见表 11。

表 11　2016 年平均期印数排名前 10 位的综合类报纸

排名	报纸名称	刊期	所在省份	2015 年排名	排名变化
1	人民日报	周七刊	北京	1	0
2	参考消息	周七刊	北京	2	0
3	南方都市报	周七刊	广东	3	0
4	新华每日电讯	周七刊	北京	4	0
5	钱江晚报	周七刊	浙江	5	0
6	半岛都市报	周七刊	山东	10	+4
7	都市快报	周七刊	浙江	8	+1
8	广州日报	周七刊	广东	9	+1
9	广州日报社区报	周一刊	广东	11	+2
10	齐鲁晚报	周七刊	山东	6	−4

与 2015 年相比，《广州日报社区报》跻身前十，《扬子晚报》退出前十；《半岛都市报》、《都市快报》和《广州日报》排名上升，《齐鲁晚报》排名下降；排名第 10 位的《齐鲁晚报》平均期印数较 2015 年排名第 10 位报纸减少 12.0 万份；平均期印数和总印数整体继续下滑。

2016 年平均期印数排名前 10 位的专业类报纸详见表 12。

表 12　2016 年平均期印数排名前 10 位的专业类报纸

排名	报纸名称	刊期	所在省份	2015 年排名	排名变化
1	英语周报	周一刊	山西	1	0
2	当代中学生报	周一刊	江西	2	0
3	学习方法报	周一刊	山西	3	0
4	中学生学习报	周一刊	河南	4	0
5	英语辅导报	周一刊	吉林	5	0
6	语文学习报	周一刊	吉林	6	0
7	学生周报	周一刊	福建	9	+2
8	快乐老人报	周二刊	湖南	8	0
9	英语测试报	周一刊	吉林	10	+1
10	学英语报	周三刊	山西	11	+1

与 2015 年相比，《学英语报》跻身前十，《语文周报》退出前十；《学生周报》和《英语测试报》排名上升；排名第 10 位的《学英语报》平均期印数较 2015 年排名第 10 位报纸减少 14.0 万份；平均期印数和总印数整体继续下滑。

三、地区结构分析

（一）各地区总体经济规模综合评价

选取营业收入、增加值、总产出、资产总额、所有者权益（净资产）、利润总额和纳税总额 7 项经济规模指标，采用主成分分析法对全国 31 个省（自治区、直辖市）及新疆生产建设兵团新闻出版业（未包括数字出版）的总体经济规模进行综合评价。

广东、山东、浙江、江苏、北京[①]、上海、河北、安徽、福建和四川依次位居全国前10位。其中，前7位均属于东部地区。与2015年相比，四川跻身前十，江西退出前十；前10位中山东排名上升，北京排名下降。详见表13。

表13　总体经济规模综合评价前10位的地区

综合排名	地区	综合评价得分	2015年排名	排名变化
1	广东	2.711 3	1	0
2	山东	1.884 4	5	+3
3	浙江	1.828 4	3	0
4	江苏	1.767 9	4	0
5	北京	1.742 1	2	−3
6	上海	0.865 6	6	0
7	河北	0.457 6	7	0
8	安徽	0.409 3	8	0
9	福建	0.306 5	9	0
10	四川	0.286 6	11	+1

说明：1. 选取营业收入、增加值、总产出、资产总额、所有者权益（净资产）、利润总额和纳税总额7项经济规模指标，采用主成分分析方法，通过SPSS直接计算所得，仅用来显示各地区的相对位置。

2. 未包括数字出版、版权贸易与代理、行业服务与其他新闻出版业务。

前10位地区营业收入合计13 328.0亿元，占全行业营业收入的74.56%，较2015年前10位地区合计所占比重降低0.1百分点（见图1）。

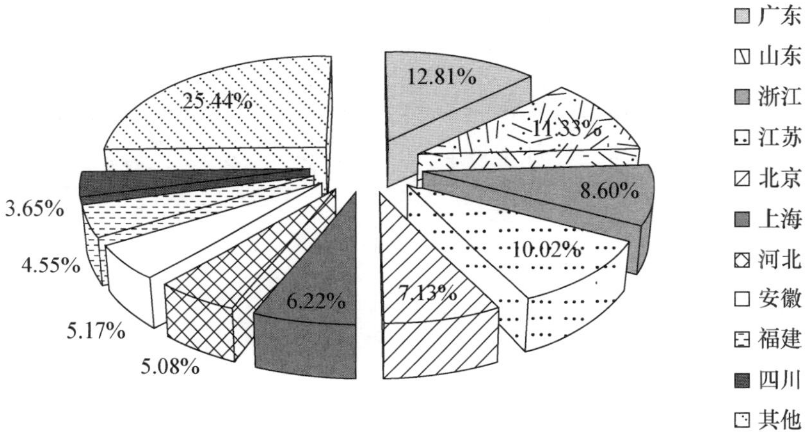

图1　营业收入的地区结构

前10位地区资产总额合计15 771.4亿元，占全行业资产总额的71.46%，提高0.3百分点（见图2）。

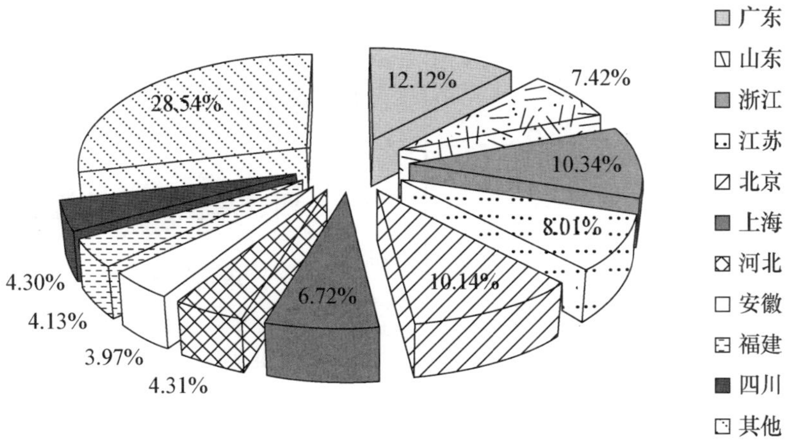

图2　资产总额的地区结构

① 包括中央在京新闻出版单位，后同。

前 10 位地区利润总额合计 931.1 亿元，占全行业利润总额的 68.26%，降低 0.1 百分点（见图 3）。

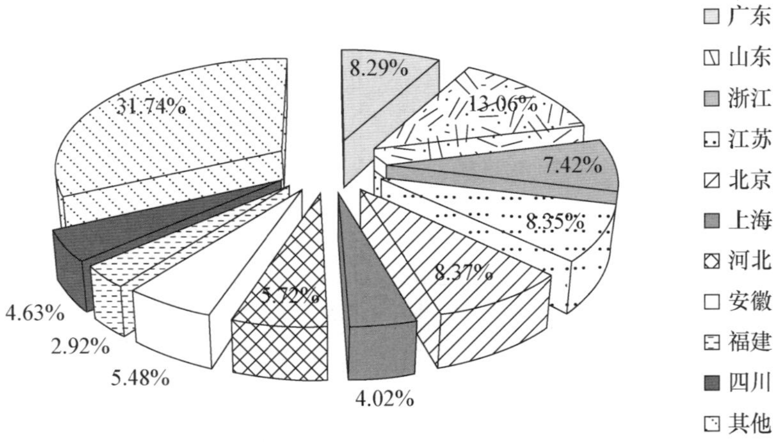

图 3　利润总额的地区结构

（二）地区增长情况

1. 增长速度

以各地区新闻出版全行业营业收入增长速度衡量，前 10 位降序依次为安徽、四川、广西、山东、天津、河北、新疆、西藏、浙江和福建（见表 14）。其中，东部地区省份（直辖市）5 个，中部地区省份 1 个，西部地区省份（自治区）4 个；安徽和四川营业收入实现两位数增长。

与 2015 年相比，东部地区省份增加 3 个，中部地区省份减少 2 个，西部地区省份减少 1 个；实现两位数增长的地区减少 4 个。

表 14　　　增长速度前 10 位的地区

排名	地区	增长速度（%）
1	安徽	13.91
2	四川	10.82
3	广西	9.59
4	山东	9.11
5	天津	6.93
6	河北	6.15
7	新疆	5.73
8	西藏	5.29
9	浙江	4.65
10	福建	4.26

2. 增长贡献

以各地区新闻出版全行业营业收入增长额和增长贡献率衡量其对全国新闻出版产业增长贡献，前 10 位按降序依次为山东、安徽、浙江、四川、广东、河北、江苏、福建、天津和广西。其中，东部地区省份（直辖市）7 个，中部地区省份 1 个，西部地区省份（自治区）2 个。

与 2015 年相比，东部地区省份增加 1 个，中部地区省份减少 2 个，西部地区省份（自治区）增加 1 个；贡献率超过 10.0% 的省份减少 1 个。详见表 15。

表 15　　　增长贡献前 10 位的地区

排名	地 区	增长额（亿元）	增长贡献率（%）
1	山东	169.05	27.14
2	安徽	113.05	18.15
3	浙江	68.33	10.97
4	四川	63.67	10.22
5	广东	58.13	9.33
6	河北	52.64	8.45
7	江苏	49.12	7.89
8	福建	33.21	5.33
9	天津	20.44	3.28
10	广西	18.48	2.97

说明：各地区增长贡献率＝（该地区本年营业收入－该地区上年营业收入）÷（各地区本年营业收入合计－各地区上年营业收入合计）×100%。

四、单位数量及就业人员情况分析

（一）单位数量与构成

2016 年，全国共有新闻出版单位 30.51 万家，较 2015 年降低 2.95%。其中，法人单位 15.23 万家，增长 1.46%，占单位总数的 49.93%，提高 2.16 百分点；非法人单位 0.86 万家，降低 1.40%，占 2.82%，提高 0.05 百分点；个体经营户 14.41 万家，降低 7.30%，占 47.25%，减少 2.21 百分点。详见表 16。

表 16　　新闻出版单位数量与构成

类型	数量（家）	增减百分比（%）	比重（%）	比重变动（百分点）
法人单位	152 334	1.46	49.93	2.16
其中：企业法人单位	149 665	1.57	—	—
非法人单位	8 597	−1.40	2.82	0.05
个体经营户	144 142	−7.30	47.25	−2.21
合计	305 073	−2.95	100.00	0.00

说明：未包括数字出版单位、版权贸易与代理单位和行业服务与从事其他新闻出版业务的单位。

（二）企业法人情况

1. 整体规模

2016 年，全行业共有企业法人单位[①] 14.97 万家，较 2015 年增长 1.57%，占全行业法人单位和非法人单位（不包括个体经营户）总数的 93.00%。企业法人单位营业收入 17 088.9 亿元，增长 3.9%，占全行业营业收入的 95.7%，提高 0.4 百分点；资产总额 20 485.9 亿元，增长 6.3%，占全行业资产总额的 93.1%，提高 0.4 百分点；利润总额1 306.5 亿元，增长 3.3%，占全行业利润总额的 95.8%，提高 0.5 百分点。

2. 所有制结构

（1）数量结构。

在 149 665 家企业法人单位中，国有全资企业 14 480 家，较 2015 年降低 5.16%，占企业法人单位数量的 9.68%，减少 0.67 百分点；民营企业 127 267 家，增长 2.79%，占 85.03%，提高 1.00 百分点（见表 17）。

表 17　　企业法人单位的所有制结构

类型	数量（家）	增减百分比（%）	比重（%）	比重变动（百分点）
国有企业	14 800	−5.16	—	—
其中：国有全资	14 480	−5.09	9.68	−0.67
集体企业	5 001	−7.61	3.34	−0.33
民营企业	127 267	2.79	85.03	1.00
外商投资企业	2 295	1.24	1.53	−0.01
港澳台商投资企业	225	4.17	0.15	0.00
混合投资企业	397	2.58	0.27	0.01
合计	149 665	—	100.00	0.00

（2）印刷复制企业。

在印刷复制企业中，国有全资企业营业收入占行业营业收入的 3.60%，较 2015 年减少 0.6 百分点；民营企业占 89.50%，提高 0.9 百分点。国有全资企业资产总额占行业资产总额的 3.59%，减少 0.5 百分点；民营企业占 89.30%，提高 0.9 百分点。国有全资企业利润总额占行业利润总额的 2.69%，减少 0.3 百分点；民营企业占 90.30%，提高 0.7 百分点（见表 18）。

表 18　　印刷复制企业法人单位的所有制结构（%）

主要指标	国有全资	集体企业	民营企业	港澳台商投资	外商投资	混合投资	合计
营业收入	3.60	3.05	89.50	0.30	3.17	0.38	100.00
资产总额	3.59	3.31	89.30	0.32	3.08	0.40	100.00
所有者权益	3.35	3.38	89.49	0.32	3.06	0.40	100.00
利润总额	2.69	3.27	90.30	0.29	3.09	0.36	100.00

（3）出版物发行企业。

在出版物发行企业中，国有全资企业营业收入占行业营业收入的 28.28%，较 2015 年减少 0.6 百分点；民营企业占 68.28%，提高 0.7 百分点。国有全资企业资产总额占行业资产总额的 30.13%，减少 0.9 百分点；民营企业占 66.70%，提高 1.0 百分点。国有全资企业利润总额占行业利润总额的 28.96%，减少 0.5 百分点；民营企业占 67.99%，提高 0.6 百分点（见表 19）。

表 19　　出版物发行企业法人单位的所有制结构（%）

主要指标	国有全资	集体企业	民营企业	港澳台商投资	外商投资	混合投资	合计
营业收入	28.28	0.99	68.28	1.67	0.09	0.69	100.00
资产总额	30.13	0.96	66.70	1.48	0.10	0.63	100.00

① 未包括数字出版、版权贸易与代理、行业服务与其他新闻出版业务企业。占比计算所用全行业数据也未包括数字出版、版权贸易与代理、行业服务与其他新闻出版业务。

续前表

主要指标	国有全资	集体企业	民营企业	港澳台商投资	外商投资	混合投资	合计
所有者权益	29.63	0.95	67.06	1.57	0.12	0.67	100.00
利润总额	28.96	0.96	67.99	1.41	0.08	0.60	100.00

（三）就业人员状况

2016 年，全国新闻出版业直接就业人数为 453.85 万人（不包含数字出版、版权贸易与服务、行业服务与其他新闻出版业务单位就业人员），较 2015 年增长 1.26%；其中男性 246.3 万人，女性 207.6 万人，分别占全行业直接就业人数的 54.3% 和 45.7%，男女比例基本平衡。

印刷复制业直接就业人数 336.09 万人，提高 3.19%；出版物发行业 77.41 万人，降低 2.70%；报纸出版业 22.35 万人，降低 7.50%；期刊出版业 10.33 万人，降低 7.01%；图书出版业 6.68 万人，降低 0.42%（见表 20）。

表 20　　就业人数的产业类别构成

产业类别	人数（万人）	增减百分比（%）	比重（%）	比重变动（百分点）
图书出版	6.68	−0.42	1.47	0.04
期刊出版	10.33	−7.01	2.28	−0.13
报纸出版	22.35	−7.50	4.92	−0.41
音像制品出版	0.42	−1.12	0.09	−0.02
电子出版物出版	0.30	10.19	0.07	0.03
印刷复制	336.09	3.19	74.05	−0.35
出版物发行	77.41	−2.70	17.06	0.84
出版物进出口	0.27	−2.96	0.06	0.00
合计	453.85	1.26	100.00	0.00

说明：未包括数字出版、版权贸易与代理、行业服务与其他新闻出版服务。

五、出版传媒集团分析

（一）总体情况

截至 2016 年底，全国共有经国务院新闻出版行政管理部门或省级新闻出版行政管理部门批准的出版传媒集团 126 家，其中图书出版集团 40 家[①]、报刊出版集团 47 家、发行集团 27 家、印刷集团 12 家。

2016 年，出版传媒集团资产规模进一步扩大，主营业务收入和利润总额显著增长。120 家图书出版、报刊出版、发行和印刷集团共实现主营业务收入 3 476.13 亿元，较 2015 年增加 474.3 亿元，增长 15.80%；拥有资产总额 6 541.45 亿元，增加 523.4 亿元，增长 8.70%；实现利润总额 296.62 亿元，增加 49.4 亿元，增长 19.99%（见表 21）。

表 21　出版传媒集团收入、资产与利润合计情况

指标	金额（亿元）	增长率（%）
主营业务收入	3 476.13	15.80
资产总额	6 541.45	8.70
所有者权益	3 540.88	11.41
利润总额	296.62	19.99

其中，108 家图书出版集团、报刊出版集团和发行集团共实现主营业务收入 3 422.1 亿元，较 2015 年增加 477.9 亿元，增长 16.2%，占全国书报刊出版和出版物发行主营业务收入的 74.5%，提高 6.9 百分点；拥有资产总额 6 432.9 亿元，增加 520.0 亿元，增长 8.8%，占全国出版发行全行业资产总额的 84.0%，提高 2.7 百分点；实现利润总额 295.6 亿元，增加 51.1 亿元，增长 20.9%，占全国出版发行全行业利润总额的 62.6%，提高 7.9 百分点。

（二）图书出版集团

1. 经济规模

2016 年，图书出版集团继续保持良好发展态势，主要经济指标均实现两位数增长。34 家图书出版集团[②]共实现主营业务收入 1 976.75 亿元，较 2015 年增加 339.9 亿元，增长 20.76%；拥有资产总额 3 386.84亿元，增加 345.4 亿元，增长 11.36%；实现利润总额 178.89 亿元，增加 30.4 亿元，增长 20.47%。

江苏凤凰出版传媒集团有限公司、江西省出版集团公司、湖南出版投资控股集团有限公司、

① 2016 年新批准成立人民卫生出版集团、中国环境出版集团有限公司、人民法院出版集团和中国健康传媒集团有限公司等 4 家图书出版集团。

② 2013 年批准成立的中国人力资源和社会保障出版集团有限公司、中国书法出版传媒有限公司及 2016 年批准成立的人民卫生出版集团、中国环境出版集团有限公司、人民法院出版集团和中国健康传媒集团有限公司等 6 家图书出版集团尚不能提供有效的集团财务数据，故参与评价的为 34 家，较 2015 年增加 1 家（中国财经出版传媒集团有限责任公司）。

浙江出版联合集团有限公司和安徽出版集团有限责任公司等5家集团资产总额、主营业务收入和所有者权益均超过100亿元，组成“三百亿”集团阵营，较2015年新增安徽出版集团有限责任公司。湖北长江出版传媒集团有限公司和河北出版传媒集团有限责任公司等2家集团资产总额、主营业务收入均超过100亿元，组成“双百亿”阵营。另有中国教育出版传媒集团有限公司、中国出版集团公司、山东出版集团有限公司和中原出版传媒投资控股集团有限公司等4家集团资产总额超过100亿元。

2. 总体经济规模排名

选取集团合并报表中的主营业务收入、资产总额、所有者权益和利润总额4项经济规模指标，采用主成分分析法，对图书出版集团的总体经济规模进行综合评价。排名前10位的图书出版集团如表22所示。

与2015年相比，中原出版传媒投资控股集团有限公司跻身前十，山东出版集团有限公司退出前十；前10位中湖北长江出版传媒集团有限公司排名上升，浙江出版联合集团有限公司、河北出版传媒集团有限责任公司和中国出版集团公司排名下降。

表22　　总体经济规模综合评价前10位的图书出版集团

综合排名	集团	综合评价得分	2015年排名	排名变化
1	江苏凤凰出版传媒集团有限公司	3.176 7	1	0
2	湖南出版投资控股集团有限公司	1.717 9	2	0
3	江西省出版集团公司	1.507 5	3	0
4	中国教育出版传媒集团有限公司	1.329 2	4	0
5	湖北长江出版传媒集团有限公司	1.310 1	10	+5
6	安徽出版集团有限责任公司	1.290 9	6	0
7	浙江出版联合集团有限公司	0.940 3	5	−2
8	河北出版传媒集团有限责任公司	0.835 2	7	−1
9	中原出版传媒投资控股集团有限公司	0.715 6	11	+2
10	中国出版集团公司	0.702 3	8	−2

说明：综合评价得分系选取主营业务收入、资产总额、所有者权益和利润总额四项指标，采用主成分分析方法，通过SPSS直接计算所得，仅用来显示各单位的相对位置，负数并不代表负面评价。

（三）报刊出版集团

1. 经济规模

2016年，报刊出版集团资产规模继续扩大；营业收入继续下滑，但降幅趋缓；得益于投资收益和营业外收入增加，利润总额大幅增长。47家报刊出版集团共实现主营业务收入382.12亿元，较2015年减少12.2亿元，降低3.09%；拥有资产总额1 619.44亿元，增加52.3亿元，增长3.34%；实现利润总额34.09亿元，增加11.6亿元，增长51.71%。

上海报业集团、成都传媒集团和浙江日报报业集团等3家集团资产总额超过100亿元。

2. 总体经济规模排名

采取同样评价方法，总体经济规模前10位的报刊出版集团如表23所示。

与2015年相比，河南日报报业集团有限公司跻身前十，四川日报报业集团退出前十；前10位中广州日报报业集团排名上升，山东大众报业（集团）有限公司、陕西华商传媒集团有限责任公司、湖北日报传媒集团、深圳报业集团和南方报业传媒集团排名下降。

表23　　总体经济规模综合评价前10位的报刊出版集团

综合排名	集团	综合评价得分	2015年排名	排名变化
1	上海报业集团	3.834 4	1	0
2	浙江日报报业集团	3.243 8	2	0
3	成都传媒集团	1.918 7	3	0
4	广州日报报业集团	1.236 9	10	+6

续前表

综合排名	集团	综合评价得分	2015 年排名	排名变化
5	山东大众报业（集团）有限公司	1.174 1	4	−1
6	陕西华商传媒集团有限责任公司	1.118 3	5	−1
7	湖北日报传媒集团	0.821 5	6	−1
8	河南日报报业集团有限公司	0.710 3	12	+4
9	深圳报业集团	0.611 2	8	−1
10	南方报业传媒集团	0.535 6	7	−3

说明：同表 22。

（四）发行集团

1. 经济规模

2016 年，发行集团继续保持良好增长态势，营业收入和利润总额快速增长。27 家发行集团实现主营业务收入 1 063.23 亿元，较 2015 年增加 150.2 亿元，增长 16.45%；拥有资产总额 1 426.59 亿元，增加 122.3 亿元，增长 9.37%；实现利润总额 82.64 亿元，增加 9.1 亿元，增长 12.45%。

安徽新华发行（集团）控股有限公司资产总额、所有者权益和主营业务收入均超过 100 亿元，由 2015 年“双百亿”集团晋级成为唯一的“三百亿”发行集团。四川新华发行集团有限公司资产总额超过 100 亿元。

2. 总体经济规模排名

采用同样评价方法，总体经济规模前 10 位的发行集团如表 24 所示。

与 2015 年相比，前 10 位发行集团保持不变但名次有所改变，山东新华书店集团有限公司、河南省新华书店发行集团有限公司和重庆新华书店集团公司排名上升，河北省新华书店有限责任公司和上海新华发行集团有限公司排名下降。

表 24　　总体经济规模综合评价前 10 位的发行集团

综合排名	集团	综合评价得分	2015 年排名	排名变化
1	安徽新华发行（集团）控股有限公司	3.894 8	1	0
2	四川新华发行集团有限公司	1.747 1	2	0
3	湖南省新华书店有限责任公司	1.030 6	3	0
4	浙江省新华书店集团有限公司	0.610 1	4	0
5	江西新华发行集团有限公司	0.607 6	5	0
6	山东新华书店集团有限公司	0.332 3	7	+1
7	河北省新华书店有限责任公司	0.281 7	6	−1
8	河南省新华书店发行集团有限公司	0.207 0	9	+1
9	重庆新华书店集团公司	0.149 7	10	+1
10	上海新华发行集团有限公司	0.120 1	8	−2

说明：同表 22。

（五）印刷集团

1. 经济规模

2016 年，印刷集团资产规模有所扩大，主营业务收入继续下滑，利润总额大幅下降。12 家印刷集团实现主营业务收入 54.03 亿元，较 2015 年减少 3.6 亿元，降低 6.17%；拥有资产总额 108.58 亿元，增加 3.4 亿元，增长 3.25%；实现利润总额 1.00 亿元，减少 1.7 亿元，降低 62.96%。

2. 总体经济规模排名

采用同样评价方法，总体经济规模前 10 位的印刷集团如表 25 所示。

与 2015 年相比，广西正泰彩印包装有限责任公司跻身前十，北京隆达印刷包装集团有限公司退出前十；前 10 位中上海印刷新技术（集团）有限公司、上海印刷（集团）有限公司和北京印刷集团有限责任公司排名上升，浙江印刷集团有限公司、辽宁新闻印刷集团有限公司和河南新华印刷集团有限公司排名下降。

表 25　总体经济规模综合评价前 10 位的印刷集团

综合排名	集团	综合评价得分	2015 年排名	排名变化
1	中国文化产业发展集团公司	1.409 0	1	0
2	江西新华印刷集团有限公司	0.917 4	2	0
3	湖南天闻新华印务有限公司	0.729 5	3	0
4	上海印刷新技术（集团）有限公司	0.323 2	6	+2
5	浙江印刷集团有限公司	0.193 5	4	−1
6	上海印刷（集团）有限公司	0.129 2	7	+1
7	辽宁新闻印刷集团有限公司	−0.272 1	5	−2
8	北京印刷集团有限责任公司	−0.492 6	9	+1
9	河南新华印刷集团有限公司	−0.540 8	8	−1
10	广西正泰彩印包装有限责任公司	−0.548 3	11	−1

说明：同表 22。

六、出版传媒上市公司分析

（一）总体情况

截至 2016 年 12 月 31 日，中国内地在境内外上市的出版传媒公司共计 37 家[①]。其中，出版公司 11 家，报业公司 7 家，发行公司 6 家，印刷公司 10 家，新媒体公司 3 家。其中在中国内地上市 33 家，在中国香港上市 4 家。详见表 26。

表 26　出版传媒上市公司的业务类型与上市地点

单位：家

业务类型	中国内地	中国香港	合计
出版公司	10	1	11
报业公司	5	2	7
发行公司	5	1	6
印刷公司	10	0	10
新媒体公司	3	0	3
合计	33	4	37

说明：出版公司包括业务内容描述为出版、出版发行和期刊的上市公司。

与 2015 年相比，新增上市公司 2 家，均在中国内地上市。其中，出版公司 1 家，为南方出版传媒股份有限公司；发行公司 1 家，为四川新华文轩出版传媒股份有限公司。详见表 27。

表 27　2016 年新增出版传媒上市公司概况

上市公司	股票简称	业务类型	上市时间	上市地点	上市方式
南方出版传媒股份有限公司	南方传媒	出版	2 月	上证 A 股	IPO
四川新华文轩出版传媒股份有限公司	新华文轩	发行	8 月	上证 A 股	IPO

（二）经济规模

1. 在中国境内外上市公司流通市值规模

以 2016 年 12 月 31 日收盘价计算，37 家在境内外上市的出版传媒上市公司股市流通市值共计 4 075.63 亿元人民币，较 2015 年同期减少 910.9 亿元，下降 18.27%。其中，在中国内地上市的 33 家公司股市流通市值共计 4 029.6 亿元人民币，减少 830.7 亿元，降低 17.1%。

各类出版传媒上市公司的股市流通市值规模，按降序依次为出版公司、印刷公司、报业公司、发行公司和新媒体公司。流通市值平均规模按降序依次为印刷公司、出版公司、新媒体公司、发行公司和报业公司。

各类出版传媒上市公司的股市流通市值增长速度，按降序依次为发行公司、印刷公司、新媒体公司、出版公司和报业公司；流通市值增长额按降序依次为发行公司、新媒体公司、印刷公司、报业公司和出版公司。详见表 28。

① 2016 年新增出版传媒上市公司 2 家。同时，湖南赛迪传媒投资股份有限公司（*ST 传媒，由北京湖南赛迪传媒投资股份有限公司更名）于 2015 年完成重大资产重组，更名为南华生物医药股份有限公司（南华生物），主要从事生物医药业务，退出传媒行业；当当网于 2016 年完成股权私有化改造，从美国纽约证券交易所退市。因此，出版传媒上市公司仍为 37 家。

表 28　　在境内外上市的出版传媒公司股市流通市值

公司类型	总金额（亿元人民币）	增长额（亿元人民币）	增长速度（%）	平均规模（亿元人民币）
出版公司	1 279.56	−369.39	−22.40	116.32
报业公司	638.47	−242.04	−27.49	91.21
发行公司	633.23	−22.09	−3.37	105.54
印刷公司	1 196.75	−217.16	−15.36	119.68
新媒体公司	327.62	−60.26	−15.54	109.21
整体	4 075.63	−910.94	−18.27	110.15

股市流通市值前10位的出版传媒公司，按降序依次为康得新、皖新传媒、中南传媒、凤凰传媒、中文传媒、浙报传媒、华闻传媒、掌趣科技、劲嘉股份和东港股份。其中，出版公司3家、报业公司2家、发行公司1家、印刷公司3家、新媒体公司1家；均在中国内地上市。详见表29。

表 29　　在境内外上市的股市流通市值前10位出版传媒上市公司　　单位：亿元人民币

排名	上市公司	股票简称	业务类型	上市地点	流通市值
1	北京康得新复合材料股份有限公司	康得新	印刷	深证A股	550.44
2	安徽新华传媒股份有限公司	皖新传媒	发行	上证A股	319.77
3	中南出版传媒集团股份有限公司	中南传媒	出版发行	上证A股	299.21
4	江苏凤凰出版传媒股份有限公司	凤凰传媒	出版发行	上证A股	266.45
5	中文天地出版传媒股份有限公司	中文传媒	出版发行	上证A股	255.31
6	浙报传媒集团股份有限公司	浙报传媒	报业	上证A股	209.85
7	华闻传媒投资集团股份有限公司	华闻传媒	报业	深证A股	206.32
8	北京掌趣科技股份有限公司	掌趣科技	新媒体	深证A股	178.92
9	深圳劲嘉彩印集团股份有限公司	劲嘉股份	印刷	深证A股	135.56
10	东港安全印刷股份有限公司	东港股份	印刷	深证A股	108.92

2. 在中国内地上市公司市值规模

（1）总体情况。

以2016年12月31日收盘价计算，在中国内地上市的33家出版传媒公司股市总市值共计5 109.22亿元，较2015年同期减少986.8亿元，降低16.19%。

各类出版传媒上市公司的股市总市值规模，按降序依次为出版公司、印刷公司、发行公司、报业公司和新媒体公司。总市值平均规模按降序依次为新媒体公司、发行公司、报业公司、出版公司和印刷公司。各类出版传媒上市公司的股市总市值增长速度，按降序依次为发行公司、印刷公司、出版公司、报业公司和新媒体公司。总市值增长额按降序依次为发行公司、印刷公司、报业公司、出版公司和新媒体公司。详见表30。

表 30　在中国内地上市的出版传媒公司股市总市值

公司类型	总金额（亿元）	增长额（亿元）	增长速度（%）	平均规模（亿元）
出版公司	1 519.60	−384.03	−20.17	151.96
报业公司	765.24	−270.26	−26.10	153.05
发行公司	821.89	254.95	44.97	164.38
印刷公司	1 390.40	−152.73	−9.90	139.04
新媒体公司	612.09	−434.72	−41.53	204.03
整体	5 109.22	−986.79	−16.19	154.82

股市总市值前10位的出版传媒公司，按降序依次为康得新、皖新传媒、中南传媒、中文传媒、凤凰传媒、掌趣科技、昆仑万维、浙报传媒、华闻传媒和新华文轩。其中，出版公司3家、报业公司2家、发行公司2家、印刷公司1家、新媒体公司2家。详见表31。

表 31　　在中国内地上市的股市总市值前10位出版传媒上市公司　　单位：亿元

排名	上市公司	股票简称	业务类型	上市地点	总市值
1	北京康得新复合材料股份有限公司	康得新	印刷	深证A股	674.35
2	安徽新华传媒股份有限公司	皖新传媒	发行	上证A股	349.50

续前表

排名	上市公司	股票简称	业务类型	上市地点	总市值
3	中南出版传媒集团股份有限公司	中南传媒	出版发行	上证 A 股	299.21
4	中文天地出版传媒股份有限公司	中文传媒	出版发行	上证 A 股	278.34
5	江苏凤凰出版传媒股份有限公司	凤凰传媒	出版发行	上证 A 股	266.45
6	北京掌趣科技股份有限公司	掌趣科技	新媒体	深证 A 股	256.03
7	北京昆仑万维科技股份有限公司	昆仑万维	新媒体	深证 A 股	243.46
8	浙报传媒集团股份有限公司	浙报传媒	报业	上证 A 股	229.92
9	华闻传媒投资集团股份有限公司	华闻传媒	报业	深证 A 股	227.76
10	四川新华文轩出版传媒股份有限公司	新华文轩	发行	上证 A 股	177.12

(2) 出版公司。

出版公司股市总市值共计 1 519.60 亿元，减少 384.0 亿元，降低 20.2%；占全体在内地上市出版传媒公司股市总市值的 29.7%。

10 家出版公司的股市总市值，按降序依次为中南传媒、中文传媒、凤凰传媒、南方传媒、大地传媒、时代出版、长江传媒、读者传媒、城市传媒和出版传媒。详见表 32。

表 32　在中国内地上市的出版公司股市总市值　单位：亿元

排名	上市公司	股票简称	上市地点	总市值
1	中南出版传媒集团股份有限公司	中南传媒	上证 A 股	299.22
2	中文天地出版传媒股份有限公司	中文传媒	上证 A 股	278.35
3	江苏凤凰出版传媒股份有限公司	凤凰传媒	上证 A 股	266.45
4	南方出版传媒股份有限公司	南方传媒	上证 A 股	128.03
5	中原大地传媒股份有限公司	大地传媒	深证 A 股	117.77
6	时代出版传媒股份有限公司	时代出版	上证 A 股	102.78
7	长江出版传媒股份有限公司	长江传媒	上证 A 股	100.85
8	读者出版传媒股份有限公司	读者传媒	上证 A 股	84.44
9	青岛城市传媒股份有限公司	城市传媒	上证 A 股	79.91
10	北方联合出版传媒（集团）股份有限公司	出版传媒	上证 A 股	61.82
—	合计	—	—	1 519.60

(3) 报业公司。

报业公司股市总市值共计 765.24 亿元，减少 270.3 亿元，降低 26.1%；占全体在内地上市出版传媒公司股市总市值的 15.0%。

5 家报业公司的股市总市值，按降序依次为浙报传媒、华闻传媒、华媒控股、博瑞传播和粤传媒。详见表 33。

表 33　在中国内地上市的报业公司股市总市值　单位：亿元

排名	上市公司	股票简称	上市地点	总市值
1	浙报传媒集团股份有限公司	浙报传媒	上证 A 股	229.92
2	华闻传媒投资集团股份有限公司	华闻传媒	深证 A 股	227.76
3	浙江华媒控股股份有限公司	华媒控股	深证 A 股	120.29
4	成都博瑞传播股份有限公司	博瑞传播	上证 A 股	95.78
5	广东广州日报传媒股份有限公司	粤传媒	深证 A 股	91.49
—	合计	—	—	765.24

(4) 发行公司。

发行公司股市总市值共计 821.89 亿元，增加 255.0 亿元，增长 45.0%；占全体在内地上市出版传媒公司股市总市值的 16.1%。

5 家发行公司的股市总市值，按降序依次为皖新传媒、新华文轩、天舟文化、新华传媒和广弘控股。详见表 34。

表 34　　在中国内地上市的发行公司股市总市值　　单位：亿元

排名	上市公司	股票简称	上市地点	总市值
1	安徽新华传媒股份有限公司	皖新传媒	上证 A 股	349.50
2	四川新华文轩出版传媒股份有限公司	新华文轩	上证 A 股	177.12
3	湖南天舟科教文化股份有限公司	天舟文化	深圳创业板	135.58
4	上海新华传媒股份有限公司	新华传媒	上证 A 股	90.80
5	广东广弘控股股份有限公司	广弘控股	深证 A 股	68.89
—	合计	—	—	821.89

（5）印刷公司。

印刷公司股市总市值共计 1 390.40 亿元，减少 152.7 亿元，下降 9.9%；占全体在内地上市出版传媒公司股市总市值的 27.2%。

10 家印刷公司的股市总市值，降序依次为康得新、劲嘉股份、东港股份、*ST 中富、紫江企业、鸿博股份、界龙实业、陕西金叶、永新股份和盛通股份。详见表 35。

表 35　　在中国内地上市的印刷公司股市总市值　　单位：亿元

排名	上市公司	股票简称	上市地点	总市值
1	北京康得新复合材料股份有限公司	康得新	深证 A 股	674.35
2	深圳劲嘉彩印集团股份有限公司	劲嘉股份	深证 A 股	136.94
3	东港安全印刷股份有限公司	东港股份	深证 A 股	108.95
4	珠海中富实业股份有限公司	*ST 中富	深证 A 股	89.48
5	上海紫江企业集团股份有限公司	紫江企业	上证 A 股	82.06
6	福建鸿博印刷股份有限公司	鸿博股份	深证 A 股	78.43
7	上海界龙实业集团股份有限公司	界龙实业	上证 A 股	57.33
8	陕西金叶科教集团股份有限公司	陕西金叶	深证 A 股	55.83
9	黄山永新股份有限公司	永新股份	深证 A 股	53.72
10	北京盛通印刷股份有限公司	盛通股份	深证 A 股	53.31
—	合计	—	—	1 390.40

（6）新媒体公司。

新媒体公司股市总市值共计 612.09 亿元，减少 434.7 亿元，降低 41.5%；占全体在内地上市出版传媒公司股市总市值的 12.0%。

3 家新媒体公司的股市总市值，降序依次为掌趣科技、昆仑万维和中文在线。详见表 36。

表 36　　在中国内地上市的新媒体公司股市总市值　　单位：亿元

排名	上市公司	股票简称	上市地点	总市值
1	北京掌趣科技股份有限公司	掌趣科技	深证 A 股	256.03
2	北京昆仑万维科技股份有限公司	昆仑万维	深证 A 股	243.47
3	中文在线数字出版集团股份有限公司	中文在线	深证 A 股	112.59
—	合计	—	—	612.09

3. 在中国内地上市公司资产规模

（1）总体情况。

截至 2016 年底，在中国内地上市的 33 家出版传媒公司资产总额共计 2 489.37 亿元，较 2015 年同期增加 520.82 亿元，增长 26.46%。

各类出版传媒上市公司的资产总额，按降序依次为出版公司、印刷公司、报业公司、发行公司和新媒体公司。资产总额平均规模按降序依次为出版公司、报业公司、发行公司、新媒体公司和印刷公司。

各类出版传媒上市公司的资产总额增长速度，按降序依次为发行公司、新媒体公司、印刷公司、出版公司和报业公司。资产总额增长额降序依次为发行公司、出版公司、印刷公司、新媒体公司和报业公司。详见表37和图4。

表37 在中国内地上市的出版传媒公司资产总额

公司类型	总金额（亿元）	增长额（亿元）	增长速度（%）	平均规模（亿元）
出版公司	1 008.40	155.48	18.23	100.84
报业公司	347.18	23.34	7.21	69.44
发行公司	337.51	179.65	113.80	67.50
印刷公司	600.69	93.21	18.37	60.07
新媒体公司	195.60	69.14	54.68	65.20
整体	2 489.37	520.82	26.46	75.44

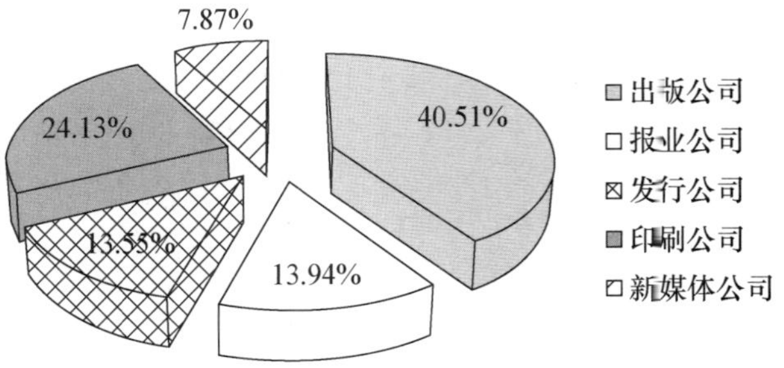

图4 资产总额的公司类型构成

资产总额前10位的出版传媒公司，按降序依次为康得新、凤凰传媒、中文传媒、中南传媒、华闻传媒、新华文轩、皖新传媒、紫江企业、掌趣科技和大地传媒。其中，出版公司4家、报业公司1家、发行公司2家、印刷公司2家、新媒体公司1家。详见表38。

表38 在中国内地上市的资产总额前10位出版传媒上市公司

单位：亿元

排名	上市公司	股票简称	业务类型	上市地点	资产总额
1	北京康得新复合材料股份有限公司	康得新	印刷	深证A股	264.25
2	江苏凤凰出版传媒股份有限公司	凤凰传媒	出版发行	上证A股	193.18
3	中文天地出版传媒股份有限公司	中文传媒	出版发行	上证A股	188.52
4	中南出版传媒集团股份有限公司	中南传媒	出版发行	上证A股	186.19
5	华闻传媒投资集团股份有限公司	华闻传媒	报业	深证A股	134.03
6	四川新华文轩出版传媒股份有限公司	新华文轩	发行	上证A股	122.55
7	安徽新华传媒股份有限公司	皖新传媒	发行	上证A股	110.14
8	上海紫江企业集团股份有限公司	紫江企业	印刷	上证A股	108.33
9	北京掌趣科技股份有限公司	掌趣科技	新媒体	深证A股	104.01
10	中原大地传媒股份有限公司	大地传媒	出版发行	深证A股	101.48

（2）出版公司。

出版公司资产总额共计1 008.40亿元，增加155.5亿元，增长18.2%；占全体在内地上市出版传媒公司资产总额的40.5%。

10家出版公司的资产总额，降序依次为凤凰传媒、中文传媒、中南传媒、大地传媒、长江传媒、南方传媒、时代出版、出版传媒、城市传媒和读者传媒。详见表39。

表39 在中国内地上市的出版公司资产总额

单位：亿元

排名	上市公司	股票简称	上市地点	资产总额
1	江苏凤凰出版传媒股份有限公司	凤凰传媒	上证A股	193.18
2	中文天地出版传媒股份有限公司	中文传媒	上证A股	188.52
3	中南出版传媒集团股份有限公司	中南传媒	上证A股	186.19
4	中原大地传媒股份有限公司	大地传媒	深证A股	101.48
5	长江出版传媒股份有限公司	长江传媒	上证A股	97.47
6	南方出版传媒股份有限公司	南方传媒	上证A股	86.09
7	时代出版传媒股份有限公司	时代出版	上证A股	76.50
8	北方联合出版传媒（集团）股份有限公司	出版传媒	上证A股	30.68
9	青岛城市传媒股份有限公司	城市传媒	上证A股	28.92
10	读者出版传媒股份有限公司	读者传媒	上证A股	19.37
—	合计	—	—	1 008.40

（3）报业公司。

报业公司资产总额共计 347.18 亿元，增加 23.3 亿元，增长 7.2%；占全体在内地上市出版传媒公司资产总额的 13.9%。

5 家报业公司的资产总额，降序依次为华闻传媒、浙报传媒、粤传媒、博瑞传播和华媒控股。详见表 40。

表 40　在中国内地上市的报业公司资产总额　单位：亿元

排名	上市公司	股票简称	上市地点	资产总额
1	华闻传媒投资集团股份有限公司	华闻传媒	深证 A 股	134.03
2	浙报传媒集团股份有限公司	浙报传媒	上证 A 股	93.20
3	广东广州日报传媒股份有限公司	粤传媒	深证 A 股	46.90
4	成都博瑞传播股份有限公司	博瑞传播	上证 A 股	43.42
5	浙江华媒控股股份有限公司	华媒控股	深证 A 股	29.63
—	合计	—	—	347.18

（4）发行公司。

发行公司资产总额共计 337.51 亿元，增加 179.7 亿元，增长 113.8%；占全体在内地上市出版传媒公司资产总额的 13.6%。

5 家发行公司的资产总额，降序依次为新华文轩、皖新传媒、天舟文化、新华传媒和广弘控股。详见表 41。

表 41　在中国内地上市的发行公司资产总额　单位：亿元

排名	上市公司	股票简称	上市地点	资产总额
1	四川新华文轩出版传媒股份有限公司	新华文轩	上证 A 股	122.55
2	安徽新华传媒股份有限公司	皖新传媒	上证 A 股	110.14
3	湖南天舟科教文化股份有限公司	天舟文化	深圳创业板	49.45
4	上海新华传媒股份有限公司	新华传媒	上证 A 股	39.49
5	广东广弘控股股份有限公司	广弘控股	深证 A 股	15.88
—	合计	—	—	337.51

（5）印刷公司。

印刷公司资产总额共计 600.69 亿元，增加 93.2 亿元，增长 18.4%；占全体在内地上市出版传媒公司资产总额的 24.1%。

10 家印刷公司的资产总额，降序依次为康得新、紫江企业、劲嘉股份、界龙实业、*ST 中富、鸿博股份、永新股份、东港股份、陕西金叶和盛通股份。详见表 42。

表 42　在中国内地上市的印刷公司资产总额　单位：亿元

排名	上市公司	股票简称	上市地点	资产总额
1	北京康得新复合材料股份有限公司	康得新	深证 A 股	264.25
2	上海紫江企业集团股份有限公司	紫江企业	上证 A 股	108.33
3	深圳劲嘉彩印集团股份有限公司	劲嘉股份	深证 A 股	66.81
4	上海界龙实业集团股份有限公司	界龙实业	上证 A 股	34.04
5	珠海中富实业股份有限公司	*ST 中富	深证 A 股	26.17
6	福建鸿博印刷股份有限公司	鸿博股份	深证 A 股	24.34
7	黄山永新股份有限公司	永新股份	深证 A 股	22.77
8	东港安全印刷股份有限公司	东港股份	深证 A 股	22.09
9	陕西金叶科教集团股份有限公司	陕西金叶	深证 A 股	17.96
10	北京盛通印刷股份有限公司	盛通股份	深证 A 股	13.93
—	合计	—	—	600.69

（6）新媒体公司。

新媒体公司资产总额共计 195.60 亿元，增加 69.1 亿元，增长 54.7%；占全体在内地上市出版传媒公司资产总额的 7.9%。

3 家新媒体公司的资产总额，降序依次为掌趣科技、昆仑万维和中文在线。详见表 43。

表 43　在中国内地上市的新媒体公司股市资产总额　单位：亿元

排名	上市公司	股票简称	上市地点	资产总额
1	北京掌趣科技股份有限公司	掌趣科技	深证 A 股	104.01
2	北京昆仑万维科技股份有限公司	昆仑万维	深证 A 股	63.06
3	中文在线数字出版集团股份有限公司	中文在线	深证 A 股	28.53
—	合计	—	—	195.60

4. 在中国内地上市公司收入规模

（1）总体情况。

2016 年，在中国内地上市的 33 家出版传媒公司营业收入共计 1 368.90 亿元，较 2015 年同期增加 235.12 亿元，增长 20.74%。

各类出版传媒上市公司的营业收入，按降序依次为出版公司、印刷公司、发行公司、报业公司和新媒体公司（见图 5）。营业收入平均规模按降序依次为出版公司、发行公司、印刷公司、报业公司和新媒体公司。

各类出版传媒上市公司的营业收入增长速度，按降序依次为发行公司、新媒体公司、出版公司、印刷公司和报业公司。营业收入增长额按降序依次为出版公司、发行公司、印刷公司、新媒体公司和报业公司。详见表 44。

表 44　在中国内地上市的出版传媒公司营业收入

公司类型	总金额（亿元）	增长额（亿元）	增长速度（%）	平均规模（亿元）
出版公司	719.54	112.72	18.58	71.95
报业公司	119.35	0.86	0.72	23.87
发行公司	183.22	76.96	72.43	36.64
印刷公司	297.98	28.80	10.70	29.80
新媒体公司	48.81	15.78	47.76	16.27
整体	1 368.90	235.12	20.74	41.48

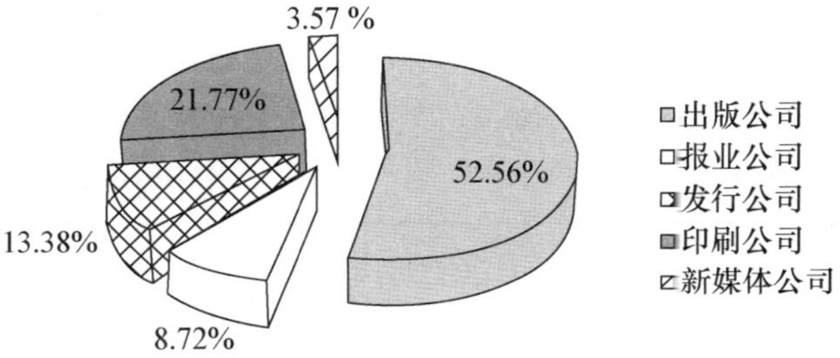

图 5　营业收入的公司类型构成

营业收入前 10 位的出版传媒公司，按降序依次为长江传媒、中文传媒、中南传媒、凤凰传媒、康得新、紫江企业、大地传媒、皖新传媒、时代出版和新华文轩。其中，出版公司 6 家、发行公司 2 家、印刷公司 2 家。详见表 45。

表 45　在中国内地上市的营业收入前 10 位出版传媒上市公司　单位：亿元

排名	上市公司	股票简称	业务类型	上市地点	营业收入
1	长江出版传媒股份有限公司	长江传媒	出版发行	上证 A 股	137.89
2	中文天地出版传媒股份有限公司	中文传媒	出版发行	上证 A 股	127.76
3	中南出版传媒集团股份有限公司	中南传媒	出版发行	上证 A 股	111.05
4	江苏凤凰出版传媒股份有限公司	凤凰传媒	出版发行	上证 A 股	105.47
5	北京康得新复合材料股份有限公司	康得新	印刷	深证 A 股	92.33
6	上海紫江企业集团股份有限公司	紫江企业	印刷	上证 A 股	83.56
7	中原大地传媒股份有限公司	大地传媒	出版发行	深证 A 股	78.90
8	安徽新华传媒股份有限公司	皖新传媒	发行	上证 A 股	75.94
9	时代出版传媒股份有限公司	时代出版	出版发行	上证 A 股	67.67
10	四川新华文轩出版传媒股份有限公司	新华文轩	发行	上证 A 股	63.56

（2）出版公司。

出版公司营业收入共计 719.54 亿元，增加 112.7 亿元，增长 18.6%；占全体在内地上市出版传媒公司营业收入的 52.6%。

10家出版公司的营业收入，按降序依次为长江传媒、中文传媒、中南传媒、凤凰传媒、大地传媒、时代出版、南方传媒、城市传媒、出版传媒和读者传媒。详见表46。

表46　　在中国内地上市的出版公司营业收入　　单位：亿元

排名	上市公司	股票简称	上市地点	营业收入
1	长江出版传媒股份有限公司	长江传媒	上证A股	137.89
2	中文天地出版传媒股份有限公司	中文传媒	上证A股	127.76
3	中南出版传媒集团股份有限公司	中南传媒	上证A股	111.05
4	江苏凤凰出版传媒股份有限公司	凤凰传媒	上证A股	105.47
5	中原大地传媒股份有限公司	大地传媒	深证A股	78.90
6	时代出版传媒股份有限公司	时代出版	上证A股	67.67
7	南方出版传媒股份有限公司	南方传媒	上证A股	49.18
8	青岛城市传媒股份有限公司	城市传媒	上证A股	17.74
9	北方联合出版传媒（集团）股份有限公司	出版传媒	上证A股	16.39
10	读者出版传媒股份有限公司	读者传媒	上证A股	7.51
—	合计	—	—	719.54

（3）报业公司。

报业公司营业收入共计119.35亿元，增加0.9亿元，增长0.7%；占全体在内地上市出版传媒公司营业收入的8.7%。

5家报业公司的营业收入，按降序依次为华闻传媒、浙报传媒、华媒控股、粤传媒和博瑞传播。详见表47。

表47　　在中国内地上市的报业公司营业收入　　单位：亿元

排名	上市公司	股票简称	上市地点	营业收入
1	华闻传媒投资集团股份有限公司	华闻传媒	深证A股	45.71
2	浙报传媒集团股份有限公司	浙报传媒	上证A股	35.50
3	浙江华媒控股股份有限公司	华媒控股	深证A股	18.24
4	广东广州日报传媒股份有限公司	粤传媒	深证A股	10.21
5	成都博瑞传播股份有限公司	博瑞传播	上证A股	9.69
—	合计	—	—	119.35

（4）发行公司。

发行公司营业收入共计183.22亿元，增加77.0亿元，增长72.4%；占全体在内地上市出版传媒公司营业收入的13.4%。

5家发行公司的营业收入，降序依次为皖新传媒、新华文轩、广弘控股、新华传媒和天舟文化。详见表48。

表48　　在中国内地上市的发行公司营业收入　　单位：亿元

排名	上市公司	股票简称	上市地点	营业收入
1	安徽新华传媒股份有限公司	皖新传媒	上证A股	75.94
2	四川新华文轩出版传媒股份有限公司	新华文轩	上证A股	63.56
3	广东广弘控股股份有限公司	广弘控股	深证A股	20.67
4	上海新华传媒股份有限公司	新华传媒	上证A股	15.25
5	湖南天舟科教文化股份有限公司	天舟文化	深圳创业板	7.80
—	合计	—	—	183.22

（5）印刷公司

印刷公司营业收入共计297.98亿元，增加28.8亿元，增长10.7%；占全体在内地上市出版传媒公司营业收入的21.8%。

10家印刷公司的营业收入，按降序依次为康得新、紫江企业、劲嘉股份、永新股份、界龙实业、

*ST中富、东港股份、陕西金叶、鸿博股份和盛通股份。详见表49。

表49　在中国内地上市的印刷公司营业收入　单位：亿元

排名	上市公司	股票简称	上市地点	营业收入
1	北京康得新复合材料股份有限公司	康得新	深证A股	92.33
2	上海紫江企业集团股份有限公司	紫江企业	上证A股	83.56
3	深圳劲嘉彩印集团股份有限公司	劲嘉股份	深证A股	27.77
4	黄山永新股份有限公司	永新股份	深证A股	19.04
5	上海界龙实业集团股份有限公司	界龙实业	上证A股	17.33
6	珠海中富实业股份有限公司	*ST中富	深证A股	16.20
7	东港安全印刷股份有限公司	东港股份	深证A股	14.91
8	陕西金叶科教集团股份有限公司	陕西金叶	深证A股	9.94
9	福建鸿博印刷股份有限公司	鸿博股份	深证A股	8.46
10	北京盛通印刷股份有限公司	盛通股份	深证A股	8.43
—	合计	—	—	297.98

（6）新媒体公司。

新媒体公司营业收入共计48.81亿元，增加15.8亿元，增长47.8%；占全体在内地上市出版传媒公司营业收入的3.6%。

3家新媒体公司的营业收入，按降序依次为昆仑万维、掌趣科技和中文在线。详见表50。

表50　在中国内地上市的新媒体公司股市营业收入　单位：亿元

排名	上市公司	股票简称	上市地点	营业收入
1	北京昆仑万维科技股份有限公司	昆仑万维	深证A股	24.25
2	北京掌趣科技股份有限公司	掌趣科技	深证A股	18.55
3	中文在线数字出版集团股份有限公司	中文在线	深证A股	6.02
—	合计	—	—	48.81

5. 在中国内地上市公司利润总额

（1）总体情况。

2016年，在中国内地上市的33家出版传媒公司利润总额共计170.56亿元，较2015年同期增加36.73亿元，增长27.44%。

各类出版传媒上市公司的利润总额，按降序依次为出版公司、印刷公司、报业公司、发行公司和新媒体公司（见图6）。利润总额平均规模按降序依次为出版公司、报业公司、发行公司、新媒体公司和印刷公司。

各类出版传媒上市公司的利润总额增长速度，按降序依次为发行公司、报业公司、新媒体公司、出版公司和印刷公司。利润总额增长额按降序依次为出版公司、报业公司、发行公司、新媒体公司和印刷公司。详见表51。

表51　在中国内地上市的出版传媒公司利润总额

公司类型	总金额（亿元）	增长额（亿元）	增长速度（%）	平均规模（亿元）
出版公司	72.52	11.70	19.24	7.25
报业公司	28.99	10.82	59.55	5.80
发行公司	22.26	10.39	87.53	4.45
印刷公司	34.87	1.77	5.35	3.49
新媒体公司	11.92	2.05	20.77	3.97
整体	170.56	36.73	27.44	5.17

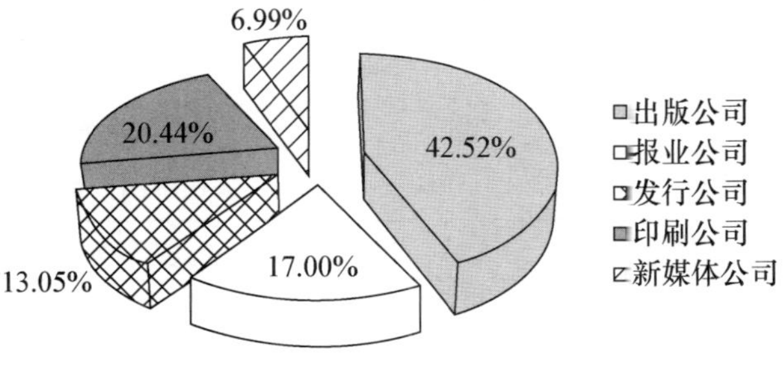

图6　利润总额的公司类型构成

利润总额前10位的出版传媒公司，按降序依次为康得新、中南传媒、中文传媒、华闻传媒、凤凰传媒、皖新传媒、浙报传媒、劲嘉股份、大地传媒和新华文轩。其中，出版公司4家、报业公司2家、发行公司2家、印刷公司2家。详见表52。

表 52　　在中国内地上市的利润总额前 10 位出版传媒上市公司　　单位：亿元

排名	上市公司	股票简称	业务类型	上市地点	利润总额
1	北京康得新复合材料股份有限公司	康得新	印刷	深证 A 股	23.02
2	中南出版传媒集团股份有限公司	中南传媒	出版发行	上证 A 股	19.33
3	中文天地出版传媒股份有限公司	中文传媒	出版发行	上证 A 股	13.70
4	华闻传媒投资集团股份有限公司	华闻传媒	报业	深证 A 股	12.35
5	江苏凤凰出版传媒股份有限公司	凤凰传媒	出版发行	上证 A 股	12.29
6	安徽新华传媒股份有限公司	皖新传媒	发行	上证 A 股	10.91
7	浙报传媒集团股份有限公司	浙报传媒	报业	上证 A 股	10.90
8	深圳劲嘉彩印集团股份有限公司	劲嘉股份	印刷	深证 A 股	7.27
9	中原大地传媒股份有限公司	大地传媒	出版发行	深证 A 股	6.97
10	四川新华文轩出版传媒股份有限公司	新华文轩	发行	上证 A 股	6.36

（2）出版公司。

出版公司利润总额共计 72.52 亿元，增加 11.7 亿元，增长 19.2%；占全体在内地上市出版传媒公司利润总额的 42.5%。

10 家出版公司的利润总额，按降序依次为中南传媒、中文传媒、凤凰传媒、大地传媒、长江传媒、南方传媒、时代出版、城市传媒、出版传媒和读者传媒。详见表 53。

表 53　　在中国内地上市的出版公司利润总额　　单位：亿元

排名	上市公司	股票简称	上市地点	利润总额
1	中南出版传媒集团股份有限公司	中南传媒	上证 A 股	19.33
2	中文天地出版传媒股份有限公司	中文传媒	上证 A 股	13.70
3	江苏凤凰出版传媒股份有限公司	凤凰传媒	上证 A 股	12.29
4	中原大地传媒股份有限公司	大地传媒	深证 A 股	6.97
5	长江出版传媒股份有限公司	长江传媒	上证 A 股	6.14
6	南方出版传媒股份有限公司	南方传媒	上证 A 股	5.05
7	时代出版传媒股份有限公司	时代出版	上证 A 股	4.13
8	青岛城市传媒股份有限公司	城市传媒	上证 A 股	2.82
9	北方联合出版传媒（集团）股份有限公司	出版传媒	上证 A 股	1.27
10	读者出版传媒股份有限公司	读者传媒	上证 A 股	0.82
—	合计	—	—	72.52

（3）报业公司。

报业公司利润总额共计 28.99 亿元，增加 10.8 亿元，增长 59.6%；占全体在内地上市出版传媒公司利润总额的 17.0%。

5 家报业公司的利润总额，按降序依次为华闻传媒、浙报传媒、华媒控股、粤传媒和博瑞传播。详见表 54。

表 54　　在中国内地上市的报业公司利润总额　　单位：亿元

排名	上市公司	股票简称	上市地点	利润总额
1	华闻传媒投资集团股份有限公司	华闻传媒	深证 A 股	12.35
2	浙报传媒集团股份有限公司	浙报传媒	上证 A 股	10.90
3	浙江华媒控股股份有限公司	华媒控股	深证 A 股	2.95
4	广东广州日报传媒股份有限公司	粤传媒	深证 A 股	1.85
5	成都博瑞传播股份有限公司	博瑞传播	上证 A 股	0.94
—	合计	—	—	28.99

（4）发行公司。

发行公司利润总额共计 22.26 亿元，增加 10.4 亿元，增长 87.5%；占全体在内地上市出版传媒公司利润总额的 13.1%。

5家发行公司的利润总额，按降序依次为皖新传媒、新华文轩、天舟文化、广弘控股和新华传媒。详见表55。

表55　在中国内地上市的发行公司利润总额　单位：亿元

排名	上市公司	股票简称	上市地点	利润总额
1	安徽新华传媒股份有限公司	皖新传媒	上证A股	10.91
2	四川新华文轩出版传媒股份有限公司	新华文轩	上证A股	6.36
3	湖南天舟科教文化股份有限公司	天舟文化	深圳创业板	3.03
4	广东广弘控股股份有限公司	广弘控股	深证A股	1.48
5	上海新华传媒股份有限公司	新华传媒	上证A股	0.49
—	合计	—	—	22.26

(5) 印刷公司。

印刷公司利润总额共计34.87亿元，增加1.8亿元，增长5.4%；占全体在内地上市出版传媒公司利润总额的20.4%。

10家印刷公司的利润总额，按降序依次为康得新、劲嘉股份、紫江企业、东港股份、永新股份、陕西金叶、鸿博股份、盛通股份、界龙实业和*ST中富。详见表56。

表56　在中国内地上市的印刷公司利润总额　单位：亿元

排名	上市公司	股票简称	上市地点	利润总额
1	北京康得新复合材料股份有限公司	康得新	深证A股	23.02
2	深圳劲嘉彩印集团股份有限公司	劲嘉股份	深证A股	7.27
3	上海紫江企业集团股份有限公司	紫江企业	上证A股	3.21
4	东港安全印刷股份有限公司	东港股份	深证A股	2.79
5	黄山永新股份有限公司	永新股份	深证A股	2.43
6	陕西金叶科教集团股份有限公司	陕西金叶	深证A股	0.75
7	福建鸿博印刷股份有限公司	鸿博股份	深证A股	0.65
8	北京盛通印刷股份有限公司	盛通股份	深证A股	0.44
9	上海界龙实业集团股份有限公司	界龙实业	上证A股	0.04
10	珠海中富实业股份有限公司	*ST中富	深证A股	−5.73
—	合计	—	—	34.87

(6) 新媒体公司。

新媒体公司利润总额共计11.92亿元，增加2.0亿元，增长20.8%；占全体在内地上市出版传媒公司利润总额的7.0%。

3家新媒体公司的利润总额，降序依次为昆仑万维、掌趣科技和中文在线。详见表57。

表57　在中国内地上市的新媒体公司利润总额　单位：亿元

排名	上市公司	股票简称	上市地点	利润总额
1	北京昆仑万维科技股份有限公司	昆仑万维	深证A股	5.69
2	北京掌趣科技股份有限公司	掌趣科技	深证A股	5.69
3	中文在线数字出版集团股份有限公司	中文在线	深证A股	0.53
—	合计	—	—	11.92

(三) 经济效益

1. 总体情况

2016年，在中国内地上市的33家出版传媒公司保持了较高的盈利能力。平均净资产收益率为10.44%，显著高于当期一年期存款基准利率（1.50%）和贷款基准利率（4.35%），表明出版传媒上市公司整体具有较强的盈利能力。

各类出版传媒上市公司的平均净资产收益率，降序依次为出版公司、报业公司、发行公司、新媒体公司和印刷公司。详见表58。

表 58　在中国内地上市的出版传媒公司平均净资产收益率

公司类型	平均净资产收益率（%）
出版公司	11.52
报业公司	10.07
发行公司	9.58
新媒体公司	9.56
印刷公司	9.50
整体	10.44

平均净资产收益率前 10 位的出版传媒公司，按降序依次为昆仑万维、康得新、浙报传媒、东港股份、华媒控股、中南传媒、新华传媒、劲嘉股份、城市传媒和南方传媒。其中，出版公司 3 家、报业公司 2 家、发行公司 1 家、印刷公司 3 家、新媒体公司 1 家。详见表 59。

表 59　在中国内地上市的平均净资产收益率前 10 位出版传媒公司

排名	上市公司	股票简称	业务类型	上市地点	收益率（%）
1	北京昆仑万维科技股份有限公司	昆仑万维	新媒体	深证 A 股	18.61
2	北京康得新复合材料股份有限公司	康得新	印刷	深证 A 股	15.75
3	浙报传媒集团股份有限公司	浙报传媒	报业	上证 A 股	15.59
4	东港安全印刷股份有限公司	东港股份	印刷	深证 A 股	15.42
5	浙江华媒控股股份有限公司	华媒控股	报业	深证 A 股	15.30
6	中南出版传媒集团股份有限公司	中南传媒	出版发行	上证 A 股	15.02
7	安徽新华传媒股份有限公司	新华传媒	发行	上证 A 股	14.75
8	深圳劲嘉彩印集团股份有限公司	劲嘉股份	印刷	深证 A 股	13.89
9	青岛城市传媒股份有限公司	城市传媒	出版发行	上证 A 股	13.59
10	南方出版传媒股份有限公司	南方传媒	出版发行	上证 A 股	13.41

2. 出版公司

出版公司平均净资产收益率 11.5%，高出出版传媒上市公司平均净资产收益率 1.1 百分点。

10 家出版公司的平均净资产收益率，按降序依次为中南传媒、城市传媒、南方传媒、中文传媒、长江传媒、大地传媒、凤凰传媒、时代出版、出版传媒和读者传媒。详见表 60。

表 60　在中国内地上市的出版公司平均净资产收益率

排名	上市公司	股票简称	上市地点	收益率（%）
1	中南出版传媒集团股份有限公司	中南传媒	上证 A 股	15.02
2	青岛城市传媒股份有限公司	城市传媒	上证 A 股	13.59
3	南方出版传媒股份有限公司	南方传媒	上证 A 股	13.41
4	中文天地出版传媒股份有限公司	中文传媒	上证 A 股	11.91
5	长江出版传媒股份有限公司	长江传媒	上证 A 股	11.18
6	中原大地传媒股份有限公司	大地传媒	深证 A 股	10.49
7	江苏凤凰出版传媒股份有限公司	凤凰传媒	上证 A 股	10.21
8	时代出版传媒股份有限公司	时代出版	上证 A 股	8.49
9	北方联合出版传媒（集团）股份有限公司	出版传媒	上证 A 股	6.40
10	读者出版传媒股份有限公司	读者传媒	上证 A 股	4.80

3. 报业公司

报业公司平均净资产收益率 10.1%，低于出版传媒上市公司平均水平 0.4 百分点。

5 家报业公司的平均净资产收益率，按降序依次为浙报传媒、华媒控股、华闻传媒、粤传媒和博瑞传播。详见表 61。

表 61　　在中国内地上市的报业公司平均净资产收益率

排名	上市公司	股票简称	上市地点	收益率（%）
1	浙报传媒集团股份有限公司	浙报传媒	上证 A 股	15.59
2	浙江华媒控股股份有限公司	华媒控股	深证 A 股	15.30
3	华闻传媒投资集团股份有限公司	华闻传媒	深证 A 股	10.70
4	广东广州日报传媒股份有限公司	粤传媒	深证 A 股	5.03
5	成都博瑞传播股份有限公司	博瑞传播	上证 A 股	1.42

4. 发行公司

发行公司的平均净资产收益率为 9.6%，低于出版传媒上市公司平均水平 0.9 百分点。

5 家发行公司的平均净资产收益率，按降序依次为皖新传媒、广弘控股、新华文轩、天舟文化、和新华传媒。详见表 62。

表 62　　在中国内地上市的发行公司平均净资产收益率

排名	上市公司	股票简称	上市地点	收益率（%）
1	安徽新华传媒股份有限公司	皖新传媒	上证 A 股	14.75
2	广东广弘控股股份有限公司	广弘控股	深证 A 股	8.94
3	新华文轩出版传媒股份有限公司	新华文轩	上证 A 股	8.11
4	天舟文化股份有限公司	天舟文化	深圳创业板	8.04
5	上海新华传媒股份有限公司	新华传媒	上证 A 股	[illegible].57

5. 印刷公司

印刷公司的平均净资产收益率为 9.5%，低于出版传媒上市公司平均水平 0.9 百分点。

10 家印刷上市公司的平均净资产收益率，按降序依次为康得新、东港股份、劲嘉股份、永新股份、盛通股份、紫江企业、陕西金叶、鸿博股份、界龙实业和 * ST 中富。界龙实业和 * ST 中富为负。详见表 63。

表 63　　在中国内地上市的印刷公司平均净资产收益率

排名	上市公司	股票简称	上市地点	收益率（%）
1	北京康得新复合材料股份有限公司	康得新	深证 A 股	15.75
2	东港安全印刷股份有限公司	东港股份	深证 A 股	15.42
3	深圳劲嘉彩印集团股份有限公司	劲嘉股份	深证 A 股	13.89
4	黄山永新股份有限公司	永新股份	深证 A 股	12.08
5	北京盛通印刷股份有限公司	盛通股份	深证 A 股	5.48
6	上海紫江企业集团股份有限公司	紫江企业	上证 A 股	5.33
7	陕西金叶科教集团股份有限公司	陕西金叶	深证 A 股	5.13
8	福建鸿博印刷股份有限公司	鸿博股份	深证 A 股	2.85
9	上海界龙实业集团股份有限公司	界龙实业	上证 A 股	−1.50
10	珠海中富实业股份有限公司	* ST 中富	深证 A 股	−77.37

6. 新媒体公司

新媒体公司的平均净资产收益率为 9.6%，低于出版传媒上市公司平均水平 0.9 百分点。

3 家新媒体公司的平均净资产收益率，按降序依次为昆仑万维、掌趣科技和中文在线。详见表 64。

表 64　　在中国内地上市的新媒体公司平均净资产收益率

排名	上市公司	股票简称	上市地点	收益率（%）
1	北京昆仑万维科技股份有限公司	昆仑万维	深证创业板	18.61
2	北京掌趣科技股份有限公司	掌趣科技	深证创业板	7.48
3	中文在线数字出版集团股份有限公司	中文在线	深证创业板	2.40

（四）业务与经营

2016 年，出版、发行、印刷业务整体呈现稳定增长态势，收入、利润稳中有升；传统报刊业务大幅下滑，报业公司经营呈现两极分化；新业态业务增长迅猛，数字出版、在线教育、新媒体、游戏娱乐、影视文化、大数据等新业态、新领域布局进一步广泛，整体发展势头良好。

1. 出版公司

出版公司主业挺拔，出版、发行、印刷继续保持核心主业地位。出版、发行、印刷业务收入在各出版上市公司营业收入中所占比重平均为 61.0%。其中 7 家公司出版、发行、印刷业务收入占比超过三分之二。

出版业务整体营业收入稳中有增，整体情况向好。读者传媒新闻出版业务收入占比最高，达到 67.4%，南方传媒、城市传媒出版业务营业收入占比超过 30%。出版上市公司出版业务收入同比增长 6.5%，9 家公司出版业务收入实现正增长；长江传媒、城市传媒增长速度达 20%左右，位居前列；个别公司出版业务营业收入和占比小幅下降。一般图书营业收入稳中有增，10 家上市公司一般图书业务收入均实现正向增长。其中，南方传媒一般图书营业收入增长速度达 18.5%，居出版上市公司之首。教材、教辅收入稳中有增，收入规模超过一般图书，仍是出版公司的重要收入来源。

发行业务整体营业收入平稳增长，占比进一步提高。除读者传媒、时代出版外，其余 8 家出版上市公司对发行业务在年报中进行了单独体现，其发行业务收入同比增长 6.4%，城市传媒、出版传媒、中南传媒等 3 家公司同比增速超过 10%。在上述 8 家出版上市公司中，4 家公司发行营业收入占比超过 50%。

印刷业务整体营业收入持平，各公司发展情况各异。除城市传媒、读者传媒外，其余 8 家出版上市公司对印刷业务在年报中进行了单独体现，增长和下滑的公司各有 4 家；印刷业务收入整体占比不高，平均仅为 3.6%，各公司均不超过 10%。出版传媒印刷业务收入同比增长 64.4%，增速居出版公司之首。

新业态业务呈现快速发展态势，但规模有限。中文传媒、凤凰传媒、中南传媒、时代出版等 4 家公司将新业态业务列入主营业务。中文传媒的新业态、中南传媒的数字出版、时代出版的数字产品收入均实现了超过 35%的高速增长。中文传媒以游戏公司智明星通为核心的新业态板块收入同比增长 45.0%，占营业收入的比重达到 38.0%，已经成为公司业务的重要支柱。不过，多数出版上市公司新业态业务收入占比不高。

2. 报业公司

传统报刊业务继续大幅下滑，发展形势依旧严峻。受新媒体持续冲击影响，除华闻传媒外，其余 4 家公司报刊发行及广告业务收入均出现不同程度下降。随着报业市场的萎缩，粤传媒和华媒控股报刊发行业务整体营业收入同比下降 27.3%和 14.6%。

面对报刊业务的严峻形势，报业公司积极推进媒体融合步伐加快，培育新的利润增长点。报业公司一方面整合传播资源，打造新媒体传播矩阵，巩固主流媒体影响力，夯实主业；另一方面布局网络游戏、大数据等相关领域，缓解主业压力。华媒控股积极拓展新媒体业务，将其列入主营业务。华闻传媒通过打造覆盖用户主要生活和工作场景的立体化现代传播体系，数字内容服务业务收入同比增长 30.9%，成为公司业务增长最快的板块。粤传媒和浙报传媒积极探索业务升级、媒体融合和跨界融合，推进产业升级转型。

3. 发行公司

发行公司营业收入和净利润稳中有增，发行业务整体呈稳步增长态势，继续保持核心地位，收入占比均在 40%以上。除广弘控股因实施发行和食品业务双主业布局，发行业务占比相对较低外，其余 4 家公司发行业务收入占比均在 50%以上。

发行公司紧密结合自身经营优势，强化业务基础，完善产业布局，拓展业务类型，积极整合线上线下资源，努力探索传统业务与数字教育、金融的融合发展。各发行公司在文教用品销售、广告报刊等发行周边业务领域，移动网络游戏、多媒体等新业态产业，食品业等业务领域的基础上，积极开展供应链及物流服务业务和出版策划及服务业务。天舟文化移动网络游戏业务收入大幅增长 37.7%，占营业收入比重接近 45%，毛利率高达 91.7%。皖新传媒积极推动与金融、科技融合，助力产业升级；打造三大物流园和物流大数据平台建设，物流金融模式发展迅速，供应链及物流服务业务全年实现营业收入 3.6 亿元，成为新的增长点。新华文轩教育服务业务板块销售收入较上年同期增长 8.8%，增加 3.0 亿元，成为拉动公司业绩大幅提升的重要动力。

4. 印刷公司

印刷公司产出和利润总体呈现增长态势，毛利率稳固提升，印刷及其相关衍生业务核心地位仍不可撼动。鉴于印刷公司各自细分业务差异较大，各分行业面临经营环境不同，个体经营差异明显。

转型升级已成为印刷公司寻求业绩增长的重要途径。部分公司紧跟行业热点，转型升级步伐较快，成效已初步显现。鸿博股份一方面充分挖掘公司现有的技术和市场资源，巩固与提升主营业务产业链，另一方面继续推进智能IC卡、物联网、电子彩票等新兴产业的发展。公司票证产品业务收入6.6亿元，占总体营业收入78.1%，同比增长39.5%。康得新投入5.4亿元研发经费用于高分子材料产品改良及调整，并将公司业务延伸至新能源汽车生态和互联网智能应用平台建设，光学膜销售收入75.2亿元，大幅提高27.2%，占主营业务收入比重超过80%，较2015年进一步提高，成为拉动公司业绩的主要动力。陕西金叶、界龙实业积极投入房地产业，房地产业营业收入占主营业务收入比重均超过40%，成为继印刷业务之外的第二大主营业务。

5. 新媒体公司

新媒体公司通过持续的业务模式创新、研发投入、市场拓展，构建泛娱乐新生态，推动业务稳定发展，产出利润保持高速增长态势。中文在线在数字出版基础上，打造IP上下游全产业链，在影视、游戏、动漫、数字阅读、有声听书等领域全面开花结果。掌趣科技专注于网络游戏尤其是移动游戏产品的开发、发行与运营。昆仑万维实行游戏开发与代理发行业务双轮驱动，着力打造“营运一体化”和“代理精品化”战略，从移动游戏到互联网工具、视频直播、亚文化领域、人工智能等方向对业务进行了全新升级，聚焦“打造海外领先的社交媒体和内容平台”，并优化商业模式，其原创西方奇幻题材的自研代表作《神魔圣域》不断拓展语言版本至多语言版本，在印尼、俄罗斯、波兰、阿根廷、巴西等多个新兴市场中长期保持游戏畅销榜前十的位置。掌趣科公司围绕游戏主业进行泛娱乐投资布局，在体育、动漫、影视、体育以及VR方面进行了一系列投资布局，开启PS及PSVR的体验项目。

七、产业基地（园区）情况分析

（一）经济总量规模

依据30家国家新闻出版产业基地（园区）报送的数据汇总，上述基地（园区）2016年共实现营业收入2 306.2亿元，利润总额309.6亿元，拥有资产总额2 934.5亿元。其中，营业收入超过百亿元的7家，资产总额过百亿的11家，利润总额超过20亿的5家。

在30家产业基地（园区）中，营业收入超过400亿元的1家，即上海张江国家数字出版基地；营业收入在200亿～300亿元之间的2家，即江苏国家数字出版基地和广东国家数字出版基地；在100亿～200亿元之间的4家，降序依次为安徽国家数字出版基地、广东国家网络游戏动漫产业发展基地、西安国家数字出版基地和杭州国家数字出版产业基地；在50亿～100亿元之间的7家，降序依次为天津国家数字出版基地、青岛国家数字出版产业基地、中国北京出版创意产业园区、中南国家数字出版基地、重庆两江新区国家数字出版基地、广东国家音乐创意产业基地和江西国家数字出版基地。上述14家基地（园区）营业收入合计占30家基地（园区）的84.8%。

营业收入不足50亿元的16家，降序依次为天津国家级新闻出版装备产业园、西安国家印刷包装产业基地、河北·廊坊国家印装产业园区、赣州吉安国家印刷包装产业基地、海峡国家数字出版产业基地、辽宁国家印刷产业基地、上海金山国家绿色创意印刷示范园区、成都国家音乐产业基地、华中国家数字出版基地、重庆市出版传媒创意区（中心）、北京国家音乐产业基地、华中国家绿色印刷包装物流产业园、辽宁国家动漫产业发展基地、黑龙江省平房国家动漫出版产业基地、上海国家音乐产业基地和北京国家数字出版基地。

上海张江国家数字出版基地、江苏国家数字出版基地、广东国家数字出版基地、安徽国家数字出版基地、广东国家网络游戏动漫产业发展基地、西安国家数字出版基地和杭州国家数字出版产业基地等7家基地（园区）资产总额和营业收入均超过100亿元，组成“双百亿”基地（园区）阵营。

（二）数字出版基地（园区）经济规模

2016年，14家国家数字出版基地（园区）共实现营业收入1 705.92亿元，较2015年增长17.4%；拥有资产总额1 759.38亿元，增长36.6%；实现利润总额271.10亿元，增长3.8%。

1. 营业收入

以营业收入衡量，14家国家数字出版基地（园区）的降序排位情况如表65所示。

在14家国家数字出版基地（园区）中，营业收入超过400亿元的1家，即上海张江国家数字出版基地；营业收入在200亿～300亿元之间的2家，即江苏国家数字出版基地和广东国家数字出版基地，新增1家；在100亿～200亿元之间的3家，即安徽国家数字出版基地、西安国家数字出版基地和杭州国家数字出版产业基地，新增 1 家；在 50 亿～100 亿元之间的 5 家，即天津国家数字出版基地、青岛国家数字出版产业基地、中南国家数字出版基地、重庆两江新区国家数字出版基地和江西国家数字出版基地；低于 50 亿元的 3 家，减少 2 家。

表 65　　国家数字出版基地（园区）的营业收入

排名	基地（园区）	营业收入（亿元）	在全体中所占比重	
			比重（%）	累计比重（%）
1	上海张江国家数字出版基地	408.00	23.92	23.92
2	江苏国家数字出版基地	255.67	14.99	38.91
3	广东国家数字出版基地	233.85	13.71	52.62
4	安徽国家数字出版基地	193.15	11.32	63.94
5	西安国家数字出版基地	113.26	6.64	70.58
6	杭州国家数字出版产业基地	101.58	5.95	76.53
7	天津国家数字出版基地	81.78	4.79	81.32
8	青岛国家数字出版产业基地	78.08	4.58	85.90
9	中南国家数字出版基地	67.31	3.95	89.85
10	重庆两江新区国家数字出版基地	62.61	3.67	93.52
11	江西国家数字出版基地	55.47	3.25	96.77
12	海峡国家数字出版产业基地	33.40	1.96	98.73
13	华中国家数字出版基地	21.53	1.26	99.99
14	北京国家数字出版基地	0.23	0.01	100.00
—	合计	1 705.92	100.00	—
—	平均	121.85	—	—

2. 资产总额

以资产总额衡量，14 家国家数字出版基地（园区）的降序排位情况如表 66 所示。

在 14 家国家数字出版基地（园区）中，资产总额超过 300 亿元的 1 家，即安徽国家数字出版基地；在 200 亿～300 亿元之间的 2 家，即上海张江国家数字出版基地和江苏国家数字出版基地；在 100 亿～200 亿元之间的 5 家，降序依次为青岛国家数字出版产业基地、广东国家数字出版基地、西安国家数字出版基地、中南国家数字出版基地和杭州国家数字出版产业基地；在 50 亿～100 亿元之间的 2 家，即重庆两江新区国家数字出版基地和天津国家数字出版基地；其余 4 家均少于 50 亿元。

表 66　　国家数字出版基地（园区）的资产总额

排名	基地（园区）	资产总额（亿元）	在全体中所占比重	
			比重（%）	累计比重（%）
1	安徽国家数字出版基地	317.15	18.03	18.03
2	上海张江国家数字出版基地	243.00	13.81	31.84
3	江苏国家数字出版基地	205.10	11.66	43.50
4	青岛国家数字出版产业基地	181.09	10.29	53.79
5	广东国家数字出版基地	172.90	9.83	63.62
6	西安国家数字出版基地	150.48	8.55	72.17
7	中南国家数字出版基地	138.73	7.89	80.06
8	杭州国家数字出版产业基地	115.38	6.56	86.62
9	重庆两江新区国家数字出版基地	87.06	4.95	91.57
10	天津国家数字出版基地	57.10	3.25	94.82
11	海峡国家数字出版产业基地	34.70	1.97	96.79

续前表

排名	基地（园区）	资产总额（亿元）	在全体中所占比重	
			比重（%）	累计比重（%）
12	江西国家数字出版基地	31.93	1.81	98.60
13	华中国家数字出版基地	23.13	1.31	99.91
14	北京国家数字出版基地	1.63	0.09	100.00
—	合计	1 759.38	100.00	—
—	平均	125.67	—	—

3. 利润总额

以利润总额衡量，14 家国家数字出版基地（园区）的降序排位情况如表 67 所示。

在 14 家国家数字出版基地（园区）中，利润总额超过 50 亿元的 1 家，即上海张江国家数字出版基地；在 30 亿～50 亿元之间的 2 家，即江西国家数字出版基地和重庆两江新区国家数字出版基地；在 20 亿～30 亿元之间的 2 家，即广东国家数字出版基地和安徽国家数字出版基地，减少 1 家；在 10 亿～20 亿元之间的 2 家，即江苏国家数字出版基地和西安国家数字出版基地，新增 1 家；其余 7 家均少于 10 亿元，其中 1 家亏损。

表 67　　国家数字出版基地（园区）的利润总额

排名	基地（园区）	利润总额（亿元）	在全体中所占比重	
			比重（%）	累计比重（%）
1	上海张江国家数字出版基地	73.60	27.15	27.15
2	江西国家数字出版基地	39.01	14.39	41.54
3	重庆两江新区国家数字出版基地	37.01	13.65	55.19
4	广东国家数字出版基地	29.94	11.04	66.23
5	安徽国家数字出版基地	23.13	8.54	74.77
6	江苏国家数字出版基地	19.27	7.11	81.88
7	西安国家数字出版基地	17.76	6.55	88.43
8	海峡国家数字出版产业基地	9.30	3.43	91.86
9	杭州国家数字出版产业基地	7.31	2.70	94.56
10	青岛国家数字出版产业基地	6.60	2.43	96.99
11	中南国家数字出版基地	3.87	1.43	98.42
12	天津国家数字出版基地	3.59	1.32	99.74
13	华中国家数字出版基地	0.77	0.28	100.02
14	北京国家数字出版基地	−0.06	−0.02	100.00
—	合计	271.10	100.00	—
—	平均	19.36	—	—

（本报告由国家新闻出版广电总局于 2017 年 7 月发布，收入年鉴时有删减）

2016—2017 年中国数字出版产业发展报告

中国数字出版产业年度报告课题组

2016 年是“十三五”开局之年，数字出版产值再创新高，数字出版产值超过 5 700 亿元；数字出版政策环境进一步趋好，政策引导力进一步加强；新闻出版业转型升级持续深化，融合发展初见成效。

一、数字出版收入规模分析

（一）整体收入规模持续增长

2016 年国内数字出版产业整体收入规模为 5 720.85 亿元，比 2015 年增长 29.91%。其中：互联网期刊收入达 17.5 亿元，电子书达 52 亿元，数字报纸（不含手机报）达 9 亿元，博客类应用达 45.3 亿元，在线音乐达 61 亿元，网络动漫达 155 亿元，移动出版（手机彩铃、铃音、移动游戏等）达 1 399.5 亿元，网络游戏达 827.85 亿元，在线教育达 251 亿元，互联网广告达 2 902.7 亿元。收入比例情况见图 1。

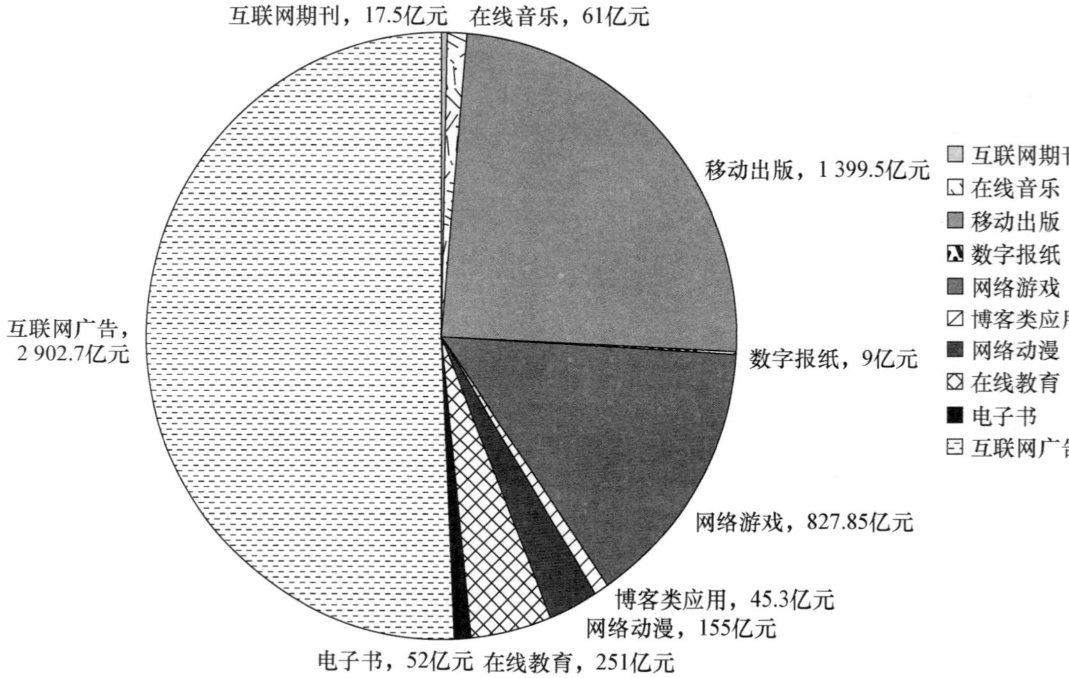

图 1　2016 年数字出版产业收入情况

（二）传统书报刊数字化占比仍在下降

2016 年互联网期刊、电子书、数字报纸的总收入为 78.5 亿元，比 2015 年增长了 5.44%，在数字出版总收入中所占比例为 1.37%，相较于 2015 年的 1.69%和 2014 年的 2.06%来说，继续呈下降趋势。这说明传统出版单位在数字化转型升级、融合发展方面仍需要加大力度，要加强转型升级，融合发展路径与方向规划，增强市场竞争能力，巩固和提升已有的市场份额。

（三）新兴板块发展强劲

2016 年，移动出版收入规模为 1 399.5 亿元，在线教育收入规模为 251 亿元，网络动漫收入规模为 155 亿元，三者占数字出版收入规模的比例为 31.56%，比 2015 年增加了 2.49 百分点，表明移动出版依然是数字出版的重要发展方向，具有雄厚的发展潜力；在线教育作为数字教育出版的核心部分，经过多年布局与市场竞争，产业取得进一步发展；网络动漫经过多年的探索与坚持，在 IP 运营日益受到重视的情况下，已经进入发展的快车道。

二、数字出版产业态势分析

（一）政策引导扶持力度进一步增强

2016年，主管部门以国家政策为依循，推动新闻出版转型升级、融合发展的政策指向性更加明确，部署更加全面、具体、细化，推进转型融合的成效日益显著。

2016年，《新闻出版广播影视业“十三五”时期发展规划》已完成编制，数字出版“十三五”时期发展规划、新闻出版业科技“十三五”时期发展规划等十多个专项规划业已出台，转型升级仍将是新闻出版业“十三五”时期的重点任务，并在全面完成转型升级的基础上，实现初步融合发展。

2016年，国家新闻出版广电总局（以下简称总局）把推进行业机构建设和智库建设作为布局重点。5月，总局发布了《关于申报出版融合发展重点实验室有关工作的通知》，并于12月底公布了20家出版融合发展重点实验室依托单位和共建名单。10月，总局发布了《关于开展首批新闻出版业科技与标准重点实验室申报工作的通知》，同样于2016年底公布了首批名单。2016年10月，总局出台了《关于加快新闻出版业实验室建设的指导意见》。2016年8月，总局发布了《关于征集新闻出版业数字化转型升级软件技术服务商的通知》，并于10月确定了《新闻出版业数字化转型升级软件技术服务商推荐名录（2016）》，此项措施为传统出版单位和技术企业之间的合作搭建了桥梁。由此可见，主管部门的服务能力、引导力有了显著提升。

（二）网络文学发展持续强劲

经过2015年的发展高峰，2016年网络文学仍然保持良好的发展势头。据《2016年数字阅读白皮书》显示，相较于2015年，2016年数字阅读内容总量增长率达到88.2%。其中，原创占比从69%上升到79.7%。

2016年，网络文学主流化进程加快。现实主义题材日益增多。越来越多的网络作家加入作协等行业组织机构，多个省市作协和行业作协相继成立网络文学组织，标志着网络作家和网络文学作品正逐渐获得全社会以及业界的身份认同和价值认同。

IP运营已成为网络文学行业的重要商业模式。随着版权环境得到显著改善，网络文学IP运作模式从一次性售卖转向对内容的深度、长线开发，产业链不断延展，带来越来越多的跨界合作。

2016年网络文学“走出去”取得重大突破。多部网络文学作品走出国门，畅销海外市场。网络文学网站纷纷开展海外市场布局，网络文学逐渐成为彰显中国文化软实力、夯实文化自信的重要文化形态。

（三）数字教育出版取得显著突破

过去一年来，在线教育、翻转课堂、MOOCs、SPOCs、数字教材、电子书包、微课等教育教学服务模式与产品不断涌现。数字教育所蕴藏着的巨大发展潜力，一方面吸引了腾讯、阿里巴巴、网易等互联网大型企业在数字教育领域的集中布局；另一方面，也先后涌现出一批如一起作业网、学科网这样的互联网教育公司。目前，传统教育出版单位转型升级渐趋深入，在政策引导与项目推动下，在学前教育、基础教育（K12）、高等教育、职业教育、在线培训等数字教育出版的不同层面，逐步找到适合自身的发展路径，思路更加清晰。加快数字资源建设步伐，依托于自身优势积极探索新的数字教育模式，提出有特色的数字教育出版实施方案，对“十三五”时期的融合发展路径，已形成了较为明确的规划目标，并已具备了一定的项目基础。

（四）知识服务取得阶段性成果

国家新闻出版广电总局遴选出28家出版社作为知识服务试点单位，在核心技术支持单位，知识体系建设、知识加工、管理技术单位，以及运营技术支持单位的选择与合作方面，提供了参考范围与指南，此举有效推进了试点单位与技术单位深度合作，推进了知识服务模式的创新性探索。2016年，总局正式批复中国新闻出版研究院筹建知识资源服务中心，为构建国家级知识资源服务体系提供基础性组织保障。

过去一年来，行业内以“知识服务”为标签的数字化产品或服务平台不断涌现，出版单位的数字化转型升级逐渐从数字出版系统搭建、资源库建设等基础环节建设过渡到搭建知识资源服务平台，向社会提供知识资源服务的建设阶段转变；逐渐从满足用户的简单文献获取需求向利用信息动态重组形成解决方案的更高层次转变，探索从“内容提供商”向“知识服务提供商”的定位转型。此外，知识服务的发展也直接推进了大数据在出版领域逐步实现落地应用。

（五）有声读物成为数字阅读新兴增长极

过去一年来，有声读物迎来发展高峰。据《2016年数字阅读白皮书》的数据显示，2016年中国有声阅读市场增长 48.3%，达到 29.1 亿元①。目前，国内已经先后涌现出 200 多个带有听书功能的移动平台，喜马拉雅 FM、蜻蜓 FM 等有声读物平台知名龙头已然兴起，市场竞争格局初步形成。在内容方面，2016 年有声平台纷纷加强与出版机构的合作，加大在有声书领域的布局。

有声读物为很多内容创业者及团队提供了机遇，财经、科技等专业垂直细分领域的内容成为有声读物发展的重点之一，有声读物有望成为知识服务的新模式。有声读物平台纷纷推出了付费精品有声内容，有声读物行业进入了内容变现阶段。与此同时，有声读物成为 IP 生态链中的一环，网络文学、影视剧、网剧等内容转化为有声读物已然非常普遍。

（六）社交媒体实现多元化发展多样化效应

微博、微信等移动端社交媒体已成为信息获取的重要渠道以及网络舆论重要源头。微博已发展成为一个综合多种细分领域的大型社交媒体平台，其话题讨论量和关注度不断创出新高，源源不断地产生新的社会热点，产生广泛的社会效应。近年来，微博不断加大对垂直领域自媒体的扶持力度。同时，实施多媒体化战略，微博的内容呈现方式更加多元化，成功转型成“文字＋图片＋视频＋直播”的综合性内容平台。微信的基础功能是即时通信，但其媒体属性也在不断增强。微信公众平台为用户提供了丰富全面的信息内容，无论是传统媒体还是新媒体都将微信公众号作为信息发布和品牌营销的重点。

新闻客户端也向社交媒体方向发展，强化社交功能。新闻客户端越来越注重自身社交属性的培养，并加大了对自媒体的培育与扶持力度，建立自己的社群关系，打造自身的媒体生态闭环。当前社交媒体不再盲目追求一时的热度，而是更加注重内容的持续效应，而随着网络直播、短视频、音频等领域的兴起，社交媒体的迭代升级多元化发展仍在继续。

（七）行业管理机制进一步健全

过去一年来，国家新闻出版广电总局加大了对数字出版的管理力度，出台了一系列管理制度与指导意见，为数字出版环境的进一步优化提供了有力保障。

2016 年 2 月 4 日，国家新闻出版广电总局、工业和信息化部联合颁布《网络出版服务管理规定》，自 2016 年 3 月 10 日起施行。该《规定》对网络出版服务许可、网络出版服务管理、监督管理、保障与奖励，以及法律责任做出说明，进一步规范了网络出版服务行为。

针对数字出版具体业务领域，主管部门也加大了管理力度。2016 年 6 月，总局出台了《关于移动游戏出版服务管理的通知》，要求对移动游戏出版进行前置审批，明确了移动游戏出版的管理流程，针对不同类型的移动游戏提出了不同的审批要求，强化了移动游戏出版服务单位的内容质量审核责任。2016 年 11 月，总局下发了《关于加强网络文学作品版权管理的通知》，进一步明确了通过信息网络提供文学作品以及提供相关网络服务的网络服务商在版权管理方面的责任义务。

（八）保障体系进一步完善

2016 年，我国数字出版产业保障体系在诸多方面得以完善与丰富。

在标准方面，数字出版标准体系族群化建设得到进一步加强。2016 年，最新修订的《出版管理条例》与《新闻出版行业标准化管理办法》，以及《标准化法》等上位法，共同构建了数字出版标准化工作的法律环境，丰富了以标准为抓手的管理手段。以《数字期刊术语》为代表的五项数字期刊标准主要涉及术语、分类与代码、核心业务流程、质量管理等，有利于夯实行业基础，提高行业运作水准。《数字出版内容卫星传输规范》系列标准的颁布，对利用卫星手段传输数字出版内容的技术方式提出了详尽的要求，有利于加强对数字出版内容卫星传输渠道与行为的规范。《中小学数字教材质量要求及检测方法》等 4 项标准不仅对数字教材和电子课本进行了明确定位，而且为中小学数字出版物进行了清晰的行业归属划分。由中国新闻出版研究院牵头研究制定的复合出版工程标准族群，有力地从技术角度支持了工程顺畅实施建设。

在数字版权保护方面，数字版权保护技术研发工程已进入全面应用推广阶段。2016 年，工程通过技术终验、财务终验与整体验收，标志着该工程的全面竣工。

数字版权保护立法工作取得新进展。2016 年 11 月发布的《电影产业促进法》对信息网络传播的公映电影进行规范。2016 年 8 月实施的《移动互联网应用程序信息服务管理规定》加强了对移动互联网应用程序（APP）信息服务领域的版权保护规范。

司法与行政保护力度加强，成效显著。各级法院受理的知识产权案件数量再创新高，审判质效稳中向好，赔偿力度有所提升。“剑网行动”成果显

① 数字阅读助推全民阅读时代 [EB/OL]. [2017-04-24]. http://media.people.com.cn/n1/2017/0424/c40606-29230126.html.

著，有效规范了网络作品的传播秩序，净化了网络版权环境。在网络文学、私人影院、APP、网络广告联盟等领域开展的专项整治行动，也取得较好效果。

社会保护获得新进展。由中国作协网络文学委员会与中国音像与数字出版协会数字阅读工作委员会于2016年7月共同发起了《网络文学行业自律倡议书》，呼吁营造网文良好发展环境。2016年9月，由主要网络文学企业和原创小说网站发起的中国网络文学版权联盟成立，联盟成员承诺积极配合政府部门开展网络反盗版维权活动，努力营造良好的网络文学版权保护社会氛围。百度、奇虎360、新浪、迅雷等企业作为网络服务提供商等纷纷针对贴吧、网盘等领域开展自查整改工作。2016年12月，首都版权产业联盟联合百度网盟推广、360广告联盟、阿里妈妈广告联盟和腾讯广告联盟发出了《网络广告联盟版权自律倡议》，共同维护健康良好的网络版权秩序。

三、数字出版产业问题与对策分析

2016年，我国数字出版产业仍存在一些突出问题：一是融合发展的思路有待进一步开拓，产品、模式有待进一步创新；二是数字出版产品内容整体水平有待提升，核心竞争力有待进一步加强；三是科技研发与应用水平和产业发展需求尚有较大差距；四是市场运营能力仍有较大提升空间。为了进一步推进新闻出版业转型升级深化，融合发展进程，未来一段时间内，要从以下几个方面予以着力。

（一）创新融合发展方式

当前新闻出版的转型升级、融合发展已经步入提挡增速的新阶段，要向深层次迈进，应当充分统筹考虑其战略地位，综合提升新闻出版的融合发展水平。要着力开拓转型升级思路，创新融合发展手段和业务模式，以切实推进融合发展提质增效、扩容提速。一是不断提升对融合发展的认识与理解。二是进行服务形态创新融合。三是加大与外部产业跨界融合。四是开放发展，加强国际交流融合。五是加强管理，及时调整融合发展的布局。

（二）提升内容生产能力

新闻出版转型升级、融合发展无论到了哪个阶段，都要把内容生产放在核心位置，始终坚持把社会效益放在首位，实现社会效益和经济效益相统一，实现内容质量和市场效应的双赢。在提升内容质量方面，企业应发扬严谨专注、精益求精、精雕细琢的工匠精神，不断提升内容品质，切实推进转型融合从数量到质量的跨越升级。同时，着力拓展题材、内容、形式、手法，推动内容和形式的有机结合；以内容主题为核心，强化IP思维，进行同一内容的全媒体版权的多元开发，最大限度地挖掘内容价值。

（三）运用技术手段推进供给优化

内容与技术的融合，不是两者简单相加。融合必须是利用先进的技术优化出版流程，实现内容与技术的相互支撑、内容与渠道的有机结合，使数字出版产品立体化传播、多样化呈现、多渠道推送，运用技术让内容优势得到充分发挥。因此，要做到科学统筹内容与技术之间的关系。技术是为内容服务的，要科学运用技术手段，推动数字内容、技术、模式和业态创新，推动有效优质供给，实现技术与内容、产品的良好适配。推动大数据技术在出版流程中的落地应用，将推动产业的供给优化。只有以数据为依据指导生产，才能在降低成本的同时，为用户提供精准的内容和服务，实现产品的优化供给。

（四）强化互联网运营能力

近年来，传统出版单位在数字化转型升级方面有了长足发展，但数字出版产品影响力仍然普遍偏低，很大程度上是源于传统出版单位缺乏在互联网环境下的运营能力。出版单位要提高互联网环境下的市场运营能力，一是强化互联网思维，提高对互联网和移动互联网的适应度和敏感度。二是要强化用户思维，充分把握用户需求，提供内容和服务的精准化、定制化推送，注重运营细节，完善用户体验。三是推进产品的市场化运作，实现运营的专业化、市场化。做到与互联网环境的真正接轨。四是树立品牌观念，综合运用各种渠道、媒介、平台进行产品推广，提升产品的市场知名度和品牌影响力。五是顺应转型需求，吸纳运营人才。

（五）加强数字内容评价体系建设

随着我国数字内容产业的迅猛发展，对数字内容评价的需求越来越迫切。当前数字内容的评价，多集中在网络文学领域，价值评估存在标准不统一的现象，从而造成版权交易中的成本浪费。当前企业大多偏重于网络文学的品牌影响力、商业价值，缺乏有关社会效益的考量。进行网络文学的价值评估应从内容、品牌、商业价值三个维度展开建立评价标准。需由主管部门出台版权价值评估操作的相关指导意见，统一术语规范，推进并完善网络文学的阅评及推介工作，并由主管部门、文学网站、科研机构、高校等从不同角度共同探讨，建立统一的网络文学评价体系。此外，不仅仅是网络文学领域，动漫游戏、数字教育、知识服务等领域都应建立起各自的评价标准体系。

（六）推动行业智库建设

当前，出版新型智库建设尚处于初级阶段，与融合发展的需求尚存在一定差距，出版领域有影响的智库数量较少。未来在建设出版智库方面，需要政府主管部门和企业的重视与投入。在研究方面，要具备高度的前瞻性、战略性、引领性；加强对发展决策的参与程度和深度；在引领行业发展方面发挥充分作用；通过打造优质团队，提升智库水平。此外，行业实验室也充当着智库的角色。在行业实验室建设方面，应紧盯前沿技术和发展趋势，大力实施新闻出版业转型升级重大项目，通过研究攻关，尽快形成一批可复制、可推广的新技术、新成果、新模式、新标准，尽快使成果转化为推动产业发展的生产力，为传统出版和新兴出版融合发展提供智力支撑、技术保障和示范经验。

四、数字出版产业趋势分析

（一）融合发展内力比拼时代即将来临

进入“十三五”时期，出版业融合发展向更深层次迈进。出版业融合发展拥有了更为扎实的基础。无论从主管部门层面，还是出版单位层面，对于转型升级融合发展都有了更加深入的思考与更为全面的布局。新闻出版单位的转型升级、融合发展将步入常态化、纵深化轨道，发展模式从单一向特色化方向发展。对于传统出版单位而言，随着转型升级步入常态化、纵深化，各家出版单位在融合发展方面的成绩和实力，也将分出伯仲，形成分水岭，考验着各家出版单位的内容生产水平、技术应用水平、运营能力以及资本运作能力。融合发展经过长时期的探索，将有望形成一批有效模式，涌现更多的新型业态。跨界融合将更紧密、更深入，培育出更多新增长点。

（二）人工智能技术重塑出版流程

人工智能技术被视为信息时代一项重大的技术变革，正在迅速渗透并颠覆各个领域，同时也正加速进入新闻出版业，在出版发行、印刷物流、数据加工、数字阅读、数字教育等领域得以应用。首先，人工智能将让出版流程实现智能化。一是语音录入稿件。当前语音识别无论是响应速度还是识别准确率都达到了较高水平，可以通过语音录入代替打字或手写稿件。二是机器协助校稿。由机器协助作者或编辑进行稿件校对，做一些基础性工作。三是机器写作，可大大缩减发稿流程，提升发稿效率。四是增强用户交互体验。此外，利用机器算法实现新闻资讯的精准化、个性化推送，已在新闻客户端广泛应用。人工智能在印刷领域同样具有广阔的发展前景，可有效淘汰落后产能，提高生产效率。

（三）IP 运营实现从量变到质变的跨越升级

2017 年，IP 市场将继续保持上升势头，但相比前两年，将从爆发期进入理性成长期。首先，业界对于 IP 的选择与运作将更加慎重，从内容质量、品牌影响力和商业价值等维度上面将有更加全面的综合考量。与此同时，市场对 IP 质量提出了更高的要求，推动 IP 的优胜劣汰。其次，未来 IP 的竞争，不仅仅是内容上的竞争，还是 IP 生命长度，即持续影响力的竞争，有关 IP 的多角度价值开发运作，让 IP 的生命力可以得到尽可能多的衍生与价值升华。再次，IP 热潮让整个文化产业认识到版权运营的重要性，多元化、深入型的 IP 全产业链开发新生态将逐步构建。同时，随着 IP 理念的深入人心，IP 这一概念已不仅仅局限在网络文学、动漫游戏、影视等领域，而是涵盖整个知识领域范畴。在教育出版和专业出版领域，知识付费兴起加速了知识 IP 化的步伐。

（四）数字教育出版生态圈逐步形成

未来一年里，数字教育出版仍将保持良好的发展势头，具有广阔的发展潜力和发展空间。在线教育在垂直领域的模式顺利发展；行为数据、学情数据、评价数据大爆发，让个性化学习成为可能；技术与内容的融合，将使得学习效率大幅提升；直播在数字教育领域广泛应用，将拓展创新在线教育应用场景和模式。

出版业在教育领域的转型升级融合发展渐趋深入，各家出版单位以优质教学资源为核心，以技术和平台数据为支撑，以数字产品为发力点，构筑完整的数字教育生态闭环。数字教育出版从内容生产到用户服务的数字教育全流程的各个环节被打通，从线上至线下的整体布局初步形成。而 BAT 等互联网企业未来在数字教育领域的布局将从前两年的攻城略地占领市场份额转向对优质教学资源的占有，以提供优质的教学内容为发展基石，构建完善的数字教育生态体系。

（五）学术期刊集群化向纵深发展

集群化发展成为学术期刊增强实力、推动转型、提升品牌的重要途径，通过搭建多学术期刊统一资源服务平台，各期刊在资源、平台、人才、运营等方面优势互补，协同发展，成为学术期刊集群化发展的新途径。学术期刊集群化发展从综合性全领域海量平台向同一垂直领域（如科技、财经等）专业平台转变。一方面，部分期刊单位旗下拥有多部期刊，多属同一专业领域，期刊单位可搭建统一平台，建立资源数据库，实现多期刊的统一管理和运营，形成集群优势，激发期刊发展内在活力，壮大期刊品牌，提升期刊的综合影响力。另一方面，期刊单位可利用自身在行业内的影响，牵头联合其他同领域的专业学术期刊。此外，由于期刊单位的技术水平、资金实力普遍较为薄弱，市场运营能力较低，行业垂直领域第三方学术期刊平台将大量涌现。

（六）知识付费渐趋兴起

过去一年来，互联网迎来了内容创业风潮，付费社区、音频问答、在线课程等知识付费产品表现抢眼，如知乎推出实时问答互动产品《知乎 live》；罗振宇的罗辑思维推出主打高效知识服务产品《得到》等，而这些较早一批进军知识付费的企业和内容创业者已取得了较好的收益。知识付费的兴起，一方面是由于内容创业者对于知识变现模式的探索，另一方面是由于用户对于互联网信息获取提出了更深层次的要求，人们更加注重知识对自身需求的实际满足。在生活节奏日益加快的今天，人们对知识获取的需求正从“大而全”逐渐转向“细而精”。从《得到》《分答》等当下知识付费热门产品来看，专业化细分领域的知识付费是未来的发展方向。

（七）网络直播行业将迎来变革期

2017 年将是网络直播的行业监管年，也是网络直播平台的洗牌之年，政策上的收紧倒逼网络直播加快迈向规范化、健康化发展的轨道。总体而言，2017 年是网络直播行业各方面迈向成熟的关键一年。在内容方面，随着人们对实用性、个性化的内容需求的日益旺盛，知识型直播成为网络直播发展的新方向。同时，直播正快速向各个垂直领域延伸，游戏＋直播、直播＋新闻、直播＋体育、直播＋教育、直播＋电商等模式将不断发展并趋于成熟。在格局方面，各类直播平台在 2017 年将会展开更为激烈的市场争夺战，行业格局渐趋明朗，将推动互联网巨头在网络直播领域的布局。在商业模式方面，除了粉丝在直播时直接打赏，网络主播孵化成为 IP，投放至其他周边产业，如广告、影视剧、娱乐活动，也将成为网络直播经济变现的重点方向之一。

（课题组组长：张立；副组长：王飚、李广宇；课题组成员：毛文思、徐瑶、郝园园、刘玉柱、孟晓明、宋迪莹、李熙）

2016 年中国广播电视产业发展报告

国家新闻出版广电总局发展研究中心

2016 年，全国各级各类广播电视传媒机构深入贯彻落实“五位一体”总体布局和“四个全面”战略布局，扎实推进媒体融合发展，播出机构职能定位进一步强化，节目制作机构规模进一步扩大，电视剧产量稳定、类型丰富，纪录片动画片精品涌现，广告创收总体保持增长态势，广播电视有线网络加快向数字化、双向化、宽带化发展，三网融合、“宽带广电”带来的新兴业务发展迅速，成为新的增长点。

一、广播电视制作播出机构发展

（一）播出机构稳步发展

截至 2016 年底，经国家新闻出版广电总局（以下简称总局）批准设立的播出机构共有 2 578 座，其中广播电台 138 座、电视台 148 座、教育电视台 40 座、广播电视台 2 252 座；开设广播电视节目 4 331 套（不含数字付费广播电视节目），其中广播频率 2 980 套，电视频道 1 351 套。

一是坚持新闻立台、导向立台，把新闻宣传放在首要。中央三台、各省级广播电视播出机构坚持以宣传为中心，不断突出强化新闻、新闻综合类频率频道建设。2016 年，全国广播节目制作量达 782.03 万小时，新闻资讯类广播节目达 145.73 万小时，同比增长 1.48%，在广播节目制作中的比重达 18.63%，同比增加 0.02 百分点；广播节目播出总量 1 456.51 万小时，同比增长 2.44%，新闻资讯类广播节目达 293.40 万小时，在广播节目播出中的比重达 20.14%，同比增加 0.15 百分点。全国电视节目制作量达 350.72 万小时，同比下降 0.37%，新闻资讯类电视节目达 98.99 万小时，在电视节目制作中的比重达 28.22%，同比增加 0.43 百分点；电视节目播出总量 1 792.44 万小时，同比增长 0.72%，新闻资讯类电视节目达 260.18 万小时，在电视节目播出中的比重达 14.52%，同比增加 0.36 百分点。

二是积极推进频率频道专业化，频率频道结构日趋优化。目前，全国地级以上 1 255 套电视频道中，共有 638 套专业频道（含各级教育电视台开办的 43 套节目），占比 50.84%。就广播来说，新闻频率、经济频率、交通频率、音乐频率市场地位进一步巩固；电视频道的专业化程度有所提升，专业频道对各类人群多样化需求的定位进一步明晰，综合频道、新闻频道、综艺频道、财经频道、体育频道、影视频道、纪录频道、青少和动画频道等占有主流地位。针对边疆地区、民族地区，近年来先后批准开办了近百套民族语频率频道，为面向边疆地区、少数民族地区的公共服务和新闻宣传提供了保障。

三是着力强化基层广播电视机构的基础作用。市县台是中国广播电视传播体系的重要组成部分，充分发挥贴近基层群众的优势，强化贴近性、针对性和服务性，成为当地党委政府实施各项工作重要工具，也是基层公共文化服务的重要主体。从 2016 年下半年开始到 2017 年 3 月底，国家新闻出版广电总局批准了青海、西藏两地共 40 个县分别设立县级广播电视台，解决了上述两地区长期以来县级广播电视播出机构建设薄弱问题，结束了西藏地区一直以来没有县级广播电视台的历史。2016 年，各省（区、市）在广电“十三五”规划中均对基层台建设做了新部署，浙江、山东等省还率先出台了促进县级广播电视台改革发展的意见，河北省和湖南省部分县、市还专门出台了扶持县级台发展的财政政策。

四是高清化、融媒化发展进程加快。各级播出机构对建设高清制播体系的重视和投入力度不断加大，越来越多的播出机构提出频道高、标清同播申请，全国高清同播频道数量稳步增加，高清电视市场规模不断扩大。截至 2016 年底，中央、省、市三级播出机构共经批准开办了 121 个高清电视频道，其中高、标清同播频道 101 个，高清开路频道 2 个，高清付费频道 18 个。此外，国家新闻出版广电总局还积极推动各级广播电视台开办的影视剧、动画、纪实、体育等专业频道的高清同播进程，截至 2016 年底，已批准中央、省、市三级播出机构开办的 58 套专业电视频道高、标清同播，进一步满足了观众对高质量、专业化、特色化节目的收视需求。2016年，广电媒体的融媒化速度也加快。各级广播电视播出机构纷纷加快云平台建设，构建“中央厨房”式的融媒体采编中心；不断健全包括频率频道、网站、客户端、微博、微信公众号在内的新型传播矩阵，以往传统频道频率单一传播运营的局面正在发生重大转变，融合媒体初步形成，中央三台、部分省台和地市台走在融媒化发展前列，传播能力大幅提升。与此同时，融合化呈现联合发展势头，比如，中央电视台（以下简称央视）2017年2月发布新的新媒体战略，推出央视新闻移动网，吸引全国37家省级和计划单列市广电机构入驻，建立了集管理、搜索、授权、引用、转发等诸多功能于一体的媒资共享机制。中央人民广播电台推动中国广播云平台项目建设，以时政新闻报道为突破口，构建“广播端+新媒体端”的音频新媒体矩阵，全国各地广播频率入驻广电云平台。中国国际广播电台立足海外传播优势，打造基于移动互联和社交媒体的新媒体矩阵。湖北台建设长江云平台，各市县广电媒体加盟，形成纵向媒体联合、横向政企对接的融媒体发展新机制。

（二）制作机构大幅增长

1. 机构规模持续扩大

截至2016年底，全国经批准设立的广播电视节目制作机构达14 389家，2016年较2015年的10 232家增加4 157家，增幅达40.63%，成为近年来增幅最大的一年。这一现象具有三个重要因素，一是国家新闻出版广电总局贯彻落实国务院商事制度改革要求，降低市场准入门槛，取消节目制作机构300万元注册金的准入标准，同时实行照证分离，先照后证，取消前置审批，促进一大批企业进入节目制作领域；二是国家鼓励大众创业、万众创新，影视制作成为创业创新的重点领域，一些地方将文化传媒产业作为经济结构优化的抓手，制定多种优惠政策促进节目制作机构发展；三是广电节目市场持续扩大，行业前景向好，吸引人才和资本纷纷进入。

民营广电节目制作机构的增长尤为突出。2016年，持有广播电视节目制作经营许可证的14 389家机构中，民营机构由2015年的8 847家增加到12 927家，增加了46.12%，且占制作机构总数的89.84%。全国拍摄完成的334部14 912集电视剧中，234部10 027集电视剧由民营机构创作完成，分别占比70.06%和67.24%；全国拍摄完成的261部9 117集动画片中，216部7 887集动画片由民营机构完成，分别占比82.76%和86.51%。

2. 专业化、区域化趋势初步形成

制作机构呈专业化发展趋势。2016年全国节目制作机构审核数据显示，同时从事电视剧、动画片、纪录片和其他节目创作生产的机构，以及既从事创作生产又从事代理交易的机构数量较少。14 389家制作机构中，1 343家以电视剧创作生产业务为主，占9.33%；825家以动画片创作生产业务为主，占5.73%；1 544家以纪录片创作生产业务为主，占10.73%；5 312家以综艺节目等其他节目创作生产为主，占36.92%。此外，还有数千家机构主要从事各类节目的版权交易、代理交易等业务，基本不开展创作生产活动。

3. 区域化集中态势明显

节目制作机构主要分布在北京、浙江、上海、广东、江苏等地区，内容创作生产日趋集中。2016年，北京有节目制作机构4 473家、浙江1 994家、上海1 343家、广东848家、江苏547家，这五省（市）的制作机构占到全国总量的63.97%。与之相比，贵州、西藏、青海、宁夏、吉林、黑龙江和内蒙古这七个省（区）的制作机构均不超过100家，累计528家，仅占全国总量的3.67%。2016年，拍摄完成的334部电视剧中，233部由北京、浙江、上海、广东、江苏五省（市）的制作机构创作完成，占比69.76%；拍摄完成的261部动画片中，178部由北京、浙江、上海、广东、江苏五省（市）的制作机构创作完成，占比68.20%。

二、电视剧创作生产

（一）电视剧产量保持稳定

电视剧创作基本保持稳定态势。2016年通过备案公示的剧目共1 208部47 802集。与2015年相比，部数增加49部，集数增加4 130集，电视剧创作仍处于活跃期。2016年，全国各类电视剧制作机构制作完成并获得发行许可的电视剧共有334部14 912集，较2015年减少60部1 628集，电视剧制作逐渐回归理性，集约化程度有所提升（见表1）。

表1　2011—2016年获得发行许可电视剧数量

类型	2011年	2012年	2013年	2014年	2015年	2016年
部数	469	506	441	429	394	334
集数	14 942	17 703	15 770	15 983	16 540	14 912

资料来源：国家新闻出版广电总局电视剧司。

当代题材仍是电视剧创作主流。2016 年，通过备案公示审核的剧目中，当代题材占公示剧目总数的 50%以上。从发行数量看，当代题材电视剧共发行 177 部 8 080 集，分别占发行总量的一半以上（见表 2）。其中，当代都市题材依旧是创作热点，共发行 136 部 6 642 集，分别占发行总量的 40.72%和 44.54%。

表 2　　2016 年获得发行许可电视剧题材比例

数量	当代题材	现代题材	近代题材	古代题材	重大题材	合计
部数	177	13	99	39	6	334
占比	52.99%	3.89%	29.64%	11.68%	1.80%	100%
集数	8 080	537	4 216	1 851	228	14 912
占比	54.18%	3.60%	28.27%	12.41%	1.53%	100%

资料来源：国家新闻出版广电总局电视剧司。

（二）电视剧类型更加丰富

在数量稳中有降的同时，电视剧质量总体提升。一批符合“三精”标准的优秀作品涌现荧屏，取得收视口碑双丰收，有力推动了行业的良性发展。

一是革命历史题材电视剧获得观众肯定。2016 年恰逢纪念建党 95 周年和红军长征胜利 80 周年的重要纪念年份，电视剧行业集中创作生产和播出了一批优秀革命历史题材电视剧，实现了新的艺术和收视突破，受到社会各界好评。《海棠依旧》《彭德怀元帅》等剧讴歌了老一辈无产阶级革命家的丰功伟绩，通过对人物形象和细节的生动刻画，充分展现了其崇高的革命精神和高尚的人格魅力，引发收视热潮。《绝命后卫师》《彝海结盟》《长征大会师》《红星照耀中国》等剧，通过不同的视角表现不朽的长征精神，激发起观众强烈的爱国主义情怀。《麻雀》《解密》等剧，用热门的类型剧，凭借鲜活的故事弘扬了民族精神和家国情怀，点燃了当代青年人观剧热情，是主旋律题材的创新实践。

二是公检法题材电视剧创作热情高涨。2016 年，一批反映公安、政法、检察等题材的电视剧在晚间黄金时段播出，这类剧弘扬正气、彰显正义，受到观众喜爱，获得积极的舆论反响，业界创作热情也逐渐升温。如《人民检察官》聚焦反腐，直面检察官工作的真实情况；《小镇大法官》深入基层，以朴素的视角展现乡村法治生活；《谜砂》全方位展现了新时代警察的精神与风貌等。这类题材电视剧侧重点各不相同，但都是用精心打磨的中国故事弘扬法治精神，传播法治价值，潜移默化地宣传了依法治国理念。

三是当代都市题材电视剧引发社会热议。2016 年，一批反映当代都市生活、经济发展变革和观念更新迭代的现实主义题材电视剧先后在一些主要省级卫视晚间黄金时段播出，引发观众广泛思考与讨论。《欢乐颂》通过对五位女性职场故事和情感的描写，折射出现代都市不同阶层青年女性的现实生活和价值追求；《小别离》直面当下教育问题，引起观众对亲子关系、升学压力等问题的讨论；《女不强大天不容》以都市报女记者自强自立的人生经历为主线，透视出五光十色的当代生活和中国传媒业变革发展的景象。这些作品根植生活、关照现实，反映当代中国都市日新月异的变化和人们真挚动人的情感，一经播出便成为热门话题，获得收视与口碑双丰收。

（三）电视剧制作主体寻求转型

截至 2016 年底，全国持有广播电视节目制作经营许可证的机构共 14 389 家，其中持有电视剧制作经营许可证（甲种）的机构 113 家，这些机构均可以进行电视剧生产发行工作。不考虑公司从属关系，2016 年申报制作数量两部以上的制作机构仅 50 余家，70%以上的公司每年仅申报发行 1 部电视剧，制作力量较为分散。同时，制作机构依旧集中在北京、浙江、上海、广东等省市。2016 年，这四个地区共制作电视剧 194 部 9 438 集，分别占年生产制作总量的 58.08%和 63.29%（见表 3）。

表 3　　电视剧产量 10 部以上的地区

序号	地区	部数	占比	集数	占比
1	北京	63	18.86%	2 655	17.80%
2	浙江	55	16.47%	2 509	16.83%
3	上海	51	15.27%	2 176	14.59%
4	广东	25	7.49%	2 098	14.07%
5	江苏	14	4.19%	595	3.99%
6	天津	14	4.19%	572	3.84%
7	陕西	11	3.29%	461	3.09%
8	湖南	10	2.99%	401	2.69%
9	重庆	10	2.99%	356	2.39%

资料来源：国家新闻出版广电总局电视剧司。

大型制作公司积极拓展业务范围。2016年，电视剧制作资源趋于集中，老牌制作公司在稳固电视剧市场的同时，不断扩展业务版图，由传统电视剧制作向电影、网络剧、综艺节目等多元业务拓展转型。华策影视仍占据较大市场份额，全年取得发行许可证的剧目共20部949集，占全年发行总量的5.99%和6.36%。同时，该公司向电影、综艺等方向布局，实现对生活场景的多维渗透。慈文传媒围绕优质内容，拓展游戏及相关业务，打造“品牌+”泛娱乐平台，取得良好的经济效益。上海新文化深化内容创意开发和制作体系的转型升级，影视剧和综艺等业务板块协同发展（见表4）。

表4　　部分电视剧制作公司业务情况

公司名称	2016年营业总收入	增幅	主营业务	2016年发行的部分电视剧
完美世界股份有限公司	61.49亿元	25.67%	游戏 电视剧 综艺	《咱们相爱吧》 《神犬小七2》 《亲爱的婚姻》
浙江华策影视股份有限公司（含克顿影视、剧酷文化等）	44.41亿元	67.12%	全网剧 电影 综艺	《解密》 《射雕英雄传》 《锦绣未央》
北京华录百纳影视股份有限公司	26.40亿元	40.04%	电视剧 综艺 体育	《深夜食堂》 《角力之城》 《乱世丽人行》
慈文传媒股份有限公司	18.31亿元	113.93%	电视剧 网络剧 游戏	《老九门》 《有一种爱叫放手》
幸福蓝海影视文化集团股份有限公司	15.38亿元	7.01%	电视剧 电影 影城院线	《最后一张签证》 《繁星四月》
长城影视股份有限公司	13.22亿元	33.09%	电视剧 广告 电影	《烽火线》 《家国恩仇记》 《大西北剿匪记》
上海新文化传媒集团股份有限公司	11.13亿元	8.47%	电视剧 电影	《长梦留痕》 《我的老爸是卧底》
浙江唐德影视股份有限公司	8.12亿元	51.04%	电视剧 电影 综艺	《天伦》 《结婚为什么》
欢瑞世纪联合股份有限公司（星美联合股份有限公司）	7.39亿元	55.69%	电视剧 艺人经纪 游戏	《大唐荣耀》 《青云志》

资料来源：营业收入及增幅源于各公司2016年度业绩快报。

中小型公司借力互联网快速成长。一部分新成立的电视剧制作公司深耕互联网资源，创新拓展内容生产模式。柠萌影业将其目标受众定义为“新大众”，从研究用户需求角度对内容生产做出前瞻性判断。2016年该公司参与出品的《小别离》《好先生》等剧获得强烈反响。耀客传媒加大对互联网渠道和年轻观众群体的开发，充分利用流行热点、热门IP，尝试打造了《幻城》《奇星记之鲜衣怒马少年时》《隐形的翅膀》等具备互联网基因的新兴剧目，为吸引年轻观众，满足个性化需求做了探索。

三、纪录片发展

（一）现象级纪录片不断涌现

2016年，纪录片的质量与数量同步提升，高品质的纪录片不断涌现。与往年现象级纪录片每年只有几部的状况不同，2016年以来现象级纪录片多达十几部。这些广受关注与好评的纪录片题材广泛，如聚焦主旋律的革命历史题材纪录片《筑梦路上》《长征》《重生》；反映十八大以来从严治党、反腐惩贪的《永远在路上》；反映国家战略的《一带一路》；传承中医中药文化价值，引领当代人探索生命和健康意义的《本草中国》；聚焦故宫文物修复师这一略显神秘职业的《我在故宫修文物》；关注生命价值，探讨大时代普通人命运的《人间世》；记录自然环境，全方位展示生态多样性的《自然的力量》；讲述普通家庭小生命降生故事的《生门》；开启空中视角、看前所未见中国的《航拍中国》。

（二）纪录片优质播出平台不断拓展

电视仍然是纪录片播出的主渠道，2016 年纪录片播出量约 4.8 万小时，多部大制作、大投入、高质量的纪录片相继在各级卫视黄金时段播出，传播效果进一步增强，口碑和收视表现不俗，体现了纪录片与电视平台的良好互动。

央视多个频道彰显主流价值，新闻频道、科教频道、纪录频道等播出优质纪录片精品，打造纪录片播出高地。纪录频道截至 2016 年 10 月的平均日收视份额达 0.56%，超额完成全年指标；观众覆盖 10.70 亿人，增幅约 3.88%，频道忠实观众群体进一步巩固扩大，纪录国际频道（CCTV—9 Documentary）在 2016 年中播出近 300 小时新节目，首播率较 2015 年增加 60 小时，在国际纪录片业界扩大了知名度与影响力，向世界讲述中国故事取得明显成效。

地方卫视 2016 年加大对纪录片的排播力度，实现了纪录片产业发展与卫视频道品牌升级的双向推动。东方卫视围绕自身定位，细分受众市场，以聚焦时代发展、关注百姓的生存状态和精神世界为出发点，推出了《急诊室故事》《上海工匠》《梦想改造家》等一批电视纪实内容，并探索出省级卫视在纪录片生产、传播和运营的新路径。浙江卫视近两年先后推出《南宋》《艺术：北纬 30 度》等优秀纪录片作品，并取得一定成绩。湖南卫视生产制作的纪录片达 60 余部，在注重时代表达的同时，选题中 80%以上记录了当代年轻人的故事，体现了“青春、向上”的频道特色。北京卫视《档案》累计播出超过 1 000 集节目，成为每周一至周四，全国省级卫视中唯一的历史纪录片自制栏目带。中国教育电视台一套、旅游卫视、河北卫视、北京纪实频道、上海纪实频道、湖南金鹰频道联合播出纪录片栏目《纪录中国》，推介优质纪录片作品，形成传播声势，扩大品牌影响，进一步深化了纪录片与卫视频道的互动模式。

（三）纪录片运营方式进一步创新升级

纪录片宣传推广方式更加多元立体。纪录片借助电视媒体、视频网站、网络社区等多种渠道进行宣传推广，扩大了传播渠道，扩大了目标受众群体，争取到更多的年轻受众，为拉升收视、赢得口碑打下良好基础。央视纪录频道结合频道无栏目、时段化播出、不设主持人的频道特点，依托互联网传播和品牌推介活动，形成线上线下一体的品牌传播体系，精心打造“央视纪录”两微一端，积极拓展新媒体平台功能，策划实施了频道官方微信的升级，强化“手机看大片”等功能，积极打造“媒体融合”创新型立体宣传架构。北京广播电视台为纪录片《大西山》专门推出《大西山》微信公众号，播出期间关注人数增长 71%。广东台着力打造了“南派纪录片”外宣微信公众号，截至 2016 年底，“南派纪录片”公众号用户超过 4 千人，阅读总次数超过 13 万。

纪录片盈利模式不断拓展。纪录片潜藏的经济效益随着纪录片土壤的肥沃日渐显现，市场运营日趋成熟。比如，《本草中国 1》广告特约赞助达到六期千万以上，另外还开辟片前片后的贴片广告、片花等多种硬广、软植方式获得商业回报。多家广告客户对节目的影响力高度认可，将《本草中国 2》纳入重点投放计划。此外，未来在商业衍生链条打造上，江苏卫视将依托“本草”这一 IP，积极整合电商平台做更多探索。这类探索正在纪录片界拓展、推广。

四、动画片发展

（一）动画片题材备案与制作发行保持良性趋势

国产动画产业继续保持产量平稳、质量不断突破的发展态势。2016 年全国电视动画片共制作完成发行 261 部 125 053 分钟，比上年 273 部 13.83 万分钟减少了 12 部 1.32 万分钟。制作发行量排在前五位的省份依次为广东 52 部、浙江 46 部、北京 30 部、江苏 23 部、上海 17 部，占全国制作发行部数的 64.37%，电视动画产业的聚集效应明显。

国产动画题材进一步丰富拓展。2016 年国产动画制作备案 383 部 211 606 分钟，比上年 399 部 29.81 万分钟减少 16 部 8.65 万分钟。经备案公示的童话题材动画片共 185 部 93 681 分钟；教育题材动画片 69 部 55 105 分钟；历史题材动画片共 29 部 17 282 分钟；科幻题材动画片共 23 部 10 317 分钟；神话题材动画片共 4 部 1 040 分钟；现实题材动画片共 23 部 12 267 分钟；其他题材动画片共 50 部 21 914 分钟。其中，涌现出优秀的现实题材动画片《棉花糖和云朵妈妈》《成长不烦恼》，军旅题材动画片《犟驴小红军》《最可爱的人》《聪明的顺溜之雄鹰小子》，传统文化题材《小济公》《中国巧姑娘之黄道婆》等。

（二）动画衍生产业持续拓展

2016 年，“动画＋相关产业”的融合创新进一步拓展，以动画片融入传统产业、新兴产业的方式推进产业转型升级，形成了动画+游戏、动画+出版、动画+教育、动画+旅游、动画+主题乐园、动画+戏曲、动画+电商、动画+传统实业、动画+互联网等衍生产业发展模式的创新探索，推动了跨行业商业模式创新和企业产品市场拓展，促进相关产业发展。

2016 年暑期，《新大头儿子和小头爸爸 2：一日成才》在全国院线上映，是近年来央视少儿频道联合央视动画全力打造核心 IP 的又一成果。金鹰卡通以动画片《爸爸去哪儿》中的卡通形象麦咭为核心，实现了中国第一个电视动漫主题乐园落地，2016 年麦咭乐园已落地两家。《虹猫蓝兔》系列动画与传统服装行业携手，推出“虹猫蓝兔”系列服饰，开启了“虹猫蓝兔”品牌新的产业化之路。北京百视文化传媒有限公司猪迪克系列动画片截至 2017 年 3 月，累计出品 1 066 分钟，出版《我的朋友猪迪克》系列同名图书 26 册。《猪迪克之古怪岛大冒险 I》在北京广播电视台卡酷少儿卫视首播平均收视率 1.28%，市场份额 5.33%。爱奇艺、优酷视频、土豆网和芒果 TV 等新媒体平台跟播，累计发行 300 余家地市级以上广播电视台，基本覆盖全部新媒体传播平台。

（三）动画创作生产国际化程度提升

2016 年，中外合拍动画片结出硕果。中捷合拍的《熊猫和小鼹鼠》、中美合拍的《半斤八两》等作品先后与观众见面。《熊猫和小鼹鼠》由中央电视台央视动画有限公司与捷克共和国捷克小鼹鼠公司共同创作，以深受孩子喜爱的中国国宝“熊猫”和捷克国家级卡通形象“小鼹鼠”共同作为主角，讲述两者之间发生的温馨、幽默、和谐的小故事，不但融入了大量中国元素，也引进了国际共通的卡通语言。《半斤八两》是 SMG 炫动传播与迪士尼公司合拍的动画项目，讲述了两只石狮子成长的故事，故事中蕴含中国文化与中国情怀。

另外，国产动画积极亮相国际影视节展。例如，北京广播电视台卡酷少儿卫视和卡酷传媒有限公司组织二十多家国内动画公司参展 2016 法国昂西国际动画电影节，推介了三十多部国产顶级动画作品，举办了多场主题活动与展览交易，并举办“北京·动画梦”主题沙龙，展示了中国最高水准的优秀动画作品，提升了中国动画在世界舞台的影响力与号召力。

五、广播电视广告发展

（一）广播电视商业广告发展平稳

1. 广播电视广告收入稳中趋降

2016 年，受整个广告市场变化和新兴媒体竞争的影响，全国广播电视商业广告收入稳中趋降。全国广播电视行业广告收入 1 547.22 亿元，同比增长 1.16%，增幅比 2015 年下降 3.28 百分点（见图 1）。

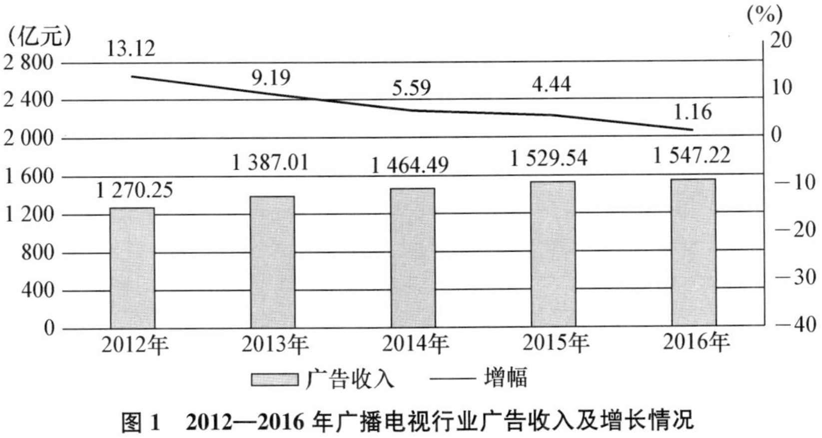

图 1　2012—2016 年广播电视行业广告收入及增长情况

资料来源：国家新闻出版广电总局财务司。

广播电视行业广告收入结构发生了明显变化，广电传统媒体广告收入比重同比下降，以新媒体广告为主的其他广告收入比重同比增加。从地域看，25%的省（区、市）行业广告收入实现增长，其余地区行业广告收入下降。广播电视行业广告收入位居前 10 名的省份如表 5 所示。

表 5　2016 年广播电视行业广告收入位居前 10 名的省份　单位：亿元

省份	北京	上海	浙江	湖南	江苏	广东	山东	安徽	四川	湖北
收入	254.93	186.64	152.7	133.98	100	62.01	48.26	34.7	26.22	24.95

资料来源：国家新闻出版广电总局财务司。

2016 年，广播广告收入 145.83 亿元，同比下降 6.77%（见图 2）。43.75%的省（区、市）广播广告收入增长，增长幅度最大是江西省，增幅达 59.44%，下降幅度最大的是陕西省，降幅达 53.04%。广播广告收入排名前 10 名的省（区、市）如表 6 所示。

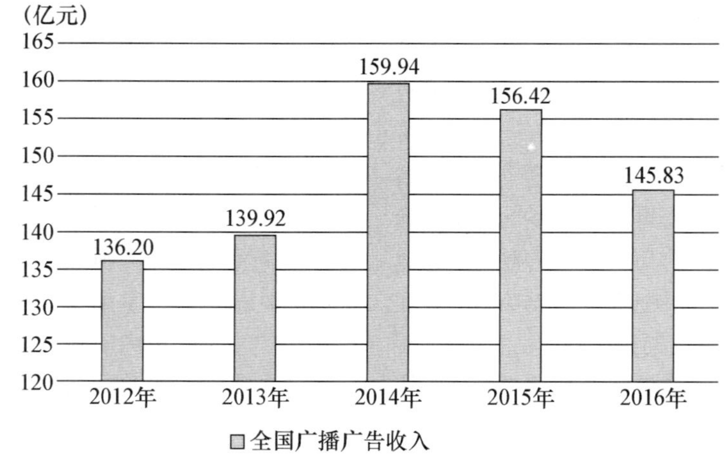

图 2　2012—2016 年全国广播广告收入情况

资料来源：国家新闻出版广电总局财务司。

表 6　**2016 年广播广告收入位居前 10 名的省份**　单位：亿元

省份	江苏	浙江	广东	山东	北京	河南	上海	辽宁	江西	黑龙江
收入	12.42	12.08	11.97	9.47	8.29	7.95	7.10	6.99	6.08	6.05

资料来源：国家新闻出版广电总局财务司。

2016 年，电视广告收入 1 004.87 亿元，同比下降 5.66%（见图 3）。87.50%的省（区、市）电视广告收入下降，下降幅度最大的达 52.62%。电视广告收入排名前 10 名的省（区、市）如表 7 所示。

图 3　2012—2016 年全国电视广告收入情况

资料来源：国家新闻出版广电总局财务司。

表 7　**2016 年电视广告收入位居前 10 名的省份**　单位：亿元

省份	湖南	浙江	江苏	上海	北京	广东	山东	安徽	湖北	四川
收入	107.35	101.95	79.34	71.21	66.24	47.01	35.79	29.11	16.15	15.82

资料来源：国家新闻出版广电总局财务司。

从收入分布情况看，中央级广播电视广告收入占比 18.92%。省级广播电视广告收入超过半数，占比达到 65.72%，比重同比增加 1.56 百分点。地市级和县级广播电视广告收入占比分别为 12.42% 和 2.94%，比重分别同比降低 1.01 百分点和 0.39 百分点（见表 8）。

表 8　　　　2011—2016 年广播电视行业广告收入分级占比情况（%）

地区	2011 年	2012 年	2013 年	2014 年	2015 年	2016 年
中央直属	24.09	24.77	24.26	21.78	19.08	18.92
省级	50.82	52.45	54.84	58.51	64.16	65.72
地市级	19.97	18.23	17.02	16.01	13.43	12.42
县级	5.12	4.55	3.88	3.70	3.33	2.94

资料来源：国家新闻出版广电总局财务司。

2. 各台多方探索创新广告经营，积极探索融媒体广告运营

2016 年全国广电广告经营实施新媒体和频率频道融合营销，强化线上线下互动、频率频道与新媒体互动，广告经营呈现新态势。比如，上海台《阿基米德》APP 相继与湖北、贵州、江西、辽宁、广西等近 60 个省（区、市）电台签署合作协议，与传统广播追求耦合发展，带动广播的“短音频”战略和直播样态的改变，通过数字化节目社区拓展传统广播的影响力空间，吸引广告客户，对接上亿广告投放进入广播市场[①]。通过融合运营，广播电视媒体一定程度上破除了在时间和空间上的局限性，强化了资源有效配置和精准投放。广电媒体努力探索基于多屏互动的智能广告生态圈，取得初步成效。比如，央视广告主打大小屏联合经营策略，用大屏销售带小屏，用小屏销售补大屏，以电视端、PC 端、移动端矩阵式资源全方位满足客户整合传播需求，创新设计融媒体广告产品，实现增量收入 1.4 亿元。全国各级广播电视台积极拓展电视广告与互联网融合运营的新模式，推动经营效益的增长。

3. 着力创新广告经营策略

面对传统广告模式的局限，各台结合自身定位，创新广电广告经营策略，促进广告增长。中央广电媒体探索广告运营从“促进销售为王”向“打造品牌为王”的转型，成效明显。2016 年，央视推出的“国家品牌计划”对以往广告招标模式实现颠覆性创新。央视把握中国经济全球化发展趋势，把广告运营与国家品牌建设结合起来，实施“国家品牌计划”，同中国的优秀企业共同成长，打造一批能够在全球市场上参与商业竞争、文化交流的国家品牌。目前这一计划已经得到了国内 29 家企业的响应。中央人民广播电台也倾力打造国家品牌战略营销，启动“2017 中国品牌集结行动”，显著拉动广告运营，有力撬动了潜在市场。对接国家发展战略、地区发展战略，这是广电广告强化供给侧结构性改革，实现转型经营升级的重要抓手，值得各级广电机构借鉴推广。

4. 推动广告产业多元发展

一是大力推进电视购物频道运营。2016 年，全国 34 家购物频道全年成交额共计 364.3 亿元，连续三年保持在 350 亿元左右，成交额保持稳定。其中，成交额超过 10 亿元的购物频道有 13 家。购物频道在微信商城、APP、实体店、电话销售、目录销售、线下活动等其他渠道的营收，平均占到总成交额的 31.80%。二是大力发展新媒体广告。比如湖南台实施台网融合计划，推动湖南卫视观众向芒果 TV 用户转化，芒果 TV 广告大幅增长[②]。截至 2016 年底，芒果 TV 全年总营收达到 20 亿元，广告营收占 50% 左右[③]。三是积极开拓市场资源。一些卫视频道深度挖掘优质节目资源，多方位开拓市场资源，推动广告收入逆势增长。北京电台广泛拓展合作渠道，改变广告招标机制，开发了 20 多套全新广告产品，拓展新的广告增长点。

（二）大力推动广播电视公益广告繁荣发展

1. 公益广告定位进一步提升

2016 年，多项举措促进广播电视公益广告创新发展。一是政策支撑有力。国家新闻出版广电总局与工商总局等部委联合下发《公益广告促进和管理暂行办法》，首次以部门规章的形式对公益广告做出规定，为广播电视公益广告发展提供政策支撑。二是全国各级电台电视台发挥主力军作用。电台电视台设立专职部门、成立专职团队开展专业化制作，提升公益广告内容质量。2016 年，全国各级电台电视台全年共制作公益广告超过 15 万条，播出 3 000 万余次，时长超过 3 000 万分钟。三是多措并举促

① 王海滨．“阿基米德”：探索广电音频传播新模式［EB/OL］．“国家广电智库”微信公众号，2017-01-25.

② 湖南广播电视台．湖南芒果 TV：从“独播”到“独特”的融合发展之路［EB/OL］．“电视剧鹰眼”微信公众号，2016-09-20.

③ 覃敏，贾华杰．芒果 TV 年收入 20 亿　广告贡献一半［EB/OL］．［2016-12-09］．http://companies.caixin.com/2016-12-09/101025154.html.

发展。总局通过完善作品库免费向各级播出机构提供优秀作品，举办2016年广播电视公益广告创作培训班，举办首届全国广播电视公益论坛暨中国广东广电公益广告大会，召开公益广告作品《我是谁》创作经验座谈会，组织开展精品公益广告创作活动等，有力促进了公益广告发展。

2. 公益广告扶持力度进一步加大

总局自2014年开始设立广播电视公益广告专项扶持资金，三年来共有313件作品和125家机构获得3 600多万元的扶持。2016年，总局专门协调相关部委对优秀作品、优秀组织机构和优秀展播机构给予资金扶持。全国有十余家省级新闻出版广电部门也设立了扶持资金，2016年扶持总金额近2 000万元。除电台电视台外，广电系统内管理部门、网络公司、台属公司，系统外的节目制作公司、广告公司、高等院校、社会工作室、社会个人，以及税务、卫生计生等方面的管理部门和机构，也更加积极参与到公益广告作品创作环节，将自行创作的作品报总局评审，最终获得扶持的作品占到总量的14%，较前两年有明显提升。

3. 国际传播成效凸显

推动优秀广播电视公益广告作品“走出去”，向世界展示中国良好形象，取得明显成效。自2015年开始，在总局指导下，中国国际广播电台每年举办环球公益广告创意大赛，围绕中华民族优秀传统文化特色主题进行创意，吸引了德国、西班牙、俄罗斯等十几个国家和地区的民众参与。广西人民广播电台在柬埔寨国家电视台每周播出的《中国剧场》栏目前，固定播出《美丽中国》等公益宣传片。内蒙古广播电视台在俄罗斯、蒙古国的频道中，每天滚动播出公益广告。2016年，总局专门协调法国华人电视台将《中国字中国年》《中国年让世界相连》等公益广告翻译成法语持续播出两周，每天播出6次，受到当地民众广泛欢迎。中央三台、省级广播电视台积极制播优秀广播电视公益广告参与对外宣传。

六、有线网络产业发展

2016年，有线网络积极落实三网融合、“宽带中国”战略和“十三五”规划的相关部署，实施供给侧结构性改革，着力推进有线网络运营转型升级。全国有线网络互联互通平台建设和整合发展实现突破，三网融合业务全面展开，产业运营总体增长。截至2016年末，全国有线电视用户达2.28亿户，全国广播电视有线网络收入910.26亿元，同比增长5.10%。三网融合业务增长迅速，收入达122.4亿元，同比增长44.80%，在网络总收入中占比达13.45%，新兴业务发展势头强劲，产业发展焕发新生机。

（一）有线网络建设与产业经营稳步推进

1. 有线网络用户首次减少，高清和双向网用户规模大幅提升

有线网络多数指标持续攀升。截至2016年末，全国有线电视用户为2.28亿户，比上年减少737万余户，同比减少3.13%，家庭渗透率为52.75%，首次出现用户数下滑情况，但数字和付费数字电视用户保持了平稳增长，高清用户规模显著提升。其中，数字电视用户超过2亿户，同比增加了381.65万户；付费数字电视用户5 817.15万户，同比增加258.07万户（见图4）；高清电视用户同比净增1 555.2万户，总量达到7 749.2万户，渗透率超过30%。多地有线电视运营商加快有线网络光网改造、

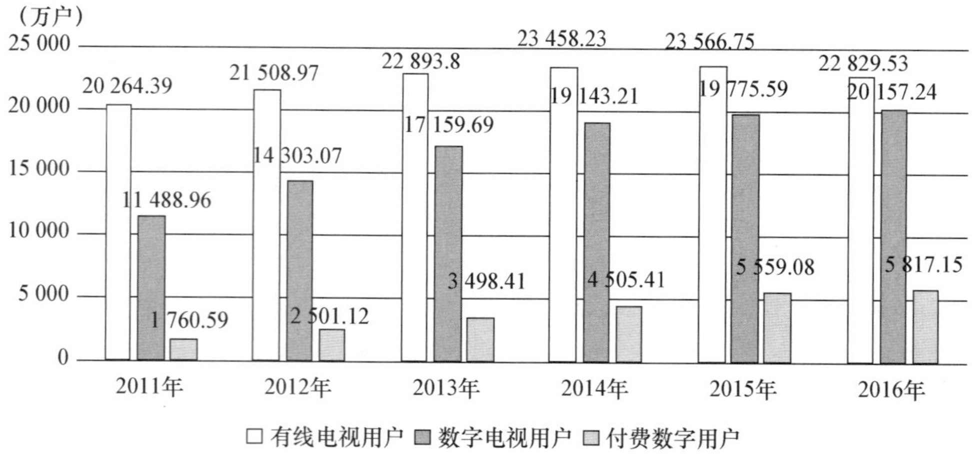

图4　2011—2016年全国有线电视用户、数字电视用户和付费数字电视用户增长情况

资料来源：国家新闻出版广电总局财务司。

大幅提升网络承载能力，推出了4K点播业务，广受用户欢迎。有线双向网改覆盖用户1.5亿户，净增1 778.4万户，有线双向覆盖率为59.93%，有线双向渗透率为26.68%，双向业务用户保持了较快增长；有线智能终端（机顶盒/网关）用户384.6万户，有线智能终端渗透率为1.52%；全国广电宽带用户数同比增长40.13%，达到2 576.9万户，渗透率为10.21%，有线网络融合业务规模不断扩大①。

有线网络进一步向乡村拓展。有条件的农村已实现有线电视全覆盖，并延伸推出多种智慧服务，对巩固农村宣传思想文化阵地，构建覆盖城乡的现代公共文化服务体系具有重要意义。在这方面，贵州、甘肃提供了很好的案例。2016年，贵州大力实施多彩贵州"广电云"村村通工程，通过有线数字化广播电视传输系统，将数字广播电视节目和政务、民生、致富信息，以及农村电子商务、天网工程、在线教育、远程医疗等多功能应用和有线宽带网，送到农村千家万户。截至2016年底，全省累计完成11 103个行政村的村村通建设任务，计划到2020年，"广电云"户户通和有线电视城乡入户率达到60%。甘肃有线网络积极落实"宽带中国"战略，2016年全面启动"宽带乡村"工程，全年完成广电光缆通乡镇达到90%以上，通行政村达到50%以上。这两个案例是全国有线网络发展的象征，显示出广阔的发展前景。

2. 有线网络收入稳中有升，三网融合业务增长迅速

有线网络行业收入稳步提升，三网融合业务收入领跑，增幅位居其他收入首位。2016年，全国有线网络总收入达910.26亿元，占全国广播电视总收入的18.06%，比2015年的866.06亿元增加了44.20亿元，同比增长5.10%，综合收入月均ARUP值（每用户平均收入）33.20元，高于上年的30.60元（见图5）。其中，有线电视收视费收入达457.92亿元，同比减少3.63%，占比超过50%；付费数字电视收入为76.44亿元，同比增长8.84%；三网融合业务收入为122.4亿元，同比增长44.80%。2016年，全国三网融合业务全面推广，广电、电信业务双向进入稳步推进。随着三网融合的普遍推开，电子商务、电视游戏、教育、生活服务等各增值业务不断扩展，三网融合业务正成为有线网络发展的重要拉动力。

图5 2011—2016年全国有线广播电视网络收入及增长情况

资料来源：国家新闻出版广电总局财务司。

3. 积极参与智慧家庭和智慧城市建设

2016年，有条件的有线网络企业积极布局智慧家庭、智慧城市建设，大力开展智慧业务。一是以新型机顶盒开发为核心，布局智慧家庭。在智慧家庭建设中，"智能网关＋智能机顶盒＋智能家居产品"支撑智慧家庭生活，而智能机顶盒的研发应用则是各省有线网络企业重点布局的领域。吉视传媒研发了国内首款光纤机顶盒，不仅能实现看电视和用电视功能，还为百姓家提供高速无线网络，甚至化身"家庭管家"，使百姓家庭真正实现智能互联。广西广电网络则以三网融合机顶盒为载体，打造电视屏和移动终端交互的新一代影视生活娱乐平台。这些探索推动了有线网络功能的升级。二是推进跨界跨领域合作，深入布局智慧城市。有线网络企业

① 中国广播电视网络有限公司，格兰研究. 2016年第四季度中国有线电视行业发展公报［R］.

积极借助用户和管理运营优势，与相关行业展开合作，快速布局智慧城市业务。如，陕西广电网络与同方股份合作，借助同方股份在智慧城市业务运营方面的经验，着力推动产业升级和转型发展；与无锡有关企业进行战略合作，探索建设智慧社区，积累了一定经验。

（二）全国有线网络整合与互联互通平台建设取得重要进展

1. 全国有线网络整合取得突破

国网公司作为全国有线网络整合的责任主体，以“一省一策”为方针，利用专项建设基金增资入股省级有线电视网络公司取得股权，再专款用于全国有线电视网络互联互通平台建设，对省网股权与业务实现整合。截至 2016 年底，已与河北、内蒙古、宁夏、青海有线网络公司签订增资入股合作协议，并加紧推进新疆、甘肃、天津、广东、辽宁、四川、黑龙江、重庆等省（区、市）的整合。网络整合发展为建成全国互联互通平台，提升网络承载能力和内容支撑能力，发展跨域、跨网、跨终端的综合信息服务和三网融合创新业务，奠定了重要基础。

2. 互联互通平台建设取得重要进展

国网公司牵头积极落实中央关于三网融合、“宽带中国”战略和“十三五”相关规划的重要部署，加快建设互联互通平台。2016 年，互联互通平台一期工程进展顺利，二期规划初步完成。一期建设已实现各省广电网络的互联互通和统一宽带通道，完成基础传输承载网络 100G 系统新建和 10G 系统扩容，基本建成北京、西安等地“广电云”基础平台数据中心，完成行业基础服务平台的开发与现网部署、面向终端用户的全业务应用开发与现网部署、智能操作系统定制研发等，宽带广电网络已具备现网运营能力。二期主要任务是建设互联互通省分平台，结合一期中央平台建设，实现全国广电网络的互联互通，平台覆盖全国有线电视用户，支撑 1 亿宽带用户。互联互通平台先导项目正式上线调试，逐步推进云平台、融合服务平台、承载网络、广电宽带数据平台、智能终端、用户支撑系统、有线无线融合平台等项目建设，并在北京、上海、江苏、河北、陕西、海南等示范省市试点，部署基于互联互通平台的全国统一运营业务。

2016年中国电影产业发展报告

国家新闻出版广电总局发展研究中心

2016年，电影系统贯彻习近平总书记在文艺工作座谈会和文联十大、作协九大开幕式上的重要讲话精神，大力推动电影业发展。电影创作水平逐年提升，电影市场化改革不断深入，电影产业进一步繁荣。中国保持全球第二大电影市场地位，电影产业多项指标增速保持全球领先地位，中国仍是全球电影产业发展的重要动力。

目前，中国电影发展重心逐渐从量的积累向质的提升转变，进入从快速增长转向平稳发展的新态势。基于中国电影产业发展过程中出现的新情况、新趋势、新问题，国家新闻出版广电总局（以下简称总局）将2017年定为"电影质量促进年"和"电影市场规范年"，加快推动电影创作从"高原"迈向"高峰"，推动电影产业发展转型升级。

一、电影市场活力持续增强

2016年，行业管理部门加大市场调控力度，电影市场多项指标继续增长，市场活力进一步增强。一些指标的增幅出现下降，标志着中国电影产业从"增量"到"提质"的转换。

（一）生产制作能力增强

电影产量平稳增长。电影生产制作热情空前高涨，各类电影生产能力持续提高，产品提质增效势头强劲。2016年全国共生产创作故事影片772部，动画片、科教片和特种影片等产量维持较高水平（见表1）。

表1　2012—2016年各类影片生产情况　　单位：部

样式		2012年	2013年	2014年	2015年	2016年
总产量		893	824	758	888	944
故事片	故事片	745	638	618	686	772
	在总产量中的占比	83.43%	77.43%	81.53%	77.25%	81.78%
其他各类影片	动画影片	33	29	40	51	49
	纪录影片	15	18	25	38	32
	科教影片	74	121	52	96	67
	特种影片	26	18	23	17	24
	在总产量中的占比	16.57%	22.57%	18.47%	22.75%	18.22%

资料来源：国家新闻出版广电总局电影局。自2012年起，供电视播出的数字电影生产数量并入故事片类计算。

电影合拍业务进一步拓展。中国电影业的快速发展，吸引越来越多的国家和地区前来合作。2016年，对外合作进一步拓展，中国与爱沙尼亚签署国家间电影和合拍协议，并更新了与加拿大在1987年签署的合拍协议。截至2017年6月，中国已与18个国家签署了电影合拍协议。2016年，通过对外合作，中国电影工业制作水平得到进一步提升，合作对象进一步增多，覆盖17个国家和地区，较往年有明显拓展。合作影片已经成为"中国制造"的重要品牌，《长城》《美人鱼》《七月与安生》等，在票房表现和艺术水平上各领风骚，并在国际上引起广泛关注。其中，《长城》是中国电影"走出去"的全新探索，开启了内地导演执导好莱坞电影的先河。

市场主体发展壮大。2016年，在行业主管部门、相关部门和市场的共同努力下，市场主体建设取得重大进展。8月，中影股份和上影股份先后在上海证券交易所挂牌上市，成为第一批上市的国有电影企业。中影股份更成为A股市场综合实力最强、影响力最大、产业链最完整的国有影视行业龙头企业第一股。幸福蓝海影视文化集团股份有限公司也在深交所创业板上市。以华谊兄弟影业、博纳影业、万达影视、光线影业、乐视影业为代表的民营公司，也获得进一步发展。一些影视企业不断探索商业电影运作并取得成功，一些影视企业与海外优质资源加强合作，提升了中国在全球电影市场的影响力。

（二）主要指标持续向好

一是电影产业主要指标继续向好（见表 2）。2016 年全国城市电影票房 492.83 亿元，保持全球第二市场地位，同比增长 11.83%，相较 2003 年以来年均逾 30%的增速显著放缓，但在全球电影大国中仍居首位。2016 年全国观影人次 13.72 亿人次，同比增长 8.89%，已超过美国，继印度之后位列全球第二。按照全国总人口计算，中国的人均年观影次数已近 1 次，在北上广深四大城市，人均年观影次数①接近或超过美国的 4.1 次。2016 年全国平均票价为 35.92 元/张，同比增长 2.69%，这个增长主要是靠网络售票环节增加的电商服务费带来的。同时，由于多方面的原因，单银幕票房产出为 119.68 万元，同比下降 14.1%。

表 2　　2012—2016 年电影产业发展基本指标一览

指标	2012 年	2013 年	2014 年	2015 年	2016 年
票房（亿元）	170.73	217.69	296.39	440.69	492.83
院线（条）	45	45	47	48	48
银幕数（块）	13 118	18 195	23 592	31 627	41 179
新增银幕数（块）	3 832	5 077	5 397	8 035	9 552
新增影院数（家）	646	1 048	1 015	1 042	1 612
观影人次（亿人）	4.66	6.17	8.34	12.6	13.72
平均票价（元）	36.25	35.28	35.54	34.98	35.92
单银幕票房产出（万元）	130.15	119.64	125.63	139.34	119.68

二是电影产品供应进一步丰富。2016 年上映国产影片 415 部，较上年的 300 余部有明显增长。国产影片日均投放市场数量已逾 1 部。进口电影供应进一步体现“多国别、多样化”。全年共上映进口电影 102 部②，数量较往年有明显增加。以第一出品国来看，进口对象国涉及 19 个国家③，进口电影对象大国仍为美国，全年共公映以美国为独立或第一出品国的影片 46 部，其中包括进口 32 部分账大片和 14 部进口买断影片④；此外还公映了 11 部以日本为独立出品国的影片。进口片涉及剧情、动画、奇幻、爱情等多种类型，这种结构调整，有利于迎接外部挑战，适应未来市场格局变化。

三是国产电影市场份额继续保持过半水平。2016 年共有 86 部影片票房过亿元，其中国产电影 45 部，进口电影 41 部。国产电影票房 287.47 亿元，市场份额为 58.33%。高品质的国产电影在市场上获得更多认可，票房前 10 名的影片中，国产电影占了 6 部，《美人鱼》更突破近年来单片票房纪录，高达 33.93 亿元⑤，显示出优质国产影片的市场影响力（见表 3）。

表 3　　2012—2016 年国产电影和进口电影市场份额情况

类别		2012 年	2013 年	2014 年	2015 年	2016 年
国产	票房（亿元）	82.73	127.67	161.55	271.36	287.47
	票房比例	48.46%	58.65%	54.51%	61.58%	58.33%
进口	票房（亿元）	88.00	90.02	134.84	169.33	205.36
	票房比例	51.54%	41.35%	45.49%	38.42%	41.67%

资料来源：国家新闻出版广电总局电影局。

① 北上广深人均年观影次数根据国家统计局和中国电影发行放映协会公布的数据计算。美国人均年观影次数根据 MPAA 公布数据计算。
② 数据来自国家新闻出版广电总局电影局。
③ 数据根据公开数据整理。
④ 美国电影协会举办答谢会展望中美合作新图景［EB/OL］.［2017-01-12］. http://ent.qq.com/a/20170112/018907.htm.
⑤ 中国电影发行放映协会. 2016 中国电影市场报告［M］. 北京：中国电影出版社，2017：311.

（三）影院建设热情空前高涨

全国城市影院市场进一步扩容，建设热情空前高涨。2016年全国拥有电影银幕41 179块，超过美国，成为全球拥有银幕数最多的国家。其中，新增银幕9 552块，日均新增银幕26.17块，日均银幕增量达到新高。全国新增影院1 612家，创近年来新增影院数量新高。影院总数达到8 011家，平均每家影院拥有5块以上银幕，影院平均体量较往年有所扩大①。城市院线总数保持48条不变，但出现了局部的兼并和重组现象，有利于优化院线资源配置。

高新科技提升影院信息化建设水平，120帧放映成为年度热点现象。上海影城、北京博纳悠唐影院是全国仅有的2家可放映120帧/4K/3D电影的影院，在120帧/4K/3D影片《比利·林恩的中场战事》排映时引发高度关注。高新技术格式银幕数量快速增长，尤其是三四线城市的高新技术格式银幕建设显著提速，激光放映加快推广。2016年，IMAX银幕总数达384块、影院数达361家，覆盖全国31个省（区、市）的138个城市；中国巨幕银幕总数达185块、影院数达158家，覆盖全国28个省（区、市）的83个城市。

（四）衍生产业快速发展

2016年，电影衍生产业快速发展，在衍生品产业、影视园区发展和大型电影节展方面均有较大突破。

在衍生品产业方面，电影企业积极拓展经营空间，提升影响力和竞争力。中影股份与美国福斯公司、香港安乐影业签署战略合作，开拓电影衍生品版权开发项目近10个，涵盖玩具、模型、家具用品、服饰鞋帽、3C数码产品、影院包材、贵金属、文具等，并开发了自有品牌“工农兵”系列产品；上影集团开拓游戏授权业务、第三方合作的衍生品开发等业务形态，自主开发经典动画电影《大闹天宫》中的孙悟空形象手办等，并与线上销售平台、肯德基等餐饮企业广泛合作，衍生品销售收入超过500万元。动画影片《大鱼海棠》的衍生品收入则超过5 000万元。

全国影视园区发展进一步加快。与此前各地重点建设影视园区不同，电影小镇和电影主题公园成为2016年新热点。重庆市打造的电影小镇项目，已吸引重庆金山文化创意产业园、华侨城大型文化旅游综合项目、重庆创意公园等项目落户。华谊兄弟已规划在14个省布局20个电影小镇。2016年，广东、江苏、河北均启动了影视主题公园项目规划，吉林省的长影世纪城营业收入达7 685万元，初步体现了影视园区的经济潜力。

在中国电影产业快速发展的推动下，大型电影节展日趋繁盛。无论是较为成熟的上海国际电影节，后发优势明显的北京国际电影节，还是起步仅三年的丝绸之路国际电影节，都具有了相当的规模和影响力。其中，2016年北京国际电影节的参展国家数、参展影片数等多项指标在2015年基础上呈倍数增长（见表4）。一些地方也积极举办区域性电影节展，促进电影文化国际交流，培育地方文化氛围，带动地方经济发展。如云南的澜沧江·湄公河流域国际电影周、甘肃的第5届中国（嘉峪关）国际短片电影展等。

表4　2015—2016年中国举办的国际电影节展基本情况

时间	国际电影节名称	届次	参赛/展映影片数（部）		参展国家数（个）	
			2015年	2016年	2015年	2016年
4月	北京国际电影节	6	360余	2 329	40余	105
6月	上海国际电影节	19	2 096	2 403	108	114
9月	丝绸之路国际电影节	3	103	242	近30	35

资料来源：根据公开数据整理。

（五）科技支撑力量更加强劲

2016年，中国全面提高电影科技创新与应用能力，科技对电影产业的支撑力量更加明显。电影拍摄制作技术水平和服务能力全面增强；电影国际化发行放映技术保障体系基本建立，影院信息化管理与服务体系全面建成，电影市场技术监管服务体系不断健全，信息化影院建设初具规模；电影高新技术相关国家重点实验室和创新工程中心逐步建立，具有自主知识产权的电影技术装备研发、生产与应用水平不断提高。电影产业链服务的大数据分析处理系统建设加强。中国电影科学技术研究所已建成电影大数据分析处理系统，通过开展大数据分析，

① 数据来自国家新闻出版广电总局电影局。

可为电影行业的剧本创作、演员选择、宣传、发行、影院排片、放映、投资等整个产业链服务。国家数据平台新一轮改造升级，有利于电影市场技术监管。VR、AR 等先进影像技术的研发与应用成为行业热点，快速推进。

二、电影“走出去”行稳致远

2016 年，中国电影全年海外销售收入 38.25 亿元，中国电影海外销售收入连续四年快速增长（见图 1）。

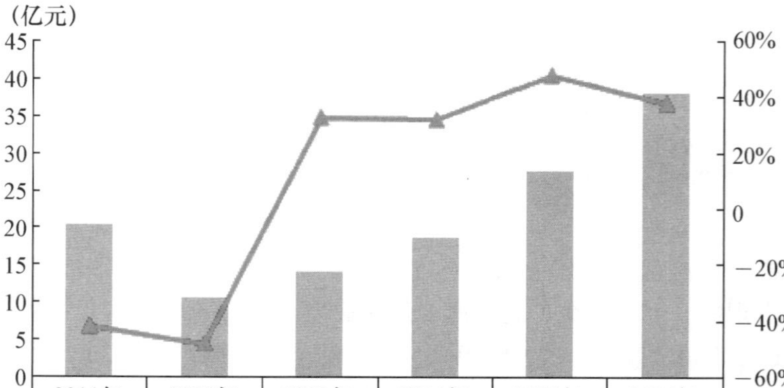

	2011年	2012年	2013年	2014年	2015年	2016年
综合收入	20.46	10.63	14.14	18.70	27.70	38.25
增长率	−41.83%	−48.04%	33.02%	32.25%	48.12%	38.09%

图 1　2011—2016 年中国电影海外综合收入情况

资料来源：国家新闻出版广电总局电影局。

电影海外销售收入的增长，得益于打通了新的有效渠道，开拓了新的销售方式。2016 年 1 月，华人文化控股集团、华狮电影发行公司共同搭建的“中国电影　普天同映”国产电影全球发行平台在北京正式启动。“普天同映”平台采用与海外院线和影院进行票房分账的市场化模式，每月至少在亚洲、欧洲、北美、大洋洲的主流影院与中国内地同步上映 1 部中国影片。经过一年多的摸索和布局，“普天同映”平台初步形成“三步走”的发展步骤：第一步是在世界重要的华人聚集区传播和放映中国电影，以获得中国电影在华人聚集区的票房份额，让海外华人共享中国电影的发展成果。第二步是通过海外华人聚集区的放映，带动所在地区的外国观众感受中国电影、中华文化的魅力，引发当地外国观众对中国电影的关注和消费。第三步是在未来逐步形成中国电影的全球营销网络。

2016 年春节期间，影片《西游记之孙悟空三打白骨精》通过“普天同映”平台，在亚洲、欧洲、北美、大洋洲共计 9 国 57 座城市的 89 座主流影院上映，并在 11 座华人聚集的海外大城市举办首映式，观影数达 11.6 万余人次，总票房 660 余万元。2016 年 4 月，华人文化成立华人影业，在全球范围开拓院线、音像、互联网和电视播映等多渠道、多层次的市场，在 10 多个国家拓展了 20 余条院线直接排片渠道，逐步建立了针对海外华人的宣发体系，尝试了《陆垚知马俐》《盗墓笔记》《一句顶一万句》《28 岁未成年》等多部新片的海外发行推广。

“普天同映”平台的建立，体现了总局对推动国产影片走向世界，增强中国电影在全球范围感召力、影响力的决心。这一平台是中国电影界积极释放内生动力、推动中国电影“走出去”的重要渠道，也开辟了传播中国故事、弘扬中国精神的新渠道，为中国电影寻找了新的增长点。

三、电影管理与政策日趋完善

2016 年，《中华人民共和国电影产业促进法》（以下简称《电影产业促进法》）的出台对中国电影产业发展具有里程碑意义，以此为契机，一系列针对性强、含金量高的政策措施相继制定发布，一个具有中国特色的电影发展政策法规体系基本建立。

（一）加强立法，为产业发展护航

2016 年，《电影产业促进法》和《中华人民共和国公共文化服务保障法》（以下简称《公共文化服务保障法》）获得全国人大常委会审议通过，是文化法治建设取得的重要进展，也为电影产业发展助力护航。

《电影产业促进法》从法律层面确立了“电影作为产业”的属性，立足于中国电影产业发展的现实需要和未来趋势，用法律的形式巩固和升华了多年来电影产业改革发展的政策措施和成功经验，并就进一步简政放权、繁荣电影创作、规范电影市场等问题明确了法律规范。对进一步优化电影产业发展环境，释放市场活力，推动创作生产出更多更好的优秀电影作品，推动电影产业进一步大力弘扬社会主义核心价值观，推动电影市场秩序进一步规范，具有重大意义。《公共文化服务保障法》中再次赋予农村电影放映工程以法律保障，并首次以法律形式明确规定了农村电影放映的基本要求。这两部法律对电影发展将产生深刻影响。

《电影产业促进法》和《公共文化保障法》是依法促进电影产业繁荣发展的新起点。当前，总局和各省（区、市）正在根据《电影产业促进法》制定配套的制度规范，对相关法条进行完善细化，推动电影进一步发展。

（二）加强扶持，促进市场健康发展

2016年，国家出台了一系列具体政策，促进电影产业进一步发展。

电影事业发展专项资金自成立以来，对电影产业发展发挥了扶持、鼓励和引导作用。2016年2月，财政部、国家新闻出版广电总局出台《中央级国家电影事业发展专项资金预算管理办法》（财教［2016］4号，以下简称新《办法》），优化电影事业发展专项资金的管理使用。2016年是按照新《办法》收缴电影事业发展专项资金的第一年，全国共收缴22.9亿元，比2015年增长了8.24%。为更好发挥电影事业发展专项资金对电影产业发展的促进作用，国家电影事业发展专项资金管理委员会先后下发了扶持国产影片的3个通知，即《关于对优秀国产影片进行奖励的通知》（电专字［2016］1号）、《关于奖励优秀国产影片海外推广工作的通知》（电专字［2016］2号）、《关于奖励放映国产影片成绩突出影院的通知》（电专字［2016］3号），对优秀国产影片生产放映进行精准扶持。

此外，总局还发布了《关于遴选优秀影视作品进行译制资助有关事宜的通知》（新广电办发［2016］17号），推动优秀影视作品对外传播。总局制定了《电影精品专项资金使用程序管理规定》《资助项目单位使用电影精品专项资金管理规定》，进一步规范电影精品专项资金管理，扶持优秀影片生产。

各省级行政管理部门出台相关措施，用好财政资金，扶持本地电影产业发展。如甘肃省修订《甘肃省影视精品资金管理办法》，福建省出台《关于支持电影发展若干经济政策实施意见》，等等。另外，一些中西部地区加大了电影业扶持力度，如，《江西省国家电影事业发展专项资金扶持电影创作生产实施细则（试行）》是江西省出台的第一个专门扶持电影创作生产的重要政策，主要有助于激励该省市场主体生产更多具有较高思想艺术水准和市场价值的电影作品。

（三）加强管理，进一步立规明矩

促进电影产业发展需要政府更好地发挥行政管理作用。2016年，行业管理部门落实全面深化改革和全面依法治国的发展要求，进一步加强电影管理，保障电影产业健康有序发展。这些管理政策的内容主要有：

一是推动行政审批改革。2016年2月，国务院出台《关于第二批取消152项中央指定地方实施行政审批事项的决定》（国发［2016］9号）取消了“电影制片单位以外的单位独立从事电影摄制业务审批”，取消了“改建、拆除电影院和放映设施审批”“电影放映单位变更业务范围或者兼并、合并、分离审批”，取消了“电影院加入院线审批”。5月，《国家新闻出版广电总局关于修改部分规章的决定》（新广电发［2016］196号）出台，废止了《电影片进出境洗印、后期制作审批管理办法》等规范性文件。这些简政放权措施在《电影产业促进法》中以法律形式固定下来。

二是严格整治市场秩序。电影行业管理部门加大对偷漏瞒报票房、盗版盗录等行为的惩处力度。2016年1月，总局电影局开展“百日电影市场专项治理活动”，中国电影发行放映协会也配合发布《关于开展电影市场秩序专项治理活动的实施方案》，重拳治理电影市场，赢得广泛好评。3月，针对《叶问3》票房异常波动等情况，总局电影局对相关各方进行严厉排查惩处，着力营造了风清气朗的行业环境。9月，湖北卫某因盗录盗播电影被判处有期徒刑10个月，罚金5 000元，该案成为中国因盗录盗播电影被判刑第一案。2017年3月，依据新实施的《电影产业促进法》，总局对全国300余家存在偷漏瞒报票房的影院及其所属院线进行了严肃处理，彰显了依法治理市场的决心。

四、电影产业转型升级面临的问题与对策

电影创作与电影产业在继续保持良好发展势头的同时，也存在一些突出问题，如部分创作存在脱离时代、脱离现实、脱离人民的现象，一些电影作品过度追求票房效应，忽视艺术品质；电影院线结构和产业结构不协调、不健全，电影市场不规范的现象仍然存在。这些现象特别是创作质量已成为严重制约中国电影发展的瓶颈。需要加大力气落实

《电影产业促进法》，加强电影管理，规范市场秩序，使之真正成为电影产业转型升级的保障。

（一）深抓创作，提升电影质量

2017 年是“电影质量促进年”。要以此为抓手，努力提升生产质量水平。深刻认识现代工业、现代科技给现代电影的叙述格局、电影语言和文本形态带来的变化和提出的要求。要在互联网背景下，彰显大银幕的特色优势，思考与探索电影应有的书写形态和视听话语体系。在继承传统的基础上，不断增强现代意识，把中国电影推向 21 世纪的崭新境界。要保持有容乃大、宽容开放的文化胸怀，给予各种类型、各种风格的电影作品以宽容的态度。要提高质量和水平，增强工匠精神，努力提升电影作品的品牌度和美誉度。

电影业不仅要有体量的增长，而且要创造质量的标杆。大力优化产品结构，发挥政府和市场两只手的作用，坚持把创作作为基础性、关键性的问题来抓，努力抓原创、出精品、攀高峰。增加有效供给，提升质量与控制增量并举，打造更多质量优秀、形式多样的电影作品。在内容方面，要以现实主义创作为重点，以弘扬社会主义核心价值观为灵魂，推进电影创作百花齐放。充分发挥现有优势，整合版权、创作、发行、播映等各方面资源，完善创作改编的协同联动机制，为推进电影高水平高质量创作创造条件。在创意方面，要实施好电影剧本孵化计划和编剧扶持计划，对一些优秀原创剧本予以资金支持，重点培养高新尖技术制作人才，促进原创力的提高。在技术方面，要在电影艺术与现代科技深度融合上下更大功夫，提升电影制作的科技水平，丰富电影表现手段，提升艺术效果。

（二）狠抓管理，营造良好产业环境

经过多年努力，电影发展的整体环境有了较大改善，电影产业“四梁八柱”的制度配套已基本到位，电影市场十分活跃。但是，电影产业也存在一些由于局部改革不彻底导致的问题，如功利浮躁现象比较突出，产业链各环节不协调、不兼容的现象时有发生。

2017 年是“电影市场规范年”。重点是要优化产业结构，推进电影的供给侧改革。一是进一步加强市场监管。加强对电影从业主体和人员的管理引导，确保法律规定的各项管理措施都能得到有效执行。着力解决偷漏瞒报票房、放映质量差等既有问题，加强对发行方、院线公司、影院和电商的监管，避免恶性竞争，维护公平有序的市场环境。加强对电影新业态的研究，针对点播影院、网络大电影等，要明确管理主体、管理职责、管理措施，加强引导，确保规范管理、有序发展。二是大力推进电影行业治理体系和治理能力现代化。建立健全科学高效的管理体系，坚持日常监管与专项治理相结合，整治行业内局部不协调、不规范的行为。积极运用高新技术，提升监测监管能力。按照简政放权、放管结合、优化服务的要求，加强管理，改进执法方式，提高执法质量。三是要推动电影供给体系结构优化，同观众需求结构相匹配。进一步积极培育和引导影院结构多样化供给，做大做优做强全国艺术电影放映联盟，完善影院市场，解决一些优秀国产艺术电影排片难的问题。

（三）稳抓落实，提供政策利好保障

法治是良法与善治的结合。要以宣传落实《电影产业促进法》和《公共文化服务保障法》为契机，切实为电影产业持续健康繁荣发展提供制度保障。2017 年是“电影普法初始年”。一是以《电影产业促进法》为依据，完善制度配套。抓紧制定和执行推动该法落实的配套法规规章，形成以该法为龙头的电影产业法律制度规范体系，使该法真正落地。二是结合电影产业实际，加强与各地各有关部门的沟通协调，制定出台相关配套措施，把各项扶持政策进一步细化具体化。三是加强督促检查。要联合有关部门，选择代表性地区，对支持电影发展政策落实情况开展督查，总结好的经验做法，推动解决存在的问题。管好用好电影专项资金，实现政府资金对电影产业引导作用的最大化。

2016 年中国动漫产业发展报告

牛兴侦

2016 年是“十三五”规划的开局之年，也是供给侧结构性改革的攻坚之年。在国家大力推进供给侧结构性改革、实施创新驱动发展战略的背景下，中国动漫产业通过深化改革、创新发展、提质增效和融合协同等多种举措，保持了又好又快的发展态势。动漫产业总产值突破 3 000 亿元，年度增长率保持在 20%以上，手机动漫和移动游戏等产品业态在移动互联网的助推下持续高速发展。依托动漫产业形成的泛娱乐产业正在逐步成熟，以 IP 为纽带推动着网络文学、动漫、游戏、音乐、影视等内容形态加快跨界融合发展。在内容产业领域协同发展的基础上，中国动漫产业还以其强大的创意设计能力和品牌版权价值日渐融入国民经济大循环，在推动文化创意产业和相关产业融合发展、支撑文化产业发展壮大等方面发挥着重要作用。

一、动漫产业：产业规模持续扩大，产业结构更加优化

（一）动漫产业规模持续扩大

2016 年，中国动漫产业维持上升态势，产业规模继续大幅提升，总产值达到 1 497.70 亿元，同比增加 283 亿元；同比增幅为 23.30%，相比 2015 年增加 5.40 百分点（见图 1）。这是中国动漫产业自 2013 年启动转型升级以来取得的最高增速。动漫产业通过淘汰落后产能、注重核心创意、提升产品质量、创新商业模式等手段达到了提质增效的目的，形成了漫画出版、影视动画、网络动漫等内容产品和动漫衍生品、动漫主题公园、动漫授权等增值业务相互融合、相互促进、协同发展的良好局面。

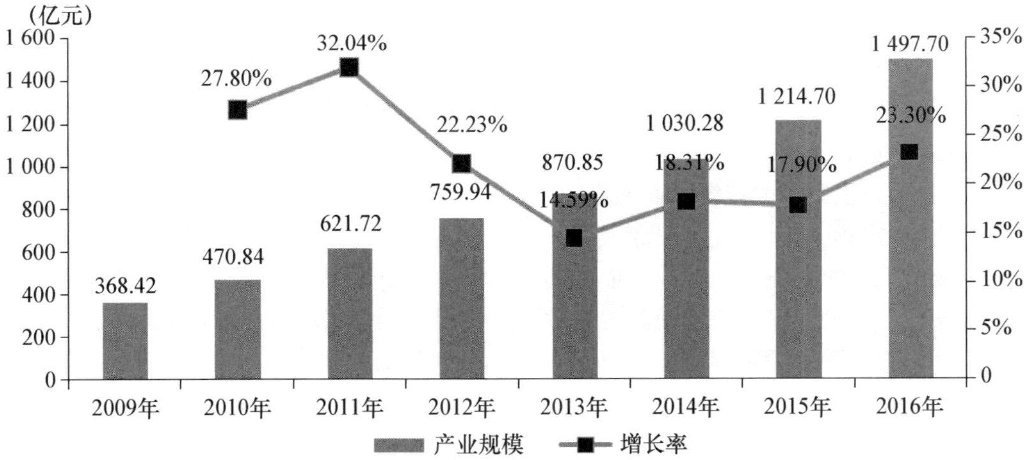

图 1　2009—2016 年中国动漫产业总产值

资料来源：文化部文化产业司、中娱智库。

（二）动漫产业结构渐趋合理

2016 年，随着动漫产业总产值的增加，动漫产业各细分领域的市场规模也相应地提高（见图 2）。其中，漫画出版产值为 64.40 亿元，占比 4.30%，传统漫画出版市场相对萎缩，互联网和手机渠道分流了部分漫画用户。影视动画产值为 202.20 亿元，占比高达 13.50%。《大鱼海棠》《熊出没之熊心归来》等国产动画电影，《你的名字》《航海王之黄金城》等日本动画电影，《疯狂动物城》《功夫熊猫 3》《愤怒的小鸟》等美国动画电影，票房成绩均出现新

突破。互联网动漫和手机动漫产值均为 70.40 亿元，快看漫画等新兴的互联网漫画平台开始崛起；二次元视频平台 Acfun 弹幕视频网和哔哩哔哩弹幕视频网，继续在粉丝互动与用户黏性层面保持独特优势。

动漫授权产值规模达到 266.60 亿元，由于包括漫画出版、影视动画、互联网动漫和手机动漫在内的上游动漫内容板块在 2016 年呈现蓬勃发展之势，大量原创和优质动漫内容提高了动漫版权的市场溢价。实体动漫经济占动漫产业的比重最高，动漫主题公园和动漫衍生品的产值分别为 350.50 亿元、392.40 亿元，分别占比 23.40%和 26.20%。动漫版权的充足供给、动漫用户消费需求的逐步打开以及版权保护机制的渐趋优化，为动漫衍生品市场的发展增强了支撑力。

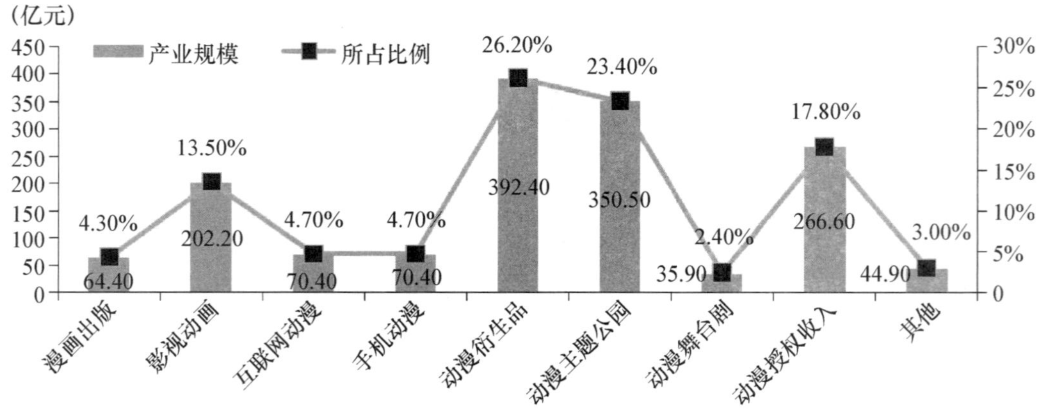

图 2　2016 年中国动漫产业各细分领域产值对比

资料来源：文化部文化产业司、中娱智库。

（三）漫画成为重要 IP 诞生源

2015 年以来，我国网络漫画平台日益增多，这主要是因为：在泛娱乐趋势下，漫画内容隶属 IP 源头，内容较为稀缺，市场机会大，各类企业争相进军漫画平台领域，有利于泛娱乐战略的布局。网络漫画平台在传媒载体上，主要分为独立网站、综合网站漫画频道和 APP 应用等主要产品形态。从参与主体来看，主要包括以“漫画＋互联网”作为发展路径的传统漫画企业、新兴漫画企业，以及以“互联网＋漫画”作为发展路径的传统互联网企业、社交平台、网络文学/视频企业、电信运营商等。

目前，网络漫画平台的三强已经形成，依崛起次序分别为：有妖气、腾讯动漫和快看漫画。通过百度指数、APP 用户规模等多项指标可以看出，有妖气在 2013 年前强势占据了国内原创漫画网络发行市场；2014 年腾讯动漫开始崛起，在 2015 年与有妖气形成了双强的局面；2016 年快看漫画凭借着在手机移动端形成的优势，与有妖气和腾讯动漫形成了三足鼎立的局面。

国内网络漫画平台普遍都推出了各自的 APP 应用，迎合了近年来持续移动互联网化的潮流趋势。根据易观千帆监测数据显示，2016 年第 4 季度中国手机漫画市场整体活跃人数达到 4 683.77 万人。其中，腾讯动漫活跃用户数达到 1 231.62 万人，位居行业第一；快看漫画以 1 120.03 万活跃用户数位居第二；咪咕动漫以 678.55 万人上升至第三位。值得注意的是，第 4 季度中国手机漫画市场整体活跃用户略有减少，前 10 名中仅腾讯动漫、快看漫画和咪咕动漫活跃用户保持增长，用户资源进一步向头部 APP 集中（见图 3）。

与网络动漫相比，漫画报刊图书出版仍保持一定规模。据统计，2016 年我国共出版动漫类图书 3 190 册（套），较 2015 年增长 3.14%，其中漫画图书 2 220 册、动画图书 972 册（交叉数量 2 册），占全年图书在版编目（CIP）数据数量（324 847 册）的 0.98%。在全国 597 家出版社中，有 275 家涉足动漫图书出版业务，中国少年儿童、江苏凤凰少年儿童、黑龙江美术、海豚、人民邮电、四川美术、北京联合出版公司、浙江人民美术、长江、新世纪等出版社出版数量较多，十大机构合计出版数量占总体的 35.10%；北京、南京、哈尔滨、成都、武汉等地出版数量较多，五大城市合计出版数量占总体的 64%，仅北京一地就出版了总体数量的 42.10%。

根据当当网统计数据显示，截止到 2016 年底，该网站在销动漫类图书共计 62 150 种，其中少儿类 23 125 种、非少儿类 39 025 种，占所有在销图书总量（11 471 400 种）的 0.54%。在 2016 年度图书畅

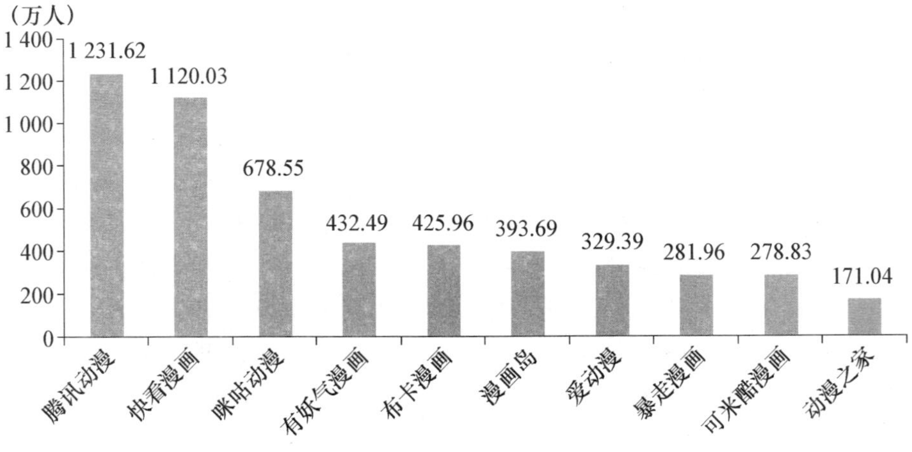

图 3　2016 年第 4 季度中国手机漫画应用活跃用户数量前 10 名

资料来源：易观网（http://www.analysys.cn/）。

销榜前 500 名中，有 14 种动漫图书上榜，包括《就喜欢你看不惯我又干不掉我的样子》、《三毛流浪记》（全集）、《你今天真好看》、《小猪佩奇》（全 10 册）、《就喜欢你看不惯我又干不掉我的样子 2》、《疯狂动物城》、《父与子全集》（精装彩色珍藏版）、《巴巴爸爸》（全 10 册）、《小猪佩奇动画故事书（第 2 辑）》（10 册套装）、《我可以咬一口吗》、《托马斯和朋友》（一、二辑套装）、《父与子全集》、《窝在角落好安心》、《就喜欢你看不惯我又干不掉我的样子》（套装全二册）等。总体来看，近几年来国产漫画所占市场份额正在稳步提升。从当当网动漫幽默类畅销图书前 500 名情况来看，中国大陆漫画作品数量所占比例为 54%，远大于欧美漫画（9.20%）和日韩漫画（9%），而在畅销榜的前 100 名中中国大陆漫画作品数量所占比例更是高达 58%。

（四）影视动画成为 IP 放大器

在政策调控和市场杠杆的双重引导下 2016 年中国电视动画行业总体上调控数量，提高质量，由数量增长转向质量提升的趋势更加明显。2016 年，全年备案公示的国产电视动画片剧目数量为 425 部 232 135 分钟，同比分别增长 6.52%和下降 22.13%（见图 4）；全国制作完成的国产电视动画片共 261 部、9 117 集、125 053 分钟，分别同比下降 4.40%、14.20%和 6.68%，创 2008 年以来最低产量纪录。但由于动画片生命周期相对较长，可循环多年持续播放，从积累数量来看仍十分惊人，目前累计数量达 1 909 871 分钟，折合约 31 831 小时。2016 年，《阿优学科学》《聪明的顺溜之雄鹰小子》《熊猫和小鼹鼠》《最可爱的人》等 46 部优秀国产动画片获得国家新闻出版广电总局推荐播出，合计 1 563 集 20 824 分钟，约占全年电视动画片总产量的 16.65%。

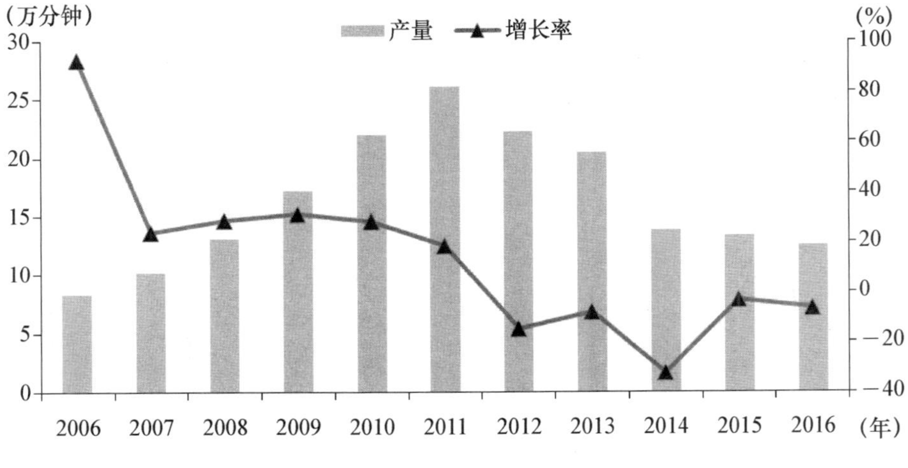

图 4　2006—2016 年国产电视动画片生产数量和增长率

资料来源：国家新闻出版广电总局。

目前，我国已形成了以 6 个少儿动画卫星频道和 33 个少儿地面频道为主体，各电视上星综合频道和各地各级电视频道动画栏目为补充的动画播映体系。除了动画专业频道、少儿频道之外，其他电视频道也是我国动画播出平台的重要组成部分。截至 2016 年 12 月，我国已经开播了中央电视台少儿频道、北京广播电视台卡酷少儿频道、上海广播电视台炫动卡通频道、江苏电视台优漫卡通频道、湖南广播电视台金鹰卡通频道、广东电视台嘉佳卡通频道等 6 个卫星频道，福建、甘肃、广东、海南、河北、黑龙江、江西、辽宁、内蒙古、宁夏、山东、山西、上海、四川、天津、新疆、云南、浙江、重庆等 19 个省（区、市），福州、广州、郑州、武汉、南京、济南、成都、乌鲁木齐、杭州等 9 个省会和首府城市，大连、宁波、厦门、深圳等 4 个计划单列市和长治 1 个地级市开播了少儿地面频道。此外，我国还有 3 套付费数字电视动画频道：新科动漫、新动漫、动漫秀场，分别由中央新闻记录电影制片厂、辽宁广播电视台、上海广播电视台开办。

截至 2016 年末，我国电视节目综合人口覆盖率为 98.9%。2015 年，全国各级电视频道动画片播出数量为 309 060 小时，其中国产片 299 405 小时、进口片 9 655 小时，与 2014 年相比，增长率分别为 1.38%、3.62%和－39.21%，国产片和进口片所占比值为 96.88∶3.12（见表 1）。动画节目电视播出数量自 2012 年以来就稳定在 30 万小时左右，现阶段播出空间已经饱和。国产电视动画片经过多年来的持续高速增长，已经从原来的数量相对稀缺转为总体数量相对过剩，这将持续要求国产动画在降低产量的同时更加注重培育精品力作，从粗放式增长向精细化经营方向发展。

表 1　　2011—2015 年全国电视动画播出数量

统计指标	2011 年	2012 年	2013 年	2014 年	2015 年	平均值
全年动画电视播出时间（小时）	280 254	304 877	293 140	304 839	309 060	298 434
进口动画电视播出时间（小时）	14 822	12 063	14 015	15 883	9 655	13 288
国产动画电视播出时间（小时）	265 432	292 814	279 125	288 955	299 405	285 146
进口动画电视播出时间所占比例	5.29%	3.96%	4.78%	5.21%	3.12%	4.45%
国产动画电视播出时间所占比例	94.71%	96.04%	95.22%	94.79%	96.88%	95.34%

资料来源：根据历年《中国社会统计年鉴》整理。

近年来，在国家发展动画产业和电影业的有利政策支撑下，我国动画电影制作和票房市场持续升温。2006 年，全年完成制作动画电影 13 部，2008 年达到 16 部，2009 年达到 27 部，2012 年达到 33 部，2006—2015 年十年间共制作完成国产动画电影 255 部。2016 年，动画电影生产和发行数量持续攀升，全年国产动画电影制作备案 194 部，制作完成并取得公映许可证的影片有 49 部。与此同时，国内动画电影票房收入急剧扩张，2006 年首次突破 1 亿元大关（包含国产片、合拍片和进口片），2009 年突破 5 亿元，2011 年猛增至 16.40 亿元，2014 年突破 30 亿元，2015 年突破 40 亿元，2016 年达到 70.68 亿元。与 2008 年的 2.55 亿元相比，八年间票房收入扩大了近 27 倍，复合增长率为 51.48%（见图 5）。在《疯狂动物城》《功夫熊猫 3》《你的名字》《大鱼海棠》《愤怒的小鸟》等中外大片的带动下，动画电影的票房收入、放映场次、观影人次等指标都有了明显的飞跃。2016 年，全国共上映动画电影 63 部，占上映影片数量的 12.48%；放映 1 257.41 万场，占总体放映场次的 16.73%；票房收入 70.68 亿元，占总体票房的 15.74%；观影人次达到 2.22 亿人次，占总观影人次的 16.39%。

图 5　2008—2016 年全国动画电影票房收入和观影人次

资料来源：中国票房网（http：//www.cbooo.cn/）。

（五）基于粉丝经济的动漫产业扩大为泛娱乐

2016年，我国动漫用户规模继续扩大，动漫用户的年龄分布呈现出年轻化特征，“90后”“95后”成为动漫用户的主力人群。动漫用户群体的基数和消费需求，为我国动漫产业的持续稳定发展提供了动力。

年轻人作为最庞大的消费群体之一，始终代表着当今时代的核心潮流趋势与消费倾向。尤其在互联网高度普及和渗透的信息化时代里，年轻人作为高新技术和一手资讯的前瞻受众，足以拥有创造时尚潮流和引领市场走向的能力。随着互联网对于经济生活的逐步渗透，互联网已经成为当前青少年重要的信息获取途径、交流沟通桥梁和休闲娱乐平台。随着互联网在青少年群体中的普及，网络文化娱乐行为在青少年日常生活中扮演的角色越来越重要。目前，以动漫游戏文化为核心，在年青群体中逐渐形成了一种独特的、具有年轻色彩的二次元文化氛围，并延伸为涵盖内容创作、平台分享和衍生品开发的二次元文化产业链。以具有架空世界观的小说、漫画、动画、游戏作为主要载体的二次元网络文化通过各类互联网娱乐应用在青少年网民中快速渗透。截至2015年12月，作为二次元文化传播载体的网络文学、视频、游戏的青少年用户规模分别达到1.3亿人、2.2亿人和1.9亿人，网络为二次元文化的传播提供了良好的基础。

随着互联网经济对娱乐传媒业的全面渗透，包括文学、动漫、游戏、电影、电视剧等在内的文化形态加速跨界融通，形成了“泛娱乐”的生态体系。以IP为核心的泛娱乐产业成为主流文化业态，为用户提供了多层次、跨媒体、跨平台的深度娱乐体验，具有更好的市场基础和更高的产业价值。网络文化娱乐产业对于IP重视程度的提高，直接推动了围绕IP为核心的文学、动漫、游戏、音乐、影视等内容形态的融合发展。

互联网对于娱乐传媒业的渗透和改变最主要体现在用户思维上，为目标用户群体提供让他们尖叫的产品。用户思维即是按照用户导向，研究分析用户需求的“痛点”，并做出极致的产品去满足他们。特别是随着移动互联网时代的到来，商业模式更是从PC互联网时代的流量经济变成了粉丝经济。这在产品生产模式上主要体现为娱乐化、IP化、互动化。

二、动漫产品：精品力作铸造超级IP

（一）优秀国产影视动画产品主导市场

根据中国广视索福瑞媒介研究（CSM）对中国电视收视的监测，对2016年全国主要城市电视台动画节目收视率及市场份额排名前20位的统计显示，共有108部作品上榜。其中，收视率较高的国产动画品牌主要有“新大头儿子和小头爸爸”“郑义门”“猪猪侠”“喜羊羊与灰太狼”“熊出没”“超级飞侠”“棉花糖和云朵妈妈”“阿优”等系列动画。以湖南电视台金鹰卡通频道播出的《新大头儿子和小头爸爸贺岁动画片马年新愿》为例，其在拉萨的收视率高达5.79%（见表2），在长沙的收视率为2.54%，在乌鲁木齐的收视率为1.11%。

表2　2016年全国主要城市电视台动画节目收视率前20位

序号	播出频道	栏目名称	节目名称	最高收视地区	最高收视率（%）
1	湖南电视台金鹰卡通频道	动画片	新大头儿子和小头爸爸贺岁动画片马年新愿	拉萨	5.79
2	浙江电视台影视娱乐频道	动画片	郑义门	杭州	3.87
3	湖南电视台金鹰卡通频道	麦咭首播剧场	猪猪侠番外篇拼装特工队上部	拉萨	3.18
4	湖南电视台金鹰卡通频道	麦咭先锋剧场	猪猪侠光明守卫者上部	兰州	2.87
5	湖南电视台金鹰卡通频道	哪鹅独播剧场	猪猪侠五灵守卫者下部	西宁	2.54
6	湖南电视台金鹰卡通频道	麦咭先锋剧场	喜羊羊与灰太狼羊羊小侦探	拉萨	2.47
7	中央电视台少儿频道	动画片	喜羊羊与灰太狼之羊羊小心愿	苏州	2.37
8	中央电视台少儿频道	银河剧场	熊出没之秋日团团转	拉萨	2.28
9	中央电视台少儿频道	动画梦工场	超级飞侠	海口	2.26
10	北京卡酷少儿频道	动画片	托马斯和朋友	西安	2.23
11	中央电视台少儿频道	动画大放映	熊出没	拉萨	2.21
12	中央电视台少儿频道	动画梦工场	超级飞侠2	海口	2.18

续前表

序号	播出频道	栏目名称	节目名称	最高收视地区	最高收视率（%）
13	优漫卡通卫视	幸福响当当	熊出没之年货	苏州	2.17
14	中央电视台综合频道	第1动画乐园	熊出没之环球大冒险	贵阳	2.16
15	中央电视台少儿频道	银河剧场	棉花糖和云朵妈妈	海口	2.15
16	中央电视台少儿频道	动画片	新大头儿子和小头爸爸之草原奇遇	苏州	2.14
17	湖南电视台金鹰卡通频道	麦咭先锋剧场	阿优之兔智来了	拉萨	2.14
18	湖南电视台金鹰卡通频道	动画连连看	熊出没之过年	西宁	2.12
19	中央电视台少儿频道	动画大放映	熊出没之环球大冒险	拉萨	2.11
20	湖南电视台金鹰卡通频道	大画连篇剧场	熊出没之过年	拉萨	2.09

资料来源：CSM 媒介研究。

随着国内电影市场的高速发展，国产动画电影也从中发展壮大起来。2016 年，全年共制作完成动画电影 49 部，有 42 部国产动画电影（含合拍片）在影院上映。中美合拍动画电影《功夫熊猫 3》累计票房收入达到 10.02 亿元，国产片《大鱼海棠》收获 5.65 亿元，《熊出没之熊心归来》收获 2.88 亿元，票房达到 5 000 万元以上的影片有《新大头儿子和小头爸爸 2：一日成才》《小门神》《神秘世界历险记 3》，票房在 1 000 万元以上的还有《摇滚藏獒》《年兽大作战》《精灵王座》《麦兜·饭宝奇兵》《超能太阳鸭》《铠甲勇士捕王》《我叫哀木涕之山口山战记》《青蛙总动员》等（见表 3）。尽管动画电影质量参差不齐，但在优秀影片的带动下，已经培养起国内动画影迷的观影热情和消费习惯。

表 3　2016 年国产动画电影（含合拍片）票房收入前十名

序号	影片名称	上映日期	国家/地区	票房（万元）	场次	人次
1	《功夫熊猫 3》	1月29日	中国/美国	100 200.38	1 137 036	28 141 951
2	《大鱼海棠》	7月8日	中国	56 520.18	692 404	16 968 522
3	《熊出没之熊心归来》	1月16日	中国	28 775.09	469 200	9 141 779
4	《新大头儿子和小头爸爸 2：一日成才》	8月19日	中国	9 021.07	212 578	3 179 110
5	《小门神》	1月1日	中国	7 280.41	112 987	2 295 146
6	《神秘世界历险记 3》	7月29日	中国	6 545.89	141 201	2 060 957
7	《摇滚藏獒》	7月8日	中国/中国香港/美国	3 964.56	83 731	1 304 170
8	《年兽大作战》	2月8日	中国	3 451.17	62 259	1 148 218
9	《精灵王座》	8月19日	中国	2 502.39	73 370	777 615
10	《麦兜·饭宝奇兵》	9月15日	中国香港/中国	1 895.97	112 034	676 494

资料来源：中国票房网（http：//www.cbooo.cn/）。

（二）优秀动画 IP 日益彰显品牌价值

根据对 2016 年百度搜索风云榜动漫榜单的统计，全年共有 182 部国产动漫上榜，搜索指数合计值为 110 505 545 次，关键词数量所占的比例为 29.69%，搜索指数合计值所占比例为 27.54%，比 2015 年略有增长。"秦时明月之君临天下""熊出没""尸兄""中国惊奇先生""爱情公寓""狐妖小红娘""王牌御史""画江湖之灵主""从前有座灵剑山""灵域""妖怪名单""十万个冷笑话""画江湖之不良人第二季""土豆侠""捏捏大爆炸""猪猪侠""喜羊羊与灰太狼""巴啦啦小魔仙""熊出没之秋日团团转""贝瓦儿歌""纳米核心"等 21 个等国产动漫品牌在网络平台上具有较高关注度、知名度和影响力，跻身 2015 年百度搜索风云榜动漫榜单前 50 名（见表 4）。在全部 182 个国产品牌中，有 53 个新上榜品牌，主要有：从前有座灵剑山、画江湖之不良人第二季、熊出没之秋日团团转、纳米核心、武庚纪、天行九歌、一人之下、熊出没之熊心归来、凹凸世界、京剧猫、熊出没之夏日连连看、魔力课堂、新葫芦兄弟、灵契、一带一路、侍灵演武、一起来看流星雨动画版、长歌行、十万个冷笑话第三季、霹雳狼烟之古原争霸、画江湖之杯莫停。

表 4　　2016 年百度搜索风云榜中国动漫榜单前 50 名

序号	关键词	搜索指数合计	序号	关键词	搜索指数合计
1	秦时明月之君临天下	12 015 775	26	勇者大冒险	1 145 039
2	熊出没	9 154 888	27	一人之下	1 138 825
3	尸兄	7 849 263	28	大头儿子小头爸爸	996 935
4	中国惊奇先生	6 513 300	29	侠岚	969 162
5	爱情公寓	4 105 146	30	黑猫警长	905 618
6	狐妖小红娘	3 399 906	31	魔晶猎人	861 968
7	王牌御史	3 160 185	32	熊出没之熊心归来	830 449
8	画江湖之灵主	3 033 076	33	铠甲勇士捕将	823 581
9	从前有座灵剑山	2 753 356	34	大耳朵图图	738 869
10	灵域	2 750 947	35	凹凸世界	671 945
11	妖怪名单	2 615 410	36	啦啦啦德玛西亚	663 111
12	十万个冷笑话	2 349 251	37	偷星九月天	646 013
13	画江湖之不良人第二季	2 317 908	38	超神游戏	645 780
14	土豆侠	1 963 004	39	熊出没之冬日乐翻天	639 197
15	捏捏大爆炸	1 847 955	40	葫芦小金刚	626 046
16	猪猪侠	1 807 650	41	马丁的早晨	566 925
17	喜羊羊与灰太狼	1 784 496	42	罗小黑战记	521 694
18	巴啦啦小魔仙	1 783 995	43	熊出没之过年	481 776
19	熊出没之秋日团团转	1 678 659	44	星游记	468 843
20	贝瓦儿歌	1 616 500	45	京剧猫	458 760
21	纳米核心	1 598 206	46	神兽金刚	445 529
22	武庚纪	1 398 486	47	斗龙战士	435 010
23	铠甲勇士	1 389 522	48	熊出没之夏日连连看	433 617
24	天行九歌	1 218 657	49	电击小子	428 374
25	择天记	1 193 276	50	逗逗迪迪爱探险	412 457

资料来源：根据百度搜索风云榜动漫榜单（http://top.baidu.com/category? c=5）每日提供的基础数据进行全年汇总，因个别日期采集遗漏，可能与官方实际数据略有出入。

（三）品牌授权助推动漫 IP 由一生万

品牌授权是指授权商将自己所拥有或代理的商标、品牌、形象等知识产权（IP），以合同的形式授予被授权商使用，从而获得许可使用费（royalty）的经营方式。据国际授权业协会数据显示，2015 年全球授权市场规模为 2 517 亿美元，我国以 76.1 亿美元的授权市场规模名列全球第五，成为全球授权市场增长最快的国家之一。中国授权市场以其发展速度和潜力吸引了诸多国际 IP 的进入，活跃在中国授权市场上的 IP 有超过 70%为国际 IP，且新的国际 IP 进入中国的速度正在加快，中国授权市场成为国内外 IP 必争之地。

根据中国玩具和婴童用品协会统计，截至 2016 年 12 月，按照企业实际开展授权业务的口径统计，活跃在我国的品牌授权企业总数为 291 家，已经开展授权业务的 IP 为 816 项。在授权 IP 品类中，娱乐 IP 授权占大多数（69%），其次为企业品牌（13%）和时尚类 IP（11%）。活跃在我国授权市场上的 IP 国别涉及 23 个国家和地区，其中主要国别为美国（35%）、中国（含港澳台）（28%）、日本（12%）、韩国（11%）。品牌授权商及其代理机构在我国主要分布地区为上海（32%）、广东（18%）、北京（18%）、香港（9%）、台湾（8%）（见表 5）。

调查还显示，我国已经开展授权业务的被授权商所在主要行业为玩具游艺（24%）、服装配饰（16%）、家居家纺（11%）、婴童用品（10%）、商业推广（9%）等。我国主要被授权商主要分布在广东（24%）、浙江（18%）、上海（14%）、江苏（14%）和北京（7%）等省份。据调查，我国活跃被授权企业意向合作的授权品牌前四类 IP 为娱乐（38%）、时尚（11%）、体育（11%）和艺术类（11%），整体趋向更为全面平衡。据被授权商企业反映，其选择与授权商合作考虑的重要因素包括 IP 的知名度和影响力（32%）、版权金费用（30%）、IP 与产品的匹配度（21%）、版权方给予被授权商的后续支持和服务（17%）等。

表 5　　我国授权产品（玩具和婴童用品类）主要 IP 品牌

序号	IP 品牌	序号	IP 品牌	序号	IP 品牌
1	AR 魔法学校	23	迪士尼公主	45	魔发精灵
2	BDuck	24	冬己	46	木奇灵
3	Duda & Dada	25	哆啦 A 梦	47	轻松熊
4	Hello Kitty	26	朵拉	48	赛车总动员
5	TOM and JERRY	27	愤怒的小鸟	49	史努比
6	阿狸	28	疯狂动物城	50	睡美人
7	阿童木	29	疯狂外星人	51	托马斯
8	巴布豆	30	钢铁侠	52	喜羊羊与灰太狼
9	巴啦啦小魔仙	31	功夫熊猫	53	咸蛋超人
10	芭比	32	怪兽大学	54	小黄人
11	宝马	33	海绵宝宝	55	小马宝莉
12	爆笑虫子	34	航海王	56	小熊维尼
13	彼得兔	35	花园宝宝	57	小猪佩奇
14	冰雪奇缘	36	加菲猫	58	小公主苏菲亚
15	布加迪	37	赛尔号	59	星球大战
16	啼隆家族	38	铠甲勇士	60	熊本熊
17	超级飞侠	39	乐高	61	熊出没
18	超能陆战队	40	漫威	62	蜘蛛侠
19	聪明的顺溜	41	美国队长	63	植物大战僵尸
20	大嘴猴	42	米菲	64	猪迪克
21	蛋蛋小子	43	米妮	65	猪猪侠
22	刀刀狗	44	米奇		

资料来源：中国玩具和婴童用品协会。

2016 年中国软件产业发展概况

孙占峰　朱　振

2016 年，欧美发达经济体复苏缓慢，中国经济面对复杂多变的国际环境和国内繁重艰巨的改革发展稳定任务，由高速增长时期进入中高速增长时期，全年国内生产总值 74.41 万亿元，比上年增长 6.7%①。软件产业虽经受国内外经济发展压力，但依托信息技术高速迭代模式，以及在国民经济中无所不在的渗透，仍保持了顽强的发展势头。

一、2016 年中国软件产业发展的宏观环境

软件产业是引领科技创新、驱动经济社会转型发展的核心力量，是建设制造强国和网络强国的核心支撑。建设强大的软件产业，是国家构建全球竞争新优势、抢占新工业革命制高点的必然选择。党的十八大和十八届三中、四中、五中、六中全会精神及习近平总书记系列重要讲话精神，坚持创新、协调、绿色、开放、共享的发展理念，顺应新一轮科技革命和产业变革趋势，充分发挥市场配置资源的决定性作用和更好发挥政府作用，以产业由大变强和支撑国家战略为出发点，以创新发展和融合发展为主线，着力突破核心技术，积极培育新兴业态，持续深化融合应用，加快构建具有国际竞争优势的软件产业生态体系，加速催生和释放创新红利、数据红利和模式红利，实现软件产业发展新跨越，全力支撑制造强国和网络强国建设。

国家连续制定并出台《中国制造 2025》、《国务院关于积极推进“互联网+”行动的指导意见》、《国务院关于深化制造业与互联网融合发展的指导意见》、《促进大数据发展行动纲要》和《国家信息化发展战略纲要》等多项国家战略。“十二五”以来，中国软件产业持续快速发展，产业规模迅速扩大，技术创新和应用水平大幅提升，对经济社会发展的支撑和引领作用显著增强。

二、2016 年中国软件产业发展的基本状况②

（一）2016 年软件产业规模情况

2016 年 1 月至 12 月，中国软件和信息技术服务业完成软件业务收入 4.9 万亿元，同比增长 14.9%，增速低于 2015 年 0.8 百分点；软件业务收入占电子信息产业比重约 29%，同比提升 1 百分点。如图 1 所示。

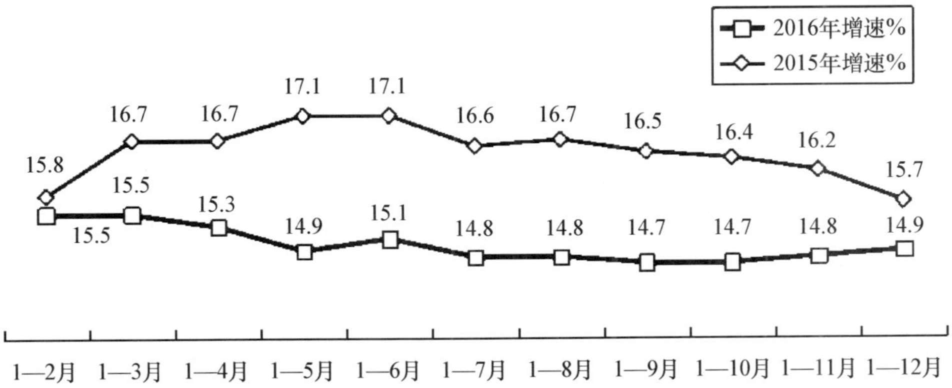

图 1　2016 年 1—12 月软件业务收入增长情况

软件业利润总额同步增长。全行业实现利润总额 6 021 亿元，同比增长 14.9%，与收入增长同步，比 2015 年回落 4.6 百分点。如图 2 所示。

① 中华人民共和国 2016 年国民经济和社会发展统计公报 [EB/OL]. [2017-08-17]. http://www.stats.gov.cn/tjsj/zxfb/201702/t20170228_1467424.html.

② 2016 年 1—12 月软件业经济运行快报 [EB/OL]. [2017-08-07]. http://miit.gov.cn/n1146312/n1146904/n1648374/c5473893/content.html.

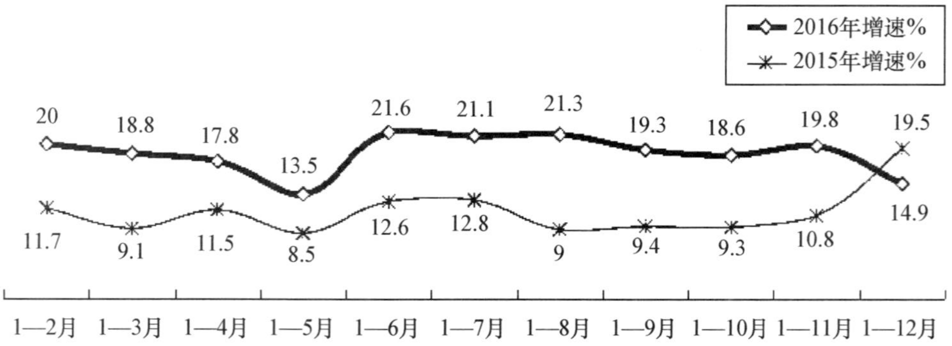

图 2　2016 年 1—12 月软件业利润总额走势

软件业出口增速稳中回升。全国软件业实现出口 519 亿美元，同比增长 5.8%，增速比 2015 年提高 4.1 百分点。其中，外包服务出口增长 5%，扭转 2015 年同期负增长局面；嵌入式系统软件出口增长 6%，增速比 2015 年回落 3 百分点。如图 3 所示。

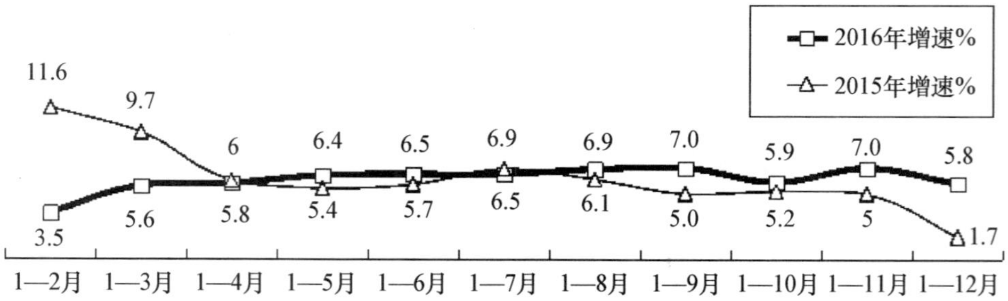

图 3　2016 年 1—12 月软件出口增长情况

随着云计算、大数据、人工智能、虚拟现实等新兴技术产业的快速发展，信息技术服务收入增长较快。2016 年，信息技术服务实现收入 25 114 亿元，同比增长 16%，增速高出全行业平均水平 1.1 百分点，但比 2015 年回落 2.7 百分点。其中，运营相关服务（包括在线软件运营服务、平台运营服务、基础设施运营服务等在内的信息技术服务）收入增长 16.1%；电子商务平台技术服务（包括在线交易平台服务、在线交易支撑服务在内的信息技术支持服务）收入增长 17.7%；集成电路设计增长 12.7%；其他信息技术服务（包括信息技术咨询设计服务、系统集成、运维服务、数据服务等）收入增长 16%。信息技术服务收入占全行业收入比重为 51.8%。

（二）分领域运行情况

软件产品收入增速低于平均水平。全年软件产品实现收入 15 400 亿元，同比增长 12.8%，增速比 2015 年提高 0.9 百分点，但低于全行业平均水平 2.1 百分点，占全行业收入比重为 31.7%。其中，信息安全产品增长 10.9%。

信息技术服务收入增长较快。信息技术服务实现收入 25 114 亿元，同比增长 16%，增速高出全行业水平 1.1 百分点，但比 2015 年回落 2.7 百分点，占全行业收入比重为 51.8%。其中，运营相关服务（包括在线软件运营服务、平台运营服务、基础设施运营服务等在内的信息技术服务）收入增长 16.1%；电子商务平台技术服务（包括在线交易平台服务、在线交易支撑服务在内的信息技术支持服务）收入增长 17.7%；集成电路设计增长 12.7%；其他信息技术服务（包括信息技术咨询设计服务、系统集成、运维服务、数据服务等）收入增长 16%。

嵌入式系统软件收入平稳。嵌入式系统软件实现收入 7 997 亿元，同比增长 15.5%，增速高出全行业平均水平 0.6 百分点，比 2015 年提高 1.4 百分点，占全行业收入比重为 16.5%（见图 4）。

（三）软件产业区域发展情况

东部和东北地区软件业增速回落，中西部地区保持较快增长。东部地区完成软件业务收入 3.8 万亿元，同比增长 14.9%，增速比 2015 年回落 2.2 百分点，占全国软件业的比重为 78.6%；中部地区完成软件业务收入 2 303 亿元，增长 20.6%，增速比 2015 年提高 0.5 百分点，占全国软件业的比重为 4.7%；西部地区完成软件业务收入 5 288 亿元，增长 17.2%，增速与 2015 年基本持平，占全国软件业的比重为 10.9%；东北地区完成软件业务收入 2 801 亿元，增长 6.3%，增速低于全国平均水平 8.6 百分点，占全国软件业的比重为 5.8%。如图 5 所示。

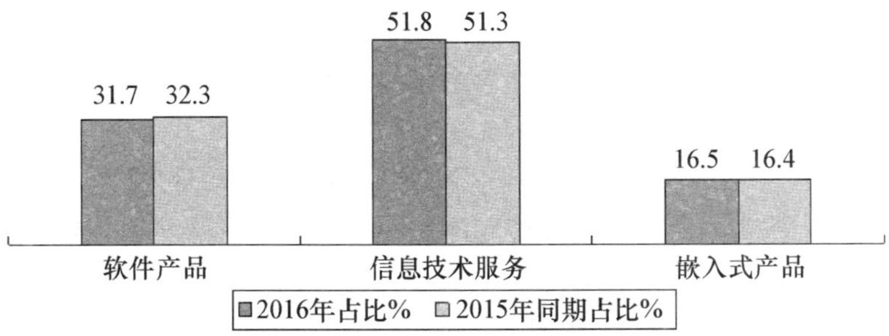

图 4　2016 年 1—12 月软件产业分类收入占比情况

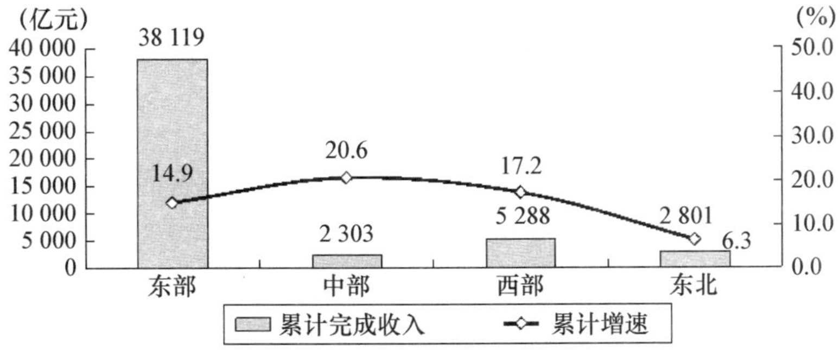

图 5　2016 年 1—12 月软件业分区域增长情况

主要软件大省保持平稳发展，部分省市增速突出。总量居前 5 名的江苏、广东、北京、山东、上海完成软件业务收入分别增长 14.4%、15.4%、11.6%、17.9%和 13.0%（见图 6）。部分中西部省市增长较快，如西部的陕西、重庆增长超过 20%，中部的安徽、湖北增长超过 25%。

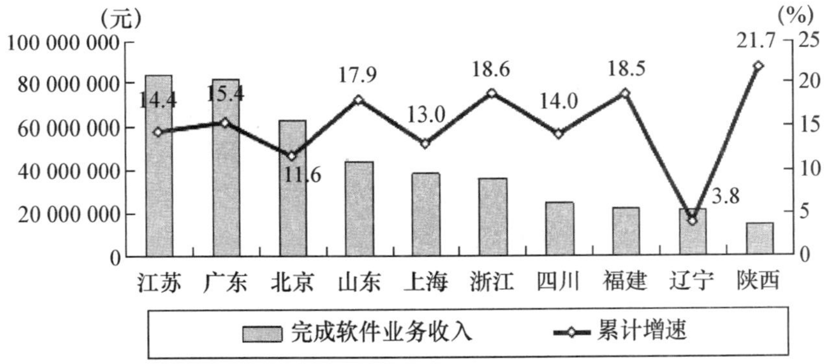

图 6　2016 年 1—12 月前十位省市软件业增长情况

中心城市增速略高于全国平均水平。全国 15 个副省级中心城市实现软件业务收入 2.7 万亿元，同比增长 15.5%，增速高出全国平均水平 0.6 百分点；中心城市的软件业规模占全国的比重为 55.3%，比 2015 年回落 1.6 百分点，同时福州、苏州、合肥等其他一些城市（非副省级）的软件业也呈快速发展态势。全国软件业务收入达到千亿元的中心城市和直辖市共 15 个，比 2015 年增加 1 个。如图 7 所示。

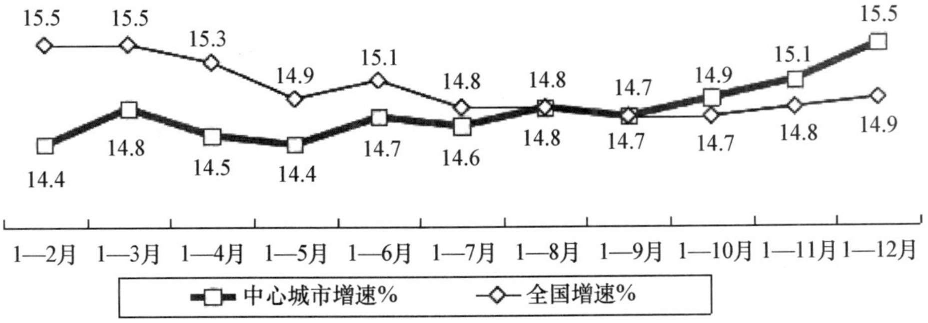

图 7　2016 年 1—12 月中心城市软件业务收入增长情况

（四）主要软件企业发展情况

根据国家统计局标准，以工业和信息化部统计的 2015 年全国软件和信息技术服务业年报数据为基础，经省市工业和信息化部门初步审核，工业和信息化部最终核定了 2016 年（第 15 届）中国软件业务收入前百家企业（以下简称软件百家企业）。

2016 年（第 15 届）软件百家企业比 2015 年多了 14 家，入围门槛为软件业务年收入 13.3 亿元，比上一届提高了 2.8 亿元，增长 26.7%。软件百家企业共完成软件业务收入 6 005 亿元，比上届增长 13.1%，占软件和信息技术服务全行业收入的 14%；实现利润总额 1 524 亿元，比上届增长 48.2%；软件业务收入超过百亿元的企业达到 7 家。部分企业增势突出，有三成左右的百家企业收入增长率超过 20%。本届软件百家企业研发投入大幅提高，共投入研发经费 1 233 亿元，比上届大幅增长 47.3%。软件百家企业研发人员近 36 万，占总从业人员的 43%，与上届相比增长了 12 百分点①。

三、2016 年中国软件产业发展的特点

2016 年，软件产业在大数据、云计算和区块链等新技术新模式创新驱动下，整体运行态势平稳，产业规模稳步扩大，行业细分和专业化进一步推进，与互联网进一步深度融合，具体呈现出如下特点：

（一）产业整体规模持续扩大，利润保持稳步增长

中国软件产业克服全球 IT 行业调整、复苏缓慢等负面因素影响，积极在大数据、云计算和区块链等新技术方面探索、深耕，进一步拓展国内市场需求，拉动国民信息消费和企业信息建设投资的升级，拓展了产业进一步发展的空间，取得了一定成效。全年运行态势平稳，收入持续两位数增长，盈利状况良好，出口较上年明显好转。其中中西部地区继续较快发展，中心城市软件业保持领先增长态势。

（二）产业细分化和专业化趋势进一步明显

软件产品的开发思路随着服务化趋势的加深正在逐步发生转变，在了解客户需求，以客户需求定制化开发软件产品、提供软件服务的过程中，软件产品的功能性划分和面对不同领域的专业化需求越来越明确，软件产业随着技术更迭和产品开发思路的转变而调整。对下游应用领域的理解程度越来越成为客户选择软件企业的重要标准之一，使得软件行业按照下游应用领域细划为越来越多的子行业，有些子行业甚至差异很大。细分化在一定程度使得软件企业较难实现横向发展，但由于对客户需求更加了解，有利于建立纵向产业链，在一定程度上提高了客户黏度，也拓展了产业范畴。

（三）产业结构布局呈现体系化趋势

操作系统、数据库、中间件和应用软件等传统概念开始相互渗透，软件向更加综合、广泛的一体化软件平台的新体系演变，硬件与软件、内容与终端、应用与服务的一体化整合速度加快。软件和信息技术服务业将围绕主流软件平台体系构造产业链，市场竞争从单一产品的竞争发展为基于平台体系的产业链竞争，产业纵向、横向整合步伐加快，围绕主流软件平台体系形成的产业生态系统将主导市场竞争。产品、资源和服务的体系化趋势日趋明显，软件即服务（SaaS）、平台即服务（PaaS）和基础设施即服务（IaaS）等基于平台的服务模式日趋成熟，移动互联网、移动智能终端、数字电视等综合平台不断涌现，基于产品、信息、客户的资源整合平台及其商业模式创新成为产业核心竞争力。

（四）产业发展与互联网结合进一步加深

计算技术的重心正逐步从计算机转向网络，软件的技术和业务创新与网络发展已深度耦合，网络成为软件开发、部署、运行和服务的主流平台。软件产品基于网络平台开发和运行、内容基于网络发布和传播、应用基于网络构架和部署、服务基于网络创新和发展成为大趋势，网络化操作系统、网络软件开发工具、网络运行管理平台、智能终端平台、远程运维等基于网络的技术、产品和服务应运而生，基于云计算、物联网、移动互联网、下一代互联网等的新兴服务将推动服务模式、商业模式不断创新。网络化趋势进一步打破了市场竞争的区域、国别界限，全面呈现出全球性竞争态势。同时，网络化环境下网络空间安全面临的挑战更加严峻，并严重影响国家经济安全、社会安全、国防安全和信息安全，提高安全保障能力成为软件和信息技术服务业的重要战略任务。

（五）产业从业群体不断壮大

从软件产业从业人员情况分析看，呈现出知识化、年轻化、高端化趋势。软件和信息技术服务业从业人员中大学生占 65%，成为我国知识性人才就业的主渠道。从产业分布来看，除 IT 领域达 35% 占主要份额外，制造、交通、教育等领域软件从业

① 工业和信息化部发布 2016 年（第 15 届）中国软件业务收入前百家企业名单及发展报告［EB/OL］.［2017-08-08］. http://www.miit.gov.cn/newweb/n1146290/n4388791/c5169086/content.html.

人员人数占比超过48%，说明软件业与制造业、服务业的融合性越来越强，也吸引更多的高端人才从事软件产业，这对于产业的发展无疑是最强有力的保障和创新实力助推器。

四、2016年中国软件正版化工作的开展情况

中国一向高度重视软件知识产权的保护，在《中华人民共和国著作权法》和《计算机软件保护条例》中对软件版权保护均有明确规定。2016年持续落实《关于计算机预装正版操作系统软件有关问题的通知》和《关于政府部门购置计算机办公设备必须采购已预装正版操作系统软件产品的通知》等相关文件要求，督促各地方严格执行并推进软件正版化工作，以营造良好的软件知识产权保护环境，维护计算机市场和软件市场秩序，推动软件自主创新活动，促进中国软件产业健康持续快速发展。

（一）提高计算机预装正版操作系统率

根据计算机预装正版操作系统软件工作要求，每年度统计国内部分品牌计算机生产商和操作系统软件提供商上年度计算机销售数量和操作系统软件的预装数量，形成年度《计算机预装正版操作系统软件情况分析报告》。随着预装正版操作系统工作的稳步推进，在计算机生产企业和软件企业的共同努力下，国内新出厂计算机正版操作系统软件的装机数量和预装率逐年提高，对推进国家软件正版化，改善国内软件知识产权保护环境发挥了积极的作用。2007年正版预装率为87.75%，之后每年均保持稳定增长，2014年正版预装率更是达到98.81%，2015年正版预装率稳定在98.57%，预装正版操作系统软件工作实施以来正版预装率提高了10.82百分点。

（二）推动软件著作权登记数量迅速增长

2016年，重点持续推动计算机预装正版操作系统工作，以政府机关作为突破口，要求使用正版操作系统和办公软件，以点带面，发挥辐射带动作用。该项工作的实施直接推动了中国软件正版化工作的进展，间接助力中国软件知识产权整体水平的提升和进步。以计算机软件著作权登记数量为参考标本，中国参与软件研发的企业越来越多，进行计算机软件著作权登记的数量也逐年增加。2016年，中国计算机软件著作权登记数量407 774件，同比增长39.48%，是自2010年以来同比增长最高的一年。从登记量地区排名上看，2016年位列全国前十位的地区分别是广东省、北京市、上海市、江苏省、浙江省、四川省、福建省、山东省、湖北省、安徽省。其中，广东省软件登记量为91 715件，约占登记总量的22.49%，高居全国榜首。前十位省市共登记了328 437件，约占登记总量的80.54%。从登记量增速情况来看，2016年增速较快的集中在西北和西南地区，宁夏回族自治区、西藏自治区、贵州省、青海省同比增长均超过110%。福建省、海南省、甘肃省、新疆维吾尔自治区、四川省、河南省同比增长均超过了50%。其中，计算机软件著作权质权登记263件，同比增长33.5%；涉及合同263个，同比增长33.5%；涉及软件作品数量1 015件，同比增长18%；涉及主债务金额285 961.82万元，同比增长62.6%；涉及担保金额291 961.68万元，同比增长87.1%①。

（三）增强版权保护工作实施力度

“剑网行动”是贯彻实施《国家知识产权战略纲要》，净化网络版权保护环境的重要部署，由国家版权局、公安部和工业和信息化部联合执法，创新手段、加大监管力度，重点任务涉及网络音乐、云存储、应用APP、网络广告联盟、网络转载等领域，从2005年开始已连续开展多年且持续保持高压态势。“剑网2016”专项行动重点对有影响的互联网企业和网站主动监管，支持指导互联网行业协会组织开展网络企业行业自律活动，协助提供查处案件涉及的网站备案信息，对经版权、公安部门认定的侵权盗版网站依法采取断开网络接入、关闭网站、吊销经营许可证等处理措施。通过专项行动治理，“剑网2016”专项行动组督导网络开发企业就其版权问题开展了自查自纠，查办了一批网络侵权盗版违法活动，有效遏制住了网络侵权盗版势头，进一步净化了中国的网络空间及网络版权环境。“剑网2016”专项行动期间，共查处行政案件514件，行政罚款467万元，移送司法机关33件，涉案金额2亿元，关闭网站290家②。

（四）软件正版化步入新常态新阶段

通过多年预装正版操作系统和软件正版化工作的扎实落实，各级政府机关软件正版率显著提高，

① 关于2016年全国著作权登记情况的通报［EB/OL］.［2017-08-08］. http://www.ncac.gov.cn/chinacopyright/contents/483/315265.html.

② “剑网2016”专项行动总结会在京召开［EB/OL］.［2017-08-08］. http://www.jsxwcbj.gov.cn/xwzx/yjdt/2016/12/ct_40642.html.

促进软件自主创新效果显著，软件正版化工作进入新阶段、新常态。为适应软件正版化工作阶段要求，进一步巩固政府机关软件正版化工作成果，推进使用正版软件工作部际联席会议建立了中央和省级机关软件正版化工作责任人数据库，指导各省（区、市）建立了市县级机关责任人数据库，推动各省（区、市）建立健全软件正版化工作考核评议制度，指导北京、天津、河北、内蒙古、福建、海南、重庆、青海、新疆等省（区、市）制定了软件正版化工作考核评议细则。各省（区、市）也开始部署和实施地方国有企业软件正版化工作，积极稳妥推进民营企业软件正版化工作。

（撰稿：孙占峰　审稿：朱　振）

2016 年中国网络游戏市场分析

易观智库

一、网络游戏的定义及产品特征

网络游戏是电子游戏的一个种类。指以互联网和移动互联网为传输媒介，以游戏运营商服务器和用户计算机（包括移动智能设备）为处理终端，以游戏客户端软件为信息交互窗口的旨在实现娱乐、休闲、交流和取得虚拟成就的具有可持续性的个体性多人在线游戏。与其他类型的电子游戏相比较，网络游戏具有实时性强、互动性强的特点。另外目前整体的网络游戏行业内在特点是随着技术不断迭代以及用户的需求口味不断变化，产品生命周期有限，网络游戏的标准也不断在改变。

二、网络游戏细分市场特征

目前网络游戏市场按地域划分主要有北美市场、欧洲市场、亚洲市场及其他地域市场。网络游戏按照所基于的网络及搭载的终端不同，分为互联网游戏和移动互联网游戏。其中互联网游戏又依据所运行模式不同分为客户端网络游戏、网页游戏两类。相互比较后，三类网络游戏细分产品具备的特征如下：

（一）客户端网络游戏

基于互联网络依托个人电脑终端运行，必须下载客户端再进行用户登录后方能使用。客户端网络游戏是目前网络游戏市场当中所占市场份额最高、盈利能力最强的细分产品类型。研发周期较长，在研发当中投入的成本以及产品推广阶段的费用都比较高。相较于网页游戏和移动互联网游戏来说，客户端网络游戏消耗游戏时间较长，用户的获取具备一定的门槛，但是用户获得以后比较稳定，流失率较低。一款客户端网络游戏的运营生命周期一般在 5 年以上。

客户端游戏市场产业链主要包括上游的游戏研发环节，中游的游戏运营环节，下游的游戏分销环节，以及提供支撑服务的设备提供商和电信运营商等。

研发环节：由于 PC 客户端游戏的研发对技术和资金的要求很高，全球范围内客户端游戏研发商的数量并不多，且顶级研发商多为集团型公司，并集中在日本、韩国和美国等地区，如 Square Enix、动视暴雪、Nexon 等，中国的网易和腾讯也是实力较强的端游研发商。

运营环节：端游产品的运营周期较长，一般需要较多人力，在本土市场端游厂商一般会选择自主运营，但在海外市场则会选择熟悉当地市场的合作伙伴代理运营。由于全球范围内客户端网络游戏行业发展萎靡，部分端游企业已经停止自研立项，专注于现有端游产品的运营。

分销环节：在端游产品的分销环节，部分运营商会通过自建官网平台，进行自主营销推广。在国内客户端游戏发展早期，网吧也是重要的推广分发平台，但随着个人电脑的普及，线下网吧衰落，网吧在客户端游戏分销中扮演的角色越来越弱。PC 单机游戏一般通过实体销售，或者通过在线 PC 游戏下载平台进行分发。

此外，在目前整体网络游戏发展的大环境中，研运一体化越来越明显，研发商与发行商相互重叠的情况是极为普遍的。另外，伴随着《英雄联盟》《DOTA2》等电子竞技端游产品在世界范围之内的流行，电子竞技也已逐渐形成较为完整的产业链，成为客户端游戏吸引核心玩家、增加变现渠道的重要方式。

（二）网页游戏

基于互联网依托于个人电脑终端运行，最大的特点是无须下载，在浏览器上即可直接进行游戏行为。目前主要分为社交游戏及休闲类网页游戏两种。研发周期短，投入成本较低，推广费用也低于客户端网络游戏。游戏所耗费的时间短于客户端网络游戏，但长于移动互联网游戏。对于网速、个人电脑硬件配置的要求较低，用户获取的成本也比较低廉，因此用户基数扩展速度比较快。但是用户获取后比较容易流失。一般网页游戏都以 RPG（角色扮演游戏）类题材居多，生命周期一般在 3 年左右。

（三）移动互联网游戏

基于移动互联网，依托于移动终端运行的游戏产品。最大的特点是不受空间的限制，可随时随地进行游戏活动。目前市场上的移动互联网游戏发展的主要促进因素是智能终端的发展，操作系统集中为 iOS 和 Android 两类。移动互联网游戏的研发周期介于客户端网络游戏和网页游戏之间，推广费用为三者最低，但未来将逐步攀升。游戏所消耗的时间也为三者最低。目前用户获取移动互联网游戏的主要手段集中于各类应用分发平台，且移动互联网游戏尚未形成明确的用户使用习惯。整体来看移动互联网游戏市场特别是智能操作系统的移动互联网游戏市场仍然处于快速发展阶段。一款移动互联网游戏的生命周期一般在 1 年左右。

（四）发展趋势

随着移动游戏便捷、随便化和智能终端的普及，以及多元化的玩法模式，它将逐渐成为比客户端游戏更受欢迎的游戏类型。并且随着客户端网络游戏市场增长瓶颈的出现以及网页游戏整体市场进入萎缩，全球范围内游戏厂商都将进行移动游戏的转型。但是目前来看，整体的网络游戏（特别是网页游戏及移动游戏）是一个快速发展的行业，市场在发展的同时也存在诸多不确定性。在全球范围内无论在哪个细分市场，产品本身的研发与游戏的内容题材与类型是吸引用户的核心因素，其他泛娱乐趋势如 IP 等因素在某些地域地区其实并不适用。

三、中国网络游戏市场规模及预测

中国是目前亚洲网络游戏最大的市场，无论是在用户规模还是营收能力方面，中国的网络游戏都有着长足的进步。中国的网络游戏厂商已经完成了从代理引入其他国家网络游戏产品，到自主研发产品为主导的市场，最后演进为将中国的网络游戏产品进行全球化发行的发展历程。特别是在网页游戏市场当中，中国也有厂商几乎垄断了东南亚地区所有的网页游戏产品供给。2016 年，中国网络游戏市场规模达到 246.06 亿美元，预计到 2020 年中国网络游戏市场达到 308.13 亿美元（见图 1）。

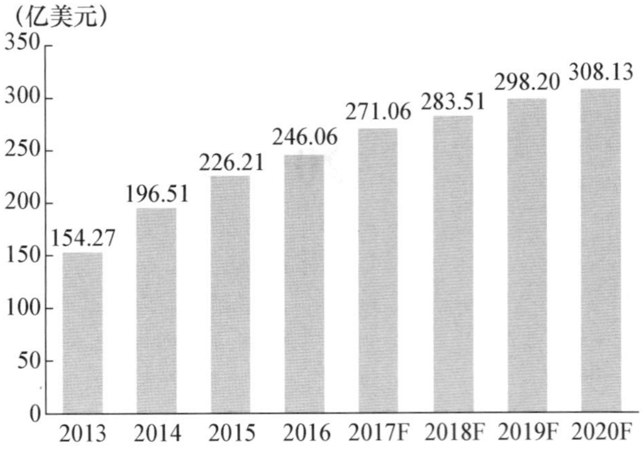

图 1　2013—2020 年中国网络游戏市场规模及预测

四、中国网络游戏细分市场分析及预测

中国客户端游戏市场保持平稳态势，市场规模基本滞涨，市场已经日趋饱和。由于竞争者的减少以及市场的逐渐成熟，企业也选择了稳健的经营策略，新游戏推出节奏减慢。受研发成本提升的影响，新产品数量降低，质量提高。

网页游戏方面，市场结束了增长态势，受到移动游戏市场的挤压，放缓趋势明显。2016 年中国网页游戏市场规达到 16.73 亿元，目前市场将出现萎缩态势。

移动游戏方面，2016 年中国移动游戏市场规模大幅超过端游，移动游戏的生命周期和可拓展性非常有限，产品产出量巨大，但经过了 2014 年的爆发，伴随着人口红利的削弱，移动游戏市场已经从单纯的获取流量，向深入挖掘用户价值转化。2016 年中国手游市场规模达到 118.60 亿美元，预计 2020 年中国移动游戏市场将达到 172.55 亿美元（见图 2）。

五、中国客户端游戏市场分析

在市场竞争格局方面，腾讯依然占有最大的市场份额，达 47.2%。在本季度，腾讯在客户端游戏方面仍致力于电子竞技产品，目前《英雄联盟》仍是世界上最吸金的客户端游戏。此外，网易客户端游戏收入有所增加，占据 24.0%的市场份额（见图 3）。这很大一部分归功于其在维护传统的《梦幻西游》等基础上，致力于打造电子竞技产品《守望先锋》的战略部署。目前我国广义的网络游戏市场，整体都受到移动游戏市场的冲击，客户端游戏市场已经形成饱和，未来在客户端游戏市场将会形成内容导向的格局。但是随着电子竞技目前成为大热产业，在一定程度上也带动了客户端游戏的市场发展。

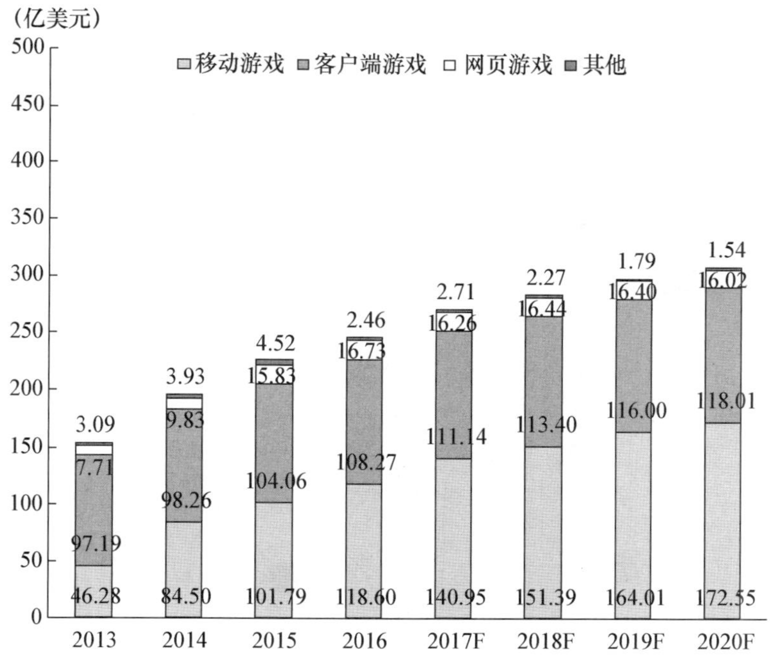

图 2　2013—2020 年中国网络游戏市场细分规模及预测

而未来“大厂控场”的状态依旧会保持下去。一些中小型客户端游戏企业将会仅仅维持旗下主力产品，而转型移动游戏领域。

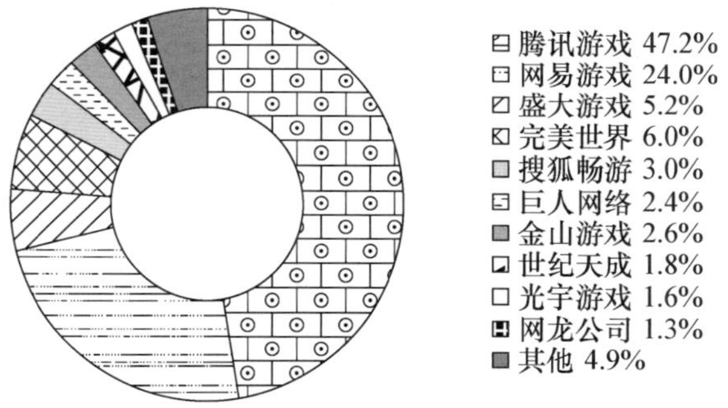

图 3　2016 年中国客户端游戏市场竞争格局

六、中国移动游戏市场分析

（一）中国移动游戏市场规模及发展特点

我国移动游戏爆发期在 2014 年，从 2013 年的 46.28 亿美元增长至 84.50 亿美元，环比增长 82.58%，在 2014 年涌现出诸多现象级产品，也带来了让许多移动游戏厂商跻身一流企业的契机，2016 年我国移动游戏产业仍然处于高速增长期，整体规模达到 118.60 亿美元，而且势头不减，预计移动游戏在 2020 年达到应用成熟期，预计规模达到 172.55 亿美元（见图 4）。

Analysys 易观分析认为，2016 年的中国移动游戏市场仍处于高速发展阶段，大型厂商囤积大量 IP，拥有强大的研发能力，同时把控发行渠道，挤压着中小创业者和新进入者的生存空间，市场准入

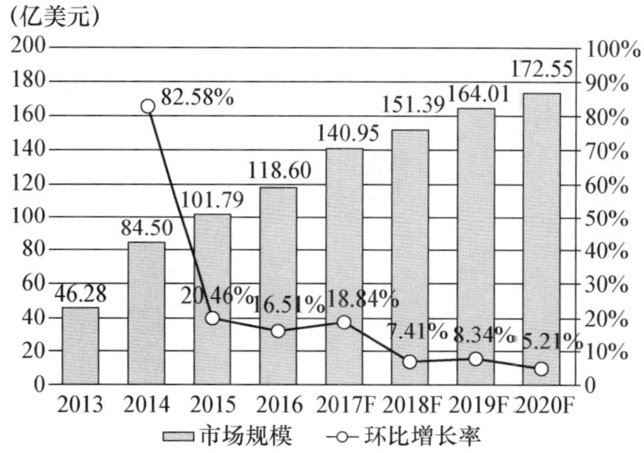

图 4　2013—2020 年中国移动游戏市场规模及预测

说明：1. 易观从 2017 第一季度度起修改数据算法，对以前中国移动游戏市场规模数据进行更新。2. 具体包括其运营及研发的移动游戏产品所创造的用户付费收入以及企业间的游戏研发与代理费用。游戏周边产品授权，内容外包与海外代理授权费用的总和。3. 上市公司财务报告、专家访谈、厂商深访以及易观推算模型得出。

门槛提高。市场竞争格局趋于稳定，腾讯、网易等大厂主宰移动游戏市场，马太效应愈发显著，行业集中度进一步提高。2016 年端游改编手游成为行业的主流产品形态，反映出玩家对游戏内容的要求日益增高。重度游戏、IP 泛娱乐化、市场细分成为移动游戏行业的三大趋势，同时由于人口红利消失和游戏转换成本增高等原因，行业对厂商精细化运营能力的要求日渐增高（见图 5）。

（二）中国移动游戏市场竞争格局

研发商市场头部企业竞争进入白热化，中国移动游戏研发企业中，市场格局依旧被腾讯游戏和网

易游戏两家主导，合计占据了 68%的市场份额，继续保持双寡头垄断的市场格局。目前整体的研发商市场除了腾讯、网易不可动摇的市场地位之外，其余厂商市场份额十分分散，竞争尤为激烈（见图 6、图 7 和图 8）。虽然游戏版号的新规对手游数量有所影响，但并不影响移动游戏厂商在年末推出大作，随着端游、页游厂商和发行商、渠道商全面拓展手游业务，流量和 IP 成为各家的重要资源，移动游戏

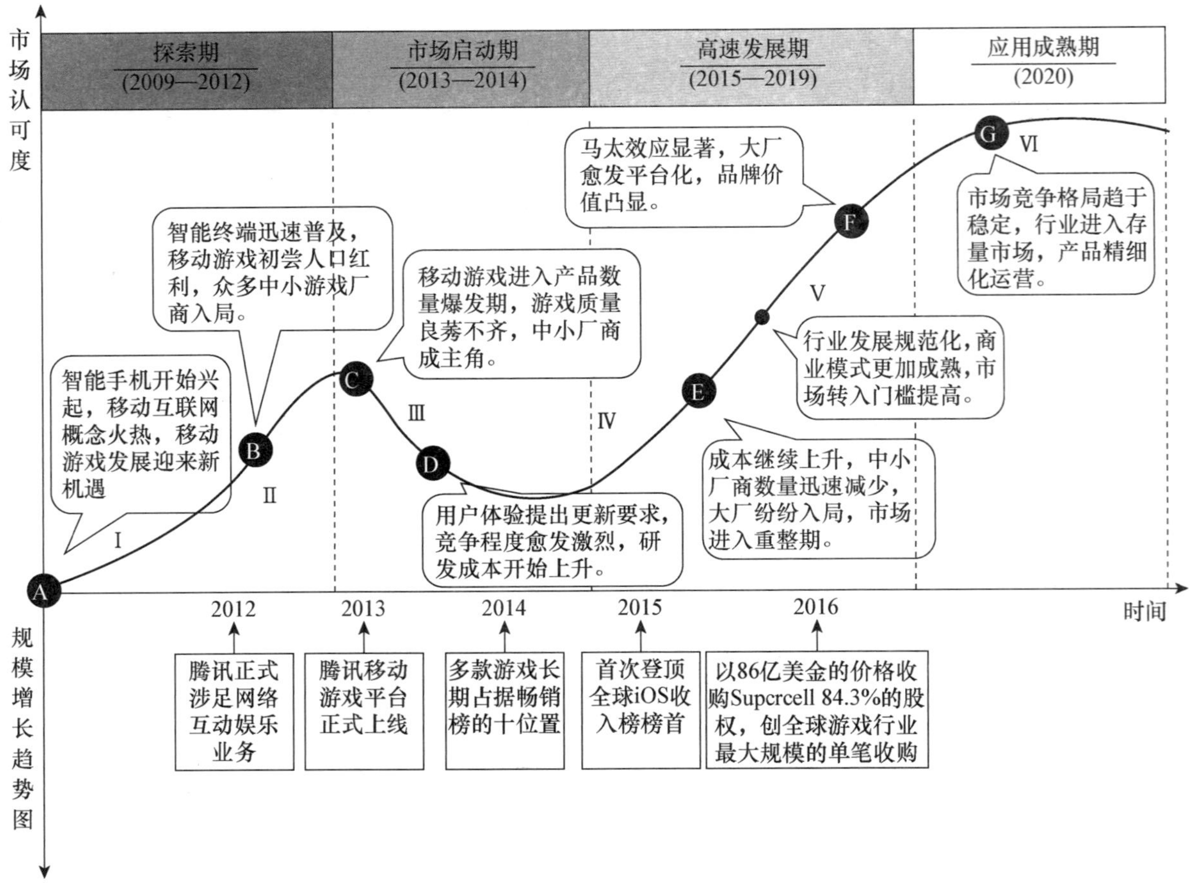

图 5　2016 年中国移动游戏市场 AMC 模型

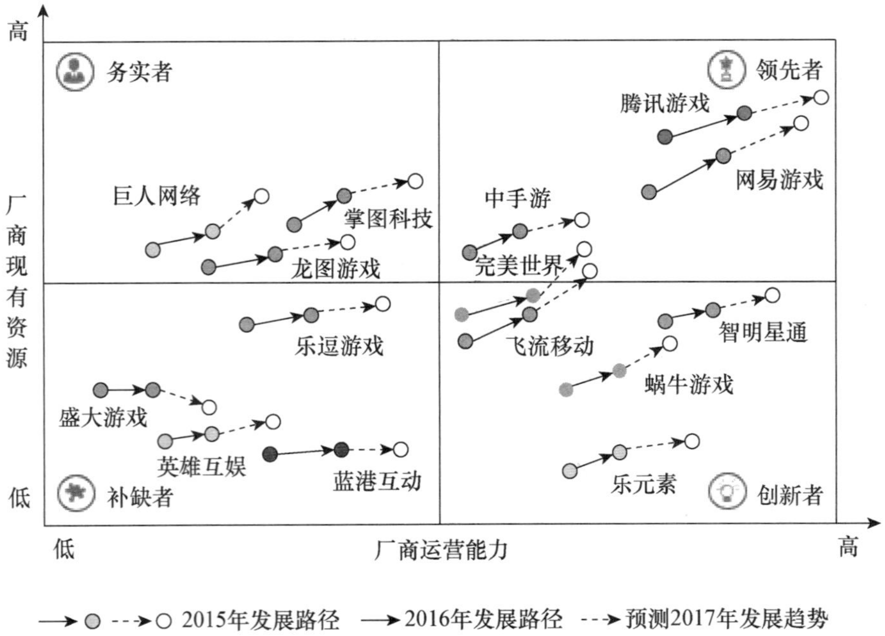

图 6　2016 年中国移动游戏市场实力矩阵

市场已经成为大厂争夺的战地。此外，相比于欧美市场，我国的整体研发人员的人工成本比较低，在欧美市场互联网巨头崛起的背景下，普通中小型开发商难以雇用高质量的研发人才。

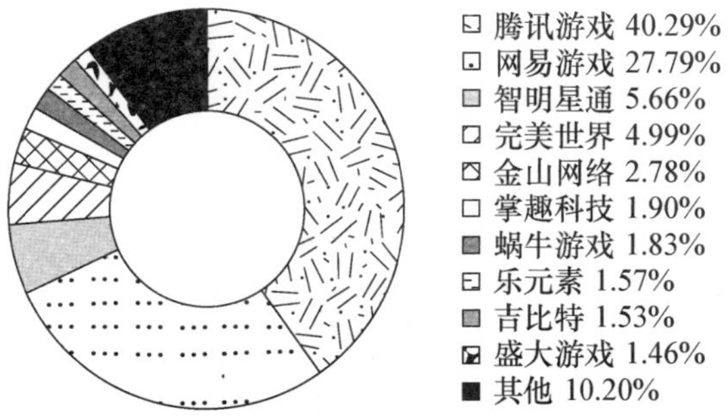

图 7　2016 年中国移动游戏研发企业市场份额

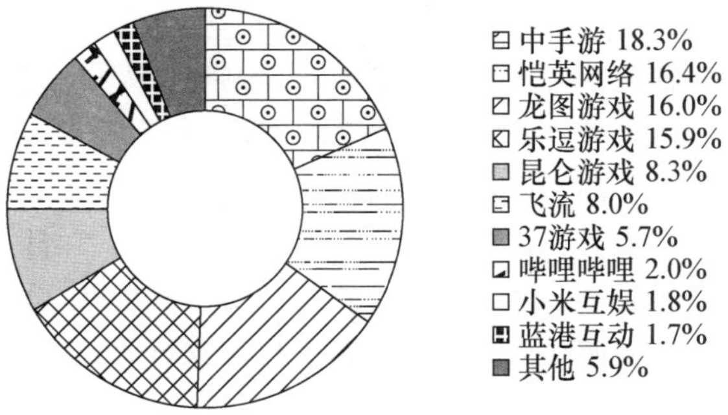

图 8　2016 年中国移动游戏发行商全平台竞争格局

从发行的市场格局变动可以看出，随着移动游戏市场规模不断扩大，页游和端游厂商、手游渠道、视频平台等移动游戏相关厂商纷纷拓展手游业务，并且已获得显著的成绩。手游内容方面，泛娱乐 IP 和 MMORPG 依然是市场热点，2017 年初各大厂商已储备大量 IP 手游，如中手游的《轩辕剑 3 手游版》、蓝港互动的《十万个冷笑话》等，而一向强于 IP 储备的飞流也将集结《全职高手》《侍魂　天下第一剑客传 3D》《三生三世十里桃花》《哆啦 A 梦》《忍者龟 OL》《樱花大战》等数款超级 IP 新品陆续与玩家见面，预计在 2017 年迎来新的爆发。

移动游戏发行商用户规模竞争格局相比上个季度变动不大。乐逗游戏依旧保持发行商市场用户规模第一，主要原因仍旧是得益于休闲手游《地铁跑酷》《神庙逃亡》等游戏一直以来具有超高的用户留存，使得乐逗游戏拥有庞大的用户基础，份额达到 28.80%。中手游凭借其大 IP 精品化战略方式保持在第二位，达到 19.00%（见图 9）。

（三）中国移动游戏产业链分析

移动游戏研发商（CP）：移动游戏的研发企业，主要以聚集产品 IP，打造产品研发的核心团队，依靠自身的智力和创意做游戏内容的创生。在此之外，

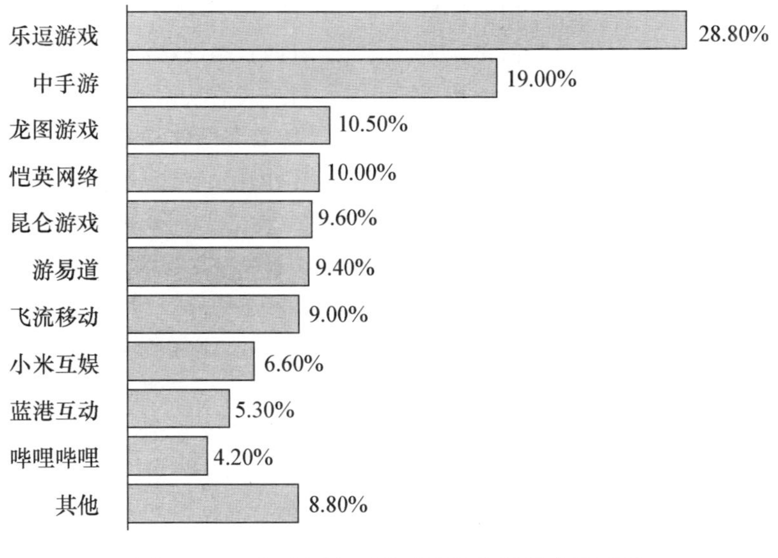

图 9　2016 年中国移动游戏发行市场用户渗透率

说明：1. 中国移动游戏发行商：以游戏代理发行为主要经营业务的中国游戏企业。通过对游戏产品的独家代理、多渠道发行，来完成其业务经营。2. 用户渗透率按厂商在中国大陆市场代理发行产品的季度活跃用户数统计。3. 上市公司财务报告、专家访谈、厂商深访以及由易观千帆数据提供综合得出。

或将自主研发的产品独家代理给发行企业，或将产品投放到移动游戏的分发渠道，做自主的运营，进而将自己的产品向产业链的下游输出（见图 10）。

移动游戏发行商：主要经营的业务为独家代理上游研发厂商的移动游戏产品，通过全渠道的发行能力、强大的市场推广能力，将代理的产品投放到多个渠道，进行产品的推广及运营。但是目前随着整体移动游戏市场节奏的加快，研运一体化的趋势愈加明显，整体的资源整合程度也高于单兵作战。

移动游戏渠道商：又称作移动游戏运营平台，直接对接用户，是用户接触移动游戏的第一个环节，也是移动游戏内容流向用户的“最后一公里”。目前

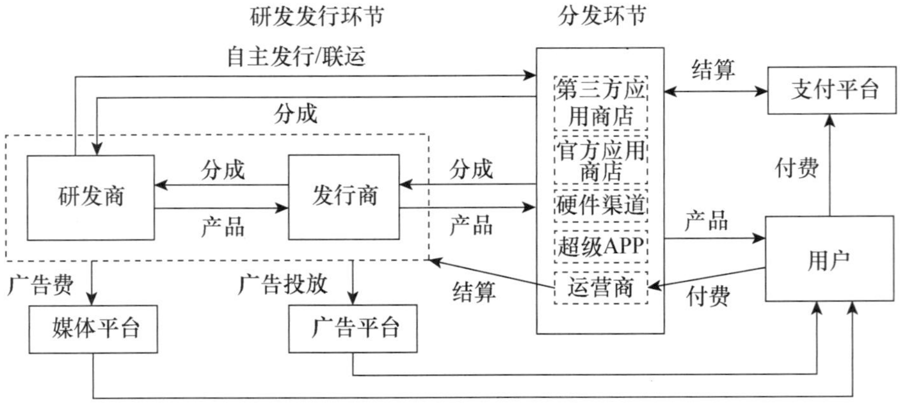

图 10 中国移动游戏产业链

全球范围内移动游戏运营平台以应用商店为主，包括官方（苹果 App Store、Google Play）与第三方应用商店。此外，还包括超级 APP、运营商渠道以及硬件厂商的应用商店。特别值得关注的是，中国市场和欧美市场在移动游戏的分发渠道上差别较大。

中国安卓平台的应用商店数量超过 200 个，如 360 手机助手、豌豆荚、91 助手等，主要是由于谷歌官方应用商店在中国市场的缺席，此外 iOS 越狱平台也有多家应用商店。但在欧美市场，官方应用商店占垄断地位，主要是 iOS 平台的 App Store 和安卓平台的 Google Play，另外还有 Windows Phone 和 Amazon 的应用商店。中国安卓平台应用商店除了作为手机游戏发行渠道之外也提供营销服务，营销服务的价格和收入分成根据产品质量决定。但欧美市场的情况相对简单，应用商店只提供用户下载渠道，并不提供营销服务。Apple 和 Google 都是从应用内购买的收入里收取 30%的服务费。

移动游戏支撑环节：包括电信网络、服务器、营销媒体、支付等环节。移动游戏作为互联网化的文化创意产品，在完成内容传达用户、实现用户交互以及用户付费的整个过程中，需要多个环节的支持，需要营销来实现产品品牌化的诉求，需要支付完成整体游戏运营的最后一环。在营销推广上，中国和海外市场也有较大差异。

国内的游戏营销主要基于社交驱动，微信、微博是手游推广重点战场。由于国内城市人口密度大，人与人之间的关系相对紧密，游戏口碑传播的比率在 200%～300%是十分正常的。但国外的游戏口碑传播的比率大大低于国内，20%～30%的口碑传播比率已经很不错了。国外网络广告经过多年的发展，RTB（实时竞价投放）、精准广告投放技术已经非常成熟，游戏开发商通过广告平台直接针对游戏玩家进行广告投放。Google 和 Apple 等应用商店厂商都有自己的移动广告平台，另外，社交渠道诸如 Facebook、Twitter 也都有各自的广告平台。

从中国移动游戏产业链来看，内容提供方是移动游戏行业的核心要素，产业的主要收入来自移动游戏研发发行环节，移动游戏市场早期人口红利优势显著，处于分发环节的渠道和平台作为流量入口，具有较大的话语权。2016 年随着人口红利减退，对游戏品质具有较高把控权的研发商在产业中的话语权逐渐提高，因此移动游戏发行商开始拓展自研业务，移动游戏渠道商开始拓展代理发行业务，全产业链布局开始成为主流发展方向，目前国内领先的研发商也具备一定的发行能力，市场趋势朝着研运一体的方向发展。

（四）中国移动游戏市场促进因素分析

1. 政府扶持

随着我国移动游戏迅猛发展，文娱行业已经成为我国国民经济发展的重要一环，我国政府大力提倡游戏游艺产业发展，许多地方政府制定政策支持产业发展，如 2016 年 10 月，文化部下发了文化娱乐行业转型升级意见，该意见主要包含鼓励引进 3D、VR、AR 等游戏设备技术升级，鼓励设立文娱场所，支持电竞赛事，鼓励资本进入文娱行业等，有利于扩大文化消费，促进游戏行业发展。

2. 经济大环境下的推动

随着我国居民收入水平提升，居民人均可支配收入不断增长，在游戏等娱乐项目上的消费能力提升。此外，移动游戏各个产业链发展成熟，大型企业加入推动产业发展，行业趋向于集中化。最后，资本催化市场热度，近年资本市场开始向移动游戏企业投入大量资金。

3. 社会主流环境认可

我国移动游戏用户群不断扩大，中国手机网民规模和智能手机用户数量快速增长，移动游戏的用户群逐渐扩大。另外，移动游戏付费习惯形成，移动游戏的收费模式以及玩家们的消费倾向正在慢慢超越许多传统行业。

4. 技术逐渐成熟提供发展土壤

移动智能设备的普及，移动互联网信息服务的蓬勃发展，推动了智能终端的迅速普及，为移动游戏的高速发展提供了土壤。流量改革助力移动游戏行业发展，工信部表示，到2017年底，将实现4G全面覆盖城市和乡村、宽带平均接入速率达到30Mbps、流量平均资费水平大幅下降三大既定目标，中国将建成全球最大的4G移动通信网络。随着流量改革的不断推进，移动游戏网络环境将有大幅改善，对强联网手游将有强力推进作用。

（五）中国移动游戏发展需注意的问题

1. 政策同时收紧对行业的监督

自2014年以来，我国政府在对整体游戏产业推动的同时，也相继出台了一系列严打措施，继视频、网络文学之后，移动游戏成为关注重点，包括文化部、国家新闻出版广电总局、体育总局等多个部门分别出台了对移动游戏相应的监察方案。其中文化部对移动游戏内容抄袭、侵权等问题十分关注，使得移动游戏产品的门槛拉高，移动游戏如何自强自律，规避法律陷阱成为严峻的必须考虑的问题。

2. 产品问题矛盾不断激化

我国移动游戏的题材与商业模式同质化十分严重，往往一款现象级产品爆发，在短时间内会被大量复制，盗版猖獗，从而快速失去活力，致使移动游戏产品的生命周期较短。同时游戏企业在移动游戏产品上获得短暂的成功之后，往往对产品的延续性做得不够到位，使得用户加速流失——研发仍是产品问题的核心因素。

3. 造假刷榜等现象仍然存在

在目前整体的移动游戏市场，侵权、抄袭、窃取源代码、盗用IP等行为仍然没有得到妥善的解决，打版权的擦边球、对热门游戏的仿制以及自充值的刷榜行为（游戏企业为提高产品在榜中位置，获得更多的流量，进行刷榜）仍然存在。另外，一些企业间接地提高自身流水收入数据，以便获取更多的资源，使得产品本身并未达到市场预期高度，破坏了移动游戏市场的生态环境以及秩序。

（六）中国移动游戏市场KSF分析

1. 注重研发能力，打造精品

随着国家对移动游戏的管理越来越规范化，优质产品逐渐大浪淘沙沉淀在最后，精品的研发已经成为整体市场竞争的重中之重。同时整体的移动游戏市场的产品门槛逐步拉升，只有精品的产品才能够最后获得成功，企业对产品后续的研发能力以及创造力都是不可缺失的，未来移动游戏产品也必将是以精品化作为主导。随着“版号”新规的实施，新游的监管和审批更为严格，政策层面对游戏质量提出越来越高的要求；以腾讯、网易为代表的厂商近些年精品战略成果显著，起到良好的标杆作用；国内移动游戏市场趋于成熟，玩家对产品品质要求越来越高，产品为王的时代到来。

2. 合理运用IP

现在我国移动游戏产品的IP化十分明显，但是IP的形成往往需要长效性，IP是一把双刃剑：一方面，随着流量购买价格上涨，泛娱乐IP的优势愈发显著，除了明显降低用户获取成本，还能因为粉丝玩家的情感溢价获得营收增加的可能；目前的IP形式以端游IP为主，而且呈现为“一个IP+多款产品”的现象，比如腾讯《梦幻诛仙》与完美世界《诛仙》手游为同IP产品。未来移动游戏的IP形式会向电影、电视剧、小说和动漫作品等泛娱乐领域拓展。另一方面，我国IP产业马太效应显著，优质成熟的IP成本普遍较高，目前IP的质量参差不齐，许多厂商太过依赖IP而不注重IP本身的质量，急功近利造成相反的效果。所以合理的运用IP才是重要的发展因素之一。

3. 中重度化得到青睐

16～25岁的年青一代作为移动游戏的核心用户，对产品的社交性和对抗性要求越来越高。轻度、休闲的手游很难为用户带来实时、沉浸式的体验；消除、棋牌等轻度手游虽然能快速覆盖大量用户，但是存在盈利能力差、生命周期短等问题，而MMO等中重度手游玩家黏性高，盈利能力强。

4. 积极出海，寻找新的增量市场

目前我国移动游戏人口红利逐渐消失，传统的流量打法受限，并且移动游戏市场日趋成熟，国内厂商基本具备出海实力，而且国内的市场竞争格局马太效应越发明显，大厂积极抱团，挤压中小企业生存空间。所以寻找新的增量市场，积极出海已经成为新的航路。

七、中国网页游戏市场分析

目前，众多页游企业已经完成转型移动游戏领域，整体的网页游戏市场，在内容上去伪存真，精品游戏产品沉淀下来，形成了整体网页游戏内容的稳定格调。一方面，在对于传统精品游戏原有的维持推广的方式下，研发精品游戏进行资源推广，仍是目前的主流做法。而另一方面，泛娱乐趋势渗透网页游戏市场，并且概念持续升级，文学、影视、综艺、明星 IP 等概念仍是网页游戏市场的追捧基调。但是在高质量的 IP 争夺中，厂商仍需注意 IP 的受众能力与改编可行性。

（一）中国网页游戏市场发展现状

2016 年，中国网页游戏市场研发格局呈现百花齐放的状态（见图 11）。这主要是因为在经过整体网页游戏市场的沉淀，市面上次级产品被淘汰，市场去伪存真留下精品产品，同时，用户仍保持较高的黏性。目前，传奇题材、仙侠题材等内容仍是网页游戏市场的主流产品背景内容。此外，RPG 类、养成类内容类型也是网页游戏市场产品类型主流。未来，在其他研发主流精品类型出现之前，这种状态也将持续很长一段时间。

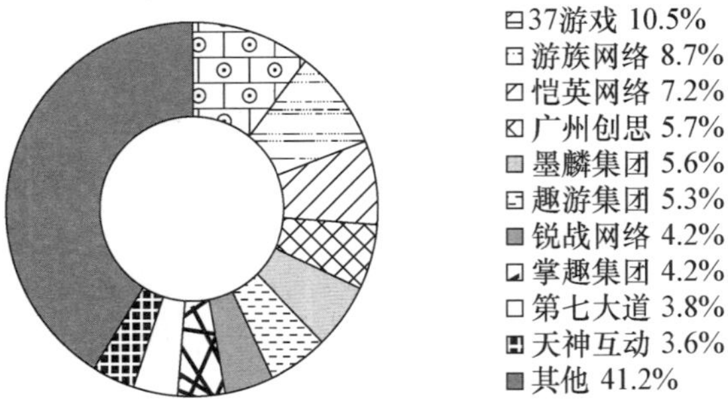

图 11　2016 年中国网页游戏市场研发格局

（二）中国网页游戏市场竞争格局

随着网页游戏市场整体格局已经稳定，整体页游市场转型趋势明显，页游运营平台更基于研运一体化的战略，渠道环境形成良好的态势，并且优秀产品层出不穷（见图 12）。此外，明星 IP 与明星代言仍是目前重要的推广手段。

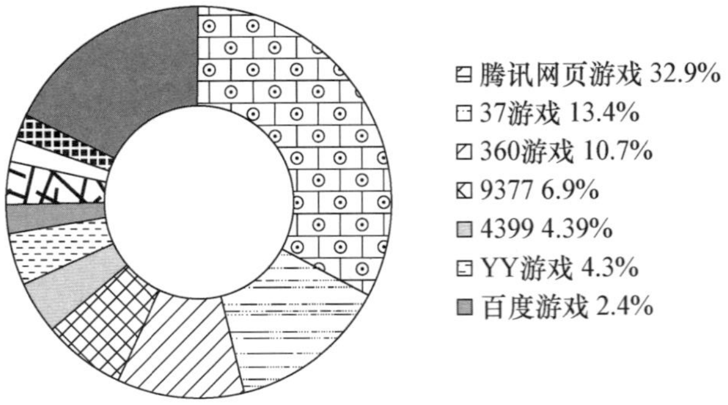

图 12　2016 年中国网页游戏市场竞争格局

（三）中国网页游戏市场产业链

网页游戏产业链也主要分为研发商、运营商、运营平台、推广渠道和其他支撑环节（见图 13）。

网页游戏研发商：主营业务为网页游戏产品的开发，将游戏产品输出给网页游戏的运营商，同时根据用户及市场的反馈，为游戏产品提供版本更新

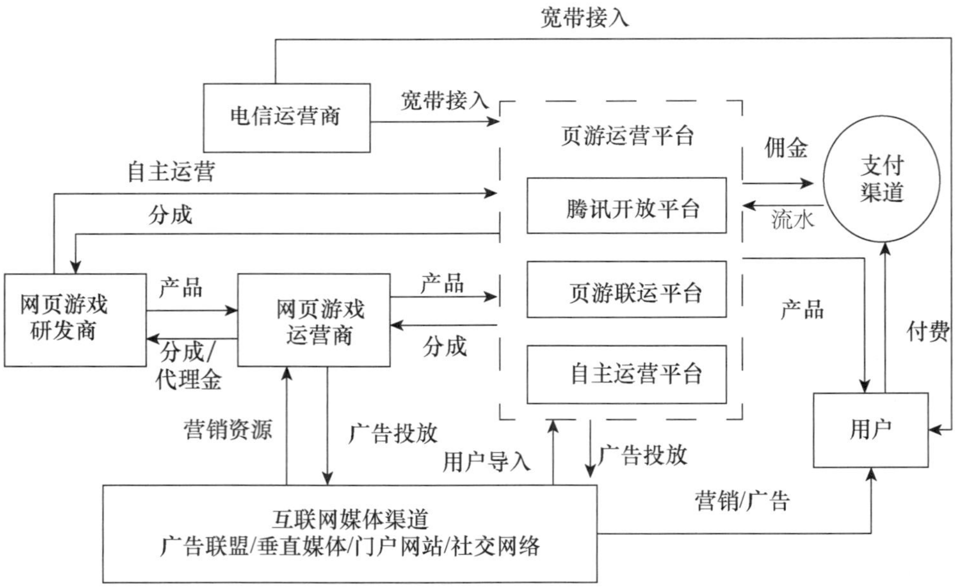

图 13　中国网页游戏市场产业链

和技术支持。网页游戏研发商是页游产业链中的初始推动环节，其研发和创意能力决定了市面上网页游戏产品的质量。

网页游戏运营商：网页游戏运营商，主要从事网页游戏的销售，包括研究用户需求、反馈指导开发、规范游戏内容并按照规定向政府主管部门报备报批游戏、选择合适的运营平台、制定开服计划、提供客服、开发游戏的其他商业价值等。网页游戏运营商既可以运营自主研发的游戏产品，也可以代理运营其他研发商的产品。在运营平台的选择上，网页游戏运营商既可以在自主运营的平台上推出游戏，也可以将产品外放，与其他第三方平台进行联运。与其他产业不同的是，整体的网页游戏市场的核心资源一般掌握在运营商中，在整体的产业链中

起到承上启下的作用。

网页游戏运营平台：导入用户的关键环节。网页游戏运营平台目前可大致分为三类：第一类，Facebook、Gree、Mobage、QQ等社交网络平台，游戏和社交的强相关使得社交网络平台具有先天的玩家导入优势。第二类，页游联运平台。页游联运平台数量较多，又可分为两类：一类是非自有流量联运平台，通过联盟广告投放的方式导入用户；另一类是自有流量联运平台，包括视频媒体、音乐播放器及其他流量巨大的综合性互联网企业，这类平台的特点是自有流量巨大，广告资源尚未饱和，会选择通过页游联运实现流量变现。第三类，自主运营平台。网页游戏运营商自主运营的平台，对于用户导入和后期运营有更精细化的运作。此外，目前欧美市场缺乏大型页游联运商，页游多依附在Facebook上由开发商直接运营。

网页游戏推广渠道：中国的页游运营平台，特别是非自有流量的联运平台对于外部线上流量入口的依赖程度较高。广告联盟、垂直媒体、门户网站以及社交网络是主要的流量来源，一般以弹窗广告的形式向用户呈现。由于流量巨大的媒体渠道开始将流量导向自有的页游联运平台，网页游戏流量的获取成本逐渐上涨。但弹窗广告的形式在欧美市场基本不存在，在欧美市场需要通过SEM/SEO在Google、Facebook等大型平台上做推广。

其他支撑环节：其他支撑环节包括支付渠道、电信运营商和服务器供应商等。支付渠道目前以网上银行，支付宝、Paypal等第三方支付，话费充值卡等方式为主。

版权

典型案件选编

DIAN XING AN JIAN XUAN BIAN

【编者按】 本栏目刊登五部分内容：1. 2017年4月24日，最高人民法院发布了2016年中国法院50件典型知识产权案例，本栏目选取其中7件著作权司法保护典型案件；2. 2017年4月26日，国家版权局在2017年中国网络版权保护大会上公布的2016年度打击侵权盗版十大案件；3. 2016年12月22日，国家版权局等四部门公布的“剑网2016”专项行动21起较为典型的网络侵权盗版案件；4. 2017年“4·26”知识产权宣传周期间，部分省、自治区、直辖市高级人民法院公布了2016年度知识产权典型案件，本栏目选取其中的著作权典型案件；5. 部分省、自治区、直辖市公布或报送的2016年度著作权行政执法案件。

2016年全国著作权司法保护典型案件

一、孙新争与马居奎侵害著作权纠纷申请再审案［山东省聊城市中级人民法院（2015）聊民三初字第333号民事判决书、山东省高级人民法院（2016）鲁民终343号民事判决书、最高人民法院（2016）最高法民申2136号民事裁定书］

【案情摘要】 再审申请人孙新争与被申请人马居奎侵害著作权纠纷一案中，孙新争主张其创作的《716预测817行情趋势方向图表》及其分析结果具有独创性。该图表作品无论是设计格局、颜色搭配、标识标注以及用途等，都具有明显的独创性。马居奎在2013年7月25日至8月25日期间使用该图表的提示，共投资了140箱鸡苗，按当时市场盈利每箱平均9 800元计算，共盈利135万元，按之前双方约定应付13.5万元作品使用费。山东省聊城市中级人民法院一审认为，本案图表是孙新争经过WPS表格软件通过输入数据完成，只是孙新争利用现有的表格软件并通过选项选择制作，其中并没有孙新争自己独立构思的内容，体现不出孙新争的创作性；对图表的数据分析不属于表现形式范畴，故不能获得著作权法保护。判决驳回孙新争的诉讼请求。孙新争不服，提起上诉。山东省高级人民法院二审判决驳回上诉、维持原判。孙新争不服，向最高人民法院申请再审。最高人民法院于2016年9月13日裁定驳回了孙新争的再审申请。

【判决结果】 最高人民法院审查认为：众所周知，著作权法保护作品及基于作品产生的权利，但并非所有作品都能成为著作权法保护的客体。只有那些符合著作权法规定的条件的作品，才能成为著作权的客体，受到著作权法的保护。我国著作权法虽未明确规定作品受保护的条件，但在《著作权法实施条例》第二条关于作品的定义中做了说明，该条规定：著作权法所称作品，是指文学、艺术和科学领域内具有独创性并能以某种有形形式复制的智力成果。这项规定表明，只有具备独创性并能以某种有形形式复制的智力成果，才是著作权去给予保护的作品。

首先，何谓独创性。如何判断一部作品是否具备独创性，在著作权理论与实践中存在不同的观点和标准。最高人民法院认为，判断作品是否具有独创性应当从以下两点把握：（1）从著作权法保护作品的历史和传统上看，著作权法之所以保护基于个人的智力劳动产生的结果，从人格权的角度，相较于体力劳动而言，智力劳动系个人运用智力、思想、认识的过程，通常被视为个人思想的延伸，作为人格延伸的智力成果应当产生归属于个人的结果，这是著作权法保护作品并赋予著作权的基础。从财产权的角度，作品系个人智力的付出，按照投入者应该从获利中得到公平回报的原则，智力劳动的结果亦应当归属于付出者。总之，无论是何种法律传统，均要求作品必须是作者独立创作完成的，因此独立创作是独创性的首要之义。独立创作通常会在作品上留下个人印迹，因此个人印迹亦是判断作品独创性的重要根据。

（2）从著作权法保护作品的目的上看，著作权法保护作品并赋予专有权的目的，正如我国《著作权法》第一条开宗明义所提到的，系为促进社会主义文化和科学事业的发展与繁荣制定该法。著作权法体现了人类对社会文化生活多样性的追求。著作权法试图推动文学艺术和科学作品的多样性与进步性的立法目的，反映在作品上，就产生了作品在客观表现形式上，至少应与公有领域和他人作品存在些许程度的差异，或者具备最低限度的创造性的要求。

综上，判断一部作品是否具有独创性，应当从是否独立创作以及在外在表现上是否与已有作品存在一定程度的差异或具备最低限度的创造性方面进行分析判断。如果一个智力成果在表现上是唯一的，那么其不符合著作权法关于独创性的要求，因为，其无法呈现出作品与已有作品的差异性或者最低的创造性，更无从寻找所谓个人的印迹，在理论上无法产生归结于作者的结果，在现实上也是无法与已有的智力劳动成果进行区分的。

其次，对有形形式应如何理解。最高人民法院认为，著作权法保护那些凝结了作者智力劳动的成果归其所有，作者的智力劳动须借助于特定的形式予以传达，否则该智力劳动他人无从知晓，智力成果也将是不确定的。因此那些仅存在于头脑中而未借助于特定形式表达的，或者那些深藏于作品内部不同的人感知到不同结果的思想与观点，将因为缺乏确定的形式而不能也无法成为著作权法调整的对象。这是作品须具备有形形式的本质含义。

再次，对本案而言，孙新争所主张的曲线图，系当事人根据客观的价格数据，通过使用 WPS 制表工具制作完成。鉴于图表所使用的数据客观存在，数量有限，WPS 为通用软件，将上述数据录入制表工具所形成的结果，尽管属于孙新争运用智力的结果，但该结果的表现形式有限，换言之，使用上述数据与工具所产生的结果缺少差异性。这种唯一或有限的表达方式，通常被排除在独创性之外。至于，孙新争所主张的线条颜色问题，在线条仅有两条的情况下对线条颜色的选择，并不能改变该图表表达有限的现状。据此，一审、二审法院认定孙新争主张的图表不构成著作权意义上的作品，认定事实清楚，适用法律正确。

最后，孙新争除主张曲线图作品外，还主张对该图表的分析利用的结果构成了作品。对此法院认为，如前所述，对说明性作品而言，即使在作品本身可以获得著作权法保护的情况下，著作权法通常也仅着重于保护作品的表达方式而非结论本身，垄断结论不符合著作权法的立法本义。本案中，孙新争主张保护的曲线图本身并不符合作品构成的要件，加之孙新争主张的所谓分析结果，并无明确确定的形式，因而无从保护。据此，一审、二审判决认为孙新争的该项主张没有依据不予支持，并无不当。

【典型意义】 此案涉及对作品构成条件，包括作品独创性、有形形式的理解，以及在司法实务中如何判断的问题。为了解决从创造性角度解释独创性的困惑，本案裁定对作品独创性除从独立性的角度予以解释外，更从立法目的出发将独创性的着眼点落于差异性，差异性重点关注的是不同，而不在于是否具有进步和创新。这种观点具有非常重要的意义，它在理论中揭示了独创性的本质，在实践中也有利于当事人举证和司法判断。另外，本案裁定还对可复制性给予了通俗易懂的解释，非常具有示范意义。

二、齐良末等与湖南美术出版社、天津市超越世纪图书商贸有限公司侵害著作权纠纷申请再审案

[天津市和平区人民法院（2014）和知民初字第0378号民事判决书、天津市第一中级人民法院（2015）一中民终字第0717号民事判决书、天津市高级人民法院（2016）津民申200号民事裁定书]

【案情摘要】 湖南美术出版社于1990年成立，2008年由全民所有制企业转制为法人独资的有限责任公司。1994年，湖南省文化厅等下发通知，确定列入国家“八五”重点出版规划的《齐白石全集》由湖南美术出版社编辑出版。在1995年和1996年间，齐白石后人齐良迟与齐佛来分别以个人名义授权湖南美术出版社出版《齐白石全集》。在此期间，湖南美术出版社与多个图书馆、博物馆及个人签订组稿协议，拍摄齐白石书画作品，并于1996年10月编辑出版了《齐白石全集》。自2004年始，齐白石继承人齐良末等就齐白石作品著作权与湖南美术出版社在全国各地法院进行多次维权诉讼。2014年7月，齐白石继承人齐良末等以湖南美术出版社在没有合法授权的情况下，以营利为目的，多年来非法出版发行包括涉案298幅美术作品在内的《齐白石全集》第三卷，侵害其著作权为由，起诉至天津和平区法院。天津和平区法院认定湖南美术出版社不构成侵权，但存在未经著作权人许可，再次印刷涉案作品的行为，依法应向齐白石继承人支付每幅作品300元的报酬。该判决生效并执行完毕后，湖南美术出版社就其中297件案件向天津高院申请再审。除以上涉及《齐白石全集》第三卷297件申请再审案件外，与《齐白石全集》第五卷有关的322件案件经天津和平区法院判决后上诉至天津一中院，另有涉及《齐白石全集》第二卷、第四卷等7件案件已经天津和平区法院做出一审判决，正在送达公告期内。

【判决结果】 天津市和平区人民法院认为，齐白石家族的人数众多，被告湖南美术出版社欲取得

涉案著作权继承人的一一授权，于现实中难以实现。齐白石继承人自该全集出版时即已知晓，一直未对出版行为提出异议。且齐白石继承人分十支，每支领取一本涉案样书，亦没有证据显示在合理期间内就被告湖南美术出版社的出版行为提出异议，故齐白石继承人的上述行为，应认定为默示授权的意思表示。被告湖南美术出版社于1996年10月出版发行《齐白石全集》的行为，既获得两位继承人的明示授权，又得到了继承人代表的默示授权。而且被告湖南美术出版社出版发行的《齐白石全集》是国家“八五”重点出版规划项目，属于继承和传播中华传统文化的行为，有助于促进优秀文化作品的推广与传承，有利于社会主义文化的发展与繁荣。因此，该出版发行行为不能认定是侵权行为。根据《中华人民共和国著作权法》第三十二条的规定，图书出版者重印、再版作品的，应当通知著作权人，并支付报酬。故被告湖南美术出版社于2001年至2004年期间，即涉案作品著作权法定保护期内，其就委托利丰雅高印刷（深圳）有限公司对涉案的《齐白石全集》进行印制的行为，应向四原告支付相应的报酬。就涉案美术作品《蜘蛛》报酬的计算标准，参考《国家版权局关于出版美术作品适用版税问题的意见》（国权办［2003］10号）中的相关规定，认定被告湖南美术出版社支付四原告其再次印制的相应报酬及维权损失，共计300元人民币。一审法院判决如下：（1）湖南美术出版社在本判决生效之日起十日内给付原告齐良末、齐秉颐、齐来欢、齐展仪涉案作品报酬及维权费用共计300元人民币，由原告齐秉颐代为领取并负责保管、分配；（2）驳回四原告其他诉讼请求。

天津市第一中级人民法院认为：《齐白石全集》由上诉人湖南美术出版社于1996年10月出版发行，系国家“八五”重点出版规划项目。该全集的出版发行促进了中华传统文化的继承与传播，发展、繁荣了社会主义文化。由于齐白石继承人人数众多、难以确定，且分散于各地。齐白石作品出版如需取得全体继承人同意，一则难以实现，二则将会导致齐白石作品在保护期内难以出版，不仅不符合包括被上诉人齐良末等四人在内的齐白石作品著作财产权继承人的利益，也有违著作权法促进文化传承与发展的精神。湖南美术出版社在出版发行《齐白石全集》时，亦取得了齐白石作品著作权继承人齐良迟、齐佛来的许可。该出版、发行行为并不会妨碍齐白石继承人对作品的正常使用，亦不会损害其合法利益。事实上，被上诉人齐良末等四人的起诉也未获得全体继承人的授权。综合考虑以上因素，认定上诉人湖南美术出版社出版、发行《齐白石全集》中使用涉案作品《蜘蛛》的行为，不构成对该作品著作权的侵害。根据《中华人民共和国著作权法》第三十二条的规定，图书出版者重印、再版作品的，应当通知著作权人，并支付报酬。上诉人湖南美术出版社在2001年至2004年间存在未经著作权人许可，再次印刷涉案作品的行为，故其依法应向齐白石作品著作财产权的合法继承人支付报酬。判决如下：驳回上诉，维持原判。

考虑到本案齐白石著作权财产权利继承人有300余人，双方当事人因齐白石作品的出版问题产生矛盾已经十余年，双方在全国其他地方均有相关诉讼，齐白石继承人的代理人将诉讼过程通过网络连续报道，引起媒体广泛关注，在天津法院一审、二审审理期间，齐白石继承人的代理人明确表示不同意调解，双方积怨较深。为了有效解决双方当事人长期形成的矛盾纠纷，以公开促公正，进一步提升司法公信力，2016年4月7日，天津高院民三庭组成由庭长咸胜强担任审判长的五人合议庭对297件再审审查案进行公开听证，专门通知一审、二审均未出庭的齐白石继承人代表齐秉颐到庭参加听证，并邀请包括来自画家群体、出版单位的部分人大代表、政协委员旁听听证。在听证过程中，齐秉颐表达了调解意愿，并希望一并解决双方尚未审结的其他案件。天津高院、天津一中院和和平区法院上下联动，在原生效裁判文书查清案件事实的基础上，使双方当事人达成一次性解决包括《齐白石全集》在内的所有湖南美术出版社出版的齐白石作品的所有争议。天津市高级人民法院调解结果：湖南美术出版社自愿给付齐白石继承人80套《齐白石全集》的价款人民币500 000元及30套《齐白石全集》，上述款项和书籍由齐白石后人齐秉颐代表全体齐白石后人保管和分配给其他齐白石后人；双方就齐白石作品及书籍著作权问题互不追究，不再有任何争议。湖南美术出版社向天津高院申请撤回297件案件的再审申请；天津一中院、和平区法院尚未生效的其他三百余件案件，齐白石继承人、湖南美术出版社分别撤回了起诉和上诉。

【典型意义】 此案是天津三级法院依据“分类施策、比例协调”司法政策，成功调解解决涉及三级法院正在审理的297件申请再审案件，322件二审上诉案件，7件一审判决已经做出、正在送达公告期内，共626件案件的典型案例。案件的处理结果既保护了齐白石后人对齐白石作品享有的著作权财产权利，同时也考虑到了湖南美术出版社作为邻接权人对文化传播做出的贡献，调解结果实现了相关方利益平衡，使双方当事人历经十余年的著作权纠纷全部得以化解，取得了良好的社会效果和法律效果。

三、上海耀宇文化传媒股份有限公司与广州斗鱼网络科技有限公司侵害著作权及不正当竞争纠纷案［上海市浦东新区人民法院（2015）浦民三（知）初字第191号民事判决、上海知识产权法院（2015）沪知民终字第641号民事判决］

【案情摘要】 完美世界（北京）网络技术有限公司是美国维尔福公司（Valve Corporation）开发的一款风靡全球的电子竞技类网络游戏 DOTA2（《刀塔2》）在中国大陆地区的代理运营商。2014年，上海耀宇文化传媒股份有限公司（以下简称耀宇公司）与游戏运营商签订战略合作协议，共同运营2015年DOTA2亚洲邀请赛，并获得该赛事在中国大陆地区的独家视频转播权，负责赛事的执行及管理工作。耀宇公司在2015年1月至2月期间举办涉案赛事，赛事分为预选赛、决赛。在赛事进行期间，耀宇公司通过火猫TV网站对比赛进行了全程、实时的视频直播，并授予虎牙独家直播/转播的权利（除火猫TV外），收取授权费用600万元。广州斗鱼网络科技有限公司（以下简称斗鱼公司）未经授权，以通过客户端旁观模式截取赛事画面配以主播点评的方式实时直播涉案赛事。耀宇公司遂提起诉讼，主张斗鱼公司侵害其合法权益。请求判令：斗鱼公司立即停止侵权、消除影响，并赔偿耀宇公司经济损失800万元以及合理费用21.1万元。

【判决结果】 上海市浦东新区人民法院认为，耀宇公司主张的视频转播权不属于法定的著作权权利，比赛画面不属于著作权法规定的作品，耀宇公司关于斗鱼公司侵害其著作权的主张不能成立。但斗鱼公司明知涉案赛事由耀宇公司举办、耀宇公司享有涉案赛事的独家视频转播权并付出了较大的办赛成本，在未取得任何授权许可的情况下，向其用户提供了涉案赛事的部分场次比赛的视频直播，其行为直接损害了耀宇公司的合法权益，损害了网络游戏直播网站行业的正常经营秩序，违反了诚实信用原则和公认的商业道德，构成对耀宇公司的不正当竞争。遂判决斗鱼公司承担消除影响、赔偿经济损失及合理费用共计110万元。斗鱼公司不服，提起上诉。上海知识产权法院认为，斗鱼公司未对涉案赛事的组织运营进行任何投入，也未取得视频转播权的许可，却免费坐享耀宇公司投入大量人力、物力、财力组织运营的赛事所产生的商业成果，为自己谋取商业利益和竞争优势，其实际上是一种“搭便车”行为，夺取了原本属于耀宇公司的观众数量，导致其网站流量严重分流，影响其广告收益能力，损害其商业机会和竞争优势，弱化其网络直播平台的增值力。因此，斗鱼公司的行为违反了反不正当竞争法中的诚实信用原则，违背了公认的商业道德，损害了耀宇公司合法权益，破坏了市场竞争秩序，具有明显的不正当性。因此，判决驳回上诉，维持原判。

【典型意义】 本案系电子竞技游戏产业日益发展过程中出现的新类型知识产权案件，涉及电子竞技游戏赛事转播权的法律保护问题。作为全国首例电竞游戏赛事直播不正当竞争纠纷案，本案重要意义在于为以电竞游戏为冲突点反映的产业更新的过渡期内版权业与互联网产业利益冲突提供了一个新的解决思路：在未确定视频转播权可以作为法定的著作权权利进行保护的情况下，从竞争关系的角度平衡双方的利益，肯定电子竞技游戏赛事的网络直播具有商品属性，赛事转播权承载着因播出行为而可以获得的商誉和经济利益，属于财产性的民事权益，并根据我国反不正当竞争法一般条款的规定对擅自转播赛事的行为予以规制。

四、江苏林芝山阳集团有限公司与磊若软件公司侵害计算机软件著作权纠纷案［江苏省无锡市中级人民法院（2015）锡知民初字第4号民事判决、江苏省高级人民法院（2015）苏知民终字第00300号民事判决］

【案情摘要】 磊若软件公司系“Serv-U”系列计算机软件作品的著作权人，其通过系统命令检测到江苏林芝山阳集团有限公司（以下简称林芝山阳公司）官方网站 www. lzsy. com 正在使用磊若软件公司一款“Serv-U FTP Server v. 6. 4”的软件，且磊若软件公司销售系统上未见林芝山阳公司购买该软件的记录。磊若软件公司认为林芝山阳公司系擅自复制、安装及商业使用上述软件，侵害了其著作权，遂提起诉讼，请求法院判令林芝山阳公司立即停止侵权并赔偿经济损失及合理费用15万元，并承担本案诉讼费。林芝山阳公司辩称，其公司网站所使用的服务器是由无锡市网之易科技有限公司（以下简称网之易公司）提供，其并非该服务器的所有人，林芝山阳公司与网之易公司签订了服务协议，公司网站由网之易公司进行管理服务。其实际也未安装涉案软件。

【判决结果】 江苏省无锡市中级人民法院认为，涉案网络服务订单未约定服务器软件安装事宜，不能推导出涉案软件系由网之易公司安装的事实。林芝山阳公司作为涉案网站的主办单位，有权对该网站进行管理，亦应对网站内容及相应服务器中的知识产权侵权行为承担责任，故认定涉案软件系林芝山阳公司安装，判决林芝山阳公司停止侵权，赔偿磊若软件公司70 000元。江苏省高级人民法院二审查明，在磊若软件公司起诉的另案（2015）锡知民初字第6号及（2015）锡知民初字第8号案件中，磊若软件公司起诉的被告服务器IP地址与本案被诉侵权服务器地址相同。二审法院认为，通过相关证据可以认定林芝山阳公司购买了网之易公司的服务器空间用以发布其公司网站。磊若软件公司在另外两个案件中起诉的被告服务器IP地址与本案被诉侵权服务器IP地址相同。因特网中的一个IP地址仅能对应一台服务器。故林芝山阳公司仅租用了网之易公司服务器中的部分空间，还有其他公司也通过该服务器发布自己的公司网站。在此情形下，林芝山阳公司不是涉案服务器的实际管理者，也无权在该服务器中安装涉案软件。磊若软件公司亦无证据证明林芝山阳公司与网之易公司有实施共同侵权的故意与行为，故二审法院认为，林芝山阳公司并未侵害磊若软件公司的计算机软件著作权，改判驳回磊若软件公司的全部诉讼请求。

【典型意义】 计算机软件著作权侵权案件中，需要厘清“网站”和“服务器”的概念区别，不能简单地认为网站的发布者、管理者就是网站所在服务器的管理者，进而推导出网站所有者需要对网站所在服务器中的侵权行为承担侵权责任的结论。关于这一点，由于涉及较为专业的计算机软件知识，许多法官及律师并不了解，导致在许多类似的案件中，律师不知道从什么角度进行合理抗辩，法官不知道两者差别从而判决错误。一个公司在因特网中发布自己公司网站主要有两种模式：一是公司购买一台服务器，将服务器在自己公司机房或者托管到电信机房接入因特网。在这种模式下，服务器的所有权属于公司所有，公司对服务器享有完整的控制权，可以随意在服务器中安装软件、更改配置。因此，如果服务器中安装有侵权软件，则相应的侵权责任应由该公司负担。二是公司到网络空间服务商处购买服务器空间，网络空间服务商负责相关服务器的连接入网以及系统软件的维护、设置，并负责将客户空间中的网站内容以web方式发布。一台服务器中的空间可以被划分为若干份分配给若干个公司。购买空间的公司对服务器没有控制权，仅对自己购买空间中的数据有上传、下载、删除等有限的操作权限。其不能在服务器中复制、安装系统软件，复制被诉侵权软件的行为不可能由网络空间购买者实施。故在空间使用者没有过错的情形下，侵权责任一般应由侵权行为实施者，即服务器的实际管理者和控制者承担。本案判决从技术上对实践中“网站”发布的两种模式进行了详细分析，并结合案件事实得出本案林芝山阳公司仅是使用被诉侵权服务器中部分空间用以发布网站内容的结论，在无其他证据证明林芝山阳公司与服务器的管理者有实施共同侵权的故意与行为的情况下，林芝山阳公司无须承担侵权责任。本案的分析及结论，对其他类似案件中侵权责任主体的认定，有一定的参考价值。

五、叶宗轼与浙江冠素堂食品有限公司著作权权属、侵权纠纷案［浙江省舟山市中级人民法院（2015）浙舟知初字第3号民事判决、浙江省高级人民法院（2016）浙民终118号民事判决］

【案情摘要】 2003年初，叶宗轼受托为筹建中的舟山市普陀山旅游食品公司（以下简称普陀山公司）开发的素食品取名并创作主题故事。叶宗轼创作完成《观音饼来历》，并建议商品定名“观音饼”，经原普陀山全山方丈戒忍审阅后，交给普陀山公司在“普陀山”牌观音饼外包装盒上印制使用。2003年10月，普陀山公司就观音饼包装盒申报外观设计专利，在该观音饼包装盒上印制了《观音饼的由来》。叶宗轼认为其系《观音饼来历》的作者，享有完整的著作权，“观音饼”三字来源于《观音饼来历》，亦应受到保护。浙江冠素堂食品有限公司（以下简称冠素堂公司）未经许可，在其生产销售的“冠素堂”牌观音饼包装盒、手提袋上改编使用叶宗轼的作品，且未注明作者，侵犯了叶宗轼对上述作品的改编权、复制权、发行权、署名权、保护作品完整权、获得报酬权等权利，在经济和精神上给叶宗轼造成了巨大损失，故向一审法院起诉请求判令冠素堂公司：（1）立即停止侵犯叶宗轼作品《观音饼来历》的改编权、复制权、发行权、保护作品完整权、署名权；（2）立即停止在其产品包装上使用“观音饼”名称，销毁其全部侵权包装及印刷模板；（3）在《浙江日报》上公开向叶宗轼道歉；（4）赔偿叶宗轼经济损失100万元，以及叶宗轼因制止侵权而发生的公证费、调查取证费2 216元，律师费1万元；（5）赔偿叶宗轼精神损害抚慰金3万元。

【判决结果】 浙江省舟山市中级人民法院一审认为，叶宗轼所创作的《观音饼来历》一文构成著作权法意义上的作品，但“观音饼”一词不构成著作权法意义上的作品。冠素堂公司的使用行为构成对上述《观音饼来历》一文的改编，侵害了叶宗轼的改编权。因此，一审判决冠素堂公司停止侵权、赔礼道歉并赔偿叶宗轼经济损失及为诉讼支出的合理费用10万元。

浙江省高级人民法院认为，一审法院关于《观音饼来历》一文构成著作权法意义上的作品，“观音饼”一词不构成著作权法意义上的作品，冠素堂公司侵害叶宗轼改编权的认定，并无不当。冠素堂公司的使用行为除构成对叶宗轼改编权的侵害外，亦构成对其署名权的侵害，但鉴于一审判决已足以弥补侵害署名权所造成的损失，二审判决维持原判。

【典型意义】 本案主要涉及根据民间宗教传说所创作的作品的保护问题。民间传说在百姓中口口相传，是我国宝贵的传统文化财富。如果创作者以公有领域的民间传说素材为基础，在再加工的过程中融入独创性的表达，完成了新的作品，那么该作品中具有独创性的表达就应当受到著作权法的保护。本案中，涉案作品《观音饼来历》虽系叶宗轼依据民间观音传说的公有素材而创作，但因其加入了作者自己想象创作的情节，并用古文体形式加以表达，故具有一定的独创性，构成我国著作权法所保护的文字作品。而“观音饼”一词系单个汉语词汇，属于思想范畴，不构成著作权法意义上的作品，且其已成为商品名称，任何人均不能禁止他人正当使用。总之，在文学、艺术领域，任何一部作品的创作都离不开对前人成果或已有素材的使用。著作权法对作品的保护是对作品表达的保护，不延及作品的思想或主题。因此，法律并不禁止创作者对前人作品的合理借鉴。但对他人作品的借鉴，应当限于对作品思想、主题或属于公有领域内容的借鉴，对他人作品中具有独创性的表达不得擅自使用。

六、上海美术电影制片厂有限公司与杭州玺匠文化创意股份有限公司侵害著作权纠纷案［浙江省杭州市中级人民法院（2016）浙01民初242号民事判决民事判决、浙江省高级人民法院（2016）浙民终590号民事判决］

【案情摘要】 2011年8月10日，速达独立创作完成了“Q版孙悟空”美术作品。2013年12月11日，上海美术电影制片厂有限公司（以下简称上海美影厂）与南京璞若广告有限公司、速达签订《“Q版孙悟空”美术作品著作权转让协议》，确认“Q版孙悟空”的全部著作权（包括复制权、发行权、出租权、展览权、表演权、放映权、广播权、信息网络传播权、摄制权、改编权、翻译权、汇编权以及著作权法规定的其他权利），自协议签署之日起永久性转让给上海美影厂。2012年1月12日，上海美影厂的电影《大闹天宫3D》上映，在电影片尾处使用了多个“Q版孙悟空”形象。新华网、搜狐新闻等媒体对《大闹天宫3D》电影进行了报道。后央广网、青岛新闻网等多家媒体就上海美影厂与肯德基合作推出“Q版美猴王”即“Q版孙悟空”玩具进行报道。2015年11月11日，上海美影厂委托代理人许乐乐向上海市徐汇公证处申请证据保全公证。在公证人员的监督下，许乐乐以普通消费者身份，在天猫网上名称为“铜师傅旗舰店”的店铺订购了“全铜摆件”3件。公证人员对购买、收件、启封过程进行公证。杭州玺匠文化创意股份有限公司（以下简称玺匠公司）确认上述铜艺产品系其生产销售。上海美影厂为本案维权支出公证费2 000元、购买商品费1 364元。上海美影厂提供了“Q版孙悟空”美术作品手绘版及彩绘版原稿，并明确其请求保护的美术作品为“Q版孙悟空”动画形象，主张涉案铜艺产品与涉案作品构成实质性相似，请求法院判令玺匠公司：（1）立即停止制造、销售侵权铜艺产品；立即销毁用于复制侵权铜艺产品的模具等专用工具。（2）在玺匠公司官方网站及天猫“铜师傅旗舰店”网站首页显著位置刊登侵权致歉声明，消除影响。（3）赔偿上海美影厂经济损失及合理费用合计30万元。（4）赔偿上海美影厂因本案的合理支出1万元。（5）承担本案的全部诉讼费用。

【判决结果】 浙江省杭州市中级人民法院一审认为，涉案“Q版孙悟空”美术作品系速达独立创作完成，表达具有一定程度的智力创造性，整体具备独创性，属于美术作品。涉案作品于2012年1月12日上映的《大闹天宫3D》电影的片尾中发布。之后上海美影厂取得作品著作权并进行商业推广和使用，涉案作品为公众所知悉，故可以认定玺匠公司有接触该作品的可能性。虽然被诉侵权作品与涉案作品相比具体神态、姿势有所不同，但二者头部特征基本相同，均有大而圆的头部，类似的帽子，面部由两个较为饱满的桃心组成，脸颊、嘴巴向外鼓，还有一双圆形招风耳等，整体上均体现出可爱的孙悟空形象，故可以认定涉案铜艺产品与涉案作品构成实质性相似。玺匠公司未经著作权人许可，制造、销售涉案铜艺产品的行为，侵犯了上海美影厂对涉案美术作品享有的复制权、发行权。因此，一审判决玺匠公司立即停止制造、销售侵权铜艺产品，并赔偿上海美影厂经济损失（含合理费用）10万元。

浙江省高级人民法院认为，“Q版孙悟空”形象在保持已有作品表达的基础上，采用现代动漫的圆萌化艺术处理手法形成卡通形象特有的造型特点，具有较高的独创性，应认定为新的作品。将被诉侵权产品和涉案作品进行比对，虽然两者在部分面貌特征上存在差异，但并不影响在主要艺术造型独创性表达部分的相似度。由于两者在身材比例、人物体貌等主要特征方面基本相同，相同之处又恰恰体现了涉案作品的独立创作部分且最具有显著性的特征部分，玺匠公司亦没有举证证明被诉侵权产品形象的创作来源，故认为两者构成实质性相似。玺匠公司将涉案角色形象造型制作成立体艺术品，是一种以立体方式再现涉案作品独创性表达的行为，构成著作权法意义上的复制。同时，玺匠公司未经著作权人许可销售被诉侵权产品，故应认定其构成对涉案作品复制权和发行权的侵害。因此，二审判决维持原判。

【典型意义】 在因对传统角色形象进行再创作而引起的著作权侵权纠纷案件中，如何正确区分传统角色形象与再创作的作品的独创性，是审判实践亟待解决的问题。本案就针对此类案件的审理，提出了在考量历史因素和现实认知的基础上，既要留存丰富的公有领域，又要尊重原作品权利人的合法权益，更要给予历史传统文化以创新空间，以利于我国传统历史文化的弘扬与发展的审理思路，具有较强的典型性。首先，要把握利益平衡规则，在对传统角色形象的创作较为成熟，留余的传统历史文化创作空间较为狭窄的情况下，结合该形象的发展历史和创作规律，对新作品所呈现出的显著性和识别性特征，应作为独创性部分予以重点关注。其次，要坚持激励创新导向，著作权侵权认定与作品独创性密切相关，给予在较窄创作空间内形成的独创性较高的作品以较强的保护，实现作品保护范围和强度与其独创性范围和尺度相适应。

七、安少康与长江文艺出版社有限公司等侵害著作权纠纷上诉案

［湖北省武汉市中级人民法院（2014）鄂武汉中知初字第612号民事判决、湖北省高级人民法院（2015）鄂民三终字第158号民事判决书］

【案情摘要】 安少康与长江文艺出版社2000年6月14日签订图书出版合同，将其翻译的《巴黎圣母院》一书授权长江文艺出版社在中国大陆、香港、台湾或其他国家和地区以图书形式出版发行；在首次出版5年内，长江文艺出版社可以自行决定重印，5年后重印应事先通知。长江文艺出版社许可第三方出版包含此作品的选集、文集、全集须另行取得书面授权。但安少康发现长江文艺出版社在首次出版5年后，即从2006年1月至2013年，未经许可，由海豚传媒股份有限公司（以下简称海豚传媒）参与策划，印刷此书12万册进行了销售，遂提起诉讼。

【判决结果】 湖北省武汉市中级人民法院一审法院认为，安少康将法国文学作品《巴黎圣母院》翻译成汉语，其对该翻译作品享有著作权。虽然安少康和长江文艺出版社就出版《巴黎圣母院》中文译本一事订立有图书出版合同，但安少康对于图书出版合同有效期内及期限届满后，长江文艺出版社、海豚传媒出版、发行其翻译作品《巴黎圣母院》的行为，选择以侵害复制权、发行权为由一并提起侵权之诉，符合法律规定。本案属侵害著作权纠纷。

涉案被控侵权图书在2006年至2013年期间的出版印刷总量为120 000册。其中，在2006年至2010年6月期间（即安少康和长江文艺出版社的图书出版合同有效期内），上述图书被出版印刷的数量为91 000册；此后（即安少康和长江文艺出版社的图书出版合同有效期届满之后），上述图书被出版印刷的数量为29 000册。长江文艺出版社在图书出版合同有效期内重印、再版91 000册图书，是图书出版合同赋予的权利，不侵犯安少康的复制权、发行权。但是，长江文艺出版社没有有效证据证明其履行了通知义务，也未按合同约定支付稿酬，违反了合同义务。长江文艺出版社应依合同约定向安少康支付91 000册图书的印数稿酬9 682.4元及相应的利息损失。长江文艺出版社在图书出版合同期限届满后继续出版图书29 000册的行为，未经安少康许可，侵害了安少康对其翻译作品的复制权、发行权，应承担停止侵害、赔偿损失等法律责任。海豚传媒因共同参与实施，应当与长江文艺出版社承担连带责任。一审法院酌定安少康所受损失按照24元（图书定价）×29 000册（合同期限届满后继续发行数）×7%（版税率）×3（倍数）的方式计算，即146 160元。一审法院判决认定长江文艺出版社、海豚传媒侵犯了安少康对其翻译作品的复制权、发行权，判令二被告停止侵权行为，判决长江文艺出版社支付稿酬9 682.4元及逾期利息1 507元，二被告连带赔

偿经济损失 146 160 元及因制止侵权所支付的合理开支 36 690 元。

湖北省高级人民法院二审认为，《图书出版合同》中约定的首次出版 5 年后，长江文艺出版社和海豚传媒未通知安少康，出版发行涉案被控侵权图书的册数应认定为 120 000 册。本案被控侵权图书是长江文艺出版社以“租型”为名，向海豚传媒收取管理费，由海豚传媒自行印刷、发行。本案被控侵权图书复制发行的主体实质上已经不是长江文艺出版社，而是海豚传媒。长江文艺出版社将从安少康处取得的《巴黎圣母院》作品专有出版权，许可海豚传媒使用，既是违反《图书出版合同》第七条约定的违约行为，也是违反著作权法规定的侵权行为。长江文艺出版社与海豚传媒对涉案被控侵权图书的复制、发行行为构成共同侵权，应连带承担停止侵害、赔偿损失等法律责任。一审法院以演绎作品版税标准的上限 7%，确定三倍的赔偿标准，虽未超出国家版权局《出版文字作品报酬规定》（1999 年）的规定，但标准偏高，二审法院将付酬的版税率从一审确定的 7%调整为 4%，再确定三倍的赔偿标准。二审判决维持一审停止侵权的判罚，改判海豚传媒股份有限公司赔偿安少康经济损失 345 600 元及因制止侵权所支付的合理开支 36 690 元。

【典型意义】 本案系一起典型的侵害翻译作品复制权、发行权的著作权案件，且法律适用问题涉及侵权责任与违约责任是否构成竞合这一民法理论难题。本案厘清了侵权责任与违约责任的界限，有效规范了出版行业的出版发行行为。二审法院在依职权查明涉案被控侵权图书是长江文艺出版社以“租型”为名，向海豚传媒收取管理费，由海豚传媒自行印刷、发行的基础上，依据《出版管理条例》、新闻出版署《关于严格禁止买卖书号、刊号、版号等问题的若干规定》等行政法规和部门规章的规定，认定被控侵权图书复制发行的实质主体是海豚传媒，而非长江文艺出版社，海豚传媒构成侵权。长江文艺出版社将从著作权人处获得的专有出版权许可第三方使用，既违反图书出版合同的约定，也违反著作权法的规定，构成违约责任与侵权责任的竞合。

“租型”，是出版行业长期以来的一大“恶疾”。少数出版单位或传媒公司认为，图书出版权的取得可以通过“缴纳管理费”“联营”“共同出版发行”等形式，从享有专有出版权的出版单位处“租型”取得，而无须经过著作权人的许可。本系列案中海豚传媒即辩称其复制权、发行权系从长江文艺出版社“租型”取得，不构成侵权。本案二审判决严格认定“租型”既是违反图书出版合同的违约行为，也是违反著作权法规定的侵权行为，厘清了侵权责任与违约责任的界限，从而为出版行业的出版发行行为提供了明晰的准则，有利于促进我国文化市场更加健康、繁荣发展。在确定侵权赔偿标准上，二审法院综合考量涉案翻译作品的知名度、印刷数量以及长江文艺出版社、海豚传媒的过错程度等因素，将付酬的版税率从一审确定的演绎作品版税标准的上限 7%调整为 4%，再确定三倍的赔偿标准，体现了对双方当事人的利益平衡。

（撰稿人：马秀荣　李嵘　廖继博　王晨）

2016年度打击侵权盗版十大案件

一、"风雨文学网"侵犯文字作品著作权案

2015年10月，江苏省张家港市文化广电新闻出版局根据权利人举报，联合公安网警大队对"风雨文学网"涉嫌侵犯著作权案进行调查。经查，2013年至2015年间，张某未经著作权人许可，将《大亨传说》等小说发布在其自建的"风雨文学网"上进行传播，并通过在网站发布广告，从百度广告联盟非法获利，非法经营额达66.7万元。

2016年12月16日，江苏省张家港市人民法院依法做出刑事判决：张某犯侵犯著作权罪，判处有期徒刑3年10个月，并处罚金人民币34万元。

【点　评】 国家版权局等四部门联合开展的"剑网2016"专项行动将整治网络文学侵权盗版列为重点任务。该案既是"剑网2016"专项行动中打击网络文学侵权盗版的一起重大案件，也是行政执法与刑事司法有效协作、合力打击侵权盗版的典型案例。

二、《echo回声》APP侵犯音乐作品信息网络传播权案

2016年4月，上海市文化市场行政执法总队根据权利人投诉，对上海青声网络科技有限公司涉嫌侵犯信息网络传播权案进行调查。经查，该公司自2014年9月开始经营客户端软件《echo回声》，日活跃用户量30万左右，下载量约1 600万。该公司未经著作权人许可，通过《echo回声》APP向用户提供《约定》《隐形的翅膀》等90部音乐录音制品的在线浏览、收听和使用服务，并通过会员充值等途径获得经营收入。

2016年6月28日，上海市文化市场行政执法总队依法对上海青声网络科技有限公司做出行政处罚：罚款人民币20万元。

【点　评】 近两年来，国家版权局大力整治网络音乐版权秩序取得良好成效。该案当事人运营的网络音乐APP，未经授权大量传播他人享有著作权的音乐作品，破坏了初步改善的网络音乐版权秩序。该案的查处，充分体现了版权行政部门维护网络音乐版权秩序的坚定决心。

三、"九九漫画"等网站侵犯漫画作品信息网络传播权案

2016年6月，江苏省常州市文化广电新闻出版局根据调查线索，对"九九漫画"等网站涉嫌侵犯信息网络传播权案进行调查。经查，张某于2010年至2016年7月间陆续开办"九九漫画""台湾漫画网""可可动漫"等漫画网站，未经著作权人许可，通过上述网站向公众提供《灌篮高手》《火影忍者》《海贼王》等351部漫画作品，涉及境内外众多权利人的作品。截至2016年7月，张某通过在网站发布广告，从广告联盟非法获利4.8万元。

2016年7月7日，江苏省常州市文化广电新闻出版局依法对张某做出行政处罚：没收违法所得，罚款人民币17万元。

【点　评】 近年来网络动漫侵权盗版呈现高发态势。该案当事人开办多个漫画网站，侵权漫画作品数量众多且涉及多个权利人，社会危害严重。该案的查处有效维护了境内外漫画作品权利人的合法权益。

四、吴某某侵犯网络游戏著作权案

2014年8月，上海市公安机关根据工作获得线索，对吴某某涉嫌侵犯网络游戏著作权案进行调查。经查，2014年5月，吴某某私自在互联网上架设服务器，推广并运营他人非法获取的网络游戏《新仙剑奇侠传ONLINE》服务器端程序，非法经营额达38万余元。

2015年10月15日，上海市普陀区人民法院依法做出刑事判决：吴某某犯侵犯著作权罪，判处有期徒刑3年3个月，并处罚金人民币6万元。后吴某某提出上诉。2016年3月28日，上海市第三中级人民法院做出终审裁定：驳回上诉，维持原判。

【点　评】 近年来互联网游戏产业规模不断扩大，但网游"私服"活动往往给投入巨额研发成本的网游公司带来重大经济损失，严重影响网游产业的健康发展。该案的一审和终审判决对网游"私服"予以重拳打击，彰显了司法部门惩治互联网领域侵犯著作权犯罪的力度。

五、汇梦影视茶吧侵犯影视作品著作权案

2015年12月，湖北省黄石市文化新闻出版广电局依法对卫某某经营的汇梦影视茶吧进行检查，发现该茶吧向顾客放映盗版《寻龙诀》等电影。2016年1月，该案依法移送公安部门。经查，卫某某于2014年10月设立汇梦影视茶吧，为获得片源，卫某某通过勾结影院内部工作人员到电影院盗录、从互联网下载、向他人购买等方式获得盗版影片，在其经营的茶吧播放，违法所得达 8.4 万余元；其间，卫某某还将以上方式获得的盗版影片通过互联网进行售卖，违法所得近 2.9 万元。

2016 年 9 月 6 日，湖北省黄石市黄石港区人民法院依法做出刑事判决：卫某某犯侵犯著作权罪，判处有期徒刑 10 个月，并处罚金人民币 5 000 元；追缴违法所得人民币 113 115 元。

【点　评】 该案是我国首例影院盗录并通过网络传播电影作品的刑事案件。盗录盗播不仅给电影产业造成巨额经济损失，也严重打击了电影从业人员的创作积极性，给我国快速发展的电影产业带来巨大破坏。该案的查处，有力震慑了盗录盗播电影的违法犯罪行为。

六、青岛约吧有限公司侵犯影视作品著作权案

2016 年 10 月，山东省青岛市文化市场行政执法局依法对青岛约吧有限公司开设的私人影院“约吧”进行检查，发现其电脑主机硬盘上共有 203 部电影。经营者郭某某无法提供作品授权文件，其未经权利人许可，擅自复制并在其经营场所为顾客提供观看和下载服务。

2016 年 12 月 5 日，山东省青岛市文化市场行政执法局依法对青岛约吧有限公司做出行政处罚：罚款人民币 17.9 万元。

【点　评】 近年来随着私人影院数量大幅增加，私人影院侵犯影视著作权的情况比较普遍。该案的查处，对规范私人影院的版权秩序具有较强的现实意义，也表明了私人影院行业必须遵守著作权法“先授权、后使用”的基本原则。

七、霍某某销售盗版图书案

2016 年 6 月，河北省保定市文化广电新闻出版局根据举报线索，查扣霍某某在其租用的保定市清苑区一库房内存放的盗版图书山东省地图出版社的《北斗地图》等共计 98 822 册，涉案码洋 270 余万元。经查，该批图书系霍某某从河南新乡李某某处购回，进行批发销售。2016 年 8 月，该案依法移送河北省保定市公安局。

2016 年 12 月 26 日，河北省保定市莲池区人民法院依法做出刑事判决：霍某某犯销售侵权复制品罪，判处有期徒刑 1 年、罚款人民币 20 万元。

【点　评】 该案侵权人以销售获利为目的购入侵权盗版图书，涉案侵权盗版作品数量巨大、涉案码洋数额较高，侵犯了多家出版社的著作权，社会危害严重。该案的判决有效维护了出版单位的合法权益。

八、巩某某等销售盗版光盘案

2015 年 4 月，山东省淄博市文化市场执法局与淄博市公安局直属分局成立专案组，对淄博市张店区天乐园商场后院一间仓库进行突击检查，现场查扣涉嫌侵权盗版光碟 2.8 万余张。经查，2011 年 1 月至 2015 年 4 月，巩某某等二人在天乐园商场销售盗版影碟和淫秽影碟，违法所得共计 46 万余元。

2016 年 12 月 6 日，山东省淄博市张店区人民法院依法做出刑事判决：巩某某犯侵犯著作权罪，判处有期徒刑 3 年 6 个月，并处罚金人民币 50 万元；犯贩卖淫秽物品牟利罪，判处有期徒刑 6 个月，并处罚金人民币 1 万元；二罪并罚，决定执行有期徒刑 3 年 6 个月，并处罚金人民币 51 万元。巩某犯侵犯著作权罪，判处有期徒刑 3 年，缓刑 3 年，并处罚金人民币 50 万元。

【点　评】 随着互联网的发展，传统的光盘盗版方式虽有所减少，但在某些地区仍很严重，仍然是版权行政执法的重要领域之一。该案的查处是版权行政执法部门配合公安部门，加强两法衔接、共同打击光盘盗版的一起典型案件。

九、邹某等制售盗版图书案

2015 年 12 月，江苏省昆山市文化广电新闻出版局联合昆山市公安局对邹某等制售盗版图书案进行调查。经查，邹某以营利为目的，未经著作权人许可，委托上海墨龙印务有限公司印刷 Kaplan 公司出版的金融分析师（CFA）图书 4 万余册，并通过网络销售，非法经营额达 55 万余元。上海墨龙印务有限公司及其负责人陈某在明知印刷品为盗版图书的情况下，通过自己印刷和分包给王某、赵某某印刷的方式，为邹某印刷上述图书。上海弘磊纸制品有限公司及其负责人吕某某在明知印刷品为盗版图书的情况下，为上海墨龙印务有限公司装订盗版书 4 万余册。

2016 年 8 月 19 日，江苏省昆山市人民法院依法做出刑事判决：因犯侵犯著作权罪，分别判处邹某有期徒刑 3 年 6 个月，并处罚金人民币 36 万元；判处上海墨龙印务有限公司罚金人民币 15 万元；判处上海弘磊纸制品有限公司罚金人民币 10 万元；判处陈某、吕某某、王某、赵某某有期徒刑缓刑，并处罚金人民币 5 万元至 10 万元不等。

【点　评】 该案涉及多个侵权主体和多种侵权行为。办案人员对印刷、分包、装订等各个侵权环节进行坚决打击，不仅对个人犯罪依法处理，同时对单位犯罪人员和犯罪单位做出刑事处罚，充分体现了刑事司法对包括国外权利人在内的著作权人的保护力度。

十、竹林新华包装材料厂盗印教辅案

2014年11月，根据举报线索，河南省巩义市公安局、巩义市文化广电新闻出版局成立联合行动组，对巩义市竹林新华包装材料厂进行检查，发现该厂正在印刷未经出版单位委托印刷的出版物，并当场查扣《中考英语》等出版物活页19万余张，《5年高考3年模拟》《小学教材全解》等多种图书共计14万余册，总码洋386万余元。2014年12月，该案依法移送巩义市公安局。

2016年2月1日，河南省郑州市中级人民法院依法做出刑事判决：徐某犯侵犯著作权罪，判处有期徒刑5年6个月，并处罚金70万元；李某犯侵犯著作权罪，判处有期徒刑4年6个月，并处罚金40万元；张某犯侵犯著作权罪，判处有期徒刑3年，并处罚金10万元；张某某犯侵犯著作权罪，判处有期徒刑3年，并处罚金10万元。后原审被告人分别提出上诉。2016年6月17日，河南省高级人民法院做出终审裁定：驳回上诉，维持原判。

【点　评】 盗版教辅不仅给权利人造成巨大损失，也严重影响学生版权保护意识的形成。该案涉案教辅图书种类、数量众多，侵权盗版规模巨大，司法部门依法从严查处，维护了出版社的合法权益，有效规范了地区教辅市场秩序，产生了较好的社会影响。

“剑网2016”专项行动21起典型案件

国家版权局与国家互联网信息办公室、工业和信息化部和公安部四部门联合开展的“剑网2016”专项行动已进入收官阶段。国家版权局等四部门于2016年12月22日公布了21起较为典型的网络侵权盗版案件。

一、北京“顶点小说网”侵犯著作权案

根据权利人投诉，北京市东城区公安部门对“顶点小说网”侵犯著作权案进行调查。经查，余某某等人未经权利人许可，在“顶点小说网”上传播非法采集的文学作品，并通过广告联盟非法获利42.8万元。2016年8月16日，北京市东城区人民法院以侵犯著作权罪判处余某某有期徒刑3年，并处罚金22万元；判处余某有期徒刑1年，缓刑1年，并处罚金3万元。

二、广西南宁“皮皮小说网”涉嫌侵犯著作权案

根据权利人投诉，广西壮族自治区版权行政执法部门会同公安部门对“皮皮小说网”涉嫌侵犯著作权案进行调查。经查，自2012年4月起，魏某某、覃某和陈某某未经权利人许可，在其开设的网站上向公众提供涉嫌侵权文字作品，并通过广告联盟非法获利获利150万余元。2016年5月，案件已移送检察机关审查起诉。

三、重庆“269小说网”涉嫌侵犯著作权案

根据举报线索，重庆市版权部门会同公安部门对“269小说网”涉嫌侵犯著作权案进行调查。经查，自2013年起，步某未经权利人许可，在其开设的网站上向公众提供2万余部涉嫌侵权文字作品，并通过广告联盟非法获利。该案正在进一步查办中。

四、江苏苏州“风雨文学网”涉嫌侵犯著作权案

根据权利人投诉，江苏省张家港市版权行政执法部门对“风雨文学网”涉嫌侵犯著作权案进行调查。经查，自2013年5月起，张某未经权利人许可，在其开设的网站上向公众提供涉嫌侵权文字作品，并通过广告联盟非法获利100余万元。该案已移交公安部门。

五、四川成都“轻之国度网”“轻之文库网”涉嫌侵犯著作权案

根据权利人投诉，四川省成都市、双流区两级版权行政执法部门会同公安部门对“轻之国度网”“轻之文库网”涉嫌侵犯著作权案进行调查。经查，该网站未经权利人许可，向公众提供涉嫌侵权小说作品5 000余部。2名犯罪嫌疑人已被批捕，案件正在进一步查办中。

六、北京《一点资讯》客户端软件侵犯著作权案

2016年8月，根据权利人投诉，北京市版权行政执法部门对北京一点网聚科技有限公司侵犯著作权案进行调查。经查，该公司未经权利人许可，通过其运营的《一点资讯》客户端软件提供文字作品的资讯阅读服务。2016年8月，北京市文化市场行政执法总队对该公司做出罚款5万元的行政处罚。

七、江苏常州“99770漫画网”等涉嫌侵犯著作权案

2016年6月，江苏省常州市版权行政执法部门对“99770漫画”等网站涉嫌侵犯著作权案进行调查。经查，张某开办“99770漫画”“可可漫画”等5个漫画网站，未经权利人许可，传播大量漫画作品，并通过广告联盟非法获利。2016年7月，江苏省常州市文化广电新闻出版局对张某做出没收违法所得、罚款17万元的行政处罚。

八、天津“吉吉影院网”涉嫌侵犯著作权案

2015年7月，根据权利人投诉，天津市版权行政执法部门会同公安部门对“吉吉影院网”涉嫌侵犯著作权案进行调查。2016年11月，办案部门锁定网站服务器地址，现场查获服务器一台及笔记本电脑、电脑主机、移动硬盘等设备。经查，该网站未经权利人许可，向公众提供涉嫌侵权影视作品近7万部，涉案金额4 000余万元，并通过广告联盟非法获利近100万元。2名犯罪嫌疑人已被刑事拘留，案件正在进一步查办中。

九、江苏淮安“BT天堂网”涉嫌侵犯著作权案

2016年7月，根据日常巡查线索，江苏省淮安市版权行政执法部门会同公安部门对“BT天堂网”涉嫌侵犯著作权案进行调查。经查，该网站未经权利人许可，向公众提供影视剧作品播放、下载服务，并通过广告联盟非法获利90余万元。犯罪嫌疑人袁某某已被抓获，案件正在进一步查办中。

十、江苏镇江“迅播影院网”涉嫌侵犯著作权案

2016年10月，根据日常巡查线索，江苏省镇江市版权行政执法部门会同公安部门对“迅播影院网”涉嫌侵犯著作权案进行调查，现场扣押电脑4台、服务器19台。经查，姜某等未经权利人许可，通过“迅播影院网”等5个网站向公众提供侵权影视剧作品2万余部，并通过广告联盟非法获利100余万元。3名犯罪嫌疑人已被刑事拘留，案件正在进一步查办中。

十一、湖北黄石“汇梦影视茶吧”侵犯著作权案

案件详情，参见本栏目“2016年度打击侵权盗版十大案件”之五(第303页)。

十二、上海《echo回声》客户端软件侵犯著作权案

案件详情，参见本栏目“2016年度打击侵权盗版十大案件”之二（第303页)。

十三、重庆《音乐一号》客户端软件侵犯著作权案

2015年12月，根据权利人投诉，重庆市版权行政执法部门对《音乐一号》客户端软件侵犯著作权案进行调查。经查，音乐一号科技有限公司自2015年9月起，未经权利人许可，通过其经营的《音乐一号》客户端软件传播大量音乐作品。2016年4月，重庆市文化市场行政执法总队对该公司做出没收非法所得3 000元、罚款3万元的行政处罚。

十四、河北保定卫某某涉嫌侵犯网络游戏著作权案

2016年9月，根据举报线索，河北省保定市公安部门对卫某某涉嫌侵犯《火影忍者OL》网络游戏著作权案进行调查，现场查获电脑、手机、银行卡等作案工具。经查，卫某某未经著作权人许可，私自架设《火影忍者OL》私服，非法获利18万元。犯罪嫌疑人卫某某已被刑事拘留，案件正在进一步查办中。

十五、重庆“8·5”系列侵犯网络游戏著作权案

2015年至2016年，根据举报线索或权利人投诉，重庆市版权行政执法部门会同公安部门对系列侵犯网络游戏著作权案进行调查。经查，林某某等私自架设《至尊合击》《回忆传奇》等多款游戏私服，并搭建游戏充值平台收取充值款，涉案金额3 000万余元；周某某等私自架设《极焰天下》等8款游戏私服，涉案金额2 500余万元；唐某某等私自架设《热血荣耀》(赤月版）游戏私服，通过第三方平台收取充值款，涉案金额260万元。犯罪嫌疑人周某某已被批捕，林某某等8名犯罪嫌疑人已被抓获，案件正在进一步查办中。

十六、福建厦门“系统大全网”侵犯著作权案

2016年8月，根据权利人投诉，福建省厦门市版权行政执法部门对“系统大全网”涉嫌侵犯著作权案进行调查。经查，黄某某未经权利人许可，通过其运营的“系统大全网”为用户免费提供Beyond Compare和Coreldraw两款软件的下载，软件点击量合计22 632次，软件下载量合计98次。2016年9月，福建省厦门市文化市场综合执法支队对黄某某做出删除侵权链接、罚款1万元的行政处罚。

十七、北京“亿梦春田”等6家淘宝网店涉嫌侵犯著作权案

2016年1月，根据举报线索，北京市版权行政执法部门会同公安部门对北京亿梦春田文化有限公司涉嫌侵权著作权案进行调查，现场查获涉嫌侵权盗版图书38种、8 140册。经查，该公司先后通过“亿梦春田”等6家淘宝网店销售侵权盗版图书，销售金额400万元。4名犯罪嫌疑人已被抓获，案件正在进一步查办中。

十八、江苏苏州“12·15”侵犯著作权案

2015年12月，根据举报线索，江苏省苏州市、昆山市版权行政执法部门会同“扫黄打非”部门和公安部门对“永恒之光777”淘宝网店涉嫌销售侵权盗版图书进行调查，捣毁一个非法出版物仓储窝点，现场查获涉嫌侵权盗版出版物3万余册，涉案金额3 000余万元。2016年8月，江苏省昆山市人民法院以侵犯著作权罪判处邹某有期徒刑3年6个月，并处罚金36万元。

十九、江苏镇江“10·26”侵犯著作权案

2015年9月，根据举报线索，江苏省镇江市公安部门对“剑锋时代图书专营店”淘宝网店涉嫌销售盗版图书案进行调查。经查，张某某等人通过网络销售盗版图书110余种、52万余册，涉案金额300余万元，现场查获盗版图书2.5万余册。江苏省版权行政执法部门会同“扫黄打非”部门和公安部门进一步调查，捣毁两处侵权盗版图书藏匿窝点，现场查获图书340余种、百万余册，及大量半成品图书。犯罪嫌疑人王某某和赵某已被批捕，其他6名犯罪嫌疑人已被刑事拘留，案件已移送检察机关审查起诉。

二十、江西南昌“6·4”侵犯著作权案

2016 年 5 月，根据浙江省杭州市余杭区市场监督管理部门移转线索，江西省南昌市版权行政执法部门会同公安部门对南昌国云科技服务有限公司涉嫌侵犯著作权案进行调查。经查，南昌国云科技服务有限公司经营的“火课旗舰店”淘宝网店未经权利人授权，销售图书电子版，供付费用户通过百度云链接下载。2015 年 3 月至案发，该网店销售 1 114 次，传播文字作品 2 万余部，销售金额超过 30 万元。犯罪嫌疑人廖某某已被批捕，案件已移送检察机关审查起诉。

二十一、广东佛山“12·23”网络批销盗版图书案

2015 年 12 月，广东省佛山市、南海区文化市场综合执法部门会同公安部门，根据相关线索对佛山市南海区大沥镇 3 个涉嫌盗版图书销售及储存窝点进行查处，现场抓获犯罪嫌疑人 12 名，查获涉嫌盗版图书 19 万余本（册），总码洋近 1 100 万元，并查获 12 台用于网络销售的电脑。2016 年 4 月，南海区检察院对 4 名犯罪嫌疑人提起公诉。

部分省（区、市）公布的2016年度著作权典型案件

北 京

1986年版《西游记》音乐作品著作权案

【简要案情】 许镜清是1986年版电视剧《西游记》中音乐作品《西游记序曲》（又名《西游记前奏曲》或《云宫迅音》）和《猪八戒背媳妇》的作者。许镜清于2015年12月初发现蓝港在线公司在其运营的网络游戏《新西游记》中使用了他作曲的两首音乐作品《西游记序曲》与《猪八戒背媳妇》，且在使用中未予署名。许镜清认为蓝港在线公司在未经许可、不加署名的情况下，在其创作并出品发行的游戏《新西游记》的配乐中使用了其享有著作权的《西游记序曲》《猪八戒背媳妇》两首作品，且该侵权配乐贯穿游戏始终。该行为侵犯了其依法享有的署名权、改编权、信息网络传播权，故起诉要求蓝港在线公司停止侵权、赔礼道歉、赔偿经济损失160万元及诉讼合理费用。

法院认为，蓝港在线公司超出授权许可使用期限，在其运营的网络游戏《新西游记》中使用涉案音乐作品，且未在使用中给许镜清署名，侵犯了许镜清享有的署名权、信息网络传播权。涉案游戏背景音乐中使用涉案音乐作品，与原曲存在一定差异，但无法确认蓝港在线公司的使用行为已经达到了改变原曲形成新作品的程度，故对侵犯改编权一节不予认定。蓝港在线公司依法应当承担消除影响、赔偿损失的民事责任。关于赔偿数额，许镜清主张经济损失按照其实际损失即合理许可使用费计算，并提供了授权他人使用涉案一首音乐作品的授权书作为计算依据，要求赔偿160万元。蓝港在线公司则以其曾获得过音著协的授权且授权数额远低于许镜清主张的数额、其系因疏忽导致侵权、涉案游戏近年处于亏损状态等为由进行抗辩，认为许镜清主张的数额过高，并提供了相关证据。由于根据上述证据，权利人的实际损失和侵权人因侵权行为的违法所得均难以确定，故本案应依法适用法定赔偿方式在50万元以下确定赔偿数额。据此，法院判决：蓝港在线公司赔偿许镜清经济损失16万元及诉讼合理支出15 488.7元。双方当事人均未上诉，一审判决生效。

【点 评】 本案是一起网络游戏侵害知名音乐作品著作权的典型案件，争议焦点集中在赔偿方式适用及赔偿数额的确定上。权利人对涉案的两首音乐作品主张按照合理许可使用费确定其实际损失，并提供了其中一首音乐作品的授权费用作为依据，要求被告赔偿160万元经济损失。被告则以其曾获得合法授权且授权数额远低于原告主张的数额、主观上系因疏忽导致侵权发生、涉案游戏近年处于亏损状态等为由进行抗辩。在双方当事人就侵权损害赔偿的确定均提供一定依据的情况下，应如何妥善确定赔偿数额，法院在本案中以充分的说理予以了明确，即权利人虽提交了涉案一首音乐作品的授权费用，但授权费用并不能证明另一涉案音乐作品当然地具有同等商业价值，在现有证据无法证明权利人的实际损失和被告因侵权行为的违法所得的情况下，应依法适用法定赔偿方式，并综合涉案音乐作品知名度、商业价值、被告主观过错程度、涉案音乐作品在涉案游戏中发挥的作用、涉案游戏的影响力、被告使用涉案音乐作品的具体方式、侵权持续时间等因素确定具体赔偿数额。在综合考虑上述因素的基础上，本案最终酌定的赔偿数额远高于同类型作品通常的赔偿标准。

天 津

一、齐白石作品著作权侵权纠纷案

案件详情，参见本栏目“2016年全国著作权司法保护典型案件”之二（第296页）。

二、国家高技术研究发展计划（“863”计划）课题成果著作权侵权纠纷案

【简要案情】 2009年6月16日，国家科学技术部（课题委托方，甲方）与吴艳兰（课题责任人，乙方）、武汉大学（课题依托单位，丙方）签订了《国家高技术研究发展计划（“863”计划）课题任务合同书》。合同约定，甲方批准由乙方依托丙方承担“863”计划地球观测与导航技术领域地球空间信息系统技术题/项目椭球上海洋划界中的比例线法技术研究课题研究开发任务。课题依托于武汉大学教育部“地理信息系统”重点实验室开展，由武汉大学提供课题的技术与条件保障。2012年11月2日，课题成果通过验收，课题成果中的专著稿《地球上自

然图形集间比例线问题及海洋划界关键技术研究报告》未正式发表，在课题验收中以《知识产权证明材料——研究报告（专著草稿）》的形式收录在课题验收材料之八当中，单独成册，约 18 万字。其中的第四章“海洋划界技术分析”为吴艳兰主张保护的涉案作品，该章节总字数为 6 625 字。被告张建辉、付瑞全是被告国家海洋信息中心的工程师，吴艳兰认为张建辉、付瑞全合作完成并发表的论文《基于GIS的海洋划界技术方法研究》，在组织结构以及其中十一部分 700 余字的表述方式和观点抄袭了其文章，故起诉请求：判令被告赔礼道歉、消除影响并赔偿损失。

法院认为，涉案作品属于课题研究成果，其著作权的归属问题，应结合该课题的具体情况加以分析。涉案课题系以武汉大学的名义申报立项，课题依托于武汉大学教育部“地理信息系统”重点实验室开展，包括吴艳兰在内的课题组成员所在单位均为武汉大学，并由武汉大学提供课题的技术与条件保障。课题任务合同书明确约定，除合同另有约定外，执行本课题形成的知识产权归属、分享和转移按照《关于国家科研计划项目研究成果知识产权管理的若干规定》等规定执行。按照该规定，科研项目研究成果及其形成的知识产权，除涉及国家安全、国家利益和重大社会公共利益的以外，国家授予科研项目承担单位。本案中，涉案作品的课题承担单位是作为课题依托单位的武汉大学。在涉案作品为“863”课题研究成果，且课题任务合同书中对课题成果的知识产权归属有明确约定的情况下，吴艳兰主张其对涉案作品享有著作权没有证据证明，故判决驳回吴艳兰的诉讼请求。

【点　评】 本案系涉及国家高技术研究发展计划（“863”计划）科研项目成果著作权的案件，涉案“863”课题科研项目从立项、实施到验收情况复杂，又因涉案作品尚未发表且无明确署名，课题承担单位武汉大学未作为本案当事人参与诉讼等因素，使得对涉案作品著作权归属的认定存在较大难度。生效判决根据著作权法的相关规定，从涉案作品与“863”课题成果的关系入手，通过对合同条款的具体分析，以抽丝剥茧的方式对涉案作品的性质、著作权归属，以及吴艳兰能否以独立完成涉案作品的唯一作者身份主张相应权利，进行了详细分析和认定，为同类案件的审理提供了参考和借鉴。在激励创新、鼓励创作的背景下，本案判决为著作权侵权纠纷中特殊职务作品权利归属及作者身份的认定提供了审理思路。

辽　宁

一、北京金铠星科技有限公司与大连市机动车污染管理处、深圳市安车检测股份有限公司侵害计算机软件著作权纠纷案

【简要案情】 原告北京金铠星科技有限公司已提供证据能够证明其对某一计算机软件享有著作权，但原告无法证明其提供给被告大连市机动车污染管理处的检测设备上运行的是案涉被侵权计算机软件。对于被告大连市机动车污染管理处、深圳市安车检测股份有限公司在被告大连市机动车污染管理处运行的设备中是否对原告早前向被告大连市机动车污染管理处提供的计算机软件擅自进行修改、复制、更改署名，原告不申请进行计算机软件程序的侵权比对鉴定，应由原告承担举证不能的法律后果，故原告的起诉没有事实依据和法律依据，应予以驳回。

【点　评】 本案的处理一方面通过正确行使释明权，充分保障了计算机软件著作权人的诉讼权利，表达出对著作权的司法保护意愿；另一方面通过对举证责任的正确分配，防止著作权人滥用诉讼权利，力图通过个案传达出鼓励创新的态度。

二、帕斯卡株式会社与大连光洋自动化液压系统有限公司著作权侵权纠纷案

【简要案情】 原告帕斯卡株式会社制作的产品说明书是原告在生产经营中，为了介绍产品、宣传企业，经过智力劳动，由有关法人、其他组织及个人创作，对其产品使用及性能独有的文字描述，以文字、绘制的示意图组合表达产品特定的内容，融入了设计者的智慧，并付出一定的金钱和劳动。被告大连光洋自动化液压系统有限公司未经原告许可，擅自使用原告享有著作权的产品说明书中图片、数据的行为，构成了对原告著作权的侵害。

【点　评】 虽然著作权法及其实施条例均没有明确把“产品说明书”列入作品范畴，但独创性应是作品的根本属性，只要是产品说明书中文学性的说明、产品设计图以及其他图片、标识符合著作权法关于作品的实质条件，就可以作为著作权客体予以保护。

吉　林

李某与吉林某农副产品公司、第三人南关区某设计工作室著作权侵权纠纷案

【简要案情】 李某多年从事民间剪纸创作，被

评为吉林省优秀民间艺术家，吉林某农副产品公司2012年6月与南关区某设计工作室签订《设计项目委托合同书》，委托其设计包装袋。同年，吉林某农副产品公司申请将该设计图中的“人鹿图案”注册为商标，并于2014年取得商标注册证。吉林某农副产品公司将该商标用于多种粮食产品的外包装上进行销售经营。李某认为吉林某农副产品公司和南关区某设计工作室的行为侵害了其著作权，遂提起告诉，要求吉林某农副产品公司按照所使用包装袋数量为计算基础，向其支付210万元的经济赔偿。

法院经审理认为：李某的作品系以民间传统艺术形式所创作的作品，而并非吉林某农副产品公司主张的传统民间文学艺术，是创作者的智力劳动成果，属于著作权法的保护范围。根据吉林某农副产品公司对于商标内容的选择，可以认定其与涉案作品有接触，并且，其所使用的图案与涉案作品实质相似，因此，认定侵权行为成立。对于权利人所主张的巨额经济赔偿的诉讼请求，人民法院在合理许可使用费用的基础上，具体考虑侵权人的使用方式以及由此而产生的非法获益，以市场的角度对权利人应得的补偿予以公平裁处，最终判决吉林某农副产品公司停止侵权，并赔偿经济损失8万元。

【点　评】　著作权人享有著作权的作品，被他人作为商标使用，其受到损害的实际上不再是对著作权复制权、发行权的侵害，而是对著作权作为转化其他智力成果的侵权。对于该种侵权的损害赔偿方式应当与侵权人的侵权行为相吻合，以相近的智力成果侵权赔偿方式为依据，而不应再以著作权的侵权赔偿方式为标准。

黑　龙　江

一、“无名缘”商标及著作权侵权纠纷案

【简要案情】　哈尔滨街上缘餐饮管理有限公司（以下简称街上缘公司）成立于2010年9月，主营米粉快餐。2011年7月6日，街上缘公司取得“无名缘”注册商标，核定服务项目为第43类：饭店、酒吧、茶馆、餐馆等。经过街上缘公司多年经营，“无名缘”米粉已成为在全国拥有近4 000家连锁加盟店的全国性快餐品牌。2013年，街上缘公司创作完成美术作品《无名缘》，并取得国家版权局颁发的著作权登记证书。哈尔滨快客餐饮管理有限公司（以下简称快客公司）成立于2007年12月10日，经核准拥有“玉名缘”注册商标，核准使用范围为第43类：饭店、酒吧、茶馆、餐馆等，期限为2012年1月7日至2022年1月6日。哈尔滨快客无名缘餐饮管理有限公司（以下简称快客无名缘公司）成立于2010年12月20日，经核准拥有“无名缘”注册商标，核准使用范围为第44类：饮食营养指导、卫生设备出租、眼镜行等，期限为2012年2月7日至2022年2月6日。自2013年起，快客公司、快客无名缘公司未经许可，授权多家加盟商使用“无名缘米粉”等字样进行经营。街上缘公司遂提起诉讼，请求判令两被告停止侵权行为，赔偿侵害商标权经济损失200万元及侵害著作权经济损失50万元，以及维权合理开支10万元。

法院经审理认为：快客公司、快客无名缘公司未经许可，擅自使用与街上缘公司“无名缘”注册商标近似的“玉名缘”商标，属于以改变显著特征方式使用注册商标，足以造成相关公众的混淆误认，侵害了街上缘公司的注册商标专用权，同时侵害了街上缘公司对《无名缘》作品享有的著作权。判令快客公司、快客无名缘公司停止侵权行为并赔偿经济损失100万元。

【点　评】　“无名缘”米粉为在全国享有较高知名度的服务商标，快客公司、快客无名缘公司未经许可，以改变注册商标显著特征、超越商标核定使用范围等方式，通过线下加盟、网上宣传等多种方式，在全国范围内吸引相关公众加盟，具有较大影响。在本案诉讼中，快客公司、快客无名缘公司几乎用尽了商标侵权诉讼的所有抗辩事由，法院均予以回应，较具典型意义。

二、KTV经营者侵犯著作权纠纷案

【简要案情】　中国音像著作权集体管理协会（简称音集协）为依法成立的著作权集体管理组织。张某经营的金莎国际娱乐会所未经许可，使用了音集协授权管理的《最炫民族风》等53首歌曲的MTV，音集协遂提起诉讼，要求张某停止侵权行为并赔偿经济损失。

法院经审理认为：音集协作为著作权集体管理组织，享有涉案《最炫民族风》等53首歌曲的著作权，张某经营的金莎国际娱乐会所未经许可，将上述歌曲用于经营活动，侵害了音集协对涉案作品享有的著作权，应根据情况承担停止侵害、消除影响、赔礼道歉、赔偿损失等民事责任。KTV点歌系统的制造、销售商未经许可使用涉案作品的行为，与张某未经许可在经营活动中使用涉案作品的行为属各自独立的行为，音集协有权选择向任何一方主张权利。KTV点歌系统的制造、销售商是否实施侵权行为并不影响张某实施侵权行为以及是否承担侵权赔偿责任

的判定。张某关于音集协应起诉KTV点歌系统的制造、销售商的上诉主张于法无据，不予支持。

【点　评】　近年来，黑龙江省法院受理的中国音像著作权集体管理协会以其管理的音乐作品著作权受到侵害为由起诉KTV经营者的案件数量逐年增长，维权范围也从哈尔滨市向省内其他各大城市扩展。此类案件多为相关KTV经营者未将音乐作品的许可使用费列为其经营成本，对支付许可使用费存有较强的抵触情绪，且极少主动缴费、重复侵权现象严重。审判实务中，KTV经营者多以所购买的KTV点歌系统（包括硬件设施及软件系统）自带卡拉OK音乐作品、已支付KTV点歌系统的价款、不应承担赔偿责任为由，抗辩不构成侵权，或主张音集协应向KTV点歌系统生产商主张权利。此案的典型意义在于KTV点歌系统的生产商并无相关音乐权利人的任何授权，KTV经营者在购买产品时即应当知晓点歌系统属侵权产品，其合法来源抗辩依法不能成立。未经许可，制造、销售、使用他人作品的行为均属侵权，权利人对于向谁主张权利拥有选择权。在权利人未申请追加被告的情况下，法院无须主动追加。

上　海

一、SAP股份公司诉朗泽企业管理咨询（上海）有限公司等侵害计算机软件著作权等纠纷案

【简要案情】　SAP公司系在德国登记设立的软件公司，主要提供企业管理和协同化商务解决方案的软件及相关服务，在中国市场享有良好的声誉。该公司享有服务器端软件ECC 6.0（IDES版本）和客户端软件GUI720的著作权，客户端软件连接服务器端软件之后，可以运行包括MM（物料管理）、HR（人力资源管理）等多项涉及标准化企业管理业务的功能模块。为帮助企业准确理解和正确应用上述软件，其以功能模块为单元，开发了SAP软件系列培训课程，并针对每一模块的功能和特点编写了软件培训教材，专门用于软件培训课程。涉案培训教材分别针对MM（物料管理）、HR（人力资源管理）模块，共计16本。朗泽公司成立于2010年12月29日，是一家主要从事SAP软件各项功能模块培训的公司。该公司在其官方网站上宣传推广自己开设的包括涉案MM（物料管理）和HR（人力资源管理）两项模块在内的十余项功能模块的培训课程，并使用SAP公司的计算机软件和培训教材进行培训。截至2014年6月，朗泽公司官方网站显示，其在上海、北京、成都、广州、深圳、大连校区十余项功能模块的培训总计毕业学员978名，网站上公布的培训费价格最低为26 800元。而根据SAP公司与其培训合作机构的授权协议，其可以从每名学员的培训费中收取40%的特许权使用费。案件审理中，朗泽公司对其网站上披露的上诉数据不予认可，但未按法院要求提供其培训学员的数量、收取的培训费等实际经营情况的证据，SAP公司认为朗泽公司的行为侵犯了其计算机软件以及培训教材的著作权，故诉至法院请求判令朗泽公司停止侵权并赔偿经济损失及合理开支。

上海知识产权法院审理后认为，朗泽公司的行为侵害了SAP公司对涉案计算机软件和培训教材享有的著作权，依法应当承担停止侵权、赔偿损失的民事责任。本案中，虽然SAP公司的实际损失和朗泽公司的违法所得均难以确定，但现有证据已经可以证明SAP公司因侵权所受到的损失超过了相关法律规定的法定赔偿数额上限50万元，故综合全案的证据情况，根据朗泽公司的培训费价格、侵权行为性质、主观状态、侵权情节及持续时间，参考SAP公司向合作机构收取特许权使用费的比例等，在法定赔偿最高限额之上酌情合理确定赔偿数额，遂判令朗泽公司停止侵权，赔偿SAP公司包括合理开支在内的经济损失共计118万元。判决后，各方当事人均未提起上诉。

【点　评】　在知识产权侵权案件审理中，当依法确定了侵权人的侵权责任后，需要遵循一定的赔偿原则确定侵权损害赔偿数额。而赔偿数额的确定，一直是案件的审理难点，也是权利人关注的焦点。本案判决的意义在于在侵权赔偿责任确定中切实贯彻全面赔偿原则，在已有证据可以证明著作权人因侵权所受到的损失已超过法定赔偿最高限额50万元的情况下，综合全案的证据情况，在法定赔偿最高限额之上酌情合理确定赔偿数额。本案判决彰显了法院对权利人合法权益的保护力度，也体现了法院不断加强知识产权司法保护的态度和决心。

二、上海耀宇文化传媒有限公司诉广州斗鱼网络科技有限公司著作权侵权及不正当竞争纠纷上诉案

案件详情，参见本栏目“2016年全国著作权司法保护典型案件”之三（第298页）。

三、上海美术电影制片厂诉浙江新影年代文化传播有限公司等著作权侵权纠纷上诉案

【简要案情】　美影厂系“葫芦娃”“黑猫警长”角色形象美术作品著作权人。新影年代公司为配合电影《80后的独立宣言》上映宣传，制作了被控侵权海报，提供给华谊兄弟公司。新影年代公司并在

其官方微博上使用了该海报。该海报上，“葫芦娃”“黑猫警长”分别居于男女主角的左右两侧，与其他背景图案大小基本相同。美影厂认为，新影年代公司等未经许可，使用“葫芦娃”和“黑猫警长”角色形象美术作品，构成对其相关著作权的侵犯，故诉至法院，请求判令新影年代公司等消除影响，停止侵权，并赔偿美影厂经济损失及维权费用。

原审法院判决驳回美影厂的诉讼请求。美影厂不服一审判决，提起上诉。

上海知识产权法院审理后认为，涉案作品在电影海报中的引用不是单纯地展现原作品的艺术美感和功能，而是反映“80后”一代曾经经历《葫芦兄弟》《黑猫警长》动画片盛播的时代年龄特征，属于转换性使用，并不影响涉案作品的正常使用，也没有不合理地损害著作权人的合法利益，故构成合理使用。因此，法院判决驳回上诉，维持原判。

【点　评】 本案中，法院在审查判断是否构成作品的合理使用时，明确了“葫芦娃”“黑猫警长”角色形象美术作品使用在涉案电影海报中属于转换性使用。所谓转换性使用，是指对原作品的使用不是单纯地再现原作品本身的文学、艺术价值，而是通过在新作品中的使用使原作品在被使用过程中具有了新的价值、功能或性质，从而改变了其原先的功能或目的。在判断转换性使用是否构成合理使用时，应当综合考察我国著作权法所规定的合理使用构成要件，即在构成转换性使用的前提下，不影响该作品的正常使用，也没有不合理地损害著作权人的合法利益。本案的审理有助于明晰合理使用的审查判断标准。

江　苏

一、网店“永恒之光777”侵犯著作权案

案件详情，参见本栏目“‘剑网2016’专项行动21起典型案件”之十八（第307页）。

二、磊若软件公司诉江苏林芝山阳集团有限公司侵害计算机软件著作权纠纷案

案件详情，参见本栏目“2016年全国著作权司法保护典型案件”之四（第298页）。

浙　江

一、杭州大头儿子文化发展有限公司与央视动画有限公司著作权侵权纠纷三案

【简要案情】 1994年，刘某某受动画片《大头儿子小头爸爸》（1995年版，以下简称95版动画片）导演崔某某委托，为其即将拍摄的95版动画片创作了“大头儿子”“小头爸爸”“围裙妈妈”三个人物形象正面图，并将底稿交给了崔某某。当时双方并未就该作品的著作权归属签署任何书面协议。后95版动画片美术创作团队在刘某某创作的人物概念设计图基础上，进行了进一步的设计和再创作，最终制作成了符合动画片标准造型的三个主要人物形象的标准设计图以及之后的转面图、比例图等。95版动画片由中央电视台（以下简称央视）和东方电视台联合摄制，在其片尾播放的演职人员列表中载明：“人物设计：刘某某”。2012年12月14日，刘某某将自己创作的涉案三幅作品的著作权转让给洪某，后洪某将上述著作权转让给杭州大头儿子文化发展有限公司（以下简称大头儿子公司）。2013年，央视动画有限公司（以下简称央视动画公司）摄制了动画片《新大头儿子小头爸爸》（以下简称2013版动画片）并在CCTV等平台上进行播放，同时对2013版动画片的人物形象进行宣传、展览，并许可中国木偶艺术剧院进行舞台剧表演。大头儿子公司认为央视动画公司在未经许可且未支付报酬的情况下，利用上述美术作品形象改编为新人物形象，并对改编后的新人物形象进行展览、宣传、制作成动画片，并发行、复制、销售、播放、网络传输该动画片，侵害了其著作权，故诉请判令央视动画公司停止侵害、赔礼道歉，并赔偿经济损失及合理费用。

杭州市滨江区人民法院经审理认为：1994年刘某某受托独立创作了“大头儿子”“小头爸爸”“围裙妈妈”三幅美术作品，因双方之间没有签订委托创作合同约定著作权归属，故刘某某作为受托人对其所创作的三幅美术作品享有完整的著作权。大头儿子公司经转让继受取得了上述作品除人身权以外的著作权。95版动画片中三个人物形象包含了刘某某原作品的独创性表达元素，整体人物造型、基本形态构成实质性相似，但央视95版动画片美术创作团队根据动画片艺术表现的需要，在原初稿基础上进行了艺术加工，增添了新的艺术创作成分。由于这种加工并没有脱离原作品中三个人物形象的“基本形态”，系由原作品派生而成，故构成对原作品的演绎作品。央视为该演绎作品的作者，对该演绎作品享有著作权。根据央视的授权，央视动画公司有权在2013版动画片中使用95版动画片中的人物形象。但央视动画公司在行使演绎作品著作权时不得侵害原作品的著作权，其未经大头儿子公司许可，

在2013版动画片以及相关的展览、宣传中以改编的方式使用大头儿子公司的作品并据此获利的行为，侵害了大头儿子公司的著作权，应承担相应的侵权责任。考虑本案创作背景等实际情况，平衡原作者、后续作品及社会公众的利益，兼顾公平原则，该院认为宜以提高赔偿额的方式作为央视动画公司停止侵害责任的替代方式。综上，该院于2015年6月30日判决：央视动画公司赔偿大头儿子公司经济损失40万元（每案）及合理费用22 040元（每案）。

一审宣判后，双方均不服，向杭州市中级人民法院提起上诉。杭州市中级人民法院经审理认为，一审事实清楚，适用法律正确，实体处理得当，遂于2016年2月22日判决：驳回上诉，维持原判。

二审判决生效后，央视动画公司向浙江省高级人民法院申请再审。浙江省高级人民法院经审查认为：央视动画公司再审申请期间提交了“刘某某签署的确认书著作权归属”书证，拟证明诉争三幅美术作品著作权并不归属刘某某，大头儿子公司无权依据相关权利转让主张央视动画公司侵权。但该证据真实性存疑，即便属实亦系出于央视维权所需，并不能由此认定央视、上海东方电视台与刘某某就诉争三幅美术作品著作权的归属达成合意。另关于央视动画公司再审申请提出刘某某“一权二卖”，应根据“先交付”的原则确认刘某某履行与央视动画公司的协议，而与洪某签订的合同则不能履行的主张，本案中，刘某某确于不同日期分别与洪某、央视动画公司签订了《著作权（角色商品化权）转让合同》、《大头儿子和小头爸爸》美术造型委托制作协议、《大头儿子和小头爸爸》美术造型委托制作协议补充协议，还有一份《说明》。上述四份文件中也均涉及刘某某对其创作的涉案三幅美术作品著作权归属的处分。但从时间上看，刘某某与洪某签署的转让合同时间在先；刘某某也在一审期间出庭作证，明确陈述其与央视动画公司签署的两份协议及《说明》均非其真实意思表示，而其与洪某签署的转让合同才系其真实意思表示；1994年刘某某受崔某某的委托，独立创作了涉案三幅美术作品，因双方之间没有签订委托创作合同约定著作权归属，故刘某某作为受托人对其所创作的三幅美术作品享有完整的著作权；刘某某将其基于受崔某某委托而创作的诉争作品底稿交付崔某某，之后央视与上海东方电视台在联合摄制95版动画片过程中，对刘某某创作的三幅诉争美术作品进行了进一步设计和再创作，且片尾播放的演职人员列表中也载明“人物设计：刘某某”，刘某某的上述行为不能视为诉争作品著作权转让的交付行为，而是刘某某基于崔某某与其之间委托创作关系而实施的交付使用行为。综上，该院于2016年11月14日裁定：驳回央视动画公司的再审申请。

【点　评】 近年来，一些经典的国产动画片被陆续翻拍，市场价值不断提升，但这些动画片在创作之初，投资方与创作者对各自的权利往往没有清晰的认识和明确的主张，对动画人物形象权利归属的激烈争议随之而来。动画人物形象属于著作权法规定的可单独使用的作品，原则上，动画人物形象的著作权归属其创作者，作者之外的主体如果要主张作品的著作权，应当与作者之间存在明确的权利归属约定。此外，在侵权成立的前提下，如果适用停止侵害的法律责任会导致公共利益严重受损的，可以在个案中通过提高赔偿数额的方式替代停止侵害责任，以突出公共利益的优先性，这符合知识产权法律制度作为公共政策产物的本质属性。

二、上海美术电影制片厂有限公司与杭州玺匠文化创意股份有限公司著作权侵权纠纷案

案件详情，参见本栏目“2016年全国著作权司法保护典型案件”之六（第300页）。

三、叶某某与浙江冠素堂食品有限公司著作权权属、侵权纠纷案

案件详情，参见本栏目“2016年全国著作权司法保护典型案件”之五（第299页）。

安　徽

一、芜湖市墨迅市场营销策划有限公司与芜湖世傲汽贸有限责任公司、繁昌县驾驶员协会侵害著作权纠纷案

【简要案情】 2015年2月至3月，芜湖世傲汽贸有限责任公司与芜湖市墨迅市场营销策划有限公司之间通过QQ聊天的形式，就墨迅策划公司为繁昌县驾驶员协会设计徽标（LOGO）一事进行了磋商。其间，墨迅策划公司向芜湖世傲汽贸公司发送了徽标（LOGO）样件（以下称引证徽标），但双方由于设计费用未协商一致，终止合作。2015年5月3日，墨迅策划公司发现繁昌县驾驶员协会在2015年4月28日的成立大会上，使用争议徽标作为标志。后墨迅策划公司向法院提起诉讼。

芜湖经开区法院审理认为，引证徽标于2015年3月17日设计完成，不是日常生活中普遍存在的徽标，系用众多元素组合而成的美术作品，具有审美意义和独创性的表达，并能以有形形式进行复制，墨迅策划公司依法对该引证徽标享有著作权。经对比，争议徽标与引证徽标两者整体设计近似。据此判决，繁昌县驾驶员协会立即停止侵权行为，芜湖世傲汽贸公司于本判决生效后十日内支付墨迅策划公司经济损失及维权费用4 500元。

【点　评】 本案关系到涉案协会千余名会员的徽标使用问题，在当地关注度较高。本案的判决，充分保护了美术作品权利人的著作权不受侵犯，也将促进相关社会团体增强保护知识产权、尊重他人智力成果的法律意识。

二、广州骇特商务咨询有限公司与安徽省远路信息科技有限公司侵害著作权纠纷案

【简要案情】 广州骇特商务咨询有限公司（以下简称骇特公司）与安徽省远路信息科技有限公司（以下简称远路公司）均从事旅游景点导览软件的开发和运营。2016年6月至7月，骇特公司发现远路公司在其《小鹿智游》APP中擅自使用了该公司创作的故宫博物院、圆明园等景点的12幅导览图，遂向各大手机软件平台发送警告函投诉侵权，并起诉要求远路公司停止侵权并赔偿损失。远路公司认为其软件所用图片是从互联网下载，非有意侵权。原告本来仅需来函和致电告知，即可实现维权，却恶意向各手机软件平台投诉，导致其软件被下架，损失严重，于是又提起反诉要求对方赔偿损失。此案经法院依法审理，判决远路公司赔偿经济损失8万元。同时，法院认定骇特公司向各手机软件平台的投诉维权方式并无不当，不应承担赔偿责任。

【点　评】 本案是安徽省首例涉及手机APP业务的著作权纠纷案件。本案在确认涉案APP使用未经授权的导览图构成侵权的基础上，认定权利人依据《信息网络传播权保护条例》第十四条实施的通知不构成权利滥用，为相关互联网新类型商业模式的发展明确了行为规则，有利于创新成果的转化和运用。

三、极致点击（北京）科技有限公司与铜陵百舟网络科技有限公司计算机软件著作权许可使用合同纠纷案

【简要案情】 2014年6月12日，作为许可方的极致点击（北京）科技有限公司（以下简称极致点击公司）与作为被许可方的铜陵百舟网络科技有限公司（以下简称百舟公司）签订了一份《网游运营许可协议》，约定许可方将最新版本的《冰火启示录》软件程序和补丁包（以下简称《冰火启示录》）北美地区英文版授权给被许可方在北美地区发行、运营，推广、营销及分发许可产品的服务给最终用户，并同意提供有限的改进、升级、文本文件、语言本地化和授权语言版本的技术支持。许可费为341 000元，被许可方分三次支付。

百舟公司按照约定，完成了第一次支付，将136 400元打入极致点击公司账户。极致点击公司按照约定交付百舟公司《冰火启示录》并完成了游戏本土化（游戏翻译成英文版），本土化完成时间是2015年1月27日。但是百舟公司拒绝完成第二次支付，也导致极致点击公司可望得到的第三次支付不能实现。原告极致点击公司要求被告百舟公司按照合同约定，承担违约责任，付给极致点击公司第二次支付和第三次支付共计204 600元。

铜陵市中级人民法院经审理后认为，极致点击公司主张《冰火启示录》本土化已经完成与查明的事实不符；双方在《网游运营许可协议》中约定的百舟公司支付第二次许可费的条件未成就，百舟公司可不予支付；极致点击公司主张百舟公司违约无事实依据。据此判决，驳回极致点击公司的诉讼请求，极致点击公司退还百舟公司许可费136 400元，并赔偿百舟公司经济损失125 132元，合计261 532元。

【点　评】 计算机软件著作权许可使用合同纠纷属于新类型案件。本案中，法院根据许可目的，综合运用解释方法，准确界定了游戏本土化的具体内涵，对计算机软件著作权许可使用合同争议条款的解释提供了参照方法。

福　建

厦门杰诗宝酒业有限公司与福建酩涛进出口贸易有限公司侵害其他著作财产权纠纷案

【简要案情】 2015年9月7日，江道济向国家版权局申请对作品《圣牛士图标》进行登记，该作品完成时间是2014年10月10日，同时江道济将上述作品授权给厦门杰诗宝酒业有限公司（以下简称杰诗宝公司）自2014年10月10日开始使用。杰诗宝公司于2014年10月在《高铁速递》杂志上刊登贴有“圣牛士”图标的葡萄酒广告。2015年12月7日，杰诗宝公司取得《圣牛士图标》的注册商标权。2015年9月8日福建酩涛进出口贸易有限公司（以下简称酩涛公司）在厦门展销会上销售贴“圣牛士”图标的葡萄酒。杰诗宝公司刊登的葡萄酒广告及在一审诉讼中提供的葡萄酒实物中文标贴均显示杰诗宝公司贴有“圣牛士”图标的葡萄酒是从西班牙“原瓶原装”进口的。酩涛公司被控侵权的葡萄酒亦是从西班牙进口。杰诗宝公司以酩涛公司侵犯其著作财产权为由诉至法院，请求停止侵权、赔礼道歉、赔偿损失。

福州市中级人民法院认为：涉案《作品登记证书》登记《圣牛士图标》的作者是江道济，江道济将该作品授权给杰诗宝公司使用，并声明杰诗宝公司有权以自己的名义提起诉讼。酩涛公司未经杰诗宝公司的许可，销售贴有涉案图标的葡萄酒，构成侵权，应承担停止侵权、赔偿损失的法律责任。

福建省高级人民法院认为：从本案查明的事实来看，最早出现涉案“圣牛士”图标是杰诗宝公司在2014年10月《高铁速递》杂志上刊登的葡萄酒广告，涉案图标被使用在葡萄酒的瓶贴上。但广告中同时标明该葡萄酒是从西班牙100%原瓶原装进口，可见该葡萄酒的瓶贴是形成于西班牙。杰诗宝公司没有提供相关的委托生产合同等证据证明前述瓶贴上的“圣牛士”图标是其提供给西班牙厂家的，亦没有提供涉案图标的创作底稿等其他证据证明该图标是由江道济独立创作完成的，所以杰诗宝公司主张江道济拥有涉案图标著作权的事实依据不足。遂改判：驳回杰诗宝公司的诉讼请求。

【点　评】 本案当事人虽然在国内对作品进行了版权登记，但当该作品最早使用于进口商品中时，并不能当然地认定该当事人即为作者。我国实行著作权自愿登记原则。根据《作品自愿登记试行办法》的规定，对于著作权的归属，主要是基于登记申请人对于著作权权属的承诺或声明，版权局并不对著作权权属及作品发表时间进行实质性审查。因此，在著作权侵权诉讼中，如果著作权主张者提交了著作权登记证书，一般可初步认为其拥有争议作品的著作权，但有相反证据时，著作权登记证书记载的著作权人应进一步举证证明其著作权利的基础合法有效。而当进行了著作权登记的作品最早出现在进口商品中时，则要分析将该作品附着于商品是形成于国外还是国内，若是形成于国外，相关当事人就需要进一步提供该作品是其创作完成并提供给国外生产商的证据，否则，将不宜直接认定《作品登记证书》中的“作者”为著作权人。

河　南

被告人何某侵犯著作权案

【简要案情】 被告人何某为谋取非法利益，从互联网上购进含有Windows、Office计算机软件的光盘及包装材料，未经微软公司许可，包装后在淘宝网网店进行销售，共计销售盗版微软软件5 606套。公安机关在何某租住处查获大量未包装的Windows、Office计算机软件光盘，COA标签和包装材料。经鉴定，上述查获的软件光盘和COA标签均系未经微软公司授权生产的盗版产品。法院认定何某犯侵犯著作权罪，判处有期徒刑3年8个月，并处罚金人民币78万元；对其违法所得人民币653 458.02元予以追缴后上缴国库；对扣押的侵权软件及相关包装材料予以没收并销毁。

【点　评】 近几年，河南省法院加强了对电子商务中知识产权侵权问题的打击力度。本案被告人从网上成批购进大量盗版操作系统和软件光盘，包装后在互联网上以正版软件的名义贩卖，侵犯了正版软件的著作权，同时严重破坏我国电子出版物市场的发展，造成软件出版、发行方面国家税收的巨额损失。本案的审理，彰显了对知识产权严格保护的原则，既对被告人处以实体刑罚，又从经济上剥夺其再犯罪的能力和条件。

湖　北

一、长江文艺出版社等侵害《巴黎圣母院》著作权纠纷案

案件详情，参见本栏目“2016年全国著作权司法保护典型案件”之七(第301页)。

二、杨修清与中工武大设计研究有限公司地图著作权确权纠纷案

【简要案情】 杨修清系报社退休干部。2011年1月，杨修清与案外人武汉大学出版社有限责任公司就涉案地图《襄阳市城区全貌图》的广告采编、征集工作签订协议书。杨修清于2011年9月将该黑白底图向版权局申请办理作品登记。协议签订后，杨修清依照约定向武汉大学出版社有限公司交付了涉案地图的黑白底图。在涉案地图出版过程中，武汉大学出版社有限公司因不具备测绘资质，依据其与中工武大设计研究有限公司之间的长期合作关系，将涉案地图的绘制及申报工作委托中工武大设计研究有限公司完成。随后，中工武大设计研究有限公司完成并办理涉案地图的绘制及申报工作。中工武大设计研究有限公司采用杨修清提供的素材和资料，通过特殊的编绘地图设备、设施和科技力量，由其工作人员使用计算机将上述内容绘制成图。其间，杨修清提供黑白底图和现实资料，核对资料有无遗漏或者错误。涉案地图的署名信息显示：编制为中工武大设计研究有限公司，出版发行为武汉大学出

版社，策划设计、编辑均为杨修清。

湖北省武汉市中级人民法院认为，中工武大设计研究有限公司对涉案地图作品享有著作权。(1) 中工武大设计研究有限公司具备编制地图的资质条件，是合法的编制普通地图的绘图机构，且涉案地图申报登记过程中，中工武大设计研究有限公司均为编绘单位、制报单位。而杨修清没有取得测绘资质证书，不具备编制地图所必需的申报条件，不是编制地图的合法主体。(2) 涉案地图由中工武大设计研究有限公司依法编制完成。杨修清主要承担了涉案地图编制、提交绘图资料、地图审核工作。(3) 涉案地图由中工武大设计研究有限公司依法署名。编制为中工武大设计研究有限公司，出版发行为武汉大学出版社，策划设计、编辑均为杨修清。中工武大设计研究有限公司作为编制者依法对涉案地图作品享有著作权。(4) 杨修清的手绘地图与涉案地图并非同一作品。通过将两者进行比对，可以确认两者仅在路网分布及地理环境上存在相同。杨修清的手绘地图与涉案地图应为素材和作品的关系，杨修清对涉案地图不享有著作权。据此，一审判决：驳回杨修清的全部诉讼请求。

杨修清不服，提起上诉。湖北省高级人民法院认为：(1) 杨修清不能依据其登记著作权的黑白地图主张涉案地图的著作权。地图中表现城市、道路的图例，表现山脉、河流、湖泊以及居民点等所在的客观位置等不受著作权法保护。地图的性质决定其提供给创作人的创作空间相对狭窄。杨修清未指出其黑白底图的独创性。并且，根据《作品自愿登记试行办法》第二条的规定，作品实行自愿登记，著作权登记机关对登记的著作权实行形式审查，杨修清主张涉案地图上标注的作品登记号与其图形作品著作权登记号相同，其对涉案地图享有著作权的理由不能成立。(2) 杨修清收集、提供的单位名称和公交线路不能体现涉案地图作品的独创性。涉案地图上标注的单位名称，系杨修清受武汉大学出版社有限公司的委托，进行的涉案地图广告认刊征集工作。杨修清按照合同约定履行义务，不能体现其创作地图作品的独创性。涉案地图上标注的公交线路，几乎涵盖了湖北省襄阳市主要的公交车线路。公交车线路属于公共资源领域的公知信息，亦不能体现杨修清创作地图作品的独创性。(3) 涉案地图由中工武大设计研究有限公司编制完成，杨修清收集和提供现实资料的行为属于辅助绘制地图的工作，不能视为著作权的创作行为。中工武大设计研究有限公司结合杨修清提供的素材和采编资料，通过特殊的绘地图设备、设施和科技力量，由其工作人员使用计算机将上述内容绘制成图，由杨修清核对上述资料有无遗漏或者错误等问题，最终绘制成涉案地图。根据《中华人民共和国著作权法实施条例》第三条的规定，杨修清提供部分素材、核对有无错漏等行为，系编制涉案地图过程中的辅助行为，不能视为著作权的创作行为。(4) 从涉案地图作品上的署名可以确认杨修清不对涉案地图作品享有著作权。涉案地图版权信息显示：编制为中工武大设计研究有限公司，出版发行为武汉大学出版社有限公司，策划设计、编辑为杨修清。根据《中华人民共和国著作权法》第十一条和《最高人民法院关于审理著作权民事纠纷案件适用法律若干问题的解释》第七条的规定，涉案地图上署名为编制单位的是地图作品的作者，而杨修清的署名为策划设计和编辑。杨修清以在涉案地图的审核图上签字的方式，对该署名情况表示认可。并且，涉案地图的编绘单位和制报单位均是中工武大设计研究有限公司。我国对从事测绘活动的单位实行测绘资质管理制度，且编绘、制印、出版地图有相应的申报、审批程序。杨修清不具备国家确认的测绘资质，也无法作为编绘单位、制报单位、编制单位或者送审单位履行地图的申报登记、送审等手续。据此，二审判决：驳回上诉，维持原判。

杨修清不服二审判决，向最高人民法院申请再审。2016年6月28日，最高人民法院做出（2016）最高法民申1226号民事裁定：驳回杨修清的再审申请。

【点　评】 本案系类型新颖的地图著作权确权纠纷。随着城市道路路网及建筑等地理信息不断更新变化，市面上出版发行着各式各样五花八门的地图。一方面，为社会公众出行提供方便、准确、快捷的地理位置向导；另一方面，地图著作权权属的确定，目前缺乏明确的法条指引和规定，司法实践中容易引发争议。本案中，涉案地图上署名的编制单位是中工武大设计研究有限公司，策划设计、编辑是杨修清，中工武大设计研究有限公司与杨修清之间不存在劳务隶属关系，杨修清依据其进行了著作权登记的黑白底图主张涉案地图的著作权。在此情况下，涉案地图著作权的归属应从以下两个方面进行考量。

(1) 划分城市道路、交通线路的公知信息与作品独创性之间的界限是审理本案的基础。地图作品应在整体构图、客观地理要素的选择和表现形式上体现独创性。公知地理信息的简单组合，不具有独创性，不构成著作权法意义上的地图作品。本案中，杨修清的黑白底图未注明地理标识、地理建筑名称、旅游景点等信息，与涉案地图相比对，两者仅在路网分布及地理环境上存在相同，而这些相同点均属于公知信息。黑白底图参考在先公开地图的地理信息并结合现有路网及建筑的地理变化进行绘制，不具有独创性。

（2）区分作者的创作行为与其他人员的辅助行为是审理本案的难点。《中华人民共和国著作权法实施条例》第三条规定："为他人创作进行组织工作，提供咨询意见、物质条件，或者进行其他辅助工作，均不视为创作。"涉案地图的编辑杨修清依据协议，为制作涉案地图收集和提供现实资料，以及核对资料有无遗漏或者错误的行为，属于辅助绘制地图的工作，不能视为创作行为。且根据涉案地图上的署名，编制单位为中工武大设计研究有限公司，出版发行为武汉大学出版社，策划设计、编辑为杨修清，可以确定涉案地图的编制单位是地图作品的作者。本案判决后，杨修清向最高人民法院申请再审，最高人民法院裁定：驳回杨修清的再审申请。本案的裁判结果得到最高人民法院的肯定，对处理类似案件具有一定的规范引导作用。

三、"好字行天下"作品著作权权属纠纷案

【简要案情】 晏秋风和潘超原系夫妻，两人共同出资设立了基石公司，法人代表晏秋风担任执行董事、总经理，潘超担任监事。基石公司自成立以来只经营"好字行天下"这一套书，公司所有的利润和开支均出自这套书。"好字行天下"系列丛书是根据义务教育阶段人教版、北师版、苏教版、语文出版社以及鄂教版的语文教材配套编写的、供学生练字用的教辅材料，涉案作品的数量多达 70 余本。自 2010 年 6 月首次出版以来，"好字行天下"系列丛书根据配套教材的修订而同步进行了修订。基石公司内设编辑部和市场部分别负责该丛书的编写和营销工作：市场部负责市场调研，根据经销商反馈的情况了解老师和学生的需求，并反馈给编辑部；编辑部负责该作品的具体编写工作，编辑人员有王应有、刘思伟等人，他们在编写过程中要听从晏秋风的安排和指导，编写内容最后要经过晏秋风的审定。"好字行天下"系列作品是在张胜华书写的字库基础上创作的，基石公司出资向张胜华购买了字库使用权。晏秋风编辑"好字行天下"作品并未单独领取过稿酬，而是与其他股东潘超一样领取工资和股东分红。"好字行天下"丛书的封面载明："主编：晏秋风　书写：张胜华　策划：基石文化"；早期版本的封面上还有"《书法报硬笔书法》编辑部组编"的字样，但《书法报硬笔书法》编辑部并未实际参与编写工作，这样表述只是为了商业宣传。晏秋风在本案诉讼前已经提起了解散基石公司的诉讼，潘超主张涉案作品著作权应归于基石公司而提起本案诉讼。

湖北省武汉东湖新技术开发区人民法院经审理认为，潘超作为基石公司的股东和监事，在其认为基石公司的著作权受到晏秋风的侵害时，为维护基石公司的利益，有权提起诉讼。涉案作品"好字行天下"字帖是一套多达 70 余本的系列丛书，是基石公司向张胜华购买字库使用权后，由晏秋风和基石公司的工作人员根据不同版本语文教材的生字顺序编排并选配相应的字格、插图及短文等形成的汇编作品。涉案作品的署名方式是"主编：晏秋风　书写：张胜华　策划：基石文化"，早期版本上还载有"《书法报硬笔书法》编辑部组编"，可见涉案作品的署名方式并不明确，特别是早期版本上"《书法报硬笔书法》编辑部组编"的署名仅仅是为了商业宣传并不实际反映创作情况，因此，涉案作品的署名方式有一定的随意性，对该作品的著作权归属应结合客观的创作证据来进行判断。潘超与晏秋风共同出资设立了基石公司，且设立公司的目的就是汇编字帖"好字行天下"并将该字帖作为出版、经营的唯一商品从事营利活动；晏秋风作为基石公司的股东和法定代表人，其主导并组织基石公司工作人员汇编"好字行天下"字帖丛书的行为是一种职务行为，体现了基石公司的意志，而不是个人从事创作的行为；"好字行天下"系列作品是在张胜华书写的字库基础上创作的，基石公司与张胜华签订作品许可使用合同获得汇编其字库的权利，是基石公司承担作品责任的体现，否则，将晏秋风个人视为"好字行天下"丛书的作者，其未获授权汇编他人作品将构成侵犯他人权利行为。综上，涉案作品符合"由法人组织支持，代表法人意志创作，并由法人承担责任"的要件，应认定为法人作品，基石公司视为作者，是涉案作品的著作权人。依照《中华人民共和国著作权法》第十一条、《中华人民共和国公司法》第一百五十一条、《中华人民共和国民事诉讼法》第一百四十二条的规定，判决：

"好字行天下"系列作品著作权属于第三人武汉基石文化传播有限公司。案件受理费人民币 500 元，由被告晏秋风负担。

【点　评】 （1）本案准确认定了涉案作品的性质及权利归属，厘清了法人作品、职务作品与个

人作品的区别，充分契合了新的修法精神。涉案“好字行天下”系列丛书是基石公司自成立以来出版、经营的唯一商品，是按照基石公司的经营策略，由基石公司提供编写人员、字库及其他相应物质条件完成的。整个编写进程受基石公司控制，并由基石公司承担法律责任。晏秋风虽为公司法定代表人，且署名为主编，但其并未单独领取报酬，故涉案作品不能认定为体现个人意志的个人作品，也不能认定为体现创作者意志且仅由单位提供物质技术条件的职务作品，而应认定为完全体现法人意志的法人作品，著作权归属法人。《中华人民共和国著作权法（修订草案送审稿）》第十五条规定，由法人或者其他组织主持或投资，代表法人或者其他组织意志创作，以法人、其他组织或者其他代表人名义发表，并由法人或者其他组织承担责任的作品，法人或者其他组织视为作者。本案对于涉案作品著作权权属的最终认定，契合了上述著作权法的修法精神。

（2）本案通过适用股东代表诉讼制度，充分维护了基石公司的合法权益。原告潘超作为公司股东，在公司利益可能受到法定代表人晏秋风侵害且公司处于晏秋风实际控制，无法行使诉讼权的情况下，以股东身份提起诉讼，保护了公司的合法权益。

（3）本案程序问题与实体问题交织，知识产权专门法与其他部门法融合，对知识产权法官综合运用法律的能力是一个考验与挑战。本案不仅涉及作品性质及权属的认定等实体问题，还涉及股东代表诉讼等程序性问题，不仅需要运用著作权法，还需要运用公司法，对知识产权法官提出了很高的要求。本案的公正判决充分体现了知识产权法官对各部门法综合运用驾轻就熟的裁判能力。

湖　南

柳子敬诉湖南潇湘数字电视有限公司、益阳市春桃花鼓戏剧团、益阳国安广播电视宽带网络有限责任公司侵害著作权纠纷案

【简要案情】　柳子敬系新编古代剧《羊皮换宰相》的作者。涉案作品《羊皮宰相》系南县实验花鼓剧团（春桃剧团的前身）、湖南文化音像出版社侵犯柳子敬《羊皮换宰相》著作权的侵权作品。潇湘公司通过网络设备对接国安公司，并输送《羊皮宰相》在益阳电视台地方戏曲频道播放。柳子敬认为该行为侵犯了其著作权，遂诉至法院，请求判令赔偿损失、赔礼道歉、消除影响，涉案作品署其名后在益阳电视台连播三天。

益阳市中级人民法院认为，涉案作品《羊皮宰相》已由在先判决确认，系侵犯柳子敬著作权的作品，人民法院已判决停止该剧出版、发行、销售，湖南文化音像出版社也依照生效判决赔偿了柳子敬损失，并登报致歉。潇湘公司应当尽到注意审查义务，不能以来源作品载有“本剧原作者不明”作为其不承担责任的抗辩。且从国安公司、潇湘公司合作协议内容来看，双方均对涉案作品有审核义务。由于双方均未尽到相应的审核义务，导致涉案作品在益阳电视台播放，侵犯了柳子敬的著作权，应共同承担侵权责任。

【点　评】　本案是一起未经权利人许可，未支付报酬的网络著作权侵权纠纷案件。潇湘公司、国安公司通过信息网络按照事先安排的时间表向公众提供作品，不允许用户选定时间，且系有线方式进行在线播放，属于单向的、点对多的作品传播方式，与点对点、交互式的信息网络传播行为有一定区别，所采用的传输信号和技术手段与广播权的外延也不相同，超出了传统广播权涵盖的范围。在《著作权法》未对此类行为的性质予以明确的情况下，法院根据《著作权法》中“应当由著作权人享有的其他权利”的兜底条款来调整，既保护了著作权人的合法权益，又对促进网络服务者树立著作权意识，改进经营模式和版权审查程序，有一定的现实意义。宣判后，当事人自觉履行了一审判决。

广　东

袁某等侵犯著作权罪纠纷案

【简要案情】　袁某等八名被告人共同设立公司，开发出《微邻友》《微邻友无验证》等计算机软件，未经腾讯公司许可，将其软件连同《微信》软件一起集合成刷机包制作刷机软件，安装、制作“搜粉智能广告机”，共销售“搜粉智能广告机”2 076台，该广告机可对任意地理位置为中心的周边微信号实现自动检测和发送消息，《微邻友无验证》可对任意地理位置为中心的周边微信号实现自动查看微信用户的详细信息，其中《微邻友》必须结合微信才能正常使用。“微系列”软件具有实现对微信软件进行自动化批量操作功能。

法院认为，被告人以营利为目的，未经著作权人许可，复制发行腾讯微信软件以销售其“搜粉智能广告机”，数量达2 076台，属情节严重，均构成侵犯著作权罪，八被告人分别被判处有期徒刑，袁

某等四被告人均各并处罚金人民币 100 万元。

【点　评】 本案被告人未经著作权人许可，复制微信软件，生产“搜粉智能广告机”，利用微信软件的定位、群发、添加好友等功能，自动添加一定范围内的微信用户好友并推送广告信息，侵害了腾讯公司的合法权益，并给广大微信用户带来侵扰，情节严重，构成侵犯著作权罪。

广　西

网络主播他人作品侵犯著作权案

【简要案情】 原告陈某系涉案作品网络小说《麻衣神相》的作者，被告薛某在“企鹅FM”网络平台向公众提供其主播的有声读物《麻衣神相》，薛某主播的有声读物与陈某享有著作权的作品内容一致，陈某认为薛某在未取得自己许可或授权的情况下，通过网络平台向公众提供涉案作品的有声读物，已构成对陈某所享有的信息网络传播权的侵害，起诉要求薛某停止侵权并赔偿损失。法院认为，尽管不能证明薛某主播他人作品存在主观恶意，也未对作品的内容进行变更、篡改，但由于薛某未经作者同意在网络平台上提供他人作品的有声读物，已构成侵犯作者的作品信息网络传播权，故应承担侵权责任。判决薛某停止侵权并赔偿损失。

【点　评】 近年来，一些播音爱好者通过网络平台提供其主播的有声读物，颇为流行。但通过网络平台向公众提供有声读物应当取得该作品著作权人的许可或授权，否则将构成对原著作权人作品信息网络传播权的侵害，承担相应的民事责任。

海　南

北京三面向版权代理有限公司诉中国（海南）改革发展研究院著作权侵权案

【简要案情】 卢福营所著的《村级治理下的村民公共参与》收录入由中国农业出版社于 2006 年 3 月出版的《中国“三农”问题研究学者文库》中。北京三面向版权代理有限公司（以下简称三面向公司）主张通过与作者卢福营签订了《委托汇编与版权转让合同书》（以下简称《合同书》）获得卢福营转让的该作品的著作权。三面向公司向法院提交了北京市海淀第二公证处 2005 年 11 月 18 日出具的（2005）京海民证字第 6100 号公证书，该公证书证明 2005 年 3 月 18 日“卢福营”与三面向公司签订的《委托汇编与版权转让合同书》的复印件与原件内容相符。《合同书》上甲方有“卢福营”的签字，下方注明的附件有：甲方（“卢福营”）身份证复印件及乙方企业法人营业执照副本复印件。《合同书》主要约定：甲方（即“卢福营”）委托乙方（即三面向公司）汇编的上述作品及汇编作品中包含的每篇文章，除署名权和本合同约定的转让金外，在合同期内版权归乙方所有；乙方在行使版权时如发现有第三方侵犯作品署名权的，由乙方直接代为主张权利；本合同自双方签字、乙方盖章之日起生效，本合同版权转让期为 10 年。

三面向公司发现，中国（海南）改革发展研究院（以下简称海南改发院）未经许可亦未支付报酬，在其网站 chinareform. org. cn 通过互联网传播三面向公司享有著作权的《村级治理下的村民公共参与》一文。海南改发院的行为已侵犯了三面向公司依法享有的著作权利。为维护自己的合法权益，三面向公司的法定代表人詹启智于 2015 年 1 月 21 日到北京市方圆公证处对海南改发院的侵权行为进行了证据保全。北京市方圆公证处出具的（2015）京方圆内经证字第 21599 号公证书及录像文件中，记录有海南改发院网站使用涉案文章的事实，海南改发院对使用涉案文章的事实亦予认可。

三面向公司以海南改发院的行为侵犯了其依法享有的著作权为由，向海南省海口市中级人民法院起诉，请求：（1）判令海南改发院赔偿三面向公司稿酬损失、合理费用合计 12 336 元；（2）诉讼费用由海南改发院承担。

海口市中级人民法院认为：根据著作权法的规定，如无相反证明，在作品上署名的公民、法人或其他组织即为作者。三面向公司提交的《村级治理下的村民公共参与》作品的署名作者为“卢福营”，据此确认《村级治理下的村民公共参与》一文的作者是卢福营。三面向公司认为其受让取得涉案文章的著作权，其提供的证据中，《委托汇编与版权转让合同书》是证明三面向公司享有涉案作品著作权并据以主张权利的主要证据，根据谁主张谁举证的原则，在海南改发院对“卢福营”的签字的真实性提出异议以及《合同书》约定的版权转让期限已届满的情况下，三面向公司对其拥有涉案作品的著作权应当负有排除任何逻辑上合理怀疑的举证责任。然而，本案《合同书》中，双方当事人约定的 10 年版权转让期于 2015 年 3 月 18 日届满，三面向公司于 2016 年 7 月 28 日提起本案诉讼，在三面向公司未提供证据证明三面向公司与卢福营续签版权转让合同的情况下，三面向公司已无权以自己的名义主张侵权，对此三面向公司应承担举证不能的法律后果。故三面向公司在没有证据证明其对涉案作品的著作权享有合法权益的情况下主张海南改发院承担侵权责任没有事实与法律依据，由此驳回北京三面向版权代理有限公司的诉讼请求。

云　南

云南绿A生物工程有限公司与昆明迈多生物科技开发有限公司侵害著作权及不正当竞争纠纷案

【简要案情】　2015年7月16日，云南绿A生物工程公司（以下简称绿A公司）发现昆明迈多生物科技开发有限公司（以下简称迈多公司）在其官网和天猫旗舰店上使用绿A公司自有天然螺旋藻原料基地图片，并标注宣称“天然螺旋藻养殖基地”“迈多螺旋藻生产基地”。而事实上迈多公司在程海湖范围内并无自有螺旋藻天然养殖基地。

2016年7月6日，云南省高级人民法院就绿A公司状告迈多公司侵害绿A著作权及不正当竞争纠纷一案做出终审判决，判决迈多公司构成侵权、不正当竞争、虚假宣传，合计赔偿各种损失共计11 000元。

新　疆

一、非法复制、汇编、发行《讲学稿》侵犯著作权案

【简要案情】　2016年4月6日，塔城地区文化市场稽查支队、沙湾县文化市场综合执法大队根据举报，对沙湾县某中学未经著作权人许可非法复制、汇编、发行《讲学稿》一案进行查处。经调查查明，自2015年3月起，沙湾县某中学组织教师从问他网、菁优网、道客巴巴、COOCO网以及精英家教网等网站下载复制由上述网站汇编的试题资料，并汇编成《讲学稿》，通过校内文印室和沙湾县某快印中心复制、发行高一高二学科地理、化学、历史等科目《讲学稿》2 480册，相关印刷费用含在教材费里向学生收取。文化市场管理部门依法做出罚款20万元的行政处罚，收缴并销毁全部《讲学稿》。

二、沈某与张某著作权权属、侵权纠纷案

【简要案情】　2015年11月26日，原告沈某发现被告张某在其经营的店铺内出售的轴承产品的外包装上使用了其俄文文字图片作品作为标识，故以被告侵犯其著作权为由诉至法院。乌鲁木齐市中级人民法院经审理查明，本案所涉作品是由俄文字母上下排列而成，并略做变形处理；且原告表示该作品是他依照国外相关品牌“伏尔加标准”的俄文文字及原图通过电脑复制而成。法院认为，本案被控侵权作品并非原告独创，不能从该图形上看到原告本人的创作思想及独特个性，缺乏我国著作权法意义上作品“独创性”的前提条件，且该“作品”不具备美术作品应具备的创作高度及艺术美感，其虽经著作权登记机构的登记，但该登记并不采用实质审查的方式。遂判决：驳回原告沈某的诉讼请求。

三、刘某销售盗版音像制品侵犯著作权案

【简要案情】　2016年6月13日，根据举报线索，喀什市文化市场稽查大队在喀什市西二环路长安郡巷内喀什市百世泉酒坊查获非法音像制品共计5 122张，其中盗版音像制品5 100张、涉嫌淫秽色情音像制品22张；7月，将案件移交喀什市公安局经侦大队。2016年10月3日，喀什市文化市场稽查大队协助市公安局在百世泉酒坊再次依法查处涉嫌盗版音像制品193张。2016年12月13日，喀什市人民法院依法判处喀什市百世泉酒坊负责人刘某有期徒刑2年4个月，并处罚金。

2016年地方著作权行政执法案件

河　北　省

一、张某某侵犯著作权案

2015年1月14日，石家庄市“扫黄”办根据省“扫黄”办移交的案件线索，联合市版权局、市文化市场行政执法大队等单位，对居住在正定县曹村的张某某家进行了检查，当场查获其未经著作权人许可擅自印刷的《习近平谈治国理政》等图书4 890册。由于案情重大，遂将该案移送公安部门处理。

2015年1月14日，张某某因涉嫌犯侵犯著作权罪被公安局刑事拘留，同年2月16日被逮捕。2015年11月30日，正定县人民法院对被告人张某某以犯侵犯著作权罪进行了一审判决，被告人不服判决，上诉至石家庄市中级人民法院。2016年4月8日，石家庄市中级人民法院根据《中华人民共和国刑法》第二百一十七条、第二百六十七条之规定做出终审判决，判决张某某犯侵犯著作权罪，判处有期徒刑3年，并处罚金5万元。

二、霍某某侵犯著作权案

2016年6月16日，保定市文化市场行政执法大队根据举报线索，对位于清苑区田各庄村实惠加油站对面的库房进行检查。经查，库房内存有陕西人民教育出版社出版的“小学教材全解”系列丛书8种共计81 000册，山东省地图出版社出版的“北斗地图”系列丛书5种共计17 822册，库房承包人霍某某承认所查获图书是从河南新乡李某某处进货，准备对外销售。后经河北省印刷产品质量监督检验站鉴定，涉案“小学教材全解”系列丛书8种、“北斗地图”系列丛书5种图书共计98 822册均为非法出版物，非法经营数额共计2 718 699.6元。

2016年12月28日，保定市莲池区人民法院依据《中华人民共和国刑法》第二百一十八条等规定对霍某某做出刑事判决，判决被告人霍某某犯销售侵权复制品罪，判处有期徒刑1年，并处罚金人民币20万元。

三、王某某等人侵犯著作权案

2015年5月，衡水市公安局开发区分局接群众举报，称衡水市桃城区某小区住户以营利为目的大量贩卖盗版光盘。根据举报人提供的信息，在网安大队的配合下，办案民警立即落地查人，迅速锁定犯罪嫌疑人王某某、霍某某。经查，犯罪嫌疑人王某某未经正常渠道，大量购进盗版CD光盘和DVD光盘，并将其中部分批发给霍某某和张某某，涉案光盘均被公安机关扣押。后经河北省印刷产品质量监督检验站鉴定，王某某被扣押的光盘中4 444张为非法出版物，霍某某被扣押的光盘中726张为非法出版物，张某某被扣押的光盘中361张为非法出版物。

2016年2月25日，衡水市桃城区人民法院依据《中华人民共和国刑法》第二百一十七条，第二十七条，第七十二条第一、第三款，第七十三条第二、第三款，第六十四条和《最高人民法院、最高人民检察院关于办理侵犯知识产权刑事案件具体应用法律若干问题的解释（二）》第一、第四条，《最高人民法院关于适用〈中华人民共和国刑事诉讼法〉的解释》第三百六十五条的规定，判决王某某犯侵犯著作权罪，判处有期徒刑1年6个月，缓刑2年，并处罚金人民币8 000元；霍某某犯侵犯著作权罪，判处罚金1 800元；扣押在案的被告人王某某的光盘4 444张、被告人霍某某的光盘726张、张某某的光盘361张，均予以没收。

四、赵某某等侵犯著作权案

2015年8月21日，衡水市桃城区何庄派出所民警在巡逻中发现，有三名男子骑三轮车销售光盘，涉嫌盗版。民警随后对三人进行跟踪调查，并在桃城区康复街技术学院家属楼发现其藏匿地点。民警迅速对该窝点进行了搜查，当场抓获赵某某、孔某某等多名嫌疑人，并查获制作盗版光盘的电脑、刻录机、打印机各一台，运输工具三轮车一辆，以及已完成刻录但未卖出的盗版光盘5 148张，空光盘2 641张。

经查，赵某某、孔某某等五人未经著作权人许可，从网络上下载歌曲，使用电脑、刻录机、空光盘等工具刻录盗版光盘进行销售，其行为已构成侵犯著作权罪。2016年4月6日，衡水市桃城区人民法院依照《中华人民共和国刑法》第二百一十七条，第二十五条第一款，第二十六条第一、第四款，第二十七条，第七十二条第一、第三款，第七十三条第二、第三款，第六十四条和《最高人民法院、最高人民检察院关于办理侵犯知识产权刑事案件具体应用法律若干问题的解释（二）》第一、第二、第

三、第四条，《最高人民法院关于适用〈中华人民共和国刑事诉讼法〉的解释》第三百六十五条的规定，判决赵某某犯侵犯著作权罪，判处有期徒刑3年，缓刑3年，并处罚金人民币7 000元；孔某某犯侵犯著作权罪，判处有期徒刑1年，缓刑1年，并处罚金人民币4 000元；辛某某犯侵犯著作权罪，判处有期徒刑10个月，缓刑1年，并处罚金人民币3 000元；季某某犯侵犯著作权罪，判处有期徒刑10个月，缓刑1年，并处罚金人民币3 000元；姜某某犯侵犯著作权罪，判处罚金人民币2 000元。

五、衡水运输集团有限公司汽车驾驶员培训学校侵犯著作权案

2016年4月5日，衡水市文化市场行政执法人员在依法对衡水运输集团有限公司汽车驾驶员培训学校进行检查时，发现该单位使用的教材《出租汽车服务规范》无书号，与人民交通出版社出版的《出租汽车服务规范图册》（ISBN 978-7-114-11236-2）内容完全一致，只是更换了封皮。经调查，涉案教材共计500册，系该驾校擅自找人印刷，未经权利人许可，属于盗版出版物。经了解，该驾校未向学员收取涉案教材的费用，因此没有非法所得，且该单位已按要求全部收回已发的《出租汽车服务规范》。该驾校的行为违反了《中华人民共和国著作权法》第十条第一款第（六）项、第三十一条的规定。

2016年4月28日，衡水市文化广电新闻出版局依据《中华人民共和国著作权法》第四十八条第一款第（一）项、《中华人民共和国著作权法实施条例》第三十六条之规定，对衡水运输集团有限公司汽车驾驶员培训学校做出如下处罚：（1）没收盗版图书500册；（2）行政罚款人民币5 000元整。

（河北省版权局）

辽 宁 省

华娱嘉恒（大连）传媒有限公司网络音乐作品侵权案

2016年7月中旬，大连市文化市场综合执法总队根据举报线索，在网络巡查中，发现域名为http://www.mvpdj.com的MVPDJ音乐网存在未经批准，擅自从事经营性互联网文化活动和通过信息网络擅自向公众提供他人作品，损害公共利益的行为，其行为涉嫌违反了《信息网络传播权保护条例》第二条之规定。2016年8月2日，经大连市文化市场综合执法总队批准立案调查。

执法人员通过工业和信息化部网站进行备案信息查询，显示该网站主办单位为华娱嘉恒（大连）传媒有限公司，经进一步远程勘验证实，该公司在未取得网络文化经营许可证的情况下，从2010年9月开始，陆续将音乐娱乐复制到其公司经营的MVPDJ网上，供网友在线收听，同时还提供会员付费下载，网站上有音乐作品近30万首。在案件调查过程中，发现该公司已办理了网络文化经营许可证。为确保证据事实有效，执法人员还在线收听并下载了其中的11首音乐作品，与华娱嘉恒（大连）传媒有限公司法定代表人宋某某当面确认，当事人均予以承认。

鉴于当事人态度端正并积极配合执法人员调查取证，并及时将未授权作品删除等情节，2016年9月18日，大连市文化市场综合执法总队根据《信息网络传播权保护条例》第十八条、《大连市文化广播影视局行政处罚自由裁量权指导标准》的基准规定以及《行政处罚法》第五条，给予华娱嘉恒（大连）传媒有限公司罚款人民币15 000元的行政处罚。

（辽宁省版权局）

吉 林 省

一、《智慧白山》手机APP客户端侵犯著作权案

2015年11月，吉林省版权局检查中发现，中国移动通信集团吉林有限公司白山分公司运营管理的《智慧白山》手机APP客户端设置了国广在线栏目链接，通过链接网络资源在线播放国内众多电视台节目及热播影视剧，其中还涉及国家版权局公布的重点预警影视作品。因未经合法授权而设置链接并通过手机APP客户端网络传播他人享有专有网络传播权的影视作品，侵犯了他人享有的专有网络传播权。

2016年3月14日，吉林省版权局依据《中华人民共和国著作权法》第四十八条、《信息网络传播权保护条例》第十八条、《著作权法实施条例》第三十六条等有关规定，对中国移动通信集团吉林有限公司白山分公司做出罚款5 000元人民币的行政处罚，并责令停止侵权行为。

二、长春市阳光计算机职业培训学校未经著作权人许可发行其作品案

2016年10月11日，长春市文化市场综合执法支队执法人员对长春市阳光计算机职业培训学校进行检查，发现该校发行《国家教师资格考试（小学）》《国家教师资格考试（中学）》《财经法规与会计职业道德》等七类培训教材 440 册，上述培训教材未经相关出版单位合法授权，侵权事实成立。

2016 年 11 月 24 日，长春市文化广电新闻出版局依据《中华人民共和国著作权法》第四十八条和《著作权法实施条例》第三十六条等规定，对长春市阳光计算机职业培训学校做出没收侵权复制品、罚款 5 000 元人民币的行政处罚。

三、吉林省吉财印务侵犯著作权案

2016 年 9 月 2 日，长春市二道区文化市场综合执法大队执法人员在检查中发现，吉林省吉财印务涉嫌印刷盗版教辅图书。经进一步调查取证，该公司未经许可盗印《中学数理化解析》《高中思想政治综合学习手册》等教辅材料，数量共计 300 余册。经与相关权利人核实，该批教辅材料为未经著作权人许可擅自印刷复制的盗版教辅材料。

根据《中华人民共和国著作权法》第四十八条、《中华人民共和国著作权法实施条例》第三十六条的规定，长春市二道区文化体育局于 2016 年 9 月 24 日决定给予吉林省吉财印务以下行政处罚：(1) 没收盗版教辅材料 300 册；(2) 行政罚款人民币 10 000 元整。

四、白某复制发行盗版图书侵权案

2016 年 6 月 24 日上午，根据群众举报，吉林市文化市场综合执法支队依法对吉林市昌邑区博远教育信息咨询服务中心进行执法检查，发现该店经销的 2016 年版全国一级建造师执业资格考试用书《建设工程法规及相关知识》等 14 种图书涉嫌盗版。调查过程中，该书经著作权人中国建筑工业出版社核对，确定为侵犯其著作权的盗版出版物，当事人白某对此事实的认定未提出异议。

2016 年 7 月 15 日，执法机关依据《中华人民共和国著作权法》第四十八条、《中华人民共和国著作权法实施条例》第三十六条等相关规定，给予当事人没收侵权复制品、罚款人民币 5 000 元的行政处罚。

五、吉林市优学网络科技有限公司发行盗版图书案

2016 年 8 月 25 日下午，根据群众举报，吉林市文化广电新闻出版局执法人员依法对吉林市优学网络科技有限公司进行检查。经查，该公司对其经销的中国税务出版社出版的《税法 Ⅰ》等 5 种图书不能提供合法来源，疑似盗版。经与该图书著作权人中国税务出版社核实，认定均为侵犯其著作权的非法出版物，依法构成侵犯著作权行为，对该事实认定当事人未提出异议。

2016 年 9 月 12 日，执法机关依据《中华人民共和国著作权法》第四十八条、《中华人民共和国著作权法实施条例》第三十六条等相关规定，给予当事人没收侵权复制品、罚款人民币 10 000 元整的行政处罚。

六、敦化市范某等网络游戏侵权案

2016 年 4 月至 7 月，经群众举报，敦化市文化广电新闻出版局执法人员分别依法检查了范某等四人经营的网络游戏工作室，发现四个网络游戏工作室均存在设置服务器，未经授权通过网络游戏室的局域网络提供韩国版《地下城与勇士》游戏，构成侵犯著作权人权益的网络传播权行为。

敦化市文广新局依据《信息网络传播权保护条例》第十八条的规定，对范某等经营的四家网络游戏工作室分别做出没收提供网络服务的设备（服务器）、罚款的行政处罚。

七、敦化市远达驾校发行盗版教材案

2016 年 8 月 9 日，敦化市文化市场综合执法大队接到举报，称敦化市远达驾校涉嫌使用《机动车驾驶人考试题库》盗版教材。执法人员依法对远达驾校进行调查。经查，该驾校使用的《机动车驾驶人考试题库》教材有定价，但无出版社名称，教材内容错别字较多，印刷质量较差，无法说明合法来源，经认定属于未经许可擅自复制的盗版制品，违法事实清楚，且发行数量较大。

执法机关责令当事人立即停止销售，并依据《中华人民共和国著作权法》第四十八条、《中华人民共和国著作权法实施条例》第三十六条等有关规定，做出没收侵权复制品、罚款 10 000 元人民币的行政处罚。

八、翰墨书苑侵犯著作权案

2016 年 7 月 22 日，四平市文化市场综合执法支队的执法人员对位于四平市铁东区新开路的翰墨书苑进行了执法检查，检查中发现该书苑销售的《小学语文》（一年级下册、八年级上册、七年级上册）等教科书无法提供出版单位签发的《发行委托书》及进货凭证，执法机关遂立案进一步调查。经与该教材著作权人长春出版社核实，认定上述教材均为未经许可擅自复制的盗版制品。

2016 年 7 月 22 日，依据《中华人民共和国著作权法》第四十八条、《中华人民共和国著作权法实施条例》第三十六条等规定，执法机关对当事人做出没收侵权复制品、罚款人民币 10 000 元整的行政处罚。

九、辉南县爱尚网咖计算机软件侵权案

2016 年 7 月 1 日，辉南县文化市场综合执法大队在日常行政执法检查时发现，该县爱尚网咖未经著作权人许可擅自在服务器和客户端里非法下载、安装多个单机游戏，总计9款，该场所102台电脑均复制安装了9款单机游戏，经认定属于盗版软件。对此事实认定该网咖负责人李某未提出异议，侵权事实成立，依法应当承担侵权责任。

2016年7月27日，执法机关依据《计算机软件保护条例》第二十四条、《中华人民共和国著作权法实施条例》第三十六条等有关规定，给予辉南县爱尚网咖罚款50 000元的行政处罚，同时责令当事人删除盗版软件。

（吉林省版权局）

上　海　市

一、斗鱼电竞游戏转播著作权侵权及不正当竞争纠纷案

案件详情，参见本栏目“2016年全国著作权司法保护典型案件”之三（第298页）。

二、易查公司、于某侵犯著作权案

【案情介绍】 被告单位北京易查无限信息技术有限公司（以下简称易查公司）于2004年2月成立，系“易查网”经营者。该网站设有小说、新闻等多个频道，通过在网页植入广告，收取广告收益分成的方式营利。被告人于某系易查公司法定代表人，并负责公司技术工作。2012年，为提高“易查网”的用户数量，被告人于某提出开发触屏版小说产品，将html格式的小说网页转码成wap格式的网页供移动终端用户阅读。后易查公司在未经著作权人上海玄霆娱乐信息科技有限公司（以下简称玄霆公司）许可的情况下，使用自行开发的爬虫软件，擅自复制、下载玄霆公司在其经营的“起点中文网”上发行的《仙傲·雾外江山》等文字作品，利用转码技术存储在易查公司服务器内，供手机用户免费搜索、阅读，再通过网站植入广告获利。经鉴定，“易查网”服务器内存储的文字作品中有588部与“起点中文网”的同名小说存在实质性相似。2016年12月，浦东新区法院做出判决，被告单位易查公司犯侵犯著作权罪，判处罚金人民币2万元，被告人于某犯侵犯著作权罪，判处拘役3个月，缓刑3个月，并处罚金人民币5 000元。

【案件点评】 “易查网”小说频道在将涉案小说转码、提供给移动端用户阅读的过程中，不仅进行了格式转换，还在其服务器中存储了经过格式转换的内容，使得用户可以直接从网站服务器中获得小说，实质上构成了在未经权利人许可的情况下，以营利为目的复制发行他人作品的侵权行为。本案系上海办理的首例利用手机JAVA技术侵犯著作权的刑事案件，关于转码及相关临时性存储行为的性质认定为日后处理同类案件提供了重要的实践参考。

三、上海海关查处进出境人员携带盗版光盘进出境系列案

【案情介绍】 2016年，上海海关结合日常监管，加强对进出境盗版光盘的监管，查处违规携带盗版光盘进出境的系列案件共28起，查处盗版光盘2 106张，取得了显著的成效。典型案件如下：

2016年2月，上海海关现场业务二处关员通过X光机检，在某外籍人员携带进境的分运行李中发现类似光盘状物品，但该外籍人员并未将光盘列入申报清单。经过海关关员查验，查获200余张盗版光盘。2016年8月，上海海关隶属车站海关关员在对香港九龙始发至上海的列车查验中，发现某外籍旅客的行李包装袋可疑，经开袋检查，在其行李衣物内查获数十张盗版光盘。

2016年12月，上海海关现场业务三处关员在对停靠上海港的一外籍集装箱货轮登船检查时，在随船入境物品中查扣盗版光盘十余张。

上述案件只是系列案件的缩影。对于进出境人员携带盗版光盘进出境案件，海关办案人员在查清案件事实后，依法对相关盗版光盘进行收缴，切实保护了相关著作权人的合法权益。

【案件点评】 旅客及相关人员进境或出境时携带盗版光盘，造成了侵权物品在国际的流通，对著作权权利人造成影响。侵权盗版光盘的流通，有别于一般的侵权货物，具有单批次数量少、隐蔽性高的特点。因此，上海海关通过加强对盗版光盘的监管，查处了一系列的案件，具有较强的示范效应，在有效保护权利人合法权益的同时，净化了上海口岸，树立了海关作为进出境渠道知识产权保护者的良好形象。

四、上海屹丰汽车模具制造有限公司侵犯计算机软件著作权案

【案情介绍】 根据CATIA系列计算机软件著作权人达索系统股份有限公司的投诉，执法人员现场检查了屹丰汽车模具制造有限公司在上海市宝山工业园区罗宁路168号研究院，发现其结构设计科办公室21台工作使用的计算机中有13台计算机内复制、安装了CATIA软件。现场提取了安装有CATIA软件的计算机的具体信息，并进行拍照取证。调查中，经著作权人核实上述软件均属侵权软件，当事人至检查之日未停止使用。因该软件主要用于查看图纸，在汽车设计环节使用，无法查证经营额和违法所得，经综合确认本案总货值为852 410元人民币。当事人侵犯了《计算机软件保护条例》第八条第一款第（四）项规定的著作权人享有的权利，违反了正常的软件市场交易秩序，同时损害了社会公共利益，构成了未经软件著作权人许可复制著作权人的软件的行为。鉴于当事人曾购买过正版CATIA软件，具有《中华人民共和国行政处罚法》第二十七条第一款第（四）项减轻处罚情形，依法责令当事人停止侵权行为，并罚款人民币426 205元。

【案件点评】 本案当事人辩称复制、使用侵权软件是员工个人行为，试图规避处罚。执法人员查实了当事人在网络招聘中要求应聘者熟练使用该软件的信息，查实了当事人的经营范围与该软件用途的一致性，以及当事人曾经购买过正版软件的事实，用确凿的证据，依法认定复制安装侵权软件的违法行为是公司行为，具有示范性和典型性。同时，本案处罚力度大，对侵权行为起到了震慑作用，充分体现了上海在科技创新中心建设中保护软件知识产权、保护创新的力度，对提高企业知识产权保护意识，促进企业软件正版化具有警示作用。

五、“葫芦娃”“黑猫警长”美术作品著作权侵权纠纷案

案件详情，参见本栏目“部分省（区、市）公布的2016年度著作权典型案件”，上海市案件之三（第312页）。

六、私人影院侵害作品信息网络传播权纠纷案

【案情简介】 某视频网站经授权享有《杀破狼2》《十万个冷笑话》等影视作品在中国大陆地区的独家信息网络传播权。某公司在其经营的私人影院中，利用计算机点播终端系统通过局域网向消费者提供有偿的视频点播服务，其中包括上述影视作品且未经著作权人许可。某视频网站向法院起诉，认为某公司经营的私人影院侵害了某视频网站享有的信息网络传播权，请求法院判令某公司停止侵权，并赔偿经济损失。杨浦区法院经审理认为，某公司未经许可将涉案影片存储在服务器终端中，通过局域网和终端点播系统，使用户能在自行选定的时间内，通过信息网络对上述涉案影片进行播放，侵害了某视频网站享有的信息网络传播权。由于诉讼中某公司自动停止侵权，法院判决某公司赔偿某视频网站经济损失及合理费用合计3万元。一审判决后，当事人均未上诉。

【案件点评】 本案是全国首例对私人影院观影模式认定侵权的案例。法院裁判明确，无论传播范围是局域网或者是广域网，都会对作品的著作权产生实质性影响，未经授权通过私人影院播放影视作品侵犯了著作权法规定的作品信息网络传播权。

七、涉深度链接的信息网络传播权纠纷案

【案情介绍】 北京某公司经独家授权获得《快乐大本营》等综艺节目的信息网络传播权。上海某公司系A网站的经营者。北京某公司发现A网站上提供了《快乐大本营》的视频点播，该视频系由A网站的注册用户将B网站上的视频投稿到A网站，具体过程为：A网站根据用户提供的视频所在播放页面的网络地址提取视频在其他网站（比如B网站）的代码后向B网站服务器发送请求，提取视频文件数据在A网站的播放器中进行播放。而北京某公司亦未授权B网站播放上述视频。故北京某公司起诉至法院，认为上海某公司侵害了其享有的信息网络传播权，应当停止侵权、赔偿损失。

浦东新区人民法院认为，上海某公司虽然未直接上传涉案作品视频到其服务器，但其对链接服务实施了人工干预，用户通过A网站可以不经由被链网站的界面直接观看该视频，被链网站存储该视频的服务器在此阶段已形同上海某公司所控制的远程服务器，且为其免费使用，A网站已经在实质上替代了被链网站向公众传播作品，使公众具有了可以在个人选定的时间或地点获得涉案作品的可能性，故应当认定上海某公司构成作品提供行为，侵害了北京某公司的信息网络传播权。因此，判令上海某公司赔偿北京某公司经济损失3 000元及合理费用2 500元。一审判决后，原、被告均不服，提起上诉。上海知识产权法院经审理认为，涉案节目实际上来源于B网站且其传播受控于B网站，上海某公司通过技术手段为涉案节目的传播提供搜索、链接服务，并未将作品置于网络中，不构成作品提供行为。但鉴于涉案节目的知名度及播放时间，上海某公司应当负有对其授权情况较高的注意义务，其主观上应当知道涉案节目具有较大侵权可能性，客观上帮助了涉案节目侵权后果的扩大，故其行为侵犯了北京某公司的信息网络传播权，应承担赔偿责任。因此，二审判决驳回上诉，维持原判。

【案件点评】 网络服务提供商通过技术手段，为作品的传播提供搜索、链接服务，且未进行网页跳转以指引用户在被链网站上观看，亦未向用户提示该作品源自其他网站，其行为本身并不构成作品提供行为，故不承担直接侵权责任。如果该链接服务商主观上明知或者应知所链接的作品侵权，客观上对于未经授权的涉案节目未采取任何预防或者避免侵权发生的措施，从而帮助了涉案节目侵权后果的扩大，构成帮助侵权，应承担赔偿责任。本案厘清了提供深度链接的网络服务提供者的侵权责任，既鼓励了网络技术发展又保护了知识产权。

八、上海驰游信息技术有限公司被非法获取计算机信息系统数据案

【案情介绍】 2016年3月，徐汇分局接到上海驰游信息技术有限公司（以下简称驰游公司）报案称，一家网站未经该公司授权，私自开设《少年三国志》网游服务器，大肆招揽玩家，导致该公司遭受巨额经济损失。徐汇分局立案侦查后，经辗转江苏、河南等地，成功抓获犯罪嫌疑人陈某、王某。经查，犯罪嫌疑人陈某、王某等人未经著作权人许可，非法从驰游公司内部人员处购买《少年三国志》网游源代码，绑定域名私自架设游戏服务器端，并在互联网上发布该游戏，大肆招揽社会玩家，该游戏私服最多时容纳1 000余名玩家同时在线游戏。陈、王二人通过游戏玩家充值账户的方式，非法获利11.8万元。2016年12月，徐汇区人民法院依法判处被告人陈某有期徒刑1年，缓刑1年，并处罚金2万元；判处被告人王某有期徒刑9个月，并处罚金人民币1万元。

【案件点评】 本案涉及侵犯著作权罪与入侵计算机信息系统罪，社会危害大；作案人员分散、作案手法隐蔽，侦办难度大。该案的成功告破，为受害公司挽回经济损失近1 000万元，有力震慑了此类犯罪，充分体现了上海公安机关打击侵权盗版犯罪的决心和能力，为保护创新企业发展、净化版权市场提供了坚实保障。

九、授权合同侵犯共有权利诉前停止侵害著作权纠纷案

【案情简介】 A公司与W公司均为韩国公司，共同拥有Mir2游戏软件的著作权，该游戏在中国大陆已运营15年。W公司于2016年6月28日与K公司签订了涉案软件的移动游戏和网页游戏授权许可合同，合同金额300亿韩元。合同签订后，K公司就此合同进行了网上公告，W公司也以书面形式通知了A公司。A公司向法院申请诉前禁令称：W公司未与其协商擅自行使不可分割的共有著作权，违反中国著作权法规定，为防止授权行为对A公司合法权益及目前该游戏的运营秩序造成不可挽回的损失，请求法院禁止W公司和K公司履行该合同。

上海知识产权法院经审查认为，A公司系涉案软件共有著作权人，W公司若未经协商对外授权，涉嫌侵害A公司的权利。鉴于合同签订后涉案软件可能投入商业运营，不及时制止将会对共有著作权人造成难以弥补的损害，法院遂裁定W公司和K公司立即停止履行该合同。法院裁定后，W公司和K公司提出复议申请，认为W公司可单独授权，A公司没有正当理由反对W公司单独对外授权，也不可能遭受不可弥补的损害；K公司已向社会公告合同事宜，如果停止合同履行将波及其股价而损害社会公共利益。上海知识产权法院复议认为：W公司不能证明其有单独对外授权的权利。涉案合同的履行必然会对共有著作权人产生实际损害后果，及时禁止合同的履行有利于合同当事人及时止损；维持公司形象不应建立在可能侵害他人权利的基础之上，因此行为保全会影响股价而侵害公共利益的观点难谓合理合法。故裁定驳回复议请求。

【案件点评】 共有权利应共同行使或协商一致后行使。未经协商擅自对外授权，所签合同可能因侵犯共有权利而无效。其他共有权利人申请禁止该合同履行，符合诉前行为保全要求的情况紧急和及时止损的法定条件。本案对侵害共有著作权权利的行为保全案件的处理具有参考价值。

十、何某侵犯著作权案

【案情介绍】 被告人何某设立“车城小说”网站（域名：checheng123.com），其通过租赁海外服务器并运行其从互联网上下载的《关关采集》抓取软件，在未获被害单位上海玄霆娱乐信息科技有限公司（以下简称玄霆公司）许可的情况下，擅自抓取复制玄霆公司具有独家信息网络传播权并发行于互联网站上的文字作品600余部，存储于自己的服务器上，供“车城小说”网站用户免费阅读。被告人何某通过在“车城小说”网站网页内刊登广告，获取广告收益，非法营利数额达19万余元。经盘石软件（上海）有限公司计算机司法鉴定所司法鉴定，被告人在“车城小说”网站上传播的涉案600余部文字作品与玄霆公司发行于“起点中文网”的同名文字作品相似度均达到90%以上。人民法院根据《中华人民共和国刑法》第二百一十七条第一款第（一）项等规定，判决被告人何某犯侵犯著作权罪，判处有期徒刑1年，罚金人民币10万元，违法所得予以追缴。

【案件点评】 近年来，随着互联网技术的迅猛发展，此类案件具有服务器虚拟化、获取盗版技术隐蔽化以及犯罪成本极小、危害后果进一步扩大的趋势。本案被告人通过软件自动控制下载文本格式或抓取网页格式，后再复制到其制作的网站，其明知下载、抓取的小说并未经过原著作权人许可的行为属侵权盗版行为。另外，执法人员严格把握司法鉴定中的“实质性相似”问题，以经鉴定相似率90%以上作为认定信息网络传播型“复制发行”的标准来统计盗版作品的数量。该案对同类案件的查处具有一定借鉴意义。

（上海市版权局）

江 苏 省

一、张家港“风雨文学网”侵犯著作权案

案件详情，参见本栏目“2016年度打击侵权盗版十大案件”之一（第303页）。

二、常州张某“九九漫画”等5个网站侵犯他人著作权案

案件详情，参见本栏目“2016年度打击侵权盗版十大案件”之三（第303页）。

三、邹某等制售盗版图书案

案件详情，参见本栏目“2016年度打击侵权盗版十大案件”之九（第304页）。

四、常州唐某架设私服侵犯他人著作权案

2015年3月，唐某在未取得上海壮游信息科技有限公司许可的情况下，架设《奇迹》游戏私服并将其命名为《寻梦奇迹》进行运营。截至2016年1月，唐某的非法经营数额共计人民币77万余元。2016年9月13日，常州市钟楼区人民法院以侵犯著作权罪判处唐某有期徒刑3年，缓刑3年，并处罚金人民币10万元。

五、镇江薛某、潘某等人架设私服侵犯他人著作权案

2016年3月，犯罪嫌疑人薛某非法侵入江苏名通信息科技有限公司服务器，通过非法获得Root权限的方式获取服务器内《热血江湖传》和《RO仙境传说》两款游戏的源代码。后犯罪嫌疑人薛某伙同潘某及谷某（另案处理）共谋，由谷某负责破解上述两款游戏源代码密码，潘某负责运营上述两款私服游戏，并收取玩家充值款牟利。截至案发，总计牟利12万元。2016年12月29日，镇江市京口区人民法院以侵犯著作权罪分别判处被告人薛某有期徒刑1年，缓刑1年，并处罚金6万元；被告人潘某有期徒刑1年，缓刑1年，并处罚金6万元。

六、张家港“2020kk电影网”侵犯著作权案

2015年3月6日，张家港市文化行政综合执法大队根据网络巡查线索，联合市公安局三兴派出所对“2020kk电影网”侵犯著作权案进行立案查处。朱某某未经著作权人许可，在2014年至案发期间，通过软件将采集的522部视频发布到其非法开设的“2020kk电影网”提供在线观看和下载，并通过发布广告非法获利74 665元。2016年6月28日，张家港市人民法院以侵犯著作权罪判处朱某某有期徒刑10个月，缓刑1年，并处罚金人民币5万元。

七、连云港赣榆区厉庄镇宏诚书店销售侵权出版物案

2016年10月23日，连云港市文化行政综合执法支队接举报，称连云港市赣榆区厉庄镇宏诚书店向赣榆第一中学、厉庄高级中学推销的《2018江苏普通高考必修科目学业水平测试考点直击·地理》涉嫌盗版。经查，涉案图书经鉴定均为盗版。连云港市版权局对该单位处以行政处罚，没收涉案图书《2018江苏普通高考必修科目学业水平测试考点直击·地理》，并处罚款人民币4万元。

八、南京某动画公司侵犯软件著作权案

2016年6月28日，南京市文化综合执法总队根据投诉，对南京某动画公司涉嫌侵犯软件著作权案进行调查。当事人南京某动画公司未经著作权人许可，擅自使用Autodesk 3ds Max、Autodesk Maya等软件共26件。2016年8月26日，南京市文广新局组织著作权纠纷行政调解并形成《行政调解协议书》。当事人与著作权人授权经销商签订采购合同，购买正版软件100套，合同总金额为人民币78.4万元；著作权人承诺，协议履行后将不再追究当事人的相关法律责任。

九、沭阳县沭城小雅书店侵犯著作权案

2016年3月30日，沭阳县文广新局根据省版权局和“扫黄打非”办的部署，对沭阳县沭城小雅书店未经著作权人许可，发行侵权作品案件进行检查，发现涉嫌侵权盗版出版物394本。2016年5月30日做出如下行政处罚：（1）没收394本侵权盗版出版物；（2）罚款8 000元整。

十、淮安某学校销售侵权盗版图书案

2016年1月12日，淮安市文化行政综合执法支队接上级线索，依法对淮安某学校进行检查。经调查取证，该校使用的《学生水平测试总复习（地理）》等6种教辅均为侵权盗版出版物。执法机关做出如下行政处罚：（1）责令该学校停止侵权行为；（2）罚款人民币8 000元整。

十一、徐州“3·11”印刷盗版图书案

2015年底，徐州市版权局收到群众举报，称云龙区三环东路附近一家印刷厂印刷大量非法图书。

经排查，锁定犯罪嫌疑人徐某。2016年3月11日，徐州市公安局治安支队、徐州市文化综合执法支队出动执法人员30多人，对该印刷厂和大龙湖办事处某工业园区一家印刷装订厂进行突击检查，当场查缴涉嫌盗版图书近70 000册，未装订盗版图书散页30 000多份，抓获犯罪嫌疑人3人，涉案金额300余万元，印刷机器5台。犯罪嫌疑人已被批捕，案件已送审。

十二、扬州某玩具商贸公司制作、销售侵权物品案

2016年11月9日，扬州市邗江区文化执法人员对扬州某玩具商贸有限公司进行检查，发现其玩具加工车间内有涉嫌侵犯他人著作权的“卡通小沙发”系列毛绒玩具若干件。11月19日，执法人员对公司法定代表人叶某某调查询问，其承认未经著作权人授权。执法机关做出如下行政处罚：没收违法制品，罚款人民币5 000元。

（江苏省版权局）

安徽省

一、萧县在线网络科技有限公司侵犯著作权案

2015年11月至12月期间，萧县在线网络科技有限公司假冒“第五季中国好声音”名义，在萧县协助、参与举办“中国好声音萧县赛区海选”活动，未经授权，擅自使用“中国好声音”“The Voice of China”名称，以及相关图形标识、LOGO标识、背景音乐等电视节目中的元素。

2016年2月5日，安徽省宿州市萧县文化广电新闻出版局对此立案调查。2016年3月25日，萧县文化广电新闻出版局依据《中华人民共和国著作权法》第四十八条、《中华人民共和国著作权法实施条例》第三十六条，依法做出行政处罚，责令停止侵权行为，销毁侵权复制品，罚款人民币1万元。

二、刘某某侵犯著作权案

合肥市版权局接到群众举报，刘某某未经著作权人许可，发行侵权复制品。经立案调查发现，刘某某未经著作权人许可非法经营侵权复制品，涉案金额为2 861.40元。

2016年8月4日，合肥市文化广电新闻出版局依据《出版物市场管理规定》第三十三条、《中华人民共和国著作权法》第四十八条第一款第（一）项、《中华人民共和国著作权法实施条例》第三十六条规定，并参照《安徽省新闻出版广播影视（版权）行政处罚自由裁量权基准》自由裁量标准，依法给予刘某某行政处罚，没收22种（共计80本）侵权出版物，罚款人民币5 000元。

（安徽省版权局）

江西省

一、南昌熊某侵犯著作案

2015年5月20日，南昌市版权局接到江西省版权局批转的案件线索，线索称不法书商在利益驱使下，公然盗印江西人民出版社出版的《南昌市2015年中等学校招生考试样卷》并在南昌市的中学进行销售，其行为严重破坏了市场经济秩序及该出版社的名誉。对此，南昌市文化市场综合执法支队依法组织调查。经查，南昌市某中学使用了上述盗版《样卷》，《样卷》是由不法书商熊某提供的，共计3 535册。

根据有关法律和司法解释规定：以营利为目的，未经著作权人许可，复制发行其文字作品，复制品数量合计在500张（份）以上的，属于《中华人民共和国刑法》第二百一十七条规定的“有其他严重情节”。按照“两法衔接”的要求，2015年9月，南昌市文化市场综合执法支队依法将此案移交南昌市公安局直属分局侦办。经公安机关侦查、检察机关起诉后，于2016年7月，南昌市东湖区人民法院依法判处被告人熊某犯侵犯著作权罪，判处有期徒刑2年，缓刑2年，并处罚金2万元整。

二、抚州市章紫光公司侵犯著作案

2016年1月28日，抚州市版权局接到江西省版权局批转的国家版权局“剑网行动”移转函，反映抚州市章紫光实业有限公司涉嫌侵犯四川华夏万卷传媒有限公司的著作权，抚州市文化市场综合执法支队介入调查。依法查明，2015年抚州市章紫光实业有限公司通过天猫、京东等网络平台，出售了近2万套《章紫光练字帖》，经国家版权鉴定部门认定字帖使用了书法家田英章老师的字体，而该公司是在没有取得授权的情况下，擅自从互联网下载制作的。因田英章与四川华夏万卷传媒有限公司存在版权合作关系，所以抚州市章紫光实业有限公司的行为侵犯了四川华夏万卷传媒有限公司的版权。在案件调查开展后，2016年5月12日，抚州市章紫光实业有限公司向四川华夏万卷传媒有限公司进行侵权赔偿并达成了谅解协议。

2016年7月2日，抚州市文化市场综合执法支队根据《著作权法》和《著作权法实施条例》的相关规定，责令抚州市章紫光实业有限公司停止侵权行为，并处罚金 5 万元。

三、江西人源职业培训学校侵犯著作案

2016 年 2 月 29 日，南昌市文化市场综合执法支队执法人员根据案件线索，对江西人源职业培训学校进行检查。检查中发现该校准备向培训人员发放的《职称英语》等教材涉嫌盗版，共计 644 册，后经鉴定为侵权复制品。该校工作人员配合执法机关调查，并承认了发放盗版图书的事实。

南昌市文化市场综合执法支队根据《著作权法》和《著作权法实施条例》的相关规定，责令江西人源职业培训学校停止侵权行为，没收盗版教材 644 册，并处罚金 3 万元。

四、景德镇市陆月茶吧（六月电影公馆）侵犯著作权案

2016 年 8 月 22 日，景德镇市文化市场综合执法支队执法人员对景德镇市陆月茶吧进行日常检查。检查中发现陆月茶吧设有 9 个包厢，其中 4 号包厢正在播放美国大片，同时发现服务器内存电影 116 部，经查，上述影片均未取得授权。

景德镇市文化市场综合执法支队根据《著作权法》和《著作权法实施条例》的相关规定，责令陆月茶吧停止侵权行为，并处罚金 3 万元。

五、于都县书香阁书店销售盗版工具书案

2015 年 9 月 23 日，于都县文化市场综合执法大队执法人员对于都县书香阁书店进行日常检查，在检查中发现该书店涉嫌销售盗版的《现代汉语词典》《古汉语常用字字典》等工具书 821 册，后经鉴定均为侵权复制品。

于都县文化市场综合执法大队根据《著作权法》和《著作权法实施条例》的相关规定，责令书香阁书店停止侵权行为，没收其侵权盗版图书 821 册，并处罚金 2 万元。

六、九江七空间咖啡屋侵犯著作权案

2015 年 12 月 25 日，九江市文化市场综合执法支队根据案件线索，对九江市七空间咖啡屋进行检查，检查中发现该咖啡屋从事电影放映业务，同时发现经营场所内的服务器内存多部影片。经营者供述所有影片均从互联网下载未取得合法授权。

2016 年 1 月 25 日，九江市文化市场综合执法支队根据《著作权法》和《著作权法实施条例》的相关规定，责令九江市七空间咖啡屋停止侵权行为，并处罚金 1 万元。

七、九江浔视界咖吧侵犯著作权案

2015 年 12 月 25 日，九江市文化市场综合执法支队的执法人员根据案件线索，对九江市浔视界咖吧进行检查，发现其从事电影放映业务，内设 18 个包厢，有投影仪、服务器设备，服务器内存《阿凡达》等多部影片，经营者无法提供影片的版权证明。

2016 年 2 月 6 日，九江市文化市场综合执法支队依据《著作权法》和《著作权法实施条例》的相关规定，责令九江市浔视界咖吧停止侵权行为，并处罚金 1 万元。

八、九江裕兴文体书店销售盗版图书案

2016 年 3 月 24 日，九江市文化市场综合执法支队的执法人员对九江市裕兴文体书店进行日常检查。检查中发现该店涉嫌销售《公共营养师》等盗版图书，执法人员现场暂扣图书 214 册，后经鉴定均为盗版图书。

九江市文化市场综合执法支队依照《著作权法》和《著作权法实施条例》的相关规定，责令九江市裕兴文体书店停止侵权行为，没收盗版图书 214 册，并处罚金 1 万元。

九、鹰潭杨某安装盗版软件案

2016 年 7 月 18 日，鹰潭市文化市场综合执法支队根据案件线索，对鹰潭市自由空间网络有限公司进行了检查。检查中执法人员发现该公司使用的电脑安装了 Windows 7 操作系统，经营者未能提供软件的合法来源。经调查发现，Windows 7 操作系统是由该公司外聘的网络维护员杨某擅自从互联网下载安装的，杨某同时还为鹰潭市暴风网络有限公司、中浩网络文化有限公司、新时尚网络有限公司等多台电脑安装操作系统，并每月从上述公司领取固定报酬。

鹰潭市文化市场综合执法支队根据《著作权法》和《著作权法实施条例》的相关规定，责令鹰潭市自由空间网络有限公司等 4 家公司删除盗版软件，责令杨某停止侵权行为，并处 1 万元罚款。

十、南昌“我的书兜”网站侵权传播网络文学作品案

2016 年 9 月 26 日，南昌市版权局接到江西省版权局转发的版权案件线索，称南昌杨某经营的“我的书兜”网站涉嫌侵权传播网络文学。经南昌市文化市场综合执法支队的执法人员依法对该网站进行调查，发现“我的书兜”网站上传了多部未经授权的网络小说，执法人员现场进行了证据固定。

依照《著作权法》和《著作权法实施条例》的相关规定，南昌市文化市场综合执法支队责令该网站停止侵权行为，并处罚金 1 万元。

（江西省版权局）

山 东 省

一、山东淄博“4·8”侵犯著作权案

2016年5月，该案被全国“扫黄”办和国家版权局列为挂牌督办案件。2015年3月，淄博市文化市场行政执法局接群众举报称张店区天乐园商场后院有人贩售大量盗版及淫秽光盘。该局迅速对该线索进行核查，发现商场后院有一处仓库具有重大涉案嫌疑。2015年4月8日，淄博市文化市场行政执法局联合淄博市公安局直属分局成立“4·8”侵犯著作权案专案组，于当日下午对该仓库进行了突击检查，当场查获涉嫌侵权复制光盘2万余张。经鉴定，侵权盗版音像制品共计28 000余张，淫秽光碟共计876张。因侵权制品数量已达到刑事犯罪案件立案标准，该案移交公安部门刑事立案查处。公安部门经过摸排侦查，于2016年1月6日，将畏罪潜逃的巩某芹、巩某清夫妇抓获，并依法对其进行刑事拘留。2016年11月7日，张店区人民检察院向张店区人民法院提起公诉，张店区人民法院于同日立案，并依法组成合议庭，公开开庭审理了此案。经审理查明，2011年1月至2015年4月，被告巩某芹、巩某清在淄博市张店区天乐园商场柜台及仓库向魏某等人销售盗版影碟和淫秽影碟，违法所得共计人民币46余万元。

根据《中华人民共和国刑法》第二百一十七条等规定，张店区人民法院于2016年12月6日依法判决被告人巩某芹犯侵犯著作权罪，判处有期徒刑3年6个月，并处罚金人民币50万元；犯贩卖淫秽物品牟利罪，判处有期徒刑6个月，并处罚金人民币1万元；二罪并罚，决定执行有期徒刑3年6个月，并处罚金人民币51万元。判决被告人巩某清犯侵犯著作权罪，判处有期徒刑3年，缓刑3年，并处罚金人民币50万元。

二、山东潍坊王某销售侵权复制品案

2015年11月，该案被国家版权局列为挂牌督办案件。2014年2月12日，山东省公安厅向潍坊市公安局通报了张银合《张博士医考红宝书临床执业含助理》一书被盗版销售的线索后，潍坊市文化市场综合执法局、公安局及时成立了专案组。专案组通过互联网络侦控，初步确认王某有销售侵权复制品犯罪嫌疑。2月18日，专案组到王某家中进行调查，在其住处现场查获各类疑似盗版书籍共计10 213本，其中《张博士医考红宝书临床执业含助理》四卷共计2 280本。依据相关规定，专案组决定，由潍坊市公安局立案并对相关物证进行查封（扣押）。通过审讯，王某供述其经营网络书店销售盗版书籍以及光盘的违法行为。

2016年2月23日，潍坊市高新技术开发区人民法院依据《中华人民共和国刑法》第二百一十七、第二百一十八条之规定，分别判处王某、秦某拘役3个月，缓刑3个月，并处罚金145 000元；没收违法所得72 740元及涉案侵权盗版出版物。

三、山东威海新航船务服务中心复制、发行侵权图书案

2015年11月，该案被国家版权局列为挂牌督办案件。2015年7月7日，威海市文化市场综合执法局执法人员依法对位于海运学院内的威海新航船务服务中心亮证检查时发现，当事人向学员销售的《航海英语》等1 285册教材均为简易装订，且无出版单位名称、无版权页、无码洋，涉嫌为侵权复制品。同年7月16日，本案经批准后以一般程序立案，同时成立专案组负责查处。12月28日，专案组赴大连海事大学出版社取得被侵权正版样书和侵权复制品《鉴定书》1份。2016年1月5日，当事人委托王某接受调查询问，其承认当事人自2015年3月采取自行复制和从网店采购的方式取得侵权教材向学员销售，违法经营额55 000元。2016年1月8日，专案组赴杭州市淘宝网总部调取了3家涉案网店的交易记录，确认了当事人采购侵权教材的事实。

2016年1月15日，本案调查终结。当事人的行为，侵犯了《中华人民共和国著作权法》第十条规定的著作权人享有的复制权和发行权。1月26日，威海市文化市场综合执法局依据《中华人民共和国著作权法》第四十八条第一款第（一）项和《中华人民共和国著作权法实施条例》第三十六条的规定，向当事人下达了《行政处罚决定书》，给予当事人没收侵权图书1 285册、罚款110 000元的行政处罚。

四、山东菏泽“4·13”志明印务侵犯著作权案

2015年11月，该案被国家版权局列为挂牌督办案件。2015年4月13日，菏泽市文化市场综合执法局接到举报后，对志明印务有限公司涉嫌盗印非法出版物依法立案进行调查，联合牡丹区公安经侦大队，成立了“4·13”专案组。涉案书籍《说明与检测》等共20 750册，案情重大。专案组通过资金调查、物流查询、话单分析等侦查手段，多次奔赴河南调查取证。

2016年10月12日，菏泽市牡丹区人民法院对“4·13”志明印务侵犯著作权案进行宣判。根据

《中华人民共和国著作权法》第四十八条，依据《中华人民共和国刑法》第二百一十七条，志明印务有限公司犯侵犯著作权罪，判处罚金人民币 20 万元；被告人张某、杨某犯侵犯著作权罪，分别判处有期徒刑 3 年，并分别处罚金人民币 8 万元。

五、山东德州张某侵犯信息网络传播权案

2016 年 3 月 7 日，德州市文化市场综合执法局在进行网络巡查时发现，一名微信用户将电影上传至其持有的百度云盘账户，通过微信收取红包获取收益的方式，向消费者持有的百度云盘账户共享影片。经德州市公安局网安大队对该微信号技术排查确定当事人信息，2016 年 6 月 17 日，德州市文化市场综合执法局对张某涉嫌未经权利人许可，通过信息网络提供他人的录像制品，获得经济利益的行为进行立案调查。

2016 年 7 月 20 日，本案调查终结，依据《信息网络传播权保护条例》第十九条第一款第（二）项规定，对当事人张某给予警告并没收违法所得的行政处罚。

六、山东青岛普生文化传播有限公司未经著作权人许可发行他人作品案

2016 年 7 月 27 日，青岛市文化市场行政执法局对青岛普生文化传播有限公司依法检查。经查，该公司未经著作权人许可，擅自销售发行“乔巴”“罗宾”“娜美”“乌索普”等动漫形象玩具，其行为违反《中华人民共和国著作权法》第四十八条第一款第（一）项之规定，2016 年 7 月 29 日予以立案。

2016 年 8 月 18 日，青岛市文化市场行政执法局对其做出罚款人民币 115 000 元的行政处罚决定。该公司于 8 月 18 日接受行政处罚，并于当日缴纳罚款。

七、山东青岛约吧有限公司未经著作权人许可复制他人作品案

2016 年 10 月 25 日，青岛市文化市场行政执法局对青岛约吧有限公司依法检查。经查，该公司未经著作权人许可，擅自复制 203 部影视作品，通过其约吧店铺观看，其行为违反《中华人民共和国著作权法》第四十八条第一款第（一）项之规定，2016 年 11 月 2 日予以立案。

2016 年 12 月 5 日，青岛市文化市场行政执法局对其做出罚款人民币 10 000 元的行政处罚决定。该公司于 12 月 5 日接受行政处罚，并于当日缴纳罚款。

八、山东泰安王某侵犯著作权案

根据某出版社现场举报，2016 年 12 月 2 日上午，泰安市文化市场综合执法支队执法人员到肥城六中进行现场检查，检查发现：随机抽查高三文科班的两位学生，正在使用涉嫌盗版的教辅《辅助教程（历史）》。当日执法人员现场对该校历史教研组组长做了《调查询问笔录》，经了解：这批书由王某发行，免费供学生使用，目的是以后买其推销的书。12 月 3 日，本案经批准后以一般程序立案。12 月 5 日经鉴定：当事人发行的 800 册图书为侵犯他人著作权的非法出版物。2016 年 12 月 12 日对王某进行调查询问，当事人承认其违法事实。

2016 年 12 月 16 日，本案调查终结。12 月 26 日，向当事人下达《行政处罚决定书》。该违法行为违反了《中华人民共和国著作权法》第四十八条第一款第（一）项之规定；依据《中华人民共和国著作权法实施条例》第三十六条给予当事人没收侵犯他人著作权非法出版物 800 册、罚款人民币112 000 元的行政处罚。

九、山东滨州“7・11”商某侵犯著作权案

2016 年 7 月 11 日，根据市场检查线索，滨州市文化市场综合执法局对商某涉嫌侵犯著作权案进行调查。经查：2016 年 7 月 4 日，商某未经著作权人许可复制《世纪金榜高中全程学习方略数学必修 1》《世纪金榜高中全程学习方略英语必修 1》等 4 种教材共计 400 册，当事人通过开设的卓越教育培训中心发放给学生当教材，收取每人培训费 1 780 元（包括培训费和资料费用），资料没有单独定价。当事人违反《中华人民共和国著作权法》的相关规定，依据《中华人民共和国著作权法》第四十八条第一款第（一）项、《中华人民共和国著作权法实施条例》第三十六条规定，给予当事人以下行政处罚：（1）没收当事人非法复制的 400 册教材；（2）罚款 55 000 元。2016 年 8 月 9 日，本案结案。

十、山东济宁“你的世界”侵犯他人网络游戏著作权案

2016 年 8 月 30 日，济宁市文化市场执法局根据举报，对某网站 ICP 备案查询，远程勘验取证并制作《远程勘验笔录》，固定相关证据，进一步了解涉案情况。经调查，《我的世界》游戏于 2014 年 11 月 6 日连同 Minecraft 游戏及 Mojang 的全部资产被微软收购。网易游戏获得了 Minecraft PC 端及 PE 端在中国的代理权。举报中的“我的世界”实际标注为“你的世界”网站（域名：www. mcndsj. com)。9 月 2 日，“你的世界”网站涉嫌侵犯权利人《我的世界》网络游戏信息网络传播权，依法予以立案。

2016 年 9 月 27 日，案件调查终结。“你的世界”

网站未经权利人许可擅自设立《我的世界》游戏私服，从事《我的世界》网络游戏经营，未经权利人许可侵犯了权利人《我的世界》网络游戏信息网络传播权，依据《中华人民共和国著作权法》第四十八条，《中华人民共和国著作权法实施条例》第三十六条，《信息网络传播权保护条例》第二条、第五条、第十八条规定，对其给予责令停止侵权网络游戏经营，并处罚款5万元的行政处罚。

（山东省版权局）

湖北省

一、武汉万某某侵犯著作权案

2011年10月份以来，万某某为牟利在青山区钢花121街北门菜场贩卖盗版光盘复制品。2012年6月10日，万某某在该地贩卖盗版光碟时，被当场抓获，现场收缴光盘复制品464种、1 106张。

该案于2012年6月11日立案侦查，同日，万某某被取保候审。2013年6月11日，因万某某擅自离开武汉市并更换手机号码，脱离了公安机关监控，严重违反取保候审规定，被列为网上追逃犯。2016年1月19日万某某到案，次日被刑事拘留。同年1月26日被批准逮捕。2016年5月9日，一审判处万某某犯侵犯著作权罪（未遂），判处拘役4个月。

二、武汉陶某、左某某、叶某某侵犯著作权案

2014年6月至2015年12月25日，左某某、叶某某为牟取非法利益，在无图书报刊印刷许可证的情况下，受陶某委托，未经权利人许可，先后印刷盗版书籍《斗罗大陆1》《斗罗大陆6》等99 140册。经审理查明，从2014年6月起至2015年12月25日，被告人左某某、叶某某为牟取非法利益，受被告人陶某委托，印刷盗版书籍99 140册。2016年7月12日，法院立案受理被告人陶某、左某某、叶某某侵犯著作权罪一案。依照《中华人民共和国刑法》第二百一十七条等规定，法院于2016年10月31日做出刑事判决：被告人陶某犯侵犯著作权罪，判处有期徒刑3年，缓刑4年，并处罚金人民币70 000元；被告人左某某犯侵犯著作权罪，判处有期徒刑3年，缓刑3年，并处罚金人民币60 000元；被告人叶某某犯侵犯著作权罪，判处有期徒刑2年，缓刑2年，并处罚金人民币40 000元。

三、黄石汇梦影视茶吧侵犯影视作品著作权案

案件详情，参见本栏目“2016年度打击侵权盗版十大案件”之五（第303页）。

四、十堰“风音音乐网”侵犯音乐作品信息网络传播权案

2015年11月24日，根据国家版权局《“剑网2015”专项行动移转函》交办，湖北省版权局向十堰市下达《案件线索移转函》，要求立案查处“风音音乐网”侵犯音乐作品信息网络传播权违法行为。

经查明，丰某某未经国际唱片业协会会员唱片公司许可，擅自将其享有录音制作者权的录音制品上传到百度云盘上，采取设置公开或私密链接等共享文件方式，将链接地址和提取码发布到“风音音乐网”上，使购买邀请码的注册会员在个人选定的时间和地点下载所需要歌曲，侵犯了国际唱片业协会会员唱片公司信息网络传播权。同时该网站以营利为目的，在没有取得网络文化经营许可证的情况下，采取收取会员注册费的方式，擅自从事经营性互联网文化活动。

受领案件查办任务后，十堰市版权局高度重视，立即组织专班，依法开展调查取证。通过远程勘验取证，执法人员发现该网站由十堰居民丰某某开办，服务器位于郑州市，网站有偿销售邀请码招募会员注册、向注册会员提供歌曲下载链接。

为合法、准确、及时固定证据，十堰市版权局购买正版屏幕录像软件，依法到市公证处做了电子证据保全公证，向公安部门调取了当事人丰某某的户籍证明材料。在湖北省版权局、河南省版权局、湖北省文化市场稽查总队、杭州市文化市场行政执法总队的大力支持和帮助下，执法人员依法调取了该网站服务器数据、ICP备案登记详细信息、支付宝交易记录等关键证据。由于前期取证工作规范有序、证据充分扎实，当事人在调查询问中全面承认了违法事实，主动关闭了网站，停止了侵权行为和擅自从事经营性互联网文化活动，自觉履行了行政处罚义务。

（湖北省版权局）

湖南省

一、永州谭某某等人侵犯软件著作权案

湖南永州市公安局零陵分局通过网上巡查发现谭某某等人涉嫌非法销售盗版软件，报省公安厅后成立专案组立案侦查。经查，谭某某等三人参与盗版侵权，现场查获各类软件光盘8 080张，各类COA标签2 432张和打印机一台。经微软公司核算该系列案所扣押的盗版软件光盘和COA标签价值

1.03 亿元，上述人员非法经营所得金额 200 余万元。

2016 年 10 月 25 日，永州市零陵区人民法院根据《中华人民共和国刑法》第二百一十七条以侵犯著作权罪做出判决。对谭某某、陈某勇、陈某梅、陈某峰判处 3 年有期徒刑，缓刑 4 年；对陈某判处 2 年有期徒刑，缓刑 3 年。并对五名犯罪人处以罚金合计 153 万元。

二、刘某侵犯网络游戏著作权案

2016 年 5 月 27 日，益阳市文化市场综合执法局根据市场巡查线索，对刘某《剑网 3》游戏代练工作室涉嫌侵权一案立案查处。经查，当事人刘某从 2015 年 11 月至 2016 年 5 月间，未经软件著作权人许可，利用《剑网 3》外挂软件，故意避开或者破坏著作权人为保护其软件而采取的技术措施，通过淘宝网为《剑网 3》网络游戏角色提供代练升级服务并从中牟利，违法经营所得共计 1 251 元整。鉴于当事人刘某主动删除了侵权软件，停止了侵权行为，决定依法给予从轻处理。

益阳市文化市场综合执法局依据《计算机软件保护条例》第二十四条第一款规定，对当事人刘某做出行政处罚：责令停止侵权行为，并处罚款人民币 1 万元。

三、衡岳公司侵犯美术作品著作权案

2016 年 4 月 12 日接权利人旷某某举报衡岳中药饮片有限公司侵犯了其美术作品著作权，并提供了相关权利证明材料。经查实，未经美术作品《祝融峰（南岳衡山）》著作权人旷某某同意，衡山县宏达塑料印刷制版厂将旷某某享有著作权的美术作品制成印刷版，由湖南恒邦彩印包装有限公司印刷在衡岳中药饮片有限公司产品的包装上，衡岳中药饮片有限公司通过渠道销售给消费者。该系列行为侵犯了权利人的制作、复制、发行权。

依据《中华人民共和国著作权法》第四十八条第一款第（一）项、《中华人民共和国著作权法实施条例》第三十六条规定，衡阳市文化市场综合执法局对侵权单位衡岳中药饮片有限公司做出罚款 9 000 元并没收侵权作品半成品 4 万份的行政处罚。

四、广济医院侵犯软件著作权案

根据 2016 年 6 月 28 日湖南“红网”《百姓呼声》栏目网民举报岳阳广济医院利用盗版软件侵犯著作权人版权的情况，岳阳市文化市场综合执法局版权执法大队立即组织开展现场检查核实。经查：该公司在其办公计算机中复制安装了微软盗版软件 200 余套。其中，复制安装的计算机 Windows XP/7 操作系统共 32 套不能提供软件权利人授权许可证明材料，已构成未经著作权人许可，复制其计算机软件行为。

岳阳市文化市场综合执法局依据《中华人民共和国著作权法》《计算机软件保护条例》做出责令停止侵权行为，并罚款 2 万元的行政处罚。

五、旅壹印象公司侵犯影视作品著作权案

2016 年 3 月 11 日，永州市文化市场综合执法局接群众举报的线索，对永州旅壹印象科技有限公司涉嫌未经著作权人许可，复制其录音录像作品用于放映案进行调查，并于 2016 年 3 月 15 日立案。经查，2016 年 2 月至 3 月间，当事人永州旅壹印象科技有限公司未经著作权人许可，从网络上复制 42 部影视作品，通过其开设的“旅壹·印象咖啡私影永州店”提供在线观看。

永州市文化市场综合执法局依据《中华人民共和国著作权法》第四十八条第一款第（一）项、《中华人民共和国著作权法实施条例》第三十六条规定，对永州旅壹印象科技有限公司做出罚款 5 000 元的行政处罚。

六、陈某侵犯软件著作权案

2016 年 10 月，怀化市文化市场综合执法局根据群众线索，成立专案组对陈某涉嫌侵犯软件著作权案进行调查。经查，当事人于 2016 年 1 月至 2016 年 8 月期间，在未经著作权人许可的情况下，先后为华桂网吧等 5 家网吧复制、安装从网络下载的盗版 Windows 7 专业版及旗舰版软件共计 490 件。当事人行为侵犯了《计算机软件保护条例》第八条第一款第（四）项关于“复制权”的规定，构成了未经软件著作权人许可，复制著作权人软件的行为；同时，违反了公平竞争原则和正常的软件市场交易秩序，损害了社会公共利益。

怀化市文体广电新闻出版局于 2016 年 11 月 16 日依据《计算机软件保护条例》第八条第一款第（四）项、第二十四条第一款第（一）项、第二十四条第二款的规定，对陈湘泉做出罚款 4.9 万元的行政处罚。

七、李某某侵犯图书著作权案

2016 年 3 月 31 日，道县文化市场综合执法大队接到群众举报：道县一中校园内在搞书展，其销售书籍疑是盗版书籍，大队领导在接到举报后立即组织执法队员赶到道县一中依法对“一届书生”书展进行调查。经查，当事人“一届书生”书展以营利为目的擅自销售盗版出版物，其销售盗版图书违法经营额 8 400 余元，违法所得 3 500 余元。

依据《中华人民共和国著作权法》第四十八条

的规定，道县文化市场综合执法大队于2016年4月8日做出以下行政处罚：没收所有盗版图书并处罚款人民币8 000元。

（湖南省版权局）

四　川　省

一、成都“爱漫画网”侵犯著作权案

2015年3月，成都市文化市场综合执法总队和成都市公安局网安支队分别接到权利人深圳腾讯计算机系统有限公司举报：“爱漫画”（www.imanhua.com）网站涉嫌侵犯其著作权。经查，2014年8月以来，叶某某、江某某共同出资成立了“深圳漫游文化科技有限公司”，并邀请胡某某担任公司法定代表人，三人在未经著作权人许可的情况下，利用江某某之前建立的“爱漫画”网站，由胡某某通过各种途径搜集他人大量漫画作品，并经其整理、编辑后上传至该网站供访客免费观看，以此提高网站访问量，同时在该网站上提供刊登收费广告服务，收取广告费。经公安机关提取并分别送交中国版权保护中心鉴定委员会、日本内容产品海外流通促进机构和韩国著作权委员会北京代表处进行鉴定和确认，该网站共计5 000余部漫画作品未经权利人许可被侵权使用。

2017年1月20日，经成都市温江区人民法院审理，下达刑事判决书“（2016）川0115刑初89号”，判处叶某某有期徒刑3年，缓刑4年，并处罚金人民币100万元；判处江某某有期徒刑3年，缓刑4年，并处罚金人民币100万元；判处胡某某有期徒刑2年，缓刑3年，并处罚金人民币50万元；没收作案工具（苹果6 plus手机3部、其他品牌手机2部、电脑4台）。

二、成都新禹书店侵犯著作权案

2015年3月26日，四川省新闻出版广电局接到权利人投诉，青羊区新禹书店涉嫌发行侵权盗版出版物。四川省新闻出版广电局联合成都市文化市场综合执法总队，依法对位于青羊区人民中路16号附1号的青羊区新禹书店和人民中路一段5号17栋1楼2号新禹书店库房进行检查。经现场检查，在该书店内及其库房内共查获涉嫌盗版出版物357种5 061册。经机械工业出版社、武汉大学出版社等13家出版单位鉴定，认定其中123种共计4 409册为侵权盗版出版物。2015年7月8日，该案移交成都市经济犯罪侦查处立案调查。

2016年2月23日，青羊区人民法院经审理，下达刑事判决书，判处李季林有期徒刑1年8个月，缓刑2年并处罚金5 000元；没收盗版出版物4 409册。

三、成都头等舱私人影院侵犯著作权案

2016年7月28日，成都市文化市场综合执法总队执法人员接群众举报后，依法对位于成都市青羊区二环路西一段155号的头等舱私人影院进行检查，现场发现该场所放映的影片有《真探第一集》等无授权证明影片39部。这些影片均由当事人通过互联网下载后存储在其自建服务器上，然后通过服务器推送到各个放映室。顾客通过《美团》《大众点评》《糯米》等客户端下单，分别以68元/场、88元/场（节假日）、158元/场不等的价格提前预约后在放映室直接点播观看。

2016年9月6日，成都市文化市场综合执法总队依据《中华人民共和国著作权法实施条例》第三十六条之规定，责令当事人停止侵权行为，并处罚款人民币5 000元整。

四、成都美映咖啡和电影影吧侵犯著作权案

2016年9月2日，成都市文化市场综合执法总队依法对成都市成华区钻石广场A座1413号的美映咖啡和电影影吧进行检查。经查，该影吧在其服务器储存电影影片1 558部供顾客观看。顾客通过百度糯米、大众点评发布团购信息或现场到店现金支付的形式取得观影资格后，用设置于该影吧包间内的平板端选取影片并直接通过包间内的投影设备进行放映观看。该影吧服务器所储存的1 558部影片，均为当事人通过土豪网、BT天堂等网站自行下载存储在服务器。该影吧开设私人影院未经著作权人许可发行其作品的行为，违反了《中华人民共和国著作权法》第四十八条第一款第（一）项之规定。

2016年10月9日，成都市版权局依据《中华人民共和国著作权法实施条例》第三十六条之规定，对成都市美映咖啡和电影影吧处罚款人民币5 000元整。

五、成都“10·31”侵犯著作权案

2016年10月31日，成都市文化市场综合执法总队接案件线索，www.wow60.com网站及其站内游戏客户端《逐风者魔兽》1.12.3涉嫌侵权，成都市文化市场综合执法总队对其立案调查。经查，当事人李某某在未获权利人授权的情况下，通过其经营的网站www.wow60.com，运营《魔兽世界》1.12.3客户端，该行为违反了《中华人民共和国著作权法》第四十八条第一款第（一）项规定。

2016年12月19日，成都市文化市场综合执法总队依据《中华人民共和国著作权法实施条例》第三十六条之规定，责令当事人停止侵权行为，并处

罚款人民币 10 000 元整。

六、德阳扬帆书店侵犯著作权案

2016 年 6 月 29 日，德阳市行政执法人员对德阳市区扬帆书店进行现场检查，发现其销售的 117 本书涉嫌为非法出版物。经立案调查，并经权利人鉴定，该批次 117 本图书为侵权盗版出版物。

2016 年 8 月 19 日，德阳市文广新局依据《出版物市场管理规定》第二十二条第二款第（三）项、第三十三条和《中华人民共和国著作权法》第四十八条第一款第（一）项之规定，依法没收侵权复制品 117 本，并处罚款人民币 10 000 元整。

七、泸州“6·15”侵犯著作权案

2016 年 5 月 26 日，泸县文体新广局接上级移交的举报材料，称泸县第四中学高三学生使用的教辅资料涉嫌为盗版图书。6 月 15 日，泸县文化市场综合执法大队对举报内容进行立案调查。经查，涉案图书系由书商李某某销售给泸县四中，共 1 种，1 043 本。经泸州市新闻出版广电局鉴定，以上 1 043 本图书为盗版，总码洋为 62 371.4 元人民币。

2016 年 12 月 23 日，泸县文体新广局依据《中华人民共和国著作权法》第四十八条和《中华人民共和国著作权法实施条例》第三十六条的规定，依法没收李某某违法所得人民币 27 861 元，并处罚款人民币 27 861 元。

八、遂宁“6·14”侵犯著作权案

2016 年 5 月 30 日，成都电子科大出版社有限责任公司向遂宁市文化市场综合执法支队举报：四川省大英中学和四川省大英县育才中学使用的《乐学七中高中数学零诊复习》为盗版，请求依法查处。6 月 14 日，遂宁市文化广电新闻出版局与大英县文化广电新闻出版局执法人员分两组对此案依法调查勘验。经权利人鉴定，四川省大英中学使用的 212 本（码洋为 10 557.6 元）《乐学七中高中数学零诊复习》，四川省大英县育才中学使用的 107 本（码洋为 5 136 元）《乐学七中高中化学必修 2》，均为盗版教辅资料，该盗版图书均为书商田某提供。

2016 年 10 月 10 日，遂宁市文广新局根据《中华人民共和国著作权法》第四十八条的规定，依法没收田某 319 本盗版教辅资料，并处罚款人民币 12 000 元整。

九、巴中海天电脑经营部侵犯著作权案

2016 年 8 月 26 日，巴中市巴州区文化市场综合执法大队执法人员在巴州区电脑城检查时发现，位于该电脑城的巴中海天电脑经营部销售的 Mastercam CAD/CAM Systems、Auto CAD 2009（开心天地）、Microsoft Visual FoxPro、友立音视频转换工具箱、最新输入法大全集、Auto CAD 2009（Microsoft for Windows）6 类共计 28 件光盘没有著作权人的许可使用合同，经查，当事人未经著作权人授权，擅自向公众发行著作权人的软件。

2016 年 9 月 18 日，巴中市巴州区文化广播影视新闻出版局依据《计算机软件保护条例》第八条第一款第（五）项，第十八条第一款和第二十四条第一款第（二）项、第二款之规定，依法没收当事人侵权软件 28 件，并处罚款人民币 2 800 元。

十、乐山“QQ190”音乐网站侵犯著作权案

2016 年 9 月 8 日，接四川省新闻出版局移送国家版权局“剑网行动”移转案件及相关初查材料，“QQ190”音乐网站未经权利人许可，擅自向公众提供大量侵权录音录像制品的下载和试听服务。乐山市文广新局于 2016 年 9 月 19 日对相关线索立案调查，通过网上远程勘验、对当事人进行调查询问等调查措施，查实卢某某未经著作权人许可，通过信息网络（自行设立的“QQ190”音乐网站）擅自向公众提供音乐作品。

2016 年 12 月 15 日，乐山市文广新局依据《信息网络传播权保护条例》第十八条第一款第（一）项之规定，责令卢某某立即停止侵权行为，并处以罚款人民币 8 000 元的行政处罚。

（四川省版权局）

陕 西 省

一、西咸新区沣西新城幕语影视咖啡厅侵犯电影作品著作权案

2016 年 12 月 12 日，陕西省版权局对西咸新区沣西新城幕语影视咖啡厅进行了现场检查，经查，自 2015 年 7 月 30 日起，当事人未经相关电影作品著作权人的许可，通过互联网擅自下载《头脑特工队》《地心引力》《忍者神龟》等 200 部电影作品存储在自备的硬盘内，经消费者点播后，在其经营场所向消费者放映，并收取费用。其行为破坏了著作权管理秩序，损害了公共利益，违反了《中华人民共和国著作权法》第四十八条第一款第（一）项规定，构成著作权侵权。根据《中华人民共和国著作权法实施条例》第三十六条规定，对其做出了停止侵权，罚款 2 万元人民币的处罚。

二、西安莱安电子科技有限公司侵犯电影作品著作权案

2016 年 11 月 14 日，陕西省版权局联合西安市文化市场行政执法总队对西安莱安电子科技有限公司经营场所进行了现场检查，对其下载电影作品的服务器进行了取证，对下载复制、放映的电影作品授权情况进行了核实。后查明：当事人未经权利人授权许可，擅自下载复制了《量子危机》《明日帝国》等60余部电影作品在公司开办的“时光影咖”包间内放映，并收取费用。其行为破坏了著作权管理秩序，损害了公共利益，违反了《中华人民共和国著作权法》第四十八条第一款第（一）项规定，构成著作权侵权。根据《中华人民共和国著作权法实施条例》第三十六条规定，对其做出了停止侵权，罚款1万元人民币的处罚。

三、西安点测网络科技有限公司软件侵权案

2016年，西安市文化市场行政执法总队按照“双打”行动精神要求积极开展“双打”工作。根据举报，西安点测网络科技有限公司所属的“蒲公英”网站，存在对手机网络游戏《斗破苍穹》的侵权行为。通过调查发现，该公司设立的“蒲公英”网站手机游戏《斗破苍穹》私服软件，侵犯了著作权人的信息网络传播权。

该案于2016年7月6日立案。2016年7月15日西安市文化市场行政执法总队依据《中华人民共和国著作权法》第四十八条第一款第（一）项，《信息网络传播权保护条例》第十八条第一款第（三）、第（五）项规定，责令西安点测网络科技有限公司停止侵权行为，并给予行政处罚35 000元人民币。

四、“天天播放”侵犯电影作品信息网络传播权案

根据陕西省“扫黄打非”办移转，按照投诉内容，陕西省版权局对“天天播放”网站（http//so.sxgkb.com）进行了远程调查取证，并及时发函陕西省通信管理局，对网站经营者的信息进行了调取。并根据陕西省通信管理局提供的信息，对该网站备案场所西安市吉祥小学门面房601进行了现场检查，发现备案场所为虚假信息。经电话与该公司法定代表人李雪玲联系，其拒不配合调查，并不再接听电话。

陕西省版权局经研究，函请陕西省通信管理局对该网站进行强行关停。2016年11月10日，该网站被关停，侵权行为被制止。

五、陕西晨星图书有限公司未经著作权人许可发行其作品案

2015年12月3日，西安市文化市场行政执法总队执法人员在陕西晨星图书有限公司检查时发现该公司销售的“植物大战僵尸2武器秘密之神奇探知历史漫画两汉时期——上”系列丛书未保留进销货票据，后经调查及中国少年儿童新闻出版总社证明，该批系列丛书为侵犯著作权的出版物。

2016年1月15日，西安市文化市场行政执法总队依据《中华人民共和国著作权法实施条例》第三十六条的规定，给予陕西晨星图书有限公司行政处罚10 700元人民币。

（陕西省版权局）

青 海 省

一、张某某经营侵权盗版音像制品案

2016年7月19日，大通县文化市场综合执法大队执法人员韩学梅、杨国伟、冯卫青对本县城关镇佰胜大街71号“云鹏钟表音像行”依法开展检查。经查，该店涉嫌销售侵权盗版音像制品，现场查获《我是特种兵之霹雳火》等音像制品254套317张。2016年7月20日，大通县文化市场综合执法大队对张某某涉嫌销售侵权盗版音像制品的行为立案调查。经青海省版权局认定，上述254套317张音像制品全部为侵权盗版产品。当事人张某某的行为违反了《中华人民共和国著作权》第四十八条第一款第（四）项的规定。依据《中华人民共和国著作权法实施条例》第三十六条，2016年9月5日，青海省西宁市大通县科技文化和旅游体育局决定对张某某给予以下行政处罚：（1）没收《我是特种兵之霹雳火》等191种254套317张侵权盗版音像制品光盘；（2）罚款人民币5 000元。

二、西宁嘉彩印刷有限公司盗印藏文书籍案

2016年6月8日，经群众举报，城东区文化旅游执法大队会同省文化和新闻出版厅发行处和省“扫黄打非”办对位于西宁经济技术开发区民和路33号创业园区的西宁嘉彩印刷有限公司进行了联合检查。现场检查发现，该场所印制疑似非法藏文出版物。6月8日，城东区文化旅游执法大队对此案进行立案调查，经过调查，证据事实清楚，该批书籍为藏文盗版书籍。依据《中华人民共和国著作权法》第四十八条第一款第（一）项、《中华人民共和国著作权法实施条例》第三十六条和《印刷业管理条例》第三十九条第一款第（三）项的规定，2016年7月29日，青海省西宁市城东区科技文体旅游局决定对该公司给予以下行政处罚：（1）警告；（2）罚款人民币30 000元整。

（青海省版权局）

版权

法律法规及规章文件

FA LYU FA GUI JI GUI ZHANG WEN JIAN

关于废止部分规章和规范性文件的决定

中华人民共和国国家版权局令

第12号

《关于废止部分规章和规范性文件的决定》已经2016年4月26日国家版权局局务会议通过，现予公布，自公布之日起施行。

局长　蔡赴朝

2016年4月29日

关于废止部分规章和规范性文件的决定

按照《国务院办公厅关于做好行政法规部门规章和文件清理工作有关事项的通知》（国办函［2016］12号）的要求，国家版权局对涉及不利于稳增长、促改革、调结构、惠民生的规章和规范性文件进行了清理。根据《规章制定程序条例》等相关规定，决定废止以下1个规章和7个规范性文件。

一、规章

1.《报刊转载、摘编法定许可付酬标准暂行规定》（国权［1993］41号）

二、规范性文件

1. 对《关于以少数民族文字翻译使用外国作品中有关著作权问题的报告》的答复（权办［1996］35号）

2. 关于贯彻实施《出版文字作品报酬规定》的意见（国权［1999］28号）

3. 关于印发《著作权行政处罚文书示范格式》的通知（国权［1999］39号）

4. 关于同意调整中国人民大学书报资料中心报刊转载作品付酬标准的复函（国权［2000］8号）

5. 计算机软件登记证书更换（国家版权局第8号公告）

6. 关于适用《出版文字作品报酬规定》的复函（国权办［2007］27号）

7. 关于《出版文字作品报酬规定》第16条适用问题的复函（国权办［2008］36号）

关于开展打击网络侵权盗版“剑网2016”专项行动的通知

国版发［2016］2号

各省（自治区、直辖市）版权局，各省（自治区、直辖市）网信办（网宣办、网管办）、通信管理局、公安厅（局），北京市、天津市、上海市、重庆市文化市场行政执法总队：

根据国务院办公厅《关于加强互联网领域侵权假冒行为治理的意见》和2016年打击侵犯知识产权和制售假冒伪劣商品工作的部署，国家版权局、国家互联网信息办公室、工业和信息化部、公安部（以下简称“国家版权局等四部门”）将于2016年7月至11月联合开展第十二次打击网络侵权盗版专项治理“剑网行动”（简称“剑网2016”专项行动）。现将有关事项通知如下：

一、工作目标

加大网络版权执法力度，提高网络版权保护水平，保障有关权利人的合法权益，维护网络版权正常秩序，营造网络版权良好生态。突出整治未经授权非法传播网络文学、新闻、影视等作品的侵权盗版行为，保障有关权利人的合法权益；重点查处通过智能移动终端第三方应用程序（APP）、电子商务平台、网络广告联盟、私人影院（小影吧）等平台进行的侵权盗版行为，维护网络版权正常秩序；进一步规范网络音乐、网络云存储空间、网络转载新闻作品的版权秩序，营造网络版权良好生态。

二、重点任务

一是开展打击网络文学侵权盗版专项整治行动。加强对文学网站的版权执法监管力度，严厉打击通过网站、贴吧、微博、微信等方式未经授权非法传播网络文学作品的侵权盗版行为，严厉打击通过电子商务平台销售盗版图书、音像制品的违法行为，规范通过浏览器、搜索引擎等方式传播文学作品的行为。

二是开展打击APP侵权盗版专项整治行动。加强对APP上传者和应用程序商店的版权执法监管，加大对聚合类APP、与网络电视棒及电视机顶盒关联的APP侵权盗版行为的打击力度，强化应用程序商店对提供文学、新闻、影视、音乐等作品APP上传者的版权监管责任。

三是开展规范网络广告联盟专项整治行动。加强对网络广告联盟在版权保护方面的监督管理，推动网络广告联盟落实企业主体责任、建立版权保护工作机制，推动版权执法监管机构与网络广告联盟建立切断侵权盗版黑色经济链条的工作机制，严厉打击故意为侵权盗版提供支持的网络广告联盟。

三、工作措施

（一）加强监测检查。各地要对传播文学、影视、音乐、新闻、游戏、软件等作品的重点网站和网络广告联盟、应用程序商店、电子商务平台、私人影院（小影吧）等进行全面清理检查，并将享有著作权的广播电台电视台节目、金融信息作品纳入版权监测范围。要组织企业开展自查自纠，查找侵权盗版问题。对发现的问题要责令企业进行限期整改，对未按期完成整改的要依法查处。

（二）突出查办案件。各级版权执法部门要发挥优势，突出重点，积极履行查办案件职责，加大对网络侵权盗版案件的行政处罚和刑事移送力度。省级版权行政执法部门要起带头作用，通过查办案件引领示范，并充分发挥中心城市及市县级版权行政执法部门查处案件的积极性。要迅速梳理一批案件线索，集中力量、快查快办；对侵权事实严重、社会影响大的侵权盗版网站，要依法从严查处；对涉嫌构成犯罪的，要及时移交公安部门立案查办。

（三）创新工作方法。要在网络文学、APP、网络广告联盟等领域建立“黑白名单”制度，树立版权保护典型企业，建立重点保护作品“白名单”库，公布侵权盗版互联网企业“黑名单”。加强侵权盗版案件信息公开，健全对互联网企业的约谈、警示、通报工作机制，推进版权领域信用体系建设。创新网络技术监测方式方法，利用第三方网络监测技术特点和优势，运用大数据分析、网络版权监管平台等新技术手段发现线索、固定证据、移交转办，提高执法打击的精准度。加强业务培训，增强利用新技术进行监管的能力。积极推动权利人及组织与互联网企业建立版权合作机制，探索建立符合互联网发展的授权模式，建立完善网站版权信息库、权利人维权绿色通道。

（四）完善工作机制。版权行政执法部门要会同通信主管部门建立快速反应机制，对从事侵权盗版活动的非法网站，依法及时制止违法行为，及时采取措施暂停网络接入。要健全常态化的联合挂牌督办机制，定期联合督办一批重点案件，做到及时督办、及时上报、及时结案。要加强行政执法与刑事司法衔接工作机制，加大刑事打击力度，充分利用集群战役模式，摧毁犯罪网络和产业链条。要不断健全区域间执法协作、协查机制，推进案件线索和信息共享，开展区域执法联动。

（五）落实主体责任。要通过专项整治，指导、督促互联网企业落实主体责任、加强行业自律。督促互联网企业加强内部版权监控和管理机制，实施侵权盗版信息巡查清理及记录留存，履行违法犯罪线索报告义务。指导提供信息存储空间或提供搜索、链接服务等网络服务提供者落实“通知—删除”义务，及时采取删除、屏蔽、断开链接等措施处理侵权盗版信息。推动应用程序商店、网络文学企业、网络广告联盟建立健全投诉举报快速处理工作机制，引导互联网企业建立共享工作机制，充分发挥打击侵权盗版的合力作用。

（六）加强宣传动员。要通过电视、广播、报纸等传统媒体和各种形式新媒体大力宣传专项行动的措施、进展和成效，积极发动权利人和广大群众投诉举报，公布电话、电子信箱、微信等投诉举报方式，鼓励社会大众积极提供案件线索。要加大对大案要案和典型案件的宣传力度，做好侵权盗版案件的信息公开工作，坚决曝光具有恶劣情节的侵权盗版互联网企业与违法犯罪分子，教育和引导广大网民树立“尊重版权、鼓励创新”的基本意识，为开展专项行动营造良好舆论环境。

四、行动步骤

（一）工作部署阶段（7月1日—7月15日）。1. 国家版权局等四部门召开新闻通气会，全面启动专项行动。2. 各地上报工作计划和实施方案。3. 各地制定宣传方案，大力宣传专项行动。

（二）清理检查阶段（7月16日—7月31日）。1. 各地组织引导重点互联网企业开展自查自纠活动，查找侵权盗版问题。2. 组织动员国内外权利人组织和社会公众积极投诉举报，搜集案件线索。3. 开展执法培训，组织各有关部门执法人员的培训工作。

（三）集中整治阶段（8月1日—10月31日）。以整治网络文学、APP、广告联盟等为重点，各地根据上级移交和自行搜集到的案件线索开展执法行动，依法加大行政处罚和刑事打击力度，集中查办一批大案要案。

（四）督查总结阶段（11月1日—11月30日）。1. 国家版权局等四部门对重点地区、重点企业进行督导检查，确保专项行动落实到位。2. 各地上报工作总结。3. 国家版权局等四部门联合召开新闻通气会，通报本次专项行动取得的成效。4. 对专项行动中表现突出的单位和个人纳入2016年度版权执法有功单位和个人奖励范围予以奖励，对重大典型案件进行专项奖励。

五、工作要求

（一）加强组织领导。各地要高度重视本次专项行动，各级版权行政管理部门要根据本地情况，协调文化综合执法、互联网信息内容、通信主管、公安等部门，召开行动部署会，制定工作计划，明确任务和责任分工。

（二）及时报送信息。省级版权局、文化市场行政执法总队要汇总本地办案信息，填写工作统计表格（见附件1、2）按月报送国家版权局。省级版权局、文化市场行政执法总队于本通知下发后15日内报送本地实施方案，12月10日前报送专项行动总结。

（三）加强协调联动。各地版权、互联网信息内容、通信主管、公安等部门要进一步加强配合，协同作战，按照分工认真开展工作。版权行政执法监管部门负责专项行动的牵头工作，具体负责组织梳理网上侵权信息，搜集案件线索，查处违法行为，移送涉嫌犯罪案件，提请通信主管部门予以暂时关闭网站直至关闭网站；开展版权监管工作。组织专项行动的宣传和奖励工作。互联网信息内容主管部门负责指导、协调、督促有关部门加强网络内容管理，有效利用各种手段加强对网络内容的监管。通信主管部门协助开展网络侵权盗版案件调查取证工作，协助提供查处网络侵权盗版案件涉及网站的备案信息；对经版权、公安部门查处且侵权盗版情节严重的网站依法吊销电信业务经营许可证或者注销网站备案，并通知相关接入服务商停止为其提供网站接入服务；组织开展行业自律活动。公安部门要加大对网络侵权盗版涉嫌犯罪案件的线索摸集、立案查处工作，及时受理版权部门移送的涉嫌犯罪的案件，进一步加大对侵权盗版犯罪案件的刑事打击力度。

特此通知。

附件：1. 工作情况统计表（略）

2. 查处案件信息表（略）

国家版权局
国家互联网信息办公室
工业和信息化部
公安部
2016年6月14日

关于规范作品登记证书的通知

国版函〔2016〕1号

各省、自治区、直辖市版权局，新疆生产建设兵团版权局，中国版权保护中心：

为进一步加强版权社会服务体系建设，完善作品登记制度，保障版权交易安全，逐步实现作品登记工作统一管理的目标，定于2016年6月1日起启用由我局统一监制的新版作品登记证书及印章，现将有关事项通知如下：

一、新版本作品登记证书由国家版权局统一监制（具体样式见附件1），该证书样本以电子形式发放，登记机构可通过国家版权局网站（www.ncac.gov.cn）下载，并严格按照样本自行印制。

二、新版本作品登记证书载有的作品登记号格式不变，为地区编号-年份-作品分类号-序号（8位起始），地区编号列表、作品分类号不变（见附件2）。

三、印章一律为圆形。直径为105px，圆边宽为2.5px，上弧为单位名称（如××省版权局），自左而右环行，中央一律刊五角星，星尖直径为35px，下弧首行一律刊“作品自愿登记”，次行为“专用章”，均自左而右环形，印文使用简化的宋体字（印章样式见附件3）。

四、各登记机构要加强新版本作品登记证书的管理，认真做好编号、登记、发放工作，做到有序、平稳过渡。

请各省、自治区、直辖市版权局，新疆生产建设兵团版权局及中国版权保护中心认真贯彻落实本通知的要求，进一步推动作品登记工作的规范化、标准化，提高作品登记工作的质量。

附件：1. 新版本作品登记证书样本（略）

2. 地区编号列表、作品分类号（略）

3. 印章样本（略）

国家版权局

2016年2月15日

关于印发《2015年推进使用正版软件工作总结》和《2016年推进使用正版软件工作计划》的通知

国版函〔2016〕2号

各省、自治区、直辖市人民政府，推进使用正版软件工作部际联席会议各成员单位：

《2015年推进使用正版软件工作总结》《2016年推进使用正版软件工作计划》已经推进使用正版软件工作部际联席会议第五次全体会议审议通过，现将上述文件印发给你们，请认真贯彻执行。请各省（区、市）制定本省（区、市）2016年推进使用正版软件工作实施方案，并于4月15日前报送至部际联席会议办公室。

推进使用正版软件工作部际联席会议

国家新闻出版广电总局（国家版权局） 代章

2016年3月16日

2015年推进使用正版软件工作总结

2015年是“十二五”规划的收官之年，也是推进使用正版软件工作进入新常态之年。2015年，在国务院的高度重视和正确领导下，推进使用正版软件工作部际联席会议（以下简称“部际联席会议”）认真贯彻落实党的十八大和十八届三中、四中、五中全会精神，加强组织领导、统筹协调和服务指导，推进使用正版软件工作取得新进展。

一、取得的成效

（一）初步建立政府机关软件正版化工作责任制度

部际联席会议推进责任落实到人，建立了中央和省级机关软件正版化工作责任人数据库，指导各省（区、市）建立了市县级机关责任人数据库。推动各省（区、市）建立健全软件正版化工作考核评议制度，指导北京、天津、河北、内蒙古、福建、海南、重庆、青海、新疆等省（区、市）制定了软件正版化工作考核评议细则。各级政府机关切实落实责任，加强软件使用管理，及时购置更新正版软件。92.63%的中央部门所属事业单位实现软件正版化。2015年，各级政府机关共采购操作系统、办公和杀毒软件95.19万套，采购金额4.92亿元；采购的办公软件中，国产软件套数占73.01%。

（二）企业软件正版化工作取得重要突破

中央企业软件正版化工作取得重大进展，98.62%的五级及以上企业实现软件正版化。大中型金融机构、新闻出版行业企业集团总部实现软件正版化。各省（区、市）制定了推进国有企业软件正版化工作实施方案，全面部署地方国有企业软件正版化工作。山西、西藏、甘肃、青海等省（区）制定了推进民营企业软件正版化工作实施方案，河北、福建、河南、湖北、宁夏等省（区）印发了关于做好推进民营企业使用正版软件工作有关事项的通知，积极稳妥推进民营企业软件正版化工作。

2015年，全国共有2 882家企业列入年度完成软件正版化工作目标，其中2 438家企业通过检查验收实现软件正版化。截至2015年底，全国累计27 001家企业通过检查验收实现软件正版化，75.35%的金融机构、93.8%的新闻出版行业企业集团下属企业实现软件正版化。2015年，中央企业和金融机构采购、升级和维护操作系统、办公和杀毒软件金额共计18.14亿元。

（三）推进软件正版化工作示范效应明显

政府机关和大中型企业带头使用正版软件，起到了示范和带动作用，软件知识产权保护环境持续改善，为软件产业发展提供了良好的市场环境和创新动力，推进了软件产业呈现繁荣发展的良好态势，也树立了中国政府保护知识产权的良好形象。2015年，软件著作权登记量达到29.24万件，同比增长33.63%。2015年，软件和信息技术服务业收入达到4.3万亿元，同比增长16.6%。世界贸易组织、世界知识产权组织等国际组织在多个场合高度评价中国政府推进软件正版化工作。

二、具体做法

（一）国务院领导高度重视，亲自部署

汪洋副总理三次主持召开打击侵权假冒工作领导小组会议，将推进软件正版化工作与打击侵权假冒工作同研究、同部署、同推进。汪洋副总理高度评价软件正版化工作取得的成绩，指出部际联席会议各成员单位齐心协力、共同努力，推进政府机关如期完成软件正版化工作任务，并把这项工作延伸到国有企业和事业单位，全面兑现推进软件正版化工作承诺，是展现中国政府保护知识产权决心和力度的标志性工程，树立了中国政府良好的国际形象，同时要求严格落实推进软件正版化工作有关政策措施，完善长效机制，巩固和扩大软件正版化工作成果。全国打击侵权假冒工作领导小组将推进软件正版化工作列入2015年打击侵权假冒重点工作，加强推进软件正版化工作的督促检查和考核评议。

（二）部际联席会议加强统筹谋划，密切协同推进

1. 科学谋划全局，共同研究推进措施。2015年2月，部际联席会议召开了第四次全体会议，从推进责任落实、规范使用管理、严格监督检查、加大推进力度、加强市场监管、做好宣传培训等六个方面，研究部署2015年推进软件正版化有关工作，制定了2015年推进软件正版化工作计划。

2. 深入基层调研，掌握政策落实情况。2015年3—4月，国家版权局会同国资委、银监会、证监会、保监会等部门组织了5个调研组，深入了解中央企业和金融机构软件正版化工作取得的成效、存在的问题，协调解决企业遇到的困难。2015年10月，以国家版权局副局长阎晓宏同志为组长，部际联席会议办公室相关同志为成员的调研组，深入基层了解推进软件正版化工作政策实施情况，增强推进软件正版化工作措施的针对性和有效性。

3. 加强过程监管，推进工作落到实处。2015年4月，部际联席会议办公室印发《关于进一步落实政府机关软件正版化工作责任的函》（国版办函［2015］20号），指导各省（区、市）建立健全软件正版化工作责任制度和考核评议办法、开展软件使用情况专项自查，加强软件使用管理和日常监督检查。2015年11月，部际联席会议办公室分别向中央各部门和各省（区、市）发出《关于请报送2015年软件正版化工作总结的函》（国版办函［2015］66号）和《关于请报送2015年推进使用正版软件工作总结的函》（国版办函［2015］67号），指导各级政府机关报送软件正版化工作年度报告，推进政府机关软件正版化工作常态化落到实处。国资委、国家版权局组建联合工作组，共同研究巩固中央企业软件正版化工作措施。

4. 明确目标任务，扩大推进工作范围。2015年4月，国资委印发《关于做好2015年推进中央企业使用正版软件工作的通知》（国资厅［2015］170号），要求中央企业加强组织领导，重点推进中央企业四级及以下企业软件正版化工作，推动中央企业实现软件正版化工作“三年目标”、积极争创企业软件正版化工作表率。2015年1月，国资委、国家版权局联合印发《关于做好推进地方国有企业使用正版软件工作有关事项的通知》（国版发［2015］1号），明确了推进地方国有企业软件正版化工作目标和时限要求。2015年6月，保监会印发《关于做好2015年保险机构推进使用正版软件有关工作的通知》（保监厅发［2015］44号），要求各保险机构从防范保险金融风险、确保信息安全的高度，加快推进软件正版化工作。2015年6月，全国工商联、国家版权局联合印发《关于做好推进民营企业使用正版软件工作有关事项的通知》（全联厅发［2015］23

号），全面启动民营企业软件正版化工作。

5. 严格监督检查，确保政策落地生效。2015 年 7 月下旬至 10 月上旬，部际联席会议办公室组织了 12 个检查组，分别由工业和信息化部、商务部、国资委、国家工商总局、国家知识产权局、国管局、国务院法制办、银监会、证监会、保监会、全国工商联和国家版权局有关部门负责同志带队，抽查了 24 家中央部门和 12 个省（区、市）的 71 家省级机关，共抽查计算机 1 587 台，并向各地区、各部门通报了检查中发现的典型经验和存在的问题。2015 年，审计署结合 42 家中央部门 2014 年度预算执行审计，对政府机关软件正版化情况进行了重点检查，审计发现的问题全部纳入了审计报告并向社会进行了公告。2015 年 11 月，国资委会同国家版权局组织了 2 个联合检查组，抽查了 10 家中央企业软件正版化工作；国家版权局组织了 5 个检查组，对各省（区、市）新闻出版行业企业集团软件正版化工作进行了全面检查。银监会、证监会、保监会、全国工商联等将软件正版化工作纳入了信息科技监管、信息化建设和信息安全检查的重要内容。

6. 提升软件能力，支撑推进工作基础。工业和信息化部加强计算机预装正版操作系统软件监管，会同有关部门研究解决微软停止 Windows XP 操作系统软件服务问题，加强软件产业发展指导，引导软件企业提升“软件能力”和“系统能力”。国产操作系统软件与国际主流操作系统软件兼容，功能、性能基本相当。国产办公软件达到国际先进水平。国产软件在典型行业和重大工程中应用，为推进软件正版化工作提供有力支撑。银监会继续推进《关于应用安全可控信息技术加强银行业网络安全和信息化建设的指导意见》（银监发［2014］39 号）的实施，组织银行业金融机构开展基于国产操作系统软件的 ATM 机客户端软件开发和应用试点，拟从根本上解决 Windows XP 操作系统软件停止服务带来的安全隐患。银监会、证监会组织开展了国产操作系统软件软硬件兼容性测试，为国产操作系统软件应用推广奠定了基础。

7. 广泛宣传培训，营造良好舆论氛围。在全国打击侵权假冒工作领导小组办公室的指导下，部际联席会议办公室举办了 4 期大型政府机关软件正版化工作培训班，各中央和国家机关、31 个省（区、市）推进软件正版化工作相关部门参加了培训。国资委、国家版权局、全国工商联分别针对各自监管企业开展了推进软件正版化工作专题培训。部际联席会议各成员单位通过新闻发布会、官方网站等方式积极宣传推进软件正版化工作成果。商务部会同有关部门在中美商贸联委会、中欧知识产权对话、亚太经合组织等多双边交流机制，以及中国知识产权海外交流活动中积极宣传中国政府推进软件正版化工作取得的进展和成效，及时回应外方关切。部际联席会议办公室通过编发专报、简报，出版《软件正版化在中国》专刊，利用中央电视台、《人民日报》、新华社、《中国新闻出版报》等权威媒体报道，以及国家版权局官方微博、微信推送消息等形式加强宣传引导。

（三）各地区落实工作责任，创新推进措施

1. 严格规范标准，加强考核评议。北京、河北、内蒙古、福建、海南、重庆、青海、新疆对省级机关和市级政府软件正版化工作进行了全面考核。北京以市政府名义通报了考核结果。河北各级机关逐级、逐人签订使用正版软件承诺书。内蒙古将软件正版化工作纳入了 2015 年度盟市厅局党政领导班子年度考核。新疆对软件正版化工作考核结果达不到优秀、良好等级的单位进行了全面复查。

2. 严把采购环节，强化审批流程。黑龙江要求各级财政部门在审核计算机办公设备采购时，要审核落实计算机设备必须预装正版操作系统软件，并有办公软件采购经费预算；对特殊用途计算机，不需要采购办公软件的，必须经同级版权管理部门审批同意后，才能批准采购计划。山东要求各级政府机关购置计算机办公设备时，对办公软件、杀毒软件一并做出购置计划。陕西要求各级财政部门在审核预算单位上报的计算机采购计划时，重点审核是否落实操作系统软件和办公软件采购预算。福建厦门要求市级机关原则上使用集中采购的场地授权办公软件，因特殊需要采购其他品种办公软件的，须经市版权局审核同意后，才能按照政府采购规定进行采购。湖南岳阳要求版权部门全程参与软件采购招标活动，防止盗版软件流入政府采购环节。

3. 加强督促检查，推进责任落实。辽宁开展了两次政府机关软件正版化工作督查，对省级机关进行了全面检查，抽查了 84 家市级机关和 216 家县级机关，共抽查计算机 2 574 台。浙江开展了两次政府机关软件正版化工作督查，推动省级机关和市级政府全部按期报送了 2015 年软件正版化工作年度报告。山东抽查了 156 家政府机关、196 家企业软件正版化工作，共抽查计算机 3 000 多台。湖北抽查了 258 家政府机关、80 家企业软件正版化工作，共抽查计算机 2 640 台。广东将 158 家企业列入重点督办单位，一一督查核实重点督办单位软件正版化工作完成情况。西藏重点督查了市县级政府机关软件正版化工作，推进列入完成软件正版化工作目标的21家国有企业和12家民营企业全部实现软件正版化。2015年，各省（区、市）共督查了3.35万家（次）政府机关软件正版化工作。

4. 改进推进方式，鼓励先进示范。江苏将版权示范创建与软件正版化工作有机结合，将完成软件正版化工作作为申报省级版权示范城市、示范单位和示范园区（基地）的必要条件。安徽将完成软件正版化工作作为评选省级诚信示范企业的重要指标，120家企业共投入5 000多万元采购正版软件实现软件正版化。贵州在四个县（区）开展国产操作系统软件应用试点，有效解决软件采购经费紧张问题。广西利用正版软件管理系统，及时、动态、准确管理全区正版软件采购和使用情况。陕西在政府机关软件正版化工作督查中提出了“六四二”争先创优标准，6家省级机关被评为“推进政府机关软件正版化工作创优示范单位”。甘肃根据完成软件正版化工作进度，以奖代补方式奖励扎实推进工作的各级党群部门，奖励资金总额达到1 000万元。新疆综合运用宣传教育、奖励补贴和督促检查等多种手段，推进企业软件正版化工作成效显著，兑现25家企业软件正版化奖补资金57.5万元。

5. 加强宣传培训，增强正版意识。北京制发了2 000余册《软件正版化宣传手册》，以漫画的形式，宣传软件正版化工作相关政策措施、标准规范和工作方法等。山西在各级机关显著位置张贴软件正版化宣传海报，强化机关工作人员使用正版软件意识。黑龙江加强县级政府机关软件正版化工作培训，举办了32期政府机关软件正版化工作培训班，参训单位2 300余家（次），参训人数2 500余人（次）。各省（区、市）通过新闻发布会、“4·26”知识产权宣传周集中宣传，利用电视、电台、报刊、公交移动媒体、互联网以及微博、微信等新媒体及时发布等方式，开展了丰富多样的软件正版化成果宣传活动。2015年，各省（区、市）共举办1 495期政府机关软件正版化工作培训班，参训单位4.24万家（次），参训人数8.86万人（次）；共举办285期企业软件正版化工作培训班，参训单位6 665家（次），参训人数1.97万人（次）。

三、存在的问题

（一）思想认识问题。一些单位软件正版化工作责任部门和责任人不明确。有的单位对推进软件正版化工作的必要性和重要意义缺乏足够的认识，软件版权保护意识还比较薄弱，软件版权保护环境尚未得到根本性改善。

（二）软件采购问题。一方面是一些单位采购计算机时，“重硬轻软”现象比较严重。有的单位采购计算机时，没有严格落实采购预装正版操作系统软件计算机的规定；有的单位新采购计算机时，没有一并购置必需的办公软件；有的单位采购软件时没有签订软件采购合同，或虽签订了采购合同，但合同中对软件的性能和售后服务要求不够细化。另一方面是一些软件厂商的销售渠道还不规范。有的软件厂商服务不到位；有的计算机销售商未按要求向用户提供预装正版操作系统软件的计算机。

（三）使用管理问题。一些单位软件使用管理制度不健全，“重购轻管”现象较为严重。有的单位软件使用管理制度流于形式，没有建立软件安装使用台账；有的单位软件安装使用台账更新不及时，台账内容与实际情况不完全一致；有的单位存在员工私自下载安装软件现象，软件安装使用日常监管不严。

（四）推进力度问题。推进软件正版化工作奖惩措施不到位，对软件侵权盗版行为的处罚力度不够，警示和震慑作用不强，难以形成强大的威慑力，在一定程度上影响了软件正版化工作的整体推进。

推进软件正版化工作是一项长期任务，对营造创新环境、推进创新驱动、保障信息安全和维护国家形象具有重要意义。2016年，部际联席会议将继续认真贯彻落实党中央、国务院的决策部署，持续深入地推进软件正版化工作，为建设法治社会、创新型国家做出应有的贡献。

2016年推进使用正版软件工作计划

2016年是“十三五”规划的开局之年，也是巩固和扩大软件正版化工作成果的关键之年。2016年的工作重点是完善长效机制，推进软件正版化工作规范化、标准化，加强软件研发指导与推广，加强督促检查和宣传培训，巩固政府机关、中央企业和大中型金融机构软件正版化工作成果，加快推进地方国有企业、中小金融机构和民营企业软件正版化工作，为实施创新驱动发展战略营造良好环境。

一、突出重点，完善推进软件正版化长效机制

（一）加强软硬件采购源头管理。研究规范计算机软硬件采购具体措施，完善计算机软硬件采购合同对软件兼容性、授权方式、使用年限、技术支持及售后服务等方面的要求。推进各地区、各部门严格落实新采购计算机时，采购预装正版操作系统软件的计算机，对需要购置的办公软件和杀毒软件一并做出购置计划，从源头上防止盗版软件流入政府机关。（财政部、国管局、中直管理局牵头）

（二）改进推进软件正版化工作管理模式。建立推进软件正版化工作信息化管理平台，通过信息化手段系统全面管理软件卫版化工作相关制度文件、进展情况、软件购置安装及使用管理等信息，提高相关信息统计分析效率，提升推进软件正版化工作水平。（国家版权局牵头）

（三）推进软件使用和管理标准化。研究制定软件使用和管理指南，建立可行性、操作性较强的软件使用和管理制度范本，以及软件安装使用台账范本。研究利用云计算等新技术创新推进措施，加快推进服务器端软件正版化工作。坚持制度与技术手段并重，推进各地区、各部门软件使用和管理标准化。（国家版权局牵头）

二、分工协作，明确推进软件正版化目标任务

（四）巩固政府机关软件正版化工作成果。推进各级政府机关完善软件正版化工作责任制度，以及软件正版化工作考核评议和责任追究制度。推动各级政府机关形成年初有计划、年中有检查、年底有总结的软件正版化工作格局。（国家版权局牵头）

（五）深入推进国有企业和金融机构软件正版化工作。巩固中央企业和大中型金融机构软件正版化工作成果，充分发挥中央企业和大中型金融机构软件正版化工作示范带动作用。研究加快推进地方国有企业和中小金融机构软件正版化工作具体措施。推进企业将软件正版化工作与业绩考核挂钩。（国资委、银监会、证监会、保监会、国家版权局分别牵头，部际联席会议办公室做好服务和配合工作）

（六）推进民营企业软件正版化工作。发挥实现软件正版化民营企业的示范带动作用，加快推进民营企业软件正版化工作。（全国工商联牵头，部际联席会议办公室做好服务和配合工作）

三、严格督查，切实推进软件正版化责任落实

（七）开展中央和国家机关、地方政府推进软件正版化工作专项督查。2016 年 6 月至 7 月，部际联席会议组织开展中央和国家机关、地方政府推进软件正版化工作督查。重点抽查中央和国家机关，省级机关，国有企业、金融机构、大中型民营企业。指导各省（区、市）督查本省（区、市）政府机关和企业软件正版化工作。推进各级政府机关和企事业单位落实软件正版化工作主体责任。（国家版权局牵头）

（八）开展行业企业软件正版化工作专项督查。适时组织开展中央企业，银行业、证券期货业、保险业、新闻出版业，以及民营企业软件正版化工作督查。（国资委、银监会、证监会、保监会、国家版权局、全国工商联分别牵头，部际联席会议办公室做好服务和配合工作）

（九）开展软件正版化审计。结合中央部门 2015 年度预算执行审计及其他审计项目，把政府机关软件正版化情况作为审计的重要内容。进一步加强对地方审计部门相关审计工作的指导。（审计署牵头）

（十）开展软件资产管理专项检查。加强中央部门软件资产管理工作监管，指导地方财政部门扎实推进软件资产管理工作。适时组织开展中央国家机关贯彻落实《财业部关于进一步规范和加强政府机关软件资产管理的意见》（财行［2011］7 号）、《政府机关办公通用软件资产配置标准（试行）》（财行［2013］98 号）、《中央行政事业单位软件资产管理暂行办法》（国管资［2011］280 号）、《中央国家机关通用办公软件配置标准》（国管资［2013］42 号）情况专项检查。（财政部、国管局分别牵头）

（十一）改进软件正版化督查方式。建立常态化随机督查制度。重视利用技术手段加强监管。建立政府主导、社会专业机构参与的督查队伍。研究建立软件使用情况监测平台，加强动态监管，增强督查工作的针对性和有效性。（国家版权局牵头）

四、夯实基础，严抓推进软件正版化日常工作

（十二）完善政府机关软件正版化责任人数据库。及时更新、完善中央和省市县四级政府机关软件正版化工作责任人数据库。推进各级政府机关进一步明确软件正版化工作责任部门和责任人，充分发挥责任部门和责任人的作用。（国家版权局牵头）

（十三）开展软件使用情况专项自查。开展政府机关和企业软件使用情况年度专项自查，指导相关单位科学合理制定软件采购计划，将软件采购资金纳入预算。（国家版权局、国资委、银监会、证监会、保监会、全国工商联分别牵头）

（十四）开展正版软件使用管理试点。在自愿的基础上，在部分政府机关和企事业单位开展软件使用管理试点工作，进一步推进相关单位软件正版化工作规范化。（国家版权局牵头）

（十五）推进通用软件集中采购。做好 2016 年党政机关软件集中采购指导服务工作。扩大中央企业软件集中采购网适用范围，建立中央国家机关正版软件采购数据库。加大中央企业软件集中采购网在中央企业下属企业的宣传力度。指导建立行业企业软件集中采购平台。充分发挥集中采购优势，协助党政机关和企事业单位降低软件采购成本。加大推广应用优秀软件产品力度。（国管局、中直管理局、国资委、国家版权局、银监会、证监会、保监会、全国工商联分别牵头，部际联席会议办公室做好服务和配合工作）

（十六）完善信息报送制度。完善政府机关和企业软件正版化信息报送范围、报送内容、报送形式和时限要求，建立动态更新的政府机关和企业软件正版化工作进展情况信息库。（国家版权局、国资委、银监会、证监会、保监会、全国工商联分别牵头，部际联席会议办公室做好服务和配合工作）

五、加强监管，维护软件市场公平竞争秩序

（十七）严厉打击软件侵权盗版行为。将打击软件侵权盗版行为作为重要内容纳入打击侵权假冒工作和打击网络侵权盗版“剑网 2016”专项行动，曝光侵犯软件著作权企业。探索将企业使用侵权盗版软件行为纳入诚信体系建设内容。（国家版权局牵头）

（十八）依法查处软件行业垄断和不正当竞争行为。加大对硬件行业等重点领域的竞争执法力度，严厉查处垄断和不正当竞争行为。维护软件市场公平竞争的市场秩序和消费者合法权益。（国家工商总局牵头）

（十九）加强计算机预装正版操作系统软件监管。加大计算机预装正版操作系统软件检查力度，开展计算机预装正版操作系统软件专项检查，督促计算机生产商和销售商落实计算机预装正版操作软件有关规定。（工业和信息化部牵头）

六、广泛宣传，营造推进软件正版化良好氛围

（二十）做好宣传培训。加大软件正版化工作宣传培训力度，建立层级化宣传培训体系，扩大宣传培训覆盖面，及时发布软件正版化工作成果，推广软件正版化典型经验做法，增强宣传培训的针对性和有效性。开展软件正版化工作示范单位评选，提高软件正版化工作先进单位的积极性。（部际联席会议各成员单位分别牵头）

（二十一）加强国际交流。利用知识产权多双边磋商和交流机制，加大软件正版化成果对外宣传力度，及时回应外方关切，营造有利于我发展的外部环境。（商务部牵头）

国家版权局关于奖励 2015 年度查处侵权盗版案件有功单位及有功个人的决定

国版函［2016］4 号

各省、自治区、直辖市版权局，新疆生产建设兵团版权局，北京、天津、上海、重庆市文化市场行政执法总队，中宣部、工业和信息化部、公安部、海关总署、工商总局办公厅，国家互联网信息办公室秘书局，高法院、高检院办公厅，全国打击侵犯知识产权和制售假冒伪劣商品工作领导小组办公室，各相关协会、新闻媒体：

为进一步调动版权相关执法部门查处侵权盗版案件的积极性和主动性，充分发挥查处侵权盗版案件先进典型的引导、示范作用，根据《国家版权局举报、查处侵权盗版行为奖励暂行办法》及实施细则的规定，国家版权局决定对在 2015 年度查处侵权盗版案件工作中做出突出贡献的 195 家有功单位及 215 名有功个人给予奖励。

各级版权相关执法部门及广大执法人员要向查处侵权盗版案件有功单位和有功个人学习，进一步加强版权执法监管工作，严厉查处各类侵权盗版行为，有效维护权利人合法权益，积极推动版权相关产业健康发展，为提升我国版权保护水平做出更大贡献。

附件：2015 年度查处侵权盗版案件有功单位及有功个人名单

国家版权局

2016 年 4 月 20 日

附件

2015 年度查处侵权盗版案件有功单位及有功个人名单

【有功单位一等奖】

1. 最高人民检察院侦查监督厅立案监督处（保护

知识产权处）
2. 公安部治安管理局一处
3. 中国版权保护中心法律部
4. 新闻出版总署信息中心互联网监测部
5. 北京市文化市场行政执法总队执法四队
6. 北京市文化市场行政执法总队执法五队
7. 河北张某某等印制盗版图书案专案组（河北省保定市“扫黄打非”领导小组办公室、河北省保定市文化市场行政执法大队、河北省保定市公安局、河北省保定市竞秀区公安分局经济犯罪侦查大队、河北省保定市竞秀区文体教育局）
8. 吉林省版权局版权处
9. 上海市版权局版权管理执法处
10. 上海市文化市场行政执法总队稽查五处
11. 上海市浦东新区人民法院民三庭（知识产权庭）
12. 上海汪某等侵犯著作权案专案组（上海市徐汇区人民法院民三庭、上海市徐汇区人民检察院金融检察科）
13. 江苏省版权局版权管理处
14. 江苏“速酷电影”网侵犯著作权案专案组（江苏省徐州市文化广电新闻出版局、江苏省徐州市公安局网安支队案件队）
15. 江苏“金火影视网”侵犯著作权案专案组（江苏省徐州市“扫黄打非”工作领导小组办公室、江苏省徐州市中级人民法院民事审判第三庭、江苏省徐州市铜山区公安局网安大队、江苏省徐州市铜山区文化广播新闻与体育局）
16. 江苏“77免费电影网”侵犯著作权案专案组（江苏省徐州市版权局、江苏省徐州市人民检察院公诉处）
17. 江苏省无锡市开发区人民检察院
18. 浙江省版权局版权处
19. 浙江省金华市中级人民法院民事审判第三庭
20. 浙江郑某等复制并通过网络销售盗版图书和软件案专案组（浙江省杭州市文化市场行政执法总队、浙江省杭州市公安局治安支队三大队（治安行动队）、浙江省杭州市拱墅区公安分局巡特警大队、浙江省杭州市拱墅区人民检察院、浙江省杭州市拱墅区人民法院刑事审判庭）
21. 安徽省版权局版权管理处
22. 安徽省合肥市文化市场综合执法大队
23. 福建省福州市文化市场综合执法支队
24. 福建省宁德市蕉城区人民检察院
25. 山东省版权局版权管理处
26. 山东省青岛市文化市场行政执法局
27. 山东“8·5”制售盗版光盘案专案组（山东省淄博市文化市场执法局、山东省淄博市公安局直属分局）
28. 山东省泰安市文化广电新闻出版局
29. 河南省版权局版权管理处
30. 河南省新乡市封丘县人民检察院侦查监督科
31. 河南徐某某等印制盗版图书案专案组（河南省焦作市文化市场综合执法支队，河南省焦作市武陟县文化市场综合执法大队，河南省焦作市武陟县人民检察院侦查监督科、公诉科）
32. 河南省安阳市滑县文化市场综合执法大队
33. 湖北省版权局版权管理处
34. 湖北省武汉市江岸区人民法院知识产权审判庭
35. 湖北省荆州市公安县公安局经济犯罪侦查大队
36. 湖南省版权局版权管理处
37. 广东省版权局版权管理处
38. 广东省中山市中级人民法院民三庭
39. 广西郑某某销售盗版音像制品案专案组（广西壮族自治区南宁市宾阳县“扫黄打非”工作小组办公室、广西壮族自治区南宁市宾阳县文化新闻出版广电和体育局、广西壮族自治区南宁市宾阳县公安局、广西壮族自治区南宁市宾阳县人民法院、广西壮族自治区南宁市宾阳县人民检察院）
40. 重庆王某某等侵犯网络游戏著作权案专案组（重庆市公安局打假总队、重庆市公安局网安总队、重庆市公安局九龙坡分局网安支队、重庆市九龙坡区文化委员会）
41. 四川“风云丝路”网侵犯著作权案专案组（四川省成都市文化市场综合执法总队、四川省成都市公安局网监支队、四川省成都市检察院侦监一处、四川省成都市检察院公诉二处、四川省成都市青羊区人民检察院）
42. 陕西胡某、路某侵犯著作权案专案组（陕西省西安市中级人民法院刑二庭、陕西省西安市中级人民检察院侦查监督一处、陕西省西安市公安局治安管理局特行处特行科、陕西省西安市文化市场行政执法总队、陕西省西安市“扫黄打非”办公室）

43. 中央电视台社会新闻部
44.《中国新闻出版广电报》出版周刊中心

【有功单位二等奖】

1. 最高人民法院刑事审判第一庭第四合议庭
2. 最高人民检察院公诉厅起诉二处
3. 公安部治安管理局九处
4. 公安部经济犯罪侦查局知识产权处
5. 工业和信息化部信息通信管理局互联网处
6. 国家互联网信息办公室网络综合协调管理和执法督查局专项行动处
7. 中央宣传部出版局出版研究处
8. 首都版权产业联盟
9. 中国新闻出版研究院政策法规研究所
10. 北京市版权局版权管理处
11. 北京市文化市场行政执法总队执法一队
12. 河北华宁印刷厂侵犯著作权案专案组（河北省石家庄市“扫黄打非”领导小组办公室、河北省石家庄市正定县文化广电新闻出版局、河北省石家庄市版权局版权出版管理处）
13. 河北叶某销售侵权复制品案专案组（河北省石家庄市版权局、河北省石家庄市文化市场行政执法大队、河北省石家庄市公安局桥西分局治安警察大队行动中队、河北省石家庄市桥西区人民检察院公诉科、河北省石家庄市桥西区人民法院刑一庭）
14. 山西省忻州市文化市场行政综合执法大队
15. 山西朔州怀仁县第十二中学非法销售、发放盗版出版物案专案组（山西省朔州市文化市场行政综合执法大队、山西省朔州市怀仁县文化市场综合执法大队）
16. 辽宁“我爱听评书”网侵犯著作权案专案组（辽宁省版权局版权管理处、辽宁省通信管理局电信管理处、国家计算机网络与信息安全管理中心辽宁分中心）
17. 辽宁省沈阳市文化市场行政执法总队直属执法四大队
18. 吉林省长春市文化市场综合执法支队
19. 吉林省敦化市文化市场综合执法大队
20. 吉林明历文化传媒有限公司盗版音像制品案专案组（吉林省通化市文化市场综合执法支队、吉林省通化市公安局治安支队、吉林省通化市东昌区人民法院）
21. 吉林省公主岭市文化市场综合执法大队
22. 黑龙江省版权局版权处
23. 上海网络案件专案组（上海市公安局嘉定分局经侦支队、上海市嘉定区人民检察院公诉科）
24. 上海市闵行区人民法院民三庭
25. 上海包某、顾某侵犯著作权案专案组（上海市普陀区人民法院知识产权庭、上海市普陀区人民检察院公诉科）
26. 江苏省委网络安全和信息化领导小组办公室网络新闻管理处
27. 江苏沈某、付某侵犯《魔域》游戏著作权案专案组（江苏省徐州市版权局版权管理处、江苏省徐州市公安局治安支队、江苏省徐州市公安局网安支队）
28. 江苏省张家港市文化广电新闻出版局
29. 浙江省义乌市市场监督管理局稽查六队
30. 浙江朱某某侵犯著作权案专案组（浙江省慈溪市文化市场行政执法大队、浙江省宁波市慈溪公安局坎墩派出所）
31. 浙江省海宁市文化市场行政执法大队
32. 安徽“拾零道人”网侵犯著作权案专案组（安徽省滁州市文化广电新闻出版局、安徽省滁州市“扫黄打非”办公室、安徽省滁州市全椒县“扫黄打非”办公室、安徽省滁州市全椒县公安局、安徽省滁州市全椒县文化广电新闻出版局）
33. 安徽省合肥市公安局网安支队
34. 福建省版权局版权管理处
35. 福建省泉州市文化市场综合执法支队
36. 山东省济南市文化市场综合行政执法局
37. 山东省济南市公安局经济文化保卫支队
38. 山东省青岛市李沧区文化市场行政执法局
39. 山东省菏泽市文化市场综合执法局
40. 山东“5·20”侵犯著作权案专案组（山东省东营市文化市场综合执法局、山东省东营市广饶县文化市场综合执法大队）
41. 山东省新泰市文化广播电视新闻出版局
42. 山东省潍坊寿光市文化市场综合执法局
43. 山东日月电脑会计职业培训学校侵犯软件著作权案专案组（山东省潍坊市文化市场综合执法局、山东省潍坊安丘市文化市场综合执法局）
44. 河南省查处侵权盗版案件联合督办组（河南省互联网信息办公室网络管理处、河南省公安厅治安总队二支队、河南省检察院侦查监督处、河南省通信管理局信息网络安全管理处）

45. 河南省驻马店市文化市场综合执法支队
46. 河南省安阳市滑县人民检察院侦查监督局
47. 湖北省通信管理局互联网管理处
48. 湖北毛某某侵犯著作权案专案组（湖北省武汉市公安局江汉区分局前进派出所、湖北省武汉市江汉区文化市场综合执法大队、湖北省武汉市人民检察院刑事审判监督部）
49. 湖北省钟祥市文化市场综合执法大队
50. 广东省高级人民法院刑二庭
51. 广东省汕头市澄海区人民法院刑二庭
52. 广东省肇庆市文化市场综合执法大队
53. 广东省深圳市市场和质量监督管理委员会福田市场监督管理局稽查科（稽查大队）
54. 广东省广州市文化市场综合行政执法总队执法二处
55. 广西博大书店销售盗版图书案专案组（广西壮族自治区南宁市文化新闻出版广电局、广西壮族自治区南宁市公安局、广西壮族自治区南宁市人民检察院、广西壮族自治区南宁市中级人民法院、广西壮族自治区南宁市文化市场综合执法支队）
56. 四川省版权局版权管理处
57. 四川省成都市文化市场综合执法总队三支队
58. 四川省绵阳市安县人民检察院
59. 四川“7·3”销售盗版音像制品系列案专案组（四川省宜宾市文广局、四川省宜宾市南溪区文广局、四川省宜宾市南溪区公安分局、四川省宜宾市南溪区人民法院刑庭）
60. 陕西省版权局版权管理处
61. 宁夏回族自治区版权局版权管理处
62. 宁夏“8·3”侵犯著作权案专案组（宁夏回族自治区银川市文广局、宁夏回族自治区吴忠市文广局、宁夏回族自治区中卫市市场综合执法队、宁夏回族自治区固原市文广局）
63. 新疆维吾尔自治区版权局版权管理处
64. 新浪微博
65. 中国知识产权报社版权周刊

【有功单位三等奖】

1. 公安部网络安全保卫局十二处
2. 国家互联网信息办公室网络应急管理和网络舆情局舆情处
3. 国家工商行政管理总局反垄断与反不正当竞争执法局反不正当竞争处
4. 海关总署政策法规司知识产权处
5. 中国互联网协会行业自律工作委员会
6. 天津市文化市场行政执法总队执法一队
7. 天津市文化市场行政执法总队执法二队
8. 天津市宝坻区文化市场行政执法大队
9. 河北省版权局版权处
10. 河北张某等侵犯《热血传奇》网络游戏著作权案专案组（河北省承德市文化广电新闻出版局、河北省承德市公安局双桥分局网络安全保卫大队、河北省承德市双桥区检察院、河北省承德市双桥区人民法院）
11. 河北省衡水市文化市场行政执法大队
12. 山西省版权局版权管理处
13. 山西省晋中市版权局
14. 内蒙古自治区版权局版权处
15. 内蒙古自治区通辽市文化市场综合执法局
16. 辽宁省大连市文化市场综合执法总队
17. 吉林省长春市二道区文化体育局
18. 吉林省长春市宽城区文化市场综合执法大队
19. 吉林省长春净月高新技术产业开发区文化稽查大队
20. 吉林省德惠市文化市场综合执法大队
21. 吉林省榆树市文化市场综合执法大队
22. 吉林省四平市文化市场综合执法支队
23. 吉林省通化市辉南县文化市场综合执法大队
24. 吉林省白城市洮北区市场综合执法大队
25. 吉林省松原市长岭县文化市场综合执法大队
26. 吉林省白山市江源区文化市场综合执法大队
27. 上海市通信管理局互联网管理处
28. 上海市互联网信息办公室网络管理处
29. 中华人民共和国上海海关法规处
30. 上海余某侵犯著作权罪案专案组（上海市杨浦区人民法院民事审判第三庭（知识产权审判庭）、上海市虹口区人民检察院航运（金融）检察科）
31. 江苏原力电脑动画制作公司侵犯著作权案专案组（江苏省南京市文化综合执法总队三支队、江苏省南京市版权局版权和出版管理处）
32. 江苏省张家港市文化行政综合执法大队
33. 浙江省丽水市文化广电新闻出版局
34. 浙江省宁波市文化市场行政执法总队
35. 浙江罗某某侵犯著作权罪案专案组（浙江省绍兴市文化市场行政执法支队、浙江省绍兴市公安局袍江分局治安大队）
36. 浙江省嘉兴市文化市场行政执法支队

37. 浙江省金华市兰溪公安局上华派出所
38. 浙江省温州市鹿城区文化广电新闻出版局
39. 安徽省“扫黄打非”工作领导小组办公室
40. 福建省福州市公安局治安支队三大队
41. 福建省厦门市文化市场综合执法支队
42. 江西省版权局版权管理处
43. 江西省上饶市余干县文化广电新闻出版（版权）局
44. 江西省九江市文化市场综合执法支队
45. 江西省萍乡市安源区文化市场综合执法大队
46. 江西省上饶市鄱阳县版权局
47. 山东省青岛平度市文化市场行政执法局
48. 山东省青岛即墨市文化市场行政执法局
49. 山东省青岛胶州市综合行政执法局
50. 山东省聊城市文化市场综合执法局
51. 山东省德州市综合文化市场执法局
52. 河南省三门峡市文化市场综合执法支队
53. 河南省周口市文化广电新闻出版局
54. 河南省驻马店市泌阳县文化市场综合执法大队
55. 河南省开封市尉氏县文化市场综合执法大队
56. 湖北省武汉市文化市场综合执法支队
57. 湖北省武汉市武昌区人民检察院侦查监督科
58. 湖北省鄂州市文化市场综合执法支队
59. 湖北省潜江市文化市场综合执法支队
60. 湖北省十堰市文化市场综合执法支队
61. 湖南省株洲市文化市场综合执法局
62. 湖南省岳阳市文化市场综合执法局
63. 湖南省长沙市文化市场综合执法局
64. 湖南省娄底市文化市场综合执法支队
65. 湖南省衡阳市文化市场综合执法局
66. 广东省惠州市惠阳区公安分局经侦大队
67. 广东省黄埔海关法规处知识产权保护科
68. 广东省广州市文化市场综合行政执法总队执法三处
69. 广西壮族自治区版权局版权处
70. 广西壮族自治区贺州市钟山县版权局
71. 海南省版权局版权处
72. 海南刘某侵犯著作权案专案组（海南省琼中县文化市场稽查队、海南省“扫黄打非”办公室）
73. 重庆市版权局版权管理处
74. 四川省通信管理局电信处
75. 四川省成都市青羊区文化广电旅游新闻出版版权行政执法大队
76. 四川阆中音像制品店销售盗版音像制品系列案专案组（四川省南充市文化广电新闻出版局、四川省阆中市文化市场综合执法大队、四川省阆中市人民检察院）
77. 四川省遂宁市文化市场综合执法支队
78. 贵州省版权局版权处
79. 贵州省贵阳市文化市场综合执法支队执法三处
80. 云南省版权局版权管理处
81. 云南省临沧市文化市场综合行政执法支队
82. 陕西省咸阳市彬县文化市场综合执法大队
83. 宁夏回族自治区银川市文化市场综合执法队
84. 新疆维吾尔自治区喀什市疏附县文化市场综合执法大队
85. 北京字节跳动科技有限公司政务信息运营部
86.《光明日报》评论部

【有功个人一等奖】

1. 罗曦（最高人民检察院公诉厅二处）
2. 李虎（最高人民检察院侦查监督厅立案监督处）
3. 徐永（公安部治安管理局一处）
4. 吕伟（公安部经济犯罪侦查局知识产权处）
5. 徐强（工业和信息化部信息通信管理局互联网处）
6. 张文瑞（全国打击侵犯知识产权和制售假冒伪劣商品工作领导小组办公室）
7. 何磊（中国版权保护中心法律部）
8. 北京一点网聚公司非法转载文字作品案专案组个人（赵红仕、邢芳英、郭东竹，北京市版权局）
9. 北京市宏泰印刷有限公司侵犯著作权案专案组个人（邢玉金、张清、戴文涛、王玉军，北京市文化市场行政执法总队执法五队；苏玥，北京市公安局通州分局张家湾派出所）
10. 北京金图创联国际科技有限公司侵犯他人著作权案专案组个人（郭涌、沈晋南、王健、高坤、熊亮，北京市文化市场行政执法总队执法五队）
11. 北京何某等侵犯网络游戏著作权案专案组个人（赵国明、熊伟，北京市文化市场行政执法总队执法五队；张志婧，北京市海淀区人民检察院知识产权检察处；崔衍亮，北京市公安局海淀分局法制处；陈维，北京市公安局海淀分局网络安全保卫总队驻区四大队）

12. 北京“阳光教育”网店销售盗版少儿出版物案专案组个人（秦永明、张博然、徐剑，北京市文化市场行政执法总队执法四队；杨岱君，北京市海淀区人民检察院知识产权检察处；翟宝宇，北京市公安局海淀分局刑侦支队）
13. 河北张某某等印制盗版图书案专案组个人（杨大勇、张海峰，河北省保定市文化市场行政执法大队；张建东、黄威，河北省保定市竞秀区公安分局；马彦飞，河北省保定市竞秀区文体教育局）
14. 薛彬（上海市版权局版权管理执法处）
15. 袁学术（江苏省版权局版权处）
16. 江苏“老调网”侵犯著作权案专案组个人（季培均，江苏省扬州市版权局；刘光明、唐海宁，江苏省扬州市文化行政综合执法支队）
17. 江苏“速酷电影”网侵犯著作权案专案组个人（高成富，江苏省徐州市版权局；艾新建，江苏省徐州市文化广电新闻出版局；郭静，江苏省徐州市公安局网安支队）
18. 浙江郑某等复制并通过网络销售盗版图书和软件案专案组个人（吕晓杰、胡孟良，浙江省杭州市文化市场行政执法总队；姚川，浙江省杭州市公安局治安支队三大队；杜倩楠，浙江省杭州市拱墅区人民检察院；石丽斐，浙江省杭州市拱墅区人民法院）
19. 晏凤志，安徽省版权局版权管理处
20. 安徽蒋某发行侵犯他人著作权出版物案专案组个人（陈江丽，安徽省合肥市版权局；江明银、戚玉生、汝梦芸、汤明，安徽省合肥市文化市场综合执法大队）
21. 高东升（山东省新闻出版广电局版权管理处）
22. 刘建峰（山东省济南市文化市场综合行政执法局）
23. 杜荣华（山东省青岛市文化市场行政执法局版权监管与执法处）
24. 山东“8·5”制售盗版光盘案专案组个人（侯本兵、孔凡军，山东省淄博市文化市场执法局；张洪强、史志伟，山东省淄博市公安局直属分局一大队）
25. 王新民（山东省泰安市文化广电新闻出版局）
26. 张安军（山东省泰安市文化广电新闻出版局）
27. 赵永磊（山东省泰安市文化市场综合执法支队）
28. 山东贾某某侵犯著作权案专案组个人（董晖、李子杰、邓作霆、张琛、吕秀兰，山东省菏泽市文化市场综合执法局）
29. “人人影视网”侵犯影视作品著作权案专案组个人（谭昕、孙玉虹、宋亮、张荣涛，湖南省新闻出版广电局版权管理处；左建建，湖南省公安厅治安总队）
30. 易瑾媛（广东省版权局版权管理处）
31. 张春节（广东省广州市黄埔区人民法院刑庭）
32. 倪天龙（广州市文化市场综合行政执法总队执法五处）
33. 黄麟渝（重庆市文化市场行政执法总队执法一处）
34. 张贺（《人民日报》政治文化部）
35. 赖名芳（《中国新闻出版广电报》出版周刊中心）

【有功个人二等奖】

1. 魏磊（最高人民法院刑一庭第四合议庭）
2. 尹春吉（公安部治安管理局十四处）
3. 韩启彬（公安部治安管理局六处）
4. 杨璠（工业和信息化部信息通信管理局）
5. 李坚（国家互联网信息办公室网络综合协调管理和执法督查局专项行动处）
6. 杨晓玫（中央宣传部出版局办公室）
7. 陈霞（新闻出版总署信息中心工程项目管理部）
8. 郁致原（新闻出版总署信息中心运行维护部）
9. 鄢韧强（国家新闻出版广电总局出版产品质量监督检测中心）
10. 北京宏文恒盛文化发展有限公司盗印出版物案专案组个人（张权、邵大明，北京市文化执法总队执法一队；高远，北京市公安局治安管理总队；白云山，北京市海淀区检察院；覃波，北京市海淀区法院）
11. 郝子谋（山西省版权局版权管理处）
12. 沙丽（内蒙古自治区版权局版权处）
13. 李安庆（辽宁省版权局版权管理处）
14. 辽宁“零点花园”网侵犯文学作品著作权案专案组个人（张志、张文利，辽宁省通信管理局电信管理处；孙大鹏，国家计算机网络与信息安全管理中心辽宁分中心；田大鹏，辽宁省版权局版权管理处）
15. 黑龙江众一图书有限公司盗版教辅材料案专案组个人（王培舒、杜宇震、田庆权，吉林省版权局版权处）

16. 黑龙江“9·3”销售侵权盗版出版物案专案组个人（赍涛、柳占林，黑龙江省哈尔滨市文化和新闻出版局发行管理处；李时强、滕相林，黑龙江省哈尔滨市公安局治安支队案件审理大队；闫晓霜，黑龙江省哈尔滨市南岗区人民法院刑事审判庭）
17. 万赟（上海市文化市场行政执法总队稽查五处）
18. 胡俊千（上海市公安局经侦总队二支队）
19. 堵雯曦（江苏省通信管理局互联网管理处）
20. 顾云（江苏省镇江市版权局）
21. 解硕群（江苏省徐州市文化广电新闻出版局版权管理处）
22. 江苏“77免费电影网”侵犯著作权案专案组个人（于湃，江苏省徐州市公安局治安支队；刘宇，江苏省徐州市检察院公诉处）
23. 江苏“金火影视网”侵犯著作权案专案组个人（颜茂苏，江苏省徐州市中级人民法院民三庭；孟繁卿，江苏省徐州市铜山区文化广电新闻出版与体育局；李恒乐，江苏省徐州市铜山区公安局网安大队）
24. 江苏打击侵权盗版杂志专项行动系列案专案组个人（陈世海、陈彩芬，江苏省张家港市文化广电新闻出版局；王黎明、朱群军、魏冉，江苏省张家港市文化行政综合执法大队）
25. 浙江杭州北洲电影院有限公司复制、放映盗版电影作品案专案组个人（艾其芬、许璐斌，浙江省杭州市余杭区文化市场行政执法大队）
26. 安徽“拾零道人”网侵犯著作权案专案组个人（刘杨、杨邦伦，安徽省滁州市全椒县公安局网安大队；关敬文，安徽省滁州市全椒县文化广电新闻出版局；许大伟，安徽省滁州市全椒县人民检察院；高红，安徽省滁州市全椒县人民法院）
27. 常桂旭（福建省版权局版权管理处）
28. 林芳（福建省人民检察院侦查监督处）
29. 李建（山东省青岛市李沧区文化市场行政执法局）
30. 山东“3·17”李某侵犯著作权案专案组个人（林志坚，山东省青岛市李沧区文化执法局；菅兴锋、孙晨光，山东省青岛市文化执法局；周正雷，山东省青岛市公安局李沧分局）
31. 马长兴（山东省青岛市即墨市文化市场行政执法局）
32. 刘肖宁（山东省潍坊市文化市场综合执法局）
33. 牛兆星（山东省潍坊市文化市场综合执法局）
34. 孟杰（山东省济宁市任城区文化市场综合执法局）
35. 山东泰安东平龙山驾驶员培训有限公司侵犯著作权案专案组个人（吕宗峰、杨红雨、孙萍，山东省泰安市文化市场综合执法支队）
36. 山东庄某某等侵犯著作权案专案组个人（赵强、荆玉涛、张守珂、李希东、蒋吉民，山东省日照市莒县文化市场综合执法局）
37. 王可志（山东省德州市文化市场综合执法局“扫黄打非”工作科）
38. 李峰（河南省版权局版权管理处）
39. 河南平舆王某某侵犯著作权案专案组个人（刘文利、申娟娟、肖宏伟、张宏图、张军瑞，河南省驻马店市文化市场综合执法支队）
40. 河南李某侵犯著作权案专案组个人（王珏，河南省安阳市人民检察院侦查监督处；郭晓娜，河南省安阳市滑县人民检察院侦查监督局；李胜标、张彦利、冯巧玲，河南省安阳市滑县文化市场综合执法大队）
41. 河南李某某制作盗版图书案专案组个人（陈红梅、贺筠，河南省焦作市武陟县人民检察院；高文波、孔丽，河南省焦作市文化市场综合执法支队；宋德勇，河南省焦作市人民法院刑三庭）
42. 卢文俊（湖北省版权局版权管理处）
43. 湖北省武汉市打击侵权盗版刑事审判专案组个人（吴燕颐、胡敏、胡慧莉、李绶波，湖北省武汉市江岸区人民法院知识产权庭）
44. 周良清（湖北省荆州市公安县公安局经侦大队）
45. 湖南衡阳周义侵犯计算机软件著作权案专案组个人（刘小平、唐能平、刘意福、尹忠国，湖南省衡阳市文化市场综合执法局）
46. 康金钟（湖南省通信管理局网络与信息安全处）
47. 骆丽莉（广东省深圳市中级人民法院知识产权庭）
48. 梁毅（广东省湛江经济技术开发区人民法院刑庭）
49. 卢芳（广东省深圳市福田区市场监督管理局稽查科）
50. 马永志（广西壮族自治区版权局版权管理处）
51. 广西郑某某销售盗版音像制品案专案组个人（梁松、韦家胜，广西壮族自治区南宁市宾阳县文化新闻出版广电和体育局；蒙立，广西壮族自治区南宁市宾阳县人民法院；蓝莉莉，广西壮族自治区南宁市宾阳县文化市场综合执法大队；思辉，广西壮族自治区南宁市宾阳县公安局城南派出所）
52. 曾伯林（海南省版权局版权处）
53. 重庆唐某销售盗版图书案专案组个人（冉凤平，重庆市大足区文化市场行政执法支队；陈炜，重庆市大足区文化市场行政执法支队）
54. 陕西高校出版物市场专项行动系列案专案组个人（张伟成、楚源、于赵磊、毛凤凤、何勇刚，陕西省西安市文化市场行政执法总队）
55. 吾拉木江·哈帕尔（新疆维吾尔自治区版权局版权管理处）
56. 曾文甫（中央电视台社会新闻部）

【有功个人三等奖】

1. 董翰飞（公安部网络安全保卫局）
2. 王宏博（工业和信息化部网络安全管理局）
3. 张伟星（国家互联网信息办公室网络综合协调管理和执法督查局综合处）
4. 张扬（国家互联网信息办公室网络应急管理和网络舆情局）
5. 罗林（中央宣传部新闻局文化新闻处）
6. 张丹（国家工商行政管理总局反垄断与反不正当竞争执法局反不正当竞争处）
7. 张芬涛（海关总署政策法规司知识产权处）
8. 北京天宫阁工艺品有限责任公司出售假冒他人署名作品案专案组个人（耿楠、马威、王泽玉，北京市西城区文化委员会执法队）
9. 安鸣（天津市文化市场行政执法总队执法二队）
10. 李冬群（河北省版权局版权管理处）
11. 杨志敏（河北省保定市莲池区文体教育局稽查队）
12. 河北星光城歌厅侵犯音乐作品著作权案专案组个人（吴杰，河北省石家庄市版权局；常志辉、王昌亮、吕素斌、李素平，河北省石家庄市赵县文化市场行政执法队）
13. 河北开元印刷厂侵权案专案组个人（李雷，河北省石家庄市版权局；郭宝珠、韩建伟、董同申、杨红，河北省石家庄市栾城区文化市场执法队）
14. 河北海潮书店案专案组个人（董岩、孙屹、杨胜利、朱小光、吴雪羽，河北省秦皇岛市海港区文化体育新闻出版局文化市场行政执法队）
15. 吉林"8·20"销售盗版教材系列案专案组个人（路野、陈哲、张文胜、朱爽、左熠琳，吉林省长春市文化市场综合执法支队）
16. 董广伟（吉林省德惠市文化市场综合执法大队）
17. 靖红艳（吉林省榆树市文化市场综合执法大队）
18. 康彤（吉林省吉林市新闻出版广电局）
19. 费泽忠（吉林省敦化市文化市场综合执法大队）
20. 左今明（吉林省四平市文化广电新闻出版局）
21. 刘丽（吉林省通化市文化市场综合执法支队）
22. 刘学国（吉林省通化市辉南县文化市场综合执法大队）
23. 邓长远（吉林省白山市靖宇县文化市场综合执法大队）
24. 吉林省延吉市璞润读书社销售盗版教辅材料案专案组个人（张国栋、高永洙、赵海波，吉林省延吉市文化市场综合执法大队）
25. 王洪云（吉林省公主岭市文化市场综合执法大队）
26. 华毓军（黑龙江省鹤岗市文化市场综合执法支队）
27. 王志斌（黑龙江省鸡西市文化广电新闻出版局新闻出版科）
28. 郭海生（黑龙江省鸡西市文化市场综合执法支队）
29. 邓兆臣（黑龙江省鸡西市文化市场综合执法支队）
30. 李鹏程（黑龙江省双鸭山市文化市场综合执法支队出版大队）
31. 张晓栋（上海市通信管理局互联网管理处）
32. 夏倩（上海市办公室网络管理处）
33. 缪赟（上海市文化市场行政执法总队稽查三处）
34. 史庭栋（上海市文化市场行政执法总队稽查三处）
35. 王浩（上海市文化市场行政执法总队稽查五处）
36. 江苏远大信息股份有限公司等5家企业侵犯软件著作权系列案专案组个人（刘峻、朱荣祥、张秋岳，江苏省张家港市版权局）
37. 王玲飞（江苏省无锡市人民检察院）

38. 王可（江苏省常州市钟楼区人民法院刑庭）
39. 浙江刘某某、邓某擅自传播他人音乐作品案专案组个人（曹剑、张辉、徐江枫、王家麟，浙江省宁波市文化市场行政执法总队）
40. 浙江家纺产业侵犯花样版权系列案专案组个人（马振宇、朱沈威、曹迪，浙江省海宁市文化市场行政执法大队）
41. 金奇烽（浙江省绍兴市文化市场行政执法支队）
42. 林汝海（浙江省公安厅治安总队行动支队）
43. 陈志勇（浙江省温州市公安局龙湾分局）
44. 李慧星（浙江省台州市黄岩区公安分局城西派出所）
45. 安徽韦某某侵犯信息网络传播权案专案组个人（杜仙林、林光莹、徐胜利，安徽省合肥市文化市场综合执法大队）
46. 安徽蒋某发行侵犯他人著作权出版物案专案组个人（陆长华、叶兆国、金强、李宏敏，安徽省合肥市文化市场综合执法大队）
47. 安徽王某销售盗版图书案专案组个人（张厚金、李敏、李德军、杨冲、费蔚晴，安徽省马鞍山市文化旅游市场综合执法支队）
48. 安徽张某某制售盗版音像制品案专案组个人（吴震宇，安徽省黄山市版权局；韦俊，安徽省黄山市版权局；张庆文，安徽省黄山市公安局治安支队）
49. 吴跃春（福建省新闻出版广电局反非法和违禁出版物处）
50. 刘洋（福建省福州市公安局治安支队）
51. 吴志诚（福建省泉州市文化市场综合执法支队直属一大队）
52. 福建“11·26”发行盗版图书案专案组个人（魏有春，福建省厦门市文化市场综合执法支队；周杰，福建省厦门市文化市场综合执法支队举报办理科；陈竑，福建省厦门市文化市场综合执法支队执法监督科；叶建福、张颖，福建省厦门市文化市场综合执法支队一大队）
53. 陈忠南，福建省厦门市文化市场综合执法支队直属二大队
54. 江西人生书店销售盗版图书案专案组个人（张玉华，江西省九江市文化广电新闻出版局；朱斌，江西省九江市文化市场综合执法支队）
55. 江西丽华书店销售盗版教辅案专案组个人（张灵，江西省上饶市文化广电新闻出版（版权）局；麻卫清，江西省上饶市余干县文化广电新闻出版（版权）局）
56. 艾华林（江西省萍乡市文化广电新闻出版局）
57. 董显祥（江西省赣州市文化广电新闻出版局文化市场科）
58. 江西向阳书院销售盗版教材教辅案专案组个人（张会昌，江西省瑞金市文化广电新闻出版局；杨振华，江西省瑞金市文化稽查大队）
59. 罗盛磊（江西省南昌市文化市场综合执法支队）
60. 刘秋华（江西省吉安市文化综合执法支队科长）
61. 山东省刘某某侵犯著作权案专案组个人（刘金祥，山东省新闻出版广电局反非法和违禁出版物处；宋涛、刘琳、张文安，山东省济南市文化市场综合行政执法局；袁大龙，山东省济南市公安局公交分局）
62. 王元昌（山东省济南市历城区文化市场综合行政执法大队）
63. 时桂琴（山东省青岛市黄岛区综合行政执法局）
64. 柴寿宁（山东省青岛市黄岛区综合行政执法局）
65. 李昌（山东省青岛即墨市文化市场行政执法局）
66. 刘成爱（山东省青岛平度市文化市场行政执法局）
67. 山东“3·27”侵犯著作权案专案组个人（李书伟，山东省青岛平度市公安局治安大队；金秉坤，山东省青岛平度市法院刑事审判庭；付晓、邹少卫、王飞，山东省青岛平度市文化市场行政执法局）
68. 王冬（山东省青岛胶州市综合行政执法局）
69. 山东省潍坊市查处非法复制计算机软件专案组个人（王启福、刘永利、杨萍，山东省潍坊市文化市场综合执法局；蔡建辉、王凯，山东省潍坊市坊子区文化市场综合执法局）
70. 山东省潍坊市查处娱乐场所侵犯著作权专案组个人（秦韶莉、王佩峰、樊恩平、贾斌，山东省潍坊市文化市场综合执法局；王洪阳，山东省诸城市文化市场综合执法局）
71. 高志强（山东省潍坊市奎文区文化市场综合执法局）
72. 山东济宁豆神动漫有限公司侵犯著作权案专

案组个人（樊存常、宋明国、龙鸿、颜廷爱、柳成林，山东省济宁市文化市场综合执法局）
73. 孙明奎（山东省济宁市梁山县文化市场综合执法局）
74. 刘培臻（山东省威海市文化市场综合执法局）
75. 徐水平（山东省威海市文化市场综合执法局）
76. 山东高某某侵犯著作权案专案组个人（于立海、马池坤，山东省日照市文化市场综合执法局；严丽丽、任晓军，山东省日照市莒县文化市场综合执法局）
77. 山东莒县友爱医院侵犯著作权案专案组个人（赵强、荆玉涛、许家同、董守国、张守珂，山东省日照市莒县文化市场综合执法局）
78. 朱文洁（山东省临沂市费县文化市场管理执法局稽查大队）
79. 万强（山东省德州市文化市场综合执法局）
80. 张玉光（山东省聊城市文化市场综合执法局）
81. 申明曾（河南省公安厅治安总队二支队）
82. 河南云海印务有限公司侵犯著作权案专案组个人（延红娟、王泽一，河南省安阳市滑县人民检察院；魏麦仲、张修建、刘翠娟，河南省安阳市滑县文化市场综合执法大队）
83. 河南泌阳二中发行盗版图书案专案组个人（殷小喜、赵飞，河南省驻马店市文化市场综合执法支队；李强，河南省驻马店市泌阳县文化市场综合执法大队）
84. 栗山（河南省南阳市文化市场综合执法支队）
85. 河南董某某销售盗版出版物案专案组个人（李民立、王建伟、王炜，河南省开封市尉氏县文化市场综合执法大队；王建坤，河南省开封市“扫黄打非”办公室；王伟，河南省开封市文化广电新闻出版局）
86. 彭骏（湖北省通信管理局互联网管理处）
87. 湖北“2·13”章某某侵犯著作权案专案组个人（杨发新，湖北省武汉市文化市场综合执法支队办公室；李斯宁、熊锦辉，湖北省武汉市文化市场综合执法支队一大队；芦险峰，湖北省武汉市公安局经侦支队六大队）
88. 王郡（湖北省潜江市文化体育旅游新闻出版局市场管理科）
89. 伍伟（湖北省仙桃市文化市场综合执法支队）
90. 李宏良（湖北省襄阳市文化市场综合执法支队）
91. 袁平（湖南省岳阳市文化市场综合执法局版权执法大队）
92. 邓洺（湖南省衡阳市文化市场综合执法局第一执法大队）
93. 湖南789私人影吧侵犯著作权系列案专案组个人（陈炜、王松林，湖南省衡阳市文化市场综合执法局）
94. 彭驰（湖南省岳阳市文化市场综合执法局）
95. 胡巍（湖南省怀化市文化市场综合执法局版权网络执法科）
96. 汤秉革（湖南省长沙市文化市场综合执法局执法四处）
97. 符超（湖南省衡阳市文化市场综合执法局执法二科）
98. 彭辉（湖南省邵阳市文化市场综合执法局执法二科）
99. 谢庆安（湖南省郴州市文化市场综合执法局网络娱乐执法大队）
100. 广东张某某销售侵权复制品案专案组个人（肖洋、刘冠成、罗文军、宋戎林、黄志强，广东省惠州市公安局经侦支队）
101. 张展雯（广东省东莞市第一市区人民检察院侦查监督科）
102. 曹慧星（广东省中山市第一人民法院民三庭）
103. 黄金生（广东省惠州市博罗县人民法院刑二庭）
104. 广东广州“6·9”制售盗版教材案专案组个人（雷小龙、唐爱民、曾卫民，广东省广州市文化市场综合行政执法总队）
105. 周文斌（广东省广州市文化市场综合行政执法总队执法三处）
106. 海南刘某侵犯著作权案专案组个人（黄俊，海南省琼中县文化市场稽查队；司安海，海南省琼中县公安局；蔡坚，海南省琼中县检察院）
107. 张德林（重庆市奉节县文化委员会）
108. 高斌（四川省版权局版权管理处）
109. 陶云（四川省通信管理局电信处）
110. 四川成都戛纳假日酒店有限责任公司侵犯著作权案专案组个人（夏应添、张林、肖梅，四川省成都市文化市场综合执法总队三支队）
111. 四川新华国际酒店有限责任公司案专案组个人（许东，四川省成都市文化市场综合执法总队一支队；闫海峰、陈志强，四川省成都市文化市场综合执法总队二支队）

112. 四川阆中市“京泰音像制品店”“同乐堂音像制品店”销售盗版音像制品系列案专案组个人（王海，四川省南充市文化广电新闻出版局；苟溪、任静、任欢，四川省阆中市文化市场综合执法大队；朱成平，四川省南充市“扫黄打非”办公室）
113. 四川金钥匙书店发行侵权盗版出版物专案组个人（陈川，四川省自贡市文化市场综合执法支队一大队；唐小珺，四川省自贡市文化市场综合执法支队二大队）
114. 李胜君（四川省简阳市文化市场综合执法大队）
115. 安定（贵州省贵阳市文化市场综合执法支队执法三处）
116. 昆明海关打击侵犯著作权专案组个人（李磊，昆明海关法规处知识产权科；刘娜，昆明海关所属打洛海关）
117. 陕西西安摩威秀云川视听技术有限公司侵犯著作权案专案组个人（张美宏、武毅、李伟、张云、李军，陕西省西安市文化市场行政执法总队）
118. 王新民（陕西省版权局版权管理处）
119. 青海董某销售盗版图书专案组个人（朱小虎、杨国伟，青海省西宁市大通县文化市场综合执法大队）
120. 宁夏“8·3”侵犯著作权案专案组个人（张秀年，宁夏回族自治区版权局；邓华，宁夏回族自治区银川市文化新闻出版广电局；孙艳琳，宁夏回族自治区中卫市文化体育新闻出版广电局；张发祥，宁夏回族自治区固原市文化市场综合执法支队；杨建忠，宁夏回族自治区吴忠市文化市场综合执法队）
121. 宁夏靓声音像部销售盗版音像制品专案组个人（罗海波、李世宁、韩静、牛丹丹，宁夏回族自治区石嘴山市文化市场综合执法队）
122. 新疆喀什查处侵犯著作权案专案组个人（杨瑞、阿力木江·巴吐尔，新疆维吾尔自治区喀什市疏附县文化市场综合执法大队）
123. 曾聪志（新疆维吾尔自治区喀什地区泽普县文化体育广播影视局文化市场）
124. 白炜（中国文化报社文化产业与市场部）

国家版权局关于公布2015年度全国打击侵权盗版十大案件的通知

国版函［2016］5号

各省、自治区、直辖市版权局，新疆生产建设兵团版权局，北京、天津、上海、重庆市文化市场行政执法总队：

2015年，按照国务院关于开展打击侵犯知识产权和制售假冒伪劣商品工作的有关部署以及国家版权局、国家互联网信息办公室、公安部、工业和信息化部联合开展的“剑网2015”专项行动的有关要求，各地区版权执法相关部门进一步加强案件查办工作，查处了一批侵权盗版案件。为集中展示版权执法相关部门查处侵权盗版案件的工作成果，充分发挥典型案例的示范引导作用，我局选定了2015年度全国打击侵权盗版十大案件。现将这些案件印发给你们，供各级版权执法相关部门在版权执法工作中参考借鉴。

特此通知。

附件：2015年度全国打击侵权盗版十大案件

国家版权局

2016年4月20日

附件

2015年度全国打击侵权盗版十大案件

一、北京金图创联国际科技有限公司侵犯信息网络传播权案

2015年6月，北京市文化市场行政执法总队根据权利人投诉，依法对北京金图创联国际科技有限公司涉嫌侵犯著作权案进行调查。经查，该公司未经权利人许可，故意删除、改变通过信息网络向公

众提供的作品的权利管理电子信息，并通过信息网络向公众提供明知或应知未经权利人许可而被删除、改变权利管理信息的作品，违法经营额 6.3 万元，违法所得 2.82 万元。

依据《信息网络传播权保护条例》第十八条、《中华人民共和国著作权法》第五十三条的规定，北京市文化市场行政执法总队于 2015 年 9 月 21 日做出行政处罚：没收违法所得人民币 2.82 万元，罚款人民币 12.6 万元。

二、广东“DJ020 网”侵犯音乐作品著作权案

2014 年 12 月，广东省广州市文化市场综合行政执法总队根据群众举报，依法对“DJ020 网”涉嫌侵犯信息网络传播权案进行调查。经查，莫某某开设“DJ020 网”，向公众提供未经授权的音乐作品达 62 286 首，且会员数量众多，仅 2015 年两个月内，在线支付的订单总金额为 6 240 元，等待付款的订单总金额达 257 547.48 元。

依据《信息网络传播权保护条例》第十八条等规定，广东省广州市文化市场综合行政执法总队于 2015 年 6 月 29 日做出行政处罚：没收网络服务器，没收违法所得人民币 6 240 元，罚款人民币 1 318 937 元，并依法移交公安机关追究其刑事责任。

三、北京天盈九州网络技术有限公司侵犯文字作品著作权案

2015 年 6 月，国家版权局根据权利人投诉，依法对北京天盈九州网络技术有限公司涉嫌侵犯文字作品著作权案进行调查。经查，该公司未经权利人许可，通过其运营的凤凰网以及苹果智能移动客户端软件《军事秘录合集》和《凤凰开卷》传播《中越战争秘录》一书，传播范围广，持续时间长，点击数量大，且系反复侵权。

依据《中华人民共和国著作权法》第四十八条，《中华人民共和国著作权法实施条例》第三十六、第三十七条，《信息网络传播权保护条例》第十八条等规定，国家版权局于 2015 年 10 月 10 日做出行政处罚：罚款人民币 25 万元。

四、“人人影视网”侵犯影视作品著作权案

2014 年 11 月，湖南省版权局根据权利人投诉，依法对“人人影视网”涉嫌侵犯著作权案立案调查。经查，网站域名所有人和负责人刘某未经著作权人授权，组织他人将包括《地心引力》在内的 467 部影视作品的对白上传至网站，供用户浏览、下载和使用。

依据《中华人民共和国著作权法》第四十八条、《信息网络传播权保护条例》第十八条、《中华人民共和国著作权法实施条例》第三十六条等规定，湖南省版权局于 2015 年 7 月 10 日做出行政处罚：罚款 5 万元；没收主要用于侵权的服务器 1 台。案发后，刘某主动关闭了涉案网站。

五、安徽蒋某等销售盗版图书案

2015 年 2 月，安徽省合肥市文化市场综合执法大队根据权利人投诉，依法对蒋某等涉嫌销售音乐类盗版图书案进行调查。经对蒋某开设的 5 家琴行进行全面检查，确定蒋某擅自从事出版物发行业务，其经营的图书中有 31 种、262 本钢琴考级教程侵犯了上海音乐出版社的著作权。

依据《中华人民共和国著作权法》第四十八条、《中华人民共和国著作权法实施条例》第三十六条等规定，安徽省合肥市文化广电新闻出版局于 2015 年 4 月 30 日做出行政处罚：没收盗版图书，罚款人民币 16.5 万元。

六、河北张某某等印制盗版图书案

2014 年 10 月，河北省保定市版权行政执法部门会同新市区公安部门依法对张某某等涉嫌印制盗版图书案进行调查。经查，张某某等 4 人未经著作权人许可，自 2014 年 4 月起印制盗版图书，各人分别负责运输、组织工人等环节。专案组现场查获盗版图书 29 种共计 67 752 册，涉及商务印书馆等 9 个出版社，涉案码洋 5 726 704 元。

依据《中华人民共和国刑法》第二百一十七条等规定，河北省保定市竞秀区人民法院于 2015 年 12 月 1 日做出刑事判决：张某某犯侵犯著作权罪，判处有期徒刑 3 年，并处罚金人民币 300 万元；朱某某犯侵犯著作权罪，判处有期徒刑 1 年，缓刑 2 年，并处罚金人民币 280 万元；王某某犯侵犯著作权罪，判处有期徒刑 1 年，缓刑 2 年，并处罚金人民币 280 万元；王某某犯侵犯著作权罪，判处拘役 6 个月，缓刑 1 年，并处罚金人民币 10 万元。

七、山东“8・5”制售盗版光盘案

2013 年 11 月，山东省淄博市版权部门会同公安部门依法对“8・5”制售盗版光盘案进行调查。经查：2013 年 4 月至 2014 年 2 月，刘某某等未经著作权人许可，制作并通过网站及淘宝店销售 33 种侵权盗版音像制品，涉案金额达 530 余万元。

依据《中华人民共和国刑法》第二百一十七条等规定，山东省淄博市高新区人民法院于 2015 年 9 月 6 日做出刑事判决：刘某某犯侵犯著作权罪，判处有期徒刑 3 年，并处罚金 3 万元；杨某、宋某犯侵犯著作权罪，分别判处有期徒刑 1 年 6 个月，缓刑 2 年，并处罚金 1 万元；孙某某犯侵犯著作权罪，判处有期徒刑 1 年，缓刑 2 年，并处罚金 5 000 元。

八、江苏“速酷电影”网侵犯影视作品著作权案

2014年，江苏省徐州市公安部门根据网络巡查线索，依法对“速酷电影”网涉嫌侵犯影视作品著作权案进行调查。经查，田某某于2010年5月开设“速酷电影”网站，自2011年7月起，田某某未经合一、乐视等著作权人许可，从互联网上采集上述公司的影视作品链接，通过“速酷电影”网站向公众传播，并在网页刊登广告收取广告费用，影视作品被点击数达1 694余万次，非法经营额122万余元。

依据《中华人民共和国刑法》第二百一十七条等规定，江苏省徐州市中级人民法院于2015年2月4日做出刑事判决：田某某犯侵犯著作权罪，判处有期徒刑3年6个月，并处罚金70万元，违法所得114万元予以追缴。

九、浙江郑某等复制并通过网络销售盗版图书和软件案

2014年6月24日，浙江省杭州市版权部门会同公安部门根据权利人投诉，依法对郑某等复制并通过网络销售盗版图书和软件案进行调查。经查，2012年至2014年期间，郑某等人以营利为目的，未经权利人许可，通过淘宝网销售自行复制的注册会计师考试复习书籍和培训材料，郑某非法获利100余万元，王某某非法获利30余万元。

依据《中华人民共和国刑法》第二百一十七条等规定，杭州市拱墅区人民法院于2015年11月3日做出刑事判决：郑某犯侵犯著作权罪，判处有期徒刑3年6个月，并处罚金人民币100万元；王某某犯侵犯著作权罪，判处有期徒刑2年10个月，并处罚金人民币30万元；郑某某犯侵犯著作权罪，判处有期徒刑2年，缓刑2年，并处罚金人民币2万元；王某某犯侵犯著作权罪，判处有期徒刑1年6个月，缓刑2年，并处罚金人民币1.5万元；何某某犯侵犯著作权罪，判处有期徒刑10个月，缓刑1年，并处罚金人民币1万元。

十、四川“风云丝路”网侵犯著作权案

2015年3月，四川省成都市版权部门根据权利人投诉，对“风云丝路”网涉嫌侵犯《新丝路传说》网络游戏著作权案进行调查。因案件涉及金额较大，成都市版权部门依法将此案移送成都市公安部门调查。经查，2013年以来，邹某某等未经权利人许可，建立网站提供名为“风云丝路”的游戏私服，并出售游戏道具，非法获利120余万元。经鉴定，《风云丝路》私服游戏与《新丝路传说》游戏存在实质性相似。

依据《中华人民共和国刑法》第二百一十七条等规定，四川省成都市青羊区人民法院于2015年12月29日做出刑事判决：邹某某、邹某犯侵犯著作权罪，分别判处有期徒刑3年，并处罚金15万元。

关于禁止未经授权通过网络传播中央电视台2016年春节联欢晚会的通知

国版办发［2016］3号

各省、自治区、直辖市版权局，北京市、天津市、上海市、重庆市文化市场行政执法总队，各相关视频、音频、网盘、社交类网络服务商：

中央电视台春节联欢晚会是深受广大人民群众喜爱、传播影响范围广泛的重要文化产品。为维护中央电视台2016年春节联欢晚会（下称“央视2016春晚”）的网络版权传播秩序，现就有关事项通知如下：

经中央电视台授权，央视国际网络有限公司（CNTV.cn/CCTV.com）独家享有通过网络向公众传播“央视2016春晚”的权利。除爱奇艺、合一（优酷土豆）、乐视和腾讯等已获央视国际网络有限公司授权的机构外，其他任何个人和机构不得以网络直播、点播、下载、IPTV等各种形式传播“央视2016春晚”。各网盘服务商应当采取有效措施，制止用户违法上传、存储并分享“央视2016春晚”，并及时受理、加快处理权利人针对“央视2016春晚”的通知和投诉；各社交类网络服务商应当采取有效措施，制止用户在博客、微博、播客、个人主页等用户共享平台传播“央视2016春晚”。

各地版权行政部门应当对本地区主要网络服务商发出针对“央视 2016 春晚”的版权预警提示，加强版权监管力度。对于未经授权通过信息网络非法传播“央视 2016 春晚”的，国家版权局并各级版权行政机构将依法进行行政查处。

特此通知。

国家版权局办公厅
2016 年 2 月 4 日

关于 2015 年全国著作权登记情况的通报

国版办发［2016］4 号

各省、自治区、直辖市版权局，新疆生产建设兵团版权局，中国版权保护中心：

2015 年，各地版权行政管理部门和著作权登记机构高度重视著作权登记工作，继续全面贯彻落实国家版权局《关于进一步规范作品登记程序等有关工作的通知》，采取有效措施，积极宣传、重点拓展、改善服务，规范化、标准化、信息化水平不断提升，登记数量持续增长，全国著作权登记工作取得新进展。现将 2015 年全国著作权登记情况通报如下：

一、总体情况

2015 年，我国著作权登记继续保持大幅度增长态势，作品登记 1 348 200 件、计算机软件著作权登记 292 360 件、著作权质权登记 606 件，著作权登记总量达 1 641 166 件，相比 2014 年的 1 211 313 件，同比增长 35.49%。

二、作品登记有关数据及排名

根据对全国 31 个省、自治区、直辖市和中国版权保护中心的作品登记信息的统计，2015 年全年，全国共完成作品登记 1 348 200 件，比 2014 年的 992 034 件增长了 35.90%。

其中，全年登记量较大的省区市分别是：北京市 601 014 件，占登记总量的 44.57%；中国版权保护中心 236 080 件，占登记总量的 17.93%；上海市 199 148 件，占登记总量的 15.12%；江苏省 109 377 件，占登记总量的 8.31%；山东省 50 218 件，占登记总量的 3.81%；重庆市 40 667 件，占登记总量的 3.09%。

从登记作品类型看，数量最多的是摄影作品 510 120 件，占登记总量的 38.74%，其次是文字作品 489 672 件，占登记总量的 37.19%；美术作品 274 431 件，占登记总量的 20.84%；影视作品 15 527 件，占登记总量的 1.18%；录像制品 8 627 件，占登记总量的 0.66%；图形作品 5 315 件，占登记总量的 0.40%；录音制品 3 998 件，占登记总量的 0.30%；音乐作品 2 834 件，占登记总量的 0.22%；模型、戏剧、舞蹈等共计 6 319 件，共占登记总量的 0.48%。

三、计算机软件著作权登记有关数据及排名

2015 年，我国计算机软件著作权登记数量再创历史新高，全年共登记软件 292 360 件，接近 30 万件，相比 2014 年的 218 783 件同比增长 33.63%，这也是自 2010 年以来，同比增长增速最高的一年。

从登记量地区排名上看，2015 年位列全国前十位的地区排名与 2014 年相比，未发生任何变化，前十位省市共登记软件 236 086 件，约占登记总量的 80.75%。与上一年度相比，上述省市登记数量增长 61 555 件，约占增长总量的 83.66%，占比近九成。其中前五位依次为：北京市、广东省、上海市、江苏省和浙江省，五地共登记软件 192 152 件，约占登记总量的 65.72%。其中，北京市登记软件 64 532 件，约占登记总量的 22.07%，继续高居全国榜首。

从登记量增速前十位排名来看，中部地区占据五席，东部地区占据三席，西部和东北部地区各占据一席。其中，广东省登记软件 61 804 件，同比增长 64.18%，增速全国最快。另外，贵州省、青海省和重庆市继续保持增速，连续进入 2014 年和 2015 年的增速排名前十位。

四、著作权质权登记有关数据

2015 年中国版权保护中心共完成著作权质权登记 606 件，同比增长 22.18%；涉及合同数量 231 个，同比下降 0.09%；涉及作品数量 1 269 件，同比增长 22.18%；涉及主债务金额 287 285 万元，同比增长 9.42%；涉及担保金额 267 542.83 万元，同比下降 6.86%。

作品著作权质权登记409件，同比上升34%；涉及合同34个，同比下降23.5%；涉及作品数量409件，同比上升34%；涉及主债务金额113 600万元，同比上升48.6%，涉及担保金额111 500万元，同比上升2.1%。

计算机软件著作权质权登记197件，同比下降3.14%；涉及合同197个，同比下降3.14%；涉及软件作品数量860件，同比增长16.21%；涉及主债务金额173 685万元，同比下降6.68%，涉及担保金额156 042.83万元，同比下降12.37%。

希望各地版权行政管理部门和著作权登记机构在进一步贯彻落实《关于进一步规范作品登记程序等有关工作的通知》的基础上，结合本地区、本部门实际，充分利用国家版权监管平台，不断提升著作权登记工作规范化、标准化、信息化水平，加强著作权登记工作队伍建设，妥善解决作品登记工作中存在的普遍性问题，全面提升著作权登记工作的效能，使著作权登记工作迈上新台阶。

国家版权局办公厅

2016年2月4日

关于国家版权监管平台（二期）第一阶段著作权登记项目运行有关事项的通知

国版办发［2016］5号

各省、自治区、直辖市版权局，中国版权保护中心：

国家版权监管平台（二期）第一阶段（以下简称"平台"）现已完成，公共服务方面开发了著作权登记项目（以下简称"项目"），具有国家版权局及各著作权登记机构的著作权登记信息在线传输、实时统计、实时发布等业务功能。项目于2014年7月通过初验后，在北京市、山东省、内蒙古自治区版权局进行了试运行，系统运行良好。

为充分发挥平台作用，定于2016年6月1日起正式运行平台项目，特作如下通知：

一、项目用户由各著作权登记机构从平台用户中指定。各省级版权局用户范围包括局长、分管副局长、版权业务处室全体人员；中国版权保护中心用户范围包括主任、分管副主任、负责汇总报送著作权登记信息等公共服务业务的经办人员。

二、各著作权登记机构应自2016年6月1日起每月10日前按照平台项目的具体栏目，完整填报上一月度的各项著作权登记信息。各著作权登记机构需使用我局统一发放的USB-Key登录平台。

三、平台支持手工录入、文件上传、系统接口等三种数据上报方式：手工录入方式适合没有著作权登记系统的机构使用，可在平台上直接录入著作权登记信息并实现著作权登记业务的流程化管理和著作权登记数据的分类汇总、统计；文件上传方式适合著作权登记量较大的机构使用，可在平台中下载著作权信息报送的Excel文件模板，根据模板格式填写著作权信息，一次上传多条著作权信息至平台；系统接口方式适合已有著作权登记系统并对现有著作权登记系统具有二次开发能力的机构使用，根据平台提供的接口开发说明文档开发数据报送接口，并通过接口自动将著作权登记数据导入平台。

四、各著作权登记机构可根据实际情况选择上述任何一种方式在规定时间内将本登记机构有关著作权登记信息录入或接入平台。

五、平台是按照国家信息安全等级保护三级标准建设的信息系统，属于非涉密信息系统，不得在平台上处理涉密信息和敏感信息。

六、各著作权登记机构仍应根据《关于进一步规范作品登记程序等有关工作的通知》（国版字［2011］14号）的要求，将相关作品登记信息报送中国版权保护中心。

七、各著作权登记机构应于2016年5月1日前指定著作权登记信息工作负责人和联络员（联络表附后），并将相关信息报送我局版权管理司。

平台项目运行过程中，如发现问题请及时与我局版权管理司或信息中心联系。

附件：著作权登记工作联络表（略）

国家版权局办公厅

2016年3月15日

关于做好 2016 年推进软件正版化有关工作的通知

国版办发［2016］7 号

各省、自治区、直辖市人民政府办公厅：

2016 年是“十三五”规划的开局之年，也是巩固和扩大软件正版化工作成果的关键之年。按照《国务院办公厅关于印发 2016 年全国打击侵犯知识产权和制售假冒伪劣商品工作要点的通知》（国办发［2016］25 号）和推进使用正版软件工作部际联席会议《2016 年推进使用正版软件工作计划》要求，2016 年推进软件正版化工作重点是巩固政府机关软件正版化工作成果，加快推进企业软件正版化工作。

一、抓住关键环节，完善推进软件正版化工作长效机制

（一）建立健全软件正版化工作责任制度。贯彻落实国务院办公厅印发的《政府机关使用正版软件管理办法》“各级政府应当将使用正版软件工作纳入年度考核，建立考核评议制度和责任追究制度，定期对使用正版软件工作进行考核、评议”要求，结合本省（区、市）实际，建立健全省级机关单位软件正版化工作考核评议和责任追究制度，制定省级机关单位软件正版化工作考核办法，建立健全本省（区、市）各级政府机关软件正版化工作责任人信息库。

（二）加强软硬件采购源头管理。严格落实国务院办公厅印发的《政府机关使用正版软件管理办法》“各级政府机关购置计算机办公设备时，应当采购预装正版操作系统软件的计算机产品，对需要购置的办公软件和杀毒软件一并作出购置计划”要求，完善计算机软硬件采购制度，规范计算机软硬件采购流程，严把源头关。审批新采购计算机办公设备时，要审核是否预装正版操作系统软件，以及是否有相应的办公软件和杀毒软件购置计划。

二、摸清底数，明确推进软件正版化工作目标任务

（一）开展软件使用情况摸底调查。组织本省（区、市）各级政府机关开展软件使用情况全面自查，重点检查操作系统软件、办公软件和杀毒软件使用情况。开展企业软件正版化工作全面自查，梳理本省（区、市）企业软件正版化工作进展情况，重点检查操作系统软件、办公软件、杀毒软件和辅助设计软件使用情况。建立维护本省（区、市）政府机关和企业软件正版化工作进展情况信息库。指导政府机关和企事业单位科学合理制订软件采购计划，将软件采购资金纳入预算。

（二）明确企业软件正版化工作目标任务。结合本省（区、市）实际，明确 2016 年推进企业软件正版化工作目标任务，研究推进企业软件正版化工作具体措施，推动企业将软件正版化工作与业绩考核挂钩。重点推进国有企业、中小金融机构软件正版化工作，加快推进民营企业软件正版化工作。

三、加强监管，落实推进软件正版化工作主体责任

（一）落实软件正版化工作主体责任。加强过程监管，指导本省（区、市）各级政府机关和企事业单位规范经费保障、使用管理、日常监管、年度报告等软件正版化工作关键环节，督促本省（区、市）各级政府机关和企事业单位落实软件正版化工作主体责任。

（二）强化责任意识落实奖惩措施。严格落实软件正版化工作奖惩措施，强化软件正版化工作责任人的责任意识，加强对软件正版化工作责任人的政策指导和业务培训，充分发挥软件正版化工作责任人的作用。

各省（区、市）要充分认识推进软件正版化工作对于我国实施创新驱动发展战略、保障信息安全和维护国家形象的重要意义。加强组织领导，创新工作方法，加强督促检查和宣传培训，持续深入推进软件正版化工作，不断巩固和扩大推进软件正版化工作成果。

请各省（区、市）通过国家版权监管平台于 5 月 31 日前报送《省级机关单位软件正版化工作责任人信息表》（附件 1）、《2015 年企业软件正版化工作完成情况统计表》（附件 2），6 月 30 日前报送《市县级机关单位软件正版化工作责任人信息表》（附件 3）、《机关单位软件使用情况统计表》（附件 4）。

附件：1. 省级机关单位软件正版化工作责任人信息表（略）

2. 2015年企业软件正版化工作完成情况统计表（略）

3. 市县级机关单位软件正版化工作责任人信息表（略）

4. 机关单位软件使用情况统计表（略）

推进使用正版软件工作部际联席会议办公室

国家版权局办公厅 代章

2016年4月20日

关于公布第一批全国版权执法监管培训师资库人员名单的通知

国版办发［2016］8号

各省（自治区、直辖市）版权局，北京、天津、上海、重庆市文化市场行政执法总队：

2015年6月30日，国家版权局下发了《关于开展全国版权执法培训师资选聘工作的通知》（国版办函［2015］39号），决定从全国各级版权行政管理部门、文化市场综合执法机构人员中选聘师资，建立全国版权执法监管培训师资库。经过资格审核、课件筛选、专家评审等程序，国家版权局决定将北京市版权局王野霏等50名同志（见附件）列入第一批全国版权执法监管培训师资库。

各级版权行政管理部门和文化市场综合执法机构要高度重视版权执法监管的教育培训工作，认真抓好对师资人员的培养锻炼，全力支持师资人员履行授课职责。入选师资库的同志要加强学习，认真准备，高质量完成培训授课任务。师资库将实行动态管理，我局将适时对师资库名单予以增减调整。

特此通知。

附件：国家版权局第一批全国版权执法监管培训师资库人员名单

国家版权局办公厅

2016年4月25日

国家版权局第一批全国版权执法监管培训师资库人员名单

序号	姓名	单位
1	王野霏	北京市版权局
2	赵红仕	北京市版权局
3	刘铁京	北京市文化市场行政执法总队
4	赵国明	北京市文化市场行政执法总队
5	杨金山	北京市文化市场行政执法总队
6	于刚建	北京市文化市场行政执法总队
7	蔡纪万	上海市版权局
8	薛　彬	上海市版权局
9	孟　晋	上海市文化市场行政执法总队

续前表

序号	姓名	单位
10	杨　勇	上海市文化市场行政执法总队
11	万　赟	上海市文化市场行政执法总队
12	谷申安	上海市文化市场行政执法总队
13	史庭栋	上海市文化市场行政执法总队
14	左图强	重庆市版权局
15	来晋军	山西省长治市文化市场行政综合执法大队
16	娄文孝	山西省晋城市文化市场行政综合执法大队
17	吴　昊	辽宁省大连市文化市场综合执法总队
18	钟　华	山东省版权局
19	张晓生	山东省版权局
20	徐增敏	山东省青岛市文化市场行政执法局
21	吾晓红	浙江省版权局
22	曹　剑	浙江省宁波市文化市场行政执法总队
23	竺兰忠	浙江省宁波市文化市场行政执法总队
24	管　静	安徽省马鞍山市文化市场综合执法大队
25	丁　钢	安徽省蚌埠市文化市场行政管理局
26	杨　阳	安徽省蚌埠市文化市场行政管理局
27	黄　翔	安徽省蚌埠市文化市场行政管理局
28	袁学术	江苏省版权局
29	张　梅	江苏省苏州市版权局
30	解硕群	江苏省徐州市版权局
31	许　生	江苏省常州市文化行政综合执法支队
32	周　俊	江苏省常州市文化行政综合执法支队
33	唐海宁	江苏省扬州市文化行政综合执法支队
34	张宏涛	江西省版权局
35	熊　焰	江西庐山市文化市场管理局
36	文国斌	湖北省潜江市文化市场综合执法支队
37	谭　昕	湖南省版权局
38	蒋斌栋	湖南省长沙市文化市场综合执法局
39	胡　巍	湖南省怀化市版权局

续前表

序号	姓名	单位
40	张同英	广东省版权局
41	江　南	广东省广州市文化市场综合行政执法总队
42	谢小特	广东省广州市文化市场综合文化执法总队
43	苏珊娜	广东省广州市文化文化市场综合执法总队

续前表

序号	姓名	单位
44	王春风	海南省文化市场行政执法总队
45	王卫武	陕西省西安市版权局
46	张创升	陕西省铜川市文化市场综合执法支队
47	吕　鑫	陕西省铜川市文化市场综合执法支队
48	孙　洁	中国版权保护中心
49	韩志宇	首都版权保护联盟
50	吴安宁	安徽省版权协会

关于印发《正版软件管理工作指南》的通知

国版办发［2016］13号

各省、自治区、直辖市人民政府办公厅，党中央有关部门办公厅（室），国务院各部委、各直属机构办公厅（室），全国人大常委会办公厅、全国政协办公厅有关部门，高法院、高检院办公厅，有关人民团体办公厅（室），各民主党派中央办公厅：

根据国务院办公厅印发的《政府机关使用正版软件管理办法》和《2016年全国打击侵犯知识产权和制售假冒伪劣商品工作要点》，为指导各级政府机关和企事业单位开展正版软件管理工作，规范使用正版软件行为，提高软件资源使用效率，保障信息系统安全高效运行，推进使用正版软件工作规范化标准化，我们编制了《正版软件管理工作指南》。现印发给你们，供参考。执行中有任何问题，请及时反馈我们。

附件：1. 正版软件管理工作指南（略）

2. 正版软件管理工作指南相关表格（略）

推进使用正版软件工作部际联席会议办公室

国家版权局办公厅　代章

2016年7月11日

关于"剑网2016"专项行动第一批网络侵权盗版案件查办情况的通报

国版办发［2016］15号

各省、自治区、直辖市版权局，北京市、天津市、上海市、重庆市文化市场行政执法总队：

国家版权局、国家互联网信息办公室、工业和信息化部和公安部四部门联合印发《关于开展打击网络侵权盗版"剑网2016"专项行动的通知》（国版发［2016］2号）以来，各地各部门及时做出工作部署、积极加强协调配合、认真开展清理检查，对已立案的网络侵权盗版案件加快查办进度，并对一批新发现的案件线索积极开展调查，形成了严厉打击网络侵权盗版的高压态势。现将近期各地查办的一批网络侵权盗版典型案件通报如下：

一、侵犯网络文学作品著作权案件

1. 江苏苏州"风雨文学网"涉嫌侵犯著作权案。2015年9月，根据权利人投诉，江苏苏州张家港市文广新局对"风雨文学网"网站涉嫌侵犯著作权案进行调查。经查，自2013年5月起，张某未经权利人许可，在其开设网站上向公众提供涉嫌侵权文字作品，并通过广告联盟获利100余万元。目前，该案已移交公安部门。

2. 重庆“269小说网”涉嫌侵犯著作权案。2015年8月，根据举报线索，重庆市版权局会同公安部门对“269小说网”涉嫌侵犯著作权案进行调查。经查，自2013年起，步某未经权利人许可，在其开设网站上向公众提供2万余部涉嫌侵权文字作品，并通过广告联盟等获利。目前，该案正在进一步查办中。

3. 四川双流“轻之国度”“轻之文库”网站涉嫌侵犯著作权案。2015年11月，根据权利人投诉，四川省成都市、双流县两级版权行政执法部门会同公安部门对“轻之国度”“轻之文库”网站涉嫌侵犯著作权案进行调查。经查，该网站未经权利人许可，向公众提供涉嫌侵权小说作品5 000余部。目前，2名犯罪嫌疑人已被批捕，案件正在进一步查办中。

4. 广西南宁“皮皮小说网”涉嫌侵犯著作权案。2015年7月，根据权利人投诉，广西壮族自治区版权行政执法部门会同公安部门对“皮皮小说网”涉嫌侵犯著作权案进行调查。经查，自2012年4月起，魏某某、覃某和陈某某未经权利人许可，在其开设网站上向公众提供涉嫌侵权文字作品，并通过广告获利。目前，该案已进入法院审理阶段。

二、侵犯网络游戏著作权案件

5. 重庆“8·6”林某某等涉嫌侵犯著作权案。2015年8月，根据群众举报线索，重庆市版权行政执法部门会同公安部门对林某某等人涉嫌侵犯著作案进行调查。经查，林某某等人非法获取权利人开发的游戏软件源代码，私自架设《至尊合击》《回忆传奇》等多款游戏，并由韦某等人搭建游戏充值平台收取充值款，涉案金额达3 000万余元。目前，林某某等8名犯罪嫌疑人已被抓获，案件正在进一步查办中。

6. 重庆《热血荣耀》（赤月版）涉嫌侵犯网络游戏著作权案。2016年7月，经权利人投诉，重庆市版权行政执法部门会同公安部门对唐某某等涉嫌侵犯网络游戏著作权案进行调查。经查，未经权利人许可，唐某某等人架设《热血荣耀》（赤月版）游戏私服，并对游戏程序进行修改用于营利。自2016年1月起，通过第三方平台收取充值款，涉案金额达260万元。目前，该案已移送公安部门。

三、通过网络平台销售盗版制品案件

7. 北京“亿梦春田”等6家淘宝店铺涉嫌侵犯著作权案。2016年1月，根据举报线索，北京市文化市场行政执法总队会同公安部门对北京亿梦春田文化有限公司涉嫌侵犯著作权案进行调查，现场查获涉嫌侵权盗版图书38种，共8 140册。经鉴定，查获图书均为侵权出版物。经查，该公司先后通过“亿梦春田”等6家淘宝店铺销售侵权盗版图书，非法销售金额达400万元。目前，4名犯罪嫌疑人已被抓获，案件正在进一步查办中。

8. 江苏镇江“10·26”制售侵权复制品案。2015年9月18日，根据举报线索，江苏省镇江市公安部门对“剑锋时代图书专营店”淘宝网店涉嫌销售盗版图书案进行调查。经查，张某某等人通过网络销售盗版图书110余种，共计52万余册，涉案金额达300余万元，现场查获盗版图书25 000余册，涉嫌侵权盗版图书60万余册。江苏省版权行政执法部门会同“扫黄打非”部门、公安部门进一步调查，捣毁两处涉嫌侵权盗版图书藏匿窝点，现场查获图书340余种共计超百万册和大量半成品图书。目前，7名犯罪嫌疑人已被抓获，案件正在进一步查办中。

国家版权局办公厅

2016年8月15日

关于同意在深圳市腾讯计算机系统有限公司设立“网络版权产业研究基地”的复函

国版办函［2016］41号

深圳市腾讯计算机系统有限公司：

你公司《关于设立国家版权局网络版权产业研究基地的建议》收悉。经研究，我局同意在你公司设立“网络版权产业研究基地”。

希望你公司以建设知识产权强国战略为指导，充分发挥作为网络产业从业者在网络版权产业发展研究和实践方面的自身优势，依托腾讯研究院深厚的研究基础和丰富的专家资源，紧密结合国际和国内网络版权产业发展新趋势，及时跟踪国内外网络版权产业发展动态，积极探索，努力实践，研究和总结网络版权产业问题应对策略，为政府部门在网络版权产业政策制定、产业管理、执法监管等方面提供实务支撑和理论支持，将基地建设成为国内重要的版权智库和网络版权产业问题研究平台。

国家版权局办公厅

2016 年 10 月 12 日

关于印发《2016 年全国新闻出版（版权）打击侵权假冒工作要点》的通知

新广出办函［2016］198 号

各省、自治区、直辖市新闻出版广电局（版权局），北京市、天津市、上海市、重庆市文化市场行政执法总队：

为贯彻落实全国打击侵犯知识产权和制售假冒伪劣商品工作领导小组第九次全体会议精神，切实做好 2016 年全国新闻出版、版权打击侵权假冒工作，总局打击侵犯知识产权和制售假冒伪劣商品工作领导小组根据《国务院办公厅关于印发 2016 年全国打击侵犯知识产权和制售假冒伪劣商品工作要点的通知》（国办发［2016］25 号）的要求，结合新闻出版、版权监管职能，制定了《2016 年全国新闻出版（版权）打击侵权假冒工作要点》。现印发给你们，请认真贯彻执行。

国家新闻出版广电总局办公厅

2016 年 6 月 2 日

2016 年全国新闻出版（版权）打击侵权假冒工作要点

2016 年，全国新闻出版（版权）系统要认真贯彻落实国务院关于打击侵权假冒工作的部署，坚持以五大发展理念为抓手，围绕推动供给侧结构性改革，加强对侵权假冒违法行为的集中整治和日常监管，为推动新闻出版、版权工作提供有力保障。

一、开展重点领域专项治理行动

（一）组织开展“剑网 2016”专项行动。深入落实《国务院办公厅关于加强互联网领域侵权假冒行为治理的意见》（国办发［2015］77 号）文件精神，严厉打击网络侵权盗版行为。今年 6 月至 11 月，国家版权局会同国家互联网信息办公室、工业和信息化部、公安部组织开展第十二次打击网络侵权盗版专项治理“剑网行动”（简称“剑网 2016”专项行动），突出整治未经授权非法传播网络文学、影视、新闻等作品的侵权盗版行为，重点查处通过智能移动终端第三方应用程序（APP）、电子商务平台、网络广告联盟、私人影院等平台进行的侵权盗版行为，进一步规范网络音乐、网络云存储空间、网络转载作品的版权秩序。

（二）组织开展部分重点城市高校及其周边复印店专项治理行动。今年 2 月至 9 月，全国“扫黄打非”工作小组办公室会同教育部、国家工商行政管理总局、国家新闻出版广电总局、国家版权局在全国范围内开展部分重点城市高校及其周边复印店专项治理行动，清查高校内部及其周边复印店，依法查处侵权盗版特别是盗印教材的行为；整治利用电脑或云盘中的教材电子文档进行盗版复印的活动；整治开展盗印、复印教材业务的网站。

（三）组织开展“秋风 2016”专项行动。将打击侵权盗版出版物工作纳入“扫黄打非·秋风 2016”专项行动，全面清查图书、音像制品、计算机软件市场，严厉打击网上网下侵权盗版活动，整治盗版重大题材出版物、畅销出版物、教材教辅等行为；加强网络环节监控，督促电子商务企业加强网上书店的审查清理，打击网上销售侵权盗版出版物等行为。

二、强化对重点环节的执法监管

（四）深入推进软件正版化工作。完善软件正版化工作责任制度，建立健全软件正版化工作考核评议细则，推进政府机关和企事业单位落实软件正版化工作主体责任。研究制定规范计算机软硬件采购具体措施，从源头上防止盗版软件流入政府机关。

在审核新采购计算机办公设备时，要审核是否预装正版操作系统软件，以及是否有相应的办公软件和杀毒软件购置计划。制定正版软件管理工作指南，提高正版软件使用效率，推进正版软件使用管理规范化标准化。加大推广使用优秀软件产品工作力度。研究加快推进企业软件正版化工作具体措施，对进展缓慢的企业进行约谈，督促企业建立软件资产管理制度，规范软件采购、登记、安装、升级等工作。加强督促检查，严格责任追究，注重利用第三方专业机构的资源和技术手段开展督查工作。加大对新出厂计算机预装正版操作系统软件的检查管理力度，将平板电脑、智能手机等纳入监管范围。

（五）加强印刷复制发行日常监管。持续加强对印刷复制发行企业监督检查力度，重点对落实管理制度情况、印制销售重大选题出版物情况、印制销售各类非法出版物情况进行检查。要在全国“两会”外专项检查行动的基础上，在国庆节前再组织一次印刷复制发行专项检查。查办一批违法违规案件，坚决打击印制销售非法出版物的行为。

（六）深入开展版权重点监管工作。利用技术手段把智能移动终端第三方应用程序（APP）、网络云存储空间、微博、微信等新型传播方式纳入监管范围，探索对新型网络侵权盗版行为的有效治理模式。在网络文学、APP、网络广告联盟等领域建立“黑白名单”制度，树立版权保护典型企业，建立重点保护作品“白名单”库，公布侵权盗版企业“黑名单”。加强侵权盗版案件信息公开，健全对互联网企业的约谈、警示、通报工作机制，推进版权领域信用体系建设，加强事中事后监管。

（七）加大版权行政与刑事双线打击力度。各级新闻出版、版权执法监管部门要坚持以查办案件为第一要务，积极履行监管职责，加大对侵权盗版案件的行政处罚和刑事移送工作力度。省级新闻出版、版权执法部门要起带头作用，通过查办案件引领示范，并充分发挥中心城市及市县级新闻出版、版权行政执法部门查处案件的积极性。积极参与“两法衔接”信息共享平台建设，加强涉嫌犯罪案件移送工作，推动司法部门依法及时侦查、起诉和审判，切实加大对侵权盗版违法犯罪行为的刑事打击力度。推动打击侵权盗版涉案物品检验鉴定体系建设。

三、夯实工作管理制度

（八）完善印刷复制发行管理机制。加快推进印刷委托书网上备案体系全国联网，提升信息化管理水平。积极开展“3·15”质检活动，加大对质量违规的查处力度。完善与重点网上书店和网络出版物销售平台的约谈机制，要求各地将网上书店纳入管理，建立沟通和应急机制，加大对网络发行活动的查处力度。

（九）健全版权执法监管工作机制。各地要进一步健全常态化的联合挂牌督办机制，定期联合督办一批重点案件，做到及时督办、及时上报、及时结案。加快推动部门间、地区间、政府与社会之间信息共享和执法协作，形成对侵权盗版违法行为的协同监管和联合惩戒。推动发展水平相近、地理位置接近的地区建立健全执法协作、协查机制，推进跨地区执法线索移转、案件会商、信息共享、案情通报、执法联动。积极推动权利人及组织与互联网企业建立版权合作机制，建立完善网站版权信息库、权利人维权绿色通道。

（十）推动侵权假冒案件信息公开。各地新闻出版、版权执法部门要认真贯彻落实《新闻出版（版权）行政执法部门依法公开制售假冒伪劣商品和侵犯知识产权行政处罚案件信息的实施细则（试行）》，按照“谁执法、谁公开”原则和行政处罚案件信息公开权限，进一步完善和落实案件信息公开管理制度，加强案件信息公开的监督检查、情况通报与考核，全面推进侵权假冒案件信息公开工作。

四、加强基础能力建设

（十一）加强版权教育培训工作。深入开展版权执法监管培训和软件正版化培训工作。继续开展对省级以下版权管理、文化执法部门的教育培训工作，全面提升基层执法人员的工作能力和业务水平。健全完善版权执法监管培训师资库，进一步提升培训工作效能。继续开展对版权、工信、财政、商务、国资、机关事务管理等省级推进软件正版化工作机制成员单位相关负责同志和政府机关软件正版化工作责任人的培训工作。开展2015年度查处侵权盗版案件有功单位和有功个人奖励工作，进一步调动相关执法部门和执法人员查处侵权盗版案件的积极性和主动性。

（十二）广泛开展宣传教育活动。要通过电视、广播、报纸等传统媒体和微信、微博等各种形式新媒体，开展打击侵权盗版集中宣传活动，提高广大公众的知识产权意识。要加大对大案要案和典型案件的宣传力度，坚决曝光具有恶劣情节的侵权盗版企业与违法犯罪分子，震慑违法者、教育从业者，教育和引导广大网民树立“尊重版权、鼓励创新”的基本意识，增强人民群众对政府打击侵权盗版的信心。

（十三）加强对打击侵权假冒工作的督导检查。总局将不定期对各地打击侵权假冒工作开展情况进行督导检查，并将检查结果纳入 2016 年全国打击侵权假冒工作考核。各省级新闻出版、版权部门要开展对各市（地）、区（县）的督导检查工作，对工作开展不力的地区和单位要予以通报并责令限期整改。

Kingbond
金版国际文化传播（北京）有限公司
立足版权 携手产业
网络新媒体 版权代理 书画艺术……
《中国版权》杂志 | 《中国版权年鉴》 | 中国版权年会 | 中国版权产业网 | 书画艺术版权网
联系电话：010-58604520

智造腾讯

腾讯版权生态和版权保护探索

作为中国领先的互联网综合服务提供商，腾讯一直秉承“一切以用户价值为依归”的经营理念，为亿级海量用户提供稳定优质的服务，始终处于稳健发展的状态。2004年6月16日，腾讯在香港联交所主板公开上市（股票代号700）。

随着科技与内容的融合，“腾讯智造”不断发力。在连接和内容产业战略的指引下，腾讯通过聚合内容资源进而聚合用户，开展内容资源的多元产品形态开发。“泛娱乐”战略初步打造了“同一明星IP、多种文化创意产品体验”的创新业态，推动文化产业共同繁荣的健康生态。为进一步支撑创新、巩固创新成果，腾讯建立了一套涵盖著作权、商标权、专利权等全方位知识产权保护体系，并通过合理的布局，实现技术与品牌的跨国保护。

腾讯不仅关注自有知识产权，更将尊重和保护第三方知识产权作为知识产权保护战略的重要组成部分，形成腾讯版权保护生态体系。在众多产品所构筑的腾讯平台上，流动的是信息，承载的是智慧。对侵权者说“不”，为创意点赞，是腾讯对创新和知识的尊重。让权利人得到应有的尊重，保护权利人的合法权益，是社会发展之必然，也是腾讯推动建立公平、开放、分享、共赢的知识产权生态的初心所在，更是践行企业社会责任的直观体现。

2017年4月15日，在上海举行的2017知识产权南湖论坛上，腾讯公司正式发布《腾讯知识产权保护白皮书》，披露腾讯在知识产权保护技术上的创新和完整的知识产权保护体系，这也是腾讯在国际知识产权保护领域一个重要的里程碑。

内容为王，连接版权产业全价值链

丰富的优质内容、中国持续进步的版权保护环境，助力腾讯数字内容业务的增长。

在“大众创业、万众创新”的国家政策指引下，在腾讯的开放平台上，移动互联网开发者掀起的大众创业浪潮持续发力，成为文创产业发展的生力军。2016年，腾讯开放平台创业公司达到600万家，帮助平台企业上市达到20家，合作伙伴总估值已突破3 000亿元，第三方总收益超100亿元。

版权运营，撬动版权增值和文化传播

优秀的作品（IP）是内容产业发展的根基，只有通过创新和推广，通过版权跨界运营，才能更好地实践版权价值增值，才能实现作品文化价值与经济价值协同发展，并以此助推文创产业发展和优秀文化的传播。

以腾讯游戏、腾讯动漫、腾讯文学、腾讯影业、企鹅影业、腾讯视频、QQ音乐等为代表的业务平台是版权创造、运用的主力军。它们不断创新商业模式，实现了正版运营模式的良好运行，满足了亿万网友健康的精神文化需求，促进了版权产业生态的繁荣和发展。

坚持创新，为数字经济注入新活力

通过大数据、人工智能等技术挖掘用户需求、偏好、兴趣等，对用户进行精准定位，进行个性化内容推荐。腾讯新闻、天天快报等新闻平台根据用户的阅读习惯推送用户感兴趣、有需求的新闻内容，同样的消费模式还存在于网络音乐、视频、文学等领域。精准的个性化消费，是未来内容消费的必然趋势。

未来，腾讯将继续通过为用户提供独家内容及利用社交关系链，发展包括网络视频、音乐及文学等数字内容业务。可以说，正是在腾讯等一批优秀的互联网内容平台的创新和运营下，真正实现了保护正版、推广正版，并推动了内容产业价值的持续提升。

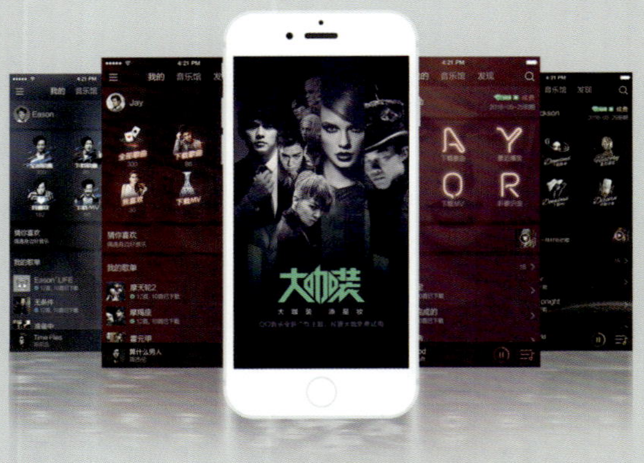

大咖装

音乐·发现杂志

设计作品来源于：QQ音乐团队

十二年的陪伴，QQ音乐已成为覆盖8亿用户群，日活跃用户破亿的国内数字音乐平台。在移动端先后推出了歌曲弹幕、歌词海报、听歌识曲、大咖装、“发现·音乐”公众号等用户口碑和体验突出的创新功能，并在PC、Mac、Pad、TV平台持续发力，成为行业内率先适配新特性和平台化运营的音乐应用，并且不断创新和优化，致力于成为用户心中更好的音乐内容产品。

个性播放页

腾讯NEXT IDEA × 故宫

2016年7月6日，腾讯与故宫博物院在故宫端门数字馆举办“腾讯NEXT IDEA × 故宫”发布会，宣布建立合作伙伴关系，开展长期合作。此次合作将以“NEXT IDEA腾讯创新大赛”为平台，故宫博物院经典IP形象或相关传统文化内容为原型，围绕赛事主题、跨界合作和创新人才培养等方面，探索传统文化IP的活化模式。

FiT FINANCIAL TECHNOLOGY
招财节

设计作品来源于：FiT金融市场部设计中心

在中国民间传说中，财神爷是主管财源的神明，招财的代表。设计周以财神为主形象，寓意FiT金融市场部是个招财的、能给用户带来好运的部门。主色调上，提取部门三大业务的颜色：QQ红包的红、理财通的蓝、QQ彩票的黄进行融合设计，反映出FiT传承部门特色的设计格调。

设计作品来源于：腾讯ISUX品牌设计中心

QQfamily是由腾讯ISUX品牌设计中心原创设计的一个IP品牌，它由一群活泼可爱的角色组成，有功夫达人Dov多福、萌货babyQ、时尚QQ、调皮Qana卡纳、自恋狂Oscar奥斯卡、K歌明星Anko安子。他们充满好奇心、喜欢新奇有趣又好玩的事物，在日常相处中不断碰撞出有趣的火花，给人积极的能量和美好生活的向往。

QQfamily角色展示

QQfamily内容展示

QQ设计演变

QQfamily内容展示

手机百度
百度一下，你就得到

双擎领航，历9弥新
百度9.0全新改版

手机百度9.0版本全新亮相，在信息呈现上，底部菜单布局从操作型按钮转变为内容频道型入口，短视频作为引力产品前置首页。关注、个人中心的外露，可以更好地引导用户与内容主动发生关联，强化用户对手机百度的归属感。与此同时，首页进一步突出搜索和Feed两大引擎。在信息消费上，手百9.0以互动为纽带，点赞、收藏、评论、分享等功能全面外露，构建出轻社交式的内容消费体验，打造内容消费到二次生产的生态闭环。

信息呈现

操作型按钮升级为内容型入口
连接信息世界

- 全新底部菜单布局，操作型按钮升级为内容型入口
- 视频入口前置，更便捷的视频获取体验
- 全新首页布局，突出搜索与Feed两大引擎

首页布局全新升级

- 强化搜索的视觉效果
- 突出搜索与Feed两大内容分发引擎
- 布局更加清晰，搜索框内增加语音搜索功能
- 金刚导航收起
- 高黏性内容类栏目（如小说）纳入Feed
- TTS功能默认外露
- 减少用户获取该服务的操作步骤
- 继续加强手百特色

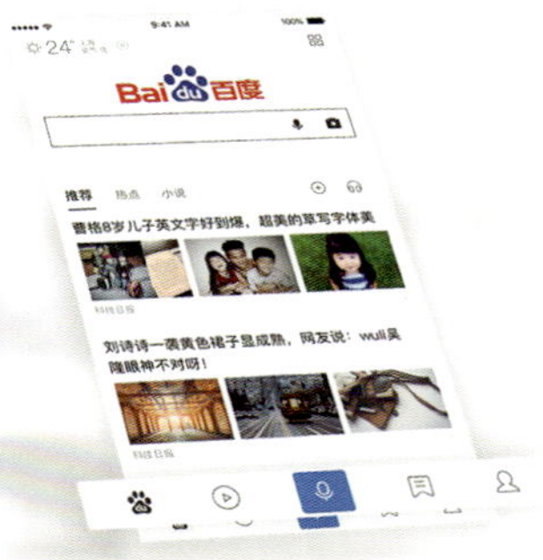

视频入口前置

获取视频内容更加便捷

- 视频入口前置底部菜单第二位
- 突出引力产品的战略重点
- 视频内容消费更加便捷

关注入口前置

强化手百连接人与号的用户认知

- 关注入口前置底部菜单第四位
- 一方面
  为用户个性化管理自己关注的内容提供了便捷的重访入口
- 另一方面
  关注关系链条的增加可以有效辅助个性化分发
  并增加内容生产者曝光，激发生产者贡献优质内容

个人中心前置底部菜单

增强用户对手百的归属感

- 个人中心下落至底部菜单第五位
- 强化用户对手百可登录和个人内容可管理的认知
- 个人中心内部功能重新梳理
- 仅外露用户自己在手百使用中的高频常见功能（如收藏、下载）
- 收起不常用功能，界面更加简洁清晰

Feed落地页

强化轻社交能力

- 底部评论、分享、收藏功能全部外露
- 用户发布评论、进行收藏和分享更加便捷，有效拉动用户参与感

手机百度9.0朝着AI化迈进了一大步。搜索+Feed双引擎是百度内容生态的总载体，接下来贴吧、知识体系、服务都可以在新版手机百度中充分体现。AI时代已来，手机百度要用AI能力进一步提升产品核心竞争力，为百度在人工智能时代的发展起到强大的推进作用。

欢迎体验全新手机百度

如需下载： 苹果手机请到APP Store　安卓手机请到各应用商店

主动调整阅读喜好，有效避免“认知窄化”

——新版搜狐新闻客户端开启个性化“阅读微公益”

八卦党，极客族，或商务范儿？你知道自己平时喜欢阅读哪一类新闻资讯吗？大数据时代用户的阅读习惯和偏好成为个性化定制新闻资讯的重要参考。而此次搜狐新闻客户端新版的“用户画像”功能，不仅致力于提升用户的个性化阅读体验，同时还为用户提供了基于个人阅读偏好的“阅读微公益”入口，将用户的每一次阅读行为，转化为向需要帮助的儿童捐赠书籍的力量。

弱水三千，该取哪瓢饮？——“用户画像”解决“信息噪音”痛点

面对现在资讯泛滥带来的无所适从，搜狐新闻客户端急需解决的痛点就是“信息噪音”，将用户不感兴趣的内容过滤掉，推荐给用户的全部是喜欢的内容。

自2014年推出智能混合推荐及“下拉一下”个性新闻操作模式以来，搜狐新闻客户端尤其注重用户的个性化阅读体验。在新版的搜狐新闻客户端中，“用户画像”功能得到了丰富与延伸。不仅能够根据用户的基本信息和阅读偏好绘制用户专属的“用户画像”，自动生成“八卦党”“观察者”“运动咖”“商务范儿”“生活达人”和“极客族”等六种不同的形象身份，还与此次搜狐新闻客户端发起的“阅读微公益”活动紧密结合。

个性形象二次校正，有效避免“认知窄化”

随着信息传播技术的赋权，针对用户进行的个性化定制和智能推荐日益突出个人对信息的传收和控制能力，但难免出现对用户的阶段性阅读偏好的误判，如驾驭不当甚至可能出现个体视野窄化、与社会日渐疏离等问题。为了防止用户在个人信息“茧房”中出现“认知窄化”的情况，端内除自动生成“用户画像”外，还可通过手动调整阅读偏好，来二次校正自己的个性化形象。“用户画像”的引入与塑造，在帮助搜狐新闻客户端更精准、快速地分析用户的阅读习惯、阅读偏好，为用户提供个性化资讯推荐的同时，也使用户更加清晰地认知自己的阅读行为，及时调整和完善自己的阅读类型和知识结构，防止因个性化定制带来的兴趣范围和知识结构上的窄化。与业界其他平台纯机器推荐内容不同，搜狐媒体平台背后有着搜狐十几年培养的媒体信任感背书，平台上的文章无论是可读性和信赖度都有明显优势。

莫小棋

母其弥雅

邓飞

赵何娟

陈静芳

何君

“阅读微公益”汇聚用户“指尖”力量，新闻获取与捐书公益良好互动

新版的“用户画像”功能，将新闻资讯的获取与捐书公益活动进行了良好的结合，用户浏览新闻即可收集捐书“能量豆”，“能量豆”集满后，系统就会根据您的“用户画像”，向需要帮助的儿童捐赠不同类型的书籍。通过点击【我】－【活动】入口，即可定制专属的用户画象，并查看自己的“能量豆”收集情况和捐赠进展。

搜狐新闻客户端相信每一位用户的力量，将用户的每一次简单的“指尖阅读”行为转化为微公益力量。个性化的“用户画像”与公益行为相结合，打通了“用户画像”基础上的个性化“掌上阅读微公益”入口，在潜移默化中培养用户的阅读习惯和“微公益”意识。

公益的践行需要每一位个体的参与，此次搜狐新闻客户端邀请“免费午餐发起人”邓飞、“钛媒体”创始人赵何娟、“中印瑜伽大使”母其弥雅、“毒舌电影”创始人何君、“金融八卦女”联合创始人陈静芳和“星座女神”莫小棋六位不同“用户画像”领域的公益传递者，携手满天星青少年公益发展中心（满天星青少年公益发展中心是一家专注儿童阅读推广的民间教育公益机构），呼吁大家一起参与“阅读微公益”活动，奉献自己微小的力量。公益从来不是一个人的事，用户在搜狐新闻客户端中的每一次阅读行为，都能聚集成微公益力量，为孩子开启更广阔的世界。

搜狐视频精品剧对抗“量产化” 原创IP《屏里狐》播放量傲人

搜狐视频原创IP“高颜值奇幻偶像剧”《屏里狐》讲述了落魄女画师郑雪景偶然间得到一只御仙笔，在屏风上解封了三个男狐仙，和他们缔结主仆契约，由此引发的奇幻故事。该片截至收官，搜狐视频总播放量已经突破3.3亿，微博“屏里狐网络剧”相关话题阅读总量6 500万，讨论量15.4万；并且剧中主人公与剧情多次登上微博话题榜和电视剧热搜榜，网友们更是为了《屏里狐》刷爆弹幕。目前，搜狐视频的日均用户为6 500万。2017年，搜狐视频将继续以高品质的原创IP，为用户提供优质的自制剧内容。搜狐集团董事局主席兼CEO、搜狐视频CEO、《屏里狐》出品人张朝阳表示，2017年，搜狐视频自制剧仍将坚持价值投资、秉承高品质差异化策略，占据精品资源，用精品战略对抗“量产化网剧”。不仅如此，搜狐视频创作团队还会一直重视网剧创作“内容为王”的原则，因此更加格外重视原创IP的开发。从《匆匆那年》《无心法师》《他来了请闭眼》，到2016年的《贴身校花》《亲爱的公主病》《法医秦明》《屏里狐》等自制剧，张朝阳说：“搜狐视频产生优质内容的决心是坚定的，制作能力和水准也较高，能够产生精品的经历是令人幸福的，我们会继续这个传统。”

搜狐荣获中国版权领域的“奥斯卡”奖——中国版权金奖之保护奖

“中国版权金奖”是我国版权领域内评选的国际性奖项。2016年“中国版权金奖”颁奖典礼上，搜狐获得中国版权金奖之保护奖。在中国互联网版权保护的历程中，搜狐是较早举起反盗版大旗的公司，自2009年至今在多个场合都为打击盗版高声呐喊，为中国版权正版化事业做出了企业应有的担当。搜狐从2009年到2014年总共发动了两场“反盗版战争”。除了上述“反盗版战争”呼吁外，搜狐在版权保护方面致力于推动立法、司法、执法上全方位的保护：第一，搜狐主导的反盗版联盟行动最终促成了因侵犯著作权而获刑责的系列刑事案件。如快播案、“2345rb.com”和“星际s电影”利用P2P技术（如百度影音、快播播放器）盗版网络视频案。第二，推动国家出台网盘监管规范。针对网盘大量传播侵权视频作品的现状，作为权利人积极向国家版权主管部门反映，国家版权主管部门发布了《关于规范网盘服务版权秩序的通知》。第三，推动司法和行政对视频聚合不正当性进行法律定性。经过数次举办研讨会和行业呼吁，司法和行政机关已经基本认定了聚合平台破坏视频网站技术保护措施，进行聚合盗链行为的不正当性。APP聚合打击列入了“剑网2016”重点工作。

今日头条

今日头条上线“维权赔付”功能，每年15亿元投入内容建设

2017年3月，今日头条与中超版权方体奥动力签署战略合作伙伴协议，成为2017—2020赛季中超联赛官方短视频合作伙伴。双方合作后，中超联赛将以头条号的形式入驻今日头条。未来四年，中超所有比赛内容，都会以短视频的形式在今日头条上进行分发。

此外，持续发力短视频的今日头条还与摔跤联盟WWE、国内娱乐内容机构芒果TV等陆续达成合作，共同尝试移动时代的内容探索。芒果TV将开放自己旗下所有综艺节目的短视频内容，通过入驻头条号的形式对节目内容进行分发；“WWE中国”的头条号上线1个多月就有超过3 400万的短视频播放量。

7月21日，今日头条与澎湃新闻签署视频战略合作伙伴协议

今日头条对内容建设的投入资金远超国内大多数信息分发平台，每年的投入成本超过15亿元人民币。

2017年7月21日，今日头条与澎湃新闻签署视频战略合作伙伴协议，澎湃新闻旗下所有原创视频内容，包括新闻短视频与新闻直播，都将入驻头条号。

今日头条已经与国内大部分主流媒体达成合作，媒体以入驻头条号的方式发布内容。截至2017年8月，今日头条合作媒体数量超过4 800家，覆盖中央、地方和行业媒体，如新华社、光明网、《解放军报》、《新京报》、澎湃新闻等。

除了与优质内容进行合作探索之外，今日头条还一直很重视版权的保护，帮助创作者进行全网维权。

2017年3月23日，今日头条头条号平台上线“维权赔付”功能，向所有头条号原创作者开放全网跨平台维权删文和追缴赔付功能。

2016头条号创作者大会上，今日头条创始人张一鸣宣布，将拿出10亿元人民币补贴短视频创作

“维权赔付”功能由第三方维权机构“快版权”“维权骑士”与头条号联合推出，作者完成维权授权签约后，快版权会对作者确认抄袭的文章进行侵权追溯，同时对侵权方沟通赔付或提起诉讼。其中，每确认一篇被抄袭文章可立案，原创作者将获得50元先行赔付金；诉讼成功后，作者可再获得100元赔付金，即每篇被抄袭文章可为作者带来累计150元赔付金。

这是继“全网监测”“快速删文”之后，头条号平台向原创作者推出的维权新功能，同时今日头条也成为国内优先可通过版权维权帮助作者获得收益的内容平台。

从2016年5月开始，今日头条就已经上线跨平台维权功能，同年年底开始小范围内测赔付功能。截至2017年7月底，平台通过全网维权和维权赔付功能，累计删文172 139篇，先后有超过300位作者获得维权赔付，甚至有头条号创作者通过维权赔付功能月入超过万元。

鳳凰網 IFENG.COM

凤凰网创建于1998年，是全球领先的跨平台网络新媒体公司，旗下拥有综合门户凤凰网、《凤凰新闻》客户端、手机凤凰网、凤凰视频等平台，依托全媒体平台优势布局风直播、凤凰号等产品，战略投资个性化资讯阅读APP《一点资讯》，秉承“中华情怀，全球视野，包容开放，进步力量”的媒体理念，为主流华人提供跨平台整合无缝衔接的新媒体优质内容与服务。

凤凰网不仅是控股的凤凰卫视传媒集团优质电视内容的网络传播渠道，更整合了众多专业媒体机构生产的内容、用户生成的内容以及自身生产的专业内容，提供含图文音视频的全方位综合新闻资讯、深度报道、观点评论、财经产品、互动应用、分享社区、在线网页游戏等服务，满足主流人群浏览、表达、交流、分享、娱乐、理财等多元化与个性化的诉求，并反向传输给凤凰卫视的电视平台，形成创新的网台联动组合传播模式，为互联网、移动互联网及视频用户提供丰富的内容与随时随地随身的服务。凤凰网目前日均覆盖用户数（UV）4 700万，月度覆盖用户数4.16亿。凤凰新闻客户端目前已达到3.29亿总安装量，日活跃用户数量（DAU）3 200万。

《凤凰新闻》客户端是一款以差异化作为立身之本的新闻APP，始终坚持提供真相和启迪思考的干货，提供简洁和适合阅读的平台，寻求认同和内心深处的共鸣，为全球亿万华人提供“就做不同”的移动阅读体验。

风直播是凤凰网旗下的直播平台，依托凤凰系，整合多方优质资源，为用户提供专业、多元的泛资讯直播内容。风直播，只为抵达，给你好看。

凤凰号是凤凰网在新型传播模式变革背景下推出的新媒体服务平台，是自媒体内容分发与品牌助推平台。目前拥有包括文化、财经、军事、历史、科技、娱乐、时尚、体育等优质账号，内容分发覆盖《凤凰新闻》客户端、凤凰网、手机凤凰网和《一点资讯》APP。

《一点资讯》是融合关键词搜索、订阅及个性化推荐的资讯聚合产品，用独创的兴趣引擎技术，将搜索整合到资讯APP中，推荐与用户搜索关键词、浏览轨迹相匹配的资讯，并在过程中帮助用户更好地发现、表达、获取和管理有价值的内容。

纵横中文网 原创精品 www.zongheng.com

熊猫看书 PANDA READER

纵横文学是以百度文学为前身，由完美世界和百度联合打造的文学平台，旗下拥有纵横中文网、熊猫看书等产品，日用户量总计突破1 400万，作品数量突破20万，是国内十分优秀的原创小说创作平台和数字内容阅读平台。依靠平台领先的内容签约和筛选能力，重点进行付费阅读、版权分销、IP孵化等版权相关业务，并通过重点作者作品的整体运营，与上下游合作伙伴联合进行小说改编影视/游戏等IP相关项目的投资开发，打造基于文学版权的泛娱乐生态圈。

年度作品

作者：烽火戏诸侯

大千世界，无奇不有。我陈平安，唯有一剑，可搬山，倒海，降妖，镇魔，敕神，摘星，断江，摧城，开天！烽火戏诸侯最新作品，初更不到10万字便有近3万的收藏，近百万的点击，连载仅三天便成为百盟作品。该书在《雪中悍刀行》完本后备受关注，可谓千呼万唤始出来。《剑来》现已成为企鹅影业重点推进项目。

作者：妖妖之心

一条祖训，一场交易！一个是天才设计师，一个是洁癖怪总裁，拼段数拼演技，爱情友情齐飞，豪门恩怨与商战穿插其中，两人携手成长，共同面对人生中的风与雨！

此文乃都市言情金牌作品，屡创女生站新高，横扫各大榜单，创造百万点击神话！受到众多读者的喜欢及追捧，在各大平台成绩非凡！作者在圈子里人气颇高，蝉联两届“纵横年度最佳女作者冠军”！

阅文集团 CHINA READING 阅世界 悦无界

一场引爆13亿人的阅读盛宴
阅文集团携手湖南卫视开启全民阅读季

长期以来，中国人均阅读率在世界排名靠后。阅读已然成为一种“潜在发展危机”，国人该如何真正面对“阅读”？第十四次全国国民阅读调查数据公布，2016年我国成年人媒介综合阅读率为79.9%，成年人人均图书阅读量仅为7.86本。

4月23日，在第二十二个“世界读书日”来临之际，阅文集团携手湖南卫视举办了一场别开生面的“2017书香中国全民阅读系列活动启动式”。何炅、黄轩、李健、易烊千玺、佟大为、关悦等多位明星登台亮相，使之成为年度颇有看点与影响力的全民共读盛会之一。

2017书香中国全民阅读系列活动启动式

全民阅读接力　另类冰桶挑战火爆全网

为了让阅读真正走入大众，QQ阅读携手湖南卫视发起“全民365共读接力”挑战，截至晚会前，微博“2017书香中国”话题量超过1.8亿，包括演员黄轩、阅文集团白金作家在内的多位名人通过朗读QQ阅读旗下作品来参与分享。QQ阅读同时线上发力，从小说到文艺经典，被名人们推荐的作品以及相关类型图书都加入了免费试读活动。

从文化咖、主持人到IP剧明星，大众潜在的读书欲被充分点燃。阅文集团更是大气“豪撒”1亿元阅读红包，进一步降低付费数字阅读门槛，造福广大读者。

坚韧的情感纽带　读书榜样展示阅读魅力

与偶像易烊千玺共读青春，与音乐诗人李健共读诗歌，与实力演员佟大为夫妇共读爱情，与老一辈艺术家共读经典，与豪山图书馆96岁高龄创始人共读理想，全民读书晚会由五大篇章组成，从不同维度展现了阅读的魅力。阅读的魅力，能够跨越岁月的长河。八位创始人，三十二年，守一座世外“书”源，启蒙数代学子。96岁的传奇老人和他的豪山村图书馆，彰显的是坚守阅读的力量。

为了帮助这图书馆继续发扬光大，阅文集团CEO吴文辉代表集团向包括豪山图书馆在内的“湖南农家书屋计划”正式捐赠图书10万册。同时，吴文辉宣布发起“你读我捐”活动，号召QQ阅读6亿用户累积阅读时长兑换公益图书，为更多爱书之人创造阅读条件。

用QQ阅读扩张“全民阅读”生力军　阅文集团勇扛阅读大旗

和豪山图书馆一样，阅文集团建立了一座更为宏伟的云端图书馆，作品储备约千万部，创作者达几百万名。除既有原创作品输出优势，阅文集团更携手两千余家出版单位运营版权引进，图书电子版权覆盖面领跑业内。而为满足“全民阅读”的多元内容需求，阅文集团内容品类已覆盖200余种。

作为一家互联网企业，阅文集团尤为善于利用互联网思维，挖掘更多“全民阅读”发展空间，例如在晚会中，利用触达6亿用户的《QQ阅读》APP，设置“共读中国梦”“全民365共读接力”等线上活动，其中全国共读《沁园春·长沙》更获得超1100万人同时响应，展现出了强大的平台影响力。

“2017书香中国全民阅读系列活动启动式”让所有热爱读书的人记住了阅文集团。而这仅仅是阅文集团不遗余力推进“全民阅读”的开始。让我们满怀憧憬，在阅文集团的引领之下，“全民阅读”进程将不断深化，越来越多的人开始读书、爱上读书。

湖南卫视何炅现场采访豪山图书馆96岁的传奇老人

“书香中国”正式启动

现场小学生们参与共读活动

展示阅读魅力

阅文集团CEO吴文辉（前排右一）为“湖南农家书屋计划”捐赠图书10万册

QQ阅读推出阅读自由主义
陈漫携手胡歌打造书香大片
有人因为好学而看书，有人因为好玩而看书；
有人像个体验者一样看书，有人像个旁观者一样看书，
一千个人心中有一千种阅读主义，
这正是阅读自由主义的意义。
胡歌这次分享的阅读体验是要自由地阅读，
那么你心目中的阅读自由主义又是怎样的？
QQ阅读

阅读自由主义　唤醒内心深处的阅读精神

青春帅气的阳光男孩、沉稳内敛的谦谦君子……过往，胡歌总是呈现着类似的形象。这一次由时尚圈内“摄影女王”陈漫为胡歌量身打造的，却是颇具英伦风范的智者形象。

熟悉胡歌的粉丝都知道，他对于阅读始终有着特别的情结。在2017年1月受邀参加阅文集团举办的“中国原创文学风云榜”时，他曾在颁奖环节巧妙地解读了自己对于“QQ阅读”的理解，即“Question”和“Quality”，这些精妙的阅读体会，与QQ阅读的理念不谋而合。于是当QQ阅读此役正式抛出阅读自由主义这一理念时，不仅获得了胡歌的高度认可，也激发了陈漫的创作灵感。

为了准确表达阅读自由主义，陈漫与胡歌不再拘泥于一般杂志拍摄的形式。在QQ阅读的鼎力支持下，二人利用大场面的场景辅助，在摄影海报中恣意传递出自己所想要表达的阅读观点。在画面与文字的力量中，传递品牌所倡导的阅读自由主义，唤醒了所有人内心深处的阅读精神。

陈漫镜头诠释胡歌新形象　引发民众围观潮

海报面世后，胡歌的全新形象迅速引发大众关注——北上广深线下的各大地铁站路人的驻足观看、线上的QQ阅读APP的截屏记录、微博和微信朋友圈的刷屏传播……一时间，大洋彼岸的胡歌再次成为大家热议的焦点。

作为QQ阅读的代言人，胡歌长久以来都在带动着年轻人多读书、多积累。虽然每个人的读书理念各不相同，阅读的习惯、场合、内容也偏好分明，但读书所带来的自由想象空间与自由体验，却是热爱读书的人们共同认可的。而拥有网络海量好书市场占比逾1/3的QQ阅读，恰能够给予读者这种自由阅读的权利，以及想读就读的广泛选择，这也是以“阅读自由主义”为主题的海报创意的诞生源头。

这种由阅读自由主义所产生的共鸣，亦使得陈漫、胡歌以及QQ阅读之间形成了高度认同。三方的协调把控，方才促成了这部作品。与其说，这是一次集合了商业属性与艺术气质的超水准作品，不如说这是对年轻人群的洞察进行了一番完美的诠释。

这也使得北上广的年轻人们，可以在出入地铁站的过程中通过陈漫所拍摄的最新胡歌海报，发自内心地感受到胡歌内心深处，对阅读自由主义的深刻理解与诠释。倘若你也想要有所感悟，不妨前往身边的地铁站找找胡歌的这组新海报，看看是否能唤醒属于你的“阅读自由主义”态度。

掌阅
《月亮与六便士》
毛姆
“那时没有谁比萝丝·沃特福德对我更好的了。她身上结合了男性的才智和女性的任性，她写的那些小说很独特，而且读后让人心绪不宁。正是在她的家里，有一天我遇见了查尔斯·斯特里克兰的妻子。那天沃特福德小姐正在举办茶会，她那小房间比平时更为拥挤，每个人似乎都在聊天，而我则安静地
我性格太内向，所以无法加入任
好像都在专注于谈论自己的事情。
相当不错的女主人，看见了我的窘态就径直朝我
“我想让你和斯特里克兰太太说会儿话，”她说
她对你的书可是推崇备至。”
I'm a Reader

塔读文学

精品原创 阅在指尖

塔读文学是天音控股旗下北京易天新动网络科技有限公司在无线阅读领域的基础平台，是中国主流的数字版权创作、聚合和分发平台。

公司是“中国版权协会常务理事单位”，拥有众多签约作家及内容产品。

截至2016年塔读注册用户数超过3.1亿，日活跃用户数420万以上，书库存量超过25万册，原创签约作者高达2 000多人。

官网：www.tadu.com

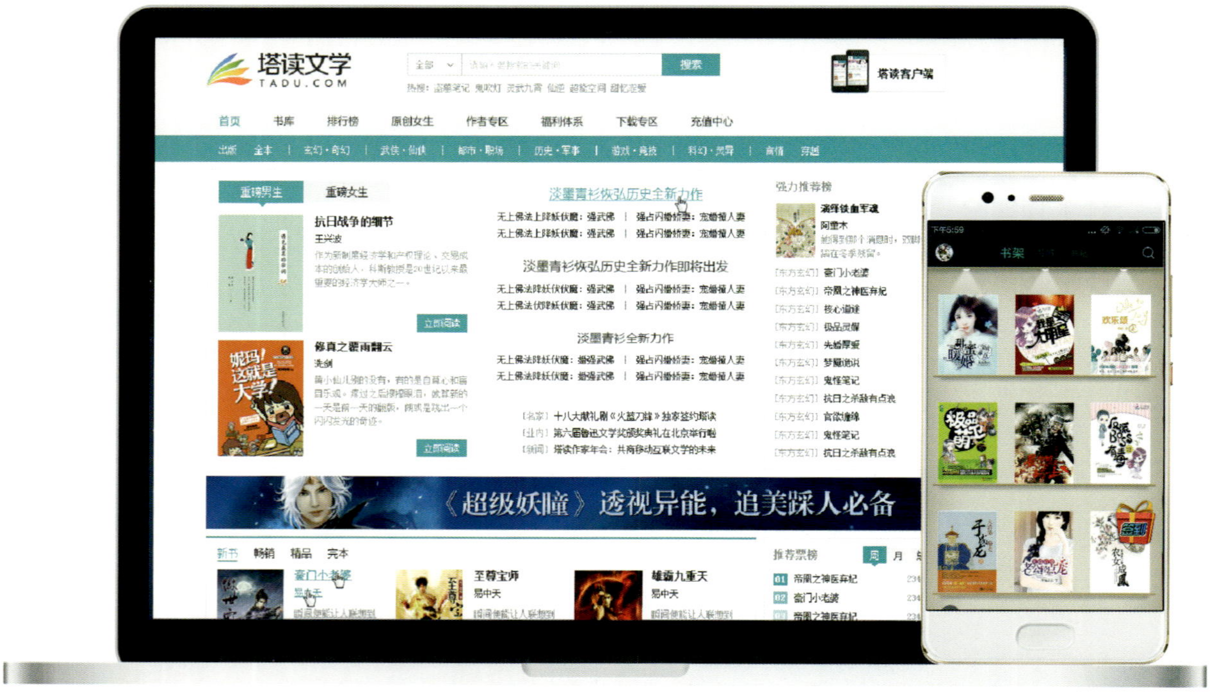

“塔读文学APP”是一款体验独特、功能强大、界面精美的在线阅读软件，拥有众多互联网及正版出版物书籍。

塔读文学
精品原创 阅在指尖
产品荣誉
2015年度
最佳手机阅读软件
塔读文学
2016年度
最佳手机阅读软件
中国APP发展论坛
最具创意奖
易观之星
O2O EXPO
互联互通 共赢全球
WORLD O2O EXPO
世界O2O博览会暨IN+2016创新大会
主办方：Organized by
WOO World O2O Organization 世界O2O组织
GMGC Global Mobile Game Confederation
光合资本 Guanghe Capital
2016年6月22日・北京国家会议中心
June 22nd, 2016 • China National Convention Center, Beijing
OSCA
2016
塔读文学
荣获
OSCA

知乎 中文互联网较大的知识讨论社区，致力于“帮助人们更有效、方便地分享与组织彼此的知识、经验和见解，并从中获得新机会”。我们期盼“知乎”能够改善人与人的沟通方式，改善人们相互了解、建立信任的方式，产生真正重要的影响。目前知乎的产品主要包括知乎问答、知乎 Live、知乎电子书店。同时，知乎电子书店还包括为激励用户和优质内容产生编辑制作的“知乎周刊”、“知乎 · 盐”、“一小时”系列电子书和出版物。“盐 Club”是知乎问答社区“盐”系列子品牌中一年一度盛大的线下活动，旨在为过去一年站内的优秀回答者们提供一个展示自我的平台，也为更多的知乎用户提供一个线下交流的机会。

知乎 CEO　周源

知乎主要产品介绍及其版权保护现状

知乎问答

知乎问答为用户提供提问、回答、赞同回答、关注问题等功能。知乎现已有大量已经被回答的问题，用户可以阅读它们，给认可的回答点赞同，回答者会收到赞许，也可以给无效的回答点反对，让更多受认可的回答排在更靠前的位置。最后，用户可以关注自己感兴趣的问题，和志同道合的人一起成长、分享。

知乎问答高度重视平台上文章内容的原创性，致力为每一位知乎用户的原创文章提供免费、便捷的版权保护。作为平台，我们一方面受理第三方权利人对知乎用户的投诉，如果权利人认为知乎上的回答涉嫌侵犯其合法权益，可以通过知乎的在线举报功能提交投诉链接，一般在 24 小时内可收到反馈；另一方面，如果第三方侵权使用知乎用户的内容作品，知乎设有专门的知乎版权团队为其提供版权问题的解答与协助。

知乎 Live

知乎 Live 是知乎推出的实时语音问答产品。主讲人对某个主题分享知识、经验或见解，听众可以实时提问并获得解答，便捷且高效地收获与交流。

知乎 Live 支持用户群体间发送消息进行实时互动，互动可以以语音、文字、图片、动态表情等方式，还支持分享短视频和视频直播。

知乎电子书店

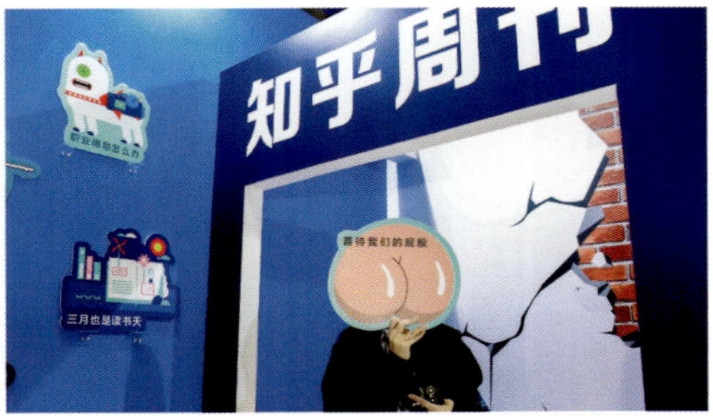

知乎电子书店是知乎推出的数字阅读产品。知乎电子书店目前可以为用户提供知乎编辑出品、其他优质出版社的作品，用户可以免费或者付费购买后阅读，在阅读过程中能够添加书签、笔记等，阅读进度和书签、笔记会同步到云端系统，获得结构化的知识，发表自己的点评和想法，和作者、其他用户交流，还可以通过分享、赠送作品将喜爱的作品推荐给其他用户。

知乎电子书店主要保护作品权利人的版权。侵权类型主要包括第三方未经权利人许可，将电子化图书通过第三方软件的方式分发、传播给其他公众，并从中谋取利益；或者未经授权传播作者数字阅读作品；或者未经授权整合、修改作者作品；或者删除原作者信息等。知乎对各类侵权类型都严厉抵制，努力为知乎电子书店的每一位作者与读者给予更优质的版权保护服务。

知乎主要产品保护措施

知乎结合各个产品的各自特点，为每一款产品都提供免费、高效、便捷的版权保护服务。一方面，知乎与平台用户签订各种规范协议，以鼓励用户发表更多原创文章、内容；另一方面，知乎平台畅通投诉渠道，特别设立知乎版权专用账号和专用邮箱以供知乎用户投诉。同时，知乎和微信团队、今日头条、搜狐等建立快速侵权投诉通道，为知乎用户提供优质的版权保护。

1.用户协议

《知乎协议》是用户注册时与知乎之间订立的协议，用于处理知乎用户和平台之间的权利义务关系。《知乎协议》明确知乎是一个信息获取、分享及传播的平台，尊重和鼓励知乎用户创作的内容，认识到保护知识产权对知乎生存与发展的重要性，承诺将保护知识产权作为知乎运营的基本原则之一。用户在知乎上传或发表的内容，应保证其为著作权人已取得合法授权，并且该内容不会侵犯任何第三方的合法权益。

《知乎 Live 用户协议》和《知乎 Live 讲者协议》是使用知乎 Live 产品的听众用户或讲者用户与知乎之间签订的专门针对知乎 Live 的协议。为尊重和保护知识产权，禁止讲者使用未经他人授权的作品，讲者必须保证在 Live 上发表的内容属于原创或已获权利人授权；未经讲者授权许可，听众用户不得以任何载体或形式使用讲者的内容。

《转载规范》是针对知乎平台内部转载行为的规范约定。知乎是一个尊重知识、尊重原创的社区，非常痛恨他人在转载、引用用户辛苦创造的内容时，抹去用户的名字和出处。更不希望知乎上发生这样的事情，鼓励每一位知乎用户和知乎一起，在中文环境中建立一种健康的转载和链接机制。

任何用户发现其他用户涉嫌不规范转载时，可以点击文后的“举报”按钮进行投诉；当用户多次涉嫌不规范转载他人内容时，知乎会对其进行处罚。

2.侵权投诉

知乎将尊重知识产权作为运营的基本原则之一，不仅保护知乎用户的原创文章、视频、语音等内容的版权，而且禁止用户的内容侵犯任何第三方的版权等知识产权合法权益。对此，知乎设有两种渠道以开展不同类型的版权侵权保护。

知乎版权团队帮助知乎用户维权

知乎为用户开辟专门团队以保护其版权等知识产权不受侵犯，当知乎原创用户认为任何第三方的相关内容侵犯其权益时可通过知乎平台私信版权团队或者发邮件至版权团队专设邮箱，授权知乎版权团队代其维权。知乎版权团队在收到用户的投诉及授权后将及时人工联系其他平台协助处理侵权内容。同时，知乎是较早提供跨平台侵权投诉产品的社区，和微信团队建立绿色投诉通道，可一次投诉多篇侵权文章。确认侵权的公众号文章将会在 24 小时内删除，整个过程由产品自动完成无须人工介入。除此以外，知乎版权团队已和今日头条、搜狐等网络平台建立了快速处理绿色通道，已建立通道的平台投诉平均处理时间在 1 个工作日内，可显著提高处理效率、降低用户的维权成本。

除了知乎用户主动投诉，知乎版权团队也会不定期清理互联网上存在的侵权内容。

知乎社区管理团队规范知乎平台内部转载行为

知乎社区管理团队规范管理知乎平台发布的问题补充说明、回答、专栏文章等，鼓励用户在使用他人作品时按照《转载规范》进行转载。如果知乎用户涉嫌不规范转载，社区管理团队则会使该回答进入“建议修改”状态；多次涉嫌不规范转载他人内容的，社区管理团队会对其账号禁言、封号。

针对版权保护，知乎还从产品层面做了一些改进：（1）在每个回答下方更加突出地展示版权声明。（2）在回答框区域增加“禁止转载”选项；当用户大段复制“禁止转载”的回答时，会收到“需要联系作者获得许可”的提醒，复制操作会被限制。

中国人
方正字
希望有中国人的地方就有方正字体
www.foundertype.com
方正字库
FOUNDERTYPE
全国直拨服务热线：
4006－516763
E-mail: font_sales@founder.com
公司地址：
北京市海淀区上地五街9号方正大厦

Media Technology
瑞德传媒

瑞德传媒荣获2016年
中国版权领域的“奥斯卡”奖
中国版权金奖

获奖理由：北京中视瑞德文化传媒股份有限公司是领先的媒体资产管理与版权管理综合服务商，视音频版权内容制作运营商，于2016年8月在“新三板”挂牌。公司主要提供版权资产管理服务、版权资产管理系统、版权资产交易系统、版权监测系统的技术开发和运维服务以及媒资管理服务、视音频版权内容制作运营服务。瑞德传媒已发展成为一家以核心技术为支撑，以版权资产管理和运营为特色的科技型文化传媒公司。公司已先后为20多家中央级媒体机构和地方传媒机构持续提供版权资产管理、运维及系统开发等服务，为促进媒体产业版权发展，提升媒体机构版权社会影响力做出突出贡献。

客户版权管家
www.rdmedia.cn

敬请关注微信 版话

证券代码：838208

一铭软件 Emindsoft

一铭软件（http://www.emindsoft.com.cn）是从事国产操作系统研发、云计算和东盟小语种智能翻译云服务的高新技术企业。2014年底，一铭软件成为在“新三板”挂牌上市的国产操作系统企业，证券代码：831266。

目前主要产品有一铭操作系统、一铭软件资产管理系统、一铭云平台、一铭翻译云等。

一铭软件是中国开源软件推进联盟副主席单位，并于2016年配合推进使用正版软件工作部际联席会议办公室开展了“国产软件应用试点”工作。一铭操作系统荣获第二十届中国国际软件博览会创新奖，开源桌面操作系统项目OPENTHOS荣获2016东北亚开源软件大奖，一铭操作系统荣获世界知识产权组织与中国国家版权主管部门联合颁发的2016中国版权金奖。

一、一铭操作系统荣获2016第二十届中国国际软件博览会创新奖

在2016年5月举办的第二十届中国国际软件博览会上，一铭操作系统荣获产品创新奖。

2016第二十届中国国际软件博览会产品创新奖证书

二、一铭桌面操作系统4.0正式发布

以用户体验为中心的一铭桌面操作系统4.0于6月正式发布。一铭桌面操作系统4.0是一铭软件基于Linux内核开发的一款国产操作系统，尊重用户习惯，确保用户向国产操作系统平台的平滑迁移，适用于正版化软件升级的政府部门、企事业单位和个人用户。

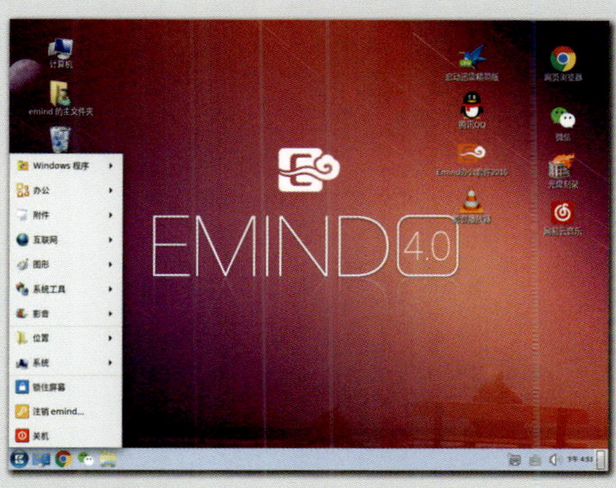

一铭桌面操作系统4. 0

三、2016中国—东盟基础软件生态战略发展研讨会

2016年7月22日，由广西软件行业协会、一铭软件主办的2016中国—东盟基础软件生态战略发展研讨会在广西南宁举办。一铭软件与东盟等国驻南宁各领事馆负责人、众多中国基础软件生态系统的企业代表以及广西壮族自治区内的用户参与了本次会议。

2016中国—东盟基础软件生态战略发展研讨会

四、国产软件应用试点选用一铭操作系统

2016年8月，推进使用正版软件工作部际联席会议办公室在贵州正式启动“国产软件应用试点工作”。一铭软件被选为该项目在贵州省黔西县、山西省平顺县和宁夏回族自治区盐池县这三个试点县中的国产操作系统厂商。

在项目启动后，为了确保三个试点县工作的顺利推广，一铭软件分别在当地成立专项技术支持团队对贵州省黔西县、山西省平顺县和宁夏回族自治区盐池县进行进了部署前期的调研工作，并根据各试点县用户的软硬件环境形成了专业的国产操作系统推广解决方案。

以推广国产软件应用为目标，实现三个试点县用户单系统运行，帮助用户平稳迁移国产操作系统为目的，在项目部署过程中，一铭软件为试点县用户解决了各种系统及应用需求。例如某些用户硬件设备因购置较早配置低，外设的早期型号打印机等设备无驱动等问题。为减少用户采购成本，使用户快速适用国产操作系统，一铭软件进行了及时应对，对产品进行了客户需求优化。此外，为保证用户真正能将国产操作系统使用起来，一铭软件在三个试点县多次举办产品应用培训及使用交流活动，保证了整体项目的顺利进行。

一铭软件以过硬的产品、专业的技术服务团队，赢得了三个试点县用户的一致好评。

一铭软件在试点县举办操作系统培训活动

五、 一铭翻译云亮相第十三届东盟博览会

2016年9月11日，一铭软件携旗下产品一铭翻译云参展了第十三届东盟博览会。

六、一铭服务器操作系统V7.0正式发布

2016年10月31日，一铭软件正式发布一铭服务器操作系统V7.0。一铭服务器操作系统V7.0可应用于金融、电信、政府、军队、能源、教育等行业和部门，为用户提供一个内聚的、统一的基础设施架构以及新的服务环境，在为各企业提供可靠保障、降低运营成本的同时加快创新。

七、一铭软件资产管理系统

一铭软件资产管理系统是一款应用于软件资产管理的专业软件。该软件在满足用户日常软件资产管理的同时，严格按照国家版权主管部门关于正版软件管理工作的相关标准定制，适用于各级政府、机关及集团企事业单位，帮助各级单位轻松实现正版软件使用过程中数据的统计、管理、分析。

八、一铭软件荣获“2016中国版权金奖”

2016年12月5日，一铭操作系统在世界知识产权组织(WIPO)和中国国家版权主管部门举办的“中国版权金奖”颁奖仪式上，荣获“中国版权金奖”。

“中国版权金奖”是我国版权领域内评选的国际性奖项。一铭操作系统为荣获“作品奖”的软件作品。

三个试点县国产软件应用试点工作启动会

一铭翻译云亮相第十三届东盟博览会

一铭软件资产管理系统

一铭操作系统荣获“中国版权金奖”

打假维权 原创保真 开发版权 弘扬精品

書畫藝術 www.cpcac.cn 版权网

书画艺术版权联合推广平台是以书画艺术版权网（www.cpcac.cn）为主体，涵括书画艺术版权微信公众号（shysbq88）、期刊纸媒、展览展示等于一体的立体跨界平台，以“打假维权、原创保真、开发版权、弘扬精品”为宗旨，为业界提供宣传推广、学术交流及书画艺术品交易等多视角、立体化的专业服务。

平台围绕书画艺术版权发展需要，依托国家文化和版权领域权威管理部门、协会团体、司法和学术部门等优势资源力量，紧密团结艺术家、藏家以及艺术经营服务机构，以权威专业的服务，促进书画艺术家和艺术版权事业发展。

艺术品鉴藏热线：
手机（微信号）：13701141048　　13070137639
座机：010-58604520 庞老师
更多详情请访问：书画艺术版权网www.cpcac.cn
欢迎投稿：shuhuabq@163.com（邮件请注明投稿）

扫一扫，关注我

版权

年度发布

NIAN DU FA BU

第五届“世界知识产权组织版权金奖（中国）”获奖名单

［**编者按**］ 2016年12月5日，中国版权金奖颁奖仪式在广州举行。“中国版权金奖”是中国国家版权局与世界知识产权组织（WIPO）开展的合作项目，每两年评选一次，是中国版权领域评选的唯一国际性奖项，也是国内版权领域的最高奖项。2016年“中国版权金奖”设有作品奖、推广运用奖、保护奖和管理奖四个奖项，共有6件作品和14家机构获奖。

一、作品奖（6个）

1.《青铜葵花》

【创作者】 曹文轩

【获奖理由】 《青铜葵花》讲述了乡村男孩青铜与城市女孩葵花的故事，字里行间无不充盈着感人肺腑、震撼人心的人间真情，无不闪耀着人道主义的光辉。2008年至今，《青铜葵花》版权输出至法国、英国、德国、意大利、韩国、越南、斯洛文尼亚7国，其中最值得一提的是，英文版《青铜葵花》于2015年由英国沃克尔公司出版，并获得“笔会奖”。在“2015伦敦中国图书节”上，江苏凤凰少年儿童出版社出版的《青铜葵花》英文版作为唯一入选的一本当代儿童文学原创长篇小说被隆重推出，并在英国各大书店展销。同时，英文版《青铜葵花》的出版也成为曹文轩获得安徒生奖的一大重要推动力。

2.《狼图腾》

【创作者】 中国电影股份有限公司等

【获奖理由】 改编自姜戎屡获殊荣的同名小说，作为具有国际影响的IP，小说《狼图腾》拥有共计39个语种版本，覆盖世界110个国家和地区。因此，《狼图腾》的电影改编在创作之初就引来了社会普遍的关注。中影在筹备的过程中，最大限度地呈现原著的精髓，最终取得了超过7亿元人民币的骄人票房成绩。《狼图腾》上映后在海外地区也得到观众的热烈反响，在法国创下了近年华语电影在法国的票房最好成绩。在北美及拉丁美洲地区影片全面上映，获得了极佳的口碑。同时，影片也获得了多项电影大奖。

3. 一铭操作系统

【创作者】 一铭软件股份有限公司

【获奖理由】 一铭国产操作系统在政府软件正版化工作中以超高的性价比和良好的售后服务，已经在全国31个省、自治区、直辖市得到不同程度的应用，尤其是在贵州省、广西壮族自治区、湖北省、宁夏回族自治区等地得到了很好的推广应用。该系统有良好的兼容性，全面适配主流硬件，支持X86、龙芯、申威、兆芯等国产芯片，外设可适配ATM、查询机、排队机等自助服务信息终端。一铭操作系统价格实惠，技术服务体系完善，是一款真正在用而且好用的国产操作系统。

4.《英汉大词典》

【创作者】 上海译文出版社

【获奖理由】 上海译文出版社出版的《英汉大词典》1991年成书，出版25年来，累计印数超过50万册，曾与台湾东华书局和香港三联书店合作，相继在台湾地区和香港地区发行《英汉大词典》繁体字版本，并以内容授权形式与卡西欧等国内外电子词典厂商合作，实现版权收益超过千万元人民币。《英汉大词典》代表着我国英汉双语辞书编纂出版的科研能力和国家水平，并替代梁实秋主编的《远东英汉大词典》成为联合国编译人员的主要英汉类工具书。

5.《海棠依旧》

【创作者】 河北电影电视剧制片中心

【获奖理由】 电视剧《海棠依旧》，自中央电视台一套黄金时间首播后，好评如潮，收视一路走高，并形成网络热议话题。专家和观众普遍认为这是一部重大革命历史题材电视剧创作的新成果，是一部力攀“高峰”的精品力作。在艺术手段上，这部剧用洁白的海棠营造了唯美的意境，用“海棠依旧”四个字蕴含着对周总理深切的思念，带来了美感也带来了回忆，是主旋律影视作品在艺术表现形式上的突破，引领观众自然而然地沉浸于历史伟人所处的时代氛围中，强化感染力和吸引力。

6.《琅琊榜》

【创作者】 海晏

【获奖理由】 2015年以来，图书《琅琊榜》在全国热销，根据该作品改编的电视剧《琅琊榜》在全国掀起观剧热潮。该书因其思想性、创新性受到广泛关注，入选了国家新闻出版广电总局2015年度“大众喜爱的50种图书”、“丝路书香工程”重点翻译资助项目和“经典中国国际出版工程”资助项目。同时，海外出版商纷纷争夺《琅琊榜》外文版权，繁体中文版、越南文版、泰文版、韩文版的出版都获得了巨大成功。截至2016年12月，《琅琊榜》在全球累计销量近30万套，一种图书实现多个国家、多个语种广泛传播，产生了显著的经济效益和社会效益。

二、推广应用奖（5个）

1. 外文出版社有限责任公司

【获奖理由】 《习近平谈治国理政》一书由国务院新闻办公室会同中共中央文献研究室、中国外文局编辑，由外文出版社以中、英、法、俄、阿、西、葡、德、日等多语种向全球出版发行，在国内外通过开展多种形式的推广活动、与国外出版机构翻译合作出版其他语种、多种渠道的营销推广工作等方式，使《习近平谈治国理政》在国际社会产生了重要影响，在图书市场上形成热销局面，截至2016年9月，发行量已突破600万册，海外发行超过40万册，发行到世界100多个国家和地区，使该书成为改革开放以来在海外最受关注、最具影响力的中国领导人著作。

2. 深圳市腾讯计算机系统有限公司

【获奖理由】 腾讯积极开发和利用版权资源，运用各种手段，特别是在网络和数字环境下，大力促进作品的创作与传播，在将版权资源转化为社会财富、实现版权作品市场价值方面做出了突出贡献，先后荣获世界知识产权组织版权金奖作品奖、十大中国著作权人、全国版权示范单位等荣誉。公司坚持版权兴业之路，通过版权的创造、推广和运用，既满足了亿万网友的精神文化需求，也使腾讯快速成长为世界领先企业。

3. 江西网络广播电视台

【获奖理由】 江西网络广播电视台积极运用各种手段开发和利用版权资源，成立专门的版权管理部门，拥有专业的版权管理团队。利用网络和数字技术，对独家授权拥有的江西广播电视台广播电视节目著作权中信息网络传播权节目资源进行运营和经营管理与使用。先后与腾讯、搜狐、爱奇艺、乐视等国内主流新媒体平台建立长期稳定的合作关系，其节目点击量、阅读量等每年增长20%以上。江西网络台还积极拓展海外市场，已在全球最大的视频网站YouTube上开设视频节目专区，同时与海外OTT平台合作，节目覆盖全球100多个国家和地区，每月点击观看的海外用户达20万多人次。

4. 时代出版传媒股份有限公司

【获奖理由】 时代传媒高度重视版权推广运用，把版权作为提高出版竞争力、抢占竞争制高点、推动文化产业发展的重要战略资源。公司大力实施文化“走出去”战略，实现了由简单版权贸易向新媒体、新业态转型，由传统合作模式向多元化国际合作转型。公司连续8年被评为“国家文化出口重点企业”，连续8年在北京国际图书博览会上版权输出全国第一。曾获“中国版权最具影响力企业”“中国最具竞争力出口企业50强”等荣誉。

5. 宁夏盛天彩数字科技股份有限公司

【获奖理由】 宁夏盛天彩数字科技股份有限公司自2008年至2013年成功策划举办了五届“宁夏（中国）动漫作品及动漫艺术家插画展”；与多家传媒公司、动漫制作公司合作开发手机动漫杂志阅读服务平台；努力推广拥有自主知识产权的品牌“嘉漫优品”，在长期的自营品牌门店经营中逐渐制定和完善了一套完整的品牌加盟体系。承办的2016年中阿国际动漫文化节促进了宁夏文化创意产业创新发展，增强了西部地区企业文化创意观念。在积极开发和利用版权资源，运用各种手段，特别是利用网络推广作品的创作、传播方面做出了突出的贡献。

三、保护奖（5个）

1. 重庆市公安局打击假冒伪劣商品犯罪侦查总队

【获奖理由】 打假总队成立于2012年9月，加挂“重庆市公安局知识产权刑事保护中心”牌子。近年来，打假总队按照公安部、国家版权局工作要求，与重庆市版权部门充分发挥互补优势，切实形成工作合力。2016年5月，重庆市公安局与重庆市文化委员会（重庆市版权局）建立了打击侵权盗版违法犯罪协作机制，将相关协作配合工作提升到新的水平。2014年至2016年共侦办侵权盗版违法犯罪案件26件，抓获犯罪嫌疑人27人，侦破“8·6”

侵犯著作权案等公安部、国家版权局等部委督办大要案件 4 起，“4·21”侵犯著作权案专案组被国家版权局、公安部评为 2015 年度全国打击侵权盗版有功单位一等奖。

2. 上海冠勇信息科技有限公司

【获奖理由】 上海冠勇信息科技有限公司以版权内容为核心，依托领先的海量音视频、图文内容搜索引擎技术、云计算、版权大数据可视化分析技术，为行业搭建了科学的版权监测保护体系、版权分账发行监测平台及版权大数据分析体系等。在强大的自主知识产权技术支持下，截至 2016 年 6 月，冠勇科技共监测影视作品逾 2 万部、音乐作品逾 100 万首、文章/游戏/图片作品近 10 万部；监测到侵权链接逾 1 500 万条；PC/APP/OTT 的侵权目标达 9 000 多家；协助发送预警函、下线函 62 000 封；侵权下线率达 95%。

3. 徐州市版权局

【获奖理由】 徐州市版权局大力实施版权强市战略，促进版权产业健康发展。特别是着力加大版权保护力度，精心组织“剑网”行动，近两年来查处侵权盗版案件 28 起，其中刑事案件 12 起、行政案件 16 起，抓获犯罪分子 30 多人。连续两年被国家版权局评为打击侵权盗版有功单位一等奖。江苏“放放影视网”侵犯著作权案、江苏“速酷电影网”侵犯著作权案，分别入选全国 2014 年、2015 年打击侵权盗版十大案件。2015 年全市荣获国家版权局表彰有功单位一等奖 3 个、二等奖 1 个，有功个人一等奖 3 人、二等奖 6 人。

4. 北京搜狐互联网信息服务有限公司

【获奖理由】 北京搜狐互联网信息服务有限公司自 2009 年至今在多个场合都为打击盗版高声呐喊，为中国版权正版化事业表现出了企业应有的担当。搜狐从 2009 年到 2014 年总共发动了两场“反盗版战争”。搜狐在版权保护方面致力于推动立法、司法、执法上全方位的保护：第一，搜狐主导的反盗版联盟行动最终促成了因侵犯著作权而获刑责的系列刑事案件。第二，推动国家出台网盘监管规范。第三，推动司法和行政对视频聚合不正当性进行法律定性。

5. 德化县人民政府

【获奖理由】 德化县先后成立福建省首个知识产权审判巡回法庭、全省第三家基层法院知识产权审判庭。较早成立县版权局，组建文化市场综合执法大队，加强版权执法监管，及时保护被侵权企业合法权益。高度重视陶瓷版权保护工作，不断加强陶瓷作品版权自愿登记工作，版权登记数量逐年上升。出台作品登记奖励措施，累计兑现版权保护等奖励政策 9 400 万元，极大提高了企业版权意识。圆满完成世界知识产权组织和中国国家版权局“全球第二个版权保护优秀案例示范点”调研项目，成为世界知识产权组织向全球发展中国家推广版权保护的“德化经验”。

四、管理奖（4 个）

1. 成都市版权局

【获奖理由】 成都市版权局按照“激励创造、有效运用、依法保护、科学管理”的基本方针，将版权工作主动服务大局，从推动产业转型升级着手，以版权公共服务为基础、以加强版权保护为手段、以促进版权转化运用为核心，构建和谐绿色版权生态系统，成效显著。形成了政府主导、媒体推动、公众参与的版权宣教格局，提升了公众版权意识和认知水平。健全调解、行政执法、司法保护等方面机制，有力地维护了市场秩序。率先开展著作权登记资助、版权经纪双证培训，举办中国国际博览会，深化了版权服务。统计调查显示，2014 年，成都版权产业经营收入 5 165.95 亿元，较 2013 年增长 12.45%。

2. 中国文字著作权协会

【获奖理由】 文著协是我国唯一的文字著作权集体管理组织，履行报刊和教科书“法定许可”稿酬收转的法定职能。文著协积极推动修改著作权法，完善文字作品付酬机制；与网络平台合作，为会员推广作品数字版权；与海外复制权组织签约，授权中文书报刊影印复制和数字化复制权；开展国际版权贸易，推动中国文化“走出去”；为出版机构解决汇编作品作者授权，为作者创造收益。同时积极宣传普法，创建了较为成熟的文字著作权集体管理体系，在维护会员权利、促进产业发展、提升集体管理组织的社会影响力等方面做出了应有的贡献。

3. 北京中视瑞德文化传媒股份有限公司

【获奖理由】 北京中视瑞德文化传媒股份有限公司是领先的媒体资产管理与版权管理综合服务商、视音频版权内容制作运营商，于 2016 年 8 月在新三板挂牌，成为新三板“影视版权管理第一股”。公司主要提供版权资产管理服务、版权资产管理系统、版权资产交易系统、版权监测系统的技术开发和运维服务以及媒资管理服务、视音频版权内容制作运营服务。瑞德传媒已发展成为一家以核心技术为支撑，以版权资产管理和运营为特色的科技型文化传媒公司。公司已先后为20多家中央级媒体机构和地方传媒机构持续提供版权资产管理、运维及系统开发等服务，为促进媒体产业版权发展，提升媒体机构版权社会影响力做出突出贡献。

4. 即墨市人民政府

【获奖理由】 近年来，即墨市政府高度重视版权工作，积极顺应新形势下版权工作的新要求，探索长效机制，版权工作成为促进地方经济增长、文化发展的重要保障。形成了版权管理“即墨模式”，主要体现在以下六个方面：第一，高度重视版权，强化组织保障。第二，突出管理服务，培育壮大产业。第三，坚持主动服务，鼓励版权创造。第四，打击侵权盗版，规范市场秩序。第五，发挥示范作用，大力推广正版。第六，强化宣传引导，增强版权意识。2015年即墨市获批创建全国版权示范城市。中央媒体采访团先后两次组织40多名记者对即墨市版权管理工作进行采访报道。

2016年中国网络版权保护年度报告

国家版权局委托中国信息通信研究院撰写

一、2016年中国网络版权[1]保护综述

（一）2016年中国网络版权保护的主要进展

1. 2016年中国网络版权保护迎来新机遇

党的十八大以来，党中央、国务院将知识产权保护工作提高到了前所未有的高度，并将其作为激励创新的重要保障，产业政策环境不断优化。

知识产权强国战略深入实施，知识产权保护政策趋向严格。2016年3月，十二届全国人大四次会议审议通过《中华人民共和国国民经济和社会发展第十三个五年规划纲要》，纲要中提出，要“实施严格的知识产权保护制度，完善有利于激励创新的知识产权归属制度，建设知识产权运营交易和服务平台，建设知识产权强国”；中共中央、国务院发布的《关于完善产权保护制度依法保护产权的意见》指明，“加大知识产权侵权行为惩治力度，提高知识产权侵权法定赔偿上限，探索建立对专利权、著作权等知识产权侵权惩罚性赔偿制度”，“将故意侵犯知识产权行为情况纳入企业和个人信用记录”，加大对知识产权的保护力度；国务院办公厅印发的《2016年全国打击侵犯知识产权和制售假冒伪劣商品工作要点》，明确指出“着力打击网上销售假冒伪劣商品和网络侵权盗版行为”，加强互联网领域侵权假冒治理；国务院知识产权战略实施工作部际联席会议办公室发布《2016年深入实施国家知识产权战略加快建设知识产权强国推进计划》，要求“突出对网络（手机）文学、音乐、影视、游戏、动漫、软件等重点领域的专项整治，加强对APP[2]、网络云存储空间、微博、微信等新型传播方式的版权监管”。

知识产权驱动创新发展，成为经济发展新常态和供给侧改革关键要素。2016年5月，中共中央、国务院印发《国家创新驱动发展战略纲要》，提出“深入实施知识产权战略行动计划，提高知识产权的创造、运用、保护和管理能力”，“强化知识产权制度对创新的基本保障作用”；12月，国务院印发《“十三五”国家战略性新兴产业发展规划》，提出到2020年，形成文化引领、技术先进、链条完整的数字创意产业发展格局，相关行业产值规模要达到8万亿元，这是数字创意产业首次纳入国家战略性新兴产业发展规划，也标志着文化产业在国民经济中的重要战略地位进一步凸显和提高。

总体来看，国家政策倡导创新、协调、绿色、开放、共享的发展新理念，要求完善产权保护制度、建设网络良好生态，在“知识产权强国”和“创新驱动发展”战略的指导下，网络版权保护迎来新的春天。

2. 2016年中国互联网内容产业发展呈现新态势

2016年，互联网经济成为驱动国民经济提质增效的关键要素，成为加速传统产业转型升级的核心动力。以互联网为基础的新兴业态密集涌现，催生和培育出新的消费需求。截至2016年12月，我国网民规模达到7.31亿，互联网普及率达到53.2%，较2015年同期增长2.9百分点。移动互联网推动消费模式共享化、设备智能化和场景多元化。其中，手机网民规模达6.95亿，网民中使用手机上网的比例由2015年底的90.1%提升至95.1%[3]。网络内容产业各领域用户规模持续增长，截至2016年12月，我国网络游戏用户规模4.17亿，网络文学用户规模3.33亿，网络视频用户规模和网络音乐用户规模均超过5亿，网络直播用户规模达到3.44亿。随着4G网络的进一步完善以及手机资费的下调，内容产业各领域移动互联网用户渗透率均达九成以上，迎来新的发展态势。移动互联网应用服务和场景不断丰富，扩展了网络版权产业细分领域，产业规模不

① 本报告所指的网络版权是著作权人对受著作权法保护的作品在互联网（包括移动互联网）环境下所享有的著作权权利。
② APP，application的缩写，指手机的软件应用程序。
③ 数据来源于CNNIC发布的第39次《中国互联网络发展状况统计报告》。

断扩大。随着产业链上下游在视频、动漫等领域以及直播、VR[①]等新业态持续发力，网络版权产业细分领域不断拓展，产业结构日趋多元，发展前景更为广阔。截至2016年底，我国网络版权产业整体产值突破5 600亿元，产业规模位居全球前三[②]。版权的经济价值和社会效益日益凸显，成为互联网生态中重要的基础性资源。

跨界融合成为内容产业变革和新经济发展重要引擎，IP[③]衍生开发和深度开发持续盛行。文化元素和数字技术连接融合现象明显，在“大众创业、万众创新”热潮的推动下，内容创新、形式创新、业态创新不断涌现，催生数字文化创意产业发展，使IP成为资本市场追逐热点。围绕IP的游戏、文学、音乐、影视、动漫等互动娱乐内容逐渐增多，内容产业商业模式逐渐由一次性售卖转向对内容的深度挖掘和长线开发，并引入越来越多的跨界合作，促进了版权内容生产的良性发展。

开放平台[④]成为“互联网＋”新业态发展的核心商业模式，内容发行和传播方式发生重大变革。互联网平台型企业大量涌现与发展，使得版权运用效率大幅提高，改变了优质版权内容的创作与传播方式，也带动了大众文娱消费习惯和内容传播渠道的变迁。内容产业正在从以复制权为中心向以传播权为中心转变，内容创作、分发和传播链条上的传统利益格局被打破和重构，网络版权保护的重心和载体也随之发生偏移。

文化产品消费方式发生改变，用户付费和广告逐渐成为内容产业收入两大主力，优质和差异化内容对用户付费吸引力增加。

随着用户对知识付费的认可、知识产权保护环境的改善和支付工具的便利，2016年，用户对数字内容的付费意愿和实际付费行为快速增长，统计数据显示[⑤]，2016年用户数字内容付费规模为2 123亿元，同比增长28%。从用户付费类型来看，用户付费内容日趋多元，游戏、直播、视频、音乐、阅读均为用户付费较大的内容[⑥]。用户付费习惯的形成，极大地促进正版化进程，净化版权环境，遏制盗版空间。

3. 2016年中国网络版权保护实现新进展

立法保护方面，相关部门在版权法律框架内以调整、解释等多种方式适应技术变革，对重点领域的立法精细化、专业化。面对网络新技术、新模式、新事物引发的新型版权问题，立法、行政、司法部门积极应对，推动新技术环境下创作、传播、使用环节的利益平衡。法律制度构建方面，全国人大常委会通过我国文化产业领域第一部法律——《电影产业促进法》，对电影知识产权保护相关问题予以法律规制；在审判规则方面，2016年4月13日，北京市高级人民法院发布的《涉及网络知识产权案件审理指南》，对涉及网络著作权中的热点、难点问题进行详尽规定；在行政监管方面，2016年11月14日，国家版权局出台《关于加强网络文学作品版权管理的通知》，该文件规定了平台服务商在传播作品时的举证责任、侵权后果和判定要素，进一步明确了网络服务商的主体责任和注意义务，为产业实践提供指引和判定标准。

司法保护方面，网络版权纠纷案件数量逐年攀升，案件的传播载体和地域广度不断扩张，从案件主体到保护客体不断泛化。总体来说，2016年网络版权司法保护呈现出以下特点：网络版权内容产业各领域的作品数量较为均衡，网络文学领域案件数量大幅上升，涉及著名影视作品网络传播的著作权纠纷案件不断增多；新技术新商业模式使得网络著作权侵权案件新情况层出不穷，侵权传播途径呈现多样化、分散化趋势，通过网站、搜索引擎、浏览器等方式进行的侵权案件数量最多；网络版权案件的地域分布呈现出相对集中适当扩散的态势，互联网产业发达地区案件量较高，知识产权法院在审理网络版权案件中作用突出，无论是案件审理的数量还是影响力都体现出知识产权法院的司法解决机制日趋完善并向着专业化方向发展。

社会保护方面，2016年网络版权社会保护体系向立体、多元、有效方向发展，社会共治机制初步建立。著作权集体管理组织充分履行维护会员权益职能，中国文字著作权协会举办“原创文字作品保

---

① 英文全称为 virtual reality，虚拟现实技术。

② 相关数据源自腾讯研究院版权研究中心的测算。

③ IP，intellectual property 的缩写，意为“知识产权”。近年来产业界将IP特指为泛娱乐产业链中具有高人气和高市场价值的文学、动漫、影视、音乐、游戏、综艺节目等作品。

④ 开放平台是由企业或第三方搭建的、以自身为核心的开放式协同体系。搭建平台的企业或第三方为平台主体，负责平台的整体支撑与运营。

⑤ 相关数据源自蓝莲花研究机构发布的报告《数字内容付费，钱景涌现》。

⑥ 例如，热播剧《太阳的后裔》拉动爱奇艺500万付费会员，会员收费近2亿元。

护月”活动，中国音乐著作权协会针对APP对音乐作品的侵权行为进行了大规模调查和维权行动；各类版权行业协会积极促进行业自律，在配合监管部门重点整治工作的同时，发布了《网络文学行业自律倡议书》《中国网络文学版权联盟自律公约》《网络广告联盟版权自律倡议》等自律公告。企业进一步落实主体责任、加强自我约束，百度、奇虎360、新浪、迅雷等企业纷纷针对贴吧、网盘等领域开展自查整改工作；腾讯、百度等各大平台均建立了较为完善的侵权投诉系统，探索主动保护机制。权利主体维权积极性不断提高、维权手段更加丰富，权利人投诉成为行政监管的重要来源，权利人委托相关机构调解来维护自身合法权益的数量逐年上升，郑渊洁、蔡明亮等知名权利人通过多种渠道维权事件也带来较大社会影响力。

行政保护方面，行政监管推动网络内容产业构建良性生态，网络版权行政执法的作用和影响得到社会普遍认可。在国家版权局积极推动下，网络文学、影视、音乐等领域大规模侵权盗版现象基本得到遏制，网络版权环境进一步净化。2016年网络版权行政保护主要呈现以下特点：一是针对互联网的传播方式和版权侵权特点，营造严格保护和重点保护交织的生态。在巩固往年重点监管领域和保护成果的基础上，2016年加强分类监管网络文学等多个领域的专项整治工作。二是创新网络版权管理模式，树立版权保护典型企业，推进版权领域信用体系建设。通过建立“黑白名单”制度，逐步探索网络版权监管的新举措、新方法。三是版权执法在打击网络侵权盗版方面承前启后，深入有效。“剑网2016”专项行动期间，各地共查处行政案件514件，行政罚款467万元，移送司法机关33件，涉案金额2亿元，关闭网站290家。四是利用社会共治这一重要手段，引导和支持市场主体创造和运用版权，推动构建全社会共同治理格局。版权监管部门与其他监管部门通力合作，指导社团组织配合协同，推动互联网主体的自律整改，网络版权的创造、运用、保护和服务水平不断提升。

（二）2016年中国网络版权保护的基本特点

1. 严格保护成为网络版权保护的总体趋势

当前我国仍处于版权矛盾和纠纷高发期，网络侵权盗版行为较为普遍、侵权形式复杂多样，网络版权环境还有待进一步优化。在此情势下，党中央、国务院高度重视知识产权保护，印发《关于完善产权保护制度依法保护产权的意见》《国家创新驱动发展战略纲要》等文件，强调加大侵犯知识产权行为的惩治力度，网络版权保护政策趋向严格。2016年，人民法院提升侵权赔偿数额，严厉打击刑事犯罪。在北京、山东作协主席诉书生公司案中，北京知识产权法院提高判赔标准；在架设私服网游《热血传奇》案中，法院判决被告有期徒刑5年，罚金高达2 500万元。版权行政管理部门继续加大版权执法监管力度，打击网络侵权盗版卓有成效。在多方的共同努力下，构建出严格的版权保护格局。

2. 互联网与版权产业的深度融合成为产业发展的重要模式

随着互联网内容新增用户人口红利的衰减，内容资源对用户黏度和流量吸引力增大，优质IP成为市场竞争的重要基础。2016年，互联网与文化娱乐深度融合共生，资本市场强势进驻IP产业链，泛文娱行业空前炙热①，各种新兴文化形态层出不穷，版权资源整合与联动现象突出，整体IP市场趋于规范化和理性化，逐渐形成网络版权健康流转模式。越来越多的网络视频、音乐、文学企业通过版权资源的运营和保护获得收益，越来越多的权利人也因此获得作品报酬。

3. 多元化治理持续推动网络版权保护环境改善

经过多年版权治理的发展，以权利人为“维权源头”、以法律法规为“维权基准”、以司法行政为“维权两翼”的立体维权体系逐渐成形，成为网络版权秩序健康有序发展的多元治理良方。行政层面，连续十二年开展的“剑网行动”等专项治理行动社会影响广泛深远，网络视频、网络音乐等曾经盗版猖獗的领域基本实现了正版化，促进了相关产业的良性循环发展②。行业组织和企业充分发挥主体作用，推动加强行业自律，畅通投诉举报渠道，使得行业、企业和社会公众成为网络版权保护重要组成部分，有力地调动社会监督资源，改变了过去单纯依靠行政手段实施事后监管的方式，形成了政府有效监管、企业自我约束、行业自律与公众监督相结合的版权保护新格局。

4. 技术手段成为解决网络环境中侵权问题的重

① 根据易观《中国IP市场专题分析2017》的数据显示：2016年中国文化娱乐产业规模达到3 505亿元，同比增长11.8%。

② 据文化部最新统计数据显示，2016年上半年，网络音乐市场营收25.4亿元。营收规模占2015年总营收的七成以上；国际唱片业协会（IFPI）在发布的《2016全球音乐报告》中称，2015年中国音乐销量上涨63.8%，达到1.7亿美元（约合10亿元人民币），其中数字收入整体上升了68.6%。

要方式

新技术环境下，传播权替代复制权成为版权产业的中心，传播技术的发展一方面降低了侵权门槛，另一方面也使得作品的可识别性、侵权证据的可追踪性大大提高。移动互联网对传播技术的倚重推动产业对技术保护措施的高度重视，监管部门利用技术手段对盗版内容和侵权行为进行有效遏制①，加速推进互联网正版化进程；越来越多的互联网企业投入大量技术资源对版权内容进行监测和管理，并通过技术创新促进商业模式创新；相关机构版权保护技术逐步产业化给网络版权保护产业打开新局面。

5. 网络文学侵权重点治理工作初见成效，网络文学版权秩序日渐规范

为重点查处打击网络文学侵权盗版行为，国家版权局发布《关于加强网络文学作品版权管理的通知》，进一步明确提供文学作品的网络服务商在版权管理方面的责任和义务。同时，在网络文学领域推行“黑白名单”制度，公布文学作品侵权盗版网络服务商“黑名单”、网络文学作品重点监管“白名单”，树立版权保护典型企业。同时将国内主要文学网站纳入国家版权局重点监管，推动网络文学企业加强行业自律。在国家版权局的协调和敦促下，国内 33 家主要网络文学企业和原创小说网站共同发起的中国网络文学版权联盟宣布成立，并签署了《中国网络文学版权联盟自律公约》，促进了网络文学作品的有序传播。

（三）2016 年中国网络版权保护存在的诸多挑战

2016 年是《信息网络传播权保护条例》颁布第十年，十年间，我国信息产业高速发展，互联网技术与内容行业的深度融合引发新的产业变革，改变了传统的创作者、传播者、使用者三方的利益分配格局，构成产业、技术与制度协同发展的现实障碍②。如何在平衡从业者利益的基础上促进产业发展，成为当前网络版权保护工作面临的重大命题。

1. 现有网络版权法律制度不能有效应对数字网络新技术带来的冲击

以数字信息技术为基础、以互动传播为特点、具有多种创新形态的新型传播方式不断冲击着现有的版权法律制度，一些新兴的文化消费热点（如游戏直播、体育赛事、内容聚合平台等）中的构成要素和传播行为的可版权性在实践中引起广泛争议，引发网络版权纠纷，反映出法律的滞后性与产业创新之间的冲突。现有的著作权法亟待做出动态调整以适应互联网发展规律，保障新形势下网络版权行为主体的利益平衡。

2. 授权机制不畅通，影响作品传播效率和版权服务水平

数字技术提升了版权运用效率，也使得版权利益被拆分过多，导致版权价格虚高、授权凌乱，影响了网络版权的运用、管理和服务水平。近年来，我国网络内容产业的市场需求、消费能力和受众群体不断扩大，优质 IP 经过传媒和互联网的多次开发，通过小说、影视剧、娱乐节目、游戏、动漫等不同形式，形成较高的增值变现能力和市场价格。一方面，实力雄厚的互联网公司独占热门作品的专有许可，将垄断 IP 资源作为竞争和营销策略，变相限制传播，引发诉讼不断；另一方面，版权授权机制的不通畅也使得需求方难以快速、低成本地获得正版授权。在创作者、传播平台和消费者之间，缺乏公平、权威、通畅和有效的版权授权平台，保障版权确权的真实性、授权规则的准确性。相关部门和企业应通过创新技术手段和管理运营模式，完善授权交易保障机制和信用机制，疏通网络版权交易渠道、明晰授权规则，并对违反信用规定、侵犯他人权利的行为形成法律、信用等多方面的惩戒措施。

3. 数字网络技术的发展降低侵权门槛，网络内容传播由专业化转向大众化

技术的发展在客观上降低了网络版权侵权难度，网络版权侵权衍生出以聚合盗链、网盘分享侵权以及盗版小网站等新型侵权形态，手段隐蔽化、产业链条化、分工专业化、人员年轻化已成为当前网络侵权盗版的突出特征，也对司法审判和行政执法提出新的要求。网络版权保护如何从行政执法、行业治理和法律规制方面与时俱进，成为我国网络版权保护体系面临的重要考验。

4. 维权成本与维权收益不成正比，制约网络内容产业发展

作为作品网络传播的主要参与者，近年来互联网公司逐步加大对版权内容的投入，但因侵权诉讼获得的损害赔偿金与作品的实际市场交易价格相去甚远，常陷入“赢了官司赔了钱”的窘境。而普通

① 2016 年，国家新闻出版广电总局出重拳打击电影盗版，总局电影质检所合作 NexGuard 公司为影片添加“数字水印”，这一技术可帮助片方检测盗版来源。这意味着今后所有在影院播出的电影都有了“身份证”，一旦发现盗版资源，可以快速查出泄露片源出自哪家影院，为片方维权提供鉴定报告。

② 田小军，柏玉珊．我国网络版权制度演化的现状、挑战与应对 [J]．中国版权，2016 (3).

权利人或缺乏维权意识，或不了解维权途径，或难进行侵权取证，自我保护和维权积极性普遍不高，直接影响后继优质内容的创作与开发。建立全方位的知识产权维权体系，亟待提高网络版权保护专业水平，提高网络版权侵权赔偿额度，优化对权利人的维权机制，完善知识产权审判机制，强化行政执法与司法的衔接。

二、2016年中国网络版权保护分述

（一）2016年中国网络版权的立法保护

2016年，党中央、国务院高度重视知识产权保护工作，国家知识产权战略持续深入推进，网络版权领域的立法呈现出精细化、专门化的特点，突出了对重点问题的规制。

1. 全国人大常委会通过《电影产业促进法》，对电影知识产权保护相关问题予以法律规制

随着电影市场的高速成长和国产电影创作力量的不断壮大，电影已经成为我国网络文化创意产业链中最活跃的领域之一。2016年11月7日，全国人大常委会第二十四次会议表决通过《电影产业促进法》，明确规定与电影有关的知识产权受法律保护，任何组织和个人不得侵犯，同时对涉及信息网络传播的公映电影进行规范。该法体现出网络版权保护在电影产业中的重要地位。

2. 国家版权局出台专门规范性文件，重点规范网络文学版权秩序

近年来，我国网络文学产业发展迅猛，但网络文学作品侵权盗版问题仍很严重，给产业良性发展造成巨大冲击。针对这一现状，2016年11月14日，国家版权局出台了《关于加强网络文学作品版权管理的通知》。《通知》按照不同类型网络服务商在传播文学作品时的特点、功能和作用，提出相应的工作要求和注意义务，要求网络服务商建立侵权处理机制、版权投诉机制、通知—删除机制和上传审核机制等四项工作机制，有效规范了网络文学作品版权秩序。

3. 国家互联网信息办公室、北京市版权局出台规范性文件，着力规范应用程序市场版权秩序

APP在提供民生服务、促进经济社会发展的同时，也为违法违规信息和侵权盗版作品的传播提供了新的途径。为此，2016年6月28日，国家互联网信息办公室发布了《移动互联网应用程序信息服务管理规定》（下文简称《规定》），明确要求“移动互联网应用程序提供者”和“互联网应用商店服务提供者”应依法严格履行相关义务和管理责任，尊重和保护知识产权。2016年11月30日，北京市版权局发布《规范软件应用市场版权秩序的通知》。该《通知》对落实上述国家网信办《规定》和国家版权局“剑网2016”专项行动工作部署做出了详细规定，明确了软件应用市场经营者应履行的“未经授权不得提供软件上架、预装和下载服务”等各项法定义务。

4. 北京市高院发布《审理指南》，对网络版权案件的审理进行指导

新业态、新领域的迅速发展催生了诸多有别于传统领域的新现象，给我国网络版权司法保护工作提出了新的挑战。为此，2016年4月13日，北京市高级人民法院发布了《涉及网络知识产权案件审理指南》（下文简称《审理指南》）。在网络版权部分，《审理指南》重点针对权利人和网络服务提供者举证证明责任的分配、网络服务提供者行为性质的认定、“分工合作”的判定方式、侵权要件与免责要件的适用关系、网页“快照”的合理使用、网络实时转播行为的法律适用等六大类问题进行了规定，加强了对司法实践的指引。

（二）2016年中国网络版权的司法保护

根据最高人民法院主办的“中国知识产权裁判文书网”、“中国裁判文书网”，以及知产宝数据库、北大法宝数据库中对于侵犯信息网络传播权的民事裁判文书的检索查询[①]，2016年全国共有4 459件网络版权相关的民事判决和裁定书。通过对这些案件状况进行分析和统计，总结出我国网络版权司法保护在2016年所呈现的一些新特点。

1. 网络内容产业各领域版权纠纷数量趋于均衡，涉及著名影视作品互联网传播的著作权纠纷案件不断增多

就公开的判决书情况来看，网络视频案件最多，占整个侵犯信息网络传播权案件数量37%左右（见图1），其中，相当一部分案件的侵权作品为基于热门IP开发的衍生产品，如《宫锁连城》《来自星星的你》《捉妖记》等，体现了网络版权的商品化诉求。

网络文学和图片作品案件数量紧随其后，网络图片作品占比与2015年基本持平，而网络文学领域案件数量比去年增加10百分点，作为泛娱乐产业链的源头，网络文学案件历年来在侵犯信息网络传播权案件中的比重较为稳定，2016年该领域案

① 查阅数据时间截止到2017年2月28日，选取数据的结案时间截止到2016年12月31日。

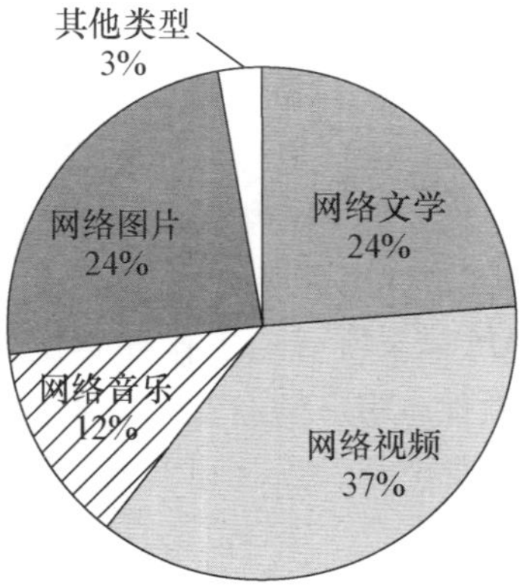

图 1　2016 年网络版权侵权案件类型分布情况

资料来源：中国信息通信研究院。

件的大幅上升更是体现出整治网络文学侵权盗版的紧迫性与必要性。此外，网络文学案件诉讼请求金额较低，被告地域分布范围较广，赔偿数额的确定仍以酌定为主，各地法院的赔偿标准仍待统一。网络音乐案件占比 12%，与去年同期相比下降 32 百分点，反映出 2015 年重拳整治之后，数字音乐版权环境的明显改善。

总体来说，2016 年网络版权案件涉诉作品类型丰富多样，数量较为均衡，相差不大，反映出内容产业各细分领域的全面发展。

2. 网络版权案件新载体、新形态不断出现，涉及的传播方式呈现多样化趋势

随着数字传播技术的发展，网络著作权侵权案件新情况不断出现，侵权传播途径出现多样化、分散化趋势。其中，一半的侵权纠纷案件通过网站、搜索引擎、浏览器等方式传播。此外，通过 APP，电视盒子，微博、微信等方式提供网络传播服务引发的侵权案件也层出不穷，分别占比 19%、16% 和 13%。贴吧和网盘引发的侵权案件数量较少，仅各占 1%（见图 2）。总体来看，随着“互联网+”的

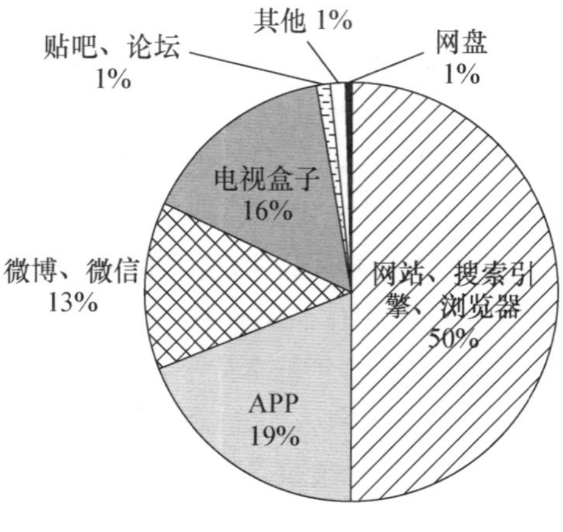

图 2　2016 年网络版权侵权案件传播方式分布情况

资料来源：中国信息通信研究院。

深入实施，市场主体技术创新活跃程度增强，由此催生了大量涉及新技术、新产业、新业态、新商业模式的知识产权纠纷，如涉及深度链接、聚合盗链、云存储空间分享等侵害作品信息网络传播权纠纷。

3. 网络版权案件的地域分布呈现出相对集中、适当扩散的态势，知识产权法院在审理网络版权案件中作用突出

从审理法院来看，法院地域分布排名前三的省份分别是北京市、浙江省和广东省（见图 3）。统计发现，地方法院审理的网络版权纠纷案件中，八成以上的案件源自这三个地区，集中体现了北京、杭州、深圳等互联网企业集聚的城市，其网络版权产业发展的活跃程度和先进水平较高。北京连续多年成为网络案件的高发地，审理了 52%的网络版权侵权案件，其中，超过半数的案件来自网络视频领域。浙江省的案件数量紧随北京市之后，连续三年排在案件数量的第一梯队，充分体现出浙江省互联网产业和信息经济的蓬勃发展。紧随浙江省之后的是广东省，以 16%的占比在法院审理案件数量的地区中排名第三。2016 年各地知识产权法院做出的网络版权民事判决共计 378 件，其中北京知识产权法院 222 件，上海知识产权法院 36 件，广州知识产权法院 120 件，分别占当地网络版权侵权案件的 31.1%、37.9%、60.6%，与上年同期相比，北京和广州知识产权法院均有近一倍的增长。作为知识产权审判的引领者和司法改革的探路者，各地知识产权法院经过对网络版权纠纷解决的不断摸索，司法解决机制日趋完善并向着专业化方向发展，审理了一批由新技术新商业模式引发的社会关注度高、影响力较大的热点案件，如腾讯诉易联伟达案、天下霸唱诉《九层妖塔》案、斗鱼直播侵权案、电影海报使用知名卡通形象案等，这些案件的审判对同类案件的示范及裁判标准的统一具有重要的指导意义。

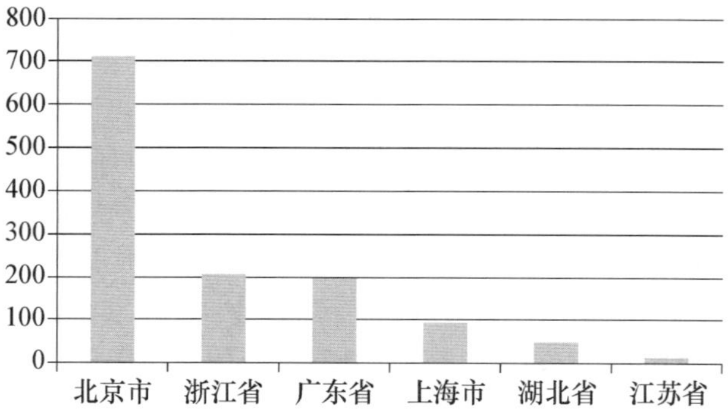

图 3　2016 年网络版权侵权案件地域分布情况

资料来源：中国信息通信研究院。

4. 刑事司法是网络版权保护的重要手段

2016年司法机关加大对网络版权的刑事保护力度，案件类型涉及网络游戏、文学、视频、音乐等多个领域。其中，网络文学和网络游戏领域的刑事案件数量最多，分别占总案件数量的42%和31%。此外，处罚金额加大是2016年网络版权刑事案件司法保护的显著特点，据统计，在已公布的有关侵犯网络著作权刑事犯罪的案件中，案件平均罚金在20万元以上，在架设私服网游《热血传奇》案中，法院判决被告有期徒刑5年，罚金高达2 500万元，有力打击和震慑了网络著作权侵权犯罪分子。

（三）2016年中国网络版权的社会保护

2016年，在国家版权局的指导和推动下，中国网络版权的社会保护更加立体、多元、有效。著作权集体管理组织充分发挥管理和服务职能，版权行业协会积极促进行业自律，企业进一步落实主体责任、加强自我约束，权利主体维权积极性不断提高、维权手段更加丰富，网络版权保护的社会共治机制初步建立。

1. 行业组织的版权保护情况

（1）著作权集体管理组织充分履行自身职能，保护会员合法权益。

2016年9月中国文字著作权协会举办“原创文字作品保护月”活动，号召原创媒体机构和原创个人对原创作品做出声明，倡导网络内容聚合平台通过在线许可获得互联网内容的使用授权，并为参与活动的机构或个人提供全面的维权服务，探索并尝试建立网络传播文字作品的版权许可与维护机制，开拓治理非法转载的维权途径。随着网络版权保护环境的持续改善，数字音乐市场发展成为主流，新媒体许可收益呈现稳步上升趋势。根据中国音乐著作权协会公布的数据，2016年歌曲版权许可总收益再创新高，达到1.84亿元，比2015年增长约8.2%。新媒体歌曲许可收益约6 845万元，首次超过表演权、广播权等其他收益，占比最大。2016年2月至11月，中国音乐著作权协会对苹果应用商店APP产品侵权使用音乐情况进行维权，共计投诉APP 166个，下架APP 56个，涵盖了众多与网络传播音乐相关的类目。

此外，2016年，中国摄影著作权协会、中国电影著作权协会等著作权集体管理组织也都积极配合国家版权行政管理部门的监管工作，举办“互联网+影像传播与运营发展”等活动，做好网络版权保护和服务的日常工作。

（2）版权行业协会积极促进行业自律，协助推进行业正版化。

2016年7月，中国作家协会网络文学委员会、中国音像与数字出版协会数字阅读工作委员会向全国网络文学界发布《网络文学行业自律倡议书》，加强行业自律，规范行业发展，自觉主动为包括青少年在内的读者营造良好的阅读环境。2016年9月，中国版权协会与掌阅、阅文等33家网络文学企业共同发起成立“中国网络文学版权联盟”，并发布《中国网络文学版权联盟自律公约》，号召网络文学服务商树立和强化版权保护意识，尊重网络文学原创作者的合法权益，自觉抵制各类侵权盗版行为，营造健康文明的行业环境。

2016年11月，首都版权产业联盟联合百度、奇虎360、阿里、腾讯等国内主要网络广告联盟共同发布《网络广告联盟版权自律倡议》，号召网络广告联盟建立健全内部版权管理制度，严格规范广告投放程序。对被国家版权局列入侵权盗版“黑名单”的网站，终止向其投放广告，并解除其会员资格，切断专门从事侵权盗版的小网站的非法利益链条，从根本上遏制小网站侵权盗版势头，有效净化网络版权环境。2016年11月，在中国互联网协会网络版权工作委员会的支持下，腾讯、掌趣、畅游等15家游戏运营企业、独立游戏制作人和游戏平台企业共同发起成立“网络游戏反盗版和产业保护联盟”，宣布建立网络游戏快速维权机制，定期组织联合维权行动，打击遏制盗版侵权行为，建立盗版预警排查机制及快速纠纷调解机制，通过维权行动和行业自律，推动行业正版化，实现健康可持续发展。

2. 互联网企业自律情况

2016年，互联网企业积极配合国家版权局的监管工作，落实企业主体责任，主动规范自身行为，不断提升企业版权保护水平。为清查网络文学盗版侵权内容，2016年5月23日，百度公司发布公告，宣布分批次暂时关闭“百度贴吧”文学目录下的全部贴吧，对其中的盗版侵权内容进行全面整顿，开设两条发帖投诉举报绿色通道“全民举报吧”和“贴吧曝光台”，一经举报即开展清查并在12小时内删除相关的盗版侵权内容。针对云盘中充斥大量侵权盗版文学、影视、音乐作品等现象，2016年，相关网盘服务商积极开展自查整改。3月9日，115网盘关停部分功能；3月18日，UC网盘宣布终止存储服务；4月25日，新浪微盘停止普通用户存储服务；4月26日，迅雷快盘停止个人用户存储服务；5月3日，华为网盘停止用户数据存储分享服务；5月27日，腾讯微云关闭文件中转站功能；2016年

10 月 20 日，360 云盘宣布停止个人云盘服务。

3. 权利主体的自我保护情况

2016 年，网络视频、网络游戏、体育赛事等热门 IP 仍是权利人的维权重点，权利人维权手段更加丰富，版权纠纷多元解决机制在探索中逐步建立。

2016 年，一系列维权热点案件产生较大的社会影响力，为相关产业的发展提供指导：在《奇迹MU》维权案中，浦东法院首次将角色扮演类网络游戏认定为“类电影作品”，对其作为有机整体享有的合法权益进行界定，对网游行业的知识产权保护具有重要的引领作用；中国首例电子竞技类游戏赛事网络直播——广州斗鱼直播案，为产业更新的过渡期内版权业与互联网产业利益冲突提供了新的解决思路；腾讯易联伟达案引发了社会各界对影视聚合平台侵权定性的关注和讨论。

除了司法维权，权利人还使用行政手段维护自身合法权益。目前，向版权行政管理部门投诉已成为权利人的重要维权手段之一。“剑网 2016”专项行动期间，国家版权局等四部门通报的 21 起典型网络侵权盗版案件中，根据权利人投诉查处的案件有 10 起，占 47.6%。权利人委托版权社会调解机构来维护自身合法权益的数量也呈逐年上升态势。

2016 年，随着“尊重原创、保护原创”等全社会权利意识的觉醒，音乐、文学、影视领域的知名权利人通过多种渠道维护自己的权利，保护和促进版权价值。4 月 26 日，百名自媒体人发出《联合维权公开信》，控诉新闻资讯应用《一点资讯》利用技术手段系统将自媒人拥有版权的原创内容，抄袭、复制到其平台和应用软件上，并要求一点咨讯支付赔偿、赔礼道歉、删除抄袭内容。8 月，由谷建芬、乔羽、三宝、小柯、刘欢、崔健等十余位知名音乐人共同发起的著作权代理机构华乐成盟，将《中国好声音》未经词曲作者授权使用作品等三起案件起诉至相关地方法院，要求被告停止侵权、赔偿损失，维护音乐人的合法权益。10 月，水木年华成员卢庚戌在京召开维权发布会，称音乐网站酷狗和虾米未经授权曝光其个人新专辑《我的生命不过是温柔的疯狂》的部分曲目，希望通过维权发布会妥善解决版权问题，警示此类音乐 APP。知名作家郑渊洁在微博发文声称其作品《舒克和贝塔》遭遇出版社严重侵权，得到国家版权局的高度重视，2016 年 8 月 17 日，在国家版权局版权管理司的推动和协调下，双方达成和解协议，郑渊洁获得 25 万元赔偿金。知名导演蔡明亮在其微博控诉多家互联网平台涉嫌侵犯版权，内地知名电影资源下载网站“蓝影网”宣布关停并道歉，“哔哩哔哩网”（B 站）被举报后两次发文致歉。

（四）2016 年中国网络版权的行政保护

2016 年，版权行政管理部门认真分析当前网络版权保护面临的新情况新问题，在做好日常监管和巩固已有的工作成果基础上，继续深入开展“剑网 2016”专项行动，进一步明确了 2016 年版权保护的工作重点，全国各级版权行政管理部门积极部署任务和责任分工，推进版权保护工作取得了一系列新成果、新进展，有效地维护了权利人的合法权益和社会公共利益。

1. 巩固往年治理成果，明确 2016 年重点整治领域，覆盖面更广泛

2016 年，版权监管部门巩固往年网络音乐、网络视频、网络云存储空间、网络转载新闻作品等重点治理领域，继续加强对大型视频网站、音乐网站版权重点监管和清理，整治了未经授权非法传播网络作品的侵权盗版行为。针对互联网治理的热点和难点，明确了网络文学、APP、广告联盟、私人影院和电子商务平台等五个重点整治领域，实施分类管理和专项整治。具体如下：

一是开展打击网络文学侵权盗版专项整治行动。针对近年来日益严重的网络文学侵权盗版问题，国家版权局在广泛调研和征集意见的基础上，于 11 月 14 日发布了《关于加强网络文学作品版权管理的通知》，针对不同类型的网络服务提供商提出相应的工作要求和注意义务，要求网络服务商建立侵权处理机制、版权投诉机制、通知—删除机制和上传审核机制等四项工作机制；并建立了网络文学作品版权“黑白名单”制度，细化了著作权法律法规的相关规定，对规范网络文学版权秩序具有重要的意义。各地先后查处了侵犯网络文学著作权的案件，包括北京“顶点小说网”、江苏苏州“风雨文学网”、重庆“269 小说网”、四川双流“轻之国度网”、广西南宁“皮皮小说网”等网络文学侵权盗版案件。

二是开展打击 APP 侵权盗版专项整治行动。北京市版权局发布《北京市版权局关于规范软件应用市场版权秩序的通知》，结合软件正版化工作对软件应用市场的经营活动进行监测并依法监管，从源头上治理 APP 侵权盗版行为，规范了软件应用市场版权秩序。在《一点资讯》客户端软件侵犯著作权案中，北京市版权行政执法部门对侵权人做出罚款 5 万元的行政处罚。各地版权执法部门也进一步加强对 APP 侵权盗版行为的打击力度，查办多起典型案例：重庆市文化执法总队针对《音乐一号》客户端

软件侵犯著作权案，对侵权人做出没收非法所得3 000元、罚款3万元的行政处罚；上海市文化执法总队针对上海《echo回声》客户端软件侵犯著作权案，对侵权人做出责令停止侵权行为、罚款20万元的行政处罚。

三是开展规范网络广告联盟专项整治行动。国家版权局加强对网络广告联盟在版权保护方面的监督管理，采取多种方式严厉打击故意为侵权盗版提供支持的网络广告联盟。国家版权局会同工商总局公布了一批与网络广告联盟有关侵权盗版网站"黑名单"，推动国内主要广告联盟开展行业自律，指导网络广告联盟建立健全内部版权机制、切实规范广告投放程序。江苏省版权局查办了非法获利近100万元的"BT天堂"盗版视频案件，以及非法传播侵权作品2万余部、非法获利100余万元的"迅播影院"案，进一步遏制了与网络广告联盟利益相关的小网站侵权盗版势头，有效净化了网络版权环境。

除此之外，国家版权局还对私人影院和电子商务平台开展了专项整治，成效显著。整治私人影院方面，江西省版权局通过开展私人影院侵权盗版专项集中整治行动，对违法传播侵权作品的10家私人影院依法进行了行政处罚，处罚金额合计8.3万元。四川省版权局组织成都、达州、资阳等地对私人影院进行排查清理，对"头等舱私人影院"等四家私人影院进行了查处。整治电子商务平台方面，国家版权局加强对电商平台侵权盗版案件查办工作，各地版权执法部门先后查处了北京"亿梦春田"等6家淘宝网店销售盗版图书案，广东佛山"12·23"网络批销盗版图书案，江苏镇江"剑锋时代图书专营店"淘宝网店销售盗版图书案等典型案件。

2. 积极回应和关注侵权高发领域，查办热点领域案件

国家版权行政管理部门重点关注贴吧、自媒体、私人影院等侵权盗版现象频发的领域，并对其涉及的版权保护的热点、难点问题进行研究，积极寻求有效的解决方案。

（1）积极回应和重点关注权利人反映的侵权纠纷高发领域。针对百度公司"百度贴吧事件"，国家版权局积极敦促百度公司切实保护好权利人的合法权益；鉴于热门电影在IP产业链中的重要地位，国家版权局先后对《陆垚知马俐》《王牌逗王牌》《湄公河行动》等国产优秀电影进行专项保护；在奥运会、欧洲杯期间，国家版权局会同中央电视台对奥运会、欧洲杯节目进行专项保护，取得了较好的成果，维护了权利人的合法利益。

（2）狠抓大案要案查办。加大对网络侵权盗版案件的行政处罚和刑事移送力度，特别是对侵权事实严重、社会影响大的侵权盗版网站，依法从严查处。国家版权局等四部门通报了包括侵犯网络文学、APP、网络广告联盟、电子商务等各重点监管领域的21起较为典型的网络侵权盗版案件。重庆市公安局打假总队联合渝中区公安分局破获"8·6"盗版游戏案，涉案金额3 000余万元，抓获8名犯罪嫌疑人；破获重庆"10·19"盗版游戏案，抓获犯罪嫌疑人2名，涉案金额达2 500多万元。辽宁省版权局对"铁甲洪流"案中链接"多玩游戏"等10余个无授权游戏网站的当事人做出行政处罚，有力地打击了侵权盗版行为，有效地保护了权利人的合法权利。

（3）加强重点监管。国家版权局要求各重点监管网站严格遵守"先授权，后使用"的原则，采取相应措施，认真开展自查整改、建立健全自律工作机制，主动下线授权到期和无授权文件的作品。根据相关网站上报的获得作品授权的情况，分七批次定期公布了2016年度重点作品版权保护预警名单。各地方版权监管部门对传播文学、影视、音乐等作品的重点网站等进行。

（4）全面清理检查：北京市版权局按月选取具有代表性的重点热门影视、音乐和综艺类节目作品，参照网站权重排名有针对性地对20家主流视频网站和12家音乐网站开展监测工作；山东省版权局深入推进"三位一体"的网络视听节目网站监管模式；海南省版权局将南海网、天涯网、凯迪网等网站列入重点监管名单。此外，各地还将享有著作权的广播电台电视台节目、金融信息作品纳入版权监测范围。

（5）针对网络版权保护中的热点难点问题组织研究探讨。在中国文字著作权协会（以下简称文著协）发起的"2016剑网行动·原创文字作品保护月"活动中，针对文字作品权利人和产业发展需要，以及网络转载、传播文字作品版权保护的难点，国家版权局要求文著协加快探索网络授权许可、盗版防范、侵权追究的有效途径和方法，推动网络规范有序传播文字作品，带动产业发展。在中国网络版权保护大会上，国家版权局结合社会关注热点难点，分别举办了网络文学版权保护、体育赛事节目与版权保护、网络转载版权保护等3个分论坛，组织专家、学者就版权热点难点问题进行研究探讨。

3. 积极探索加强网络版权保护工作的新举措新办法

（1）推进约谈工作机制。国家版权局在"双十

一”前夕，对部分电子商务平台企业进行了约谈，要求电子商务平台企业按照著作权法要求，落实好主体责任，配合执法部门查处平台上的侵权盗版经营者。北京市版权局对侵权和盗版链接较为严重的网站采取了“线上通知”“线下约谈”的工作模式，约谈了网易、腾讯、乐视等企业，有效净化了首都地区版权市场秩序。上海市文化执法总队约谈“城通网盘”，要求其彻底关闭“城通网盘”用户的“主动开启文件分享”功能。上海市网信办针对财经资讯类网站存在的超范围转载时政类新闻等问题，依法约谈东方财富网、证券之星、每日经济新闻网、华尔街见闻、环球老虎财经 5 家网站，效果明显。

（2）推进预警工作机制。国家版权局根据相关网站上报的获得作品授权的情况，公布了 7 批共计 284 部热播、热映的重点影视作品预警名单。福建省版权局公布网络文学、影视、游戏、动漫等重点作品版权保护“白名单”42 件。北京市文化执法总队对于社会关注、盗版行为频发的网络视频领域试行了版权保护预警机制，受理搜狐、乐视、腾讯等企业的版权保护申请，开通版权保护绿色通道。预警工作机制为减少网络侵权盗版发挥了重要作用。

（4）建立“黑白名单”制度。2016 年，国家版权局在网络文学、广告联盟、APP 等领域推行“黑白名单”制度。一方面，将从事侵权盗版的网站纳入“黑名单”，切断专门从事盗版网站的非法利益链条，从源头上遏制侵权盗版势头；另一方面，通过公布重点监管作品“白名单”，明确热门文学作品等领域的授权链条，解决版权纠纷中的“明知”“应知”问题。该举措对于树立版权保护典型企业，健全网络作品版权使用传播的长效机制，推进版权领域信用体系建设具有重要创新意义。

（5）加强部门联动。专项行动期间，各级版权执法监管部门加强联动，进一步完善多部门协调办案工作机制，通过联席会议、督办督查、信息共享、开展区域合作交流，与互联网信息管理、通信管理、“扫黄打非”以及公检法等部门积极开展合作，取得了显著成果。国家版权局督办 4 批共计 31 起侵犯著作权案件。重庆市公安局和重庆市版权局成立打击侵权盗版违法犯罪工作联席会，各成员单位在重点整治领域建立“黑白名单”（重点保护作品“白名单”、侵权盗版互联网企业“黑名单”）。广州市文化执法总队协助吉林省版权局、江西省版权局、北京市执法总队、天津执法总队和银川市执法队办理了一系列网络侵权案，联合青岛、武汉长沙、清远等地市开展执法人员培训工作。

（6）加大宣传力度。国家版权局通过举办“中国网络版权保护大会”“数字环境下影视产业版权保护圆桌会议”，发布了“2015 年度打击侵权盗版十大案件”和《2015 年中国网络版权保护年度报告》；与中央电视台《热线 12》栏目联合制作以“网络版权保护”为主题的“聚焦世界知识产权日”特别节目；举办“版权相关热点问题媒体培训班”走进重庆、广州等地；同时积极拓展宣传工作渠道，通过网站、微博、微信、新闻客户端等方式，扩大版权社会影响，提高社会公众版权意识。

三、结语

回顾 2016 年，随着数字技术的发展和国家政策的强力推动，数字文化创意产业日益成为培育经济发展的新动能、引领消费供给的新引擎。我国版权创造、运用、保护、管理和服务水平不断提高，网络版权保护迎来新局面：网络版权法律构建趋向严格、重点突出；司法部门对新技术新业态引发的纠纷规制边界明晰、导向明确；网络版权社会服务管理多元有效、协同共治；网络版权行政监管创新形式，力度不断加大，网络文学治理初见成效，网络版权保护环境日益清朗。面对技术快速发展带来多重利益冲突的愈加复杂的形势，网络版权保护工作依然任重道远。展望未来，中国网络版权保护事业将在经济转型升级、创新驱动发展的新形势下不断前进，为建成中国特色、世界水平的版权强国奠定坚实基础。

2016 年度查处侵权盗版案件有功单位及个人

［编者按］ 2017 年 5 月 26 日，国家版权局印发《关于奖励 2016 年度查处侵权盗版案件有功单位及有功个人的决定》，对在 2016 年度查处侵权盗版案件工作中做出突出贡献的 208 家有功单位及 243 名有功个人给予奖励。

【有功单位一等奖】

1. 公安部治安管理局一处
2. 公安部经济犯罪侦查局九处
3. 最高人民检察院侦查监督厅立案监督处（保护知识产权处）
4. 河北保定霍某某销售侵权复制品案专案组（河北省保定市“扫黄打非”领导小组办公室、河北省保定市人民检察院侦查监督部、河北省保定市公安局莲池区公安分局治安大队、河北省保定市文化市场行政执法大队、河北省保定市莲池区人民检察院侦监科）
5. 河北石家庄张某某侵犯著作权案专案组（河北省石家庄市“扫黄打非”领导小组办公室、河北省石家庄市版权局、河北省石家庄市公安局治安警察支队行动大队、河北省石家庄市中级人民法院刑二庭、河北省石家庄市文化市场行政执法大队）
6. 吉林省版权局版权处
7. 上海吴某某侵犯著作权案专案组（上海市第三中级人民法院刑庭、上海市普陀区人民法院知识产权庭、上海市普陀区人民检察院公诉科）
8. 上海市版权局版权管理执法处
9. 江苏省版权局版权管理处
10. 江苏昆山“12·15”制售侵权盗版图书案专案组（江苏省昆山市文化行政综合执法大队、江苏省昆山市公安局治安警察大队、江苏省昆山市人民法院知识产权庭）
11. 江苏张家港“风雨文学网”侵犯著作权案专案组（江苏省苏州张家港市文化广电新闻出版局、江苏省苏州张家港市公安局网络警察大队）
12. 江苏徐州“猪猪影院”侵犯著作权案专案组（江苏省徐州市版权局、江苏省徐州市中级人民法院民三庭）
13. 浙江省版权局版权处
14. 浙江省金华市文化广电新闻出版局
15. 福建省版权局版权管理处
16. 江西省新闻出版广电局版权管理处
17. 山东省新闻出版广电局版权管理处
18. 山东省青岛市文化市场行政执法局
19. 山东淄博“4·8”侵犯著作权案专案组（山东省淄博市文化市场执法局、山东省淄博市公安局直属分局）
20. 山东省泰安市文化市场综合执法支队
21. 山东省威海市文化市场综合执法局
22. 河南巩义“11·17”竹林新华印刷厂侵犯著作权案专案组（河南省巩义市文化广电新闻出版局、河南省巩义市公安局、河南省郑州市人民检察院公诉三处）
23. 河南焦作“12·1”侵权案专案组（河南省焦作市武陟县文化广电新闻出版局、河南省焦作市文化市场综合执法支队、河南省焦作市文化广电新闻出版局）
24. 湖北省版权局版权管理处
25. 广东省中山市中级人民法院民事审判第三庭
26. 广东省广州市文化市场综合行政执法总队执法五处
27. 重庆市两江新区知识产权法庭
28. 四川省版权局版权管理处
29. 陕西省版权局版权管理处
30. 新疆塔城“4·6”侵权盗版案专案组（新疆维吾尔自治区塔城地区文化市场稽查支队、新疆维吾尔自治区塔城地区沙湾县文化市场综合执法大队）
31. 《中国新闻出版广电报》出版周刊中心

【有功单位二等奖】

1. 中宣部出版局出版研究处
2. 工业和信息化部信息通信管理局互联网处
3. 公安部网络安全保卫局二处
4. 国家互联网信息办公室网络综合协调管理和执法督查局执法督查处
5. 最高人民法院刑事审判第一庭第四合议庭
6. 全国打击侵权假冒工作领导小组办公室法规信息组
7. 北京市版权局版权管理处
8. 河北省版权局版权管理处
9. 河北衡水赵某某等侵犯著作权案专案组（河北省衡水市“扫黄打非”领导小组办公室、河北省衡水市公安局桃城分局何家庄派出所）
10. 内蒙古自治区赤峰市文化市场综合执法局
11. 内蒙古自治区版权局版权管理处
12. 辽宁省版权局版权管理处
13. 辽宁省沈阳市文化市场行政执法总队直属执法四大队
14. 吉林省长春市文化市场综合执法支队
15. 吉林省公主岭市文化市场综合执法大队
16. 吉林省通化市辉南县文化市场综合执法大队
17. 黑龙江张某某侵犯著作权案专案组（黑龙江省哈尔滨市文化广电新闻出版局印刷发行版权处、黑龙江省哈尔滨市南岗区人民法院刑事审判庭）
18. 黑龙江省哈尔滨市中级人民法院刑事审判二庭
19. 上海市文化市场行政执法总队稽查三处
20. 上海市文化市场行政执法总队稽查五处
21. 上海市人民检察院金融检察处
22. 上海市通信管理局互联网管理处
23. 中共江苏省委网信办网络新闻管理处
24. 浙江省义乌市市场监督管理局
25. 安徽省版权局版权管理处
26. 江西省抚州市文化综合执法支队
27. 山东省泰安市宁阳县文化市场综合执法大队
28. 河南省版权局版权管理处
29. 河南省公安厅治安总队二支队
30. 河南郑州“1·26”侵权案专案组（河南省郑州市荥阳市人民检察院侦查监督科、河南省郑州市荥阳市文化广播电视新闻出版局）
31. 湖北省通信管理局网络安全管理处
32. 湖北省武汉市江岸区人民法院知识产权审判庭
33. 湖北汇梦影视茶吧侵犯电影著作权案专案组（湖北省黄石市文化新闻出版广电局、湖北省黄石市公安局）
34. 湖南省新闻出版广电（版权）局版权管理处
35. 湖南省永州市道县文化市场综合执法大队
36. 湖南省永州市宁远县文化市场综合执法大队
37. 广东省版权局版权管理处
38. 广东省佛山市南海区人民法院未成年人案件审判庭
39. 广东省深圳市市场和质量监督管理委员会南山区市场监督管理局知识产权科
40. 广东省东莞市文化市场综合执法大队
41. 广东佛山“12·23”网络批销盗版图书案专案组（广东省佛山市文化市场综合执法大队、广东省佛山市南海区文体旅游综合执法队、广东省佛山市南海区大沥镇文化站、广东省佛山市公安局南海分局治安管理大队、广东省佛山市公安局南海分局盐步派出所）
42. 广西壮族自治区版权局版权管理处
43. 重庆市版权局版权管理处
44. 重庆市石柱土家族自治县文化委员会
45. 贵州省贵阳市文化市场综合执法支队
46. 新疆维吾尔自治区乌鲁木齐市文化市场稽查支队
47. 新疆维吾尔自治区版权局版权处
48. 新疆刘某某侵犯著作权案专案组（新疆维吾尔自治区喀什市文化市场稽查大队、新疆维吾尔自治区喀什市公安局经侦大队）
49. 国家新闻出版广电总局信息中心互联网监测部
50. 中国版权保护中心法律部
51. 中国日报社特刊编辑部

【有功单位三等奖】

1. 中宣部新闻局文化新闻处
2. 海关总署政法司知识产权保护处
3. 国家工商总局反垄断与反不正当竞争执法局经济检查处
4. 国家互联网信息办公室移动网络管理局行业监管处
5. 中国互联网协会备案部
6. 天津市文化市场行政执法总队执法二队
7. 河北省衡水市公安局经济开发区分局
8. 河北省衡水市文化市场行政执法大队
9. 山西省版权局版权管理处

10. 内蒙古自治区呼和浩特市文化市场综合执法局
11. 辽宁省通信管理局电信管理处
12. 辽宁省沈阳市文化市场行政执法总队直属执法一大队
13. 辽宁省沈阳市文化市场行政执法总队和平区大队
14. 吉林省长春市宽城区文化市场综合执法大队
15. 吉林省长春市二道区文化体育局
16. 吉林省长春市榆树市文化市场综合执法大队
17. 吉林省吉林市文化市场综合执法支队
18. 吉林省延边州敦化市文化市场综合执法大队
19. 吉林省四平市文化市场综合执法支队
20. 吉林省四平市梨树县文化市场综合执法大队
21. 吉林省通化市文化市场综合执法支队
22. 吉林省梅河口市文化市场综合行政执法大队
23. 吉林省白城市洮南市文化市场综合执法大队
24. 吉林省松原市前郭县文化市场综合执法大队
25. 黑龙江省哈尔滨市文化市场行政执法局
26. 黑龙江省鹤岗市文化市场综合执法支队
27. 上海陈某某等侵犯网络游戏著作权案专案组（上海市公安局经侦总队二支队、上海市公安局徐汇分局经侦支队、上海市公安局徐汇分局康健新村派出所、上海市徐汇区人民法院民三庭）
28. 上海海关法规处
29. 上海市嘉定区人民检察院公诉科
30. 上海“易查小说网”侵犯著作权案专案组（上海市公安局治安总队食品药品犯罪侦查支队、上海市公安局网安总队三队、上海市浦东新区人民检察院公诉二处、上海市浦东新区人民法院知识产权审判庭）
31. 上海罗某某、欧某某侵犯著作权案专案组（上海市杨浦区人民法院知识产权庭、上海市杨浦区人民检察院金融检察科、上海市公安局杨浦分局中原路派出所）
32. 上海市互联网信息办公室网络管理处
33. 江苏省南通市公安局开发区分局经侦大队
34. 江苏省连云港市文化行政综合执法支队
35. 江苏省常州市文化行政综合执法支队
36. 江苏省南京市文化综合执法总队三支队
37. 江苏省镇江市版权局
38. 江苏省淮安市文化行政综合执法支队
39. 江苏省淮安市版权局
40. 江苏省宿迁市文化行政综合执法支队
41. 浙江省温州市苍南县公安局治安二大队
42. 浙江省东阳市公安局千祥派出所
43. 浙江省嘉兴市文化广电新闻出版局
44. 浙江省海宁市文化市场行政执法大队
45. 浙江丽水郑某某侵犯著作权案专案组（浙江省丽水市文化广电新闻出版局、浙江省丽水市莲都区文化广电新闻出版局）
46. 浙江省温州市鹿城区文化广电新闻出版局
47. 浙江宁波“12·8”侵犯著作权案专案组（浙江省宁波市文化市场行政执法总队、浙江省余姚市文化广电新闻出版局）
48. 浙江省温州市公安局龙湾区分局永中派出所
49. 安徽省“扫黄打非”领导小组办公室
50. 福建省泉州市文化市场综合执法支队
51. 福建省厦门市文化市场综合执法支队
52. 福建省福州市仓山区人民检察院
53. 福建省泉州市德化县版权局
54. 福建省泉州市版权局
55. 福建省通信管理局信息通信管理处（互联网管理处）
56. 江西省南昌市文化市场综合执法支队一大队
57. 江西省南昌市文化市场综合执法支队二大队
58. 江西省南昌市文化市场综合执法支队四大队
59. 江西省九江市文化市场综合执法支队
60. 江西省萍乡市文化市场综合执法支队
61. 江西省新余市文化市场综合执法支队
62. 江西省鹰潭市文化市场综合执法支队
63. 江西省赣州市安远县文化市场管理办公室
64. 江西省赣州市于都县文化市场综合执法大队
65. 江西省赣州市兴国县文化广电新闻出版局
66. 江西省上饶市文化市场综合执法支队
67. 江西省上饶市万年县文化广电新闻出版局
68. 江西省上饶市弋阳县文化广电新闻出版局
69. 江西省鄱阳县版权局
70. 江西省新闻出版广电稽查总队
71. 江西省新闻出版广电监管中心
72. 山东潍坊王某某销售侵权复制品案专案组（山东省潍坊市文化市场综合执法局、山东省潍坊市公安局治安支队）
73. 山东济宁江某某等著作权案专案组（山东省济宁市公安局、山东省济宁市公安局市中区分局治安管理大队、山东省济宁市文化市场综合执法局）
74. 山东省平度市文化市场行政执法局
75. 山东省潍坊市坊子区文化市场综合执法局

76. 山东省潍坊市奎文区文化市场综合执法局
77. 山东省东营市文化市场综合执法局
78. 山东省德州市文化市场综合执法局“扫黄打非”工作科
79. 山东省聊城市文化市场综合执法局
80. 山东省青岛市黄岛区综合行政执法局
81. 山东省即墨市文化市场行政执法局
82. 山东省潍坊市安丘市文化市场综合执法局
83. 河南省“扫黄打非”办公室
84. 河南省检察院侦查监督处
85. 河南省驻马店市文化市场综合执法支队
86. 河南省驻马店市汝南县文化市场综合执法大队
87. 湖北省文化厅文化市场处
88. 湖北省公安厅治安总队
89. 湖北省武汉市人民检察院审查批捕部
90. 湖北省十堰市文化市场综合执法支队
91. 湖北省互联网信息办公室网络管理处
92. 湖南省湘西土家族苗族自治州凤凰县文化市场综合执法局
93. 湖南省益阳市文化市场综合执法局
94. 湖南省永州市文化市场综合执法局
95. 湖南省岳阳市文化市场综合执法局版权执法大队
96. 湖南省长沙市宁乡县文化市场综合执法局
97. 湖南省长沙市知识产权局
98. 湖南省株洲市文化市场综合执法局
99. 湖南省衡阳市文化市场综合执法局
100. 广东省深圳市宝安区人民法院民事审判第四庭
101. 广东省珠海市文化市场综合执法支队
102. 广东省汕头市文化市场综合执法大队
103. 广西壮族自治区南宁市文化新闻出版广电局
104. 广西壮族自治区桂林市全州县文化市场综合执法大队
105. 广西壮族自治区桂林市资源县文化新闻出版广播电视体育局
106. 广西壮族自治区钦州市钦南区文化体育广电局
107. 重庆市渝中区文化市场行政执法大队
108. 重庆市大足区文化市场行政执法支队
109. 重庆市奉节县文化市场行政执法大队
110. 四川省通信管理局信息通信管理处
111. 四川“6·14”田某侵犯著作权案专案组（四川省遂宁市文化市场综合执法支队、四川省遂宁市大英县文化体育广播电影电视局）
112. 四川省德阳市文化市场综合执法支队
113. 四川省德阳市旌阳区文化市场综合执法大队
114. 四川省泸州市泸县文化市场综合执法大队
115. 贵州省版权局版权处
116. 云南省新闻出版广电局版权管理处
117. 云南省曲靖市文化市场综合行政执法支队
118. 昆明海关所属打洛海关
119. 陕西省西安市文化市场行政执法总队
120. 陕西省通信管理局网络安全管理处
121. 甘肃省兰州市文化市场行政执法支队
122. 宁夏回族自治区版权局版权管理处
123. 新疆维吾尔自治区石河子市文化市场执法大队
124. 新疆维吾尔自治区阿勒泰市文化市场稽查大队
125. 新疆维吾尔自治区巴州文化体育广播影视局
126. 中国文化报社

【有功个人一等奖】

1. 张牙（工业和信息化部信息通信管理局）
2. 刘晓飞（公安部治安管理局一处）
3. 吕伟（公安部经济犯罪侦查局九处）
4. 宿海涛（国家网信办网络综合协调管理和执法督查局专项行动处）
5. 孙勇（全国打击侵权假冒工作领导小组办公室督察联络组）
6. 尹志军（河北省版权局版权管理处）
7. 河北保定霍某某销售侵权复制品案专案组个人（王辉，河北省保定市市委政法委执法监督一处；范立新，河北省保定市公安局治安支队；衡国柱，河北省保定市文化市场行政执法大队；甄明辉，河北省保定市文化市场行政执法大队综合处；马世珍，河北省保定市文化市场行政执法大队）
8. 吉林《智慧白山》手机 APP 客户端侵犯著作权案专案组个人（杜宇震、王春和，吉林省版权局版权管理处）
9. 上海青声网络科技有限公司侵犯信息网络传播权案专案组个人（王浩、万赟、陈启光，上海市文化市场行政执法总队稽查五处）
10. 王骞（上海市版权局版权管理执法处）
11. 余列（江苏省版权局版权管理处）
12. 江苏昆山“12·15”制售侵权盗版图书案专

案组个人（王斌、朱益新、陶亮亮，江苏省昆山市文化行政综合执法大队；朱屹峰，江苏省昆山市公安局治安警察大队三中队；徐华，江苏省昆山市人民法院知识产权庭）
13. 江苏张家港“风雨文学网”侵犯著作权案专案组个人（陈世海、陈彩芬，江苏省苏州张家港市文化广电新闻出版局；李明，江苏省苏州张家港市文化行政综合执法大队；俞李杨，江苏省苏州张家港市公安局网络警察大队；李海光，江苏省苏州张家港市公安局塘市派出所）
14. 周俊（江苏省常州市文化行政综合执法支队）
15. 福建福州“1·22”赖某某销售盗版光盘案专案组个人（刘超、刘莹、余洪亮，福建省福州市文化市场综合执法支队；郑必凤，福建省福州市公安局台江分局新港派出所；王明亮，福建省福州市鼓楼区法院知识产权庭）
16. 李青（山东省新闻出版广电局版权管理处）
17. 高振江（山东省新闻出版广电局反非法和违禁出版物处）
18. 杜荣华（山东省青岛市文化市场行政执法局）
19. 孙晨光（山东省青岛市文化市场行政执法局）
20. 山东淄博“4·8”侵犯著作权案专案组个人（徐海涛、张伟，山东省淄博市文化市场执法支队；李志强，山东省淄博市人民检察院；史志伟、张洪强，山东省淄博市公安局直属分局）
21. 张安军（山东省泰安市文化广电新闻出版局）
22. 山东威海新航船务服务中心复制、发行侵权图书案专案组个人（张海舰，山东省威海市文化市场综合执法局；韩兵，山东省威海市文化市场综合执法局稽查二队）
23. 山东菏泽“4·13”志明印务侵犯著作权案专案组个人（邓作霆、张琛、吕秀兰，山东省菏泽市文化市场综合执法局；段强，山东省菏泽市公安局牡丹区分局经济侦查大队）
24. 河南“11·17”侵权案专案组个人（逯熙鹏，河南省巩义市文化广电新闻出版局；杨成国，河南省巩义市“扫黄打非”工作领导小组办公室；钟利明，河南省巩义市文化新闻出版管理办公室；薛锦，河南省郑州市人民检察院公诉三处；张德庆，河南省巩义市公安局经侦大队）
25. 陕西西安莱安电子科技有限公司侵犯电影作品著作权案专案组个人（陈选康、孙涛，陕西省版权局版权管理处）
26. 郁致原（国家新闻出版广电总局信息中心运行维护部）
27. 雍婷婷（中国版权保护中心法律部）
28. 张贺（人民日报社）
29. 曾文甫（中央电视台社会新闻部）
30. 史竞男（新华社中央新闻采访中心政文采访室）
31. 赖名芳（中国新闻出版广电报社）

【有功个人二等奖】

1. 梁振东（中央宣传部出版局）
2. 魏磊（最高人民法院刑一庭）
3. 贝金欣（最高人民检察院公诉厅）
4. 北京一点网聚科技有限公司侵犯著作权案专案组个人（刘立新、熊伟、孙琦健，北京市文化市场行政执法总队执法五队）
5. 郝炜（内蒙古自治区版权局版权处）
6. 林明富（上海市文化市场行政执法总队稽查三处）
7. 谷申安（上海市文化市场行政执法总队稽查三处）
8. 江春明（上海市文化市场行政执法总队稽查三处）
9. 沈畅（上海市长宁区人民检察院公诉科）
10. 王海岸（江苏省常州市钟楼区人民法院知识产权案件综合审判庭）
11. 孙飞（江苏省常州市钟楼公安分局网络安全保卫大队）
12. 江苏“CHD网”侵犯著作权案专案组个人（唐海宁，江苏省扬州市文化行政综合执法支队；刘翀、薛康，江苏省扬州市公安局治安警察支队治安行动大队；许杰，江苏省扬州市公安局治安警察支队办公室；梅健，江苏省扬州市公安局治安警察支队场所行业管理大队）
13. 杨敏（浙江省台州市公安局治安支队）
14. 汪闻敏（安徽省版权局版权管理处）
15. 谢振芳（福建省版权局版权管理处）
16. 游冰峰（福建省人民检察院侦查监督处）
17. 福建福州“3·16”揭某某非法销售盗版光盘案专案组个人（许庆安、陈四兴，福建省福州市文化市场综合执法支队；陈椿，福建省福州市公安局台江分局新港派出所；谢国志，福建省福州市鼓楼区法院知识产权庭）

18. 杨旭（江西省新闻出版广电局版权管理处）
19. 杨雨露（江西省赣州市兴国县文化市场综合执法大队）
20. 江西南昌打击教育机构侵犯著作权案专案组个人（邹爱强、罗盛磊、赵扬超，江西省南昌市文化市场综合执法支队）
21. 江西打击私人影院侵犯著作权案专案组个人（饶兴奇、王小林、魏勇兵，江西省南昌市文化市场综合执法支队）
22. 山东潍坊王某某销售侵权复制品案专案组个人（刘肖宁、高增光，山东省潍坊市文化市场综合执法局；薛林、尹高峰，山东省潍坊市公安局）
23. 山东泰安石某某侵犯著作权案专案组个人（吕宗峰、杨红雨，山东省泰安市文化市场综合执法支队执法二科）
24. 山东泰安中天建筑书店侵犯著作权案专案组个人（赵永磊，山东省泰安市文化市场综合执法支队；刘绍强，山东省泰安市文化广电新闻出版局版权科）
25. 山东威海天骄书店出售假冒他人署名作品案专案组个人（辛进波、王华栋，山东省威海市文化市场综合执法局稽查二队）
26. 山东滨州“7·11”商某某侵犯著作权案专案组个人（吕金生、王文静、冯天翔，山东省滨州市文化市场综合执法局）
27. 江尔玉（山东省潍坊市昌乐县文化市场综合行政执法局）
28. 山东“你的世界网”侵犯网络游戏著作权案专案组个人（张兆鸿、孟杰、田阳，山东省济宁市任城区文化市场综合执法局）
29. 李峰（河南省版权局版权管理处）
30. 陈红梅（河南省焦作市武陟县人民检察院侦查监督科）
31. 河南“1·26”侵犯知识产权案专案组个人（王星，河南省郑州市荥阳市文化广播电视新闻出版局；卢凯鹏、李鑫鑫、姬小静，河南省郑州市荥阳市人民检察院侦查监督科）
32. 河南南阳系列侵犯著作权案专案组个人（栗山、佘向东、赵万刚，河南省南阳市文化市场综合执法支队）
33. 董全生（河南省南阳市文化市场综合执法支队）
34. 胡先阳（湖北省版权局版权管理处）
35. 方植（湖北省公安厅网络安全保卫总队）
36. 湖南谭某某等侵犯著作权案专案组个人（左建建，湖南省公安厅治安总队；唐志刚、潘高军、盘贤力，湖南省永州市公安局零陵分局治安大队）
37. 费晓（广东省深圳市中级人民法院知识产权审判庭）
38. 陈铃铃（广东省深圳市福田区人民法院知识产权审判庭）
39. 广东合富辉煌（中国）房地产顾问有限公司侵犯著作权案专案组个人（黄俊禧、梁斯洛，广东省广州市文化市场综合行政执法总队执法五处）
40. 何玲（广东省深圳市市场和质量监督管理委员会福田市场监督管理局稽查科稽查大队）
41. 阎桦泽（广西壮族自治区版权局版权管理处）
42. 曾伯林（海南省版权局版权处）
43. 海南王某某侵犯著作权案专案组个人（牛金虎，海南省“扫黄打非”领导小组办公室；宋小怡、林世龙，海南省海口市公安局龙华分局滨海派出所；杜伟，海南省海口市人民检察院；陈孝诚，海南省海口市龙华区人民检察院）
44. 王志坚（四川省版权局版权管理处）
45. 周海滨（贵州省贵阳市文化市场综合执法支队三处）
46. 施晓娟（新疆维吾尔自治区版权局版权处）
47. 新疆常某侵犯著作权案专案组个人（陈新平，新疆维吾尔自治区乌鲁木齐市新闻出版局；王合生、邵威钧、李新革，新疆维吾尔自治区乌鲁木齐市文化市场稽查支队；王中锋，新疆维吾尔自治区乌鲁木齐市水磨沟区公安分局南湖南路派出所）
48. 樊国斌（国家新闻出版广电总局出版产品质量监督检测中心出版物鉴定室）
49. 郑直（中央电视台版权和法律事务室）
50. 王志艳（新华网）
51. 张红兵（法制日报社）
52. 成琪（中国经济网）
53. 郑晓红（《中国版权》杂志社）
54. 刘仁（中国知识产权报社）

【有功个人三等奖】

1. 赵江涛（中央宣传部新闻局）
2. 庞文建（公安部互联网违法犯罪信息中心）
3. 吴思洁（文化部文化市场司执法指导监督处）

4. 解新红（海关总署政策法规司知识产权处）
5. 宁军红（国家工商总局反垄断与反不正当竞争执法局经济检查处）
6. 王健兵（国家互联网信息办公室网络应急管理和网络舆情局）
7. 李明（商务部条约法律司知识产权法律处）
8. 鹿原（中国互联网络信息中心）
9. 北京创新伙伴教育科技有限公司侵犯著作权人作品案专案组个人（史曙亮，北京市文化市场行政执法总队执法五队；王辉、张少帅，北京市文化市场行政执法总队法制监督处）
10. 天津育人书店侵犯著作权案专案组个人（吕学军、张永军，天津市文化市场行政执法总队）
11. 天津新天空外国语培训学校侵犯著作权案专案组个人（李利强、艾沙提、李连胜，天津市河西区文化市场行政执法大队）
12. 天津市职业大学侵犯著作权案专案组个人（王哲、安鸣，天津市文化市场行政执法总队）
13. 李文卫（天津市版权局版权处）
14. 刘柏汛（河北省通信管理局网络安全管理处）
15. 狄月清（山西省版权局版权管理处）
16. 内蒙古通辽销售盗版工具书案专案组个人（吴忠利、王刚、杨秋萧，内蒙古自治区通辽市文化市场综合执法局）
17. 内蒙古鄂尔多斯博物馆造型音乐盒侵权案专案组个人（郭栋、辛晨环、石瑞，内蒙古自治区鄂尔多斯市文化市场综合执法局）
18. 辽宁“钢甲洪流网”侵犯著作权案专案组个人（李安庆、田大鹏、周沫，辽宁省版权局版权管理处；张志、张文利，辽宁省通信管理局电信管理处）
19. 辽宁沈阳法库县东湖二中侵犯著作权案专案组个人（任东晖、张洋，辽宁省沈阳市文化行政执法总队直属执法四大队）
20. 辽宁沈阳龙生源书店侵犯著作权案专案组个人（刘曙光、汤景海、孙丹阳，辽宁省沈阳市文化行政执法总队直属执法四大队）
21. 华娱嘉恒（大连）传媒有限公司侵犯著作权案专案组个人（吴浩、王吉庆、阎寒，辽宁省大连市文化市场综合执法总队指挥调度中心）
22. 张丽（辽宁省大连市金州区人民法院）
23. 高翔（辽宁省大连市经济技术开发区人民检察院）
24. 陈哲（吉林省长春市文化市场综合执法支队）
25. 吉林长春丁某侵犯著作权案专案组个人（朱爽、李洋、付伟峰，吉林省长春市文化市场综合执法支队）
26. 文春怀（吉林省长春市二道区文化市场综合执法大队）
27. 吉林优学网络科技有限公司侵犯著作权案专案组个人（常恭赫、金玉柱、闫海春，吉林省吉林市文化广电新闻出版局）
28. 吉林敦化远达驾校复制盗版教材案专案组个人（费泽忠、刘中华、王立明，吉林省延边朝鲜族自治州敦化市文化市场综合执法大队）
29. 孟立夫（吉林省四平市文化市场综合执法支队）
30. 梁洪臣（吉林省四平市梨树县文化市场综合执法大队）
31. 李树平（吉林省公主岭市文化广电新闻出版局）
32. 吉林公主岭系列网吧网络游戏侵权案专案组个人（杨易丽、于锋、赵新宇，吉林省公主岭市文化市场综合执法大队）
33. 吉林通化乐尚网城游戏软件侵权案专案组个人（刘丽、徐波、张东辉，吉林省通化市文化市场综合执法支队）
34. 刘洋（吉林省通化市辉南县文化市场综合执法大队）
35. 吉林辉南伟丹网络时空侵犯著作权案专案组个人（付冠桦、姜德刚，吉林省通化市辉南县文化市场综合执法大队）
36. 吉林盛大网络中心侵犯著作权案专案组个人（刘学国、马连海，吉林省通化市辉南县文化市场综合执法大队）
37. 马洪新（吉林省梅河口市文化市场综合行政执法大队）
38. 吉林洮南博联网吧侵犯著作权案专案组个人（孙伟东、彭广宇、周相东，吉林省白城市洮南市文化市场综合执法大队）
39. 吉林洮南极速网吧侵犯著作权案专案组个人（曹春林、王立军，吉林省白城市洮南市文化市场综合执法大队）
40. 吉林松原诚信学生书局侵犯著作权案专案组个人（高文生、姜英华，吉林省松原市文化市场综合执法支队）
41. 白淑杰（吉林省白山市江源区文化广电新闻

出版局）
42. 于海航（黑龙江省哈尔滨市文化市场行政执法局）
43. 崔森（黑龙江省工商局竞争执法处）
44. 华毓军（黑龙江省鹤岗市文化市场综合执法支队）
45. 黑龙江“5·12”齐齐哈尔疯趴私人影院侵权播放影视作品案专案组个人（刘国强，黑龙江省齐齐哈尔市文广新局；张胜西、张延军、王宇，黑龙江省齐齐哈尔市文化市场综合执法支队）
46. 上海海关查处外籍人员携带盗版物品进出境专项整治专案组个人（何良君，上海车站海关旅检科；钱佳俊，上海海关现场业务二处海运行李物品监管科；卢金涛，上海海关现场业务三处船舶调研科）
47. 王蛟（上海市通信管理局互联网管理处）
48. 顾擎天（上海市互联网信息办公室网络管理处）
49. 孙青浩（江苏省南通市公安局开发区分局经侦大队）
50. 刘明芳（江苏省通信管理局网络安全管理处）
51. 邓华（江苏省公安厅网络安全保卫总队案件查处科）
52. 江苏张家港“2020kk 电影网”侵犯著作权案专案组个人（葛显平、蔡平，江苏省苏州张家港市文化行政综合执法大队；杨芬，江苏省苏州张家港市公安局网络警察大队；赵小竹，江苏省苏州张家港市公安局三兴派出所；刘艺琳，江苏省苏州张家港市人民法院民三庭）
53. 江苏南京侵犯软件著作权系列案专案组个人（蔡健，江苏省南京市文化综合执法总队；曹岚、汪庆平，江苏省南京市文化综合执法总队三支队；张红伟，江苏省南京市版权局版权管理处）
54. 江苏如皋慧轩书店侵犯著作权案专案组个人（冒曙光、陈建军，江苏省南通如皋市文体旅游综合执法大队）
55. 胡艳艳（江苏省沭阳县文化行政综合执法大队）
56. 李海辉（江苏省常州市文化行政综合执法支队）
57. 谢万能（江苏省南京市江宁区文化综合执法大队）
58. 舒茂森（江苏省沭阳县文化行政综合执法大队）
59. 浙江嘉兴系列侵犯著作权案专案组个人（顾天存、陆冰，浙江省嘉兴市文化市场行政执法支队）
60. 浙江海宁美术作品系列侵犯著作权案专案组个人（金珂星、李琴、史艳红，浙江省海宁市文化市场行政执法大队）
61. 浙江宁波爱沐文化交流中心通过网络向公众传播侵权作品案专案组个人（潘剑武、宫卫波、柳伟，浙江省宁波市海曙区文化市场行政执法大队）
62. 徐庆宵（浙江省金华市公安局治安支队）
63. 郭林（浙江省公安厅治安监督管理总队）
64. 方胜（浙江省金华市文化行政综合执法支队）
65. 安徽萧县在线网络科技公司侵犯著作权案专案组（陈志强、吕维爱，安徽省宿州市文化市场综合执法支队；陈从记、杨同站、刘龙，安徽省宿州市萧县文化市场综合执法大队）
66. 安徽刘某某侵犯著作权案专案组个人（陈江丽、陈勇、秦家香、史继华，安徽省合肥市文化市场综合执法支队）
67. 王林霞（安徽省通信管理局网络安全管理处）
68. 孙德勇（安徽省公安厅治安总队）
69. 福建“8·22”非法销售盗版光盘案专案组（曾朝晖，福建省泉州市文化市场综合执法支队；陈能贤，福建省泉州市文化市场综合执法支队直属执法二大队；吴艺敏，福建省泉州晋江市文化市场综合执法大队；陈梓龙，福建省泉州晋江市公安局滨江派出所；许江洪，福建省泉州晋江市公安局滨江派出所）
70. 林卯聪（福建省漳州市芗城区人民法院刑二庭）
71. 福建厦门市游动网络公司侵犯动漫作品纠纷案专案组个人（陈忠南、林翔莺，福建省厦门市文化市场综合执法支队二大队；洪露，福建省厦门市文化市场综合执法支队执法监督科）
72. 福建厦门兴才职业技术学院擅自销售盗版教材案专案组个人（颜耿逸，福建省厦门市文化市场综合执法支队执法监督科；蔡云斌、林启森，福建省厦门市文化市场综合执法支队二大队）
73. 江西熊某侵犯著作权案专案组个人（涂晓斌、

龚文其，江西省南昌市公安局直属分局三大队）
74. 江西人源职业培训学校侵犯著作权案专案组个人（黄一洋、张雪梅、胥辉，江西省南昌市文化市场综合执法支队）
75. 江西“144电影网”影视作品侵权案专案组个人（陈小毛、秦刚、徐洪钧，江西省南昌市文化市场综合执法支队）
76. 江西九江裕兴文体书店销售侵权出版物案专案组个人（沈师、赵金星，江西省九江市文化市场综合执法支队）
77. 江西九江浔阳区浔视界私人咖吧放映侵权影片案专案组个人（朱斌、法亮，江西省九江市文化市场综合执法支队）
78. 金耀武（江西省九江市文化市场综合执法支队）
79. 江西九江市创业培训中心侵权盗版案专案组个人（潘骏、张磊、丁峰，江西省九江市文化市场综合执法支队）
80. 谭涛（江西省景德镇市文化市场综合执法支队稽查一科）
81. 贾峰（江西省萍乡市安源区文化市场综合执法大队）
82. 江西新余朱某某侵犯著作权案专案组个人（蓝波、张小安、刘刚，江西省新余市文化市场综合执法支队）
83. 董显祥（江西省赣州市文化广电新闻出版局）
84. 尧飞武（江西省赣州市安远县文化市场管理办公室）
85. 谭春森（江西省赣州市于都县文广新局执法大队）
86. 江西吉安步步高书店侵权盗版出版物案专案组个人（张平，江西省吉安市文广新局；王敏杰、周建忠，江西省吉安市永新县文广新局；尹迈仔、彭翠，江西省吉安市永新县文广新局文化市场综合执法大队）
87. 江西抚州日月书城侵权盗版案专案组个人（胡光斌、杨慧建、付峻峰，江西省抚州市文化综合执法支队）
88. 江西瑞金大润发侵权盗版案等5起案件专案组个人（杨振华、黄庚明，江西省瑞金市文化广电新闻出版局）
89. 江西省鄱阳阳光书店侵权盗版案等5起案件专案组个人（徐邦平、黄礼芳、王福斌，江西省鄱阳县版权局）
90. 山东济宁江某某销售侵权盗版图书案专案组个人（樊存常、王天湖、颜廷爱，山东省济宁市文化市场综合执法局；宗恩峰，山东省济宁市公安局治安警察支队；张亚斌，山东省济宁市公安局市中区分局治安管理大队）
91. 柴寿宁（山东省青岛市黄岛区综合行政执法局）
92. 刘成爱（山东省平度市文化市场行政执法局）
93. 王子清（山东省安丘市文化市场综合执法局）
94. 孙天舒（山东省商务厅）
95. 朱全明（山东省青岛市市北区综合行政执法局）
96. 邱永伟（山东省青岛即墨市文化市场行政执法局）
97. 李昌（山东省青岛即墨市文化市场行政执法局）
98. 山东平度“3·16”侵犯著作权专案组个人（李书伟，山东省青岛市平度市公安局治安大队；金秉坤，山东省青岛市平度市法院刑事审判庭；付晓、王五生、邹少卫，山东省青岛市平度市文化市场行政执法局）
99. 丁文清（山东省潍坊市奎文区文化市场综合执法局）
100. 张龙华（山东省诸城市文化市场综合执法局）
101. 王立国（山东省安丘市文化市场综合执法局）
102. 谭相忍（山东省聊城市东昌府区文化广电新闻出版局）
103. 申明曾（河南省公安厅治安总队二支队）
104. 毛志广（河南省新闻出版广电局反非法和违禁出版物处）
105. 河南徐某某销售盗版出版物专案组（李乾、梁广益、王宏博，河南省开封市杞县文化广电新闻出版局；王建坤，河南省开封市“扫黄打非”办公室；王伟，河南省开封市文化广电新闻出版局）
106. 周来来（湖北省互联网信息办公室网络管理处）
107. 陈倩（湖北省通信管理局网络安全管理处）
108. 纪永康（湖北省公安厅经侦总队）
109. 江光成（湖北省公安厅治安总队治安管理支队）
110. 丁晓锡（湖北省潜江市文化体育旅游新闻出版局）

111. 湖南田某某侵犯影视作品著作权案专案组个人（龙伟、张希、王宴，湖南省湘西土家族苗族自治州凤凰县文化市场综合执法局）
112. 湖南衡岳公司侵犯美术作品著作权案专案组个人（刘意福、尹忠国、沈蓓，湖南省衡阳市文化市场综合执法局）
113. 陈炜（湖南省衡阳市文化市场综合执法局）
114. 符超（湖南省衡阳市文化市场综合执法局）
115. 王松林（湖南省衡阳市文化市场综合执法局）
116. 湖南啡影公司侵犯影视作品著作权案专案组个人（胡文艺、钟淙，湖南省衡阳市文化市场综合执法局）
117. 湖南大影咖啡馆侵犯影视作品著作权案专案组个人（尹承丽、张宇、谭啸，湖南省长沙市知识产权局）
118. 娄卫华（湖南省长沙市宁乡县文化市场综合执法局）
119. 贺远（湖南省长沙市宁乡县文化市场综合执法局）
120. 湖南陈某侵犯著作权案专案组个人（刘立新、胡巍、张建华，湖南省怀化市文化市场综合执法局）
121. 湖南壹捌玖伍主题咖啡厅影片侵权案专案组个人（谭琪琳、王建文、谢建明，湖南省娄底市文化市场综合执法大队）
122. 湖南岳阳市侵犯软件著作权系列专案组（刘伟、李军、曾利宏，湖南省岳阳市文化市场综合执法局）
123. 湖南华某某侵犯影视作品著作权案专案组个人（李灵钧、张德文、唐庆平，湖南省永州市文化市场综合执法局）
124. 颜桂元（湖南省株洲市文化市场综合执法局）
125. 郭宁（广东省中山市第二人民法院民三庭）
126. 孙寒梅（广东省人民检察院）
127. 刘立（广东省深圳市市场和质量监督管理委员会南山市场监督管理局知识产权科）
128. 傅民（广东省珠海市文化市场综合执法支队）
129. 钟科念（广西壮族自治区南宁市文化市场综合执法支队）
130. 梁艳（广西壮族自治区南宁市兴宁区文化市场综合执法大队）
131. 广西柳州掌上网络科技有限公司网络侵犯录像制品著作权案专案组个人（刘川华，广西壮族自治区柳州市文化新闻出版广电局；潘星池，广西壮族自治区柳州市文化市场综合执法支队；李兵，广西壮族自治区柳州市文化市场综合执法支队）
132. 田源（重庆市文化市场行政执法总队）
133. 金义汉（重庆市奉节县文化委员会）
134. 陶云（四川省通信管理局信息通信管理处）
135. 四川“3·26”新禹书店侵权盗版案专案组个人（刘永黴，四川省出版物市场稽查总队；肖梅，四川省成都市文化市场综合执法总队；王黎莉，四川省成都市人民检察院公诉二处）
136. 四川李某某侵权案专案组个人（黄晓楠、黄光有，四川省成都市文化市场综合执法总队）
137. 四川德阳扬帆书店发行侵犯他人著作权案专案组个人（邓爱明、黄泽强，四川省德阳市文化市场综合执法支队）
138. 四川卢某某侵犯网络音乐作品著作权案专案组个人（周毅、刘锦宇、兰燕，四川省乐山市文化市场综合执法支队）
139. 四川邹某某、骆某侵犯网络游戏著作权案专案组个人（江媛，四川省宜宾市公安局南溪区分局网安大队；程松，四川省宜宾市南溪区人民检察院）
140. 四川叶某某侵犯著作权案专案组个人（林万平、黎姣，四川省广元市文化市场综合执法支队）
141. 张璐（云南省孟连海关监管科）
142. 陕西晨星图书有限公司侵犯著作权案专案组个人（张宗立、程原力、郑国强、于赵磊、毛凤凤，陕西省西安市文化市场行政执法总队）
143. 刘健（陕西省通信管理局网络安全管理处）
144. 王永生（甘肃省定西市岷县文化广播影视局）
145. 芦世宏（甘肃省兰州市文化市场行政执法支队直属执法大队）
146. 袁娅洲（甘肃省兰州市文化和旅游局出版版权处）
147. 青海张某某销售盗版音像制品案专案组个人（韩学梅、冯卫青，青海省西宁市大通县文化市场综合执法大队）
148. 青海西宁嘉彩印刷有限公司盗印藏文书籍案

专案组个人（王生琦，青海省西宁市城东区文化旅游执法大队；李鹏程，青海省“扫黄打非”领导小组办公室；付成久，青海省版权局版权管理处）

149. 张宁学（宁夏回族自治区版权局版权管理处）

150. 卓莉萍（新疆维吾尔自治区新闻出版广电局出版物市场稽查队）

151. 杨博云（新疆维吾尔自治区阿克苏地区温宿县文化市场稽查大队）

152. 新疆乌鲁木齐名师三人行考试书店侵犯著作权案专案组个人（王文贵，新疆维吾尔自治区乌鲁木齐市新闻出版局；秦晓东、古力娜·马木提、刘涛，新疆维吾尔自治区乌鲁木齐市文化市场稽查支队）

153. 刘志军（新疆维吾尔自治区石河子市文化市场执法大队）

154. 何源（中央人民广播电台中国之声）

155. 李苑（光明日报社）

156. 王座桥（中国互联网新闻中心）

157. 韩莉（河北日报报业集团）

158. 虞伟（南方都市报社）

2016 年中国版权十件大事

［编者按］ 2017 年 3 月 9 日，国家版权局评选出"2016 年中国版权十件大事"。

1. "剑网 2016"专项行动成果显著

2016 年 7 月至 12 月，国家版权局、国家网信办、工信部、公安部联合开展打击网络侵权盗版"剑网 2016"专项行动，重点整治网络文学版权秩序。此次专项行动成果显著，全国共查处网络侵权盗版行政案件 514 件，罚款 294 万元，关闭侵权网站 391 家，涉案金额 2 亿元。通过此次专项行动，我国网络版权秩序持续好转，网络版权生态不断优化。

2. 我国版权产业对 GDP 贡献达 7.28%

2016 年 4 月 27 日，中国新闻出版研究院发布了 2014 年中国版权产业的经济贡献调研结果：2014 年我国版权产业的行业增加值为 46 287.81 亿元人民币，占全国 GDP 的 7.28%。调研结果显示，近年来我国版权产业保持平稳发展态势，版权产业对促进经济社会发展的重要作用日益凸显。

3. 版权司法保护力度不断加大

2016 年 11 月 27 日，中共中央、国务院正式发布《关于完善产权保护制度依法保护产权的意见》，强调加大侵犯知识产权行为的惩治力度。12 月 14 日，北京知识产权法院就北京作协主席刘冠军、山东省作协主席张炜诉书生公司案做出终审判决，变更一审法院仅判赔 1 万元的判决，赔偿数额按照原创稿酬高限每千字 300 元的标准计算。2016 年，人民法院继续提升侵权赔偿数额，加大了版权司法保护力度。

4. 推进《视听表演北京条约》生效取得重大进展

2016 年 7 月 21 日至 22 日，"一带一路"数十个国家代表汇聚北京，举行知识产权高级别会议，其间就《视听表演北京条约》召开专门会议，呼吁各国携手推进《视听表演北京条约》早日生效，为建立公正合理的国际版权制度不懈努力。到 2016 年底，已有 15 个国家批准或加入《视听表演北京条约》，推进条约生效工作取得重大进展。

5. 全国著作权登记总量突破 200 万件

2016 年，我国著作权登记总量达 2 007 698 件，首次突破 200 万件大关，相比 2015 年增长 22.33%。其中，软件著作权登记突破 40 万件。随着我国推进版权强国建设、创新驱动发展战略的有效实施，著作权登记工作实现了新跨越，著作权登记量的大幅增长彰显了我国创新能力的迅速提高。

6. 经中央批准的首届中国版权金奖颁发

2016 年 12 月 5 日，国家版权局与世界知识产权组织在广州举办中国版权金奖颁发仪式，这是经中央批准后举行的首届中国版权金奖。此次中国版权金奖共有《青铜葵花》等 6 个作品奖、腾讯公司等 5 个推广运用奖、重庆市公安局打击假冒伪劣商品犯罪侦查总队等 5 个保护奖和成都市版权局等 4 个管理奖。中国版权金奖是我国版权领域最高奖项，对提升版权创作、运用、保护和管理能力，推动版权强国建设具有显著激励作用。

7. "德化经验"全球共享

2016 年 11 月 14 日至 18 日，中国国家版权局在瑞士日内瓦世界知识产权组织总部举办中国德化陶瓷版权保护优秀成果展，并发布《版权保护促进中国德化陶瓷产业发展的研究》（英文版），向全球推广德化在陶瓷产业版权保护方面的成功经验。"德化经验"对于发展中国家探索版权保护和经济发展的密切关系有重要指导和借鉴作用。

8. 5 家著作权集体管理组织被列入全国性行业协会脱钩试点名单

2016 年 6 月，按照中央关于全国性行业协会与行政机关脱钩的部署与要求，中国音乐著作权协会、中国音像著作权集体管理协会、中国文字著作权协会、中国摄影著作权协会和中国电影著作权协会被列入全国性行业协会脱钩试点名单，开始进行脱钩试点。根据中央规定和实施方案，著作权集体管理组织将厘清与主管机关的关系，强化权利人组织的定位，起到更好为权利人服务的作用。国家版权局继续对著作权集体管理组织履行法定职责，监督、支持其开展活动。

9. 互联网企业积极履行版权保护主体责任

2016年5月23日，百度公司宣布分批次暂时关闭“百度贴吧”文学目录下的全部贴吧，全面整顿和清查其中的盗版侵权内容；10月20日，奇虎360科技有限公司宣布停止个人云盘服务，以强化版权保护。2016年，互联网企业更加重视版权保护，主动规范自身行为，积极履行企业主体责任，与社会各界共同努力促进网络版权秩序不断好转。

10. “网络版权产业研究基地”在腾讯公司设立

2016年10月，国家版权局批准腾讯公司申请，在该公司设立我国首家“网络版权产业研究基地”。该基地将研究总结国内外网络版权产业发展的新趋势、新动态及应对策略，为发展我国网络版权产业提供支持。该基地的成立，体现出大型互联网公司对版权工作的高度重视，表明了版权在网络产业中的重要地位。

2016 CPCC 十大中国著作权人

［编者按］ 2017 年 2 月 22 日，由中国版权保护中心（CPCC）主办的 2017 CPCC 中国版权服务年会开幕，“2016 CPCC 十大中国著作权人”年度评选结果当天揭晓，沈阳机床股份有限公司、北京香橙互动网络科技有限公司、中国歌剧舞剧院、天津春天影业投资发展有限公司、中青新影文化传媒（北京）有限公司、成都盛世尚品文化传播有限责任公司、广联达科技股份有限公司、薛文静、阿尔斯别克·努汉、武汉斗鱼网络科技有限公司被评为 2016 CPCC 十大中国著作权人。

1. 沈阳机床股份有限公司

沈阳机床股份有限公司（以下简称沈阳机床），是沈阳机床（集团）有限责任公司旗下控股的子公司。2016 年在中国版权保护中心登记了 4 件作品。

沈阳机床在推进供给侧结构性改革的大潮中，坚持自主创新，从顶层设计入手，开启了从核心软件到智能制造的新型工业化道路，设计开发出了具有智能、互联特征的数控系统“i5”智能控制系统，并以此为核心制造出世界第一台智能机床——“i5”智能机床，打破了国际高端机床的垄断，实现了数控机床的突破，成为高端制造业创新的典范。

“i5”智能机床是沈阳机床智能产品的代表。作为基于互联网的智能终端，实现了操作、编程、维护和管理的完全智能化。目前，“i5”智能控制系统已经集成搭载到十余款数控机床上，得到市场的高度认可，原创价值得到巨大提升。在全球行业低迷的当下，沈阳机床的“i5”智能机床风景这边独好，市场订单和出货量呈现爆发式增长，出口到 80 多个国家和地区，营销规模超越了久负盛名的日本马扎克和德国的德玛吉公司，为中国的制造业赢得了世界同行的赞誉。

沈阳机床在融合创新发展中，充分认识到版权保护是软件产品开发利用的生命线，不断强化版权保护力度，主动登记，明确权属关系，规避侵权盗版风险，促进智能高端机床的设计研发，增强了企业产品研发升级动力，为实现企业结构优化和有效供给提供了重要保证。

2. 北京香橙互动网络科技有限公司

北京香橙互动网络科技有限公司（以下简称香橙互动）是一家致力于智能快餐厅整体解决方案研发的移动互联网公司。香橙互动用信息化带动商业模式的创新，通过打造全新的信息化服务平台，提升了快餐业的品质，成为快餐业的新业态代表。2016 年在中国版权保护中心登记了 4 件软件作品。

香橙互动独自设计开发的《香橙智能餐厅系统 4.5》《香橙智能餐厅系统——进销存系统 1.0》等软件，在其“人人湘”店中推广应用，有效优化了餐厅成本结构，提升了餐厅运营效益，带动了快餐业的转型升级。在信息平台的助力下，打磨出了全球首家无收银员、无服务员、无采购员、无大厨的“四无未来餐厅”，受到了青年人的喜爱，引导了快餐业的消费潮流，成为互联网＋快餐的领军企业。

香橙互动 2016 年将自主研发的香橙智能快餐厅成套系统销售到 30 多家连锁快餐业，有效解决了困扰餐饮企业的多项经营及管理痛点，改造并降低了餐饮成本结构，得到了行业的认同和可观回报。其建造的餐饮云 SaaS 平台，助力了快餐业的更新换代，受到海外媒体 CNN 的关注和报道。

香橙互动在发展中十分重视版权保护和版权价值的开发利用，积极引领快餐业互联网信息化和消费升级。

3. 中国歌剧舞剧院

中国歌剧舞剧院是中央直属的国家级艺术剧院，曾创作演出了《白毛女》《小二黑结婚》《宝莲灯》《红楼梦》等经典舞台作品，享誉海内外。2016 年在中国版权保护中心登记了民族舞剧《孔子》《昭君》等 7 件作品。

中国歌剧舞剧院随时代而行，坚定文化自信，勇攀高峰，在继承创新中，努力挖掘传统经典，赋予其新的时代内涵和现代表达形式，激活了传统新价值，不断满足文化市场需求，奉献了更多更好的舞台作品。新编舞剧《孔子》《昭君》融合剧院各类作品创意，从人物造型、舞美设计、场面呈现到剧情发展，运用唯美的现代舞台表达，展现了高雅艺术的酷炫，让观众感受到了中国传统文化的魅力，成为传统再造的新史诗。《孔子》应邀多次到海外演出，向海外电视台输出版权，向世界传播中国文化精髓。《昭君》以唯美的舞蹈，现代视觉诠释了王昭君“和亲宁边”的大爱情怀，受邀到北京电视台《传承者之中国意象》展演后，大获热赞，用创新融合的新艺术、新经典感动了观众。

中国歌剧舞剧院十分重视版权保护，主动把优秀作品《孔子》《昭君》进行著作权登记，彰显出其对精品文化的保护意识，为不断挖掘民族舞剧经典的版权价值，传播高雅艺术，提升观众的审美水平，奠定了基础。

4. 天津春天影业投资发展有限公司

天津春天影业投资发展有限公司（以下简称春天影业），是集拍摄、制作、发行、演员经纪等业务于一体的综合性影视文化产业公司。在市场竞争中，坚持拍摄讴歌主旋律的影视剧，凭借《可可西里》《南京南京》《中国合伙人》《为爱坚守》《生死兄弟情》等一系列脍炙人口佳作，赢得了业界好评和观众认可。在中国版权保护中心登记了 34 件作品。

春天影业与时代同频共振，重视原创，努力创新，把最好资源投入到接地气、传播正能量的精品力作上，讲好中国故事，集聚起《妈妈别走》《啊，父老乡亲》《美丽乡村》《京港爱情故事》《于无声处》《摩登 50》《后生》等一批有温度贴民心的影视版权资源，提升了供给能力，在观众心中树立起“春天影业”的品牌，彰显其文化自觉、文化自信、文化自强。融资金、融人才、融资源，吸引越来越多的合作者加盟，为做大做强奠定了坚实基础。

2017 年播映的《啊，父老乡亲》，把镜头聚焦从严治党、农村反腐的社会热点，塑造了一个心中有党、心中有责，为群众办事，敢于同黑恶势力做斗争的基层党员干部形象，成为社会高度关注的年度大戏。

春天影业主动将拥有的版权资源进行著作权登记，明确权属关系，为版权价值的释放衍生保驾护航，成为促进公司融合发展的新动能。

5. 中青新影文化传媒（北京）有限公司

中青新影文化传媒（北京）有限公司（以下简称中青新影）是集影视剧策划、制作、文化艺术交流、公益活动于一体的综合性公司。先后在中国版权保护中心登记了 5 件作品。

中青新影立足未来发展，积极构建促进青年电影人才成长的平台，引导青年人投身反映社会热点的精品创作中，推动公司在电影领域的迅速崛起。他们联合北京电影学院共同扶持年轻导演，以年轻人为主，担纲拍摄的电影《盛先生的花儿》，讲述了家人为患有老年痴呆症的父亲找来一位保姆照料起居，但老人常常把保姆当成过世妻子的故事。透过年轻导演的独特视觉，用电影语言及表达方式，引导社会关注中国老龄化的严重问题，呼唤人们对养老问题的重视；又因是青年人自觉提出爱老、助老的重大民生问题，所以格外引人注目，让影片两次进入微博热门话题，阅读量超过千万人次。在新片扎堆上映的残酷竞争中，该片脱颖而出，获得口碑，发挥了电影在弘扬中华优秀传统上的独特作用。众望所归，在 2016 第十九届上海电影节上，此片收获了最受传媒关注影片、新人导演等大奖，并在首届意大利中国电影节上斩获了最佳编剧奖，让观众终于呼吸到了中国艺术电影的春天气息。

中青新影作为一家充满活力、蓬勃发展的影视新锐公司，自觉将版权保护和发展战略有机融合，主动进行著作权登记，希望通过版权资产的管理，助力公司的快速发展。

6. 成都盛世尚品文化传播有限责任公司

成都盛世尚品文化传播有限责任公司（以下简称盛世尚品），是一家致力于以“中国梦”IP 化运营为手段，实践“版权＋定制＋营销”的平台型文化企业。2016 年在中国版权保护中心登记了 6 件作品。

盛世尚品创作完成的《“中国梦”IP 可行性分析及商业实战初探》，以打造中高端奢侈品牌为目的，构建“魅力东方　理想之家”体验店为载体，提升“东家”品牌价值为突破点，反向布局，聚拢手工艺传承者，融合匠心、匠艺，弘扬地方文化，实现手工艺者“中国梦”的创意蓝图。通过“东家”独特的孵化方式，系统展示具有地方特色的文化产品，带动越来越多衍生品的私人定制，将“工匠精品”和“高端市场”相融合，架构起“创意＋营销模式＋技艺＋实体店（展示平台）＋衍生品”产业链，促进现代消费的转型升级，提升中国品牌的国际影响力。

盛世尚品赋予了“东家”诚信的新内涵，增强了消费者对中国制造和中国品质的信心和消费欲望，为中国品牌走出去打下坚实基础，让创新创造者的成果得到越来越多的回报。

7. 广联达科技股份有限公司

广联达科技股份有限公司（以下简称广联达），作为建筑产业互联网平台服务商，是建筑工程领域信息化产业首家上市公司。2016 年在中国版权保护中心登记了 26 件软件作品。

广联达构建了建筑产业互联网的一站式服务模式，通过软件产品开发、大数据服务和解决方案的提供，积极打造智能化、信息化、网络化的建筑产业服务平台。以融合创新、集成创新为导向，撬动了建筑产业的转型升级，推进了建筑工程领域信息化，规范了建筑工程领域相关标准。围绕工程项目的全生命周期，为建筑全产业链提供信息化工具。

广联达开发的《广联达云计价平台成本测算软件 V5.0》等云计价平台软件是建筑工程造价管理整体解决方案中的核心产品。它采用统一管理平台，追求造价专业分析精细化，用信息技术帮助建筑业内从业人员完成了工程造价、工程施工、工程项目管理等专业工作，大大提升了工作效率，降低了工程成本，促进了行业技术与管理进步。公司以 BIM、云计算为技术支撑，产品从单一的预算软件扩展到包含工程造价、产业金融等九大业务，近百款产品，已为 17 万家企业用户、百万专业工程技术和管理人员提供了专业应用软件。

广联达高度重视版权保护工作，积极主动登记，通过对软件著作权价值的挖掘，带动了传统建筑产业的绿色转型升级。

8. 薛文静

薛文静，家具产品设计师。她在中国版权保护中心登记的“木攻记”，把中国传统技艺榫卯运用到现代家具设计制作中，提升了家具品质，丰富了家具品种，一跃成为实用家具艺术品的新宠。

薛文静在家具设计制作中，融合了传统智慧和现代技艺，大胆打破了传统榫卯的构造方式，重新设计每一个节点，通过两种不同的材质表达榫头和卯眼的咬合关系，将隐藏在家具之内的结构显露在家具之外，并在造型中引入曲面的概念，创新打造了深获行业称赞、收藏家青睐的纯手工系列家具品牌“木攻记”。她的代表作《高背椅》和《脚摇凳》不用一根钉子一抹胶，整件作品就像“鲁班锁”，抽离一根销，便可以将家具完全拆解开来，让使用者获得从未有过的全新体验和视觉享受。榫卯结构在家具设计里的再造，不再仅仅是一种结构，而是一种功能、一种装饰、一种传统技艺和现代创意的完美融合，成为当代家具设计的创新示范，为传统榫卯工艺开辟了新天地。

薛文静在家具设计探索中十分注重创作成果的版权保护，主动将自己设计的作品申请著作权登记，为创作成果保驾护航。

9. 阿尔斯别克·努汉

阿尔斯别克·努汉，是一位来自新疆阿勒泰的哈萨克族年轻动画制作者。2016 年，他在中国版权保护中心登记的动画片《我，来自草原》先后获得了北京大学生电影节最佳动画短片奖、第 11 届亚洲国际青少年电影节最佳动画片奖，并作为海外学生组唯一入围的中国学生作品，获得了第 43 届学生奥斯卡电影奖最佳外语动画短片组提名。

作为北京电影学院动画学院的研究生毕业作品，动画片《我，来自草原》用朴实无华的画风与简洁流畅的线条，描绘和叙述了新疆哈萨克族牧民热爱自然、勇敢坚定、豁达包容的精神世界和感人故事。《我，来自草原》将传统电影的叙事手法与极具哈萨克民族特色的象征手法完美融合，呈现出人与自然和谐相处的意境。

《我，来自草原》用国际化的表达方式，传达了中国文化价值，讲好了中国故事，实现了少数民族文化与现代艺术形式有机融合，丰富了少数民族题材动画片的内容和形式，为创作、发展少数民族动画片提振了信心，更为新疆动画产业的发展增添了一抹亮丽的色彩。

10. 武汉斗鱼网络科技有限公司

武汉斗鱼网络科技有限公司（以下简称斗鱼网络），是国内首家弹幕式直播分享网站。2016 年在中国版权保护中心登记了 19 件软件作品。

斗鱼网络以游戏直播为主，涵盖体育赛事、科技金融、综艺娱乐等多种直播内容，打造新型的网络文化交流共享平台，致力于建立中国最大的视频直播生态产业链，培育供给侧结构性改革的新动能。

斗鱼网络创新了直播平台的商业模式，凸显了“平台经济”和“网红经济”的吸金能力，实现了销售收入 6.2 亿元，为当地贡献税收 6 000 多万元，形成了众多主播、公司、经纪人及观众参与互动的生态链，营造出了以斗鱼直播平台为核心的娱乐集群，打通了“草根”到“艺人”的通道，使任何人都可以在平台上实现零成本创业。基于此，平台日活跃人数达到了 1 500 万，月活跃用户已超过 2 亿人。

斗鱼网络凭借原创内容和融合创新，实现了企业的快速发展，提高了企业对版权保护的认识，强化了企业运用、挖掘版权价值的积极性。

2016年（第九届）全国大学生版权征文获奖名单

［编者按］ 由国家版权局主办，《中国版权》杂志社承办的第九届全国大学生版权征文活动圆满结束。本届征文活动共收到征文2 131篇，其中，本科生组1 445篇，研究生组686篇。经专家评审，最终评选出本科生组：一等奖10名，二等奖30名，三等奖40名，鼓励奖80名；研究生组：一等奖9名，二等奖19名，三等奖31名，鼓励奖60名；组织奖：20名。

一、本科生组获奖名单（排名不分先后）

一等奖（10名）

曹嫣然　南开大学
薛　钰　华东政法大学
熊加玲　华东政法大学
周静平　北京理工大学
郑茗予　湖南大学
王泽钧　中南财经政法大学
秦梦圆　华中师范大学
徐青格　中南民族大学
黄彦霈　中南财经政法大学
范　鑫　西南政法大学

二等奖（30名）

吴　清　扬州大学
曹　磊　天津医科大学
陈　迪　太原师范学院
黄杨昊宇　南开大学
吴思琦　南开大学
邓　策　南开大学
胡正东　北京印刷学院
张思罡　华东政法大学
查汝玲　华东政法大学
张芷璇　华东政法大学
邓若楠　北京理工大学
王宏宇　广东外语外贸大学
王靖文　广东外语外贸大学
曹孔龙　河南科技大学
郭怡萌　河南科技大学
李　坪　江苏师范大学
马艺萌　南京理工大学
胡心怡　南开大学
李　凡　西北政法大学
赵璐妮　上海商学院
程　娅　河南科技大学
高紫琼　华南理工大学
陈明辉　集美大学
郑　菁　重庆理工大学
史明婷　重庆工商大学
朱文洁　中南民族大学
王　静　中南大学
曾　诚　广东外语外贸大学
陈　洁　中南财经政法大学
李　靖　武汉理工大学

三等奖（40名）

陈益华　扬州大学
房　平　南开大学
于　婷　南开大学
李宜楠　南开大学
苗奕凡　南开大学
邓慧杰　南开大学
武宇佳　南开大学
张淑雅　河北大学
吴育伦　华东政法大学
刘　海　华东政法大学
王　莹　华东政法大学
曹宇琦　北京理工大学
白翊婷　北京理工大学
李　鑫　北京印刷学院
赖燕霞　广东外语外贸大学
牛奇川　广西师范大学
冯纪元　河南科技大学

马　赛　江苏师范大学
袁雨祥　江苏师范大学
王熙伦　南京审计大学
吕雪薇　南方医科大学
刘倩倩　南京财经大学
郭明瑞　南京财经大学
贺　煜　南京理工大学
吴林天池　南京大学
姚　叶　西南政法大学
陈嘉伦　湖北文理学院
俞子奇　华中科技大学
卢桧冰　华中师范大学
吴娉婷　集美大学
曹锐涛　兰州大学
倪国伟　南京师范大学
张志鼎　南京师范大学
张茗颖　重庆工商大学
谭燕竺　重庆工商大学
刘灵睿　中南民族大学
郑浩冉　中南民族大学
潘柏华　中南大学
薛桃安　中南财经政法大学
杨　婕　中南财经政法大学

鼓励奖（80 名）

王熙恒　扬州大学
吴　清　扬州大学
刘正翰　西北大学
陈逸宽　西北大学
王东旭　西北大学
李泽岚　太原师范学院
卢　桐　苏州大学
郭　宸　苏州大学
胡　岚　上海大学
王歆玥　山东政法学院
廉春雨　燕山大学
田　然　燕山大学
李文月　南开大学
吴晨銮　南开大学
王志鹏　北京印刷学院
蒋采薇　中原工学院
刘锦璘　北京印刷学院
王林盼　北京印刷学院
李骄阳　北京印刷学院
王梦楠　华北电力大学
王逸娴　华东政法大学
戴文盈　安徽大学
江宗娟　安徽大学
梁新意　安徽大学
李杰昕　北方工业大学
向　鱼　北方工业大学
王鹏宇　北京理工大学
杨雪娟　北京理工大学
洪靓勤　湖南师范大学
彭玉叶　广东外语外贸大学
蔡园欣　广东外语外贸大学
龙柯芯　广东外语外贸大学
杜敏华　广东外语外贸大学
孙云皓　杭州电子科技大学
胡小雅　河南科技大学
廖　翔　河南科技大学
赵亚真　河南科技大学
王卓奇　河南科技大学
王晨蔚　河南科技大学
张　琰　吉林大学
陶　璐　江苏师范大学
彭　娟　江苏师范大学
刘梦笛　南方医科大学
张馨升　南京理工大学
王　仪　南京理工大学
马金仪　西南政法大学
陈　翰　西南政法大学
王天丛　西北政法大学
赵娟念　上海商学院
姚意伦　上海商学院
张琪晨　上海商学院
余佩诗　华南农业大学
曾其五　集美大学
李亚兰　兰州大学
秦燕婷　南京师范大学
梁若琳　南京师范大学
施凌波　南京师范大学
陈　宇　重庆理工大学
徐广辉　重庆理工大学
胡　轶　重庆工商大学
郑成希　重庆工商大学
王　优　重庆工商大学
李国洋　中原工学院
卢　艺　中南民族大学
田梦赟　中南民族大学
邓栩健　中南大学

曾　卓　中南财经政法大学
陈启凡　中南财经政法大学
刘　果　中南财经政法大学
陆晶晶　中南财经政法大学
郑新月　中国传媒大学
王润迪　中国传媒大学
马　泽　云南大学
李健婕　湘潭大学
高　逸　湘潭大学
任祖梁　湘潭大学
吴　磊　西南科技大学
陈　曦　中国政法大学
鲁声遥　中国传媒大学
夏浩胜　西南科技大学

二、研究生组获奖名单（排名不分先后）

一等奖（9名）

王志鹏　华东政法大学
戴　哲　华东政法大学
龚　超　北京外国语大学
王玉凯　中国人民大学
王树磊　南京理工大学
刁　舜　西南交通大学
邵树杰　中国政法大学
文育娟　中南财经政法大学
章倩玲　华中师范大学

二等奖（19名）

李旭颖　华东政法大学
韩倩艺　北京理工大学
高掉梅　北京理工大学
刘　增　北方工业大学
胡谦益　北京外国语大学
杨　珊　重庆理工大学
郑华超　兰州大学
陈帅君　南京理工大学
李　谦　南京师范大学
钟炜杰　西南政法大学
邓思迪　西南政法大学
沈天文　重庆工商大学
彭　瑶　湘潭大学
鞠文杰　山东大学
孙　笑　江苏师范大学
王一如　江苏师范大学
区婉珊　暨南大学
储天阳　东南大学
朱晓睿　清华大学

三等奖（31名）

张　涛　中国政法大学
华忆昕　中国政法大学
刘子银　华东政法大学
阮文楚　华东政法大学
游宛儒　华东政法大学
周梦秋　华东政法大学
罗媛媛　北京理工大学
黄大鹏　北京外国语大学
卓　丽　北京外国语大学
叶东山　暨南大学
吴乙婕　武汉理工大学
王思璐　西北大学
宋天骐　烟台大学
赵　霞　南京理工大学
张芳芳　南京理工大学
祝瑜敏　华中师范大学
张芸芝　法国奥尔良大学
范俊琴　中南大学
牛　巍　中南财经政法大学
王平利　西北政法大学
方　姮　武汉大学
卢惊涛　南京师范大学
张　轩　南京师范大学
刘亚川琦　南京师范大学
蒋美谊　云南大学
张玉菡　江苏师范大学
朱飞宇　江苏师范大学
何淑平　南开大学
张　暄　北京印刷学院
高家伟　扬州大学
刘　辉　湘潭大学

鼓励奖（60名）

黄　斌　中南大学
袁兰娣　中国传媒大学
刘诗蕾　西南政法大学
程烁宇　同济大学
陈秋汝　同济大学
黄　艳　上海大学
李汶蔚　上海交通大学
王　雯　上海交通大学
梁　辰　上海理工大学
安昱睿　天津商业大学
邢王霞　西北政法大学

李　浩　　西北政法大学
杨立孚　　中国政法大学
千　倩　　中国政法大学
李宝霞　　中国政法大学
张　昊　　扬州大学
张　健　　扬州大学
毕海鸥　　扬州大学
郑　栋　　中南财经政法大学
王若邻　　中南财经政法大学
赵燕飞　　中南财经政法大学
李钰龄　　中南财经政法大学
苏恒瑶　　中南财经政法大学
周星宇　　中南财经政法大学
陈珂然　　中南财经政法大学
林明语　　中南财经政法大学
易　磊　　中南财经政法大学
刘　桢　　西安交通大学
苏伦格　　北京印刷学院
王熙元　　北京印刷学院
方月悦　　华东政法大学
张雨林　　华东政法大学
沈一萍　　华东政法大学
何雨菁　　华东政法大学
唐　倩　　华东政法大学
陆梦仙　　华东政法大学
季冬梅　　北京大学
曾令峰　　北京理工大学
郑创新　　北京理工大学
翁　翔　　北京外国语大学
吴小亚　　重庆理工大学
王佩玉　　重庆理工大学
俞　昊　　广东财经大学
胡安栋　　河北经贸大学
刘　思　　河北经贸大学
潘　倩　　华南理工大学
林玉娟　　华侨大学
陈倩蓉　　暨南大学
卢敏明　　南京理工大学
韩文斌　　南京理工大学
阚山湄　　南京理工大学
方　芳　　南开大学
周　梦　　宁波大学
李学文　　厦门大学
康　鑫　　山东大学
姚宏涛　　西北大学
吴晶晶　　浙江工商大学
李　杨　　江苏师范大学
李美静　　江苏师范大学
胡德畅　　中央民族大学

三、组织奖获奖名单（排名不分先后）

南开大学
河南科技大学
扬州大学
江苏师范大学
广东外语外贸大学
北京印刷学院
华东政法大学
华中师范大学
中南财经政法大学
南京师范大学
中南民族大学
北京理工大学
重庆理工大学
西南政法大学
南京理工大学
上海商学院
湖北文理学院
中南大学
燕山大学
云南大学

第十五届输出版、引进版优秀图书推介活动获奖名单

为鼓励引进国外优秀读物，促进输出中华民族优秀文化，推动“走出去”战略的实施，中国版协国际合作出版工作委员会、中国新闻出版研究院、出版参考杂志社联合发起主办了年度输出版、引进版优秀图书推介活动，引起了国内外出版界的广泛关注和好评。

第十五届输出版、引进版优秀图书推介活动从2016年2月份启动，国内各出版单位踊跃报名。经过初评、复评等评审环节，共评出2015年度输出版优秀图书100种，引进版优秀图书78种，年度典型人物4名，年度优秀版权经理人9名。

第十五届输出版、引进版优秀图书推介活动

输出版图书

出版社	书名
外文出版社有限责任公司	习近平谈治国理政
外文出版社有限责任公司	中共十八大：中国梦与世界
人民出版社	学习习近平总书记重要讲话
上海交通大学出版社有限公司	平易近人：习近平的语言力量
五洲传播出版社	中国巨变
广东人民出版社	从耶鲁到东京
中国人民大学出版社	当代中国政治理论读本
人民出版社	改革是中国最大的红利
人民出版社	中国金融体制改革30年回顾与展望
中信出版集团股份有限公司	中国新趋势
中信出版集团股份有限公司	人民币国际化之路
译林出版社	中国经济的现代化
中国社会科学出版社	中国社会巨变和治理
译林出版社	中国未来十年改革之路
中国人民大学出版社	大道之行：中国共产党与中国社会主义
中国社会科学出版社	新中国人权保障发展六十年
商务印书馆有限公司	中欧智慧城市比较研究报告（2014年）
商务印书馆有限公司	中国语言生活状况报告2014
新星出版社有限责任公司	西藏的变迁
新星出版社有限责任公司	见证中国：爱泼斯坦回忆录
复旦大学出版社	博雅教育
中译出版社	中国新生代农民工（英文版）
浙江人民出版社	这就是马云
中信出版集团股份有限公司	参与感：小米口碑营销内部手册
新星出版社有限责任公司	从鸦片战争到解放
社会科学文献出版社	当代中国史研究
中国社会科学出版社	中国历史学30年（1978—2008）
社会科学文献出版社	苏联专家在中国（1948—1960）
上海交通大学出版社有限公司	基于语料库的翻译文体研究
外语教学与研究出版社	论契合——中西文学与翻译
外语教学与研究出版社	中国历史文化导论
商务印书馆有限公司	中国特色社会主义审计理论研究（修订版）

中国人民大学出版社	走向历史的深处——马克思历史观研究
复旦大学出版社	国史概要
辽宁美术出版社有限责任公司	丝绸之路与石窟艺术
北京大学出版社有限公司	本体与常无：经济学方法对话
北京大学出版社有限公司	生态移民政策与地方政府实践：以敖鲁古雅鄂温克生态移民为例
中华书局有限公司	曲院风荷
社会科学文献出版社	日本右翼问题研究
华东师范大学出版社	上海数学・一课一练（第 1 册、第 2 册）
江西人民出版社有限责任公司	中国文化 ABC
安徽美术出版社	中国国家博物馆古代艺术系列丛书（5 册）
中国水利水电出版社	漫画技法圣经（3 册）
江苏人民出版社	图说中国传统艺术（8 卷本）
中国大百科全书出版社有限公司	中华文化百科丛书（10 册）
中国轻工业出版社	近代汉族民间服饰全集
中华书局有限公司	中日论语四十八篇
外语教学与研究出版社	中国雕塑
安徽人民出版社	中国节庆文化丛书（10 册）
广东教育出版社有限公司	岭南文化十大名片（10 册）
生活・读书・新知三联书店	何处是江南
生活・读书・新知三联书店	中国建筑史
生活・读书・新知三联书店	中国雕塑史
上海人民出版社有限责任公司	中国饮食文化史
上海人民出版社有限责任公司	中国园林文化史
上海人民出版社有限责任公司	中国长城史
中华书局有限公司	裂变中的传承
江苏凤凰文艺出版社有限公司	依偎
中国教育图书进出口有限公司 湖南科学技术出版社有限责任公司	三体
安徽文艺出版社	国剧英译系列
北京出版集团	笔尖下的北京城
中国美术出版总社	南京的陷落
五洲传播出版社	追梦中国：商界领袖系列
中华书局有限公司	陶渊明传
宁夏人民教育出版社	拒绝遗忘
四川文艺出版社	琅琊榜
人民文学出版社	隐身衣
山东文艺出版社有限公司	卷卷向前冲
希望出版社	牛肚子里的旅行
新疆青少年出版社	故宫
浙江少年儿童出版社有限公司	中国原创绘本精品系列（6 册）
二十一世纪出版社集团有限公司	熊猫的故事
二十一世纪出版社集团有限公司	孔子学堂
中国美术出版总社	漫画中国历史（繁体）
接力出版社	中国汉字听写大会
江苏凤凰少年儿童出版社有限公司	青铜葵花
江苏凤凰少年儿童出版社有限公司	小水的除夕
四川少年儿童出版社有限公司	奇迹之旅之《万里长城的奥义》
中国少年儿童新闻出版总社	伟大也要有人懂：少年读马克思
机械工业出版社	风资源与微观选址：理论基础与工程应用

高等教育出版社有限公司	群作用手册（第Ⅰ卷、第Ⅱ卷）
高等教育出版社有限公司	可持续生物能源
国防工业出版社	航天智能发射技术——测试、控制与决策
国防工业出版社	飞行器测控与信息传输理论与技术
成都西南交大出版社有限公司	高速铁路道岔设计理论与实践
人民交通出版社股份有限公司	公路生态工程学
人民交通出版社股份有限公司	桥梁概念设计
中国科技出版传媒股份有限公司	中国植物
中国科技出版传媒股份有限公司	非线性超分辨纳米光学及应用
中国科技出版传媒股份有限公司	中国大陆科学钻探工程
中国建筑工业出版社	中国建筑史·中国民居艺术
清华大学出版社	纳米材料与器件导论
化学工业出版社	于康：吃好每天3顿饭
人民邮电出版社	大数据安全技术与应用
浙江大学出版社有限责任公司	口腔微生物学图谱
上海交通大学出版社有限公司	结构生物信息学
上海交通大学出版社有限公司	精神疾病的神经外科治疗
人民卫生出版社有限公司	实用传染病影像学（上、下册）
人民卫生出版社有限公司	腹腔镜胃癌根治术淋巴结清扫技巧
人民卫生出版社有限公司	阻击埃博拉（大众版）（葡萄牙文版）（英文版）

第十五届输出版、引进版优秀图书推介活动
引进版图书

出版单位	书名
上海古籍出版社	考古学：理论、方法与实践（第六版）
四川人民出版社有限公司、中国方正出版社	历史的教训
社会科学文献出版社	野蛮大陆
人民教育出版社有限公司	育人三部曲
新世界出版社	中国，被遗忘的盟友：西方人眼中的抗日战争全史（精装）
北京美术摄影出版社	艺术的力量
浙江大学出版社有限责任公司	道德的起源：美德、利他、羞耻的演化
生活·读书·新知三联书店	武梁祠：中国古代画像艺术的思想性
大象出版社有限公司	全球帝国史——帖木儿之后帝国的兴与衰（1400—2000）
中信出版集团股份有限公司	世界秩序
上海人民出版社有限责任公司	大屠杀：根源、历史与余波
江苏人民出版社	仪式、政治与权力
上海交通大学出版社有限公司	远东国际军事法庭判决书
中国人民大学出版社	大洗牌：全球金融秩序最后角力
复旦大学出版社	世界电影史（全三册）
译林出版社	这受难的国度：死亡与美国内战
中央编译出版社	民主的阴暗面
湖南科学技术出版社有限责任公司	国家为什么会失败
党建读物出版社	权力的任性——人类历史上最糟糕的决策（1～2）
浙江人民出版社	共享经济
中国科技出版传媒股份有限公司	科学的认知基础
重庆出版社	没有我们的世界
四川人民出版社有限公司	激流男孩
安徽文艺出版社	巴尔卡尼亚浴室
广东花城出版社有限公司	第二空间——米沃什诗选

南方出版社	仲冬血液
漓江出版社	姜的味道是热的
中信出版集团股份有限公司	所有我们看不见的光
中华书局有限公司	海豚湾
译林出版社	一个市民的自白
湖南文艺出版社有限责任公司	伯吉斯家的男孩们
黑龙江少年儿童出版社有限公司	我的将军
上海译文出版社	悲伤与理智
重庆出版社	坚不可摧
人民文学出版社	倒带人生
希望出版社	池上池下
明天出版社有限公司	世界插画大师昆廷・布莱克绘本（11 册）
新疆青少年出版社	偷书贼
浙江少年儿童出版社有限公司	不列颠少儿百科全书（4 册）
贵州人民出版社有限公司	地下水下
二十一世纪出版社集团有限公司	不一样的卡梅拉 13
长江少年儿童出版社（集团）有限公司	我的小小烦恼系列（7 册）
知识出版社	看得见的文明史（12 册）
接力出版社	灾难求生系列（8 册）
江苏凤凰少年儿童出版社	小树苗译系列（6 册）
四川少年儿童出版社有限公司	最后的狗武士（3 册）
上海世纪出版股份有限公司少年儿童出版社	小宝贝大世界（幼幼成长图画书纸板书 9 册套装）
中国少年儿童新闻出版总社	瑞典儿童文学大师马丁・维德马克畅销作品：怪怪特工记（1～11）
机械工业出版社	工业 4.0（实践版）：开启未来工业的新模式、新策略和新思维
高等教育出版社有限公司	城市遥感：城市环境监测、集成与建模
西安交通大学出版社有限责任公司	风能利用——理论、设计和应用（第 2 版）
国防工业出版社	稀疏与冗余表示——理论及其在信号与图像处理中的应用
中国水利水电出版社	河流演变学
中航出版传媒有限责任公司	燃气涡轮原理（第 6 版）
电子工业出版社	Python 黑帽子：黑客与渗透测试编程之道
上海世纪出版股份有限公司科学技术出版社	水 4.0
清华大学出版社	概率图模型
华中科技大学出版社有限责任公司	极端非线性光学
上海交通大学出版社有限公司	飞行控制系统设计和实现中的问题
北京大学医学出版社有限公司	克氏外科学（第 19 版）
化学工业出版社	现代分子光化学（1～2）
中国建筑工业出版社	西方建筑理论经典文库・帕拉第奥建筑四书
中国建筑工业出版社	国外城市设计丛书・公共空间与城市空间
中国建筑工业出版社	城市用水与节水手册
中国科技出版传媒股份有限公司	国家信息基础设施的安全保护
人民邮电出版社	视觉之旅：化学世界的分子奥秘（彩色典藏版）
人民邮电出版社	贝叶斯思维：统计建模的 Python 学习法
中国农业科学技术出版社	农业技术转移决策支持系统（DSSAT）在改进非洲施肥技术方面的应用
中国林业出版社	蘑菇病虫害防控彩图手册
上海世纪出版股份有限公司科学技术出版社	胸部影像学
北京大学医学出版社有限公司	凯利风湿病学（第 9 版）
中国农业出版社	默克兽医手册（第 10 版）
化学工业出版社	农药手册

中国科技出版传媒股份有限公司	安德鲁斯临床皮肤病学（原书第 11 版）
人民卫生出版社有限公司	曼氏足踝外科学
人民卫生出版社有限公司	奈特人体解剖学彩色图谱
天津科技翻译出版有限公司	妇科恶性肿瘤手术图谱
天津科技翻译出版有限公司	经自然腔道内镜外科学

第十五届输出版、引进版优秀图书推介活动
推动版权引进输出的典型人物（4 名）

姓　名	单　位
李永强	中国人民大学出版社
李艳辉	北京师范大学出版社（集团）有限公司
张海鸥	新世界出版社有限责任公司
黄和平	安徽科学技术出版社

第十五届输出版、引进版优秀图书推介活动
优秀版权经理人（9 名）

姓　名	单　位
赵欣	北京大学出版社有限公司
张亚男	中信出版集团股份有限公司
李旦	上海交通大学出版社有限公司
安晓露	商务印书馆有限公司
孙玮	生活·读书·新知三联书店
率琦	中国建筑工业出版社
欧阳伟萍	外文出版社有限责任公司
姜珊	五洲传播出版社
潘竞翔	吉林科学技术出版社有限责任公司

版

理论研究

LI LUN YAN JIU

权

2016年著作权法研究综述

向　波*

一、关于著作权法基础理论问题的研究

有学者认为，网络技术的出现，改变了信息拥有者、传播者、使用者三者之间的利益格局，对传统版权制度带来挑战。传播技术创新所引发的版权制度创新，其面临的主要问题包括：明确新的主体界定标准；承认新的客体利用方式；审视新的作品保护措施；增设新的侵权认定规则等①。另有学者认为，信息自由在伦理上、法理上和文化渊源上有其正当性理据，但它与现行版权法之间存在冲突。在互联网条件下，版权法的改革势在必行，可以考虑的改革措施包括：确立一般性的默示许可规则；扩大合理使用的适用范围；取消复制权和演绎权，使版权人仅仅保留控制作品传播的权利②。

有学者通过理论分析与实证检验发现版权经济不仅具有显著的经济增长效应，而且能促进技术进步，对创意环境治理、解决市场经济中信用缺失问题也有积极作用。其经济增长效应作用路径有两条：一是版权资源要素以直接生产投入要素参与社会生产，提高产出；二是版权资源要素作为间接生产投入要素参与社会生产，通过发挥对技术进步以及劳动生产率的溢出效应促进经济增长③。而关于文化创意产业，它是最契合信息时代的产业组织形式，即是以个人的创意和智慧为依托，以版权保护制度为保障，以生产、经营文化产品和文化服务为主要业务范围，以满足人类社会的精神文化生活需求为本质内容的社会生产组织形式。文化创意产业的核心内容是版权产业，版权保护制度正是通过对版权产业的直接调整从而最终影响到整个文化创意产业的存在和发展④。

还有学者认为，思想与表达二分法设计的初衷在于，在保障作者获得报酬的利益和对激励社会公众创新的利益之间寻找一个平衡点。而作者获得报酬的利益主要来源于其对作品独创性的劳动付出，因此，法律保护的基础是作品的独创性。基于该立法设计初衷，在思想与表达二分法的适用过程中，可以辅之以作品的独创性来明确"思想"与"表达"的界限⑤。

二、关于著作权权利内容问题的研究

1. 著作人身权

有学者认为，著作人身权的立法理由，按大陆法系的经典表述，就是作者通过作品实现精神表达，作品包含并反映作者的人格利益，所以有保护作者在作品中体现出来的人身利益的必要。大陆法系之所以产生这样的理论，原因在于18世纪发轫于德国的浪漫主义运动对文学艺术作品与作者天才创作内在关系的认识，从理论到司法再到立法，著作人身权得以确立和受到保护⑥。还有学者认为，未经作者许可，破坏作者与作品之间的"父子"关系，割裂作者与作品之间的特定联系的行为，构成对作者署名权的侵权。署名权存在权利的边界，一是仅在著作权法意义上的作品使用行为中才涉及侵害署名权与否的问题，二是署名权应局限于在物理意义上可以署名、惯例上予以署名的情形⑦。

有学者认为，追续权是对艺术作品"传播性"使用的补偿，追续权的权利与义务所共同指向的对象是作品，而非作品载体。设立追续权基于的是艺术作品在作品载体上的不可复制性和唯一性，追续权的客体应为在载体上具备稀缺性的艺术作品。基于此，在我

---

* 向波，法学博士，南开大学法学院副教授，从事知识产权法学研究。

① 吴汉东. 网络版权的技术革命、产业变革与制度创新 [J]. 中国版权，2016 (6)：5-8.

② 胡波. 信息自由与版权法的变革 [J]. 现代法学，2016，38 (6)：78-86.

③ 张苏秋. 版权资源的经济增长效应及其作用路径：基于版权经济解释的定量分析 [J]. 广东财经大学学报，2016，31 (1)：60-69.

④ 同③.

⑤ 张春艳，张玉蕊. 思想与表达的理论困境与实践突破：琼瑶诉于正案引发的思考 [J]. 中国版权，2016 (5)：31-34.

⑥ 刘金萍. 论著作人身权的产生 [J]. 政法论丛，2016 (4)：44-52.

⑦ 董文涛. 电影海报与署名权：兼评《爵迹》电影海报争议 [J]. 中国版权，2016 (6)：33-37.

国，追续权客体应当限于美术作品①。美国一直都是坚定的追续权制度的反对者，但美国在 2013 年改变了立场，转而支持在联邦层面引入追续权制度。我国《著作权法》第三次修改中新增了追续权条款，我国可以从美国追续权立法实践以及讨论中获得启示。在追续权制度的实施上，我国应当采用著作权集体管理模式，并且规定信息获取权，探索建立艺术市场登记制度。在追续权的权利限制上，追续权不应适用于特定情形下作品原件的初次转售②。该学者还认为，德国追续权立法极具特色，其在世界上首创信息获取权，采用强制性集体管理模式实施追续权制度，并专设条款规定对外国作者进行追续权保护。我国《著作权法》可以借鉴德国追续权制度，在追续权运行上采用强制性集体管理模式，创设信息获取权，还可以借鉴德国追续金的分配模式，提升追续金的效用③。还有学者认为，法国是世界上第一个确立追续权的国家，追续权制度自 1920 年诞生以来，经历了两次重大的变革，其历史嬗变的过程具有典型性。两次变革的结果使得法国追续权制度更加具体化、规范化，更具可操作性。我国可以借鉴在《著作权法》中构建追续权制度④。但是，也有学者认为追续权入法所赖以成立的三个假说却无一能被确证，其入法的必要性、可能性、理论体系的合逻辑性和实践展开的可操作性均存疑问，应当谨慎对待追续权的入法问题，在未获充分论证的情况下宜暂缓入法以节约有限的立法资源，有效推进《著作权法》的第三次修改⑤。

2. 著作财产权

有学者认为，在现行著作权法体系下，录像制作者权以及广播组织权均无法规制网络实时转播行为，只能通过作品的著作权进行规制。对于初始传播方式为广播的视听节目的实时转播行为，存在两种规制方案：一是将网络实时转播纳入广播权的控制范围；二是将同样适用兜底权利条款进行调整。上述方案均有一定合理性，但从便于实践操作以及统一裁判标准的角度，当前宜采用第二种方案，即对网络实时转播他人作品的行为均适用兜底权利条款进行调整⑥。另有学者认为，复制权作为著作权人享有的首要经济权利，其由于技术的发展面临着在互联网环境中扩张的趋势。著作权法需要解决复制权扩张给既有法律体系带来的挑战，其中包括对于临时复制的定位⑦。

3. 邻接权

关于表演者权，有学者认为，在界定著作权法中的“表演者”及“表演”概念时，应从表演行为、表演对象和表演主体三个层面着眼，从而实现社会福利的最大化。还需要考量是否应当将具有一定艺术表现力和独创性的文体活动界定为表演活动或者作品，从而激励创作和投资；视听作品中演员的二次获酬权是否与中国相关行业的惯例相悖，从而有可能增加交易的成本，阻碍创意产业的健康发展⑧。还有学者认为，为保护广播组织的正当利益并在立法上实现技术中立，应当对广播组织的转播权进行扩张，使之能够控制通过任何技术手段和媒介实施的同步传播行为。国际著作权和邻接权条约并不干预成员国如何保护本国国民的权益，转播权的扩张无须以国际条约为立法依据。因我国已参加的国际条约将邻接权国民待遇原则适用的范围仅限于条约专门规定的权利，故外国广播组织在我国不能必然地享有扩张后的转播权权益⑨。而关于版式设计权，有学者认为，我国《著作权法》中出版者权的权利客体“图书、期刊的版式设计”存在歧义，对出版者权的相关研究和纠纷解决造成混乱，而建议以“图书、期刊的版面”作为出版者权客体⑩。该学者还认为，我国《著作权法》为出版者规定的版式设计权没有明确规定是否适用于网络传播的使用情形。为保护出版者的正当利益，应当对出版者的版式设计权进行扩张，使之能够控制通过任何技术手段和媒介实施的使用行为⑪。

三、关于著作权对象问题的研究

有学者认为，“独创性”“固定”“智力成果”这

① 戴哲. 论追续权之客体［J］. 中国版权，2016（6）：57-61.
② 戴哲. 美国追续权立法研究：兼谈对我国追续权立法的影响与启示［J］. 电子知识产权，2016（8）：35-46.
③ 戴哲. 德国追续权立法及其启示研究［J］. 德国研究，2016，31（2）：44-56.
④ 何蓉. 法国追续权制度研究及借鉴［J］. 电子知识产权，2016（6）：66-74.
⑤ 孙山. 追续权入法的三个假说及其检验［J］. 法律科学（西北政法大学学报），2016，34（6）：107-118.
⑥ 苏志甫. 从著作权法适用的角度谈对网络实时转播行为的规制［J］. 知识产权，2016（8）：29-35.
⑦ 孟兆平. 比较与选择：互联网环境中作品复制权的重构：以临时复制为视角［J］. 河北法学，2016，34（5）：96-103.
⑧ 熊文聪. 论著作权法中的“表演”与“表演者”［J］. 法商研究，2016，33（6）：180-187.
⑨ 王迁. 论广播组织转播权的扩张：兼评《著作权法修订草案（送审稿）》第 42 条［J］. 法商研究，2016，33（1）：177-182.
⑩ 于文. 论我国著作权法中出版者权的客体重置［J］. 科技与出版，2016（4）：60-63.
⑪ 于文. 论网络环境下版式设计权的扩张［J］. 编辑学刊，2016（3）：29-33.

三个要素都未能展现作品的本质属性，应当将著作权法上的作品定义为“文学、艺术和科学领域内具有创造性的表达”，同时规定“著作权法保护已经固定在有形载体上并具有独创性的作品”①。还有学者认为，作品结构是作品的重要构成元素，按抽象层级的不同，可以界分为抽象性结构与具体性结构。后者属于由作品的文本表达所直接限定的元素，在具备原创性要件时应受著作权法保护。两个作品具体性结构的近似是证成其构成实质性相似的重要考量因素。在基于作品结构进行作品之间是否具有实质性相似的判定时，也应将作品结构放置在作品整体中进行考量②。而随着信息产权的提出与发展，具有精神功能的符号组合或者非实用性的信息被解释为作品的本质。这将认识作品本质的基本范畴从主客体关系推向了主体关系，蕴含着怀疑主义的危险。基于法学共识，作品本质是在泛关系网络与著作权社会关系网络中生成的，是在文学艺术与科学领域内社会公众共同接受的引起利益分配的形式③。

1. 孤儿作品

有学者认为，版权登记的缺失是孤儿作品产生的主要原因。通过鼓励版权私人登记组织发展以及赋予版权受让人登记义务，从版权初始登记和变更登记两个方面来完善版权登记制度，有利于扩大作品登记数量和范围，建立版权公示信息数据库，为孤儿作品利用模式提供“勤勉查找”范围，减少未来孤儿作品的数量④。还有学者认为，孤儿作品利用的传统版权保护模式主要包括延伸性版权集体管理、强制许可、法定许可和限制责任模式。伴随人类社会迈入大数据时代，图书馆孤儿作品利用的版权保护也体现出了新趋势，孤儿作品利用的传统版权保护模式已无法在新的环境中充分发挥作用。应以法定许可和强制许可为保护模式的主要表现形态、以延伸性版权集体管理为保护模式的必要补充，构建完备的大数据综合版权保护配套制度⑤。世界范围内对孤儿作品版权保护的三大模式虽然在效用上各有优劣，但均较能有效地保护孤儿作品的版权，并能在一定程度上推进孤儿作品的合理使用。其中，扩展性集体授权模式和非自愿许可模式对我国可能更具借鉴意义⑥。还有学者在比较美国立法的基础上，认为孤儿作品立法应围绕权利许可而展开，基于利益衡平理念，丰富合理使用的制度内涵，实现“勤勉查找”之主观标准客观化，将孤儿作品纳入集体管理制度的管理范围并引入延伸性集体许可制度⑦。

2. 体育赛事

有学者认为，体育赛事转播权是随着体育与媒体结合而产生的新兴权利。在国外，就体育赛事转播权的法律属性，存在着运动场准入权说、娱乐服务提供说和企业权利说等各种理论，在我国，存在着传统知识产权说和财产权说两种观点。体育赛事转播权的享有主体是体育赛事主办方。而在传媒机构通过转让合同获得体育赛事转播授权后，体育赛事转播权衍生出了新的权利：传媒机构因制作体育赛事节目而获得的著作权⑧。基于中国立法在体育赛事网络转播保护方面还存在很多漏洞，有学者认为立法需要遵循新技术的特点，明确规定体育赛事转播权，规定该权利的具体内容；完善《著作权法》中的著作邻接权制度，增设能够涵盖通过各种技术手段传播信息的转播权，规定广播组织对其播放的体育赛事节目信号享有全面的控制权；确定体育赛事网络转播主体享有广播组织权，使网络转播主体有权控制他人在互联网上转播体育赛事节目⑨。在我国《著作权法》第三次修改中，应借鉴发达国家协调新旧技术传播者间冲突的经验，将体育赛事节目纳入著作权法保护的视听作品范畴。针对网络实时直播，立法上应摒弃技术思维，确立传播权；司法上借鉴技术中立和整体效果原则；管理上为新旧传播技术运营商营造公平竞争环境⑩。为充分保障体育赛事产业的发展，应在体育赛事产业的现场比赛阶段与传播阶段分别以体育赛事组织者与体育赛事传播者为基础配置权利。体育赛事组织者应具有对门票、广告

① 戴哲. 论著作权法上的作品概念 [J]. 编辑之友，2016 (5)：89-94.

② 卢海君. 论著作权法语境中的作品结构：以中小学教辅对教材进行“结构性使用”为例 [J]. 社会科学，2016 (12)：92-98.

③ 付继存. 著作权法的作品观：从本质主义到建构主义 [J]. 知识产权，2016 (1)：51-56.

④ 张颖. 探索孤儿作品问题的解决之道：以完善版权登记制度为视角 [J]. 编辑之友，2016 (1)：65-68.

⑤ 欧阳爱辉，谭泽林. 大数据时代图书馆孤儿作品利用的版权保护模式研究 [J]. 图书馆建设，2016 (9)：4-9.

⑥ 卢家银，段莉. 孤儿作品版权保护的三大模式评析 [J]. 编辑之友，2016 (1)：59-64.

⑦ 肖少启，张保红. 美国孤儿作品的版权立法及其对我国的启示 [J]. 图书情报工作，2016，60 (14)：67-74.

⑧ 冯春. 体育赛事转播权的法律属性研究 [J]. 社会科学家，2016 (3)：117-121.

⑨ 姚鹤徽. 体育赛事网络转播法律保护制度的缺陷与完善 [J]. 天津体育学院学报，2016，31 (3)：198-203.

⑩ 刘友华，朱蕾. 体育赛事节目流媒体传播的著作权挑战与应对 [J]. 中国体育科技，2016，52 (4)：44-50.

以及传播的专有权利，而体育赛事传播者应对传播体育赛事的信号以及传播形成成果享有专有权①。另有学者认为，体育赛事组织者只能凭借对赛事场所的物权设定他人入场并进行直播的条件，不能根据自身的章程原始取得对直播画面的著作权或邻接权。由于在对体育赛事进行直播时，摄像机的设置需要遵循一定规范，且导播对画面的选择需要满足观众的稳定预期，因此独创性程度有限。降低对独创性的要求、将直播画面认定为作品，将在很大程度上降低广播组织权的意义。因此对现场直播画面的保护，应当通过完善《著作权法》对广播组织权的规定加以实现②。

3. 游戏作品

有学者认为，游戏作品的表现形态千变万化，著作权法应区别对待它的“文本”本身固定的内容与游戏运行过程中临时呈现的内容，进而在必要时将它视为多种类型的传统作品的集合体，而没有必要创设特殊的作品类型。游戏用户的行为同样不能简单定性，需要根据游戏的具体情况判断游戏用户是否构成游戏画面的演绎作者。用户公开播放或通过网络传播游戏画面的行为落入游戏开发者的多项著作权权能的覆盖范围③。从解释论和立法论两个方面剖析网络游戏直播画面的著作权保护问题，将游戏画面与其他元素一起，作为整体归入具体作品类型进行保护，有利于明晰产权边界、保护权利人的合法利益④。剖析作品的本质并与网络游戏比赛画面进行对比后，另有学者发现虽较之于传统比赛画面，网络游戏比赛画面存在诸多特殊性，但这并无碍网络游戏比赛画面的作品属性，而网络游戏版权方是权利人，直播方可以通过与版权方签订协议获得传播网络游戏比赛画面的权利，比赛中的玩家虽然使用了网络游戏中的素材，但并不是权利人⑤。还有学者认为，尽管网络游戏并不是知识产权法域明确规定的某一类保护客体，但是网络游戏中涵盖的各个要素可以分别纳入现有知识产权法律体系进行保护⑥。

还有学者分别讨论了民间文学艺术作品⑦、电视节目⑧、字体⑨、实用艺术作品⑩、专利说明书⑪、摄影作品⑫、无主作品⑬、文身作品⑭、计算机程序⑮、广告语⑯、特殊作品⑰、时事新闻⑱、网页快照⑲、违

① 刘铁光，张路路. 体育赛事的权利配置及其法律选择：基于体育赛事产业发展的充分保障 [J]. 体育科学，2016，36 (2)：72-79.

② 王迁. 论体育赛事现场直播画面的著作权保护：兼评“凤凰网赛事转播案” [J]. 法律科学（西北政法大学学报），2016，34 (1)：182-191.

③ 崔国斌. 认真对待游戏著作权 [J]. 知识产权，2016 (2)：3-18.

④ 储翔. 网络游戏直播著作权保护困境与出路 [J]. 中国出版，2016 (24)：8-11.

⑤ 徐书林. 网络游戏比赛画面的法律性质探讨：基于耀宇公司诉斗鱼公司一案的分析 [J]. 北京邮电大学学报（社会科学版），2016，18 (6)：45-51.

⑥ 郝敏. 网络游戏要素的知识产权保护 [J]. 知识产权，2016 (1)：69-77.

⑦ 管育鹰. 民间文学艺术作品的保护机制探讨 [J]. 法律科学（西北政法大学学报），2016，34 (4)：101-113；胡光. 我国民间文学艺术作品的版权保护 [J]. 编辑学刊，2016 (2)：107-112；贾丽萍. 慕课（MOOCs）使用民间文学艺术作品版权限制与例外制度研究：兼评《民间文学艺术作品著作权保护条例（征求意见稿）》第十四条之规定 [J]. 福建论坛（人文社会科学版），2016 (4)：187-194；杨怡悦. 论我国民间音乐的知识产权保护：基于陕西传统戏曲、民歌的特征 [J]. 西北大学学报（哲学社会科学版），2016，46 (4)：118-123.

⑧ 朱慧. 电视节目模板可版权性的经济学分析 [J]. 广东社会科学，2016 (4)：37-47；杨海生. 电视节目版权价值评估方法的创新研究 [J]. 中国版权，2016 (6)：53-56.

⑨ 李海侨，张乾良. 从方正字体侵权案谈字体著作权保护的四个问题 [J]. 中国版权，2016 (6)：30-32.

⑩ 吕炳斌. 实用艺术作品交叉保护的证成与潜在风险之化解 [J]. 法律科学（西北政法大学学报），2016，34 (2)：137-147；徐棣枫，邱奎霖. 实用艺术作品双重保护问题及裁判路径探讨 [J]. 知识产权，2016 (12)：47-51.

⑪ 郭鹏鹏. 专利说明书著作权问题研究 [J]. 中国版权，2016 (5)：47-51.

⑫ 马一德. 再现型摄影作品之著作权认定 [J]. 法学研究，2016，38 (4)：137-151.

⑬ 肖少启. 我国无主作品著作权保护的路径选择与制度构建 [J]. 政治与法律，2016 (8)：112-125；王果. 无主作品著作权归属的“公”“私”之争 [J]. 中国版权，2016 (4)：53-56.

⑭ 张体锐. 纹身著作权保护问题研究 [J]. 知识产权，2016 (7)：35-40.

⑮ 刘汉霞. 对计算机程序保护中“同一作品”原则的质疑：兼评《著作权法（修订草案送审稿）》第 5 条第 15 项 [J]. 知识产权，2016 (6)：54-61.

⑯ 傅姚璐. 广告语著作权保护的实证分析 [J]. 中国版权，2016 (6)：62-66.

⑰ 季峰. 特殊作品的著作权特点和著作权法律保护：兼析 2015 年出版专业职业资格考试著作权综合题 [J]. 科技与出版，2016 (4)：20-25.

⑱ 刘文杰. 探析著作权法中的“时事新闻”：翻译引发的著作权法疑难问题 [J]. 新闻与传播研究，2016，23 (3)：18-37.

⑲ 詹启智. 网页快照作品提供行为的合理使用性研究：基于民事案件司法审判实践 [J]. 法学杂志，2016，37 (10)：80-87.

禁作品①、舞蹈作品②的性质和保护问题。

四、关于著作权交易问题的研究

有学者归纳出，有些人建议将版权从作者授权制度转化为单纯的收费制度，使用者在支付法定费用之后无须授权就可以使用作品，从而取消版权交易的必要性；另一种建议则旨在进一步促进市场交易，为权利人公开版权管理信息提供激励，并为市场参与者版权许可模式的创新和完善提供发展空间。相比较而言，法定许可类制度会大大削弱市场主体提高经营效率和进行技术创新的经济动力。立法者不能以降低交易成本的名义，彻底取消市场交易，取消市场作为社会资源配置的主要机制③。

1. 著作权登记

有学者认为，版权公示信息的缺失导致公示外部性影响扩大，阻碍了作品的利用效率，而在现有的自动保护原则下，版权公共登记又难以向市场充分供给作为公共产品的版权公示信息。私人无法充分提供公共产品，版权公示信息的生产与提供应采取公私合作模式。版权管理部门应该转变职能，成为登记服务的审批者和监管者，并将登记权限下放至符合从事登记服务资格的第三方组织，包括公共登记机构和私人登记组织④。而且，著作权登记不仅可以给著作权人提供权属的初步证明，还可以为降低交易风险、避免权属争议提供制度保障⑤。有学者则认为，《著作权法（修订草案送审稿）》"未经登记的权利，不得对抗善意第三人"的规定采用的是登记对抗规则，因我国版权登记或版权转让登记缺乏公信力，这一规则不仅与我国物权变更生效主义不一致，而且也不符合民事权利有权处分规则⑥。

2. 著作权集体管理

有学者认为，著作权集体管理组织的市场支配力因其集中权利来源的功能而形成，且被一直视为自然垄断的结果和反垄断规制的例外。然而，该市场支配力在显著提高著作权市场交易效率的同时，也因其带来的社会成本而遭到权利人和使用者的质疑。我国需要首先通过放松规制的方法，允许产业主体自行创设集体管理组织；其次通过强化规制的方法，要求集体管理组织为使用者提供多元化的许可类型选择，避免集体管理组织市场支配力的不当利用⑦。该学者还认为应调整强制规则，允许权利人在集体管理组织之外独立实施许可，不但能为解决集中许可版税标准争议提供参照，而且能促进不同许可主体和许可机制的良性竞争⑧。

关于集体管理组织的垄断性问题，有学者认为，在理论上著作权集体管理是具有自然垄断特点的行业。著作权集体管理组织在相关领域内的垄断地位乃是实现其多元功能的前提和保障。建议以著作权集体管理组织多元的功能定位为讨论基础，辩证理解民法基本原则所追求的价值目标，在肯定垄断式集体管理组织存在正当性的前提下，着力完善《著作权法》和《著作权集体管理条例》的制度建设⑨。还有学者认为，关于著作权集体管理组织的设立模式，竞争将增加交易成本、阻碍作品的传播与使用；而法定垄断则将导致管理效率低下、滥用垄断地位等问题。作为该问题的立法对策，应删除《著作权集体管理条例》第七条第二款第（二）项的规定，取消法定垄断，引入竞争，并新增一条，控制竞争规模，建立有限竞争、相对集中的著作权集体管理模式⑩。

关于著作权集体管理的延伸性问题，有学者认为，在数字网络时代著作权授权模式多元化的背景下，延伸性集体许可模式在回应大规模用户海量许可的产业诉求和尊重著作权人的意思自治方面有其独特优势。我国应引进延伸性集体许可模式，完善著作权集体管理制度，以推动我国机构知识库的建设⑪。另有学者则在比较英国相应制度的基础上，

① 李岩. 违禁作品法益性质的界定及保护模式构建［J］. 东北大学学报（社会科学版），2016，18（4）：405-411.

② 刘洁. 当前中国舞蹈作品著作权保护的现状及对策研究［J］. 北京舞蹈学院学报，2016（6）：13-18；王军. 论舞蹈作品知识产权的保护策略［J］. 北京舞蹈学院学报，2016（6）：1-7.

③ 刘家瑞. 论著作权法修改的市场经济导向：兼论集体管理、法定许可与孤儿作品［J］. 知识产权，2016（5）：40-51.

④ 张颖. 论版权登记组织的私人创制［J］. 华中科技大学学报（社会科学版），2016，30（1）：67-73.

⑤ 赵玺. 论著作权登记写入著作权法的必要性［J］. 出版发行研究，2016（5）：67-69.

⑥ 董美根. 论版权转让登记的对抗效力：评著作权法修改草案（送审稿）第59条［J］. 知识产权，2016（4）：37-42.

⑦ 熊琦. 著作权集体管理组织市场支配力的法律规制［J］. 法律科学（西北政法大学学报），2016，34（1）：92-103.

⑧ 熊琦. 著作权集体管理中的集中许可强制规则［J］. 比较法研究，2016（4）：46-59.

⑨ 李陶. 垄断性著作权集体管理组织的价值基础与监督完善［J］. 知识产权，2016（6）：39-46.

⑩ 林秀芹，黄钱欣. 我国著作权集体管理组织的模式选择［J］. 知识产权，2016（9）：53-59.

⑪ 陈化琴，陈雨杏. 著作权延伸性集体许可对我国机构知识库建设的启示：从我国《著作权法》第三次修改谈起［J］. 图书馆学研究，2016（7）：89-93. 类似的观点还有：刘平. 我国建立著作权延伸集体管理制度的必要性分析［J］. 知识产权，2016（1）：104-111.

主张我国应该学习英国采取较为缓和的折中模式，先将延伸性集体管理在强烈需要的著作权产业领域确定下来后，逐步完善配套法规制度，建议如下：一是在国家知识产权局内设立专门的部门围绕知识产权政策的制定展开对社会经济和产业状况的专门性研究，为立法设计提供足够的信息；二是构建著作权领域的反垄断机制，避免著作权管理组织在运营过程中排斥其他竞争模式的引入；三是学习英国构建专门的报酬争议解决机制，提供多渠道的解决思路；四是学习英国构建著作权集体管理数字化平台①。

还有学者对著作权许可协议②、著作人身权的转让③、作品增值利益的分配④、网络转载许可⑤等问题展开了讨论分析。

五、关于著作权限制问题的研究

1. 一般问题

作为权利限制制度的合理使用，有学者认为，立法时不应当存在一种可以通过事后解释的方式而创设的权利限制方式，将其适用到司法实践中也会引发向一般条款逃逸等不合理现象，兜底条款的创设更会使合理使用制度的展开欠缺正当性⑥。还有学者认为，我国已签署《马拉喀什条约》，亟须对著作权法中的限制与例外条款进行修改和调整。一是要扩大“受益人”和“无障碍格式版”的范围，缩小“被授权实体”的范围；二是明确规定“无障碍格式版”作品的范围；三是明确规定著作权例外所包含的权利范围；四是制定为视力和阅读障碍者利益而规避技术措施的例外⑦。

2. 合理使用

从美国以往判例看，在合理使用的判断中，转化性使用处于核心地位，如果使用作品的行为构成转化性使用，不会取代原作品市场，有助于公共利益的实现，则构成合理使用。中国《著作权法》合理使用模式过于僵化，应引入美国合理使用的弹性判断标准，并明确规定转化性使用规则⑧。有学者认为，美国法院对“转换性使用”的解释呈现逐步扩大的趋势，在判断“转换性使用”的程度时会重点关注经济层面的影响。我国在立法时可以参考美国制度背后的原理和内核，制定适合我国司法土壤的原则性标准，再在司法实践中灵活解释运用原则，以适应不断变化的社会现实⑨。还有学者认为，美国的变型使用规则是美国法院在适用合理使用制度时逐步发展出来的一个规则，使得构成变型使用的二次创作行为有可能因符合合理使用而被排除出侵权行为之外。建议在我国著作权法上重构一个独立的可供当事人选择适用的补偿型变型使用制度⑩。

有学者认为，谷歌侵权案促使法律对“合理使用”做出新的诠释：判定受版权保护作品之“使用的目的和性质”时，关键要看对内容的使用是否具有“转变性”；倾向于将“合理使用”看作积极权利；“合理使用”的判决并不意味着合理的利益关系⑪。还有学者认为，可以考虑在条件成熟时颁行司法解释，以“合目的性”和“可预见性”重塑“三步检验法”的“第一步”，增加其开放性：修改“修订草案送审稿”第四十三条第一款第（十三）项，令其符合三步检验法“第一步”的正当解释；建议借用“合理使用”四大标准来引申和丰富“三步检验法”的“第二步”和“第三步”，同时引入“比例原则”补强其均衡性⑫。另有学者认为，对于个人使用例外，应当从以下四个方面进行考虑：限定例外的受益者和使用地点；限定例外所允许的行为；限

① 陈可欣，林秀芹．英国引入延伸性集体管理的论争及其启示［J］．东南学术，2016（6）：172-179.

② 刘强，陈舜翊．开放源代码硬件许可协议知识产权问题研究：以 3D 打印为视角［J］．北京理工大学学报（社会科学版），2016，18（1）：134-141；张天浩．试论信息网络传播权许可使用合同中特殊限制性条款的有效性［J］．知识产权，2016（5）：63-67；黄先蓉，刘玲武．媒介融合背景下版权授权机制探析［J］．数字图书馆论坛，2016（7）：2-8.

③ 吴珂．著作人身权转让问题研究［J］．西安电子科技大学学报（社会科学版），2016，26（3）：54-60.

④ 曾青未．论作品增值利益的分配［J］．苏州大学学报（哲学社会科学版），2016，37（6）：67-75.

⑤ 彭桂兵．网络转载许可制度研究：版权生态学与法哲学的视角［J］．南京社会科学，2016（6）：113-119.

⑥ 孙山．合理使用“一般条款”驳［J］．知识产权，2016（10）：56-63.

⑦ 华劼．《马拉喀什条约》对我国著作权权利限制与例外制度的影响［J］．同济大学学报（社会科学版），2016，27（6）：117-124.

⑧ 姚鹤徽．从美国谷歌图书馆案看网络时代版权合理使用制度的完善［J］．图书馆，2016（11）：86-91.

⑨ 晏凌煜．美国司法实践中的“转换性使用”规则及其启示［J］．知识产权，2016（6）：123-128.

⑩ 唐艳．论二次创作的著作权法规制与保障［J］．知识产权，2016（11）：46-52.

⑪ 张大伟，于成．“谷歌侵权案”判决中的“合理使用”：新技术、新市场与利益再平衡［J］．新闻大学，2016（6）：117-124.

⑫ 张陈果．解读“三步检验法”与“合理使用”：《著作权法（修订送审稿）》第 43 条研究［J］．环球法律评论，2016，38（5）：5-24.

定著作权客体的来源；限定例外的目的①。还有学者讨论了图书馆或者数字图书馆的合理使用问题②。

六、关于著作权法律保护问题的研究

1. 著作权的民法保护

有学者认为，禁令救济与关系型版权结构难以兼容，不加限制地适用禁令救济会加大作品后续创作渠道被阻滞的风险、助推投机性版权诉讼的出现以及阻碍作品的有效利用。为此，可以通过充分发挥财产性救济的替代功能来弱化版权禁令救济无限制适用的内在动力③。还有学者认为，在著作权剽窃侵权案件中，接触要件有其独立的程序意义和实质意义，不应沦为实质相似性要件的附庸。在程序上，接触要件平衡了原告和被告之间的举证责任；在实质方面，接触要件阻止了新颖性取代独创性在著作权制度中的地位④。另有学者认为，“整体概念与感觉测试法”提供了一个解决方案，但需要进一步明晰美术作品的思想与表达。美术作品的画面构成包括内容和形式，对应于思想与表达。在著作权保护范围内应当考虑的表达要素有组织结构、形象词汇、抽象词汇，但同时不应忽略其他部分做整体考究。要素对比与整体感觉缺一不可⑤。而在侵犯影视作品信息网络传播权的案件中，权利人对赔偿范围面临着极大的因果关系证明难题，以至于无法有效根据传统民法的“差额理论”主张赔偿。有鉴于此，法定赔偿不应被定位于一种尽力使权利人回复至侵权未曾发生时的应然境况的判赔方法，其功能在于，为因侵权而处于不利益状态的权利人提供一种带有“保底性质”的救济⑥。

有学者认为，无论从现有立法规定、网络中立还是从激励理论角度探讨，网络服务提供者都不适宜承担连带责任。事实上，过重的责任负担容易阻碍网络产业的发展。网络服务提供者是网络空间的传播者和守护者，其在职责范围内对网络社会生活场域充当着类似安全保护角色，这为网络服务提供者承担相应的补充责任奠定了基础和提供了可行的路径⑦。还有学者认为，“通知—删除”前置能够降低网络版权保护总成本，节约宝贵司法资源，有助于责任划分。“通知”的主体可以包括独占被许可人以及特定情形下的排他被许可人与普通被许可人。“删除”的期限应当考虑权利人要求的期限与ISP承诺的期限⑧。另有学者提出，欧盟法院在审理Tobias Mc Fadden v Sony案时明确提出避风港原则适用于Wi-Fi提供者，但版权人可以申请禁令救济以防止侵权行为继续发生，禁令可以要求Wi-Fi提供者设置访问密码以让用户表明身份信息⑨。还有学者认为，网盘存储服务商在本质上仍属于信息存储空间服务商，基于法律的规定以及操作性和运营成本考量，网盘存储服务商不应承担用户存储或分享内容的版权审查义务，但是应尽到相应的注意义务，即根据“通知—删除”规则要求，及时删除侵权内容和断开侵权分享链接，同时采取必要技术措施筛查明显的侵权内容，监控用户账号异常登录和流量的异常变化，及时采取应对处理⑩。

2. 技术措施

为有效防范和规制版权技术保护措施所带来的信息安全风险，美国和德国对此采取了不同模式加以应对。有学者通过比较两国信息安全遵从模式，认为美国版权立法的反规避条款例外规定是规制技术保护措施信息安全风险的主要模式，而德国赋予版权人强制的独立义务适应了数字时代版权技术保护措施安全应用的需求，也显示了完善版权技术保护措施法律规章制度的立法趋势⑪。为平衡版权人

---

① 胡超. 国际法视野下的著作权个人使用例外［J］. 知识产权，2016（9）：110-116.

② 屈华. 我国图书馆版权合理使用制度的重构［J］. 图书馆理论与实践，2016（9）：6-10；张军华，韩全会. 数字网络环境下我国图书馆合理使用制度的反思与重构［J］. 图书馆建设，2016（9）：14-21；高军，王文敏. 数字图书馆合理使用规则新发展：美国HathiTrust案与Google Books案的比较［J］. 图书馆论坛，2016，36（6）：43-49；谢光旗. 数字时代公共图书馆合理使用制度：《公共图书馆法（征求意见稿）》的完善［J］. 图书馆，2016（9）：7-11.

③ 杨红军. 版权禁令救济无限制适用的反思与调适［J］. 法商研究，2016，33（3）：184-192.

④ 周小舟. 论接触要件在剽窃案中的程序和实质意义：从《小站》案切入［J］. 华东政法大学学报，2016，19（2）：108-118.

⑤ 杨雄文，王沁荷. 美术作品的表达及其实质相似的认定［J］. 知识产权，2016（1）：44-50.

⑥ 徐聪颖. 侵犯影视作品信息网络传播权的司法判赔问题研究：以414件民事判决为样本的实证分析［J］. 河北法学，2016，34（11）：61-78.

⑦ 王晋. 不作为的网络服务提供者著作权侵权承担补充责任的提出［J］. 学术探索，2016（12）：70-77.

⑧ 徐明. 避风港原则前沿问题研究：以“通知—删除”作为诉讼前置程序为展开［J］. 东方法学，2016（5）：28-36.

⑨ 孙雷. 浅析Wi-Fi提供者的版权侵权责任：评Tobias Mc Fadden v Sony案［J］. 中国版权，2016（6）：81-84.

⑩ 刘鹏. 网盘存储服务商的版权义务探析［J］. 知识产权，2016（6）：47-53.

⑪ 赵丽莉. 版权技术保护措施信息安全遵从模式比较分析：以美国和德国为主要研究对象［J］. 河北法学，2016，34（4）：86-96.

与公众间的利益，美国《数字千年版权法》率先将技术措施纳入保护范围，开创性地规定禁止规避技术措施的一般例外与临时例外。临时例外经五次修改，整体上呈现出例外情形数量和类型递增、应用范围日广的演进态势。演进特点有二：临时例外的增删与新技术的应用如影相随；各方博弈焦点与国会图书馆意志共同左右其走向。我国宜结合因素主义与规则主义两种立法模式，在规定一般例外情形基础上，重点补充图书馆档案馆等合理使用类例外①。还有学者认为，版权法应当保护版权利益，要求技术措施与版权保护的关联是必要的，但不能要求规避行为与版权侵权的关联；同时应当赋予被告一项抗辩——被规避的技术措施根本不是出于版权保护之目的②。

3. 著作权的刑法保护

域外典型案件表明，不同 P2P 技术架构下网络服务商在著作权侵害中所起的作用、对用户侵害著作权的知悉可能性以及对于用户的监督控制能力大相径庭，因而是采取集中或混合式架构还是分散式架构对于 P2P 网络商的责任评价可能产生不同影响，有必要针对其提供 P2P 软件和服务的行为，就教唆犯与帮助犯各自的成立条件基于不同的技术架构予以仔细分析③。有学者认为，美国正在进行版权法的修订，其刑事责任条款以严惩非法实施流传播行为为主要内容。流传播技术所带来的盗版困境和版权营利模式的改变，是推动美国版权法修订的事实因素。在以保护复制、发行权为中心构建的美国传统版权法无法规制侵犯作品表演权的犯罪行为是推动美国版权法修订的直接原因。美国希望通过将侵犯作品表演权的行为纳入刑法重罪规制范围的方式达到保护其版权的目的④。

有学者认为，当前网络著作权刑事保护面临着运动式执法、地区分布不均、知识产权法律保护“重民轻刑”“重行轻刑”、缓刑适用比例低且随意性较大、罚金刑适用偏执且任意等问题。完善我国的网络著作权刑法保护，必须推进刑事立法创新，优化司法资源配置，探索建立知识产权法院，完善著作权刑罚体系及严格、科学的知识产权管理和监督机制，使执法常态化、制度化⑤。还有学者认为，司法解释均将“网络传播行为”硬性解释为“复制发行行为”存在诸多问题。因为网络传播行为与复制发行行为存在本质不同，它当属于类推解释而非扩大解释，有违罪刑法定原则。在未来刑事立法中应将严重的网络传播侵权行为规定为一种独立的犯罪行为，但以“点击量”作为其情节严重的认定标准仍然存在不足，可以“实际侵权作品的数量”来替代⑥。

七、关于新技术条件下著作权法律保护问题的研究

1. 3D 打印技术

由于 CAD 文档不构成专利权保护下的技术方案，知识产权直接侵权规则无法适用于专利产品 CAD 文档的制作、销售与传播；CAD 文档的非物质性使得前述行为游离于帮助侵权规则之外；非生产经营实施例外为 CAD 文档制作等行为开启了免责之门；著作权法“思想与表达二分法”规则也无助于保护实用性功能⑦。基于 3D 打印技术原理，有学者将其分为输入和输出两个环节。在输入环节，对 CAD 文件的作品类型进行规制，采用视觉标准界定立体作品，并以“美术作品＋模型作品”的思路进行综合保护；在输出环节，3D 打印属于复制，且可以实现从平面到立体和从立体到立体的复制形态，复制权的控制范围应不限于现行法律所列举的方式。针对 3D 打印技术在网络传播中的侵权风险，应对合理使用中的私人复制予以限制，灵活运用“三步检验标准”对合理性进行审查⑧。

2. 视频聚合

有学者根据其行为手段及所采取的技术手段的不同，将视频聚合平台又分为采用一般深度链接手段的聚合平台及采用盗链手段的聚合平台。其中，采用盗链手段的视频聚合平台违背被盗链的视频网

---

① 肖冬梅，方舟之. 美国禁止规避技术措施例外制度的缘起、演进与启示［J］. 图书馆论坛，2016，36（6）：1-9.

② 覃斌武. 评美国版权法技术措施规则的司法分歧［J］. 知识产权，2016（11）：98-104.

③ 杨彩霞. P2P 软件和服务提供商著作权侵害刑事责任探究：以 P2P 技术架构为切入点［J］. 政治与法律，2016（3）：42-53.

④ 张燕龙. 美国版权法案中刑事责任条款的修订及其启示：以美国对非法实施流传播行为的刑法规制为例［J］. 法商研究，2016，33（1）：156-165.

⑤ 张先昌，鲁宽. 近十年网络著作权犯罪案件的实证研究［J］. 知识产权，2016（9）：76-80.

⑥ 仝其宪. 网络著作权犯罪刑事立法的反思与完善［J］. 西安电子科技大学学报（社会科学版），2016，26（2）：79-84.

⑦ 刘文琦. 3D 打印中 CAD 文档侵权问题研究：理论逻辑与立法反思［J］. 浙江工商大学学报，2016（5）：47-52.

⑧ 李永明，郑金晶. 3D 打印中 CAD 文件的定性与复制问题研究［J］. 浙江大学学报（人文社会科学版），2016，46（2）：147-159.

站的意志，通过技术破解措施，直接盗链视频网站的资源，达到向用户提供作品的目的。上述盗链行为，应在著作权法上认定为信息网络传播权的直接侵权行为①。还有学者认为，网络传播行为可以观念上区分为信息网络提供行为与作品展示行为，而聚合行为应当被视为通过网络平台公开展示作品的直接侵权行为。将聚合行为与转播行为相对比，能够凸显将聚合行为视为直接侵权行为的合理性②。而对深度链接法律性质的认定，主要有服务器标准、用户感知标准和链接不替代标准。服务器标准倾向于认定设链行为是网络服务提供行为，其虽更符合立法出发点，但亦存在诸多弊端，需要立法重新调整以实现利益平衡。有学者认为将深度链接行为纳入信息网络传播权的权利调整范围之中，从而限制设链网站通过深度链接获得不正当竞争优势和商业利益③。对此种观点，另有学者认为，任何著作权法意义上的传播行为都应当形成"传播源"，使作品从该"传播源"向公众传送。"深层链接"通常只是为用户提供了从同一"传播源"获得作品的不同途径，并未形成新的"传播源"，因此不构成"信息网络传播行为"。对于破解其他网站的技术措施并相应地提供"深层链接"的行为，著作权法中禁止规避技术措施的条款可进行规制④。也有学者根据公开传播权理论，认为设链网站提供的是作品的网络地址，而非作品本身，所以设链行为并非网络传播行为。将破坏技术措施的设链行为认定为不正当竞争行为，不会影响版权人获得行政、民事救济⑤。

八、结语

从上文收集、整理的论文内容来看，2016年我国著作权法研究的特点主要表现在以下三个方面：第一，追踪学术、司法热点问题。除了一些比较零散的论文主题以外，2016年我国学者分别对追续权、视频聚合、著作权的集体管理、体育赛事与体育赛事节目、孤儿作品等主题展开了各个角度的研究讨论，并在一定程度上深化了对于相关问题的认识和理解。第二，著作权法的基础理论研究还不够深入。从相关的论文主题来看，大部分论文主要围绕着当年的热点问题而展开，缺乏持续性的、系统性的基础理论研究成果。第三，仍然欠缺与民法制度的沟通与衔接。我国已启动民法典的制定工作，作为民法的部分内容，有必要对包括著作权法在内的知识产权法与民法之间的关系问题展开多角度的深入研究。而从上文的内容来看，我国知识产权学者仍然关注于对具体问题、热点问题的应对和解答。

① 林子英，崔树磊. 视频聚合平台运行模式在著作权法规制下的司法认定［J］. 知识产权，2016（8）：36-48.
② 崔国斌. 得形忘意的服务器标准［J］. 知识产权，2016（8）：3-19.
③ 谢兰芳，付强. 深度链接行为的侵权判定标准探讨［J］. 知识产权，2016（11）：41-45.
④ 王迁. 论提供"深层链接"行为的法律定性及其规制［J］. 法学，2016（10）：23-39.
⑤ 陈绍玲. 再论网络中设链行为的法律定性：兼与崔国斌先生商榷［J］. 知识产权，2016（10）：17-24.

2016年著作权热点问题研究

民间文学艺术作品的保护机制探讨

管育鹰

本文尝试就我国民间文学艺术作品保护机制的建立与运行提出自己的建议，以期进一步推动相关研究和立法。需要指出的是，本文对民间文学艺术作品保护机制的分析和评述仅为个人的观点和方案设计。如需了解立法进展，可以比对研究国家版权局于2014年9月2日公布的《民间文学艺术作品著作权保护条例（征求意见稿）》（以下简称《条例》）。

一、民间文学艺术作品之概念与理解

民间文学艺术作品指由特定的地区或族群共同创作，通过口头或动作传授、模仿等方式长期传承的反映其社会生活特征与文化特性的民间文学艺术具体表现形式[①]。

首先，一方面，民间文学艺术作品是个集合概念，包括所有无法追溯创造时间和具体创作者的民间文学艺术作品的总和，而不是当代作者根据民间文学艺术作品演绎创作的民间文学艺术改编作品。另一方面，民间文学艺术作品在客观表现形式上与受著作权法保护的当代作品并无差别，比如应当是可构成歌曲的完整曲调或者有具体情节内容的故事等，而不仅仅是笼统的民间文艺类别或流派、简单的主题等。其次，民间文学艺术作品与现代作品的主体、保护期不同。多数情形下，某一具体的民间文学艺术作品，其流传的地区、族群等来源是可以确定的，其创作和受益主体可以被推定为相应的地区、族群全体成员；在某些情况下，民间文学艺术作品可能同时由几个地区、族群共同传承，其创作源头经专业人士论证也不能确定，这时可以考虑设定该作品由这些地区或族群共有[②]；有些民间文学艺术作品由于流传太广，已经成了中国传统文化的代表符号的，应当推定为全国人民共有。民间文艺具有集体性、口头性、变异性、传承性[③]，由于其创作一般被推定为代代相传、呈持续的动态性和变异性，某一民间文学艺术作品如果还在传承，则推定其一直还处于动态的集体创作过程中，现行著作权制度为作品设定的保护期就不应当适用。

笔者认为，民间文学艺术作品包括但不限于以下类型：

（1）口头言语、文字符号类表现形式，如民间故事、史诗、传说、谚语等；

（2）音乐、曲调的表现形式，如民歌、器乐的曲调等；

（3）动作、表演类表现形式，如民间舞蹈、戏剧等；

（4）平面或立体的美术、建筑类有形的表现形式，如民间绘画、传统工艺品、建筑等。

由于民间文学艺术作品客体的复杂性，在《著作权法》第三次修改之际，国家版权局接受知识产权学界多数专家的意见，将《著作权法》第六条的“民间文学艺术作品”术语改为“民间文学艺术表达”，并删掉了“著作权”的限定[④]，该草案送审稿已经于2014年6月6日由国务院法制办公布征求意见；同时，2014年以来国家版权局又一次启动了民间文学艺术表达保护的立法工作；当然，限于《著作权法》本身尚未修改，草案的名称仍然只能依据现行法第六条草拟，仍称为《民间文学艺术作品著作权保护条例（草案）》。

二、民间文学艺术作品的保护机制

笔者认为，要实质性推进我国民间文学艺术表达法律保护制度的建立，应当考虑一套合理的、可行的方案。在设立我国民间文学艺术作品保护机制

---

① 本定义参考了WIPO《保护传统文化表达：政策目标与核心原则（草案）》，与国家版权局草案略有差异。

② 这里有两种情况，一种是可以明确为同一民族传承的，比如《格萨尔王传》史诗传说同时流传于西藏、青海、四川、甘肃等藏族聚居地，则该作品属于全体藏族共有，刘三姐的故事也同样可以认定为壮族共有；另一种是可以明确为几个地区或族群共同传承的，比如植根于汉族民间曲艺文化的东北二人转传统剧目，由辽宁、吉林、黑龙江三省和内蒙古东部三市一盟的全体人民共有。

③ 钟敬文. 民间文学概论［M］. 上海：上海文艺出版社，1980：23-46.

④ 《中华人民共和国著作权法（修订草案送审稿）》第十条：民间文学艺术表达的保护办法由国务院另行规定。

时需要考虑以下方面的问题：

（一）民间文学艺术作品的权利内容

民间文学艺术作品的著作权属于共同创作并世代传承体现其传统观念和文化价值的民间文学艺术作品的民族、族群或者地区全体人民。民间文学艺术作品的权利主体享有精神权利和经济权利：首要的是精神权利，其内容是指明来源，包括署名权、发表权和禁止歪曲篡改权；其次是经济权利，即民间文学艺术作品主体就主体群体之外的人以复制、发行、表演、改编或者向公众传播等方式商业化使用其作品获得报酬的权利。

笔者认为，与世界上最早规定原住民对其传统知识享有"集体知识产权"，并赋予原住民从防御性和主动性两个方面行使该权利的巴拿马法律相比①，我国现行《著作权法》框架下拟设定的经济权利内容应该要窄，这是因为权利客体仅涉及能确定为作品的部分。在选择著作权模式保护民间文学艺术作品的国家，法律赋予权利人的经济权利内容也与著作权大同小异，或者直接对民间文学艺术作品适用著作权法保护。比如加纳2005年的著作权法第四条规定："本法保护民间文学艺术表达不被复制、通过表演向公众传播、通过有线或其他任何方式发行、改编、翻译或其他任何使用"②。

笔者建议，民间文学艺术作品的权利仅针对习惯法之外的"商业性使用"。为避免不确定性，可以在立法上对经济权利采取笼统的规定，即"以复制、发行、表演、改编或者向公众传播等方式使用"，同时在"例外与限制"中明确规定主体的群体成员之"未超出传统习惯和范围的使用"不属于法律适用对象。

（二）民间文学艺术作品的保护机制

1. 以使用登记和付费为前提的法定许可模式

笔者认为，应当明确建立一种有别于传统、典型的著作权之事先许可的授权模式，不应要求使用者事先需要获得许可，而仅应规范作品的使用方式和使用人与民间文学艺术作品权利人之间的利益分享。换言之，对民间文学艺术作品的商业性使用，采取严格的附条件的法定许可模式更符合民间文学艺术传承的长远需要。此方案的主要特点在于：民间文学艺术作品的使用者不需要事先获得许可，但需要在规定期间登记并支付报酬，否则将依法承担法律责任。设立这一附条件的许可模式的主要原因是，我国民间文学艺术作品种类繁多，且权利主体多处于偏远闭塞地区，族群没有受到西方文化和法律思维的影响，也没有非政府组织活动的渗透、帮助，缺乏相应的权利意识和依法事先进行登记的能力。这一具体国情与非洲、东南亚、大洋洲等地区传统族群所处的境地不同（这些地区的族群成员因原先的殖民地历史，甚至能够掌握英国、法国、葡萄牙或西班牙等宗主国的语言），因此在民间文学艺术作品使用的授权模式上不可能完全照搬这些地方的事先登记和授权许可使用模式。另外，我国民间文艺界长期以来形成的既有观念和做法是鼓励当代创作者和使用人深入这些条件艰苦的不发达地区，采集、开发民间文学艺术作品，或者据此创作新的作品，要求使用人事先经过权利人许可和付费才能使用的方案在实践中是难以实施的。

2. 民间文学艺术改编作品的使用问题

很多情况下，商业使用人使用的是有具体现代作者的民间文学艺术改编作品，而不是民间文学艺术作品本身。笔者认为，既然对民间文学艺术作品本身采取法定许可保护模式，则要求民间文学艺术改编作品的使用人须获得民间文学艺术作品权利人的事先许可也就不必要了；也即，使用人仅需依据《著作权法》获得改编作品著作权人的许可。但是，鉴于民间文学艺术作品与改编作品之间"源与流"上的关系，使用人仍应当依法进行使用登记，并参照市场上原作与改编作品的使用费比例交纳民间文学艺术作品的使用费。

3. 记录人、口述人、表演者的权益问题

记录人忠实的记录活动不仅需要比较艰苦的劳动和投入，有时还需要具备特别的技能。关于记录

① Panama. Law No. 20 of June 26，2000 on Special System for the Collective Intellectual Property Rights of Indigenous Peoples for the Protection and Defense of Their Cultural Identity and Their Traditional Knowledge [EB/OL]. WIPO网站，http://www.wipo.int/wipolex/en/details.jsp?id=3400，2016年1月访问。其中第二条译文为：原住民的习俗、传统、信仰、灵性、宗教、宇宙观、民俗表达、艺术表现形式、传统知识及其他传统的表现形式，是其文化遗产的组成部分，其他人未经原住民的明确授权不得通过知识产权制度，如版权、外观设计、商业标志、地理标志或其他标记等将上述内容作为自己专有权的客体。不过，根据现有立法已获得的以上权利不受影响并应得到尊重。第六条译文为：本法赋予传统族群对其可依本法登记注册的可受保护的物品享有集体权利，以保证这些物品来源正宗和真实。

② Tunisia. Law No. 94-36 of February 24，1994 on Literary and Artistic Property [EB/OL]；Sri Lanka. Intellectual Property Act (Act No. 36 of 2003)；Ghana. Copyright Act，2005 (Act 690) [EB/OL]. WIPO网站，http://www.wipo.int/wipolex/en/，最后访问日期：2016-01.

人的权益，主要是署名权和劳务报酬权。《条例》应当明确记录人的署名权和获得报酬的权利，即使用人使用记录人搜集、记录的民间文学艺术作品的，应当指明记录人的身份，并向其就其劳务支付相应的报酬（但这不等同于民间文学艺术作品的使用费），使用人不履行这一义务应当承担相应法律责任。另外，即使《条例》不做规定，民间文学艺术作品的表演者也可以根据现行《著作权法》第三十八条获得保护。口述人的地位与表演者类似，都是来自相应主体的成员，但一般说来口述人更加资深，有的甚至是根据族群习惯法确定的唯一或极少数传承人。在根据族群习惯法不得外传的情形下，相关的民间文学艺术作品处于未公开状态、仅限于内部传承使用的范围，使用人如果将表演或口述内容公开发表和获利的，表演者和口述人将依法承担共同侵权责任。

（三）民间文学艺术作品的登记制度

笔者认为，可以采取将登记与确权、登记与使用费收转分配两个重要问题分开的思路，即由民间文学艺术作品专门管理机构建立两套登记系统：权属登记和使用登记。

1. 建立民间文学艺术作品的权属登记和确权机制

笔者认为要求民间文学艺术作品主体事先进行权属登记既不现实也无必要，转换思维，不要将权属登记（包括之后的使用费收转分配）这一高度复杂的问题设置为使用民间文学艺术作品的第一道障碍，将其与使用人在一定期限内依法进行的使用登记分开更为可行。当然，考虑到目前我国有些民间文学艺术作品的主体已经有了较强的法律意识，《条例》也应当规定相关主体的代表机构可以就其具体的民间文学艺术作品事先进行登记；不过，关于主体、客体的事先登记需要满足一定条件才可发生效力（即登记的主体代表机构有权收取和支配民间文学艺术作品专门管理机构收转的使用费）。具体的登记、公告和权属争议程序由《条例》之外的细则或办法另行制定。

2. 建立民间文艺作品使用登记和付费机制

我国的民间文学艺术长期传承，不同地区或族群的民间文学艺术作品形成了各自的特色，一般来说使用人都知道自己使用了民间文学艺术作品，也大致知晓使用的是哪个地方哪个族群的作品。《条例》应当规定民间文学艺术作品的使用者必须在一定期限内到指定机构进行登记并支付相应的使用费，且不能以其已经向民间文学艺术作品的表演者、传承人支付了采风或表演等劳务费用为抗辩（正如向歌手付费不等于向作曲家付费）；为保证使用人履行此义务，《条例》后面应配合制定相应的条款予以追责。

3. 进一步明确和细化民间文学艺术作品登记制度的主要内容

具体来说，民间文学艺术作品登记包括两个相互独立的系统：权属登记和使用登记。

其一，权属登记。民间文学艺术作品的权属登记，可以设计为一个由主体代表机构代为申请的机制，并辅以公告、争议程序，对主体代表机构资格、民间文学艺术作品的内容及归属等可能产生的争议进行协商解决；同时，考虑到民间文学艺术作品的主体多地处偏远、权利意识普遍欠缺等因素，登记的公告、争议解决方式，以及期间的设定等都应当相对宽松。另外，由于民间文艺文学艺术作品的特殊性，为了避免《条例》通过后法院的压力突增，可以规定民间文学艺术作品专门管理机构设立的纠纷调解委员会的听证和裁决程序为诉前的必要前置程序，以便对可能诉争到法院的案件之原告、被告的适格性，以及被使用的民间文学艺术作品本身的内容等问题事先进行判定，无程序瑕疵的委员会裁决可以作为法院判决的优势证据。民间文学艺术作品专门管理机构应当根据生效的裁决或判决进行公告登记。

其二，使用登记。民间文学艺术作品的商业使用人应当主动在使用之前，或者接到主管专门管理机构的通知后一年内到民间文学艺术作品专门管理机构就使用情况进行登记，并交纳使用费。使用人可以在使用之前自己了解，也可以根据文化部门名录事先查询（或通过其他方式知晓）其使用的民间文学艺术作品基本信息并据此进行登记。民间文学艺术作品专门管理机构应当设立民间文学艺术作品使用情况登记和公告机制，公告已经登记的被使用的民间文学艺术作品之主体、客体、使用费收取等细节；专门管理机构还应设立民间文学艺术作品使用通知登记制度，对收到通知后没有主动进行登记的使用人采取书面公告通知，限定其在一年内进行登记和交费；《条例》应规定对于逾期不登记交费的使用人，专门管理机构有权代为追诉。在规定时期内若没有收到对所使用的民间文学艺术作品、作品的主体及其代表机构等方面的争议，民间文学艺术作品专门管理机构在扣除一定的管理费后，将民间文学艺术作品的使用费转付所登记的相应的主体代表机构，由其按照族群内部规约或习惯法分配或使用。如果对民间文学艺术作品、作品的主体或其代表机构有争议并在规定期限内提出的，民间文学艺术作品专门管理机构将留存该使用费，待相关民间文学艺术作品、作品的主体及代表机构的争议纠纷最终解决后转付。另外，对于民间文学艺术改编作品的商业性使用，使用人除了依照《著作权法》与改编作品著作权人事先协商外，也应当到民间文学艺术作品专门管理机构参照以上方式进行使用登记，并比照民间文学艺术作品本身的使用减交一定比例费用；民间文学艺术改编作品著作权保护期已满的并不解除使用人依法登记并交纳一定比例民间文学艺术作品使用费的义务。

（四）民间文学艺术作品保护的受益人

民间文学艺术作品保护机制最终落脚点，在于专门管理机构代为收取的民间文学艺术作品法定许可使用费如何转付给其主体，具体可采取以下措施：

1. 使用情况登记及其公示

使用人使用民间文学艺术作品的，应当在被使用的内容投放市场后的一年内到民间文学艺术专门管理机构登记，民间文学艺术专门管理机构也可以主动或应第三人请求通知使用人进行登记。民间文学艺术专门管理机构还应当实时更新并向社会公示已登记的民间文学艺术作品的使用信息；考虑一定的滞后性，公示应当在使用登记完成之日起一个月内发布。

2. 基于权属登记的使用费收转

事先没有登记的民间文学艺术作品权利人，在民间文学艺术作品专门管理机构将使用登记情况公示后的两年内，应当向该机构进行权属登记，以便该机构将其收取的使用费分配给相应的主体（民族、族群或者地区全体人民）或其代表机构。

3. 民间文艺作品权属和使用登记数据库的建立与查询

民间文学艺术作品专门管理机构应当建立数据库，向社会公示民间文学艺术作品权属登记、使用登记以及使用费收转等相关情况并随时更新。

三、结语

如何有效保护民间文学艺术作品，应明确的思路是通过立法建立起一套可操作的保护机制，为我国民间文学艺术中那些具有作品表现形式的内容提供类似著作权的保护。笔者认为，建立以严格的使用登记并以公告程序相配套的法定许可模式，并辅以允许权利人选择事先或事后的权属登记的确权程序，可以达到通过让权利人或受益人分享到其民间文学艺术作品商业性使用获益的方式来鼓励其保持民间文艺传承的目的。有一点需要强调：鉴于现实中民间文学艺术作品权利人主动主张权利极其困难，立法拟设立的专门管理机构在民间文学艺术作品保护中具有特别重要的作用，应赋予其通知使用人按期进行登记，以及以自己的名义对违法者依法提起诉讼的权利。

（本文原发表于《法律科学（西北政法大学学报）》2016 年第 4 期。
作者单位：中国社会科学院法学研究所）

参考文献

[1] 郑成思. 版权法（修订本）[M]. 北京：中国人民大学出版社，1997.

[2] 钟敬文. 民间文学概论 [M]. 上海：上海文艺出版社，1980.

[3] 世界知识产权组织（WIPO）网站，http://www.wipo.int.

[4] 民间文学艺术作品著作权保护条例（征求意见稿）[EB/OL]. 国家版权局网站，http://www.ncac.gov.cn/chinacopyright/contents/483/225066.html，2016 年 1 月访问.

[5] 中华人民共和国著作权法（修订草案送审稿）[EB/OL]. 国务院法制办网站，http://www.chinalaw.gov.cn/article/cazjgg/201406/20140600396188.shtml，最后访问日期：2016-01.

从知识产权司法需求论我国民法典的编纂*

李 琛

在我国民法典的制定过程中，知识产权的安置是焦点问题之一①。立法最主要的功能是作为裁判依据，从知识产权司法的需求角度考量知识产权在民法典的地位，应当是一个重要的视角。法典化的首要意义在于实现立法的体系化。“取向于目的、设定所期功能，将知识或事务根据其存在上之关系、作用组织起来的方法，便是体系化。”② 法作为一种文化现象，不可避免地受到文化信念的影响。但是法作为调整社会生活的实用工具，设计它的技术不可能完全由一种文化偏好所支撑。体系化以及作为体系化

* 本成果受到中国人民大学“中央高校建设世界一流大学（学科）和特色发展引导专项资金”支持，项目批准号：15XNLG06。

① 李琛. 论中国民法典设立知识产权编的必要性 [J]. 苏州大学学报（法学版），2015（4）：75-82.

② 黄茂荣. 法学方法论与现代民法 [M]. 北京：中国政法大学出版社，2001：458.

之表达形式的法典始终未被离弃，是有其实用性理由的。本文将从体系化的工具价值出发，探讨体系化思维对当前知识产权审判的特别意义，以此论证民法典的体系形式回应知识产权司法需求的必要性。

一、体系化的工具价值与民法典的功能

法典化作为一种立法技术的意义，主要是基于体系化思维的实践价值。法典乃是体系化思维在立法中的外化。体系化的实践功能示例如下：

（一）说服价值

无论是立法还是司法裁判，其权威性都不能仅仅来源于国家强制力，必须以其合理性赢得民众的认可与接受。内部逻辑的一致性是法律文件合理性的组成部分。

体系化反映出“人类力求将公平正义以可靠而且可以理解的方法实现在人间的努力”[①]，法的体系化程度越高、呈现的逻辑自足性越强，其说服力也就越强。尽管法律之中的利益导向是不可避免的，但至少在效果上，体系化的形式比无章可循的形式具有更大的亲和力。当制度形成一个有序的、科学的体系时，仿佛人类社会的应然秩序与实然秩序融为一体。为了强化自身的正当性，法典的体系建构总是尽量地汲取当时最新的认知成果。一旦法典找到了一个具有说服力的前提作为体系的脉络，具体的制度设计、司法判决都成为这种前提运用的结果。因此，体系化有助于强化新秩序的正当性、对抗旧制度的影响。

民法典的制定者在确定体例编制时，总是依据某种被公认为比较合理的线索。例如，对于法国民法典的三编制顺序，学者的解释是：人显然应当在物之前，物是人所有或受益的对象。物应当规定在取得它们的方式之前，只有界定了物，人们才能利用物建立各种法律关系[②]。可见，法典的体系总是具有某种逻辑基础，无论该逻辑的具体模式如何，这种合逻辑性本身就具有一种说服公众的价值。

（二）普及价值

一部逻辑清晰、结构合理的法典，最易于在民众中普及。1791 年《普鲁士民法典》的公布规则中对法典的普及价值有明白的论述：“全部法律将按照一定的条理层次，用民族语言制定，用一种大众能理解的方式表达，以使本国的任何居民，只要其自然能力经受过教育，哪怕是只有中等水平，自己便能阅读法律，弄懂法律，在将来的案件里尊重这些规定，他应当按照法律行事，并应当接受法律的审判。”我国学者也认为，法典对于民众心理的影响不可小视[③]。

法的体系化结构，也容易被采纳为司法判决、理论研究和法学教育的思维模式，从而使新制度不断在现实中得到推广。例如，德国民法典的总则—分则模式，非常符合司法活动从一般到具体的推理习惯；法典的体系化在逻辑上越完善，越容易被采纳为法学著述和法学教育的体系。显然，立法的体系化程度越高，这种理想越有可能实现。当立法体系在司法、学术、教育中被推广之后，就会成为整个法律共同体的语言规则。相反，一部体系混乱的立法常常成为法学教育与学术批评的对象，从法学院走出来的法官们也容易规避他们自认为不妥当的立法，各行其是地寻找裁判依据，从而造成法律共同体内部语言的分裂与裁判的不统一，使立法在实际适用中的影响力被大大减损。

法典的体系化形式对于民众与法律共同体的信念与思维方式具有很强的塑造作用。法典作为司法的文本依据，体系化的文本形式对于裁判思维具有极其重要的指引作用。

二、法典的体系化形式对裁判思维的影响

（一）减轻说理与找法的负担

体系化的主要功能之一，在于储藏人类理解法律的经验。法律体系的基本单位是法律概念。“作为人类的行为规范，法律的制定或接受既然本来便是‘有所为’而来，则在法律之制定、接受或甚至在探讨时，人们对之莫不‘有所期待’……”[④] 因此，概念形成时便融入了特定社会的价值观。一般情况下，只要正确运用概念，便符合概念之后的价值取向，因此裁判者不必重复论证概念的合理性，不必详细剖析概念背后的考量，可以减轻裁判者的思维负担及说服任务。裁判者通过查找与案件事实相关的概念在体系中的定位，就可以发现此概念可适用的规则，而不必盲目地从头再来。例如，尽管知识产权单行法对权利许可规定得非常简略，但只要知道许可合同是合同之一种，就可以在合同法的规则中寻找裁判依据。如果民法典把知识产权许可与合同的联系揭示出来，就可以清晰地指引法官找法。

（二）促进裁判标准的统一

合乎体系是说服力的重要来源，司法裁判的证

① 黄茂荣．法学方法论与现代民法［M］．北京：中国政法大学出版社，2001：406．

② Levasseur A. On the structure of a civil code［J］. Tulane Law Review，1970：697．

③ 尹田．民法典总则之理论与立法研究［M］．北京：法律出版社，2010：16．

④ 黄茂荣．法学方法论与现代民法［M］．北京：中国政法大学出版社，2001：45．

立也不例外。“一种根本没有潜在指涉某个体系的法律证立是一种特别证立。它不符合普遍性与一般性的前提，因而也不符合正义的基本要求。这个句子是有效的：正义要求将法律证立置入一个尽可能融贯的体系之中。”① 当立法体系清晰展现之后，法官会首先在体系中寻找法律概念的依归，而不是任意地创设新的概念与原则，从而起到促进裁判标准的作用。当知识产权的专门规范没有给出明确答案时，法官会上溯至民事权利的通用规范，如果还不能解决，则继续上溯至民法的总则性规定，包括民法的基本原则。

（三）提供新问题的解决思路

按照体系化的方法，面对新问题而缺少直接相应的具体规则时，法官可以从既有规则回溯至规则背后的原则与价值，而后推演出适合新情况的规则。

知识产权界对知识产权救济中停止侵害责任的认识过程就是一个很好的例子。侵害知识产权的归责原则一度成为法学界争论的问题，后来学者们发现，物权救济中的物上请求权行使是无须考虑过错的。回溯物上请求权制度的理据，物权请求权的效力来自物权的绝对性。一切支配权都具有绝对效力，由“物权派生物上请求权”之原理，可以推出“一切支配权派生回复其效力圆满状态之请求权”。所以，民法学者认为，“凡属支配性质之权利，均具有与物上请求权相关之请求权”②。知识产权作为支配性财产权也不例外。于是学者借助物上请求权理论解释知识产权保护中“停止侵害请求权”的性质，并逐渐为实务界认可。这是利用已有的物权原理解决后来出现的知识产权问题，是典型的体系化的思维方法，反映了体系化思维的“温故知新”功能。

三、非体系化思维对我国知识产权审判的制约

相比其他法律领域，知识产权的理论与实务在体系化方面的欠缺更为严重。知识产权审判中非体系化的弊端的主要表现如下：

（一）浪费已有经验

在知识产权实务中，有些民法中已经解决的问题，却被当作新问题重新讨论。最典型的例子当属对侵害防止请求权的误解。所谓侵害防止，是指侵害尚未实际发生时给予的消除侵害危险的权利救济，学界将“侵害之虞”称为“即发侵权”。不少人认为“即发侵权”挑战了传统民法理论，因为民法理论中的侵权构成应当包含实际的侵权行为，从而认为侵害知识产权有别于一般的民事侵权③。在“北京天朝公司诉北京通州运河化工厂”案中④，为了预防侵害商标权的行为发生，法院判令被告销毁已经购买的带有原告商标标识的包装桶，该案被称为“国内即发侵权第一例”。因为此案中被告的侵权行为尚未发生，所以该判决被奉为对传统民法中“侵权四要件”理论的新突破。

以体系化思维观之，“即发侵权”是为了预防侵害的发生，侵害防止并非知识产权特有的救济方式，作为物上请求权类型之一的“妨害预防请求权”即属于侵害防止。侵害防止请求权属于支配力回复请求权，类似于物上请求权，与侵权请求权无关，当然不必满足“侵权四要件”，突破之说无从谈起。此类司法创新，实为经验浪费。

（二）裁判语言与标准的不统一

由于欠缺体系化思维，无法认清体系内已经存储的经验，容易盲目地引入各种新概念，导致裁判语言的混乱。一个成熟的法律共同体，应当尽量保证立法语言、学术语言与裁判语言的统一性。由于脱离了对整个民法体系的观照，知识产权的理论与实务界从其他法域引入了大量与我国民法术语体系不相容的概念。例如，《民法通则》和《著作权法》中只有“著作人身权”的表述，而不少司法文书中却使用“精神权利”的表述。有判决行文如下：“著作权是一系列精神权利和财产权利的集合……《中华人民共和国著作权法》第十条规定的精神权利包括发表权、署名权、修改权和保护作品完整权四项。”⑤ 看不出有何特别理由需要回避立法中的“著作人身权”表述。我国经典教科书认为：“主观的东西不可能受到侵犯，任何人都不能对他的主张享有垄断的支配力，法律既无须也无法为‘精神’设置权利。我国民法理论和民事立法称之为著作人身权，这种称谓符合我国的立法传统，也易于被人理解。”⑥

能够在现有的立法术语体系内找到裁判的依据，是法官说理能力的体现。任意地引入新概念，绝不是值得鼓励的司法创新，这恰恰是欠缺体系化思维、找法能力薄弱的反映。

---

① 罗伯特·阿列克西. 法：作为理性的制度化［M］. 雷磊，译. 北京：中国法制出版社，2012：127.

② 谢在全. 物权法论［M］. 北京：中国政法大学出版社，1999：40.

③ 孙玉. 即发侵权与知识产权保护［N］. 人民法院报，2002-01-28.

④ 北京市二中院（1998）二中初字第124号民事判决书.

⑤ 广西壮族自治区高级人民法院（2013）桂民三终字第65号民事判决书.

⑥ 刘春田. 知识产权法［M］. 5版. 北京：中国人民大学出版社，2014：69.

裁判语言的分裂并不仅仅是一个形式问题，也会在实质上造成裁判标准的不统一。因为“新概念”的表象会使法官错认为这是一个独立于现有概念体系的新问题，从而忽视了本应遵守的体系约束。例如，不少判决书随意地使用“商品化权”“商业秘密权”“包装装潢权”等概念，这些原本局限于个案解决的表述，一旦形成风气，就可能使知识产权审判在整体上疏离了划分权利与法益的民法价值，从而助长司法的任意设权。由于缺乏一致的体系认同，裁判标准必然会不统一。

（三）欠缺温故知新的能力

技术发展迅速以及相应的法律新问题频发，是知识产权法学质疑体系化价值的主要理由。事实上正好相反，越是新问题频发的领域，越要重视体系化。由于人的预见力有限，专门针对新问题的特别规则只能是事后发展起来的。在特别规则颁布之前，裁判者最佳的解决途径就是在体系中寻找已有的规则或原则，用类比或演绎的方式得出解决方案。因此，越是变动频繁的领域，越依赖体系的发展新知的功能。

例如，委托创作合同的纠纷日渐增多，而《著作权法》相关的条文非常简单，实务中不得不参照《合同法》。应当参照哪一种有名合同的规范，是正确找法的前提。不少判决书把委托创作合同称为“委托合同”，显然是错误的。委托合同的标的是完成一定的事务，而委托创作合同的标的是作品，应当属于定作合同。当然，传统的定作合同规则是以“物”作为标的预设的，在适用时可能需要根据物与作品的差异做适当的变通。但只要正确地运用体系化思维，就可以推陈出新。

相比知识产权法，民法的历史悠久，有着比较成熟与完整的概念体系，其中大量的规则与原则都是对民事法律关系的抽象与总结。现象的复杂并不改变社会关系的本质，知识产权领域的新问题未必都是本质性的“前所未有”。

四、知识产权司法需求与民法典的回应

综上所述，从知识产权司法需求的角度考虑，我国的民法典很有必要设立知识产权编。在立法的过程中，可以梳理、审视已有的知识产权规则与民法典的相容性。例如著作人身权与人身权的关系，著作人身权是否具有专属性，对于著作人身权的特别规定如何做出合理的解释①。又如，司法解释对侵害知识产权之诉的诉讼时效做出了特别规定，该规定如何与民法衔接。以著作权为例，根据《最高人民法院关于审理著作权民事纠纷案件适用法律若干问题的解释》第二十八条：“侵犯著作权的诉讼时效为二年，自著作权人知道或者应当知道侵权行为之日起计算。权利人超过二年起诉的，如果侵权行为在起诉时仍在持续，在该著作权保护期内，人民法院应当判决被告停止侵权行为；侵权损害赔偿数额应当自权利人向人民法院起诉之日起向前推算二年计算。”物上请求权不罹于消灭时效，是民法学已有的理论，同一性质的停止侵害请求权类比适用，尚有法理依据。但损害赔偿请求权作为债权请求权，不适用消灭时效的法理依据何在，值得讨论。“在我国民法学说以及民事习惯法上遵循诚实信用原则得到认可的失权期间，即可对其发挥限制功能。”② 虽然知识产权不适用取得时效，若在民法视角下整体审视，裁判者当注意知识产权保护与已有利益关系的稳定性之间的权衡，对于发生时间较长的侵权行为，或许会依据个案更为谨慎地对待停止侵害救济。

把知识产权纳入民法典，会深刻地影响司法者的裁判思维，引导司法者体系性地找法，并且在概念与规则运用方面受到体系约束。同时，针对新技术带来的挑战，司法者也会逐渐养成从体系中推演新知的良好习惯。

裁判思维与裁判语言的统一，才是促进裁判统一的根本途径，而这一目标的达成，最终要仰仗法教义学的成熟。法教义学的主要任务是“认识现行法，体系化地整理现行法和现行法规范背后的道理，用其来沟通和交流，以指导法律实践”③。现实中立法的体系化程度越高，法教义学的建构就越容易，各种法学理论之间的分歧也越小。受过成熟的法教义学熏陶的法官之间，话语与思维的一致性程度也较高。民法典的体例必将影响民法与知识产权教科书的编纂体例以及民法与知识产权法课程的讲授模式，经由法学教育而塑造法官的话语体系与思维模式。同时，不被主流教科书与法学理论接纳的指导性案例或经典案例，起不到太大的影响作用。那些随意运用概念、创设所谓新规则的案例，即便被评选为经典案例或指导性案例，在法学教育和法学研究中也只能作为批判对象而存在，无法通过法教义学的

① 在司法实践中，对于委托创作合同能否约定著作人身权的归属，态度不一。陈锦川．著作权审判：原理解读与实务指导［M］．北京：法律出版社，2014：71.

② 王轶．民法原理与民法学方法［M］．北京：法律出版社，2009：79.

③ 纪海龙．法教义学：力量与弱点［J］．交大法学，2015（2）：90-104.

认可而真正地获得权威性。立法体系依归、符合体系化语言规则与思维规则的先例，也就是与立法、学说契合度最高的先例，才能真正地发挥指导作用。

知识产权裁判已经出现了比较严重的不统一现象[①]。通过在民法典中设置知识产权编，推进知识产权法教义学的发展，深刻影响裁判者的思维方式与表达习惯，缩小立法、司法与学术之间的语言分歧，引导裁判者在体系依托中寻求裁判的正当性与说服力，节制无根基的所谓“司法创新”，才能从根本上推进知识产权裁判的统一性。

（本文原发表于《法律适用》2016年12期，收入时有删减。
作者单位：中国人民大学法学院）

竞争与垄断：我国著作权集体管理组织的模式选择

林秀芹　黄钱欣

一、前言

近年来，我国社会上屡有批评著作权集体管理组织法定垄断地位的声音，如有音乐界人士认为音乐著作权协会（以下简称“音著协”）滥用垄断地位、收费不合理、维权不到位等等[②]。而世界上至今仍然并存着法定垄断与自由竞争两种著作权集体管理模式，孰优孰劣，尚无定论。于我国而言，应综合域外经验、我国实际，选择最适合我国的方案。目前，我国正在修订《中华人民共和国著作权法》（2010年修订，以下简称《著作权法》）与《中华人民共和国著作权集体管理条例》（2005年实施，以下简称《著作权集体管理条例》），因此，探讨我国著作权集体管理组织垄断与竞争问题，必要且迫切。本文将从著作权集体管理组织自由竞争制的弊端、我国著作权集体管理法定垄断实施中的问题以及域外经验等角度进行探讨，并借鉴南非和我国台湾地区的立法模式，对《著作权集体管理条例》有关条文进行修改，实现有限竞争、相对集中的著作权集体管理模式。

二、著作权集体管理组织的竞争与垄断之争

著作权集体管理组织应采用竞争或是垄断模式，从理论到实践，都存有争议。从理论上看，支持著作权集体管理组织应采用竞争模式的理由主要有：法定垄断将导致著作权集体管理组织滥用其市场支配地位，损害权利人和使用者利益，故应引入竞争[③]；引入竞争，可以提高许可效率和发挥市场机制的作用[④]，还将有利于尊重权利人的自主选择权，符合著作权私权自治的理念[⑤]等等。也有学者认为应采用垄断模式，主张以下几点理由：垄断可以降低交易成本[⑥]；垄断是著作权集体管理组织实现成本控制、捍卫作者根本利益、促进作品传播与保存文化多样性功能的前提和基础[⑦]；垄断可以让管理更加高效和具有权威性[⑧]等。从各国家或地区立法情况来看，有的国家或地区规定著作权集体管理组织应以垄断形式存在，比如匈牙利[⑨]、印度[⑩]。而有的国家或地区则未规定著作权集体管理组织应以垄断形式存在，换言之，是允许竞争的，比如美国、加拿大、法国、德国、日本、保加利亚[⑪]、巴西[⑫]等。

---

① 李琛．论商标禁止注册事由概括性条款的解释冲突［J］．知识产权，2015（8）：3-9．

② 李欣．音著协自定标准收版权费涉嫌垄断？［EB/OL］．http://ip.people.com.cn/GB/8573419.html，最后访问日期：2015-06-29；新浪娱乐．宋柯刘欢提著作权法修改意见　打破音著协垄断［EB/OL］．http://ent.sina.com.cn/c/2012-04-16/17563607059.shtml，最后访问日期：2015-06-29；小西：著作权法草案引争议　律师：音著协不应垄断市场［EB/OL］．http://ent.qq.com/a/20120407/000017.htm，最后访问日期：2015-06-29．

③ 崔国斌．著作权集体管理组织的反垄断控制［J］．清华法学，2005（2）：113．

④ 熊琦．著作权集中许可机制的正当性与立法完善［J］．法学，2011（8）：109．

⑤ 王慧．我国音乐作品著作权维权困境的制度反思：以著作权集体管理制度为视角［J］．电子知识产权，2015（4）：47．

⑥ 常青．论著作权集体管理制度：法经济学的视角［J］．法学杂志，2006（6）：104．

⑦ 李陶．论著作权集体管理组织的反垄断规制［J］．知识产权，2015（2）：40．

⑧ 蒋万来．论我国著作权集体管理制度的完善［J］．电子知识产权，2003（11）：16．

⑨ 匈牙利2007年修订的《版权法》第86条第2款规定：“关于以下每一种作品和制品的著作权和相关权，在全国范围内只允许有一个集体管理组织进行管理。”

⑩ 印度1957年颁布的《著作权法》第33条第3款规定：“中央政府通常不得登记一个以上的著作权协会处理同类作品的业务。”十二国著作权法［M］．《十二国著作权法》翻译组，译．北京：清华大学出版社，2011：240．

⑪ 保加利亚2011年修订的《著作权和相关权法》第40条第1款明确规定：“作者可以根据其自身意愿建立著作权集体管理组织。”

⑫ 巴西1998年颁布的《著作权法》第97条第1项规定：“作者和邻接权权利人……不能同时加入多个对同一种类的权利进行集体管理的协会。”（十二国著作权法［M］．《十二国著作权法》翻译组，译．北京：清华大学出版社，2011：22．）这从侧面反映出巴西是允许针对同一种类的权利存在多个集体管理组织的。

可见关于著作权集体管理组织应采用法定垄断还是自由竞争模式，尚无定论。然而，就中国而言，以上两种模式均不理想，而应采用有限竞争、相对集中的模式。

三、自由竞争模式的负面影响

（一）理论层面上自由竞争模式的弊端

第一，自由竞争模式将导致著作权集体管理效益的流失。在自由竞争状态下，存在多家集体管理机构，使用者和权利人都要面对众多的著作权集体管理组织，特别是对于使用者，需要在多家著作权集体管理组织中搜寻和取得许可，因此竞争的多家著作权集体管理机构不能解决交易成本问题①。

从成本与收益的角度来说，著作权集体管理组织也天然地具有倾向垄断、排除自由竞争的性质（但不代表必须要实行法定垄断）。因为著作权集体管理将产生较高的固定成本和相对较低的边际成本，因此这种规模经济效应就将导致更大规模的著作权集体管理组织能运行得更好②。更大规模的著作权集体管理组织可以将固定成本分摊到更多的权利人身上，这样每个权利人所需承担的运行成本就会更低，从而其收入就相对地得以提高③。

第二，竞争模式导致的“叠床架屋”式的著作权集体管理组织将不适应互联网时代海量作品快速流通。著作权集体管理组织建立在当今“碎片化”的权利基础上，各个集体管理组织专司某个领域或某个权利的管理与许可④。于是，随着权利“碎片化”的发展，著作权集体管理组织也渐呈“叠床架屋”之势，各自业务范围错综复杂。而在网络环境下，信息流量极大、流速极快，数字化的版权作品形态呈现多样性及碎片化⑤。在这种情况下，面对“叠床架屋”的著作权集体管理组织体系，作品的创作往往不得不寻求多家著作权集体管理组织的许可，若有任何一家著作权集体管理组织拒绝许可，作品的创作都将可能受到阻碍。虽然“身为事实或法定垄断者的著作权集体管理组织通常不能拒绝许可”⑥，但这至少存在被拒绝许可的风险，提高了使用和创作的难度。即使最终取得了所有许可，但使用者或创作者辗转于各个著作权集体管理组织进行逐个的许可谈判，可能导致最终作品使用或创作累积成本过高⑦。

因此，著作权集体管理组织若可自由设立，则著作权集体管理组织将有“叠床架屋”之虞，作品使用许可往往需辗转于庞杂的著作权集体管理组织体系，既增加成本，又影响效率，不利于互联网时代海量作品的高速流通。

（二）现实层面上自由竞争模式的缺陷

著作权集体管理组织自由竞争制，不仅理论上会出现上述问题，在现实中，也产生了不少问题。这里以法国为例。

法国著作权集体管理组织实行自由竞争制，其国内著作权集体管理组织林立，如表1所示。

表1　　法国主要著作权集体管理组织及业务范围

活动 组织	电视播放	广播播放	在线与移动服务	音乐作品	机械复制/录制内容	面向公众的播放或租赁	舞台现场表演	实物产品	其他
SCAM	N	Y	Y	N	Y	N	N	N	N
SCPP	N	N	Y	Y	N	Y	Y	Y	Y
SPRE	Y	Y	N	N	N	Y	N	N	N
SPPF	Y	N	Y	N	N	Y	N	Y	Y
SDRM	Y	Y	Y	N	Y	Y	N	N	Y

---

① 常青．论著作权集体管理制度：法经济学的视角［J］．法学杂志，2006（6）：104.

② Josef Drexl，Sylvie Nerisson，Felix Trumpke，Reto M. Hilty. Comments of the max planck institute for intellectual property and competition law on the proposal for a directive of the european parliament and of the council on collective management of copyright and related rights and multi-territorial licensing of rights in musical works for online uses in the internal market COM（2012）372［J］. International Review of Intellectual Property and Competition Law，2013，44（3）：325.

③ Gerd Numitor. Max planck institute for intellectual property and competition law［M］. Munich：Flu Press，2013：216.

④ 罗向京．著作权集体管理组织的发展与变异［M］．北京：知识产权出版社，2011：196.

⑤ 陈凤兰．CCC版权运营模式及启示［J］．科技与出版，2014（11）：84.

⑥ Gervais，Daniel. Collective management of copyright：theory and practice in the digital age. Collective Management of Copyright and Related Rights［M］. The Netherlands：Kluwer Law International BV，2010：13.

⑦ European Commission. Copyright and related rights in the information society［M］.［S. l.］：Green Paper of European Commission，1995.

续前表

组织＼活动	电视播放	广播播放	在线与移动服务	音乐作品	机械复制/录制内容	面向公众的播放或租赁	舞台现场表演	实物产品	其他
SACD	Y	Y	Y	N	N	N	Y	Y	N
SACEM	Y	Y	Y	Y	Y	Y	Y	Y	N

资料来源：WIPO，Baker & McKenzie. Collecting societies handbook 2014 [EB/OL]. http://t.im/11p4n，最后访问日期：2015-08-16.

说明：表中所用组织名称为简称，由于该表主要目的是表明法国著作权集体管理组织体系的复杂性，所以就不对组织的全称再进行翻译。表中"N"和"Y"分别表示相应组织未从事和从事表中对应业务活动。该表仅仅列举了法国几个主要的著作权集体管理组织，实际上法国的著作权集体管理组织远超比表中所列，多达26家（Nathalie Piaskowski. Collective management of copyright in france，in Daniel Gervais. Collective management of copyright and related rights [M]. Alphen aan den Rijn：Kluwer Law International，2010：209-213.）。而仅就该表而言，就已十分复杂。

横向看，同一著作权集体管理组织，往往涉及多项业务活动；纵向看，同一业务活动，也往往涉及多个不同的著作权集体管理组织。举例而言，若有使用者想进行音乐作品的广播，那么在音乐作品的许可环节，他就应当向SCPP和SACEM这两家著作权集体管理组织寻求音乐作品的许可；在广播环节，他又将向SCAM、SPRE、SDRM、SACD和SACEM这五家组织寻求取得许可。这样，仅仅一项日常的音乐作品广播活动，就需要使用者做出如此巨大的搜寻努力，产生如此巨大的搜寻成本，堪称"走迷宫"①，势必影响作品的使用和传播。法国文学艺术财产委员会（Conseil Supérieur de la Propriété Littéraire et Artistique）也指出：现存的搜寻和确认权利人的复杂体系，导致有必要建立一个更为简化的体系，以利于囊括更多样和广泛的作品及制品的使用②。

我国虽未实行竞争制的著作权集体管理组织模式，但可想见，若实行自由竞争制，不仅上述问题可能出现，而且将可能有两家以上著作权集体管理组织有权向同一使用人收取使用费，而从我国国情出发，集中管理机制容易被社会接受，分头收费容易使人反感③，给广大使用人带来困扰。

就著作权集体管理制度而言，世界上尚未有成熟的"最佳实践"，各国均应根据自己的国情进行探索，寻求符合本国国情并能促进作品有效流通的桥梁。根据以上分析，著作权集体管理组织实行自由竞争，将与著作权集体管理所要求的规模经济效应矛盾，不适合互联网时代海量作品的高速流通，对我国而言，自由竞争所导致的多头收费甚至还将引起社会的普遍不满。因此，在我国，著作权集体管理组织不宜采用自由竞争模式。

四、法定垄断的缺陷

《著作权集体管理条例》第七条第二款第（二）项④确立了我国著作权集体管理组织的法定垄断地位。而法定垄断，将可能导致著作权集体管理组织滥用市场支配地位，损害权利人和使用者的利益⑤；熊琦认为克服著作权集体管理组织垄断地位的滥用，是实现著作权集中许可机制交易效率的保证⑥，因此也可以由此认为法定垄断将对著作权的集中许可机制和交易效率产生负面作用；而王慧还认为，实行竞争制，有利于尊重权利人的自主选择权，符合著作权私权自治的理念⑦，这也就从反面看出法定垄断会限制权利人（当然包括使用人）的自主选择权，也不利于著作权集体管理组织自身管理水平的提高。而欧盟的竞争法也禁止著作权集体管理组织滥用市场支配地位⑧。

具体而言，法定垄断具有如下缺陷：

第一，从著作权集体管理的原理来说，法定垄断可能导致著作权集体管理组织滥用市场支配地位，损害权利人和使用者的利益。滥用市场支配地位不

① Daniel Gervais. Collective management of copyright：theory and practice in the digital age，in Daniel Gervais. Collective management of copyright and related rights [M]. Alphen aan den Rijn：Kluwer Law International，2010：11-13.

② Nathalie Piaskowski. Collective management of copyright in France，in Daniel Gervais. Collective management of copyright and related rights [M]. Alphen aan den Rijn：Kluwer Law International，2010：209-213.

③ 许超. 多家著作权集体管理组织统一收费：由音像组织同卡拉OK厅纠纷引发的思考 [J]. 电子知识产权，2004（11）：60.

④ 《著作权集体管理条例》第七条第二款规定："设立著作权集体管理组织，应当具备下列条件：……不与已经依法登记的著作权集体管理组织的业务范围交叉、重合……"

⑤ 崔国斌. 著作权集体管理组织的反垄断控制 [J]. 清华法学，2005（2）：113.

⑥ 熊琦. 著作权集中许可机制的正当性与立法完善 [J]. 法学，2011（8）：101.

⑦ 王慧. 我国音乐作品著作权维权困境的制度反思：以著作权集体管理制度为视角 [J]. 电子知识产权，2015（4）：47.

⑧ Dehin，Violaine. The future of legal online music services in the European Union：a review of the EU commission's recent nitiatives in cross-border copyright management [J]. European Intellectual Property Review，2010，32（5）：223.

仅是著作权集体管理领域的问题，而且是反垄断法领域常见的问题，背后的原理在此便不赘述。由于法定垄断是以法律的形式规定了著作权集体管理组织的垄断地位，所以著作权集体管理组织在缺乏竞争压力的条件下，很可能滥用其市场支配地位，损害权利人和使用者的利益。具体损害权利人和使用者利益的做法主要有：限制会员退出、歧视会员、强迫接受一揽子许可、索要高额许可费以及其他行为①。虽然可以依靠反垄断相关法律法规进行规制，但我国反垄断法律法规起步较晚，实践尚不成熟，对著作权集体管理组织的反垄断规制效果尚有待观察。

第二，就我国情况而言，法定垄断还需注意到许可效率低下的问题。熊琦认为，由于我国著作权集体管理组织实行法定垄断制度，而有能力一次性在全国范围内取得代理权的，只有官方性机构，实际上排除了私人创制集体管理组织的可能，所以集体管理组织并非由权利人创制，而仅供权利人加入，导致其缺乏提高许可效率的经济诱因，因此既不会根据市场情势为使用者提供最优许可方案，也不会积极提高自身的运作效率，因此使用者在许可条件的设计和选择上只能接受无效率的结果②。虽然将我国著作权集体管理组织的性质归为“官方机构”的说法有些绝对，但我国著作权集体管理组织常常受到来自权利人和使用者两方的指责，这与其许可效率不高、收费定价难以反映权利人和使用者的需求是有很大关系的。

所以，著作权集体管理组织的垄断，容易导致著作权集体管理组织滥用市场支配地位，损害权利人和使用者的利益，导致许可和管理效率低下等问题。而法定垄断以法律形式固定了垄断地位，从法律上取消了著作权集体管理组织竞争的可能性，更加容易出现上述负面影响。

五、日本著作权集体管理组织竞争与垄断演变路径及反思

日本在著作权集体管理制度建立之初，情况也和我国类似，在同一业务范围内只允许有一家著作权集体管理组织③，后来放开了著作权集体管理组织的竞争，直至今日。其走过的道路，既有值得肯定之处，也存在着一系列问题。我国目前也正面临日本当年类似的情况，因此，日本走过的道路对我国具有借鉴意义。

日本在2001年颁布了《著作权等管理事业法》，将著作权集体管理组织的设立方式由“许可制”④改为“登录制”⑤，根据其规定，只要符合注册条件，著作权集体管理组织就可以设立，由此著作权集体管理组织的设立转为竞争模式，其后日本的著作权集体管理组织由许可制条件下的4家增加到如今的31家⑥。

这项改革给日本著作权集体管理带来了一系列的改观，如扩大了权利人的选择面，潜在的竞争压力促使著作权集体管理组织精简管理费用、提高服务品质、改善经营等⑦。

但同时也应看到，即使在自由竞争制下，著作权集体管理组织仍处于事实垄断的状态。仅以2004年为例，日本音乐著作权协会所收取的使用费占所有音乐作品著作权集体管理所收取使用费的99.25%，而其他有关音乐作品的著作权集体管理组织所收取的使用费仅占所有音乐作品著作权集体管理所收取使用费的0.75%⑧。在表演权的管理领域，由于需要很大的组织能力和管理成本，事实上只有日本音乐著作权协会在进行管理⑨。

另外，日本的著作权集体管理组织和法国一样，也存在“叠床架屋”的问题，同一种作品类型，往往有多家著作权集体管理组织管理，仅以文字作品为例，就有多达15家的著作权集体管理组织从事文字作品的管理业务；而同一家著作权集体管理组织也往往管理数种作品类型，如“教学图书协会”“出版物出租管理中心”等。权利人和使用者面对众多著作权集体管理组织，将产生较高的许可交易成本，不利于著作权集体管理制度目的的实现。日本许多

---

① 崔国斌．著作权集体管理组织的反垄断控制［J］．清华法学，2005（2）：124-132.

② 熊琦．论著作权集体管理中的私人自治［J］．法律科学，2013（1）：147.

③ Koji Okumura. Collective management of copyright and neighbouring rights in Japan, in Daniel Gervais. Collective management of copyright and related rights［M］. Alphen aan den Rijn：Kluwer Law International，2010：385-386.

④ 许可制类似于我国的审批制，但由于两国法律制度不同，所以此处还是采用日文名称——“许可制”，直译为许可制。

⑤ 登录制类似于我国的注册制，但由于两国法律制度不同，所以此处还是采用日本名称——“登録制”，直译为登录制。

⑥ 著作权等管理事业者登录状况一览（平成27年5月1日现在）［EB/OL］．http://www.bunka.go.jp/seisaku/chosakuken/seido-kaisetsu/kanrijigyoho/toroku_jokyo/pdf/toroku_jokyo.pdf，最后访问日期：2015-08-16.

⑦ 文化审议会著作权分科会报告书［R］．文化审议会著作权分科会，2006：193.

⑧ 同⑦178.

⑨ 同⑦183.

团体对集体管理组织的种种弊端提出强烈的疑问与批评，认为在同一业务范围内存在多家著作权集体管理组织，带来了许可手续复杂化、有些著作权集体管理组织信赖度低等问题，要求强化对著作权集体管理组织的规制①。另外，在2010年，日本存在37家著作权集体管理组织②，而到了2015年，则降为31家，说明其中有一些规模较小的组织被竞争所淘汰，这也体现了著作权集体管理所需的规模经济效应，而那些较小的组织被淘汰，不仅将给权利人和使用者带来不便，也将浪费社会资源。

所以，纵览日本著作权集体管理制度的发展路径，可以看到上述优缺点。而且由于著作权集体管理的特殊性，导致即使实行自由竞争，也仍会出现事实垄断，并不能期待依靠自由竞争模式摆脱滥用市场支配地位的阴影。

对于竞争所带来的问题，日本采取的是让市场自行解决的做法，而非在法律上限制竞争③，然而，我国人口众多，区域发展极不平衡，而且作为版权制度后发国家，历史进程以数十倍于以往的速度在前进，是否还容许市场以十年磨一剑的工夫实现自我调整，这确实令人深思④。所以，我国不应再重蹈日本的覆辙，而应在立法上做出更为精妙的设计，一方面顾及著作权集体管理的自然垄断性，采取相对集中的模式，减少或者避免完全放开竞争所带来的弊端，另一方面又适当引入有限竞争，减少或者避免法定垄断所致的积弊，在立法上体现出有限竞争、相对集中的著作权集体管理组织设立制度。

六、我国著作权集体管理组织有限竞争、相对集中的立法设计

我国建立有限竞争、相对集中的著作权集体管理制度，具体而言，可做如下设计：首先，删除现行《著作权集体管理条例》第七条第二款第（二）项的规定；同时，新增一项作为著作权集体管理组织设立的消极条件："申请设立的著作权集体管理组织，其业务范围与已经批准设立的著作权集体管理组织业务范围全部或部分重复的，如果已经批准设立的著作权集体管理组织已能够充分有效发挥著作权集体管理的作用，国务院著作权管理部门对该重复部分的申请，可以不予批准。"通过上述修改，有限竞争、相对集中的著作权集体管理将分为两个方面理解。

首先，取消《著作权集体管理条例》第七条第二款第（二）项，意味着在同一业务范围内，允许设立一家以上的著作权集体管理组织，从而取消了法定垄断的壁垒，著作权集体管理组织的竞争就有了可能，这将有利于克服垄断所导致的弊端，促使著作权集体管理组织提升管理水平。

其次，新增一项作为著作权集体管理组织设立的消极条件。该规定参考了我国台湾地区2010年修订的"著作权集体管理团体条例"第8条第2款⑤和南非2006年颁布的《关于在音乐产业建立著作权集体管理组织的规定》第3条第3款第g项⑥。这项设计提供了是否批准设立著作权集体管理组织的判断标准，即"已经批准设立的著作权集体管理组织已能够充分有效发挥著作权集体管理的作用"。这就将著作权集体管理组织设立的目的置于优先地位，著作权集体管理组织的设立，是为了能够充分有效地发挥著作权集体管理的作用，若现存的著作权集体管理组织已能实现该目的，国务院著作权管理部门就将可能不再批准设立新的著作权集体管理组织。而国务院著作权管理部门也可根据各业务范围自然垄断强度的不同，灵活判断设立的著作权集体管理组织的数量，垄断性强的，则数量可能少一些，垄断性弱的，则数量可能多一些。所以，采用上述标准判断批准设立与否，是较合理的。

由此，从积极和消极条件两方面，设计出有限竞争、相对集中的著作权集体管理制度，既能够引入有限竞争，克服法定垄断带来的弊端，又能将竞

① 文化审议会著作权分科会报告书［R］. 文化审议会著作权分科会，2006：193-194.

② Koji Okumura. Collective management of copyright and neighbouring rights in Japan，in Daniel Gervais. Collective management of copyright and related rights［M］. Alphen aan den Rijn：Kluwer Law International，2010：391.

③ 文化审议会著作权分科报告书中所提到，"由于竞争的效果还未显现"，所以才造成现实运行当中使用者所反映的问题，"没必要对现行法律（指《著作权等管理事业法》——笔者注）进行修改，而应由文化厅加强指导监督"。文化审议会著作权分科会报告书［R］. 文化审议会著作权分科会，2006：194.

④ 文化审议会著作权分科会报告书［R］. 文化审议会著作权分科会，2006：234.

⑤ 我国台湾地区"著作权集体管理团体条例"第8条第2款规定："申请管理之范围与业经许可之集管团体之管理著作类别及权利范围有全部或一部重复者，如业经许可之集管团体已足以发挥集体管理之功能，著作权专责机关就该重复之部分，得不予许可。"

⑥ 南非《关于在音乐产业建立著作权集体管理组织的规定》第3条第3款第g项规定："除非申请者满足下列条件，否则登记注册将不被允许：……对申请者予以登记注册，不会与业已存在的著作权集体管理组织所进行的足够的、有效的和有影响的集体管理活动产生冲突。"

争限制在有限范围内，减少或避免过度竞争所可能导致的缺陷，这对我国而言，可以说是一种比较理想的立法设计。

七、结论

综上所述，面对由来已久的著作权集体管理组织的竞争与垄断问题之争，我国既不应实行完全自由竞争的模式，也不应继续法定垄断的道路，而应兼顾著作权集体管理的天然垄断特性和竞争所具备的优点，建立有限竞争、相对集中的著作权集体管理模式。当然，其中竞争和集中的界限应当划在何处，则有待今后理论和实践进一步探讨。

（本文原发表于《知识产权》2016 年第 5 期，为 2014 年国家版权局政策法制司委托项目“《著作权集体管理条例》修订设计”阶段性研究成果。作者林秀芹系厦门大学法学院、知识产权研究院教授，黄钱欣系厦门大学知识产权研究院博士研究生）

论著作权法语境中的作品结构

——以中小学教辅对教材进行“结构性使用”为例

卢海君

一、问题的提出

在作品的非文字性要素中，作品结构是重要一环，其可版权性地位很早都被确立①，在知识产权理论界也普遍被认可②。虽然如此，围绕作品结构的著作权争议频发，例如在我国著作权司法实践中，围绕同步教辅“延用”中小学教材的结构所引发的著作权争议此起彼伏。其根本原因在于，应受著作权法保护的作品结构并未被正确认识，该结构在著作权法中的地位也未被清晰阐述。现有对教材教辅版权争议所进行的理论解读就是典型。中小学教材大多数是汇集已有事实和材料（包括作品），并在这些事实和材料的基础之上进行选择与编排之后所形成的作品，属于典型的汇编作品③。教材编写者如果在事实和材料的选择或编排上具有个性，则最终可以形成具有原创性的汇编作品，其原创性集中体现在作者个性的选择或编排所最终形成的表达形式上，而这些表达形式往往集中表现为教材原创性的结构。基于此，本文将以教材教辅有关作品结构的著作权争议为例，研习著作权法语境中的作品结构的真实所指，并以此为基础，对教材教辅有关作品结构的著作权争议进行解析，以期折射出作品结构著作权保护的一般原理。

二、作品结构的著作权法地位

作品结构即作品各个组成部分的排列组合方式，例如，普通文字作品中章、节、段之间的排列组合方式，软件作品中各模块之间的排列组合方式等。作品结构是作品的重要构成元素，在特定类型作品（例如，汇编作品）中甚至有可能是唯一可受著作权法保护的元素④。作品结构的著作权法地位不仅体现在其价值之上，而且体现在作者所付出的创造性劳动之上⑤。作品结构著作权法地位的确立，不仅在作品之间是否基于作品结构的近似而构成实质性相似的判定时有意义，而且，作品结构的可单独利用性也在不少作品类型中予以突出体现。例如，在软件作品中，他人可以对软件作品进行反向工程，解析出其中的软件结构，并在此基础之上创作出代码不同的软件。甚至，软件结构可以脱离软件成为独立的交易客体。在此意义上，至少是在特定的作品类型中，作品结构有脱离作品而获得独立著作权法地位的端倪。

（一）作品结构的存在形式

版权法应该保护作者的创作成果，通俗而言被称为作品，本质是一种表达形式，具体表现为意义符号的排列组合（例如，作品的文本表达）以及能够被这些排列组合所直接限定的表达元素（例如，作品的情节、结构、角色等）⑥。整个作品表现为不应受版权保护的思想、应受版权保护的由作品的文本表达所能够直接限定的元素（例如，作品的具体性结构）和应受版权保护的文本表达的三元结构，该结构就如同一个金字塔，抽象思想处于金字塔的顶端，具体的文本表达处于金字塔的底端，应受版

---

① Whelan Associates Inc. v. Jaslow Dental Laboratory, Inc. , et al. 797 F. 2d 1222, 230 USPQ 481.

② Melville B. Nimmer, David Nimmer. Nimmer on copyright [A]. New York: Matthew & Bender Company, Inc. , 2009, 13. 03 [A] [1].

③ Alfred Bell & Co. v. Catalda Fine Arts, Inc. , 191 F. 2d 99, 102 (2d Cir. 1951).

④ Feist Publications, Inc. v. Rural Tel. Serv. Co. , 111 S. Ct. 1289. (interimed. 1991).

⑤ 例如，在软件作品中，作品结构是作品至关重要的构成元素，是软件价值的重要决定因素，同时也是软件作品创作中最为困难的环节。反倒是，软件代码即软件的文字性要素的创作较为简单。Lotus Dev. Corp. v. Paperback Software Int'l, 740 F. Supp. 37, 56 (D. Mass. 1990).

⑥ 卢海君. 版权客体论：第 2 版 [M]. 北京：知识产权出版社，2014：111.

权保护的由作品的文本表达所直接限定的元素处于中间。在这个三元结构中，抽象思想好比作品的灵魂，由作品的文本表达所直接限定的元素好比作品的骨架，文本表达好比作品的血肉，灵魂、骨架与血肉有机联系构成整体性的作品。由思想表达两分法[①]可知，处于金字塔顶端的抽象思想并不受版权法保护；处于金字塔底端的文本表达在满足原创性要件时应受版权法保护；处于金字塔中间的由文本表达所直接限定的元素有可能受版权法保护，也有可能不受版权法保护，衡量其是否具有可版权性的关键在于这些元素是否细致到一定程度以至于演变成作者的创作成果。换言之，由作品的文本表达所能够直接限定的元素本身可被界分成不同的抽象层次，在这些抽象层次中，存在一个临界点，临界点之上的部分属于不应受版权法保护的思想，临界点之下的部分属于应受版权法保护的表达。具体到作品结构，其可以界分为概括性结构与具体性结构，只有细致到一定程度的具体性结构才可受版权法保护。

（二）作品结构的正确界定

作品结构是整体作品的有机组成部分，作品具体性结构的界定需要结合作品内容进行。作品具体性结构应指将特定内容放在特定位置所呈现出来的作品各个组成部分的独特排列组合方式，此方式从较高的抽象层级来看，可能表现为时间顺序、逻辑顺序等，但处于较高抽象层级的方式并不具有可版权性。以中小学语文教材为例，教材的结构即构成教材整体的各个被选作品的编排，此编排可能反映的是一种“时间顺序”。“时间顺序”显然属于不应受版权法保护的思想，只有由各个被选作品所构成的具体性编排才属于应受版权法保护的结构。按照中小学语文教材所编写的同步教辅的结构在较高的抽象层次上必然也是“时间顺序”，但该顺序不受版权法保护毋庸置疑；在较低的抽象层次上，其结构表现为构成教辅整体的每部分解析的编排，此编排为应受版权法保护的具体性编排。由此可见，尽管教材与同步教辅的结构在较高抽象层次上具有同一性，但在具体性结构层面并不相同。上述有关作品结构界定的方式具有普适性。例如，对于事实性汇编作品，如电话号码簿。两部电话号码簿，其一为甲城市居民的，其二为乙城市居民的，尽管两者都按照字母顺序进行排列，但两者的具体性结构并不相同，因为前者的具体性结构为将甲城市居民的电话号码按照字母顺序排列所形成的排列组合方式，而后者的具体性结构为将乙城市居民的电话号码按照字母顺序排列所形成的排列组合方式。又如，对于普通文学作品，如报道文学作品。两部报道文学作品，其一是有关甲的，其二是有关乙的，尽管两部文学作品都是按照时间顺序进行顺叙，但两者的具体性结构并不相同，因为前者的具体性结构为将有关甲的情节片段按照时间顺序进行顺叙所形成的排列组合方式，而后者的具体性结构为将有关乙的情节片段按照时间顺序进行顺叙所形成的排列组合方式。

（三）作品结构原创性的判定

著作权法保护思想的表达形式，并不保护思想本身，但只有原创性的表达形式才能够获得著作权法保护。表达形式是否具有个性是衡量其是否满足原创性的根本标准[②]。作品结构是作品的构成要素，具体性的作品结构是一种表达形式，在其满足原创性要件时应受著作权法保护。以教材结构为例，从创作过程的演进来看，当作者所构思的作品结构达到一定的细致程度，即从思想转化成表达[③]，可能演变成应受版权法保护的客体。例如，“按照时间顺序编排文章”是不应受版权法保护的思想，但贯彻此种思想安排特定的文章放在特定的章节所形成的特定结构却是应受版权法保护的表达。如果特定的教材结构是作者个性思想的产物，该教材结构即满足了原创性，从而可以获得版权法保护。在教材的编写过程中，编写者需要考虑的因素至少包括但不限于下列几个方面：规划的贯彻落实、学习的循序渐进、知识的逻辑关系、学生的兴趣爱好等。通常而言，越是优秀的教材，编写者所考量的因素越多。基于此，一部教材尤其是优秀教材的结构通常是作者个性创作的产物，从而可以满足原创性要件而受版权法保护。同教材创作类似，对于其他类型作品，作品结构的安排对整个作品的形成至关重要，在文学作品的创作中，数个相同的情节片段以不同的顺序进行不同的排列组合（例如顺叙与倒叙），形成不同的作品，带来不同的欣赏体验。在事实性汇编作品中，结构的安排关乎读者信息获取的效率，数个

① 思想表达两分法是著作权法的基本原理，是整个著作权法规则的基石，意指著作权法只保护思想的表达方式，并不保护思想本身。Baker v. Selden, 101 U.S. 99 (1879).

② Bleistein v. Donaldson Lithographing Co. 188 U.S. 239, 23 S. Ct. 298, 47 L. Ed. 460.

③ 作者的创作行为事实上是从思想到表达的转化过程。卢海君. 版权客体论［M］. 北京：知识产权出版，2011：46-48.

电话号码以不同的结构（例如按照字母顺序和按照行业排序）进行编排所带来的便捷性并不相同。在功能性作品（譬如软件作品）的创作过程中，结构关乎作品的效率，数个相同的模块进行不同的排列组合，运行的效率可能迥然不同。作品结构的合理安排甚至是提高作品审美价值的重要决定性因素①。因此，在作品的创作过程中，作者通常会下大功夫"雕作"作品结构，以期通过作品的结构美实现整个作品的形式美。作者在设计作品结构时，其独特的思想与观念随着作品创作过程的演进最终转化成个性的表达形式，从而满足原创性要件而取得可版权性地位②。

（四）基于作品结构进行作品实质性相似的判定

由上述作品的三元结构之间的关系可知，如果作品的文本表达相同，作品的结构必然相同，当作品的文本表达相同之时，证成作品之间构成版权侵权关系当无疑问。但反过来，如果作品的文本表达不同，作品的结构不一定有差异，此时，欲判定两部作品之间是否构成版权侵权关系就需要从作品的实质性部分（substantial part）③（包括作品结构）入手。"字面侵权"（literal copying）并不产生理论难题，在版权司法实践中也属少见。通常而言，欲证成两部作品之间构成版权侵权关系，须满足接触与实质性相似（substantial similarity）两项要件。实质性相似理论在"字面侵权"中并无意义，通常只有在作品的文本表达不同，但同时包括作品结构在内的其他作品的实质性部分相同或相近时才会凸显其价值。作品的实质性部分实际上就是构成作品的个性表达元素，包括但不限于结构、情节、角色等。因此，两部作品的结构近似是证成其间构成实质性相似的重要考量因素。需要注意的是，判断两部作品是否具有实质性相似时，所应比较的是两部作品受版权保护的部分④，即如果以作品结构相同或相近为依据判定实质性相似是否构成，必须在应受版权法保护的具体性结构的基础之上进行。反之，在抽象性结构相似的基础之上得出两部作品构成版权侵权关系的结论必然为假，因为抽象性结构根本不应受著作权法保护。例如，一部语文教材与一部数学教材遵循的都是循序渐进的学习规律，此即为抽象结构上的近似，但很难下结论认为两部教材之间构成实质性相似。所以，在进行实质性相似的判定中首先要解决的问题是，特定作品具体性结构的真实所指。如果没有正确解决该问题，混淆了"此结构"与"彼结构"，容易得出错误结论。上述有关教材教辅的著作权争议的解决方案之所以不尽如人意，个中原因之一便是没有认清这一问题，混淆了教材与教辅两种不同种类作品的不同结构。尽管教材原创性的具体性结构应受著作权法保护，但实际上，教辅所沿用的教材的结构并非教材应受版权保护的具体性结构，而是处于较高抽象层次不应受版权法保护的结构。

作品结构只是构成作品的表达元素之一，尽管在有些情形之下（例如上文所述电话号码簿），作品结构为作品中唯一的原创性因素，在基于作品结构进行作品之间是否具有实质性相似的判定时，也应将作品结构放置在作品整体中进行考量。一般而言，不同种类作品尤其是不同类型作品之间，很难证成其间存在实质性相似。对于不同种类作品，例如，教辅与教材，尽管两者都属于文字作品，尽管两者具有密切联系，在沿用教材结构编写教辅的场合，即便有人认为教辅的结构同教材的结构完全相同（从上文的论述可以看出，教辅同教材在结构上的相似之处处于较高的抽象层次，从而不应受版权法保护），不论从整体概念与感觉原则⑤出发，还是基于约减主义⑥的路径⑦，通常也很难证成同步教辅同教材之间构成实质性相似，因为两者是不相同的两类作品，就好比人与狗，虽然都是生物，都有四肢与五脏六腑，但很难就此得出结论认为人与狗为同一物。对于不同类型作品，例如，雕塑作品与舞蹈作品，即使两者神似，很明显，也难以下结论认为两者构成实质性相似。

三、合并原则对作品结构版权保护的限制

合并原则是著作权法的基本原则之一，此原则在作品的任何层级的表达元素中都具有可适用性，申言之，其不仅在作品的文字性要素中适用，也适用于作品的非文字性要素。由此，作品的结构选择如果具有唯一性或者有限性，该作品的结构即使属

① 刘颖．作品结构与形式美探论［J］．东北师大学报（哲学社会科学版），2011（2）．

② Burrow-Giles Lithographic Co. v. Sarony111 U. S. 53，4 S. Ct. 279，28 L. Ed. 349.

③ Lionel Bently，Brad Sherman. Intellectual Property Law（4th edition）［M］. Oxford：Oxford University Press，2014：195.

④ Nichols v. Universal Pictures Corp. 45 F. 2d 119，121（2d Cir. 1930）.

⑤ Roth Greeting Cards v. United Card Co. 429 F. 2d 1106，1110（9th Cir. 1970）.

⑥ Nichols v. Universal Pictures Corp.，45 F. 2d 119，121（2d Cir. 1930）.

⑦ 卢海君．论作品实质性相似和版权侵权判定的路径选择：约减主义与整体概念和感觉原则［J］．政法论丛，2015（1）．

于抽象层次较低的具体性结构，也不应该获得著作权法保护。正确认识到合并原则在作品结构版权保护中的可适用性，前述有关教材教辅的著作权争议便可迎刃而解。申言之，虽然教材的原创性结构应受版权法保护，但此只能够说明按照教材的具体性结构编写教材应该获得原教材版权人的许可，否则构成版权侵权；而并不能够说明按照教材的结构编写教辅，教辅即构成对教材的版权侵权的结论，因为，如上所述，教辅同教材本属两类作品，并且两者相似的结构处于较高的抽象层次，难以证明教辅同教材构成实质性相似。在较为极端的情形中，教材版权人自己也编写了教辅，其以他人所创作的教辅侵犯其教辅版权为由阻碍他人沿用教材结构编写教辅，此种诉讼主张仍然不能够成立，其根本原因就在于合并原则在沿用教材结构编写教辅的情形中适用。具体而言，从教辅的性质及其同教材的关系出发，教辅的功能是辅助学生理解和学习教材内容，这一功能决定了教辅的整体概括性结构必然同于教材的整体概括性结构，否则，教辅的功能不能够圆满实现。在这一整体概括性结构的基础之上，教辅编写者将特定解析内容放置在整体概括性结构之中，形成具体性结构，由于两部作品都是教辅，所以，在这一整体概括性结构的基础之上所形成的具体性结构也必然相近。因此，利用教材结构编写教辅尤其是同步教辅，在教辅整体概括性结构和具体性结构的选择上，仅有唯一或有限表达，也即“按照教材整体结构编写教辅”这一思想仅有唯一或有限的表达方式。依据合并原则，该唯一或有限的表达不应该受到版权法保护，否则会产生思想垄断的后果，教辅市场进而会被垄断。因此，即使他人所编写的教辅同教材版权人自己所编写的教辅在具体性结构上完全相同，也并不能认为两部作品之间构成实质性相似，因为，该结构为受合并原则限制的唯一或有限表达，本不应受版权法的保护，以不受版权法保护的要素被他人作品利用为由主张版权侵权岂不怪哉？

教辅结构之所以会受合并原则限制而处于不受著作权法保护的地位，根本原因在于，教辅结构的创作受到各种因素的制约进而可发挥的空间有限。在其他类型作品结构的创作过程中，只要是结构创作受到特定因素的制约而受限，其结构的可版权性就可能存在问题。例如，在电话号码簿的编排中，如果在电话号码的取舍上并没有体现作者的原创性，按照字母顺序对电话号码所进行的编排可能是唯一实用的方式[①]，该编排方式如果受到著作权法保护，显然是不合理的。不同种类的作品，作品结构的创作空间可能并不一样。相对于普通文字作品，功能性作品的结构创作受限因素更多，受合并原则限制的可能性更大。例如，软件结构的设计可能受到诸多外部因素的影响，这些因素包括数据格式、机器规格、兼容性要求、效率等，从而软件的潜在表达范围有限[②]，在软件结构的版权保护中，相对于普通文字作品的结构，合并原则适用的可能性更大，软件结构的保护范围应当较窄一些。即便都为非功能性的文字作品，语文教材与数学教材结构的创作空间都不一样，相对而言，受循序渐进学习规律的限制，数学教材结构的创作空间更小一些，受合并原则限制的可能性更大一些。

四、结论

纵观著作权法的发展历史，著作权的保护范围不断向纵深方向发展，突出表现就是，作品受著作权保护的范围从文字性要素向诸如结构、情节等非文字性要素扩张[③]。原创性的作品文字性要素当然是作者的创作成果，理应受著作权法保护；原创性的作品结构、情节等非文字性要素亦为作者的创作成果，同理，也应受著作权法保护。不过，相对于作品的文字性要素，作品的非文字性要素更难以精确界定，因此，著作权法保护范围的理性扩张应该仰赖对作品非文字性要素的确切认知。作品构成要素的组成犹如一个金字塔，抽象思想处于金字塔的顶端，具体的文本表达处于金字塔的底端，由作品的文本表达所直接限定的元素处于中间。抽象思想不应受著作权法保护，具体的文本表达在满足原创性要件时应受著作权法保护，处于较低抽象层级上的由作品的文本表达所直接限定的表达元素在满足原创性要件时也应受著作权法保护。作品结构是作品的有机组成部分，属于作品的非文字性要素，按照其具体性程度的不同，作品结构可以界分为抽象性结构与具体性结构两个层级，抽象性的作品结构属于思想的范畴，不受著作权法保护，具体性的作品结构属于处于较低抽象层级的由作品的文本表达

① BellSouth Advertising & Publishing Corp. v. Donnelley Information Publishing. 999 F. 2d 1436 (11th Cir. 1993) (en banc), cert. denied, 114 S. Ct. 943 (1994).

② 尽管一部软件作品可能有众多可能的表达方式，但往往只有有限的经济上实用的表达。

③ 卢海君. 版权客体论［M］. 北京：知识产权出版社，2014：19.

所直接限定的表达元素，在满足原创性要件的前提之下应受著作权法保护。作品的结构设计是否具有个性是评判其是否能够满足原创性要件的根本标准。当作者在进行结构设计时其独特的思想与观念随着作品创作过程的演进最终转化成个性的表达形式时，该结构即获得可版权性地位。作品之间是否构成实质性相似的判定应该基于作品中应受版权法保护的具体性结构。作品是其各个构成要素所组成的有机整体，界定某部作品中应受著作权法保护的结构应该考虑作品的不同种类并结合作品内容进行。如同作品的文本表达，对作品结构的著作权法保护也应该放在整体的著作权法制视野中进行考察。也即，对作品结构的著作权法保护也应受各种著作权限制制度的约束。由此，依据思想表达两分法与合并原则，当按照特定思想所创作的作品结构具有唯一性或有限性时，该作品结构同不受著作权法保护的思想合并，从而不应受著作权法保护。

（本文原发表于《社会科学》2016年第12期，收入时内容有删减。
作者单位：对外经济贸易大学法学院）

实用艺术作品交叉保护的证成与潜在风险之化解

吕炳斌

一、引言

正在进行的著作权法修改拟明确将“实用艺术作品”增列为著作权（版权）保护的客体。《中华人民共和国著作权法（修订草案送审稿）》第五条第二款第（九）项规定：“实用艺术作品，是指玩具、家具、饰品等具有实用功能并有审美意义的平面或者立体的造型艺术作品”。实用艺术作品明列为著作权保护客体是此次著作权法修改的亮点之一。

在以往法律实践中，我国法院已有将实用艺术品作为美术作品提供著作权保护的先例，但遇到的一个难题是实用艺术作品著作权和外观设计专利权之间的竞合和冲突。本次著作权法修改拟新增实用艺术作品这一类型，对实用艺术作品的著作权和外观设计专利权的关系问题却避而不答，仍给未来的司法实践留下不确定性。随着技术的发展，艺术和技术的结合变得容易。这种结合增添了产品的顾客吸引力，从本质上符合人们日益增长的精神文化需求。

那么，实用艺术作品著作权和外观设计专利权的关系到底该如何正确定位？交叉保护是否会导致扩大保护的风险？如何避免可能存在的制度风险？这些在逻辑上紧密相关的问题值得进行前瞻性研究。

二、实用艺术作品的交叉保护

（一）专利和版权之间的模糊地带

实用艺术作品位于技术与艺术的十字路口，处于专利和版权之间的模糊地带。实用艺术作品在很大程度上可能与外观设计发生交叉，有可能获得交叉保护甚至重叠保护。

基于实用艺术作品和外观设计之间的模糊关系，相关知识产权国际条约都承认实用艺术作品和工业品外观设计为应受知识产权保护的客体，但并未强制要求成员方以专利权或版权等明确的方式对其加以保护。在知识产权的国际法框架下，成员方有义务保护工业品外观设计和实用艺术作品，有权选择以何种方式对其提供保护，如采用版权法、专利法或自成一体的专门法。

基于实用艺术作品的特殊性、国际条约协调的模糊性，在我国法律实践中，对实用艺术作品著作权和外观设计专利权均可进行保护，但对其关系产生了“双重保护”和“非此即彼”之争。

（二）“双重保护”和“非此即彼”之争

1. 双重保护说

双重保护是我国司法实践中的一种立场，典型案例如英特莱格公司诉可高公司著作权纠纷案①。有法官撰文指出，即使外观设计在专利权失效后，如果仍然符合著作权法规定的保护条件，不能仅仅因为其曾经受到专利法保护的事实而拒绝继续给予著作权法保护，并认为这种双重保护不会破坏知识产权制度本应具有的公益目标，而是全面充分保护权利人利益的必然要求②。

2. 非此即彼说

非此即彼说（选择论）认为，如果权利人选择外观设计专利权进行保护，进入公有领域后，该设计不应再享有其他类型知识产权的保护，否则将有违外观设计专利制度的本意③。

---

① 北京市高级人民法院（2002）高民终字第279号民事判决书。
② 凌宗亮. 失效的外观设计仍受著作权法保护［J］. 人民司法·案例，2010（4）：86-89.
③ 徐晓雁，张鹏. 外观设计专利权与实用艺术品著作权竞合冲突问题与对策研究［J］. 中国发明与专利，2014（8）：87.

非此即彼说的核心在于一旦权利人选择专利权保护，专利权失效后的外观设计不再受到著作权保护。这种立场也反映在我国司法实践中。典型案例如三茂公司诉永隆商行著作权侵权纠纷案。在该案中，法院认为三茂公司自愿选择将涉案标贴申请外观设计专利权进行保护，在专利权失效之后，该设计就进入公有领域，社会公众均可自由使用，不能再受到著作权法保护①。又如，在谢新林诉叶根木、海宁市明扬食品公司著作权侵权纠纷案中，法院认为他人对失效的外观设计的实施不会侵犯外观设计中的著作权，理由是认定侵权将有违专利法的立法宗旨，也将影响社会公众对专利公示效力的信赖利益②。

（三）正确定位：交叉保护及其正当性

1. 本文观点：交叉保护

本文倾向于双重保护说，但双重保护、重叠保护这样的术语易使人产生误解，以为同一客体可以在一般意义上获得外观设计专利权和实用艺术作品著作权的同时保护。其实不然，两者的关系严格而言是“交叉保护”，而非“双重保护”。两者取得条件各异，只有当一个客体同时符合各自条件时，才能获得双重保护。交叉保护实为一种有条件的重叠保护。

外观设计专利权保护立足于产品之上，要求其美感设计必须与产品相结合，是对产品设计方案的创新，在设计的美感上要具有新颖性。外观设计还要求具有工业应用性。实用艺术作品只有当在工业上能批量生产时，才可作为工业品外观设计获得专利权保护；若仅能以手工制作，则无法归入工业品外观设计③。然而，一个外观设计可否获得著作权保护，取决于是否满足著作权法规定的实质性条件。著作权保护的关键在于产品上体现出来的美感表达，要求在表达上具有独创性。专利保护和著作权保护的条件存在差异，其交叉保护只存在于其交集之中。

2. 交叉保护的正当性：基于知识产权法原理的考察

（1）根源所在：思想表达两分法。

交叉保护在理论上具有正当性和圆融性。实用艺术作品著作权和外观设计专利权的交叉保护的根源在于思想表达两分法。从原理上而言，专利法保护的是创意或思想，通过专利法对外观设计进行保护也是旨在保护这种设计的美学思想，而非美感表达；与之相反，著作权法保护的是创意的表达。专利权和著作权的保护客体存在差别。而实用艺术作品和外观设计很可能指向同一对象。实用艺术作品具有实用性、功能性，与产品相结合，就可能同时落入外观设计的范畴。

在思想表达两分法下，外观设计专利权期满之后，其设计的思想进入公有领域，但其设计的美感表达仍受著作权法保护。他人如要使用该外观设计，需要在该设计的形状、图案或者其结合以及色彩与形状、图案的结合上做表达形式上的变更。如将一个外观设计的颜色做变更，在专利权保护期内，仍可能因为等同侵权、实质性相似而构成侵权，在专利权到期后，如果不构成对具有独创性的表达形式的复制或实质性复制，就不属于同一表达形式，将不会侵犯著作权。

（2）契约论对额外的专利保护的解释。

实用艺术作品交叉保护的本质在于：实用艺术作品一旦创作完成，就自动享有版权保护，然而，如果申请并获得了专利，就在版权保护之上添加了一个专利保护。本文认为，这一添加的专利保护是创作者或设计者通过专利制度公开其作品或设计的对价。契约论可以为之提供很好的理论诠释。

实用艺术作品的交叉保护本质上是在符合专利法和著作权法各自条件的情形下，在自动保护的著作权之上添加一个需要经过申请获得的专利权。这一额外的专利保护在理论上可以被视为创作者通过专利申请这一权威且具有较高公信力的程序向全社会较早地公开其设计方案的对价。添加的专利保护以公开为对价，并不需要以消灭版权保护为对价。以公开作为获得专利保护的对价契合知识产权法基本原理，而以消灭版权保护作为专利保护的对价在实体法上和理论上都找不到依据。

（3）激励创新论视野下的交叉保护。

作为公开的对价，知识产权制度给予实用艺术作品创作者一个额外的专利权，但这种专利权的保护期限相比著作权保护期限而言较短，较好地实现了利益平衡。在专利权保护期届满之后，他人即可以利用其创意，创作出新的表达形式，这有利于促进实用艺术品的持续创新。可以享有版权保护的实用艺术作品的创意和思想对应的表达形式应当较多，从而存在进一步设计、创新的空间。

在外观设计专利权届满后，在实用艺术作品著作权保护期内，他人可以充分地利用表达形式的创

① 广东省高级人民法院（2005）粤高法民三终字第236号民事判决书。

② 浙江省嘉兴市中级人民法院（2013）浙嘉知终字第5号民事判决书。

③ 吕炳斌. 实用艺术作品可版权性的理论逻辑［J］. 比较法研究，2014（3）：70-71.

作空间，利用已存在的设计创意，发挥想象，不断创作出新的表达形式。这样的制度安排本质上是有利于激励艺术和创作的不断发展的。

（4）知识产权制度的逻辑自洽性。

如果一个实用艺术作品不申请专利保护，可以享有较长的知识产权保护期限，而一旦创作者花费成本，去申请并获得专利权保护，其可享有的知识产权保护期限却被缩减。这在逻辑上将产生明显的悖论，无法自洽。

在非此即彼的选择论下，还可能产生一个在逻辑上无法自圆的问题。如果一个创作者对其创作或设计选择进行专利保护，但其专利申请由于不符合新颖性要求以失败告终，如果严格按照选择论的逻辑，创作者已经选择专利保护而放弃了版权保护，这意味着其作品无法受到本可享有的版权保护。这样的制度安排存在明显的不公之处，给创作者的选择施加了过高的风险。著作权法对版权保护的条件自有其体系，将满足独创性要求的作品排除出版权保护，将破坏著作权法在体系上的一致性。

三、交叉保护可能导致的制度风险及其避免措施

（一）交叉保护可能导致的扩大保护之制度风险

尽管实用艺术作品的交叉保护有其正当性，但不可否认，交叉保护在某种程度上将导致扩大保护的制度风险。这种现象主要发生在一个客体同时满足专利权和著作权保护的条件从而同时享有两种权利的场合。正如有论者指出，交叉保护使权利人在相应期限内的权利垄断性强于单一模式保护①。

本文的观点是正视两者的交叉保护，并进行两项权利之间的平衡架构，采取措施尽可能避免实用艺术作品的扩大保护。

（二）避免实用艺术作品扩大保护的纠正措施

1. 实质性条件的限制

（1）可分离性原则的把关。

可分离性原则源于思想表达两分法，意在将实用艺术作品中的实用性和艺术性进行分离。只有当艺术性可以从产品的实用功能中分离出来时，这种艺术表达才具有独立性，才可以作为版权保护的客体进行评价从而可能获得版权保护。否则，如果艺术设计和实用功能水乳交融、难解难分，这种具有审美特征的产品只能通过外观设计专利权进行保护，无法获得版权保护。可分离性标准扎根于思想表达两分法，契合著作权法基本原理，可以作为实用艺术作品可版权性判断的一个基本原则。

可分离性原则的典型立法例见于美国。在我国司法实践中，法院在关于实用艺术作品著作权保护的裁判中已经引入可分离性原则。

基于可分离性原则在实践中已被我国法院接受，但其判断又颇具难度，尤其是观念上的可分离性判断更是难以把握，有必要探寻一种尽可能符合著作权法基本原理又在客观上具有可行性的判断方法。笔者建议采用“显著的艺术性＋价值判断法”，具体分为两步：第一，站在普通观察者的立场，以一般人的眼光对该作品本身进行日常性的观察，判断其是否具有较为显著的艺术性和美感表达；第二，这种较为显著的艺术性是否具有独立存在的价值，进一步地可分析艺术性的存在是否使作品的价值得以提升，换言之，如果去除这种艺术性成分，并不妨碍该物品作为一种实用品而使用②。对于可分离性的判断，吸收不同的考量因素中的合理成分，并进行适当的融合，将更具有客观性和可行性。

通过可分离性原则的把关，会使得很多实用艺术品无法获得版权保护，将从实质性条件上限制实用艺术作品的保护，避免扩大保护的制度风险。

（2）美感表达和艺术上的独创性的把关。

美感表达和艺术上的独创性可从另一方面对实用艺术作品的保护进行实质性条件上的限制。在实用艺术作品的独创性判断上，就理论上和比较法上而言，可有两种模式：第一，施行“一元基准”，对所有的作品采用同样的独创性要求；第二，施行“更高标准”，要求实用艺术作品满足更高的独创性。

上述两种独创性的理论模式在本质上并不矛盾。从本质上而言，独创性的判断标准应当是统一的，实用艺术作品的独创性要求应当和美术作品的独创性要求一致。但实用艺术作品的创作空间受制于实用性和功能性的考虑，事实上将会导致在艺术创作和美感表达上的创作难度的提升。因此，即使采用基于作者个性的“一元基准”来衡量实用艺术作品的独创性，其独创性要求在事实上也将较高。“一元基准”更多是基于原理上的考虑，而“更高标准”则是纳入了现实因素考量后的方案。

通过独创性的把关，并不是所有的实用艺术品

① 高亦鹏. 我国实用艺术作品保护的困境突破［J］. 社会科学辑刊，2013（6）：80-83.

② 吕炳斌. 实用艺术作品可版权性的理论逻辑［J］. 比较法研究，2014（3）：68-80.

都能获得著作权保护。只有当存在多个表达形式的可能时，创作者才有足够的空间去发挥艺术想象，体现作者个性，在美感表达上进行创作。这实际上是功能性作品的共性。工程设计图、示意图、地图等功能性作品在事实上也因为表达形式有限而需要满足较高的独创性①。对实用艺术作品的独创性施加“更高标准”的要求，将有效地避免实用艺术品的扩大保护，维持著作权保护的利益平衡机制。

2. 私人复制和合理使用规则的利用

私人复制问题由来已久，但该问题的凸显却是在数字技术发达之后。消费者行为研究的结论支持这样的假设：随着技术发展，复制越来越方便，私人复制在增加而不是减少②。实用艺术作品的复制将随着3D打印技术的发展变得容易。3D打印技术的发展给私人复制的争议在理论上和实践上注入了新的内涵。

对3D打印新技术背景下的实用艺术作品私人复制应持比较宽松的态度，但也并非允许私人无限制地通过相关设备复制实用艺术作品。无论法律如何修改，私人复制最主要的是要符合判断著作权限制和例外的“三步检测法”。在“三步检测法”下，著作权的例外和限制应仅限于法律规定的特定情形，并且这种使用不得对作品的正常使用造成不利影响，也不得对权利人的合法利益造成不合理损害。我国著作权法此次修改也拟在法律文本中明文规定“三步检测法”，配之以著作权法合理使用兜底条款规定的“其他情形”，我国未来的著作权合理使用规则将具有一定的灵活性。在这种灵活性下，法官在未来可能涉及实用艺术作品的私人复制纠纷中，应当充分考虑鼓励和支持新技术发展这一因素，在允许范围内放宽私人复制的适用条件和适用范围。一般而言，个人利用3D打印机等设备印制实用艺术作品，其数量极为有限，不会对作品的正常使用造成不利影响，也不会对权利人的合法利益造成不合理损害，应属于合理使用的范围。

3. 知识产权诉讼规则的限制

即使一个作品符合专利法和著作权法规定的条件，可享有专利权和著作权的双重保护，这并不意味着权利人可以在诉讼中同时主张专利权保护和著作权保护。

在一个诉讼中，权利人需要对外观设计专利权或著作权进行选择从而提出相应的权利主张，两种主张是非此即彼的关系③。在外观设计专利权保护期内，权利人提起专利侵权之诉将具有优势，主要原因在于前述的专利权的排他性较强，不需要证明“接触”。当然，也会有权利人在同时享有外观设计专利权和著作权的情况下选择起诉著作权侵权，尤其是在作品的独创性较强，以著作权侵权起诉具有较大胜诉把握时④。

通过知识产权诉讼规则的限制，实用艺术作品双重保护、扩大保护在实践中将大大减小。进一步地，实用艺术作品交叉保护的潜在制度风险将得以避免。

四、结语

实用艺术作品是一种特殊类型的作品，对符合专利法和著作权法各自条件的实用艺术作品给予交叉保护具有正当性。交叉保护是一种有条件的重叠保护，本质上需要施加一定的限制性条件。“实用艺术品”能否成为版权法意义上的“实用艺术作品”而获得版权保护，关键在于是否符合版权保护的实质性条件。可分离性原则、独创性都将在法律技术意义上起到把关作用。这些限制条件有助于避免实用艺术作品的扩大保护，从而取得版权法的平衡架构。本文对外观设计专利权和实用艺术作品著作权进行界分的努力无非是为了使知识产权法的激励机制处于恰当状态，使权利人、使用者和产业之间的利益位于平衡点，从而取得版权制度的平衡架构。

（本文原发表于《法律科学》2016年第2期。
作者单位：南京大学法学院）

比较与选择：互联网环境中作品复制权的重构

——以临时复制为视角

孟兆平

一、互联网环境中著作权经济权利的变革与复制权的扩张

（一）著作权经济权利的变革

互联网创造了作品创作、传播和使用的全新技

① 徐棣枫，解亘，李友根. 知识产权法［M］. 北京：科学出版社，2011：146.

② Stiching de Thuiskopie，WIPO. International survey on private copying，Law & Practice 2012［EB/OL］. pp. 3-9，http://www.wipo.int/freepublications/en/copyright/1037/wipo_pub_1037. pdf，最后访问日期：2014-12-22.

③ 姚建军，冉崇高，赵克. 实用艺术作品保护中著作权与外观设计专利权的竞合与冲突［J］. 民事法律文件解读，2011（8） 87.

④ 比如：代仁军与张景强著作权纠纷案，浙江省高级人民法院（2014）浙知终字第168号民事判决书。

术环境，这个新的技术环境对作品流通的全过程造成了影响，由此对于在出版技术和模拟技术基础上形成的传统著作权法带来了全面而又深刻的冲击。新技术的冲击形成了一系列互联网环境中著作权保护体系更新的难题，诸如：第一，如何在互联网环境中创建新的维持“公益”和“私益”平衡的机制是法律规制必须解决的一个关键问题；第二，数字技术和网络技术的发展使得互联网应用普及化，社会公众的作品复制能力较互联网产生之前有了极大的提升，因此而出现了许多新的法律问题，譬如在互联网环境中复制权概念的扩张、私人复制行为的法律规制问题等；第三，伴随数字技术和互联网技术发展而产生的大规模复制行为，使得权利人对其作品的控制力削弱，权利人在互联网环境中如何通过法律规制实现自身利益成为权利人关注的焦点问题。这些难题都涉及著作权法体系中的基本理论问题，而这些问题的解决需要法律对于技术的发展做出积极的回应，通过扩张权利人的经济权利，以构筑互联网环境中作品创作、传播和使用的法治秩序。

回应互联网环境下的变革，以对复制权、发行权和传播权的扩张最为典型：第一，数字技术的出现使得作品的复制不再需要依赖物质载体，作品可以二进制代码的方式存在并通过互联网在全球范围内快速传输，权利人已经很难控制作品的复制，因此复制权范围的扩张成为必然；第二，传统环境中作品发行权用尽原则不适用于互联网环境，权利人无法控制作品数字化发行后作品后续的任何使用或处置行为；第三，互联网环境中多对多的传播模式使得作者无力控制作品的传播行为，传播权必须根据传播模式的变动进行扩张，使权利人能够控制信息在互联网环境中的传播行为。

（二）复制权在互联网环境中的扩张

作品的传播和使用离不开对作品的复制，所以各国均将复制权视为著作权人享有的首要经济权利。互联网时代的来临对于传统复制权的法律规制模式构成重大冲击，复制权必须因应技术的发展做出应对。

作品在互联网环境中不再需要附着在“实体物”上，私人复制成本和难度都相应地大为降低，社会公众可以在互联网环境中实现对作品低成本、高质量的复制，因此“复制行为变得不需投入大量资本任何人都可以进行时，由于复制人数的激增，谈判成本变得高昂，从而使现行法以禁止复制这样的形式来收取对价的前提受到了挑战”①。在这种情况下，国际社会和各国均努力改革在传统技术环境中确立的复制权规则，扩大复制权的范围，以实现权利人对互联网环境中作品复制行为的控制。其核心在于作品在传播和使用过程中的临时复制行为。

单纯地扩张著作权人的复制权将是不可取的方案，因为如果直接或不经思考地将著作权人控制复制的权利直接适用于网络空间中的行为，很可能造成反效果，权利的限制此时就成为一种可行的方案——将某些情况下的临时复制行为排除在复制权的范围之外，从而既能保障权利人权益的实现，又能保障互联网作为信息传播媒介的重要功能。

二、国际公约层面的讨论：互联网条约的态度

在理论层面，关于临时复制的法律地位，联合国教科文组织编撰的《版权法导论》认为由于数字技术发展而出现的临时复制行为（例如：缓存）仅具有技术上意义而无独立的经济价值，所以应被认为不属于复制行为②。但是这种见解并未体现在《伯尔尼公约》和由世界知识产权组织（WIPO）主导制定的互联网条约中。

《伯尔尼公约》斯德哥尔摩文本是最早明文确定复制权的著作权国际公约，在其中关于复制权的界定及其后发布的官方指南中对于复制权均采用最广泛的定义。但是由于议定《伯尔尼公约》1971 年巴黎文本的斯德哥尔摩会议发生在 1967 年，互联网技术彼时尚未进入实用阶段，与会代表不可能在议定相关文本时能够预见到未来技术的发展以及相关技术对复制权的影响，所以直到 1996 年互联网条约制定时，国际社会才有机会在 WIPO 框架内尝试界定临时复制在著作权法律体系中的地位。

WIPO 制定的《世界知识产权组织版权条约》（WCT）基础提案中采取的规制模式是规定一个范围广泛的复制权，将临时复制纳入复制权的范围之内；紧接着在基础提案的第 7 条第 2 款中提出特定情形下的临时复制行为应属于复制权规制的例外，如临时复制的目的单纯是为了使作品的使用者能够感知相关作品。WCT 基础提案的内容由于在缔结条约的外交会议中遭到多数发展中国家的反对而未能通过，取而代之的是由美国为主的一些国家提出的

① 田村善之．日本知识产权法［M］．周超，等译．北京：知识产权出版社，2011：441.

② 联合国教科文组织．版权法导论［M］．张雨泽，译．北京：知识产权出版社，2009：69.

关于WCT第1条第4款的议定声明，该议定声明阐明了《伯尔尼公约》在传统技术环境内所确立的复制权及其例外制度可以在数字环境下适用。作为互联网条约组成部分的WPPT做出了与WCT上述议定声明相似的规定。

WCT最终文本的议定声明实质上是对复制权在互联网环境中的确认，但是并没有为各缔约方解决“临时复制”的法律地位问题提供可资参考的意见，实质上是由各缔约方根据本国或本地区的实际情况自行选择用立法或司法的方式解决该问题[①]；在明确复制权将适用于互联网环境的情况下，为保证著作权法律体系中占有规则与传播规则之间的平衡，将《伯尔尼公约》第9条第2款所确立的复制权限制规则进行延伸适用，但是WCT同样没有为各缔约方在互联网环境中应针对临时复制行为设置何种例外规则做出必要的指引。

虽然各国制度的具体设计不同，但是有一点是相通的，即适应互联网技术的发展，在给予“临时复制”必要规制保障著作权人利益的同时，畅通互联网环境中作品传播的必要方式，实现对公众利益和互联网产业利益的平衡保护。

三、美国模式的讨论：判例法的角度

关于作品权利产生的机制，美国特别强调相关原创性表达必须固定（fixation）在复制品和录音制品中。“固定”是判断作品的使用行为是否构成美国法下复制行为的关键，在具体判断过程中应通过以下两个要件进行判断：其一是媒介要件（embodiment requirement），是指作品必须附着在一定的媒介之上，之后借由附着的媒介可以被感知、复制或传播；其二是时间要件（duration requirement），是指作品在媒介上的存续时间必须是非短暂的[②]。

在互联网时代来临之前，美国法上关于相关作品的使用行为是否构成复制的判断主要集中在媒介要件的判断上。随着计算机及互联网应用的普及，数字化的作品在传输过程中在计算机内存中的临时复制是否属于版权法意义上的“复制”的讨论则成为美国版权法理论和实践领域的焦点问题。关于临时复制法律地位的讨论始于国会关于1976年版权法的报告，报告中指出现行版权法中有关“固定”的定义将像在电脑内存中的暂时复制行为那样易逝的（evanescent）或短暂的（transient）的复制排除在外，所以此种行为不构成版权法规制的复制行为[③]。在报告发布的同时，美国国会组成了新科技使用委员会（the Commission on New Technology Uses，CONTU）对因计算机技术发展而产生的版权法问题进行研究，在CONTU发布的最终报告中却认为计算机内存对作品的使用行为应受美国版权法规定的复制权规制[④]。

美国法院最先在MAI Systems Corp. v. Peak Computer Inc.[⑤]一案中采纳了CONTU报告中提出的观点。在MAI案中，原告MAI主要提供计算机及计算机之上运行的软件，其同时为客户提供售后服务；被告Peak主要为运行MAI计算机系统的客户提供日常和紧急维护工作。在Peak为客户提供服务过程中，其雇员不可避免地需要将MAI操作系统程序调用至电脑的内存中。MAI认为Peak雇员实施的行为构成对其拥有版权的软件的复制行为，因此构成侵权。第九巡回上诉法院认为被告Peak将相关软件调至计算机内存运行以及根据运行结果检查系统的行为，客观结果是使计算机内存中形成了对MAI享有版权的软件的复制件，相关复制件可以在非短暂的时间内为公众所感知、复制或传播，所以据此认定Peak的相关行为满足了美国版权法中有关“固定”的要求，侵犯了MAI公司对其软件享有的版权[⑥]。其后，美国国会在1998年《数字千年版权法》（DMCA）中推翻了MAI案的判决，增加了第117（c）条，根据该条规定，如果软件的复制是为了启动安装有该计算机软件的计算机及进行日常维护，计算机所有人或承租人复制或授权复制计算机软件的行为不构成侵权。根据该条，任何主体再从事与Peak公司类似的行为就不构成侵权行为，但是从该条规定我们亦可看出美国实质上已经接受了计算机内存中的临时复制应受版权法复制权规制的观点，因为第117（c）条是关于复制权限制的规定，该条规定仅是豁免了计算机所有人或承租人的复制权侵权责任。

进入2001年，美国版权局在关于DMCA的报

① 郑成思．两个新的国际版权条约评介［J］．外国法译评，1997（4）．

② Cartoon Network LP，LLLP v. CSC Holding，Inc.，536 F. 3d 121，127（2d Cir. N. Y. 2008）．

③ H. R. Rep. No. 94-1476，94th Cong. 2d Sess. at 53（1976）．

④ National Comm'n on New Technological Uses of Copyrighted Works，Final Report（July 31，1978）．

⑤ MAI Systems Corp. v. Peak Computer Inc.，991 F. 2d 511（9th Cir. 1993）．

⑥ MAI Systems Corp. v. Peak Computer Inc.，991 F. 2d 511，518（9th Cir. 1993）．

告中具体分析了关于临时复制的法律问题，该报告指出计算机内存中的复制应受版权法的规制①。报告以相关临时复制件的形成是否会对权利人的经济利益造成损害为构建基础，充分体现了英美法系版权法律体系中对于经济权利的重视。这一原则指引了 2008 年第二巡回上诉法院在 Cartoon Network 一案中对于版权法第 101 条中关于“非短暂的存续期间”的定义做出的说明。在 Cartoon Network 一案中，该案的原告 Cartoon Network 向用户提供一种名为 RS-DVR 的服务，这种服务与传统的 DVR 服务不同：RS-DVR 服务允许用户在由 Cartoon Network 运营的中央服务器中存储相关的数字视频并在节目播出后观看，用户可以在任何时间运用该远程控制系统获取及回放其选择的视频。Cartoon Network 提供的服务是将内容提供者提供的节目数据流分隔成两组，其中一组数据流即时传输给用户，而另一组数据流进入特定的技术设备，该设备对数据信息进行缓存、重新格式化后将格式化的信息传输至由公司维持运营的服务器系统内，这个服务器主要是由两个数据缓冲器和若干高容量的硬盘组成。当数据流经过第一个数据缓冲器（主数据缓冲器）时，系统监测到由用户订阅了相关电视节目的情况下，相关数据流将经过主数据缓冲器进入辅助数据缓冲器，并最终存入高容量硬盘中为特定用户预留的空间。当新的数据流通过主数据缓冲器时，它们就会覆盖原先存储在缓冲器中的信息。在任一时刻，主数据缓冲器中对于相关数据的存储时间都不超过十分之一秒，因此每十分之一秒，主数据缓冲器中的信息将自动清除和替换。针对 Cartoon Network 运营的系统对视频片段的暂时性存储是否侵犯复制权，第二巡回上诉法院指出：“信息在缓冲存储器中的存储均没有超过 1.2 秒，而且任何信息在系统运作过程中均自动快速地为其他信息所覆盖。这些事实充分证明了涉案的作品仅在缓冲存储器中存在很短的时间，不满足法律关于复制的时间要件要求。因此，RS-DVR 服务中数据缓冲器中对于作品的复制不构成对版权人复制权的侵害”。

综上，目前在大规模地修正 1976 年版权法之前，美国对临时复制问题采取的应对方式是交由法院在个案中对版权法中与临时复制规制相关的条款进行解读。对于临时复制的规制，美国法肯定临时复制应受复制权的规制，但这种规制有一定的例外：如果相关临时复制行为中所形成的复制件仅能存在一段相当短暂的时间，仅仅是相关技术流程的附属产物，不具有任何经济意义，那么就不构成侵犯复制权的行为。

四、欧盟模式的讨论：成文法的角度

与美国采取的应对模式不同的是，欧盟主要以订立成文法的方式应对技术发展对著作权法律制度提出的挑战。欧盟对复制权扩张的基本态度是规定一个范围最大的复制权，以期对于作品的任何复制行为都进行规制，但又规定一系列的例外②。

《欧盟信息社会著作权指令》为应对互联网技术发展对复制权做出扩张界定。根据《欧盟信息社会著作权指令》第 2 条的规定，复制权是指著作权人授权或者禁止他人“采取任何措施、以任何形式、直接或者间接、临时或者永久性地”复制其作品或制品的全部或者一部分的专有权。在将临时复制行为纳入复制权规制范围的同时，该指令认为复制的专有权应当受到限制，即允许某些临时性复制行为的例外。同时指令前言第 33 段认为如果在作品传播过程中产生了临时复制行为，这种复制也仅是短暂的或偶然的复制，是数字环境下作品传播在技术实现过程中必要的组成部分，而且相关临时复制行为是为了使网络服务提供者能够顺利地完成作品的传播行为，或是为了公众能够合法使用③作品或其他客体。除了以上对临时复制行为的要求外，相关段落中也认为临时复制行为不应具有独立的经济价值。综合以上，欧盟对临时复制行为的限制主要是为了实现互联网的信息传输功能和保护合法的作品使用行为。

五、中国复制权变革的路径选择

中国《著作权法》在 1990 年的法律文本中认为应归属于《著作权法》中规定的复制权规制的行为类型包括印刷、复印、拓印、录音、录像、翻录、翻拍等。随着技术的发展及互联网的商业化，作品逐步摆脱物质载体的限制，而以数字化的形式在网

① DMCA Section 104 Report [EB/OL]. http://www.china.com.cn/chinese/PI-c/1233148.htm. http://www.copyright.gov/reports/studies/dmca/sec-104-report-vol-1.pdf，最后访问日期：2016-01-01.

② 有学者将这种立法模式称为“大圆圈套小方块”的立法模式。薛虹. 网络时代的知识产权法 [M]. 北京：法律出版社，2000：148.

③ 《欧盟信息社会著作权指令》对“合法使用”做出界定，即“由权利人授权的使用或不为法律所禁止的使用，就应当被认为是合法的使用”。

络中传播。

为了应对技术发展对法律滞后性提出的挑战，在《著作权法》2001年修订之前，最高人民法院以司法解释的形式把作品的数字化确认为“复制”的一种方式，并对数字化作品的保护做出了明确规定。《著作权法》2001年修订时，有关复制权的条款并未做出变更，因此法律中并未对作品的数字化形式的地位做出明确，但是司法机关仍然延续了法律修订之前对于作品数字化形式的性质认定。经由以上，在中国的著作权法律体系中，传统技术环境中确立的复制权规则已延伸适用于作品在互联网环境中传播过程中必经的上传和下载行为。

对于临时复制的法律定性问题，《著作权法》2001年修订时虽然考虑到技术发展对著作权保护提出的挑战，增设了相关的制度，但是没有对临时复制做出明确的定性。作为规制作品网络传播的重要法律文件，国务院制定并颁布的《信息网络传播权保护条例》对于临时复制也没有做出准确的定性。条例起草者认为，中国当时的著作权法及其实施条例、最高院的相关司法解释中关于复制权的相关界定已可解决实际生活中发生的与临时复制相关的法律问题，因此对临时复制不做特别规定。

目前，中国的著作权法律体系在解决临时复制问题时所采取的方式是回避对于临时复制的明确法律定性，但是对于特定的临时复制行为做出权利限制的规定，豁免行为人的法律责任。这些权利限制的规定主要包括：第一，合法作品使用的例外。这种例外规定在《计算机软件保护条例》中，条例中有关于软件合法复制品所有人对于软件作品复制行为的特别例外规定，例如应用或改进之必要修改例外、学习和研究例外。条例允许持有人实施临时复制行为，只要这些临时复制行为符合法律规定的要件。第二，信息传输保障的例外。《信息网络传播权保护条例》中为保证互联网作为信息传输媒介功能的实现，规定了提供自动传输服务或缓存服务的网络服务提供者的避风港制度。如果这些网络服务提供者在提供自动传输服务或缓存服务中对作品实施的临时复制行为符合条例中规定的要件，网络服务提供者即可免于承担赔偿责任。

六、结语

中国著作权法律体系采取回避法律定性的方式处理临时复制问题，但是由于互联网已经发展成为信息社会作品流通的主要媒介，在传播和使用两个环节中临时复制行为是客观存在的。如果继续现行的法律处置方式，那么类似美国 Cartoon Network 的案件发生在中国域内，司法机构在现时的法律规制模式下将可以采取两种解决方法：

一种解决方法是将传播过程中的临时复制行为根据其客观表现认定为是以数字化方式复制作品。由于中国现有的法律体系中对于复制的时间要件并没有做出要求，复制的成立与作品复制件能够存续多久没有必然的联系，可以是持久的，也可以是暂时的。采取这样的界定方法符合现有的法律规定，但是却将所有的临时复制行为纳入权利范围，不论其存续时间长短以及是否能够为人所感知、传播或使用。这样宽泛的权利界定方法将使信息的传播者和使用者时时面临侵权的法律风险，不利于互联网产业商业模式的创新以及社会公众利益的保护，有悖于著作权法固有的利益平衡精神。

另一种解决方法是参照现有欧美著作权产业发达国家的立法或判例，在承认临时复制行为应受复制权规制的同时，将某些短暂的及不具有独立经济价值的临时复制行为设定为例外。此种解决方法虽有利于产业发展，但却需要法官在没有法律明文规定的情况下创设临时复制行为限制的判定标准，这在一定程度上有悖于中国大陆法系的传统。而司法个案的解决方式在中国目前的司法体系下亦具有明显的弊端，个案的裁判仅在极为有限的情况下方可对其他法院的类似案例具有指导的意义，但即使具有了指导意义，亦不能改变中国司法体制下判例不能成为法源的事实。

以上两种解决方法很难在权利人权益保障与社会公众利益维护之间取得平衡，将使司法机关在司法政策的选择上出现两难的境地。因此随着《著作权法》第三次修订工作的启动，中国著作权法律体系必须对临时复制的法律地位做出明确的界定。

（本文原发表于《河北法学》2016年第34卷第5期。作者单位：阿里巴巴集团平台治理部）

论二次创作的著作权法规制与保障

唐　艳

一、原始创作激励与二次创作自由在新的技术条件下的关系紧张

目前我国主流的著作权法基本理念通常预设这样一个制度功能：通过赋予著作权人对其作品排他的支配权和获益权，激励作者从事创作性劳动，从而达到繁荣文学艺术发展的目的。然而，这种理念主要强调的是对原始创作作品的激励，并不能有效应对二次创作的相关规制与激励。已有学者指出“版权涉及两个经济现象”①，一方面，需要保护原创者最初的创作和投资，否则“不加限制的模仿会使得创作者的利益和经济激励化为乌有”。但在另一方面，“版权又会压抑二次创作者的使用”②，因为二次创作者的作品可能建立在对原始作品的修改、提升、再创作之上③。当“知识和学习通过创作更多的作品得以促进时，知识和学习也要通过更有效地获取和使用他人的作品得以提升”④。所以，从这个意义上，仅仅保护原始创作者或者仅仅保护二次创作者的排他性利益都是片面的，我们需要考虑的是，如何在制度层面上协调好原始创作者与二次创作者之间的相互关系及利益平衡，以实现社会福利的最大化。

如果说在以前的技术条件下，原始创作激励与二次创作自由之间的矛盾在现有的著作权制度框架下还不那么明显的话，那么自20世纪90年代以来，随着数字技术及互联网的发展，这二者之间的矛盾已在不断加剧。新的技术已经使得二次创作变得非常简单和方便，再加之互联网的普及，社交平台上共享着越来越多的图片、音乐和视频素材，正如费舍尔所说，“新技术部分潜在优势是有助于普通消费者修改手中的文化作品并将修改后的版本再行传播”⑤。在这样一个技术发达、素材丰富的时代，人们是否可以满怀欣喜地期待出现风格更加多元、数量更加繁多、内容更加丰富的作品？我想我们至少应当做一些制度建构上的努力促使这一结果发生，而不是让制度成为技术发展的桎梏。

二、中美著作权法对二次创作的态度

我国现行著作权法将一系列与二次创作相关的权利都赋予了著作权人，包括修改权、保护作品完整权、改编权、翻译权、汇编权等，也就是说，二次创作者如需在原始作品的基础上进行创作，则需要经过原始作者的许可，否则将构成侵权。例外的是合理使用制度，在合理使用制度中，与二次创作相关的是第二十二条第一款第（二）项规定的“为介绍、评论某一作品或者说明某一问题，在作品中适当引用他人已经发表的作品”这一情形。由于我国的合理使用制度并未规定兜底性条款，所以我国著作权法并不存在抽象意义上平衡原始创作与二次创作紧张关系的一般性制度。

与此相较，美国的版权法，一方面，给著作权人规定了演绎权，也即意味着原则上二次创作者如需在前人作品基础上从事二次创作，需要得到原始作品的著作权人许可，但在另一方面，其合理使用制度又给二次创作者的某些创作行为开了一个小口，这便是合理使用制度中所涉及的“变型使用”（transformative use），也就是说，如果二次创作涉及变型使用的话，则未经授权的对原始作品的使用行为将有可能被认为合理使用而不被认为是侵权。

三、美国著作权法上变型使用规则的确立及发展

（一）合理使用制度与变型使用规则

说到美国著作权法上的变型使用规则，就离不开美国的合理使用制度，它确立了判断合理使用的四因素检测法，这四个因素中的第一个因素是：该使用的目的和性质，包括该使用是否具有商业性质或者是为了非营利的教学目的⑥。

该考量因素涉及新作品本身，现今已演化为对两个问题的回答：第一，第二作品是商业性的还是非商业性的。第二，第二作品对原创作品的使用是不是变型使用。而这个演化过程，在近二十年的时间里，使用的商业属性曾经是第一因素中最重要的部分考量内容，然而，通过1994年标志性的Campbell v. Acuff-Rose Music案，最高法院确立了变型使用规则⑦。

（二）变型使用规则的产生

“变型使用”思想其实脱胎于“生产性使用”（productive use）这一概念，这出现在Sony Corp. of America v. Universal City Studios, Inc. 一案中⑧。

① 迈克尔·A. 艾因霍恩. 媒体技术和版权：经济和法律的融合［M］. 赵启杉，译. 北京：北京大学出版社，2012：17.

② 同①.

③ “没有法律上的专用权，就不会有多少的信息被创造出来，但是有了法律上的专有权又不会有太多的信息被使用。”迈克尔·A. 艾因霍恩. 媒体技术和版权：经济与法律的融合［M］. 赵启杉，译. 北京：北京大学出版社，2012：50.

④ L. P. Loren. Redefining the market failure approach to fair use in an era of copyright permission system［J］. Journal of Intellectual Property Law，1997（1）：6.

⑤ 威廉·W. 费舍尔. 说话算数：技术、法律以及娱乐的未来［M］. 李旭，译. 上海：上海三联书店，2008：27.

⑥ 17U. S. C&107（1976）.

⑦ Ashten Kimbrough. Transformative use vs market impact：why the fourth fair use factor should not be supplanted by transformative use as the most important element in a fair use analysis［J］. Alabama Law Review，2012（63）：625.

⑧ 同⑦.

“变型”这个概念的正式提出是在1990年，Pierre N. Leval法官在《哈佛法律评论》上发表了一篇很有影响力的论文。文中，Leval法官强调法院必须判断第二作品是否具有变型性以及变型的程度①。

后来，在1994年，美国最高法院采纳了Leval法官的建议，在Campbell v. Acuff-Rose Music一案中，使用了“变型使用”的分析，并使得“变型使用”成为合理使用制度第一因素的考量内容。该案中，原告阿库夫-罗斯音乐公司（Acuff-Rose Music）是歌曲《哦，漂亮女人》（“Oh, Pretty Women”）的音乐出版商及著作权人，该首歌的原唱为罗伊·奥比逊（Roy Orbison）。原告起诉被告说唱乐队2 Live Crew，是因为被告未经原告的许可，将该首歌曲戏谑性改编后推出了自己的演唱版本，原告认为其行为构成了版权侵权。法院最后认为被告的滑稽模仿行为属于合理使用。法院的分析中最关键的一点就是被告是如何改变原创歌曲的——也即滑稽模仿中的“变型”特征。对此，Souter法官认为，为了决定第一因素中的“使用的性质”，有必要考查该使用是不是变型的，也即第二作品是否“增加了一些新东西，具有新的目的或不同的特点，用新的表达、含义或信息改变了原始作品”②。

（三）变型使用规则的相对定型及发展

Campbell案之后，变型使用规则对合理使用制度产生了重大影响。法院判决较为严格地适用了Leval法官关于变型使用的界定，这使得在合理使用制度的适用过程中形成了一个形式化的、三个层级的分类系统。

这个分类系统的第一层级包括这样一些第二作品，即被告未能对原始作品增加任何额外的创作性价值。这样的作品因不包含明确的额外的创作性价值而不被认为是变型使用。

第二层级包括这样的一些第二作品，它们不是简单的复制，被告以某种方式改变了原始作品，这些作品一般能够满足法律关于演绎作品的定义，但也有可能构成变型使用。这是最有争议、最难处理的一个领域。

第三层级包括在Campbell案中明确讨论了的一些作品：批评、滑稽模仿和学术作品。由于这类作品被告已经对原始作品贡献了新颖的、独创的表达，所以，这类作品本身便构成了变型使用③。

该种分类系统是存在问题的，学界认为分类太机械，未进行功能性考虑，随后，法院将变型使用描述为“将受版权保护的表达与原始的表达结合起来以产生一个新的具有创造性的作品”或者是“将一个受版权保护的作品用于一个新的语境中，实现不同于原始作品的新的功能”④。

四、美国学界对变型使用规则的探讨及批判

美国学界对变型使用规则有过一些探讨和批判，了解这些探讨和批判将有助于我们加深对变型使用规则的理解。

（一）探讨：演绎作品与变型使用的区分

由于演绎作品和变型使用都涉及原始作品与二次创作的关系，而前者未经著作权人许可将构成侵权，后者则有可能因符合合理使用而不构成侵权，故而二者的区分既是一个难点又非常重要。

美国学界对二者的区分大致存在三个角度的探讨：

其一，从二者功能的角度。一般而言，演绎作品是与原始作品具有相同市场功能的作品，而变型使用则与原始作品具有不同的市场功能。

其二，从二者自身性质的角度。演绎作品是那些“重铸（recast）、改变（transform）、改编（adapt）成另一种媒介、模式、语言或修改版本，但同时仍然代表原作品”⑤的作品。而变型使用并非代表原作品。

其三，从对市场影响的角度。新的使用是否应被认为是演绎的，仍然取决于市场分析，需要判断新的使用是否干预了第一作品的潜在市场⑥。

（二）批判：变型使用在司法实践中适用不统一

学者指出，变型使用的概念在司法实践中并未得到统一的适用，而且对于该概念的界定并没有明确的指南。

① Pieer N. Leval. Toward a fair use standard [J]. HARV. L. REV., 1990 (103): 1105.

② Campbell v. Acuff-Rose Music, Inc., U.S., 1994, 510: 569, 579.

③ Jeremy Kudon. From over function: expanding the transformative use test for fair use [J]. B. U. L. Rev., 2000 (80): 579.

④ Ashten Kimbrough. Transformative use vs market impact: why the fourth fair use factor should not be supplanted by transformative use as the most important element in a fair use analysis [J]. Alabama Law Review, 2012 (63): 625.

⑤ 同④.

⑥ 同④.

（三）批判：应在合理使用制度之外增设独立的变型使用规则

还有学者走得更远，艾因霍恩就认为版权保护与合理使用制度让“法官必须在两个同样极端的立场上进行选择——禁止还是免费使用”①。

基于此，该学者建议在保留合理使用制度的前提下，额外增设一个独立的可供选择适用的建立在赔偿机制而非禁令基础上的变型使用规则，并以市场基准作为赔偿基础②。

五、变型使用规则与我国二次创作的法律规制

为了避免盲目的制度借鉴，我们仍需先回到本国现有法学理论及基本法律框架下，运用理性分析，对变型使用规则所涉及的一些根本性问题理清思路。

（一）原始作品的著作人格权保护问题

美国版权法上之所以有变型使用规则，实际上与英美法系国家对著作权的精神权利的非强化保护是有关系的。

在大陆法系国家，其著作权法理论一般认为，作品当中蕴含着作者独特的人格利益。基于该理论，大陆法系国家的著作权法往往将保护作者人格权放在首位，将作者的财产权放在其次。

而在英美法系国家，版权体系同样保护人格利益，但这种保护被置于著作权法之外。也就是说，作者的人格利益源自“作者是人”这一前提，法律并没有为作者专设特别的人格权③。

具体到我国的情况，笔者认为，基于我国大陆法系传统，著作人格权仍然需要保护，但著作人格权不应过强保护。原因主要在于：首先，从理念角度，“作品反映人格”作为一种文化信仰已经受到冲击④。其次，从实用角度，如果作品与作者的关联过于紧密，必将影响作品的传播与最大效用的利用。甚至有学者提出，著作人格权是对自由市场运作的不合理的法律干预⑤。而将作者与作品之间的关系做些弱化，则“不仅是对创作集团化这一事实的承认，也是对艺术实践的尊重；不仅仅是调整作品与投资者的关系之所需，也是调整创作者之间关系之所需”⑥。

笔者认为，具体而言，像署名权这样的接近于自然权利的权利，仍然可以保留，而对于修改权、保护作品完整权这样的强化作者对作品控制的权利可以适度弱化，从而为引入变型使用规则留下空间。

（二）原始作品作者与变型作品作者的利益平衡问题

美国著作权法实际上通过将变型使用纳入合理使用制度的方式，采用了一种绝对化的全有或全无模式，也即在二次创作不属于变型使用不能构成合理使用的情形——这往往属于原始作者的演绎权所涵盖的范围——二次创作者的行为将构成侵权，不能保有其创作带来的任何利益（须损害赔偿），而如果二次创作属于变型使用从而符合合理使用制度，则二次创作者能享有其创作带来的所有收益，即便其利用了原始作品，原始作品的作者也不能从中分一杯羹，而这在二次创作属于商业利用并赢得巨大收益时显得尤为不公。美国 Cariou v. Prince 一案便引发了较多争议。被告 Prince 未经许可利用了原告 Cariou 的照片画成油画，只做了少量修改，最终被认定为属于合理使用，不用承担任何责任。被告其实是一个画家，其作品售价非常高⑦。如果我们先抛开美国具体的法律制度，不探讨该案本身适用法律是否正确，光从案件结果来说，利益的分配似乎对原告并非公平，因为被告的高价画作无疑有从原告处受益的成分。

正是因为这种全有全无的模式，二次创作行为到底属于演绎行为还是属于变型使用就显得尤为重要，从上文中，我们可以看到美国学界对该问题的讨论非常激烈，但并未达成共识，而在司法实践中，法院系统对二者的区分也并未形成一个清晰明确的分界线，由此，何为变型使用也总显得扑朔迷离，并常被指责为适用不连贯不统一。

由此，笔者认为，这种将变型使用纳入到合理使用制度之中的全有全无模式并非一个理想的模式。艾因霍恩教授提出的在合理使用制度之外设立一个建立在赔偿机制而非禁令基础上的变型使用规则，

---

① 迈克尔·A. 艾因霍恩. 媒体技术和版权：经济和法律的融合［M］. 赵启杉，译. 北京：北京大学出版社，2012：17.

② 同①18.

③ 李琛. 著作权基本理论批判［M］. 北京：知识产权出版社，2013：184.

④ 同③.

⑤ Lionel Bently, Brad Sherman. Intellectual property law［M］. Oxford: Oxford University Press, 2001: 235.

⑥ 同③.

⑦ Liz Brown. Remixing transformative use: a three part proposal for reform［J］, N. Y. U. J. of Intell. Prop. Law, 2014 (4): 139.

这种思路倒是非常值得推崇。

六、代结论：变型使用规则在我国法律中的借鉴

首先，对于变型使用的定义，可以界定为：在二次创作中，增加了一些新的内容，用新的表达、含义或信息改变了原始作品，使其具有不同于原始作品的新的目的或新的特点，或者将一个受版权保护的作品用于一个新的语境中，实现不同于原始作品的新的功能。

其次，关于变型使用的法律后果。变型使用不得侵害原始作品作者的署名权，须在作品中指明原始作品的作者、作品名称、出处等信息。在符合上述要求时，变型使用不构成侵权，但变型使用人须向原始作者进行经济上的补偿，补偿的数额考虑变型使用人的获益、原始作品的贡献与变型使用贡献的比例，以实现公平的利益分配。

再次，变型使用与其他制度的衔接问题。变型使用制度与合理使用制度一样，都作为对著作权行使的限制和例外，但发挥作用的领域不同，变型使用制度只体现在二次创作领域，实现原始作者和二次创作作者的利益平衡。该制度作为当事人可供选择的一种新方案。即便变型使用制度与合理使用制度适用的情形可能存在些许重合，但也可因当事人的选择适用而避开矛盾。具体而言，对于被控著作权侵权的二次创作人而言，其既可以选择传统的合理使用制度作为抗辩，以达到不用赔偿的目的，也可以在不符合前者要求或是否符合不明朗情况下，直接选择变型使用作为抗辩，以寻求只需补偿而不被禁止的法律后果。对于原始作品的著作权人而言，其既可以选择著作权侵权诉讼，以达到发布禁令和获得损害赔偿的法律后果，也可以选择放弃上述诉求，只选择以变型使用而追索补偿费而起诉。法官则需根据当事人的诉求在各自的制度框架下来判断。

总而言之，在新的技术发展为文学艺术带来新的创作活力之际，笔者通过介绍美国著作权法上的变型使用规则，并吸取其有益的精华，试图通过增设一个独立的可供当事人选择适用的补偿型变型使用制度，以适度解放二次创作空间，并通过补偿机制在原始作品作者与二次创作作者之间实现利益平衡。

（本文原发表于《知识产权》2016年第11期。作者单位：重庆理工大学重庆知识产权学院）

论体育赛事现场直播画面的著作权保护

——兼评“凤凰网赛事转播案”

王　迁

近日，北京市朝阳区人民法院在“北京新浪互联信息服务有限公司诉北京天盈九州网络技术有限公司案”（以下简称此案为“凤凰网赛事转播案”）中认定，对体育赛事进行现场直播形成的画面构成作品，被告未经许可进行转播，侵犯了“赛事画面作品”的著作权①。此案的判决结果受到了已获得体育赛事播放授权的电视台和网站的欢迎。这是因为，一方面，《著作权法》第四十二条虽然规定录像制作者享有“通过信息网络向公众传播”的权利，但该权利实际上仅限于交互式网络传播权，即公众在其个人选定的时间和地点获得的权利，而不能涵盖网播等非交互式传播的行为②；另一方面，《著作权法》第四十六条仅规定电视台播放他人的录像应当取得录像制作者许可，并没有规定网站播放也应当取得许可。如果某一网站未经许可截取了电视台或其他网站现场直播信号或数据流之后进行了转播，并不会构成录像制作者权的侵权。

在这种情况下，经过授权的电视台和网站要阻止他人未经许可通过网络转播其对赛事的现场直播，只可能借助《著作权法》第四十五条为广播组织权规定的“转播权”或《反不正当竞争法》第二条规定的一般原则。但对于法院是否能够超出立法原意将《著作权法》中广播组织权的“转播权”扩张解释为可以涵盖通过互联网进行的转播存在意见分歧，以往法院判决也多持否定观点③。《反不正当竞争法》的功能并不是为广播组织规定专有权利，而是维护公平竞争的市场秩序，适用一般原则条款有其不确定性。

应当承认，对体育赛事的现场直播往往需要不菲的投资，未经许可对直播进行转播会分流观众、

① 参见北京市朝阳区人民法院民事判决书（2014）朝民（知）初字第40334号。虽然该案判决书没有明确说明涉案直播画面构成何种类型的作品，但它只可能被归入“以类似摄制电影的方法创作的作品”。

② 王迁．网络环境中的著作权保护研究［M］．北京：法律出版社，2012：132-135.

③ 参见浙江省嘉兴市南湖区人民法院民事判决书（2011）嘉南知初字第24号，浙江省嘉兴市中级人民法院民事判决书（2012）浙嘉知终字第7号。许福忠．广播组织权中的转播权不应延伸至互联网领域［J］．人民司法，2013（2）．

减少广告收入，损害显而易见[①]。因此需要对此类行为进行规制并不存在太大的争议，问题在于如何规制。

一、现场直播画面的权利来源

在“凤凰网赛事转播案”中，原告举证证明，涉案体育赛事的组织者——中国足球协会根据自身章程证明自己是原始权利人[②]，以及原告从中国足协的代理人处获得了在网络中传播赛事视频的专有许可。对此，该案法院认为：

依据《国际足联章程》以及《中国足球协会章程》的规定，中国足球协会当然地拥有各项足球赛事的权利；其权利包括……视听和广播录制、复制和播放版权，多媒体版权……在此前提下，依据……中国足球协会出具的授权书，可以确认中超公司有权代理中国足球协会开发经营中超联赛的电视、广播、互联网及各种多媒体版权……上述章程及授权手续，可以认定……中超公司向新浪互联公司出具授权书的有效性[③]。

笔者认为：无论是否将现场直播画面认定为作品，在著作权侵权诉讼中，法院对权利来源的这一认定都是值得商榷的。

（一）赛事组织者的章程不能创设民事权利

狭义著作权和邻接权均为典型的绝对权，具有对世效力，权利人可以排斥其他人以特定方式利用受保护的客体。包括知识产权在内的绝对权必须法定[④]，不能由民事主体自行创设是民法的一项基本原则。无论是国际足联还是中国足协都是一个民事主体，其章程只能对其会员产生合同法意义上的约束力，而不能约束第三人。

《中华人民共和国著作权法》第九条规定：“著作权人包括：（一）作者；（二）其他依照本法享有著作权的公民、法人或者其他组织”。据此，如果赛事组织者并未以自己的名义拍摄比赛过程，则除非由此形成的作品属于《著作权法》规定的委托作品，并由约定作品著作权归属于作为缔约一方的赛事组织者[⑤]，或者属于法人作品[⑥]、特殊职务作品[⑦]，赛事组织者不能成为著作财产权原始权利人。同样，如果赛事组织者自身没有对比赛过程进行录制，也不能成为《著作权法》规定的录像制作者[⑧]。同时，除非赛事组织者自己就是电台、电视台并且播放了比赛的实况，否则赛事组织者也不享有广播组织权。如果赛事组织者又没有通过与原始权利人签订合同而受让权利，则赛事组织者对拍摄而成的连续画面或载有该画面的信号并不享有任何著作权法意义上的权利。这一状况，是著作权与邻接权作为绝对权必须由法律规定的必然结果，不能由赛事组织者的章程加以改变。

国内外案例也不承认包括体育赛事在内的各类活动组织者可以凭借单方意愿或章程取得与活动有关的照片或录影的著作权、邻接权或其他财产权利。比如在比利时发生的“赛车协会诉 Costich 案”中，赛车协会声称，摄影师们只有经其许可才能拍照，而且还必须与其签订合同，承诺不得未经赛车协会许可对照片进行商业化利用。而一名摄影师未经赛车协会许可，拍摄了比赛的场景并对照片进行了商业化利用。由于该名摄影师未曾与赛车协会签订合同，赛车协会无法起诉其违约，于是起诉其侵犯了赛车协会的知识产权。比利时阿尔隆地方法院驳回了赛车协会的诉讼请求，认为比利时《著作权法》并没有赋予赛事组织者一项控制他人利用赛事照片的权利[⑨]。

我国法院也在涉及亚洲杯足球赛网络传播的系列诉讼中做出了正确的认定。在“体奥动力诉土豆网案”中，法院指出：

---

① 需要指出的是：未经许可将电视台或网站的体育赛事现场直播画面录制之后，择期播出的行为（又称为“播放实况录像”），虽然也会对经过授权的电视台或网站的利益产生一定影响，但这种影响并不大。这是因为体育赛事具有极强的时效性，比赛结束之后对观众的吸引力会大大降低。与此同时，由于《著作权法》第四十二条为录像制作者规定了“复制权”，第四十五条为广播组织规定了“录制权”，即使不将直播画面认定为作品，摄制者、广播组织和其专有被许可人仍然可以获得一定保护。因此对于“播放实况录像”的问题并不是业界关注的焦点。

② 《中国足球协会章程》第 49 条“赛事权利”的内容为：“……本会为中国足球运动的管理机构，是本会管辖的各项赛事所产生的所有权利的最初所有者。这些权利包括各种财务权利，视听和广播录制、复制和播放版权，多媒体版权，市场开发和推广权利以及无形资产如徽章和版权等”。

③ 北京市朝阳区人民法院民事判决书（2014）朝民（知）初字第 40334 号。

④ 郑胜利. 论知识产权法定主义//北大知识产权评论（第二卷）[M]. 北京：法律出版社，2004：65.

⑤ 《著作权法》第十七条。

⑥ 《著作权法》第十一条第三款。

⑦ 《著作权法》第十六条第二款。

⑧ 《著作权法实施条例》第五条第（五）项规定：“录像制作者，是指录像制品的首次制作人”。

⑨ Olivier Vrins. Court finds no sui generis IP rights for sporting event organisers [EB/OL]. http://www.internationallawoffice.com/newsletters/detail.aspx?g=f604c2f2-336a-4918-af7a-0c6ed5402d27.

我国目前并无相关法律对体育赛事“转播权”做出规定，此项权利不是一项法定的权利。……体育赛事节目和体育赛事两者产生的权利性质并不相同，并且体育赛事转播权的权利主体一般为赛事组织者，而体育赛事节目的著作权或邻接权的主体往往对应节目制作单位、电视广播组织者等，当然，赛事组织者与节目制作单位或电视广播组织者有特别约定的除外①。

由此可见，在“凤凰网赛事转播案”中，法院有关“依据章程享有相关著作权”的观点恐难成立。

（二）法律可为赛事组织者创设特殊民事权利或邻接权

绝对权应由法律创设。如果一国立法已为体育赛事组织者创设了对体育赛事及有关体育赛事的照片、视频和直播信号的民事权利，则可以使体育赛事组织者得以控制他人的相关行为。匈牙利和法国是通过专门立法创设此类权利的典型代表。匈牙利《体育法》第36条第1款规定：对体育活动和比赛进行录制或通过电视、广播和其他电子或数字手段进行传播以及对上述行为进行商业许可的权利属于组织这些活动和比赛的体育协会②。法国于1984年通过“有关组织和促进体育运动”的专门规定，后被纳入法国《体育法典》，其中第L333-1条规定体育联盟和比赛组织者享有其主办的体育比赛的利用权③。法国最高法院据此在2004年认定，有关体育比赛照片的拍摄和传播，应当经过体育联盟和比赛组织者的授权④。无论是否将这种权利解释为一种知识产权，它都是由立法所明确规定的，而不是由比赛组织者章程创设的。

意大利则在《著作权法》中专门为体育赛事组织者规定了一项邻接权——“体育视听权”⑤，并由《体育视听权归属及管理条例》具体实施⑥。其核心内容是：“体育视听权”由赛事组织者享有⑦，包括对体育赛事的向公众传播权、录制权；对录制品的再复制权、交互式点播权、发行权、出租权、出借权；对赛事广播的录制权、重播权和转播权以及为进行促销、广告宣传、博彩而使用赛事照片的权利等⑧。

由于我国既不像匈牙利、法国在体育法等专门立法中为赛事组织者规定针对赛事照片、视频和直播信号的民事权利，也不像意大利在《著作权法》中创设此项邻接权并规定其优先于影视作品或录像权利归属条款的地位，体育赛事组织者在我国不能在缺乏合同约定的情况下，对他人拍摄的照片、视频和传播的信号直接享有民事权利。如果立法者希望加强对体育赛事组织者的保护，则应考虑借鉴上述国家的立法。

二、现场直播画面的独创性

对体育赛事现场直播画面著作权保护问题的最大争议，是直播画面是否构成作品。直播画面的特殊性，在于它是对进行中的比赛即时拍摄并实况直播的，而不是先在赛场完成摄制，再进行后期剪辑、特效制作之后播出，明显有别于对影视剧的拍摄。但是，许多赛事直播涉及在现场设置十几个甚至几十个摄像机位，导播必须面对众多摄像机传回的画面在瞬间进行选择，其过程又有别于通过一台摄像机进行的简单而机械的拍摄。因此，其究竟属于“电影作品和以类似摄制电影的方法创作的作品”还是“录像”，难以在现行立法中找到答案。“凤凰网赛事转播案”判决书引起的争议，实际上就是有关认定作品所需的独创性标准之争。

（一）英美法系国家的独创性标准缺乏参考价值

“凤凰网赛事转播案”判决书中最引人注目的一点，就是认为对足球比赛的直播画面具有充分的独创性，因此可以被认定为作品。法院认为：

赛事的转播⑨、制作是通过设置不确定的数台或数十台或数几十台固定的、不固定的录制设备作为基础进行拍摄录制……上述的画面的形成，是编导通过对镜头的选取，即对多台设备拍摄的多个镜头的选择、编排的结果。而这个过程，……应当认

---

① 上海市第一中级人民法院民事判决书（2013）沪一中民五（知）终字第59号。

② Asser International Sports Law Centre. Study on sports organisers' rights in the European Union [EB/OL], 2014: 40.

③ Id, p. 38.

④ Andros v. Motor Presse France, 02-12771, Decision No. 542 of 17 March 2004, Supreme Court-Commercial Division.

⑤ 意大利《著作权法》第78条之四。

⑥ 该条例全称为《2008年1月第9号法令：体育视听权归属及管理条例》。

⑦ 该条例还区分了体育赛事的整体组织者和其中具体竞争比赛项目的组织者并规定了权利如何在二者之间进行分配，见意大利《体育视听权归属及管理条例》第3、4条。

⑧ 意大利《体育视听权归属及管理条例》第2条第1款第（n）项。

⑨ 判决书此处的“转播”，显然不是指《著作权法》第十条第一款第（十一）项广播权定义中的“转播”——接收到载有作品的无线信号之后，以无线或有线的方式进行同步播放，而是指在导播的指挥下，对赛事进行实时的视听传播，即本文所说的“直播”。

为是对赛事录制镜头的选择、编排，形成可供观赏的新的画面，无疑是一种创作性劳动，且该创作性因不同的选择、不同的制作会产生不同的画面效果，这恰恰反映了其独创性①。

可以看出，法院认定涉案的足球比赛直播画面构成作品的主要理由，在于该画面的形成需要经过导播对源自多台摄像机画面的选择与编排②。应当指出的是：对于构成作品所需要的独创性在许多情况下并不是有和无，而是程度高与低的问题。需要进行选择与判断才能形成的成果是否属于作品，取决于从著作权法的结构和逻辑关系中反映出的对智力创造程度的要求。

以口述作品为例，《伯尔尼公约》第 2 条第 1 款列举的作品类型中，包括“授课、演讲、布道和其他相同性质的作品”，即以口述方式表达的作品。应当承认，人类的口头表达非常丰富，且具有个性化的特征。这就是为何对同样的主题和观点，不同人的口头表达会有很大区别。但《伯尔尼公约》只将“授课、演讲、布道”列为作品。虽然“其他具有相同性质的作品”的用语有兜底性质，但“相同性质”自然是与“授课、演讲、布道”的性质相同。“授课、演讲、布道”都是面对听众的较为正式的语言表达③，其中的遣词造句经过了一定程度的准备和思考，且具有一定长度。我国《著作权法实施条例》将“口述作品”定义为“即兴的演说、授课、法庭辩论等以口头语言形式表现的作品”④，也体现了对口述作品较高的独创性要求。

对于直播形成的连续画面，在对智力创造程度要求较低的英美法系国家，当然可以认为它们是作品。例如，美国《版权法》中只规定了“视听作品”(audiovisual work)⑤，而没有像大陆法系国家那样规定作为邻接权客体的“活动画面”(类似于我国的“录像”)，因此对“视听作品”采取了较低的独创性标准。在美国的司法实践中，除了纯粹由机器自动拍摄和纯粹翻拍这两种情况之外，几乎所有的录影都被承认为视听作品，体育赛事的直播画面也不例外。

在至今仍然采用“额头流汗”规则的英国以及以英国法为立法参照的新西兰等国，同样采取了较低的独创性标准。英国《版权法》将作品分为三类，第一类是独创性文字、戏剧、音乐或艺术作品；第二类是录音、影片（film）⑥ 或广播；第三类是出版物的版式设计⑦。可见，英国《版权法》是将大陆法系国家邻接权的一些客体，如录音和版式设计作为作品提供保护的。体育赛事直播画面如果被直播者固定在物质载体上，可作为“影片”受到保护。

有观点认为，我国对体育赛事直播的保护“与国际通行做法存在显著差距”，并以“美国众议院在对《1976 版权法》的解释中亦明确体育赛事直播节目构成具有独创性的作品”作为参照之一⑧。

从著作权法的结构和各类保护的逻辑关系来看，英美法系国家将体育赛事直播画面作为作品提供保护的做法对我国基本没有借鉴意义。我国参照大陆法系国家的传统，以相关成果的智力创造程度划分作品与邻接权的客体，并不承认表演、录音和录像为作品。而美国和英国《版权法》均将录音规定为一种法定作品类型⑨，美国在司法实践中还将对音乐作品的表演认定为演绎作品⑩。同时，两国《版权法》也并未创设“录像制作者权”和“广播组织权”这两类邻接权。以英美版权法要求的独创性标准作为在我国认定直播画面性质的参考是不适当的。

（二）赛事现场直播的特征决定了其画面独创性有限

对于体育赛事直播画面而言，其独创性主要体现在对机位的设置和对多台摄像机所拍画面的取舍与编排。的确，由不同的直播团队进行直播，或者由不同的人担任导播，呈现的赛事直播画面会有所

① 北京市朝阳区人民法院民事判决书（2014）朝民（知）初字第 40334 号。

② 该观点也得到了一些学者的赞同。丛立先. 体育赛事直播节目的版权问题析论 [J]. 中国版权，2015 (4).

③ Sam Ricketson, Jane C. Ginsburg. International copyright and neighbouring rights: the berne convention and beyond [M]. 2nd Edition. Oxford: Oxford University Press, 2006: 418, para. 8. 19.

④《著作权法实施条例》第四条第一款第（二）项。

⑤ 在美国《版权法》中，“影视作品”(motion pictures) 属于“视听作品”的一种，见美国《版权法》第 101 条。

⑥ 英国《版权法》中的“film”不仅包括我国《著作权法》中的“电影和以类似摄制电影的方法创作的作品”，还包括我国《著作权法》中的“录像”，为避免混淆，本文并不将其译成“电影”，而是译成“影片”。

⑦ UK Copyright Act, Section 1 (1).

⑧ 见第十二届全国政协第三次会议提案：《关于加强体育赛事直播节目法律保护，发展体育赛事转播业的提案》。

⑨ 17 USC 102 (7), UK Copyright Act, Section 1.

⑩ Capitol Records, Inc. v. Mercury Records Corp., 221 F. 2d 657, 664 (2d Cir. 1955). Melvile B. Nimmer, David Nimmer. Nimmer on copyright [M]. [S. l.]: Matthew Bender & Company, Inc., 2003: § 2. 10 A (2) (b).

区别，这体现了直播过程中的个性因素。而不同的人完成同一工作形成的结果不同，也确实是认定独创性的因素之一。例如，小说的译文被认定为作品的理由之一即是不同的译者完成的翻译在文字组合上并不相同。然而，这并非认定独创性的唯一因素。“因人而异”是判断一种成果是否构成作品的“必要但非充分”条件——作品必然是个性化创作的结果，但并非所有个性化、因人而异的成果都是作品。

对于体育比赛的现场直播而言，观众在特定时刻对于看到何种角度拍摄的画面通常有较为稳定的预期。对于熟练的体育比赛现场导播而言，在哪一时刻应当采用哪个机位拍摄的画面，是有规律可循的。如果有多名达到一定技术水准的导播面对相同的、从不同角度拍摄的比赛画面进行实时的选择，差距并不会过于显著，因为他们都知道其选择必须符合观众稳定的预期。例如，对于足球比赛的进球场景，导播一般先选择能够反映最后阶段传球与射门进球全过程的全景，再回放以在球门各个侧面的机位拍摄的慢镜头，这几乎成为直播的常规。观众对直播画面的预期和直播的常规决定了导播工作的个性化程度是有限的。这种程度在英美法系国家已足以使直播画面成为作品，但在区分“影视作品”与“活动画面”的大陆法系国家，体育赛事的直播画面尚难以达到作品所需要的独创性程度。

既然我国《著作权法》采用了大陆法系国家著作权立法的“二分法”、区分“电影作品和以类似摄制电影的方法创作的作品”和“录像”，我国法院适用大陆法系国家的独创性标准，将反映体育比赛本身过程的现场直播画面认定为“录像”更为合理。笔者更为赞同近期另一法院对体育赛事（涉案体育赛事为巴西世界杯足球赛）现场直播画面所做的定性：

摄制者在拍摄过程中并非处于主导地位，其对于比赛进程的控制、拍摄内容的选择、解说内容的编排以及在机位设置、镜头选择、编导参与等方面，能够按照其意志做出的选择和表达非常有限，因此由国际足联拍摄、经央视制作播出的“2014巴西世界杯”赛事电视节目所体现的独创性，尚不足以达到构成我国著作权法所规定的以类似摄制电影的方法创作的作品的高度①。

三、对现场直播的著作权保护与广播组织权保护

在我国和其他大陆法系国家，由于规定了“广播组织权”，将独创性较低的体育赛事直播画面认定为作品，会导致著作权法中不同保护机制之间的协调问题。

（一）认定现场直播画面为作品将降低广播组织权的意义

在大陆法系国家，创设邻接权的主要目的就是使某些不构成作品的成果也能受到著作权法的保护。随着电视广播技术的进步，电视台在制作和播出节目时，已极少使用纯粹机械式、毫无独创性的摄制方式了，即使是拍摄新闻发布会或教师的授课，也往往有数个机位的摄像机同时拍摄。如果电视台播出的独创性较低的连续画面都可以作为作品受到保护，《著作权法》赋予电视台对载有连续画面的信号以“广播组织权”的意义就会大大降低②。《世界知识产权组织版权条约》第8条已经以技术中立的方式规定了“向公众传播权”，可以规制以各种技术手段传播作品，包括对载有作品的信号进行转播的行为。既然电视台可以用“向公众传播权”保护自己那些被认定为作品的连续画面，以“转播权”为核心的广播组织权的价值也就寥寥无几了③。

英国《版权法》的规定可为此提供佐证。英国《版权法》同时将“录音”、“影片”和“广播”列为法定作品客体。那么，为什么在对“录音”和“影片”不要求独创性的情况下又规定了“广播”这种作品类型呢？其中的原因之一就是要对现场直播提供保护。根据英国《版权法》的规定，“录音”和“影片”是指在物质载体上录制的画面或声音④。而现场直播中声音和画面并非先录制之后再播放（“播放实况录像”），而是实时传送，因此在英国并不被认为是在制作或利用“录音”或“影片”。由此可见，如果直播画面可以作为“影片”受到保护，则

① 北京市石景山区人民法院民事判决书（2015）石民（知）初字第752号。

② 当然，如果播送信号的电视台不是相关节目的创作者或制作者，也不是专有被许可人，则著作权法对作品或录像的保护是无法保护该电视台的，但这种情形毕竟并不多见。

③ 在世界知识产权组织讨论的《世界知识产权组织保护广播组织条约》在广播组织究竟应当享有何种权利的问题的一直存在分歧，但无论是哪一个提案或草案、工作文件，“转播权”始终都在其中。典型实例是迄今仍然作为讨论基础的《保护广播组织条约工作文件》，其第9条规定了广播组织权的内容，虽然该条“备选方案A”和“备选方案B”的内容相去甚远，但都规定了“转播权”。SCCR/27/2 REV，Working Document for a Treaty on the Protection of Broadcasting Organizations，Article 9. 这就印证了“转播权”在广播组织权中的核心地位。

④ UK Copyright Act 5A（1），5B（1）.

英国《版权法》将“广播”列为法定作品类型的做法，也将在很大程度上失去意义。

美国《版权法》从另一角度阐释了这一问题。美国《版权法》虽将“固定在物质载体上”作为作品受保护的条件①，但并未将“广播”列为法定作品类型，也未像大陆法系国家那样规定“广播组织权”，但这正是因为美国国会在对1976年《版权法》的报告中明确指出：只要向公众进行实时传播的同时进行了录制，作品应当在物质载体上被“固定”的要求就得到了满足，被实时传送的连续画面就可以作为电影作品受到保护②。显然，由于美国《版权法》对“视听作品”的独创性要求极低，录音又被规定为法定作品类型，同时边播边录的现场直播又可以符合作品被“固定”的要求，使得广播电台的现场直播可以作为“录音”作品受到保护，电视台的现场直播可以作为“视听作品”受到保护，美国《版权法》没有必要再像英国一样将“广播”规定为一类作品，或者像大陆法系国家一样规定“广播组织权”。

（二）对现场直播的保护应通过对广播组织权的完善

我国《著作权法》一方面规定了“广播组织权”，另一方面并没有将“固定在物质载体上”作为作品受到保护的前提条件③。在这种情况下，我国《著作权法》对连续画面的独创性要求不应太低，否则会在很大程度上影响“广播组织权”存在的意义。

由国家版权局报送国务院法制办公室，并公开征求意见的《著作权法（修订草案送审稿）》已经以技术中立的方式为广播组织规定了“转播权”④，使之可以规制以各种技术手段，包括通过互联网实施的转播行为。倘若现在降低对作品独创性的要求，使包括赛事直播画面等绝大多数的连续画面都可以作为作品受到保护，则《著作权法（修订草案送审稿）》完善“广播组织权”也就无太大意义了。

与此同时，无论国际上对于是否将直接通过互联网实施传播的网站纳入《世界知识产权组织广播组织保护条约》存在何种争议，我国都可以将网播组织纳入《著作权法》中“广播组织”的范围提供保护，这既是因为一个主权国家的著作权法对一项权利的规定并不需要以国际条约为依据，也是因为在缺乏条约义务的情况下，我国不需要将此种保护给予其他国家的网播组织⑤，其实际效果将是仅对我国的网播组织提供保护。由此可见，对体育赛事直播画面的保护，应当依靠对广播组织权的尽快完善，而非通过降低对独创性的要求而扩大作品的范围。从这个角度看，“凤凰网赛事转播案”保护直播者利益的价值取向值得赞许，但具体手段尚可讨论。在目前的法律机制中，认定未经许可通过网络转播的行为构成不正当竞争是更为可取的方法⑥。

（本文原发表于《法律科学（西北政法大学学报）》2016年第1期，为国家社会科学基金重大项目“互联网领域知识产权重大立法问题研究”的研究成果（编号：14ZDC020）。
作者单位：华东政法大学）

参考文献

［1］郑成思．版权法：修订本［M］．北京：中国人民大学出版社，1997.

［2］胡康生．中华人民共和国著作权法释义［M］．北京：法律出版社，2011.

［3］姚红．中华人民共和国著作权法释解［M］．北京：群众出版社，2001.

［4］世界知识产权组织．罗马公约和录音制品公约指南［M］．刘波林，译．北京：中国人民大学出版社，2002.

［5］M．雷炳德．著作权法［M］．张恩民，译．北京：法律出版社，2004.

［6］Sam Ricketson，Jane C．Ginsburg．International copyright and neighbouring rights：the berne convention

① See 17 USC 102（a）.

② See the House Report on the Copyright Act of 1976，H. R. REP. 94-1476，p. 52；Paul Goldstein. Copyright［M］. 2nd Edition. ［S. l.］：Aspen Law & Business，2002：§ 2.4

③ 我国不仅没有像美国等国那样，在《著作权法》中将“作品被固定在物质载体上”规定为作品受保护的条件，同时还明确将“口述作品”列为受保护的一类作品，这就充分说明我国《著作权法》并不要求受保护的作品必须被“固定在物质载体上”。

④ 该法第四十二条规定：“广播电台、电视台对其播放的广播电视节目享有下列权利：（一）许可他人以无线或者有线方式转播其广播电视节目；……”

⑤ 在我国加入的各项国际知识产权条约中，只有《与贸易有关的知识产权协定》（TRIPs）规定了对广播组织权的保护。该条约第3条规定：就表演者、录音制品制作者和广播组织而言，每一成员给予其他成员国民“国民待遇”的义务“仅适用于本协定规定的权利”。同时该条约第14条第3款规定，广播组织享有“转播权”仅限于无线转播权。这就意味着，如果未来我国《著作权法》将“网播组织”纳入广播组织的范围并享有通过互联网转播的权利，由于该项权利并非是TRIPs规定的权利，对外国广播组织不适用“国民待遇”。

⑥ 适用《反不正当竞争法》制止未经许可互联网转播的案例见北京市海淀区人民法院民事判决书（2013）海民初字第21470号。

and beyond [M]. 2nd Edition. Oxford: Oxford University Press, 2006.

[7] Hugh Laddie, Peter Prescott, Mary Vitoria. The modern law of copyright and designs [M]. 4th Edition. [S. l.]: Butterworths, 2011.

[8] Melvile B. Nimmer, David Nimmer. Nimmer on copyright [M]. [S. l.]: Matthew Bender & Company, Inc., 2003.

[9] Asser International Sports Law Centre. Study on sports organisers' rights in the European Union [EB/OL]. 2014.

[10] Silke von Lewinski. International copyright law and policy [M]. Oxford: Oxford University Press, 2008.

避风港原则前沿问题研究

——以"通知—删除"作为诉讼前置程序展开

徐　明

近年来，网络领域出现了五种典型的商业模式，正改变着信息传播的方式。第一，信息聚合模式；第二，深度链接模式；第三，转码传播模式；第四，云计算模式；第五，大数据分析模式。网络领域的知识产权纠纷已经不再局限于网站转载未获授权的作品而被诉侵权等形态，而是随着新兴商业模式的产生发展出了诸多新型的著作权纠纷形态。以"避风港"原则为核心的侵权判定方式是否仍适用于新的商业模式？是否需要对其实体、程序性要求进行调整或进一步明确以便更贴合产业发展的实际需要？学术界、司法界、产业界不仅高度关注，更是争议不断，有必要对避风港原则适用中的前沿问题加以探讨。

一、避风港原则的产生与法律规定

（一）避风港原则的产生

避风港原则的雏形出现在《世界知识产权组织版权条约》①与《世界知识产权组织表演和录音制品条约》②之中，正式形成于美国《数字千年版权法》③，根据其中第512条的规定："网络服务提供者使用信息定位工具。包括目录、索引、超文本链接、在线存储网站，如果由于其链接、存储的相关内容涉嫌侵权，在其能够证明自己并无恶意，并且及时删除侵权链接或者内容的情况下，网络服务提供者不承担赔偿责任。"由于其核心在于网络服务提供者收到权利人通知后及时删除侵权信息，所以避风港原则又被称为"通知—删除"原则（Notice-Take down Procedure）。

（二）我国有关避风港原则的法律规定

尽管我国法律条文上并没有"避风港"这一法律术语，但其立法精神已经先后体现于法律、行政法规、司法解释之中，如表1所示。

表1　我国有关避风港原则的法律规定

年份	性质	名称
2000年	司法解释	《最高人民法院关于审理涉及计算机网络著作权纠纷案件适用法律若干问题的解释》第五条
2005年	行政法规	《互联网著作权行政保护办法》第十二条
2006年	行政法规	《信息网络传播权保护条例》（2006年公布，2013年施行）第二十三条
2009年	法律	《侵权责任法》第三十六条第二款
2012年	司法解释	《最高人民法院关于审理侵害信息网络传播权民事纠纷案件适用法律若干问题的规定》第六条
2014年	司法解释	《最高人民法院关于审理利用信息网络侵害人身权益民事纠纷案件适用法律若干问题的规定》第六条

在2009年通过并实施的《侵权责任法》中规定了接到通知但并未移除侵权内容所应当承担的法律责任。2013年新修订的《信息网络传播权保护条例》中避风港原则仍然得以延续和适用。

二、避风港原则的一般适用规则

（一）法律主体与法律关系

互联网信息服务产生了"设备供应商—基础网络运营商—内容收集者和生产者—业务提供者—用户"的链条。通常情况下，设备供应商不需要承担任何责任，因为其根本无法知道也不能阻止侵权行为的发生。基础网络运营商仅提供了互联网的接入带宽，也不需要承担法律责任。由于用户不以盈利为目的，而只是自己观看或学习，通常也不会构成侵权。因此，与避风港原则有直接关系的主体涉及内容收集者和生产者、业务提供者之间。

① World Intellectual Property Organization Copyright Treaty, WCT.

② WIPO Performances and Phonograms Treaty, WPPT.

③ Digital Millennium Copyright Act, DMCA.

在法律主体方面，避风港原则对网络服务提供商（ISP）与网络内容提供商（ICP）两个法律主体进行区分①，其中 ISP 即向广大用户综合提供互联网接入业务、信息业务和增值业务的电信运营商，ICP 是向广大用户综合提供互联网信息业务和增值业务的电信运营商。从目前我国的立法来看，权利人、ISP、ICP 的权利义务关系主要包括：权利人拥有通知 ISP 的权利。权利人可以自主决定是否将侵权情况通知 ISP。ISP 在收到权利人通知后，有及时审查的义务，以及当作品侵权时删除相应信息或断开侵权信息链接的义务。当作品侵权时，ICP 应当承担侵权的直接责任。

（二）避风港原则的适用条件

对于 ICP 而言，避风港原则并不适用。例如，对于在微信公众号中发布信息的法律主体，其本身就是信息的上传者，对于信息的正当来源与否应当有着清晰的认识，不能以避风港原则加以免责。由于 ICP 直接接触内容，一旦其公开的信息侵犯了他人的著作权，则根据现有法律能够认定为直接侵权，避风港原则为 ISP 提供了免责事由，而并非为 ICP 提供免责事由。

对于 ISP 而言，通过避风港原则免除自己的责任必须同时满足以下四个条件：第一，主观上 ISP 不知道也不应当知道其平台上所公开的信息构成侵权。第二，客观上 ISP 在收到侵权通知后及时删除或断开了侵权信息的链接，使其无法通过互联网得以访问。第三，ISP 有能力和权利控制侵权内容的访问权限。第四，ISP 没有从侵权内容中获得直接的经济收益。

三、避风港原则的前沿问题及建议

（一）权利人针对 ISP 的诉讼是否应当以“通知—删除”程序为前提

避风港原则中的“通知—删除”程序是一种抗辩事由还是一种诉讼前置程序，目前我国的法律中尚未明确规定，但其中的差异直接影响着网络产业的发展效率。实践中，“通知—删除”程序中的“通知”是证明 ISP 已经处于“知道”或“应当知道”侵权信息存在的一种手段，而诉讼却被作为“通知”的一种形式。如果缺少了“通知”的环节，除非侵权事实非常明显②，ISP 是否知道侵权信息的存在将取决于其应当尽到多大程度的“注意义务”。

但实际上，由于网络带来了信息的爆炸式增长，将海量信息的审核义务强加于 ISP 之上，虽然能够最大限度地保护知识产权权利人的利益，却极大地遏制了信息传播的速度与效率。正因为缺乏明确的规定，实践中许多著作权人跳过了“通知”环节直接将 ISP 起诉至法院，其理由是 ISP 没有尽到适当的注意义务而导致了侵权损害的扩大，再由 ISP 举证自己尽到了注意义务且并未收到权利人的“通知”。避风港原则产生的目的是尽快弥补权利人的财产利益，节约宝贵的司法资源，实践中以诉讼作为通知的情形，不仅使避风港原则处于极其尴尬的地位，也存在着滥诉、滥用司法资源的可能性。

为了解决这一难题，笔者认为，尽管在实体法上规定了知识产权权利人拥有向法院起诉的权利，但是可以考虑在程序法上增加将“通知—删除”前置的要求，最晚在提出诉讼时行使通知的权利，以使得避风港原则在具体执行过程中更有效率。

第一，“通知—删除”前置能够降低网络产业中的总成本。法律规则的设定必须对产业的整体发展具有好处，如果将权利人和 ISP 作为一个整体来看待，权利人用于“通知”的成本将远低于 ISP 尽到最大审核义务的成本，即采用“通知—删除”前置的规则能够在双方产生合作之余，权利人的权益能够得到保障，ISP 也能够节省因过度的注意义务所支出的成本③。

第二，“通知—删除”前置能够节约宝贵的司法资源。对于大部分 ISP 来说，接到权利人的通知后，其主观方面已经处于“知道”的状态，如果仍然不采用行动，那么在将来的司法诉讼中将面临着极高的败诉风险，此时采用删除侵权信息或断开侵权信息链接的做法无疑是优选的策略，甚至支付一定金额的补偿，权利人在能够实现权利救济的基础上将不会选择成本更高的诉讼④。

第三，不“通知”而直接起诉，有放任侵权范围扩大之嫌。避风港原则设立的目的之一是让那些主观上无过错的 ISP 及时阻止侵权范围的扩大⑤，ISP 收到通知后及时删除了侵权内容，就能够阻止侵权信

① 网络服务提供商，即 internet service provider，简称“ISP”；网络内容提供商，即 internet content provider，简称“ICP”。

② 对于侵权事实特别明显的情形，一般适用“红旗原则”。

③ 此处仅指“过度的注意义务”，因为 ISP 本身应当尽到合理的注意义务，而非零注意义务。

④ 此时排除了商业目的诉讼的可能性，例如有时诉讼是为了实现另一种广告效益，这种情况在本研究报告中不予考虑。

⑤ 如果不及时阻止，将承担侵权后果，因此 ISP 会选择及时阻止。

息传播范围的进一步扩大，这也符合权利人的利益和立法的目的。而向法院起诉往往需要准备起诉材料，甚至聘请律师，这将花费额外的时间，此时由于权利人未履行“通知”程序而导致侵权范围的扩大，变相加剧了侵权所产生的不利后果，如果让 ISP 承担因未及时通知而加重的所有后果，有失公平。

第四，“通知—删除”程序前置有助于双方积极行使权利、履行义务，也有助于责任的划分。当权利人发现侵权事实之后，如果“通知”了 ISP 但后者并未“删除”，则 ISP 既不能免责也要承担“通知”之后侵权范围扩大所导致的更严重的后果，如果未“通知”ISP 而直接向法院诉讼，则 ISP 能够以自己“不知道”而免责，且不用承担权利人发现侵权事实之后的全部后果[①]，权利人没有及时采用“通知—删除”规则来维护自己的权利，法律也不应当代替其实现这部分的权利救济。

（二）“通知”的主体是否应当包括著作权的被许可人

向 ISP 发出通知的主体通常是享有著作权的权利人，那么，是否应当包括著作权的被许可人呢？笔者认为应当区分来看。

第一，独占许可的情形下，在许可期间内被许可人应当拥有权利人“通知”的权利。在独占许可的情形下，被许可人虽然不享有作品的所有权，但却是市场中基于该作品收益的唯一主体，因此，被许可人必定会付出极大的努力从而使自己的收益最大化，未经许可的 ISP 对该作品的传播直接侵害了被许可方的经济利益，而享有所有权的权利人却可能因为没有直接利益受损从而怠于行使“通知”的权利，此时，应当从法律规定中直接赋予独占许可的被许可人拥有与权利人一致的“通知”权利，从而使得避风港原则的运行更有效率。

第二，排他许可的情形下，在许可期间内如果权利人怠于行使或放弃行使“通知”的权利，被许可人可以单独行使“通知”的权利。如果发生 ISP 未经许可传播作品的情形，首先应当由权利人行使“通知”的权利，如果权利人尚不知道传播的情况，被许可人应当及时通知权利人。如果权利人怠于行使甚至明确表示放弃行使“通知”的权利，而导致了该作品传播范围的进一步扩大，被许可人经济利益的受损，此时，笔者认为被许可人可以单独行使“通知”的权利，要求 ISP 删除侵权作品。

第三，普通许可的情形下，被许可人并不当然拥有“通知”的权利，除非获得了权利人的明确授权。被许可人只是拥有了合法使用作品进行收益的权利，并没有排除他人未经授权使用作品的权利，该项权利应当由权利人行使。被许可人发现了 ISP 未经授权传播作品的情况，可以选择通知权利人，再由权利人通知 ISP。在得到权利人明确授权的情况下，特定的普通被许可人才能拥有“通知”的权利。

（三）收到通知后，ISP“删除”作品的期限应当加以明确

按照我国《信息网络传播权保护条例》第十五条规定，网络服务商接到权利人通知后，应当“立即”删除涉嫌侵权的内容或链接。那么，ISP 删除作品的期限是否应当由法律明确规定呢？笔者认为给定一个法定的删除期限并不妥当，该期限过长则会导致 ISP 对避风港原则的滥用，该期限过短则会导致 ISP 支出过多的人力和技术成本，不利于产业的发展。并且，删除期限也因个案而异，无法给出明确的法定数字。那么，《信息网络传播保护条例》中的“立即”应当如何理解呢？笔者认为应当分情况对待。

第一，权利人的通知中给定明确期限的，应当以该期限为限，期限过短的，可以要求延长。当权利人通知中有给定的期限时，该期限以通知到达 ISP 时开始起算，ISP 应当在给定的期限内加以审核和处理，如果期限过短无法对权利人的真实性或者作品是否构成侵权加以判断，可以协商延长期限，但延长期限内 ISP 有义务不让作品的传播范围更加扩大。

第二，权利人的通知中未给定明确期限的，ISP 的删除期限应当符合合理期限的要求，即综合考虑该作品的知名度、传播范围等因素后确定的期限。当作品的知名程度较高、传播较广时，ISP 的处理时间应当更加迅速。尤其是一些热播的电影、电视剧，一旦不能及时删除侵权内容和链接，对权利人造成的损失将是难以估量的。

第三，如果 ISP 在其服务协议中明确给出删除期限的，应当认定为最晚删除期限，除非权利人同意延长。实践中，有些 ISP 为了表达对知识产权的重视，主动在其服务协议中对外表明接到权利人通知后的删除期限，此时则构成单方承诺，具有法律约束力。

① 因为权利人对于侵权范围的扩大也有一定放任之嫌疑。

（四）避风港原则中“非盈利”的条件应当以具体情形加以区分

基于前文避风港原则适用条件的分析，其中ISP没有从侵权内容中获得直接的经济收益是其适用避风港原则的要件之一，也就是说，一旦ISP依靠侵权内容获得利益，就不能够得到避风港原则的免责保护。但是，在商业社会中，任何网络服务的提供者都是以盈利为目的加以运营，没有通过侵权内容直接获得利益的规定应当做出进一步具体的明确。笔者认为，根据盈利渠道和模式的不同，可以分为以下几种情况加以区分：

第一，付费点播模式，构成直接盈利，不能得到避风港原则的保护。从某种意义上看，ISP对该作品是否构成侵权应当有了足够的判定，付费点播的费用直接成为ISP获得利益的渠道，因此不满足避风港原则适用的条件。并且，该付费的形式应当是多样化的，通过货币形式直接付费以及通过网站点数购买等，都应当认为是付费的形式。

第二，会员制费用，是否构成直接盈利应当以非会员是否能够观看侵权作品而加以区分。对于一些视频网站而言，采用会员费的方式进行盈利，此时，如果非会员无法访问侵权作品的链接，那么相当于该笔费用被用于侵权作品的点播，构成直接盈利；如果非会员仍然能够获得侵权作品的链接并能够正常观看，那么该笔会员费不能够被认定为基于该侵权作品的直接盈利。

第三，广告贴片费用，不能够认定为基于侵权作品的直接盈利，除非该广告仅针对侵权作品单一播放。此时，ISP虽然通过侵权作品前的广告获得了广告费，但由于该笔费用并不是用户为观看侵权作品而支付的直接费用，因此，并不能够认定为ISP的直接盈利。但是，ISP基于热门侵权影视剧植入的特定广告，应当认定为直接盈利。

四、结语

目前的互联网版权保护案件已经不再局限于被诉网站转载未经授权的作品，而是呈现出多样化的形态，避风港原则作为判定ISP是否承担侵权责任的核心，其实体与程序上应该不断调整，以更加适合产业的发展趋势。基于上述研究，笔者认为“通知—删除”程序可以有四方面调整。第一，将“通知—删除”程序作为权利人针对ISP的诉讼的前置程序；第二，除著作权人外，“通知”的主体可以包括独占被许可人以及特定情形下的排他被许可人与普通被许可人；第三，“删除”的期限应当考虑权利人要求的期限与ISP承诺的期限；第四，付费点播模式构成直接盈利，会员制费用是否构成直接盈利应当以非会员是否能够观看侵权作品而加以区分，广告贴片费用则不能够认定为基于侵权作品的直接盈利，除非该广告仅针对侵权作品单一播放。

（本文原发表于《东方法学》2016年第5期，为上海市法学会2015年理论法学研究课题“网络领域知识产权保护法律问题研究”研究成果之一。
作者单位：华东理工大学法学院）

美术作品的表达及其实质相似的认定

杨雄文　王沁荷

著作权制度主要发端于文字作品保护，而对美术作品的保护相对滞后。随着科技发展，特别是电脑技术的发达，通过扫描、下载图片、软件处理等新的手段，美术作品可以被轻松复制，相关纠纷层出不穷。这不仅仅是因为美术作品与文字作品存在很大差别，而且后现代艺术、行为艺术、装置艺术等艺术创新都会为美术作品相关的司法裁判带来很大的困难。目前美术作品剽窃裁判缺乏有效的理论和方法支持，严重制约了美术创新发展以及美术作品的市场化、商品化。

一、美术作品实质相似认定的方法及其不足

作品剽窃认定的重心是判定作品是否构成实质相似。抽象测试法（abstract teat）适用于文字作品，尤其是小说类作品。“在判定图形、摄影、美术、视听等具有艺术性或美感性的著作是否抄袭时，如使用与文字著作相同的分析解构方法为细节对比，往往有其困难度或可能失去公平。”[①] 美国1970年在一个美术作品剽窃案审判中，法院认定被告的商品捕捉（capture）原告享有著作权的贺年卡的“整体概念与感觉”，包括绘画方式、组合方式和文字编排等方面，造成了原被告作品间存在着明显的相似[②]。这一裁判方法被称为“整体概念与感觉测试法”（total concept and feel），其特点在于“判断构想与表达之区别时，原告与被告之著作自整体观察所得之观感或著作权所予人之意境，亦属于‘表达’

① 台湾最高法院1995年度台上字第6398号刑事判决。

② Roth Greeting Cards v. United Card Co.，429F. 2d 1106（9th Cir. 1970）.

之范畴，可为著作权保护之标的”[①]。其主旨是在美术作品实质相似的判断的时候，由于美术作品呈现的方式和人的视觉感官具有密切的关系，所以需要把两个作品拿来做整体的观感和细部的观察，以它们对人的视觉发生什么样的作用来评价是否实质相似。但我国境内法院对于美术作品的审查还是参酌抽象测试法更为普遍。

截至2015年4月，在北大法宝中查到美术作品剽窃的案例有177个。从这些案件可以看出，除了和解的案件以外，司法判决很少对美术作品的思想与表达进行适用前的区分。《次仁卓玛》案中法院认为“作品画面所呈现的构图、光线对比、人物细微的姿势、神态、服饰以及物品摆放的状态等属于作品表达的有机组成部分”[②]。《葫芦娃》案判决书中描述：“无论是‘葫芦娃’角色造型的线条、轮廓、色彩还是服饰、颈饰、腰饰、葫芦冠等的选择都体现了作者个人的构思、选择和表达。”[③] 暂且先不说这些断言是否正确，对于为什么这样认定，怎么认定，法官也并未说明。不同的法官尽管对于“思想还是表达”的范畴抉择可以说是尚未统一，但他们之间还是有个比较一致的做法，就是在判决书措辞中避免对思想还是表达进行具体分析，而是在结合个案作品的具体形态的描述后直接断言其为思想或者表达。这个做法对于美术作品侵权认定的缺点在于：其一，实质相似的对比中混入了思想成分，容易导致相识度偏高；其二，纠结于“独创性”的认定，却没有适当的认定方法去明晰独创性界限。这种裁判文书上自说自话的态度带来的结果是艺术工作者与法律工作者互不认同，最常见的上诉理由是上诉方认为法院判决混淆了美术专业上的创意概念与法律上的主题思想[④]。

不过，西方国家流行的“整体概念与感觉测试法”在实践中仍有局限性，主要不足在于：用语模糊、思想与表达的区分不清晰造成使用混乱，最后仍然归结于法官或者专家的感性认定，缺乏理论依据让大众信服。有批评观点认为，“整体概念与感觉测试法”并不能自动实现对于思想及表达的区分，其适用结果不过是造成另一种的名词混乱，而对于著作权侵权的存在与否的进一步分析却没有什么帮助[⑤]。

继Krofft案遭受“不当扩大了对表达的保护范围”的批评之后，美国第九巡回上诉法院随后对“整体概念与感觉测试法”的适用进行了局部修正，提出了“作品在整体观念和感觉上是否存在实质性相似并不重要，重要的是作品中受到保护的表达部分与诉称侵权作品中的等同部分是否构成实质性相似”[⑥]。这意味着美国法院主张在适用普通理性观察者的标准之前，应当先行分离出思想与表达。

二、美术鉴赏：划分美术作品思想与表达的工具

有观点认为，“美术著作抄袭之判断，不应与文字著作为相同处理，无法采取分析解构之方式为细节比较”[⑦]。甚至极端观点主张“在美术作品中是不存在抄袭或者剽窃问题的”[⑧]。其实不然。前面提到的判例，无一不是使用画面要素进行美术作品相似性的对比。从国内外的相关司法实践来看，业界对于美术作品的相似性判断还是坚守思想/表达二分法的原则。通过什么样的正确而便利的方法提取美术作品中的表达，或者说归属为美术作品的思想还是表达的判断依据是什么，是目前存在的一个难点，亟待解决。

文字作品是用文字等构成要素有序组合而成，美术作品没有文字要素，但这并不意味美术作品就没有自己的构成要素。一些研究成果在分析美术作品的时候提到作品的结构、对比角度与设计元素[⑨]，认为美术作品的表达性要素包括明暗、色彩、点、线面的结合与分配，其物质要素包括画布、颜料、石块等[⑩]。这些构成要素从何而来，是否能覆盖美术作品表达的内容，并无定论。

可见，对于是否存在美术作品侵权行为的分析，

① 罗明通．著作权法论（Ⅱ）［M］．7版．台北：群彦图书股份有限公司，2009：362．

② 北京市第二中级人民法院（2011）二中民终字第21796号。

③ 上海市第二中级人民法院（2011）沪二中民五（知）终字第62号。

④ 北京市第二中级人民法院（1999）二中知初字第145号。

⑤ Howard B. Abrams. The law of copyright［M］．［S. l.］：Clark Boardman Callaghan，1993：vol. Ⅱ，§14.03（G）．

⑥ Cooling Systems & Flexibles，Inc. v. Stuart Radiator，Inc.，777 F. 2d 485（9th Cir. 1985）．

⑦ 姚信安．双鱼罗生门：论美术著作之抄袭：从智慧财产法院100年度刑智上诉字第39号判决谈起［J］．月旦法学杂志，2013（217）．

⑧ 崔勃，阮莹．油画《重庆大轰炸》被扯上法庭［J］．民主与法，2004（12月下半月刊）：54-55．

⑨ 邓燕谊，关晓海．从商标图案纠纷看美术作品的侵权认定［N］．中国知识产权报，2014-06-13．

⑩ 龙云辉．美术作品侵权判断的特殊性问题研究［J］．学海，2008（4）：185．

离不开对美术作品进行解构，抽析其表达的工作。美术作品的表现方式千变万化，旧的表现手法不停地被新的创作形式突破，一些传统的观念也在不断改变，但是美术鉴赏的基本原理也一直维持着稳定。美术鉴赏理论提供了一个很好的解构与归类美术作品的思想与表达的手段。

美术鉴赏是指人们对美术作品艺术形象进行感受、理解和评判的过程，是观众凭借美术作品而展开的一种积极、主动的审美再创造活动①。美术作品的画面构成包括内容和形式，对应于思想与表达的二分法，内容属于思想范畴，形式则属于表达的领域。

我们可以选取美术鉴赏理论中的基本概念来解构美术作品，从美术作品的构成要素这一角度筛选可用于美术作品抄袭判定的内容。利用鉴赏理论连接艺术与法律，将解构后的美术作品要素融入抄袭的认定依据是一种理性的选择。通过这种方法，可以实现对美术作品思想与表达的区分，再将区分出来的表达部分进行是否实质相似的对比。

美术鉴赏理论将美术作品的画面构成区分为内容和形式两个方面（见图 1）。

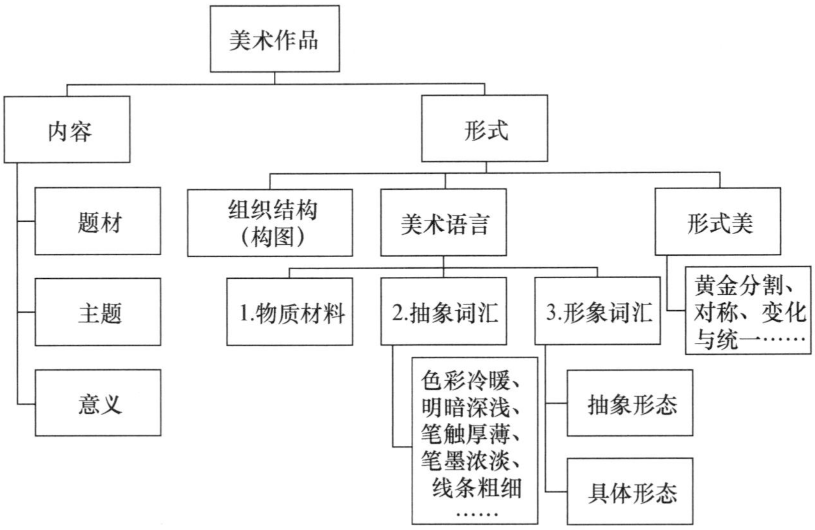

图 1　美术作品的画面构成

具体而言，美术作品的内容包括题材、主题、意义②，这些选择与主题的选择都体现了作者的眼界和智慧，但是在著作权法体系里应属于不被保护的思想部分。在凡·高创作了油画作品《向日葵》之后，莫奈也同样以向日葵为内容创作了一幅同样名为《向日葵》的油画作品，没有人说这是表达的抄袭。

三、美术作品的形式及其与表达的对应

美术作品的形式即艺术创作的表现状态，是思想内容的存在方式。根据鉴赏理论，美术作品形式的构成要素可分为内部形式、外部形式和形式美。在著作权保护范围内应当考虑的作为表达要素的有内部形式和外部形式中的形象词汇、抽象词汇两种要素，但同时应当注意结合其他要素进行整体的考究。

（一）美术作品的内部形式

美术作品的内部形式，亦称“构图”“组织结构”。这一词汇源于西方，在我国国画理论中也叫布局。它是指美术作品的骨架，是点、线、面的结合，相当于文字作品的大纲，是美术作品表达形式中非常重要的一部分。如凡·高的《吃土豆的人》，在画面的最前面凡·高以一个背影来衬托后面其他人的表情，就是一种构图能力的体现。在《重庆大轰炸》美术作品侵权问题的案件中，两个审级的人民法院均认定如美术作品的构图和刻画手法相同，就会构成侵权③。因此，组织结构自然会是判定侵权的考察内容。

（二）美术作品的外部形式

美术作品的外部形式，又称“美术语言”，可以分为三个方面：物质材料、抽象词汇、形象词汇。

1. 物质材料

物质材料指的是绘画采用的材料。美术作品作

① 陈慧钧. 美术鉴赏［M］. 北京：清华大学出版社，2013：19.
② 钱初熹. 美术鉴赏及其教学［M］. 北京：人民美术出版社，2007：30.
③ 重庆市高级人民法院（2006）渝高法民终字第 129 号。

者在创作作品时，一般会选择自己擅长的一种或者几种材料，这样选择更像是一种习惯的趋势，并不能算成智慧的成果。犹如某人想要表达一个创意故事，小说家会用小说来表达，戏剧工作者会用舞台剧来表达，电影导演会用电影来表达，一般会从自己擅长的表达方式考虑。

不同物质材料的转变。如果一幅版画作品与一幅油画作品看上去一模一样，因其材质发生了较大的改变，可能是演绎作品问题，侵犯了其演绎权。“因为演绎权所控制的行为，正是以不同的表达形式表现同一内容的行为。”① 美术作品的种类多样，物质材料的变化可以参考专利保护中同等替换原理。

总之，物质材料的不同并不是作品表达的不同，在抄袭侵权认定的时候不应该作为相似的对比因素，但应考虑其物质变化带来的表达形式变化。

2. 抽象词汇

抽象词汇指的是色彩冷暖、明暗深浅、笔触厚薄、笔墨浓淡、线条粗细等等②。抽象词汇包含的内容很多，一般会有一种或者几种抽象词汇包含在作品中。如黑白的作品有明暗的深浅却没有色彩冷暖，漫画作品有线条粗细却没有笔触的厚薄。这些都是创作者在运用美术技巧表达感情，如俄罗斯画家列宾在作品《伊凡·雷帝杀子》中用黑色、红色和黄色搭配，形成惶恐紧张的情绪。不同的组合有不同感受，细腻的感情表达离不开创作者经验的累积和智慧的劳动。抽象词汇是我们最变化多端的表达，必然属于判断美术作品侵权与否的考虑要素。

3. 形象词汇

形象词汇可以分为抽象和具象两种形态，是作者所绘内容的具体呈现。运用形象词汇进行艺术表达需要具有一定的艺术修养。如同要求没有经过训练的人用油画材料画一个苹果，会很难下笔，更不知道怎么画出立体感。再下一步到底是表达出怎样的苹果，哪种词汇适合表达创作者的情感，这肯定是经过思考的。作者想要画雄伟的山水，而观众从画中感受到了是雄伟的山水，这就是具象形态的表现，虽然抽象的形态形成的抽象作品不一定每个人都看得明白，但形象词汇无疑是最接近版权意义上表达定位的要素。

（三）形式美

美术作品的形式的最后一部分是形式美，指的是符合美术语言规律的目的性组合，如黄金分割、蛇形线、对称、变化与统一等。形式美指的是古往今来都认可的一些美感的构成，是种有限的固定形式，符合思想与表达合并原则，并不适合享有著作权。

四、美术作品实质相似的判断

美术作品的素材多半是动物、植物、风景文化素材或别人的作品等已经存在的东西，所以实务上常常使人感到苦恼，一个作品似乎来自某种已经存在的物象（也可能是别人的作品）。该如何处理？一般而言，对于作品创作性的判定必须结合相关行业的背景、传统习惯综合认定。

（一）美术作品实质相似判断的主体

艺术家创作出来的美术作品必须通过鉴赏主体的鉴赏活动，才能真正实现它的社会意义和美学价值③。这一美术作品是否构成实质相似的判断所需的审美能力，应以一般大众的感受或印象还是专业人士的鉴定为判断基准？

美术作品最大的受众还是大众，过度的专业化只会让美术作品的侵权判定脱离一般大众的审美。对于有人认同的“作品”——无论这些人品位是高还是低，他们是嬉皮士、先锋派还是小资，是成年人还是少年——我们都应当承认它们属于版权法意义上的艺术品④。美国 Holmes 法官在判决中就谈道：“如果美术作品能够博得任何公众的兴趣，那么它们就是具有商业价值的，任何一种公众的喜好都不应被鄙视。”⑤ 笔者认为，在判断美术作品的独创性这个问题上，当我们进行抽象词汇比对的时候可以借鉴“两阶段判断法”中听取专家意见的环节，而在感觉测试环节则应以“一般理性观察者”的角度判断。

（二）美术作品实质相似认定的质与量的标准

两个作品间是否实质相似，并非依两作品的实质部分加以比较，而是以被告引用或近似原告作品的部分在原告的作品中是否达到实质而定⑥。一般情况下，是否构成实质相似可以从质与量两个方面

① 王迁. 知识产权法教程［M］. 北京：中国人民大学出版社，2010：46.

② 钱初熹. 美术鉴赏及其教学［M］. 北京：人民美术出版社，2007：31.

③ 陈慧钧. 美术鉴赏［M］. 北京：清华大学出版社，2013：20.

④ Melvile B. Nimmer, David Nimmer. Nimmer on Copyright［M］. Mattew Bender & Company, Inc., 2003：2.08（B）（1）.

⑤ 杨明. 文字作品 v. 美术作品对几个基本理论问题的反思［J］. 中外法学，2009（2）：256.

⑥ 曾腾珍，洪维拓. 智慧财产权权法专论：著作权之抄袭与侵害［M］. 台北：五楠图书有限公司，2013：97.

分别进行分析。如果美术作品中无法用数字来准确估算抄袭“量”的抄袭，那么对于“质”的方面的抄袭在实质相似的判断分量就更重。

（三）美术作品对于“创”的要求

我国著作权法规定了作品需具备独创性，但对“创”需要达到的高度却没有明确说明。在美术作品的定义上所强调的审美意义，实质上是对“创”的一种要求。美学之父鲍姆嘉通说过：“美学是感性认识的科学。”① 美的独创性也是一种直觉经验下的感性认识。我国美术文化的发展正处于高产低质的时期，为了避免阻碍国家文化发展的目的，需要结合艺术与法制的发展对美术作品的独创性要件从严解释。

在对“创”的判断过程中，要注意以下几个方面：

（1）对于通过单个要素判断实质相似与否的，相似程度要求高。这是实质性相似判断因素“质”与“量”结合的体现。

（2）对于通过多个要素判断实质相似与否的，相似程度要求低。对多个要素相似的情况，相似程度的要求不应过分苛刻，否则会让艺术创作环境出现与文字创作环境中东拼西凑、混作一团的相似的抄袭现象。

（3）要素对比与整体感觉缺一不可。无论怎么解构，美术作品仍然是个注重要素之间关系的作品类型，不能不考虑整体感觉就把这种感性艺术所具有的融合美活生生抹去。例如，如果两个美术作品多要素达到实质相似，但整体给一般理性大众的感觉完全不同，这一定是个在表达创新上达到突破的作品，值得我们去保护。

鉴于法律与艺术的协调，以及理性与感性的融合，要素对比与整体感觉都必须列入实质相似判断方法的考虑范围。

五、结语

立体主义画家毕加索曾说：“好的艺术家懂得抄袭，伟大的艺术家善于盗取”（Good artists copy, great aritists steal）。在这样令人迷惑的美术作品的创作之路上，如何正确划分合理借鉴与非法剽窃是个难题。利用鉴赏理论对美术作品解构的基本概念与分类，能够将具体个案中的美术作品解析出相关构成要素，这就类似于文字作品的解构了，甚至在思想与表达的区分上比文字作品更明朗。正是这样对美术作品的要素的提取，并进而结合“整体概念与感觉测试法”，有望取得美术作品实质相似判断方法的完善。

由于美术作品的种类繁多，上述做法也可以与商标、外观设计、摄影作品等类别的实质相似判断挂钩，甚至可以完全利用于商标作品的侵权判定。

另外，美术作品还存在用典的侵权例外情形。用典，亦称挪用艺术。因其作为一种美术语言意义上的类似于文字作品的引注方式，被认为是适当的。如爱德华·马奈《奥林匹克》的构图几乎完全抄袭意大利画家提香·韦切利奥的《乌尔比诺的维纳斯》。这些也值得我们关注。

（本文原发表于《知识产权》2016年第1期，本文写作得到中央高校基本科研业务费专项资金（编号2015XZD24）资助。
作者单位：华南理工大学）

网络著作权侵权中“直接侵权主体”判断的规范构成

——以“私人复制例外”的合法范围确定为中心

张　鹏

一、问题的提出

在著作权法理论中，始终存在着“直接侵权行为”与“间接侵权行为”的划分，而这种划分就根源于著作权侵权构成的特殊构造之上，即著作权法并不是对于作品的一切利用行为赋予排他权，而仅仅针对法定的某些利用行为设置了“专属领地”，只有未经许可实施这些法定利用行为，并在缺乏法律上免责事由的情况下，才构成著作权“直接侵权”。如果脱离了直接侵权行为的违法性而追究间接行为侵权构成的话，将会突破著作权法上以法定利用行为作为侵权要件的构造，使得第三人丧失对于自身行为违法与否的可预见性，进而阻碍促进作品复制与流通的创新性活动的开展②。

伴随着数字化技术的发展，对作品的复制行为更加简便，多功能数字载体的普及也使得均还原成二进制数字代码的复制品与原件在质量上几乎不存在任何差距，复制成本更加微乎其微，加之互联网技术的勃兴，使得在前数字时代不可想象的跨越“时间”、“地点”与“载体”的作品利用行为成为现实。不可否认的是在这一过程中更多地包含了服务提供商的贡献，并体现出了难以清晰区分最终用户

① 朱立元．西方美术家论美和美感［M］．台北：昭明出版社，2001：23．

② 田村善之．著作権の间接侵害//著作権法の新论点［M］．商事法务，2008：259-306．

"直接行为"与服务商"间接行为"界限的商业模式。如果放任此种服务的存在将导致权利人通过排他权设置价格差别的手段难以奏效，因此比较法上也存在将服务提供商拟制为"直接行为主体"，使得其无法适用"私人复制例外"的做法。但是此种做法旨在阻止为最终用户提供技术便利与网络服务的商业活动，最终也将导致利用者本应享受的作品效率性地跨越"时际"、"区际"与"载体"的利用活动难以实现。

本文将以网络著作权侵权判断中的"直接行为主体"为切入点，探讨其认定上的规范模式，并在此基础上探求我国著作权侵权判断中"直接行为主体"的规范含义。

二、"直接行为主体"判断问题上"从属说"适用难题的克服

区别于诱发"直接侵权行为"大量发生的中介服务，扩张私人对于作品利用范围的服务模式主要集中在"时际"、"区际"以及"载体"转移之上，对于上述以"私人复制例外"为基础建构的商业模式，如何追及服务提供商的侵权责任成为问题的焦点。如果直接利用者的行为属于合理使用行为，服务提供者的行为既不构成共同侵权行为，也不构成独立的侵权行为，因而必须寻求其他解决之道。从既有学说角度看，具体方案不外乎三种：其一是针对各类型商业模式通过立法做出特别规定，将其视为独立的著作权侵权行为；其二是要求提供具备实质非侵权用途的数字复制载体的生产者或者提供者向著作权人或者邻接权人支付适当复制补偿金；其三是将服务提供商拟制为"直接行为主体"，进而免于著作权限制规定的适用。

其中第三种方案直接涉及"直接行为主体"的判断问题。各国司法实践也较为积极地采取了此种模式。即由于服务提供商在商业实践中深度参与了"直接行为人"的复制行为，因此在满足一定要件的前提下，通过扩张解释"直接行为主体"的范围，将物理意义上的"直接行为主体"判断，即何者在物理意义上亲自实施了作品的复制，扩张到经济价值或社会通识意义上的判断，即何者可以拟制为直接行为人。

对于"直接行为主体"进行扩大性拟制的手法是解决上述问题的较为朴素的想法，而且也在比较法上被普遍使用，区别只在于拟制的程度上。其中日本通过"卡拉OK"法理的运用全面地拟制性判断"直接侵权主体"，而德国则是在维持以物理意义判断"直接行为主体"的原则下，例外性质地拟制了"直接行为主体"。但是事实上这一模式的最大弊端就在于"拟制"的扩大倾向导致的可预见性降低，进而对于新技术下商业模式的创新带来抑制效果。

扩大性拟制"直接行为主体"的实质在于：某一行为由于行为主体的不同直接导致了侵权判断上的本质差异。既有认定"直接行为主体"的方案不管是依据物理意义标准还是实质参与性标准，都忽略了"直接行为主体"认定与著作权限制规定的实质性关联，均以"私人复制例外"作为判断的前提，在此基础上认为对于私人范围内的复制行为如果认定私人为"直接复制主体"的话，就不存在间接侵权存在的可能性，故而需要拟制"直接行为主体"为服务提供商。

三、"私人复制例外"的合法范围与"直接行为主体"判断

传统上对于"私人复制例外"的理解存在两种不同的合理化基础：一种是认为在个人、家庭以及类似闭锁范围内微量作品利用行为应予免责。也就是说本来私人复制行为也应纳入著作权人排他权范围之内，未经著作权人许可的利用行为也构成侵权行为，但是考虑到权利行使成本过高等市场失败现象，而通过立法放弃对此领域的规制。一旦私人复制对于著作权人造成的损害不再是轻微程度，抑或在私人复制的权利处理费用由于数字化许可模式的发展而骤减的情况下，理应废除"私人复制例外"。另一种是认为对于利用者已经支付过对价的作品为确保其后续私人范围内的利用自由。也就是说私人复制行为本身并不是违法行为，而是维护私人自由活动空间的体现，即使由于损害的积聚或交易成本的降低使得私人复制可以为排他权控制的情况下，也应在一定范围内维持其存在。

两种理由在处理建立在"私人复制例外"基础之上的服务提供商侵权责任判定上也存在实质性的区别。如果认为"私人复制例外"的理论基础是在于轻微损害与交易成本过高的话，间接性服务提供商的服务提供使得个别性轻微损害易于产生积聚效果，此时私人复制行为对于权利人造成的损害不再是轻微程度，而且通过对于服务提供商的"一网打尽"就可以避免对各个私人复制主体行使权利的交易成本过高问题，因此通过限缩"私人复制例外"的范围，使得权利人容易找到直接侵权主体，进而根据间接侵权判定规则①追究服务商的责任，或者

① 学说上多主张使用民法上的共同侵权责任。崔国斌. 网络服务商共同侵权制度之重塑［J］. 法学研究，2013（4）.

通过将数字网络服务商拟制为直接行为主体，就可以避免在数字时代对于“私人复制例外”的继续维持；如果认为“私人复制例外”的理论基础在于维护使用者对于已经支付过对价的私人空间作品利用自由的话，问题的关键就集中在利用者是否实际对于其所利用的作品支付过对价以及利用者是否自主地决定所利用作品的范围与内容，并且此种利用行为也在权利人预想范围之内，而对于服务提供商的行为，也因为不存在直接侵权行为，而无法进行间接侵权责任追及。

采用第一种正当化理由背后主要是认识到数字时代“私人复制例外”对于著作权人可能带来更大的损害，因此应通过维护作为价格差别工具的著作权保护体系，限缩性适用“私人复制例外”。著作权法中事实上存在着诸多以较低价格向某些支付能力较低的用户提供作品的机制，诸如思想表现二分法、著作权权利限制等，这些规定可依合同予以变更，因此仅仅是预设规则的集合，而不属于不可通过合同僭越的强制性规则。同理各种排除用户复制及接触的技术措施，也可以视作通过合同约定维持价格差别的工具，因此有必要通过法律予以保障。数字时代使得作品的交易成本显著降低，因此应创设价格差别的实现条件，即市场是独占性的，著作权人享有法定的独占权，并可以控制价格；市场的消费者间存在高低不同的信息费用；禁止不同价格意愿和能力的消费者间的套利行为，进而实现效率性。

但是自从作为价格差别的著作权理论诞生之后，对于其质疑之声不断。特别是对于价格差别性设定下著作权人获得的消费者剩余来说，其中不仅包含了对于著作权人创作的激励效用，还包含了对于作品具有较高价格支付能力的消费者通过作品演绎利用的再生产效用，以及通过二手市场与私人复制领域的例外规定，低收入消费者与对作品价格低支付能力的消费者由于得以接触到作品，从而可能转变成新的作者的效用。因此如果承认著作权人通过价格差别战略获取消费者剩余的话，损害的将是分散化主体分享作品效用下新作品创造的激励①。与上述价格差别理论相反，第二种正当化理由则认为相比于著作权人中央集权式的价格差别战略行使，保留较为广泛的权利限制与例外，从而允许消费者间私人领域自生的作品共享机制，将更具有效率性②。也就是对于利用者已经支付过对价的作品确保其后续私人范围内利用自由。著作权人仅对于作品首次使用行为中的复制、传播等法定利用行为实施排他权，并取得相应对价，而对于后续其交易时可预想的私人复制行为不再控制。

在“私人复制例外”的第二种正当化理由的构造下，认定“直接行为主体”的首要标准是就复制作品范围由何者决定且是否支付过一次对价后行使权利人预想范围的作品利用行为③。只有支付了对价并决定作品种类的利用者才可以被评价为不必再度支付对价而在私人领域内行使法定利用行为的主体。

有关作品利用的不同商业模式下，“直接行为主体”判断是否满足首要标准的判断也会有所不同。对于书籍与音乐等一次性销售的商品，只要利用者购买该类商品，对其后续的私人范围内的“时际”、“区际”以及“载体”转移行为应该认定其构成“直接行为主体”，而在复制以及电子化的标的是由服务提供商自行购买并提供给用户的话，即使物理上、技术上是由最终用户亲自操作的，也应将服务提供商认定为“直接行为主体”。较为复杂的是对于电视节目等商业模式是建立在通过广告的重复播放分次取得对价的处理，该类作品的盈利模式不是对于作品的一次性对价取得，而是通过广告的播放实现多次收益。对于服务提供商所提供的电视节目跨地域复制及传送服务，到底是将其视为用户已经支付了对价并在其指示下进行复制与传送，还是将其视为服务提供商自己复制了节目并向用户兜售，两种认识将产生质的区别，即前者用户将被评价为“直接行为主体”，后者服务提供商将被评价为“直接行为主体”。

总之，对于“直接行为主体”的认定不应脱离“私人复制例外”这一免责规定的宗旨，只有这样才能对物理意义上的“直接行为主体”与社会通识意义上的“直接行为主体”进行有意义的区分，进而拟制的“直接行为主体”不会因为缺乏预见可能性而阻碍新型商业模式的发展。

四、我国著作权法上“直接侵权主体”判断的模式选择

如果我国著作权侵权判断在构造上需要满足法

① 田村善之. 効率性・多様性・自由―インターネット時代の著作権制度のあり方［J］，北大法学論集，2002，53（4）：42-61.

② Michael J. Meurer. Copyright law and price discrimination［J］. Cardozo L. Rev，2001（23）：55.

③ 前田健. 著作権の間接侵害論と私的な利用に関する権利制限の意義についての考察［J］. 知的財産法政策学研究，2012（40）：177-212.

定利用行为要求的话，那么就应该按照“从属说”来对“间接”行为追究侵权责任①。在此基础上寻找“直接侵权主体”成为追究间接行为主体的必要步骤。如果过度限缩“私人复制例外”的范围，的确可以轻易地寻找到可资评价的直接侵权行为，进而圆满地解决“从属说”对于间接行为者的责任追及问题。这样的话，刻意进行“直接行为主体”的规范性认定也是多余的。

另外，对于侵权来源的作品能否适用“私人复制例外”的问题，有学者认为如果最终用户在主张“私人复制例外”时都必须举证证明其作品来源于合法渠道的话，那么“私人复制例外”的适用将会被大大限制②。更重要的是私人复制的作品来源于违法复制件的行为仅仅是证明对于“三步检验标准”第二步骤“与作品正常使用相冲突”的指示性条件，而不是决定性条件。其理由在于根据“正常使用”的规范性解释，仅仅证明了最终用户复制所使用的作品不是其购买的，或者不是通过合法渠道获得的，并不能证明著作权人丧失了对作品使用所享有的市场。因此单纯强调最终用户在适用私人复制例外时必须合法取得作品的做法并不是“三步检验标准”所强制要求的要件，不区分合法与非法来源作品一概适用与私人复制例外的做法并不与“三步检验标准”相冲突。而解决P2P软件上违法作品泛滥并极大损害权利人利益的更加有效的方法是对于向公众上传作品的传播者进行有效规制，同时对于为上述行为提供场所、道具以及系统的第三人，应在间接侵权独立说的模式下追究诱发私人复制广泛发生行为的侵权构成。

因此从结论上看，应强调对于服务提供商侵权判断的两步法：第一步是对于“私人复制例外”的范围，判断何者为“直接行为主体”，这一过程中主要强调利用人至少进行一次对价支付，而对于违法作品的私人复制应持否定性见解。而在此基础上第二步则是对于间接行为者的责任追及，即对于由最终用户支付过对价并自主决定复制作品的内容与种类的行为，即使服务提供商在技术上较高程度地参与了复制与传播的过程，也应该维护最终用户在私人范围内的行动自由；而对于不满足“私人复制例外”的“直接侵权行为”的诱发与帮助性间接行为则应根据“间接侵权”的规则予以判定。

五、结语

综上，本文认为应该结合“私人复制例外”的宗旨与适用范围探讨“直接行为主体”的判断问题。对作品初次支付过对价并自主决定所要复制及传播的作品内容和种类的情况，不应将深度参与技术性辅助的服务提供商拟制为“直接行为主体”。而对于我国在立法论上限缩“私人复制例外”范围的做法应予以警惕，该做法会造成对于私人用户提供技术性辅助的行为陷入违法责任追及的境地，不利于新型商业模式的开展。因此从维护私人领域行动自由的宗旨出发，对于我国法律上的个人使用例外应扩大解释，以期从解释论上一以贯之地促进私人作品共享的宗旨。

（本文原发表于《华东政法大学学报》2016年第1期。

作者单位：中国社会科学院法学研究所）

① 王迁. 网络环境中的著作权保护研究［M］. 北京：法律出版社，2011：147.

② Christophe Geiger. Legal or illegal—that is the question! private copying and downloading on the internet［J］. IIC. 2008，39（5）：597-603.

2016年著作权相关图书简介

《中华人民共和国国家知识产权局公报》(2015年英文版)，国家知识产权局办公室编，北京：知识产权出版社，2016年12月。

该书是面向国内外公开发行的政府出版物，其主要刊载内容为：全国人民代表大会及其常务委员会通过的涉及知识产权的法律；国务院发布的涉及知识产权的法规和法规性文件；国家知识产权局发布的规章、公告、重要文件、统计数据以及其他需要公告的事项。其上刊登的国家知识产权局规章、规范性文件为标准文本。

《网络知识产权法：制度体系与原理规范》，梅术文著，北京：知识产权出版社，2016年12月。

该书聚焦网络环境中的著作权、商标权、专利权、技术措施、权利管理电子信息、域名、软件、数据库、集成电路布图设计的权利保护和不正当竞争等问题，设定总论，细化分论，初步建构起网络知识产权法的总论框架，就现代信息技术发展、网络对知识产权影响、网络知识产权立法和制度体系等内容进行总体分析。同时，建立起较为全面的知识产权分论内容，针对现代信息技术所带来的知识产权问题，系统探讨网络著作权、网络专利权、网络商标权、网络环境下新型知识产权保护、网络知识产权侵权救济、网络服务提供者的侵权责任、网络反不正当竞争对知识产权的兜底保护等分论部分，而且尽量细化讨论相应的制度规范。通过网络环境中知识产权保护的原理，解读网络环境知识产权保护的规则，同时注重将理论探索与司法判例、热点实例综合起来，使得原理、规范和实例紧密结合，具有实证性和针对性。该书紧跟网络技术的发展，及时进行知识更新，反映新的立法动态和司法理念，具有前瞻性和时代感。在研究方法上注重实证案例和最新的技术发展带来的实际影响，通过实证分析和规则分析的结合，运用新案例解读复杂的社会关系。同时，在研究方法上注重国际规则和比较研究，探讨美国、欧盟、日本、韩国等最新的立法进展和司法案例。

《知识产权法学》(第三版)，曹新明著，北京：中国人民大学出版社，2016年12月。

该书共有五编，分别是第一编“知识产权总论”，第二编“著作权制度”，第三编“商标制度”，第四编“专利制度”和第五编“其他知识产权制度”，将整个知识产权体系清晰、完整、全面地呈现给读者。为了让读者能够尽快地进入知识产权学习状态，该书在每一章以“导言”开篇，提出本章的中心内容，然后进入正文，再以“案例与思考”结束。

《著作权纠纷案例与实务》，李俊平、曾芳芳著，北京：清华大学出版社，2016年11月。

该书共分5章，主要包括著作权概述、著作权侵权纠纷、邻接权纠纷、著作权合同纠纷和网络著作权纠纷。该书立足于著作权法律实践，精选39个著作权典型案例，每个案例由案情简介和案例评析两部分组成。其中案例评析部分对著作权纠纷中涉及的主要法律问题进行分析，系统全面地解读我国著作权相关法律规定。该书所选案例紧扣著作权实务，结合相关法律规范，具有针对性、示范性和指导性，既可以作为普通消费者了解和掌握著作权法相关知识的启蒙读本，也可以作为从事著作权纠纷处理的法官、政府工作人员、律师、企业法律顾问的参考用书。

《威科法律译丛：全球信息经济下的美国版权法》，[美]朱莉·E. 科恩等著，王迁等译，北京：商务印书馆，2016年11月。

该书建立了一个完整的美国版权法体系，覆盖了美国国内和国际版权法领域的几乎所有基本问题，特别强调法律、技术革新与全球化之间的关系，突出立法和公共政策的变化和争议，指出了版权法并不仅是一个私法制度，而且与公共利益息息相关。通过精心挑选的案例，探讨了包括版权法的目的和渊源、获得版权保护的要求、版权侵权的相关问题和技术变革对于版权保护和责任的影响等重要主题，能够培养读者在整个版权法体系中发现争议问题的关键、进行批判性思考的能力。

《知识产权研究(第24卷)》，周林著，北京：知识产权出版社，2016年10月。

该书为中国社会科学院知识产权中心不定期学术文集第24卷，收录国内外知识产权研究领域前沿理论、学术观点、问题探讨、案例分析和实证调研，跟踪展示知识产权领域的主要问题和研究水平。

《著作权法第三次修正下的“限制与例外”制度应用研究》，曾琳著，北京：中国政法大学出版社，2016年10月。

全书主体内容共三章：第一章是“合理使用制度研究”，对我国及国际上的合理使用制度进行分析介绍；第二章是“法定许可制度应用研究”，涉及现行法定许可存在的问题以及在网络环境下的重构；第三章是“著作权强制许可制度”，涉及其他国家以及国际上对著作权强制许可的规定以及我国著作权强制许可的重构。最后的附件部分是“著作权合理使用案件数据检索及统计”。

《中国著作权法：判例综述与规范解释》，何怀文著，北京：北京大学出版社，2016年10月。

通过对二十余年来中国各级各地法院的司法实践的系统分析来阐释我国著作权法的基本原理、法律概念和法律规范，通过大规模系统的著作权判例，尽力刻画我国著作权法司法实践的全貌，进而探讨现有著作权法理论和实践，对著作权法理论体系进行有的放矢的深入讨论。

《中国著作权案例精读》，罗东川主编，北京：商务印书馆，2016年9月。

该书所选案例，集中反映了我国在著作权领域司法保护的成果，体现了当今著作权审判注重平衡著作权人、网络服务提供者和社会公众三方面利益的价值取向。通过大量涉及新技术、新商业模式案例的选取，探讨了司法实践亟须指导的问题，极富时代感。

该书由人民法院资深大法官担任主编，编写团队的成员均为来自全国法院系统的知识产权法官。撰稿人丰富的审判实践经验和扎实的理论功底，有效地保证了该书所选案例的前沿性、典型性和对案例所涉法理解读的权威性、实践指导性。每篇案例的“评析”部分，有支持、有反对、有附议、有对抗，具有很强的可读性。

《中外网络版权经典案例评析》，许超著，北京：人民出版社，2016年9月。

互联网涉及版权问题的国内外案件数量巨大，有些是传统环境下鲜见的，有些案件已成定论，有些在学界、司法界和企业界争论不一。该书旨在系统整理中外案件，选其中有代表性、典型性的24件案件进行梳理，对有争议的案件进行分析和评论，最终形成既有理论高度又具实践意义的文献。该书按照网络发展的阶段编写：第一阶段，以WCT和WPPT为代表，确认网络环境下版权也受保护，以及技术保护措施和权利管理信息受保护；第二阶段，以DMCA、欧盟两个指令和我国《信息网络传播权保护条例》为代表的避风港制度；第三阶段，P2P技术对网络版权保护提出的挑战；第四阶段，后P2P技术引发的案例；第五阶段，澄清一些基本概念。重点在后三个阶段，特别是近五年发生的案件。该书编写以案为引，辅以评述，以判决为核心部分；评述既具有理论高度，又具有实际意义，涉及历史背景、与主案相关的旁案（案中案）介绍、法官思路、结论产生过程、解决的特殊问题、判决的合法合理性、法条与法律渊源的关系，以及不同看法等。

《民间文学艺术权利主体问题研究》，张洋著，北京：中国政法大学出版社，2016年9月。

民间文学艺术的保护日益为人们所关注，但是对于民间文学艺术的权利主体以及相关主体问题于立法层面尚欠缺明确的规定，于理论层面尚未形成通说的观点。想要对民间文学艺术进行周到的保护，首先需要解决的是权利主体问题，否则，主体尚且不知为何人，遑论对民间文学艺术的保护。该书从理论上探讨了民间文学艺术的权利主体等问题。

《最高人民法院知识产权司法解释理解与适用》（最新增订版），最高人民法院知识产权审判庭编，北京：中国法制出版社，2016年7月。

为准确适用知识产权和竞争实体法和有关程序法，正确审理知识产权和竞争纠纷案件，最高人民法院在不断总结各级人民法院审判经验的基础上，及时制定司法解释和有关指导性文件，由此建立和完善了一系列重要的知识产权和竞争审判制度及裁判案件的法律适用原则，对于指导各级人民法院正确审理知识产权和竞争纠纷案件，发挥了十分重要的作用。

该书收录了2001年至2016年公布的知识产权和竞争纠纷方面的相关司法解释和指导性文件，以及最高人民法院知识产权审判庭负责人或者相关文件起草人在文件发布后的权威解读，对于研究和解决相关问题具有重要参考作用。

《最高人民法院知识产权审判案例指导（第8辑）》，最高人民法院知识产权审判庭编，北京：中国法制出版社，2016年7月。

该书收录了最高人民法院每年发布的知识产权年度报告全文和该报告所涉及的所有裁判文书。该报告已经成为最高人民法院指导知识产权审判工作的重要载体和社会公众了解最高人民法院知识产权审判发展动态的重要渠道。

该书第一部分公布了最高人民法院知识产权案件年度报告（2015）及其所涉及的33个典型案例裁判文书全文，共归纳出38个具有普遍指导意义的法律适用问题，总结和梳理了最高人民法院在知识产权和竞争审判领域处理新型、疑难、复杂案件的审判标准、裁判方法和司法导向。第二部分全面收录年度报告所涉及的所有裁判文书全文，全面准确展现案件裁判全貌。

《迈向知识产权强国之路——知识产权强国建设基本问题研究》，申长雨主编，北京：知识产权出版社，2016年6月。

该书由国家知识产权局保护协调司、国家知识产权局知识产权发展研究中心组织编写，国家知识产权局局长申长雨主编，集中探讨了知识产权强国的概念与特征、知识产权强国建设的国际国内形势、知识产权强国建设的战略任务、知识产权强国建设的关键举措等问题，旨在为知识产权强国建设提供理论指导和智力支撑。本书分为理论篇、形势篇、任务篇和政策篇，便于各位读者更好地了解知识产权强国建设的基本理论和任务思路。

《中国知识产权发展报告2015》，中国人民大学知识产权教学与研究中心编，北京：清华大学出版社，2016年6月。

该书由中国人民大学知识产权教学与研究中心根据2015年及2015年以前中国知识产权发展的现状、存在的主要问题以及未来发展的目标而编写，报告包括总论、著作权法、专利法、商标法、反不正当竞争法、商业秘密等11章内容。报告以中英文两种文字出版，是详述中国知识产权发展的作品。

《中国知识产权指导案例评注（第7辑）》，最高人民法院知识产权审判庭编，北京：中国法制出版社，2016年6月。

该书以案例评析方式进行编写，每个案例一般包括阅读提示和裁判要旨、案情和裁判、法官评述三个部分。阅读提示同时体现在目录和正文中，有助于读者根据目录迅速判断出案例所涉法律或者其他裁判问题；裁判要旨在于展现法官在裁判具体案件过程中对法律适用、裁判方法、司法理念等案件焦点问题的精要评述。案情和裁判反映了当事人的诉辩主张、争议焦点，法院审理查明的事实、裁判理由和裁判结果等内容。法官评述包括对本案争议焦点和不同意见、裁判思路和方法的深入分析，以及对本案纠纷发生的社会背景、裁判结果的社会影响和效果的介绍等内容。

《著作权技术保护措施信息安全遵从制度研究》，赵丽莉著，武汉：武汉大学出版社，2016年6月。

该书介绍了在互联网时代著作权技术保护措施的必要性，同时指明这些保护措施有可能对用户信息造成的危害，提出了以“协同治理”作为其法律规范调整的基本原则之一，并提出了具体法律治理机制。

《现场直播节目版权问题研究》，严波著，北京：法律出版社，2016年6月。

该书对现场直播节目的版权问题进行了国内学术界较为全面和深入的分析和研究。内容上，系统而有针对性地提出了立法完善方案与建议，为现场直播节目等视听作品法律性质的界定奠定了创新的理论基础；形式上，创造性地将法律分析方法与媒体创作艺术理论结合起来，为著作权作品性质的判定从研究方法的创新上做出贡献。

《版权法的经济分析》，王素玉著，北京：经济科学出版社，2016年6月。

在全球经济中，版权构成了诸多行业的基础，并影响着很多其他的经济活动。版权作为一个有力的经济增长源泉，创造了就业机会并激励了行业发展。研究现有版权制度的经济学原理，以制定高效率的版权制度就具有特别的现实意义。该书较系统地论述了版权法律制度的经济学理论基础并对此做出评述，剖析经济理论对于政策制定的指导意义，并分析了版权的范围，公平使用制度和集体管理制度的经济学原理。该书还运用规范分析、成本收益分析、博弈论、激励分析的方法，较全面和具体地考察研究了版权法的产权激励理论、平衡理论和价格歧视理论，指出版权作为产权仅仅是纠正失市场失灵的一种可能的干预形式，是针对生产不足问题的一种重要的手段。

《文化创意知识产权典型案例评析》，宿迟、梅松编，北京：法律出版社，2016年6月。

该书收集知识产权各类案件审判实践中具有典型性的疑难、新型案例，总结提炼出解决这些问题涉及的法理上和适用法律相关的事实上的关键词，阐明法学理论、争议观点、法律适用，旨在解决审判实践中疑难、新型问题的法律适用问题，从而为初级法官、律师办理案件提供有效指引。

《网络环境中著作权保护体系的重构》，孟兆平著，北京：北京大学出版社，2016年5月。

从社会发展以及公众需求角度来看，互联网技术的不断进步大大加速了信息传播。如何平衡版权人、传播者、社会公共等主体之间的诉求，如何协调版权保护与技术发展之间的关系，如何构建合理的版权确权与授权机制、利益分配机制成为迫在眉睫又不可回避的问题。面对互联网环境下的版权难题，该书通过研究互联网技术进步与版权保护之间的张力，厘清互联网与版权制度之间的"复杂关系"，并着眼于新技术、新商业模式不断涌现的状况，构建合理有效的版权确权、授权模式与利益分配机制，进而实现权利人保护、互联网创新发展、社会繁荣进步的有机统一。该书对于网络著作权的发展和相关法规的制定具有一定的意义。

《版权和相关权国际法律文件集》，裘安曼著，北京：中国书籍出版社，2016年5月。

版权和相关权国际法律文件，即是各种版权国际公约、版权国际条约、版权国际协定等。从1886年签署的《保护文学和艺术作品伯尔尼公约》，到2013年签署的《关于为盲人、视力障碍者或其他印刷品阅读障碍者获得已出版作品提供便利的马拉喀什条约》，在120多年中，我国一共签署了14部国际条约。这14部国际版权公约、条约协定的法律文件的中英文，都包括在该书之中，非常全面。

《知识产权刑事司法：中国特色实证研究》，贺志军著，北京大学出版社，2016年5月。

该书从年度司法数据实证、司法案例实证、司法解释规范文本实证三个方面展开具体运用：一是司法统计数据实证分析，对该机制十余年运行实效的各年度统计数据进行定量分析和比较解读；二是司法案例实证分析，对北大法意等网站收录的1 617份知识产权刑事判决建立案件数据库，采用SPSS软件进行定量分析和比较解读；三是司法解释实证分析，对有关知识产权刑事司法的31个文件、130个规范建立文本数据库，进行法律文本实证分析，从事实层面归纳揭示其若干特点。该书内容包含大量数据、图表（近60幅），可为相关研究人员及从业人员提供翔实的参考资料。

《知识产权保护与信息自由的冲突与协调》，蔡祖国著，北京：知识产权出版社，2016年5月。

该书认为，无论是从价值层面、规范层面还是从历史层面来看，知识产权保护与信息自由之间难以避免地存在矛盾和冲突。随着技术的发展以及资本的深度介入，知识产权保护与信息自由之间的冲突愈显突出，传统上通过知识产权内部规范予以平衡的制度安排已不能有效地协调二者间的冲突关系，有必要在内部规范平衡的基础上，将知识产权保护纳入宪法审查的范畴，建立起内部协调与外部协调相统一的平衡机制。

《网络服务提供者著作权侵权责任研究》，王晋著，北京：知识产权出版社，2016年5月。

该书从网络空间中的网络传播特性入手，以引入激励理论的利益平衡原则为主线，借鉴美国等国外的立法规定及司法判例，重点研究我国网络服务提供者著作权侵权的归责原则和责任形态，提出在网络服务提供者不作为和网络用户直接侵权的情况下承担补充责任的观点。为探讨我国各类别的网络服务提供者著作权侵权典型案例，选取北京市海淀区人民法院2012年1月到2014年6月两年半间的，以视频网站为被告的网络服务提供者著作权侵权的352件案例进行实证统计分析，结合视频网站的市场，以生动鲜活的案例完善了该书观点，发现我国网络服务提供者承担宽泛和严的责任，但却没有英美国家避风港原则的庇护。

在网络著作权侵权的热点研究领域里，有关网络服务提供者著作权侵权的著作几乎凤毛麟角，因此该书无论从理论研究意义还是市场前景均具有重要价值。

《论著作权的正当性》，陈杰著，北京：知识产权出版社，2016年5月。

知识产权法哲学的核心问题是知识产权的正当性。不同类型的知识产权是否具有相同的正当性事由是需要证明的，其在未证明之前只能被默认为不同。现有的著作权的正当性理论主要有劳动理论、人格理论和功利主义三类。各种著作权的正当性理论都可以成功解释一部分知识产权的问题，但又各有缺陷。不同的著作权正当性的理论存在着相互竞争的关系，通过证伪的方式可以进行优胜劣汰。该书提出了两种证伪的方法，一为作品的属性；一为著作权的"古今之问"。

《中国著作权观念的历史解读》，杨华权著，北京：北京大学出版社，2016 年 5 月。

该书从社会结构出发，把中国社会经济结构、政治结构和文化结构作为一个完整对象进行分析，结合中国著作权制度发展过程，考察中国著作权观念产生和发展历程，分析中国著作权观念依赖的政治、经济和文化基础，系统研究政府、传播者、作者和使用者的著作权观念，提炼出著作权制度功效的发挥需要社会整体尤其是政府著作权观念的提升，并决定于社会结构变革的结论。对于了解我国著作权的历史发展具有一定的意义。

《网络环境下中国著作权刑事保护研究》，杨彩霞著，北京：中国社会科学出版社，2016 年 5 月。

该书旨在通过研究我国当前网络环境下著作权违法犯罪行为，寻求既不妨害互联网发展又不损害著作权人及相关权利人利益的对策。全书直面网络环境下著作权扩张带来的著作权刑事保护的挑战，论证了网络环境下著作权刑事保护正当性的根基；在域外比较考察的基础上，重点对 P2P 软件和服务提供商的著作权刑事责任、搜索引擎引发的网络著作权刑事保护问题、规避著作权技术措施行为的刑法规制以及私人复制分享行为的刑法考量等疑难争议问题进行了深入探讨；最后在刑事一体化思想的指导下，结合实证调研所反映的公众网络著作权意识水平和网络环境下侵犯著作权行为的社会危害性的评估结果，从实体和程序两方面对我国网络著作权犯罪提出了具体的规制对策和建议。

《网络知识产权保护热点疑难问题解析》，宿迟、陈锦川、杨柏勇著，北京：中国法制出版社，2016 年 5 月。

互联网的发展使各种资源的共享更加便捷，传播更加迅速，与此同时，知识产权的保护也不断面临着新的挑战，新问题层出不穷。该书由北京市高级人民法院、北京市知识产权法研究会组织编写，内容紧密结合网络知识产权的前沿实践问题，所收录的文章，为法院、代表企业和学者三方面的知识产权专家对互联网环境下的知识产权法律问题所进行的研究成果，大多是一线法官和法务人员的经验心得，对于广大知识产权法官和企业法务具有较好的参考作用。该书通过列举典型案例，将热点疑难问题归纳梳理，提出焦点问题，引起读者思考和探究，具有非常积极的意义。

《著作权法故事汇》，刘勇著，北京：中国政法大学出版社，2016 年 5 月。

该书立足普法，运用大众化的语言将公民常用的《著作权法》法律知识编成 84 篇小故事，对我国著作权法律制度进行简要讲解，将创新性、实践性、知识性、教育性、娱乐性融为一体，寓法于案、寓理于事，是广大人民群众了解著作权法、增长著作权法律知识、提高版权意识、增强维权能力的好帮手。

《中国法院 2016 年度案例：知识产权纠纷》，国家法官学院案例开发研究中心著，北京：中国法制出版社，2016 年 4 月。

该书汇集全国各地法院审结的典型案例，分卷分类编排；高度提炼案情和裁判要旨，突出争议焦点，剔除无效信息。主审法官撰写"法官后语"，展现法律适用方法和裁判思路。该书内容易于运用，无论是对法官、检察官、执法人员，还是对律师、法律顾问、案件当事人，该书都力求为读者节约查找和阅读案例的时间，使读者获得真正有用的信息。

《中国知识产权蓝皮书（2014—2015）》，吴汉东著，北京：知识产权出版社，2016 年 4 月。

该书秉承"民间视野、学者观点"的编写方针，依托理论，注重实证，力求精深，兼顾广博，旨在汇集中国知识产权界的智力资源，展示中国知识产权事业的发展成果。全书分为特稿、研究报告、专题研究报告、热点关注和大事纪要五部分，以翔实的材料、深入的分析、独特的视角和准确的概括，记录 2014—2015 年内我国知识产权事业发展的脉络和轨迹，为建设知识产权强国提供智力支撑和决策参考。

《知识产权论丛（第2卷）》，苏平编，北京：法律出版社，2016年4月。

该书在传统“基础理论专题”“专利专题”、“著作权专题”“商标专题”等栏目的基础上，新增了“知识产权政策研究专题”、“人才培养专题”以及“实务讲坛”三大栏目。“知识产权政策研究专题”从宏观政策视角切入知识产权研究，“人才培养专题”探讨知识产权人才培育这一实践意义重大的论题，而“实务讲坛”则收录了实务界专家的相关前沿讲座。该期论丛在坚持必要的理论厚重与学术底蕴的基础上，同时着重关注实践并为知识产权实践提供必要的智识支撑。

《中国知识产权法律制度》，管荣齐著，北京：知识产权出版社，2016年4月。

该书内容共分五编：第一编为总论，阐释中国知识产权法律制度的客体、历史和环境；第二编为著作权法律制度，阐释著作权的创造、运用、保护、管理；第三编为专利法律制度，阐释专利权的创造、运用、保护；第四编为商标法律制度，阐释商标权的创造、运用、保护；第五编为其他知识产权法律制度，阐释制止不正当竞争权、植物新品种权、集成电路布图设计专有权的创造、运用、保护。其中，“环境”主要论述国家知识产权战略、知识产权强国建设两项大政方针，“创造”从相应知识产权的主体、客体、取得三个方面展开论述，“运用”从相应知识产权的内容与限制以及转让、许可和出质两个方面展开论述，“保护”从相应知识产权的民事保护、行政保护、刑事保护三个方面展开论述。

《2016中华人民共和国知识产权法律法规全书》，法律出版社法规中心编，北京：法律出版社，2016年4月。

该书以知识产权相关法律法规及司法解释、司法文件、行政规章、规范性文件等为主要内容，涵盖了著作权、商标权、专利权三大传统知识产权以及植物新品种权、集成电路布图设计等新兴知识产权，以及中国加入的国际公约等，并收录了最高人民法院发布的知识产权方面的典型案例，以及现行有效的全部知识产权法律、行政法规、司法解释，重要的部门规章、相关政策规定，全面覆盖知识产权法律的方方面面。法规编排注重其相互间的关联性、逻辑性，体系清晰、方便查询。该书各部分特设“导读”栏目，对核心主体法进行解读；该书对重点法律附加“条旨”，可指引读者迅速找到自己需要的条文；书中还收录人民法院公布的知识产权相关指导案例和典型案例，对法官判案具有深刻的指导作用。

《解读最高人民法院司法解释·指导性案例·知识产权卷》，陶凯元主编，北京：人民法院出版社，2016年4月。

该书为人民法院出版社于2003年起推出的“解读最高人民法院司法释丛书”的第五版，收录截至2016年4月最高人民法院公布的司法解释374件，指导性案例56件。该书收录了审判工作中常用的司法解释、指导性案例及司法文件，并由起草司法解释的最高人民法院法官撰写解读，对民事司法解释和指导性案例中的难点、疑点问题以及实务中应注意的问题等进行了精准阐释，具有高度的权威性和专业性。该书集最高人民法院现行有效的司法解释、指导性案例与重要司法文件之大成，系最高人民法院公布的法释系列司法解释理解与适用的全面分类汇编。

《知识产权审判思路与办案技巧》，袁博著，北京：法律出版社，2016年4月。

该书共分四个部分，即商标法编、专利法编、版权法编和反不正当竞争法·综合编。每编所选择的文章大多为热门问题或经典案例，通过对这些热门问题或案例的解读、阐释、拓展，充分展示了知识产权法的内涵和魅力。

《北大知识产权评论（2014/2015年卷）》，刘银良主编，北京：北京大学出版社，2016年3月。

当今世界经济飞速发展，知识产权相关问题正日益凸显，对其进行研究的价值也日益提高。为了跟进理论前沿，北大知识产权学院收集了近年来学术界、实务界对于知识产权法学理论、法律制度和有关案例的研究成果，组织编撰了该书，以供广大知识产权界业内人士、各级领导干部、企事业单位管理人员、科研人员、高等院校师生以及其他感兴趣的人士阅读和探讨。该书对读者了解知识产权学科的发展具有很大帮助。

《公开传播权研究》，陈绍玲著，北京：法律出版社，2016年3月。

该书认为，公开传播权区别于复制、演绎权和发行、出租权，是著作权人享有的以不转移作品有形载体所有权或占有的方式向公众传播作品，使公众得以欣赏或者使用作品内容的权利。在此基础上，该书分析了公开传播权的产生规律、发展规律和构成要件的演进规律。最后该书认为，现行《著作权法》中应引入公开传播权的定义，将“在公众传播权”统一为公开表演权，以解决该类权利过于分散的问题，同时还应扩大“向公众传播权”的控制范围，使其与国际条约保持一致。

《知识产权法》，丁丽瑛著，北京：厦门大学出版社，2016 年 3 月。

近年来，我国知识产权纠纷及案件数量上升，各种典型案例涌现，知识产权法律关系更加复杂多样，知识产权行政保护和司法保护的水平也不断提高，相关指导性判例及司法解释逐步发布，北京、上海、广州三个知识产权法院设立并运行良好。这些都对知识产权法学研究及教材的修订提出了新的要求，并提供了新的内容。为确保教材的出版质量和教学的使用要求，作者对该书进行了第四版修订。该书系统阐述了我国知识产权保护的相关法律法规的基本原理和有关规定，共分 6 编 27 章，先阐述了知识产权和知识产权法的基本概念、基本理论等，然后分编阐述了著作权法、专利法、商标法、反不正当竞争法、集成电路布图设计保护制度、植物新品种保护制度、知识产权的国际保护等基本理论和规定。

《版权法》(全 2 册)，郑成思著，北京：社会科学文献出版社，2016 年 3 月。

《版权法》是我国最早的，也是至今最完善的一部版权法专著。该书全面系统地介绍了西方版权法的基本原理、基本功能和版权保护制度，并以此为关照，深入探讨了我国版权法的立法工作。《版权法》的创作始于上世纪 70 年代末，历时十多年之久，该书旁征博引，洞见迭出，与枯燥的理论著作截然不同，该书在详细论述了各国先进版权制度的同时，叙述评析了大量具体生动的判例，还不时出现妙趣横生的比喻、翔实丰富的史料。《版权法》一经问世，就受到法学界的广泛赞誉，成为众多版权学者和实践者的必备书，其诸多研究成果有相当一部分至今仍在启发着版权界的进一步研究与争论，而另一些已经转化为立法和司法实践，成为知识产权发展史的见证。

《知识产权损害赔偿评估》，王景、高燕梅著，北京：知识产权出版社，2016 年 1 月。

知识产权在现实经济中具有重要地位与作用，各种利益主体对知识产权各种形式进行了激烈争夺，有关知识产权的纠纷有日益增加之势。知识产权纠纷领域也明显拓宽，不仅涉及诉前临时措施、网络著作权和网络域名、驰名商标认定、植物新品种等案件，而且涉及集成电路布图设计、民间文学艺术、地理标志、确认不侵权、特许经营合同、反垄断等纠纷。知识产权纠纷案件的持续大幅增长，随之而来最棘手的就是知识产权侵权所造成的损害赔偿评估问题。知识产权受到不法侵害如何进行赔偿是当前知识产权侵权损害案件审判的难点问题，也是知识产权侵权行为经济与法理研究急需进行的重点课题。该书针对目前知识产权损害赔偿领域缺乏系统的理论指导、缺乏科学规范的操作规则，以及缺乏行业监管的现状，系统开展知识产权损害评估有关理论与法律问题、评估方法与操作规范、评估实务具体问题解决途径，以及配套监管制度等方面的研究工作，形成具有可操作性和实用性的研究成果，为知识产权损害赔偿评估行业提供系统的理论与实务指导，为规范知识产权损害赔偿评估行为、制定相关政策法规和进行宏观管理提供咨询意见。

《欧盟版权法之未来》，［英］埃斯特尔·德克雷著，徐红菊译，北京：知识产权出版社，2016 年 1 月。

该书收录了英国知识产权领域知名专家的 24 篇研究论文，详细介绍了欧盟版权法一体化进程的若干成果和待解决的问题，为我国著作权法的发展以及与国际版权法的同步化提供了积极的借鉴。该书适用于那些致力于版权一体化的各成员国及欧共体立法机构与行政机构的开拓者，以及那些引发、创造并继续为一体化而努力的法官们。

《知识产权法学》(第二版)，杨巧著，北京：中国政法大学出版社，2016 年 1 月。

该书在第一版的基础上对我国现行《专利法》《著作权法》《商标法》的内容做了新的解读，尤其是对 2013 年《商标法》修订的部分做了修改；对知识产权法基本原理的内容也增添了新的理解；在“知识产权国际保护”部分融入了新的国际条约；还对各编其他内容进行了补充修正。该书既包含对基本知识、基本原理的阐述，也包含“延伸阅读”和“参考阅读”，还选取了“典型案例”来帮助读者巩固理论知识。

《中华人民共和国知识产权法典·注释法典·7》（第三版），国务院法制办公室编，北京：中国法制出版社，2016年1月。

该书涵盖知识产权领域重要的法律、行政法规、部门规章、规范性文件、司法解释以及法律法规规章的适用解释及函复。全面反映近年来国家大规模法律文件清理工作的成果。收录经提炼的法律流程图、诉讼文书、纠纷处理常用数据等内容，帮助读者大大提高处理法律事务的效率。对重难点法条进行条文注释，帮助读者理解和把握法律规定的精髓。收录最高人民法院公报案例及其他权威出版物、各高级人民法院判决公布的典型案例，全面展示解决法律问题的实例。文件效力层级清晰；正文提供相关且有效的条文援引；特设“典型案例索引”，迅速定位案例资源，最大限度地提高该书的即查即用性。

版

统计资料

TONG JI ZI LIAO

权

2016年中国版权统计资料

2016年全国作品登记情况统计

单位：件

	1月	2月	3月	4月	5月	6月	7月	8月	9月	10月	11月	12月	总计
合　计	**87 677**	**60 739**	**114 567**	**115 327**	**149 074**	**133 618**	**149 289**	**140 544**	**144 260**	**126 495**	**144 630**	**233 377**	**1 599 597**
北　京	34 755	16 110	59 733	45 853	73 428	59 431	64 041	56 371	55 555	52 050	61 180	114 914	693 421
天　津	12	13	12	14	4	32	86	0	72	7	35	169	456
河　北	22	10	23	47	26	20	46	5	14	44	10	111	378
山　西	8	6	20	31	5	4	11	16	9	219	3	24	356
内蒙古	45	8	14	7	5	11	20	4	15	5	82	0	216
辽　宁	676	147	181	395	41	40	61	294	152	92	5 438	727	8 244
吉　林	59	105	57	38	168	38	214	103	90	351	119	88	1 430
黑龙江	23	33	29	37	64	23	60	161	66	31	38	92	657
上　海	15 720	15 160	19 390	18 120	19 120	19 140	19 160	19 160	19 095	15 099	19 037	19 048	217 249
江　苏	10 370	6 744	9 217	10 555	13 698	18 542	20 546	22 974	20 737	15 204	14 955	17 767	181 309
浙　江	1 409	1 242	1 104	1 310	1 208	1 082	1 477	2 046	1 217	1 402	1 904	2 383	17 784
安　徽	18	8	68	30	39	36	217	66	73	62	168	3 657	4 442
福　建	3 474	2 022	2 001	3 692	3 506	5 363	4 609	3 730	3 934	4 256	5 204	5 540	47 331
江　西	89	141	973	611	238	513	265	630	644	740	612	663	6 125
山　东	908	238	1 219	10 310	10 922	1 066	11 756	1 749	11 919	4 005	2 379	14 507	70 978
河　南	82	12	59	75	76	25	79	57	29	50	152	153	848
湖　北	1 217	785	805	1 175	988	3 192	931	1 234	575	1 756	2 536	1 067	16 261
湖　南	56	29	28	177	444	694	350	231	427	898	757	263	4 354
广　东	1 140	1 528	1 716	1 255	2 473	2 417	3 339	3 522	4 138	3 924	4 116	5 925	35 493
广　西	14	7	11	3	15	20	16	14	11	4	27	47	189
海　南	7	13	7	19	8	5	10	7	15	16	21	10	138
重　庆	4 075	3 918	4 154	4 504	3 925	1 709	5 577	4 190	5 919	6 975	9 590	17 300	71 836
四　川	498	3 764	4 347	6 702	7 948	10 019	8 221	6 229	6 090	3 737	4 234	13 589	75 378
贵　州	24	0	12	13	11	29	18	55	28	24	20	37	271
云　南	19	3	8	11	34	17	32	13	13	2	4	7	163
西　藏	0	0	0	0	0	0	0	0	0	0	0	0	0
陕　西	25	31	134	49	83	144	108	544	1 114	251	185	254	2 922
甘　肃	9	0	20	0	0	35	25	0	52	5	37	32	215
青　海	2	0	1	1	47	0	0	0	0	17	0	2	70
宁　夏	4	42	11	5	19	23	12	60	3	17	12	11	219
新　疆	206	87	108	164	38	33	27	80	29	51	36	77	936
中国版权保护中心	12 711	8 533	9 105	10 124	10 493	9 915	7 975	16 999	12 225	15 201	11 739	14 908	139 928

注：中国版权保护中心共登记出证87 988件/系列，涉及作品139 928件。

2016 年全国版权合同情况统计

单位：份

	合计	图书	期刊	音像制品	电子出版物	软件	电影	电视节目	其他
合　计	**19 744**	**16 755**	**99**	**1 790**	**238**	**686**	**1**	**2**	**173**
中国版权保护中心	**1 674**			1 604		70			
北　京	**10 281**	9 994	96		188	3			
天　津	**462**	420			13	29			
河　北	**88**	85				3			
山　西	**45**	45							
内蒙古									
辽　宁	**262**	262							
吉　林	**141**	141							
黑龙江	**119**	119							
上　海	**1 025**	861		129	35				
江　苏	**375**					375			
浙　江	**663**	480	2	57		124			
安　徽	**101**	98				3			
福　建	**77**	76				1			
江　西	**414**	414							
山　东	**313**	313							
河　南	**437**	437							
湖　北	**567**	480				77			10
湖　南	**220**	218	1				1		
广　东	**423**	255			2	1		2	163
广　西	**510**	510							
海　南	**204**	204							
重　庆	**301**	301							
四　川	**495**	495							
贵　州	**18**	18							
云　南	**150**	150							
西　藏									
陕　西	**292**	292							
甘　肃	**5**	5							
青　海									
宁　夏	**30**	30							
新　疆	**52**	52							

2016 年全国版权执法情况统计

案件查处情况				收缴盗版品情况			
项目	上年度数量	本年度数量	同比增减(%)	项目	上年度数量	本年度数量	同比增减(%)
行政处罚数量（件）	3 477	3 065	－11.85	书刊	5 396 752	10 042 515	86.08
案件移送数量（件）	160	189	18.13	软件	368 499	378 021	2.58
检查经营单位数量（个）	846 140	878 013	3.77	音像制品	3 734 808	1 953 899	－47.68
取缔违法经营单位数量（个）	9 340	6 243	－33.16	电子出版物	177 506	162 048	－8.71
查获地下窝点数量（个）	392	325	－17.09	其他	1 743 364	383 264	－78.02
其中：地下光盘生产线（条）	0	1		未分类项			
违法经营网站服务器（个）	475	709	49.26	合计	11 420 929	12 919 747	13.12
罚款金额（人民币元）	9 746 538	13 406 043	37.55				

2016 年版权输出地汇总表

计量单位：册、盒、张、件、部、集

版权输出项目 版权输出的国家或地区	合计	图书	录音制品	录像制品	电子出版物	软件	电影	电视节目	其他
总计（项）	**11 133**	**8 328**	**201**	**18**	**1 264**		**16**	**1 249**	**57**
美国	1 483	932			446		2	103	
英国	353	290			5			54	4
德国	346	262			30			54	
法国	164	110						54	
俄罗斯	360	356	4						
加拿大	143	87						56	
新加坡	403	184			118		2	96	3
日本	356	353					2	1	
韩国	719	576	46		93		2	2	
香港地区	710	486	99		5		2	110	8
澳门地区	179	56		12			2	108	1
台湾地区	2 110	1 848	19		148		2	61	32
其他	3 807	2 788	33	6	419		2	550	9

2016 年版权引进地汇总表

计量单位：册、盒、张、件、部、集

版权引进项目 / 原版权所在国家或地区	合计	图书	录音制品	录像制品	电子出版物	软件	电影	电视节目	其他
总计（项）	**17 252**	**16 587**	**119**	**251**	**217**	**8**	**4**	**66**	
美国	5 461	5 201	41	174	17	2	1	25	
英国	2 966	2 873	10	15	38	1	1	28	
德国	895	888	2	1	3	1			
法国	1 100	1 069	7	12	11			1	
俄罗斯	104	101		3					
加拿大	152	142	1	6	3				
新加坡	262	260		1				1	
日本	1 952	1 911	8	6	25			2	
韩国	1 067	1 024		12	27	3		1	
香港地区	248	208	26	1	12	1			
澳门地区	1	1							
台湾地区	979	949	15		15				
其他	2 065	1 960	9	20	66		2	8	

2016年中国新闻出版产业统计资料

2016 年全国各地区图书出版总量

	图书总计											
	种数（种）			总印数（万册、张）			总印张（千印张）			定价总金额（万元）		
	合计	初版	租型	合计	初版	租型	合计	初版	租型	合计	初版	租型
全国总计	**499 884**	**262 415**	**11 629**	**903 682**	**240 835**	**150 995**	**77 721 102**	**24 163 518**	**11 065 358**	**15 809 598**	**6 814 149**	**1 165 038**
中　央	**199 701**	**106 901**	**17**	**241 215**	**83 828**	**198**	**26 290 309**	**10 112 055**	**14 765**	**5 965 734**	**2 995 337**	**1 475**
地　方	**300 183**	**155 514**	**11 612**	**662 467**	**157 007**	**150 797**	**51 430 793**	**14 051 463**	**1 105 0593**	**9 843 864**	**3 818 812**	**1 163 563**
北　京	13 712	7 310		28 144	8 122		2 389 696	884 281		564 823	244 244	
天　津	6 789	4 507	204	6 425	2 397	1 077	561 438	239 837	79 475	165 854	92 618	8 382
河　北	9 263	3 254	418	26 865	4 709	6 988	2 040 127	389 031	536 306	350 303	97 278	54 281
山　西	3 513	2 264	263	9 860	3 198	3 571	980 272	465 006	274 185	168 369	86 793	29 378
内蒙古	3 249	1 791	384	6 172	943	3 347	503 711	108 257	278 045	75 862	32 415	28 742
辽　宁	10 385	4 993	308	14 758	3 944	2 816	1 176 157	339 229	216 463	229 012	88 046	21 550
吉　林	26 919	16 516	557	23 922	8 944	3 664	1 927 029	778 890	266 275	424 882	214 075	30 475
黑龙江	7 336	5 541	533	7 694	2 119	3 226	666 381	208 594	240 209	118 962	50 619	26 811
上　海	27 481	13 907	4	41 806	16 656	54	3 612 034	1 312 898	3 391	916 221	479 251	832
江　苏	27 569	13 647	472	62 656	14 880	9 492	4 513 855	1 275 563	650 544	856 653	350 028	69 648
浙　江	14 165	6 853	485	39 900	9 676	8 048	2 911 230	778 742	587 076	576 972	222 647	62 665
安　徽	9 441	5 212	703	24 892	7 442	6 300	1 827 684	526 764	481 036	354 293	144 881	54 093
福　建	3 954	2 620	200	9 710	2 310	3 309	793 481	240 883	246 575	143 426	63 506	2 3827
江　西	7 491	4 345	224	21 423	4 890	6 028	1 439 798	377 884	488 612	271 533	101 981	45 713
山　东	15 925	5 618	887	53 037	6 518	13 186	3 500 830	501 195	738 029	593 363	145 342	92 485
河　南	8 588	4 598	278	24 608	3 943	9 647	1 930 044	303 953	766 329	278 925	80 848	72 715
湖　北	15 105	7 911	449	27 044	8 669	6 247	2 236 384	834 961	448 153	480 284	235 516	51 923
湖　南	12 618	5 137	446	51 704	13 917	10 205	3 932 076	1 213 374	665 629	739 615	257 020	76 003
广　东	10 841	6 367	147	31 196	4 684	7 010	2 419 153	488 720	553 430	383 020	136 559	50 319
广　西	7 406	3 067	549	29 197	4 082	7 768	2 075 167	328 362	601 279	346 993	91 539	59 774
海　南	3 797	1 483	204	5 717	1 233	999	424 989	115 278	69 825	82 891	29 755	8 305
重　庆	5 685	2 195	249	12 751	2 202	2 702	887 150	190 155	182 414	162 977	47 827	23 471
四　川	10 878	6 332	470	24 296	4 699	6 932	1 967 670	463 183	516 881	327 175	119 804	55 867
贵　州	1 013	742	612	8 823	589	7 320	660 392	55 681	549 237	83 357	14 715	55 731
云　南	8 563	4 436	314	15 244	3 457	5 477	1 335 854	384 523	449 002	222 941	86 451	42 638
西　藏	588	260	324	1 497	85	856	108 359	13 110	61 069	15 576	3 419	7 325
陕　西	10 284	5 271	559	19 304	3 953	4 693	1 688 853	425 824	376 345	341 364	114 853	35 842
甘　肃	3 484	2 149	250	7 541	2 079	2 994	611 132	184 402	23 1694	96 423	35 973	21 654
青　海	613	306	223	1 030	90	699	87 068	10 552	54 075	11 266	4 233	5 196
宁　夏	3 098	1 645	192	4 552	1 139	800	462 796	122 354	60 127	95 490	31 668	7 098
新　疆	9 975	4 846	704	20 316	5 181	5 342	1 717 187	461 584	378 883	351 496	105 421	40 820
新疆生产建设兵团	455	391		383	257		42 796	28 393		13 543	9 417	

2016 年全国各级报纸出版数量

	合计					中央及省、自治区、直辖市级					地、市级					县级				
	种数（种）	平均期印数（万份）	总印数（万份）	总印张（千印张）	总金额（万元）	种数（种）	平均期印数（万份）	总印数（万份）	总印张（千印张）	总金额（万元）	种数（种）	平均期印数（万份）	总印数（万份）	总印张（千印张）	总金额（万元）	种数（种）	平均期印数（万份）	总印数（万份）	总印张（千印张）	总金额（万元）
全国总计	**1 894**	**19 494.94**	**3 900 666**	**126 726 967**	**4 082 042**	**997**	**14 685.11**	**2 643 309**	**83 928 443**	**2 891 113**	**878**	**4 780.59**	**1 249 274**	**42 632 264**	**1 184 440**	**19**	**29.24**	**8 083**	**166 260**	**6 489**
中　央	**217**	**3 029.57**	**787 648**	**22 538 698**	**892 631**	**217**	**3 029.57**	**787 648**	**22 538 698**	**892 631**										
地　方	**1 677**	**16 465.37**	**3 113 017**	**104 188 269**	**3 189 410**	**780**	**11 655.53**	**1 855 661**	**61 389 745**	**1 998 481**	**878**	**4 780.59**	**1 249 274**	**42 632 264**	**1 184 440**	**19**	**29.24**	**8 083**	**166 260**	**6 489**
北　京	35	267.64	72 308	339 4385	75 493	35	267.64	72 308	3 394 385	75 493										
天　津	24	175.53	49 324	1 673 895	49 322	24	175.53	49 324	1 673 895	49 322										
河　北	64	520.13	128 177	2 849 598	121 678	28	349.59	81 503	1 412 910	80 013	35	169.24	46 362	1 430 448	41 303	1	1.30	312	6 240	362
山　西	60	2 412.93	201 619	2 015 550	196 110	36	2 285.56	176 218	1 505 721	173 382	23	127.04	25 371	509 523	22 670	1	0.32	31	307	58
内蒙古	58	127.85	30 227	691 819	29 829	23	72.38	14 766	387 483	15 814	32	54.16	15 264	302 449	13 849	3	1.30	198	1 888	166
辽　宁	68	529.37	103 862	3 808 361	76 054	19	337.58	54 169	2 169 132	37 502	46	190.10	49 403	1 637 777	38 271	3	1.70	290	1 451	281
吉　林	51	861.95	78 857	2 046 263	102 095	24	783.80	59 559	1 541 593	82 047	27	78.15	19 298	504 670	20 049					
黑龙江	68	356.80	62 387	1 455 702	60 113	27	154.41	32 716	697 272	24 068	41	202.39	29 671	758 430	36 044					
上　海	70	455.47	100 393	4 567 195	112 522	70	455.47	100 393	4 567 195	112 522										
江　苏	81	1 127.83	232 495	8 131 138	223 899	30	697.45	124 434	4 565 754	113 667	51	430.39	108 061	3 565 384	110 232					
浙　江	67	925.91	261 247	9 617 286	233 660	21	380.10	102 473	3 466 811	101 447	43	530.67	153 390	6 014 355	128 035	3	15.14	5 384	136 120	4 178
安　徽	51	363.25	79 488	2 012 609	74 574	19	196.90	40 441	808 416	38 923	32	166.34	39 047	1 204 193	35 651					
福　建	42	429.08	90 608	3 415 302	95 278	19	299.08	46 974	1 832 406	48 846	23	130.00	43 634	1 582 896	46 433					
江　西	41	1 052.92	107 365	2 278 902	101 798	19	953.40	74 385	1 214 308	72 141	20	96.23	32 449	1 059 279	29 219	2	3.29	531	5 314	439
山　东	87	894.56	262 037	11 986 237	236 121	29	470.45	143 886	7 997 126	133 608	58	424.11	118 151	3 989 111	102 512					

续前表

	合计					中央及省、自治区、直辖市级					地、市级					县级				
	种数（种）	平均期印数（万份）	总印数（万份）	总印张（千印张）	总金额（万元）	种数（种）	平均期印数（万份）	总印数（万份）	总印张（千印张）	总金额（万元）	种数（种）	平均期印数（万份）	总印数（万份）	总印张（千印张）	总金额（万元）	种数（种）	平均期印数（万份）	总印数（万份）	总印张（千印张）	总金额（万元）
河　南	77	1 476.40	192 109	4 949 801	203 683	31	1 211.58	126 718	3 050 621	134 866	46	264.81	65 391	1 899 180	68 817					
湖　北	73	522.35	122 128	3 479 620	136 029	27	189.12	47 124	1 455 914	57 520	43	328.68	73 870	2 012 372	77 671	3	4.55	1 134	11 335	837
湖　南	48	567.33	98 425	2 829 882	94 685	22	425.94	59 587	1 878 774	68 909	26	141.39	38 838	951 108	25 776					
广　东	99	1 151.85	298 845	16 595 386	442 454	32	522.58	138 361	8 015 687	257 836	67	629.27	160 484	8 579 699	184 618					
广　西	53	223.29	64 275	1 738 851	60 281	20	121.51	31 362	945 495	29 566	33	101.78	32 913	793 357	30 716					
海　南	14	73.96	21 536	694 276	23 555	10	54.38	16 467	537 433	17 710	4	19.58	5 069	156 843	5 845					
重　庆	27	221.90	44 041	1 917 096	50 311	24	213.80	41 746	1 858 558	48 505	3	8.10	2 294	58 538	1 806					
四　川	85	592.52	152 764	5 157 271	158 361	37	334.50	75 078	2 470 745	87 591	48	258.02	77 686	2 686 527	70 770					
贵　州	30	108.38	30 224	822 155	28 474	13	50.45	13 413	390 279	13 685	17	57.93	16 811	431 875	14 789					
云　南	42	151.05	40 062	1 012 112	37 100	17	100.78	25 078	743 240	25 972	25	50.27	14 983	268 872	11 128					
西　藏	25	39.49	7 972	205 006	5 762	11	25.67	5 454	116 550	3 404	14	13.81	2 518	88 456	2 358					
陕　西	43	242.99	57 328	1 632 654	55 875	27	151.14	34 474	1 083 413	32 880	16	91.85	22 854	549 240	22 995					
甘　肃	50	250.84	50 207	1 037 892	42 484	23	174.07	27 134	473 587	27 292	27	76.77	23 074	564 305	15 192					
青　海	26	37.61	9 566	313 133	6 829	15	23.27	5 525	162 595	4 654	9	12.92	3 860	147 043	2 020	2	1.43	181	3 495	155
宁　夏	14	46.03	10 439	273 247	11 457	8	34.34	6 992	189 899	7 954	6	11.68	3 448	83 348	3 503					
新　疆	85	225.76	46 121	1 480 752	36 302	35	124.37	23 235	700 731	16 308	49	101.17	22 863	779 911	19 981	1	0.22	22	110	13
新疆生产建设兵团	19	32.41	6 582	104 894	7 220	5	18.66	4 364	81 818	5 033	14	13.75	2 219	23 076	2 186					

2016 年全国各地区各类期刊出版的种数、印数、总印张、总金额（1）

	合计					综合					哲学、社会科学				
	种数（种）	平均期印数（万册）	总印数（万册）	总印张（千印张）	总金额（万元）	种数（种）	平均期印数（万册）	总印数（万册）	总印张（千印张）	总金额（万元）	种数（种）	平均期印数（万册）	总印数（万册）	总印张（千印张）	总金额（万元）
全国总计	**10 084**	**13 904.97**	**269 669**	**15 195 298**	**2 324 154**	**365**	**850.99**	**18 230**	**968 323**	**123 111**	**2 664**	**6 860.61**	**126 966**	**6 490 942**	**1 046 737**
中　央	**3 047**	**5 294.25**	**87 501**	**6 075 179**	**977 729**	**67**	**95.89**	**2 297**	**150 953**	**25 008**	**925**	**3 566.34**	**60 241**	**3 217 117**	**567 524**
地　方	**7 037**	**8 610.71**	**182 168**	**9 120 119**	**1 346 426**	**298**	**755.10**	**15 934**	**817 369**	**98 103**	**1 739**	**3 294.26**	**66 724**	**3 273 825**	**479 214**
北　京	174	176.91	3 371	247 130	39 233	2	0.35	1	203	77	50	69.45	1 513	95 749	14 535
天　津	254	199.01	3 100	161 877	31 358	3	1.80	21	1 323	206	50	54.62	978	48 249	8 255
河　北	227	207.09	4 605	209 252	32 121	9	2.38	29	1 761	500	59	90.10	1 870	81 463	12 158
山　西	202	127.93	2 421	150 409	25 102	3	0.95	28	2 115	552	52	52.81	887	48 419	8 547
内蒙古	147	82.77	1 714	90 217	10 723	3	0.85	9	605	90	51	47.41	803	38 621	4 874
辽　宁	321	473.45	8 767	364 339	52 641	6	5.45	78	4 927	492	72	271.00	5 649	225 445	29 961
吉　林	240	245.19	7 731	362 689	50 167	3	1.60	36	2 593	596	63	57.84	1 597	74 164	10 118
黑龙江	314	206.84	4 340	245 976	34 870	8	3.13	30	2 064	410	76	98.65	1 851	95 149	13 301
上　海	637	652.87	11 205	626 093	94 970	14	12.50	335	16 394	2 493	143	216.90	4 361	226 356	35 179
江　苏	470	399.70	11 954	523 319	101 456	18	5.81	101	5 211	1 741	104	146.66	4 370	191 840	35 828
浙　江	226	515.00	7 690	336 176	55 838	21	3.47	23	1 566	324	48	114.55	1 997	106 398	16 974
安　徽	186	291.20	5 017	233 049	43 785	24	2.48	12	1 336	226	34	69.58	1 218	58 401	9 989
福　建	176	197.15	4 215	201 196	27 487	8	4.40	49	2 097	610	55	136.23	3 137	138 106	17 269
江　西	165	261.29	7 291	222 830	30 931	6	3.87	108	6 290	719	47	79.96	1 716	58 796	8 565
山　东	270	442.27	10 241	470 314	62 399	19	10.35	329	15 865	2 818	75	238.12	3 938	229 639	28 655

续前表

	合计					综合					哲学、社会科学				
	种数（种）	平均期印数（万册）	总印数（万册）	总印张（千印张）	总金额（万元）	种数（种）	平均期印数（万册）	总印数（万册）	总印张（千印张）	总金额（万元）	种数（种）	平均期印数（万册）	总印数（万册）	总印张（千印张）	总金额（万元）
河　南	248	333.43	8 166	388 579	50 997	22	2.89	17	1 653	271	68	163.70	3 915	198 479	23 971
湖　北	429	763.37	18 544	1 027 425	120 801	21	282.39	5 519	238 903	24 786	104	197.22	4 835	215 272	30 883
湖　南	256	591.73	13 966	641 469	88 012	13	2.12	14	1 173	215	54	148.66	3 288	147 051	19 765
广　东	388	621.55	12 270	663 517	101 761	27	26.16	353	21 883	3 816	99	283.69	5 791	320 640	45 433
广　西	184	180.85	4 236	180 387	30 869	12	6.40	172	8 395	1 360	49	74.00	1 378	66 388	9 726
海　南	44	40.10	718	50 292	7 657	2	6.20	72	7 247	1 360	13	11.23	140	8 060	1 324
重　庆	138	217.89	4 854	284 443	49 181	4	2.20	74	5 988	1 530	32	132.87	2 183	111 393	19 834
四　川	359	316.36	5 045	290 004	50 662	14	23.46	674	20 007	4 580	78	140.71	2 079	111 016	19 072
贵　州	90	80.14	1 713	87 897	16 445	6	2.39	34	2 090	617	27	53.37	1 171	64 785	11 948
云　南	127	186.93	3 387	177 410	24 240	6	1.04	14	1 113	287	38	94.42	1 232	74 665	9 509
西　藏	37	19.55	233	14 823	2 297	1	0.30	1	100	6	12	10.54	91	4 664	689
陕　西	287	176.14	3 067	190 713	29 301	6	4.70	86	5 042	822	57	79.71	1 491	82 409	11 317
甘　肃	134	429.60	9 562	520 777	57 329	7	327.85	7 622	433 508	46 096	34	66.72	1 324	50 562	5 998
青　海	54	20.67	318	21 422	2 996	0	0	0	0	0	19	7.83	133	5 372	796
宁　夏	37	29.06	669	52 375	8 181	1	0.50	6	818	240	14	20.45	564	42 563	5 863
新　疆	199	113.72	1 625	77 661	11 512	8	7.09	84	5 088	264	56	60.58	1 133	49 547	8 299
新疆生产建设兵团	17	10.92	135	6 060	1 104	1	0.03	0.10	9	0.40	6	4.71	91	4 164	579

说明：含高校学报、公报、政报、年鉴 1 586 种，平均期印数 351 万册，总印数 4 677 万册，总印张 745 574 千印张。

2016 年全国各地区各类期刊出版的种数、印数、总印张、总金额（2）

	自然科学、技术					文化、教育					文学、艺术				
	种数（种）	平均期印数（万册）	总印数（万册）	总印张（千印张）	总金额（万元）	种数（种）	平均期印数（万册）	总印数（万册）	总印张（千印张）	总金额（万元）	种数（种）	平均期印数（万册）	总印数（万册）	总印张（千印张）	总金额（万元）
全国总计	**5 014**	**2 495.78**	**36 920**	**3 040 433**	**456 385**	**1 383**	**2 678.98**	**61 745**	**3 198 073**	**483 020**	**658**	**1 018.60**	**25 808**	**1 497 528**	**214 901**
中　央	**1 560**	**950.92**	**12 542**	**1 584 830**	**214 846**	**353**	**525.57**	**9 164**	**909 139**	**128 162**	**142**	**155.53**	**3 257**	**213 141**	**42 190**
地　方	**3 454**	**1 544.85**	**24 378**	**1 455 604**	**241 540**	**1 030**	**2 153.42**	**52 581**	**2 288 934**	**354 857**	**516**	**863.07**	**22 551**	**1 284 387**	**172 712**
北　京	78	34.65	469	38 053	6 960	32	63.70	1 266	100 683	15 991	12	8.77	122	12 442	1 669
天　津	147	63.30	801	45 512	10 454	34	31.94	591	25 976	5 151	20	47.35	709	40 817	7 292
河　北	110	50.10	763	52 691	10 220	35	52.07	1 714	57 136	7 194	14	12.44	229	16 202	2 049
山　西	91	32.71	417	32 179	4 981	35	25.95	820	52 033	7 997	21	15.51	269	15 664	3 025
内蒙古	49	11.83	211	14 453	1 736	21	8.21	219	11 437	1 172	23	14.47	472	25 101	2 852
辽　宁	180	91.14	1 185	66 377	11 861	45	94.62	1 633	52 894	7 919	18	11.24	222	14 695	2 408
吉　林	104	23.55	378	36 235	6 077	43	43.47	1 174	45 083	7 730	27	118.74	4 546	204 613	25 646
黑龙江	161	43.23	856	44 501	6 732	50	38.47	1 125	72 968	11 135	19	23.36	478	31 294	3 292
上　海	364	170.76	2 084	170 180	25 125	77	103.50	1 493	87 756	15 655	39	149.20	2 931	125 406	16 518
江　苏	263	125.50	2 676	109 888	21 675	57	93.40	4 079	181 724	34 728	28	28.33	728	34 657	7 485
浙　江	109	43.41	442	25 946	5 136	32	326.31	4 773	177 382	28 851	16	27.26	454	24 885	4 553
安　徽	88	52.87	636	42 830	5 591	27	143.65	2 792	96 244	13 577	13	22.61	358	34 237	14 401
福　建	72	23.57	214	19 227	3 212	29	23.59	678	33 570	4 709	12	9.35	137	8 195	1 687
江　西	71	19.99	281	14 371	2 352	32	149.66	4 972	135 402	17 855	9	7.81	214	7 971	1 440
山　东	131	54.10	1 213	64 266	8 975	31	119.56	4 092	141 598	18 634	14	20.14	669	18 948	3 318

续前表

	自然科学、技术					文化、教育					文学、艺术				
	种数（种）	平均期印数（万册）	总印数（万册）	总印张（千印张）	总金额（万元）	种数（种）	平均期印数（万册）	总印数（万册）	总印张（千印张）	总金额（万元）	种数（种）	平均期印数（万册）	总印数（万册）	总印张（千印张）	总金额（万元）
河　南	114	46.94	1 120	57 067	8 870	25	88.99	2 138	88 571	10 295	19	30.92	975	42 808	7 589
湖　北	211	75.28	1 058	75 691	14 250	63	62.40	1 624	76 452	11 593	30	146.08	5 508	421 106	39 288
湖　南	131	111.00	1 647	81 047	13 210	42	291.84	7 909	347 423	47 976	16	38.11	1 109	64 775	6 846
广　东	183	217.50	4 351	213 860	30 336	47	69.88	1 349	78 092	17 132	32	24.31	427	29 042	5 043
广　西	78	37.79	644	29 681	5 398	30	57.83	2 005	73 582	13 997	15	4.84	37	2 341	388
海　南	15	7.75	148	8 404	1 138	11	13.87	349	25 808	3 728	3	1.05	9	775	109
重　庆	80	28.53	594	47 218	8 665	19	53.39	1 996	119 423	19 095	3	0.89	7	421	57
四　川	205	73.07	895	75 301	12 766	44	71.19	1 200	65 692	11 603	18	7.93	196	17 989	2 641
贵　州	34	6.62	65	4 883	917	16	14.77	380	9 918	1 875	7	3.00	63	6 221	1 089
云　南	50	17.35	295	15 551	2 667	21	19.96	582	30 516	4 107	12	54.17	1 264	55 564	7 670
西　藏	6	0.44	2	124	14	13	7.37	135	9 657	1 552	5	0.90	4	278	35
陕　西	173	44.13	577	45 091	8 024	37	36.39	684	43 168	6 393	14	11.20	229	15 003	2 744
甘　肃	66	12.88	133	11 797	1 923	20	21.09	476	24 304	3 237	7	1.07	8	605	74
青　海	18	2.09	11	672	98	9	6.24	116	11 373	1 609	8	4.51	57	4 005	493
宁　夏	11	2.99	28	1 990	377	7	3.92	57	5 683	1 585	4	1.21	13	1 321	117
新　疆	55	17.54	164	9 412	1 624	45	16.11	161	7 370	778	35	12.41	83	6 242	548
新疆生产建设兵团	6	2.23	21	1 105	177	1	0.06	0.36	19	2	3	3.90	23	764	346

说明：含高校学报、公报、政报、年鉴 1 586 种，平均期印数 351 万册，总印数 4 677 万册，总印张 745 574 千印张。

2016 年全国各地区录音制品出版品种、数量及发行总量（按载体形式分类）

单位：种、万盒、万张

	录音制品					录音带（AT）				激光唱盘（CD）				高密度激光唱盘（DVD-A）				其他载体			
	合计		其中：新版		发行数量	合计		其中：新版		合计		其中：新版		合计		其中：新版		合计		其中：新版	
	种数	数量	种数	数量		种数	数量	种数	数量	种数	数量	种数	数量	种数	数量	种数	数量	种数	数量	种数	数量
全国总计	**8 713**	**21 358.42**	**3 450**	**2 045.93**	**18 831.61**	**1 526**	**11 450.56**	**395**	**336.20**	**5 844**	**7 755.36**	**2 611**	**1 465.84**	**178**	**80.03**	**149**	**54.93**	**1 165**	**2 072.46**	**295**	**188.97**
中　央	**3 151**	**13 601.67**	**1 098**	**532.13**	**12 304.74**	**747**	**7 917.21**	**144**	**55.53**	**1 612**	**4 617.70**	**783**	**378.13**	**46**	**18.34**	**38**	**13.09**	**746**	**1 048.41**	**133**	**85.38**
地　方	**5 562**	**7 756.75**	**2 352**	**1 513.80**	**6 526.87**	**779**	**3 533.35**	**251**	**280.66**	**4 232**	**3 137.66**	**1 828**	**1 087.71**	**132**	**61.69**	**111**	**41.84**	**419**	**1 024.05**	**162**	**103.59**
北　京	168	40.55	164	38.75	15.16	18	1.82	18	1.82	126	29.43	126	29.43	23	8.60	19	6.80	1	0.70	1	0.70
天　津	69	48.80	36	21.75	46.79	30	26.65			19	15.00	18	14.90	10	2.70	8	2.40	10	4.45	10	4.45
河　北	131	587.59	26	25.09	572.67	104	514.82	15	19.39	27	72.78	11	5.70								
山　西	168	331.30	168	331.30	331.30					168	331.30	168	331.30								
内蒙古	37	9.72	37	9.72	15.59					37	9.72	37	9.72								
辽　宁	193	89.65	103	39.50	153.26					190	88.90	102	39.35	3	0.76	1	0.15				
吉　林	125	172.83	75	27.82	489.58	52	93.05	34	21.38	73	79.78	41	6.44								
黑龙江	5	0.12	5	0.12	1.32					4	0.10	4	0.10	1	0.02	1	0.02				
上　海	2 538	2 989.82	495	428.96	2 200.39	184	1 163.74	18	97.65	2 025	1 093.24	334	237.26	15	17.54	6	2.33	314	715.30	137	91.72
江　苏	189	1 047.67	73	51.33	1 047.49	68	918.86	27	21.20	118	128.36	43	29.68	3	0.45	3	0.45				
浙　江	141	299.01	73	23.37	284.54	34	95.25			55	188.16	21	7.77	52	15.60	52	15.60				
安　徽	47	22.72	43	19.88	29.46	15	10.02	13	9.58	32	12.71	30	10.31								
福　建	32	9.60	32	9.60	26.47					31	8.80	31	8.80	1	0.80	1	0.80				
江　西	168	69.93	66	27.15	57.53	33	6.90	33	6.90	125	52.23	23	9.45	10	10.80	10	10.80				
山　东	134	21.21	118	16.72	17.71	19	1.76	12	0.60	115	19.45	106	16.12								
河　南	2	0.90	2	0.90	0.90					2	0.90	2	0.90								
湖　北	60	15.43	43	9.47	16.36	2	2.46	1	0.06	56	12.58	41	9.32	2	0.39	1	0.09				

续前表

	录音制品					录音带（AT）				激光唱盘（CD）				高密度激光唱盘（DVD-A）				其他载体			
	合计		其中：新版		发行数量	合计		其中：新版		合计		其中：新版		合计		其中：新版		合计		其中：新版	
	种数	数量	种数	数量		种数	数量	种数	数量	种数	数量	种数	数量	种数	数量	种数	数量	种数	数量	种数	数量
湖　南	162	464.31	58	59.82	280.46	21	32.91	20	32.22	111	242.76	37	26.11					30	188.64	1	1.50
广　东	709	1 342.22	443	265.07	733.23	134	638.70	30	64.56	539	596.30	408	198.85	4	2.03	1	0.40	32	105.18	4	1.27
广　西	132	56.03	77	34.26	51.05					132	56.03	77	34.26								
海　南	27	4.29	27	4.29	4.29	14	1.29	14	1.29	7	1.20	7	1.20	6	1.80	6	1.80				
重　庆	56	19.78	7	0.87	21.81	16	1.25	3	0.32	31	15.18	4	0.55					9	3.35		
四　川	14	1.77	11	1.41	0.86					14	1.77	11	1.41								
贵　州																					
云　南	77	37.49	56	36.76	16.76	10	0.55			67	36.94	56	36.76								
西　藏	41	11.70	41	11.70	8.40	13	3.70	13	3.70	26	7.80	26	7.80	2	0.20	2	0.20				
陕　西	90	39.49	33	10.15	40.27	12	19.63			55	13.43	24	6.20					23	6.43	9	3.95
甘　肃	1	0.50	1	0.50	0.50					1	0.50	1	0.50								
青　海	1	0.50	1	0.50	0					1	0.50	1	0.50								
宁　夏	12	2.71	12	2.71	23.69					12	2.71	12	2.71								
新　疆	33	19.11	26	4.31	39.05					33	19.11	26	4.31								
新疆生产建设兵团																					

2016 年全国各地区录像制品出版品种、数量及发行总量（按载体形式分类）

单位：种、万盒、万张

	录像制品					录像带（AT）				数码激光视盘（VCD）				高密度激光视盘（DVD-V）				其他载体			
	合计		其中：新版		发行数量	合计		其中：新版		合计		其中：新版		合计		其中：新版		合计		其中：新版	
	种数	数量	种数	数量		种数	数量	种数	数量	种数	数量	种数	数量	种数	数量	种数	数量	种数	数量	种数	数量
全国总计	**5 671**	**6 226.20**	**3 715**	**3 408.82**	**5 339.30**					**792**	**1 479.69**	**270**	**432.68**	**4 725**	**4 712.67**	**3 299**	**2 948.19**	**154**	**33.85**	**146**	**27.95**
中 央	**2 625**	**3 123.55**	**1 578**	**1 350.84**	**2 283.79**					**357**	**1 182.47**	**47**	**299.12**	**2 150**	**1 919.39**	**1 416**	**1 032.33**	**118**	**21.68**	**115**	**19.38**
地 方	**3 046**	**3 102.66**	**2 137**	**2 057.99**	**3 055.51**					**435**	**297.22**	**223**	**133.56**	**2 575**	**2 793.27**	**1 883**	**1 915.86**	**36**	**12.17**	**31**	**8.57**
北 京	65	21.16	61	18.37	2.41									65	21.16	61	18.37				
天 津	3	1.10	3	1.10	0.52									3	1.10	3	1.10				
河 北	17	8.70	4	0.60	5.99					10	7.40			7	1.30	4	0.60				
山 西	36	6.61	36	6.61	26.93									32	6.22	32	6.22	4	0.39	4	0.39
内蒙古	27	2.20	27	2.20	6.19									27	2.20	27	2.20				
辽 宁	127	48.44	121	47.74	43.88					11	3.68	11	3.68	111	44.41	105	43.71	5	0.35	5	0.35
吉 林	110	58.31	108	57.21	72.65					5	0.50	5	0.50	105	57.81	103	56.71				
黑龙江	3	0.14	3	0.14	0.14									3	0.14	3	0.14				
上 海	751	1 931.65	252	1 078.97	1 887.59					183	138.55	63	35.45	556	1 785.38	180	1 036.86	12	7.72	9	6.67
江 苏	92	151.72	64	124.09	147.88					16	7.33	11	5.15	74	144.01	51	118.56	2	0.38	2	0.38
浙 江	95	40.10	75	25.72	38.84					25	13.94	12	3.68	70	26.16	63	22.03				
安 徽	43	19.20	36	17.85	22.17					3	3.61	3	3.61	38	15.36	31	14.01	2	0.23	2	0.23
福 建	43	7.53	43	7.53	8.05									43	7.53	43	7.53				
江 西	80	43.87	54	15.85	45.17					53	29.11	40	12.00	27	14.76	14	3.85				
山 东	206	98.48	206	98.48	174.80									206	98.48	206	98.48				
河 南	51	21.52	49	15.29	10.10									51	21.52	49	15.29				
湖 北	83	23.88	78	22.93	21.82					18	5.00	16	4.80	65	18.88	62	18.13				

续前表

	录像制品					录像带（AT）				数码激光视盘（VCD）				高密度激光视盘（DVD-V）				其他载体			
	合计		其中：新版		发行数量	合计		其中：新版		合计		其中：新版		合计		其中：新版		合计		其中：新版	
	种数	数量	种数	数量		种数	数量	种数	数量	种数	数量	种数	数量	种数	数量	种数	数量	种数	数量	种数	数量
湖　南	223	111.19	79	68.80	168.89					59	54.24	21	36.46	163	56.40	58	32.34	1	0.55		
广　东	342	127.40	215	86.26	46.20					10	7.30	10	7.30	332	120.10	205	78.96				
广　西	26	13.71	24	9.03	3.60					1	0.20	1	0.20	25	13.51	23	8.83				
海　南	4	0.60	4	0.60	0.60									4	0.60	4	0.60				
重　庆	38	10.68	33	8.08	32.03					4	2.20			34	8.48	33	8.08				
四　川	73	54.52	70	52.26	55.58									65	52.17	63	51.91	8	2.35	7	0.35
贵　州	1	0.50	1	0.50	0.50									1	0.50	1	0.50				
云　南	149	81.21	147	80.86	67.06					16	5.20	16	5.20	131	75.81	129	75.46	2	0.20	2	0.20
西　藏	62	69.30	62	69.30	39.34					2	0.60	2	0.60	60	68.70	60	68.70				
陕　西	111	16.55	103	13.08	87.90					7	3.42			104	13.13	103	13.08				
甘　肃	37	7.75	37	7.75	8.15									37	7.75	37	7.75				
青　海	21	32.90	21	32.90	0									21	32.90	21	32.90				
宁　夏	6	0.60	6	0.60	0.90									6	0.60	6	0.60				
新　疆	121	91.14	115	87.29	29.64					12	14.93	12	14.93	109	76.21	103	72.36				
新疆生产建设兵团																					

2016 年全国新华书店系统、出版社自办发行单位出版物发行进、销、存情况

单位：万册（张、份、盒）、万元

	购进		销售		库存	
	数量	金额	数量	金额	数量	金额
全国总计	**2 077 831**	**28 571 116**	**2 082 656**	**27 713 353**	**657 455**	**11 430 050**
中　央	**244 150**	**6 272 887**	**247 738**	**5 810 167**	**135 928**	**4 418 011**
地　方	**1 833 681**	**22 298 229**	**1 834 919**	**21 903 186**	**521 526**	**7 012 039**
北　京	14 007	393 276	13 249	366 419	8 370	269 185
天　津	12 504	188 928	12 450	186 892	4 842	105 557
河　北	97 610	1 205 918	100 225	1 202 341	56 533	172 283
山　西	45 038	559 457	45 437	563 797	16 480	216 963
内蒙古	16 464	207 865	16 869	202 601	3 640	39 420
辽　宁	23 562	321 643	23 171	315 589	9 611	204 746
吉　林	19 400	316 584	20 024	316 159	6 199	123 880
黑龙江	22 455	308 279	23 267	308 669	5 323	89 424
上　海	46 540	1 106 486	44 274	1 025 661	21 175	632 256
江　苏	200 430	2 084 793	192 089	1 985 503	67 739	886 063
浙　江	126 382	1 850 357	132 438	1 893 859	50 052	871 332
安　徽	114 528	1 351 613	116 438	1 324 892	18 314	283 248
福　建	38 717	405 126	38 416	404 868	7 989	83 567
江　西	88 136	1 087 667	85 762	1 052 983	9 792	161 099
山　东	138 708	1 450 691	144 885	1 492 716	56 624	462 755
河　南	153 680	1 273 074	153 229	1 260 126	15 671	199 268
湖　北	72 666	897 178	72 657	840 621	9 981	267 788
湖　南	147 923	1 978 369	148 751	1 944 037	41 742	488 833
广　东	71 998	815 594	71 594	804 718	30 922	323 809
广　西	58 281	520 764	58 158	521 022	6 872	89 954
海　南	13 703	162 943	13 645	155 368	1 696	29 723
重　庆	30 426	424 928	30 640	422 413	10 722	189 118
四　川	67 027	924 898	66 489	896 623	14 522	291 631
贵　州	34 694	319 498	34 384	311 968	3 244	31 948
云　南	41 621	556 162	41 820	551 674	6 505	109 420
西　藏	1 843	24 758	2 571	24 274	1 500	7 916
陕　西	63 805	658 299	60 579	640 448	21 803	212 536
甘　肃	34 237	373 231	33 354	363 382	4 229	51 287
青　海	2 051	32 996	2 319	34 201	1 147	11 497
宁　夏	4 777	70 115	4 818	67 686	576	15 351
新　疆	30 468	426 736	30 917	421 677	7 709	90 180

说明：1. 本表中购进、销售为总购进、总销售（按国家商品流通企业统计口径，包括新华书店系统内购销）。
2. 销售金额：指向读者实际销售的出版物以及直接向国外出口的出版物的销售额。

2016年全国图书、期刊、报纸进出口情况

载体	类别	出口		进口	
		数量（万册、万份）	金额（万美元）	数量（万册、万份）	金额（万美元）
总计		**1 765.52**	**5 886.67**	**3 108.18**	**30 051.73**
图书	合计	1 450.28	5 407.37	1 551.63	14 421.60
	哲学、社会科学	146.00	1 826.43	61.70	1 828.11
	文化 、教育	158.03	763.35	296.78	3 035.78
	文学、艺术	189.19	960.36	170.95	1 745.86
	自然、科学技术	49.36	296.58	56.30	2 336.71
	少儿读物	729.87	653.26	510.40	1 671.76
	综合性图书	177.83	907.39	455.50	3 803.38
期刊		265.69	443.78	338.37	14 137.21
报纸		49.55	35.52	1 218.18	1 492.92

说明：以上数据为全国有出版物进口经营许可证的出版物进出口经营单位数据。

2016年全国音像、电子出版物、数字出版物进出口情况

载体	类别	出口		进口	
		数量（盒、张）	金额（万美元）	数量（盒、张）	金额（万美元）
总计		**13 270**	**156.43**	**108 096**	**25 859.38**
录音	合计	11 975	34.67	98 261	95.92
	录音带（AT）				
	激光唱片（CD）			98 261	95.92
	数码激光唱盘（DVD-A）	11 975	34.67		
录像	合计	1 295	1.11	9 835	17.32
	录像带（VT）				
	数码激光视盘（DVD-V）	1 295	1.11	9 835	17.32
	数码激光视盘（VCD）				
电子出版物					
数字出版物			120.65		25 745.14

说明：以上数据为全国有出版物进口经营许可证的出版物进出口经营单位数据。

2016 年全国广播电视发展主要指标一览表（1）

	节目制播情况								覆盖情况				有线广播电视发展情况				
	广播节目播出时间	增长率	电视节目播出时间	增长率	广播节目制作时间	增长率	电视节目制作时间	增长率	广播综合人口覆盖率	电视综合人口覆盖率	无线广播综合人口覆盖率	无线电视综合人口覆盖率	有线广播电视用户	数字电视用户	付费数字电视用户	有线广播电视用户占本地区总户数比重	有线广播电视网络传输干线总长
	(万小时)	(%)	(万小时)	(%)	(万小时)	(%)	(万小时)	(%)	(%)	(%)	(%)	(%)	(万户)	(万户)	(万户)	(%)	(万公里)
全国合计	1 456.51	2.44	1 792.44	0.72	782.03	1.32	350.72	−0.37	98.37	98.88	97.11	96.68	22 829.53	20 157.24	5 817.15	52.75	477.61
总局直属	27.06	2.90	40.00	11.14	24.09	−9.18	18.32	18.13	—	—	—	—	—	—	—	—	4.36
北京	18.06	5.21	13.19	2.90	22.26	24.46	15.15	−15.71	100.00	100.00	100.00	99.75	580.42	529.15	76.40	109.66	19.41
天津	13.91	−5.58	18.00	6.69	7.84	−4.01	3.34	0.67	100.00	100.00	100.00	100.00	358.45	335.05	76.95	96.73	0.68
河北	65.93	1.00	81.05	1.09	35.78	0.6	18.77	3.84	99.35	99.28	98.43	96.96	857.22	755.60	110.73	36.23	20.43
山西	41.58	0.62	48.90	0.20	19.45	−0.75	8.53	1.04	98.61	99.41	98.61	99.39	455.96	358.83	20.57	35.14	10.79
内蒙古	66.53	−2.71	63.41	−1.94	25.08	2.75	8.14	10.99	99.09	99.19	98.87	94.90	339.15	301.36	22.78	40.59	3.56
辽宁	68.80	1.24	74.38	0.15	38.77	0.77	18.02	3.98	99.05	99.13	98.91	97.64	842.14	747.53	48.23	55.69	13.54
吉林	50.07	1.12	52.98	0.73	26.03	−1.96	10.60	−1.72	98.68	98.77	98.40	93.91	526.41	493.20	209.46	52.13	9.85
黑龙江	53.65	9.80	63.42	4.82	23.95	8.92	11.51	18.15	99.21	99.00	99.21	98.88	651.40	642.63	193.09	48.42	6.44
上海	14.52	6.70	17.90	0.33	7.67	−10.8	6.35	−13.52	100.00	100.00	100.00	100.00	522.97	492.42	171.63	97.43	4.71
江苏	78.62	0.79	77.47	−1.28	60.88	3.31	19.50	2.96	100.00	100.00	100.00	100.00	2 068.64	1 754.10	514.13	84.80	40.28
浙江	77.86	2.20	75.60	0.29	53.05	3.24	15.50	−4.36	99.65	99.72	99.25	99.40	1 526.08	1 507.17	438.76	92.92	29.59
安徽	52.57	−2.73	59.59	−2.93	16.28	−4.1	7.25	−6.38	98.89	99.03	98.89	98.96	878.10	585.21	61.69	41.19	6.21

续前表

	节目制播情况								覆盖情况				有线广播电视发展情况				
	广播节目播出时间	增长率	电视节目播出时间	增长率	广播节目制作时间	增长率	电视节目制作时间	增长率	广播综合人口覆盖率	电视综合人口覆盖率	无线广播综合人口覆盖率	无线电视综合人口覆盖率	有线广播电视用户	数字电视用户	付费数字电视用户	有线广播电视用户占本地区总户数比重	有线广播电视网络传输干线总长
	(万小时)	(%)	(万小时)	(%)	(万小时)	(%)	(万小时)	(%)	(%)	(%)	(%)	(%)	(万户)	(万户)	(万户)	(%)	(万公里)
福　建	52.34	−0.14	36.92	1.19	25.84	1.83	6.90	−6.77	98.96	99.12	97.82	96.37	738.89	715.37	305.52	69.25	14.69
江　西	41.05	0.61	67.13	−0.39	18.17	−7.24	9.35	−6.39	98.04	98.83	97.61	98.36	662.66	585.94	163.13	52.31	15.85
山　东	95.71	1.96	115.54	0.07	56.02	5.02	23.31	5.23	98.98	98.62	98.48	96.62	1 848.07	1 762.67	702.00	61.49	39.14
河　南	67.90	0.58	91.14	0.31	31.92	0.49	13.91	−1.08	98.43	98.64	98.38	98.55	1 056.49	777.24	58.55	32.61	21.73
湖　北	48.13	0.79	67.44	−0.25	26.71	8.45	10.99	1.98	99.33	99.15	98.91	98.61	1 060.75	1 003.25	379.75	51.45	27.74
湖　南	42.51	3.32	76.07	0.13	20.83	8.64	13.27	−2.59	94.68	98.26	93.09	96.51	1 267.30	1 090.30	277.61	61.59	13.81
广　东	81.56	9.17	74.01	1.64	62.09	−8.48	31.79	−5.02	99.90	99.90	99.43	99.39	2 017.08	1 755.87	113.67	89.44	26.70
广　西	40.12	6.44	59.58	3.39	23.27	5.36	8.26	−15.34	96.90	98.40	94.87	96.28	690.42	510.47	222.10	43.82	16.68
海　南	13.12	7.10	9.47	6.12	5.66	−1.45	2.68	−14.71	96.82	95.78	96.64	95.49	115.15	106.17	10.05	43.71	1.31
重　庆	17.93	6.77	29.72	0.52	8.20	1.13	6.43	5.32	98.86	99.19	90.76	90.80	415.33	357.25	185.38	33.11	17.56
四　川	68.95	4.76	114.01	−0.58	26.68	6.82	14.33	−11.31	97.19	98.29	95.36	96.16	1 132.53	1 004.52	642.10	35.48	58.57
贵　州	24.87	−1.83	25.53	−6.31	14.27	3.29	3.81	−10.59	93.02	96.13	80.06	69.84	457.00	452.75	136.01	35.01	21.27
云　南	33.12	8.25	83.42	2.76	16.55	−3.68	8.70	−4.20	97.37	98.24	95.48	95.47	405.36	393.18	264.81	27.23	12.51
西　藏	6.34	8.88	8.26	1.84	3.66	0.14	1.57	12.77	95.21	96.32	93.79	94.39	24.71	18.39	1.61	32.64	0.45
陕　西	47.15	0.26	60.55	1.77	24.16	−1.78	12.78	8.49	98.27	98.87	97.24	97.49	720.37	598.29	177.47	56.81	3.88
甘　肃	35.75	4.53	49.97	2.56	14.27	6.74	7.53	11.74	98.12	98.55	94.61	94.80	206.14	171.37	103.39	24.70	8.12
青　海	9.50	0.10	10.11	−9.88	4.64	−0.22	1.82	51.17	98.22	98.21	98.13	98.06	54.73	54.10	29.35	30.67	0.66
宁　夏	11.64	0.51	16.62	−3.42	6.14	5.09	2.66	−6.42	96.72	99.34	96.50	98.74	104.71	104.71	31.06	49.75	1.31
新　疆	89.65	4.65	111.07	1.65	31.82	2.58	9.66	3.33	96.82	97.25	96.31	96.45	198.40	193.17	69.18	29.99	4.28
新疆生产建设兵团	—	—	—	—	—	—	—	—	97.19	98.04	—	—	46.54	—	—	—	1.50

2016 年全国广播电视发展主要指标一览表（2）

	总收入（亿元）	增长率（%）	实际创收收入（亿元）	增长率（%）	广告收入（亿元）	增长率（%）	广播广告收入（亿元）	增长率（%）	电视广告收入（亿元）	增长率（%）	网络收入（亿元）	增长率（%）	收视费收入（亿元）	增长率（%）	付费数字电视收入（亿元）	增长率（%）	三网融合业务收入（亿元）	资产总额（亿元）	增长率（%）
全国合计	5 039.77	8.74	4 322.40	9.37	1 547.22	1.16	145.83	−6.77	1 004.87	−5.66	910.26	5.10	457.92	−3.63	76.44	8.83	122.40	13 320.31	13.46
总局直属	713.49	1.15	625.31	2.65	292.72	0.31	8.16	0.51	276.21	−0.24	38.10	24.68	10.32	−6.34	3.70	−2.78	18.65	2 003.54	11.30
北　京	761.35	33.23	691.44	40.08	254.93	18.37	8.29	−34.75	66.24	6.83	34.65	32.42	10.95	−4.88	2.50	337.95	9.13	2 140.37	32.97
天　津	31.21	−21.90	25.99	−23.53	8.23	−35.96	3.12	−14.78	4.91	−44.20	12.62	15.23	4.54	−5.25	1.03	53.24	3.72	135.73	−0.34
河　北	79.36	8.44	62.69	6.58	18.44	−7.48	5.25	8.06	12.41	−6.00	30.05	8.24	16.77	−9.42	1.02	8.48	3.36	201.57	10.75
山　西	46.47	6.40	33.00	10.94	7.57	−21.82	2.14	−9.56	5.19	−26.79	10.59	−9.81	7.94	−12.11	0.92	−5.60	0.17	117.32	10.26
内蒙古	49.09	−0.50	20.82	−2.24	3.83	−2.06	1.32	12.26	2.50	−8.21	16.17	−1.33	10.88	−3.54	0.60	149.60	—	98.77	41.21
辽　宁	70.64	−8.37	55.96	−14.37	21.04	−16.56	6.99	1.30	13.88	−23.29	26.53	−13.99	21.19	−11.37	0.71	−52.80	1.15	201.24	−0.68
吉　林	49.15	−13.38	34.20	−2.79	11.76	−4.88	2.70	−11.66	8.98	−3.18	21.57	0.09	12.32	−0.28	3.05	20.60	0.39	264.95	4.74
黑龙江	63.21	9.44	52.99	10.17	19.59	−5.50	6.05	−0.75	13.00	−6.87	23.81	3.75	18.91	27.19	2.55	68.64	1.05	172.14	52.96
上　海	560.31	21.40	536.87	21.44	186.64	31.71	7.10	−21.39	71.21	21.35	39.90	15.01	15.38	−2.12	5.60	23.20	6.57	1 009.26	11.35
江　苏	291.03	−1.42	273.38	−3.05	100.00	−7.12	12.42	2.00	79.34	−8.71	84.11	1.99	39.33	−1.75	5.64	8.46	8.99	1 133.51	11.91
浙　江	457.15	−0.84	435.23	0.13	152.70	3.56	12.08	−8.61	101.95	−3.35	74.70	5.89	31.81	−1.45	5.07	13.26	16.79	1 453.14	14.53
安　徽	90.83	5.09	75.02	4.75	34.70	−0.82	3.28	8.62	29.11	−3.41	16.31	3.20	9.51	−2.81	1.46	3.31	0.79	159.11	5.13
福　建	105.80	6.51	74.33	3.30	17.40	−12.35	3.74	−7.75	10.77	−21.16	28.87	10.54	11.27	0.23	5.19	29.28	1.38	220.78	1.01
江　西	70.90	0.83	56.79	−6.58	19.71	5.24	6.08	59.44	13.17	−9.59	19.26	−5.17	12.01	−7.71	0.87	−40.57	0.36	103.66	−2.93
山　东	159.79	−7.27	142.91	−7.79	48.26	−18.67	9.47	0.24	35.79	−22.26	61.59	−1.38	34.62	−10.75	5.08	−16.94	3.52	411.94	−2.06
河　南	68.92	−0.31	53.24	−4.41	23.95	−10.21	7.95	4.96	15.33	−16.04	18.59	−5.46	12.89	−9.52	1.15	97.99	0.59	209.24	9.77

续前表

	总收入	增长率	实际创收收入	增长率	广告收入	增长率	广播广告收入	增长率	电视广告收入	增长率	网络收入	增长率	收视费收入	增长率	付费数字电视收入	增长率	三网融合业务收入	资产总额	增长率
	(亿元)	(%)	(亿元)	(%)	(亿元)	(%)	(亿元)	(%)	(亿元)	(%)	(亿元)	(%)	(亿元)	(%)	(亿元)	(%)	(亿元)	(亿元)	(%)
湖北	110.05	4.99	91.26	2.08	24.95	−6.67	4.96	10.16	16.15	−18.51	39.16	10.81	23.18	5.02	3.11	39.10	4.97	319.26	3.03
湖南	286.29	14.82	265.81	14.34	133.98	4.95	5.30	−3.05	107.35	−4.18	40.82	15.43	19.08	−5.85	3.32	−11.97	8.39	614.55	5.14
广东	268.65	2.82	246.54	3.76	62.01	−24.52	11.97	−4.74	47.01	−13.47	75.56	−2.82	42.62	−11.12	5.19	−7.00	4.06	752.50	7.38
广西	64.13	−0.50	44.42	5.60	8.08	−24.25	1.43	−14.69	6.23	−26.69	27.77	14.09	10.05	2.13	1.31	1.56	2.77	165.47	26.93
海南	16.50	0.37	11.20	−7.40	3.64	−51.04	0.44	−34.50	3.20	−52.62	3.93	−0.12	2.63	−4.05	0.23	−8.72	—	37.36	4.25
重庆	57.43	8.02	47.28	5.23	10.15	−9.53	1.77	−20.46	8.01	−7.53	26.98	8.04	11.90	−5.17	2.33	16.57	6.06	133.62	6.38
四川	203.74	44.60	136.79	48.54	26.22	2.36	4.44	−0.41	15.82	−16.44	52.08	2.86	22.99	−0.46	4.56	18.36	9.85	469.32	36.89
贵州	92.94	10.88	82.10	12.08	21.76	1.14	1.82	1.96	15.22	4.09	19.96	11.11	8.83	−0.35	3.15	0.73	1.99	171.83	36.63
云南	64.62	14.58	33.74	−10.12	9.16	−24.19	1.00	−51.12	7.58	−22.29	18.07	−4.17	9.87	−5.70	2.18	−11.77	1.74	177.48	−11.57
西藏	13.04	7.62	1.47	−7.98	0.66	−11.14	0.02	8.79	0.62	−13.23	0.54	−0.21	0.50	3.03	0.01	−42.86	—	22.96	18.39
陕西	81.51	−3.61	64.85	−8.66	11.80	−42.38	2.87	−53.04	8.89	−38.07	22.64	9.67	11.39	14.65	1.86	−2.14	4.45	126.89	−27.20
甘肃	40.61	9.39	16.49	3.16	3.79	−19.03	0.96	1.81	2.62	−27.09	9.59	15.10	5.22	2.81	0.59	−19.02	1.10	146.10	42.51
青海	12.75	−25.67	4.03	−17.51	1.04	24.93	0.26	29.91	0.76	23.12	2.48	4.86	1.53	0.49	0.28	−24.86	0.02	20.87	17.39
宁夏	16.97	−2.12	9.05	−12.53	2.32	−14.28	0.28	−12.26	1.35	−34.87	3.37	−17.80	2.08	−2.52	0.75	−1.71	0.17	47.06	5.16
新疆	39.36	−5.25	15.50	−2.89	5.47	−5.46	2.16	0.37	3.30	−8.42	8.96	−0.17	4.48	−6.71	1.41	8.59	0.20	78.80	2.38
新疆生产建设兵团	2.47	−40.82	1.70	−14.28	0.77	−24.87	—	—	0.77	−27.00	0.94	−4.34	0.94	−4.34	—	—	—	—	—

2016年中国软件产业统计资料

2016年全国软件产业统计数据

单位：万元

	企业个数（个）	软件业务收入（年度累计）	软件产品收入（年度累计）	信息技术服务收入（年度累计）	嵌入式系统软件收入（年度累计）
合　计	**32 310**	**482 322 235**	**150 278 252**	**260 904 233**	**71 139 750**
北　京	2 879	64 160 228	24 448 314	39 571 159	140 755
天　津	465	11 858 459	2 824 402	7 568 853	1 465 203
河　北	204	2 101 822	365 043	1 721 880	14 899
山　西	85	239 172	104 621	125 911	8 640
内蒙古	72	279 598	163 399	115 023	1 176
辽　宁	1 892	18 903 341	7 906 035	10 340 257	657 048
吉　林	900	5 110 867	1 668 621	2 708 275	733 970
黑龙江	502	1 679 761	608 601	940 402	130 758
上　海	1 479	38 158 600	11 922 807	24 385 984	1 849 808
江　苏	4 844	81 656 015	18 513 795	37 455 568	25 686 652
浙　江	1 492	36 000 230	10 866 988	21 893 586	3 239 656
安　徽	298	2 600 306	909 752	1 488 655	201 899
福　建	2 563	21 578 985	7 776 170	12 307 126	1 495 689
江　西	113	870 067	338 927	520 876	10 263
山　东	3 965	42 610 828	15 610 362	18 912 595	8 087 871
河　南	178	2 963 543	1 117 252	1 834 942	11 348
湖　北	2 547	13 305 111	6 937 091	5 711 966	656 054
湖　南	355	3 960 107	1 140 827	2 283 922	535 359
广　东	3 631	82 233 915	19 612 172	38 958 597	23 663 145
广　西	163	729 215	100 953	622 851	5 410
海　南	143	767 042	261 981	505 061	0
四　川	1 201	24 230 870	9 586 500	14 487 056	157 313
贵　州	222	1 278 329	502 687	767 758	7 884
云　南	91	502 951	123 645	377 760	1 546
重　庆	1 158	10 249 597	2 386 354	6 596 127	1 267 116
陕　西	580	13 001 964	4 204 166	7 702 833	1 094 964
甘　肃	93	414 210	105 954	303 776	4 481
青　海	15	11 541	3 983	6 691	867
宁　夏	51	132 037	61 855	61 419	8 764
新　疆	129	733 527	104 994	627 323	1 210

说明：西藏暂未纳入统计。

版权名录

MING LU

版权行政管理部门

国家版权局

局　长：聂辰席

副局长：周慧琳

地　址：北京市西城区复兴门外大街 2 号；宣武门外大街 40 号

邮　编：100052

电　话：010-86093114，83138036

传　真：010-83138737

邮　箱：copyright@ncac. gov. cn

网　址：www. ncac. gov. cn

北京市版权局

局　长：杨　烁

副局长：王野霏

版权管理处处长：卢志鹏

地　址：北京市东城区朝内大街 55 号

邮　编：100010

电　话：010-64081208

传　真：010-65159068

邮　箱：webmaster@bjcab. gov. cn

网　址：www. bjcab. gov. cn

天津市版权局

局　长：王建存

分管副局长：梁淳久

版权处处长：张露娜

地　址：天津市河西区尖山路 82 号

邮　编：300211

电　话：022-28335745

传　真：022-28335745

邮　箱：tjsbqj@163. com

网　址：www. tjsppb. gov. cn

河北省版权局

局　长：李晓明

分管副局长：王　智

版权管理处处长：尹志军

地　址：石家庄市建华南大街 100 号

邮　编：050031

电　话：0311-87116309

传　真：0311-85081417

邮　箱：hbbq206@163. com

网　址：www. hbcbgd. gov. cn

山西省版权局

局　长：李海渊

分管副局长：田奇越

版权管理处处长：杨志云

地　址：太原市迎泽大街 318 号

邮　编：030001

电　话：0351-8301523

传　真：0351-8301523

邮　箱：sxsbqj@163. com

网　址：www. sxrt. gov. cn

内蒙古自治区版权局

局　长：姜伯彦

专职副局长：乌恩奇

版权管理处处长：沙　力

地　址：呼和浩特市回民区成吉思汗西街 1 号

邮　编：010050

电　话：0471-4590193

传　真：0471-3288042

邮　箱：nmgbqjbqc@163. com

网　址：www. nmgxwcbgdj. gov. cn

辽宁省版权局

局　长：刘向阳

分管副局长：季秉学

版权管理处处长：李安庆

地　址：沈阳市和平区北一马路 108 号

邮　编：110001

电　话：024-23261003

传　真：024-23261003

邮　箱：lnsbqj@163. com

网　址：www. lnxcgd. gov. cn

吉林省版权局

局　长：许云鹏
分管副局长：姚玉和
版权管理处处长：王培舒
地　址：长春市卫星路 2066 号
邮　编：130033
电　话：0431-85810270
传　真：0431-85816273
邮　箱：jlbqj@sina. com
网　址：www. gdj. jl. gov. cn

黑龙江省版权局

局　长：赵洪生
专职副局长：朱德宝
版权管理处处长：周美胜
地　址：哈尔滨市南岗区汉水路 333 号
邮　编：150090
电　话：0451-82898560
传　真：0451-82898560
邮　箱：hljbanquanju@163. com
网　址：www. hljxwcbgd. gov. cn

上海市版权局

局　长：徐　炯
专职副局长：蔡纪万
版权管理执法处处长：薛　彬
版权产业促进处处长：陈琳琳
地　址：上海市绍兴路 5 号
邮　编：200020
电　话：021-64332452
传　真：021-64332452
邮　箱：bqc@sppa. gov. cn
网　址：www. cbj. sh. gov. cn

江苏省版权局

局　长：焦建俊
分管副局长：于国民
版权管理处处长：陈　晔
地　址：南京市中山东路 132 号
邮　编：210009
电　话：025-58500713
传　真：025-58500730
邮　箱：jsbq2013@126. com
网　址：www. jsxwcbj. gov. cn

浙江省版权局

局　长：寿剑刚
分管副局长：单　烈
版权管理处处长：严庆荣
地　址：杭州市体育场路 178 号
邮　编：310039
电　话：0571-87163108
传　真：0571-87163107
网　址：www. zrt. gov. cn

安徽省版权局

局　长：车敦安
分管副局长：董　荣
版权管理处处长：杨　剑
地　址：合肥市桐城南路 355 号
邮　编：230022
电　话：0551-62846150
传　真：0551-62850751
邮　箱：anhuibanquan@126. com
网　址：www. ahgd. gov. cn

福建省版权局

局　长：陈立华
分管副局长：蒋达德
版权管理处处长：邱建宏
地　址：福州市东水路 76 号
邮　编：350001
电　话：0591-87532711
传　真：0591-87532711
邮　箱：fjbq001@163. com
网　址：www. fjxwgd. gov. cn

江西省版权局

局　长：杨六华
专职副局长：兰丽华
版权管理处处长：阙米秋
地　址：南昌市红谷滩区翠林路 339 号
邮　编：330038
电　话：0791-86895383
传　真：0791-86895383
邮　箱：349354270@qq. com
网　址：www. jxxgj. gov. cn

山东省版权局

局　长：司安民

分管副局长：钟　华
版权管理处处长：张晓生
地　址：济南市经十路18567号
邮　编：250011
电　话：0531-85036507
传　真：0531-85038149
邮　箱：sdbq8606@126. com
网　址：www. sdxg. gov. cn

河南省版权局

局　长：李宏伟
分管副局长：赵　艳
版权管理处处长：李清彬
地　址：郑州市农业路3号
邮　编：450002
电　话：0371-65887227
传　真：0371-65887227
邮　箱：hnsbqj@163. com
网　址：www. hnppb. gov. cn

湖北省版权局

局　长：张良成
专职副局长：胡　伟
版权管理处处长：卢文俊
地　址：武汉市武昌区黄鹂路39号
邮　编：430077
电　话：027-68892414
传　真：027-68892414
网　址：www. hbnp. gov. cn

湖南省版权局

局　长：朱建纲
分管副局长：蒋强先
版权管理处处长：王军湘
地　址：长沙市金鹰影视文化城
邮　编：410003
电　话：0731-84801000
传　真：0731-84801888
邮　箱：hncopyright@126. com
网　址：www. hnxwcbgd. gov. cn

广东省版权局

局　长：白　洁
专职副局长：陈春怀
版权管理处处长：张同英
地　址：广州市环市东路331号广电中心二期
邮　编：510066
电　话：020-37605967
传　真：020-37604405
邮　箱：gdsbqj@126. com
网　址：www. xwcbgdj. gd. gov. cn

广西壮族自治区版权局

局　长：彭　钢
专职副局长：李承武
版权管理处处长：马永志
地　址：南宁市金湖路53号
邮　编：530028
电　话：0771-5516174
传　真：0771-5516087
邮　箱：gxbq123@163. com
网　址：www. gxpprft. gov. cn

海南省版权局

局　长：丁　晖
版权处处长：曾伯林
地　址：海口市海府路59号
邮　编：570203
电　话：0898-65399213
传　真：0898-65399213
邮　箱：wtt. tuyin@hainan. gov. cn
网　址：www. wtt. hainan. gov. cn

重庆市版权局

局　长：张洪斌
巡视员：雷　平
版权管理处处长：左图强
地　址：重庆市江北区鸿恩路25号
邮　编：400020
电　话：023-67502723
传　真：023-67502722
网　址：www. cqwhw. gov. cn

四川省版权局

局　长：邹吉祥
分管副局长：周　青
版权管理处处长：张万富
地　址：成都市红星路二段119号
邮　编：610072
电　话：028-86697076

传　真：028-86696803
邮　箱：sccopyright@163. com
网　址：www. scppa. gov. cn

贵州省版权局
局　长：朱新武
专职副局长：王贤赓
版权管理处处长：傅　琳
地　址：贵阳市延安中路 5～9 号
邮　编：550002
电　话：0851-85813428
传　真：0851-85813428
邮　箱：2534243157@qq. com
网　址：www. gzpp. gov. cn

云南省版权局
局　长：梁宗华
分管副局长：洪耀星
版权管理处处长：张　雯
地　址：昆明市人民西路 182 号
邮　编：650031
电　话：0871-65310920
传　真：0871-65310920
邮　箱：bqj@ynppb. gov. cn
网　址：www. ynxgj. gov. cn

西藏自治区版权局
局　长：韩　辉
分管副局长：刘　俐
版权管理处处长：张百忍
地　址：拉萨市江冲路 7 号
邮　编：850000
电　话：0891-6356150
传　真：0891-6356150

陕西省版权局
局　长：钱远刚
专职副局长：沙庆超
地　址：西安市长安南路 336 号
邮　编：710061
电　话：029-85496118
传　真：029-85496158
邮　箱：sxbqc@163. com
网　址：www. srftd. gov. cn

甘肃省版权局
局　长：管钰年
副巡视员：武志元
版权管理处处长：夏　玲
地　址：兰州市东岗西路 226 号
邮　编：730000
电　话：0931-8539060
传　真：0931-8539408
邮　箱：gsbqh@163. com
网　址：www. gsgd. gov. cn

青海省版权局
局　长：高玉峰
分管副局长：周　宇
政策法规（版权）处处长：朱桂英
地　址：西宁市同仁路 10 号
邮　编：810001
电　话：0971-6141050，6143650
传　真：0971-6143650
邮　箱：qhsbqc@163. com

宁夏回族自治区版权局
局　长：马宇桢
分管副局长：黄占宝
地　址：银川市金凤区北京中路 66 号
邮　编：750001
电　话：0951-5117173
传　真：0951-5117173
邮　箱：nxbqj815@163. com
网　址：www. nxgdj. gov. cn

新疆维吾尔自治区版权局
局　长：古力先・吐拉洪
版权管理处处长：施晓娟
地　址：乌鲁木齐市北京南路 591 号
邮　编：830011
电　话：0991-2385490
传　真：0991-3637555
邮　箱：xjbqj@sina. cn
网　址：www. xjgdj. gov. cn

版权公共服务机构

中国版权保护中心
主 任：段桂鉴
副主任：索来军 魏 红 范继红
地 址：北京市西城区天桥南大街1号天桥艺术大厦A座
电 话：010-68003887
邮 编：100050
网 址：www.ccopyright.com

北京版权保护中心
主 任：薛 峰
地 址：北京市东城区朝阳门内大街55号新闻出版大厦
邮 编：100010
电 话：010-64081206
传 真：010-64081900
邮 箱：bcpc@bjcab.gov.cn
网 址：www.bjcopyright.org.cn

北京计算机软件登记中心
主 任：崔玉军
地 址：北京市东城区朝阳门内大街55号新闻出版大厦
邮 编：100010
电 话：010-64081391
传 真：010-64081204
邮 箱：bcpc@bjcab.gov.cn
网 址：www.bjcab.gov.cnjsjrjdjzx2009110915682.html

河北省版权保护中心
主 任：刘 浏
地 址：石家庄市和平西路新文里8号
邮 编：050071
电 话：0311-67561197
传 真：0311-67561176
网 址：www.hebeibanquan.gov.cn/new

浙江省版权服务中心
主 任：张蓓君
地 址：杭州市庆春路219号601～603室
邮 编：310006
电 话：0571-88137853
传 真：0571-85062879
网 址：www.zjbanquan.org

江西省版权保护中心
主 任：赖政兵
调研员：聂文星
地 址：南昌市红谷滩区翠林路339号
邮 编：330038
电 话：0791-86894610
传 真：0791-86895220
网 址：www.jxbq.gov.cn

湖北省版权保护中心
主 任：郑凌辉
地 址：武汉市武昌区公正路9号
邮 编：430071
电 话：027-87329148
传 真：027-87329148
网 址：www.ccct.net.cn

重庆市版权保护中心
副主任：王 京
地 址：重庆市江北区洋河一村78号
邮 编：400020
电 话：023-67708231
传 真：023-67708231
邮 箱：cpc1604@yahoo.com.cn
网 址：www.cqca.com.cn

山西版权保护中心
主 任：王克冰
地 址：太原市并州北路31号
邮 编：030001
电 话：0351-4088107
传 真：0351-4113046
邮 箱：sxbanquan@163.com

版权协会

中国版权协会

理事长：阎晓宏

驻会副理事长：王自强

秘书长：孙　悦

地　址：北京市朝阳区焦化路甲 18 号北京出版产业创意园先导区 3 层 335 室

邮　编：100023

电　话：010-68003910

传　真：010-68003910

邮　箱：csc68003910@163. com

网　址：www. csccn. org. cn

北京市版权保护协会

负责人：刘志伟

地　址：北京市朝阳区呼家楼北里 2 号楼 4 门 303

邮　编：100026

电　话：010-64460903

邮　箱：bjbqbhxh@163. com

天津市版权保护协会

会　长：李树仁

秘书长：陈燕丽

地　址：天津市河西区卫津路 241 号金桥国际宾馆

邮　编：300074

电　话：022-23377538

传　真：022-23377538

邮　箱：tca2011@126. com

河北省版权协会

会　长：陈建英

秘书长：刘　浏

地　址：石家庄市和平西路新文里 8 号

邮　编：050071

电　话：0311-67561177

传　真：0311-67561112

邮　箱：hebeibanquan@126. com

网　址：www. hebeibanquan. gov. cn

山西省版权协会

会　长：张金柱

副会长：杨志云

秘书长：王　琦

地　址：太原市建设南路 21 号

邮　编：030012

电　话：0351-4956162

传　真：0351-4956162

邮　箱：3523482@163. com

内蒙古自治区版权保护协会

会　长：高金祥

秘书长：志　民

地　址：呼和浩特市新城区老缸房街 18 号印刷物资楼 202

邮　编：010010

电　话：0471-4967453

传　真：0471-4967453

邮　箱：1371951119@qq. com

辽宁省版权保护协会

负责人：李安庆

地　址：沈阳市和平区北一马路 108 号

邮　编：110001

电　话：024-23261003

传　真：024-23261003

吉林省版权保护协会

会　长：朱　彤

秘书长：李长江

地　址：长春市卫星路 2066 号

邮　编：130033

电　话：0431-85816284

传　真：0431-85644760

邮　箱：brli@163. com

黑龙江省版权保护协会

秘书长：周美胜

地　址：哈尔滨市南岗区汉水路 333 号

邮　编：150090

电　话：0451-88622758
传　真：0451-82898560
邮　箱：hljbanquanju@163.com

黑龙江省反盗版联合会
秘书长：周美胜
地　址：哈尔滨市道里区森林街 68 号
邮　编：150010
电　话：0451-88622758
传　真：0451-82898560
邮　箱：hljbanquanju@163.com

上海版权协会
会　长：胡大卫
秘书长：张　宏
地　址：上海市张江路 69 号 612
电　话：021-50278103
传　真：021-50278103

江苏省版权协会
会　长：傅杰三
常务副会长：于国民
地　址：南京市鼓楼区高云岭 56 号
邮　编：210009
电　话：025-83207838
传　真：025-83207838
电子邮箱：jssbqxh@163.com

浙江省版权协会
会　长：单　烈
秘书长：吾晓红
地　址：杭州市庆春路 219 号 6 楼
邮　编：310006
电　话：0571-88137853
传　真：0571-88137853

安徽省版权保护协会
理事长：李金华
秘书长：杨　剑
地　址：合肥市桐城南路 355 号 A 座 1705
邮　编：230022
电　话：0551-64399912，62850753
传　真：0551-62850751
邮　箱：anhuibanquan@126.com

福建省版权协会
会　长：白京兆
秘书长：刘行宇
地　址：福州市东水路 76 号
邮　编：350001
电　话：0591-87535956
传　真：0591-87535956
邮　箱：fjsbqxh@163.com

山东省版权协会
地　址：济南市经十路 18567 号旧楼 1414
邮　编：250062
电　话：0531-85038149
传　真：0531-85038149

河南省版权协会
负责人：赵　艳
秘书长：李清彬
地　址：郑州市农业路 3 号
邮　编：450002
电　话：0371-65887627
传　真：0371-65887227
邮　箱：hnsbqj@163.com

湖北省版权保护协会
会　长：陈　锋
秘书长：赵文福
地　址：武汉市武昌区黄鹂路 39 号
电　话：027-68892562

湖南省版权保护协会（湖南省反盗版联盟）
会　长：张树青
秘书长：张树青
地　址：长沙市营盘东路 3 号
邮　编：410005
电　话：0731-82231655
传　真：0731-82231655

广东省版权保护联合会（广东省版权事务所）
常务副会长：陈冬云
秘书长：梁守坚
地　址：广州市环市东水荫路 44 号 2 楼
邮　编：510075
电　话：020-37667333，37638239
传　真：020-37638192

邮　箱：gdcopyright@gdpg. com. cn

广西壮族自治区版权保护协会

会　长：于开金
秘书长：石　卫
地　址：南宁市金湖路 53 号
邮　编：530028
电　话：0771-5516087
传　真：0771-5516087
邮　箱：gxbqbhxh@163. com

海南省版权协会

会　长：王　琦
秘书长：唐　俐
地　址：海口市海南大学社科联楼 708
邮　编：570228
电　话：0898-66259079
传　真：0898-66259079
邮　箱：18907526181@189. cn

四川省版权保护协会

负责人：李正培
地　址：成都市红星路二段 119 号
邮　编：610075
电　话：028-86697076
传　真：028-86696803

云南省著作权保护协会

会　长：艾罕炳
秘书长：马云虹
地　址：昆明市环城西路 609 号新闻出版大楼
邮　编：650034
电　话：0871-64110371
传　真：0871-64110371

陕西省版权协会

会　长：曹先觉
秘书长：党　雷
地　址：西安市雁塔区曲江行政商务区陕西文化大厦 B 座
电　话：029-89131695
传　真：029-89131698

新疆维吾尔自治区版权协会

会　长：古力先·吐拉洪
秘书长：施晓娟
地　址：乌鲁木齐市北京南路 591 号
邮　编：830011
电　话：0991-3637542
传　真：0991-3637555

深圳市版权协会

会　长：詹培明
秘书长：陈　彦
地　址：深圳市福田区梅林路 19 号斯达大厦 6 楼 602
邮　编：518106
电　话：0755-86185519
传　真：0755-86185516
邮　箱：szcopyright@163. com
网　址：www. scs. org. cn

宁波市版权协会

会　长：陆开江
地　址：宁波市江东区兴宁路 53 号
邮　编：315000
电　话：0574-89187806
传　真：0574-89187806
邮　箱：nbbq2011@126. com
网　址：www. nbbqxh. com

苏州市版权协会

会　长：张　梅
秘书长：冯　坚
地　址：苏州市干将路 178 号苏州大学北校区科技园 309（中）
邮　编：215004
电　话：0512-65156801
传　真：0512-65156801

青岛市版权保护协会

会　长：张　焱
秘书长：封红雨
地　址：青岛市市北区郑州路 43 号 A 栋 125
邮　编：266045
电　话：0532-67773267
邮　箱：gy1@rubbervalley. com
网　址：bqbh. org. cn/n23734668/index. html

大连市版权保护协会
会　长：李东平
秘书长：李毅男
地　址：大连市西安路107号
邮　编：116021
电　话：0411-84522067
传　真：0411-84522067
邮　箱：wgj_dcpa@dl.gov.cn
网　址：www.dcpa.org.cn

南京市版权保护协会
会　长：江　飞
常务副会长：杜维鸣
秘书长：陈　锷
地　址：南京市秦淮区瑞金北村57幢5楼
邮　编：210016
电　话：025-85659022，84645491
传　真：025-85659011
邮　箱：1148694563@qq.com
网　址：www.njbq.org.cn

郑州市版权协会
会　长：董现仓
秘书长：倪天礼
地　址：郑州市西太康路19号郑州购书中心820
邮　编：450018
电　话：0371-66280990
网　址：www.zzbq.org

厦门市版权协会
秘书长：詹朝晖
地　址：厦门市软件园二期望海路6号303
邮　编：361008
电　话：0592-5914419
传　真：0592-2070020-807
邮　箱：412324212@qq.com

著作权集体管理组织

中国音乐著作权协会
主　席：赵季平
总干事：屈景明
地　址：北京市东单三条33号京纺大厦5层
邮　编：100005
电　话：010-65232656
传　真：010-65232657
网　址：www.mcsc.com.cn

中国音像著作权集体管理协会
理事长：周建潮
常务理事长兼总干事：邹建华
地　址：北京市朝阳区呼家楼京广中心商务楼401
邮　编：100020
电　话：010-66086468
传　真：010-66086475
邮　箱：cavca@cavca.org
网　址：www.cavca.org

中国文字著作权协会
会　长：陈建功
总干事：张洪波
地　址：北京市西城区珠市口西大街太丰惠中大厦1027～1036
邮　编：100050
电　话：010-65978905
传　真：010-65978926
邮　箱：wenzhuxie@126.com
网　址：www.prccopyright.org.cn

中国电影著作权协会
理事长：任仲伦
副秘书长：史文霞
地　址：北京市西城区北展北街5号楼F座5层
邮　编：100044
电　话：010-62364640
传　真：010-62369799
邮　箱：cfcac2009@163.com

网　址：www. cfca-c. org

中国摄影著作权协会

主　席：李前光
副总干事：林涛
地　址：北京市东城区东四 12 条 48 号
邮　编：100007
电　话：010-65978100
传　真：010-65595720
邮　箱：hyb@icschina. net
网　址：www. icsc1839. org

版权相关行业协会

中国互联网协会网络版权工作委员会

主　任：高卢麟
秘书长：石现升
地　址：北京市海淀区板井路曙光花园智业园 B 座 6E
邮　编：100097
电　话：010-88466861-815
传　真：010-88546086
网　址：www. iscu. cn

中国音像与数字出版协会

理事长：孙寿山
常务副理事长兼秘书长：王　炬
地　址：北京市西城区莲花池东路 102 号天莲大厦 17 层
邮　编：100055
电　话：010-65122882
传　真：010-65127030
邮　箱：cava2008@163. com
网　址：www. cadpa. org. cn

版权代理公司

中华版权代理总公司

总经理：贺传军
地　址：北京市西城区天桥南大街 1 号天桥艺术大厦 A 座 4 层
邮　编：100050
电　话：010-68003887，84195154
传　真：010-84195860
网　址：www. ccopyrightagency. com. cn

中国图书进出口（集团）总公司版权部

主　任：雷建华
地　址：北京市朝阳区工体东路 16 号
邮　编：100020
电　话：010-65069500
邮　箱：publishing@cnpiec. com. cn

中国出版对外贸易总公司

地　址：北京市朝阳区安定门外安华里 504 号
邮　编：100011
电　话：010-64210403
传　真：010-64214540
网　址：www. cnpitc. com. cn

中国国际电视总公司

地　址：北京市海淀区羊坊店路 9 号京门大厦
邮　编：100038
电　话：010-63950016
传　真：010-63955916
邮　箱：office@citvc. com
网　址：www. citvc. com. cn

九洲音像出版公司版权贸易部

负责人：吕艺鸥
地　址：北京市朝阳区外馆斜街甲 1 号泰利明苑 A 座 510
邮　编：100011

电　话：010-85285083

北京版权代理有限责任公司

负责人：刘志伟

地　址：北京市海淀区知春路 23 号量子银座 1403

邮　编：100191

电　话：010-82915383

湖南省版权代理公司

负责人：张树清

地　址：长沙市营盘东路 3 号

邮　编：410005

电　话：0731-82231655

重庆市版权代理有限公司

负责人：王　京

地　址：重庆市江北区洋河一村 78 号国际商会大厦 10 楼

邮　编：400020

电　话：023-67708231

传　真：023-67708231

邮　箱：934986845@qq. com

国家级版权交易机构

中国人民大学国家版权贸易基地

执行主任：白连永

地　址：北京市海淀区中关村大街甲 59 号文化大厦 403

邮　编：100872

电　话：010-62513050

传　真：010-82509959

邮　箱：copyrightyb@163. com

网　址：www. copyrightmall. com

北京国际版权交易中心

董事长：李　蘅

地　址：北京市朝阳区京广中心商务楼 2 层

邮　编：100020

电　话：010-65974890（总机）

传　真：010-65978017

邮　箱：kf@icfea. com

网　址：www. e-bq. com

东方雍和国际版权交易中心

董事长：殷秩松

地　址：北京市东城区安定门东大街 28 号雍和大厦 E 座 208

邮　编：100007

电　话：010-64097700

传　真：010-84195406

邮　箱：public@cbice. com

网　址：www. cbice. com

华中国家版权交易中心

主　任：郑凌辉

地　址：武汉市武昌区公正路 9 号

邮　编：430077

电　话：027-68892430

传　真：027-68892414

网　址：www. ccct. net

成都国家版权交易中心

执行主任：杨　蛟

地　址：成都市高新区世纪城南路 599 号 2 栋 1 层 103、104 号

邮　编：610213

电　话：028-61375595

网　址：www. cdice. com. cn

国家版权贸易基地（上海）

负责人：任义彪

地　址：中国（上海）自由贸易试验区马吉路 2 号 33 层

邮　编：200131

电　话：021-58697777

传　真：021-58698366

邮　箱：fenglan@soict. com. cn

网　址：www. soict. com. cn

广州市越秀区国家版权贸易基地

董事长：黎伟成

地　址：广州市越秀区文德北路 68 号
邮　编：510030
电　话：020-83349123
邮　箱：123@banquanmaoyi. com
网　址：www. cnscee. com

台儿庄国家版权贸易基地
管理办公室主任：黄　伟
地　址：枣庄市台儿庄区文化路 258 号
邮　编：277400
电　话：0632-6611762
传　真：0632-6611762

青岛国际版权交易中心
总经理：封红雨
地　址：青岛市郑州路 43 号橡胶谷 A 栋 134
邮　编：266045
电　话：0532-81638255
传　真：0532-68662009
邮　箱：lijs@rubbervalley. com
网　址：www. nctcqd. com

国家海峡版权交易中心
总经理：王　斌
地　址：厦门市软件园二期望海路 6 号 2 层
邮　编：361008
电　话：0592-5953686
传　真：0592-5953687

邮　箱：contact@hxnce. net
网　址：www. hxnce. net

西部国家版权交易中心
总经理：党　雷
地　址：西安市雁塔区雁塔南路陕西文化大厦 B 座 6 楼
邮　编：710061
电　话：029-89131653
传　真：029-89131698
邮　箱：ctvtc _ china@163. com
网　址：www. xtce. cn

横琴国际版权交易中心
负责人：陈钦禄
地　址：珠海市香洲区海洲路 8 号九昌大厦 6C
邮　编：519015
电　话：0756-3211668
传　真：0765-3210567

国家版权交易中心联盟
负责人：李　蘅
地　址：北京市朝阳区京广中心商务楼 2 层
邮　编：100020
电　话：010-65974890
传　真：010-65978017
邮　箱：kf@icfea. com

知识产权教学与研究机构

中国人民大学知识产权学院
地　址：北京市海淀区中关村大街甲 59 号中国人民大学明德法学楼 612
邮　编：100872
电　话：010-82500369
传　真：010-62514365
邮　箱：law612@126. com
网　址：www. law. ruc. edu. cn

北京大学知识产权学院
地　址：北京大学凯原楼 309
邮　编：100871
电　话：010-62751268
邮　箱：zscq@pku. edu. cn
网　址：www. iplaw. pku. edu. cn

中国社会科学院知识产权中心
地　址：北京市东城区沙滩北街 15 号
邮　编：100720
电　话：010-64054144
传　真：010-64014045
邮　箱：ipstudies@163. com
网　址：www. iolaw. org. cn

中国政法大学民商法经济法学院知识产权研究所
地　址：北京市昌平区府学路 27 号
邮　编：102249
电　话：010-58909336
网　址：msjjfxy. cupl. edu. cn

中南财经政法大学知识产权学院
地　址：武汉市东湖高新技术开发区南湖大道 182 号
邮　编：430073
电　话：027-88386364
网　址：www. iprcn. com

上海大学知识产权学院
地　址：上海市上大路 99 号
邮　编：200444
电　话：021-66133937
传　真：021-66133938
网　址：www. ips. shu. edu. cn

华中科技大学科技法与知识产权系
地　址：武汉市洪山区珞瑜路 1037 号东 4 楼
邮　编：430074
电　话：87545438
传　真：027-87542228
邮　箱：stud201@hust. edu. cn
网　址：www. hust. edu. cn

复旦大学知识产权研究中心
地　址：上海市淞沪路 2005 号法学楼 410
邮　编：200438
电　话：021-51630042
传　真：021-51630112
邮　箱：zhangng@fudan. edu. cn
网　址：www. ipcenter. fudan. edu. cn

华东政法大学知识产权学院
地　址：上海市松江区龙源路 555 号
邮　编：201620
电　话：021-57090083
邮　箱：zsb@ecupl. edu. cn
网　址：www. ipschool. ecupl. edu. cn

暨南大学知识产权学院
地　址：广州市黄埔大道西 601 号
邮　编：510632
电　话：020-85228561
邮　箱：ozsb@jnu. edu. cn
网　址：law. jnu. edu. cn

同济大学知识产权学院
地　址：上海市四平路 1239 号同济大学综合楼 1001
邮　编：200092
电　话：021-65983113
邮　箱：sicip@mail. tongji. edu. cn
网　址：law. tongji. edu. cn

武汉大学知识产权高级研究中心
地　址：武汉市武昌区珞珈山街 16 号
邮　编：430072
电　话：027-68753447
邮　箱：wdzsb@whu. edu. cn
网　址：www. whu. edu. cn

西安交通大学知识产权学院
地　址：西安市咸宁西路 28 号
邮　编：710049
电　话：029-82665824
邮　箱：xjtuzs@mail. xjtu. edu. cn
网　址：fxy. xjtu. edu. cn

中国科学技术大学知识产权研究中心
地　址：合肥市金寨路 96 号
邮　编：230026
电　话：0551-63492241
邮　箱：songlan@ustc. edu. cn
网　址：pas. ustc. edu. cn

西北大学知识产权学院
地　址：西安市长安学府大道 1 号
邮　编：710127
电　话：029-029-88308080
传　真：029-88308079
邮　箱：lawdep@nwu. edu. cn
网　址：fxy. nwu. edu. cn

华南理工大学知识产权学院
地　址：广州市广州大学城华南理工大学 B9
邮　编：510006

电　话：020-39380308
传　真：020-39380308
邮　箱：scutg06@scut. edu. cn
网　址：www. scut. edu. cn/iplaw

南京理工大学知识产权学院

地　址：南京市孝陵卫 200 号
邮　编：210094
电　话：025-84303386
传　真：025-84303386
网　址：ip. njust. edu. cn

中山大学知识产权学院

地　址：广州市新港西路 135 号
邮　编：510275
电　话：020-84113148
网　址：www. law. sysu. edu. cn

重庆知识产权学院（重庆理工大学知识产权学院）

地　址：重庆市巴南区李家沱红光大道 69 号重庆理工大学花溪校区
邮　编：400054
电　话：023-62563375
传　真：023-62563375
邮　箱：cgzs@cqut. edu. cn
网　址：ipschool. cqut. edu. cn

湘潭大学知识产权学院

地　址：湘潭市雨湖区湘潭大学法学院知识产权学院
邮　编：411105
电　话：0731-58292281
邮　箱：zscqxy@xtu. edu. cn
网　址：ipf. xtu. edu. cn

厦门大学知识产权研究院

地　址：厦门市思明南路 422 号
邮　编：361005
电　话：0592-2182729
传　真：0592-2182729
邮　箱：ip@xmu. edu. cn
网　址：www. iprixmu. com

西南政法大学知识产权研究中心（民商法学院）

地　址：重庆市渝北区宝圣大道 301 号西南政法大学集美楼 3 楼
邮　编：401120
电　话：023-67258430
邮　箱：xsczsb@supsl. cn
网　址：ccls. swupl. edu. cn

深圳大学知识产权学院

地　址：深圳市南山区南海大道 3688 号
邮　编：518060
电　话：0755-26534171
传　真：0755-26535115
邮　箱：szu _ ip@163. com
网　址：www. law. szu. edu. cn

中南大学知识产权研究院

地　址：长沙市麓山南路 932 号
邮　编：410012
电　话：0731-88660480
传　真：0731-88660291
邮　箱：admis@mail. csu. edu. cn
网　址：law. csu. edu. cn/zscq/

附录：国际版权动态

FU LU：GUO JI BAN QUAN DONG TAI

著作权在数字时代的保护与限制

——2016 年国际著作权法制发展回顾

郭　禾　吕凌锐

随着以计算机技术为基础的数字技术和网络技术的普及运用和迅猛发展，作品的利用和传播变得更为便捷。这一方面导致了利用数字技术和网络环境侵犯著作权的活动在全球范围变得日益猖獗，如视听作品、音乐作品及软件作品常常在网络环境中被非法传播，严重损害了著作权人的利益。另一方面，由于诸多涉网行为在相关法律规定中的界定尚不清晰，致使图书馆、博物馆等公共机构及科研机构在利用数字和网络技术复制、传播作品信息的同时，亦面临承担侵犯著作权责任的风险。2016 年，世界上的主要国家和与知识产权相关的国际组织在著作权立法和司法方面的主要工作，无不是为了适应数字时代的发展，围绕打击网络环境中的盗版行为、保护著作权人的利益，并同时为捍卫公众的言论或信息传播自由而在一定程度上扩大公共机构、科研机构在著作权限制或例外的范围而展开的。

一、网络环境下的著作权保护的强化

（一）避风港原则与网络中立原则

在数字互联网背景下，侵犯著作权行为一般都需要技术平台的支持才能完成，这种帮助行为在侵权过程中的地位和作用正逐渐为大家所认知。如何规制平台的行为，以及准确划分其与直接侵权行为人之间的责任就成为一项重要的课题。由于提供技术帮助行为在现实中越来越普遍，对技术帮助行为的定性也越来越困难。为应对数字技术时代的挑战而创建的避风港原则是否应当适用、应如何适用再度成为一个重要问题。目前，国际上应对网络环境下侵犯著作权行为的规则主要是“通知—删除”规则，它最早出现于美国《数字千年版权法》（DMCA）第 512 条中，即当著作权人发现网上有侵权作品时，需要向该网站的网络服务提供商发出侵权通知，请求删除侵权作品或屏蔽、断开链接，网络服务提供商在接到通知后应采取必要的措施。尽管该规则在保护著作权人利益方面发挥了一定的作用，但在实践中也存在如下问题：例如，一些网络服务提供商故意纵容网络用户上传侵权作品，在著作权人要求追究其责任时，却以未收到侵权通知、主观上不知道为由逃避法律责任，从而使著作权人的利益难以得到保护。另外，虽然反通知制度一定程度上弱化了著作权人错发移除通知所产生的后果，但其并不能根本解决著作权人滥用“通知—删除”程序的问题。滥用这种“通知—删除”手段不仅有损于公众言论自由和获得信息的公共利益，而且也给网络服务商带来过重的负担。有鉴于此，目前以欧美为代表的发达国家正在考虑对“通知—删除”规则和网络中立原则做适当调整使其更加完善。

2016 年 10 月 31 日，美国版权局发布了对指定版权代理建立电子系统的新规则，这一规则旨在利用避风港条款使得网络服务提供商豁免侵权。根据《美国法典 17》第 5 章第 512 条，网络服务提供商通常是指任何提供在线服务（如网站、电子邮件服务、讨论论坛或聊天室）的运营商；版权代理人通常是指网络服务提供商为接收侵犯著作权之类的通知而指定的代理人，该代理人的联系方式应当提供给版权局。在新的电子系统下，2016 年 12 月 1 日起所有网络服务提供商（包括已经向版权局指定过代理人的网络服务提供商）基于第 512 条的规定寻求避风港保护时，必须通过该电子系统提交指定代理人信息，版权局将不再接受纸质系统的指定。之前提交过纸质版信息的必须在 2017 年 12 月 31 日前在电子系统中提交新的指定代理人信息，否则将不受避风港规则的保护。不仅如此，版权指定代理人信息每三年至少更新一次，注册及后续更新费用

为 6 美元/次[①]。由此，美国新的版权代理电子申请注册系统将逐步全面取代基于纸张的申请系统。美国版权信息中心（The Center for Copyright Information，CCI）宣布，截至 2016 年 12 月 31 日，经过四年来消费者广泛的参与及对消费者的教育，将结束版权预警系统（Copyright Alert System，CAS）[②]的使命，备受争议的“六振”版权预警系统将不再适用[③]。

此外，网络链接行为的法律属性也在这期间成为业界关注的重点问题。其中主要涉及平台服务商在何等程度上需要对链接行为承担侵犯著作权的责任。欧盟法院（CJEU）在 2016 年 9 月 8 日处理了一起人们期待已久的关于链接未经授权的内容的侵权纠纷[④]。法院认为，如果涉链行为涉及营利目的，则涉链人有义务了解被链内容是否属于合法上传。而此前的 Sevennson 案[⑤]已经确立了若链接为得到作者同意的已出版内容则不侵权。与此同时欧盟法院还在审理一个关于零售商是否可以不加任何保护地为其顾客提供免费的 Wi-Fi 网络接入服务的案件。该案件的争议在于当顾客自己访问了一些未经作者同意而被传上网的作品后，该零售商提供免费接入网络的服务行为是否构成侵犯著作权[⑥]。

所有这些案件的焦点都涉及网络平台在侵犯著作权行为中的地位和作用。法律上是否应当将网络平台作为侵犯著作权的共同行为人？很显然，如果没有平台的帮助，侵权行为是不可能完成的。但平台在这个过程中是否存在侵权的故意，无论直接故意还是间接故意，都将成为判定平台是否应当承担责任的重要考量因素。当然对于什么是平台，在现实中亦有不同的界定。但在这些案件中，无论是网络接入服务的提供者，还是链接他人网站的设链者，其面临的法律问题在性质上是相同的。这直接涉及如何理解技术中立或网络中立原则。更进一步就是如何适用避风港原则。从各国近年来的司法实践和法律解释看，强化互联网环境下的著作权的保护已经成为总体趋势。

2015 年 12 月美国弗吉尼亚州的一个联邦陪审团裁定互联网服务提供商 Cox Communications 对其用户的侵犯著作权的行为负有责任的案件就是一个例证。这个互联网服务提供商因没有适当地封锁重复侵权行为人的账号而不能获得安全港保护，并被认为应承担主观故意的共同侵权责任。Cox 公司提起上诉，希望能推翻 2 500 万美元赔偿的判决，音乐出版商 BMG 版权管理却支持该判决。Cox 公司的主张已获得了若干行业协会、学术机构以及电子前沿基金会（EFF）的支持。2016 年 12 月，电子前沿基金会（EFF）再次强调了本案判决结果的重要性。这些组织认为，接入互联网应被视为一项人的基本权利，它不应该被著作权人所控制。著作权人不应该基于侵犯著作权的主张而享有禁止他人接入互联网的权利。EFF 承认《数字千年版权法》要求互联网服务提供商应当有应对重复侵权行为的政策。然而，DMCA 并没有明确单方的盗版指控就足以导致如此结果。EFF 指出：“没有人应当由于不确定的指控而忍受被切断与互联网连接的忧虑和恐惧。实践中，著作权人的指控并不总是准确的。即使跟踪到正确的 IP 地址，也并不意味着账户所有人就是分享侵权材料的人。是否是重复侵权行为人不应当由通过不作为获取利润的盗版检测结构决定，而应当由法庭来决定。”[⑦]

（二）网络环境下侵犯著作权犯罪刑事责任

2016 年，相关国家的著作权立法有加重网络版权犯罪的刑事责任的趋势。随着数字技术的进步，英美等国家试图通过强化侵犯著作权罪制度进一步规制数字时代的盗版行为。2016 年 7 月，英国政府提出了《英国数字经济法案》。法案内容之一是加强

---

① Digital millennium copyright act：new DMCA safe harbor copyright agent requirements for online services providers [EB/OL]. http://www.natlawreview.com/article/digital-millennium-copyright-act-new-dmca-safe-harbor-copyright-agent-requirements，2016－11－03.

② 作为美国电话电报公司（AT&T）、康卡斯特、时代华纳有线电视公司等主要互联网服务提供商之间订立的自愿协议结果，CAS 由三层级的警报构成，每一层级又包括两个独立的警报，共计六次警报。警告一到警告四是教育和确认警告，其目的是教育网民观看盗版内容是非法的，并通知他们通过合法途径来获取内容。网民持续性的行为将导致警告升级，并可能招致连接速度受限的惩罚措施。警告五和六是缓解警告，要求订阅者与其网络服务提供商联系或在线观看更多的反盗版教育材料。

③ Controversial “six strikes” Copyright Alert System laid to rest in the US [EB/OL]. http://www.techspot.com/news/67947-controversial-ix-strikes-copyright-alert-system-laid-rest.html，2017－01－29.

④ GS Media v. Sanoma (Case 160/15).

⑤ Nils Svensson and others v. Retriever Sverige AB (C-466/12).

⑥ McFadden v. Sony Music Entertainment Germany GmbH (C-484/14).

⑦ Unfounded piracy claims shouldn't lead to internet cut-offs [EB/OL]. https://torrentfreak.com/unfounded-piracy-claims-shouldnt-lead-to-internet-cut-offs-161213/，2016－12－13.

对网络知识产权的保护①。其中最具争议的决定是将网络环境下侵犯著作权刑事犯罪的最高监禁期从2年提高到10年②。类似地，美国在《反电子盗窃法案》、《数字千年版权法》及《作者权利及反盗版法案》等一系列重要的法律出台之后，在侵犯著作权犯罪构成的主观目的、客观罪状、量刑指南改革等多领域完成了相应的改革，使其侵犯著作权犯罪刑事责任体系正式进入了数字技术时代。2015年11月5日，由美国主导的《跨太平洋伙伴关系协议》（TPP）草案公之于众。协议稿的知识产权条款明显体现了“TRIPs-plus”特征，构建出更高的知识产权国际保护标准。从TPP的刑事条款中可以看到，美国是将本国关于版权法的刑事责任定罪条款、刑事处罚内容以及《联邦量刑指南》的规定等普遍化为各缔约国均应该遵守的内容，从而提出了一个侵犯版权犯罪刑事责任体系领域的“美国标准”。在此基础上在某些具体问题上（如入罪门槛）甚至提出了比本国更高的版权保护标准。尽管由于2016年美国政府的换届导致美国退出《跨太平洋伙伴关系协议》谈判，但是美国并没有改变通过这一协议所反映出的打击盗版犯罪的态度和在相关国家国掀起打击盗版犯罪行动的决心。有学者认为这一标准可能会成为其国内法中的刑事条款，进而实施更为严格的盗版犯罪刑事惩治的法律体系③。鉴于侵犯著作权犯罪的定罪门槛不断降低，普通社会主体涉嫌实施侵犯著作权犯罪的案件时有发生。例如，基于《在下坂本，有何贵干?》《未来日记》《进击的巨人》《暗杀教室》《浪客剑心》等各类知名漫画的出版社和著作权人的控告，日本京都府警方在2016年11月30日逮捕了一名经营“扫描书籍”店铺的男子，并准备首次对书籍扫描的营业者提起刑事诉讼。据报道，该男子将顾客送来的书籍在自己的扫描仪上将其电子化，然后通过网盘传输交付顾客。该店铺不仅就书籍电子化这一步骤收取费用，还应顾客的请求将电子数据直接复制到光盘进行贩卖。根据警方的调查，该名男子自2011年左右开始经营“扫描书籍”店铺，截至案发大约受理了2.6万点（大约17万本档案）的扫描书记申请，至少实现了750万日元的营业额④。

二、适度扩大网络环境下的著作权限制

（一）图书馆、档案馆的侵权责任豁免

数字化时代为图书馆和档案馆等存储和传播信息打开了一扇新的大门。但是，在从事信息的保存和传播活动时，图书馆和档案馆时常面临侵犯著作权的风险。因此它们要求世界知识产权组织（WIPO）版权委员会不仅要为它们制定一些版权例外，而且要为它们制定一些规避责任的保护措施。WIPO版权及相关权常设委员会（SCCR）于2016年11月14日至18日召开会议，讨论图书馆与档案馆版权例外与限制。11月17日，图书管理员与档案管理员的代表在发言中解释了他们需要的保护其免于承担侵犯版权责任的国际标准。他们认为，“图书馆和档案馆都是遵纪守法的组织，它们一直努力尊重版权，但今天的法律太过复杂难以驾驭，图书管理员和档案管理员无意间就侵犯了版权”⑤。美国档案管理员协会的代表认为：“现有技术可以在全球范围让档案管理员发挥其影响力，但侵权的风险让我们对数字时代望而却步。”该代表指出，档案不应当是被珍藏起来的物品，而应当是日常用品，如同信件、报告、照片和计算机文件等。档案管理员并不要求为所欲为，仅仅希望确保其在履行基本职责时不会因承担法律诉讼费或罚款，耗尽他们微薄的预算。“我们需要避风港，我们会善意地开展我们的工作。”国际图书馆协会联合会（IFLA）也表示，版权法非常复杂，图书管理员和档案管理员是训练有素的专业人士，但并非律师。许多图书馆和档案馆都在按照政府的指令实施数字保存计划，但常常为了完成任务而置身侵权风险之下。因此，图书馆电子信息联盟主张，“为了给图书管理员和档案管理员的行为在法律上留出空间，应当将法律责任加以限制。具体而言，在判定为帮助侵犯版权的情形下，图书馆或者档案馆不用承担责任”。图书馆电子信息

① UK proposes to tighten IP protections online [EB/OL]. http://www.ip-watch.org/2016/07/06/uk-proposes-to-tighten-ip-protections-online/, 2016-07-06.

② Bill documents—Digital Economy Act 2017 [EB/OL]. http://services.parliament.uk/bills/2016-17/digitaleconomy/documents.html. 根据《1988年版权、外观设计和专利法案》规定，主要“实体”版权刑事罪行可判处的最高刑期为10年，网络侵权条例规定的监禁期为两年。

③ 张燕龙. 数字技术时代我国版权保护的刑事路径思考：以美国版权犯罪立法的转型为参照［J］. 政治与法律，2017（4）.

④ 自炊代行業の男性、著作権法違反容疑で逮捕、データの使い回しや古書店への転売も行っており「極めて悪質」[EB/OL]. http://internet.watch.impress.co.jp/docs/news/1032544.html. 2016-11-30.

⑤ Librarians, Archivists. Call on WIPO members to create safe harbour against copyright liability [EB/OL]. http://www.ip-watch.org/2016/11/18/librarians-archivists-call-wipo-members-create-safe-harbour-copyright-liability/, 2016-11-18.

联盟还表示，几乎没有图书管理员接受过正式的法律培训，绝大多数人没有获取专业法律建议的途径。欧洲图书情报和文献协会管理局（EBLIDA）表示，在面对著作权法时，即便在没有充分法律保护的情况下，图书管理员也必须将自己置身于公共利益一边。欧洲的代表引用了《欧盟议会和理事会关于协调信息社会中著作权和相关权某些方面的指令》，指令中包括了20个可选择的例外列表，欧盟各成员可以自主地选择，并可以在其国内法中以不同的方式来施行①。非洲集团中的一些国家以及巴西也表示，图书馆和档案馆的善意行为可适用侵犯著作权责任的限制。美国解释了其国内法的例外规定，并表示成员国应支持图书馆、档案馆和其他相关机构的善意行为可适用某些金钱赔偿责任豁免。欧盟表示，欧盟版权框架没有讨论图书馆与档案馆责任问题，但可通过成员国国家层面和其他领域的法律加以解决。

同时，国际博物馆理事会（ICOM）表示，博物馆也应被加入SCCR图书馆和档案馆著作权例外提案的受益者名单中，包括责任的限制。国际博物馆理事会代表认为，博物馆藏品包括档案材料和图书馆藏品，博物馆与图书馆、档案馆有着相似的学术追求，从事的交流活动亦与图书馆和档案馆类似，常见的如博物馆藏品和工艺品的复制等。

图书管理员善意地犯了错误，绝不应当被当作罪犯。当一个机构以有限的预算来运营时，法律诉讼对其是致命的。澳大利亚学校国际版权主任和澳大利亚知识共享组织共同领导人德莉娅·布朗代表知识共享组织指出："自愿许可机制永远不是也不可能是一个全面的解决方案。政府和其他部门就需要起到领导作用，在例外和限制的框架范围内来保证教导者和学习者可以利用世界范围内的知识而不用担心侵权。因为这个原因，知识共享组织坚信基本法律和法规的改革是必要的。不管知识共享的许可协议有多么成功以及它为建设一个更公平、合理、公正的世界所起到多大的促进作用，我们均支持强制、灵活的版权例外，以维持教育和研究。"②

澳大利亚政府于同年12月发布了生产力委员会关于澳大利亚知识产权规划的报告。报告指出："知识产权法，包括版权法和专利法在内，必须十分审慎地调整。如果法律太弱势，那么投资者们将很难收回花费在将新的发明、书籍、音乐以及电影投入市场的成本费用；但如果法律太过强势，则会限制知识的创新和获取，这将阻止人们进行新的发明或创造新的作品——因为获取现有的资料变得太过昂贵和困难。对消费者而言，法律的强势将使得他们接触知识、了解文化的成本更加高昂，并且会成为进行教育和满足弱势群体正当需求的障碍。"生产力委员会在回顾这些证据的基础上说明，"目前的版权法并未平衡各方利益，……太过偏向于版权人，而对消费者和居于中间的传播用户造成了损害"。目前对于版权的例外"太过确定和狭窄，它没能完全反映现如今人们对知识的消费和利用方式，也并不乐意迎合对版权资料的正当使用"。

（二）对科研机构的侵权责任豁免

在版权现代化改革中，欧盟为在数字和跨境环境下使用版权作品设置了三项例外，其中包含了文本数据挖掘（TDM），但仅仅限于科研机构（research organizations）为了科学研究进行文本与数据挖掘③的情形，可以对其合法获得的作品进行复制（reproduction）和提取（extraction）。2016年末，欧洲的研究组织声明，欧洲立法者应该在欧盟版权指令修正案有关数字单一市场的规定里加强对研究人员和教育工作者的保护。此外还指出，"立法者和政策制定者必须重新考虑文本和数据挖掘的规定，以及在数字和跨境教学中使用作品的例外情况"。欧洲研究图书馆协会执行董事苏珊·赖利（Susan Reilly）号召大家："团结起来，我们是成千上万的研究人员、教育家、创新者、图书馆和学术机构的呐喊者。研究人员、教育家、创新者以及图书馆馆员是创造知识、捍卫知识、从知识上成长并帮助别人前进的人。因此，我们强烈建议保护那些创造知识投入的人以及那些进一步推动其产生价值的人。文本和数据挖掘使得研究人员能够从机器可读材料中获取信息，同时也是其处理大量数据和出版物所必需的。"

此外，针对拟议的新版权指令引入了文本和数

① 张燕龙．数字技术时代我国版权保护的刑事路径思考：以美国版权犯罪立法的转型为参照［J］．政治与法律，2017（4）．

② Creative commons at WIPO：supporting a more fair copyright for teaching and learning［EB/OL］．https://creativecommons.org/2016/11/24/creative-commons-wipo-supporting-fair-copyright-teaching-learning/，2016－11－24．

③ 文本数据挖掘大致相当于文本分析，是一个从文本中提取高质量信息的过程。文本数据挖掘需要：首先，构造输入文本，包括解析语法、提取语言特征、删除不相关内容、导入数据库等过程；其次，从输入的文本中提取出所需的信息或信息模式；最后，对提取出的结果进行评估和解释。高质量的信息通常是指那些兼具相关性、新颖性和趣味性的信息。典型的文本数据挖掘包括文本分类、文本聚类、概念提取、情感分析、文件概要和实体概念建模等。

据挖掘豁免的主体要求，限定了主体是研究机构，以科学研究为目的，研究组织认为应当重新起草指令，允许任何个人或组织合法使用内容来利用数字技术开发这些内容。迈克尔·桑德斯基（Michael Sadowski，来自Brand24的首席执行官）和迈克尔·布莱兹克（Michael Brzezicki，来自SentiOne的创始人）共同认为，“欧盟委员会提出的版权改革措施阻碍了初创公司充分合法地使用文本和数据挖掘技术”。这两位科技公司的年轻创始人在联合发布的声明中指出：“我们生活在数字经济时代。数据无处不在，包括设备、服务、商业、用户在内的一切事物都可以构成数据。欧盟委员会关于版权改革的措施可能会导致大量的年轻创新企业逃离欧洲，数千家成功的创新公司将会被迫迁址或面临倒闭。对于欧盟来说，在未来出现像Skype、Spotify或者Pipedrive这样具有竞争力的公司将变得更加困难，其在与硅谷的竞争中也难以取得上风。”芬兰阿尔托艺术大学法律顾问玛丽亚·伊丽莎白·雷宾德表示，“扩大文本数据挖掘的豁免，比如对研究人员和初创企业的豁免，非常符合欧洲的福利政策”。文本数据挖掘的豁免是被迫切需要的，“挖掘的权利就是阅读的权利”，这项豁免将允许我们阅读学术出版物中的原始文本、数据和表格，允许我们对这些内容进行深入的研究①。

据报道，2016年1月13日，欧盟委员会作为欧盟区域内的政府间组织，正在呼吁欧洲各国政府在国家层面上捍卫网络中立原则，改变限制用户言论自由的违宪规定。相关成员国亦接受了这个旨在进一步确立与网络中立相关的表达自由权和隐私权的欧盟委员会指南。《部长委员会对成员国在保护和促进网络中立相关的表达自由权和生活隐私权方面的建议CM/Rec（2016）1》（部长委员会在2016年1月13日于部长代表会议第1244次会议通过）的主要内容包括：在信息社会中个人的自由表达，包括接收、传递相关信息和观点的权利以及对民主生活的参与，正在逐步依赖于网络连接的可获得性和质量。网络连接服务的供应商拥有管理网络信息和数据流量的技术能力。它们可能为了特定法律目的参与网络流量管理，如保护网络的统一性和安全性。它们可能采取措施以防止非法或者有害信息的获取或者传播，如通过与公权力合作建立的自我规范系统。然而，其他对网络流量的干涉会影响为用户提供的网络服务的质量，并且可能导致屏蔽、歧视，或者特定种类内容、应用或服务的优先。在这种情况下使用技术手段对通信的检查或者监控会降低用户对网络的信任。这些问题引发了人们对隐私权和表达自由权的保护和促进的关注，这两项权利分别由欧洲人权公约（ETS No.5，后文简称公约）的第8条和第10条予以保护。这些问题也可能会对网络丰富和多元的信息以及公共服务媒体内容的获得产生影响，而这些信息又是民主和文化多样性的基础。自由表达的权利，包括接收和传递信息，并不是一项绝对权。但是，任何对该权利行使的限制必须符合该公约第10条的规定。网络中立原则巩固了网络流量的非歧视原则以及用户接受传递信息、使用自己选择的设备的权利。它促进了表达自由权的充分行使和享受，因为该公约第10条不仅仅适用于信息的内容，而且适用于其传播的方式。网络中立原则也能够促进科技创新和经济增长。此外，为了保护隐私权和表达自由权能够根据公约第8条和第10条的规定充分行使，促进网络公共服务价值的充分实现，部长委员会根据欧盟委员会法典第15条的规定，建议成员国：（1）采取所有必要的措施，与所有的利益相关者进行合作，来保障它们政策框架中的网络中立原则与本建议附录里规定的指南相一致。（2）在其他处理有关网络中立原则事务的国际和区域法庭中促进此指南的实施。由此可见，网络中立原则在法律中所涉及的问题并非仅仅局限于著作权领域。如何把握这一原则的适用关系到人类社会中认定相互关系的定位，也关系到网络产业的发展。

三、美国大选年及英国脱欧对著作权法治和相关产业政策的影响

2016年全球范围的“黑天鹅”事件屡见不鲜，无论是特朗普当选美国总统还是英国脱欧都将对世界知识产权制度包括著作权法治产生重大影响。尽管英国脱欧的程序尚未全面启动，但一些可以预见的效应已经摆在人们的面前。前述欧盟在2016年9月提出的关于版权改革，尤其是关于文本和数据挖掘的例外，以及印刷出版业的20年相关权、作者与表演者取得公平报酬的方法等如何适用于英国？我们固然可以期待在漫长的英国与欧盟的脱欧谈判中，那些原本已经由英国议会通过的涉及知识产权的欧盟或欧共体条约可以以某种形式转换成英国的国内法，故而保证英国国内知识产权制度的稳定性。尽

① Europe needs more successful data mining startups [EB/OL]. https://www.euractiv.com/section/digital/opinion/europe-needs-more-successful-data-mining-startups，2017-04-03.

管英国知识产权局对于前述欧盟的立法建议已经开始征询意见，但对于新近通过的欧盟知识产权法如何被引入英国还有很多不甚明朗的地方。

同样地，美国方面也因总统更替出现了一系列不确定因素。2016 年 8 月，唐纳德·特朗普、希拉里·克林顿都不满意颇具争议的 TPP。在短短几个月的时间内，TPP 的通过就从一件确定的事演变成了一件处于危机中的事。奥巴马总统仍然是 TPP 最忠实的支持者之一，他希望在大选日之后立即通过该协议，如果不成功，协议的通过将交由下一届国会和美国总统负责。然而两大党的候选人都反对 TPP 条约。对两名美国总统候选人而言，反对该协议的理由是政治原因；但对代表新西兰艺术家和唱片公司利益的 Recorded Music 组织而言，问题在于版权，尤其是如何以及何时延长版权保护期。数字监督机构电子前沿基金会（EFF）称，将版权保护期从死后 50 年延长至死后 70 年是“陷阱”，只有少数成功的作者可以受益。“增加的 20 年版权保护期会限制原本已公共领域作品的利用，禁止以既有作品为基础创造新作品，并使孤儿作品问题恶化。”美国版权局也认为版权保护期太长了，并提出了缓解不良影响的方法。

2016 年 9 月，《好莱坞报道》（*Hollywood Reporter*）的记者与美国负责知识产权的商务部副部长兼专利和商标局局长——米歇尔·李就当前知识产权改革和新一届政府将会带来哪些影响进行了深度访谈。谈及政府换届对于当前众议院司法委员会所进行的著作权改革可能产生的影响时，米歇尔·李指出：“著作权从来不是一个党派争议话题，因此没有理由相信政府的换届会是著作权政策改变的一个信号。当然，立法首先需要通过国会，而当前国会的领导局面并不会改变。我认为古德拉特主席仍将联合两党的力量去领导立法委员会推进著作权法律的更新。美国自建立以来就意识到了著作权对于促进创造性表达的重要性，并致力于通过激励民众创造并分享作品来促使美国在文化和经济产出中占据主导地位。我相信美国专利商标局会一直从事著作权政策工作，确保我们的著作权制度继续适应、促进和深化宪法中‘促进科学和使用艺术进步’的宗旨。”[①] 由此可知，作为知识产权大国，美国官方在整体上依旧持亲知识产权的态度。这一点不会因大选或政党更替而有任何变化。

2016 年 12 月 6 日，美国国际知识产权联盟（International Intellectual Property Alliance，IIPA），发布了《美国经济中的版权产业：2016 年度报告》（以下简称《报告》）。与往年一样，2016 年的《报告》还是聚焦在版权产业、版权产业增加值、版权产业的就业、在国际市场上的美国版权内容以及结论等五个部分。该《报告》显示，美国全部版权产业为美国经济贡献了近 2.1 万亿美元的增加值，是无可争议的美国经济支柱产业。美国核心版权产业[②]在美国 GDP 中的比例一直超过 6%，并且逐年增加，如果计算全部版权产业增加值，则会占据美国 GDP 的 11%以上。同样，美国版权产业也为美国提供了巨大的就业市场，美国核心版权对美国的就业贡献率近 4%；以全部版权产业计，则将近 8%。再从薪酬角度来看，美国版权产业从业人员的薪酬水平遥遥领先于美国平均水平。2015 年，美国核心版权产业人员平均薪酬高达 93 221.45 美元，是美国人均薪酬水平的 1.38 倍[③]。

2016 年 12 月 13 日，包括经营基督音乐、古典乐、节奏布鲁斯以及电影原声音乐的 19 家音乐产业集团，一致致信美国当选总统唐纳德·特朗普，要求当其在 12 月 14 日会见科技产业领袖时，将音乐作品的版权利益纳入考虑范围。“当您在明天会见一些世界主要技术公司的高管的时候，我们希望强调一些观点以保证作为美国国家财富的音乐行业能够继续保持活力。”[④] 信中主要内容包括音乐产业带来的经济增长、驱动创新以及科技公司对音乐作品权利人利益的负面影响。“搜索引擎、用户上传平台、服务提供商以及域名登记注册机构均应当依照判例规制，有效阻止盗窃以及保障音乐作品使用费的公平支付”。此外，音乐组织认为“当下广泛存在‘价值攫取’现象，即一些公司利用法律漏洞达到减少支付给作者的报酬的效果，进而弱化美国创作

① Obama's IP advisor talks reform efforts and a new administration [EB/OL]. http://www.billboard.com/articles/business/7633171/obamas-ip-advisor-talks-reform-efforts-and-a-new-administration，2016-12-23.

② 美国的版权产业由核心版权产业、部分版权产业、交叉版权产业、版权相关产业四个部分组成。核心版权产业（core industries）是指主要目的是创作、生产、传播和展览版权内容的产业，主要包括图书、报纸、期刊、电影、电视剧、音乐、广播和电视广播，以及所有格式的软件，包括视频游戏。

③ https://iipa.org.

④ Music industry groups in harmony in calling for support from trump [EB/OL]. https://www.ip-watch.org/2016/12/14/music-industry-groups-harmony-calling-support-trump/，2016-12-04.

者的版权，损害作为美国经济和就业引擎之一的音乐产业”①。

2016年12月21日，美国贸易代表办公室(USTR)发布了该年度“恶名市场”报告。这份报告列出了对美国文化创意产业最具威胁的线上和线下市场，并且在其中特别强调了窃取流媒体资源的新趋势。报告引用了国际唱片工业联合会的一份研究报告，该研究表明对流媒体资源的窃取行为在全球领先的音乐市场中愈演愈烈，30%的网络用户通过盗版服务获得了未授权的音乐产品。“对流媒体资源的窃取行为直接威胁了数字产品的增长，因为它减弱了用户对正版服务的需求，从而剥夺了艺人和唱片公司的这一重要收入来源。”美国贸易代表办公室这样阐述，“付费下载网站以及合法的流媒体服务同时受到了损害，而且开发和推出新一代合法流媒体服务的激励机制也被削弱”②。在这份报告中，作为美国和国际权利人的“重点关注”，中国C2C交易平台淘宝网同样被点出。淘宝网的经营“对打击泛滥的假冒、盗版商品形成了持续的严重挑战”③。

四、小结

无论是加强著作权保护的措施，还是适当限制著作权效力的观点，其出发点都是因为数字时代的到来或者网络技术的普及。因此回顾著作权法治的发展，这两个方面都面临新技术带来的冲击。

首先，实现网络环境下的版权保护及如何界定相应网络服务提供者的义务范围、网络版权犯罪刑事责任的规制等问题受到英美等国家的持续关注。出现网络版权保护问题的根源在于科技进步，直接动力则是西方发达国家文化产业的发展刺激了社会对版权法的需求，正是文化产业的发达程度直接决定了版权的发展进程。同时，文化产业对立法的影响作用也是显而易见的，大量的民间行业自治组织如美国电影协会、音乐协会等机构通过专业咨询、游说，甚至直接参与司法委员会的听证会等方式，向有关国家的国会或立法者发表意见。

自1997年出台《反电子盗窃法案》开始，美国相继通过了《数字千年版权法》《作者权利及反盗版法案》等来专门规制网络侵犯版权的行为。通过这些法案的出台，美国构建了较为完善的版权犯罪刑事责任体系，也在全球树立了用刑事手段保护版权的“美国标准”。随着知识经济的进一步发展，以美国为首的西方发达国家认为世界贸易组织《知识产权协议》的内容已经跟不上数字网络技术的发展，它们希望能够出台一个更加先进的保护知识产权的协议，TPP应运而生。虽然由于特朗普上台导致TPP前途渺茫，但总体上讲，在“美国标准”的影响下，各国著作权法刑事责任条款的发展，延续了保护对象不断扩大、规制行为种类不断增多、处罚加重的趋势。目前，各国著作权法刑事责任条款的发展逐渐呈现出两种并存的趋势。一是维持传统刑事责任条款以规制非法复制和发行行为为中心，并在其基础上进行数字网络时代改良的刑法体系。二是希望通过规制如规避技术措施等前置行为来预防、打击网络版权犯罪。到目前为止，平台规制、个人合法行为与合理使用行为的界限依旧不清晰，以及实施行为模糊化、共同犯罪复杂化、预防性措施不断前移以及主观目的多元化等一系列问题，仍是未来数字时代各国著作权保护和立法的世界性难题。

其次，在保证技术中立原则的基础上强调数字技术发展下图书馆等公共机构以及教育研究机构使用作品的例外以及确立这种例外的必要性。数字技术的传播速度引起了权利人对图书馆利用电子技术传播作品的例外的恐慌。但是从公共利益的角度，尤其是本年度WIPO版权及相关权常设委员会会议上反映出的各国代表所强调的扩大图书馆、博物馆和档案馆等公共机构的例外限制范围的必要性，以便公众有包括通过包括网络平台在内的更广泛的途径获得文化信息的需求，的确影响着著作权制度的另一个侧面。欧盟已经认识到图书馆作为获得知识的渠道的重要性，并且号召委员会评估如下情况：允许公共或研究型图书馆通过网络或者图书馆局域网，以电子格式向公众合法地出借作品，在限定期限内归个人使用，这样有助于图书馆高效行使向公众传播知识的公共职能。同时建议作者应该因电子借阅获得合理的补偿；在获得了阅读作品的允许的

① A letter to United States President-Elect Donald Trump [EB/OL]. https://www.ip-watch.org/weblog/wp-content/uploads/2016/12/Music-Community-Letter-to-POTUSE-121316.pdf，2016-12-13.

② U.S. trade report highlights stream ripping as piracy concern [EB/OL]. http://rainnews.com/u-s-trade-report-highlights-stream-ripping-as-piracy-concern/，2016-12-22.

③ 阿里巴巴声称，在截至2016年8月底的12个月内，它已经主动地移除了超过3.8亿件上架商品和关闭了大约18万个淘宝商店。阿里巴巴前瞻性地宣布从四振出局到三振出局政策，以及旨在扩大其前瞻性的执行力度的联合动力系统。U.S. trade rep condemns stream ripping，calls out Alibaba in new “notorious markets” report [EB/OL]. http://www.billboard.com/articles/news/7632451/us-trade-representative-stream-ripping-notorious-markets-report，2016-12-21.

前提下，为了科研目的而使用自动化分析技术挖掘文本、数据和内容。欧盟试图在利用数字技术传播知识和补偿作者之间达成平衡，这些权利例外的实施效果还取决于能否制定规则以有效地管控电子出借的过程，防止大规模盗版的出现。可见讨论权利例外依旧是为了实现制度的平衡。所谓的“平衡”是相对的平衡，或者说矫正过去着重于保护作者权利的不平衡，此次欧盟着重保护社会公共利益，尤其是获得知识权、言论自由以及人道主义关怀。

当然，著作权的核心还是财产权。在市场经济条件中，无论环境怎样千变万化，著作权法治一定会沿着市场经济所指引的轨道前行，无论在什么国家都无不如此。只是不同国家因其著作权利益所在方位有所不同，故而在立法和司法上有各自的关切和侧重。未来的世界纵有各种变数，但不变的是市场规则。所以中国的著作权法治只要在大方向上不违背市场经济规律，就不会出大问题，除非技术更新导致作品不再具有财产性。近来人工智能技术的进步让人产生了这种担忧，但到目前为止还仅仅是一种担忧而已。

（作者单位：中国人民大学知识产权学院）

2016年国际版权动态

◆ 立法与行政

【2016年度美国版权政策概览】

美国国会对版权法案进行了三年的审查，然而更多的是空谈而不是行动。

2016年初，美国商务部发布了它令人期待已久的版权改革议案，并且，春季的时候，版权局向前推进了三个主要的版权政策研究，奥巴马总统向参议院递交两条国际版权公约以获得批准，并且白宫呼吁更多的影子监管。

国会图书馆和版权局都做了知名度高的人员调整，版权局为网页持有者制定了一条危险的新规则，并且一些反规避豁免生效。

公众仍然不知道版权法的大修改是否迫在眉睫，但是2016年肯定为有趣的2017年设定了一张表。

三年："下一个大的版权"审查过程

2016年是美国版权法国会审查的第三年，这一审查从2013年开始，当时负责版权登记的人员玛丽亚·帕兰特呼吁国会在"下一个大的版权法"中修改版权法。2016年，这一审查还将继续推进，版权局对有争议的版权法领域进行三项政策研究。虽然版权法早已由几个强大的行业塑造，但是电子前沿基金会（EFF）在努力确保如果国会提出进一步修改法案，公众将不会被排除在过程之外。

为自由向法案修改者作斗争

EFF在2016年启动，督促美国版权局确保其向国会提出的建议保护用户真正拥有自己的设备的能力——使用、修改、调整、修理和销售生活中司空见惯的基于软件的产品。EEF鼓励版权局支持修改法律，以改变版权局用有限许可打破《数字千年版权法》一揽子禁止的坏方法，进而真正改变第1201条限制用户言论自由的违宪限制。2016年秋天，EFF和11 000名支持者出于安全研究、修理和可用性的目的，敦促版权局支持永久免除第1201条下的责任。

美国版权局于2016年12月15日发布了关于软件使用设备的研究结果，很明显它没有采纳EFF和其他有公共利益集团提出的建议。

（信息搜集、翻译：赵玲。

资料来源：http://beforeitsnews.com/libertarian/2016/12/this-year-in-u-s-copyright-policy-2016-in-review-2666670.html）

【欧盟委员会（COE）保护表达自由和隐私的网络中立指南】

2016年1月13日，欧盟委员会呼吁欧洲各国政府在国家层面上保护网络中立原则。诸成员国亦接受了这个旨在保护和促进与网络中立相关的表达自由权和隐私权的欧盟委员会指南。

全文如下：

欧盟部长委员会对成员国在保护和促进网络中立相关的表达自由权和生活隐私权方面的建议CM/Rec（2016）1（部长委员会在2016年1月13日于部长代表会议第1244次会议通过）。

（1）在信息社会，个人的自由表达权的行使和享受，包括接收、传递信息和观点的权利，以及他们对民主生活的参与，正在逐步依赖于网络连接的可获得性和质量。

（2）网络连接服务的供应商拥有通过它们运营的网络管理信息和数据流（网络流量）的技术能力。它们可能为了特定法律目的参与网络流量管理，如保护网络的完整性和安全性。它们也可能采取措施以防止非法和有害信息的获取与传播，如通过与公权力合作建立的自我规范系统。然而，其他对网络流量的干涉会影响为用户提供的网络服务的质量，并且可能导致屏蔽、歧视，或者将特定种类内容、应用或服务的优先。此外，在这种情况下使用的一些技术手段会产生对通信的检查或者监控行为，这种行为会降低用户对网络的信任。

（3）这些问题引发了人们对隐私权和表达自由权的保护和促进的关注，这两项权利分别由欧洲人权公约的第8条和第10条予以保护（ETS No. 5，后文简称公约），此外，关于个人数据自动处理的个人保护公约也对此进行了规定（ETS No. 18）。此外，这些问题也可能会对网络丰富和多元的信息以及公共服务媒体内容的获得产生影响，而这些信息又是民主和文化多样性的基础。自由表达的权利，包括接收和传递信息，并不是一项绝对权。但是，任何对该权利行使的限制必须符合该公约第10条的规定。

（4）网络中立原则巩固了网络流量的非歧视原则以及用户接受传递信息、使用自己选择的设备的权利。它促进了表达自由权的充分行使和享受，因为该公约的第10条不仅仅适用于信息的内容，而且适用于其传播的方式。同时，网络中立原则也能够促进科技创新和经济增长。

（5）为了保护和促进隐私权和表达自由权能够根据公约第 8 条和第 10 条的规定充分行使，同时促进网络公共服务价值的充分实现，部长委员会根据欧盟委员会法典第 15 条的规定，建议成员国：采取所有必要的措施，与所有的利益相关者进行合作，来保障它们政策框架中的网络中立原则与本建议附录里规定的指南相一致。在其他处理有关网络中立原则事务的国际和区域法庭中促进此指南的实施。

（信息搜集、编译：连雨晴。

资料来源：http://www.ip-watch.org/2016/01/13/council-of-europe-guidelines-for-network-neutrality-to-protect-freedom-of-expression-privacy/；http://www.ip-watch.org/2014/05/13/new-eu-human-rights-guidelines-on-freedom-of-expression-offline-and-online/；http://www.ip-watch.org/2016/04/01/council-of-europe-internet-governance-strategy-2016-2019-stresses-human-rights/）

【欧盟法院：链接到盗版内容的行为本身不侵犯著作权】

根据欧盟著作权指令，通过链接到公众已经可以得知的盗版内容不被看作侵犯著作权。这是佐审官梅尔吉奥·沃斯雷特于 2016 年 4 月提交到欧盟法院的建议，这可能是一个里程碑式的建议。

近年来，欧盟法院也被要求就几个有关超链接的案件进行裁决，以认定对其他网站进行链接的行为是否侵犯著作权。以前，欧盟法院认为如果版权人将其作品公之于众，则对受著作权保护的作品进行链接的行为不侵犯著作权，同样的情形也适用于受著作权保护的影像资料。但如果链接指向的是没有经过版权人许可的作品，这种行为仍然被允许吗？根据欧盟法院佐审官梅尔吉奥·沃斯雷特的观点，答案是肯定的。

在其一份递交欧盟法院的建议报告中，梅尔吉奥·沃斯雷特评论了先前的花花公子网站（Playboy）与荷兰名为吉恩的博客网站（GreenStijl.nl）之间的纠纷。在 2011 年 10 月，吉恩网站发布了一张海报，链接到了花花公子网站存储在文件访问服务器中的照片。这些图片的上传发布者请求花花公子网站移除了主机服务器上的照片，但是吉恩网站仍然链接到了其他能够接触到这些照片的网站。荷兰法院请求欧盟法院裁决这些链接是否能够被认为是欧盟著作权指令第 3 条第 1 款的“向公众传播”行为，并认定其是否构成帮助侵权。

在梅尔吉奥·沃斯雷特看来，尽管这种链接有助于受保护的作品被更多人发现，使其更容易被获得，但是这种行为仍然不构成著作权侵权。“当受保护的作品本身已经在其他网站可为公众获得的时候，对这些作品的链接，无论直接与否，都不构成‘公之于众’，并且仅仅是帮助他们被公众发现而已”，欧盟法院在评论梅尔吉奥·沃斯雷特提出的建议时这样写道。此外，梅尔吉奥·沃斯雷特论证道，链接行为与使作品处于可得而知的状态不同，后者只是适用于最初上传的人。这意味着吉恩网站的行为不能被定性为侵犯著作权。

法院解释道，“实际‘使作品处于可得而知的状态的行为’是指进行了最初的传播行为的人。因此，对于已经被公布在网站上，并且可免费为公众获取的版权作品进行链接的行为，不能被定义为欧盟法令下的传播行为”。事实上，在吉恩网站的案件中，网站所有者设置链接的行为，对于涉案作品处于为网络用户可得而知的状态并非不可或缺的。

严格意义上说，大多数侵权网站包括海盗湾在内，大都将链接设置在已经为公众可得而知的版权作品中，但是在这些案件中，网站的目的也是应当考虑的一个重要因素。也就是说，欧盟法院的这次裁决对于那些新兴的网站、博客和社会公众而言是好消息，因为对一些相关的已被公开的版权作品进行链接在大多数情况下应当是被允许的。

（信息搜集、编译：宋璇。

资料来源：https://torrentfreak.com/linking-to-pirated-content-is-not-copyright-infringement-160407；http://in.reuters.com/article/internet-copyright-eu-court-idINKCN0X40VE?hs = true；http://intellectualpropertyblog.fieldfisher.com/2016/hyperlinking-to-unlicensed-playboy-photos-is-not-copyright-infringement-says-advocate-general/）

【英国提议加强网络知识产权保护】

2016 年 7 月，英国政府提出了《英国数字经济法案》。英国政府在官方文件中表示，该法案旨在“为公民和企业提供快速的数字通信服务，实现对数字通信基础设施的投资，塑造一个为儿童、消费者和企业造福的新兴数字世界，同时为政府的数字化转型提供支持，以提供更优的公共服务、世界领先的研究和更精确的统计数据”。

法案内容之一是加强对网络知识产权的保护。

知识产权相关规定中最具争议的决定是将网络版权刑事犯罪的最高监禁期从 2 年提高到 10 年，并将其适用于实际侵权中。

“如果该法案正式通过，它将帮助版权所有者和警方打击网络盗版”，霍金路伟（伦敦）律师事务所知识产权、媒体与技术实践组成员阿拉斯泰尔·肖（Alastair Shaw）这样说道。开放权利集团执行董事吉姆·基洛克（Jim Killock）则表示：“这个提议可能意味着分享文件或提供文件链接的人会被判入狱，这是一种过度的惩罚。”

英国政府认为，《1988 年版权、外观设计和专利法案》（后文简称《1988 年法案》）规定主要“实体”版权刑事罪行可判处的最高刑期为 10 年，而规范网络侵权条例规定的监禁期仅为 2 年，该条例是 2003 年英国将欧盟信息社会指令纳入本国法的过程中引入的。2015 年经过协商后，政府决定将可能判处的最高刑罚定为 10 年，与《1988 年法案》保持一致。

该法案还修订了《1949 年注册外观设计法》，使得设计所有人有权选择使用将产品与注册外观设计编号相链接的网站地址作为产品的标记。这给予了设计所有人另一种提供所需推定告知的方法，以防止侵权人事后声称他不知道该设计已被注册而要求豁免其对设计所有人的损害赔偿。

政府文件中提到的第三个变化涉及《1988 年法案》第 73 条，该条规定使 Virgin Media 等有线电视运营商在转发核心公共服务广播机构频道时无须再缴付版权牌照费。这项豁免旨在支持 80 年代和 90 年代鼓励发展有线电视基础设施的具体政策目标。文件中也提到，由于以卫星、地面和互联网为平台的多频道和数字电视的发展，这种豁免已不再适用。

该法案废除第 73 条的原因是政府认为在数百万有线电视用户中，许多用户对服务的使用不仅限于电视，“如今，发展有限基础设施的目标通过诸如电子通信代码改革（这也是该法案的一部分）等其他立法措施同样可以实现”。

潜在的“过度”制裁?

阿拉斯泰尔·肖认为，刑事制裁修正案和在线注册设计标志的规定“表明英国正在努力使版权和外观设计法更充分地融入 21 世纪”。

盗版磁带和光盘的日子还没有过去，如今互联网上却发生了最严重的版权侵害行为。“将最高刑期调整为 10 年以及提高可能的罚款使得权利持有人和执法机构在与网络侵权的战斗中拥有更强的火力。”肖在电子邮件中写道。

“版权需要被保护，但该提议可能意味着分享文件或提供文件链接的个人将要面临监禁刑罚，即使他们没有获得任何经济利益。”开放权利集团执行董事吉姆·基洛克在电子邮件中写道。他认为这种处罚是过度的，它意味着在线共享文件可能导致比实物盗窃更长的刑期。

（信息搜集、编译：李梦颖。

资料来源：http://www.ip-watch.org/2016/07/06/uk-proposes-to-tighten-ip-protections-online；http://services.parliament.uk/bills/2016-17/digitaleconomy/documents.html）

【欧盟有权批准《马拉喀什条约》的意见或将被打破】

欧盟法院法律顾问发现，欧盟在批准《马拉喀什条约》为视觉障碍人群的版权例外规定上具有专属权力。这一结论为视障群体的代表们所乐于接受，会加速欧盟批准该条约的进程。

2013 年，世界知识产权组织的成员国通过了旨在促进为盲人、视觉障碍或印刷品阅读障碍者查阅已出版作品的《马拉喀什条约》。来自欧盟法院的“9 月 8 日意见”表明，欧盟在缔结该条约上具有专属职权。

包括法国、芬兰和匈牙利在内的部分欧盟成员国以多种理由挑战欧盟专属权，这些理由均被欧盟法院法律顾问尼尔斯·瓦尔驳回。

根据欧盟发言人对“知识产权观察”的回答，“法律顾问的结论是法院得出最终意见程序中的第一步，为尽快做出最终批准条约的决定，目前欧盟委员会正迫切等候着这一意见”。

欧盟法院法律顾问的意见表明，捷克、芬兰、法国、立陶宛、匈牙利、罗马尼亚和英国“认为欧盟在缔结《马拉喀什条约》上不享有专属权力，尤其需要指出的是，上述国家的政府都辩称目前并不具备《欧盟运行条约》第 3 条第 2 款主张的欧盟享有专属权的条件”。

《欧盟运行条约》第 3 条第 2 款规定，“当缔结一项国际条约是联盟的立法活动，或该条约在联盟行使外部职权上必不可少，或该条约的缔结将影响联盟的共同规范或改变其范围时，联盟需具有缔结该项国际条约的专属职权”。

然而，上述国家的政府在欧盟不享有专属职权的理由上看法各异。

例如，辅佐法官指出，“捷克、法国、匈牙利和芬兰政府拒绝接受无障碍版式副本的跨境交换发生在商业框架内”。但是，他发现“这些政党似乎认为‘知识产权的公益性’概念包括了非营利基础之上的商品交换，从而导致后者独立于共同的商业政策”。

此外，他认为这种观点是对《欧盟运行条约》第 207 条的误解。他说，“该条款并未将非营利活动排除在外。事实上，部分商品或服务在特定情况下能够基于某些非营利的目的进行交换（比如，包括当其被免费供应时），这并不意味着这些商品或服务并未进行交易”。“《欧盟运行条约》第 207 条排除的仅仅是知识产权的非营利性。这表明，知识产权法律的各个部分并非直接地与国际贸易相关联，这明显是一个辅助的层面”。

有法律顾问认为，知识产权规则意在授予“使用智慧创造成果的专属权利以促进创新”。这些专属性权利“仅仅是有可能限制商品或服务自由流转的垄断的特有形式”。因此，立足于它们最根本的属性，“知识产权规则在绝大程度上与贸易相关”。

法国、匈牙利、罗马尼亚和芬兰政府强调《马拉喀什条约》是在世界知识产权组织这一联合国的代理机构框架内达成的，而世界知识产权组织并不具有促进贸易自由化的任务。

法律顾问说，“匈牙利和英国政府也无可辩驳地指出了《马拉喀什条约》和《与贸易有关的知识产权协议》之间联系极其微弱的事实”。

瓦尔说，共同的商业政策是欧盟与世界关系核心的其中一环。根据《欧盟运行条约》第 207 条第 1 款，他指出，“政策必须基于共同的原则，尤其当涉及关税税率调整时，有关商品和服务贸易、知识产权的商业化、外方直接投资、实现自由化的统一措施、出口政策和保护贸易措施相关的关税和贸易协定应当在发生倾销或补贴的情况下缔结”。

9 月 8 日意见认为，《马拉喀什条约》的许多核心条款，例如跨境交流、进口无障碍版式副本等，均和国际贸易有着明确的联系。条约的其他条款，特别是第 4 条（关于无障碍版式副本限制和例外规定的国内法）也旨在通过在缔约多方间将知识产权的可即性、范围和使用规则标准化以促进国际贸易。

法律顾问认为，《马拉喀什条约》向《与贸易有关的知识产权协议》靠拢的目的之一是意在通过商品的特殊形态之一——无障碍版式副本，来提高、促进和主导贸易。

根据该意见，“《马拉喀什条约》的缔结明白无误地要求欧盟立法机构修正《欧盟版权指令》的第 5 条（例外及限制）”。《欧洲版权指令》解决了信息社会中版权的特定层面和相关权利间的协调问题。

“目前，该条款的第三段（b）让成员国去解决在‘有利于残疾人在特殊障碍的情况下为了弥补障碍而直接、非营利性使用’的情况下是否设定例外或限制规定”。

意见认为，“因此，为了符合《马拉喀什条约》中包含的规则，基于特定缺陷人群（盲人、视觉障碍者或其他印刷品阅读障碍者）的利益考虑，设定例外和限制规定不应是选择性的而应是义务性的”。

欧盟委员会发言人娜塔莉·范迪斯塔特说，《马拉喀什条约》目前因专属批准权的分歧悬而未决，欧盟委员会正寻求迅速批准该条约的方式。“欧盟委员会在 2014 年 10 月的批准议案因少数成员国的阻挠而未能在理事会通过，”她说，“为了有助于终结现在的僵局，欧盟委员会已经要求欧洲法院在该议题上给出法律意见。”

范迪斯塔特说，“法律顾问做出的结论是得出法院意见的第一步，目前欧盟委员会正迫切等候该意见，以便尽快做出批准条约的决定”。

除此之外，欧盟委员会将及时提出以欧盟法律执行该条约的议案，这一进程独立于批准条约，旨在促进《马拉喀什条约》要求的内容和欧盟法律相适应的目标。

（信息搜集、编译：唐少敏。

资料来源：http://www.ip-watch.org/2016/09/14/judges-opinion-that-eu-is-competent-to-ratify-marrakesh-treaty-might-break-standstill/）

【澳大利亚生产力委员会提倡合理使用，重新激起版权大战】

澳大利亚政府于 2016 年 12 月发布了生产力委员会关于澳大利亚知识产权规划的报告。这份报告为版权领域的改革提供了一个严谨的、有证据支持的案例，是一份对澳大利亚知识产权法在法律效力、效率、适应性及责任认定诸方面进行评估的研究报告。学者们纷纷称赞这是一个独立而系统的研究。

我们对于知识产权法在实务中的运行情况有时是很难跟踪评测的，知识产权法包括版权法和专利法在内，必须十分审慎地调整。如果法律太弱势，那么投资者们将很难收回花费在将新的发明、书籍、音乐以及电影投入市场的成本费用；但如果法律太过强势，则会限制知识的创新和获取，这将阻止人们进行新的发明或创造新的作品——因为获取现有的资料变得太过昂贵和困难。对消费者而言，法律的强势将使得他们接触知识、了解文化的成本更加高昂，并且会成为教育和满足弱势群体正当需求的障碍。

多年来，学者们一致认为知识的保护和获取之间的最佳平衡点很难被精确定位，因此知识产权政策是一个极具争议性的、极为敏感的领域。在过去，知识产权政策的决定大都建立在企业的大力游说、本能、直觉以及猜测的基础上。在这种情况下，生产力委员会的报告则显得尤为重要，因为这份报告回顾了知识产权法实施情况的现有证据，并提供了能够改善澳大利亚知识产权法的建议方案。澳大利亚委员会在回顾这些证据的基础上，认为目前的版权法并未平衡各方利益，他们认为澳大利亚的法律“太过偏向于版权人，而对消费者和居于中间的传播用户造成了损害”。

让澳大利亚版权法变得“公平”

具有重大意义同时也是最具争议的一个建议是，在版权侵权中引进“合理使用”这一例外。合理使用允许人们不需要事先获得许可就可以以合理的方式使用版权作品，这一制度在美国的各行各业都具有极其重要的作用。制片人利用这一制度制作纪录片，图书馆用它来数字化其藏品并保存，学者用它来做数据和文本的深度研究，搜索引擎用它来索引网页等。

生产力委员会的报告仅仅是一系列要求引入合理使用制度的例外中最新的一个，报告认为澳大利亚目前对于版权的例外“太过确定和狭窄，它没能完全反映如今人们对知识的消费和利用方式，也并不乐意迎合对版权材料的正当使用”。

其他建议

这份报告是详细而全面的，涵盖的范围很广泛。生产力委员会为澳大利亚版权法的现代化提出了许多其他的建议，包括：

（1）禁止版权人通过限制性条款否认消费者的权利；

（2）允许消费者破解那些阻止合法活动的（保证汽车安全的）数字锁（如修理一台拖拉机）；

（3）解决运行长达十年之久的避风港制度，这个制度使得本土与 YouTube 或者社交媒体平台类似的媒体很难掌握作品内容；

（4）澄清法律规定，确保澳大利亚的消费者可以使用 VPN 访问其他国家的合法内容；

（5）保证在开放获取政策下，公共资助的研究成果能为社会公众免费获取；

（6）从竞争法中移除允许软件公司签订独占性许可和其他限制性许可条款的例外，否则将会带来反竞争的后果。

（信息搜集、编译：宋璇。

资料来源：https://theconversation.com/productivity-commission-re-ignites-copyright-wars-by-recommending-fair-use-70708；http://www.gizmodo.com.au/2016/12/australian-productivity-commission-re-ignites-copyright-wars-by-recommending-fair-use）

◆ 司法判例

【威秀集团与福斯电视台为屏蔽盗版网站提起诉讼】

威秀影业（Village Roadshow）在澳大利亚对福斯电视台（Foxtel）提起诉讼，请求其屏蔽盗版网站。该消息得到福斯电视台和澳大利亚联邦法院的确认。

美国广播公司称，威秀影业于 2016 年 2 月 18 日向澳大利亚联邦法院提起的诉讼依据的是 2015 年 6 月通过的《打击盗版法》。该法规定版权所有者可以向法院提出要求网络服务提供商禁止用户访问具有促进或意图侵犯版权的网站的申请。

福斯电视台发言人说：“福斯电视台打算用法律屏蔽盗版网站，并期望迅速实现。”联邦法院发言人说，威秀集团和其他公司起诉的是网络服务提供商和在新南威尔士注册的其他网络服务提供商。美国广播公司称，版权权利人和澳大利亚几个最大的网络服务提供者在过去几个月中一直在讨论网站屏蔽进程的问题。

屏蔽盗版网站可通过阻止域名系统将网站名称转化为 IP 地址予以实现，也可通过将网站流量重新指向另一个网站的缓存污染技术来实现。

知识产权律师戴维·斯图尔特认为，此案意义重大，因为一旦成功，威秀影业和福斯电视台将成为第一批在发行之时就能及时处理盗版的媒体企业，这比起诉单个的盗版者效率要高。起诉单个盗版者的版权所有人就如同使用长柄大锤砸花生，既浪费精力，又浪费诉讼时间。

斯图尔特说：“域名管理机构有时会非正式地利用缓存污染技术以减少诈骗和刑事犯罪活动的风险。”他说屏蔽盗版网站会有人为失误的风险，也会偶然屏蔽并非被视为盗版目标的 IP 地址从而导致网络用户不能访问合法网站。

通信部部长的发言人米奇·法依菲尔德说，“2015 年 6 月通过的法律旨在帮助版权所有人克服使其很难对外国侵权在线服务行使权利的法律障碍。

为了保护他人合法获取在线内容，法律为版权权利人规定了更高的门槛，即只有满足条件才能获得法院下达的屏蔽网站的禁令。该法律只适用于那些在海外运作并且主要目的是侵犯版权或协助侵权的网络地址”。

（信息搜集、编译：姜琳浩。

资料来源：http://www.theguardian.com/international）

【澳大利亚联邦法院认定数字数据信号不受版权保护】

2016 年 7 月，澳大利亚联邦法院合议庭已经确认，澳大利亚《版权法》不保护代表直播内容声音和图像的数字数据流。

在大型体育比赛直播时，其声音和图像通常都是数字数据流，获得并播放该数据流的价格是非常昂贵的。在澳大利亚税务局局长（Commissioner of Taxation）诉 Seven Network Limited 案中，澳大利亚联邦法院确认，澳大利亚《版权法》不保护声音和图像的即时数字转让，这些声音和图像被组合在一起实现直播。

该案中的争点是，是否 Seven 公司向国际奥委会（IOC）支付的广播权费用属于版税且因此由于 IOC 支付预扣税的义务而导致 Seven 公司有义务保留部分付费数额。

问题的关键在于：Seven 公司用于广播奥林匹克比赛的国际视听信号（ITVR 信号）是否具有版权？使用或有权使用该信号是否包括使用或有权使用一个“财产或权利”？如果以上任何问题的回答都为“是”的话，Seven 公司就有预扣税义务。

在一审中，贝内特法官认定，数字数据信号不具有版权，IOC 授予 Seven 公司的权利不是一种“财产或权利”，所以 Seven 公司向 IOC 支付的使用 ITVR 信号的费用不是版税，不会根据《澳大利亚和瑞士避免重复征收所得税协议》产生版税预扣税。

合议庭维持了贝内特法官的判决。ITVR 信号并不来自任何之前录制的版本；ITVR 信号是由东道主广播机构生成并通过电磁力传输的数字信号，在任何时刻该信号只能传输比赛声音和图像的一小部分；没有技术可以允许不使用接收设备来复制该信息；在传输该信号的铜线中没有录制或永久保存图片、图像和声音；独家播放付费不等于“财产或权利”的许可使用费用。

联邦法院维持贝内特法官的判决，认定 Seven 公司为其独家广播权支付的费用不是版税，因此，Seven 公司就没有义务因为 IOC 的预扣税义务而预扣税。该判决表明，使用数字技术的内容使用方和开发方应该检查一下自己是否受到目前有效的任何知识产权立法的保护，比如，代表直播体育赛事（比如奥林匹克比赛）声音和图像的数字数据流就不受知识产权保护，除非该信号本身是版权作品的复制品。通常情况下，该信号进行首次广播后才会产生版权。如果对于是否存在法律保护有怀疑的话，各当事人应该确保通过合同充分保护自己的权利。

（信息搜集、编译：隋川。

资料来源：http://www.lexology.com/library/detail.aspx?g=4111cea5-93e5-4390-a175-cc9505e8a4f4）

【美国：联邦版权法不能取代对商业秘密的保护】

在 GlobeRanger 公司诉 Software AG US 公司案（GlobeRanger Corporation v. Software AG US, Inc., Case No. 15-1012 1 (5th Cir., Sept. 7, 2016) (Costa, J).）中，美国第五巡回上诉法院肯定了地区法院的判决，认为联邦版权法不能排除原告对商业秘密的主张，因为美国版权法与有关商业秘密的主张是对不同权利的保护。

GlobeRanger 公司是一家专业从事用于库存管理的射频识别技术实施的软件公司。2007 年，GlobeRanger 公司签订了一份为美国海军建造实施一项 RFID（射频识别）技术的合同。在海军决定建立一个可以由单一位置运行而非需要各地都有服务器的整体系统之前，GlobeRanger 公司向海军提供了三种解决方案的建议。但海军在 GlobeRanger 公司和 Software AG 公司的提议中决定采用 Software AG 公司的建议。Software AG 公司在履行与海军间的合同时，使用了 GlobeRanger 公司的若干数据资料、指南和软件。GlobeRanger 公司提起诉讼称，Software AG 公司在接管 GlobeRanger 公司的技术转包时盗用了 GlobeRanger 公司的技术。

地区法院陪审团认为 Software AG 公司盗用了 GlobeRanger 公司的商业秘密，并要求被告给予原告 1 500 万美元的补偿性赔偿。地区法院还认为，GlobeRanger 公司没有证明 Software AG 公司存在主观恶意，因此不应有惩罚性赔偿。Software AG 公司随后上诉。

上诉过程中，Software AG 公司声称联邦版权法应取排除 GlobeRanger 公司有关商业秘密的主张，本案应发回州法院。第五巡回上述法院并不赞成，解释说，商业秘密索赔与联邦版权法相比寻求保护的是不同的权利。对商业秘密盗用行为的索赔，要求原告证明被保护的商业信息是通过不正当的手段或破坏秘密状态的方式获得的，而这一因素是侵犯版权的索赔所不包含的。因为侵权方面与版权相比对相关权利提供了实质性不同的保护，并不能取代。这一判决在这个问题上与其他 10 个区域的法院观点是相一致的。

（信息搜集、编译：白宇嘉。

资料来源：http://www.natlawreview.com/article/federal-copyright-law-does-not-preempt-trade-secret-claim）

【纽约州法院：天狼星公司无须向 1972 年之前的音乐的表演者付费】

2016 年 12 月 20 日，纽约州法院裁定：天狼星公司不必向 1972 年之前的录音中的表演者支付版税。这一系列的诉讼由 Flo&Eddie 公司提出。该公司是由 The Turtles 乐队的两名初始成员马克·佛曼和霍华·凯兰成立的。The Turtles 乐队最出名的歌曲当属“Happy Together”，这首歌是 20 世纪 60 年代的热门前 40 首之一。即便是联邦法院也认为，这个案件的结果将会有“重要的经济意义”，因为它将不仅适用于 The Turtles 乐队的录音制品，还将适用于披头士、路易斯·阿姆斯特朗和其他无数表演者的录音制品。

然而 1972 年出台的联邦版权法对在这之后的录音制品提供了有限的保护，任何先前的录音制品在 1972 年之后都受到州版权法的制约。对于 Flo&Eddie 发起的诉讼，多数法官认为，要“创建一个以前没有存在的普通法权利”。“我们认为，纽约普通法不承认 1972 年前录音制作者的公开表演权。”斯坦特法官写道。

但是这并不意味着 Flo&Eddie 得不到任何东西。根据许多媒体的报道，音乐家和天狼星公司在上个月达成了有条件的解决方案，即使他们败诉，诉讼人也将获得至少 2 500 万美元，如果他们胜诉，最多获得 4 000 万美元。天狼星公司还同意支付未来 10 年的许可费，最高可达 5 900 万美元。亨利在一份声明中说：无论如何，今天的三个上诉案件的结果并不会改变最近在加利福尼亚州达成的至少 2 500 万美元、最高 9 900 万美元补偿金的解决方案。

根据法庭文件，天狼星公司称会向音乐作品的所有者支付版权费，但是不包括 Flo&Eddie 公司以及在 1972 年之前的其他录音所有者。其主张称，当这些人的录音制品被播放时，他们并没有法律上要求付款的权利。

天狼星公司的律师并没有回复这条评论。

（信息搜集、编译：范瑞。

资料来源：http://www.newsday.com/long-island/politics/spin-cycle/ny-court-sirius-xm-doesn-t-have-to-pay-artists-for-pre-1972-music-1.12783148；https://1.next.westlaw.com/Document/Iabaa0b40c75e11e6885cf17f25a92dbe/View/FullText.html?transitionType=SearchItem&contextData=(sc.Search)）

【日本“扫描书籍”营业者，因涉嫌侵犯著作权被逮捕】

日本京都府警方在 2016 年 11 月 30 日逮捕了一名经营“扫描书籍”店铺的男子。该男子在没有得到著作权人许可的情况下，将书籍电子化后复制到 DVD 光盘中，后又将复制后的光盘转让给他人，涉嫌著作权侵权。一般社团法人——电脑软件著作权协会在同一天发布了这个新闻。

该男子将两名顾客送交的漫画电子化处理后复制到自己的电脑中，该行为侵犯了复制权，与此同时，又将该电子化处理后的书籍转让给该两名顾客合计收取了 5 700 日元，这一行为也涉嫌侵犯了转让权。

根据警方的调查，这名男子自 2011 年左右开始经营“扫描书籍”店铺，截至 2016 年 11 月 30 日大约受理了 2.6 万点（大约 17 万本档案）的扫描书籍申请，至少实现了 750 万日元的营业额。

京都府的搜查员是通过发现该男子经营店铺的网站才发现了该店铺的行为。发行《在下坂本，有何贵干?》《未来日记》《进击的巨人》《暗杀教室》《浪客剑心》等各类漫画的知名出版社和各类作品的著作权人纷纷控告了此类行为。

该男子将顾客送来的书籍在自己的扫描仪上进行电子化，然后通过网盘传输给顾客。然后，不仅是将书籍电子化这一步骤要收取费用，还应顾客的请求将电子数据直接复制到光盘进行贩卖。

像这样既可以将电子数据重复利用多次贩卖获利之外，当顾客送往的书籍有重复的情况下，还可以将多余书籍不经允许直接贩卖给旧书店获利的行为，各个出版社称之为“极端恶劣的行为”，决定对其进行刑事诉讼，并且表示“将凝聚着著作权人心血的作品以正确的形式呈现在读者的面前，这是出版社的职责所在。为了尽到这样的职责，今后对于恶劣的侵犯著作权行为要严肃处理”。

根据京都府警官的描述，自从 2016 年 3 月结束了对“扫描书籍”营业者进行停止损害民事诉讼以来，针对这类行为本身的刑事诉讼还是首次。

（信息搜集、编译：宋璧如。

资料来源：http://internet.watch.impress.co.jp/docs/news/1032544.html；http://wenku.baidu.com/link?url=LUVFPCHBQlrJiXYPt5PsMeEABQa8b51XzHslRVfLt1JBM2QhwZe4ckW8WdmLiWZxRwNhTZs1O817UpfovAGqbiRu6_qDamcT3GwDzsZFdYW；http://www.xsjedu.org/riyu/Show/88322/）

◆ 业界动态

【知识共享组织：版权的另一面是什么？】

2016年2月，知识共享组织发言人称：合理使用周来临了，知识共享组织非常高兴能与其他同样认为灵活例外对著作权法十分重要的组织和个人一起来庆祝它的到来。

现在有超过10亿CC许可证的作品可用，这些免费的作品可以供任何人使用和分享。CC许可证之所以有效，是现有的著作权范围所决定的。作者们有时候会抱怨著作权集体规则中大量的负面影响——比如不合理的长期规定、不相称的侵权惩罚、普遍的文化限制。同时，著作权法的一些特质也需要被支持和扩大，正是它们使大众有更多的机会去获取信息、参加教育以及进行自由的表达。作者们也可以利用CC许可证去创建作者自己的内容共享活动，让信息可以被重复利用以及共享。但是，作者们仍然依赖于著作权法基础的审查以及平衡而不能仅仅使用公开许可。这就是为什么我们要举办合理使用周。

合理使用“允许在一定范围内不经过权利人的许可而使用著作权作品……包括评述、搜索引擎、批判、戏剧、新闻报道、科研、教学、图书馆归档和学术领域”。合理使用被视为一种著作权人排他性权利的例外，合理使用并不是一种侵犯著作权的行为。

法律上合理使用的规定变得越来越强大。在美国，有判例表明为了科学研究可将对享有著作权的作品的复制视为合理使用。在纪录片的摄制等学术和创意领域，都依靠协同开发的“最佳实践指南”来指导人们在各自领域合理使用一些作品。合理使用原则的背后暗含的力量是灵活性，正是这种灵活性可以顾及技术的改变，以及如何在教育、学习、创造性的成果中使用著作权作品，当然也包括在研究和新闻领域新技术的使用。

现在仍然有一些障碍让人们没有意识到版权灵活限制和例外的全部潜力。比如，现在的一些贸易协定中减少了版权限制的重要性，与保证强制性限制和在TPP下版权使用的例外不同，这些贸易协定中所有的条款都强调公共权利的自愿性，因为几乎所有的保证权利人权利的条款都涵盖在里面。一些学术出版者正试图以许可证的方式来限制研究者进行文本和数据挖掘。这些许可证和协议有一定的问题，因为它们试图要求法律之下的允许，然而这些允许都是不必要的。

很明显的是，合理使用以及其他的限制和例外对一个健全的著作权系统来说至关重要。在合理使用周以及2016年其他的活动中，知识共享组织会继续支持和扩大使用者的这些重要的权利。

（信息搜集、编译：刘笑晗。

资料来源：https://blog.creativecommons.org/2016/02/23/the-flip-side-of-copyright）

【贝宝出于版权问题考量停止支持VPN和智能DNS服务提供商的支付功能】

2016年2月，美国贝宝公司（PayPal）宣布停止对加拿大VPN和智能DNS服务提供商Uno Telly支付功能的支持，因为Uno Telly的这类服务很可能是被用于著作权侵权活动。

由于版权问题，各个国家或地区网络平台提供的影片数量不一，因此会有大量的互联网用户借助VPN翻墙，以此突破地区限制。而往往快速稳定的VPN服务需要付费，因此就需要借助在线支付服务来购买。尽管使用VPN本身并不违法，但其经常被用于作品著作权的侵犯。

VPN服务可以用来规避地域限制，这样就可能违反贝宝的禁止任何“在没有著作权人许可的情况下，规避、越过、删除、化解或削弱技术保护措施”的情形。而智能DNS服务是“由流媒体网站删除了地域限制，允许用户无论在何地都可以观看频道”。

贝宝在一份电子邮件中写道，“在贝宝的使用规则中，使用贝宝服务不得用于发送或接收与侵犯版权、商标权、公开权、隐私权或其他受法律保护的权利有关的付款项”。因此，贝宝决定停止对VPN、智能DNS服务提供商提供支付服务。

Uno Telly则表示，其为全球客户提供DNS解析和安全的VPN服务，是连接世界各地的人们的网络继电器，其对于贝宝在没有事先警告的情况下单方面解除提供支付服务协议的行为感到失望，而且贝宝暗示不允许其提供开放和无限制网络存取服务。

Uno Telly告诉客户，其无法控制贝宝的决定，并且为给客户带来的不便而道歉。

（信息搜集、编译：高雪。

资料来源：http://arstechnica.com/tech-policy/2016/02/paypal-blocks-vpn-smartdns-providers-payments-over-copyright-violations/；https://torrentfreak.com/paypal-starts-banning-vpn-and-smartdns-services-160205；http://www.gizmodo.com.au/2016/02/paypal-is-blocking-payments-to-vpn-providers）

【知识产权及创新等事项被纳入TRIPs理事会例会议程】

TRIPs理事会是面向WTO所有成员，负责TRIPs实施及监控的组织，其例会于2016年3月1日至2日举行。理事会新任主席是来自坦桑尼亚的大使莫德斯特·乔纳森·梅罗先生。

数年来，WTO的成员们，尤其是发达国家已经向TRIPs理事会介绍有关知识产权及创新的讨论事项。此次大会，澳大利亚、欧盟、瑞士以及美国则提出有关教育及其传播的讨论建议，此份提议得到了日本、秘鲁、俄罗斯以及新加坡的共同支持，瑞士甚至提交文件详细介绍了该国的国情及经验。该文件显示，瑞士政府对于国内创新文化的孕育一直给予了高度重视，从而实现了商业、经济、教育体系内创新概念的一体化。

文件还指出，提供介绍知识产权原理及其运行的教育与培训，是促进改革和创新的知识产权体系效用最大化的关键。瑞士政府相信，针对不同年龄阶段的人群，需要提供不同层次的知识产权教育。例如，针对小学生，应当着重版权问题的教育；而对于中学生，则应当赋予其有关知识产权及创新的特殊实践课程的选择权。

有关知识产权及创新的事项被列入大会议程，将为成员们深入讨论培养创新精神、促进经济发展的知识产权保护体系提供良好契机。另外，一同被纳入大会议程的事项还包括，TIPRs协定与联合国生物多样性公约（以下简称CBD）的关系，及对传统知识与民间文学的保护，当然，此二者已不是第一次被列入理事会的议程之中。有来自WTO的消息称，WTO成员们提出的两份建议已经得到部分成员的支持。建议一是，由WTO秘书处更新总结了过去若干次讨论中各成员代表团观点的备注信息；建议二是，由CBD秘书处向TRIPs理事会简要报告于2015年起施行的名古屋议定书的相关情况。

此外，成员们还将就永久性禁止知识产权非违反之诉的可能性进行深入讨论。非违反之诉指代如下情况：如果某一成员实施的某项措施，致使另一成员依照WTO协定而合理预期的利益受到损害，即使该项措施并没有违反WTO协定，利益受到损害的一方仍然有权依照WTO争端解决程序提起申诉。现行TRIPs框架下的中止令禁止知识产权相关的非违反之诉，而这一禁止令每隔两年得以延长一次。于2013年举办的部长级会议即要求TRIPs理事会就是否无限期延长知识产权中止令达成一致意见。然而，大多数成员赞成无限期延长该项中止令，美国和瑞士则持反对态度，这一分歧至今仍未消除。该份中止令已被延长至2017年，而在2016年3月举办的TRIPs理事会例会上，WTO成员们就该分歧重新进行了讨论。

（信息搜集、编译：罗文君。

资料来源：http://www.ip-watch.org/2016/02/26/ip-and-innovation-non-violation-complaints-on-trips-council-menu-next-week/；https://www.wto.org/english/tratop_e/trips_e/intel6_e.htm）

【联合国教科文组织关于文化贸易的报道】

2016年3月，联合国一项新报告提供了大量关于全球文化贸易流量增加的细节。新报告题为《文化贸易的全球化：消费的转变；文化产品和服务2004—2013年的国际流动》，由总部位于巴黎的联合国教育科学及文化组织（UNESCO）发布。此报告由联合国教科文组织统计研究所的丽迪雅在何塞·佩索阿的指导下撰写，并在丽莎·巴博萨的协助下准备数据和制作地图。

该报告介绍了多年来文化产品和服务的市场变化，尤其在互联网的兴起之后。该报告依赖于行业统计，并表示几乎所有的音乐收入来自版权，但它似乎没有考虑到提高开放接入的经济收入，它也不研究可能涉及的文化产品，如传统知识或者商标或专利等知识产权。

尽管如此，近200页的报告充满了数据和分析，并要求做更多的研究工作。报告中写道："总之，当谈到在数字化和互联网的背景下评估著作权法，统计学家和经济学家面前存在大量研究任务，包括作曲家、创作者、表演者和其他人之间在网上的价值和分销链之间复杂的联系，收入方式的分割以及在一个新的数字环境中对创作的复杂测量"。

（信息搜集、编译：潘梦琦。

资料来源：http://www.ip-watch.org/2016/03/15/unesco-report-on-globalisation-of-cultural-trade）

【《我们要战胜一切》歌曲版权争议】

2016 年 4 月 12 日，致力于帮扶孤儿和贫穷人群的非营利组织“我们要战胜一切”基金会，在几次尝试获得授权在电影中使用歌曲《我们要战胜一切》均遭到拒绝之后，对声称享有该歌曲版权的音乐出版商提出诉讼。该基金会希望借助法院判决对下列内容形成确认性的声明，即该歌曲不受著作权法保护，应当属于公共领域的范围。

现该案件正在美国曼哈顿联邦地区法院进行审理。原告诉求出版商里士满组织（the Richmond Organization）和勒德落音乐（Ludlow Music）返还因歌曲的使用获得的具体数额不详的版权费用。

正如“祝你生日快乐歌”案一样，“我们要战胜一切”案所涉及的著名歌曲《我们要战胜一切》，其早期历史较为模糊、著作权权属登记繁杂，增加了案件审理的难度。

根据原告对事实的陈述，歌曲《我们要战胜一切》是对灵歌《我们将战胜一切》的改编；该灵歌在 1909 年第一次被美国煤矿工人报以印刷的方式公之于众，被称为“那首美丽的老歌”；到 20 世纪中期，该灵歌被确立为游行圣歌；同时，其作为美国黑人民权运动的颂歌直到今天仍然被美国国会图书馆称为“20 世纪最具影响力的歌曲”。

原告主张歌曲《我们要战胜一切》的版权范围并不像出版商声称的那样广泛，并且其版权已经超过保护期限。皮特·西格在 1948 年发行了《我们将战胜一切》版本歌曲，但其本人也不能清晰地解释该歌曲歌名变化的原因，即歌名由“我们将战胜一切”变为“我们要战胜一切”（皮特·西格先生已于 2014 年去世）。

出版商勒德落音乐于 1960 年对歌曲《我们要战胜一切》进行了版权注册，但原告认为其注册范围仅包括对歌曲《我们将战胜一切》的改编以及额外的段落。原告引用一名应其请求对该歌曲历史进行研究的音乐学家的研究结果，证明歌曲《我们要战胜一切》的版本与于 1948 年发行的最原始的歌曲《我们将战胜一切》相同。因此，歌曲《我们要战胜一切》的版权保护期限应截止于 1976 年。

（信息搜集、编译：赵悦。

资料来源：http://www.nytimes.com/2016/04/13/business/media/we-shall-overcome-copyright-may-be-overcome-one-day.html? _r=1）

【WIPO 召开知识产权及发展里程碑会议】

2016 年 4 月 7 日至 8 日，有关知识产权及发展的国际会议于瑞士日内瓦举行。作为世界知识产权组织（WIPO）的一次里程碑式会议，本次大会成为不同国家、地区及国际观点相互交融的平台。本次会议上，来自发达国家及发展中国家的学者、政府机构官员及国际组织代表们汇聚一堂，共同讨论知识产权在经济、社会及文化发展中的作用。

WIPO 总干事弗朗西斯·高锐主持召开本次大会，指出 WIPO 是在公共和私营部门合作的基础上成立的一个政府间国际组织。WIPO 是一种独特而珍贵的合作伙伴关系，因为 WIPO 97%的收入来源于私营部门提供服务获得的费用，而 WIPO 支出费用的 21%则用于发展和能力建设活动。他还指出，在变幻莫测的世界环境下，本次会议举办得非常及时。知识产权已不再处于经济体系的边缘地带，而是成为经济发展的关键核心。大多数政府将创新作为经济策略的主要元素，以及创建可持续经济的重要工具。然而，如何建立创建市场交易激励机制与社会大众享受创新所带来利益之间的平衡，则是至关重要的。

关于知识产权对于创新产生的积极影响，美国科罗拉多大学经济学院社科系副系主任凯斯·马斯库斯说道：“对此，我们能够证明的还太少了。与国际知识产权体系相比，贫困经济体系的创新性难以被量化，故通过重建知识产权体系未必就能够对经济增长和发展产生积极影响，只能说采用整体分析的方法，这样的目标将更有可能实现。此外，根据 TRIPs 签订以来的证据显示，知识产权体系的全球一体化并未给发达国家带来更多的创新性。”

大会上，希腊版权组织总干事、希腊文化和体育部部长伊里尼·斯塔穆托蒂被要求就版权及公有领域问题发表讲话。相关人士透露，斯塔穆托蒂已被提名为 WIPO 版权部部长候选人，该职位自 2015 年秋天起一直处于空缺状态。斯塔穆托蒂指出，版权是促进和维持创意产业创新及投资的基本工具，同时起到了平衡的作用。至于公有领域，通常被定义为不受版权法保护的客体，例如已经超过保护期的作品，或者作者放弃权利的作品，又例如知识共享中的零许可。他还指出，公有领域的存在是为了平衡版权的保护，国际、国家以及地区的版权法应当提供相应的灵活性。

（信息搜集、编译：罗文君。

资料来源：http://www.ip-watch.org/2016/04/08/landmark-wipo-conference-on-ip-and-development-kicks-off；http://www.wipo.int/meetings/en/2016/ip_development_conference.html）

【世界知识产权组织传统知识委员会同意就修订的草案做进一步讨论】

2016 年 11 月 28 日至 12 月 2 日，世界知识产权组织代表商定了一套修订的草案条款，将在传统知识委员会（该委员会主要致力于制定一项保护传统知识的潜在条约，以下简称委员会）的下届会议上做进一步讨论。对于该草案，各界看法不一。

该约束条款的支持者认为，这个草案反映了修订者对于该问题有了更好的理解，并且一些差异性也有所减少。然而，一些不支持该条款的发达国家则认为，差异性仍旧很大，还需要继续做大量的工作。

在 11 月 28 日至 12 月 2 日举行的知识产权与遗传资源、传统知识和民间文学艺术政府间委员会（IGC）第 32 届会议的最后一天，委员会发布了一份新的条款草案修订案。两个协调人在会议期间与成员国举行非正式会议，以形成反映所有立场的文本，同时保持观点清晰。11 月 30 日，委员会对该案文进行了第一次修订。

一些赞成该约束性条约的国家的代表认为差异性的减少主要是由于非洲集团和一些观点相近的国家集团的立场趋同，包括非洲集团、亚洲和太平洋国家集团以及拉丁美洲和加勒比国家集团。

一些发达国家及地区，包括美国、韩国、欧盟和加拿大的代表，在会议结束时说，对于该草案的一些核心问题的理解仍有许多工作要做。这些核心问题包括受益人是否应包括洲和国家，以及该文本的范围。

第二次修订的主要变化。

在草案的政策目标部分（第 1 条）中，增加了一个新的备选方案："无论是否商业化，都鼓励和保护基于传统的创造和创新"，但其中没有"以传统为基础"这样的字眼。

在文本的第一次修订（Rev 1）中被删除的语言也被重新引入。这些重新引入的语言是备选方案的第二点，即关于防止对传统知识（TK）授予错误的知识产权。

文本的主题有一个新的备选案文（备选案文 4）。该备选案文是由智利提交的，在关于资格标准方面与备选案文 3 是一样的，但没有提到时间标准。而备选方案 3 则为资格标准规定了时间限制，即传统知识（如果想要受到保护的话）代代相传的年限不得低于 50 年或五代。

条文 5 的保护范围被重新组织了，但是仍然有 3 个备选方案。备选案文 2 的起首部分目前包括了所提到新的第 14 条（不减损），该第 14 条现在已在另一条中加以规定，该规定指出，文书中的任何内容不得解释为削弱或剥夺土著或者当地社区群众现在已经取得或者将来可能取得的权利。这是由土著小组会议提出的并且得到了一些成员国的支持。

该草案的第 5 条新增了第 2 款的规定（数据库，补充和防御性保护），新增的第 2 款的内容包括有三种不同类型的传统知识志愿数据库保护的部分，以及一个关于补充/防御性保护的部分。

一些发展中国家的代表指出，第 5 条第 2 款应当作为一个独立的条款提出，因为他们认为它与该条的其余部分会产生混淆。他们还对目前提议作为积极保护的范围插入第 5 条的标题提出了否定意见。他们认为"积极保护"一词应该删除。

在目前的第 6 条（制裁，补救和权利的行使/适用）的第二个备选案文中增加了一个新段落。第 7 款规定，如果该文本所保护的权利确定被侵犯了，可根据侵权的性质和影响，考虑将制裁纳入恢复性司法措施。

第 7 条（公开要求）的内容，直到第二次修订才被协调人重新审查，目前该条款被分成了 4 个备选方案。第一个备选方案是成员国新提出的，其内容如下：根据国家法律的要求，传统知识的使用者应遵守有关传统知识的来源和来源的要求。

第 13 条（与其他国际文书的关系）中，涉及不减损土著人民权利的内容被放在了第 14 条。同时又增加了两个涉及"联合国土著权利宣言"的新段落。

（信息搜集、编译：卢岩。

资料来源：http://www.ip-watch.org/2016/12/05/wipo-committee-traditional-knowledge-agrees-revised-text-discussions；http://www.ip-watch.org/2012/07/13/wipo-governments-push-on-folklore-treaty-text-indigenous-peoples-disappointed；http://www.ip-watch.org/2016/12/05/wipo-committee-traditional-knowledge-agrees-revised-text-discussions；http://www.ip-watch.org/2016/09/23/wipo-traditional-knowledge-text-passes-committee-approval-goes-to-next-session/?relatedposts_hit=1&relatedposts_origin=51284&relatedposts_position=2）

【新西兰音乐产业要求改变 TPP 中的版权条款】

2016 年 8 月，唐纳德·特朗普、希拉里·克林顿达成共识，都不满意颇具争议的《跨太平洋伙伴关系协议》（TPP）。对两名美国总统候选人而言，反对该协议的理由是政治原因，但对代表新西兰艺术家和唱片公司利益的 Recorded Music 组织而言，问题在于版权，尤其是如何以及何时延长版权保护期。

在参加新西兰议会委员会的会议时，Recorded Music 首席执行官达米安·沃恩（Damian Vaughan）说，其组织支持 TPP 协议中将作品保护期统一为作者有生之年加死后 70 年的条款（新西兰是几个现有保护期为作者有生之年加死后 50 年的成员国之一）。但是，沃恩认为，让国家升级到 70 年的准备阶段是不必要的，对权利人而言是沉重的负担。他说："对音乐用户或公众而言，TPP 中的版权规定晦涩难懂，程序更加复杂。权利组织和版权所有人将被迫执行新程序……我们发现我们付出的代价比任何节省的成本要多得多。"

在 TPP 的 12 个谈判国中，各个国家的现有版权保护期是作者有生之年加死后一定年限：美国（50 年）、日本（50 年）、澳大利亚（70 年）、秘鲁（70 年）、马来西亚（50 年）、越南（50 年）、新西兰（50 年）、智利（70 年）、新加坡（70 年）、加拿大（50 年）、墨西哥（100 年/2003 年 7 月前为 75 年）、文莱（50 年）。

数字监督机构电子前沿基金会（EFF）称，将版权保护期从死后 50 年延长至死后 70 年是"陷阱"，只有少数成功的作者可以受益。增加的 20 年版权保护期会导致公共领域盗用作品，禁止以之前的作品为基础创造新作品并使孤儿作品问题恶化。美国版权局也认为版权保护期太长了，并提出了缓解不良影响的方法。

除了知识产权章节，TPP 还包含金融服务、电信和环境等方面的协议。仅仅几个月的时间，TPP 的通过就从一件确定的事演变成了一件处于危机中的事。奥巴马总统仍然是最忠实的支持者之一，他希望在大选日之后的"跛脚鸭"会期通过该协议，但如果不成功，将由下一届国会和美国总统决定，两大党的候选人都反对 TPP。

美国通过 TPP 存在的不确定性让一些新西兰人纳闷为何美国政府还要让国会批准 TPP。

（信息搜集、编译：隋川。

资料来源：http://www. billboard. com/articles/business/7476914/new-zealand-tpp-copyright-extension-rules）

【美国《数字千年版权法》对网络服务提供商提出的避风港版权代理新要求】

2016 年 10 月 31 日，美国版权局发布了对指定版权代理商建立电子系统的新规则，这一规则旨在利用避风港原则使得网络服务提供商豁免侵权。根据《美国法典 17》第 5 章第 512 节，网络服务提供商通常是指任何提供在线服务（如网站、电子邮件服务、讨论论坛或聊天室）的运营商；版权代理商通常是指网络服务提供商为接收版权侵权等通知而指定的代理人，该代理人的联系方式应当提供给版权局。

在新的电子系统下，2016 年 12 月 1 日起所有网络服务提供商（包括已经向版权局指定过代理人的网络服务提供商）基于第 512 节的规定寻求避风港保护时，必须通过该电子系统提交指定代理人信息，版权局将不再接受纸质系统的指定。之前提交过纸质版信息的必须在 2017 年 12 月 31 日前在电子系统中提交新的指定代理人信息，否则将不受避风港规则的保护。并且，版权指定代理人信息每三年至少更新一次，注册及后续更新费用指定为每次 6 美元。由此，美国新的版权代理电子申请注册系统将逐步完全取代基于纸张的申请系统。

（信息搜集、编译：白宇嘉。

资料来源：http://www. natlawreview. com/article/digital-millennium-copyright-act-new-dmca-safe-harbor-copyright-agent-requirements；http://www. ipr. gov. cn/article/gjxw/lfdt/mj/bqmj/201612/1899044. html）

【图书馆和档案馆呼吁 WIPO 成员制定避风港规则】

数字化时代为图书馆和档案馆等传播信息打开了一扇新的大门。但是，在跨境活动中，图书馆和档案馆时常面临承担版权侵权责任的风险。图书馆和档案馆要求世界知识产权组织（WIPO）版权及相关权常设委员会（SCCR）不仅要为它们制定一些版权例外，而且还要为它们制定一些规避责任的保护措施。

WIPO 版权及相关权常设委员会会议于 2016 年 11 月 14 日至 18 日举行。议项是图书馆与档案馆版权例外与限制。11 月 17 日，图书管理员与档案管理员代表在发言中解释了他们需要保护其免于承担版权侵权责任的国际标准。

图书馆和档案馆的代表对 SCCR 说，图书馆和档案馆都是遵纪守法的组织，它们尽力尊重版权，但法律太过复杂难以驾驭，图书管理员和档案管理员可能会无意识地侵犯版权。

美国档案管理员协会的代表说，现有技术可让档案管理员发挥全球影响力，但诉讼的风险“让我们对数字时代望而却步”。

美国档案管理员协会的代表指出，档案并不是封锁起来的珍品，而是包含信件、报告、照片和计算机文件等日常用品。制定避风港规则并不代表档案管理员可以为所欲为，而是旨在确保履行基本工作不会让他们承担法律诉讼费或罚款，耗尽他们“微薄的预算”。

美国档案管理员协会的代表说：“我们需要避风港，我们会善意地开展我们的工作。”

国际图书馆协会联合会（IFLA）表示，版权法非常复杂，图书管理员和档案管理员是训练有素的专业人士，但并非律师，许多图书馆和档案馆都在按照政府的指令实施数字保存计划，有时候为了完成使命却要冒侵权风险。

IFLA指出，责任限制将为图书管理员和档案管理员提供宝贵的法律空间，即使在帮助侵犯版权的情况下他们也不用承担责任。

图书馆电子信息联盟（EIFL）也表示，几乎没有图书管理员接受过正式的培训，绝大多数并没有获取专业法律建议的途径。EIFL说它已经研发出一种称作核心库异常检查表的新资源来帮助图书管理员。

德国图书馆协会称，版权法“极其复杂”，版权限制与例外更是如此。德国规定的版权例外适用于文献传递，如将作品数字化并公布在专门的终端上或提供给阅读室，将作品的部分内容用于课堂教学。但是，当图书管理员使用这些例外时，他们会面临详细的法律辩论和诉讼。德国图书馆协会代表说，关于报酬以及在例外范围内使用作品的进一步条件的讨论仍在继续。

欧洲图书情报和文献协会管理局（EBLIDA）表示，在面对著作权法时，即便在没有充分法律保护的情况下，图书管理员也必须将自己置身于公共利益一边。其代表引用了《欧盟议会和理事会关于协调信息社会中著作权和相关权某些方面的指令》。

EBLIDA的代表说道，指令包括了20个可选择的例外列表，欧盟各成员可以自主地选择，并可以在其国内法中以不同的方式来施行。

国际档案馆理事会（ICA）指出，虽然版权制度规定了次要责任，但档案馆和图书馆应免于对用户的行为承担责任。苏格兰档案馆理事会（SCA）表示，档案管理员经常发现版权制度复杂得让人困惑并令人生畏，关于版权制度的国际文本更是如此。

SCA代表也呼吁避风港，这使档案员和图书管理员能够有信心地、凭借其诚信来“解释”和“适用”法律。

最近被授权作为SCCR观察员的非洲图书馆信息协会与机构联合会（AFLIA）指出他们的成员致力于以平衡的方式提供获取知识的价值，为权利人提供公平的报酬，以最大限度地实现书籍和学习、创造和发展方面的其他资源的价值。

AFLIA的代表说道，当图书管理员犯了诚实的错误，他们不应当被当作罪犯。她说，“如果法律是清楚的，那么就不需要律师了。当一个机构以有限的预算来运营时，法律诉讼对其是致命的。如果让在传达一种平衡的、合法的和可持续的著作权体系中是重要的合作者的图书管理员被第一个受到责备，打击盗版是不会成功的”。

博物馆也需要避风港制度

同时，国际博物馆理事会（ICOM）表示，博物馆也应被加入SCCR图书馆和档案馆著作权例外提案的受益者名单中，包括责任的限制。

ICOM的代表说，博物馆藏品包括档案材料和图书馆藏品，博物馆从事与图书馆和档案馆相似的学术追求和交流活动，图书馆和档案馆经常藏有类似博物馆的物品和工艺品。

记者：世界需要独立的记者

国际记者联合会（IFJ）指出，世界需要道德新闻。尽管一些报纸在这方面存在不足，个人和独立记者的工作仍然是反对专断权力的最好堡垒。IFJ代表说，图书馆、档案馆和教育机构应该享有法律确定性，方便它们在保证公民知情方面发挥至关重要的作用，并呼吁这些机构可以获得充足的资金支持，以便作者获得作品使用补偿，因为随着图书馆上线以及图书馆与“某些互联网公司”建立合作伙伴关系，它们的活动在某些方面接近出版，影响了作者的收入。

非洲集团中的一些国家以及巴西也表示，图书馆和档案馆的善意行为可适用版权侵权责任限制。美国解释了其国内的例外规定，并表示成员国应支持图书馆、档案馆和其他相关机构善意行事可适用某些金钱赔偿责任限制。欧盟表示，欧盟版权框架没有讨论图书馆与档案馆责任问题，但可通过成员国国家层面和其他领域的法律解决。

限制与例外仍存在明显的分歧

SCCR的限制和例外问题仍未解决。一些发展中国家要求制定一项条约，为图书馆和档案馆、教育和研究机构以及视力障碍以外的残疾人制定例外和限制。一些发达国家及地区，如欧盟、中欧和波罗的海国家，都表示国际版权法中包含的例外和限制可以在国家层面适用。这些国家赞成为了所有成员国的利益交流国家经验。代表非洲集团的尼日利亚于 2016 年 11 月 17 日表示，SCCR 的讨论结果已经超越了交流国家经验的范畴。

（信息搜集、编译：潘梦琦。

资料来源：http://www.ip-watch.org/2016/11/18/librarians-archivists-call-wipo-members-create-safe-harbour-copyright-liability/；http://www.ip-watch.org/2016/11/18/librarians-archivists-call-wipo-members-create-safe-harbour-copyright-liability/；http://www.ip-watch.org/2016/11/18/librarians-archivists-call-wipo-members-create-safe-harbour-copyright-liability/；http://ipr.gov.cn/article/gjxw/guojizuzhi/201611/1898376.html）

【俄罗斯网络盗版力争上游之下的力量角逐】

俄罗斯知识产权业爆出一个新的丑闻。俄罗斯作家协会（Russian Authors' Society，RAS）负责人谢尔盖·费多托夫（Sergey Fedotov）被逮捕后，俄罗斯警方指控俄罗斯作家协会也即俄罗斯主要的知识产权公共保护协会的会长受贿几百万卢布，警方宣称已经对马克西姆·雷亚布科（Maxim Ryabyko）启动刑事诉讼程序，雷亚布科是俄罗斯网络版权保护协会（RAPCI）的会长。

RAPCI 专注于对互联网版权所有者权利的保护，尤其是对遭受盗版和其他知识产权权利侵犯的作者和公司提供法律支持。与此同时，RAPCI 分析师称，对俄罗斯那里的专门从事知识产权保护的协会的持续攻击是由在盗版者协助下的人士以及支持他们利益的政府工作人员组织的，这是由于他们近年来在俄罗斯对非法内容的销售和分配利润已经明显下降。

这也源于最新旨在打击盗版的举措，这些措施由 RAPCI 和 RAS 专家设计，随后受到俄罗斯政府支持。

俄罗斯的知识产权保护状况一直都不乐观。俄罗斯内务部官方数据显示，2015 年来自知识产权非法使用的年利润高达 4 亿美元。但是，近年来这种情况已经明显得到改善，主要是由于在俄罗斯知识产权行业内国家改革的开始以及版权保护领域国家立法的收紧。

弗拉季斯拉夫·沃罗特尼科夫（Vladislav Vorotnikov）是俄罗斯财政部财务管理部门的资深专家以及版权保护领域的权威分析师之一，他称，雷亚布科以俄罗斯互联网盗版的主要打击者之一闻名。因此对他启动诉讼程序以及对 RAO（俄国作家协会，Russian Authors' Organization）最近的攻击可能是盗版者以及犯罪者对于他们在俄罗斯持续受到的打击做出的一个反应。盗版者的特别关注（根据俄罗斯联邦安全局称，其中很多受到俄罗斯国家机构和执法机构中腐败官员的协助）与版权保护领域内的最新举措相关，这些措施已经由 RAPCI 提出并得到 RAO 的支持。

其中一个倡议包括强制性要求网站所有者在俄罗斯境内注册为法人，并进一步将他们与互联网地址连接在一起。部分的计划是将这些网站纳入法律实体的国家注册中，不包括在注册内的网站将被禁止植入广告。

据专家介绍，这个计划在 2016 年 11 月生效。实施这个计划将不仅进一步防止广告在盗版网络资源上盈利，还包括在所有的国外网站上。盗版网站的广告是网站收入的主要来源。由于匿名问题以及俄罗斯刑法启动刑事诉讼程序，盗版网站在俄罗斯再也无法作为法律实体注册。

根据俄罗斯内务部推测，由于盗版者不需要购买合法内容，盗版资源的平均利润率约为 95%。RAO 分析师预计费多托夫的逮捕和对于雷亚布科刑事诉讼程序的启动可能会抹黑这两个协会的活动，同时导致它们计划的暂停实施，尤其是那些旨在打击俄罗斯盗版的计划。

（信息搜集、编译：曾雪。

资料来源：http://www.ip-watch.org/2016/10/31/power-struggle-russia-internet-pirates-vie-upper-hand）

【澳大利亚学校因避风港计划出错而违反 TPP 版权规则】

避风港原则由来及释义

避风港原则来自美国 1998 年制定的《数字千年版权法》，最早适用于著作权领域，后来由于网络中介服务商没有能力进行事先内容审查，一般事先对侵权信息的存在不知情，所以，采取“通知—删除”规则，是对网络中介服务商间接侵权责任的限制。即“网络服务提供者使用信息定位工具。包括目录、索引、超文本链接、在线存储网站，如果由于其链接、存储的相关内容涉嫌侵权，在其能够证明自己并无恶意，并且及时删除侵权链接或者内容的情况下，网络服务提供者不承担赔偿责任”。

避风港计划在澳大利亚的适用受到限制

2016年10月，澳大利亚版权顾问组（CAG）的版权主任迪莉娅·布朗（Delia Browne）对澳大利亚议会条约委员会说，澳大利亚现有的避风港计划是以美国的相似计划为基础，是在签署《美澳自由贸易协议》时被要求采纳的。

但是，澳大利亚的避风港计划仅适用于商业化的网络服务提供商，并不适用于提供网络服务的学校、大学和图书馆，这是一个“粗心的错误”所造成的局面。布朗说：“这意味着商业性的网络服务提供商在履行版权侵权删除通知时能得到合法保护。”

布朗对议会条约委员会说，如果澳大利亚既要符合《美澳自由贸易协议》，也要符合《跨太平洋伙伴关系协议》，避风港计划的措辞就要调整。《版权修正（无障碍获取与其他措施）法案》草案已完成。布朗说：“我们敦促委员会将法案推荐给议会，尤其是有关避风港的条款。”

CAG负责澳大利亚学校的版权事务。澳大利亚数字联盟的执行官杰西卡·科茨（Jessica Coates）对议会条约委员会说，小型的互联网初创企业不受避风港计划保护。科茨说：“这让我们的初创企业在与国际同行竞争时处于商业劣势，严重抑制技术企业在澳大利亚建立主机托管业务以及其他新的技术服务，增加了同那些同领域国际机构相比的企业的风险。”

TPP将规范澳大利亚、美国、新西兰、加拿大、新加坡、越南、马来西亚、日本、墨西哥、秘鲁、文莱和智利之间的贸易。

（信息搜集、编译：隋川。

资料来源：http://www.out-law.com/en/articles/2016/october/australian-schools-could-breach-tpp-copyright-rules-due-to-error-in-safe-harbour-agreement）

【知识共享组织在WIPO：支持更公平的教学研究版权政策】

2016年11月在日内瓦，知识共享组织（Creative Commons，CC）参加了世界知识产权组织版权及相关权常设委员会双年度会议。

从2011年开始，CC在WIPO就享有“观察者”的地位，这就意味着它可以参与诉讼并且可以在某些时候就委员会的活动提供书面或口头的反馈。

WIPO的议程中至少包含了一些关于教学和研究中著作权的限制和例外的讨论——主要是如何建立一个法律或规范机制，来提升对受版权保护作品的使用，从而为教学和学习服务。

虽然CC继续坚持宣传和拓展教育开放政策的内容，但是CC一直明白自愿许可机制永远不是也不可能是一个全面的解决方案。那么政府和其他部门就需要起到领导作用，在例外和限制的框架范围内来保证教导者和学习者可以利用世界范围内的知识而不用担心侵权。因此，CC坚信基本法律和法规的改革是必要的，不管CC牌照有多么成功以及它为建设一个更公平、合理、公正的世界所起到多大的促进作用，CC支持强制、灵活的版权例外，以维持以及授权给教育和研究。

澳大利亚学校国际版权主任和澳大利亚知识共享组织共同领导人迪莉娅·布朗代表CC参与了此次会议。她在会议上的演讲内容如下文所述。同时，公共财产组织也参与了WIPO以教育的限制和例外为议题的一系列会议，知识共享组织也是公共财产组织的成员之一。

另外，WIPO宣布它将会使用一种开放接触政策“以支持其分享和传播知识的承诺，以使其出版物容易地提供给尽可能广泛的受众”。通过这个声明，WIPO加入了诸如联合国教科文组织、世界银行以及英联邦学习共同体等政府间组织，以使其出版物可以在开放许可证的条件下被他人获得。CC祝贺WIPO和这些政府间组织，并呼吁其他公共机构支持开放获取和分发他们开发的作品。

2016年11月18日，迪莉娅·布朗题为《知识共享组织——关于教育限制和例外的声明》的演讲主要内容如下：

首先感谢主席先生，今天我代表的是知识共享组织，这个组织是世界范围内的非营利性组织，它致力于在符合版权规则的情况下，让人们更容易地分享以及在别人智力成果的基础上开展工作。我们非常热烈欢迎和祝贺WIPO的新开放获取政策，这将使其所有出版物在知识共享政府间组织（IGO）许可证下提供。我们欢迎WIPO致力于使其出版物尽可能广泛地被获取，我们很高兴能够在这里听取WIPO周三公布的公告。

我们还感谢主席先生提供了极为有用的关于教育限制和例外的图表，我们将非常感兴趣地加以考虑。知识共享组织相信，在数字化的年代，普及教育是可能的。为此，我们正在与政府、教育机构、公司和个人广泛合作，共享免费许可证和法律工具，促进获取知识和信息。

知识共享许可证支持数以百万计开放获取和开放教育资源，从学术论文到优质教育视频、高等教育课程，政府和慈善组织越来越多地要求研究成果授权公开许可，以换取资金支持。

知识共享组织公共域标记用于标记分享平台上的版权保护之外的数以百万计的作品，比如 Europeana 分享平台。

政府和组织正积极将 CC 0 牌照（CC 0 是 CC 项目下一种知识共享方式）使用于数据集，以消除会阻碍研究的版权限制。

我们为知识共享资源提供的机会感到骄傲，但是我们也感受到，只有共享许可不能也不可能是全部的解决办法。知识共享许可仅适用于一小部分必要的教育资源，创作者有意识地决定公开许可他们的工作。许可，开放或其他方式，都不能取代教育例外和限制的基本工作。

因此，知识共享组织支持教育限制和例外的强制性最低标准。我们祝贺 Seng 教授关于教育活动的版权限制和例外的研究取得进展。虽然我们理解在审查 189 个成员立法之前仍有进一步的工作要做，但已经出现了三个关键点：

这是一个广泛的协议，教育领域的例外和限制是必要的；

如何保护教育权利以及哪些确切权利受到保护之间存在分歧；

许多国家的例外没有跟上技术进步的步伐——虽然一些较旧的例外已经设法去适应新技术，在新权利所有者权已经被引入的领域，比如技术保护措施领域相应的教育保护没有跟上。

知识共享组织相信有进一步探讨此建议如何支持强制性最低标准以保护版权限制和例外的工作的余地。

（信息搜集、编译：刘笑晗。

资料来源：https://creativecommons.org/2016/11/24/creative-commons-wipo-supporting-fair-copyright-teaching-learning/）

【WIPO：追续权——纠正版权收入不平衡的方式】

2016 年 11 月 13 日至 17 日，WIPO 版权及相关权常设委员会于瑞士日内瓦举行了第 35 届会议。作为大会讨论主题之一的追续权，经由塞内加尔和刚果的提案提出。11 月 18 日，墨尔本大学法学院知识产权法研究联合主任萨姆·里基森教授就追续权这一议题做了一般性的介绍。

追续权于 1920 年首次在法国引入，它指的是视觉艺术家，如画家，在他们的作品被转售后得到的版税。视觉艺术家每卖出一份作品将获得一定的收入。一旦作品以更高的价钱被转售出去，一些国家则赋予这些艺术家追续权。而在其他国家，这种权利并不存在，使视觉艺术家处于不利的境地，特别是本土艺术家，因为他们的作品在国际艺术市场上可能变得非常有价值。

追续权本是《保护文学和艺术作品伯尔尼公约》布鲁塞尔文本（1948 年）的一项选择性义务。但在过去的 20 年中，各国采用追续权制度的速度大大加快。据萨姆·里基森教授称，截至 2016 年 11 月，已有 81 个国家对于追续权予以保护，包括通过 2001 年欧盟指令 2001/84/EC 以保护原作艺术作者利益的所有欧盟成员。澳大利亚的原住民社区中有着许许多多创造着伟大艺术品的创作者，他们的作品被本土及海外的收藏者及画廊所收藏。利益被剥削引发了本土艺术家寻求保护的共鸣。出于对本土艺术家利益的关注，澳大利亚于 2009 年颁布了追续权立法。此外，许多其他国家也对追续权感兴趣，特别是当传统的艺术作品在国家和国际艺术市场上具有价值时。

“调查显示，与其他类别的创作者相比（如作家或计算机程序员等），视觉艺术家的地位不平衡，其平均收入低于其他类别艺术家，视觉艺术家应当通过转售继续利用他的作品。”萨姆·里基森说道。各国对于追续权采取了不同的立法模式，而根据其对于不同国家法律的研究发现，实施追续权最为有效的方式是通过集体行政管理。

据一位任职加拿大版权研究所的艺术家称，视觉艺术家们为争取追续权已奋斗多年。艺术家在加拿大很穷，其中视觉艺术家是最为贫困的。他强调了退休的视觉艺术家正处于水深火热之中，尽管他们的作品的价值在转售市场上随着时间的推移而增加。因无法再进行创造工作，他们正挣扎于极度的贫困之中，而加拿大的中间商却从事着以更高的价格转售本土作品的工作。关于追续权的立法可以纠正这种情况，他说，现在是时候让这样一项权利成为普遍性的权利了。

（信息搜集、编译：罗文君。

资料来源：http://www.ip-watch.org/2016/11/22/resale-royalty-right-way-redress-imbalance-copyright-revenue-wipo-told；http://www.wipo.int/meetings/en/details.jsp? meeting_id=42304）

【WIPO 对自身所有出版物使用知识共享许可】

知识产权的最重要的国际机构——联合国世界

知识产权组织（WIPO），于2016年11月16日宣布，它将通过创作共享许可证的方式来提供自己所有的出版物，这一举动旨在与其他组织共发展。WIPO和其他主要国际组织的这一行动，使得它的出版物能够尽可能广泛地被读者获得，也间接地指出版权制度存在的限制性。

该公告是在WIPO版权及相关权常设委员会（SCCR）为期一周的会议期间发布的。

世界知识产权组织宣布了其新的开放式获取政策，以促进公众尽可能广泛地使用其出版物，促进本组织对传播和分享知识的承诺。

作为知产相关信息的参考来源，WIPO收藏了全面的出版物，包括研究报告、指南和其他学习资源。开放获取政策有助于政策制定者、研究人员、从业人员和任何希望使用这些资源的人更方便地获得这些资源。

“WIPO的出版物是珍贵信息的精品合集，”WIPO的总干事弗朗西斯·高锐说，“我们的开放获取政策是为了确保这笔宝贵的知识财富更容易被每个人使用。”

为了支持开放获取政策的实施，WIPO将使用知识共享政府间组织（IGO）的一系列许可证，它曾在2013年帮助一些国际组织行使相关权利。创作共用许可证是一种广泛使用且易于理解的成套的版权工具和协议，促进获取和使用创意内容。

从现在开始，由WIPO创建和全权拥有的新出版物以及一些现有出版物将根据CC-BY 3.0 IGO许可证或知识共享IGO套件中的其他许可证获得许可。WIPO的出版物能够在知识共享许可下获得，这些出版物在WIPO网站的出版物范围内可以被清楚地识别和搜寻。

WIPO目前还支持开放存档倡议，通过如上的广泛使用方式。这一倡议主要通过协同性标准和高效的许可计划促进内容的传播。

（信息搜集、编译：陈早璟。

资料来源：http://www.ip-watch.org/2016/11/16/wipo-use-creative-commons-licences-publications；http://www.ruanyifeng.com/blog/2008/04/creative_commons_licenses.html；http://www.ip-watch.org/2015/09/17/did-wipo-get-cool-un-ipr-agency-joins-creative-commons-initiative）

【欧盟理事会同意消除电子商务地域屏蔽】

欧盟理事会于2016年11月28日就防止跨境电子商务封锁法律草案达成一致意见，不过草案中著作权限制或将保留。

“地域屏蔽是一种歧视性的做法，这种做法阻碍了线上用户从其他成员国网站上获取和购买商品或服务。”欧盟理事会在其发布的通讯中解释道。通讯同时谈到，这份法律草案将形成理事会共同立场，以此启动与欧盟议会和欧盟委员会的磋商机制。

通讯中说：“新规与欧盟著作权保护相关规定一致，将在著作权限制方面例外。”其解释道：

根据新规，在三种情况下，商人在销售商品和提供服务时，将不能就其所提供的包括价格在内的一般交易条件对顾客进行区别对待，这三种情况是当商人：

（1）销售在其承担送货义务的成员国中运送的商品，或者与顾客约定地点交货的商品时。

（2）提供以电子方式供应的服务，如云服务、数据库存服务、虚拟主机服务、网络防火墙服务时。本款不适用于以提供受著作权保护作品（或其他受保护主体）的使用权或获取路径为主要特征，或以销售受著作权保护的非实体作品（如电子书和在线音乐）为主要特征的服务。

（3）提供顾客于该商人营业地所在国接受的服务时。这些服务包括酒店住宿、体育赛事、汽车租赁、音乐节或休闲公园的门票等。

与价格歧视不同，价格差异化将不被禁止。因此，针对某一地域范围内的特定消费者人群，商人仍旧可以提供包括价格差异在内的不同交易条件。

此外，在提供送货服务的成员国之外，商人没有送货义务。

（信息搜集、编译：侯旭烽。

资料来源：http://www.ip-watch.org/2016/11/28/eu-council-agrees-remove-geo-blocking-barriers-e-commerce；https://ec.europa.eu/digital-single-market/en/news/proposal-regulation-geo-blocking；http://www.lexology.com/library/detail.aspx?g=7c413f1e-833f-40c9-a7fc-83e15fef8442；http://www.klgates.com/new-rules-and-prohibitions-to-promote-e-commerce-in-europe-06-14-2016）

【关于ASKA的未发表歌曲的作曲泄露问题之著作权法上的思考】

2016年11月，涉嫌吸毒而被逮捕的日本歌手ASKA尚未发布的作曲在电视节目中播放一事引发热议。根据日本《著作权法》第18条第1款的规定：作者享有将自己尚未发表的作品（包括未取得作者同意已经发表的作品，下款同）复制、向公众提供的权利。尚未发布的作曲在电视中公开播放，侵犯了作者人格权中的发表权。此外，还可能侵犯著作财产权（信息网络传播权、广播组织权等）。关于此案的分析如下：

首先，如果 ASKA 事先已向日本音乐著作权协会转让登记该作品，则应视为同意发表。根据日本《著作权法》第 18 条第 2 款的规定：作者转让著作权则推定为同意发表。但是，如今由于被擅自发布的作曲属于暂时未附歌词且未经处理的母带，因此不可能发生转让，故推测不成立。

其次，有关权利限制的规定。日本《著作权法》第 32 条第 1 项规定：已经发表的作品可以以引用的方式加以利用。此时的引用，要符合正当性原则，并且必须是在报道、评论、研究以及其他属于正当目的范围内进行引用。在判断是否是出于正当目的的引用之前，首先要判断引用的对象。根据第 32 条规定，正当引用的对象限于“已经发表的作品”，可以认定尚未发表的作品不属于正当引用的对象。故媒体的行为不构成正当引用。另外，关于时事新闻报道中的“利用行为”。日本《著作权法》第 41 条规定：当使用照片、视频、广播及以其他方式报道的时事新闻的情形下，相关作品组成或者再现事件过程，或者报道时无意中摄入的作品，可在正当目的范围内进行复制及报道该相关事件时加以利用。该条规定适用对象并不限于已经发表的作品。本案的问题关键在于该未发表的作曲是不是“组成或者再现事件过程的相关作品”及是否属于“出于正当目的而使用报道的范围”。如果在时事报道中称“若即使吸毒仍能创作出如此优秀的乐曲”，则可能符合该条规定的情况。

此外，根据第 41 条规定，关于未发表的作品能否被报道的情况，例如，某知名画家在创作过程中逝世，在报道中介绍作品应该适用该条规定。（由于作者已经去世，发表权在一定程度上受到限制。）（编者注：涉嫌吸毒的 ASKA 在被捕前乘坐出租车回家，出租车内的行车记录仪拍摄到 ASKA，并被媒体曝光。该曝光行为被谴责侵犯了社会公众个人隐私。）对于被警察逮捕的嫌疑人，以前的主流观点认为，不论大众传媒报道什么，民众都会接受，但是如今这样的观点却不得不加以转变。

（信息搜集、编译：兰鉴。

资料来源：http://bylines.news.yahoo.co.jp/kuriharakiyoshi/20161202-00065052/；http://www.nikkansports.com/entertainment/news/1745454.html）

【音乐产业集团一致呼吁特朗普的支持】

19 家音乐产业集团，业务范围涉及从基督音乐到古典乐，从节奏布鲁斯到电影原声，一致致信美国当选总统唐纳德·特朗普，要求当其在 2016 年 12 月 14 日会见科技产业领袖时，将它们的知识产权纳入考虑之中。

“当您在明天会见一些世界主要技术公司的高管的时候，我们希望强调一些观点以保证作为美国国家财富的音乐行业能够继续保持活力。”19 家音乐产业集团公司在信中写道。

关于音乐行业的争论话题包括“音乐产业的经济增长”、“驱动创新”以及“科技公司不要总是拿走权利持有人的利益”。

“搜索引擎，用户上传平台，服务提供商以及域名登记注册机构应当依照其他案例以有效阻止盗窃以及保障公平支付。”它们说。此外，音乐组织补充道，“现在存在着大量的‘价值攫取’现象，即一些公司通过利用法律漏洞的方式，滥用美国法律达到减少支付给作者的报酬的效果，以弱化美国创作者的知识产权，进而损害作为美国经济和就业引擎之一的音乐产业”。

它们说：“在基于自由市场所设立的音乐价格的公平支付以及对于非法访问的禁止等方面，作为全球最有优秀的技术公司当然可以做得更好。”

（信息搜集、编译：梁瑞元。

资料来源：http://www.ip-watch.org/2016/12/14/music-industry-groups-harmony-calling-support-trump/）

【未确定的盗版索赔不应导致切断互联网】

据 2016 年 12 月的相关报道，电子前沿基金会（EFF）关注到一个令人忧心的发展趋势，互联网服务提供商仅因为盗版行为的指控即被迫切断与互联网用户的联系。EFF 将互联网的连接视为一项基本权利，而不是版权所有者应该控制的权利。

2015 年 12 月，美国弗吉尼亚的一个联邦陪审团裁定互联网服务提供商 Cox Communications 对其用户的版权侵权行为负有责任。这个互联网服务提供商因没有适当地封锁重复侵权行为人的账号而不能获得安全港保护，并被认为应承担主观故意的共同侵权责任。Cox 公司提起上诉，希望能推翻 2 500 万美元赔偿的判决。截止到 2016 年 12 月，Cox 公司已获得了几个行业协会、学术机构以及 EFF 的支持。2016 年 12 月，EFF 再次强调了本案的重要性。根据数字权利组织所称，版权所有者不应该享有基于侵犯版权的主张而切断互联网的权利。“没有人应当承担由于不确定的指控而失去互联网连接的忧虑恐惧。”EFF的克里·希恩（Kerry Sheehan）写道。

EFF承认《数字千年版权法》（DMCA）要求互联网服务提供商应当有应对重复侵权行为的政策。然而，DMCA并没有说片面的盗版指控就足够导致这样的结果。EFF指出，当时的情形已表明来自著作权人的指控并不总是准确的。即使跟踪到正确的IP地址，也并不意味着账户所有人是分享侵权材料的人。是不是重复侵权行为人不应当由通过不作为的人来获取利润的盗版检测结构决定，而应当由法庭来决定。EFF希望上诉法院认识到可能导致范围过宽的监测和过滤行为，并且将切断互联网络作为最后选择而不是通常选择的措施。

（信息搜集、编译：白宇嘉。

资料来源：https://torrentfreak.com/unfounded-piracy-claims-shouldnt-lead-to-internet-cut-offs-161213/）

【USTR谴责窃取流媒体资源的行为，新的“恶名市场”报告点名阿里巴巴】

美国贸易代表办公室（USTR）在2016年12月21日发布了它的年度“恶名市场”报告。这份报告列出了对美国文化创意产业最具威胁的线上和线下市场，并且在其中特别强调了窃取流媒体资源的新趋势。

报告引用了国际唱片工业联合会的一份研究。研究表明对流媒体资源的窃取行为在全球领先的音乐市场中愈演愈烈，30%的网络用户通过盗版服务获得了未授权的音乐产品。正如在数字音乐销售中，流媒体传播下载音乐那样，盗版手段通过窃取潮流的下载音乐，模仿了这种趋势并将其作为窃取音乐的首选方法。

“对流媒体资源的窃取行为直接威胁了数字产品的增长，因为它减弱了用户对正版服务的需求，从而剥夺了艺人和唱片公司的这一重要收入来源。”美国贸易代表办公室的恶名市场报告这样阐述，“付费下载网站以及合法的流媒体服务同时受到了损害，而且开发和推出新一代合法流媒体服务的激励机制也被削弱。”

尽管美国贸易代表办公室及其引用的研究将窃取流媒体资源的行为描述为音乐产业数字收入的重要威胁，但并没有从任何经济角度评价它的总体影响，而是关注了这种行为方式的增长。它们忽略了一个更大的趋势，即越来越少的人对“拥有”音乐感兴趣，无论是购买正版还是盗版，因为流媒体才是新的王道（2016年，即使是唱片，其销量也超过了数字下载）。至于它们是否夸大了窃取流媒体资源行为对音乐产业的实际影响，这并不清楚。

美国唱片工业协会回应了美国贸易代表办公室对窃取流媒体资源行为的确认，董事长兼首席执行官卡里·谢尔曼（Cary Sherman）发表声明表示支持。“这个新报告正确及时地曝光了这种特殊类型的恶名市场。它抢走了词曲作家们、艺人们以及唱片公司本应可以从正版流媒体服务中可以获得的版税收入。”谢尔曼说。

在这份报告中，作为美国和国际权利人的“重点关注”，中国C2C交易平台淘宝网同样被点出。淘宝网的经营“对打击泛滥的假冒、盗版商品形成了持续的严重挑战”。淘宝网的母公司阿里巴巴则声称，截至2016年8月，它在12个月内清除了近4亿产品清单并关停了18万个淘宝网店。阿里巴巴也改变了它的强制政策，原来对商家的“四振出局”变成了“三振出局”。

（信息搜集、编译：张瑜。

资料来源：http://www.billboard.com/articles/news/7632451/us-trade-representative-stream-ripping-notorious-markets-report；http://www.billboard.com/files/styles/article_main_image/public/media/internet-piracy-stock-biz-2015-billboard-1548.jpg；http://rainnews.com/u-s-trade-report-highlights-stream-ripping-as-piracy-concern/）

索　引

0～9

2006—2015 年中国版权产业的城镇单位就业人数及占全国 GDP 比重（图） 215
2006—2015 年中国版权产业的商品出口额及占全国 GDP 比重（图） 216
2006—2015 年中国版权产业的行业增加值及占全国 GDP 比重（图） 214
2006—2015 年中国核心版权产业的行业增加值及占全国 GDP 比重（图） 215
2006—2015 年中国核心版权产业、全部版权产业行业增加值与 GDP 的年均增长率对比图（图） 214a
2006—2015 年中国核心版权产业行业增加值占全部版权产业的比重（图） 214b
2006—2015 年中国与美国版权产业行业增加值占全国 GDP 比重的比较（图） 216
2006—2016 年国产电视动画片生产数量和增长率（图） 271
2008—2016 年全国动画电影票房收入和观影人次（图） 272
2009—2016 年中国动漫产业总产值（图） 269
2011—2015 年全国电视动画播出数量（表） 272
2011—2016 年广播电视行业广告收入分级占比情况（表） 259
2011—2016 年获得发行许可电视剧数量（表） 253
2011—2016 年全国有线电视用户、数字电视用户和付费数字电视用户增长情况（图） 260
2011—2016 年全国有线广播电视网络收入及增长情况（图） 261
2011—2016 年中国电影海外综合收入情况（图） 266
2012—2016 年电影产业发展基本指标一览（表） 264
2012—2016 年各类影片生产情况（表） 263
2012—2016 年广播电视行业广告收入及增长情况（图） 257
2012—2016 年国产电影和进口电影市场份额情况（表） 264
2012—2016 年全国电视广告收入情况（图） 258
2012—2016 年全国广播广告收入情况（图） 258
2013—2020 年中国网络游戏市场规模及预测（图） 284b
2013—2020 年中国网络游戏市场细分规模及预测（图） 285
2013—2020 年中国移动游戏市场规模及预测（图） 285b
2015—2016 年中国举办的国际电影节展基本情况（表） 265
2015CPCC 十大中国著作权人评选揭晓 156a
《2015 年北京知识产权保护状况白皮书》发布 148a
《2015 年新闻出版产业分析报告》发布 159b
2015 年中国版权产业的经济贡献 213
2015 年中国版权产业的经济贡献（表） 213
《2015 年中国网络版权保护年度报告》发布 157a
2015 年中国游戏产业规模达到 1 407 亿元 198b
2015 年中国知识产权发展状况发布会举行 148a
2015 年专利、商标、版权质押融资达 931.72 亿元 199a
2016—2017 年中国数字出版产业发展报告 246
2016 CPCC 十大中国著作权人 400
2016CPCC 中国版权服务年会在京举行 163b
2016 版权宣传周宣传资料发布 158a
2016 第一届“文化＋”新创意新业态新经济论坛举办 170a
2016 海峡两岸知识产权法学论坛成果报道 209a
“2016 剑网行动·原创文字作品保护月”正式启动 181b
2016 美国书展中国展团盛装参展 188a
2016 年 1—12 月前十位省市软件业增长情况（图） 279
2016 年 1—12 月软件产业分类收入占比情况（图） 279
2016 年 1—12 月软件出口增长情况（图） 278

2016 年 1—12 月软件业分区域增长情况（图） 279
2016 年 1—12 月软件业利润总额走势（图） 278
2016 年 1—12 月软件业务收入增长情况（图） 277
2016 年 1—12 月中心城市软件业务收入增长情况（图） 279
2016 年 BIBF 国际版权贸易高级研修班在京举行 169a
2016 年百度搜索风云榜中国动漫榜单前 50 名（表） 275
2016 年版权公共服务机构与社会服务组织工作（版权工作概览） 103
2016 年版权输出地汇总表 481
2016 年版权引进地汇总表 482
2016 年单品种累计印数排名前 10 位的图书（表） 221a
2016 年地方版权工作（版权工作概览） 45
2016 年地方著作权行政执法案件（典型案件选编） 322
2016 年第 4 季度中国手机漫画应用活跃用户数量前 10 名（图） 271
2016 年（第九届）全国大学生版权征文获奖名单 403
2016 年电视广告收入位居前 10 名的省份（表） 258
2016 年度查处侵权盗版案件有功单位及个人 387
2016 年度美国版权政策概览 527a
2016 年度打击侵权盗版十大案件（典型案件选编） 303
2016 年广播电视行业广告收入位居前 10 名的省份（表） 257
2016 年广播广告收入位居前 10 名的省份（表） 258
2016 年国产动画电影（含合拍片）票房收入前十名（表） 274
2016 年国际版权动态 527
2016 年国际版权论坛聚焦“版权 创新 发展” 194a
2016 年获得发行许可电视剧题材比例（表） 254
2016 年平均期印数排名前 10 位的期刊（表） 221b
2016 年平均期印数排名前 10 位的专业类报纸（表） 222b
2016 年平均期印数排名前 10 位的综合类报纸（表） 222b
2016 年全国版权工作（版权工作概览） 39
2016 年全国版权合同情况统计 480
2016 年全国版权社会服务工作交流会在广州召开 172a
2016 年全国版权司法保护工作（版权工作概览） 42
2016 年全国版权行政管理工作（版权工作概览） 39
2016 年全国版权执法情况统计 481
2016 年全国各地区各类期刊出版的种数、印数、总印张、总金额（1） 486
2016 年全国各地区各类期刊出版的种数、印数、总印张、总金额（2） 488
2016 年全国各地区录像制品出版品种、数量及发行总量（按载体形式分类） 492
2016 年全国各地区录音制品出版品种、数量及发行总量（按载体形式分类） 490
2016 年全国各地区图书出版总量 483
2016 年全国各级报纸出版数量 484
2016 年全国广播电视发展主要指标一览表（1） 496
2016 年全国广播电视发展主要指标一览表（2） 498
2016 年全国软件产业统计数据 500
2016 年全国图书、期刊、报纸进出口情况 495
2016 年全国新华书店系统、出版社自办发行单位出版物发行进、销、存情况 494
2016 年全国音像、电子出版物、数字出版物进出口情况 495
《2016 年全国知识产权系统执法维权工作方案》印发 147b
2016 年全国主要城市电视台动画节目收视率前 20 位（表） 273
2016 年全国著作权司法保护典型案件（典型案件选编） 295
2016 年全国作品登记工作培训班在京举行 159a
2016 年全国作品登记情况统计 479
2016 年数字出版产业收入情况（图） 246
2016 年网络版权侵权案件传播方式分布情况（图） 382
2016 年网络版权侵权案件地域分布情况（图） 382
2016 年网络版权侵权案件类型分布情况（图） 382
2016 年新增出版传媒上市公司概况（表） 229
2016 年中国版权十件大事 398
2016 年中国版权统计资料 479
2016 年中国电影产业发展报告 263
2016 年中国动漫产业发展报告 269
2016 年中国动漫产业各细分领域产值对比

（图） 270
2016 年中国广播电视产业发展报告 252
2016 年中国广播影视产业统计资料 496
2016 年中国客户端游戏市场竞争格局（图） 285a
2016 年中国软件产业发展概况 277
2016 年中国软件产业统计资料 500
2016 年中国网络版权保护年度报告 377
2016 年中国网络游戏市场分析 283
2016 年中国网页游戏市场竞争格局（图） 290b
2016 年中国网页游戏市场研发格局（图） 290a
2016 年中国新闻出版产业分析报告 218
2016 年中国新闻出版产业统计资料 483
2016 年中国移动游戏发行商全平台竞争格局（图） 287a
2016 年中国移动游戏发行市场用户渗透率（图） 287
2016 年中国移动游戏市场 AMC 模型（图） 286
2016 年中国移动游戏市场实力矩阵（图） 286
2016 年中国移动游戏研发企业市场份额（图） 287a
2016 年著作权法研究综述 415
2016 年著作权热点问题研究 424
2016 年著作权相关图书简介 468
《2016 体育创业白皮书》关注电竞媒体赛事版权 158b
2016 新德里世界书展中国代表团版权贸易成果丰硕 186a
2016 移动互联网创新大会关注版权开发 166b
2016 中国版权金奖在广州颁发 162a
2016 中国互联网法治大会在京召开 169b
《2016 中国音乐产业发展报告》发布 205a
“2016 中韩出版合作论坛”在京举行 190b
467 种中国新书亮相第 23 届东京国际书展 191b
4 家游戏公司被指侵犯金庸作品改编权 141b
750 部电视剧亮相 2016 春季北京电视节目交易会 198a

A

AIPPI 中国分会版权热点论坛举行 172b
“APP 及广告联盟相关版权侵权问题研讨会”在京举行 168b
IFPI 2016 全球音乐报告发布 198b
《QQ 阅读》借势营销《明妃传》被叫停 132b
USTR 谴责窃取流媒体资源的行为，新的“恶名市场”报告点名阿里巴巴 545a
WIPO 对自身所有出版物使用知识共享许可 542b
WIPO 召开知识产权及发展里程碑会议 536a
WIPO：追续权——纠正版权收入不平衡的方式 542a
阿里巴巴 238 亿元收购优酷土豆所有股份 197a
阿里巴巴海外购得独家版权 205b
阿里影业投资大地影院 199b
爱奇艺诉华数传媒侵权索赔 30 万元 135b
爱奇艺与 20 世纪福克斯合作拓展网络版权 195a
安徽（典型案件选编） 314b
安徽省版权保护协会选举换届 174a
安徽省（版权工作概览） 65b
安徽省版权局下发《关于开展广播电视节目版权专项检查活动的通知》 146a
安徽省（典型案件选编） 329a
澳大利亚联邦法院认定数字数据信号不受版权保护 532a
澳大利亚生产力委员会提倡合理使用，重新激起版权大战 530b
澳大利亚学校因避风港计划出错而违反 TPP 版权规则 540b
澳门 209b
澳门贸促局促中小企业利用知识产权优势勇闯内地市场 209b

B

百度关闭文学类贴吧清查盗版侵权获国家版权局肯定 178a
百度开放云助力国家新闻出版打造智能数字出版体系 202b
百度云盘擅传《金陵十三钗》被判赔偿 135b
版权代理公司（名录） 512
版权工作概览 37
版权公共服务机构（名录） 507
“版权和相关权热点问题亚太地区研讨会”在西安举行 188b
版权界动态 129
版权人沙龙聚焦互联网内容平台版权保护与管理 164a
版权：仍然任重道远 28
版权扫描 127
版权师培养计划在京启动 177a
版权为桥——有声出版火起来 203b
版权相关产业与版权贸易 211
版权相关热点问题媒体研修班在北京开班 165b
版权相关行业协会（名录） 512
版权协会（名录） 508

版权行政管理部门（名录） 503
“版权云北京之夜暨 426so 平台上线周年庆”在京召开 176b
“保护视听表演对文化和创意产业发展的重要性圆桌会议”在京举行 167a
报纸的层级结构（表） 222a
报纸的内容结构（表） 222a
暴风体育获得中超新媒体版权 201a
北京“12318”查扣非法出版物、盗版光盘逾 200 万件 147b
北京版权保护协会成立“网络工委” 175b
北京查获特大网络销售盗版图书案 144b
北京打通动漫游戏产业链 201b
北京（典型案件选编） 309a
北京国数与北青社合力打造数字产业服务平台 199b
北京三男子因架设“私服”侵犯游戏《笑傲江湖 OL》著作权罪被判刑 130a
北京市 2016 年国家机关软件正版化工作全面启动 150b
北京市（版权工作概览） 45a
北京市版权局再次联合业内企业打击侵权盗版手游 153a
贝宝出于版权问题考量停止支持 VPN 和智能 DNS 服务提供商的支付功能 534b
《奔跑吧兄弟》官微涉著作权纠纷 129b
比较与选择：互联网环境中作品复制权的重构 443b
避风港原则前沿问题研究 457a
标准推广与标准版权保护推进会在厦门举行 170b
部分电视剧制作公司业务情况（表） 255
部分省（区、市）公布的 2016 年度著作权典型案件（典型案件选编） 309

C

蔡赴朝会见世界知识产权组织总干事高锐一行 189b
产业发展 194b
长沙市举办网络著作权行政执法培训班 156b
长沙市举办网络著作权行政执法培训班 175b
成都市建立首批版权服务工作站 182a
成都在全国率先培训出“双证”文创人才 159a
出版传媒集团收入、资产与利润合计情况（表） 226b
出版传媒上市公司的业务类型与上市地点（表） 229a
出版物对外版权贸易构成（表） 219a
出版物发行企业法人单位的所有制结构（表） 225
出口视听著作及代工激光唱片不用申请核验文件 208b
楚楚街与乐视斥资亿元共建音乐产业新生态 197b
“创意广州·梦想飞翔”2016 版权宣传活动在穗举行 157a
从知识产权司法需求论我国民法典的编纂 427b
重庆版权交易中心揭牌 178a
重庆市（版权工作概览） 86b
重庆市文化委、公安局协作打击侵权盗版 150b
重庆文创协会版权登记服务中心成立 181b

D

“大数据安全·互联网新闻出版和数字资产沙龙”举行 170b
“大头儿子”著作权案二审央视胜诉 131a
大优酷与东方梦工厂达成顶级家庭娱乐内容版权合作协议 206b
导航地图侵权案新进展：第三方公司称奇虎已获授权 136b
德化经验　全球共享 192b
迪士尼等起诉国产动画电影《汽车人总动员》侵权 137b
第 23 届北京国际图书博览会闭幕 204a
第 29 届莫斯科国际书展中俄出版机构达成多项合作 191b
第八届中国国际影视动漫版权保护和贸易博览会闭幕 160b
第九届中国版权年会在京召开 171a
第九届中国国际漫画节落幕 204b
第九届中国家纺画稿交易会在南通举行 205a
第十二届中国国际动漫节交易额逾 151 亿元 199b
第十二届中韩版权研讨会在韩举行 188b
第十五届输出版、引进版优秀图书推介活动获奖名单 407
第十五届输出版引进版优秀图书推介活动名单公布 185a
第十五届输出版、引进版优秀图书推介活动输出版图书（表） 407
第十五届输出版、引进版优秀图书推介活动推动版权引进输出的典型人物（4 名）（表） 411
第十五届输出版、引进版优秀图书推介活动引进版图书（表） 409
第十五届输出版、引进版优秀图书推介活动优秀版权经理人（9 名）（表） 411
第四届青岛市版权年会暨版权培训会召开 155b

第五届“世界知识产权组织版权金奖（中国）”获奖名单 373
典型案件选编 293
电视剧产量 10 部以上的地区（表） 254b
豆瓣阅读开卖原创故事作品影视改编权 200b
多位文艺创作者获“中国版权卓越成就者”奖 162a
“哆啦 A 梦”诉《叮咚小区》侵权败诉 140a

E

俄罗斯网络盗版力争上游之下的力量角逐 540a

F

法国主要著作权集体管理组织及业务范围（表） 432
法律法规及规章文件 339
泛珠三角区域深化知识产权合作协议 208a
福建（典型案件选编） 315b
福建省（版权工作概览） 67b
附录：国际版权动态 517

G

甘肃省（版权工作概览） 95b
港澳台版权信息 207
公众号著作权侵权投诉文字作品超六成 155a
关于 2015 年全国著作权登记情况的通报（国版办发［2016］4 号） 362
关于 ASKA 的未发表歌曲的作曲泄露问题之著作权法上的思考 543b
关于废止部分规章和规范性文件的决定（中华人民共和国国家版权局令第 12 号） 341
关于公布第一批全国版权执法监管培训师资库人员名单的通知（国版办发［2016］8 号） 365
关于规范作品登记证书的通知（国版函［2016］1 号） 343
关于国家版权监管平台（二期）第一阶段著作权登记项目运行有关事项的通知（国版办发［2016］5 号） 363
关于“剑网 2016”专项行动第一批网络侵权盗版案件查办情况的通报（国版办发［2016］15 号） 366
关于禁止未经授权通过网络传播中央电视台 2016 年春节联欢晚会的通知（国版办发［2016］3 号） 361
关于开展打击网络侵权盗版“剑网 2016”专项行动的通知（国版发［2016］2 号） 341
关于同意在深圳市腾讯计算机系统有限公司设立“网络版权产业研究基地”的复函（国版办函［2016］41 号） 367
《关于完善产权保护制度依法保护产权的意见》发布 153b
关于印发《2015 年推进使用正版软件工作总结》和《2016 年推进使用正版软件工作计划》的通知（国版函［2016］2 号） 344
关于印发《2016 年全国新闻出版（版权）打击侵权假冒工作要点》的通知（新广出办函［2016］198 号） 368
关于印发《正版软件管理工作指南》的通知（国版办发［2016］13 号） 366
关于做好 2016 年推进软件正版化有关工作的通知（国版办发［2016］7 号） 364
光影音乐网站正式上线 196b
广电总局发布《关于进一步明确进口用于出版的音像制品审批工作相关要求的通知》 151b
广东（典型案件选编） 319b
广东省（版权工作概览） 79b
广东省新闻出版广播影视（版权）工作会议在穗举行 174a
广西（典型案件选编） 320a
广西举行版权进校园活动 156b
广西：下放版权登记权限　桂林人可在本市申请版权 176a
广西壮族自治区（版权工作概览） 82a
广州首聘版权咨询专家 177a
规章文件 341
贵州省（版权工作概览） 91a
国产电影全球发行平台启动 195a
国际版权贸易培训班在京举办 158b
国际交流与合作 185b
国家版权局 2016 年共发布七批重点（影视）作品预警名单 144b
国家版权局等四部门通报 21 起“剑网 2016”专项行动典型网络侵权盗版案件 154b
国家版权局第一批全国版权执法监管培训师资库人员名单（表） 365
国家版权局发布《关于加强网络文学作品版权管理的通知》 153b
国家版权局公布 2015 年中国版权十件大事 146a
国家版权局公布打击侵权盗版年度十大案件 150a
国家版权局关于公布 2015 年度全国打击侵权盗版十大案件的通知（国版函［2016］5 号） 359
国家版权局关于奖励 2015 年度查处侵权盗版

案件有功单位及有功个人的决定（国版函〔2016〕4号） 349
国家版权局奖励查处侵权盗版案件有功单位及个人 149a
国家版权局率17家中央媒体记者学习交流重报集团版权维权工作 161b
国家版权局召开“网络广告联盟服务版权保护工作座谈会” 171b
国家版权贸易基地（越秀）打造版权综合服务平台 173b
国家级版权交易机构（名录） 513
国家数字出版基地（园区）的利润总额（表） 245
国家数字出版基地（园区）的营业收入（表） 244
国家数字出版基地（园区）的资产总额（表） 244
国家新闻出版广电总局发布通知规范移动游戏管理 151a
国家新闻出版广电总局发出《关于大力推动广播电视节目自主创新工作的通知》 151b
国家新闻出版广电总局引入水印技术，强化电影版权保护 153b
国务院办公厅关于印发知识产权综合管理改革试点总体方案的通知（国办发〔2016〕106号） 21
国务院办公厅印发《2016年全国打击侵犯知识产权和制售假冒伪劣商品工作要点》 148b
国务院办公厅印发《国务院关于新形势下加快知识产权强国建设的若干意见》重点任务分工方案的通知（国办函〔2016〕66号） 14
国务院关于印发“十三五”国家知识产权保护和运用规划的通知（国发〔2016〕86号） 3
国务院同意建立知识产权战略实施工作部际联席会议制度 129a

H

“哈利·波特”系列电子书首次在中国发售 203a
海淀法院：影视聚合平台盗链行为不属于合理使用 131a
海南（典型案件选编） 320a
海南省（版权工作概览） 84b
合肥开展“2016扫霾”专项突击检查行动 147b
河北省（版权工作概览） 48a
河北省版权局、河北省版权保护中心在曲阳设立版权服务站 183b
河北省（典型案件选编） 322a
河南（典型案件选编） 316a
河南省（版权工作概览） 75a
黑龙江（典型案件选编） 311a
黑龙江省（版权工作概览） 58b
胡巴款定制T恤引发侵权纠纷 142b
湖北（典型案件选编） 316b
湖北省（版权工作概览） 76b
湖北省（典型案件选编） 333a
湖南（典型案件选编） 319a
湖南省（版权工作概览） 78b
湖南省（典型案件选编） 333b
互联网版权保护与运营新媒体论坛在京举行 166a
“互联网环境下传统出版版权保护与国际版权贸易高级研修班”在沪举办 163b
华人文化入股好莱坞 196b
华为被诉侵犯漫画作品版权 142a
华中国际版权高峰论坛聚焦现代版权产业发展 192a

J

吉林（典型案件选编） 310b
吉林省（版权工作概览） 56a
吉林省（典型案件选编） 323b
《吉林省加强互联网领域侵权假冒行为治理实施方案》下发 146b
“剑网2016”专项行动21起典型案件（典型案件选编） 306
“剑网2016”专项行动总结会在京召开 154a
江苏（典型案件选编） 313a
江苏省（版权工作概览） 61b
江苏省（典型案件选编） 328a
江苏省镇江市警方破获特大网络制售盗版图书侵权案 150a
江苏泰州开展摄影作品著作权保护培训 155b
江苏张家港推两项版权评审奖励办法 175a
江西省（版权工作概览） 69b
江西省成立首家知识产权仲裁中心 175a
江西省（典型案件选编） 329b
交流研讨 163a
今日头条战略投资东方IC 203a
京津冀知识产权发展联盟正式成立 176a
经济新常态下知识产权的创新、驱动与发展 32
竞争与垄断：我国著作权集体管理组织的模式选择 431a
《九层妖塔》侵权案宣判：未侵犯保护作品完整权 138a
就业人数的产业类别构成（表） 226a

K

《开心消消乐》游戏引发系列权利纷争 136a

L

《老爷车中国行》羊城举行版权授权仪式 173b
乐动卓越起诉昆仑万维“MT 游戏”侵权，法院判决昆仑万维停止不正当竞争行为 132a
乐视 20 亿美金收购美国最大智能电视厂商 202b
乐视成立 CDLA 产业联盟 201b
乐视票务平台多元运营挖掘体育赛事版权价值 200a
乐视诉电视猫“盗链”侵权获赔 50 万元 139b
乐视云发布多款云产品 203b
理论研究 413
立法 129a
立法与行政 527a
利润总额的地区结构（图） 224
利润总额的公司类型构成（图） 237b
联合国教科文组织关于文化贸易的报道 535b
辽宁（典型案件选编） 310b
辽宁省（版权工作概览） 54a
辽宁省版权局与京版十五社反盗版联盟签署战略合作协议 149b
辽宁省（典型案件选编） 323a
论二次创作的著作权法规制与保障 447b
论体育赛事现场直播画面的著作权保护 451b
论著作权法语境中的作品结构 436a

M

漫画《蜡笔小新》遭盗播　权利人起诉 133b
美国：联邦版权法不能取代对商业秘密的保护 532b
美国《数字千年版权法》对网络服务提供商提出的避风港版权代理新要求 538a
《美人制造》著作权纠纷案宣判 143b
美术作品的表达及其实质相似的认定 460b
美术作品的画面构成（图） 462
美团猫眼电影首推电影票在线改签　覆盖近 2 000 家影院 195b
《芈月传》编剧署名纠纷案一审宣判 143b
民间文学艺术作品的保护机制探讨 424a
民进中央召开两会新闻通气会　拟提交版权相关提案 174b
名录 501

N

南北两大影视版权交易平台达成战略合作 196a
内蒙古鄂托克旗开展侵权盗版及非法出版物集中销毁活动 152a
内蒙古自治区（版权工作概览） 52a
年度发布 371
聂辰席任国家新闻出版广电总局局长、国家版权局局长 153a
宁夏回族自治区（版权工作概览） 100a
宁夏举办全区党政机关软件正版化工作培训班 158a
纽约州法院：天狼星公司无须向 1972 年之前的音乐的表演者付费 533a
《女医·明妃传》陷版权纠纷　掌阅告阅文索赔 100 万元 141b

O

欧盟法院：链接到盗版内容的行为本身不侵犯著作权 528a
欧盟理事会同意消除电子商务地域屏蔽 543a
欧盟有权批准《马拉喀什条约》的意见或将被打破 529b
欧盟委员会（COE）保护表达自由和隐私的网络中立指南 527b

Q

期刊产品结构（表） 221b
齐白石后人与湖南美术出版社著作权系列纠纷案达成和解 134b
企业法人单位的所有制结构（表） 225b
侵权网站 BT 天堂站长被刑拘 143a
青岛“5·16”非法期刊经营案告破 144a
青岛出版集团成功并购日本渡边淳一文学馆 204b
青海省（版权工作概览） 98a
青海省（典型案件选编） 337b
蜻蜓 FM《香火》被判侵权 140b
全国“版权云”体验店授牌仪式在太原举行 181b
全国出版物对外贸易情况（表） 219
全球创作者论坛在京举办 193b

R

人民网与各党报新媒体发起党报新媒体版权联盟 206a
日本“扫描书籍”营业者，因涉嫌侵犯著作权被逮捕 533b

S

三家著作权集体管理组织走进清华研讨热点

话题 165a
三男子印刷逾25万册高仿盗版教辅书　案值超700万元 137a
山东省（版权工作概览） 72a
山东省（典型案件选编） 331a
山东省即墨市启动首届优秀版权作品大赛 161a
山西省（版权工作概览） 50a
陕西建成线上代理版权登记平台 178b
陕西省（版权工作概览） 95a
陕西省（典型案件选编） 336b
擅用金庸武侠作品元素　游戏公司败诉赔偿百万元 134a
上海宝山区版权服务工作站揭牌 179b
上海（典型案件选编） 312a
上海市（版权工作概览） 60a
上海市（典型案件选编） 325a
上海召开推进使用正版软件工作会议 147a
少儿出版反盗版联盟在北京成立 181a
社会管理与服务 173a
摄著协推出“摄影家银行卡”加强摄影作品版权保护 182b
“深圳版权金奖”举行颁奖典礼 162b
深圳罗湖区政府与中国版权保护中心签约设立粤港澳版权登记大厅 183a
“十二五”期间中国完成软件著作权登记92万余件 157b
“十三五”知识产权保护和运用主要指标（表） 5
实用艺术作品交叉保护的证成与潜在风险之化解 440a
世界知识产权组织传统知识委员会同意就修订的草案做进一步讨论 537a
手游公司擅用金庸小说内容被判侵权 131b
手游《幻想江湖》被判侵犯著作权 130b
首份产经媒体融合发展报告发布 205b
首个国家网络版权产业研究基地落户腾讯 184a
首个民族文化版权交易中心落户顺义 179b
首个中国主题图书翻译出版中心在蒙古国成立 192b
首届中国知识产权保护高层论坛举办 164a
首例电竞直播侵权案终审宣判 135a
数字版权保护技术研发工程竣工 184b
数字版权保护技术研发工程应用在京签约 180a
“数字环境下影视产业版权保护圆桌会议”在北京举行 187b
司法 129b
司法判例 531b
四部门启动“剑网2016”专项活动 152a
四川部分市实行作品登记免费服务 173a
四川省（版权工作概览） 88b
四川省（典型案件选编） 335a
四川省发布《关于加强互联网领域侵权假冒行为治理的实施意见》 145b
四川省阆中市审结两起制售盗版音像制品刑事案 130a
四川为蜀绣作品免费登记著作权 155a
苏州市版权培训基地揭牌成立 182b
苏州市吴江区成立首个市级版权工作站 182a

T

台湾 208b
唐德影视购买好声音版权 195a
特辑 1
腾讯86亿美元收购Supercell，开拓网游大时代 201a
腾讯泛娱乐开发深挖儿童出版内容版权价值 200b
腾讯“芒种计划”打造媒体生态圈 196b
腾讯、微影8 500万美元投资韩国YG娱乐 200b
天津IPTV被诉侵权　遭索赔2 000万元 138b
天津（典型案件选编） 309b
天津市（版权工作概览） 46b
天涯社区携手中大中文系打造全国大学生影视剧本创作平台 196a
“童话大王”郑渊洁声讨网络店铺侵权 139a
统计资料 477
图书馆和档案馆呼吁WIPO成员制定避风港规则 538b
推进使用正版软件工作部际联席会议第五次全体会议在京召开 146b

W

外文出版社伦敦书展版权输出成绩显著 187b
万达35亿美元并购美国传奇影业 194b
网店售卖画像复制品侵权　卖家被判赔尝著作权人4.5万元 134a
“网络音乐版权保护与商业模式”研讨会在京召开 163a
网络游戏反盗版和产业保护联盟在京成立 206a
网络著作权侵权中“直接侵权主体”判断的规范构成 464b
威秀集团与福斯电视台为屏蔽盗版网站提起诉讼 531b
未确定的盗版索赔不应导致切断互联网 544b

文著协与《读者》签订稿酬收转协议 180a
我国出版版权输出总量 8 年增 3 倍 201a
我国视频付费市场规模突破 10 亿元大关 206b
我国授权产品（玩具和婴童用品类）主要 IP 品牌（表） 276
我国数字出版产业规模突破 4 400 亿元 202a
我国有关避风港原则的法律规定（表） 457
《我们要战胜一切》歌曲版权争议 536a
五部门联合下发通知：严打高校周边复印店盗版活动 145a
五起《漫画帮》著作权侵权案宣判 141a
武汉开展高校版权专题辩论赛 156b

X

"西部丝路版权交易平台"在京正式启动 181a
西藏自治区（版权工作概览） 93a
熙颐影业收购国际版权销售公司 196a
县城影院呈现超速度增长势头 195b
香港 207a
香港海关打击分发侵权课程教材 207b
香港海关侦破"点对点"发放怀疑侵权电视节目案件 207a
香港政府建议修订《仲裁条例》 207b
新版图书与重印图书品种、总印数结构（表） 220
新疆（典型案件选编） 321a
新疆维吾尔自治区（版权工作概览） 101b
新闻出版产业结构（表） 218a
新闻出版单位数量与构成（表） 225a
新西兰音乐产业要求改变 TPP 中的版权条款 537b
行政管理 144b
宣传教育 155a

Y

烟台建立山东首个著作权纠纷诉调对接机制 177b
阎晓宏赴上海美术电影制片厂调研 153b
阎晓宏会见查德·康斯坦德、洪伟典一行 190a
阎晓宏会见英国能源及知识产权国务大臣娜薇尔·露芙一行 191a
阎晓宏率代表团访问埃及并参加开罗国际书展 186a
业界动态 534a
页游《青云志》被诉侵犯《诛仙》游戏改编权 143a
"一带一路"高峰合作论坛推版权输出 169b
"一带一路"知识产权高级别会议召开 167a
一铭软件推动中国—东盟基础软件生态合作 202b
移动 APP 第三方证书签名与版权登记联合服务平台正式上线 174b
艺恩咨询发布《2015—2016 中国电影产业报告》 198a
音乐产业集团一致呼吁特朗普的支持 544b
音乐剧《断桥》版权之争结束 133a
银川破获全国首起手游侵犯著作权案 133b
印刷复制的内部构成（表） 218
英国提议加强网络知识产权保护 528b
《婴儿画报》《幼儿画报》向美国输出版权 192a
营业收入的地区结构（图） 223
营业收入的公司类型构成（图） 235b
"影视创作从依法保护原创开始"座谈会在京举办 163a
逾 6 800 万美元国际动漫版权合作协议在苏州签署 194a
阅文集团报告显示"90 后"网络作家逐渐崛起 155b
粤港保护知识产权合作专责小组第十五次会议在广州召开 152b
云南（典型案件选编） 321a
云南省（版权工作概览） 92a

Z

在境内外上市的出版传媒公司股市流通市值（表） 230
在境内外上市的股市流通市值前 10 位出版传媒上市公司（表） 230
在"全球创作者论坛"上的书面致辞 27
在中国内地上市的报业公司股市总市值（表） 231
在中国内地上市的报业公司利润总额（表） 238
在中国内地上市的报业公司平均净资产收益率（表） 241
在中国内地上市的报业公司营业收入（表） 236
在中国内地上市的报业公司资产总额（表） 234
在中国内地上市的出版传媒公司股市总市值（表） 230b
在中国内地上市的出版传媒公司利润总额（表） 237a
在中国内地上市的出版传媒公司平均净资产收益率（表） 240a
在中国内地上市的出版传媒公司营业收入（表） 235a
在中国内地上市的出版传媒公司资产总额（表） 233a
在中国内地上市的出版公司股市总市值（表） 231
在中国内地上市的出版公司利润总额（表） 238

在中国内地上市的出版公司平均净资产收益率（表） 240
在中国内地上市的出版公司营业收入（表） 236
在中国内地上市的出版公司资产总额（表） 233
在中国内地上市的发行公司股市总市值（表） 232
在中国内地上市的发行公司利润总额（表） 239
在中国内地上市的发行公司平均净资产收益率（表） 241
在中国内地上市的发行公司营业收入（表） 236
在中国内地上市的发行公司资产总额（表） 234
在中国内地上市的股市总市值前 10 位出版传媒上市公司（表） 230
在中国内地上市的利润总额前 10 位出版传媒上市公司（表） 238
在中国内地上市的平均净资产收益率前 10 位出版传媒公司（表） 240
在中国内地上市的新媒体公司股市营业收入（表） 237
在中国内地上市的新媒体公司股市资产总额（表） 235
在中国内地上市的新媒体公司股市总市值（表） 232
在中国内地上市的新媒体公司利润总额（表） 239
在中国内地上市的新媒体公司平均净资产收益率（表） 241
在中国内地上市的印刷公司股市总市值（表） 232
在中国内地上市的印刷公司利润总额（表） 239
在中国内地上市的印刷公司平均净资产收益率（表） 241
在中国内地上市的印刷公司营业收入（表） 237
在中国内地上市的印刷公司资产总额（表） 234
在中国内地上市的营业收入前 10 位出版传媒上市公司（表） 235
在中国内地上市的资产总额前 10 位出版传媒上市公司（表） 233
增长贡献前 10 位的地区（表） 224b
增长速度前 10 位的地区（表） 224a
掌阅科技与时尚集团开展版权合作 202a
浙江（典型案件选编） 313a
浙江省（版权工作概览） 63b
知识产权及创新等事项被纳入 TRIPs 理事会例会议程 535a
知识产权教学与研究机构（名录） 514
知识产权署推出有关版权保护新电视宣传短片 207a
知识共享组织：版权的另一面是什么？ 534a
知识共享组织在 WIPO：支持更公平的教学研究版权政策 541a
中超天价版权催生“网台联动” 199a
中俄两大电影节在俄签署战略合作仪式 189a
中国版权保护中心 DCI 体系再拓新应用 177b
中国版权保护中心（版权工作概览） 103a
中国版权保护中心西南版权登记大厅在成都开业运行 178b
中国版权协会 2016 年第一期版权培训班成功举办 159b
中国版权协会（版权工作概览） 108a
中国版权协会艺术品版权工作委员会成立 179a
中国版权协会与冠勇科技签署战略合作意向书 180a
中国出版亮相罗马尼亚 193a
中国出版数字资源国际交易平台启动 180b
中国出版协会六届六次常务理事会召开 173a
中国电影衍生品产业联盟成立 200a
中国电影著作权协会（版权工作概览） 121b
《中国好声音》版权纠纷激化　影响唐德影视业绩 137b
中国互联网协会网络版权联盟（版权工作概览） 122b
中国取代美国成为最大文化产品出口国 197a
中国摄影著作权协会（版权工作概览） 119b
中国图书受突尼斯读者欢迎 187a
中国网络版权保护大会在北京召开 165a
中国网络文学版权联盟成立 204b
中国网页游戏市场产业链（图） 290
中国文字著作权协会（版权工作概览） 115a
中国移动游戏产业链（图） 288
中国音乐著作权协会（版权工作概览） 110b
中国音像著作权集体管理协会（版权工作概览） 113b
中国展团重磅亮相博洛尼亚童书展 187a
中国资本拿下英国足球版权巨头 200a
中韩图书版权交易会在南昌举行 189a
中捷建立战略伙伴关系共同保护知识产权 186b
中罗文字著作权集体管理组织展开合作 194b
中美著作权最新发展研讨会在京召开 190a
中南传媒搭建 IP 全版权运营平台 197b
中日著作权研讨会在沪举行 168a
中山市设立版权专项资金 184a
中摄权协受邀参加国务院修法研讨会 129a
中以签署文学和翻译领域合作谅解备忘录 185b
中英探索建立双语侵权举报平台 188a

Z

“助力原创　保护版权”全球公共艺术倡议行动启动　160b
著作权集体管理组织（名录）　511
著作权在数字时代的保护与限制　519
专文　25
资产总额的地区结构（图）　223
资产总额的公司类型构成（图）　233b
总体经济规模综合评价前 10 位的报刊出版集团（表）　227
总体经济规模综合评价前 10 位的地区（表）　223a
总体经济规模综合评价前 10 位的发行集团（表）　228
总体经济规模综合评价前 10 位的图书出版集团（表）　227
总体经济规模综合评价前 10 位的印刷集团（表）　229
综述　519
作家刘心武诉世纪超星侵权　142b